KLEPPNER'S

17th Edition

Advertising Procedure

W. Ronald Lane
University of Georgia, Emeritus

Karen Whitehill King
University of Georgia

J. Thomas Russell
University of Georgia, Emeritus

PEARSON

Prentice Hall

Upper Saddle River, New Jersey 07458

Library of Congress Cataloging-in-Publication Data

Lane, W. Ronald
  Kleppner's advertising procedure / W. Ronald Lane, Karen Whitehill King, J. Thomas Russell. —
Seventeenth ed.
    p. cm.
  Includes bibliographical references and index.
  ISBN 978-0-13-230829-8
  1. Advertising. I. King, Karen Whitehill. II. Russel, Thomas, III. Title. IV. Title:
Advertising procedure.
HF5823.K45 2008
659.1—dc22

2007021990

Editor-in-Chief: David Parker
Product Development Manager: Ashley Santora
Project Manager, Editorial: Melissa Pellerano
Editorial Assistant: Christine Ietto
Assistant Editor, Media: Ashley Lulling
Marketing Manager: Jodi Bassett
Marketing Assistant: Ian Gold
Senior Managing Editor: Judy Leale
Project Manager, Production: Kevin H. Holm
Permissions Project Manager: Charles Morris
Permissions Researcher: Marcy Lunetta
Senior Operations Supervisor: Arnold Vila
Art Director: Suzanne Duda
Interior Design: Suzanne Duda
Cover Design: Suzanne Duda
Cover Illustration/Photo: tom white.images
Illustration (Interior): Carlisle Publishing Services
Director, Image Resource Center: Melinda Patelli
Manager, Rights and Permissions: Zina Arabia
Manager: Visual Research: Beth Brenzel
Manager, Cover Visual Research & Permissions: Karen Sanatar
Image Permission Coordinator: Ang'john Ferreri
Composition: Carlisle Publishing Services
Full-Service Project Management: Lynn Steines, Carlisle Publishing Services
Printer/Binder: C J Krehbiel / Phoenix Color Corp.
Typeface: 10/12.5 Utopia

Credits and acknowledgments borrowed from other sources and reproduced, with permission, in this textbook appear on appropriate page within text.

Pearson Education LTD.
Pearson Education Singapore, Pte. Ltd
Pearson Education, Canada, Ltd
Pearson Education–Japan

Pearson Education Australia PTY, Limited
Pearson Education North Asia Ltd
Pearson Educación de Mexico, S.A. de C.V.
Pearson Education Malaysia, Pte. Ltd.

10 9 8 7 6 5 4 3 2 1
ISBN-13: 978-0-13-230829-8
ISBN-10: 0-13-230829-0

BRIEF CONTENTS

CONTENTS

PREFACE

WHAT MAKES THIS BOOK UNIQUE?

The objective of *Kleppner's Advertising Procedure* is to provide a basic introduction to the planning and execution of advertising and promotio within the context of marketing goals and objectives. It is primarily intended for undergraduate students majoring in advertising, marketing, and management. In addition, the text would be beneficial to students majoring in the social sciences, especially psychology and sociology. The text also has proven valuable as a resource for advertising and business practitioners.

MAJOR OBJECTIVES OF THE TEXT

The text offers a clear and comprehensive examination of the roles that advertising practitioners play from three perspectives: (1) a firm's marketing and advertising department; (2) as an advertising agency professional; and finally (3) from the perspective of media executives who provide the bridge between a company's products and its target audience. More than ever, the text recognizes that the skill set needed for a successful advertising career has never been more complex. In this regard, the authors have brought together contemporary information from the fields of marketing, communication, psychology, sociology, anthropology, and social science research as they relate to the practice of advertising. The current edition also recognizes the growing importance of global marketing and new communication technology and addresses both of these areas in depth.

PRINCIPAL POINTS OF DISTINCTION

1. The text introduces students to the following areas:
   - The changing role of global marketing and advertising with an emphasis on steps that U.S. companies are taking to contend with foreign competitors.
   - The evolving role of the marketing communication channel and the role of permission marketing with consumers are increasing using the Internet and other emerging technologies.
   - Changing management roles in an environment of mega mergers amount media, ad agencies, and their clients.
2. The 17th edition continues the tradition of introducing students to the latest information from the fields of marketing communication and advertising through:
   - **Viewpoints** that discuss contemporary issues in marketing and advertising from the standpoint of some of the leading executives in the field.
   - **Exhibits** that are virtually all new for this edition and which highlight the best advertisements and promotional techniques.
3. The 17th edition maintains its 80+ year tradition of providing new material reflecting the dramatic changes impacting the planning and execution of advertising. Among the most important additions to this edition are:
   - New technology discussion—advertisers are increasing using new technology from computer design to cell phones

KLEPPNER VIEWPOINT 3.1

Brad Majors
Former CEO, SOCOH Marketing LLC; Senior Vice President, Lintas Worldwide
Brand Development Demystified

There is a lot of talk about "branding" or "brand development" these days, as if it is the next "new thing" in marketing and sales. "Brand development" is not a new phenomenon. It has been around for at least 100 years.

Any marketer or ad agency worth its salt practices "brand development" every time they perform any marketing function. The history of advertising in America is, essentially, the history of branding. That is what good advertising (and the other communication disciplines) does—create good and consistent reputations for products or services and this consistent imagery is what converts a product into a "brand."

I say "consistent" because one of the greatest sins of marketing these days (especially for smaller businesses) is a lack of "integrated marketing." By this I mean that there may be mixed messages (from media advertising, public relations, the Web site, package copy, or whatever) that go out to consumers from a brand. And with these inconsistent messages comes an inconsistent image for the brand. Developing integrated marketing communications is one of the most important activities that can be done to enhance the value of a client's brand. It is nearly impossible to build a brand with inconsistencies in your marketing communications mix.

Business schools teach "the Marketing Mix," which is pretty basic stuff, but bear with me. This Marketing Mix includes the Four P's of marketing: the Product itself (and its structural packaging), the Price of the product, the Place (of distribution) where the product can be purchased, and the Promotion of the product. Interestingly, the fourth P, Promotion, is simply the communication of aspects of the first three P's.

What else is critical to the sale other than what the product does, how much it costs, and where you can get it? Only one more "element" I can think of.

Enter the "Fifth P" which isn't discussed in B-School textbooks, but I doubt the idea is mine alone. What does the Fifth P stand for? The Prospect. The person who is going to buy this product or service, based on perceived needs and wants.

If the Fourth P, Promotion, connects Product, Price, and Place, it also performs another valuable function. Good Promotion, be it in the form of media advertising, packaging graphics, public relations, or in-store merchandising, also has the responsibility of connecting the Prospect to the Product, its Price, and the Place it can be found. In essence, the product is just a collection of features and attributes until the Prospect arrives on the scene. When

the Prospect's needs and wants begin to surface, so do the brand's marketing possibilities.

As the Prospect evaluates all the information he or she knows about the product (what it does, what it costs, where it can be purchased), a relationship may begin to form. However, this will only happen if the brand imagery has been consistently presented. This relationship is based on how the Prospect feels the product (or service) will meet his or her needs and wants. I call this "personal relevance." How does the Prospect relate emotionally to those rational product attributes? This "personal relevance" is not a new concept in marketing either. Marketers have been trying to figure out how to achieve the emotional bond between Prospect and brand since the 1920s when Motivational Research was first used by ad agencies. And we are still trying to crack the code on why consumers make the brand choices they make.

A final comment in the Brand Development Demystification process: Sometimes the term *brand development* can suggest some type of inexpensive shortcut in marketing. I have spoken with entrepreneurs who wanted to do "brand development" because they didn't have money for advertising. Sorry, it doesn't really work that way. While media advertising may not be the only way to promote your brand, developing a brand takes time and money. Strong brands do not come cheaply. Fortunately, if the "brand development" process is successful, that investment will pay out big as you go down the marketing road. ▪ ▪ ▪

Brad Majors

as consumer media. For example, Chapter 13 discusses the role of new media in reaching a "in control consumers" and Chapter 18 discusses the role of computer technology in the production of advertisements.

- **The best of contemporary advertising**—throughout the text, virtually every advertisement exhibit is new to this edition, demonstrating the best of today's commercial messages.
- **Advertising integrated into the business environment**—throughout the text, advertising and promotion is discussed with the total business context recognizing that advertising decisions are rarely made in a business vacuum. The text also reflects the fact that the contemporary business environment increasingly must deal with a global perspective which is reflected throughout this edition.
- **Expanded discussion of legal and ethical considerations**—advertising must function within a strict matrix of both legal and ethical restraints and additional information is devoted to these issues, particularly in Chapter 24.

WHY A NEW EDITION

There are few areas of business and marketing that operate in a more dynamic atmosphere than advertising and promotion. The process of new product and target audience research, branding and product development, executing creative sales approaches, and selecting media and non-traditional marketing communication placement are part of an evolving development that is undergoing dramatic change. The primary reason for publication of this new edition is to reflect this environment.

These important changes in the advertising profession are reflected throughout the text while keeping the basic structure similar to past editions. The 17th edition is organized as follows:

PART I

The authors strongly believe that contemporary advertising should be studied from the perspective of the social, cultural, and economic foundations that created modern marketing and promotion. Part one offers an historical overview.

- **Chapter 1** examines how advertising and marketing developed as part of the larger society including the Industrial Revolution, a rising middle class, and the introduction of democratic principles in both politics and economics. The chapter brings the personalities and events which created the modern American marketing system to life.

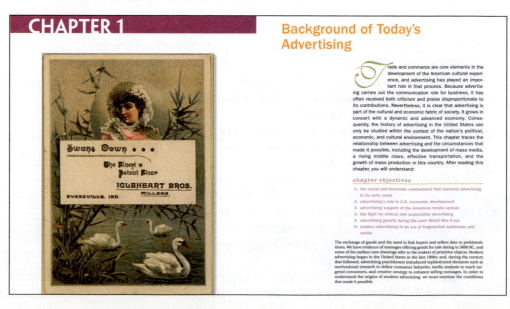

■ **Chapter 2** offers an overview of the multitude of channels currently being used to reach prospective buyers and demonstrates the ways that advertising and marketing communication are used by advertisers as small as the neighborhood retailer and as large as global multinational corporations.

PART II

This section introduces fundamentals of advertising planning and brand research on which virtually all sucessful advertising is based.

■ **Chapter 3** introduces the concept of the advertising spiral and the strategies needed to keep brands vigorous in a changing marketplace.

■ **Chapter 4** outlines the fundamentals of identifying and understanding target markets who are most interested and profitable for specific products.

PART III

This section of the text emphasizes the business operations of advertising and the sometimes fragile and contentious relationships between agencies and clients.

■ **Chapters 5 and 6** explore how the advertising and management function have become more complex. Today, advertising is more likely to be integrated into a total marketing communication program resulting in management and relationship changes from the past. The text also discusses the organization of the advertising industry from both advertiser and agency perspectives.

PART IV

In this section, the authors discuss the methods of reaching consumers with sales messages. The chapters in this part examine both traditional media and emerging methods of reaching customers and future prospects.

■ **Chapter 7** begins the consideration of media with an overview of the media planning function and the role of the media planner in delivering advertising messages to consumers.

■ **Chapters 8 to 14** discuss each of the basic media and communication methods used to reach consumers. "Media" as diverse as Web sites, iPods, and cell phones are included in the examination. This section also addresses the communication strengths and weaknesses of each medium and how these media are converging as consumers embrace new technology and media companies merge to form large multimedia conglomerates.

PART V

Ultimately, prospects are converted to buyers with the introduction of stong product benefits that solve consumer problems. The discussion of the creative function in this section highlights the need for creative ideas based on research that offers insight into consumer needs, product selection, and media preferences.

■ **Chapters 15 to 22** emphasize the need for planning and research to bring rough ideas to fruition as a finished ad. Contrary to popular opinion, great advertising is rarely a result of spontaneous brilliance, but rather is the byproduct of hours of hard work and study.

PART VI

■ **Chapter 23** underscores the global nature of advertising and marketing. Globalization is no longer a theory, but rather part of the everyday strategy of companies throughout the world. While the United States continues to be the major player in international marketing and advertising, its share of advertising and sales continues to shrink as competitors from around the world produce products and advertising that are often equal to the best the U.S. has to offer. It no longer dominates the global economy as it did in much of the last century.

■ **Chapter 24** stresses that fact that advertising is constrained by a number of legal, regulatory, and ethical considerations as the public demands greater candor from advertisers and protections from governmental agencies. More than a discussion of rules and regulations, Chapter 24 emphasizes the new environment of public responsibility that major advertisers have embraced over the last half-century. More and more the public is demanding that advertisers be sensitive to the societal and cultural dimensions in the messages they distribute. For their part, advertisers are finding that doing what is right is also good business.

INSTRUCTOR RESOURCES

Many of the following supplements can also be downloaded via our password-protected Instructor's Resource Center (IRC). Visit www.prenhall.com/lane to access these resources.

Instructor's Manual The instructor's handbook for this text includes chapter objectives, a chapter overview, a detailed chapter outline, and answers to review questions in the textbook. Also included within each chapter is a section that offers suggestions for class projects and exercises, which serve to enhance the learning experience in the classroom.

Test Item File Featuring more than 2,600 questions, 110 questions per chapter, this Test Item File has been written specifically for the seventeenth edition. Each chapter consists of multiple-choice, true/false, matching, completion, and essay questions, with page references and difficulty level provided for each question.

TestGen Test Generating Software Prentice Hall's test-generating software is available from the *IRC Online* (www.prenhall.com/lane) or from the *IRC on CD-ROM*.

■ PC/Mac compatible; preloaded with all of the Test Item File questions.
■ Manually or randomly view test bank questions and drag-and-drop to create a test.
■ Add or modify test bank questions using the built-in Question Editor.
■ Print up to 25 variations of a single test and deliver the test on a local area network using the built-in QuizMaster feature.

■ Free customer support is available at media.support@pearsoned.com or call 1-800-6-PROFESSOR between 8:00 A.M. and 5:00 P.M. CST.

PowerPoints A set of PowerPoint slides is available on the IRC on CD. The slides include a chapter outline, discussion questions, images from inside and outside the book, and Web links.

Instructor's Resource Center Register. Redeem. Login.

www.prenhall.com/irc is where instructors can access a variety of print, media, and presentation resources available with this text in downloadable, digital format. For most texts, resources are also available for course management platforms such as Blackboard, WebCT, and Course Compass.

It gets better. Once you register, you will not have additional forms to fill out, or multiple usernames and passwords to remember to access new titles and/or editions. As a registered faculty member, you can log in directly to download resource files, and receive immediate access and instructions for installing Course Management content to your campus server.

Need help? Our dedicated technical support team is ready to assist instructors with questions about the media supplements that accompany this text. Visit: http://247.prenhall.com/ for answers to frequently asked questions and toll-free user support phone numbers.

All instructor resources in one place. It's your choice. Available via a password-protected site at www.prenhall.com/lane or on CD-ROM. Resources include:

■ *Instructor's Manual:* View chapter-by-chapter or download the entire manual as a .zip file.
■ *Test Item File:* View chapter-by-chapter or download the entire test item file as a .zip file.
■ *TestGen EQ for PC/Mac:* Download this easy-to-use software; it's preloaded with the twelfth edition test questions and a user's manual.
■ *Image bank (on CD only):* Access many of the ads and illustrations featured in the text. Ideal for PowerPoint customization.
■ *PowerPoints (on CD only):* A set of slides to accompany your lecture.

Video Gallery 17 segments on DVD, all covering various topics in advertising, are offered. These segments, all 8–12 minutes in length, are geared around well-known companies and their advertising practices. A video guide and correlation grid are included in the Instructor's Manual.

AdCritic.com Prentice Hall and AdAge are bringing the most current ads and commentary from advertising experts into your classroom. Only Prentice Hall can offer students 16 weeks of access to a special AdCritic.com site that includes AdAge's encyclopedia of articles at a deeply discounted rate. An access code is available only when shrink-wrapped with a Prentice Hall text, so be sure and specify the appropriate package with your local bookstore in advance. Please visit www.prenhall.com/marketing for a tour of the AdCritic site.

STUDENT RESOURCES

Announcing SafariX Textbooks Online—Where the Web meets textbooks for student savings! *Kleppner's Advertising Procedure*, 17th edition, is also available as a WebBook! SafariX WebBooks offer study advantages no print textbook can match. With an Internet-enhanced SafariX WebBook, students can search the entire text for key concepts; navigate easily to a page number, reading assignment, or chapter; or bookmark important pages or sections for quick review at a later date. Some key features:

- Digital textbook delivery that saves students off the print edition's suggested list price.
- Internet-based service making textbook content available anytime, anywhere there is a Web connection.
- Easy navigation, which makes finding pages and completing assignments easy and efficient.
- Search, bookmark, and note-taking tools that save study time and reduce frustration by making critical information immediately accessible. Organizing study notes has never been easier!
- Ability to print pages on the fly making critical content available for offline study and review. Prentice Hall is pleased to be the first publisher to offer students a new choice in how they purchase and access required or recommended course textbooks. For details and a demonstration, visit www.prenhall.com/safarix.

VangoNotes Study on the go with VangoNotes—chapter reviews from your text in downloadable mp3 format. Now wherever you are—whatever you're doing—you can study by listening to the following for each chapter of your textbook:

- *Big Ideas:* Your "need to know" for each chapter
- *Practice Test:* A gut check for the Big Ideas—tells you if you need to keep studying
- *Key Terms:* Audio "flashcards" to help you review key concepts and terms
- *Rapid Review:* A quick drill session—use it right before your test

VangoNotes are **flexible**; download all the material directly to your player, or only the chapters you need. And they're **efficient**. Use them in your car, at the gym, walking to class, or wherever. So get yours today. And get studying.

VangoNotes.com.

ACKNOWLEDGMENTS

Mark Baldwin, Chick-fil-A, Atlanta

Sheri Bevil, Lane Bevil+Partners, Atlanta

David Botsford, The Botsford Group, Atlanta

Pat Buckley, The Johnson Group, Chattanooga, TN

Chisholm Burbage, Charleston Area Convention & Visitors Bureau, Charleston, SC

Mary Beth Burner, Cooking Light/Southern Progress, Birmingham, AL

Kelly Caffarelli, Home Depot Foundation, Atlanta

Steve Caffarelli, Office of the Treasury, State of Georgia

Mike Casey, Cohn, Overstreet & Parrish, Atlanta

Frank Compton, Blattner Brunner, Atlanta

Julie Dombrowski, The Daniel Island Co., Daniel Island, SC

Judy Franks, EnergyBBDO, Chicago

Steven Guyer, G2 Direct & Digital, New York

Chris Hooper, Fitzgerald+Co., Atlanta

Ron Huey, Huey+Partners, Atlanta

Steven Jones, McRae Communications, Atlanta

Gilad Kat, Grey Tel Aviv, Israel

Alice Kendrick, Southern Methodist University, Dallas

Jason Kreher, Messner Vetere Burger McNamee Schmetter Euro RSCG/New York

Peggy Kreshel, Ph.D., Grady College, The University of Georgia, Athens, GA

Karen Kuchenbecker, Charleston Regional Development Alliance, Charleston, SC

Steven Lang, Southern Broadcasting Corp., Athens, GA

Donna LeBlond, Grady College, The University of Georgia

Thomas Lentz, Broyhill Furniture Industries, Lenoir, N.C.

Amy Lokken, McRae Communications, Atlanta

Brad Majors, GTC, Greenville, S.C.

Tim Mapes, Delta Airlines, Atlanta

Hugh J. Martin, Ph.D., Grady College, The University of Georgia

Michael Martin, Employees, Atlanta

Vicki Mills, Imedia, Inc., Macon, GA

Bruce Murdy, Rawle Murdy, Charleston, SC

Gregory Nyilasy, Ph.D., Hall and Partners, New York

Lynne J. Omlie, DISCUSS, Washington, DC

Daniel Partich, PACTIV, Atlanta

Charles M. Penuel, Georgia Higher Education Savings Plan

Don Perry, Chick-fil-A, Atlanta

John Robertson, VitroRobertson, San Diego

Tom Robinson, Robinson & Associates, Tupelo

Charles Van Rysselberge, Charleston Metro Chamber of Commerce, Charleston, SC

Sunayana Sarkar, Starcom MediaVest Group, New York

Scott Scaggs, Trone Advertising, High Point, NC

Shannon Scott, Applebee's, Overland Park, KS

Megan Sovern, Leo Burnett, Chicago

Jeanne Spencer, Idea Engineering, Santa Barbara, CA

Alana Stephenson, The Johnson Group, Chattanooga, TN

Peggy Sullivan, Pathway Communities, Atlanta

Emily Watts, Charleston Metro Chamber of Commerce, Charleston, SC

Robert Willett, Grady College, The University of Georgia, Athens, GA

ABOUT THE AUTHORS

OTTO KLEPPNER
(1899-1982)

A graduate of New York University, Otto Kleppner started out in advertising as a copywriter. After several such jobs, he became advertising manager at Prentice Hall, where he began to think that he, too, "could write a book." Some years later, he also thought that he could run his own advertising agency, and both ideas materialized eminently. His highly successful agency handled advertising for leading accounts (Dewar's Scotch Whisky, I. W. Harper Bourbon and other Schenley brands, Saab Cars, Doubleday Book Clubs, and others). His book became a bible for advertising students, and his writings have been published in eight languages.

Active in the American Association of Advertising Agencies, Mr. Kleppner served as a director, a member of the Control Committee, chairman of the Committee of Government, Public and Educator Relations, and a governor of the New York Council. He was awarded the Nichols Cup (now the Crain Cup) for distinguished service to the teaching of advertising.

W. RONALD LANE

Ron has worked in all aspects of advertising. He began in advertising and promotion for a drug manufacturer. Later he was marketing manager for a drug store chain. He has worked in creative and account services for clients including Coca-Cola, National Broiler Council, Minute-Maid, and for small clients like Western North Carolina Tourism and Callaway Gardens Country Store.

He was presented with the American Advertising Federation Distinguished Advertising Educator Award for service to advertising education and industry. He was coordinator of the Institute of Advanced Advertising Studies sponsored by the American Association of Advertising Agencies for six years. He was a partner in SLRS Communications, an advertising-marketing firm. He served 20 years on the American Advertising Federation's (AAF) Academic Committee. He has

(L to R) W. Ronald Lane, Karen Whitehill King, J. Thomas Russell

been AAF Academic Division Chair, a member of the AAF Board of Directors, Council of Governors, Executive Committee and the AAF Foundation. He has been an ADDY Awards judge numerous times, and been a member of the Advertising Age Creative Workshop faculty. He has also served as a member of the ACEMJC Accrediting Council.

Currently, Ron is a senior partner at Lane Bevil+Partners.

KAREN WHITEHILL KING

Karen King is a professor of advertising and the Head of the Department of Advertising and Public Relations in the Grady College of Journalism and Mass Communication at the University of Georgia. She received her Ph.D. in communications from the University of Illinois. While on the faculty at UGA, she has been a visiting communication researcher at the Centers for Disease Control and Prevention in Atlanta, working on their AIDS public service campaign, and a visiting professor at Lintas in New York.

Karen's research interests include advertising industry issues and health communication. She has published her research in leading academic journals including: *Journal of Advertising, Journal of Advertising Research, Journal of Public Policy and Marketing, Journal of Current Issues and Research in Advertising, Journalism and Mass Communication Quarterly, Journal of Newspaper Research, Journal of Health Care Marketing and Journalism*, and *Mass Communication Educator*. She was the editor of the *1994 Proceedings of the American Academy of Advertising Conference* and she co-authored a textbook supplement, *Media Buying Simulation*.

Prior to joining the Grady College, Karen was a research supervisor and a media planner/buyer at FCB Chicago. Her clients included Kraft, Coors, Sears, Sunbeam, and International Harvester. In 1999, Karen was named the Donald G. Hileman Educator of the Year by the American Advertising Federation's Seventh District for her work with the UGA Ad Club and its AAF campaign competition team.

J. THOMAS RUSSELL

Thomas Russell is Dean Emeritus of the College of Journalism and Mass Communication at the University of Georgia. Tom received his Ph.D. in communications from the University of Illinois and has taught and conducted research in a number of areas of advertising and marketing. He was formerly editor of the *Journal of Advertising*.

In addition to his academic endeavor, Tom has worked as a retail copywriter as well as serving as a partner in his own advertising agency. He also served as a faculty member and lecturer for the Institute of Advanced Advertising Studies sponsored by the American Association of Advertising Agencies.

KLEPPNER'S

17th Edition

Advertising Procedure

PART ONE

The Place of Advertising

CHAPTER 1

Background of Today's Advertising

*T*rade and commerce are core elements in the development of the American cultural experience, and advertising has played an important role in that process. Because advertising carries out the communication role for business, it has often received both criticism and praise disproportionate to its contributions. Nevertheless, it is clear that advertising is part of the cultural and economic fabric of society. It grows in concert with a dynamic and advanced economy. Consequently, the history of advertising in the United States can only be studied within the context of the nation's political, economic, and cultural environment. This chapter traces the relationship between advertising and the circumstances that made it possible, including the development of mass media, a rising middle class, effective transportation, and the growth of mass production in this country. After reading this chapter, you will understand:

chapter objectives

1. the social and economic environment that nurtured advertising in its early years
2. advertising's role in U.S. economic development
3. advertising support of the American media system
4. the fight for ethical and responsible advertising
5. advertising growth during the post–World War II era
6. modern advertising in an era of fragmented audiences and media

The exchange of goods and the need to link buyers and sellers date to prehistoric times. We have evidence of messages offering goods for sale dating to 5000 BC, and some of the earliest cave drawings refer to the makers of primitive objects. Modern advertising began in the United States in the late 1800s; and, during the century that followed, advertising practitioners introduced sophisticated elements such as motivational research to define consumer behavior, media analysis to reach targeted consumers, and creative strategy to enhance selling messages. In order to understand the origins of modern advertising, we must examine the conditions that made it possible.

At the outset, it is necessary to understand that advertising is a communications tool that functions most efficiently in combination with two primary components:

centralized exchange
A system of trade and marketing through specialized intermediaries rather than direct exchange of goods between buyers and producers.

1. **Centralized exchange.** When goods and services moved from a system of decentralized exchange in which buyers and sellers dealt directly with each other to one in which merchants functioned as intermediaries, advertising was needed to make potential consumers aware of the availability of goods.
2. *An economy in which supply surpasses demand.* The primary purpose of advertising is to create demand by introducing new products or suggesting how consumers can solve some problem with existing products. When consumers' problem(s) are obvious (demand) and a particular product is the clear solution to the problem, advertising's role is largely limited to letting buyers know the location and price of goods. However, in an economy with numerous brands fighting for the consumer dollar, advertising must not only inform and persuade potential customers that these products exist but also give consumers reasons to purchase one brand over those of competitors. "Societies of scarcity . . . need not advertise anything. Their people sign up to buy a car, wait three years or more and then gladly take whatever is assigned them. Their people line up to buy bread; they cannot shop among enriched and homogenized and white and pumpernickel and rye."[1]

While centralized exchange and excess supply were necessary ingredients for advertising, a number of other factors came together in the 50 years after the Civil War to create the foundations for this multibillion-dollar industry. The first was the beginning of the fulfillment of democratic ideals. Although eighteenth-century America had far to go before basic rights such as women's suffrage and full citizenship for Americans of African descent were a reality, public education was creating a literate population and interest in the political process created both the need and support for newspapers and magazines.

Second, advertising prospered as the Industrial Revolution swept across the United States during the latter part of the nineteenth century. Not only did mass production allow the efficient manufacturing of goods, but this same technological expertise created the high-speed presses that enabled the publishing of mass circulation magazines and newspapers that carried the advertising that provided the media's financial foundations. Just as important, industrialization created the need for skilled workers who earned higher wages and moved from the farm to urban centers bringing with them the need for information provided by a growing print media.

Mass production efficiencies could only be realized if manufacturers were able to distribute goods beyond a limited geographic area. The introduction of the railroad not only created unity among a formerly divided country but also created a means of national distribution for the products of a growing manufacturing sector. The railroad, combined with instant telegraph communication, connected the country economically and culturally. However, it wasn't until the introduction of national brands that advertising and marketing began to fulfill their promise.

National brands, supported by a coast-to-coast system of railroad distribution and national magazines to advertise them, provided the impetus for a sophisticated advertising and marketing structure based on product differentiation and consumer loyalty to individual brands. Nationally branded goods changed the relationship between buyers and sellers from one of commodity goods to that of a marketing system based on consistent product quality and identification, and they gave manufacturers leverage over retailers that would continue for the next 100 years until the rise of mega-retailers during the 1990s.

The era of national brands and the advertising and distribution systems to sell and market them cannot be underestimated. Although advertising did not create the centralized, efficient system of national marketing, it did provide one of the

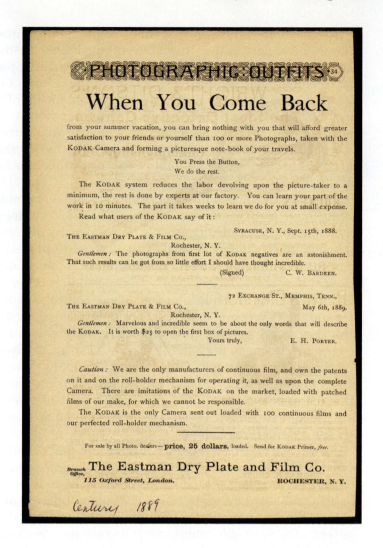

EXHIBIT 1.1

By the late 1880s, modern advertising techniques were evolving.

Courtesy of Eastman Kodak Company. From John W. Hartman Center for Sales, Advertising & Marketing History; Duke University Rare Book, Manuscript, and Special Collections Library; http://scriptorium.lib.duke.edu/eaa/.

primary ingredients to make such a strategy practical. Entrepreneurs rushed to benefit from the advantages of being the first in the marketplace with branded goods. Quaker Oats cereal is generally considered to be the first national marketer, but men such as Daniel Gerber, Dr. William Scholl, Gail Borden, Richard Sears, and Frederick Maytag have all left their legacies through the brands they established. A Kodak camera advertisement (see Exhibit 1.1) published in 1889 demonstrates a sophisticated approach to advertising including testimonials from satisfied customers.

The convergence of the availability of branded products, the ability to provide national distribution, and a growing middle class with the income to provide a market for these products had evolved sufficiently by 1920 to support the creation of an advertising industry that demonstrated many of the basic functions found among modern agencies and corporate advertising departments today.

ADVERTISING'S MODERN ERA: RESEARCH AND RESPONSIBILITY

The two elements missing in most advertising during the early years of the twentieth century were:

1. an ethical framework for creating promotional messages
2. valid and reliable research to measure advertising effects

At first glance, these may seem to be unrelated concerns. However, from a philosophical perspective, they are very much linked. Advertising was part of a rising democratic movement with foundations in Europe's eighteenth-century Age of Enlightenment, during which for the first time, a philosophy was introduced that held that the individual was fully capable of discerning truth from falsehood. In this open marketplace of ideas, falsehoods would be identified and rejected as part of some natural process. In such an environment, there would be little need for regulation of information. Furthermore, research to find underlying consumer motivations would be of scant value in influencing totally "rational" buyers.

However, by the late nineteenth century, public opinion shifted to a position calling for greater consumer protection. The initial battleground centered on the regulation of patent medicines. Not only did many of these concoctions provide no benefit to consumers in need of medical help, but in many cases they actually were harmful. With products containing high levels of alcohol, opium, and cocaine, they created a group of legal drug addicts rather than curing legitimate ailments. There is little question that greater control and regulation of these products and the advertising that promoted them were needed. However, many of the most zealous proponents of advertising regulation were as extreme in their criticism of advertising as the fraudulent advertisers themselves. These critics continued their condemnations of advertising throughout most of the twentieth century. Promoting false fears of the power of techniques such as subliminal advertising and motivational research, a host of advertising commentators demanded that both advertising research and the messages that resulted from it be curtailed or greatly limited.

As we look back on the period, it is obvious that the advertising research of the period held little danger of mind control, subliminal or otherwise, for the average consumer. If anything, most of the early research was almost laughable in its lack of sophistication. For example, "Several agencies boasted of . . . research into consumer attitudes in the late 1920s, but their crude, slapdash methods made these 'surveys' of questionable value in providing accurate feedback. One agency reported that it could obtain quick, inexpensive results . . . by having all members of the staff send questionnaires to their friends."[2]

Despite the rather primitive research methods of the period, a few advertising executives such as Claude Hopkins were conducting direct-mail and coupon-response research in the 1920s to gather information about effective advertising messages. Pond's was among a few enlightened advertisers that were analyzing audience response to advertising (see Exhibit 1.2). However, it would not be until the 1950s that sophisticated advertising research gained widespread acceptance.

BEGINNINGS

The urge to advertise seems to be a part of human nature, evidenced since ancient times. Of the 5,000-year recorded history of advertising right up to the current satellite age, the period that is most significant begins when the United States emerged as a great manufacturing nation about 100 years ago. The early history of advertising, however, is far too fascinating to pass by without a glance.

Perhaps the earliest known evidence of advertising is a Babylonian clay tablet dating to 3000 BC, which bears inscriptions for an ointment dealer, a scribe, and a shoemaker. Papyri exhumed from the ruins of Thebes show that the ancient Egyptians had a better medium on which to write their messages. (Regrettably, the announcements preserved in papyrus offer rewards for the return of runaway

EXHIBIT 1.2

Basic advertising research was introduced by the 1920s.

Courtesy of Unilever. From John W. Hartman Center for Sales, Advertising & Marketing History; Duke University Rare Book, Manuscript, and Special Collections Library; http://scriptorium.lib.duke.edu/eaa/.

slaves.) The Greeks were among those who relied on town criers to chant the arrival of ships with cargoes of wines, spices, and metals. Often a crier was accompanied by a musician who kept him in the right key. Town criers later became the earliest medium for public announcements in many European countries, and they continued to be used for centuries. (At this point, we must digress to tell about a promotion idea used by innkeepers in France around AD 1100 to tout their fine wines: They would have the town crier blow a horn, gather a group, and offer samples!)

Roman merchants, too, had a sense of advertising. The ruins of Pompeii contain signs in stone or terra-cotta, advertising what the shops were selling: a row of hams for a butcher shop, a cow for a dairy, a boot for a shoemaker. The Pompeiians also knew the art of telling their story to the public by means of painted wall signs. These and other forms of outdoor advertising have proved to be some of the most enduring forms of advertising. Outdoor advertising survived the decline of the Roman Empire and became the decorative art of European inns in the seventeenth and eighteenth centuries. That was still an age of widespread illiteracy, so inns vied with one another in creating attractive signs that all could recognize. This explains the distinctive names of old inns, especially in England, such as the Three Squirrels,

EXHIBIT **1.3**
Signs outside
seventeenth-century
inns.

Hog in Armour

Three Squirrels

King's Porter and Dwarf

The Ape

Harrow and Doublet

Barley Mow

Hole in the Wall
"A Guide for Malt Worms"

Bull and Mouth

Man in the Moon

Goose and Gridiron

the Man in the Moon, and the Hole in the Wall (see Exhibit 1.3). In 1614, England passed a law, probably the earliest pertaining to advertising, that prohibited signs from extending more than 8 feet out from a building. (Longer signs pulled down too many house fronts.) Another law required signs to be high enough to give clearance to an armored man on horseback. In 1740, the first printed outdoor poster—referred to as a **hoarding**—appeared in London.

hoarding
First printed outdoor signs—the forerunner of modern outdoor advertising.

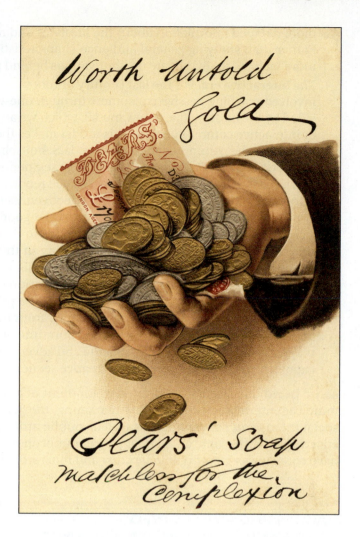

EXHIBIT 1.4
Advertisers begin to offer specific consumer benefits in the early 1900s.

From the on-line databases of the John W. Hartman Center for Sales, Advertising & Marketing History, Duke University. http://library. duke.edu/specialcollections/ hartman/index.html.

We begin our discussion of the foundations of modern advertising by examining its history, which we divide into four broad periods:

1. *The* **premarketing era**. From the start of product exchange in prehistoric times to the middle of the seventeenth century, buyers and sellers communicated in very primitive ways. For most of this period, "media" such as clay tablets, town criers, and tavern signs were the best ways to reach potential prospects for a product or service. Only in the latter decades of the period did primitive printing appear as the forerunner of modern mass media.

2. *The* **mass communication era**. From the 1700s to the early decades of the 1900s, advertisers were increasingly able to reach larger and larger segments of the population. Mass newspapers first appeared in the 1830s, quickly followed by a number of national magazines. By the 1920s, radio had ushered in the broadcast era when advertising was delivered free to virtually every American household. The mass communication era also saw advertisers beginning to differentiate their brands with specific consumer benefits (see Exhibit 1.4).

3. *The* **research era**. Beginning in the 1920s, advertisers used a number of techniques to reach and motivate mass audiences. From the 1990s to the present, reflecting the more personalized nature of media, advertisers have shifted their focus to ever more sophisticated techniques for identifying and reaching narrowly targeted audiences with messages prepared specifically for specific groups or individuals. Early advertising research emphasized general information concerning broad demographic information such as age, sex, and geographic location of consumers. Today, advertising research includes much

premarketing era
The period from prehistoric times to the eighteenth century. During this time, buyers and sellers communicated in very primitive ways.

mass communication era
From the 1700s to the early decades of the last century, advertisers were able to reach large segments of the population through the mass media.

research era
In recent years, advertisers increasingly have been able to identify narrowly defined audience segments through sophisticated research methods.

more detailed information about the lifestyles and motivations of consumers. Rather than studying general audience characteristics, advertising research is more inclined to investigate the motivations behind purchase behavior.

4. *The* **interactive era**. For the last century or more, the typical advertising model involved reaching passive consumers through one-way communications provided by the mass media. A new model, which we are just embarking on, is one of interactive communication. This model makes the consumer an active participant in the communication process. U.S. household Internet usage is close to 80 percent with even formerly low-usage segments such as over-50-year-olds and households with incomes below $30,000 reporting 60 percent access. More important, advertisers are seeing the effectiveness of interactive promotions. For example, mainstream consumer package-goods marketers are diverting significant money from television advertising to the Internet. It was estimated that from 2005 to 2006, Internet advertising in the package-goods category would rise by more than 20 percent to $470 million.[3] The cell phone has also become a significant means of communication, especially for teens (see Exhibit 1.5), and in coming years it will become a primary means of delivering marketing messages. Obviously, the change from media to consumer control and the development of one-to-one communication channels will require major changes by both the mass media and advertisers. We discuss these implications throughout the media and creative sections of the text.

As we begin our discussion of the development of advertising, we must keep in mind the interrelationships among marketing, the general business climate, and social mores and conventions, as well as public attitudes toward advertising. As advertising has become an integral part of our economy, advertising practitioners have come under closer public scrutiny and must work within a complex legal and

EXHIBIT 1.5

From Bradley Johnson, "Connected and Craving: Teens Hungry for Latest Cell Phone Technology," *Advertising Age*, March 20, 2006, pg. 36. Copyright © 2006 Crain Communication Inc. Reprinted with permission.

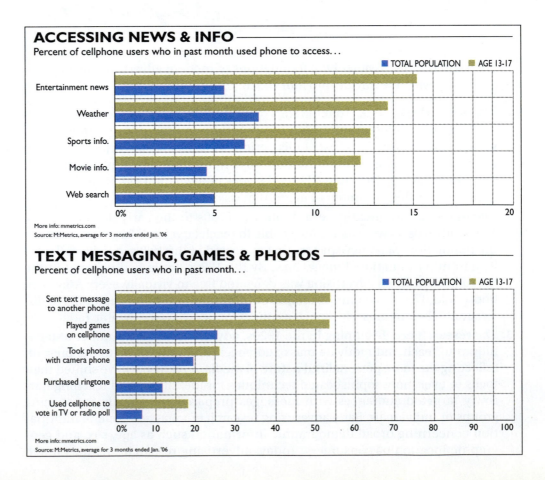

regulatory framework. Perhaps the most important change in the business climate during the last 20 years has been the growing sense of social responsibility within the advertising community. Many advertising practices that were routine a century ago are universally condemned by the industry today. Advertisers realize that public trust is a key to successful advertising. Throughout the remainder of this chapter, we discuss the forces that have shaped contemporary advertising.

THE MOVE TO CREATIVITY IN ADVERTISING

As we discuss in a later section, the original advertising companies were really no more than media space brokers—buying bulk space from newspapers and reselling small space allotments to advertisers. However, significant changes in the economic environment forced both agencies and their clients to emphasize the creative function. The first two decades of the twentieth century were marked by an emphasis on persuading consumers through creative advertising messages. Several factors led to the growing importance of persuasive advertising during the early decades of the century:

1. By 1900, the industrial output of products had reached a point at which serious brand competition was taking place in a number of product categories such as soap and food. Led by major companies such as Procter & Gamble, Kellogg, and H. J. Heinz, the shift from commodity products to branded goods was well established in a number of consumer goods categories. The competition among brands for the first time saw strong promotional offers accompanying product advertising (see Exhibit 1.6), as well as the introduction of emotional appeals.

2. Innovative marketers such as John Wannamaker of Wannamaker Department Store in New York City saw the need to sell products on the basis of style and luxury rather than simple utility. He hired John Powers, considered by many to be the first true copywriter. By the turn of the century, agencies were emphasizing their creative expertise as they moved toward providing full-service advertising to their clients.

3. Advertising was beginning to draw from social science research to determine the most effective means of reaching consumers. In 1921, J. Walter Thompson hired John Watson from Johns Hopkins. Watson, the "father of **behavioral research**," was one of the earliest researchers to study the underlying motivations of consumer purchasing. Even at this early stage, agencies such as Thompson recognized the need to understand the needs and wants of consumers (see Exhibit 1.7).

behavioral research
Market research that attempts to determine the underlying nature of purchase behavior.

4. Building on the work of Watson and others, Alfred Sloan Jr. made General Motors (GM) the preeminent carmaker by surpassing his major rival Henry Ford. Sloan viewed the automobile as a symbol of status, and GM advertising sought to transform Ford's idea of the car as low-cost transportation to one in which consumers were encouraged to trade up to buy the newest tailfins and other cosmetic changes as automobiles introduced model changes from year to year. Sloan is credited with introducing the idea of planned obsolescence in which products would be discarded not because of a loss of utility but because of a loss of status.

By the 1950s, virtually all national companies had accepted the concept that it was the position that a brand held in the mind of consumers more than real product superiority that would determine which firms would be successful. "If sales were not dependent either upon ever lower prices or real technological improvements but on status perceptions, artificial needs and superficial change, then focusing on the brand, rather than individual products, might prove the best way for a marketer to achieve lasting profitability. Products, after all, had life cycles and died. Brands, properly managed, could last forever."[4]

EXHIBIT 1.6

As competition increased, promotion became an important element in advertising.

From the on-line databases of the John W. Hartman Center for Sales, Advertising & Marketing History, Duke University. http://library. duke.edu/specialcollections/ hartman/index.html.

THE DEVELOPMENT OF PRINT MEDIA

Although product availability and compelling selling messages are certainly necessary components for the growth of advertising, neither can be successful without a readily available means of reaching consumers and prospects with information concerning the quality, price, and availability of goods and services. The early history of advertising cannot be separated from the early print media that carried its messages. From our discussion, it will become obvious that the relationship between advertising and the mass media is a symbiotic one with growing media circulations allowing advertisers to reach more and more buyers and increasing advertising dollars enabling the media to prosper in an environment largely free from government and special interest control.

The Newspaper as an Advertising Medium

Newspapers have historically been the primary medium for information and advertising. It has only been in the last century that other communication media have challenged the preeminent position of newspapers. As early as 59 BC, the Romans posted daily government-published news sheets known as *acta diurna*;

and the forerunners of modern want ads were **siquis**, which were notices posted by clergy seeking positions. The name comes from the Latin *si quis* ("if anyone"), which was the way the notices usually began. The name *siquis* continued for many years, although soon these notices covered a variety of subjects, including lost-and-found objects, runaway apprentices, and so on, much in the mode of many modern classified advertisements.[5]

While the Chinese probably developed some form of printing as early as the eighth century AD, it was *Johannes Gutenberg*'s invention of movable type that introduced printing to the West in 1440. Within a decade of Gutenberg's introduction of the printing press, forerunners of the newspaper in the form of pamphlets and broadsides opened the door to more formal publications. The first English newspaper, *The Oxford Gazette*, was published in 1665. The first colonial newspaper, Benjamin Harris's *Publick Occurrences*, was published in Boston in 1690 and was promptly banned by the governor after one issue. The first American newspaper to carry advertising was the *Boston Newsletter*, published in 1704. Soon newspapers were common throughout the colonies, and by 1800 every major city in the United States had several daily or weekly publications.

siquis
Handwritten posters in sixteenth- and seventeenth-century England—forerunners of modern advertising.

penny press
Forerunner of the mass newspaper in the United States that first appeared in the 1830s.

With the introduction of Richard Hoe's rotary press during the 1830s, Benjamin Day's *The New York Sun* ushered in the era of the so-called **penny press**, which provided inexpensive newspapers to the general population. For the first time, both readers and advertisers had extensive access to a mass medium. The Civil War created an unprecedented demand for current news and information, and by the 1880s more than 11,000 newspapers were being published in the United States (compared to approximately 8,000 daily and weekly newspapers today). By 1900, newspapers such as the *New York World* and the *Chicago Tribune* had circulations of more than 500,000. These high-circulation publications were supported by advertisers seeking more and more buyers for their goods. The newspapers of the era established the model for financial support from advertising that continues for the majority of media to the present.

Magazines

The earliest colonial magazines gave little promise that they would grow into a major communication medium. The first magazine in America was published by William Bradford in 1741. Aptly named the *American Magazine*, it lasted all of three issues. Its major competitor, Benjamin Franklin's *General Magazine* started in the same year, died a quiet death after only six issues.

Despite the barriers to financial success for magazines, a number of publications emerged during the latter part of the eighteenth century. By 1800, there were more than 100 magazines serving an educated and wealthy elite with articles and essays on matters of literary, political, or religious interest. Unlike newspapers, magazines were national or regional in scope and, therefore, poor transportation and high cost further prohibited the rapid growth of magazines. Although legislation providing low-cost mailing rates for magazines had passed Congress as early as 1794, it was not until the Postal Act of 1879 that magazines enjoyed significant mail discounts.

Despite the hurdles for magazines, publications such as *Harper's Monthly*, *Atlantic Monthly*, and *Century* were widely read and some, such as *The Saturday Evening Post*, provided content of a more popular nature. However, the editorial and advertising foundations of the modern consumer magazines did not take shape until the latter part of the nineteenth century. Using the business plan developed by Benjamin Day and other publishers of penny newspapers and supporting a populist agenda, many magazines of the day began to speak to the concerns of the American family with articles on health, fashion, and food. In addition, some of the major writers of the time such as Mark Twain and Sir Arthur Conan Doyle were frequent contributors to these magazines. Unlike their newspaper counterparts, these magazines had a national audience with influence beyond the borders of a particular city.

In many respects, the magazine was a unifying means of communication and, serving as a slower version of the telegraph, gave the far-flung country a sense of common purpose after the Civil War. "The magazine was a vehicle which could present simultaneously identical facts, uniformly treated, in every locality. Men and women, North, South, East, and West, could read and judge the same materials, instead of forming their beliefs and reaching their decisions on the basis of varied accounts published in different sections and often distorted by regional prejudice."[6]

By the turn of the century, *Ladies Home Journal* passed a milestone with a circulation of 1 million and other major magazines such as *Munsey's* and *McClure's* had circulations of more than a half million. Many of the major publishers of the day also embarked on campaigns to address the abuses of patent medicine advertising as well as social reforms in industries such as meatpacking and industrial monopolies.

Advertising support for these publications came from manufacturers that were enjoying success with the distribution of national brands such as Quaker Oats and Uneeda Biscuit. It was very common for magazines of the time to carry 100 pages or more of advertising. For manufacturers, magazines provided the only means of reaching buyers throughout the country. Advertising was crucial to the success of most magazines; because subscription prices covered only a small portion of the costs of publishing, advertising was required to make up the revenue shortfall. During the 1920s, high-quality color advertisements were commonplace in most major publications. By 1923, when Henry Luce and Briton Hadden founded *Time*, magazines were the preeminent medium for national advertisers. They offered national circulation, both editorial and advertising credibility, color availability, and an extremely low-cost means of reaching millions of readers.

Mass Production Matures

By the mid-1700s, primitive forms of **mass production** were being introduced into English textile industries. In America, the manufacture of firearms during the Revolutionary War was one of the earliest examples of production using interchangeable parts. By the end of the Civil War, American industry was rapidly adopting many of the techniques of mass production as factories produced an array of goods such as textiles, furniture, and even food. For example, by the 1850s, Gail Borden was selling purified, airtight, sealed milk from his Connecticut plant.

Although the beginnings of mass production in this country were impressive, it was the introduction of the automobile that created the foundations of American industry (see Exhibit 1.8). Innovators such as Henry Leland, who built the first Cadillac; Louis Chevrolet; Albert Champion; Walter Chrysler; and John and Horace Dodge all contributed to the growth of the automotive industry. However, it was Henry Ford and his Model T, selling for less than $600, that put a car within the reach of the ordinary family. The first Model T sold 10,000 cars in 1908; and by 1913, sales passed 250,000. Ford was a visionary who saw that mass production was based on high volume, affordable price, and mass selling through advertising. Throughout the early 1900s, American industry was quick to adapt to the successful formula of Henry Ford.

The move to a manufacturing economy had dramatic effects on politics, culture, and society. The availability of goods created significant improvements in the lifestyle and standard of living of almost every American family. Virtually anyone could afford to own products that would have been available to only the wealthiest classes a few years before. A growing manufacturing sector required more and more consumption to keep factories humming. "To encourage such consumption, the advertising industry grew while rapid improvements in transportation, warehousing, and distribution led to giant department store chains and supermarkets. American society moved from a culture of 'Yankee thrift' to one of extravagant consumerism."[7]

mass production
A manufacturing technique utilizing specialization and interchangeable parts to achieve production efficiencies.

The Advertising Agency

Volney Palmer is generally given credit for starting the first advertising agency in 1841. In reality, he was little more than a space broker, buying bulk newspaper space at a discount and selling it to individual advertisers at a profit. In 1869, George Rowell published *Rowell's American Newspaper Directory*, which provided

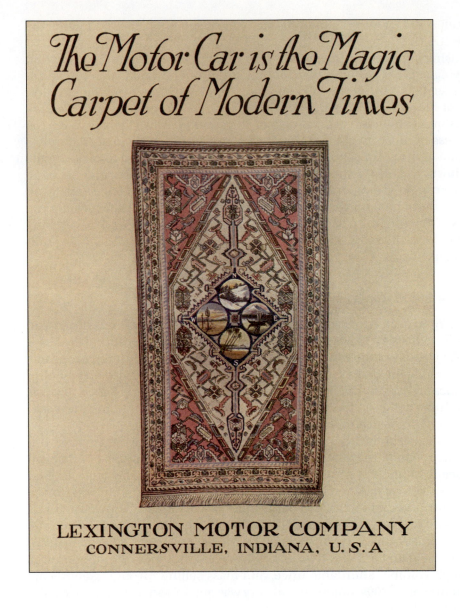

The Motor Car is the Magic Carpet of Modern Times

LEXINGTON MOTOR COMPANY
CONNERSVILLE, INDIANA, U.S.A

newspaper circulation estimates and started the movement toward published rate cards and verified circulation. In the fractured world of media, we are seeing a limited return to the brokerage model. In 2005, Google announced that it would buy bulk pages in a number of magazines and make them available to online customers. The magazine advertisements will then carry a Web address or toll-free phone number that will allow both a comprehensive relationship with customers and a means of tracking response unavailable in print advertisements alone.[8] More recently, a number of companies have announced plans to introduce online buying opportunities for broadcast media.

By the end of the nineteenth century, major agencies such as J. Walter Thompson, N. W. Ayer & Sons, and Batten and Company (the forerunner of BBDO) were providing creative services, media placement, and basic research and developing the functions of the full-service agencies of the future. In 1917, the **American Association of Advertising Agencies (AAAA, 4As)** was founded with 111 charter members. Today, the 4As has more than 500 member agencies that place approximately 75 percent of all advertising dollars. By the 1930s, agencies such as McCann-Erickson and J. Walter Thompson had established overseas

American Association of Advertising Agencies (AAAA, 4As)
The national organization of advertising agencies.

offices to begin the movement to global advertising. Marion Harper, a legendary advertising innovator, founded the Interpublic Group in 1954, which sought to provide a holding company for separate agencies that could then serve competing accounts. By 1960, Interpublic not only controlled a number of agencies but also owned subsidiaries that conducted research, provided television production, and handled the public relations needs of clients. At the time, *Advertising Age* wrote that Harper's plan "may be a wholly new tactic for the agency business."[9] Certainly, Interpublic represented the first formal move to integrated marketing by a major advertising company. We devote Chapter 5 to the role of the contemporary advertising agency.

AMERICA ENTERS THE TWENTIETH CENTURY

The changes in American industry, advertising, and society during the nineteenth century were remarkable by any standard. In that short 100 years, the country saw a movement to urbanization, the abolition of the blight of slavery, railroads and instantaneous communication spanning the continent, and the emergence of the United States as a world power. However, as impressive as these changes were, they were only a harbinger of greater developments to come. In 1900, 60 percent of Americans resided on farms, including 2,000 within New York City. In 1895, the city had perhaps 300 automobiles—a figure that grew to 78,000 by 1905.[10] Neither American society nor business would ever be the same.

However, all the changes during the period were not positive. In the decades after the Civil War, a business atmosphere emerged that reflected laissez-faire policies in the extreme. The administration of Ulysses S. Grant (1869–1877) is still considered one of the most corrupt in American history. By the dawn of the twentieth century, the excesses of big business and the advertising that contributed to the environment of immorality reached a stage where both the public and Congress demanded stricter regulation of advertising and other business practices.

The Pure Food and Drug Act (1906)

Concerns about public safety in the food supply date to colonial times. However, it wasn't until after the Civil War that serious efforts were mounted for national legislation to protect consumers. As Americans moved from farms to cities, for the first time a majority of people were dependent on others for their food. While mass production was bringing a host of economically priced products to American consumers, many food and drug products were notably lacking in purity and often placed the health of consumers in jeopardy.

Furthermore, the advertising claims for these products were often outrageous (see Exhibit 1.9). A number of media had taken up the challenge of exposing the problem. Some, such as the *New York Herald Tribune* and the *Ladies Home Journal*, restricted or completely banned medical advertising. The primary catalyst for reform is often credited to *Colliers* magazine, which in 1905 published a ten-part investigative report of the patent medicine industry entitled "The Great American Fraud." These media were joined by industry leaders such as H. J. Heinz who made food safety a primary attribute of all his products. He was among the first to sell products in clear glass jars to demonstrate to buyers that they were buying untainted food. By 1906, public opinion had reached the point that Congress moved to protect public health with passage of the **Pure Food and Drug Act**. President Theodore Roosevelt signed the Act on June 30, 1906.

Pure Food and Drug Act
Passed in 1906 by legislation, it was one of the earliest attempts by the federal government to protect consumers.

Although the 1906 Act did much to protect the public health, it failed to address a number of important issues. For example, product content information on labels had to be truthful, but there was no requirement that such labels had to be used. In addition, false claims for patent medicines were outlawed, but enforcement required that the government had to prove that the manufacturer intended to swindle buyers. In other words, if defendants asserted that they believed the claims, no matter how absurd, there was little the government could do. In addition, apathetic enforcement and minor penalties for breach of Food and Drug Administration (FDA) regulations did little to control the problem. For example, Robert Harper, maker of a headache remedy called Cuforhedak Brane-Fude, was the first person cited under the Act for instilling his product with caffeine and abundant amounts of alcohol—hardly a wise headache remedy. After a 16-day trial, he was found guilty and fined $700 despite having made some $2 million on the sale of the product.[11]

The modern era of food and drug enforcement began with passage of the Federal Food, Drug, and Cosmetic Act, which was signed by President Franklin Roosevelt on June 25, 1938. Among the several provisions of the 1938 Act, drug manufacturers were required to provide scientific proof of new product safety and proof of fraud was no longer required to stop false claims for drugs. Since that time, a number of amendments including those dealing with pesticide, food additives, and color additives have continued to strengthen the role of the FDA in production and labeling of food, drug, and cosmetic products.[12]

The Federal Trade Commission Act (1914)

The original mandate of the **Federal Trade Commission (FTC)** was to protect one business owner from the unscrupulous practices of another. In 1914, when the Federal Trade Commission Act was passed, Congress and the public were increasingly alarmed over antitrust violations by big business. It was clear by the early 1900s that the antitrust actions of John D. Rockefeller and other business titans would soon drive their smaller competitors into bankruptcy and create monopolies in vital industries such as oil and steel. Basically, the law said that unfair business-to-business practices were now illegal and would no longer be tolerated.

In 1938, the Wheeler-Lea Act extended the FTC's original mission to offer protection to consumers as well as businesses. By combining both business and consumer protection activities, the FTC "seeks to ensure that the nation's markets function competitively, and are vigorous, efficient, and free of undue restrictions. The Commission also works to enhance the smooth operation of the marketplace by eliminating acts or practices that are unfair or deceptive."[13] Today, the FTC is the primary federal enforcement agency to ensure that advertising claims and sales practices meet reasonable standards for honesty and truthfulness.

In Chapter 24, we discuss in detail not only the role of the FTC but also other regulatory and legal bodies that are concerned with truthful advertising. In addition, the advertising industry's self-regulatory mechanisms are examined and a number of criticisms of advertising's social effects are addressed.

Federal Trade Commission (FTC)
The agency of the federal government empowered to prevent unfair competition and to prevent fraudulent, misleading, or deceptive advertising in interstate commerce.

ADVERTISING COMES OF AGE

By 1900, both the public and legislators were increasingly concerned about unscrupulous businesses and the deceptive advertising they used to take advantage of consumers. It was during this time that a number of advertising executives recognized the need for the industry to do more to ensure honest advertising and to regain consumer confidence lost due to decades of fraudulent claims and inferior products. They gathered with like-minded peers in their communities to form advertising clubs to support truthful advertising.

These clubs subsequently became the Associated Advertising Clubs of the World (now the American Advertising Federation). In 1911, they launched a campaign to promote truth in advertising. In 1916, they formed vigilance committees that developed into today's **Council of Better Business Bureaus**, which continues to deal with many problems of unfair and deceptive business practices. In 1971, the bureaus became part of the National Advertising Review Council, an all-industry effort at curbing misleading advertising. The main constituency of the American Advertising Federation continues to be the local advertising clubs. On its board are officers of the other advertising associations.

In 1910, the Association of National Advertising Managers was born. It is now known as the Association of National Advertisers (ANA) and has about 500 members,

Council of Better Business Bureaus
National organization that coordinates a number of local and national initiatives to protect consumers.

including most major national advertisers. Its purpose is to improve the effectiveness of advertising from the viewpoint of the advertiser. In 1917, the American Association of Advertising Agencies was formed to improve the effectiveness of advertising and the advertising agency operation. More than 75 percent of all national advertising is currently placed by its members, both large and small.

In 1911, *Printers' Ink*, the leading advertising trade paper of the day, prepared a model statute for state regulation of advertising, designed to "punish untrue, deceptive or misleading advertising." The ***Printers' Ink* Model Statute** has been adopted in its original or modified form by a number of states, where it is still operative.

Up to 1914, many publishers routinely exaggerated their circulation claims. In the absence of reliable figures, advertisers had no way of verifying what they got for their money. However, in that year, a group of advertisers, agencies, and publishers established an independent auditing organization, the **Audit Bureau of Circulations (ABC)**, which conducts its own audits and issues its own reports of circulation. Most major publications belong to the ABC, and an ABC circulation statement is highly regarded in media circles. As advertising has become international, similar auditing organizations are operating throughout the world. In June 1916, President Woodrow Wilson, addressing the Associated Advertising Clubs of the World convention in Philadelphia, was the first president to give public recognition to the importance of advertising. Advertising had come of age!

***Printers' Ink* Model Statute (1911)**
The Act directed at fraudulent advertising, prepared and sponsored by *Printers' Ink*, which was the pioneer advertising magazine.

Audit Bureau of Circulations (ABC)
The organization sponsored by publishers, agencies, and advertisers for securing accurate circulation statements.

Advertising in World War I

When the United States entered World War I, advertising was called upon to support the war effort across a broad spectrum of initiatives. Advertising agencies turned from selling consumer goods to arousing patriotic sentiment, selling government bonds, encouraging conservation, and promoting a number of other war-related activities. One of the largest agencies of the era, N. W. Ayer & Sons, prepared and placed advertisements for the first three Liberty Loan drives and donated much of its commission to the effort.[14] The success of these initiatives demonstrated that advertising could be used effectively to sell products or as an instrument of direct social action. By the end of the war, these efforts by individual agencies were coordinated by the Division of Advertising of the Committee of Public Information, a World War I government propaganda office.

The 1920s

Throughout most of the 1920s, America experienced enormous economic growth fueled by postwar euphoria and unprecedented business expansion. When World War I drew to an end, manufacturers of war goods turned to the task of meeting unfulfilled consumer demand built up during the war. A newly created highway system fueled the need for personal automobiles, and demand for commercial trucks skyrocketed as overland transportation became an effective means of product distribution. Firestone spent $2 million promoting the generic "Ship by Truck" campaign. With truck manufacturers profiting by the good roads that had been built, production jumped from 92,000 trucks in 1916 to 322,000 in 1920. Door-to-door delivery from manufacturer to retailer spurred the growth of chain stores, which led, in turn, to supermarkets and self-service stores. Transportation was only one of the multitude of product categories that boomed during this period. New products appeared in profusion: electric refrigerators, electric washing machines, electric shavers, and—most incredible of all—the radio. Installment selling made hard goods available to all. And all the products needed advertising. Unfortunately, the good times of the 1920s would come to a sudden halt with the devastation of a worldwide depression.

Radio was among the very few industries that actually grew during the Depression. Radio was invented by Guglielmo Marconi in 1895 as the first practical system of wireless communication. In the early years, radio was viewed as a means of maritime communication using Morse code and, with the first voice transmission in 1906, as a diversion for hobbyists. Prior to 1920, few investors saw any commercial potential for the medium. KDKA, the first commercial station, was established in Pittsburgh by Westinghouse Corporation to provide programming to buyers of its radio sets.

The modern era of radio can be traced to the broadcast of the Harding-Cox presidential election results in 1920. Soon radio was broadcasting sporting events such as the 1921 heavyweight title fight between Jack Dempsey and Georges Carpentier and various local entertainment shows.[15] By 1922, there were more than 500 licensed stations on the air, but fewer than 2 million homes owned radio sets and the medium was still in the novelty stage (see Exhibit 1.10).

EXHIBIT **1.10**

In the 1920s, radio ushered in a new form of mass communication and advertising.

From John W. Hartman Center for Sales, Advertising & Marketing History; Duke University Rare Book, Manuscript, and Special Collections Library; http://scriptorium.lib. duke.edu/eaa/.

By the mid-1920s, the emphasis was shifting away from local radio to networks where several stations could simultaneously broadcast programs. In 1926, the Radio Corporation of America (RCA) established two NBC networks with twenty-four stations; and a year later, William Paley founded CBS with sixteen stations.

Unlike most advertising media of the period, radio advertising revenues demonstrated healthy growth rising from $18.7 million in 1929 to more than $80 million by 1939.[16] Likewise, as the cost of radio sets became more affordable and listeners sought radio's free entertainment in a period of economic hardship, set ownership increased from 12 million households in 1930 to more than 28 million in 1939.[17] Regular programming featuring news, drama, and comedy was becoming standard at both the local and network levels. Radio came under government regulation with formation of the Federal Communication Commission (FCC) in 1934. By 1939, there were 1,464 stations in the United States; and by the end of World War II, 95 percent of households owned at least one radio.[18] Today, Americans average more than five radio sets per household and it is difficult to find an automobile or workplace without a radio. From its noncommercial beginnings, radio advertisers now spend approximately $18 billion annually.

The Great Depression of the 1930s

The rapid growth of advertising was temporarily slowed by the Great Depression, beginning with the stock market crash of 1929 and continuing through much of the 1930s. The crash had a shattering effect on our entire economy: Millions of people were thrown out of work; business failures were widespread; banks were closing all over the country. Breadlines and high unemployment eventually moved the government to establish the Works Progress Administration (WPA) to put people to work on public service projects. However, even this extraordinary step offered only partial relief to a country in crisis.

Some of the major causes for the Depression, that is, excess industrial capacity, heavy consumer debt, and declining price levels, combined to discourage consumer spending and manufacturing output with a resulting negative impact on advertising. With few exceptions, the Depression was a time of catastrophe for advertising, businesses, and society in general. With the start of World War II, the economy recovered. However, wartime restrictions on consumer goods would not permit a rejuvenation of advertising until after the war.

Advertising During World War II

World War II saw a replay of the practices of World War I, only played on a larger scale and with even greater homeland sacrifices. As consumer goods turned to war goods, virtually all civilian material was rationed or in short supply. Although there were limited sales of household goods, many companies continued to advertise to keep their brand names before the public as they looked to a future of peacetime normalcy. Most advertising, even messages promoting specific brands, was created to encourage Americans to cooperate in the war effort through conservation and volunteerism.

However, the government needed the public to do more than simply adhere to the letter of rationing regulations. "Food, clothing and a variety of essential items were to be used wisely. Avoiding purchasing items through a black market and acting in the interest of the greater community were strongly encouraged, both to hold down inflation and to ensure that scarce items would be available for

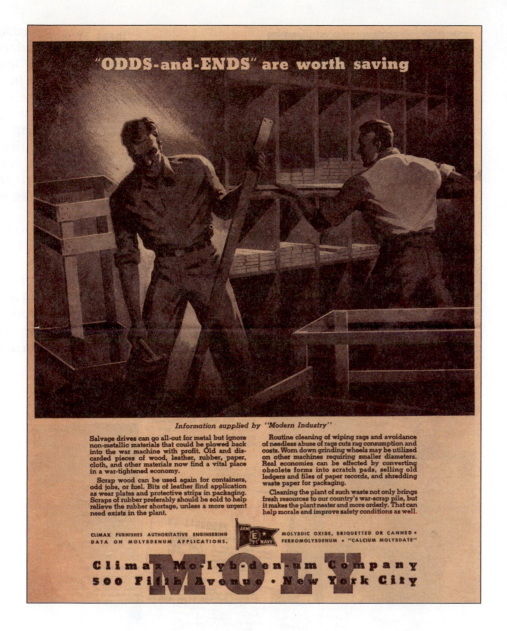

everyone."[19] The majority of these advertising messages were sponsored by the government, but many private companies also joined in helping disseminate similar information (see Exhibit 1.11).

THE WAR ADVERTISING COUNCIL

In November 1941, at a meeting of advertising executives, James Webb Young of the J. Walter Thompson advertising agency suggested the idea that ". . . a greater use of advertising for social, political and philanthropic purposes will help immeasurably to remove the distaste for advertising that now exists."[20] With the Japanese attack on Pearl Harbor 3 weeks later, the advertising industry began this mission with the beginning of World War II.

War Advertising Council
Founded in 1942 to promote World War II mobilization, it later evolved into the Advertising Council.

Advertising Council
A nonprofit network of agencies, media, and advertisers dedicated to promoting social programs through advertising.

With the support and cooperation of the government, the **War Advertising Council** was formed in 1942. The first campaign from the Council was developed by J. Walter Thompson to encourage women to enter the workforce. The "Rosie the Riveter" campaign successfully overcame prejudices toward women in the workforce and added significantly to a labor pool depleted by wartime service. Among the many themes and projects promoted by the Council were conservation of items such as fuel, fat, and tires; planting victory gardens; buying war bonds; promoting rationing; encouraging communications from home to our troops; and reminding Americans not to reveal sensitive information. With the cooperation of advertising and media, the Council was able to place advertisements encouraging the initiatives that covered virtually every aspect of the war effort (see Exhibit 1.12).

Advertising's success during the war moved President Franklin Roosevelt to urge peacetime continuance of the organization as the **Advertising Council**. Today, the Council annually produces more than thirty-five campaigns ranging from environmental issues to educational concerns, family preservation, and antidrinking promotions. Each year member advertising agencies create campaigns on a pro bono basis and media outlets donate more than $1 billion in time and space for Council messages. During the last 25 years, Council campaigns have been instrumental in addressing crucial issues to Americans. In doing so, it has created a num-

EXHIBIT 1.12

The War Advertising Council supported numerous efforts to bring the war to a close.

From John W. Hartman Center for Sales, Advertising & Marketing History; Duke University Rare Book, Manuscript, and Special Collections Library; http://scriptorium.lib.duke.edu/adaccess.

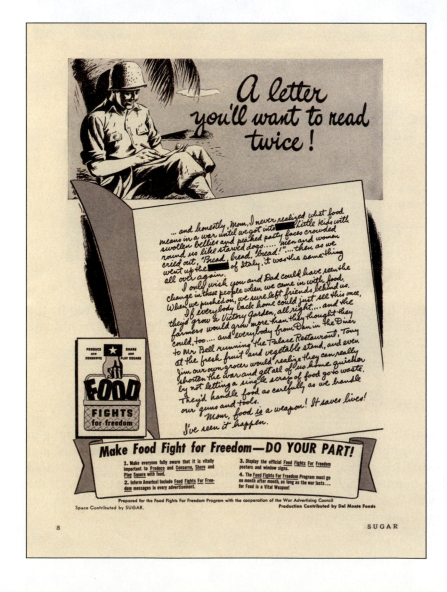

ber of slogans and characters that have become advertising icons such as Smokey the Bear and McGruff the Crime Dog.

Advertising After World War II to 1975: The Word Was Growth

On August 15, 1945, the Allied powers declared victory over Japan and ushered in a period of extraordinary economic prosperity. Advertising, like every aspect of American society, had taken a backseat to the war during the early 1940s. With the end of World War II, advertising and consumer goods makers began to reach out to a public ready to get on with their lives and spend, spend, spend. With "the end of the war pent-up demand led to an unprecedented acceleration in the rate of growth of advertising media investment—so much so that ad media volume by 1950 was almost three times what it had been only ten years earlier!"[21] By 1950, Americans were living better than at any time in their history. Moreover, it is doubtful that any nation had ever experienced the same rate of economic expansion as the United States did during the decade after World War II. Consumer goods purchases grew at an unprecedented rate, and advertising was the fuel that fed this consumer buying spree.

During the first years after the war, pent-up demand provided sales for virtually any product offered to consumers. However, by the mid-1950s, consumers had met most of their basic needs and now had to be persuaded to buy products that were more wants than necessities. Advertisers were called upon to encourage consumers to replace products that still had utility with the latest tailfin or new color. Companies were contantly seeking to differentiate their products from competing brands with concepts such as the "unique selling proposition."

The introduction of television coincided with this surge in marketing. From its novelty status in the late 1940s, television reached 90 percent of households by 1960. Equally impressive was its growth as an advertising medium. In 1951, advertisers invested $128 million dollars in television. In just 4 years, the figure rose to more than $1 billion.[22] Television changed not only advertising and marketing but society as a whole as millions of viewers gave up playing bridge, going to the movies, and even talking to each other to tune in to Milton Berle and *The $64,000 Question*.

Perhaps the most significant influence of television was on sports and politics. In its insatiable appetite for programming, television brought thousands of hours of sports into the living room. It was the lure of television dollars that created the American Football League and the American Basketball Association, and it allowed even mediocre players to become millionaires. But perhaps television had its greatest impact on politics during the 1950s. As television's popularity continued to grow, it soon became apparent to politicians that the same formula used so successfully in selling soap and cigarettes might be adapted to selling candidates. Rosser Reeves is generally credited with introducing the 60-second commercial to American politics during the 1960 presidential campaign of Dwight Eisenhower. In a series of commercials, Reeves converted the reserved, rather stiff and awkward candidate into the personable "Man from Abilene." For better or worse, politics would never be the same again.

The Figures Also Said Growth Between 1950 and 1973, the U.S. population increased by 38 percent, while disposable personal income increased by 327 percent. New housing starts went up by 47 percent, energy consumption by 121 percent, college enrollments by 136 percent, automobile registrations by 151 percent, telephones in use by 221 percent, number of outboard motors sold by 242 percent, retail sales by 250 percent, families owning two or more cars by 300 percent, frozen-food production by 655 percent, number of airline passengers by 963 percent, homes with dishwashers by 1,043 percent, and homes with room air conditioners by 3,662 percent.

EXHIBIT 1.13

Humor became a vital part of many advertising compaigns.

From © Unilever, Inc. Used with permission. Image provided by John W. Hartman Center for Sales, Advertising & Marketing History; Duke University Rare Book, Manuscript, and Special Collections Library. http://library.duke.edu/specialcollections/hartman/index.html.

Advertising not only contributed to the growth but also was part of it, rising from an expenditure of $5,780 million in 1950 to $28,320 million in 1975—a growth of 490 percent. There were many developments in advertising during this time:

- In 1956, the Department of Justice ruled that advertising agencies could negotiate fees with clients rather than adhere to the 15 percent commission that had been required on all media placed. This encouraged the growth of specialized companies, such as independent media-buying services, creative-only agencies, and in-house agencies owned by advertisers.

- Creativity, including humor, became a hallmark of advertising during the period (see Exhibit 1.13).

- The consumer movement spurred Congress to limit advertising. Legislation limited outdoor advertising along interstate highways and banned cigarette advertising from television.

- The FTC introduced corrective advertising demanding greater accountability for those companies which had made false or misleading claims. Comparison advertising (mentioning competitors by name) was deemed an acceptable form of advertising.

- The magazine-publishing world saw the disappearance of the old dinosaurs—*The Saturday Evening Post*, *Collier's*, and *Women's Home Companion*. There was no vacuum at the newsstand, however, for there was an immediate upsurge in magazines devoted to special interests.

■ Newspapers felt the effect of the shift of metropolitan populations to the suburbs. Freestanding inserts became an important part of newspaper billings.

■ Radio took a dive when television came along. The story of how it came out of that drastic decline is a good example of turning disadvantages into advantages.

■ Direct-response advertising soared from $900 million in 1950 to $8 billion in 1980, reflecting the growth of direct marketing.

■ The two biggest developments to emerge were television and electronic data processing. Television changed life in America as well as in the world of advertising. Data-processing systems brought management a wealth of organized information. This information explosion, together with syndicated research services, revolutionized the entire marketing process and the advertising-media operation.

Advertising in the Fragmented 1980s

As we have seen in this chapter, advertising is a volatile business. It must constantly adapt to changes in economic conditions, technology, and the social and cultural environment. In some cases, it has a role in causing these changes; in others, it simply follows. The decade of the 1980s was a period of significant transformations in American society, and certainly advertising was affected by many of these changes.

Let's briefly discuss some of the major developments during this period:

1. *New technology.* Changes in technology and diversification of the communication system had profound effects on advertising during this period. Cable television, home video recorders, a proliferation of specialized magazines, the success of direct mail and home shopping techniques, and the growth of sales promotion changed the practice of advertising in fundamental ways. The advertising practitioners of today are much more likely than their predecessors to be marketing generalists, competent in evaluating research and understanding the psychology of consumer behavior as well as executing advertising.

2. **Audience fragmentation**. The 1980s was a watershed decade for many changes in marketing and advertising. Of greatest significance, it marked the beginning of the end of the traditional mass market strategies that had dominated American business for almost a century. Advertisers began to identify customers more as individuals rather than by households or homogeneous groups. The period set the stage for technological, research, and creative options that characterize contemporary advertising; and the move from mass to individualized media had its genesis in this period. While the diverse universe of cell phones, computers, digital video recorders, iPods, and Blackberrys was still some years away, the foundation of a system of shared control of media content and the flow of information, entertainment, and advertising was starting to be set in place.

3. *Consolidation.* Paradoxically, as media and audiences proliferated, ownership of brands, advertising agencies, and media were consolidated among a few giant companies. Firms such as Procter & Gamble (now even bigger with the acquisition of Gillette), American Home Products, and PepsiCo provided corporate umbrellas for dozens, even hundreds, of separate brands. With their billion-dollar-plus budgets, they exercised significant leverage over the total advertising enterprise including the advertising agencies vying for their accounts and the media carrying their messages.

audience fragmentation
The segmenting of mass-media audiences into smaller groups because of diversity of media outlets.

Like their clients, advertising agencies also merged into so-called mega-agencies or holding companies designed to offer greater service to these giant conglomerates, usually on a global basis. Often as not, these agency mergers led to as many headaches as benefits, starting with awkward client conflicts. Like both corporations and agencies, media increasingly came under the control of fewer and fewer communication companies. The establishment of the Turner cable empire; Time Warner's ownership of a bewildering array of print, broadcast, and media production outlets; and Gannett's interest in everything from newspapers to the outdoors were only a few examples of the changing media landscape during the 1980s.

4. *Credit.* Perhaps the greatest long-term legacy of the 1980s was the "buy now, pay later" mentality that pervaded every facet of American life from the federal government to the individual household budget. The leveraged buyouts of corporate America and the overuse of consumer credit created an atmosphere in which living within one's income was an illusion. By the late 1990s, when companies and consumers began the slow process of paying for the excesses of the past decade, advertising was often the first victim of any cutbacks. Media saw advertising revenues fall; advertising was harder to sell even with deep discounts; merchants began to deal with a reluctant consumer more interested in deals than fancy advertising; and some of the most famous names in American business faced serious trouble, if not outright bankruptcy.

America Becomes a Service Economy

Earlier in the chapter, we discussed the numerous changes in nineteenth-century American society that transformed the country from the Jeffersonian ideal of a rural nation to an urbanized country where manufacturing ran the economic engine.[23] During the last 50 years, another equally momentous conversion of the American economy has taken place. A nation, once respected around the world for its technical and production expertise, has been transformed into one focused on the providing of services. This conversion was underscored in 2001 when Wal-Mart became the largest company in the United States, for a time replacing General Motors and Exxon Mobil for the top spot. It was the first time in history that a service company held the number-one position.

While Wal-Mart, barely 40 years old, is a phenomenon by any standard, the movement to a service-oriented society is a long time trend. As recently as 1955, the Fortune 500 was dominated by companies such as Western Electric, Corn Products Refining, U.S. Plywood, and Shoe Corporation of America. As household income increased, the percentage spent on basics declined and there were greater opportunities to indulge in travel, movies, and more expensive houses. Today, manufacturing, with a significantly smaller workforce, accounts for the same dollar share of the economy as it did in 1955. Technology and production efficiency have allowed manufacturers to replace marginal workers and marginal operations. In their place is a sophisticated workforce of engineers and computer specialists with more and more functions being outsourced abroad.

As Harvard economist Claudia Goldin points out, the twentieth-century move to a service economy is the continuation of a process that began in the 1800s when numerous small-town mills and slaughterhouses were replaced by men such as Pillsbury, Armour, and Swift whose large operations soon made these small operations obsolete.[24] Wal-Mart did the same to many mom-and-pop stores. In fact, manufacturing's share of employment peaked in 1953 when 35 percent of the workforce was employed in producing goods. Over the last five decades, the industrial share of workers has steadily declined. The U.S. Bureau of Labor Statistics predicts that by 2010, service employment will outpace manufacturing by a five-to-one margin.

Advertising and the Twenty-First Century

The 2000s have been marked by two significant developments in marketing and advertising:

1. *Defining and utilizing the new technology to reach prospects.* Advertisers are working in a marketing environment vastly different from that of only a decade ago. Technology has created a consumer empowered with interactive, two-way communication devices that allow them to determine when, where, and if they will invite advertisers to deliver their message. This era of *permission marketing* is requiring companies to rewrite the old rules of marketing and fundamentally redefine exactly what constitutes advertising.

   One example of this new media landscape is so-called "third screen" or mobile advertising. Many marketers view the cell phone as a unique means of connecting with niche prospects through text messaging, music, and videos. Although mobile marketing is still in its beginning stages, a number of major advertisers are already finding success with the opportunities afforded by the technique. Brands such as Coca-Cola, McDonald's, Nestle, and Kraft are developing techniques to involve the mobile audiences with games, music downloads, free ring tones and a variety of other promotions.[25] While the specific promotions demonstrate a wide variety of uses, they have a number of elements in common. First, they offer a creative message that relates to the interests of specific audiences—particularly teens and young adults. Second, they realize that audience involvement is the key to their success so they function as participatory communications—that is, talking with consumers rather than talking at them.

2. *Related to the changes in how we reach prospects is the related problem of measuring the value of investing in various communication channels.* Since the beginning of mass advertising in the late 1980s, measuring the return on investment (ROI) of advertising dollars has been a major problem. The prevailing media measurement technique during the last century has been the delivery of audience—that is, broadcast ratings and print media circulation. Advertisers knew that these metrics were rough estimates at best. However, given the limited media outlets during most of that period, audience delivery seemed the best and most economical means of comparing competing advertising vehicles.

   As we entered the twenty-first century, advertisers knew that a system that worked marginally during a period of limited media was woefully inadequate in this era of expanded communication opportunities. "Continued media fragmentation and consumers' increased control over how, when and where they receive ad messages caused advertisers to look for new avenues. Strategies included product integration . . . viral marketing and contextual Internet advertising, out-of-home media, and co-branding and branded entertainment."[26]

The transition from mass to class media saw huge increases in costs to reach customers. For example, in 1994, it cost $7.64 to reach 1,000 households with a prime-time television commercial. In 2004, it cost $19.85 to reach an equivalent number of households. During the last decade, the television audience has declined approximately 2 percent annually. At the same time, computer usage and broadband household penetration has increased dramatically since 2000. However, new media audiences tend to be individualized and expensive to reach. Consequently, audience measures based on media delivery (as contrasted to some minimum communication) make these new communication vehicles appear prohibitively expensive compared to traditional "old media."

Perhaps the most apparent aspect of the transition from old to new media will be a change in advertisers' mindset concerning audience measurement. It is a given that reaching individual consumers will continue to be more expensive. However, while they are resigned to accepting a higher expense ratio, advertisers are demanding that media offer evidence concerning audience engagement and outcomes of advertising. Simply counting eyeballs tuned to a network program or purchasers of a magazine or newspaper is no longer adequate to prove the value and efficiency of a company's advertising investment. A number of companies are developing media research models to measure audience involvement, attention, and/or media loyalty as an alternative to audience delivery.

Communication media are in a period of rapid transition. However, while the old media are clearly in decline, a fully implemented new order is some years off. Regardless of what the future holds, both advertisers and media know that content is king. As one media executive pointed out, "The key for us is to be able to come up with that unique, signature, compelling content for the Internet, the way television has been able to do over the years."[27] Bob Garfield, *Advertising Age* columnist, has coined the term "The Chaos Scenario" to refer to the current period of media transition. It will be interesting in coming years to see if media, advertising agencies, and clients can bring order to this chaos.

At one time, most observers viewed media consolidation and content convergence as a movement that would typify the current century. The proponents of convergence predicted great advantages for huge companies blending technologies such as television, cable, and the computer to create Internet interactivity with the technical speed of cable and the sight, sound, and motion of television. According to its proponents, convergence was going to offer advertisers the ability to reach audiences on a one-to-one basis with individualized commercial messages tailored specifically for their needs.

In recent years, many of the mega media companies are finding that some of the benefits of these consolidations were more illusion than reality. Clearly, the consolidation of media is a reality. Over the last 20 years, fostered by liberalized laws and regulations that allow almost unlimited ownership of broadcast stations, more and more media are owned by fewer and fewer corporations. Companies such as General Electric (NBC, Telemundo, Universal Pictures, and approximately thirty television stations), Disney (ESPN cable networks, online services and ESPN the Magazine, ABC, Disney Channel), Time Warner (AOL, CNN, local cable systems, and more than 150 magazines) increasingly brought numerous media outlets under their control. However, many of the optimistic predictions of greater profitability and efficiencies of cross-media advertising have not come to fruition or have not created profit centers for the parent companies. In many cases, overlapping media ownership has created competitive problems rather than cooperation among units. Companies have found that managing divisions that have historically been in competition with each other and that have very different corporate cultures can be difficult. For example, how do top executives of these mega-corporations deal with the problem of their recording divisions being at odds with their online counterparts over downloading music from the Web? Or how do they corporately reconcile between their program production studios negotiating fees with their own cable and network entities with one trying to maximize program fees and the other negotiating the lowest possible costs?

There will be no return to a model of media ownership characterized by relatively small companies each owning a few newspapers, magazines, or broadcast stations. However, we are seeing a recognition that media companies may be best served by concentrating in specific areas of expertise rather than trying to manage communication outlets with little in common in terms of audiences, content, or advertising. For example, in January 2006, Viacom formally split into two companies—CBS Corporation, which will control the network, radio, and outdoor units, and Viacom, which owns a number of cable networks such as MTV, Nickelodeon, TV Land, and Comedy Central, as well as movie production through Paramount. Likewise, Time Warner has begun to view each of its units (e.g., cable channels TNT and TBS, AOL, its magazine group including *Time* and *Sports Illustrated*) as separate profit centers rather than emphasizing corporatewide synergy. Other media conglomerates such as News Corp and Disney also are rumored to be exploring various types of unit independence or spinoffs.

Another aspect of advertising in the twenty-first century will be a return to strong branding with companies searching for means to differentiate their products and a move away from price competition and generic selling. For those products that can successfully build their brand images, they will enjoy the luxury of fewer price-based promotions. With consumers increasingly in control of the communication channel, companies will find that strong brands are more important than ever. After all, we don't invite strangers into our house; and likewise, unknown brands will find it difficult to get an invitation in a consumer-controlled environment. It will be harder for companies to develop new markets by sheer weight of advertising, and we will probably see more brand extensions in the future to take advantage of established brand names. On the other hand, smaller companies with superior products may find that customized communication may make entry to the market possible at a lower cost than they might pay using traditional mass-media outlets.

Finally, marketing in this century will be a period of globalization and diversity. One only has to look at the population projections for Latin America, the Far East, and Africa to see the potential for sales of virtually any goods but particularly consumer products. The smallest increase in the market share of Coca-Cola, Tide detergent, Huggies diapers, Gerber Baby Food, or Charmin toilet tissue in India or China would create a profit windfall for these brands.

Understanding the language, culture, economy, and political environment of countries throughout the world is already a prerequisite for most marketing executives. It will become even more important as new areas of the globe are opened to foreign investment. Multinational marketers will find that a locally oriented strategy for global marketing is essential. Corporations such as Coca-Cola, Sony, Ford, and Procter & Gamble will continue to increase their expansion into every part of the world. However, global strategies will increasingly be geared to each country or region.

An advertiser does not have to go abroad to see the necessity for marketing plans that consider a diversified marketplace. Marketing executives and advertisers must realize that in our own country, Hispanic, Asian American, and African American consumers are part of the fabric of our society and they must be reached through messages that are sensitive to their needs. This sensitivity means supporting minority media owners with advertising dollars; hiring a diverse workforce in the advertising industry; creating advertising and commercials that fairly reflect the various ethnic and cultural groups within this country; and, when appropriate, developing products specifically for these markets. In Chapter 23, we discuss the globalization of advertising as well as the need for greater sensitivity to the issue of diversity in domestic advertising.

SUMMARY ✺

If the study of advertising history tells us anything, it is that change is the norm. Every period of advertising has seen remarkable changes in the structure of the industry, whether media, creative, or account planning. In addition, the public perception of advertising also changes from one generation to the next with resulting differences in its effectiveness and importance within the marketing communication matrix. As we write this text, advertising is continuing to demonstrate its affinity for change. For example, the development of e-commerce, or Internet selling, has already had major effects on marketing, promotion, and selling. In 2005, Internet advertising revenues reached almost $16 billion, a level placing it competitively with radio and consumer magazines. Of more far-reaching significance, the development of new technology that allows advertisers to reach prospects on a more personal basis is having a major impact on the way we communicate with consumers. We are beginning to look at consumers as individuals as opposed to large groups of buyers.

As we conclude this opening chapter, we should make three points about advertising, past and future:

1. While modern advertising with its sophisticated, segmented media and billion-dollar expenditures is primarily a creation of the last 100 years, the idea of using persuasive communication to sell goods and services is as old as trade and commerce.

2. Advertising cannot be studied in the abstract. Virtually any development in advertising is the result of some advance in technology (e.g., printing presses, radio, television, the Internet), research (advances in psychology, sociology, and anthropology to better understand human behavior), or society as a whole (the acceptance of capitalism and consumerism by the majority of the American population). In the United States, advertising prospered because of a unique situation that included a democratic government, unfettered business institutions, sophisticated technology, an inexpensive media, and a receptive culture. The move from an agrarian to an industrialized society brought with it unprecedented specialization. However, the efficiencies of mass production and specialization could only be achieved with effective use of mass advertising and promotion.

3. It is obvious that advertising and promotion are no longer confined to the traditional media that dominated during the last century. As we have noted, persuasive communication will take numerous forms in coming decades. Advertising and brand identification are ubiquitous. Commercial messages, to the chagrin of many critics, can be found in venues as diverse as NASCAR races; product placement in movies, television shows, and video games; and on practically every cap and T-shirt. As we will see in our later discussions, the definition and implementation of traditional advertising have undergone and will continue to undergo dramatic changes in coming years.

While we can't be certain about the specific advertising trends during the coming decades, we can predict that the twenty-first century will be a time of fundamental changes in marketing and mass communication not seen since the advent of high-speed presses and the introduction of broadcasting. As audiences take greater control of communication channels, advertisers will need to view themselves as invited guests rather than opportunistic intruders. Likewise, advertisers will have to adapt creative messages to the specific needs of smaller groups of homogeneous consumers. The Internet will be only one piece of the marketing puzzle. Marketers will have to coordinate a host of available communication and distribution channels to reach evermore demanding buyers. Traditional retailers will increasingly utilize direct-selling techniques such as the Internet while e-commerce companies and catalogers will establish retail outlets to serve specific segments of their prime prospects.

REVIEW ✺

1. What factors contributed to the rise of modern advertising during the last 100 years?
2. Advertising can rarely be successful in an economy in which demand is greater than supply. Why?
3. Discuss the importance of the introduction of national brands to the growth of advertising.

4. How has the so-called "interactive era" brought fundamental changes to the advertiser/customer relationship?

5. Discuss some of the factors that caused the emphasis on creativity in advertising during the early 1900s.

6. Briefly trace the development of the advertising agency from Volney Palmer to the early 1900s.

7. What societal changes led to passage of the Federal Trade Commission Act and the Pure Food and Drug Act?

8. Discuss the role of the War Advertising Council.

9. How did the Great Depression support the growth of radio?

10. How has new technology contributed to more personal relationships between advertisers and customers?

TAKE IT TO THE WEB ✹

The John W. Hartman Center for Sales, Advertising, and Marketing History is housed in Duke University's Rare Book, Manuscript, and Special Collections Library (http://scriptorium.lib.duke.edu/hartman/brochure.html). Compare early advertisements with modern ones for similar products and brands.

Review how the topics of the Ad Council (www.adcouncil.org) have changed over the last 50 years. Pay particular attention to the advertisements produced during the years of the War Advertising Council when most consumer products were unavailable or in short supply.

The history of the Federal Food and Drug Administration (www.fda.gov/opacom/backgrounders/miles.html) provides a useful insight into the development of consumer protection in the United States.

CHAPTER 2

Roles of Advertising

As we discussed in the previous chapter, advertising has undergone significant changes in the last two decades. Fueled by new technology and demands from clients for more accountability for their advertising expenditures, media companies and advertising agencies have seen a number of modifications in the practice and execution of advertising. However, regardless of the revolutionary changes in mass communication and marketing, advertising's primary role continues to be to convey truthful information about products, services, or ideas to a targeted audience.

There is no question that new consumer-controlled communication technology will force advertisers to alter both the methods of reaching consumers and their messages. There is vigorous debate as to whether the traditional advertising plan comprised of 30-second commercials supported by print and direct response is still viable. We can predict with some certainty that the media that carry advertising will continue to change and specific advertising executions will become more targeted as we become better able to identify and reach small groups of customers or even individual buyers—often at their invitation. However, the basic communication goals of good advertising will remain constant whether they are used by companies to reach customers on a global basis or around the corner. After reading this chapter, you will understand:

chapter objectives

1. **primary goals and objectives of advertising**
2. **changing roles of advertising within the marketing communication mix**
3. **value of advertising and measuring return-on-investment (ROI)**
4. **various categories of advertising**
5. **advertising and building brand equity**
6. **advertising of ideas and nonprofit organizations**

ADVERTISING AND THE CHANGING COMMUNICATION ENVIRONMENT

convergence
The blending of various facets of marketing functions and communication technology to create more efficient and expanded synergies.

Historians may look back on the early years of the 2000s as an era of convergence. The term **convergence** means coming together or intersecting different components of some related system. In mass communication, the term has come to refer to three distinct though related areas:

1. *Technological convergence.* For example, listening to radio programs over your home computer or watching movies through a DVD player connected to your television set.
2. *Business convergence.* Usually referred to as consolidation, one of the dominant trends of modern business is the merging of company after company, including, as we discuss later in the text, advertising agencies and media companies.
3. *Content convergence.* Content is the primary expense of most communication companies. Whether it is a network showing reruns to amortize its investment in its programs or an advertising agency using clip art or sharing footage with its global partners, companies try to stretch the use of communication content.

Nowhere is convergence more apparent than in advertising communication. Reaching elusive consumers with meaningful messages at a reasonable cost has become more and more difficult. Advertisers are in a period in which the old rules don't work and they have yet to find new ones that guarantee success. "If marketers learned one key point . . . it is that reaching consumers by traditional means—TV, magazines and newspapers—is getting harder. . . . They are seeking information from a broader range of sources than ever and, in the process, filtering out messages that don't resonate or speak to their specific needs."[1] Finding a cost-efficient plan for reaching increasingly in-control and demanding consumers is the major challenge of contemporary advertising. As we discuss the functions and procedures of advertising, we will see that the forces of convergence and consolidation dominate virtually every advertising, promotion, and marketing decision.

Advertisers find they have a dual problem. On the one hand, they must choose a media plan from an ever-expanding number of options. At the same time, they must develop advertising messages that consumers will invite to share their time. "Advertising was once a simple mass-market media buy; now it is a dialog between a seller of soup, sneakers or cell phones and a particular media outlet's narrow audience. That media outlet is just as likely to be a computer screen or a mobile device as a television set. . . ."[2]

Some have coined this new relationship between advertisers and consumers as *citizen media* implying more control by users of communication rather than by providers.[3] Another step in citizen media is participatory media in which the audience takes an active role in creating media content. So-called blogs, which began as informal communication links among individuals with similar interests, have become an important part of the marketing plans of companies such as General Motors and Procter & Gamble. Commercially sponsored blogs not only provide an exciting means of reaching fragmented audience segments but also provide companies with information and research about their brands at virtually no cost. They might be characterized as an electronic focus group without boundaries.

Since the 1970s, futurists have predicted a communication revolution. But in the future, we might look back on 2000 as the benchmark when the revolution first

Survey respondents were asked which media will receive a greater/smaller percentage of the marketing budget in three years as they navigate a changed media environment.

Medium	More	Less
Network TV	5%	69%
Cable TV	34%	29%
Print	18%	29%
Radio	26%	29%
Outdoor	31%	22%
Internet	86%	1%
Other interactive tech.	88%	0%
Branded entertainment	74%	3%
Point of sale	61%	3%
Event marketing	66%	5%
Direct marketing	75%	6%
Public relations	69%	4%
Incentives	30%	25%

EXHIBIT 2.1

Three-year Forecast

From James B. Arndorfer, "More Consumer Control Forces Shift in Spending," *Advertising Age*, March 7, 2005, p. 10. Copyright © 2005 Crain Communications, Inc. Used with permission.

became commercially viable. In 1985, cell phones cost approximately $1,000 and calls were 45 cents per minute. The worldwide universe of cell phones was perhaps 200,000, including military and public safety officials. By 2009, it is projected that some 2.6 billion cell phones will be in use, serving a third of the world's population.[4] The term *phone* is already becoming a misnomer as mobile technology is used for everything from music downloads to text messaging—with much of the content sponsored by one or more brands.

Advertisers vote with their dollars, and no better evidence exists of the importance of new technology than the shift in financial support by major advertisers away from traditional media to new and, especially, interactive technology (see Exhibit 2.1). It is obvious from the data that marketers are anticipating dramatic changes in the way they spend promotional dollars over the next 3 years. Given the popularity of network television over the last 25 years, it is remarkable that only 5 percent of respondents see an increase in their future network allocations as compared to 86 and 88 percent increases in Internet and interactive technology respectively over the same period.

Advertising as a Communication Tool

With the significant changes in advertising practice, it is tempting to lose sight of the fact that advertising remains a communication tool. Regardless of the specific advertising plan or goals of a particular strategy, successful advertising depends on utilization of effective communication (see Exhibit 2.2). Advertising objectives must be viewed from a *communication* perspective; advertising rarely can accomplish tasks that are not related to communication. The fundamental principle of good advertising is that it must be built around the overall marketing plan and execute the communication elements of a more far-reaching marketing program. For example, increasing a dealer network by 10 percent is a marketing goal; increasing awareness of a brand by 25 percent among retailers is an advertising goal that we would expect to contribute to achieving a growth in dealers of 10 percent.

Because advertising objectives must complement the marketing plan, let's look at the primary factors in a typical marketing plan. As we do, consider those aspects

that can be addressed by marketing communication and in what ways communication could complement the implementation of the plan:[5]

1. *Overall goal(s) of the plan.* Marketing goals are often expressed in financial terms such as expected sales revenues at the end of the first year or percentage increases over previous years.

2. *Marketing objectives.* Marketing objectives should be clearly stated and measurable. For example, we may want to show a significant increase in market share relative to specific competitors over a set time period.

3. *Marketing strategy.* The strategy outlines the general course of action to achieve our goals and objectives. These will include what each element of the marketing function (e.g., advertising and promotion, distribution, pricing) should contribute to achieving our goals.

4. *Situational analysis.* This analysis is a statement of the product benefits as well as data concerning sales trends, competitive environment, and industry forecasts.

5. *Problems and opportunities.* At this point, we outline the major current and anticipated future problems and opportunities facing the brand.

6. *Financial plan.* The financial plan is an outline of the expected profit or loss over various time frames. Projections are made concerning needed investments in various marketing functions before a product is profitable.

7. *Research.* Marketing planning is based on both secondary and primary research. This section outlines the data needed, where they can be obtained, their cost, and time frame for availability.

With the marketing plan providing our blueprint, we begin to plan the advertising implementation needed to accomplish the communication tasks specific to brand and company objectives.

a. *Prospect identification.* The guiding principle of the advertising plan is detailed identification of a company's prime prospects including who they are (e.g., basic demographic data) and the social, cultural, and psychological characteristics that predict purchase behavior.

b. *Consumer motivations.* Accurate insights about our core consumers will greatly enhance our chances of success as we move to determine the role that advertising can play in channeling consumer needs, wants, and aspirations into purchases of general product categories and, more important, specific brands of goods and services.

c. *Advertising execution.* Once we identify the role of advertising within the context of the marketing program, our next step is to develop overall creative themes and media plans that effectively deliver messages to set our brand apart from its competitors, recognizing that advertising does not communicate in a void; rather, it benefits from a synergism between message and medium.

d. *The advertising budget and allocation.* The share of the marketing program designated for advertising will be included in the marketing plan. However, allocation of the advertising budget to specific media, creative executions, and production will normally be a part of the advertising plan.

For the remainder of this chapter, we examine the many aspects of advertising and the planning and executions that result in success or failure for the companies that advertise.

ADVERTISING AND PROFITABILITY

The critical evaluation for any business activity is its contribution to profitability. The value of a particular marketing function is often expressed as **return-on-investment (ROI)**, that is, how many dollars are produced for every dollar spent. A number of research studies indicate a strong correlation among brand awareness, market share, and profits (see Exhibit 2.3). A leading marketing executive summed up the importance of advertising's role in profitability, ". . . [W]e believe that brand building is about sustaining price premiums. . . . [O]ur experience is that advertising influences price more than sales. And yield improvements go straight to the bottom line."[6] With this emphasis on brand building, clients are increasingly demanding that

return-on-investment (ROI)
One measure of the efficiency of a company is the rate of return (profits) achieved by a certain level of investment on various business functions including advertising.

EXHIBIT 2.3

How brand awareness aids profitability (the sequence of events).

Used with permission. *Cahners Advertising Research Report*, No. 2000.6, p. 6.

Previous Level of Brand Awareness	+	Changes in Brand Awareness	=	Current Level of Brand Awareness	×	Conversion Rate of Brand Awareness into Market Share	=	Level of Achieved Market Share	which strongly influences	ROI or Profitability
This is the net result of all past successes and failures.		Brand awareness decreases by the normal decay process, and increases by (a) doing an above-par volume of Marketing Expenditures/Sales (b) having a higher-than-average level of Advertising/Sales (c) being successful (recently) in converting previous brand awareness into market share.				The conversion rate is aided by (a) having available or developing new production capacity, and (b) advertising (and other actions) that establish product or company differentiation.			See Exhibit 2.3	

media and advertising agencies measure advertising success on the basis of effective communication rather than on audience exposure (i.e., circulation or ratings).

In 2005, a joint task force of major advertising trade associations announced an initiative that would replace the concept of audience delivery with one that measured audience engagement. While there is general agreement on the need to estimate audience involvement, there is a lack of consensus on how to define and/or measure it. As one advertising executive pointed out, "The issue is whether we can agree on what [audience] engagement is. . . . There are different levels of engagement and different levels of effectiveness."[7]

The demand for accountability and a focus on ROI are already becoming part of the media/advertiser relationship. For example, in the fall 2006 television season, Court TV guaranteed a certain audience level but also offered to rebate advertisers if the network fell short of a previously guaranteed level of *engaged viewers*. The figure was determined by a formula that included measures of viewer attentiveness, engagement, and recall.[8] The Weather Channel also announced a similar plan based on slightly different measurement techniques.

Despite these attempts to change the method of buying and measuring the audience of various media, we are far from a consistent model for determining audience value across the hundreds of communication vehicles currently used by advertisers—not to mention those that will come online in future years. Advertising researchers realize that each communication outlet presents its own unique challenges for measuring audience response (see Exhibit 2.4). In addition, there are concerns by some media directors that the emphasis on short-term audience involvement runs the risk of devaluing the long-term value of advertising. Because brand building is a continuing process that often takes years to accomplish, involvement-based ROI measures may give advertising less than its full worth in the marketing process. Despite some misgivings on the part of media and advertising agencies, it is the client that will ultimately prevail in the application of ROI management. Perhaps A. G. Lafley, chairman-CEO of Procter & Gamble, summed up the widespread sentiment of advertisers, "Every brand in every country that has done . . . marketing ROI [analysis] has improved the productivity of its marketing spending without exception."[9]

INTEGRATED MARKETING

marketing mix
Combination of marketing functions, including advertising, used to sell a product.

Marketing consists of four primary elements: product, price, distribution, and communication. These are the primary elements in what is known as the **marketing mix**.[10] The communication component of marketing is further divided into four primary categories:

1. *Personal selling*. Personal communication is the most effective means of persuading someone. However, it is also the most expensive and, because of its expense, usually impractical at the initial stages of mass selling. The days of door-to-door selling at the retail level are largely over. As a primary technique, personal selling is most often used in business-to-business marketing. Even then, it is frequently employed as a follow-up to advertising to close a sale or develop a long-term relationship that will eventually result in a sale. In business-to-business marketing, advertising opens doors for personal salespeople, and in consumer marketing it introduces brands and retailers, which allows salespeople to make the final sale. While traditional personal selling is a minor part of the promotional strategy of most companies selling directly to consumers, its techniques are becoming important factors in many selling tactics across a number of media platforms. For example, direct response and the Internet both incorporate the strengths of personal selling in communicating personalized messages and anticipating consumer resistance to sales approaches.

The groundswell of marketer demand for methods to measure the value of their advertising has hit an unprecedented level. *Ad Age* asked Aegis Group's Marketing Management Analytics to rate the measurability for ROI of various marketing media.

Medium	The Measurement Challenge	ROI Measurability Rating
Direct Response	Direct mail, telemarketing and other forms are the most measurable of media listed here. Direct can have a synergistic feel, especially on pharma, telecom and financial services.	5
Sales Promotion	Offers such as coupons and discounts generate a lot of consumer response and therefore a bounty of data. The data lend themselves to measurement, especially for package goods via syndicated scanner data. Free-standing inserts generate much valuable data.	5
Internet	The Internet can be very influential for big-ticket purchases like cars. Very measurable, with the cautionary note that "Internet is a very broad net," ranging from search engines to ads in content to Web sites such as in the auto market, where such marques as Saab (r.) get lots of hits, and all should be looked at separately. The goal is to understand how the consumer is interacting online with the brand.	5
TV	While promotions have very pronounced, short-term effects that allow precise measurement, TV has a more subtle and gradual effect that may show greater variability. But ROI can be measured with a high degree of accuracy, and there's no excuse for TV not to show a measurable effect. MMA clients have been using a lot more analysis to create a better mix between :15s and :30s, and better allocation across dayparts.	4 1/2
Print	The experts can slice and dice print by weekly vs. monthly publications, by targeted vs. general market, by promotional ads vs. equity-building. Print promotional materials, like free-standing inserts, are a separate—and much more measurable—matter. As with all other media, accuracy and timing of the data are crucial in determining how measurable the medium is. Print can play a strong role in expanding the reach of the media mix.	4 1/2
Public Relations	There are companies that specialize in the measurement of PR campaigns' quality; they can measure the number of impressions delivered—via positive or negative PR—for a brand name or category. PR can have a measurable impact on sales (think trans fats in food). The problem: Many marketers aren't buying these PR data.	4
Video Games	Whether the game is played online or offline is crucial. An ad embedded in a game cartridge is very hard to measure because there's no way to know how often it's played. Though there's no denying "True Crime's" Nick Kang (r.) is a big hit. With online games, there are great data available through the Internet.	Online: 4 Offline: 1
Radio	The available data typically aren't as strong as those for its traditional-media colleagues of TV and print, and this hampers radio.	3
Cinema	Movie advertising can be measured by the number of impressions delivered, much like outdoor or kiosk advertising would be measured.	3
Sponsored Events	Measurability depends on whether sponsorship is likely to spark short-term effect. A major recurring event like the Olympics is very measurable. Others can be difficult to measure short term. Measurement can be complex because events have so many pieces, including how the event is advertised, the PR buzz, signage and the recollection of event itself.	3
Product Placement in Content	There are companies that measure quality of placement as well as the quantity of exposures. Treated much like TV advertising, with the caveat that not every product placement is the same. Fox's "American Idol" is a great example: AT&T Wireless's tie-in, which involved voting by text message, is interactive—even part of the entertainment—while Paula Abdul drinking from a Coke cup (l.) is not. (P.S. AT&T Wireless, now owned by Cingular, isn't an MMA client.) So the question becomes: How do you score the quality of placement?	3
Outdoor	Available data are limited due to the nature of outdoor advertising; there's no syndicated vendor that sells the needed data on outdoor. And outdoor lacks "variance"—the billboard is up X number of months and is seen by an unchanging X number of people each day.	2
Guerrilla Marketing	Hard to measure if the variable you're using is sales. If 10,000 people at an event get free T-shirts, it's difficult to measure the effect on the 400,000 people living in that market. Because guerrilla can encompass so many different kinds of tactics, getting useful data can be a problem—it depends on how measurable the response is. Marketers' ROI expectations for guerrilla are lower than for other media, so the urgency to measure is less. Not to mention they spend a lot less on guerrilla than on traditional media like TV.	1

EXHIBIT 2.4

Rating Media for Their Accountability

From Dan Lippe, "Media Scorecard: How ROI Adds Up," *Advertising Age*, June 20, 2005, pg. 5–6. Copyright © 2005 Crain Communications, Inc. Used with permission.

sales promotion
(1) Sales activities that supplement both personal selling and marketing, coordinate the two, and help to make them effective. For example, displays are sales promotions. (2) More loosely, the combination of personal selling, advertising, and all supplementary selling activities.

public relations
Communication with various internal and external publics to create an image for a product or corporation.

2. **Sales promotion**. Sales promotion is an extra incentive for a customer to make an immediate purchase. It is by far the most extensive category of promotional spending. Sales promotion may consist of a special sales price, a cents-off coupon, a colorful point-of-purchase display, or a chance to win a trip to Hawaii in a sweepstakes. The largest categories of promotions, those directed to wholesalers and retailers, are rarely seen by consumers. These promotions, known as *trade promotions*, are used to persuade the distributors to carry a brand or give it an advantage such as favorable shelf space. One of the fears, especially during recessionary periods, is that an overuse of short-term promotions such as coupons and various trade deals will not only cut into profits but also harm long-term brand equity by placing a major emphasis on price. Marketers are well aware of the potential downside of promotional offers, and the most astute companies incorporate strong brand messages in their promotions. By doing so, they ensure that promotions remain short-term sales incentives rather than having consumers rely on them for their primary means of brand assessment. Promotional offers such as automobile rebates have created price competition that contributed to an erosion in brand loyalty and profitability for a number of carmakers.

3. **Public relations**. According to the Public Relations Society of America, "Public relations helps an organization and its publics adapt mutually to each other." In the last decade, public relations has become one of the fastest-growing sectors of marketing communication. A primary benefit of public relations is that it is perceived as having higher audience credibility than advertising. For most of its existence, public relations, as practiced by most companies, consisted primarily of issuing an occasional press release with little or no follow-up, coordination with other marketing elements, and virtually no attempt to measure either its short- or long-term value to profitability. In the last decade, the regard for public relations among major marketers has increased dramatically and public relations has been fully integrated into the marketing communication plans of most major companies. Exhibit 2.5 reviews the numerous ways in which public relations can potentially function within marketing communication.

Since the 1930s, researchers have known that word-of-mouth endorsements by influential peers are an important method of getting ideas adopted by a greater population. Early work by researchers such as Paul Lazarsfeld and Elihu Katz demonstrated the relationship between media and personal influence in the political arena. In what is known as the *two-step flow*, the media provided information to opinion leaders who, in turn, influenced the opinions of less-involved voters. Contemporary marketers have adopted many of the techniques of the two-step flow and other public-relations practices to develop similar programs of influencing the purchase of brands.

In recent years, terms such as *buzz*, *guerilla marketing*, and *word-of-mouth marketing* have been added to the business lexicon. The techniques have many characteristics, including product placement in movies and television shows, company-sponsored blogs, having a book reviewed by Oprah, event marketing, and hundreds of other techniques to engage consumers. Regardless of their names, the key to success of word-of-mouth marketing is to engage marketplace influencers. Faced with negative public opinion toward pharmaceutical companies, industry giant GlaxoSmithKline enlisted its 8,000-member sales force as public-relations ambassadors. The aim of the campaign was to have these local representatives speak to civic clubs, senior citizen groups, and local media to spread the word about the work of drug companies. A company executive noted that information from rank-and-file employees would be more trusted than the same information imparted through formal communication media from company executives.[11]

In which roles do you consider public relations effective?

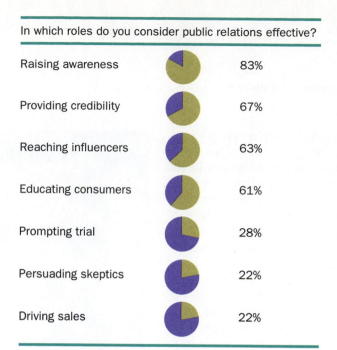

Raising awareness	83%
Providing credibility	67%
Reaching influencers	63%
Educating consumers	61%
Prompting trial	28%
Persuading skeptics	22%
Driving sales	22%

EXHIBIT 2.5

PR Effectiveness and Functionality

Firms are increasing their use of public relations as a marketing tool.

From Paul Holmes, "Senior Marketers Are Sharply Divided About the Role of PR in the Overall Mix," *Advertising Age,* January 24, 2005, pg. C1. Copyright © 2005 Crain Communications, Inc. Used with permission.

The key to successful public relations is to view it as a complement rather than a competitor to advertising. Ideally, advertising and public relations should work in concert to get the brand message to as many prospects as possible. For example, Chick-fil-A has greatly enhanced the value of its advertising through public-relations techniques related to its "eat more chicken" bovines. Because public relations is usually seen as news, it has credibility that is lacking in most advertising. On the other hand, even a unique product is news for only a short period of time. Public relations and especially word-of-mouth advertising tend to work best at the introductory stage of building brand awareness with advertising taking over to build long-term brand loyalty.

Best Buy introduced its in-home technical support unit with Geekmobiles on high-traffic roads; Microsoft created buzz for the Xbox 360 by creating *Colony*, a community-based game; and Procter & Gamble scored a coup by having Super Bowl winning quarterback Ben Roethlisberger shave his beard on the *Late Show with David Letterman* the week following his big win using the just-introduced five-bladed Fusion razor. Furthermore, unlike advertising, a public-relations message is ultimately controlled by the media. The media make decisions concerning when, where, and if a particular product story will be carried. The elements of message control and credibility most distinguish public relations and advertising.

4. **Advertising**. Advertising is a message paid for by an identified sponsor and usually delivered through some medium of mass communication. Advertising is persuasive communication. It is not neutral; it is not unbiased; it says: "I am going to attempt to sell you a product or an idea." As in the case with other forms of marketing communication, advertising is undergoing dramatic changes as it adapts to new technologies—including those allowing the audience to delete advertisements. Throughout the remainder of this text, we discuss not only the principles of advertising but also how advertising interacts with other forms of marketing communication.

During the early development of modern marketing and advertising, marketing communication components were regarded as more or less discrete functions.

advertising
Advertising consists of paid notices from identified sponsors normally offered through communication media.

Don Perry
Vice President of Public Relations, Chick-fil-A
Leveraging Public Relations

Throughout Chick-fil-A's history, public relations has played a critical role in building, maintaining, and protecting the brand. In fact, Truett Cathy himself could be considered the company's first "PR man." In addition to being a born entrepreneur, Cathy also was a natural showman. Although he had no formal marketing training, Cathy was a natural brand-builder, not to mention a natural public-relations practitioner and somewhat of a publicity hound.

Before the chain's inception, Cathy relied on his innate salesmanship and publicity-driving skills as he created the name for his new product, licensed his product, and eventually built a chain of restaurants around it. The early marketing efforts for the Chick-fil-A chain were predominantly public-relations-driven:

- Grand openings of new Chick-fil-A restaurants
- Development of the Leadership Scholarships ($1,000 scholarships provided to qualified restaurant team members)
- Creation of the "Symbol of Success" award (through a partnership with Lincoln and Ford, Cathy offered cars as incentives for Operators to reach aggressive sales goals)

As the company continued to grow, the strength of the Chick-fil-A brand—and the need to formalize a public-relations function to protect and enhance the brand—continued to grow along with it. By the early 1980s, Chick-fil-A was achieving annual sales of more than $100 million.

Competitors were beginning to take notice of the success Chick-fil-A was enjoying, and one by one they began to introduce their own version of a chicken sandwich. These competitors included the major players—the members of the Big Three fast-food restaurants, which had multi-million-dollar advertising budgets to support

Don Perry

their efforts. Chick-fil-A's advertising budget was—and still is—relatively minute in comparison to what its competitors spend. With no way to compete dollar for dollar for ad exposure, the chain relied predominantly on local marketing and public relations.

In 1983, with 281 stores spread out in malls from New Jersey to Atlanta to California that produced $136 million in total sales, Chick-fil-A hired Don Perry as its first public relations manager. As Perry recalls, "My directive from Steve Robinson was simple: put Truett Cathy and Chick-fil-A on the map."

Perry spent his first several years at Chick-fil-A on the road with Cathy, telling the Chick-fil-A story and sampling the food, as the company spread its reach (both in terms of restaurants and publicity/brand building) beyond its original Southeast footprint.

Cathy made an effort to attend every opening and to conduct media interviews in each city. As Perry reflects,

Each had its own manager, and coordination of the various functions was not always as rigorous as it should have been. Today, many see the use of various elements of the marketing mix as a first step in changing the core mission of advertising agencies. An executive at a major agency said that his agency should look upon itself not as an advertising agency but as a media-arts company.[12] By that he meant that brand messages should be woven into the culture in such a way that art and

it was a public-relations manager's dream to have the founder so available and so willing to work with the media.

As the chain increased its geographic reach and number of restaurants, it was necessary for the public-relations function to adapt as well. Traveling with Truett to every grand opening was a logistical impossibility, with more and more slated each year. The size of the home office support staff was growing at a steady pace to keep up with the chain's continued growth.

With growth came the need for structure and processes. Amid all this change in the chain as a whole, the role of public relations during this time went through a transition as well.

Public-relations efforts in the early days at Chick-fil-A could generally be divided into three distinct categories:

- Acting as "publicist" for Cathy
- Event marketing logistics (primarily Grand Openings)
- Early stages of brand publicity (scholarships, product publicity)

Those categories quickly expanded to include a whole host of issues, initiatives, activities, and events that all require public relations support to maximize positive impact on the chain's customers:

- Between sixty and seventy new restaurant openings per year
- Increased role and visibility of other Cathy family members involved in the business
- Marketing initiatives
  - Event marketing (*Chick-fil-A Bowl*; sponsorship of the ACC, SEC, and Big 12 conferences; and the *Chick-fil-A Kyle Petty Charity Ride*)
  - Family and kids marketing (Kids Meal program, *Core Essentials* and *Shake This Planet* character education programs)
  - Brand development (New Products, Brand expression)
  - Business development (licensing, outside sales)
  - Store marketing (systemwide promotions, in-store/ local store marketing)
- Corporate initiatives (annual meeting, Operator awards, etc.)
- HR initiatives support (scholarships, trends, etc.)
- Issues management (crisis communications)

One area of support that has had a prominent place in Chick-fil-A's public-relations plans since 1995 has been the "Eat Mor Chikin" Cows. The impact of the Cow billboard campaign—and the significant role public relations would play in supporting it—was realized early on when one of the fiberglass Cows was stolen in Chattanooga, Tennessee, by a group of bored teenagers. The "Cow-napping" and subsequent "Cow hunt" made national news. Perry's public-relations team was on site to manage and disseminate the message through all media channels. From then on, the Cows remained a pubic-relations/branding staple for the chain.

The Cows quickly became a key component in the chain's efforts to generate public awareness and to solidify the bond between the Chick-fil-A brand and its customers. Perry's team quickly learned to leverage the Cows in many other ways to help enhance current programs. Costumed Cow mascots were created to support all of Chick-fil-A's local marketing and event marketing efforts. Over time, the Cows became a focal point for a majority of Chick-fil-A's marketing efforts (sports sponsorships, product launches, Grand Openings, merchandising and branding, their very own calendar, even the title of Cathy's second book—*Eat Mor Chikin: Inspire More People*).

Public relations' place in Chick-fil-A's marketing mix is all but secured as the company continues to grow. Now in thirty-seven states and Washington, D.C., Chick-fil-A is moving ever closer to being a truly national brand—especially with its expansion into western markets (e.g., Southern California).

Consider where the brand is heading with the support of public relations:

- Mentioned on the *Regis & Kelly* show (During her pregnancy, Kelly Ripa spent several minutes during her show discussing her cravings for a Chick-fil-A Chicken Sandwich.)
- Truett Cathy was recently listed among the *Forbes* 400 richest people.
- Cathy has published four books and currently is working on a fifth book.
- WebMD profiled Chick-fil-A as an example to consumers on its segment about making healthy choices when dining out at quick-service restaurants.
- Chick-fil-A was named a "Customer Oriented Leader" by *Fast Company* magazine.

In just over four decades, Chick-fil-A has grown to truly become part of the popular culture. While much of the credit for this accomplishment rightly goes to Truett Cathy and to the success of the Cows campaign, public relations has played a pivotal role in telling the Chick-fil-A story every step of the way. ▪ ▪ ▪

commerce are seamless, using all aspects of communication technology to focus on consumer needs. More important, the various elements of marketing communication, as they become more personal and move from mass to one-to-one contacts, can more accurately measure a campaign's ROI. The reliance on marketing mix strategy allows evaluations that view promotion as a coordinated mix of elements rather than judging each independently. In the past, a lack of coordination led many companies to address their customers with several different and sometimes confusing and contradictory messages. However, in recent years, companies have begun to move toward a consolidation of all areas of the marketing function, especially marketing communication.

The complexity of contemporary marketing communication plans has resulted in a demand for programs that *speak with one voice*, which refers to the fact that companies are demanding that all communication from their letterheads to product packaging demonstrate a consistent look and theme. The need for coordinating marketing communication is apparent when one realizes that 75 percent of *Fortune* 1,000 companies have more than 100 brands. As one marketing executive said, "Today's environment has created an overabundance of brands, messages, and delivery channels, and brand portfolios that fail at driving business performance. Unless someone is charged with 'minding the store,' individual brand management will remain as brand fiefdoms and brand proliferation will continue to drag the business down."[13]

integrated marketing communication (IMC)

The joint planning, execution, and coordination of all areas of marketing communication.

For approximately 20 years, companies have moved to organize the total communication program under the general heading of **integrated marketing communication (IMC)**. While the application of IMC differs with each company, a primary outcome of the approach is less concern with how a message is delivered (e.g., advertising, public relations) and more emphasis on the effectiveness of the total marketing communication plan. The need for coordination and integration of marketing communication is apparent when you realize that a company like Toyota has seventeen unique marketing plans for each of its models. "Each plan is designed to package information in the way customers want to get it and have it delivered when they need it."[14] Yet, within these targeted plans, there needs to be a consumer awareness that each is a member of the "Toyota family." Integrated marketing communication also has had significant implications for the way advertising agencies deal with clients. For example, one of the world's largest agencies, Ogilvy & Mather, has combined its advertising, direct marketing, public relations, health care, and sales promotion agencies into a single reporting structure and profit-and-loss statement.[15]

Today, major marketers are much more interested in the efficiency and benefits of their total marketing communication program than with the specific means of achieving these results. "Whatever the disciplines used . . . they all must work together to give a unified message to consumers. It is relationships with consumers that matter, and these are built by ideas that transcend individual media."[16] In coming years, some form of IMC will be even more the norm in the marketing plans of virtually every company (see Exhibit 2.6). Demands for marketing efficiency combined with new marketing communication channels and an increasingly diverse audience will combine to force greater integration and coordination of all aspects of the marketing function, especially those involved in the communication process.

As integration of the various promotional functions becomes more typical, the advertising professional of the future will be required to make decisions about the role that both advertising and other promotional tools will play in any particular campaign. This assessment will include an evaluation of marketing goals and strategies, identification of prime prospects, product characteristics, and the budget available for all areas of the communication mix. Although the benefits of IMC are apparent, the implementation of the strategy can be extremely difficult, especially for multibrand companies with numerous target customers. In later chapters, we discuss in more detail the execution of IMC.

ADVERTISING: AN INSTITUTIONAL APPROACH

Society establishes institutions to bring order to vital activities. Social institutions control various behaviors within a society by setting certain standards and guidelines for what are both appropriate and required to promote the goals of a society

Traditional Wool
Cruiser Jacket
from $159

Hunting Wabbits?

For all things classic or new,
call 1-800-609-2326 or shop llbean.com

L.L.Bean
DIRECT FROM
FREEPORT, MAINE™

EXHIBIT 2.6

Companies reach out to consumers in a number of different venues.

Courtesy of © 2004, L.L. Bean, Inc.

(or at least goals agreed upon by the majority). Institutions can be regarded as "evolving to address the separate needs of society (e.g., the military institution out of the need for defense; the family out of social needs for procreation, socialization and intimacy). . . ."[17] Some would argue that advertising is not a stand-alone institution such as religion. However, an institutional consideration of advertising permits us to see that it is a logical—some would say necessary—requirement for a capitalistic economic system. To the extent that advertising is an institution, it is ". . . primarily designed to provide information on economic goods and services, but which now, under the impact of modern conditions, finds broader, noneconomic applications."[18]

Advertising is viewed from two related perspectives: (1) its economic role and (2) its social and cultural role in communicating not only product information but also social values. The cultural role of advertising is often referred to as its *inadvertent role.* With the exception of advertising overtly intended to foster some idea or initiative, many of advertising's social consequences are often unintended by sponsors. One of the major criticisms of contemporary advertising is its effect on the behavior of children. Advertising is so ubiquitous that children begin to develop strong brand preferences by the age of 2 and babies as young as 6 months are able to recognize certain corporate logos and mascots.[19] Critics charge that the epidemic of childhood obesity is a direct result of the advertising of unhealthy food to children, but their complaints go far beyond this hot-button topic. ". . . [J]unk food isn't the only potentially harmful product being marketed directly to children. Each day children are bombarded with sophisticated marketing for alcohol, tobacco, violent media, and precociously sexualized clothes, toys and accessories as well.[20]

Under the current level of scrutiny, advertisers must be aware of both economic and social aspects of their advertising. The public has proven itself to be unforgiving when it perceives that certain advertising is exploitive (whether the exploitation is intended or not).

Most economists agree that advertising has a utilitarian function in the marketing system. That is, the basic economic functions of advertising—to disseminate product information that allows consumers to know that products exist, to give consumers information about competing brands, and to permit consumers to make intelligent choices among product options—are accepted by most observers. However, the effects of advertising, beyond these strictly functional characteristics, are viewed with suspicion in many quarters. Increasingly, critics and advertisers alike are examining advertising messages from a social perspective. Issues such as truthful messages; the inclusion and portrayal of women, ethnic groups, and the elderly; and the need for responsible consumption are among the issues contemporary advertising must confront that were minor considerations in the past. The current controversy about advertising to children is only one example that demonstrates that advertising is regarded by many as an institution that communicates social as well as economic messages even when the social aspects of advertising may be both unintended and undesirable from the advertiser's perspective.

The majority of both practitioners and consumers accept the fact that advertising has an ethical and moral responsibility to provide product information that is both truthful and socially appropriate. On the other hand, it is obvious that consumers make purchase decisions on the basis of psychological and social factors as well as strictly utilitarian considerations. People buy Cadillacs instead of Chevrolets, not just for basic differences in transportation needs but also because the Cadillac brand satisfies a need for prestige, social status, and a number of other psychological factors. It can be argued that advertising creates these wants (as opposed to needs). But, in fact, advertising mirrors the society in which it functions while over time it probably contributes to subtle changes in the mores and behavior of the public that is exposed to it.

Advertising's role as an institution has been studied by both critics and proponents. These perspectives about the roles of advertising generally fall into one of the following three categories.

What Advertising Does for Consumers

Consumer behavior is need driven. That is, we assume that a purchase is the culmination of a process that begins with the recognition that some problem can be solved by a particular product or service. The *problem* may be utilitarian (we buy a new car for transportation) or hedonistic (we buy a new car to impress our neighbors). To a large degree, our purchases have elements of both and consumers search for products that satisfy their needs and wants on both levels. Advertising's role in this process is to provide information as efficiently and economically as possible to potential buyers. Advertising is particularly proficient in providing information and introducing consumers to new products and services. The value of advertising tends to decrease the longer a product has been on the market and the higher the consumer usage. With the advent of specialized media that can reach narrowly segmented audiences, advertising has an enhanced ability to provide even better information to selected consumers about products.

Closely related to the function of consumer information is the belief that advertising promotes greater choice for the consumer. Effective communication provides a means for new products to enter the marketplace and, therefore, increases the number of products available to consumers. In the future, as technology and interactive media increase the practicality for consumer feedback, buyers will have even greater input into the marketing process. In 2006, when Ford Motor Company announced a restructuring of the company, its press release used the word *customer* twenty-four times. CEO William Clay Ford Jr. said, "From now on, our products will be designed and built to satisfy the customer, not just fill the plant."[21] The key to the new strategy is for Ford to build cars that are innovative and distinctive with the consumer in mind.

What Advertising Does for Business

Advertising is one element in a fundamental marketing process known as *exchange theory*. Simply put, exchange theory suggests that market transactions will take place only to the extent that both buyers and sellers see value in the process. From an advertising perspective, we can hypothesize that consumers will continue to search for information only if they believe that additional facts will increase the benefit accrued from an eventual purchase. One of the myths perpetrated by advertising critics is that there is an adversarial relationship between businesses selling goods and consumers buying them with each side trying to "beat" the other. To the contrary, exchange theory suggests that the long-term success of a business is built on a positive and mutually beneficial relationship with its consumers. This relationship can only be maintained if consumers perceive value in the goods they purchase and the business enjoys a reasonable profit for its efforts.

Just as mass production provides economies of scale in production, advertising provides similar efficiencies in communicating to mass audiences. Despite the introduction of specialized media reaching smaller and smaller audience segments, there remains a demand for mass advertising to promote widely distributed products and services. Without advertising, many businesses would not be able to bring new products to the attention of enough consumers fast enough to make the enormous cost of creating, developing, manufacturing, and distributing these products practical. In other words, advertising is both a tool and requirement of an abundant economy. For businesses, one of the primary roles of advertising is its contribution in launching new products, increasing consumer brand loyalty for existing brands, and maintaining the sale of mature brands.

What Advertising Does for Society

If we accept the fact that advertising is a social institution (or at least interacts strongly with many other institutions), then its role in society should be considered. As we discussed earlier, advertisers convey subtle messages about society by the manner in which their advertising portrays products and services. In the current environment of social change and diversity, advertisers are hard-pressed to present effective sales messages that are at the same time compelling to the audience and noncontroversial to all segments of the population. In the United States, where people are continually undergoing changes in values and mores, advertisers are constantly challenged to develop effective marketing programs. Three challenges for contemporary marketing stand out:

1. Monitoring changes so that a company is aware of what is happening in society
2. Creating products and services compatible with changing values
3. Designing marketing messages that reflect and build on the values target markets and individual customers hold[22]

In a landscape of fragmented media and diverse audiences, it is more and more difficult to develop messages that appeal to specific target audiences without exposure to unintended consumers. For example, in 2005, Carl's Jr. promoted its BBQ Six Dollar Burger with racy advertisements featuring Paris Hilton. While the advertisements were created for a target audience of young males, the advertisements drew criticism from a number of groups who took exception to the messages. Obviously, the intended purpose of advertising is to contribute to the profitable sale of products and a continuing economic expansion that presumably is a benefit for society as a whole. In addition to its economic role, advertising benefits society by providing revenues to support a diverse and independent press system protected from government and special interest control.

However, in carrying out these goals, advertising must be aware of its responsibility as a mirror and monitor of society. From a pragmatic standpoint, advertisers realize that "Consumers' reactions to a product are also influenced by their evaluations of its advertising, over and above their feelings about the product itself. Our evaluation of a product can be determined solely by our appraisal of how it's depicted in marketing communications—we don't hesitate to form attitudes toward products we're never seen in person much less used."[23]

Clearly, there are numerous opinions regarding the proper role of advertising as it relates to the overall social good. However, there is little question that advertisers have a new and different responsibility to society in the way they sell their products and services. New technology and sophisticated research methods have only increased the importance of issues such as consumer privacy and the potentially intrusive nature of advertising.

ADVERTISING TO DIVERSE PUBLICS

Most advertising is created for a relatively small group of current and potential buyers. However, few advertisements and commercials are seen only by the target audience for which they are intended. Companies must consider the effect of their messages on a number of publics beyond the narrow scope of the intended recipients. Advertising, regardless of its intended recipients, communicates a message to various groups and individuals who in turn interpret this message in the context of their own interests.

When designing an advertisement or advertising campaign, firms must consider the many publics that will be reached by their messages and take into account how specific messages will be received. For example, a company's advertising intended to demonstrate to consumers that it is a responsible corporate citizen by publicizing a lucrative employee health care program may raise questions among stockholders about expenditures of funds that could be used to raise dividends. Tyson Foods made available a free book of prayers entitled *Giving Thanks at Mealtime*. The booklet contained messages from a variety of religions from Christianity to Islam and was intended to carry out the company's mission statement as a "faith-friendly company." In the first month of the offer, the company had more than 25,000 requests for the booklet. It also gained a good deal of criticism that it was commercializing religion. While advertisers must be aware that they reach unintended audiences, they also often use a single advertising campaign to reach several publics at once. A single advertisement might be directed to a number of publics:

distribution channel
The various intermediaries, such as retailers, that control the flow of goods from manufacturers to consumers.

1. *The* **distribution channel**. With the growth of huge national retailers such as Wal-Mart and Kmart, national advertisers often use consumer advertising to demonstrate to retailers that they are offering brands with high consumer demand and ones they are willing to support with significant advertising dollars at the consumer level. In fact, large retailers often demand a certain level of consumer advertising support before they will agree to stock a brand.

2. *Employees*. The most important assets of any company are its employees, and it is important to build loyalty and teamwork among rank-and-file workers. An advertising message may carry an overt appeal to employees by mentioning the quality workmanship that goes into a product or featuring company employees in advertising. More often, the message to employees is subtler but nevertheless can be an important function of advertising.

3. *Current and potential customers.* Obviously, the key to success for most companies is building brand awareness among new customers and enhancing brand loyalty among current buyers. Advertising is often the most efficient means of gaining both objectives.

4. *Stockholders.* Approximately 50 percent of American households currently own stock, up from 19 percent in 1983. For the first time in history, the majority of ordinary customers hold ownership in many of the companies they patronize. Not surprisingly, studies have shown that high brand awareness and a company's positive reputation are contributing factors to keeping stock prices higher than might otherwise be the case.

5. *The community at large.* Many companies operate local plants throughout the country. Advertising is often used to influence public opinion so that when the inevitable disputes about local tax assessments, excessive noise, or zoning ordinances arise, the company is viewed as a good neighbor.

Too often, firms take a short-term, narrow view of advertising. These companies view advertising from the perspective of the immediate (and intended) communication effects on the primary market for their products. However, advertising functions within a matrix of political, legal, economic, and cultural environments. Within each of these categories are interested parties who are judging companies and their products by the advertising messages they disseminate. It is important to consider the entire range of publics when developing a particular advertisement, commercial, or advertising campaign.

THE COMPONENTS OF ADVERTISING STRATEGY

With this section, we begin to discuss the fundamentals of advertising procedure. As we will see, the application of advertising techniques often demonstrates markedly different approaches from one company to another. Advertising should be designed to reach those consumers who are interested in the particular product features and benefits that a brand offers. The most successful brands are those with features and benefits unique within a product category and, consequently, those that hold a differentiated position in the minds of consumers. It is advertising's job to turn product benefits into an attention-getting story that appeals to prospective buyers. In this section, we discuss some of the primary elements of successful advertising. In subsequent chapters, we examine the various executions of these basic principles that set one brand apart from its competitors.

Brand Name

An established **brand name** that customers recognize and respect is one of the most valued assets of a company. Studies have shown that anywhere from one-third to one-half of the value of some companies comes from the brand names they own. One of the principal uses of advertising is to enhance brand familiarity awareness in the minds of consumers by emphasizing consumer benefits of a product. James Spaeth, past president of the Advertising Research Foundation, said that "A brand name is the intangible benefit that differentiates an otherwise readily substitutable product in a highly consumer relevant way." For example, a primary difference between McDonald's and the thousands of other fast-food restaurants that compete for consumers' dollars is its name.

Although high brand recognition is important for any product, it is especially critical for product categories that have little inherent product differentiation; that is, soft drinks, beer, cigarettes, and similar products are easily duplicated by competitors from a functional standpoint. What competitors cannot duplicate are the years of successful brand building, primarily through advertising, that the parent

brand name
The written or spoken part of a trademark, in contrast to the pictorial mark; a trademark word.

A study of 25 popular product categories and their leading brands shows that branding was an important concept over 80 years ago. And brands that were built then are still the dominant brands in the business today. Source: Proprietary research by Jack Trout, based on industry share data.

Rank	25 product categories	The leading brands in 1923	The leading brands of today	Only five lost their leadership
1	Bacon	Swift	Swift	Swift
2	Batteries	Eveready	Duracell	Eveready
3	Breakfast Cereal	Kellogg's Corn Flakes	Cheerios	Kellogg's Corn Flakes
4	Cameras	Kodak	Kodak	Kodak
5	Canned Fruit	Del Monte	Del Monte	Del Monte
6	Canned milk	Carnation	Carnation	Carnation
7	Chewing gum	Wrigley's	Wrigley's	Wrigley's
8	Chocolate	Hershey's	Hershey's	Hershey's
9	Crackers	Nabisco	Nabisco	Nabisco
10	Flour	Gold Medal	Gold Medal	Gold Medal
11	Mint candies	Life Savers	Life Savers	Life Savers
12	Paint	Sherwin-Williams	Sherwin-Williams	Sherwin-Williams
13	Paper	Hammermill	Hammermill	Hammermill
14	Pipe Tobacco	Prince Albert	Prince Albert	Prince Albert
15	Razors	Gillette	Gillette	Gillette
16	Sewing machines	Singer	Singer	Singer
17	Shirts	Manhattan	Arrow	Manhattan
18	Soap	Ivory	Dove	Ivory
19	Soft Drinks	Coca-Cola	Coca-Cola	Coca-Cola
20	Soup	Campbell's	Campbell's	Campbell's
21	Shortening	Crisco	Crisco	Crisco
22	Tea	Lipton	Lipton	Lipton
23	Tires	Goodyear	Goodyear	Goodyear
24	Toilet soap	Palmolive	Dial	Palmolive
25	Toothpaste	Colgate	Colgate	Colgate

EXHIBIT 2.7

Solid Foundations

companies have invested in their brands. Exhibit 2.7 demonstrates how difficult it is for competitors to compete against established brands. As the table points out, only five product category leaders have been replaced among twenty-five product types over the last 80 years. Even among the five displaced leaders, several remain popular names in the marketplace.

In the global market, companies are finding that overcoming entrenched local brands is very difficult as they expand into new markets. Although Asian companies dominate the manufacture of home appliances and electronics, they often lack the name recognition of American brands. In the automotive sector, Japanese carmakers such as Nissan, Toyota, and Honda have a strong presence, but it is one that has taken more than 25 years to achieve. Hoping to jump-start the process, many foreign companies have bought U.S. brands or even entire companies. Familiar American brands now owned by foreign manufacturers include IBM personal computers (Lenovo of China) and Zenith Electronics (LG Electronics of Korea). When China's Haier Group bid more than $1 billion to take over Maytag—including brands such as Amana, Hoover, and Jenn-Air—the primary motivation was acquisition of the brand names.[24] Although Maytag was eventually bought by Whirlpool Corporation, the Haier bid demonstrated the importance and value of brands. As new companies enter the global marketplace, brands will take on even more importance as a competitive tool to differentiate one product from another.

The fierce competition and the difficulty of entering new markets—either geographic or target market based—have caused many companies to consider

brand extension rather than brand innovation as a strategy for product introduction. As we have seen, high-profile brands are a major resource for companies in a competitive environment. Obviously, the cost and financial risk of introducing a new product under an established name are much less than under a completely new name. For example, once Bic became an established brand with its ballpoint pens, it was much more efficient to market disposable lighters and razors under the Bic name than building new brands. The problem faced by contemporary marketers is to determine when excessive brand extension begins to harm core brands that, in some cases, have been nurtured for a century or more.

brand extension
These are new product introductions under an existing brand to take advantage of existing brand equity.

"If you chase two rabbits, both will escape."

ANONYMOUS

Brand extensions are sometimes like the hunter chasing two rabbits. Companies want to keep their core audience while using an established brand to reach new markets. Soft drinks and automobiles have been among the most persistent users of brand extensions. As established brands such as Coca-Cola Classic and Pepsi demonstrate flat sales trends, the companies have moved to give sales a boost by introducing numerous products under some version of the core brand. Since 2000, Coca-Cola and Pepsi together introduced approximately twenty new beverages using some version of these brand names.

The decision to use a brand extension or introduce an entirely new product is not a trivial one. Major soft-drink makers know that many of these brand extensions will fail. A major consideration is whether or not a product failure will hurt the core brand in the minds of consumers. "There's also the danger of cannibalizing sales of existing brands when new products are pushed hard. Finally, ". . . companies also run the risk of confusing consumers by introducing too many products."[25]

An overriding problem of brand extensions is that successful brands have defined a special niche in the minds of consumers. When companies attempt to significantly enlarge or alter the scope of these brand positions, it leads consumers to question the values and benefits of the original brand. For example, the Volkswagen Phaeton luxury model (with prices starting in the mid-$60,000 range) met with lukewarm interest from consumers accustomed to seeing the brand sell in the $20,000 range. While brand extensions present challenges, most successful brands reach a point of saturation among their core consumers and see some form of brand extension—either through new products or different advertising positioning—as the only way to expand their markets.

In 1991, reacting to the healthy eating movement, executives at Kentucky Fried Chicken changed the name to simply KFC. To many, the change took an established brand that held a specific position in the marketplace—and in the minds of consumers—and substituted a meaningless set of initials that meant nothing to its market. Fast-forward to 2005: the company brought back the Kentucky Fried Chicken name along with its "Finger Lickin' Good" tagline in a fifty-store test. The KFC experience underscores a fundamental tenet of branding; "KFC violated basic rules that ailing marketers often forget when a business and market are in flux. Marketers need to be what they are, be authentic, be real. If you sell a product, make it the best you can, be proud of it, and don't waffle. . . ."[26]

As tempting as brand extensions can be, many companies take a more conservative approach, fearing any diminution of value in its core brands. For example, Nike has long wanted to enter the lower-priced shoe market to broaden its market and enhance overall profits. With the high-end athletic shoe market stagnant, it became even more imperative to develop new markets for less expensive footwear. In an innovative deal with Wal-Mart, Nike agreed to provide a running shoe for approximately $40. However, there will be no Nike name or swoosh logo in sight. The shoes will be marketed under the "Starter" brand with no observable connection to Nike. The introduction represents a test for both Nike and Wal-Mart. Nike will determine if it can profitably market a shoe that sells for significantly less than its other sneakers, and Wal-Mart will see if there is demand among its customers for a shoe that sells for considerably more than its current inventory.[27]

We can summarize our discussion of brand extension by looking at advantages and disadvantages of the strategy.

Advantages of a brand-extension strategy are:

1. Saving money by not needing to build awareness for a new and unknown brand name
2. Adding equity to an existing brand name with a successful extension

Disadvantages of a brand-extension strategy are:

1. Damaging a core brand in the minds of loyal consumers with a failed introduction
2. Losing marketing focus on your existing brand and/or diluting marketing efforts and budget across several brands

From these examples, we can see that no single brand strategy is right for every company. However, regardless of the approach, the development, protection, and maintenance of brand value will continue to be one of the driving forces in modern advertising. Building brand value or equity is one of the most important elements of advertising. Whether introducing a new product or maintaining the vitality of a mature one, brand identity is crucial to a product's success. Products are concrete objects; brands, on the other hand, represent attitudes and feelings about products.

A GOOD PRODUCT THAT MEETS A PERCEIVED NEED

The fundamental job of most businesses is to develop products that meet the need of some consumer segment (see Exhibit 2.8). Successful products are those that solve a consumer problem better and/or more economically than an available alternative. Products and services must also lend themselves to efficient promotion, distribution, and production that will produce a profit for the manufacturer or provider. The difficulty of the task of introducing successful products is underscored by the estimates that only one in seven product ideas that enter the developmental process are successful and nearly half of the dollars allocated to new product introductions go to products that either fail or are abandoned.[28]

If there is any doubt about the odds against new products, a trip to the closeout chain Big Lots provides a sobering experience. "Closeout retailer Big Lots is a microcosm of corporate America's mistakes, missteps and ambitions. The seemingly endless supply of new packaged-goods products—1,561 in 2004, according to Information Resources, Inc.—not to mention brand extensions—up 94% last year—has turned Big Lots into a \$4.3 billion brand with 1,500 stores."[29] One of the goals of product planning may be to stay off the shelves of Big Lots!

To create one of the relatively few products that will be successful in the marketplace, companies must start with the premise that they are offering not a physical object but, rather, the means of solving a problem. The late Harvard Professor Theodore Levitt is quoted as saying that "People don't want a quarter-inch drill. They want a quarter-inch hole!" "When people find themselves with a job to be done, they essentially *hire* products to do that for them. Following this model, then, the marketer's fundamental task is not so much to understand the *customer* as it is to understand what *jobs* customers need to do—and build products that serve those specific purposes."[30] The more closely a brand is associated with a specific job, the more likely it will be the first choice of consumers faced with a particular task.

When evaluating the marketing potential for innovative products or product line expansions, firms often have to determine the social and psychological ten-

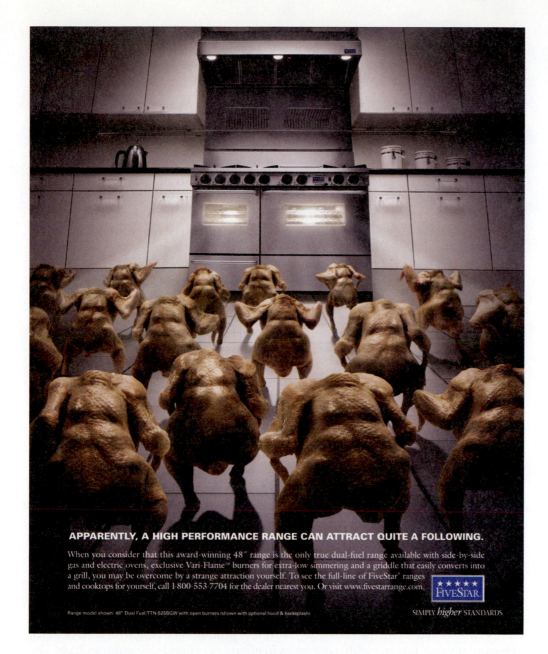

dencies of their prospects before moving ahead. For more than a century, Kodak dominated the home photography market by appealing to women emphasizing emotional appeals of "The Kodak Moment" rather than product technology. However, in the 1990s, the introduction of digital photography was a disaster for Kodak. Studies showed that, while women had the aptitude to deal with digital photography, many women indicated that they simply were not interested in dealing with the hardware necessary to take digital pictures.

Kodak could have changed its marketing strategy and competed against digital camera leaders such as Sony and Canon on a technological basis. Instead, Kodak chose to emphasize the simplicity of its digital cameras and associated computer software. At the same time, it continued to emphasize the female market as the family "keeper of memories." The strategy has been so successful that Kodak moved from the number three seller of digital cameras in 2002 to the number one position by mid-2005.[31] The Kodak experience underscored the fact that the product benefit (and how that benefit is achieved) is more important than the product itself. Successful products are those that are *perceived* by consumers as being best for a task, not necessarily those that are considered the winner according to some objective standard. For example, blind taste tests for soft drinks and beer have been notoriously unreliable in predicting what consumers will do in the marketplace.

One of the fundamental problems of product development addressed throughout the text is the fragmentation of both products and audiences. In their quest to gain market share and meet the demands of every market niche, companies have presented consumers with an array of oftentimes confusing alternatives. The variations of toothpaste, coffee, cereal, and virtually every other common household product can be overwhelming. Likewise, technology has created alternatives to accomplishing even the simplest tasks—with major implications for a variety of products. Up until a few years ago, if you wanted to see what time it was, you looked at your wristwatch. While there were a vast variety of timepieces in assorted prices and styles, the basic product remained the same for more than a century. Today, many young people have given up their watches although not the need to know the time. With cell phones, iPods, and laptops standard equipment for many young adults, a watch has become for many of them an unnecessary appliance. Watches appealing to younger market segments declined more than 10 percent from 2004 to 2005. Meanwhile, watchmakers are busy designing "watches" that do much more than tell time to meet this change in consumer preference. They have come up with everything from watches with music files, compasses, and thermometers to watches on charm bracelets and even ear buds that play digital music.[32]

Of course, attempting to determine the needs of consumers and actually doing so are two different things. For one thing, consumers may know their problems but not be able to enunciate the type of products that would solve these problems. This is particularly true of yet-to-be-marketed pioneering products. For example, before the invention of the microwave oven, consumers couldn't say they wanted a device that would stir up water molecules and provide a hot dinner in minutes. They could say that when they were tired and hungry they didn't want to wait 45 minutes for a conventional oven.[33]

It is not unusual for products to face changing preferences in the marketplace. The problem for marketing and advertising is how to adapt to these shifts in consumer attitudes without alienating current customers. The fundamental premise of fast-food outlets is the promise of speed and convenience—some would argue that these attributes are even more important than the food itself. Currently, Starbucks Corporation, a company founded on the premises of quality and premium pricing with an ambiance of leisure sipping, is faced with a dilemma in efforts to expand its customer base. The basic question facing Starbucks is whether or not it can keep its upscale image and at the same time move to drive-through pick-up windows. On the one hand, drive-through service offers the potential of increasing its breakfast business, especially in new suburban stores. On the other hand, some customers think that drive-through service cheapens the brand image and reduces it to just another fast-food outlet. There seems to be no consensus on the part of customers, with some suggesting they would not take the time to patronize a Starbucks without the drive-through convenience while others think that it cheapens the brand and makes it more aligned with McDonald's and Dunkin' Donuts.[34] The Starbucks example demonstrates that a brand is more than the physical characteristics of a product. Rather, it is a complex combination of product, price, distribution methods, and communication, which creates a sociological, psychological, and physical experience for users.

Mercedes-Benz has found that rebuilding consumers' trust in a brand is much harder than gaining it in the first place. Long known for its quality, the carmaker experienced some quality-control problems during the early 2000s. Mercedes found that it was able to correct many of the defects relatively quickly. However, it may take much longer to win back consumers lost by the mechanical problems. In

2006, Mercedes launched an extensive advertising campaign aimed at explaining the steps it took to correct the problems while at the same time countering Mercedes' negative brand perceptions among many car buyers.[35]

A key ingredient in determining product success is reliable research. Companies constantly employ a host of research techniques to discover the most appealing products, advertising and promotional messages that will be most interesting to target prospects, and even information about pricing and distribution preferences. In a survey in the *Wall Street Journal*, readers were asked, "What factor is most important to you when buying a car?" Among the almost 3,500 respondents, no more than 20 percent cited a single reason (price and style tied for first).[36] The survey only reinforced what researchers have known for years—that product purchase decisions are a result of numerous factors. Research also has shown that buyers often say that they want an array of product features but that they are uncertain about the priority they assign to these features and the price that they would be willing to pay for them.

Over the last 20 years, a research technique known as **conjoint analysis** has been developed to address the numerous ways a consumer considers a product. "The rationale underlying the technique is that consumers weigh all the many elements of a product or service—such as price, ingredients, packaging, technical specifications, and on and on—when choosing, say, a sweater, airline ticket, stereo system."[37] Consumers may prefer a particular airline, but scheduling (one stop versus nonstop) or bargain pricing may move them to another normally less preferred carrier.

Conjoint analysis considers the many individual elements that together determine consumer preference. By placing a value on these elements, it offers insight into the way consumers actually weigh considerations in making purchases. Done correctly, conjoint analysis can prevent costly mistakes when companies emphasize product characteristics that are of little value to consumers. By the same token, the technique allows product designers and marketers to concentrate on those factors that determine the characteristics of a "good product" in the minds of target prospects.

As we have seen in these examples, the key to successful advertising begins with product development and marketing from the consumer's perspective. For many companies, the idea of consumer empowerment in the marketing process has been given more than lip service. Procter & Gamble, the world's largest maker of consumer goods, has instituted an annual "Consumer is Boss" event. As part of Procter and Gamble's consumer emphasis, executives are required to man call-center phones to interact with customers and spend time with consumers in their homes or on shopping trips.[38] Procter & Gamble is not alone in adopting a bottom-up, consumer-centric model of product development and maintenance as opposed to the top-down model of providing customers with products companies hoped they would buy. Obviously, the failure rate for the latter demonstrated that this new approach was long overdue.

conjoint analysis
A research technique designed to determine what consumers perceive as a product's most important benefits.

Sales, Revenues, and Profit Potential

Marketing's contribution to profitability is achieved through a complex balance among sales, market share, promotional expenditures, and cost efficiency. Despite the contemporary demand for marketing accountability, there is no easy answer to the equation. For example, while strict accounting of expenditures and, when appropriate, making significant cuts in marketing and promotional outlays may contribute to immediate profits, no company achieves continuing success through protracted cost cutting. Likewise, gains in market share and gross sales may look good on the short-term balance sheet, but they can be misleading if this growth is not related to profitability. The cleverest advertisement or the most humorous, memorable television commercial is totally worthless unless it contributes directly to company profitability.

While only the most unsophisticated marketing executives would emphasize sales and revenue goals to the detriment of profits, a number of strategies are used to attain profitability. In this section, we examine three major approaches used by established companies to achieve long-term revenues and profits:

1. *Developing and expanding new-product niches to reach current customers.* In the early 1990s, JCPenney's advertising was driven by sales and price promotions with little attention given to the JCPenny brand. Other than bargain pricing, there was little reason for a customer to shop at JCPenney because it offered little differentiation from other retailers. Beginning in 2000, JCPenney began a centralized branding strategy to set the chain apart from competitors such as Target and Macy's. The approach combined centralized control of advertising with the introduction of a number of private-label brands marketed exclusively through JCPenney. The JCPenney program was driven by a process known as "gap analysis." Simply put, the store looked for gaps in the style preferences of customers and then developed private-branded clothing to fill those gaps. Today, JCPenney is among the most profitable clothing retailers, and it has established a reputation for exclusivity with its in-house brands.[39]

   Wal-Mart, unlike JCPenney, has long had a distinctive and dominant brand image. However, with 93 percent of households shopping at Wal-Mart at least once a year, the company held such a high level of market share that future increases in profitability were difficult to achieve. A recently announced strategy is to move upscale customers who are currently purchasing household goods and underwear at Wal-Mart to think of the chain as a place to buy fashion clothing. Toward this end, Wal-Mart ran advertisements in *Vogue* featuring real customers but in much more stylish settings than in previous advertising. While results are still out on the success of the campaign, most observers think that it holds little risk for the company of losing its current customer base. As one marketing consultant said, "You are never in danger when you make what you sell appealing."[40]

2. *Emphasizing profits over sales volume.* On January 23, 2006, Ford Motor Company Chairman William Clay Ford Jr. announced a 20 percent reduction in its workforce and the closing of fourteen plants. In his announcement, Mr. Ford said that the company was moving away from a philosophy of "if you build it, they will buy it," in which product planning was driven by available production capacity. The new plan drastically cut production to match demand; furthermore, Mr. Ford indicated that "From now on, our vehicles will be designed to satisfy the customer, not just fill a factory."[41] Ford is redesigning and introducing a number of new models with a strategy of giving emphasis to revenue and profitability over sales and market share. The move once again underscores the fact that gross revenue and sales volume can be a misleading gauge of a company's success. Similarly, General Motors followed Ford's announcement by declaring its intention to cut back on marginally profitable sales such as fleet transactions and emphasize high-profit models even at the expense of overall market share.[42]

3. *Emphasizing short-term market share rather than profitability.* Faced with significant increases in advertising and promotion from arch rival Procter & Gamble, Colgate-Palmolive made the decision that it had to reduce profit levels in coming years in order to protect market share in a number of product categories. In commenting on the battle between Procter & Gamble and Colgate-Palmolive, the *Wall Street Journal* reported, ". . . a struggle for market share

between big consumer goods companies will likely erode profit growth for the next several years."[43] The Colgate-Palmolive example underscores the need to take a long-term perspective in developing a marketing strategy.

4. *Customer tracking—are all customers created equal?* Among the goals of advertising is to grow the customer base of a firm. However, we also need to bear in mind that some customers may be a detriment to a company's bottom line. Some companies have long discouraged continued patronage from some of their buyers. For example, insurers cancel policies for those that "use" the product too often and banks impose significantly higher fees for customers who maintain low balances or write excessive checks. Now other mainline companies are beginning to identify and reward their best customers (i.e., most profitable) while discouraging less-valuable buyers with a number of tactics.

Obviously, retailers do not refuse to sell to a customer; and, unlike insurance companies, they can't cancel their buying privileges. On the other hand, retailers initiate restrictive return policies for those who frequently take back merchandise; delete less-profitable buyers from direct mail and Internet promotion lists; and, with checkout scanning technology, provide coupons for future purchases only to A-list customers. As one marketing consultant pointed out, "It is controversial to redline [eliminate] customers. But done correctly, it really is simply about saying I have a limited pool of money, and I need as a business person to spend that money where I can get the most return."[44]

The emphasis on profit-based accountability in all areas of advertising and promotion has created major changes in many areas of advertising. For example, advertising agencies are being compensated on how their work contributes to a client's bottom line, not whether they produce award-winning advertisements, and media buys are evaluated from the perspective of their return on investment. At the corporate level, all marketing and promotional functions are being given much greater scrutiny than ever before and are increasingly being judged on the basis of return on investment.

This move to more precisely measure the contributions of advertising has led to a broader view of what advertising can and should accomplish. For example, advertisers are focusing on the role of advertising in *maintaining* sales and market share as a goal of equal importance to *increasing* sales. It is difficult to measure the value of advertising in terms of sales not lost versus sales gained. However, given the cost involved in finding new customers versus keeping present ones, the overall contributions to profitability may actually be greater in the former case. The emphasis on profitability and accountability—and the technology that allows them to be more precisely measured—has largely eliminated past mistakes made by viewing sales and revenues as substitutes for profits. A review of the last decade demonstrates that some of the largest companies in America (in terms of sales volume) experienced the largest financial losses. Anyone can devise a marketing plan that will result in greater sales if profits are not considered.

Product Timing

Successful business ventures, including advertising, often depend on proper timing. From a strategic standpoint, advertising timing involves the interaction between stages of product development known as the **product life cycle** and the probability of marketplace acceptance. For example, the current growth in Internet selling was only possible when household computer usage reached a certain level. Likewise, consumers had to be convinced that transactions could be completed in a secure environment where credit card and other personal information was protected. Finally, the introduction of online selling by major brands and retailers and

product life cycle
The process of a brand moving from introductions to maturity and, eventually, to either adaptation or demise.

new companies such as Amazon came together to create a comfort level for a computer marketplace. As we discuss more fully in the next chapter, the level of product maturity is a critical timing issue in marketing and advertising decisions. Advertising functions differently at various stages of the product life cycle. During the introduction and growth phase of a product, businesses advertise to establish a beachhead against competition and to gain a level of consumer awareness. As products enter more mature stages of development, advertising strategies take longer perspectives and their goals are likely to be involved in brand equity and a longer horizon for sales development. With this in mind, businesses constantly evaluate their brands based, in part, on the maturity of the brands.

Product introduction and the advertising that accompanies it are among the most important decisions that determine the long-term success of a company. Few companies enjoy long-term survival without a steady flow of new products and product innovations. Likewise, how these improvements are communicated and to what market segments they are offered can have a major influence on their acceptance. The key is not just to spot new trends but, rather, to creatively develop products and services to take advantage of them in the marketplace. "Don't confuse real trends with what's simply trendy. Trends are long-term economic, sociological, anthropological changes in the way people behave or believe."[45] Research conducted by Procter & Gamble found that men wanted to protect their skin but viewed most skin-care products as feminine. The company marketed a line of skin-care products under the Boss Skin brand. A crucial part of the introduction was print and television advertising that was decidedly manly with black backdrops and the tagline "Tested by Men."[46]

In many cases, the trend spotting is relatively easy, especially that associated with future demographic changes. For example, we know that during the next 20 years the United States will see growing numbers of people who are single, elderly, and of various ethnic minorities. These changes will have an impact on all consumer markets but especially on the food industry. More meals will be eaten out of the home, there will be a demand for smaller packages, consumers will purchase more health-oriented foods, and manufacturers will offer much more diversity in food choices in both the restaurant and grocery categories. We will see products entering the mainstream that were formerly niche products. However, turning these trends into winning products that will best the competition is the key to success.

One of the great frustrations of marketers is that no matter how good a product is, it can rarely be forced on consumers before they are ready to accept it. Fuel-efficient automobiles have become a major area of competition in the last few years. However, without the current spikes in gasoline prices and more awareness of environmental issues by the public, it is doubtful that these cars would have been accepted. In fact, in a very short period, fuel economy has moved from a fringe benefit for many buyers to a major marketing tool. Virtually every domestic and foreign carmaker is marketing a fuel-efficient car and making conservation a key theme in its advertising. As a spokesman for Daimler-Chrysler said, "We've definitely stepped up efforts to advertise our fuel economy. You will see more on it in the future."[47]

Demonstrating that fuel conservation is not a fad nor is it confined just to the car industry, we are seeing a number of other products touting energy savings. Products including lawn mowers, home furnaces and air conditioners, and a number of home appliances are emphasizing fuel economy in their advertising and product development. "Responding to public sentiment in the wake of soaring gas prices, marketers of all stripes are pitching energy conservation and efficiency in their marketing messages."[48] The question is how marketers can take advantage of the trend toward conservation to connect with consumers with products that buyers perceive will meet their demand for achieving responsible consumption.

Let's look at a couple of other examples, one a "trend" that turned out to be decidedly a fad and another an example of products in development hoping to catch a trend. First, low-carb eating was going to revolutionize weight maintenance and create a new food industry built on a high-protein, low-carb diet. Developed by Dr. Robert C. Atkins, the Atkins diet and a host of related eating plans generated hundreds of products for followers of the plan. However, many people thought the diet was too restrictive for the long term, and soon one food maker after another withdrew low-carb products from grocers' shelves. While many dieters gave up the Atkins plan, they didn't forsake their desire to lose weight. To cater to this audience, a number of companies are introducing "portion-control" products that allow eaters to indulge their cravings but still closely count calories. Nestlé and Hershey's have introduced 90-calorie candy products that attempt to cater to both weight consciousness and indulgence. As one marketing consultant observed, "Better-for-you eating is becoming a more consistent lifestyle choice for more people and rather than face the headwinds, many companies are trying to offer products that show how you can responsibly fit some indulgence into a weight-management program."[49] Only time will tell whether these product will resonate with consumers.

Another example of trend spotting that marketers hope will lead to new-product success is eating on the run. We have already seen the first phase with the introduction by food manufacturers and fast-food outlets of a variety of "one-handed, drive-friendly" food. From soup to tacos to chips, eat-on-the-run enthusiasts have numerous options to fill up on the road—according to Productscan, 405 food brands with the word "Go" were introduced in 2004. Dining mobility carries with it the inevitable result that food often ends up on ties, trousers, and blouses just as drivers are ready to make their next sales call or interview. Procter & Gamble, hoping to profit from the in-car eating trend, introduced Tide to Go stain-removal stick. The stick was developed to work on freshly spilled food and drink and looks like a small highlighter pen.[50] While it is too soon to determine if Tide to Go will be a success, it demonstrates the way trends evolve into an array of products and the importance of timing in the introduction of most new products.

Market timing may be a matter of doing something first rather than doing something different. For example, makers of baby products know that their prime market is mothers of newborns. In the past, most strategies to reach this market involved contact with mothers shortly after the birth of their children. For example, mothers might be given a gift sampler of baby products when leaving the hospital. Kimberly-Clark Corporation, maker of Huggies disposable diapers, decided to get a jump on the competition by developing a relationship with expectant mothers shortly after they became pregnant. The key to the strategy was an expanded Internet presence that offered expectant mothers not just an introduction to the company's baby's products but answers to questions and solutions to problems common to all new mothers and mothers-to-be. The company's ". . . $7 million marketing effort [is] designed to befriend women as soon as they get pregnant. The idea is to build a relationship so that Huggies will be top of mind as new moms buy their first package of diapers."[51]

Timing is often strategic, involving long-term decisions by both customers and marketers. However, timing can also be tactical, involving sales related to specific events or occasions. For example, a major department store often substituted an umbrella and rainwear advertisement in the next day's newspaper when rain was predicted. Super Bowl Sunday is the biggest day for pizza delivery, especially in the cities whose teams are participating in the game. To accommodate sales that are sometimes 400 percent higher than normal, stores cancel vacations for drivers, stock extra supplies of dough and chicken wings, and pay workers overtime. Some stores reduce absenteeism by providing drivers with satellite radios so they don't miss the game during deliveries. Domino's stores provide television sets in stores so employees can anticipate orders, which spike during commercials and halftime.[52]

Timing also is a major factor in the everyday function of advertising. Agency media planners deal with timing issues every day. Should television commercials be placed in prime time? Daytime? Late night? Should they be 30-second or 1-minute commercials? Should newspaper advertisements run on weekends or in midweek? Are magazine advertisements more effective in monthly or weekly publications; and, in either case, what is the most effective placement schedule? Every issue? Every fourth issue? Timing, in all its variations, is one of the most important decisions in advertising.

Finally, advertising may contribute to changing consumers' normal buying season for a product category. For example, over the years, marketers have found that seasonal products such as soft drinks and soup can effectively expand the life of a product from a niche category to one with year-round potential. In fact, "off timing" from competitive advertising patterns is a method of differentiation if consumers will purchase during nontraditional periods. Still, it is rare for any product category to have consistent sales throughout the year and advertisers are taking a major risk when they run counter to established consumer buying patterns and preferences.

Product Differentiation

product differentiation
Unique product attributes that set off one brand from another.

Product differentiation is the circumstance in which a target audience regards a product as different from others in the category. While this difference may be the result of some tangible attribute of the physical product, it also is often based on some intangible elements about the product including a brand image created in part by advertising. "The consumer's perception of brand value comes from many sources, but essentially it is based on ideas—rational or emotional—that set the brand apart from competitive brands."[53] Meaningful product differentiation exists only if it is perceived as an important distinction by consumers. If consumers *think* a product is better, then it is—regardless of any objective judgments to the contrary.

In the absence of a strong brand identity built on meaningful differentiation, buyers tend to view all brands in a category as interchangeable. When there are no real or perceived differences among brands, products are viewed as commodities and purchase decisions tend to be based on price. To the extent that price is the primary differentiating factor, profitability suffers as brands offer deeper and deeper price cuts to maintain market share. That is why brands built on an exclusive product attribute have such an advantage in the marketplace. As we mentioned earlier, attribute exclusivity is a matter of consumer perception. For example, if you did a survey and asked potential car buyers what brand is most closely associated with "safety," a majority of respondents would probably answer Volvo. In fact, the brand is so closely associated with safety that the carmaker felt safe in expanding its positioning to include performance and styling. In order to appeal to a broader customer base, Volvo introduced a new theme for its 2006 models: "Safety is a beautiful thing, especially when it's beautiful." As a Volvo executive commented, while its advertising may push other features, ". . . safety is always going to be part of our message."[54]

Products with well-defined positions find that their differentiating characteristics also can play major roles in brand extensions if the differentiation is transferable to new products. For example, Procter & Gamble introduced Febreze Fabric Refresher as a laundry accessory to give clothes a fresh scent. While the brand was the category leader, it was obvious that there was limited growth potential given the number of consumers who used fresheners as part of their laundry routine. Based on consumer research, Procter & Gamble extended the brand with the introduction of Febreze Air Effects, its brand of air freshener. The new product was an immediate hit and built the combined Febreze brand into a billion-dollar juggernaut and demonstrated once again that brand equities can be broader than a single product category.[55]

One of the most important elements of differentiation is keeping an open mind about how to achieve it. If a product is a bundle of benefits, we must look at the entire bundle when searching for a meaningful differentiation. Product differentiation often involves minor changes in either a product or the position communicated by advertising. For example, in a marketplace with a deli or sandwich shop on every corner, Quiznos created a distinctive position with toasted sandwiches. From its start in 1981, Quiznos now has more than 3,000 stores in the United States and fifteen foreign countries. One problem that the chain faces is that its distinctive toasted sandwich is being offered by larger chains such as Subway and a number of other franchises. Whether Quiznos can continue to "own" toasted sandwiches as a distinctive differentiation in the face of growing competition remains to be seen. The situation does point up the problem of product differentiation based on features that can be duplicated by competitors in a reasonably short period.

Too often when companies search for product differentiation they concentrate on product function. A product category facing major problems of brand differentiation is cell phones. Surveys indicate that most users are quite satisfied with their cell phones, provider service, and the calling area for their phones. In this type of product environment, price becomes the overriding motivation for selecting a brand—at the expense of corporate profits. Motorola, one of the major players in the cell-phone industry, decided that because service and function were regarded as equal by consumers, it would compete on the basis of design. The RAZR cell phone was intended to capture the youth market. Its name adopted spelling used in text and Internet messaging shorthand. The RAZR propelled Motorola from a distant second in 2001 to the number one position with 36 percent of the market in the United States while making strong gains in international markets.[56] The RAZR example shows that any part of the "benefit package" is open to examination when searching for unique differentiations.

The key motivation in the product-differentiation strategy is to reduce the competition for your brand. Competition is usually present but not something to be embraced. In the contemporary marketing environment, one of the major challenges for businesses is to separate their products from those of competitors in the minds of consumers. The more consumers see your product as meaningfully different from competing brands, the less the competition. W. Chan Kim and Renée Mauborgne in their book *Blue Ocean Strategy* argue that competition is both a waste of time and a strain on scarce resources. Their suggestion to firms is: "Don't compete in an existing market space; create a new one without any competition. Don't try to fight for demonstrated demand; build new demand."[57] Remember that just being different is not enough. It is not even sufficient that consumers perceive that the product is different. The key is that prospects see a brand as differentiated in a manner that is important to solve their specific problems.

Before we leave the topic of product differentiation, we should mention two important elements involved in the process. First, as companies set about to differentiate their products, they should remember that product differentiation is also a means of target marketing. As they position their brands to appeal to a specific market segment, they often simultaneously surrender those consumers looking for features not emphasized in their brands to other manufacturers. A carmaker who markets a sports model that features high-performance handling, fancy design, glitzy colors, and an ornamental trim will eliminate cost-conscious, family-oriented buyers as it appeals more directly to the high-performance car market. Before embarking on a specific product-differentiation strategy, companies must make sure that their brand position is important to enough prospects that they will be able to sustain a profitable niche.

Finally, firms have a special responsibility as they develop a brand-differentiation strategy. Advertisers have an obligation to promote meaningful product differences. Much of the criticism of modern advertising is that it tries to make obscure and inconsequential product variations important. There is no question that some advertising promotes unimportant product features. However, the best and most successful products demonstrate valuable differences from their competitors.

Price

"Pricing power has long been the ultimate arbiter of brand value—a marketer's ability to charge consumers more than it costs them to provide a product or service is largely determined by perception of their product."[58] In this sense, price is closely related to product differentiation. "One useful way to look at what a company does is to think of it as a translation device between what the customer needs and what [the company] can do. A marketer's task is to get the translation just right, so that the price you charge represents fair compensation for the value you create."[59] Obviously, the cost of producing and marketing a product has to play a role in pricing strategy, but pricing strategy is much more complicated than simply covering costs and providing a reasonable profit. In fact, price is most often dictated by favorable consumer perceptions of the value of a product—a perception that is created in part by advertising. In many instances, the value of a brand has little to do with its objective worth. In fact, a primary function of advertising is to create, or enhance, a positive gap between the price of a product and the value the average consumer assigns to the product. The greater this **value gap**, the more insulated the product is from price competition. The concept of the value gap emphasizes the notion that price alone is not a particularly safe means of establishing a long-term, competitive advantage.

A major part of positioning a product in the market and in the minds of consumers is setting the price. At least some segment of consumers in each product category equates price with value; and, especially at the retail level, price plays an important role in maintaining sales (see Exhibit 2.9). These consumers gain a psychological benefit by the mere fact of paying more for a product. Price also defines

value gap
The perceived difference between the price of a product and the value ascribed to it by consumers.

EXHIBIT 2.9

Price is usually only one factor in creating demand.

Courtesy of Johnson Group.

who your competitors are. For example, the price-conscious buyers of the Ford Escort are not in the same market as customers for luxury-model BMWs or Mercedes. Rather than viewing pricing strategy as solely a means of covering costs, it should also be seen as an integral part of overall marketing strategy. ". . . [S]hould you charge more than your competitors? Or price below them? Should you pass cost increases along? And what message do these alternatives convey about you and your company?"[60] One only has to compare the advertising for a discounter such as Wal-Mart and an upscale retailer like Nieman-Marcus to see how price positioning dictates the tone and content of the message.

While price has long been a major topic of concern for marketers, new technology is allowing them to be more flexible and precise in relating price to specific market segments, seasonal selling, and particular items within a product line. Many marketers have long used a strategy known as **yield management** to even out supply and demand. Hotels offer special weekend rates to offset the loss of business travelers. Car-rental companies offer specials based on seasonal demand, and telephone companies cut long-distance rates on weekends and evenings as a form of yield management. Too often these pricing strategies were hit or miss, based more on instinct than solid data. However, with software programs that identify consumer segments in terms of their sensitivity to price, the process has become much more sophisticated and reliable. At the retail level, research technology allows managers to analyze each store as its own discrete market. Known as *variable pricing strategy*, it offers "each customer a different price at a different point in time."[61] The goal is to neither lose sales by offering price-sensitive customers merchandise at too high a cost nor lose profits by selling goods below what premium buyers would be willing to pay.

yield management
A product pricing strategy to control supply and demand.

We should make it clear that we are not disparaging a low-price strategy as a legitimate marketing tool and advertising strategy. It can be an important element in the marketing process. Many successful products cater to the low end of the price spectrum within a category. In fact, store brands, one of the fastest-growing segments of grocery and home products, are almost exclusively marketed as low-cost alternatives to name brand competitors. Depending on the product type, pricing strategy can be both a means of market entry for new products and a means of product differentiation for mature products. A new product can gain immediate visibility with a price advantage. For example, KIA cars and Men's Wearhouse owe much of their initial success to their low prices. Likewise, for both new and mature products, price is an important point of differentiation. However, in recent years, companies as diverse as Kohl's department stores, Southwest Airlines, and Suave shampoo have found that low-price strategies must be augmented by a strong consumer promise to be successful.

Pricing is one of the most studied areas of marketing and advertising. Proper pricing strategy is necessary for profitability and the continued existence of a business. However, it is a rare circumstance when a brand enjoys long-term success with a low-price strategy in the absence of some other brand value positioning. Price also plays a major role in advertising strategy. It is very difficult for an advertising creative plan to ignore the basic price/value perception held by a target audience. The pricing strategy for a brand determines to a significant degree the type of marketing strategy that can be used and the success that advertising will have in promoting and selling a specific brand.

VARIATIONS IN THE IMPORTANCE OF ADVERTISING

Because companies differ in terms of their marketing goals, competitive situation, product line, and customer base, we would expect that advertising plans demonstrate markedly different approaches from one company to another. Exhibit 2.10 demonstrates the wide variance among major companies in terms of advertising-

EXHIBIT **2.10**

Reliance on advertising.

From Bradley Johnson, "R&D vs. Ads in Battle for Bucks," *Advertising Age,* May 1, 2006, pg. 1. Copyright © 2006 Crain Communications, Inc. Used with permission.

Advertising's share of worldwide revenue for selected 100 LNA marketers. Beauty seller Estee Lauder is at the top; Wal-Mart is most efficient.

Least Reliant			Most Reliant		
LNA RNK[1]	Marketer	'05 AD Spend. as % of Rev.	LNA RNK[1]	Marketer	'05 AD Spend. as % of Rev.
30	Estee Lauder Cos.[2]	28.6	40	Wal-Mart Stores	0.5
100	Molson Coors Brewing Co.	13.2	37	Hewlett-Packard Co.	1.3
20	Unilever	12.6	23	Home Depot	1.3
78	Mattel	12.1	48	Dell Inc.	1.4
3	Time Warner	11.8	57	IBM Corp.	1.4
65	Nike	11.7	86	BellSouth Corp.	1.5
41	Gillette Co.[3]	11.5	6	DaimlerChrysler	1.7
61	Diaego	11.3	5	AT&T Inc.	1.9
68	Coca-Cola Co.	10.7	36	Target Corp.	2.0
2	Procter & Gamble Co.	10.4	13	Toyota Motor Corp.	2.0

Figures for most recent available calendar or fiscal year for 100 LNA marketers that disclosed ad spending. 1. *Ad Age*'s '04 Leading National Advertisers, 2. Includes promotions, 3. 2004; P&G bought Gillette in '05.

to-revenue ratios. Even within the same industry, companies often demonstrate large discrepancies in the use of advertising (see Exhibit 2.11). Advertising investments fall along a continuum from the rare company that uses none to the equally unusual business that allocates its entire marketing communication budget to advertising.

Most firms use advertising in concert with a number of other promotional activities. The role that advertising plays in a company's promotional strategy depends on a number of factors including:

1. *Corporate preference for various segments of marketing communication channels.* In an era of greatly expanding communication options, marketers

EXHIBIT **2.11**

Even products in the same class often demonstrate wide variance in levels of advertising spending.

From Bradley Johnson, "Toyota Gets the Best Bang for Its Ad Bucks," *Advertising Age,* March 13, 2006, pg. 39. Copyright © 2006 Crain Communications, Inc. Used with permission.

Measured ad spending by auto marketers; excludes dealer associations and dealer advertising Corporate and multibrand spending apportioned to brands based on sales.

Vehicle	'05 Ad Spend	Vehicle	'05 Ad Spend
Scion	$284	Subaru	$863
Isuzu	$293	Lexus	$875
Ford	$369	Hyundai	$932
Toyota	$422	Lincoln & Mercury	$965
Chevrolet	$454	Saturn	$1,012
Mini	$458	Acura	$1,050
Honda	$482	Cadillac	$1,088
BMW	$507	Suzuki	$1,161
Volvo	$599	Audi	$1,221
Chrysler, Dodge, Jeep	$619	Volkswagen	$1,431
Bentley	$632	Infiniti	$1,545
Porsche	$648	Mitsubishi	$1,557
Mercedes-Benz	$660	Maserati	$1,968
Pontiac	$671	Rolls-Royce	$2,044
GMC	$681	Saab	$2,116
Buick	$751	Hummer	$2,343
Kia	$785	Land Rover	$2,406
Mazda	$807	Jaguar	$2,517
Nissan	$861	Aston Martin	$3,698

have more choices than ever before to effectively reach their target audiences. For example, the top five airlines reduced advertising spending by one-third from 1994 to 2004, opting instead for one-on-one communication with their best customers. "With a wide range of information about their customers—where they travel and how often, for starters—carriers can issue finely tuned offers to loyalty-program members."[62] Procter & Gamble, a company synonymous with the 30-second television commercial, has begun to shift significant spending from television commercials to product placement—paying to have its products on various television shows. Likewise, General Mills reduced its advertising budget as a percentage of sales from 4.8 percent in 2002 to 3.3 percent in 2005. According to the company, the reduction was a result of utilizing nontraditional and new media approaches including the Internet and tests with cell-phone messaging.[63] As a number of major companies experiment with marketing through the Internet, event marketing, word-of-mouth advertising, and public relations, we will continue to see a trend to supplement or replace dollars previously spent in traditional advertising media. Molson Coors' national rollout of its Blue Moon beer represented an extreme example of this move away from advertising. The company relied entirely on word-of-mouth advertising to build brand awareness. Noting the fact that consumers tended to "discover" Blue Moon through recommendations from friends, a spokeswoman for the brand said that television and radio advertisements were contrary to what the Blue Moon brand is about.[64]

2. *High sales volume tends to lower advertising to sales ratios.* Companies with high sales volumes tend to spend less on advertising as a percentage of sales. In part, the consumers of these companies have often been saturated over a number of years with the brand story and need only to be reminded of the brand, not "sold" on it. In addition, the brands with the highest sales are also the most dominant in the market and the cost of attaining new customers through additional advertising may be nonproductive.

3. *Industries with a number of competing firms and/or extensive competition.* The acknowledged leader in the snack-food segment is Pepsico's Frito-Lay division. In addition to the flagship Frito brand, Lay's, Cheetos, Doritos, and Tostitos are among the iconic brand names that allow the company to dominate the salty snack category. In spite of its dominant position in the category, Frito-Lay announced a 50 percent increase in its advertising budget in 2005.[65] The company's rationale for the increase was that a number of companies such as Nabisco have entered the market with snack-size packages of popular cookies, crackers, and candy. By introducing new lines of snacks and increasing advertising support for its core brands, Frito-Lay hopes to prevent loss of market share by recognizing that competition in the snack category is not confined to salty snacks, which it dominates, but potentially comes from any snack product.

4. *Product categories with widespread competition and little perceived product differentiation.* In the first 6 months of 2005, carmakers ranked number one among all advertisers in total advertising spending. The high level of expenditures in the industry reflects the degree of competition among major manufacturers as they try to maintain or enhance market share. Interestingly, the number two spending category is telecommunications companies that face many of the same marketing challenges. With the recently announced mergers of major telecom companies, it will be interesting to see if less competition results in a decrease in advertising dollars in the future.

5. *Reversing sales or market share declines.* Advertising is generally seen as a tool to increase sales and expand customer usage. However, advertising also

is used as a defensive weapon to halt declines in market share and sales volume. As we discuss in Chapter Six, often smaller brands in a category must allocate a significantly higher percentage of sales to advertising to compete with larger competitors. Companies such as Burger King and Wendy's spend at very high levels compared with most industries, but their dollars are dwarfed by McDonald's.

This list is not intended to include all the factors that might determine the level of advertising expenditures in a specific marketing communication plan. However, it does demonstrate the many variables that must be considered when a business is deciding the role that advertising will play. Companies, even those with similar product lines, not only use different levels of advertising as part of their marketing communication mix but also utilize vastly different advertising plans in terms of media used, scheduling of advertising placements, and the messages communicated. The allocation of advertising dollars is a continually changing dynamic of marketing management. Sometimes changes in advertising's role are made simply to avoid audience wearout after being exposed to the same marketing communication mix over a long period of time. However, most often, advertising is altered according to some specific change in the marketing environment.

ADVERTISING AND THE MARKETING CHANNEL

One of the most important aspects of marketing is the development of the marketing channel. Exhibit 2.12 presents a traditional marketing channel model in which both products and communication flow from manufacturers to ultimate consumers. A well-organized marketing channel creates efficiencies through specialization in the movement of goods from producers, wholesalers, and retailers to ultimate consumers. Crucial to market channel efficiency is effective communication, including advertising. Most of the advertising that we see every day is called *consumer advertising* because it is directed to end-of-channel customers. However, advertising also plays a major role in moving products through the various levels of production and distribution in the marketing channel.

For most of the last century, the fundamentals of the marketing channel remained unchanged. Each product and service developed certain distribution methods for reaching consumers that were relatively consistent within an industry. However, in the last decade, new technology has started to change even longtime relationships among various elements of the marketing channel. For example, travel agents have seen their business drop as more and more travelers buy tickets directly from airline and hotel websites. Digital cameras are quickly doing away with the need for film and film processing. More and more consumers are producing pictures on their home computer, sending them by e-mail and bypassing hard copy prints altogether. Likewise, the ability to down-

EXHIBIT 2.12

The traditional marketing channel is undergoing significant changes.

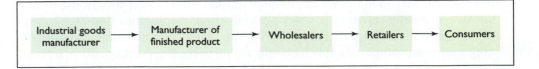

load music has affected all levels of the music marketing channel from major recording studios to the local music store. As we discuss the distribution channel, we should be aware that the "traditional" marketing channel has largely been replaced by distribution and marketing communication systems that are unique to each seller.

One of the fundamental changes has been the control of both marketing and communication channels by the consumer. For example, 68 percent of new-car buyers use nonmanufacturer-owned websites to gain information and 37 percent of new-car sales are the direct result of online purchase decisions.[66] Research studies underscore the importance of the Internet as a marketing communications tool across a number of product categories and market segments. More than half of electronic goods buyers report they gathered information online before making a purchase, and approximately 25 percent spent as long as 3 hours researching their purchase. As one electronic marketer commented, "People are using the Internet not only to gather information about brands, but about product selection and variations of products and pricing."[67] A decade ago, the Internet was overwhelmingly a male-dominated communication channel. However, in recent years, that has changed dramatically as more and more women are using the convenience of Internet commerce. New mothers report that they have reduced their out-of-home shopping with the Internet, and 32 percent report fewer trips to shopping malls. Overall, 78 percent of women report they use the Internet to obtain product information.[68]

While the Internet has had profound effects on consumer behavior, its use is even more dramatic among business-to-business (B2B or B-T-B) buyers. Given the relatively small number of B2B buyers in any particular industry, traditional media have rarely been efficient as sales tools in this market. The Internet, with its ability to identify and communicate on a one-to-one basis, allows B2B sellers to customize their sales messages to the unique needs of each customer. Research shows that the Web is an excellent means of reaching B2B decision makers (see Exhibit 2.13), but more important, it is the best way to influence purchases (see Exhibit 2.14).

While the Internet has increased the options for communicating and selling, it has not changed the fundamental decision-making process. Marketing strategy not only determines the role of advertising and its budget but also plays a major part in

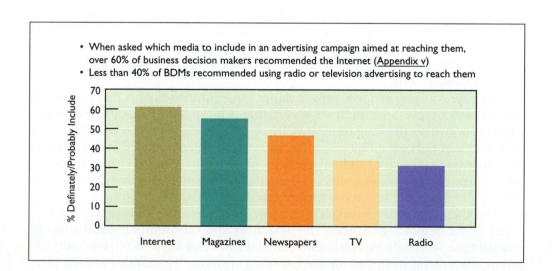

- When asked which media to include in an advertising campaign aimed at reaching them, over 60% of business decision makers recommended the Internet (Appendix v)
- Less than 40% of BDMs recommended using radio or television advertising to reach them

EXHIBIT 2.13

The Web is the best place to reach decision makers.

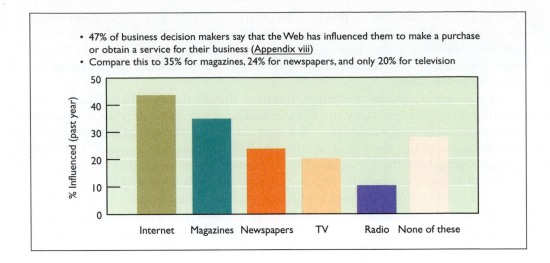

- 47% of business decision makers say that the Web has influenced them to make a purchase or obtain a service for their business (Appendix viii)
- Compare this to 35% for magazines, 24% for newspapers, and only 20% for television

decisions concerning media choices. For example, a plan to use a coupon promotion will probably dictate a print media strategy. A decision to demonstrate product features may mean that television or the Internet will get the call. A complex sales message may take us to magazines, and a localized advertising strategy may move our message into newspapers or radio.

In the remainder of this chapter, we examine some of the ways advertising functions in various industries and stages of the marketing channel. Although you are most familiar with consumer advertising, it is only one of a number of categories that are used to bring products to market. Regardless of its audience, effective advertising must be successful on two levels: (1) communicating and (2) carrying out marketing goals.

Perhaps the easiest way to evaluate advertising's role in the marketing process is to evaluate the *directness* of the intended communication effect and the anticipated *time* over which that effect is supposed to function. In other words, how much of the total selling job should be accomplished by advertising and over what time frame should we expect that task to be accomplished?

Advertising designed to produce an immediate response in the form of product purchase is called *direct-action, short-term* advertising. Most retail advertising falls into this category. An advertisement that runs in the newspaper this morning should sell some jeans this afternoon. Advertising used as a direct-sales tool but designed to operate over a longer time frame is called *direct-action, long-term* advertising. This advertising category is used with high-ticket items (washers and tires) in which the purchase decision is a result of many factors and the purchase cycle is relatively long.

Another category of advertising includes those advertisements that are used as indirect sales tools. Such indirect advertising is intended to affect the sales of a product only over the long term, usually by promoting general attributes of the manufacturer rather than specific product characteristics. Included in this category are most institutional or public-relations advertising. The exception would be remedial public-relations advertising designed to overcome some immediate negative publicity concerning product safety, labor problems, and so on.

The aim of most advertising is to move a product or service through the various levels of the marketing channel. The objectives and execution of advertising will change from level to level. The intended target audience will result in markedly different advertising strategies. In the following sections, we examine several categories of advertising to both consumers and businesses.

ADVERTISING TO THE CONSUMER

National Advertising

The term **national advertising** has a special nongeographic meaning in advertising: It refers to advertising by the owner of a trademarked product (brand) or service sold through different distributors or stores. Thus, advertising for the dozens of regional beer brands is considered national advertising even though distribution might be confined to a single state or small area. Regardless of whether we are discussing a small regional company or a global brand such as Tide, Chevrolet, or Nike, all national advertising has a number of characteristics in common. For example, national advertising tends to be general in terms of product information. Because retailers often have varying policies and business practices, information concerning price, retail availability, and even service and installation is often omitted from national advertising or mentioned only in general terms. Conversely, **retail advertising** often includes price information, service and return policies, store locations, and hours of operation—information that national advertisers usually cannot provide. However, the need to communicate more closely with targeted consumers has caused national advertising to take on a more personalized tone during the last decade.

Beginning in the late 1980s, many national advertisers began to target their advertising on a geographic basis—first regionally and, increasingly, on a market-by-market basis. More recently, with a combination of better consumer research and advances in technology, national advertisers have begun to identify and reach more narrowly defined market segments and, in some cases, individual consumers. Growth of Internet household penetration in concert with scanner data at the retail level allows national advertisers to offer specifically tailored messages to consumers based on individual lifestyle and product usage characteristics.

national advertising
Advertising by a marketer of a trademarked product or service sold through different outlets, in contrast to local advertising.

retail advertising
Advertising by a merchant who sells directly to the consumer.

Retail (Local) Advertising

Retailing has undergone dramatic changes in the last 20 years, and these changes are reflected in its advertising and promotion. Without question, the most important change in retailing is the move from local and regional stores with anywhere from one to a dozen outlets to national chains operating throughout the country with more than 1,000 stores. The consolidation of the retail industry has changed many of the retail practices of the last century. Consolidation has not only had the obvious effect of driving many locally owned, independent stores out of business; it also has had pronounced effects on the way retail marketing is conducted.

More and more, retail categories are dominated by one or two retailers. Rather than patronizing several independent retailers, customers more and more are doing "one-stop shopping," in which they can buy everything from groceries to eyewear, get a haircut, and service the family sedan under one roof. The new retail landscape makes it difficult to even categorize retailers. Does Wal-Mart more closely compete with Kroger as a grocery store or Target as a clothing store? Is Kroger a florist or a druggist? They sell more cut flowers and are the leading prescription drug seller in many markets. Is Target a high-end discounter or a low-end department store? Does a department store still fit that category if it employs shopping carts, centralized checkout, and few sales associates?

A highly publicized shift away from traditional retailing was the announcement in 2005 by Federated Department Stores, Inc., that it would adopt the Macy's name for all its regional department store chains. In short order, we saw the demise of some of the icons of American retailing. No more could customers frequent Marshall Fields in Chicago, Rich's in Atlanta, or Kaufman's in Pittsburgh. In their place Federated would offer only Macy's (and Bloomingdale's in selected markets). The brand consolidation allowed Federated to implement national advertising strategies—an approach that was impossible if it was promoting more than a dozen local store brands. The move also provided Federated the opportunity to move into national media such as television and magazines and promote its in-store, exclusive brands on a national basis.

The move to national retailing also has significant ramifications for newspapers and local radio stations. Newspapers, in particular, are seeing dramatic advertising spending shifts as retailers move to national promotional plans. A continuing trend over the last decade has seen declines in advertising pages in most major newspapers. Few observers see a quick turnaround given the continuing consolidation across virtually every segment of the retail industry. As we discuss later in the text, retail consolidation has also changed relationships between retailers and manufacturers. It has become so important for manufacturers to gain entry to these mega-stores that they often provide a number of product, merchandising, and promotional services specific to each retailer. For example, some products are manufactured to an individual retailer's specifications and both in-store promotions and advertising may be unique to a particular chain. At the same time, manufacturers find themselves increasingly competing with in-store brands. In effect, they are accommodating some of their strongest competitors.

End-Product Advertising

end-product advertising
Building consumer demand by promoting ingredients in a product, for example, Teflon and Nutrasweet.

What do products such as Intel computer chips, Lycra, and Nutrasweet have in common? They are rarely purchased directly by consumers. Instead, they are bought as ingredients in other products. The promotion of such products is called **end-product advertising** (or *branded ingredient advertising*). End-product advertising is most commonly employed by manufacturers of ingredients used in consumer products. Successful end-product advertising builds consumer demand for an ingredient that will help in the sale of a product. The knowledge that consumer demand is being created by the manufacturer will encourage companies to use these ingredients in their consumer products.

End-product advertising began in the 1940s when DuPont began promoting its Teflon nonstick coatings. Soon consumers began to associate Teflon with a special benefit in cookware, and merchandise with the Teflon seal was marketed at a premium price and quickly built a loyal following among buyers. Despite the obvious benefits to the manufacturer, building demand through end-product advertising is not easy. It took Intel almost 5 years before computer buyers started actively seeking out the Intel brand when shopping for a computer. Regardless of the superiority of an ingredient, consumers must be convinced that it offers an added value to the final product. The selling task is made even more difficult by the fact that such ingredients usually are not obvious in the product; therefore, extensive advertising is required to make consumers aware of their advantages. Successful end-product advertisements are those that create meaningful differentiation for consumer purchase decisions. End-product advertising is a small part of total advertising, but it is extremely important in a number of product categories.

Direct-Response Advertising

direct-response advertising
Any form of advertising done in direct marketing. Uses all types of media: direct mail, television, magazines, newspapers, radio. Term replaces mail-order advertising. See direct marketing.

Direct marketing and **direct-response advertising** are not new. In this country, Benjamin Franklin is credited with the first direct-sales catalog, published in 1744, to sell scientific and academic books. The modern era of direct selling was ushered in with the publication of the Montgomery Ward catalog in 1872. The techniques and media of direct-response advertising have changed dramatically since those early days. However, what has not changed is the necessity to reach consumers with personal messages with offers designed to meet their specific needs. While it has grown steadily throughout the last 50 years, the twenty-first century will be the era of direct-response marketing.

As more and more advertisers have shifted dollars from traditional mass media to more targeted vehicles, direct-response advertising has grown to more than $170 billion or almost half of all advertising expenditures. Consumer direct response accounts for 54 percent of the total with the remainder spent on B2B advertising.[69] The largest sector of direct-response advertising is direct mail, which accounts for almost one-third of the total. Not unexpectedly, the fastest-growing area is Internet advertising. While spending in telemarketing is still strong, it remains to be seen how the Do-Not-Call list will impact the long-term health of the industry. With more than 90 million households signing up, it appears that consumer telemarketing may face serious hurdles in the future

New technology, such as the Internet and other interactive media, provides a catalyst for future growth of direct response. In addition, advertisers in traditional media will increasingly adopt direct-response techniques. For example, it is quite common for advertisements and commercials to include 800-numbers to provide consumers with a way to buy directly or to obtain additional information about a product. In addition, cable television shopping channels and videocassettes give consumers the opportunity to see merchandise "live" before ordering it from their living rooms. The future holds great promise for various forms of interactive media that will provide even more innovative ways of communicating with prospects.

ADVERTISING TO BUSINESS AND PROFESSIONS

The average person doesn't see a very important portion of advertising, because it is aimed at retail stores, doctors, home builders, wholesalers, and others who operate at various stages of the marketing channel. However, B2B is one of the fastest-growing categories of advertising and it requires a much different strategy than consumer advertising. Although business publications remain a primary tool of B2B marketing, personal selling, telemarketing and other forms of direct response, and the Internet occupy a much higher share of expenditures directed to businesses compared to traditional media.

Another major difference between B2B and consumer advertising is the messages used in each. Although all advertising has to gain the audience's interest and attention, B2B tends to be fact-oriented with few of the emotional appeals found in consumer advertising. Business-to-business messages are addressed not only to specific industries but also often to particular job classifications within these industries. In addition, B2B advertising appeals tend to be profit-oriented with few, if any, emotional appeals. How a product will eliminate downtime, how it will decrease customer complaints, how it can save time and money, and how it can contribute to the overall efficiency and profitability of a business are among the primary themes of B2B marketing.

Business-to-business advertising also has to consider major differences in the buying process compared to consumer purchase behavior. Consumer purchases tend to be fairly straightforward. There may be some external influences on the purchase decision, such as children determining a family's fast-food or cereal preferences, but these causal relationships have little similarity with the formal purchasing models used in many B2B buys. The typical B2B purchase decisions tend to have distinct differences compared to typical consumer purchases. For example:

1. Purchase decisions made by companies frequently involve many people, including those who do the actual buying, those who directly or indirectly influence this decision, and the employees who will actually use the product or service.
2. Organizational and industrial products are often bought according to precise, technical specifications that require significant knowledge about the product category on the part of both buyers and sellers.
3. Impulse buying is rare (industrial buyers do not suddenly get an "urge to splurge" on heavy machinery or silicon chips).
4. The dollar volume of purchases is often substantial, dwarfing most individual consumer grocery bills or mortgage payments.[70]

CATEGORIES OF BUSINESS ADVERTISING

Trade Advertising

trade advertising
Advertising directed to the wholesale or retail merchants or sales agencies through whom the product is sold.

Trade advertising is normally created by manufacturers and directed to middle components of the marketing channel—usually wholesalers and retailers. Trade advertising emphasizes product profitability and the consumer advertising support retailers will receive from manufacturers. In addition, trade advertising promotes products and services that retailers need to operate their businesses. Advertising for shelving, cleaning services, and cash registers, as well as the actual consumer products stocked for consumer purchase, is part of trade advertising.

Trade advertising has several objectives:

1. *Gain additional distribution.* Manufacturers are interested in increasing the number of wholesale and retail outlets that carry their brands.
2. *Increase trade support.* Manufacturers compete for shelf space and dealer support with countless other brands. Trade advertising can encourage retailers to give prominent position to products or to use a manufacturer's point-of-purchase material.
3. *Announce consumer promotions.* Many trade advertisements offer a schedule of future consumer promotions and demonstrate to retailers that manufacturers are supporting brands with their advertising.

There are approximately 9,000 trade publications—several for virtually every category of retail business. The average consumer probably has not heard of most of these publications, but trade journals such as *Progressive Grocer* and *Drug Topics* play an important role in the advertising plans of many national advertisers.

Industrial Advertising

industrial advertising
Advertising addressed to manufacturers who buy machinery, equipment, raw materials, and the components needed to produce goods they sell.

A manufacturer is a buyer of machinery, equipment, raw materials, and components used in producing the goods it sells. Companies selling to manufacturers most often address their advertising to them in appropriate industry publications, direct mail, telemarketing, and personal selling. This method is quite unlike consumer advertising and is referred to as **industrial advertising**. Industrial advertising is directed at a very specialized and relatively small audience. Examples of industrial magazines are *Plant Services*, *Rubber World*, and *Valve World*—only a few of the hundreds of publications that make up this category.

Industrial advertising rarely seeks to sell a product directly. The purchase of industrial equipment is usually a complex process that includes a number of decision makers. Often, industrial advertising is a means of introducing a product or gaining brand name awareness to make it easier for follow-ups from company sales representatives to close a sale.

Professional Advertising

The primary difference between **professional advertising** and other trade advertising is the degree of control exercised by professionals over the purchase decisions of their clients. Whereas a grocery store encourages consumer purchases of certain goods by the brands it stocks, people can go to another store with more variety, lower prices, or better-quality merchandise. On the other hand, a person rarely will change doctors because a physician doesn't prescribe a certain brand of drugs, change banks because the bank orders checks for its customers from a particular printer, or choose an architect based on how designs are reproduced. Publications in this category include the *ABA Journal* published by the American Bar Association, the *AMA Journal* published by the American Medical Association, *Public School Administrator*, and so on.

professional advertising
Advertising directed at those in professions such as medicine, law, or architecture who are in a position to recommend the use of a particular product or service to their clients.

Corporate or Institutional Advertising

To the average consumer, giant conglomerates such as United Technologies, Conagra, and Unilever bring to mind few specific brands. However, these same consumers are very familiar with Dove soap, Lipton tea, and Birds Eye frozen food, all products of Unilever. Likewise, Healthy Choice, Chef Boyardee, and Orville Redenbacher's (Conagra) and Otis elevators, Pratt & Whitney engines, and Carrier air conditioners (United Technologies) are household names. While institutional advertising remains a long-term image-building technique, in recent years it has taken on a decided sales orientation in terms of the audiences reached and intent of communication. More and more, companies are attempting to bring their diverse inventory of products and brand names under a single corporate identity. In doing so, they are attempting to accomplish a number of corporate objectives, including:

institutional advertising
Advertising done by an organization speaking of its work views, and problems as a whole, to gain public goodwill and support rather than to sell a specific product. Sometimes called public-relations advertising.

- Establishing a public identity
- Explaining a company's diverse missions
- Boosting corporate identity and image
- Gaining awareness with target audiences for sales across a number of brands
- Associating a company's brands with some distinctive corporate character

These are only a few examples of possible corporate advertising objectives. The competitive environment of recent years has brought about dramatic changes in corporate advertising.

NONPRODUCT ADVERTISING

Idea Advertising

It is not surprising that the same marketing techniques so successful in selling products would be used to promote ideas. We are living in a period of conflicting ideas and special interest groups. Marketing concepts and advertising have become important elements in swaying public opinion. As we saw in Chapter 1, advertising propaganda is not a new phenomenon. What is new are the number of public interest groups using advertising and the sophistication of the communication techniques being employed. In recent years, issues such as gun control, abortion, animal rights, and the environment have been debated in mass advertising.

idea advertising
Advertising used to
promote an idea or cause
rather than to sell a
product or service.

Idea advertising is often controversial. Apart from the emotionalism of many of the topics being espoused, there are critics who think that advertising messages are too short and superficial to fully debate many of these issues. Proponents counter that advertising is the only practical way to get their messages before a mass audience. They point out that idea advertising may be the most practical means for these groups to use their First Amendment privileges. Regardless of one's position on idea advertising, the increasing ability of media to narrowly target audiences, by ideology as well as product preference, will make this type of advertising more prevalent in the future.

Service Advertising

service advertising
Advertising that promotes
a service rather than a
product.

We are becoming a nation of specialists with more and more Americans seeking advice and services for everything from financial planning to child care. Because service providers are basically people enterprises, **service advertising** almost always has a strong institutional component. Service companies tend to keep the same slogan, theme, or identifying mark over long periods of time to increase consumer awareness. Because service industries are so similar (and often legally regulated), it is difficult to develop a distinct differentiation among competitors. Banks and insurance companies have a particularly difficult time establishing an effective identity.

Fundamentals of good advertising are the same regardless of whether a product or service is being promoted. However, many marketing experts point out that differences between the two categories require some care in the manner in which service messages are handled. Some basic principles of service advertising include:

1. *Feature tangibles.* Because service advertising has no tangible product to feature, it should be personalized in some way. For example, service advertisements often use testimonials. Service messages should show the benefits of the service, such as an on-time plane trip that results in closing a deal or a contented older couple as a result of good investment advice by their broker.

2. *Feature employees.* Because the value of a service largely depends on the quality of a firm's employees, it is important to make them feel an important part of the company and develop trust with customers. Often, service messages feature real employees in their advertisements. This approach has the advantage of personalizing the service to customers and building employee morale.

3. *Stress quality.* Because the quality and performance of services are sometimes more difficult to measure than products, advertisements should emphasize consistency and high levels of competency. Hospitals use words such as *caring, professional,* and *convenient* in their advertising.

GOVERNMENT ADVERTISING

All levels of government in this country have created various forms of propaganda and public policy messages since the Revolutionary War era. However, in the last 20 years, the growth of government services and programs has resulted in a greater use of traditional advertising by government agencies. The federal government spends millions of dollars each year promoting an array of agencies including the volunteer armed forces, consumer-protection programs, and environment and health initiatives. The new Medicare prescription drug program was launched with massive spending aimed at educating senior citizens about the options available to them. State governmental agencies also have seen the advantage of advertising in reaching the citizens with beneficial services such as savings plans for higher education (see Exhibit 2.15).

Every year brings them closer to college.

Are you ready?

- **Anyone can open an account** – Parents, grandparents, relatives and friends at any income level, regardless of where they live in the U.S., may open an account and contribute to the Plan for a beneficiary.

- **Tax advantages** – Contributions grow free from federal and state income tax until withdrawn. When you withdraw the money to pay for qualified higher education expenses, you pay no federal or Georgia income taxes. The law allowing federal tax-free qualified withdrawals is set to expire on December 31, 2010. Congress may or may not extend the law beyond this date. Withdrawals for qualified higher education expenses are free of Georgia income tax after the account has been open for a year.

- **You may be eligible for a Georgia tax deduction for contributions of up to $2,000 per year per child** – The only 529 plan to offer a Georgia state tax deduction. Contributions may be deductible from Georgia taxable income up to a maximum of $2,000 a year per beneficiary. The maximum deduction for each beneficiary decreases by $400 for each $1,000 of federal adjusted gross income over $100,000 for a joint return or $50,000 for a single return, and is available when itemized Georgia and federal income tax returns are filed. The tax deduction is available to parents or guardians who own an account for a beneficiary who is claimed as a dependent. Rollover contributions from other 529 plans do not qualify for the Georgia income tax deduction.

- **Savings can be used at virtually any college in the U.S.** – Your beneficiary can use the funds at eligible schools in Georgia, around the U.S. and abroad.

- **Choose among five investment options** – Select an option or a combination of options that best fits your needs and investment philosophy.

- **It takes just $25 to start** – You can start with a small investment and change contributions over time based on your savings goals or financial situation.

- **It's a smart complement to Georgia's HOPE Scholarship** – Savings can be used for qualified expenses not covered under a HOPE Scholarship. Or should your child attend college outside Georgia, the savings can be used for tuition as well as other qualified expenses.

For more information or to enroll online go to **www.gasavings4college.com** or call toll-free **866-549-6541**.

C34180

GA0508School

SUMMARY ✺

The roles of advertising are many, varied, and ever changing. The options open to advertisers have never been greater, and the costs of errors are significantly magnified compared to only a few years ago. With fragmented audiences and media, higher costs of reaching prospects, and the challenges of effectively using new media technology, the demands on advertisers and their agencies have never been greater. However, regardless of the changes in the advertising process, two fundamentals for successful advertising will remain constant:

1. Effective advertising can only function within the context of an organized marketing plan.
2. Advertising is a marketing communication tool and rarely will be successful if directed at noncommunication problems. It is difficult, if not impossible, for advertising to overcome deficiencies in the core marketing program.

An effective advertising plan is an extension of the marketing goals of a firm. Advertising typically is asked to help develop or maintain product awareness, build company and brand image, and provide product information that differentiates one brand from another. The execution of advertising will vary by the stage in the trade channel to which it is directed (e.g., retail, consumer, industrial, or professional). Furthermore, it can adapt to the primary product benefits and express them in a number of ways (e.g., testimonials, demonstrations, or long copy). Advertising also is modified according to budgetary considerations, as well as the corporate philosophy concerning the value of advertising within the marketing plan.

It is clear that advertising is only one of a number of possible sales tools. The advertising executive of the future will be a marketing communicator who is able to utilize an array of marketing communication elements including promotion, public relations, and personal selling in a coordinated fashion to bring synergy and unity to the overall corporate message.

Although major changes in advertising are on the horizon, the key to its success will continue to be the ability to develop an interesting message that will reach potential customers in an appropriate environment at the most opportune time. During the remainder of the text, we discuss the techniques of advertising against a backdrop of marketing, research, and planning.

REVIEW ✺

1. How has the emphasis on return on investment changed the relationship between advertising and the media?
2. Compare and contrast the three types of convergence discussed in this chapter and their effect on advertising.
3. How does advertising complement other elements of marketing communication?
4. Discuss public relations from the standpoint of audience credibility and message control.
5. What role does brand equity play in a product's long-term success?
6. Why has integrated marketing communication become even more important in a period of media fragmentation?
7. Discuss the primary advantages and disadvantages of brand extension.
8. A product is a bundle of benefits. Discuss.
9. Discuss product differentiation in terms of target market segmentation.

10. Discuss price strategy as a means of marketing strategy.

11. Compare and contrast business-to-business and consumer advertising in terms of audiences, media, and promotional techniques.

TAKE IT TO THE WEB ✻

The Public Relations Society of America (www.prsa.org/) is the leading professional organization dedicated to the improvement of the field. Note the far-reaching programs of the society and how they interact with both marketing and advertising.

The American Association of Advertising Agencies (www.aaaa.org/) provides a great deal of information about the current practice of advertising. What are some of the primary topics of interest to the association and its agency members?

One of the keys to successful advertising is the ability to integrate all aspects of the marketing communication program. How do various advertisers use IMC to reach all their diverse target markets (http://marketing.about.com/)?

PART TWO

Planning the Advertising

CHAPTER THREE

SWEET.
NOT SISSY.

INTRODUCING OUR NEW *SWEET & Spicy* PEPPER SAUCE.
Its Asian-inspired flavor is perfect on everything
from fries to chicken fingers to Moo Goo Gai Pan.

www.TABASCO.com

The Advertising Spiral
and Brand Planning

ne of the critical aspects of marketing communications decision making is developing a strategy. It has been said that strategy is everything. After reading this chapter, you will understand:

chapter objectives

1. **the importance of understanding the product life cycle**
2. **the relationship of the advertising spiral**
3. **the birth and basics of branding**
4. **brands and integrated marketing**
5. **brand equity**
6. **strategic planning methods**

Advertisers and their agencies don't agree on a lot of issues, but almost everyone agrees that brands are a company's most valuable assets.

Today's consumers control the power because of their ability to turn us off and on easier than ever before; therefore, it is no longer enough for a brand to distinguish itself only through an advertising campaign. Brands such as Apple, Google, IKEA, and Starbucks are considered global leaders not because of their sleek logos but because of the relevant and unique experiences they offer to customers—be it online, in the retail shop, or through the products and services themselves.[1] People remember the things that excite them, and every marketer wants his or her brand to be one of them.

Consumers are more sophisticated than ever before about marketing efforts. Yet, they are continually confused by the deluge of brand names, subbrands, and minibrands directed at them. At the same time, manufacturers are having trouble finding substantial and long-term ways of differentiating their products and services. It is a complex environment. If companies or brands set up false or unachievable objectives, they are likely to have failures. How do you differentiate your product and manage and protect your most important asset—your brand? How do you know what kind of strategic message is needed? How do you manage advertising or branding for success?

Consumers are rapidly using the multitude of new fragmented media choices available to them, which is forcing marketers and agencies to scramble in their attempt to keep up. Brands are reaching out with integrated messages throughout a number of media touch points. New emphasis is being placed on ways to integrate brand communications (also called integrated marketing communication), build brand equity, and build better strategies for marketing products. It doesn't matter what the product category is—new marketing is new marketing. Great importance is placed on the development of a product and its marketing objectives as part of a brand's strategic plan prior to creating advertisements. Here we examine several aspects and their advertising implications that are important to creating the strategic plan. Despite many marketing practices being challenged today, one of the constants

EXHIBIT **3.1**

Primary Stages of the Life-Cycle Model

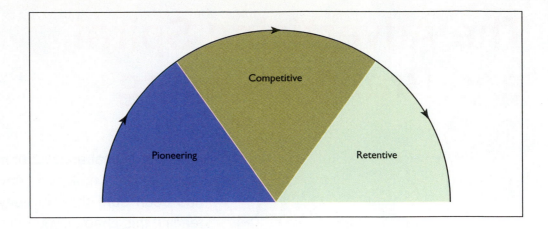

is the need to have a clear understanding of the product and consumer wants and needs when making strategic advertising decisions.

Think about the many stages in life. We are born; we grow up, mature, grow old, and at some point expire. You have already gone through a number of stages of development in your life with more to come. Products also pass through a number of stages. The developmental stage of a product determines the advertising message. As products pass through a number of stages—from introduction to dominance to ultimate demise—the manner in which advertising presents the product to consumers depends largely on the degree of acceptance the product has earned with consumers. The degree of acceptance can be identified as the product passes through its life cycle. *It is this degree of acceptance that determines the advertising stage of the product.* The life-cycle model discussed in this chapter consists of three primary stages (see Exhibit 3.1):

- Pioneering stage
- Competitive stage
- Retentive stage

The nature and extent of each stage are discussed in the next sections.

PIONEERING STAGE

Every year, there are some 20,000 new products introduced to consumers in this country. Many are simply advertisers trying to get a piece of the pie in an established product category. The failure rate is staggering. Over the past 25 years, almost 60 percent of the companies appearing on the *Fortune* 500 list have been replaced by new companies. These new companies' success is because they have created new markets or reinvented existing ones. One way of accomplishing this is to create new products or new product categories. Companies like Procter & Gamble (P&G) have grown because of their ability to launch new products and create new product categories successfully. Procter & Gamble introduced Tide in 1941. It also introduced a new product category—the disposable diaper, or Pampers—in 1961, which became a billion-dollar product. In 1986, Procter & Gamble introduced the first shampoo-conditioner combination. It also introduced the successful Swiffer mop.[2] And Febreze Fabric Refresher. Procter & Gamble had to convince consumers that they needed a kind of product they had never heard of.

When manufacturers create revolutionary new products, they may think consumers will flock to buy them. Many times manufacturers have trouble accepting the fact that despite all the money spent in developing and then promoting their product, consumers pay little or no attention to it. There are no guarantees that consumers will see a need for the product. It may never have occurred to consumers that they need or want the product, and as a result they don't feel compelled to buy it.

Will consumers flock to these products whose creators are trying to start a new category?

■ Baby Gender Mentor Home DNA testing kit marketed by Acu-Gen Biolabs, which answers the eternal mysteries of the sex of an unborn baby. It requires no prescription and is 99 percent accurate.

■ Greens Gluten Free Discovery Beer. Gluten-free foods and beverages grew 78 percent in the past year. They are great alternatives for those suffering from celiac disease allergies. Do you want some?

And of course there is a long list of products not attracting consumers:

■ In January 1993, Crystal Pepsi was launched. It was clear cola and tasted much like regular Pepsi. It attempted to create a "clear cola" category for those more health-conscious consumers. It lasted about a year in the United States. Oops.

■ H. J. Heinz pitched funky fries—chocolate-flavored, blue-colored french fries— in 2002. Kids didn't think they were cool, and a year later Heinz pulled them off the shelves.

■ And how many of you rode a Segway scooter today?

Until people appreciate the fact that they need it, a product is in the **pioneering stage**.

Advertising in the pioneering stage introduces an idea that makes previous conceptions appear antiquated. It must show that methods once accepted as the only ones possible have been improved and that the limitations long tolerated as normal have now been overcome. It may be difficult to believe, but consumers didn't rush out to buy the first deodorants. Many consumers who were concerned with body odor simply used baking soda under their arms. So we can't take for granted that consumers will change their habits. Advertising in this stage must do more than simply present a product—it must implant a new custom, change habits, develop new usage, or cultivate new standards of living. In short, advertising in the pioneering stage of a product's life cycle must educate the consumer to the new product or service.

In 1973, Fleischmann's introduced Egg Beaters, a frozen egg alternative made from real eggs but without the yolks. The company had to convince consumers that they needed an egg alternative. It had to convert egg eaters into Egg Beaters customers. Its market was concerned about the high cholesterol and fat of egg yolks. Fleischmann's had to change attitudes and habits to be successful. By accomplishing this, it became the dominating force in this new-product segment. In the early 1990s, Egg Beaters tried to expand the market with an advertising campaign built around the theme "When the Recipe Calls for Eggs" (see Exhibit 3.2). These advertisements tried to sell Egg Beaters as a substitute in cooking "because you're using the healthiest part of real eggs. No cholesterol. No fat." Do you and your family use Egg Beaters or egg substitutes?

The purposes of the pioneering stage of a product's life cycle, reduced to their simplest terms, are:

■ to educate consumers about the new product or service
■ to show that people have a need they did not appreciate before and that the advertised product fulfills that need
■ to show that a product now exists that is actually capable of meeting a need that already had been recognized but could not have been fulfilled before

pioneering stage
The advertising stage of a product in which the need for such a product is not recognized and must be established or in which the need has been established but the success of a commodity in filling that need has to be established. See competitive stage, retentive stage.

Pioneering advertising generally stresses what the product can do, offer, or provide that could not have been done, offered, or provided by any product before.

A true pioneering product offers more than a minor improvement. It is important for the advertiser to remember that what determines the stage of the advertising is consumer perception of the product. In the pioneering stage, the consumer is trying to answer the question "What is the product for?" It does not really matter what the manufacturer thinks. Does the consumer think the improved changes in the product are significant? Or, does the product really offer a better way of doing things?

Often the copy focuses on the generic aspect of the product category in an attempt to educate or inform the consumer. In the late 1980s, Interplak introduced a revolutionary new home dental product—an automatic instrument that removed plaque using two rows of counterrotating oscillating brushes. Interplak had to convince consumers that this product cleaned teeth better than any kind of toothbrush—electric or otherwise (see Exhibit 3.3). This was no easy task because the product cost about $100 at introduction. The pioneering Interplak advertisements suggested that "Plaque is the real villain in oral hygiene. If not removed daily, its bacterial film can lead to early gum disease and tooth decay. But clinical studies have shown that manual brushing removes only some of the plaque buildup."

Finally. A sophisticated weapon in the war against plaque.

These days, it seems like every product from mouthwash to toothpaste wants to help you fight plaque. And for very good reason. Plaque buildup is a leading cause of gum disease which can have a number of very serious complications.

But among the so-called "plaque attackers," the INTERPLAK Home Plaque Removal Instrument stands out as a true technological breakthrough.

The INTERPLAK Home Plaque Removal Instrument cleans teeth virtually plaque-free.

If plaque is not removed daily, its bacterial film can lead to gingivitis, an early stage of gum disease, and tooth decay. But clinical studies have shown that manual brushing removes only some of the plaque buildup. Those same studies, on the other hand, show the INTERPLAK instrument cleans teeth and gums virtually plaque-free.

How the INTERPLAK instrument cleans circles around ordinary brushing.

With manual or even electric toothbrushes, you move the bristles up and down or back and forth. But with the INTERPLAK instrument's patented design, the brush remains still while the bristles rotate. Ten tufts of bristles rotate 4,200 times a minute, reversing direction 46 times a second. They literally scour off plaque and stimulate your gums. And at the precise moment they reverse direction, the tufts fully extend to clean deep between teeth and under gums. Yet because the bristles are four times softer than the softest toothbrush, the INTERPLAK device is no more abrasive than manual brushing with toothpaste.

Dental professionals approve.

The INTERPLAK Home Plaque Removal Instrument has received rave reviews from dentists and periodontists across the country.

"I am recommending the INTER-PLAK Home Plaque Removal Instrument to all my patients." —Dr. L. K. Yorn, Cedar Grove, NJ

Bristles rotating 4,200 times a minute literally scour plaque off your teeth.

"At last, my patients enjoy using a product which we recommend." —Dr. J.W. Blackman, III, Winston-Salem, NC

"Since my patients have been using the INTERPLAK instrument, I have seen a dramatic improvement in the health of their teeth and gums." —Dr. S.G. Newhart, Orthodontist, Beverly Hills, CA

"The INTERPLAK Home Plaque Removal Instrument is a technical breakthrough in home dental care." —Dr. Alan Kushner, Chicago, IL

Ask your own dentist about the benefits of using the INTERPLAK instrument.

Serious plaque removal for the whole family.

Each INTERPLAK Home Plaque Removal Instrument comes with two interchangeable brush heads. You can purchase additional brush heads so every family member can benefit from cleaner teeth and gums. The INTERPLAK instrument is also cordless, recharging between uses in its own stand.

For more information or the name of a retailer near you, call toll-free **1-800-537-1600**, and ask for **Operator 188.**

Do it soon. Because if you are really serious about fighting the war against plaque, you couldn't have a stronger ally.

INTERPLAK®
HOME PLAQUE REMOVAL Instrument

© Dental Research Corporation, 198?
INTERPLAK® is the registered trademark of Dental Research Corporation.

Twenty years later, Interplak is still trying to get the average household to try its product. And, of course, there is a new generation of less-expensive electric and battery-operated toothbrushes using the same idea.

Consumer acceptance and understanding may take a long period of time—a few months, a number of years, or perhaps never. Yahoo! was introduced in 1994 as the first search engine. Both eBay and Amazon.com were introduced in 1995 as the first auction site and online bookstore. Priceline.com came along in 1998 selling airline tickets on the Internet with a "name-your-own-price" selling system. These selling concepts became accepted rather rapidly considering they were new business and technology types. Of course, they were enhanced by all the attention to the Web and their leadership.

Snapple was created in 1972 as an all-natural juice drink line to be sold primarily in health-food stores. It didn't become a national beverage company until 1992. Originally, few consumers were interested in natural beverages and the idea took time to grow. Today, almost everyone buys bottled water products like Aquafina or Dasani. This concept wasn't accepted overnight either. But once it was accepted by many consumers, along came products like Propel offering enhanced water with vitamins and/or flavors. As an interesting contrast, Coca-Cola had a disastrous introduction of Dasani water in the United Kingdom in 2004. The drink was panned by the British media as recycled tap water and was withdrawn from shelves within weeks.

Manufacturers may produce a product that does something many consumers instantly desire—an iPod, a DVD player/recorder, a cellular phone, a laptop computer, or a Palm personal digital assistant (PDA). For these products, advertising will not exhort consumers to raise their standards of acceptance but rather will aim at convincing them that they can now accomplish something they couldn't before, through the use of the new product. For instance, the cellular phone industry told businesswomen that the cellular phone could not only keep them in touch with their clients but also could be used as a security device—especially if they had car trouble or were threatened in some way. Now it is more a matter of deciding on design, color, or size and other features than if they should own one. For many people today, a cell phone is one of life's necessities.

Usually during the early introduction of a new product, heavy advertising and promotional expenses are required to create awareness and acquaint the target with the product's benefits. To expand, the manufacturer must gain new distribution, generate consumer trial, and increase geographic markets. The product in the pioneering stage is not usually profitable. In other words, there can be a number of factors involved in the acceptance and purchase. According to a U.S. study by Ernst & Young, there is a 67 percent failure rate among the truly new products that create a new product category.[3] Other studies say it may be higher in specific categories.

Purell Instant Hand Sanitizer was introduced in 1997 with a $15 million advertising budget. This was a new concept for consumers who may have used antibacterial soaps to kill germs. When a new pain product called Aleve, containing naproxen, was introduced, it created a new category in a very mature analgesic market. Consumers had many analgesic choices to fight pain: Aspirin was the first major product (i.e., Bayer) to fight pain, then came aspirin compounds (Anacin, BC tablets, among others), then acetaminophen (Tylenol), then ibuprofen (Advil, Nuprin), and then naproxen. Aleve's advertising support for the introduction was about $50 million. As you can see, pioneering advertisers incur heavy expenses in the process of educating the public about the advantages of a new type of product. If the advertiser has some success with the new idea, one or more competitors will quickly jump into the market and try to grab share from the pioneer.

Usually, the main advantage of being a pioneer is that you become the leader with a substantial head start over others. So a pioneering effort can secure customers before the competition can even get started. "When you're the market leader," says Ivan Seidenberg, Verizon CEO, "part of your responsibility is to reinvent the market."[4]

COMPETITIVE STAGE

Once a pioneering product becomes accepted by consumers, there is going to be competition. The consumer now knows what the product is and how it can be used. At this point, the main question the consumer asks is, "Which brand shall I buy?" When this happens, the product has entered the **competitive stage**, and the advertising for it is referred to as *competitive advertising*. (Note that this is a restrictive meaning of the term, not to be confused with the broader meaning that all advertisements are competitive with each other.)

In the short term, the pioneer usually has an advantage of leadership that can give dominance in the market. Red Bull started the caffeine-stoked energy drinks category decades ago in Europe. In 2006, more than 500 new energy drinks were launched worldwide to get a piece of the action. There are 7.6 million teens in this

competitive stage
The advertising stage a product reaches when its general usefulness is recognized but its superiority over similar brands has to be established in order to gain preference. See pioneering stage, retentive stage.

country who claim to drink them. Generally, in the early competitive stage, the combined impact of many competitors, each spending to gain a substantial market position, creates significant growth for the whole product category. If the pioneer can maintain market share in this category during the initial period of competitors' growth, it can more than make up for the earlier expense associated with its pioneering efforts.

Among the many everyday products in the competitive stages are deodorants, soaps, toothpaste, cars, detergents, headache remedies, shaving creams, shampoos, televisions, DVD players, cat food, computers, and packaged foods. The purpose of competitive stage advertising is to communicate the product's position or differentiate it to the consumer; the advertising features the differences of the product.

Competitive headlines include the following:

It's not expensive to look expensive. HP color Laserjets starting at $399.

HEWLETT-PACKARD

Keep your food garden fresh longer.

GE PROFILE

**Built for the coldest, most miserable places on earth—
Like your driveway in January.**

L.L. BEAN

**Plump, gorgeous lips, instantly
(no needles, no waiting, no kidding).**

LIP FUSION

How to tell a pair of quality sunglasses from high-priced junk.

COSTA DEL MAR

These heads don't educate you as to the product category advantages; they are taken for granted. Instead, each headline and the copy that follows set out to tell you why you should select that particular brand. The Johnson Group, Chattanooga, created an advertisement for Litespeed aluminum road bikes (see Exhibit 3.4) that said, "They're built for all-out, go-for-the-jugular speed. Crafted with our exclusive Alite alloy, they are available in ultra-light compact and standard geometries. Plus, the Lite TEC Titanium Enhanced Carbon monostay and butted tubing provide a ride that's as smooth as the paint job." The advertisement gives serious riders significant information.

RETENTIVE STAGE

Products reaching maturity and wide-scale acceptance may enter the **retentive stage**, or reminder stage, of advertising.

If a product is accepted and used by consumers, there may not be a need for competitive advertising. At this point, everybody knows about this product and likes or dislikes it—why advertise? The chief goal of advertising may be to hold on to those customers. Over the years, many manufacturers of successful products have stopped advertising and have seen the public quickly forget about them. Most advertisers try to retain their customers by keeping the brand name before them. The third stage through which a product might pass is called *reminder advertising*—it simply reminds consumers that the brand exists. This kind of advertising is usually highly visual and is basically name advertising, meaning that the advertisement gives little reason to buy the product. Most reminder advertisements

retentive stage
The third advertising stage of a product, reached when its general usefulness is widely known, its individual qualities are thoroughly appreciated, and it is satisfied to retain its patronage merely on the strength of its past reputation. See pioneering stage, competitive stage.

EXHIBIT **3.4**

Litespeed road bikes
talk about competitive
advantages.

Courtesy of The Johnson Group
and Litespeed Lunaris.

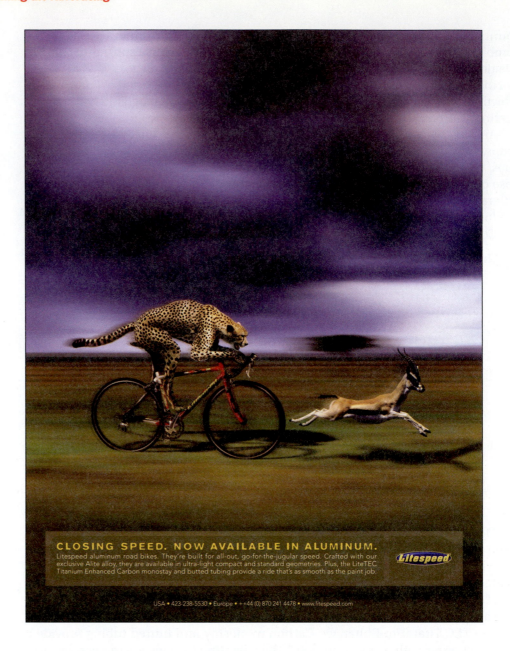

look like posters—they have a dominant illustration of the product and a few words. Generally, there is little or no body copy because there is no need to give consumers this kind of information.

Few products are entirely in the reminder stage. There usually are other products in the pioneering and competitive stages challenging their leadership position. In fact, if your product is truly all alone in the retentive stage, that may be cause for alarm. It may mean the product category is in decline, and the competition sees little future in challenging you for consumers.

The advertiser's goal in the retentive stage is to maintain market share and ward off consumer trial of other products. Products in the retentive stage do not necessarily cut back on their advertising expenditures, but they adopt different marketing and promotional strategies than those used in the pioneering and competitive stages. When a brand is used by a large portion of the market, its advertising is intended to keep present customers and increase the total market, on the assumption that the most prominent brand will get the largest share of the increase.

Generally, products in the retentive stage are at their most profitable levels because developmental costs have been amortized, distribution channels established, and sales contacts made. The development of advertising and promotion may often be routine at this stage. Obviously, companies like to maintain their products in the retentive stage as long as possible.

THE ADVERTISING SPIRAL

The advertising spiral (see Exhibit 3.5) is an expanded version of the advertising stages of products just discussed. The spiral provides a point of reference for determining which stage or stages a product has reached at a given time in a given market and what the thrust of the advertising message should be. This can be important information for deciding on strategy and giving the creative team a clear perspective on what information it needs to communicate to prospects. In many respects, the advertising spiral parallels the life cycle of the product.

Comparison of Stages

Naturally, there are fewer products in the pioneering stage than in the competitive stage. The development of new types of products or categories does not take place frequently. Most advertising is for products in the competitive stage. As already pointed out, such advertising often introduces features of a new product that is in the pioneering stage and gets the spotlight for a period of time.

In using the advertising spiral, we deal with one group of consumers at a time. The advertising depends on the attitude of that group toward the product. A product in the competitive stage may have to use pioneering advertising aimed at other groups of consumers to expand its markets. Thus, pioneering and competitive advertising could be going on simultaneously. Each series of advertisements, or each part of one advertisement, will be aimed at a different audience for this same product.

Products in the retentive stage usually get the least amount of advertising. This stage, however, represents a critical moment in the life cycle of a product when important management decisions must be made. Hence, it is important to create effective advertising in this stage.

Product in Competitive Stage, Improvement in Pioneering Stage It is not unusual for a new brand to enter the competitive stage without doing any pioneering advertising. A new product entering an established product category must hit the ground

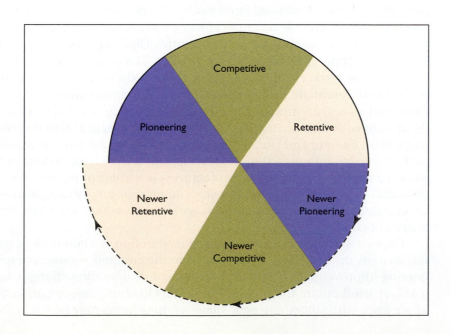

EXHIBIT **3.5**

The Advertising Spiral

running to differentiate itself from the competition. Every new brand thus enjoys whatever pioneering advertising has already been done in the product category. Despite the new product failure rates, marketers obviously see the value of new products. New brands entering an existing category experience a 50 percent failure rate and, perhaps most surprising, an 84 percent failure rate among brand extensions. Ernst & Young cited a fundamental lack of competitive differentiation as the reason for line extension failure.[5]

Earlier we said the consumer is the one who determines the stage of a product. What stage would you place Coca-Cola Zero? Coca-Cola Zero—a sugar-free cola designed to taste like ordinary Coca-Cola—was described by the company as its most important new product since Diet Coke was launched in 1984. After introducing Coca-Cola Zero, several modifications to the advertising were made. It was introduced with advertisements with a tagline, "Everybody Chill." The key advertisement, called "Chilltop," was a remake of the famous Hilltop advertisement used for Coca-Cola in the1970s. The intro advertisements did not precisely tell consumers what the product was about, and consumers didn't understand the product proposition. Later, they added an explanatory line: "Real Coca-Cola Taste Plus Nothing." Another commercial showed Coca-Cola morphing into a bottle of Coca-Cola Zero, and the copy read: "Real Coca-Cola Taste, Zero Calories, No Compromise." It has not attracted a huge share of the soft-drink market. But we do not know Coca-Cola's share goals. Do consumers understand the product premise today? Or care? Sales will tell.

Where in this process is Microsoft's Zune? It was introduced in late 2006 and positioned as the anti-iPod. "Welcome to the social," was the Zune's introductory tagline. In contrast to iPod's iconic, solitary silhouette, Zune is all about company. "The player will live or die based on its qualities, intrinsic and intangible, that will be rapidly assessed and exchanged among the universe of potential users. For instance, Zune has more functionality than the iPod, but that comes at the cost of simplicity," said Bob Garfield of *Advertising Age*.[6]

Can bread be white and whole grain at the same time? Earthgrain, owned by Sara Lee, developed Soft & Smooth, a combination of whole grains that would appeal to white-bread lovers. It quickly became one of the best sellers, generating sales over $50 million. As you've guessed, since Soft & Smooth was so successful, the rivals rushed in—Wonder Made, for one.[7]

Gold Bond Foot Swabs created a new way to deliver athlete's foot relief (see Exhibit 3.6), the end of the messy athlete's foot creams. "Introducing Gold Bond Foot Swabs. Just snap and release . . . the only medicine proven to cure and prevent most athlete's foot. New Gold Bond swabs. The no-mess, no-touch cure."

A few years ago, manufacturers placed 150 new deodorant and antiperspirant products on store shelves within 12 months. Unilever brought its successful Axe line from Europe, sparking competitive sales. The category quadrupled. New formulas hit the market in all forms—gels, creams, sticks, and sprays. Manufacturers rushed to differentiate new products. Procter & Gamble created a "soft solid" that came out as a gritty mush that melted on the skin. Herbal Care introduced a deodorant with "anti-irritant and antioxidant" properties, aimed at women's sensitive skin. Gillette and Unilever introduced "odor-blocking technology." Take a look at the deodorant section the next time you're in a mass discounter, grocery store, or drugstore. See how manufacturers are attempting to differentiate their products. As you can see, simply selling deodorant is very competitive. Most new deodorants start in the competitive stage even when they are attempting to create a new subcategory.

Change is a continuum: As long as the operation of a competitive product does not change, the product continues to be in the competitive stage, despite any pioneering improvements. Once the principle of its operation changes, however, the product itself enters the pioneering stage. Obviously, electronics change every other week with something new. However, new items may be costly for old prod-

EXHIBIT **3.6**

"Gold Bond Foot Swabs—just snap and release, with no-mess, no-touch cure."

Courtesy of The Johnson Group, Chattanooga and Gold Bond.

ucts. Flat panel TVs have replaced the 30-year-old technology of the CRT as consumers move toward LCD and plasma televisions. By 2010, it is expected that CRTs will account for only 2.1 million of the 44 million televisions sold.

When a product begins to move into more than one stage, the changes are not always easy to categorize. Whenever a brand in the competitive stage is revitalized with a new feature aimed at differentiating it, pioneering advertising may be needed to make consumers appreciate the new feature. Toyota introduced the Prius sedan using electric power steering and sensors that help guide the car when it reverses into a parking space.

Scramblers and Better 'n Eggs, Healthy Choice eggs, and Simply Eggs created nonfrozen egg substitutes to compete with Egg Beaters' frozen product. Egg Beaters

EXHIBIT **3.7**

Egg Beaters expanded beyond the freezer with its refrigerated version. Advertisements told consumers where in the store they could find the product.

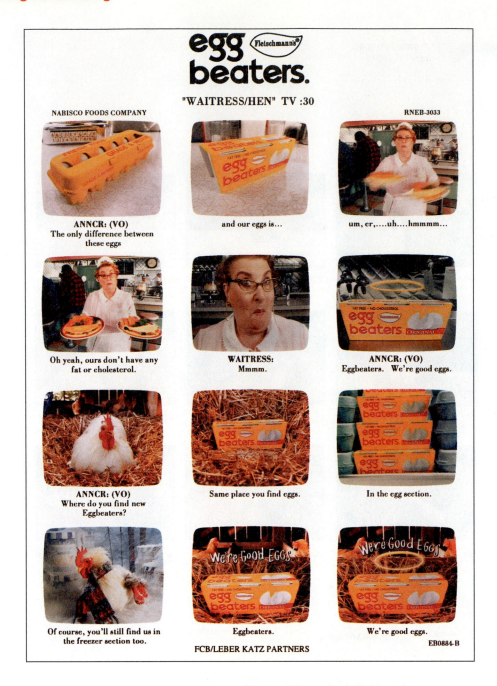

developed a refrigerated version to go with its frozen product. Exhibit 3.7 shows a television commercial that tells consumers they can find Egg Beaters in either the frozen food section or the egg section of their grocery. Was this new Egg Beaters in the competitive stage, the pioneering stage, or both?

Gillette has been a master of creating new products with new features in its razors. It turns out many successful new products with new product wrinkles—Venus, Gillette Fusion, M3Power, Satin Care, and so on. That's quite an investment by the marketer.

The Retentive Stage

The life of a product does not cease when it reaches the retentive stage. In fact, it may then be at the height of its popularity, and its manufacturer may feel it can just coast along. But a product can coast for only a short time before declining. No business can rely only on its old customers over a period of time and survive.

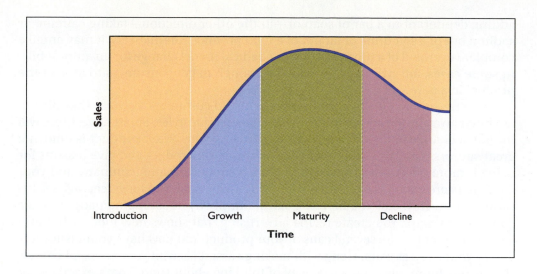

EXHIBIT **3.8**
A Typical Life-Cycle Model

As noted earlier, the retentive stage is the most profitable one for the product. But all good things must come to an end. A manufacturer has a choice between two strategies when the product nears the end of the retentive stage.

In the first strategy, the manufacturer determines that the product has outlived its effective market life and should be allowed to die. In most cases, the product is not immediately pulled from the market. Rather, the manufacturer simply quits advertising it and withdraws other types of support. During this period, the product gradually loses market share but remains profitable because expenses have been sharply curtailed. This strategy is the one typically presented in textbook descriptions of the product life cycle, but it is not necessarily the one that corresponds to actual product development.

The problem with the typical life-cycle model in Exhibit 3.8 is that it portrays an inevitable decline in the product life cycle, whereas most long-term products go through a number of cycles of varying peaks and duration before they are finally taken off the market. The advertising spiral depicted in Exhibit 3.5 shows these cycles. The advertising spiral—the second strategy for a product nearing the end of the retentive stage—does not accept the fact that a product must decline. Instead, it seeks to expand the market into a newer pioneering stage. General Mills' CEO's advice is, "Do not believe in the product life cycle. Innovate constantly." Tide detergent was introduced in 1946. Since then, Tide has gone through more than sixty product upgrades.

As a product approaches the retentive stage, management must make some important decisions:

■ Can it make some significant improvements in the present product so that it virtually represents a new type of product or category (e.g., Clorox Cleaner)?
■ Is there a possibility for line extensions (e.g., Diet Coke)?

As we have seen, the life cycle of a product can be affected by many conditions. If, however, the product is to continue to be marketed, its own advertising stage should be identified before its advertising goals are set.

The three basic stages of the spiral (pioneering, competitive, and retentive) are straightforward and easy to understand. However, the stages in the bottom half (newer pioneering, newer competitive, and newer retentive) are trickier. To continue to market an established product successfully and profitably, creative marketing is necessary.

The newer pioneering stage attempts to get more people to use the product. Basically, there are two ways to enter this new stage. The first is making a product change. This can be minor, such as adding a new ingredient to a detergent or adding deodorant to a bar of soap or—in the other direction—taking caffeine or sodium out of a soft drink or fat out of a food product. Alternatively, it may entail a complete overhaul of a product, such as a radical model change for an automobile. In some cases, advertising alone may be enough to get consumers to look at the product in a new light.

Advertisers cannot afford to simply rely on old customers, because they die off, are lured away by the competition, or change their lifestyles. Smart advertisers will initiate a change in direction of their advertising when their product is enjoying great success. They will show new ways of using the product and give reasons for using it more often. For instance, if you are a successful soup company and your customers are eating your canned soup with every meal, you have reached a saturation point. How can you increase sales? Simply by encouraging people to use soup in new ways. You create recipe advertising that shows new food dishes and casseroles that require several cans of your product. You now have your customers eating your soup as soup, along with making casseroles with your soup. Of course, this means more sales and a new way of thinking about soup. That's exactly what Egg Beaters did once the manufacturer got consumers to switch from eggs to Egg Beaters for breakfast. Then the company tried to get cooks to use Egg Beaters in their next recipe and emphasize taste.

New Pioneering Stage and Beyond

A product entering the new pioneering stage is actually in different stages in different markets. Longtime consumers will perceive the product to be in the competitive or retentive stage. New consumers will perceive it as being a pioneer. At this point, the advertising spiral will have entered still another cycle (see Exhibit 3.9), which we will call the *newest* pioneering stage, in which the focus is on getting more people to use this type of product. Today, the maker of Egg Beaters still advertises, "They taste like real eggs, because they are real eggs." The copy adds, "Look for Garden Vegetable and Southwestern with real vegetables and special seasonings." The new "Garden Vegetable" adds a blend of green and red peppers, onions, celery, and seasonings, whereas the "Southwestern" adds red and green peppers, onions, chilies, and southwestern spices for burritos and omelets. It is also now part of ConAgra Foods (see Exhibit 3.10).

EXHIBIT 3.9

Expanded Advertising Spiral

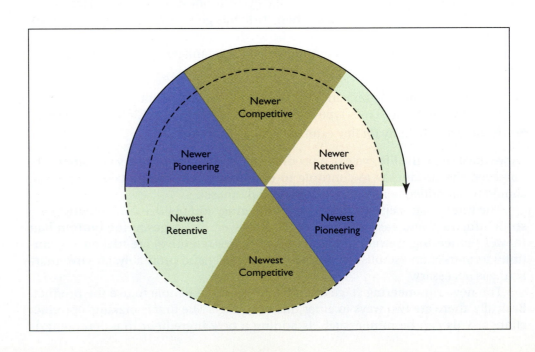

The product in this stage is faced with new problems and opportunities. Can you convince segments of your market not using your product that they should? Obviously, you have to understand why consumers were not interested in the product earlier. Creative marketing and a flexible product help this process.

McDonald's, Nike, Jell-O, Pepsi-Cola, Mountain Dew, Budweiser, Disney, ESPN, Google, and Gillette are a few of the brands that reached the retentive stage and began to look for ways to move beyond it. All of these companies moved into new pioneering with product innovations. Hence, products such as Diet Coke, Coke Zero, Cherry Coke, Diet Pepsi, Diet Mountain Dew, and Bud Light were born. New pioneering can be the result of reworking the original product or a line extension—with a new formula and name—that is related to the original version of the product. What about Anheuser-Busch and Miller Brewing? They produce several "energy beers" containing caffeine. Bartenders have created Friday Flatteners, which have been made with Red Bull and vodka for a number of years.

Creating product innovation does not always translate into brand share. Royal Crown Cola has been an industry innovator—first with national distribution of soft drinks in cans (1954), then a low-calorie diet cola (1962), then a caffeine-free diet cola (1980), and then a sodium-free diet cola (1983).[8] It had the innovation but didn't effectively manage its advertising against the larger companies of Coca-Cola and Pepsi, nor did it effectively communicate with consumers.

Since its 2001 launch, Kellogg's Special K Red Berries sales were so strong the company asked grocers not to promote it because the company couldn't keep up with the demand. As Special K has expanded in recent years to include new flavors and new forms, including bars, snack bites, and waffles, spending has also increased. Kellogg laid out about $45 million in measured media for the brand in 2005. In late 2006, it rolled out a line of protein wafers and protein bars for the diet section. It also launched Special K Chocolate Delight to help assuage dieters' cravings come diet season in January 2007.[9] Targeting the improved product by new pioneering advertising increased the total brand's performance in the marketplace.

As with the pioneering stage, once an established product in the competitive stage begins to innovate successfully in a newer pioneering stage, competition isn't far behind. In January 2003, General Mills answered Kellogg's Special K Red Berries by adding freeze-dried berries to its Cheerios, creating Cheerios Berry Burst cereals. Cheerios Berry Burst jumped to a 2 percent share of the total cereal market in its first month. Other cereal manufacturers like Post and McKee Foods followed with berry entries of their own.[10]

The idea for Special K Red Berries grew out of Kellogg's European operations, where French focus groups told the cereal maker they craved fruit on their flakes. Because there wasn't a mass market for freeze-dried berries in Europe, Kellogg uses a produce broker to match Polish berry growers with European freeze-dried coffee producers. In 1999, Kellogg's Special K Red Berries, which included strawberries, raspberries, and cherries, was launched in France and the United Kingdom and took off like a rocket, according to Jeff Montie, vice president of innovation in Europe for Kellogg's.

The advertising focus in the newer pioneering stage must be on getting consumers to understand what the product is about. Advertising in the newer competitive stage aims at getting more people to buy the brand. Moving through these stages—newer pioneering, newer competitive, newer retentive—is not easy. It requires the manufacturer to develop either product innovations or advertising positioning strategies that make the product different in consumers' eyes. Also, as we move to the newer stages of the spiral, there are usually fewer prospects for the product. Therefore, a company must become most efficient at targeting smaller groups of prospects. H. J. Heinz Company introduced EZ Squirt, a line of colored, vitamin-C-fortified ketchup in packaging especially designed for kids. EZ Squirt was developed from insight that kids under age 12 are the biggest ketchup consumers. The advertising promoted the green-colored ketchup variety plus the product's easy-to-grip, squeezable bottles with a cap that allows kids to control the ketchup stream for drawing.[11]

Since Bayer introduced and sold the first aspirin product in the late 1800s (first in powder form, then in 1915 as a tablet), it has become both a medical and marketing marvel. Its new pioneering stages have been endless. It has been sold for headaches, toothaches, muscle aches, back pain, and more recently to stave off first and repeat heart attacks. The Food and Drug Administration recently officially approved new uses, recommending aspirin for the prevention of heart problems, angina (severe chest pain), and stroke. In 2003, research showed daily aspirin use significantly reduced incidence of colorectal tumors. Another study among postmenopausal women suggested the use of aspirin may reduce their risk of developing breast cancer by 21 percent. Each time a new use for the product is found, a new advertising campaign promotes the product to an appropriate group of consumers.

Just take the statement of Emory University professor and cardiologist, John Douglas. "Aspirin is the standard treatment for any person who has coronary heart disease," he said. "It should be standard therapy for anyone who's had a heart attack, has angina or coronary atherosclerosis—hardening of the arteries." Such comments are a marketer's dream. Obviously, most products aren't as versatile as this miracle product. But if marketers can find new uses for their products, then a new stage of pioneering advertising may result.[12]

New Pioneering It is easy to understand the need for pioneering advertising when a new wrinkle in a product category is created. Just think of all the new technology advances over the past few years. Think of the recent changes in cell-phone uses beyond talking. The cell phone has become an entertainment medium offering photos, games, music, and information. In these cases, a marketer must simply educate consumers about what the product will do for them. And think of the impact of Apple's iPod and iTunes. Many consumers are eagerly waiting for the advances in this product category.

As another example, look at the evolution of Procter & Gamble's Crest toothpaste.

Crest was launched in 1955.

Crest received American Dental Association approval in 1960.

Crest Gel was introduced in 1980.

Crest Tartar Control was introduced in 1985.

Crest Sparkle for Kids was launched in 1988.

Crest Multicare was introduced in 1996.

The Advertising Spiral as a Management Decision Tool

A product may try to hold on to its consumers in one competitive area while it seeks new markets with pioneering advertising aimed at other groups. We must remember that products do not move through each stage at the same speed. In some instances, a product may go quickly from one stage in one cycle to a newer stage in another cycle. This change may also be a matter of corporate strategy. A company may believe it can obtain a greater share of business at less cost by utilizing pioneering advertising that promotes new uses for the product. It is possible that the same results could be obtained by continuing to battle at a small profit margin in a highly competitive market. A retentive advertiser may suddenly find its market slipping and plunge into a new competitive war without any new pioneering work. Like a compass, the spiral indicates direction; it does not dictate management decisions.

Before attempting to create new ideas for advertising a product, the advertiser should use the spiral to answer the following questions:

■ In which stage is the product?
■ Should we use pioneering advertising to attract new users to this type of product?
■ Should we work harder at competitive advertising to obtain a larger share of the existing market?
■ What portion of our advertising should be pioneering? What portion competitive?
■ Are we simply coasting in the retentive stage? If so, should we be more aggressive?

So far we've shown how the life cycle of a product or brand may be affected by many conditions. If the brand is to continue to be marketed, its advertising stage must be identified before its advertising goals can be set. Next, we examine how to expand on what we have learned to develop a strategic plan for a brand.

Your cookies should be so lucky.

MAYFIELD Milk

EXHIBIT 3.11

Mayfield milk has the reputation of a pure quality brand . . . even for cookies.

Courtesy of The Johnson Group, Chattanooga, and Mayfield.

brand
A name, term, sign, design, or a unifying combination of them, intended to identify and distinguish the product or service from competing products or services.

Building Strong Brands and Equity

Brands are the most valuable assets a marketer has, so we need to understand a little about them. The product is *not* the brand. A product is manufactured; a **brand** is created. A product may change over time, but the brand remains. A brand exists only through communication. Landor Associates' Antonio Marazza said, "A brand represents the most powerful link between the offer and consumer. What else is a brand if not what consumers (or more generally, stakeholders) perceive it to be? Familiarity, image, and trust drive a brand's reason to be and thus they are the building blocks of its capacity to generate value. It follows that to value a brand, you have to investigate not only within the company walls (or accounts), but above all else the mind of the consumer, where the real value of the brand resides." Landor's brand pioneer Walter Landor argued that "products are made in the factory, but brands are created in the mind."[13] Milk isn't exactly made in a factory, but it does have a clear place in consumer minds (see Exhibit 3.11).

Every product, service, or company with a recognized brand name stands for something slightly different from anything else in the same product category. If the difference is a desirable one and is known and understood by consumers, the brand will be the category leader. Today, more than ever before, the perception of a quality difference is essential for survival in the marketplace.[14]

The Origin of Branding In the mid-1880s, there were no brands and little quality control by manufacturers. Wholesalers held power over both manufacturers and retailers. Manufacturers had to offer the best deals to wholesalers to get their products distributed. This created a squeeze of profits. As a result of this profit squeeze, some manufacturers decided to differentiate their products from the competition. They gave their products names, obtained patents to protect their exclusivity, and used advertising to take the news about them to customers over the heads of the wholesalers and retailers. Thus, the concept of branding was born. Among the early brands still viable today are Levi's (1873), Maxwell House Coffee (1873), Budweiser (1876), Ivory (1879), Coca-Cola (1886), Campbell Soup (1893), and Hershey's Chocolate (1900).[15] In 1923, a study showed that brands with "mental dominance" with consumers included Ivory (soaps), Gold Medal (flour), Coca-Cola (soft drinks), B.V.D. (underwear), Kellogg's Cornflakes (breakfast food), Ford (automobiles), Del Monte (canned fruit), and Goodyear (tires). Today, we have a whole new generation of brands fighting for value and a permanent place in consumers' lives, including TiVo, Starbucks, Panera, America Online, Swiffer, eBay, ThermaCare, Febreze, Amazon.com, and others.

Brand Connections Since brands started advertising in the mid-nineteenth century in newspapers, mass-media advertising has been about making connections. As technology brings areas of the modern world closer together, advertising is becoming more disconnected from its historical base, including its business models and its changing audiences. Thanks to all the digital changes and the Internet, advertising is going through its first true paradigm shift with the advent of television. As a result, there is a revolutionary change in media tools—the promise of IPTV (Internet Protocol Television) that married television to the Internet—and a whole new way to connect. Brands remain about connecting.[16]

Branding as a Financial Decision

Howard, Merrell & Partners of Raleigh, North Carolina, an IPG unit, introduces itself to clients by saying, "Branding isn't an advertising decision. It's a financial decision. We have learned that creating brand leverage is about dealing correctly with strategic issues and financial commitments at the top management level— then taking the risks necessary to deliver category-dominating creative. It is about risk management. It is about a deep understanding of a brand's one-on-one relationship with people, considered in the context of a macro-competitive environment. We believe that perhaps our most important role is assisting our client partners to achieve the alignment needed to reinforce brand values at all points of human contact. . . ."[17]

Consumer Environment

Consumers control communication access. Consumers set the terms of their marketplace relationships because they have more access to information than ever before, and a lot more communication channels, which seems to be increasing daily. Consumers look for product information on the Web prior to making major purchases. Advertisers talk in terms of *person-to-person*. Relationship marketers talk in terms of *customer satisfaction*. Information specialists talk in terms of *smart systems*. This is a new era for brands. It is about consumers telling marketers what they want and marketers responding. It is about interactive, continuous, real-time dialogue replacing traditional models of advertising and consumer communication. Yet consumers have consistently said year after year in Yankelovich's MONITOR research that once they find a brand they like, "it is difficult to get them to change."[18]

Habit is also a marketing challenge. Generally, past experiences with a brand are consistently the most important factors in consumers' future choices. Despite all the talk about quality, past experiences followed by price, quality, and recommendations from other people lead the reasons people buy a brand. These factors haven't significantly changed over the past two decades; however, price has become more important. Yes, psychological motivations are important, but a brand's most powerful advantage is rooted in the human tendency to form habits and stick to routines. Most people will buy the same brand over and over again if it continues to satisfy their needs.

For marketers to succeed, they must answer three questions: Who buys the brand? What do they want from it? Why do they keep coming back? According to the Roper Organization, many people buy familiar brands even if they believe the product does not have an actual advantage. Only half of Americans think that a specific brand of mayonnaise is different or better than others and worth a higher price. However, 62 percent know what brand of mayonnaise they want when they walk into the store. Another 22 percent look around for the best price on a well-known brand. Brand behavior is complex. Not everyone is brand conscious, and not all brand-conscious people are truly brand driven.[19] Private-label store brands from Publix, CVS, Wal-Mart, and Target are gaining credibility in terms of quality, price, and market share. Once these were looked at as generic brands, but they are a force for national brands to deal with.

KLEPPNER VIEWPOINT 3.1

Brad Majors

Former CEO, SOCOH Marketing LLC; Senior Vice President, Lintas Worldwide
Brand Development Demystified

There is a lot of talk about "branding" or "brand development" these days, as if it is the next "new thing" in marketing and sales. "Brand development" is not a new phenomenon. It has been around for at least 100 years.

Any marketer or ad agency worth its salt practices "brand development" every time they perform any marketing function. The history of advertising in America is, essentially, the history of branding. That is what good advertising (and the other communication disciplines) does—create good and consistent reputations for products or services and this consistent imagery is what converts a product into a "brand."

I say "consistent" because one of the greatest sins of marketing these days (especially for smaller businesses) is a lack of "integrated marketing." By this I mean that there may be mixed messages (from media advertising, public relations, the Web site, package copy, or whatever) that go out to consumers from a brand. And with these inconsistent messages comes an inconsistent image for the brand. Developing integrated marketing communications is one of the most important activities that can be done to enhance the value of a client's brand. It is nearly impossible to build a brand with inconsistencies in your marketing communications mix.

Business schools teach "the Marketing Mix," which is pretty basic stuff, but bear with me. This Marketing Mix includes the Four P's of marketing: the Product itself (and its structural packaging), the Price of the product, the Place (of distribution) where the product can be purchased, and the Promotion of the product. Interestingly, the fourth P, Promotion, is simply the communication of aspects of the first three P's.

What else is critical to the sale other than what the product does, how much it costs, and where you can get it? Only one more "element" I can think of.

Enter the "Fifth P," which isn't discussed in B-School textbooks, but I doubt the idea is mine alone. What does the Fifth P stand for? The Prospect. The person who is going to buy this product or service, based on perceived needs and wants.

If the Fourth P, Promotion, connects Product, Price, and Place, it also performs another valuable function. Good Promotion, be it in the form of media advertising, packaging graphics, public relations, or in-store merchandising, also has the responsibility of connecting the Prospect to the Product, its Price, and the Place it can be found. In essence, the product is just a collection of features and attributes until the Prospect arrives on the scene. When

Brad Majors

the Prospect's needs and wants begin to surface, so do the brand's marketing possibilities.

As the Prospect evaluates all the information he or she knows about the product (what it does, what it costs, where it can be purchased), a relationship may begin to form. However, this will only happen if the brand imagery has been consistently presented. This relationship is based on how the Prospect feels the product (or service) will meet his or her needs and wants. I call this "personal relevance." How does the Prospect relate emotionally to those rational product attributes? This "personal relevance" is not a new concept in marketing either. Marketers have been trying to figure out how to achieve the emotional bond between Prospect and brand since the 1920s when Motivational Research was first used by ad agencies. And we are still trying to crack the code on why consumers make the brand choices they make.

A final comment in the Brand Development Demystification process: Sometimes the term *brand development* can suggest some type of inexpensive shortcut in marketing. I have spoken with entrepreneurs who wanted to do "brand development" because they didn't have money for advertising. Sorry, it doesn't really work that way. While media advertising may not be the only way to promote your brand, developing a brand takes time and money. Strong brands do not come cheaply. Fortunately, if the "brand development" process is successful, that investment will pay out big as you go down the marketing road. ■ ■ ■

Marketers need to be aware that as consumers' needs change, their purchase behaviors also may change. It is not unusual for needs to change when a life stage changes. For example, a couple may trade in their sports car for a van or SUV when they have a child. A recently divorced parent may be forced to change buying patterns due to less income. Interestingly, 40 percent of the people who move to a new address change their toothpaste. Yes, we need to understand consumers and their relationship to brands. Technology companies live in an ever-faster-changing world. Their products change quickly and often live in a compressed life cycle. Technology changes, and consumer needs change just as quickly.

Brands and Integrated Communication

Integrated marketing communications (IMC) could be called simply *common sense*. In the past, many marketing functions—advertising, promotion, packaging, direct marketing, public relations, events—were created and managed independently in most organizations. Today, a brand's equity is best strengthened through the integrated use of all marketing communication tools working from a single strategy. It is imperative to project a single, cohesive brand image into the marketplace and into the consumer's mind. The result has been what is labeled *integrated marketing communications*.

Integrated marketing communications refers to all the messages directed to a consumer on behalf of the brand: media advertising, promotion, public relations, direct response, events, packaging, Web, and so forth. Each message must be integrated or dovetailed in order to support all the other messages or impressions about the brand. If this process is successful, it will build a brand's equity by communicating the same brand message to consumers.

"Brand integration doesn't mean ensuring that your logo and end line are always the same. It doesn't mean persuading half a dozen agencies to work together. It is a result, not a process. When customers have a coherent experience whenever and wherever they come across your brand you have achieved integration," says Charlie Wrench of Landor Associates.[20] Ideas that can be captured in a nutshell can be more easily understood.

There are those who say integration has been around for decades and decades, but it wasn't as important or formal an issue as it is today.

Many marketers milked their brands during the 1980s for short-term profits instead of protecting and nurturing their brands. Brand building became fashionable again in the 1990s. Today, marketers realize the brand is their most important asset. Because integrated programs and brand building are so important, we discuss a system of integrated communications that builds brand equity. The most important factor in determining the actual value of a brand is its equity in the market. We can define **brand equity** as the value of how people such as consumers, distributors, and salespeople think and feel about a brand relative to its competition.

Let us look at how Young & Rubicam assesses brand equity's value.

brand equity
The value of how such people as consumers, distributors, and salespeople think and feel about a brand relative to its competition over a period of time.

Young & Rubicam's Brand Asset Valuator (BAV)

One of the most respected proprietary tools in the industry for assessing a brand's stature among consumers is the Brand Asset Valuator (BAV) created by Young & Rubicam (Y&R). It is a diagnostic tool for determining how a brand is performing relative to all other brands. It explains the strengths and weaknesses of brands on measures of stature and vitality. It believes the relationship between these two factors tells the true story about the health of brand equity and can help diagnose problems and solutions.

The Brand Asset Valuator demonstrates that brands are built in a very specific progression of four primary consumer perceptions: differentiation, relevance, esteem, and knowledge.

- Differentiation is the basis for choice: the essence of the brand, source of margin.
- Relevance relates to usage and subsumes the five P's of marketing related to sales.
- Esteem deals with consumer respect, regard, and reputation and relates to the fulfillment of perceived consumer promise.
- Knowledge is the culmination of brand-building efforts and relates to consumer experiences.

A brand's vitality lies in a combination of differentiation and relevance. A brand must be distinct, or it simply isn't a brand. But the fact that a brand is highly differentiated doesn't necessarily mean consumers have the desire or means to buy it. Unless a brand is also relevant, the consumer has no reason to select it. The lack of relevance is the reason so many fads come and go.

The two components of brand stature are esteem and familiarity, that is, whether people know and understand your brand and whether they like it. A brand that more consumers know than like is a clear warning signal. Similarly, a brand that is held in high esteem but ranks lower in familiarity suggests that increasing awareness is an appropriate objective.

Steve Owen, chief strategic officer at McGarry Bowen and who helped create BAV, says BAV looks at brands from a logical perspective. The key challenge a brand has is how to increase its dominance. The most interesting thing about BAV is that it's based upon the fact that almost every successful brand begins by being very simple. "It doesn't try to sell to everyone. It begins by selling one thing to a few people and ensures that it's different and better in a meaningful way."[21]

One of the keys to understanding brand equity is to recognize that there are differences between product categories.

From this discussion, you should be getting the sense that developing advertising strategy and building brand equity deal with many complex issues. Despite being a little deep, this discussion has given you a feel for the many issues and terms advertising practitioners face daily. Despite this complexity, the development of advertising isn't brain surgery. It is understanding all the ramifications in the market and the consumer's mind, so we can integrate communication and build brand equity better.

Brand Equity and Developing Integrated Marketing Communications Strategic Plans

Before you start to think about creating advertisements for a brand, you need a strategic plan. Before you can develop a strategy, you need an understanding of the marketing situation and a clear understanding of the brand's equity. There are four logical steps in this process resulting in the creative brief or plan:

1. Brand equity audit analysis
2. Strategic options and recommendations
3. Brand equity research
4. Creative brief

Of course, these generally would be followed by evaluation or assessment of some nature. An outline of a strategic planning process is presented next to give you insight into what is required. Some of the concepts and terms are discussed in more detail throughout the text.

Brand Equity Audit Analysis

There are a number of areas to examine in the first step, brand equity audit analysis. For instance, the context of the market, strengths and weaknesses, consumer attitude descriptions, and competitive strategies and tactics are of importance here.

Market Context We begin by examining the existing situation of both the market and the consumer. What we are looking for are clues and factors that positively or negatively affect brand equity. The whole purpose is to set the scene. The types of questions that are asked include the following:

- What is our market and with whom do we compete?
- What are other brands and product categories?
- What makes the market tick?
- How is the market structured?
- Is the market segmented? If so, how? What segment are we in?
- What is the status of store and generic brands?
- Are products highly differentiated?
- What kind of person buys products in this category? The Piggly Wiggly advertisement (see Exhibit 3.12) illustrates that there may be different levels of consumer interest.

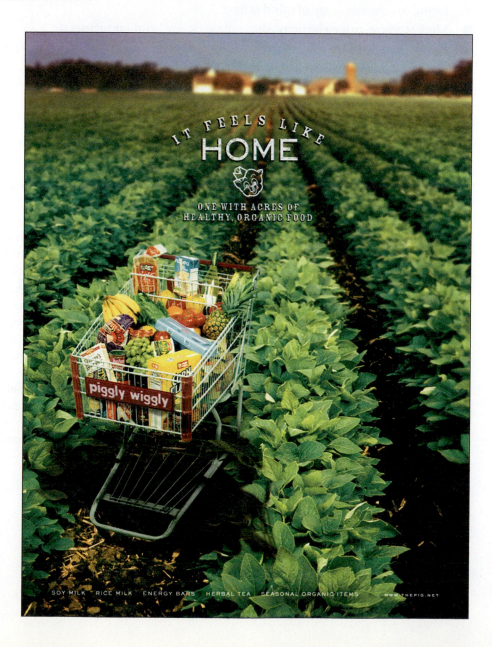

EXHIBIT 3.12

Piggly Wiggly supermarkets branding advertisement offers lots of organic foods.

Courtesy of Rawle-Murdy Associates, Charleston, and Piggly Wiggly Carolina Co.

■ In the minds of these consumers, what drives the market or holds it back (needs, obstacles, and so forth)? What are the key motivators?

■ Do consumers perceive the brands as very much alike or different?

■ Is the product bought on impulse?

■ How interested are consumers in the product?

■ Do consumers tend to be brand loyal?

These questions should help us understand the status and role of brands in a given market. For example, when the market is made up of a few brands, the consumer will likely be more brand sensitive than if the market is split up into many brands.

We must look at the market from varying angles and select only the relevant ones, so that we can set the scene for understanding and building brand equity.

Brand Equity Weaknesses and Strengths Now we have a better understanding of the market context and are ready to examine the current brand equity—how strong or weak consumer bias is toward our brand relative to other brands. The following is a list of weakness and strength indicators often used.

■ Brand awareness—top of mind is best

■ Market share, price elasticity, share of voice, and similar factors

■ Brand sensitivity—the relative importance of the brand to other factors involved in the purchase, such as price, pack size, model

■ Consistency of the brand's communication over time

■ Image attribute ratings or ranking attributes

■ Distribution, pricing, product quality, and product information

■ Brand loyalty—the strength of a brand lies in the customers who buy it as a brand rather than just as a product

Once the key weakness and strength indicators have been identified, they are used for future tracking purposes.

market
A group of people who can be identified by some common characteristic, interest, or problem; use a certain product to advantage; afford to buy it; and be reached through some medium.

Brand Equity Descriptions Now that we understand the **market** in which our brand operates and have a clear understanding of the strengths and weaknesses of our brand equity, we need to identify and describe consumers' thoughts and feelings that result in their bias toward our brand relative to other brands. This personal relationship between the consumer and the brand provides the most meaningful description of brand equity. To accomplish this, we need to analyze from two points of view.

First, we need to review all the available research to get as close a feeling as possible on how consumers view the brand and how they feel about it. Second, we must analyze in depth our brand's and its competitors' communications over a period of time. It is from these communications that most of consumers' feelings (emotional elements) and opinions (rational elements) about the brand are derived (see Exhibit 3.13).

A brand equity description for the Golf GTI automobile might be as follows:

Emotional Elements	**Rational Elements**
My little sports car	Inexpensive
Sets me free	High gas mileage
It makes me feel and look good	Retains value
Simple	Durable
It's there when I want it	Dependable
I'm in control	Handles well
	Easy to park—small

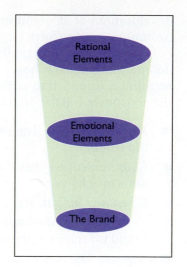

EXHIBIT **3.13**
**The Basic Elements
of a Brand**

Competitive Strategies and Tactics This area of the audit is designed to provide a clear summary of the current communication strategies and tactics of our brand and of key competitors. It should include an analysis of all integrated communications in relation to brand equity. Is the strategy designed to reinforce current brand equity? Who is the target audience? Are there different target audiences? What are the themes and executional approach? How are the marketing funds being spent (e.g., consumer pull versus trade push, advertising, promotions, direct marketing, others)? An assessment of problems and opportunities is also in order here.

Strategic Options and Recommendations

The second step draws on the conclusions from the analysis to develop a viable recommendation plan. The strategic options include:

- *Communication objectives.* What is the primary goal the message aims to achieve?
- *Audience.* To whom are we speaking?
- *Source of business.* Where are the customers going to come from—brand(s) or product categories?
- *Brand positioning and benefits.* How are we to position the brand, and what are the benefits that will build brand equity?
- *Marketing mix.* What is the recommended mix of advertising, public relations, promotion, direct response, and so on?
- *Rationale.* How does the recommended strategy relate to, and what effect is it expected to have on, brand equity?

Brand Equity Research

In the third step, we do the proprietary, qualitative research. It is exploratory and task-oriented research. Here, we need to determine which elements or elements of brand equity must be created, altered, or reinforced to achieve our recommended strategy and how far we can stretch each of these components without risking the brand's credibility. This may give us a revised list of rational and emotional elements that describe how we want consumers to think and feel about our brand in the future.

Creative Brief

The final step is a written creative brief (or work plan) for all communications. We synthesize all the information and understanding into an action plan for the development of all communications for the brand: advertising, public relations, promotion, and so forth.

The creative strategy (brief or work plan) is a short statement that clearly defines our audience, how consumers think or feel and behave, what the communication is intended to achieve, and the promise that will create a bond between the consumer and the brand. A typical strategy would include the following:

- *Key observations.* The most important market/consumer factor that dictates the strategy
- *Communication objective.* The primary goal the advertising or communication aims to achieve
- *Consumer insight.* The consumer "hot button" our communication will trigger
- *Promise.* What the brand should represent in the consumer's mind; what the brand is promising the consumer
- *Support.* The reason the promise is true
- *Audience.* To whom we are speaking and how they feel about the brand

There may be a need for an additional element:

- *Mandatories.* Items used as compulsory constraints, for example, a specific legal requirement or corporate policy that impacts the direction of the strategy

Other Examples of Strategic Planning

It is important to understand that there isn't just one approach to developing an integrated strategic plan for a brand. The basic steps are similar, but each agency approaches the process with a little different wrinkle. Let us take a look at the basics of a couple of other strategic planning approaches.

Avrett, Free & Ginsberg's Planning Cycle   Avrett, Free & Ginsberg (AFG) uses a seven-step planning cycle that helps create strategic advertising. It uses the discipline of account planning at each stage of developing strategy. Briefly, the framework for its strategic planning cycle (see Exhibit 3.14) involves the following steps:

1. *Brand/market status.* AFG evaluates where the brand is in its marketplace and determines strengths, weaknesses, opportunities, and threats.
2. *Brand mission.* After determining brand status, AFG proposes and agrees on brand goals, that is, where it can take the brand.

EXHIBIT 3.14

AFG Planning Cycle

Courtesy of Avrett Free & Ginsberg.

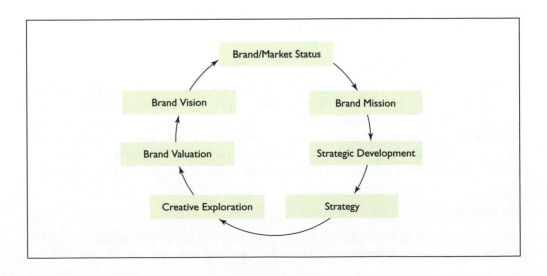

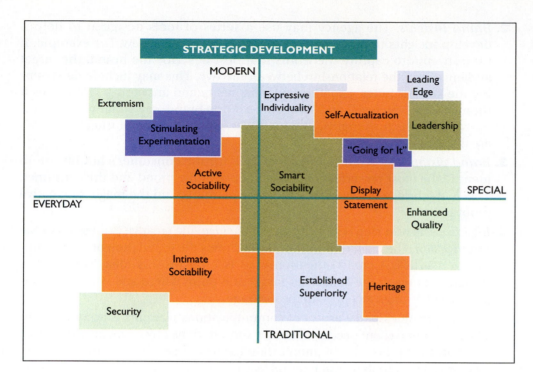

EXHIBIT 3.15

An Example of AFG's Need-Mapping Process
Courtesy of Avrett Free & Ginsberg.

3. *Strategic development.* Here, AFG explores various options to determine which of several strategies will empower the brand to achieve the mission. AFG uses a process called *needs mapping* (see Exhibit 3.15). The basic principle is that people respond or bond to products based on a wide range of psychological and rational needs. This process is loosely based on Maslow's hierarchy of needs.

4. *Strategy.* AFG formulates a tight strategy to be used in developing a fully integrated marketing communication program.

5. *Creative exploration.* AFG develops, explores, and evaluates a range of executions to ensure that it maximizes the relevancy, distinctiveness, and persuasiveness of the strategy and final execution.

6. *Brand valuation.* AFG tracks marketplace performance and progress because it believes it must be accountable for the results its work generates. AFG constantly fine-tunes and improves communications in response to changing market conditions.

7. *Brand vision.* In building equities for a brand through effective communications, AFG plots long-range expansion plans for the base brand. AFG determines if the emerging brand equities can be line extended or translated to serve needs in other related categories.

These seven steps are constantly pursued in the evaluation of a brand's life cycle to ensure long-term growth and brand equity.

Another View of the Planning Process Following are some of the typical steps agencies and clients take in the planning process.

1. *Current brand status.* In this step, there is an attempt to evaluate the brand's overall appeal. The brand is examined in the context of its marketplace, in its consumers' view, and in relation to its competitors. It answers: Where do we stand in the marketplace? Who are our real competitors? What is the consumer attitude toward our brand? The category? Who are the consumers?

2. *Brand insights.* The agency may use a series of tools designed to help it develop insights to better understand the consumer's view. For example, it may attempt to capture the words that best describe the brand, the target audience, and the relationship between the two. This may include determining the key attributes, benefits, and personality and answering: "How does it (brand) make you feel?" and "What does it (the brand) say about you?" This is the step in which strengths, opportunities, weaknesses, and threats (SWOT) are determined.

3. *Brand vision.* The strategic planners look for the consumer's hot button to identify the most powerful connection between the brand and the consumer. This is the bridge between the insight of planning and the magic of creative innovation.

4. *Big idea.* The next step is identifying the *big idea*, the creative expression of the *brand vision*. The *big idea* for branding becomes the foundation of all communication briefs. A communication plan is built on this idea. This plan is designed to reach the consumer target at a point where and when the consumer will be most receptive to the message.

5. *Evaluation.* An essential aspect of communications planning is accountability. The agency and client need to determine how well the objectives have been met and how to improve the communication the next time. Agencies may use their own proprietary tools to evaluate and learn from their performance, or they may use outside sources to accomplish this measurement.

Every agency has its own version of strategic brand building and understanding the consumer. After all, agencies have to differentiate themselves to attract clients:

- The word *disruption* and the TBWA agency have become synonymous with one another. Disruption helps TBWA define brands for its clients. The process challenges the underlying conventions that shape communication and marketing on every level in an attempt to break the status quo.

- Euro RSCG Worldwide looks at the marketer's need for ideas that apply to its business strategy. This strategic integration goes beyond advertising into such areas as "buzz" or word-of-mouth advertising that transfers brand information through social networks. This buzz concentrates not on the traditional trendsetters of society but on a group defined as *trend spreaders*. So when we talk about a strategic approach, it may include approaching the brand problem or solution from a different direction.

- Ogilvy & Mather takes a holistic look at communications and uses "what is necessary from each of the disciples . . . to build a brand." Ogilvy calls this 360 Degree Branding. Under 360, every point of contact builds the brand. Building the brand is no longer solely the job of traditional advertising but also includes direct marketing, public relations, sponsorships, interactive services, customer relationship management, consulting, and promotion.

In short, the consumer (target) has to be an important part of the strategic planning process. How the advertiser engages consumers is critical to the process. In the past, marketers spoke and consumers listened. Today's consumers are proactive and speak loudly, and marketers have learned they need to listen. You can't plan integrated communications effectively without understanding the target more wisely than ever before.

What Great Brands Do

Scott Bedbury, former senior vice president of marketing at Starbucks Coffee, said, "I walked through a hardware store last night and I came across 50 brands I didn't know existed. They may be great products, but they're not great brands." Scott should know brands. He's the man who gave the world "Just Do It," Nike's branding campaign. A few of Bedbury's brand-building principles are examined here:[22]

■ *A great brand is in it for the long haul.* For decades, there were brands based on solid value propositions—they had established their worth in the consumers' minds. Then, in the 1980s and 1990s, companies focused on short-term economic returns and diminished long-term brand-building programs. As a result, there were a lot of products with very little differentiation. Today a great brand is a necessity, not a luxury. The Zippo lighter, for example, was created in the early 1930s (see Exhibit 3.16). By using a long-term approach, a great brand can travel worldwide, speak to multiple consumer segments simultaneously, and create economies of scale by which you can earn solid margins over the long term.

■ *A great brand can be anything.* Some categories lend themselves to branding better than others, but anything is brandable. For example, Starbucks focuses on how coffee has woven itself into the fabric of people's lives, and that's an opportunity for emotional leverage. Almost any product offers an opportunity to create a frame of mind that is unique. Do you know what Intel computer processors do, how they work, or why they are superior to their competitor? All most people know is that they want to own a computer with "Intel Inside."

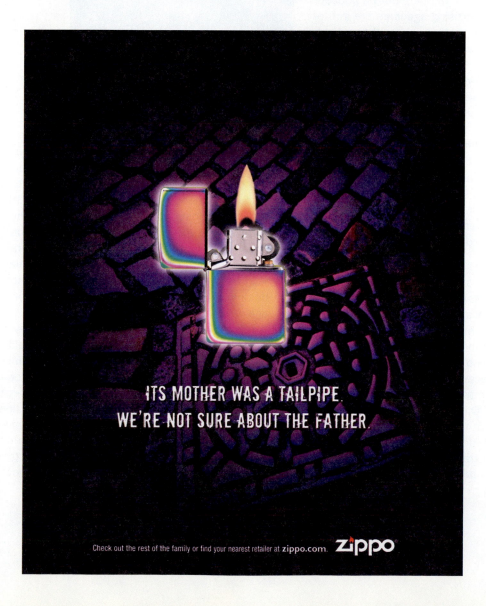

EXHIBIT 3.16

A Creative Branding Approach

Courtesy of Blattner Brunner and Zippo.

ITS MOTHER WAS A TAILPIPE.
WE'RE NOT SURE ABOUT THE FATHER.

Check out the rest of the family or find your nearest retailer at zippo.com. **Zippo**

KLEPPNER VIEWPOINT 3.2

Frank Compton

Chief Creative Ambassador, *Blattner Brunner*
The Quest for Great Advertising

The advertising agency world today covers a broad spectrum of businesses that, in some form or fashion, create perceptions of brands or awareness for products or services. These entities go about doing it in a variety of ways, some developing specialties and proprietary processes. But in the end, however, the goal is to sell something, and, ultimately, it's all about the business of creativity.

Yet, of the literally thousands of businesses called advertising agencies, a very small number of those actually become recognized for their creativity. These agencies stand out from the pack for their ability to consistently present relevant marketing messages in ways that are so unique and different they can't help but be noticed in the marketplace. So, if advertising agencies are in the business of creativity, what distinguishes those that seem to have this creative magic from those that simply do "good work"?

At Sawyer Riley Compton, we did "good work" for many years. We grew and we helped clients grow their businesses as well. But all the while, there was a yearning, a passion from within, to really create for our clients that cutting-edge work that truly stands out in an extraordinary way. And we simply set out to do it.

A decade later we're now included in a group of agencies known within the industry and among a certain genre of clients for our creative work. So, how did that happen? What does it take to consistently produce a level of creative thinking that is recognized as a cut above? These are some things we believe.

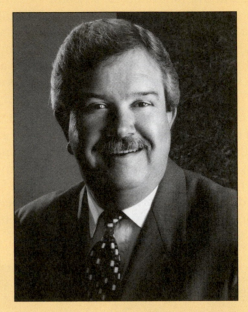

Frank Compton

1. **It begins at the top.** Unless it's a passion and a commitment by the people responsible for the vision and financial success of the agency, it simply can't happen. For a while, it's a huge investment with little return. Old clients leave because that's not why they hired you. New clients who expect great creative work won't come on board because you haven't proved you can do it yet. There's staff turnover because some don't share the vision. Others are simply not willing to make the commitment to go beyond where they've been. And others simply don't have the talent. So, for years, the agency is in transition resulting in inordinate emotional and financial stress, loss of identity and, in general, chaos.

2. **Great creative is just good business.** Louis Sawyer describes truly great creative work as "smart work." Not only is there a wonderful idea at the center but also you immediately recognize it as having true relevance and doing an extraordinary job for the client. The power of the idea multiplies the media budget. It finds its way into the streets. It shows up in conversations around water coolers. And ultimately, it works—something is sold! Then it becomes good business for the agency as well. The phone rings again with clients who want what we do.

3. **It takes a very special group of clients.** They may be within a corporate giant or a rising, privately held organization. But you find each other. And when you meet, you know. The chemistry is there. You have big ideas and they have the courage to see the potential. They flatten their organizations to give you access to decision makers. They take you inside the tent to help them wrestle with all strategic issues relating to success in the marketplace. In turn, you become obsessed with their success. You challenge them; they challenge you. Trust grows. And so does substantial progress.

4. **The whole agency is the creative department.** Sure, we have copywriters and art directors but one would have a hard time putting our people in traditional agency pigeonholes. The account managers are very creative. The copywriters and art directors think strategically. Media, PR, and interactive people contribute ideas that may very well become ads. Or vice versa. Production people are fanatical about the crafting of the idea in every tactical execution. And improvement to the idea never ends. Someone is constantly working to make it better. Even the financial staff realizes their importance in making ideas soar and brands successful. The passion to do better work becomes cult-like.

5. **Find the talent.** I'm convinced creativity is like athleticism. Some people have an inordinate amount while others have less. We work hard to find the ones who have a lot. This means looking beyond a résumé to see the talent or the potential. As an agency's creative notoriety spreads, finding great talent becomes somewhat easier. The people who have it seek out places where they can use it. And they come to us.

6. **No prima donnas.** No prima donnas and great creative talent—an oxymoron? Not so. It's a matter of confidence, I believe. When ad people are really good and they know it, they don't have to exhibit the stereotypical trappings ranging from "the look" to temper tantrums. There are nice people who possess amazing creative talent and we work hard to find them.

   Peer selection and peer management are very important tools we use to avoid the prima donna trap. Interviews and portfolio reviews involve numerous team members from multiple disciplines. When someone becomes part of the SRC team, she or he has been thoroughly run through the proverbial ringer by a group of peers. This results in respect among the team that means accountability to the whole. Everyone not only wants to do their best for the others; they also readily solicit the critique of their ideas from their peers. Everyone makes everyone else's work better.

7. **Respect the culture.** Yes, we have a culture. And so do our clients. Respecting both is essential to great work. Seldom do we have a fully developed idea summarily rejected by a client. If it's off strategy, the team detects it before it gets that far. But creating within each client's culture is equally important. The culture of The Ritz-Carlton is totally different from the culture of Dow. Thus, the approaches we'd take for each are totally different as well.

   Internally, our own culture is based on respect. There is no distinction between how people are treated by "management" versus how people are treated by each other. They are one and the same. There is no doubt about a passion for the work and an undying determination to constantly make it better. But beyond this, there's also a realization that we are also husbands and wives, fathers and mothers, girlfriends, golfers, runners, gardeners, and any number of descriptors that indicate there's a personal life outside of advertising. And it's often in real life where ideas begin anyway.

8. **Unstructured structure.** This involves everything from office space to managing the clock. A total lack of structure means chaos but some amount of managed chaos is good. Within our office space, for example, there are no doors. So, it gets noisy. People aren't compartmentalized either. An art director is neighbor to a media planner. As a result, people overhear ideas for a brand's strategic direction or a campaign in the hallways. They come out and join in. Before you know it, a myriad of people is contributing. And the idea gets better.

   There's also freedom to disagree, challenge, take charge, or even make mistakes. Certainly there are systems and procedures in place to manage the chaos. But the real accountability in a truly creative environment is to each other.

9. **There's no substitute for hard work.** It begins long before a creative team ever starts to conceptualize. Observing. In homes. In stores. On sales calls. Great insights come from involvement with the brand and people who buy and use the brand. Research adds further clarification. Client and agency teams are meeting throughout. Pushing. Challenging. Progressing. Then it comes down to really smart creative people being prolific. Walls are plastered with good ideas. Then replaced by better ideas. Then more of the same. Ultimately, the idea gels. Is it smart? Does it surprise? Yes, but there's something better. Let's find it.

10. **Celebrate the work.** Never get comfortable. We challenge ourselves by constantly reviewing what other agencies we admire are doing. We review award show reels and annuals. And we submit our work to the premier creative shows. When it's awarded, we unashamedly celebrate. When it's not, we try harder. Otherwise how do we know where our creative bar stands as compared to the work considered the best in the world?

   So, as you can see, there is no magic. It's more about uncompromising vision and truly believing great work creates better value for clients. I'd have to say it's also about personal satisfaction in knowing we did our absolute best and we've been part of something pretty special. I can live with that.

Courtesy Sawyer Riley Compton. ■ ■ ■

- *A great brand knows itself.* The real starting point is to go out to consumers and find out what they like or dislike about this brand and what they associate as the very core of the brand concept. To keep a brand alive over the long haul, to keep it vital, you have to do something new, something unexpected. It has to relate to the brand's core position.

- *A great brand invents or reinvents an entire category.* The common ground that you find among brands such as Disney, Apple, Nike, and Starbucks is that these companies made it an explicit goal to be the protagonists for each of their entire categories. Disney is the protagonist for fun family entertainment and family values. A great brand raises the bar—it adds a greater sense of purpose to the experience.

- *A great brand taps into emotions.* The common ground among companies that have built great brands is not just performance. They realize consumers live in an emotional world. Emotions drive most, if not all, of our decisions. It is an emotional connection that transcends the product. And transcending the product is the brand.

- *A great brand is a story that's never completely told.* A brand is a metaphorical story that is evolving all the time. This connects with something very deep. People have always needed to make sense of things at a higher level. Levi's has a story that goes all the way back to the gold rush. It has photos of miners wearing Levi's dungarees. Stories create connections for people. Stories create the emotional context people need to locate themselves in a larger experience.

- *A great brand is relevant.* A lot of brands are trying to position themselves as "cool," but most of them fail. The larger idea is to be relevant. It meets what people want; it performs the way people want it to. In the past couple of decades, a lot of brands promised consumers things they couldn't deliver. Consumers are looking for something that has lasting value. There is a quest for quality, not quantity.

SUMMARY ✹

Products pass through a number of stages—from introduction to ultimate demise—known as the product life cycle. Advertising plays a different role in each stage of product development. Until consumers appreciate the fact that they need a product, that product is in the pioneering stage of advertising. In the competitive stage, an advertiser tries to differentiate its product from that of the competition. The retentive stage calls for reminder advertising.

A product's age has little to do with the stage it is in at any given time. Rather, consumer attitude or perception determines the stage of a product. As consumer perception changes, moving it from one stage to another, the advertising message should also change. In fact, the advertising may be in more than one stage at any given time. Creative marketing may propel a product through new pioneering, new competitive, and new retentive stages. And it is even possible for a product to continue on into the newest pioneering, newest competitive, and newest retentive stages. As a product ages, so do its users, which is why no product can survive without attracting new customers. Long-term success depends on keeping current customers while constantly attracting new ones.

In the mid-1880s, there were no brands. Manufacturers differentiated their products and gave them names as the concept of branding was born. Brands are now among the most valuable assets a marketer owns. The product is not the brand. A product is manufactured; a brand is created and is made up of both rational and emotional elements. In today's marketing environment, it is essential that every communication reinforces brand personality in the same manner: advertising, public relations, promotion, packaging, direct marketing, and so forth. The most important factor in determining the actual value of a brand is its equity in the market: how consumers think and feel about the brand.

Avrett, Free & Ginsberg (AFG) uses a seven-step planning cycle that helps create strategic advertising. It uses the discipline of account planning at each stage of developing a campaign: brand/marketing status, brand mission, strategic development, creative exploitation, brand valuation, and brand vision.

REVIEW ✹

1. Briefly identify each stage in the first half of the advertising spiral.
2. What determines the stage of a product?
3. What is the essence of the advertising message in each stage of the spiral?
4. What is brand equity?
5. What are the elements of the creative brief?
6. What are the key elements in the AFG planning cycle?

CHAPTER 4

Target Marketing

Advertisers have been forced to get creative in reaching target demographics in such a fragmented market. In Chapter 3, we examined the brand in the context of its market and consumers. In the creative brief, we were asked, "Whom are we speaking to?" Here, we speak to answering your options and understanding changes taking place in society and their impact on business. After reading this chapter, you will understand:

chapter objectives

1. defining prime prospects
2. the importance of target marketing information
3. the marketing concept
4. planning the advertising
5. niche marketing and positioning
6. beyond demographics: psychographics

Change is absolutely everywhere: The kinds of people advertisers are trying to reach, their behavior, and the way we reach them are only part of the story. Even consumers are bewildered by the rate of change. Advertisers must keep up with the trends around them. If they don't understand their brands' environment, their advertising won't be on trend and to the right people.

Who do we think is going to buy our product? Men? Women? Teenagers? College students? Men and women? Seniors? Twenty-five- to forty-nine-year-olds? Primarily Hispanic people? To whom are we going to aim our advertising? Is it going to be profitable? What is our rationale for selecting this target? Have there been any changes in this target? There are a lot of questions to be answered. We need a lot of answers. In the process, does that mean we don't aim at everybody who has money? We know that won't work—that's a shotgun approach. We need to be focused and direct, like a rifle shot, to hit our target.

The monolithic mass market of the mid-twentieth century has long been laid to rest, and smaller mass markets have taken its place. Coming up with new targeting approaches is critical to many advertisers. For example, Yahoo! developed approaches that allowed it to identify actual product or category purchases. They do this by matching the behavior of certain consumers with the Nielsen HomeScan database that captures consumers' actual buying habits (thus making advertising more relevant), and Yahoo! does this with full permission of these consumers. Yahoo! is then able to look for that Web-user behavior pattern online, and it serves advertisements to those anonymous consumers. There is a high enough correlation with the Web behavior and the purchasing of certain products.[1]

MARKETING GENERALIZATION

As we discuss many factors and groups used by marketers, a word of caution is in order. We talk about baby boomers; Seniors; and generations X, Y, and Z or limit discussions to demographics (age, income, sex) as if each is a uniform group of people who live, think, and act exactly the same. Do all 20-year-old women think and act alike? Do all Hispanic people? Do all Boomers? Virtually no generalization encompasses an entire consumer segment, especially age groups. If we stop to think about it, we know better than to generalize. Consider that Seniors or Matures can be wealthy or not, love the outdoors or not, be inclined to travel or be homebodies, own a vacation home or live in a mobile home. The same considerations apply to virtually every one of these catchall categories. Of course, these groupings or segments can be very useful in assessing potential markets; after all, they do have group behavior and lifestyle commonalities. These segments should be considered, but remember that they stereotype groups of people. We all know that all Russians drink vodka, Germans drink beer, and the French drink wine, right? Or that all Southerners eat grits? It is okay to start with a premise in narrowing to one of these groups, but it is important to dig deeper and create an understanding.

A cardinal rule in marketing has always been to know your market. That doesn't mean segmenting young and old or rich and poor. It means defining your target in as much detail as circumstances allow and necessity requires. There is a reason that reliable market research looks at multiple factors such as age, gender, income, net worth, ethnicity, geography, lifestyle, and family status. It is very appropriate to use "families" as a partial descriptor of a given market, as long as it doesn't become a synonym for the market itself.[2] Now that we have sent up a red flag, let us look at some factors and segments used in target marketing. When possible, today's marketing aims at the individual and not at the mass market.

Once you ask the obvious questions, you must determine which answers are critical to your decision making. Do you need more information to reach your prospects successfully? Do you understand their problems? Have you thought about what you want people to think and feel about your brand as a result of being exposed to your advertising?

DEFINING PRIME PROSPECTS

target marketing
Identifying and communicating with groups of prime prospects.

One of the decisions critical to success is defining prime prospects so you do not waste time and money advertising your product to people unlikely to buy it or people you can't make a profit by attracting. This search for the best prospects among all consumers is called **target marketing**.

The process of finding prime prospects is not limited to products; services, cities, almost any organization may need to target prospects. The Charleston Regional Development Alliance advertisement says, "The world is your market. More business happens in an hour than once happened in a day. Casual Fridays last all week. And you no longer have to stay in the city to stay on top. The rules of business have changed. So has the address." (See Exhibit 4.1.) Obviously, this advertisement is not targeted at everyone.

Where Do We Start?

Different agencies and companies approach the process a little differently, as we saw in the last chapter, but all have to answer the same important questions before advertising can be created. Brand equity research, for instance, seeks to answer a

EXHIBIT **4.1**

Charleston, South Carolina

"The world is your market. . . . The rules of business have changed."

Courtesy of the Charleston Regional Development Alliance.

number of questions and examine the existing state of the brand in the context of market and consumers. Today, marketers have a host of informational sources to help plan integrated marketing programs aimed at individual users or groups. Let us look at some of the information sources and trends in America and their implications for advertising planning.

Census Data

Marketing executives must adapt to a constantly changing environment, especially shifts in demographics and lifestyles. Census data offer marketers a wealth of information about people and how they live in the United States. Much of the database is online. The Topologically Integrated Geographic Encoding and Referencing system, known as TIGER, is one of the more sophisticated tools. This coding of the country's natural, political, and statistical boundaries includes every street, road, and subdivision. TIGER provides the data for computer maps to plan sales territories and pinpoint direct-marketing prospects. This information can be linked to a number of relevant characteristics, such as age, income, and race. Custom research companies using these data have developed software for marketers to access geodemographic databases. The 2006 First Edition TIGER/Line files contain updates to street features and/or address ranges from the Census 2000 versions of the TIGER/Line files.

Now advertisers have a number of geodemographic sources that claim unprecedented precision and details about consumers and their purchasing behavior based on their home addresses. These services using 2000 Census data clusters promise advertisers that classifying geodemographics has grown from an art to a science. Each service organizes America's households into forty to seventy number-coded nicknames (Blue Bloods, Trailblazers, Penny Pinchers, Shotguns, and Pickups) to identify lifestyle segmentation. Claritas' PRIZM, for example, steps beyond ZIP Code + 4 level of detail, a geographic area that encompasses ten to twelve households, as opposed to blocks, which have 340 households, and ZIP Codes, which include 3,600 households. These companies can zero in on smaller segments of the population than was previously possible. They also overlay precise demographic information with consumer behavior information giving advertisers a better consumer picture. Depending on the level of information, these geodemographic services can cost an advertiser from $500 to $100,000. Some of the services described here are discussed later in the text:[3]

- *Aciom.* Aciom has a life-stage-driven, household-level, consumer segmentation system representing approximately 110 million U.S. households.
- *Claritas.* By segmenting customers using demographic and behavioral traits, Claritas can identify who the best customers are, what they are like, and where to find them.
- *ESRI.* ESRI provides a demographic and lifestyle picture of neighborhoods, enabling businesses to profile their best customers.
- *Experian.* Experian is a global segmentation product accessing resources including automotive, retail, and catalog transactional information, household demographics, and so on.
- *MapInfo.* MapInfo ties location to behaviors and characteristics of the population, helping advertisers make decisions about market and product potential and store placement. Pollo Tropical® has sixty-four Florida locations. Prior to working with MapInfo, the company relied on "gut and instincts" to determine new real estate locations. MapInfo's press release says that Pollo Tropical realized that to successfully expand in its core markets of south and central Florida, as well as to break into new areas of the country, it would need more fact-based geodemographic research.

Population

In October 2006, the Census Bureau reported the U.S. population grew to 300 million people. We'll talk about the significance of that increase shortly. In the United States, marketers have always had to deal with population growth and shifts that influence advertisers' markets in some way. Obviously, we need to know who is out there in the marketplace. How many of them? Where and how do they live? What do they need? What are their buying patterns? We can't easily reach people if we don't know where they are. But population is more than simple numbers of people. Society tends to group people by age, ethnicity, generation, or some other factor. For instance, *American Demographics* breaks down the generations living in 2000:

GI Generation, 71+ years old (9.1 percent); Depression, 61–70 years old (6.5 percent); War Babies, 55–60 years old (5.7 percent); Baby Boomers, 36–54 years old (28.2 percent); Generation X, 22–34 years old (16.4 percent); Generation Y, 6–23 years old (25.8 percent); and Millennials, 0–5 years old (8.3 percent).[4] How they think, act, and spend influences marketers. An advertiser must understand these people beyond the numbers.

The U.S. Census Bureau data projections indicate that by the year 2025, 70 percent of the growth will take place in the South and West. By 2025, there will be moderate growth for New York, New Jersey, Pennsylvania, Ohio, and Michigan. California will double its population from the year 1990 to 2040. But that is only part of the story. California gained 1.3 million immigrants while losing 1.5 million natives to surrounding states. So numbers alone don't tell the picture. But the numbers themselves indicate change.

Selected Census State Population Projections

The following is a look at the ten most populous states and their populations in 2000 and the population projections for the ten states projected to have the most people by 2030:

2000

1.	California	33,871,648
2.	Texas	20,851,820
3.	New York	18,976,457
4.	Florida	15,982,378
5.	Illinois	12,419,293
6.	Pennsylvania	12,281,054
7.	Ohio	11,353,140
8.	Michigan	9,938,444
9.	New Jersey	8,414,350
10.	Georgia	8,186,453

2030

1.	California	46,444,861
2.	Texas	33,317,744
3.	Florida	28,685,769
4.	New York	19,477,429
5.	Illinois	13,432,892
6.	Pennsylvania	12,768,184
7.	North Carolina	12,227,739
8.	Georgia	12,017,838
9.	Ohio	11,550,528
10.	Arizona	10,712,397

Source: Estimated U.S. Census Bureau projections.

Marketers may look at specific markets for numbers of people in a market or making media decisions. A narrower look might be using Metropolitan Statistical Area (MSA) data, which are population estimates. These data examine the metropolitan areas where people actually live. You could also look at each of these MSAs by a number of demographic characteristics discussed later.

Selected Rankings of U.S. Metropolitan Statistical Area (2005) Population Estimates

1.	New York–Northern New Jersey–Long Island, NY–NJ–PA	18,747,320
2.	Los Angeles–Long Beach–Santa Ana	12,923,547
3.	Chicago–Naperville–Joliet, IL–IN–WI	9,443,356
4.	Philadelphia–Camden–Wilmington, PA–NJ–DE–MD	5,823,233
5.	Dallas–Fort Worth–Arlington, TX	5,819,475
6.	Miami–Fort Lauderdale–Miami Beach, FL	5,422,200
7.	Houston–Sugar Land–Baytown, TX	5,280,077
8.	Washington–Arlington–Alexandria, DC–VA–MD–WV	5,214,666
9.	Atlanta–Sandy Springs–Marietta, GA	4,917,717
10.	Detroit–Warren–Livonia, MI	4,488,335
14.	Phoenix–Mesa–Scottsdale, AZ	3,865,077
16.	Minneapolis–St. Paul–Bloomington, MN–WI	3,142,779
22.	Denver–Aurora, CO	2,359,994
25.	Cincinnati–Middletown, OH–KY–IN	2,070,441
36.	Charlotte–Gastonia–Concord, NC–SC	1,521,278
50.	Salt Lake City, UT	1,034,484

Change, Change, Change

American Demographics says the population for the next quarter century will be larger, older, and more diverse, one with many opportunities and challenges for business. Of course, it is difficult to accurately predict the future. The demographics are easy because they are alive today. Speculation about the social and cultural—and even political aspects—is not so clear. By 2025, the U.S. population is expected to exceed 350 million. As this population grows, niche markets may become unwieldy for businesses to target with a single strategy. The niche market of today may become a mass market in its own right, segmented not only by nationality but also by spending behavior and other psychographic characteristics. This trend is called *beehiving*, says Vickie Abrahamson of Iconoculture, a trend consulting firm. Beehiving is the growth of tight-knit, alternative communities sharing common values and passions. Abrahamson says, "Marketers must tap in to beehive rituals, customs and language to build trust and patronage."[5]

A large opportunity for marketers in the next few decades will be in the age 65 and older set. The baby boomers group will almost double in size. In addition to being focused on youth, marketers will also pay more attention outside the youth market. The clue in the future will be how to establish brands that attract older consumers without alienating younger ones.

We are not going to attempt to cover all the demographics that may be important, but these items should give you something to think about. Keep in mind that these may or may not be important to a specific marketing situation. It is imperative to get a handle on what data are important.

Multicultural Overview

Defining the multicultural market appears to be a problem for some. "We tend to forget that a culture means a culture, not necessarily a different language," says Lynn Adrian-Hsing, Asian segments marketing manager, multicultural marketing integration at Bank of America.[6] She encourages advertisers to "think outside the traditional 'multicultural box'" to include gay and lesbian consumers, senior consumers, and members of Generation X and Generation Y (*Gen X* and *Gen Y*, respectively). "These are cultural markets, not ethnic." Bank of America placed 25 percent of its advertising budget to win business from African American, Hispanic, and Asian American consumers. The campaign's objective was to add mortgages and about a million new checking accounts over a 12-month period. Citigroup and JPMorgan Chase are other banking corporations that tailor campaigns to specific ethnic groups. The Census indicates that the minority population totaled 98 million, or about 30 percent of the total population. If a marketer included gay and lesbian people in the population mix, they would account for another 20 million potential consumers.[7]

Today's multicultural marketing has evolved since the term *minority marketing* was used to describe targeting African American potential consumers during the 1960s. As marketers included Hispanic American efforts, it was called *ethnic marketing*. Today, many marketers prefer the term *multicultural marketing*, because it encompasses not only a range of ethnicities but also lifestyle-related targets such as the gay and lesbian markets.

Selected Demographic Snapshots

The American Community Survey, a Census Bureau program, released its first findings in the summer of 2006. Among the new data were the following:

Ancestry. Seventeen percent of Americans say their roots are German, the largest ancestral group; 12 percent say their background is Irish; those saying their background is English (10 percent) rank third; and ranking fourth, 7 percent of the population say their ancestral background is "American."

Immigrants. One in eight residents (12.4 percent) are immigrants, up from 11 percent in 2000. Latin American residents account for more than half (53 percent) of the immigrant population; 27 percent came from Asian/Pacific areas. Nearly one-third (31 percent) of immigrants are from Mexico; there are an estimated 11 million Mexican-born residents in the United States, which is greater than the population of all but seven states.

Age and household. Utah has the nation's youngest median age (28.5), the highest percentage of households with children (44 percent), and the largest families (average 3.1 people). The oldest state is Maine (median age of 41.2). In Florida, 29 percent of households have residents age 65+, the highest in the nation; but the Sunshine State ranks sixth in median age (39.5). The nation's median age is 36.4.

Education. Twenty-seven percent of U.S. adults (age 25+) have a bachelor's degree; 10 percent have an advanced degree. Massachusetts scores first among states in percentage of residents with a bachelor's (37 percent) or advanced degree (16 percent). Among large cities, San Francisco is by far the most educated: 50 percent of its residents are college graduates.

The African American Population The mid-decade Census report indicates that African American people make up 13.4 percent of the U.S. population, or 36.6 million. According to the Census, there are 11.8 million African American children under the age of 18 in the United States. Some 54 percent of the African American population lives in the South. The median age for the African American population is 29.5 years, which is both younger and faster growing than the white population. There are also 823,500 African American–owned businesses generating $71 billion in revenues. Women own 38 percent of the nation's African American businesses, a higher percentage than that of any other minority ethnic group. There are 5.7 million African Americans who own their homes, which represents 46 percent of the

African American population. The top five African American population cities are New York, Chicago, Detroit, Philadelphia, and Houston.

The median income of all African American families was $30,134 compared to that of Caucasian families at $48,977. However, married-couple African American families' median income was similar to the income of Caucasian families, at $49,752 versus $59,025. Between 2001 and 2010, there will be a slight decline in African American students ages 5 to 9 in schools and a decrease of 9 percent for children ages 10 to 14. Census data indicate that 55.3 percent of U.S. African American people live in the South, 18.1 percent live in the Northeast, 18.1 percent live in the Midwest, and about only 8.6 percent live in the West.

About 30 percent of African American households have achieved middle- and upper-income status. *American Demographics* reports that in areas such as Middlesex, New Jersey, and Nassau-Suffolk, New York, home of many commuting New Yorkers, and in San José and Orange County, California, home of suburbanizing Los Angelinos, more than half of all African American households earn more than $50,000 a year. The number of African American college graduates has increased significantly over the past two decades adding to the middle-class impact. Today, there is a greater tendency for Gen X and Gen Y African American students to graduate from college and enter professional careers. How do advertisers reach them effectively as they become more mobile across the nation? "A number of marketers still tend to think African-Americans are darker versions of white people, that they don't have to do anything different to reach them," says Howard Buford, CEO of Prime Access, a multicultural agency.[8]

The Hispanic Population The U.S. Hispanic population, including immigrants and those born in the United States, totaled 41.9 million, or 14.5 percent of the nation's population, in the mid-decade Census study. The median age of members of the U.S. Hispanic population is 27.2 (26.8 for males, 27.6 for females), which is 9 years younger than the U.S. median (36.4). One-third of the U.S. Hispanic population (34 percent, or 14 million) are under age 18. People of Mexican origin make up 64 percent of the U.S. Hispanic population; 9 percent of the Hispanic population in the United States have roots in Puerto Rico, 7 percent in Central America, 5 percent in South America, and 3 percent each in Cuba and the Dominican Republic. The Census Bureau uses the "non-Hispanic white" designation because Hispanics can be of any race. The Census Bureau says the term Hispanic is an ethnic classification. Hispanic purchasing power reached $736 billion in 2005 and is projected to reach one $1 trillion by 2010, or almost 10 percent of the nation's buying power.

Remember our warning about generalizations. Home Depot, for example, successfully introduced a paint palette called Colores Origenes with vibrant colors and names that are not just in Spanish but evoke familiar Latin foods and images. Even chambers of commerce are very much aware of the changing landscape (see Exhibit 4.2).

EXHIBIT 4.2

"Muchas Conexiones," says the Charleston Metro Chamber of Commerce.

Courtesy of the Charleston Metro Chamber of Commerce.

muchas conexiones

mi cámara es su cámara   charlestonchamber.net

Coors' Hispanic marketing chief, Carl Kravetz, speaking to an ANA multicultural marketing conference, hammered home the findings of a market study that paints a much more sophisticated, multifaceted, and nuanced picture of the country's broad Hispanic community. Kravetz said that the study's in-depth research found that traditional demographic markers such as Spanish-language usage, country of origin, and length of time in the United States are becoming much less relevant as the number of bilingual, bicultural households grows quickly. "If the heart is the core of Latino identity, then the four chambers [that] are responsible for its functioning are interpersonal orientation, time and space perception, spirituality, and gender perception. Interpersonal orientation is the way we live our relationships with other people, and is . . . radically different from non-Latinos," he said. For instance, individualism is important to Anglos, whereas Latinos have a collectivist culture that favors cooperation and values family needs over those of the individual.[9]

For marketers, that means understanding the family as a unit, including group decision making, and avoiding conflict between individual needs and group expectations. Latino individuals perceive time and space very differently. They change plans easily, are more present- and past-oriented and value friends and family more than privacy. In contrast, non-Hispanic people are future-oriented, have a rigid sense of space and privacy, and focus on results. Religion and spirituality affect how Latino individuals see the world and create a love of rituals and celebrations. Gender roles are also radically different. Machismo is about protecting and providing for the family.[10]

The Asian and Pacific Islander Population In 2005, the Census reported 12.5 million Asian and Pacific Islander people living in the United States, representing 4.8 percent of the population. Of the total, 51 percent live in the West, 19 percent live in the South, 12 percent live in the Midwest, and 19 percent live in the Northeast with 95 percent living in metropolitan areas. In 2002, members of the Asian population were younger than those of the non-Hispanic white population: 26 percent of the Asian populations were under age 18, compared with 23 percent of the non-Hispanic white population. A high value is placed on education: 51 percent of Asian men and 44 percent of Asian women earned at least a bachelor's degree compared to 32 percent of non-Hispanic white men and 27 percent of non-Hispanic white women. A glance at income in 2001 indicates that 40 percent of all Asian families had incomes of $75,000 or more, compared with 35 percent of non-Hispanic white families. However, 17 percent of Asian families had incomes less than $25,000, compared with 15 percent of non-Hispanic white families. Members of the Asian American population belong to at least one of fifteen distinct ethnic groups and national origins, including Bangladesh, Cambodian, Chinese, Filipino, Indian, Indonesian, Japanese, Korean, Laotian, Malaysian, Pakistani, Sri Lankian, Taiwanese, Thai and Vietnamese, and others differing in culture, language, and history. Each factor drives what will be the most effective channel for reaching these consumers. The percentage increase in numbers of Asian children rises faster than Hispanics; ages 5 to 9 will increase by 22 percent by 2010, and those ages 10 to 14 will increase by 31 percent. "The Asian market will become increasingly more important over the next decade," says Bank of America's Ms. Adrian-Hsing, especially for high-end products. "It is slowly being discovered that this is an extremely wealthy, extremely affluent segment that is relatively untapped."[11]

Gilbert Davila, vice president–multicultural market for The Walt Disney Co., puts all of this into a marketing perspective, saying, "Multicultural marketing is not a fad. When you take a look at everything that's happening, at all the projections from the census, America is only going to become increasingly diverse, which will place more challenges on companies to figure out how to better market, be more relevant and target these constituencies."[12]

Other Target Influences

As you can see, there is a lot of information for marketers to digest. There are many additional factors a marketer can examine that might influence basic marketing decisions. For example, Home Depot may target women, do-it-yourselfers, contractors, and gardeners, requiring an understanding of many groups and lifestyles. Applebee's Carside To Go outdoor advertisement understands today's busy lifestyle (see Exhibit 4.3). Again, we'll sample some of the typical information available to marketers.

Household Income The Bureau of Labor Statistics' Consumer Expenditure Survey produces annual estimates of household spending on hundreds of items, cross-tabulated by demographic characteristics. As with most data, you need to use these data wisely. In addition to looking at household income, advertisers often look at disposable and discretionary income. Disposable income is after-tax income. Discretionary income is the amount of money consumers have after paying taxes and buying necessities such as food and housing.

Spending *American Demographics* found that the average U.S. metropolitan household devotes 16 percent of its spending for shelter, 17 percent for transportation, 14 percent for food, 6 percent for utilities, 6 percent for apparel, 5 percent for entertainment, 3 percent for household operations, and 11 percent for personal insurance. Spending patterns depend strongly on the unique age and income characteristics of individual markets.[13] Many products and services depend on disposable income of consumers for their existence.

Marrieds The U.S. Census Bureau reported in 1999 that 110.6 million Americans ages 18 and over were married. That is 56 percent of the adult population. The report indicates that the median age for men at first marriage was 26.7, compared to 26.1 in 1976. For women, it was 25.0, the highest median age for first marriage. Some 19.4 million adults are currently divorced. There were 1,348,000 interracially married couples. Nearly 6 percent of all children under age 18 live with grandparents. Clearly, this decline has had social and marketing ramifications.

Birthrate To marketers, the number of births in a given year can be important in projecting market size. The birthrate in the United States has been in decline for decades. In 1960, the rate was 23.7 per thousand population; and it was 13.9 per thousand in 2002, the lowest since government records have been kept. There were 4,019,280 recorded births in America in 2002. Just think of the significance to companies selling baby items. If marketers marry knowledge of fluctuations in the

EXHIBIT 4.4
The Georgia Higher Education Savings Plan aims at those family members or friends that might consider setting up a 529 Savings Plan for a youngster as a gift.

Courtesy of The Georgia Higher Education Savings Plan.

birthrate with an understanding of how consumers tend to act at different stages of their lives, they can get a rough picture of the market challenges that lie in the future.

In recent years, there were slightly fewer than 4 million babies born per year; about one-third of children in 1997 were of ethnic minorities, and roughly 62 percent of married mothers with preschoolers were in the workforce (in 1965, only 23 percent of married mothers worked). Despite the declining numbers, this may be a terrific market for more than baby products, such as selling 529 Savings Plans. This Georgia website says, "Give the Gift of Education" (see Exhibit 4.4).

Aging In 2003, one in eight Americans were 65 years or older. It is estimated that by 2020, one in every six Americans will be 65+. Census estimates indicate that the seniors segment of the population will more than double by 2050. This will have a significant implication for both marketers and society as a whole.

Women For starters, there are 110 million women in this country. They account for 47 percent of all workers and 51 percent of management positions. Women with kids under age 18 account for nearly one-third of U.S. households, according to the Census Bureau, and are a rich target for marketers. According to the U.S. Department of Education, in every state, in every income bracket, and in every racial and ethnic group, women earn close to 60 percent of the bachelor's degrees and master's degrees in this country.[14]

Women purchase or influence 85 percent of all products. The demands on marketers will increase as women increase their wealth, education, and longevity. For decades, marketers have known that women drive all the obvious categories of food, beauty, and household products. Bridget Brennan, founder of Female Factor Communications, says that marketing to women as your leader is the way of the future in almost every product category. Mary Lou Quinlan, in her book *Just Ask a Woman*, tries to answer a number of questions marketers have. What does it mean? Do they want different products than men? Do they want marketers to feminize advertising?[15] And, of course, are there major differences among African American, Hispanic, Asian, Italian, Greek, and other women? Or does everybody think the same? This is another example of having to really understand the target because

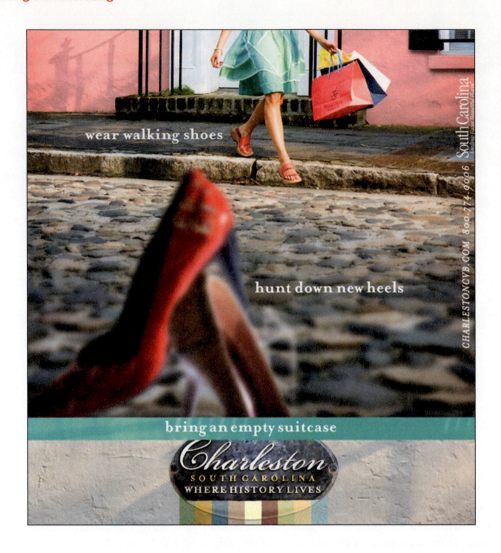

numbers don't always tell the whole story. Charleston's Convention and Visitors Bureau appeals to the women's shopping instinct (see Exhibit 4.5). As you see, there are a lot of organizations promoting Charleston to different audiences, which is typical of most metropolitan cities.

Men Recently, advertisers and media buyers were wondering where the 18- to 34-year-old men had gone. They weren't in front of the television set. The answer was simply that their media habits had changed. This disturbed advertisers because single males have relatively high disposable incomes, are still forming brand loyalties, and are important to a number of product categories—electronics, automobiles, beer, and personal items. Marketers have courted women more aggressively than men because women either buy or influence more purchases. *The Future of Man*, coauthored by an advertising man, looks at the stereotypes and changes taking place in the male culture.

Single-Person Households In 2005, the Census Bureau reported that single-adult households have displaced two-parent families with children as the most common kind of U.S. household. They project this group to total 34 million by the year 2010. The report indicated that people are most likely to live alone at either end of the life cycle—in youth or as senior citizens.

Apparently, most Americans still believe the typical household consists of a "mom, pop, and two kids." This nuclear-family household was the most common as recently as 1990, when there were 25 million such households. They are now the second largest group. Married households without children remained third, with 20 million in 1990 and 22 million in 2000.

Understanding these numbers can be a complex issue. Peter Francese, who tracks trends for Ogilvy & Mather, says not all of those adults living alone are living completely alone. "There are many professional, commuter couples living alone during the week, but share weekends together. Single parents might regularly have their children in the home, and single adults might have lengthy visits from friends or lovers. There is a tremendous diversity in the living-alone group."

"The people who choose to live alone are creating their own communities without regret or unwanted claims made on their lives."[16]

Marketers need to realize that despite the potential of this group, like the others we have discussed, it is not a homogeneous target audience. For example, Looking Glass, Inc., lists eight of its thirty-plus key consumer segments that are likely to live as one-person households. Among them are upscale mature women (56 percent of the segment lives alone), working-class women (63 percent), fit and stylish students (52 percent), well-to-do gentlemen (76 percent), and working-class men (78 percent).[17]

GENERATIONAL MARKETING

The consumer society is really a twentieth-century phenomenon; and for the past century or so, many businesses have made decisions based on the assumption that one generation will grow up and make the same kinds of choices made by the group that went before it at the same stages of life.

Modern marketing's definition of *generation* is composed of two disparate parts. First, there's the traditional definition used by demographers as the number of people in any age group and what that portends about the size and shape of tomorrow's markets. Second, there's the issue of shared attitudes, a common history, and formative experiences. Both definitions are important to marketers of life. Most agree that a *generation* usually is defined as 30 years and extends past a single decade. However, if you look at the history of generations, you'll find some that are very short. Demographers are beginning to agree that Gen Xers were born between 1964 and 1984.

Marketers think experiences bind people that are born in continuous years into a *cohort*—a group of individuals who have a demographic statistic in common. Demographers like to package things in a way that's easy to measure, and date of birth is the easiest way to define generations. Generational marketing people take the statistical analysis of births and overlay major world events that occurred during a generation's formative years to construct a picture of a generation's personality.[18] Knowing how many babies are born and then tracing the numbers through different stages of their lives give marketers a rough idea of the challenges and opportunities over 10, 20, and even 30 years.

Target Generations

Researchers have concentrated on four generations mentioned earlier (Matures, Boomers, and Generations X and Y) and are beginning to learn about the Millennials (Gen Z). There are distinct differences in how each generation thinks and buys.

The values of Matures are close to what are considered classic American values: They favor a kind of Puritan work ethic, with plenty of self-sacrifice, teamwork, conformity for the common good, and so forth.

The Boomers, on the other hand, are self-assured and self-absorbed. They are much better educated than any generation before them, and they are aware of this. They think they are more sophisticated and believe they know better than their predecessors. They are very self-conscious about changing the world and fixing things. They are fighting the concept of *old*.

Generation X The Gen Xers were born in the post–baby boom in the 1963 to 1978 time period. This generation was a longtime media whipping post, once decried as overeducated slackers, with a distrust for social institutions, politics, and religion. Recent Yankelovich Partners research finds Xers to be self-reliant, entrepreneurial, techno focused, media savvy, socially tolerant, and—slowly, but surely—parents. Growing up with skyrocketing divorce rates and with less than family stability, Gen Xers have been more cautious about entering the life stage of family formation. As a result, today's Xers are reinventing the traditionalism they are bringing to family life. Generation X is not a life stage; it is a birth group ultimately moving through life stages.

Research indicates they are much more likely than their Boomer counterparts were some 20 years ago to want to return to traditional standards across a number of domains, especially family life. Marketers have begun shifting their views as these changing self-concepts evolve from carefree kids to obligation-bound parents. A recent advertising campaign cleverly highlighted markers of this life-stage transition, focusing on events such as the first time a man is called "Sir" and the first time one doesn't get carded at a bar; the advertisement touts sporty cars that will "make the other soccer moms talk." It seems that every generation is a catalyst for change as it moves through a new life stage. The visual in Exhibit 4.6, for example, indicates that it is appealing to serious golfers of several generations with a little humor, "You'll feel like you're cheating."

Generation Y (Echo Boomers, Millennials, iGeneration) Although demographers debate cutoff dates, most calculations place Generation Y as those born from 1979 to 1995. By 2010, the 12 to 19 age group will have expanded to a historic peak of 35 million. However, members of this group outspend all previous generations. According to *USA Today*, they're techno savvy, coddled, optimistic, prone to abrupt shifts in taste, and tough to pigeonhole.[19]

Generation Y is the first generation to come along that's big enough to hurt a Boomer brand simply by giving it a cold shoulder. This generation is more racially diverse: One in three is not Caucasian. Marketers will have to learn to think like they do—and not like the Boomer parents.[20]

According to a new *Los Angeles Times*/Bloomberg poll that surveyed the habits of 12- to 24-year-olds, girls ages 12 to 14 are the most deeply motivated by television: 65 percent say they are influenced by a television show or network, are more likely to

EXHIBIT 4.6

Mizuno Golf Clubs

The slice-of-life advertisement appeals to serious golfers from several generations.

Courtesy of Huey+Partners and Mizuno.

multitask than boys of their age group and are easily bored; 41 percent say there are too few choices of entertainment. These kids are known by economists, sociologists, and marketing experts as optimistic team players and rule followers, born into "child-centered" families and raised as part of the most celebrated, protected, and overscheduled generation in memory. Technology has been so much a part of their lives that, to them, life before e-mail and the Internet was "the Stone Age."[21]

Looking ahead to the next generation of potential customers, Toyota introduced its inexpensive boxy Scion line to appeal to buyers in their 20s. It appears to be working. The average buyer's age for Toyota is 47, and the Toyota Scion's average buyer is significantly lower at 39. All automobile producers understand that if they misfire with Generation Y, they will miss the largest cohort of consumers to come along since the post–World War II baby boom.[22] Toyota realizes that its average customer is among the oldest in the industry.

Generation Z This generation is said to have begun with people born in the late 1990s or early 2000s and is expected to run through about 2017. (Keep in mind that there is rarely agreement as to when a generation officially begins or ends or sometimes even its name as it moves through time.) This generation will come from a wider mix of backgrounds and will bring different experiences for marketers to understand. By 2010, marketers will have to start all over again to figure out how to impress this new generation.

Why is all of this important to advertising people?

No company provides a better object lesson in the importance of staying relevant than Levi Strauss & Co., one of America's great brands. Levi's lost more than half its share of the American jeans market during the 1990s. According to John Hancock Financial's CEO David D'Alessandro, Levi's failed to invest in Gen X and the Echo Boom. It didn't keep tuned to what kids wanted to wear. It didn't offer this target market anything of value to distinguish its potential consumers from the previous generation.[23] Without an accurate view of generations, you are likely to misinterpret what you see in the marketplace. Marketers need to know all about generations. The consumer marketplace is no longer the homogeneous marketplace of the 1950s and early 1960s that was dominated by Matures. The Xers' view of convenience has moved from the Matures' "do it quickly" and the Boomers' "do it efficiently" to their own "eliminate the task."[24]

Marketing Concept and Targeting

Companies cannot operate in every market and satisfy every consumer need. Companies generally find that it is necessary to divide the market into major market segments, evaluate them, and then target those segments they can best serve. This focus on specific groups of buyers is called *market segmentation* (discussed later in this chapter). It is an extension of the **marketing concept**, defined by Philip Kotler, that achieving organizational goals depends on determining the needs and wants of target markets and delivering the desired satisfactions more effectively and efficiently than competitors. This idea has been stated as "find a need and fill it" or "make what you can sell instead of trying to sell what you can make." Advertisers have expressed this concept in colorful ways; for example, marketers at Burger King said, "Have It Your Way."

The old marketing concept—the management philosophy first articulated in the 1950s—is a relic of an earlier period of economic history. Most of its assumptions are no longer appropriate in the competitive global markets of today. The world is rapidly moving toward a pattern of economic activity based on long-term relationships and partnerships among economic factors in the loose coalition frameworks of network organizations. The concept of customer value is at the heart of the new marketing concept and must be the central element of all business strategy.

marketing concept
A management orientation that views the needs of consumers as primary to the success of a firm.

As we look at the differences, the old marketing concept had the objective of making a sale, whereas under the new marketing concept, the objective is to develop a customer relationship in which the sale is only the beginning. Under both marketing concepts, market segmentation, market targeting, and positioning are essential requirements for effective strategic planning. In the new marketing concept, the focus is sharpened by adding the idea of the value proposition.[25]

Market-driven companies need to understand how customer needs and company capabilities converge to form the customer's definition of value. This includes more than monitoring data. It includes listening to the consumer because they now control the communication process. That means using all the research techniques discussed in later chapters. It also means being attuned to the "blogosphere" and other informational technology and tracking systems. This is more than a philosophy; it is a way of doing business. It includes customer orientation, market intelligence, distinctive competencies, value delivery, market targeting and the value proposition, customer-defined total quality management, profitability rather than sales volume, relationship management, continuous improvement, and a customer-focused organizational structure.[26]

The technology of marketing databases is helping companies deliver one-to-one relationships not previously available. These databases include comprehensive data about individual customers' and prospects' sales histories, as well as demographics and psychographics. Interest by marketers has changed from simply getting people to switch brands to figuring ways to keep from losing current customers by continually trying to meet their needs.

Radio frequency identification (RFID) tags, sometimes controversial among consumer groups, are a new type of bar code with tremendous data implications for tracking products and understanding how they are used by consumers. An RFID tag is a small strip of plastic containing a computer chip and a radio antenna. The chip holds up to ninety-six characters and identifies the article to which it is attached. The antenna sends information to a receiver, which transfers the information to a computer for tracking analysis. It is a very advanced bar code. The long-term implication is enormous because the tag might tell companies what is being bought and where the product goes once bought. Down the road, stores may be able to track products beyond store shelves—perhaps learning which clothes you wear to work, which you wear to party, and where your clothes go.[27] The world of marketing is constantly changing.

What Is a Product?

Seems like a silly question, doesn't it? Let us define a *product* as a bundle of ingredients put together for sale as something useful to a consumer. People don't go into a store to buy alcohol denat., PPG-15 stearyl ether, butylenes glycol, aqua/water, propylene glycol, dipropylene glycol, cyclopean tasiloxane, and so on. Many people seeking a sunless tanning product do, however, go into a store and buy L'Oreal Sublime Bronze Any Angle Self-Tanning Spray. It is more than a physical object. It represents a bundle of satisfactions—a product that gives someone concerned about skin cancer (or because they work from 9 to 5) a chance to show up at the pool on the weekend with a tan.

Some of these satisfactions are purely functional—a watch to tell time or a car for transportation. Some of the satisfactions are psychological—a car may represent status and a watch may represent a piece of beautiful jewelry. Different people have different ideas about which satisfactions are important. Literally, a white respondent to a self-tanning suntan product said, "I work all day and can't get out in the sun, and when I go to the pool on the weekend, I want to be any shade other than white." Products are often designed with satisfactions to match the interests of a particular group of consumers. We are also judged in large measure by our physical possessions—think of your attitude toward Mercedes, BMW, Jaguar, or a BlackBerry or our 120-inch plasma television and so on. The products that we purchase say something about us and group us with people who seek similar satisfactions from life and products. As we match people and benefits, we create product loyalty that insulates us against competitive attack.

The yearly some 20,000-plus new products have a difficult time finding a place in the market. Manufacturers must be selective in defining the most profitable market segments because the cost of introducing a new product can be expensive. New products need to be well thought out, and a key is to innovate brands that are sustainable. One innovation failure in the soft-drink industry is Surge, Coca-Cola's much-hyped rival to Mountain Dew. Surge was introduced in 1997, and sales soared to 70 million cases. A half-dozen years later, Surge had almost faded out of the U.S. market. There are numerous ways to estimate the chances of getting a heavy user of another brand to try a new brand. One technique is to define market segments according to their brand loyalty and preference for national over private brands. Studies of packaged goods brand loyalty found six such segments:[28]

1. *National-brand loyal.* Members of this segment buy primarily a single national brand at its regular price.

2. *National-brand deal.* This segment is similar to the national-brand-loyal segment, except that most of its purchases are made on deal (that is, the consumer is loyal to only national brands but chooses the least expensive one). To buy the preferred national brand on deal, the consumer engages in considerable store switching.

3. *Private-label loyal.* Consumers in this segment primarily buy the private label offered by the store in which they shop (for example, CVS, Wal-Mart, Target, Publix, and other store brands).

4. *Private-label deal.* This segment shops at many stores and buys the private label of each store, usually on a deal.

5. *National-brand switcher.* Members of this segment tend not to buy private labels. Instead, they switch regularly among the various national brands on the market.

6. *Private-label switcher.* This segment is similar to the private-label-deal segment, except that the members are not very deal prone and purchase the private labels at their regular price.

Price, product distribution, and promotion also affect the share of market coming from each competing brand. However, a new national brand would expect to gain most of its initial sales from segments 2 and 5, whereas segments 1 and 3 would normally be poor prospects to try a new brand. There are many factors to consider. But remember: today, a camera is not just a camera; markets change with the product, and products change with the market.

What Is a Market?

All advertising and marketing people could easily answer this question, but you might get different answers, depending on their perspectives. For our purposes, a *market* can be defined as a group of people who can be identified by some common characteristic, interest, or problem—who could use our product to advantage, who could afford to buy it, and who can be reached through some medium.

Markets can be defined differently and broadly or narrowly. Examples of potential markets are weight watchers, golfers, mothers of young children, singles, Matures, newly marrieds, skiers, tennis players, Hispanic teens, do-it-yourselfers, runners, seniors, and tourists. The *majority fallacy* is a term applied to the assumption, once frequently made, that every product should be aimed at and acceptable to a majority of all consumers. Research tells us that brands aimed at the majority of consumers in a given market will tend to have rather similar characteristics and will neglect an opportunity to serve the needs of consumer minorities. Take, for example, chocolate cake mixes. A good-size group of consumers would prefer a light-chocolate cake or a very-dark-chocolate cake, but the majority choice is a medium-chocolate cake. So, although several initial cake mix products would do best to market a medium-chocolate cake to appeal to the broadest group of consumers, later entrants might gain a larger share by supplying the smaller but significant group with its preference. What if the dark-chocolate cake was both calorie and fat free?

What Is Competition?

Stroll down the aisles of your favorite supermarket or drugstore and look at the toothpaste choices—brighteners, abrasives, fresh breath, fluorides, pastes, gels, peroxides, and so on. Or look in the analgesic section. You will find many brands competing for your attention—Bayer, Aleve, Advil, Tylenol, Ascriptin, Empirin, Vanquish, Motrin IB, Goody's, BC, Excedrin—and the list goes on. Why does one consumer choose one brand and another consumer something else? How does one even get on the shelf to compete? These are very important questions to the makers of these products.

We are speaking of competition in the broadest sense to include all the forces that are inhibiting the sales of a product. They may be products in the same subclass as your product or in the same product class, or they may be forces outside the category of your product. Our list of analgesics includes products in different subcategories: Bayer, Tylenol, Aleve, and Advil are each in different analgesic categories, such as aspirin, acetaminophen, naproxen, and ibuprofen. Advil and Nuprin are in the same subcategory. Does that mean they compete with only themselves? The answer is generally no. Many consumers don't even consider the subclasses; they only think in terms of pain relief. If consumers are considering only the benefits of an ibuprofen product, then the answer is yes. Advil, Motrin IB, and Excedrin IB would all compete. The point is that advertisers and marketers need to try to find the answers as to which products in what categories compete for the consumer's attention and dollar. It may sound confusing because you don't know the category, but the seasoned marketer for these products knows its category and the products and the reasons people buy.

Marketers for all kinds of products and services must ask: Who are our competitors? What are their brands? What are other product categories? Are there many brands or only a few? Which are strong? Which are vulnerable? What impact, if any, do store brands and generics have? Are there any strong, long-established brands, or is the market volatile?

PLANNING THE ADVERTISING

Market Segmentation

Marketers can't efficiently reach every person who has a dollar to spend. It is about maximizing your potential in the marketplace by targeting your product to certain segments of the population with similar behaviors, such as people your age, your gender, and with a similar lifestyle. From a communication standpoint, it is usually more difficult than you would imagine. You must understand each segment's cultural nuances and choose the right message so you don't stereotype the service or product you're selling as one designed only for that segment. It has been said, "If you try to talk to everyone, you'll end up talking to nobody." The division of an entire market of consumers into groups whose similarity makes them a market for products servicing their special needs is called **market segmentation**.

This classifying of consumers is generally one of the tasks of a marketing plan's **situation analysis** section, which consists of four components: a description of the current situation; an analysis of strengths, weaknesses, opportunities, and threats (SWOT); major issues; and assumptions about the future. The Cub Cadet Commercial lawn mower reeks of toughness (see Exhibit 4.7): "Enough steel to build a tank. Wait, we did." And the body copy says, ". . . For more common-sense machines that can help you get more work out of your workday, visit www.cubcommercial.com. . . ."

market segmentation
The division of an entire market of consumers into groups whose similarity makes them a market for products serving their special needs.

situation analysis
The part of the advertising plan that answers the questions: Where are we today and how did we get here? It deals with the past and present.

EXHIBIT 4.7

Cub Cadet Commercial

This machine is targeted to those who need a tough machine.

Courtesy of Blattner Brunner, Pittsburgh, Atlanta, Washington.

Typically, the market-segmentation process runs through a number of steps:

Segment your market.

Target a segment.

Position your product for that segment.

Communicate your positioning.

A number of factors need to be considered in planning advertising to take advantage of market segmentation. The first step is to determine the variable to use for dividing a market. In addition to demographics, the major means of market segmentation are geographic, product-user, and lifestyle segmentation. It is common for marketers to combine more than one segmentation variable in seeking their target. Of course, the segment has to be large enough in size to justify the marketing effort.

Geographic Segmentation This, the oldest form of segmentation, designates customers by geographic area. It dates back to earlier days when distribution was the primary concern of manufacturers. Today, geomarketing is of particular importance to media planners in deciding on national, regional, and local advertising campaigns. It is only recently that geomarketing has been elevated to a marketing discipline the way demographics was in the 1950s and psychographics was in the 1970s. In this instance, consumers haven't changed but marketers' awareness of regional and global marketing has. Geodemographical marketing is just another way of segmenting the market for companies in search of growth.

There has been a "data explosion" on local markets. Some of the information comes from an abundant number of research services for use on merchandising and buying decisions. Many retail companies such as supermarkets or fast-food feeders practice *micromarketing*—treating each individual store as its own market and trading area. Often, this approach translates into different advertisements for different markets. When thinking about geographic segmentation, advertisers have a number of categories to explore:

- census trace data/areas of dominant influence (ADI)
- ZIP Codes/states
- counties/census regions
- metropolitan statistical areas/total United States

Companies that lack national distribution may consider geographic segmentation. Pro Balanced dog food is distributed primarily in the South but has to compete against national brands to survive. There are many local or regional brands that must be successful in their geographic areas to survive. Cheerwine is a cherry-cola-like soft drink that is strong in its home area but would have problems in areas wherein its history and tradition were unknown. In the past, Cheerwine used a slogan that said, "It's a Carolina Thing." Cheerwine products can be purchased in grocery and convenience stores in North Carolina and South Carolina, as well as some places in Alabama, Georgia, Illinois, Indiana, Iowa, Kansas, Kentucky, Minnesota, Missouri, Nebraska, Tennessee, Virginia, West Virginia, and Wisconsin. In this case, geographic segmentation is a distribution strategy rather than a promotional one. Despite being small, Cheerwine is innovative with blogs, Web games, road trips, and so on to help connect to prospects.

It is not unusual for national companies to divide their advertising and marketing efforts into regional units to respond better to the competition. McDonald's uses a major advertising agency (and media planning and buying agency) to handle its national advertising and numerous (generally smaller) agencies to handle franchise and regional efforts supplementing the national effort. Of course, we didn't mention their multicultural agencies that serve minority marketing. When McDonald's launched "i'm lovin' it," a global advertising campaign using Justin Timberlake, they used a German agency. This gives McDonald's the ability to react to the marketplace by cities, regions, or individual stores as well as globally.

Product-User Segmentation **Product-user segmentation** is a strategy based on the amount of usage and/or consumption patterns of a brand or category. The advertiser is interested in product usage rather than consumer characteristics. As a practical matter, most user-segmentation methods are combined with demographic or lifestyle consumer identification. Here, the advertiser is interested in market segments with the highest sales potential. Typically, a market segment is first divided into all users and then subdivided into heavy, medium, light users and nonusers of the product. For example, let us look at the frequency of weekly use of fast foods:

Frequency	Adults	Men	Women
Heavy (4+ visits)	11.4%	14.8%	8.3%
Medium (1–3 visits)	44.9	46.5	43.3
Light (less than weekly)	22.8	20.6	24.8

The definition of usage varies with the product category. For example, heavy fast-food use may be defined as four or more times per week; heavy luxury-restaurant use as once a week; and heavy seafood-restaurant use as once a week. As you can see, product-user segmentation can get quite complex, but these kinds of data allow marketers to use a rifle instead of a shotgun.

Lifestyle Segmentation **Lifestyle segmentation** makes the assumption that if you live a certain way, so do your neighbors and, therefore, any smart marketer would want to target clusters filled with these clones. Lifestyle clusters are more accurate characterizations of people than any single variable would be.

The concept of lifestyle segmentation is a viable one; however, researchers are having to adjust to a sea of changes taking place among America's shopping public. For example, old attitudes toward work and leisure or fitness don't fit today's realities. As a result, segmentation researchers are changing how they view many of the new lifestyle characteristics driving this new era.[29]

Marketers have used specialized segmentation techniques to find the most fruitful target audiences since PRIZM (Potential Rating Index for ZIP Markets) in 1974 grouped people who had similar demographics and lifestyles into neighborhood clusters on the theory that "birds of a feather flock together." A number of similar programs have popped up since—such as SRI's **Values and Lifestyle System (VALS)**—all based on the premise that people in the same ZIP Code or neighborhood tend to buy the same products. Each research company has its own terminology for the various clusters it identifies. Recently, Yankelovich Partners Inc. developed a psychographic-segmentation system called MONITOR MindBase. Its premise is the idea of segmenting individuals by values, attitudes,

product-user segmentation
Identifying consumers by the amount of product usage.

lifestyle segmentation
Identifying consumers by combining several demographics and lifestyles.

Values and Lifestyle System (VALS)
Developed by SRI International to cluster consumers according to several variables in order to predict consumer behavior.

The joys of SummerGrove will turn you into a kid again.

All it takes is one swing on the 18-hole golf course. You'll forget the busy life you lead and remember how much fun it is to have, well, fun. And it won't stop there. You'll play at the pools and tennis courts. Go boating on the 100-acre lake. Then remember the simple pleasures of a day at the park or a trip down the lazy river. You'll also experience the joy of finding just the right home. We've got a variety of styles to choose from by some of the area's best builders. Including golf course homes from the low $200s and custom lake homes from the $300s. Come to SummerGrove. Your second childhood is waiting.

Homes from the $130s to $700s • Information Center open Daily 11-6, Sunday 1-6 • 770-252-9000 • www.summergrove.com

I-85 South to Exit 47 (Newnan). Left on Hwy. 34, one mile. Turn right on Shenandoah Blvd. Continue 1.4 miles to SummerGrove. Follow signs to Information Center.

and mind-sets rather than by geography, demographics, and consumption patterns. It segments people into categories of consumers with varying degrees of materialism, ambition, orientation to family life, cynicism, openness to technology, and other elements.[30]

SummerGrove homes (see Exhibit 4.8) range from $130,000s to $700,000s and are convenient to Atlanta and the airport. If you can afford them, those are good attributes, but copywriter Amy Lokken knew the lifestyle appeal is what it is about, "All it takes is one swing on the 18-hole golf course. You'll forget the busy life you lead and remember how much fun it is to have, well, fun." And she ends with, "Your second childhood is waiting."

Researchers Kevin Clancy and Robert Shulman argue that "off-the-shelf segmentation studies cannot be as good as customized segmentation done with a specific product or service in mind. VALS will help break up the world into pieces, but the pieces may or may not have any relevance for any one brand."[31]

One approach to determining lifestyle characteristics is to identify consumers' activities, interests, and opinions (AIO). Typical AIO measures are:

- *Activities:* Hobbies or leisure-time preferences, community involvement, and preferences for social events
- *Interests:* Family orientation, sports interests, and media usage
- *Opinions:* Political preferences and views on various social issues

Benefits and Attitude Segmentation Not everyone wants the same thing from a product. There isn't just a single toothpaste, because some people are interested in taste, or fresh breath, or whiteness of their teeth, or decay prevention, or tartar control for gums, or value, and so on. The objective here is to cluster people into groups based on what they want in a product.

Segmentation Risks Although segmentation is very important to successful advertising, it isn't without risks. One problem is that once the outer limits of the niche are reached, sales growth will be limited unless the company can expand beyond its niche. By too narrowly defining a market—that is, by excessive segmenting—a marketer can become inefficient in media buying, creating different advertisements, and obtaining alternative distribution channels. A few years ago, Taco Bell was the first fast-food chain to target people with its Value Menu. It was so successful that most other fast-food companies followed with their own value menus. As a result of this competition, the pool of value-conscious consumers was split among numerous companies, diluting the profit.

Target Market Sacrifice

Consultant Jack Trout says that staying focused on one target segment in a category enables your product to be different by becoming the preferred product by the segment: Pepsi for the younger generation, Corvette for the generation that wants to be young, Corona beer for the yuppies on their way up, Porsche for the yuppies who have made it. When you chase after another target segment, chances are you'll chase away your original customer. Whatever you do, you should not get greedy but stay true to your product type, your attribute, or your segment.[32]

Niche Marketing

Niche marketing can serve at least two purposes. It can gain a product entry into a larger market by attacking a small part of it not being served by the competition. It can also cater to latent needs that existing products do not adequately satisfy.

In segmentation, marketers may slice the population very narrowly to find very specific groups. Niches usually are smaller groups of consumers with more narrowly defined needs or unique combinations. But *niche marketing* is not another buzzword for marketing segmentation, says Alvin Achenbaum.[33] It is essentially a flanking strategy, the essence of which is to engage competitors in those product markets where they are weak or, preferably, have little or no presence. The guiding principle of niche marketing is to pit your strength against the competitor's weakness. No-frill motels did not exist for many years, but they were

niche marketing
A combination of product and target market strategy. It is a flanking strategy that focuses on niches or comparatively narrow windows of opportunity within a broad product market or industry. Its guiding principle is to pit your strength against their weakness.

logical means of competing against other motel segments. Red Roof Inn opened its motels with an advertisement claiming "Sleep Cheap" and positioned itself to value consumers not wanting to pay high prices for a place to sleep. Later, they even made fun of hotels placing a chocolate mint on your pillow for an extra $30 or $40. Today, most major hotel chains have moved into that niche with their own no-frills express motels.

Heart Attack Niche Niche marketers may create a specific product through variations of their product to meet a specific niche's needs. For example, Bayer Aspirin created an adult low-strength tablet for aspirin regimen users. As you know, research indicated that second heart attacks were greatly reduced by simply taking an aspirin daily. The only problem was that regular use of aspirin by some people resulted in stomach problems. A regular aspirin tablet consisted of 325 milligrams. The doctor-recommended daily therapy for patients having suffered an initial heart attack was 81 milligrams. Adults started taking children's aspirin, which was 81 milligrams, to prevent stomach problems and yet get the advantage of heart attack protection. As a result of this consumer action, Bayer introduced Bayer Enteric Aspirin, which is 81 milligrams and protects the stomach.

Social-Networking Niches When Facebook and MySpace websites became broad based, niche sites appealed to advertisers. For example, LinkedIn aimed at career-oriented professionals, *BlackPlanet* attracted blacks, MiGente and AsianAvenue attracted Hispanics and Asians. These niches attracted people of similar interests.

Brand marketers seeking new niche opportunities should pay attention to marketing basics: changing shopping trends, demographics, marketing strategy, and delivery on commitments.[34]

Each niche offers challenges for advertisers. When trying to develop niche marketing to Asians, understanding of cultural and language issues is required, as we have indicated. Does the advertisement promoting Georgia tourism in Exhibit 4.9 aim at the "Civil War history buff"? Is this niche advertising?

Companies can build growth out of finding small niches to serve consumers' needs. For example, Kimberly-Clark launched Huggies Pull-Ups training pants in 1989. In 1994, it launched Goodnites for older children who wet the bed. In 1997, it introduced Huggies Little Swimmers designed to survive swimming. The niche for Huggies Little Swimmers is a very narrow category segment. Originally, Procter & Gamble said the training pants niche was too small, but it has grown to a $400 million segment within the disposable diaper category.[35]

Bobos Another example niche segmentation is *Bobos*, which is short for Bourgeois Bohemian. David Brooks coined this term in 2000 in his book *Bobos in Paradise*. Professor Richard Florida writes about Bobos in *The Rise of the Creative Class*. In defining Bobos, these creative people seem to have combined the countercultural 1960s and the achieving 1980s into one social ethos. This group is about 40 million strong. These people work in a range of fields from science to entertainment, but their jobs are to create new ideas, new technology, and new content. Typically, these people don't work 9-to-5 jobs because they are working on projects with deadlines. Generally, age isn't a defining factor and Bobos are highly educated. Doug Cameron, strategist at Amalgamated advertising agency, says that Bobos go for the functionally extreme; rather than buying any refrigerator, they'll buy an $8,000 Sub-Zero. Their individual incomes exceed $75,000 annually with many earning above $150,000. The group favors brands such as JetBlue Airways, Volkswagen, and Apple Computer. The top ten Bobo markets include San

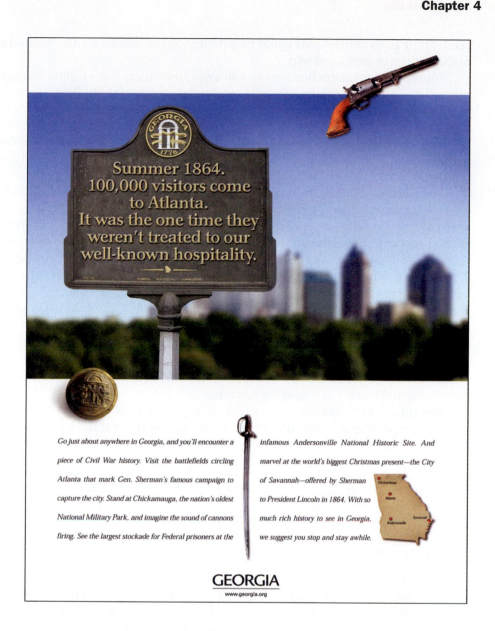

Summer 1864.
100,000 visitors come
to Atlanta.
It was the one time they
weren't treated to our
well-known hospitality.

Go just about anywhere in Georgia, and you'll encounter a piece of Civil War history. Visit the battlefields circling Atlanta that mark Gen. Sherman's famous campaign to capture the city. Stand at Chickamauga, the nation's oldest National Military Park, and imagine the sound of cannons firing. See the largest stockade for Federal prisoners at the infamous Andersonville National Historic Site. And marvel at the world's biggest Christmas present—the City of Savannah—offered by Sherman to President Lincoln in 1864. With so much rich history to see in Georgia, we suggest you stop and stay awhile.

GEORGIA
www.georgia.org

EXHIBIT 4.9

Despite being part of the state's tourism advertising, is this advertisement aimed at those people who are Civil War history buffs? Would you consider that a niche?

Courtesy of McRae Communication and Georgia Department of Economic Development.

Francisco; Seattle; Boston; Austin; San Diego; Washington, D.C.; Chapel Hill–Raleigh–Durham, North Carolina; New York; Minneapolis; and Denver.[36] One method marketers use to find Bobos is looking at educational levels and Starbucks per capita, culled from census data.

POSITIONING

Positioning has to be done with a target in mind. You position a product in the mind of a specific prospect. **Positioning** is another term for fitting the product into the lifestyle of the buyer. It refers to segmenting a market by either or both of two ways: (1) creating a product to meet the needs of a specialized group, and/or (2) identifying and advertising a feature of an existing product that meets the needs of a specialized group. The Coke Zero position was a new "Coca-Cola" drink with a great "Coke" taste but Zero Sugar; "Coca-Cola" Zero sits alongside "Coke" and "Diet Coke," offering consumers a new, third way to enjoy "Coke."

Estrovite vitamins recognized a potential problem among women on birth-control pills and created a product positioned to fulfill that need. The headline

positioning
Segmenting a market by creating a product to meet the needs of a select group or by using a distinctive advertising appeal to meet the needs of a specialized group, without making changes in the physical product.

read, "Your birth control pills could be robbing you of essential vitamins and minerals." The copy explained why.

Sometimes products don't quite work out in testing. The original Nyquil was created as a superior daytime cough suppressant. It had a slight flaw. The product made people drowsy. In an attempt to regain product-development costs, the side effect of drowsiness was transformed into a powerful positioning strategy. It became "the nighttime, coughing, sniffling, sneezing so you can rest" medicine. As a result, Nyquil created a new category resulting in the ownership of the nighttime cold remedy market.

The purpose of positioning is giving a product a meaning that distinguishes it from other products and induces people to want to buy it. Positioning is what you do to the mind of the consumer. Specifically, you position the product in the mind of the prospect. You want your positioning to be in harmony with the lifestyles and values we have discussed. It is necessary to understand what motivates people to buy in the product category—what explains their behavior. It is also necessary to understand the degree to which the product satisfies the target's needs.[37] One automobile may be positioned as a sports car, another as a luxury sports car, another as the safest family car, and still another as a high-performance vehicle.

It is possible for some products to successfully hold different positions at the same time. ARM & HAMMER baking soda has been positioned as a deodorizer for refrigerators, an antacid, a freezer deodorizer, and a bath skin cleanser without losing its original market as a cooking ingredient.

You might try to get the following reactions from consumers to a new line of frozen entrees that are low in calories, sodium, and fat and have larger servings than the competition's. Before seeing your advertising, the consumer thinks:

> I like the convenience and taste of today's frozen foods, but I don't usually get enough of the main course to eat. I would like to try a brand that gives me plenty to eat but is still light and healthy—and, most important, it has to taste great.

After being exposed to your advertising, the consumer thinks:

> I may buy Ru's Frozen Food entrees. They taste great and I get plenty to eat, and they are still low enough in calories that I don't feel I'm overeating. They're better for me because they have less sodium and fat than others. Also, there is enough variety so that I can eat the foods I like without getting bored by the same old thing.

HOW TO APPROACH A POSITIONING PROBLEM

As you would expect, not all products lend themselves to the type of positioning discussed here. The advertiser must be careful not to damage current product image by changing appeals and prematurely expanding into new markets. Jack Trout and Al Ries, who have written about positioning for several decades, say that the advertiser who is thinking about positioning should ask the following questions:[38]

- What position, if any, do we already own in the prospect's mind?
- What position do we want to own?
- What companies must be outgunned if we are to establish that position?
- Do we have enough marketing money to occupy and hold that position?
- Do we have the guts to stick with one consistent positioning concept?
- Does our creative approach match our positioning strategy?

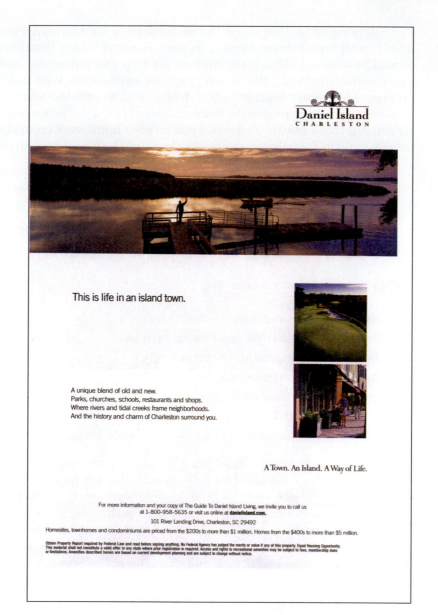

This is life in an island town.

A unique blend of old and new.
Parks, churches, schools, restaurants and shops.
Where rivers and tidal creeks frame neighborhoods.
And the history and charm of Charleston surround you.

A Town. An Island. A Way of Life.

For more information and your copy of The Guide To Daniel Island Living, we invite you to call us
at 1-800-958-5635 or visit us online at **danielisland.com.**
101 River Landing Drive, Charleston, SC 29492
Homesites, townhomes and condominiums are priced from the $200s to more than $1 million. Homes from the $400s to more than $5 million.

Obtain Property Report required by Federal Law and read before signing anything. No Federal Agency has judged the merits or value if any of this property. Equal Housing Opportunity. This material shall not constitute a valid offer in any state where prior registration is required. Access and rights to recreational amenities may be subject to fees, membership dues or limitations. Amenities described herein are based on current development planning and are subject to change without notice.

EXHIBIT 4.10

This unique planned development is positioned as "A Town. An Island. A Way of Life."

Courtesy of Daniel Island.

According to David Aaker, the most-used positioning strategy is to associate an object with a product attribute or characteristic. Daniel Island (see Exhibit 4.10) is a planned community blending old and new, parks, churches, schools, restaurants, shops, where rivers and tidal creeks frame neighborhoods. Its advertising is primarily lifestyle. Its positioning is "A Town. An Island. A Way of Life." Developing such associations is effective because when the attribute is meaningful, the association can directly translate into reasons to buy the brand. Crest toothpaste became the leader by building a strong association with cavity control, in part created by an endorsement of the American Dental Association. BMW has talked about performance with its tagline: "The Ultimate Driving Machine." Mercedes? "The Ultimate Engineered Car." Hyundai? "Cars That Make Sense." The positioning problem is usually finding an attribute important to a major segment and not already claimed by a competitor.[39] Philip Kotler says that many companies advertise a major, single-benefit position, for example, best quality, best performance, most durable, fastest, least expensive, and so on. In automobiles, Mercedes owns the "most prestigious" position, BMW owns the "best driving performance," Hyundai owns the "least expensive," and Volvo owns the "safest." Volvo also claims to be one of the most durable.[40]

Following up on this, David Martin, founder of the Martin Agency, says to think about Volvo for a minute. What is its core identity? Which benefits stand out and should be featured? What is the emotion the target feels from the brand? Would you agree with Volvo being the "safest" car? The car handles well and has speed and styling, with many built-in safety features that include sturdy construction. Reassurance is an appeal to the basic instinct of fear. *I feel better because my daughter drives a Volvo.* Martin also says if you do your homework on the brand, you may be able to fill in the following blanks for developing a brand positioning statement.[41]

> To the (*target market*), (*brand name here*) is the brand of (*frame of reference*) with (*benefits and attributes*) that is (*sustainable and emotional point of difference*).

> To the *car owner*, *Volvo* is the brand of *automobile* with *all the style, power, and comfort you want* that is *built to be safe*.

POSITIONING EXAMPLES

- Dove soap is the moisturizing beauty bar.
- Allstate insurance is the good hands people.
- Cheer is the detergent for all temperatures.
- Intel is the computer inside.
- Ace hardware is the helpful place.
- It's not TV. It's HBO.
- Milk-Bone dog biscuits clean teeth and freshen breath.

Some marketers frequently alter a brand's positioning for the sake of change. This is especially unfortunate for those brands that are firmly entrenched and successful because their reason for being is widely accepted. In the past, a number of positioning statements were successful but were dropped; "Good to the Last Drop," "Pepperidge Farm Remembers," and "Two Mints in One" are examples. These campaigns were revised long after they were discontinued because they truly represented the consumer end benefit and character of the brand.[42]

Profile of the Market

market profile
A demographic and psychographic description of the people or the households of a product's market. It may also include economic and retailing information about a territory.

Up to this point, we have discussed market segments. Now we examine the overall **market profile** for a product. First, we determine the overall usage of the product type. This is usually defined in terms of dollars, sales, number of units sold, or percentage of households that use such a product. Then we determine if the category is growing, stagnant, or declining. We compare our share of the market to the competition. Next we ask what the market share trends have been over the past several years. Finally, we want to know the chief product advantage featured by each brand.

When you look at market share, beware as to whether you are looking at a brand's share or a company's share. The Coca-Cola Company has a 43.1 percent market share, Pepsi-Cola has a 31.4 percent share, and Cadbury Schweppes's has a 14.6 percent share. In the soft-drink convenience store market, Coke Classic had a 15.7 percent share; Pepsi-Cola had a 15.3 percent share; Mountain Dew was third with 12.4 percent; and Dr Pepper, with a 7.9 percent share, was fourth. Is this the whole picture? Obviously not. Coca-Cola dominates distribution in fountain sales in restaurants. The total market share reflects their brands' domination in this area with Coke Classic with a 17.6 percent share of market, Pepsi with an 11.2 percent share, Diet Coke with a 9.8 percent share, Mountain Dew with a 6.5 percent share, and Diet Pepsi with a 6.0 percent share. A marketer with a leading share in a product category and a marketer with a very small share will probably approach advertising

Michael Martin

Director of Marketing Programs, Employease
Using the Net to Target Customers

We're a different kind of company. Before we talk about how we do marketing, I'll tell you what we are about. Based in Atlanta, Employease is an Internet provider of human resources benefits and payroll solutions. Employease takes full advantage of the Internet's power to facilitate communication and connectivity between employers, employees, managers, benefits carriers, and service providers. For example, our clients view their employees' work-related data to process hirings, promotions, and terminations with HR approval. Similarly, employees enroll in benefits programs and update contact information online. HR manages and reports on data while controlling all access. Employease helps over 1,000 customers reduce administrative costs, improve service to employees and, most importantly, increase focus on strategic HR.

Our first marketing effort sent out e-mails soliciting business, with little response. We went back and tweaked the message and received over 1,500 replies in several hours—that's direct response.

What we do here is different from what the industry has traditionally done in marketing to prospects. My previous agency and corporate advertising and marketing jobs required that we plan marketing programs well in advance of implementation. Of course, we then had to produce the materials and deliver them to the appropriate targets. Once you had one of your marketing programs operating you could easily justify the program, but it was difficult to adjust an ongoing program. You just didn't have a lot of marketing flexibility.

Today, my job is to develop campaigns that create interest in our products and drive sales. Most of our programs are electronically focused using e-mail, online seminars, and reference forums.

One of the most cost-effective tools we use is online seminars. They are similar to a talk-radio show where you can listen to a live interview with one of our customers and

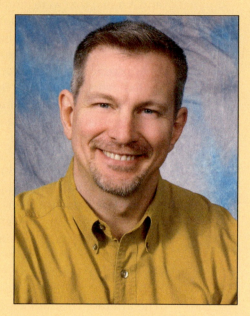

Michael Martin

then ask questions yourself. It is similar to the testimonial copy technique. The listener can find out what our customer's situation was before we were hired and how we solved their problems. It really works well.

The technology offers solutions more effectively than many of the practices in the past, where you rented a hotel or resort meeting room, flew in special entertainment, and spent lots of money. Today our clients can simply go to our Web site, saving time and travel. This is a new way of doing business-to-business marketing. It is evidence that we're in a changing world.

In my job I have to rely on my past experiences and gut, but I have to test and monitor everything I do. As with any marketing communication, you must know your target's issues so you can understand their needs. ■ ■ ■

in very different ways. Remember Cheerwine. It spends roughly $1 million on marketing with a 0.01 percent share, and Diet Coke spends roughly $60 million to promote the brand with almost a 10 percent share. A lot of factors must be considered when evaluating a situation.

It is important for the advertiser to know not only the characteristics of the product's market but also similar information about media alternatives. In fact, approaching the market as media neutral is a good idea in the world of today's changing media habits. Most major interactive companies, newspapers, magazines, movies, and broadcast media provide demographic and product-user data for numerous product categories. Database marketing is giving the marketer an abundance of information on which to base integrated promotional decisions.

Profile of the Buyer

Earlier in this chapter, we highlighted ethnic groups (Hispanics, African Americans, and Asians) that were largely ignored by advertisers in the past, but their increasing numbers demand attention in today's marketplace. The Xers, Boomers, teenagers, college students, and the 50+ markets are all studied by smart advertisers to understand their potential for specific products and services. As indicated, these groups of consumers are not necessarily easy to understand or reach with effective integrated programs. Not all Boomers act the same, and all Gen Yers don't respond to messages in the same manner.

Advertisers have to look at demographics and lifestyles, for starters, to understand any market.

Let's look at women ages 50 to 70. Why are marketers obsessed with youth when women between 50 and 70 are the golden bull's-eye of target marketing? The U.S. Census Bureau predicts a 72 percent increase in adults 50+ between 2000 and 2020 and a slight decrease in adults under 50. Adults 50+ control 77 percent of the country's assets. Women are responsible for 80 percent of household spending. Per capita spending is 2.5 times the national average in 50+ households. And because women live longer, this population will skew increasingly female. MassMutual created a Web seminar, "Ten Financial Questions and Answers for Women." It could be accessed at the consumer's convenience, 24-7. The interactive audio learning experience addressed the older female consumer's financial concerns. The solutions and planning tools are aligned with her life's stages and milestones, as well as tips for retirement and estate planning. It delivered exactly what women of this age group need in a format that speaks effectively to them. Women nurture lots of people. MassMutual acknowledged these relationships by offering planning segments for them as well their spouse, parents, and children. Women recognize that circumstances often change quickly and are likely to go with the flow when things change unexpectedly. MassMutual's tagline was right on target, "You can't predict. You can prepare."[43]

Demography is the study of vital economic and sociological statistics about people. In advertising, demographic reports refer to those facts relevant to a person's use of a product. Exhibit 4.11 presents a snippet of average weekly regular soft-drink demographics.

EXHIBIT 4.11

Selected Demographics of Regular Soft Drink Average Weekly Consumption for Specific Types (in Percentages)

Courtesy of www.usda.gov.

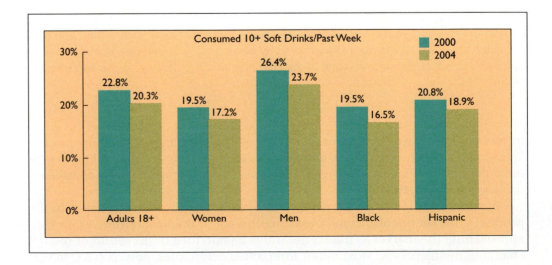

The selected soft-drink demographics probably offer few surprises to you. However, be sure to examine the differences in regular and diet consumption between males and females or between consumers ages 18 to 24 and older, and compare regional differences for starters. You can begin to understand how demographic differences could be important factors in advertising strategy and expenditure decisions.

Heavy Users

Take any product category and you will find that a small percentage of users is responsible for a disproportionately large share of sales. The principle of heavy usage is sometimes referred to as the 80/20 rule—that is, 80 percent of the units sold are purchased by only 20 percent of the consumers. Few products meet this exactly, but Kraft's Miracle Whip comes fairly close. And the most avid Miracle Whip customers live in the Midwest. So Kraft knows who buys the most and where they live. Of course, the exact figure varies with each product and product category, but the 80/20 rule is representative of most product sales. In the case of Diet Coke, what if 8 percent of the households account for 84 percent of the volume. This is rather significant information. Keeping that small segment loyal to Diet Coke is smart marketing, pure and simple. Heavy users are identified not only by who they are but also by when they buy and where they are located. Of course, another issue for marketers is not only how to reach these consumers but also what to say or do once they make contact.

The following table shows that the heavy users of brand X are women ages 55 and older. In addition, the most effective selling is done from January through June in the East Central and Pacific regions. Obviously, heavy users are an important part of the market; however, they are also the group most advertisers are trying to target and, therefore, the competition can be fierce and expensive. Some advertisers find that aiming for a less lucrative segment—medium or light users—may offer more reasonable expectations. A marketer cannot just assume the best prospects are 18- to 49-year-old women, heavy users, or people similar to current customers. Instead, marketers need to carefully study their target audience in great depth. In defining their market, then, they must determine who the heavy users are and identify their similarities, which would define the marketing goal.

USERS OF BRAND X

1. Target Audience: Current Consumers

Women	Pop. (%)	Consumption (%)	Index (100 = national (%) average)
18–24	17.5	5.0	29
25–34	21.9	10.1	46
35–54	30.1	24.0	80
55+	30.5	61.0	200
Total	100.0	100.0	

2. Geography: Current Sales

Area	Pop. (%)	Consumption (%)	Index
Northeast	24	22	92
East Central	15	18	120
West Central	17	16	94
South	27	24	89
Pacific	17	20	118
Total	100	100	

---

3. Seasonality

Period	Jan–Mar	Apr–Jun	Jul–Sept	Oct–Nov
Consumption (%)	30	36	20	14
Index	120	144	80	—

BEYOND DEMOGRAPHICS: PSYCHOGRAPHICS

When driving through any suburban area past modest-size yards of middle-class homes, one is struck first by their similarity. But a harder look is more illuminating, for behind the similarities lie differences that reflect the interests, personalities, and family situations of those who live in such homes. One yard has been transformed into a carefully manicured garden. Another includes some shrubs and bushes, but most of the yard serves as a relaxation area, with outdoor barbecue equipment and the like. A third yard is almost entirely a playground, with swings, trapezes, and slides. A swimming pool occupies almost all the space in another yard. A tennis court occupies yet another. Still another has simply been allowed to go to seed and is overgrown and untended by its obviously indoor-oriented owners.

psychographics
A description of a market based on factors such as attitudes, opinions, interests, perceptions, and lifestyles of consumers comprising that market.

Although the neighborhood consists of homes of similar style, age, and value, the people are not all the same. If you want to advertise to this neighborhood, you would be speaking to people with different interests and different tastes. There may be a big difference in the nature and extent of purchases between any two groups of buyers that have the same demographic characteristics. The attempt to explain the significance of such differences has led to an inquiry beyond demographics into psychographics. **Psychographics**—studying lifestyles—sharpens the search for prospects beyond demographic data. It has been said that lifestyle information gives the soul of the person. Good creative people can devise copy that appeals to a specific segment's lifestyle interest. The media are then selected, and advertising is directed to that special target group or groups. Put very simply, lifestyle information gives the soul of a person; demographics alone gives only a skeleton and not a whole person.

Target Audience: Beyond Demographics

Let us look at an example of a travel advertiser's defined target. This profile is based on the advertiser's research that helped define those people most likely to visit the area.

Research indicated that the basic demographic guideline for the consumer target is households with a combined household income of $40,000 or more. Households with less than $40,000 combined income simply do not have the discretionary income necessary for vacation travel.

target audience
That group that composes the present and potential prospects for a product or service.

The other qualifiers in defining a consumer **target audience** are lifestyle and geography:

Primary vacation travelers: These are vacation travelers who take a 1-week-plus vacation during the primary season (summer).

Weekend travelers: These people live in states within close proximity who can be attracted during the fall, winter, and spring seasons.

Mature market (50+): These people have both the discretionary income and available time to travel.

Business travelers: These are businesspeople coming to an area on business who can be encouraged to either extend their stay for pleasure travel purposes or to bring their spouse and family along.

International travelers: Canada provides an enormous influx of visitors. Also, the increasing number of international flights to and from the area provide increasing opportunities.

Psychographic Research

Today, there is much more refined information available. Agency research information includes syndicated research from outside sources, the client's research, and the agency's own resources. Syndicated research services specialize in different types of information on what types of products people buy and which brands, who buys them and their demographic and psychographic distinctions, a comparison of heavy and light users, how people react to products and to advertisements, and people's styles of buying and what media reach them.

Lifestyle categories are numerous. Data categories are available through syndicated research to advertisers and their agencies to help them select the target market. This information is available on a market-by-market basis defining both demographic and lifestyle information. Some of the categories indicating the percentage of household activities include:

- Credit card usage for travel and entertainment, bank cards, gas and department store usage
- Good life activities, which include such activities as attending cultural or arts events, foreign travel, gourmet cooking and fine food interests, stock investments, antique interest, interest in wines (see Exhibit 4.12)
- High-tech activities and usage, which involve home computers, watching cable television, VOD and viewing, photography interests
- Sports and leisure activities by households, which include activities such as bicycling, boating, golf, bowling, tennis, and jogging
- Outdoor activities, which include the number of households in a specific market involved in camping, fishing, motorcycling, environmental interests
- Domestic activities such as gardening, Bible and devotional reading, coin collecting, pet care, sewing, crafting, and reading

Test Marketing

Although extremely helpful, psychographic research cannot replace market testing as the ultimate guide to successful advertising and marketing. Manufacturers seldom introduce new products without doing some prior testing. This kind of testing helps determine if consumers will really purchase a product or react to specific advertising and promotional activities.

It is difficult to say which cities are best for testing. Ira Weinblatt, a Saatchi & Saatchi senior vice president, says, "You can't say one place represents everything because there are so many different lifestyles." Some cities are historically popular for test marketing. The Midwest has been popular because,

EXHIBIT 4.12

This Piggly Wiggly advertisement touts its wine selection including boutique and vintage wines, limited bottlings, and special orders.

Courtesy of Rawle-Murdy and Piggly Wiggly Carolinas.

geographically, it is the heartland of America. Each test market represents a kind of microcosm of America. Saatchi & Saatchi ranks the top-performing test markets. To make the list:[44]

A city's demographics must fall within 20 percent of the national average.

The city should be somewhat isolated.

Local media should be relatively inexpensive.

Citizens should not be extremely loyal to any particular brand.

Supermarkets should be impartial enough to give new products good display on their shelves.

Milwaukee, one of the test market cities that historically makes the list, is popular because the newspapers offer marketers the flexibility to split production runs. This allows advertisers to test up to four advertisements at a time and to experi-

KLEPPNER VIEWPOINT 4.2

Chris Hooper
Senior Vice President, Fitzgerald+CO
"So, why do you want to work in advertising?"

Chris Hooper

That's probably the most common question asked of folks interviewing for entry level jobs at agencies. It's a good question. And the answer really does matter—not so much the answer you give in the interview, but the reason you want to be in this business has to be a good one if you hope to succeed.

Bad answers, and reasons, abound. "I'm really creative" is a clear signal to most agency veterans that you are probably not. "I love to watch television for the commercials" is odd behavior, at best. "It seems like a fun business" is certainly true some of the time but only if you're in it for the right reason.

There is one good reason to work for an agency—*it's the love of ideas*. It's the one trait that is common to those who excel in the business. If you're a person who loves ideas, it's probably a love that is bigger than just advertising. You'll love ideas in many areas from the arts to pop culture to politics to the sciences. Any time you come across a fresh perspective or a novel way to think about or look at any subject, you find it interesting and stimulating. It's a part of who you are that holds the key to what you can do with your career.

Star performers, in good agencies, not only love ideas but they are skilled at helping generate them or nurture them or sell them or implement them in the marketplace. Being able to play a role in bringing ideas to life is the common thread between the very best art directors, media planners, writers, account managers, producers, and brand planners. And it's what binds people from the different disciplines into the best teams who do the best work. Ideas are a constant in the ever-changing agency business and now more than ever, change is rampant. Television may become secondary to interactive and in-store plasma screens may become the new media frontier. No one knows what the future really holds. But ideas always have been and always will be the life blood of the business. If you enter the business for the love of ideas and can find your role in birthing and growing them, change will simply make your career more interesting.

So if you're interested in the agency business because of glamorous TV shoots, you may be disappointed. But if your heart races and your spirits lift over new ways of looking at the world around you, you have every reason to expect a great career in an advertising agency, built on your love of ideas. ■ ■ ■

ment with run-of-the-paper color or freestanding inserts. Typically, researchers examine purchases for a number of weeks before advertisements run, during the period of the test, and afterward.

Acxiom® Corporation, a database services company, ranks American's top 150 Metropolitan Statistical Areas (MSAs) based on their overall characteristics as a consumer test market. "If it plays in Peoria, it will play anywhere" is a traditional American marketing adage, but today's advertisers and direct marketers may want to look 800 miles farther east, to Albany, New York.[45]

The top ten test market cities, which represent American consumers as a whole, are:

1. Albany–Schenectady–Troy, New York
2. Rochester, New York
3. Greensboro–Winston-Salem–High Point, North Carolina
4. Birmingham, Alabama
5. Syracuse, New York
6. Charlotte–Gastonia–Rock Hill, North Carolina–South Carolina
7. Nashville, Tennessee
8. Eugene–Springfield, Oregon
9. Wichita, Kansas
10. Richmond–Petersburg, Virginia

The least favorable test markets, or cities that least represent American consumers, are:

141. El Paso, Texas
142. Columbia, Missouri
143. Tallahassee, Florida
144. Brownsville–Harlingen–San Benito, Texas
145. Provo–Orem, Utah
146. Ocala, Florida
147. McAllen–Edinburg–Mission, Texas
148. Honolulu, Hawaii
149. San Francisco, California
150. New York, New York

The perils of introducing a product nationally without test marketing include failure. This can be extremely expensive, and most marketers are not willing to take that risk without some type of testing. In the late 1990s, PepsiCo took its lemon-lime Storm into eleven test markets over 2 years without success. PepsiCo also tested a lemon-lime cola called Pepsi Twist in mid-2000. The test was in Minneapolis and San Antonio using television and FSI (freestanding inserts) support. What makes Twist an interesting product is the fact that it was viewed as a possible in-and-out seasonal product and continues to be a niche product today. PepsiCo replaced Storm with caffeine-free Sierra Mist, which is now available nationally.

SUMMARY ✳

The accurate identification of current and prospective users of a product will often mean the difference between success and failure. The targeting of advertising to these prospects in an efficient media plan with appropriate creativity is critical.

This chapter has concentrated on fundamentals: Who are the prospects? What is a market? What about competition? Positioning? Numerous methods of examining segmentation and other important considerations in planning integrated marketing programs have been discussed. Understanding these basic concerns through research is part of the process. Research is the key to successful target marketing. Market research to define prime market segments, product research to meet the needs of these segments, and advertising research to devise the most appropriate messages are mandatory for the success of a firm in a competitive environment. Also, we need to be familiar with the multitude of research services providing data for aiding our planning.

Advertisements are aimed at consumers with a rifle approach instead of a shotgun approach. It is becoming easier to tailor messages through a variety of special-interest media vehicles.

Advertisers place more importance on lifestyle characteristics than on demographic factors. Advertisers recognize that purchase behavior is the result of a number of complex psychological and sociological factors that cannot be explained by a superficial list of age, sex, income, or occupational characteristics.

Finally, we need to keep abreast of changes in population and better understand such important segments as Hispanic, Asian, and African American populations as well as generational groups. This kind of knowledge will lead to better communications and targeting. We need to know more than simply numbers and location. We need to understand consumer lifestyles, identities, and motivations.

REVIEW

1. What is target marketing?
2. What is market segmentation?
3. What is multicultural marketing?
4. What is positioning?
5. What is the 80/20 rule as it relates to target marketing?

PART THREE

Managing
the Advertising

CHAPTER 5

The Advertising Agency, Media Services, and Other Services

Advertising agencies create most national and international advertising. The agency role and relationships are changing. After reading this chapter, you will understand:

chapter objectives

1. the agency
2. the history of the agency business
3. the full-service agency
4. global advertising agencies
5. agency and client relationships
6. forms of agency compensation
7. other advertising services

Agencies are pressured today to lead the way in communication through all the new channels and to react in the marketer's interest in figuring out how to deal with the new control that consumers have, especially the Connected Generation. This group covers a huge blanket of people (those from ages 9 to 41) linked by attitude and is empowered with the new tools and highly networked technology that have reshaped them from the inside out. And they are reshaping marketing. And agencies are being asked by their clients, "How do we connect with these multitasking creatures?" And everyone is trying to figure this out.

The self-description of Santa Monica's Ignited Minds speaks to many of the issues faced by today's agencies.

Ignited Minds is not an advertising agency.

We're not in the business of creating advertising. We are in the business of making our clients part of the cultural dialogue and the collective consciousness.

The means by which we accomplish this can take any form—from a two-dollar T-shirt to a million dollar TV spot. It could be a web site, an event, a reality show, a contest, a stunt, a store, a documentary, or anything else you can dream up. And each is equally important. In that sense, we are more of an idea studio than an ad agency.

And Jeff Hicks, president of Crispin Porter+Bogusk, says, "Everything Crispin does for a client is with an eye toward gaining media attention for the brand, which is why it insists that clients break down corporate silos separating advertising, public relations, and other units. The agency turns away clients that don't give it access to every part of a company.[1] Crispin Porter+Bogusky's description of advertising is:

Most people think in terms of magazines, television commercials and billboards. We think it's anything that makes our clients famous. That is our job.

And we make creative content that makes that happen. Then we think of ways to distribute that creative content. It may be through an online film, an event on the street, a book or something we can't imagine yet.

To us, it's all advertising.

OK, agencies don't publicly agree on what advertising covers today. Some of us believe more in the Crispin view, that anything created for a client comes under the umbrella of advertising. It isn't worth arguing about. We're talking about delivering marketing communication for clients in many forms. Despite these arguments and pressures, agencies continue to be the most significant companies in the development of advertising and marketing, not only in the United States but globally. During a time when every business is being reinvented, agencies are grappling with a number of issues: media proliferation and fragmentation, compensation, client loyalty, short-term pressures on the bottom line, lean structures, use of talent, reorganization, and how to make integrated communication really work the way it was envisioned. And, yes, the new consumer is yet another issue.

The changes in corporations have pressured agencies to become stronger partners in reaching advertisers' marketing and sales goals. Agencies have undergone their own reengineering, adapting to the environment in which they operate and to the clients they serve. Not only have agencies changed their structures, but also many have gobbled up specialty firms such as health care, online, mail-order, interactive, and promotion companies and other units involved in integrated communication. Make no mistake about it—it's not business as usual. Roles and relationships are changing. "We've been here before," says Keith Reinhard, chairman emeritus of DDB Worldwide, of the challenges presented to the advertising industry by new technologies like the Internet. "You have to focus on human beings. You can't forget that you're trying to reach someone who has age-old desires to be noticed, admired, and loved."[2]

THE AGENCY

An advertising agency, as defined by the American Association of Advertising Agencies, is an independent business, composed of creative and business people, who develop, prepare, and place advertising in advertising media for sellers seeking to find customers for their goods or services.

According to the U.S. Census Bureau, there are more than 10,000 agencies in operation in this country. The *LexisNexis Red Book of Advertising Agencies* (also known as the "Agency Red Book") lists over 5,000 agency profiles, including full-service agencies, house agencies, media-buying services, sales promotion agencies, cyberagencies, and public relations firms. The *Adweek Agency Directory* lists more than 6,000 agencies, public-relations firms, and media-buying services, plus 26,000 personnel listings. There are about 2,000 agencies listed in the New York Yellow Pages alone. Unfortunately, there isn't a single printed or online directory listing every agency throughout the country.

The majority of agencies are small one- to ten-person shops (we talk about size and services later in this chapter). You will see advertisements for many specialized products and services throughout this text—from consumer, industrial products, and services to pro-bono causes—in which the agency had to become an expert in marketing as well as writing the advertisement.

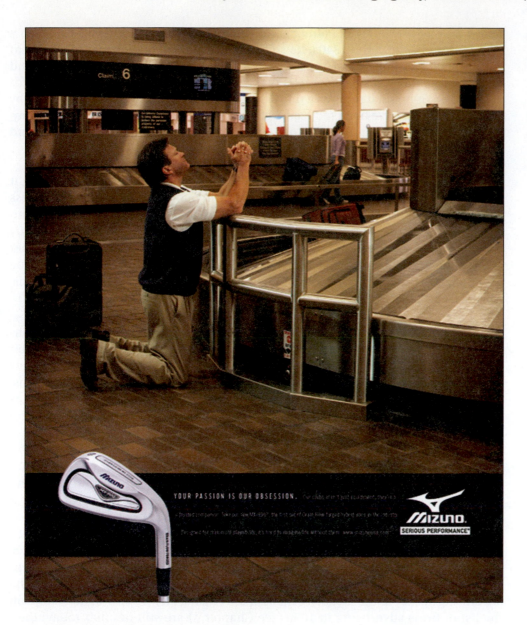

HOW AGENCIES DEVELOPED

Before we discuss present-day agencies further, let us take a look at how advertising agencies got started and how they developed into worldwide organizations that play such a prominent role in the marketing and advertising process.

The Early Age (Colonial Times to 1917)

It is not generally known that the first Americans to act as advertising agents were colonial postmasters:

> In many localities advertisements for Colonial papers might be left at the post offices. William Bradford, publisher of the first Colonial weekly in New York, made an arrangement with Richard Nichols, postmaster in 1727, whereby the latter accepted advertisements for the *New York Gazette* at regular rates.[3]

Space Salesmen Volney B. Palmer is the first person known to have worked on a commission basis. In the 1840s, he solicited advertisements for newspapers that had difficulty getting out-of-town advertising. Palmer contacted publishers and offered to get them business for a 50 percent commission, but he often settled for less. There was no such thing as a rate card in those days. A first demand for $500 by the papers might have been reduced, before the bargain was struck, to $50. (Today, we call that negotiation.) Palmer opened offices in Philadelphia, New York, and Boston. Soon there were more agents, offering various deals.

Space Wholesalers During the 1850s in Philadelphia, George P. Rowell bought large blocks of space for cash (most welcome) from publishers at very low rates, less agents' commissions. He would sell the space in small "squares"—one column wide—at his own retail rate. Rowell next contracted with 100 newspapers to buy one column of space a month and sold the space in his total list at a fixed rate per line for the whole list: "an inch of space a month in one hundred papers for one hundred dollars." Selling by list became widespread. Each wholesaler's list was his private stock in trade. (This was the original media package deal.)

The First Rate Directory In 1869, Rowell shocked the advertising world by publishing a directory of newspapers with their card rates and his own estimates of their circulation. Other agents accused him of giving away their trade secrets; publishers howled, too, because his estimates of circulation were lower than their claims. Nevertheless, Rowell persisted in offering advertisers an estimate of space costs based on those published rates for whatever markets they wanted. This was the beginning of the media estimate.

The Agency Becomes a Creative Center In the early 1870s, writer Charles Austin Bates began writing advertisements and selling his services to whoever wanted them, whether advertisers or agents. Among his employees were Earnest Elmo Calkins and Ralph Holden, who in the 1890s founded their own agency, famous for 50 years under the name of Calkins and Holden. These men did more than write advertisements. They brought together planning, copy, and art, showing the way to combine all three into effective advertising. Not only was their agency one of the most successful agencies for half a century, but also the influence of their work helped to establish the advertising agency as the creative center for advertising ideas. Many of the names on the list of firms advertising in 1890 (see Chapter 1) are still familiar today; their longevity can be attributed to the effectiveness of that generation of agency people who developed the new power of advertising agency services. The business had changed from one of salesmen going out to sell advertising space to one of agencies that created the plan, the ideas, the copy, and the artwork; produced the plates; and then placed the advertising in publications from which they received a commission.

To this day, the unique contribution to business for which agencies are most respected is their ability to create effective advertisements.

Agency-Client Relationship Established In 1875, Francis Ayer established N. W. Ayer & Son (one of the larger advertising agencies today). Ayer proposed to bill advertisers for what he actually paid the publishers (that is, the rate paid the publisher less the commission), adding a fixed charge in lieu of a commission. In exchange, advertisers would agree to place all their advertising through Ayer's agents. This innovation established the relationship of advertisers as clients of agencies rather than as customers who might give their business to various salespeople, never knowing whether they were paying the best price.

The Curtis No-Rebating Rule In 1891, the Curtis Publishing Company announced that it would pay commissions to agencies only if they agreed to collect the full price from advertisers, a rule later adopted by the Magazine Publishers of America. This was the forerunner of no-rebating agreements, which were an important part of the agency business for more than 50 years. (Agency commissions, however, ranged from 10 to 25 percent in both magazines and newspapers.)

Standard Commissions for Recognized Agencies Established   In 1917, newspaper publishers, through their associations, set 15 percent as the standard agency commission, a percentage that remains in effect for all media to this day (except local advertising, for which the media deal directly with the stores and pay no commission). The commission would be granted, however, only to agencies that the publishers' associations "recognized." One of the important conditions for recognition was an agency's agreement to charge the client the full rate (no rebating). Other criteria for recognition were that the agency must have business to place, must have shown competence in handling advertising, and must be financially sound. These three conditions are still in effect. Anyone may claim to be an agency, but only agencies that are recognized are allowed to charge a commission.

Today's agencies still receive commissions from the media for space they buy for clients. However, artwork and the cost of production are generally billed by the agency to the advertiser, plus a service charge—usually 17.65 percent of the net, which is equivalent to 15 percent of the gross. By preagreement, a charge is made for other services.

The American Association of Advertising Agencies   Founded in 1917, the **American Association of Advertising Agencies** (sometimes known as **AAAA** or **4As**), is the national trade association representing the advertising agency business in the United States. Its membership produces approximately 75 percent of the total advertising volume placed by agencies nationwide. Although virtually all of the large, multinational agencies are members of the AAAA, more than 60 percent of its membership bill less than $10 million per year. It is a management-oriented association that offers its members the broadest possible services, expertise, and information regarding the advertising agency business. The typical AAAA agency has been a member for more than 20 years.

> **American Association of Advertising Agencies (AAAA, 4As)** The national organization of advertising agencies.

The No-Rebate Age (1918–1956)

The events of this era that left their mark on today's agency world are summarized here.

Radio   One of the main events of 1925 was the notorious *Scopes* trial, and the main advent was radio. They did a lot for each other. Radio dramatized evolution-on-trial in Tennessee; it brought the issue of teaching scientific evolution home to Americans, and it brought people closer to their radios. Tuning in to radio soon became a major part of American life, especially during the Great Depression and World War II. Radio established itself as a prime news vehicle. It also gave advertising a vital new medium and helped pull agencies through those troubled years. A number of agencies handled the entire production of a radio program as well as its commercials. By 1942, agencies were billing more for radio advertising ($188 million) than they were for newspaper advertising ($144 million). The radio boom lasted until television came along.

Television   Television became popular after 1952, when nationwide network broadcasts began. Between 1950 and 1956, television was the fastest-growing medium. It became the major medium for many agencies. National advertisers spent more on television than they did on any other medium. Television expenditures grew from $171 million in 1950 to $1,225 million in 1956.

John Robertson

Founder, Co-Creative Director, VitroRobertson, San Diego
Taking Responsibility

*W*e believe that when a group of people get together and decide to open an advertising agency, that decision carries with it a group of responsibilities.

The agencies that, over the long term, neglect those responsibilities will struggle and make foolish compromises and allow their creative product to erode until those agencies themselves erode.

The agencies that never lose sight of those responsibilities and that try to live up to them every day are the agencies that will be respected and do outstanding work and will prosper in even the most competitive of environments.

At least that's our theory. Here are the responsibilities we try to live up to.

Our Responsibilities to Consumers

We have a responsibility to show them a good time. They have better things to do than to pay attention to advertising messages. We'll reward them for their time by making it an interesting, entertaining experience.

We have a responsibility to tell them what they want or need to know. We won't be all style and no substance. We won't waste their time.

We will be nice. We won't be obnoxious, rude, or inappropriate in our advertising. If they like the advertising, they'll like the company. And, if they like the company, they'll want to do business with it.

Our Responsibilities to Clients

We will listen. Carefully. We will never forget that they know a lot more about their business, their customers, and their

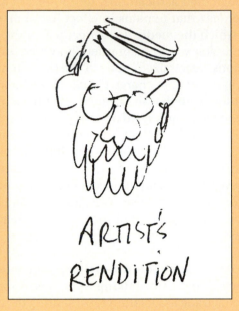

John Robertson

market than we do. Our job is to pay attention and make sure that they don't get caught up in too much "inside-out" thinking.

We will NOT do everything we're told. We will make it our responsibility to bring them ideas they didn't ask for and to keep solving problems in new and different ways.

We will argue for what we believe in, but we won't be jerks about it. There are enough jerks in the world already.

Electronic Data Processing The computer entered advertising through the accounting department. By 1956, the computer was already changing the lives of the media department, the marketing department, and the research department—all having grown in competence with the increasing number of syndicated research services. Agencies prided themselves on their research knowledge and were spending hundreds of thousands of dollars for research every year to service their clients better.

Business was good, and American consumers were attaining a better standard of living than they had ever previously enjoyed. The period from 1950 to 1956 proved to be the beginning of the biggest boom advertising ever had. Total expenditures jumped from $4.5 billion in 1950 to $9.9 billion in 1956. More than 60 percent of this spending was national advertising placed by advertising agencies. And the agency business was good, too.

The Age of Negotiation (1956–1990)

Consent Decrees In 1956, a change occurred in the advertiser-agency relationship. The U.S. Department of Justice held that the no-rebating provision between media

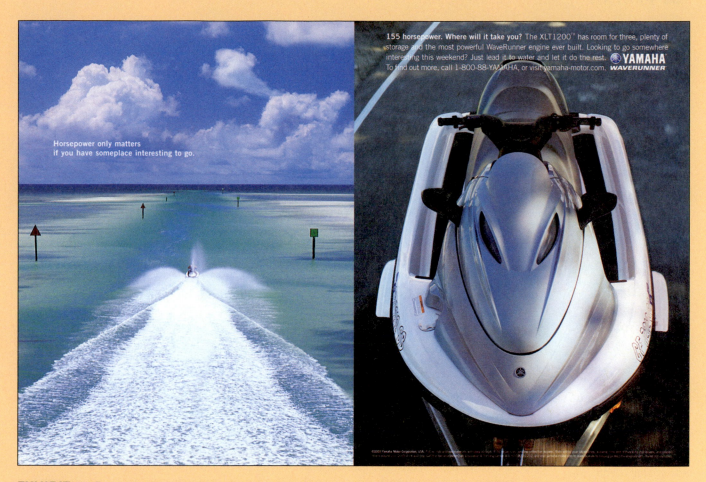

EXHIBIT 5.2

Who is Yamaha WaveRunner trying to reach with this ad?

Courtesy of VitroRobertson, Inc., Yamaha Watercraft, and Robert Holland, photographer.

In addition to being nice to the consumer, we will be nice to them, too.

We think they deserve our full attention and our best thinking.

Perhaps most importantly, we'll respect their product and their brand. We'll treat it very carefully, because we know how much it's worth.

When we went into business more than 10 years ago, this was what we believed in. And we still do today. ■ ■ ■

associations and agencies limited the ability to negotiate between buyer and seller and, therefore, was in restraint of trade and in violation of antitrust laws. Consent decrees to stop no-rebating provisions were entered into by all media associations on behalf of their members.

Although the Justice Department's ruling in no way affected the 15 percent that commission agencies were accustomed to getting from the media, it opened the way to review the total compensation an agency should receive for its services, with the 15 percent commission a basic part of the negotiations. Later we look at the effects this has had on the agency-client relationship.

The Reengineering Age (1990–2000)

Mergers During the 1980s, many corporations had merged, creating giant corporations. To be more competitive, agencies followed suit, many merging because of financial pressures to serve larger clients.

Integrated Services The decade of the 1990s was about agencies reevaluating how they operate. *Integrated services* has been a buzzword relating to efforts to coordinate a client's entire marketing mix, including public relations, promotion, direct marketing, package design, and so on. Some agencies have expanded their communication services to clients by expanding departments or buying or creating subsidiary companies that enable them to offer sales promotion, public relations, direct marketing, logo and packaging design, and even television programming. One of the reasons is financial—clients have been moving dollars from advertising to promotion, and clients want their communications integrated. Agencies are trying to change to supply those needs.

Media and the Digital Age (Since 2000)

Agency holding companies created mega-media buying and planning agencies (also called *media services agencies*) that became profit centers to attract global clients in an effort to become more efficient and cost-effective. As a result, many clients unbundled their media from their agencies and gave them to a single-media agency to buy and place. Interactive agencies have risen in importance as clients have attempted to deal with the mobile, Web, iPod, blog, BlackBerry, consumer-generated advertising world.

THE FULL-SERVICE AGENCY

full-service agency
An agency that handles planning, creation, production, and placement of advertising for advertising clients. May also handle sales promotion and other related services as needed by client.

In the simplest terms, the **full-service agency** offers clients all the services necessary to handle the total advertising function—planning, creation, production, placement, and evaluation. Many have expanded this to include the management of all integrated marketing communications through a variety of disciplines—advertising, promotion, direct marketing, public relations, and so forth—with a tight strategic marketing focus so that the brand image is reinforced every time the consumer is exposed to a communication.

Almost everyone has taken to heart clients' needs to change the way they do business, which, of course, means that agencies have to change their model to survive. This typical attitude was reflected in a recent website-redesign message from Luckie Advertising's agency, which said:

> Rethink everything. . . . Stay tuned for the most radical agency transformation in the history of radical agency transformations.

The large agencies, especially, need a new concept of the role and responsibilities to meet the demands of their large clients. A new mission will demand a different organization. Some agencies have undergone a restructuring or reengineering in recent years, more than once. Small agencies are loving it, because they can adjust more quickly than the large agencies and this becomes a selling point.

Most agencies believe that brand building is impossible without creative, persuasive advertising, which is with few exceptions the most potent component in the marketing communication mix. Despite the restructuring, most marketers will find familiar unit names in most agency restructuring: account management, creative, media, research or account planning, and administration. But many of these agencies have changed how they operationalize the work. It still isn't brain surgery, but it does require a managed process.

Today, there isn't a universal agency structure model, because agencies have clients with specific needs. One structure doesn't fit all. That said, let's take a look at the functions full-service agencies perform. When a new account or a new product is assigned to a full-service agency, work on it will generally proceed along the following lines.

Diagnosing the Marketing and Brand Strategy

The process begins with the collection of all that you know about the product category, the brand, and its competitors. Research or brand planning takes the lead, looking at consumer attitudes to develop penetrating insights into the prospects and defining the brand's core: Who are the prime prospects? Where are they? What are their demographics and psychographic characteristics? How does the product fit into their lifestyles? How do they regard this type of product, this particular brand, and competitive products? What one benefit do consumers seek from this product and this particular brand? In what distinctive way can the product solve the prime prospects' problems? What media will best reach your market? What will it take to reach this audience? Some advertising agencies use their research capability to attract clients. An agency self-advertisement said, ". . . It's understandable that when you advertise, you tend to do it from your own perspective . . . we don't promote who you think you want to be. We explore through research who consumers will let you become. Then we apply that knowledge to the most important part of any communication plan, the ad itself." Exhibit 5.3 shows a highly targeted advertisement. There is little question as to the target.

Setting Objectives and Developing Strategy

Using the answers to the questions asked in the previous section, a strategy is formulated that positions the product in relation to the prime-prospect customer and emphasizes the attribute that will appeal to the prime prospect. Account management is responsible for leading this phase. Here, you define what is to be accomplished strategically, such as intensifying brand imagery and recapturing

EXHIBIT 5.3

Reed & Barton advertisements target prospects.

Courtesy of Blattner Brunner, Pittsburgh, Atlanta, Washington.

prior users, and plan how to carry it out. These strategic dialogues involve teams of account, creative, media, and research people.

Creating the Communication

Once the overall strategy is determined, you decide on the creative strategy, write copy, and prepare rough layouts and storyboards. In advertising, the creative impulse is always disciplined—an imaginative and persuasive expression of the selling strategy and the character of the brand.

The Media Plan Large clients may have separated the media function to a separate media service agency. In this event, both the creative and media agencies have to collaborate in developing the media plan. Either way, you define media strategy, checking objectives to ensure that they parallel your marketing objectives. Then you select media. All traditional and nontraditional options are explored, the goal being to avoid mere execution and add value instead. Media schedules are prepared with costs. At this stage, you seek to coordinate all elements of the marketing communication mix to ensure maximum exposure. The choice of media leads the process by developing an environment that multiplies the impact of the creative team. This step may be implemented by the agency or by an independent media agency or buying service.

The Total Plan You present roughs of the copy, layouts, and production costs, along with the media schedules and costs—all leading to the total cost.

Evaluation Plan The evaluation step in this process is both the end and the beginning. It is the moment of reckoning for the creative work, based on the objectives set in the beginning, and provides the evidence needed to refine and advance future efforts. As such, it is an accountable system.

Notify Trade of Forthcoming Campaign

For many product categories, you would inform dealers and retailers of the campaign details early enough so that they can get ready to take advantage of the advertising campaign.

Billing and Payments

When advertisements are run, you take care of billing the client and paying the bills to the media and production vendors. As an example of the billing procedure, let us say that through your agency an advertiser has ordered an advertisement in *Leisure Gourmet* magazine for one page costing $10,000. When the advertisement appears, the bill your agency gets from the publisher will read something like this:

1 page, August *Leisure Gourmet* magazine	$10,000
Agency commission @ 15% (cash discount omitted for convenience)	1,500
Balance Due	$8,500

Your agency will then bill the advertiser for $10,000, retain the $1,500 as compensation, and pay the publisher $8,500.

The agency commission applies only to the cost of space or time. In addition, as mentioned earlier, your agency will send the advertiser a bill for production costs for such items as the following:

finished artwork	reproduction prints/films
typography (typesetting)	recording studios
photography	broadcast production
printing collateral	

The items are billed at actual cost plus a service charge, usually 17.65 percent (which is equivalent to 15 percent of the net).

THE TRADITIONAL AGENCY ORGANIZATION

In this section, we first examine the traditional approach to the full-service agency structure, and then we look at the reengineering of this process.

Advertising agencies come in all sizes and shapes. The largest employ hundreds of people and bill thousands of millions of dollars every year. The smallest are one- or two-person operations (usually a creative person and an account manager). As they grow, they generally must add to their organizational structure to handle all the functions of a full-service agency.

All agencies do not structure themselves in exactly the same manner. For discussion purposes, we have chosen a typical traditional organizational structure under the command of major executives: the vice presidents of (1) the creative department, (2) account services, (3) marketing services, and (4) management and finance (see Exhibit 5.4). We discuss briefly how each department is organized.

Creative Department

Ken Roman, former chairman of Ogilvy & Mather Worldwide, says, "Agencies are generally hired on the basis of their creative abilities—the promise that they can create campaigns that will build business for the client." Every agency that exists is concerned with creating good advertising.[4] Yet, only a small number of agencies are known for their creative work. Later, in Chapter 16, Frank Compton takes a look at defining the requirements to creating more than fundamentally basic advertisements. In almost every agency, the agency creative director is almost a mythical, often legendary creature positioned near the top of the agency totem pole. The creative director is considered to be responsible for the care and feeding of its most prized possession—the creative product. Today, more than ever before, success is measured

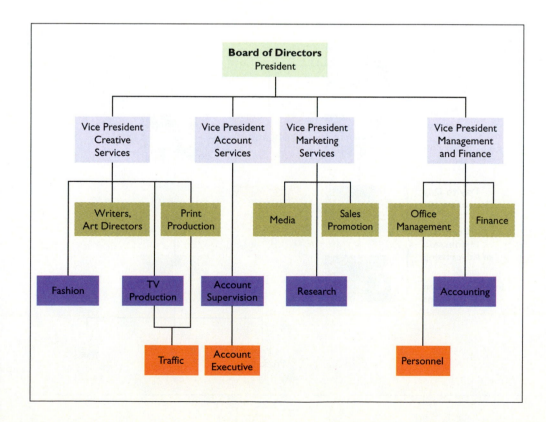

EXHIBIT 5.4

Organization of a Typical Full-Service Agency

by the client's results. The creative director is expected to have an opinion on everything Interactive to promotion to public relations. In addition to den mother, psychologist, cheerleader, arbiter of taste, basketball coach, team player, historian, jack-of-all-trades, showman, social convener, architect, designer, and Renaissance person, today's more evolved species is also required to be a strategist, businessperson, planner, financier, and new-product developer. Bill Westbrook, on taking over as creative head of Fallon McElligott, stressed the importance of strategy: "If it's not a great strategy, it isn't a great campaign." Lee Chow, chairman and chief creative officer of TBWA/Chiat Day, says, "Managing an integrated campaign is different from doing just ads, as creative directors we've become joined at the hip with account planners."[5]

At first, all writers and artists will work right under one creative director; but as the business grows, various creative directors will take over the writing and art activities of different brands. A traffic department will be set up to keep the work flowing on schedule.

The print production director and the television manager also report to the creative director, who is ultimately responsible for the finished product—advertisements and commercials.

Account Services

The vice president in charge of account services is responsible for the relationship between the agency and the client and is indeed a person of two worlds: the client's business and advertising (see Exhibit 5.5). This vice president must be knowledgeable about the client's business, profit goals, marketing problems, and advertising objectives. He or she is responsible for helping to formulate the basic advertising strategy recommended by the agency, for seeing that the proposed advertising prepared by the agency is on target, and for presenting the total proposal—media schedules, budget, and rough advertisements or storyboards—to the client for approval. Then comes the task of making sure that the agency produces the work to the client's satisfaction.

EXHIBIT 5.5

Typical Team Responsibilities

In some agencies, the account planner works directly with creative to provide consumer insights and research.

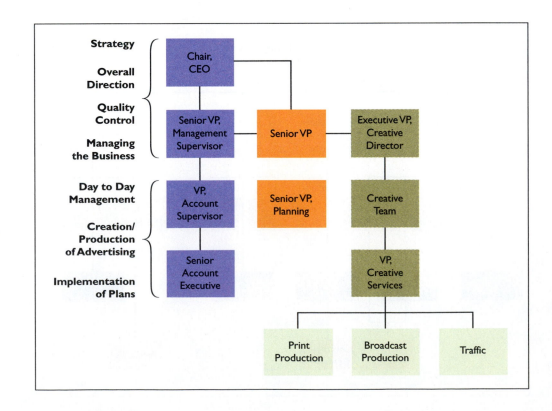

Alana Stephenson

Account Services, The Johnson Group, Chattanooga
A day in the life of an Account Executive

At my agency, our account service department is divided into Account Executives and Project Managers. The Account Executive is the main client contact and handles presenting agency ideas to the client and client ideas to the agency. The Project Manager is the internal communicator for the client. Each client has an Account Executive and a Project Manager assigned to them. This way, each client has at least 2 contacts within the agency and should always be able to reach someone. I am a Project Manager.

As a Project Manager, my job is to make sure that the client's needs are being met within the agency. I keep up with due dates and make sure that jobs travel through the appropriate channels before being sent out of the office.

When the client or the agency has an idea for a project, my first action is to open a job in our system for that project. Jobs are assigned a number, which is how it is referenced internally and how the project is archived. After a job is opened, I arrange a meeting with everyone who will work on the job. This includes the Account Executive, Creative Director, Art Director, Production Artist and Production Manager. The purpose of this meeting is to determine the direction we will take and to leave the meeting with everyone knowing what they need to do. We call this our download meeting.

After the download, work begins on a job. My role is to make sure that the time spent on the job is within the amount of time we estimated. When the creative department has the job to a point where it is ready to show the client, we first have an internal review. This gathers the people from the original download together again and we reexamine to make sure we are on target with our concept. Once everyone from the agency is on board, the Account Executive presents the job to the client.

Once the client has seen the job they may suggest changes or give feedback. This feedback is brought back to the creative department and any revisions are made and resubmitted to the client.

Alana Stephenson

Once the client approves the job, it is my responsibility to get the final product out the door. If the job is a print ad, I make sure the ad meets the publications specs (size, color, bleed, etc.) and then send the ad to the publication in the format they request. If the job is a radio or TV ad, I send the spot(s) along with traffic instructions to the station. Traffic instructions are all information the station needs about how and when to run spots. After the ad has been sent to the station or publication, I file a copy of the finished product in the agency archive.

Every day in an advertising agency is different. The year begins with planning meetings to decide the direction of the campaign. This involves a lot of strategic thinking. Once the campaign direction is decided, there is production time for all pieces of the campaign. After the campaign pieces are completed, they must all be sent out to the media outlets. Once the campaign is out and running, it's about time to start planning the next campaign. ■ ■ ■

As the business grows and takes on many clients, an account supervisor will appoint account executives to serve as the individual contacts with the various accounts. Account executives must be skillful at both communications and follow-up. Their biggest contribution is keeping the agency ahead of its client's needs. But the account supervisor will continue the overall review of account handling, maintaining contacts with a counterpart at the client's office.

Marketing Services

The vice president in charge of marketing services is responsible for media planning and buying (if the creative agency handles media), for research, and for sales promotion. The media director is responsible for the philosophy and planning of the use of media, for the selection of specific media, and for buying space and time. As the agency grows, there will be a staff of media buyers, grouped according to media (print, television, or radio or Interactive), accounts, or territory. The media staff will include an estimating department and an ordering department, as well as a department to handle residual payments due to performers. The media head may use independent media services, especially in the purchase of television and radio time.

The research director (or planning director) will help define marketing and copy goals. Agencies usually use outside research organizations for fieldwork, but in some agencies, research and media planning are coordinated under one person. The division of work among the executives may vary with the agency.

The promotion director takes care of premiums, coupons, event marketings, and all types of promotions.

Management and Finance

Like all businesses, an advertising agency needs an administrative head to take charge of financial and accounting control, office management, and personnel (including trainees).

THE CONTINUING EVOLUTION OF THE AGENCY

Decades ago, clients sought the agency powerhouse talents of Leo Burnett, Bill Bernbach, David Ogilvy, Rosser Reeves, Howard Gossage, and Mary Wells. This was followed by agencies that were less driven by famous individuals and more often driven by a collection of bright talent. There has always been some sort of agency evolution taking place. In the 1980s, agencies followed the trend of clients and they merged and restructured to be more financially competitive. The 1990s brought a major agency reengineering as agencies changed to better serve the integrated and Web needs of clients, and some no longer called themselves "advertising agencies." Peter Arnell, chairman of Arnell Group, says "The term ad agency needs a true and sincere facelift." He does complicate it by defining his agency as a "brand-ideation and experience-marketing company specializing in integrated branding, strategy and communication solutions."[6]

For example, J. Walter Thompson says it is a "brand communication company." It is now simply called JWT. The result is an integrated company with a number of companion companies offering marketing expertise beyond traditional advertising and marketing. In early 2005, it held a funeral around the world at its many offices. In Paris, the staff lit a bonfire made of old campaigns. In Tokyo, its founder Commodore J. Walter Thompson received a mock burial at sea to symbolize that the advertising agency was dead!

Traditionally, agencies were trusted partners in the stewardship of the brand. They would be key in developing products, serving as marketing and media experts and visionaries. Today, most major corporate marketing departments have the ability to manage these functions. Many agencies feel they are treated more like vendor–order takers than partners as clients seek solutions from any place, once the exclusive territory of agencies.

Under the traditional structure, an account person met regularly with creatives to discuss strategy and advertising copy, or with media people to review scheduling, or separately with the public-relations person. Rarely did everyone meet together. In most reengineered operations the key people on the team meet on a regular basis so that everyone knows what is going on in every aspect of the account. For example, key people meet every Monday morning to review the week's work—and meet again when necessary. This means the sales-promotion person knows about the public-relations work, and the art director knows about media planning, and everyone knows about the Interactive film. If necessary, the client participates in the review. In theory, a client could call anyone on the team to get an answer.

A few years ago, Jay Chiat, a pioneer in agency reengineering, said:

> We believe the hierarchical structure [of the traditional agency], if not obsolete at present, is on its way. The traditional pyramid is about personal power and focuses on how to run a business. Most of the decisions are about the organization's needs—fiscal and administrative issues. An agency is a service organization whose sole existence depends on satisfying client needs.[7]

In traditional agencies, senior managers spend 15 to 20 percent of their time on client business. In reengineered agencies, they spend about 60 percent of their time in the trenches working on client business. Middle managers in reengineered agencies act as coaches, team leaders, and quality-control managers. One of the significant changes is that creative staff, account managers, and media planners must work together as a team—a team of people working together to rapidly solve problems. Most agency reengineers say their teams consist of eight to twelve people, although some use teams of about twenty people. Most agencies' reengineered structure is somewhat similar to traditional structure. *It is how business works that is different.* People don't do their thing in isolation; they approach problem solving together. The team concept often helps younger people because it allows them to work side by side with senior people.

As with any new management trend, traditional agencies will copy and modify those reengineering structures that have been successful to meet their specific needs. There is little doubt that the agency structure in the future will not be a copy of today's.

Specialty Agencies

Most advertising agencies are primarily general consumer agencies. However, some agencies primarily specialize in certain kinds of business. Some examples are: business-to-business (B2B) accounts, health care (Grey Healthcare, Cline Davis, Euro RSCG Life), entertainment, or tourism; and other business specialties like Maximum Design & Advertising (Exhibit 5.6), which specializes in real estate marketing. Then you have the multicultural agencies: the Asian market, the African American market, the Hispanic market, and other groups such as the Arab market. And a big growth area includes Interactive agencies (Euro RSCG 4D, Grey Digital, Ogilvy Interactive, Avenue A/Razorfish). Each of these operate pretty much as any other agency, but their expertise is more narrow than reaching all consumers.

Agency Size

Some agencies are run by one or two people, others by hundreds or thousands. There has always been an argument that large agencies offer more services and expensive star talent. The negative is that they generally charge more and aren't very flexible because of their size. Small agencies promote that small-to-medium clients can be serviced by the agency's senior management and creative.

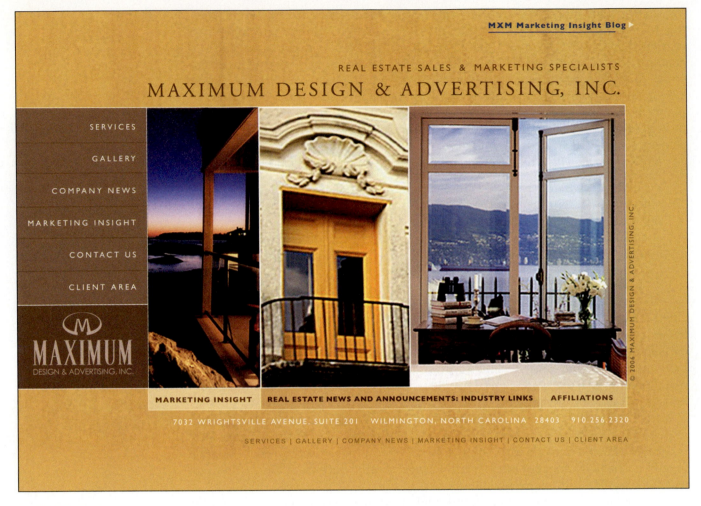

EXHIBIT 5.6

Maximum specializes in real estate development advertising.

Courtesy of © 2006 Maximum Design. Used with permission.

Brad Majors, former president of Socoh Marketing who has worked for agencies of all sizes in senior positions, offers these thoughts about size of agency:

- Large/public agencies will, more than ever, be confined to large, multinational accounts. It will be nearly impossible for them to profitably service smaller clients. And since there will continue to be large multinational clients (with growth primarily from the acquisitions of smaller competitors' brands), there should be room for the larger agencies to profitably handle them.

- Medium-size agencies, which have been the greatest source of creativity historically, will exist but will remain in the state of flux we see today. As they grow, they will have the resources to hire strong talent. Much of this talent, without the cumbrances of public ownership, will continue to produce provocative work. As the work is noticed and clients and prospects become more interested, these medium-size agencies will become attractive to larger agencies as an acquisition target. As the principals of the agency age, an immediate cash-rich buyout may seem more attractive than a deal with the next generation of the agency's management. Thus, the newly acquired agency will not be medium size any longer but will become only a part of the larger whole. Once acquired, it will be important for it to remain in the niche prescribed for it by the parent agency.

■ Interestingly, smaller agencies not only will exist but also will thrive, if managed prudently. Historically, small agencies have either fared very well or gone under. To some extent, small agency success has been determined by how strong the agency's financial management was. Managing cash flow and accounts receivables has been a critical issue for most small agencies and it will continue to be so. But given the instability expected in medium-size agencies, there should be great opportunities for smaller agencies that combine a marketing-driven creative product with sound financial management.

COMPETING ACCOUNTS

The client-agency relationship is a professional one. It may involve new product strategies, new promotions, sales data, profit or loss information, and new marketing strategies—information that is sensitive and confidential. As a result, most clients will not approve of an agency's handling companies or products in direct competition; Coca-Cola isn't going to allow its agencies to handle Pepsi products. In some cases, agencies will handle accounts for the same type of product or service if they do not compete directly—for example, banks that do not compete in the same market. Many agency-client conflicts result from mergers in which one merger partner handles an account for a product that competes with a product being handled by the other merger partner. When agencies consider merging, the first question is, "Will any of our accounts conflict?" There are a number of large national agencies with independent offices around the country that hope clients will not view the same type of account in another office as a conflict.

CLIENT-AGENCY RELATIONSHIP LENGTH

Clients generally retain agencies as long as the relationship seems to be working. However, most contracts allow for a 90-day cancellation by either party if the relationship goes sour. At the same time, agencies can resign an account if they differ with the client's goals and the account isn't profitable. American Association of Advertising Agencies research has indicated that the average tenure of client-agency relationships has declined from 7.2 years to 5 years since 1984. Yet today, some clients have been with their agencies for decades. For example, GE (1920), Hormel Foods (1931), and DaimlerChrysler (1926) have been clients of BBDO Worldwide for many years.

AGENCY OF RECORD

The agency-of-record relationship offers marketers an advertising team to work solely on their brand, creating a stable team of experts in that particular industry. Global agencies claim they are capable of providing multiple services to a client, which enables marketers to respond quickly to changes in the global business environment.[8]

In some instances, large advertisers may employ a number of agencies to handle their advertising for various divisions and products. To coordinate the total media buy and the programming of products in a network buy, the advertiser will appoint one agency as the agency of record. This lead agency will make

ADVANTAGE POINT

Huey+Partners

*A*dvertising agencies, like brands, need a clear and distinguishable point of difference. With that in mind, Ron Huey and partner, Joe Paprocki, opened the doors of their Atlanta agency in 1997. Their distinguishable point of difference? Very simply: Creative work that sets their clients' brands apart and grows their business. It was that sole focus on crafting emotionally-compelling, arresting creative work that moved *Ad Age's Creativity* to name them one of the country's "Top 20 Agencies to Watch" in 2000. Over their first four years, the agency's work was recognized with over 300 ADDY awards—more than any other Atlanta agency in that time. In the Fall of 2004, *Communication Arts* featured the agency in an 8-page profile—one of only four agencies worldwide to be featured that year.

What's the secret behind their success? Agency founder, Ron Huey, explains that he took the best of what he'd learned at some of the country's most-acclaimed shops including The Martin Agency and Team One Advertising where Ron's creative work for Lexus helped establish the brand as the number one luxury automobile in America. However, unlike larger shops, Huey+Partners is able to deliver that level of big brand and big agency experience to their clients in a much leaner, more responsive agency model.

Today, Huey+Partners continues their steadfast belief that creativity is the key to setting brands apart. Its an approach that has yielded great results for their clients. In the agency's five-year relationship with Mizuno USA, the client has seen their market share in golf irons literally double. Thanks, in part, to a quirky, untraditional advertising campaign that recognizes the passion golfers share for the game. Meanwhile, other clients such as Hitachi Power Tools, WeatherBug, The Daily Report and Russell Athletic have also reaped the benefits of Huey+Partners' dedication to a singular mission: the work. ■ ■ ■

Courtesy of Huey+Partners.

the corporate contracts under which other agencies will issue their orders, keep a record of all the advertising placed, and communicate management's decisions on the allotment of time and space in a schedule. For this service, the other agencies pay a small part of their commissions (usually 15 percent of 15 percent is negotiated) to the agency of record.

AGENCY MULTIPLE OFFICES

Many major agencies have offices in cities throughout the United States. McCann-Erickson is typical, with major offices in New York; Los Angeles; San Francisco; and Birmingham, Michigan. JWT USA operates major agencies in Atlanta, Chicago, Detroit, and Houston, with its headquarters in New York. It also has a number of JWT Specialized Communication offices in a number of other cities, as well as other offices throughout the world. BBDO has regional headquarters in Atlanta, Chicago, Detroit, Miami, Minneapolis, San Francisco, and Los Angeles, in addition to its New York worldwide headquarters. For the most part, each office functions as an autonomous agency that serves different clients and is able to draw on the talents and services of the other offices. As a rule, these offices don't normally work on the same project for the same client. Whereas the parent organizations are busily marketing themselves as global networks, each local office fiercely tries to protect its unique culture. Recently, BBDO's chairman says, "It's no secret that BBDO in Los Angeles is our best agency in terms of print creative. Why shouldn't we make that expertise available to clients from other offices?"[9] It may be said that because each office handles different kinds of accounts, each office has different specialties that could be leveraged on behalf of all clients. But, as a general rule, each office works primarily on its own accounts.

Keep in mind that the large media services agencies also have multiple offices in many of the same cities.

GLOBAL AGENCIES AND GLOBAL MARKETS

Globalization has become a necessary part of business and advertising. The demands on marketers to survive in a global economy place pressures on large- and medium-size agencies to become global partners. Companies and agencies need to learn cultural and market patterns to understand consumers from a global perspective. Someone trying to sell burgers, fries, and soft drinks outside of the United States may think there is no competition because there are no other burger outlets. The local version of fast food may not include hamburgers at all; the real competition may be a rice shop or a tacqueria. Unless marketers understand competing sources for that same dollar, they won't be successful.[10]

Many small- to medium-size agencies that don't have the resources for international offices have made affiliations with agencies or independent agency networks throughout the world to service clients and give advice. If you're a Jacksonville agency without foreign offices, you might turn to one of the independent network agencies in Hong Kong for help marketing in Hong Kong. If an agency doesn't have the resources (offices or network) to help clients engage in international marketing, then the client is likely to turn to agencies that do have the resources and knowledge, or the client may seek a local agency in the country where it is doing business. Major agencies have been global in nature for many decades to service their clients' international needs.

JWT opened its first office outside the United States in 1891 in London. It now has 315 offices in ninety countries. Following is a list of its non–North American offices.

JWT Global Agency Network

Latin America	Asia Pacific	Europe	Africa	Middle East
Argentina	Australia	Austria	Ghana	Egypt
Bolivia	Bangladesh	Belgium	Ivory Coast	Israel
Brazil	China	Bosnia-	Kenya	Jordan
Colombia	Hong Kong	Herzegovina	Mozambique	Kuwait
Costa Rica	India	Bulgaria	South Africa	Lebanon
Dominican	Indonesia	Croatia		Morocco
Republic	Japan	Czech Republic		Saudi Arabia
Ecuador	Korea	Denmark		Syria
El Salvador	Malaysia	Estonia		UAE
Guatemala	Nepal	Finland		
Honduras	New Zealand	France		
Mexico	Pakistan	Germany		
Nicaragua	Philippines	Greece		
Panama	Singapore	Hungary		
Paraguay	Sri Lanka	Ireland		
Peru	Taiwan	Italy		
Puerto Rico	Thailand	Latvia		
Uruguay	Vietnam	Macedonia		
Venezuela		Netherlands		
		Norway		
		Poland		
		Portugal		
		Romania		
		Russia		
		Slovenia		
		Spain		
		Switzerland		
		Turkey		
		Ukraine		
		United Kingdom		
		Yugoslavia		

JWT Worldwide has had a system to manage a client's global business that includes the following:

1. *Global teams.* JWT can help clients achieve their communications objectives virtually anywhere in the world.

2. *Director-in-charge system.* JWT uses an account director, who is the director-in-charge (DIC) on a global scale. These people operate as heads of an "agency within the agency," working with all offices to service global clients. The DICs work closely with their regional directors, local office CEOs, and account directors in each country to make sure the agency's network comes together seamlessly to execute a multinational advertiser's global communications efforts to build its business.

3. *Regional directors.* JWT regional directors have the responsibility for a specific group of countries. The CEOs of JWT's offices in that region report to the regional director.

4. *Global directors.* Each worldwide client is represented by a global business director, who sits on the JWT worldwide executive group. The DIC reports to the global business director, whose role is to ensure that the full resources of the JWT global network are brought to bear in servicing multinational accounts.

WWP, the parent of JWT, sponsors BrandZ, a research study that interviews some 70,000 people around the world. This study asks consumers questions in fifty categories to understand how consumers view 3,500 brands. These insights are available to JWT clients.

Most global agencies have similar operations to JWT. For instance, DDB has 206 offices in ninety-six countries. BBDO has 316 offices in seventy-seven countries. Sometimes agency offices are opened in a country because a client wants to do business there.

In Chapter 23, we deal extensively with international operations.

Global Ad Centers

The leading international advertising cities ranked in terms of local advertising billings are New York and Tokyo—fighting neck and neck for world leadership. Other major advertising centers include London, Paris, Chicago, Los Angeles, Detroit, San Francisco, Minneapolis, Frankfurt, São Paulo, Düsseldorf, Madrid, and Seoul. Almost every country has an advertising agency center. Exhibit 5.7 shows a Korean utility advertisement. For U.S. agencies, setting up a foreign office can be very complex. Each country is a different market, with its own language, buying habits, ways of living, mores, business methods, marketing traditions, and laws. So instead of trying to organize new agencies with American personnel, most U.S. agencies purchase a majority

EXHIBIT 5.7

Megapass

The Korean Telecom advertisement's banner says, "Congratulations Megapass! Investment from foreign customers!" The bottom copy says, "Thank you for contracts! Three million customers! Megapass Summer special event."

Courtesy of Korean Telecom and Chang Hwan Shin.

or minority interest in a successful foreign agency. Key members of the international offices regularly meet for intensive seminars on the philosophy and operation of the agency and share success stories. Remember, good marketing ideas can come from any place. The United States doesn't have a lock on great ideas.

Global Marketing

Companies are continually attempting to become more globally integrated. Sometimes these efforts don't work as smoothly as the company wishes. As with U.S. advertising, success often stems from a product or positioning that is relevant to consumer needs, which often vary by culture. Although cultures and habits vary, people's emotions are remarkably similar. People are very much alike in their attitudes regarding love, hate, fear, greed, envy, joy, patriotism, material comforts, and family. Ogilvy & Mather has found that strategies can and do move worldwide, but it is usually best to create advertising locally from a worldwide plan and strategy to maintain the desired brand image. If there is a local reason to vary strategy, it should be worked out in advance. For smaller companies, the promise of global branding has been a bumpy road. Global players face a common problem—virtually every global strategy now has a full complement of strong multinational and regional competitors. The promise of managing marketing from a single headquarters hasn't worked the way it was planned.[11] Jerry Judge, former CEO of Lowe Worldwide, says, "There really isn't much global marketing. There are companies that market globally." According to Ken Kaess of DDB Worldwide, "The benefit is consistency of product image or message, which is particularly true of service marketers like American Express, McDonald's, or Exxon Mobil. They have the same core values around the world."[12]

It is only logical that multinational clients want their agencies to know how to develop great advertising campaigns that can run across all the principal markets of the world. As the world gets smaller, there needs to be brand consistency so people don't get confused as they move from market [country] to market.[13] The result of this need is pressure on U.S. agencies to produce, place, and research global advertising.

Global Production Efficiencies

Cost efficiencies in production of global advertising motivate advertisers to seek a single world execution for advertising concepts. A single execution also helps build the same global brand equity. However, "every international brand starts out as a successful local brand . . . reproduced many times."[14] Being a global advertiser and having one global campaign sound easy. But it is not. Despite being a global advertiser for many decades, Coca-Cola didn't launch its first global advertising campaign until 1992 with all the advertisements being similar in each country. Exhibit 5.8 shows an advertisement developed by Coca-Cola Company–Japan.

A brand and its advertising must be presented in relevant and meaningful ways in the context of local environments, or consumers won't care. As many experienced multinational marketers know, for any given brand, advertising that elicits the same response from consumers across borders matters much more than running the same advertising across borders. That may mean using the same brand concept or advertising concept and similar production format across borders, but the executions need to be customized to local markets so the consumers can relate to and empathize with the advertising. Simply translating American advertisements into foreign languages has proved dangerous. Perdue's (Chicken) Spanish translation of "It takes a tough man to make a tender chicken," actually said, "It takes a sexually excited man to make a chick affectionate." Language can be a barrier; for example, "Come alive with the Pepsi Generation" translated in Chinese as "Pepsi brings your ancestors back from the grave."

AGENCY NETWORKS

Many small- and medium-size agencies that have working agreements with each other to help with information gathering from different markets and sharing are called *agency networks*. Usually there is only one network member in each market or region. Agency networks provide information and financial skills to enhance agency operations.

The Mega-Agency Holding Companies

Marion Harper set out his holding company vision for Interpublic Group of companies in 1960. He understood that once an agency reached a certain size, account conflicts hindered the agency's growth. His solution was to create an organization that would own individual agencies that could handle competing brands. Each of these agencies would operate freely and independently. The definition still holds true today, by and large, but not quite as Harper envisioned. There are still account conflict problems. And how is the integration of these agency brands working? Do clients really prefer one-stop shopping? Some of the holding companies are selling integrated services to a number of clients successfully.[15]

Mega-agency holding companies have huge networks of their agencies and support companies around the world to serve clients. The modern version of the mega-agency holding company started in 1986 when a small London agency, Saatchi & Saatchi PLC, systematically grew over a 2-year period to become a mega-agency network with capitalized billings of more than $13.5 billion. Not a bad growth pattern. As a result, it became the world's largest advertising organization for a brief period and truly changed global advertising. Today, the largest organizations are Dentsu (Tokyo), WWP Group (London), Omnicom Group (New York), and Publicis Groupe (Paris). These and other mega-agency organizations own many advertising agencies and marketing service companies throughout the world. Some of the holdings of the Omnicom Group, founded in 1986, are listed in the Advantage Point on page 182.

ADVANTAGE POINT

Omnicom Group

Founded in 1986, Omnicom Group is a strategic holding company that manages a portfolio of global market leaders. Omnicom companies operate in the disciplines of advertising, marketing services, specialty communications, interactive/digital media, and media buying services. Omnicom Group includes:

Omnicom's Three Global Advertising Brands

BBDO Worldwide, New York

DDB Worldwide, New York

TBWA Worldwide, New York

Leading U.S.-Based National Advertising Agencies

Arnell Group, New York

Element 79 Partners, Chicago

Goodby, Silverstein & Partners, San Francisco

GSD&M, Austin

Martin|Williams, Minneapolis

Merkley Newman Harty|Partners, New York

Zimmerman Partners, Fort Lauderdale

Omnicom Media Group (OMG)

- *OMD Worldwide.* This is one of the largest media communications companies in the world. It was initially formed out of the media departments of three of Omnicom's global advertising agencies: BBDO, DDB, and TBWA. OMD is headquartered in New York, with more than 140 offices in eighty countries.
- *PHD Network.* This London-based media firm has long been a leading media services company in the United Kingdom and North America that is widely recognized for its pioneering and innovative work for clients.
- *Prometheus Media Services.* This firm was spun off of OMD in 2005 and has quickly become a market leader with strength in ROI and accountable media. Headquartered in Chicago, Prometheus also has offices in New York and London.

Diversified Agency Services (DAS)

DAS consists of a global enterprise of more than 160 companies, which operate through more than 700 offices in seventy-one countries. They provide marketing services in direct marketing/consultancy, public relations, promotional marketing, and specialty communications. DAS companies operate through a combination of networks and regional organizations. They serve international and local clients. A few examples follow:

- *Public Relations/Public Affairs* DAS includes three of the top seven public relations firms in the world—Fleishman-Hillard, Ketchum, and Porter Novelli—as well as specialist agencies including Brodeur Worldwide, Clark & Weinstock, Gavin Anderson & Company, and Cone.
- *Specialty Communications* DAS has built an influential global health-care franchise, of which six health-care communications companies are ranked in the top twenty-five. DAS also includes Bernard Hodes Group and the premier business, corporate, and financial advertising agency, Doremus.

Following are some other business categories and Omincom brands that serve them:

Customer Relationship Management

Branding/Consultants/Design

AvreaFoster

Design Forum

Hall & Partners

Hornall Anderson Design Works

Interbrand

Direct Marketing/Relationship Marketing

Direct Partners

FSA Communications

Rapp Collins Worldwide

Targetbase

Entertainment, Event & Sports Marketing

AWE

Davie Brown Entertainment

Horrow Sports Ventures

Kaleidoscope

Radiate Sports & Entertainment Group

Serino Coyne Inc.

Field/Channel Marketing

CPM

Creative Channel Services

National In-Store

U.S. Marketing & Promotions

Interactive Services

AGENCY.COM

Critical Mass

EVB

Organic

Nonprofit Marketing

Changing Our World

Grizzard Communications Group

Promotional Marketing

Alcone Marketing Group

TIC TOC

TracyLocke

Retail Marketing

Gotocustomer Services

Research

M/A/R/C Research

Point Of Sale/Merchandising

Integrated Merchandising Systems

Source: © Omnicom Group, Inc., 2007. ■ ■ ■

Mega agencies claim several advantages to their clients other than sheer size. Among the most important are a greater reservoir of talent and an ability to shift portions of accounts from one agency to another without going through the time-consuming, and often confusing, agency review. (Several Omnicom clients switched brand assignments from one of their national agencies to another, keeping the business in the family.) There are also some disadvantages for clients, the most important of which is conflicts with competing accounts.

Size, in itself, doesn't have significant advantages or disadvantages in developing the advertisments themselves. All agencies—large or small—consist of small units or teams that work on an assigned account or group of accounts. The ability of the team and the dedication to creative and professional excellence are dictated by the talent and innovative abilities of individuals, not the size of their company. Obviously, size and structure of an agency will attract or repel clients, depending on what level and quality of services they are seeking. The agency business is simply mirroring business in general by diversifying, economizing, and becoming more efficient and profitable.

Publicis Groupe Chairman-CEO Maurice Levy recently changed the holding-company-as-superagency model to give its agency networks a distinct identity. "Each has its own individual character that is not artificial," he said. Mr. Levy described the Leo Burnett network as the agency strongly associated to heartland American brands such as McDonald's Corp. and the U.S. Army, whereas Saatchi has an edgier British origin and is known as an ideas company. Publicis is differentiated by its French origin and strong integrated approach to communication.[16]

Despite using agency holding companies, not all advertisers think they are perfect partners. Executives have complained that agency holding companies are "flabby" organizations that have become "more revenue models than consumer-solution models."[17]

OTHER ADVERTISING SERVICES

New services are continually springing up in competition with advertising agencies. Each new service is designed to serve clients' needs a little differently. This competition has impacted agency structure and operations. Today, we're seeing a lot of innovation related to gaming, mobile, and Interactive services.

Talent and Production Agencies Creating Creative

A relatively new resource for clients is the melding of talent sources to develop advertising concepts. Creative Artists Agency (CAA), a production and talent agency involving entertainment stars, writers, directors, and others, made inroads with Coca-Cola in 1991 as a working partner with Coca-Cola's advertising agencies, in some cases independently developing advertising concepts and commercials. A number of other talent agencies have had working agreements with marketers and their advertising agencies to provide creative and talent services. Later, Coca-Cola returned the creative duties primarily to a new agency. CAA restructured and is responsible for bringing Coca-Cola and Fox network together with the producer of *American Idol*. As a result, the soft drink got aboard the show's first season. "The receptivity to *American Idol* was far more overwhelming than we expected," said David Raines, vice president of integrated communications at Coca-Cola. "It facilitated social connection, access to behind-the-scenes. It was fun, relevant and somewhat organic—it didn't feel forced. It provided branded experience rather than brand exposure."[18] Some industry insiders believe such talent agency relationships can add another dimension to the advertising agency and client resources.

Agency-holding company WPP's Mediaedge bought a stake in The Leverage Group, an entertainment company. Omnicom Group bought Davie Brown entertainment consultancy, and other agency-holding companies are including more Hollywood assets to offer clients.

Independent Creative Services

Some advertisers seek top creative talent on a freelance, per-job basis. Many creative people do freelance work in their off hours. Some make it a full-time job and open their own creative shop or creative boutique. In general, the creative boutique has no media department, no researchers, and no account executives. Its purpose is strictly to develop creative ideas for its clients.

À La Carte Agency

There are agencies that offer for a fee just the part of their services that advertisers want. The à la carte arrangement is used mostly for creative services and for media planning and placement. Many agencies have spun off their media departments into independent divisions to seek clients interested only in media handling. Handling only the media portion of an account typically brings commissions that range from 3 to 5 percent.

In-House Agency

When advertisers found that all the services an agency could offer could be purchased on a piecemeal basis, they began setting up their own internal agencies, referred to as *in-house agencies*. The **in-house agency** can employ a creative service to originate advertising for a fee or markup. It can buy the space or time itself or employ a media-buying service to buy time or space and place the advertisements. As a rule, the in-house agency is an administrative center that gathers and directs varying outside services for its operation and has a minimum staff.

Folks, Inc., an Atlanta restaurant company, had an agency. Then it created an in-house agency, which developed all creative concepts, copy, layout ideas, radio scripts, and so forth. It primarily used art studios and graphic design services to produce the finished art and used broadcast production companies for its broadcasts. It brought all print media in-house and used a media-buying service to place its broadcast buys. It also developed all direct mail, store marketing, public relations, and promotion. Later, it found a need for strategic marketing services and hired Cole Henderson & Drake advertising to assist in strategic development for one of its restaurant concepts. The agency then created advertisements, produced advertising, and bought media. When the agency contract expired, the company turned to its former marketing director Sheri Bevil, now CEO of Lane Bevil+Partners, for its marketing communication. Exhibit 5.9 is a promotional advertisement for Folks Southern Kitchen.

When Tom Lentz came to head Broyhill Furniture's marketing, he soon found that this account wasn't big enough to demand major attention from larger national agencies, and the turnover of personnel in small- to medium-size agencies often made it difficult to work with knowledgeable people. He constantly had to educate account people about the furniture business. Broyhill solved its problem by building a strong in-house agency (see Exhibit 5.10). In-house agencies are generally created to save money or give advertisers more control over every aspect of their business. Many industrial companies have highly technical products that constantly undergo technological changes and advances; it may well be more efficient to have in-house technical people prepare advertisements. When the companies place their advertisements, they use their in-house agency or a media-buying service.

Rolodex Agency

An agency run by several advertising specialists, usually account and/or creative people, that has no basic staff is called a *Rolodex agency*. It hires specialists—in marketing, media planning, creative strategy, writing, and art direction, for example—who work on a project basis. The concept is similar to hiring freelance creative people to execute advertisements, except that the experts are hired as needed. The Rolodex agency claims to be able to give advertisers expertise that small full-service agencies cannot match.

in-house agency
An arrangement whereby the advertiser handles the total agency function by buying individually, on a fee basis, the needed services (for example, creative, media services, and placement) under the direction of an assigned advertising director.

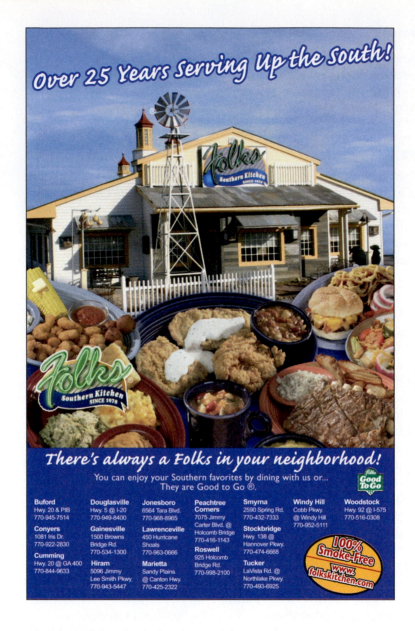

Media-Buying Services

There have been major changes in how advertisers handle their media since the mid-1990s. As all the new media developed, everyone had to be more creative in developing plans to meet the consumer's changing media habits. Some major advertisers chose to unbundle media or give their media buys to independent media-buying services or new media agencies to try to gain buying efficiencies. At the same time, some agencies reinvented their media operations to remain competitive with the growing number of media-buying services and to develop their media operations as a stand-alone profit center.

Many of the large agencies have made their media services independent of other agency services to better compete. Remember, for example, Omnicom's major national agencies BBDO, DDB, and TBWA. Each of these had its own media-planning and buying department for its clients. The holding company, Omnicom, pulled together the media departments into a single, more-efficient, separate company called Omnicom Media Group (OMD is one of the Media Services Agencies). Being huge, it has more negotiating clout and resources.

JWT and Ogilvy, two global agencies owned by the same parent WPP, followed the trend of creating joint media alliances and formed MindShare, a mega-media

EXHIBIT 5.10
This was created by Broyhill's in-house agency.
Courtesy of Broyhill Furniture Industries.

planning and buying agency to serve advertisers better. Both the Omnicom Media agency and WPP's media agency are free to seek clients that want to consolidate their media regardless of who handles their creative. "It is simply big business."

In order to be more efficient and deal with this new terrain, many agencies are spinning off their media departments into separate profit centers. However, there is now talk among some agencies of rebundling media back within the agency. Some executives are concerned that media and creative aren't working together efficiently as separate companies. Remember, we said everyone is reinventing themselves to better serve client needs.

The original reasons for creating separate media companies included the following: media agencies are stronger, with better resources to explore new areas within media; second, the fragmentation of target audiences and media vehicles has made media more important than ever before; third, a media company has the potential to be a major profit center. If the agency loses the creative responsibilities of a client, the media agency could continue serving the client because it is separate. Finally, the reciprocal action allows media agencies to acquire accounts that work with other parent agencies for their creative work.[19] One of the reasons for the consolidation is the fact that mega-advertisers have consolidated their multiple accounts to obtain better rates in their media buying.

Coca-Cola, as in the case of many large corporations, shifted its U.S. media planning and buying to a single media agency. Coca-Cola's domestic media buying and planning had been handled previously by Universal McCann and Starcom MediaVest. The accounts were worth about $350 million. Coca-Cola said the changes were spurred by an ongoing integration of Coca-Cola's three big North American units: Coca-Cola North America, Coca-Cola Fountain, and Minute Maid. Keep in mind that many smaller agencies still have their media departments within the agency walls.

In-House Media Services

A few large advertisers have taken the media-buying function in-house so they will have more control over the buying operation. It is more likely that advertisers will keep a seasoned media consultant on staff to ride herd on their agency or media service's performance.

FORMS OF AGENCY COMPENSATION

Historically, agency compensation has been fairly standardized since the 1930s. An agency received a commission from the media for advertising placed by the agency. The commission would cover the agency's copywriting and account services charges. This method of compensation has been unsatisfactory during recent years due to the changing nature of business. The straight 15 percent remains in theory, but in most instances there are fixed commissions less than 15 percent (most large advertisers have negotiated a rate closer to 10 percent), sliding scales based on client expenditures, flat-fee arrangements agreed on by clients and agency, performance-based systems, and labor-based fee-plus-profit arrangements. Crispin Porter+Bogusky negotiated stock from clients in return for work. In other words, compensation arrangements now take many forms. Despite this change, there are only two basic forms of advertising agency compensation: commissions and fees.

- *Media commissions.* The traditional 15 percent commission remains a form of agency income, especially for modestly budgeted accounts. Clients and agency may agree to a relationship in which the rate is fixed at less than 15 percent. This generally applies to large-budget accounts—the larger the budget, the lower the rate for the agency. With a sliding-scale commission agreement, the agency receives a fixed commission based on a certain expenditure. After that level of spending, the commission is reduced (there may be a 14 percent commission for the first $20 million spent by the client and a 7 percent commission on the next $15 million). Media payment is complicated by the independent media agency arrangements, but most of these negotiated contracts are similar to the foregoing. The combinations are endless.

- *Production commissions or markups.* As indicated earlier, agencies subcontract production work (all outside purchases such as type, photography, or illustrators) and charge the client the cost plus a commission—17.65 percent is the norm (see Exhibit 5.11). The RainDrop Man collector's edition twelve-page promotion comic was created by the McRae Communications agency, not an outside firm.

- *Fee arrangements.* At times, the 15 percent commission is not enough for agencies to make a fair profit. For example, it may cost an agency more to serve a small client than a large one. The agency and client may negotiate a fee arrangement. In some cases, it is a commission plus a fee. There are a number of options: A cost-based fee includes the agency's cost for servicing the account plus a markup; a cost-plus fee covers the agency cost and a fixed profit; a fixed fee is an agreed-upon payment based on the type of work being done (for example, copywriting at hourly fixed rates, artwork charges based on the salary of the involved personnel); and a sliding fee is based on a number of agreed-

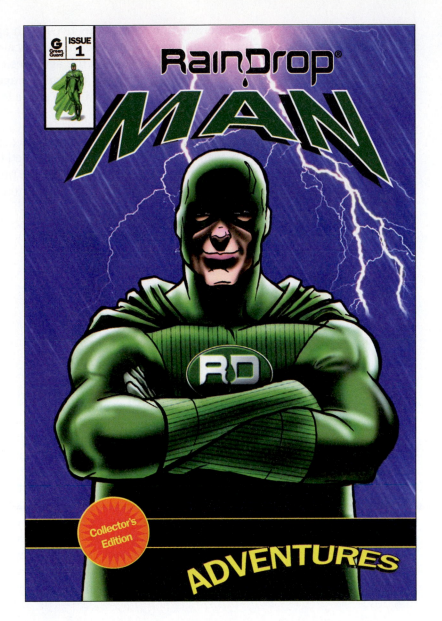

EXHIBIT 5.11

This unique housewrap product was promoted with a twelve-page comic.

Courtesy of McRae Communication.

upon parameters. Again, there are many possibilities based on agency and client needs.

■ *Performance fees.* A predetermined performance goal may determine the compensation fee. For example, advertisingt-recall scores, unit sales, or market share may determine the level of compensation. If the agency meets the goals, compensation may be at the 15 percent level; if it exceeds them, a bonus could give the agency a 20 percent level. If it fails to meet the goals, compensation could be much less than 15 percent.

In 2002, the American Association of Advertising Agencies and the Association of National Advertisers, Inc., released a joint position paper outlining a set of guidelines covering compensation agreements between agencies and advertisers. The Guidelines for Effective Advertiser/Agency Compensation Agreements is divided into two sections: "Guiding Principles" and "Best and Worst Practices."

Many marketers have replaced the traditional commission system of paying media commissions with performance-based compensation. Agency payments are calculated on predetermined, measurable goals like growth in sales, increasing awareness of a brand, or gaining broad distribution for a new product. In some agreements, compensation is determined by sales objectives, with agencies being paid more if a brand's sales increase and less if sales decline. All Coca-Cola agencies are on fees plus bonuses. This payment system allows the agencies not to worry if Coca-Cola cuts its advertising budget; it is designed to give the agency the best return on investment it can get. An example of a commission plus a fee is described in the following agency contract copy:

> Internal creative services provided by [agency] shall be applied against the monthly agency fee at the prevailing hourly rates [as distinguished from services bought outside our organization]. Such services include preparation of print, radio, television production, storyboards, special comprehensive layouts, booklets, catalogues, direct mail, sales representations, extraordinary research, package design, collateral materials, etc.

Agency Function	Hourly Rates
Creative director	$175
Copywriter	120
Art director	120
Production supervisor	95
Computer design	150
Type and composition	130
Computer artwork	130
Research/planning	130

Most agencies aim for a 20 percent profit on each account to cover personnel and overhead costs plus a profit. The president of Campbell Mithun Esty says, "There's a broad acceptance among clients that it's in their best interest that their account be profitable for their agency. The smarter client understands that's what gets it the best people on their account. That's what gets it the best service."[20]

An advertising management consultant suggests that the key flaw of compensation based on the price of traditional media is the lack of a consistent relationship between income generated and the cost of providing services required by the clients. This will continue to be a problem as new media techniques are developed. He suggests that agencies align their compensation with their roles as salespeople, not buyers of media, and link agency profit goals to agreed-upon performance standards.[21]

OTHER SERVICES

Barter

barter
Acquisition of broadcast time by an advertiser or an agency in exchange for operating capital or merchandise. No cash is involved.

One way for an advertiser or agency to buy media below the rate card price, especially in radio or television, is **barter**. Some agency-holding companies own barter companies as part of their integrated offerings to clients. The Atlanta Convention and Visitors Bureau (ACVB) bartered for commercial time from television and broadcast stations to advertise the city's accommodations, restaurants, and attractions. Its agency offered hotel rooms, tickets to local attractions, and meals at Atlanta area restaurants. The ACVB was able to turn a $165,000 budget into $1.5 million in promotions. A typical prize would be a 3-day trip to Atlanta for a family of four with tickets to four attractions; according to Bill Howard of the ACVB, more than 900 packages were offered in exchange for airtime.[22]

Barter houses often become brokers or wholesalers of broadcast time. They build inventories of time accumulated in various barter deals. These inventories are called *time banks,* which are made available to advertisers or agencies seeking to stretch their broadcast dollars.

One of the drawbacks of barter is that the weaker stations in a market are more apt to use it the most. Some stations will not accept barter business from advertisers already on the air in the market. Generally, the airtime is poor time, although it is generally a good value at the low rate paid.

Research Services

The advertiser, the agency, or an independent research firm can conduct any needed original research. Large agencies may have substantial in-house research departments. In some, the research title has been replaced by the account planner. Account planning has a crucial role during strategy development, driving it from the consumer's point of view. The account planners are responsible for all research, including quantitative research (usage and attitude studies, tracking studies, advertisement testing, and sales data) as well as qualitative research (talking face-to-face to their target). On the other hand, many smaller agencies offer little in-house research staffing, although many agencies have moved to add account planners.

In addition to the syndicated research previously discussed, which regularly reports the latest findings on buyers of a product—who and where they are; how they live and buy; and what media they read, watch, and listen to—these research companies offer many custom-made research reports to advertisers and their agencies, answering their questions about their own products and advertising. Studies cover such subjects as technology use, advertising effectiveness, advertising testing, customer satisfaction, concept and product testing, premium or package design testing, image and positioning, brand equity measurement, market segmentation, strategic research, media preferences, purchasing patterns, and similar problems affecting product and advertising decisions.

A fascinating variety of techniques is available to gather such information, including consumer field surveys (using personal or telephone interviews or self-administered questionnaires), focus groups, consumer panels, continuous tracking studies, cable testing of commercials, image studies, electronic questionnaires, opinion surveys, shopping center intercepts, and media-mix tests. (Research techniques are discussed in Chapter 15.) Regardless of the technique used in collecting data for a research report, its real value lies in the creative interpretation and use made of its findings.

Managing Integrated Brands

A brand needs a single architect, someone who will implement and coordinate a cohesive strategy across multiple media and markets. According to David Aaker, the advertising agency is often a strong candidate for this role.[23] It regularly develops brand strategy and gains insights due to exposure to different brand contexts. An advertising agency inherently provides a strong link between strategy and executions because both functions are housed under the same roof. Strategy development in an agency is more likely to include issues of implementation. On the downside, many agencies still have a bias toward media advertising, and their experience at managing event sponsorships, direct marketing, or interactive advertising may be limited.

The challenge for today's agency is to be able to develop an integrated program that accesses and employs a wide range of communication vehicles. There are several approaches to managing this.

Agency Conglomerate Many agencies have approached the integrated communication program by acquiring companies with complementary capabilities. The usual mix includes promotions, corporate design, Interactive, direct marketing, marketing research, package design, public relations, trade shows, and even event marketing. The hope is that advertisers will buy one-stop coordinated communications. The general consensus is that this approach doesn't work well because the units that make up the conglomerate often don't blend well with each other and are rivals for the advertiser's budget, and each unit within the conglomerate isn't necessarily best suited to solve the problem at hand.

Jason Kreher

Account Guy/Creative Guy, EURO RSCG MVBMS Partners/New York
How to Be an Account Person/How to Be a Creative Person

*Y*ou know the steps to *becoming* either an account person or a creative person, but what do you need to know once you get there? This simple primer gets to the core of the most important aspects of your new career in advertising.

Word Choice

Account: This is very easy. You need only use these crucial seven phrases: synergies, value-add, testing results, out-of-the-box, closing the loop, holistic branding, client POV. Mix and match! All you need are a few linking verbs and you're ready to go.

Creative: If you are a writer, remember this rule of thumb: Copywriting is a showcase for your vocabulary, nothing more. A good tip is to write copy, and then use the thesaurus on your computer to change every word to its longer, more cumbersome synonym. Remember to sigh dramatically when the account people ask you to change it back.

Note: If you are an art director, don't worry about words. Just pick the prettiest colors and stay within the lines.

Wardrobe

Account

- *Male:* Variety is the order of the day for the well-dressed account man. Make sure to have a colorful spectrum of oxford button-ups, from off-white to bone to ecru and everything in between. Spice up your khaki collection with an occasional pleat. And never forget—the icon on your breast pocket makes the man. The little polo player or the tiny alligator? Choose carefully, young friends.
- *Female:* Break out the Banana Republic credit cards, ladies! Your all-black, business-casual attire should exude confidence, style, and a willingness to compromise everything you believe in for a single nod of approval from the client. And remember—the higher the heel on your shoe, the more respect you will command. It's that simple.

Creative: Be you male, female, or "curious," tight, ironic T-shirts are crucial in communicating your status on

Jason Kreher

the fringe of counterculture. "I'm no one's puppet," you'll say, adjusting your clunky, black-frame glasses and sporting your brand-new "Don't Mess with Texas" ringer tee from Urban Outfitters. Spend 20 minutes making sure your hair looks like it's never been combed.

Desk/Office

Account: Fill your workspace with pictures of your family and children. If you are not married or do not have children, how about several framed pictures of your dog? Yeah, that's not pathetic at all.

Creative: Ensure your desk is completely free of impediments to creativity like folders, paper clips or Post-it Notes. Cover its surface in a chaotic jumble of action figures, magic 8 balls, snow globes, liquor bottles, obscure French design magazines, and unopened "Final Notice" bills. This will help you be creative.

Note: Jason Kreher spent his first two years at EuroRSCG MVBMS Partners as an account executive on the Intel business and then subsequently transitioned to a junior copywriter position on brands such as Intel, Volvo, Evian, and New Balance. He is currently considering another switch and wants to become a high school principal. ■ ■ ■

In-House Generalist Agency Another option is to expand the agency's capabilities to include such functions as promotions and public relations. Brand teams spanning communication vehicles can then deal with the coordination issue. Hal Riney & Partners exemplified this approach with its set of promotional programs designed for Saturn. Riney was named guardian of the Saturn brand and created advertisements, promotions, and a website and even helped design a retail concept. This approach works if the agency has the talent to handle the new services or has the clients or revenues to support such a diverse staff.

Service Cluster A service-cluster team is a group of people drawn together from all the agency affiliate organizations. Strategically, the cluster's purpose is to service client needs, and the cluster has the flexibility to change with the needs of the client. A key characteristic of the service-cluster team is that it focuses on creating ideas rather than advertisements.

Communication Integrator In this approach, the agency draws from sources outside the agency and integrates these services for the brands.

Brand Strategy In-House

Many advertisers choose not to rely on the agency at all for managing brand strategy. Their view may be that agencies may be great at creating advertisements, but brand strategy may be better planned by the brand-management team. If outside help is needed, their view may be that the agency may not be the best source—particularly if it has limited research resources. Some clients have found it beneficial to employ a team of specialized communication firms, each of which is the best in what it does. The advertiser may develop specialized expertise—including research, media buying, and strategy consulting.

SUMMARY ✺

The advertising agency is in a period of transition. It is being reevaluated and reengineered to be more responsive to clients' needs.

A full-service agency works on many aspects of a client's marketing problems: strategy, creative response, media planning, and trade campaigns. Many agencies are organized into four divisions: account services, marketing services, creative services, and management and finance. Some agencies have a domestic network of offices or affiliates to service their large accounts better. The growing importance of global marketing to some clients has led agencies to expand internationally. Clients usually pay agencies by commission, fees, or a combination of the two.

Other types of advertising services beside the traditional advertising agency include in-house agencies, à la carte agencies, creative boutiques, Rolodex agencies, and media-buying services. Agencies usually cannot and will not handle two accounts that compete in the same market.

REVIEW ✺

1. What is a full-service agency?
2. Give an example of a global agency network.
3. What is an agency of record?

CHAPTER 6

The Advertiser's Marketing/ Advertising Operation

*T*oday, the changing world of new technology is challenging marketers and their companies. They are learning to navigate the nontraditional landscape where the consumer is basically in control, not marketers. That's right, consumers control how they consume media and marketing. As marketers understand these changes, their companies have restructured their marketing operations to be more competitive in an attempt to make all of their consumer communication efforts speak with one voice—and in many cases, communicating with consumers one-on-one. Here, we learn about some fundamentals about marketing structure in a time of change. After reading this chapter, you will understand:

chapter objectives

1. the marketing service system
2. integrated marketing brand management
3. how advertising budgets are set
4. advertising goals versus marketing goals
5. agency-client relationships

We've written and read about a lot of change—even used words like revolution. Yes, consumers are changing, but they have always been in evolution. What makes this so different is the shift of control to consumers—and the speed of media vehicles and degree of media fragmentation, which is discussed in detail in later chapters. "Research has demonstrated most people overestimate the speed of change in the marketplace and underestimate the significance of the changes taking place. Markets and consumer behavior don't change overnight, but over time these changes can be dramatic," says Ken Bernhardt, author and marketing professor.[1] What are the implications of these consumer and media changes? Simply put, it will be harder and harder to reach consumers with communication messages. Marketers are attempting to integrate these problems and opportunities into their advertising and marketing organizational structure. In simple terms, we must always remember that advertising is a business. It is a marketing tool used by companies to reach consumers. It has a structure and an organization and must be managed, just like any business. Advertising is a financial investment in the brand or company.

THE DIGITAL REVOLUTION IS MAINSTREAM

Major marketers and media have finally come to terms with this fact: The methods by which consumers absorb information and entertainment—the ways consumers perceive, retain, and engage with brands and brand messages—have changed. Marketing communication is being reborn as a consumer-centered craft. This is creating an in-house renovation for many companies. The Association of National Advertisers and consultant Booz Allen Hamilton found that nearly 70 percent of all companies have recently reorganized their marketing department. Companies need new expertise in digital technology, relationship marketing, and media innovation to supplement their traditional brand-management apparatus. Many believe they need to integrate their marketing system across a broader network of partners and media alternatives. To accomplish this, companies need to experiment with new advertising models and integrated media solutions and need to redefine skills and companies.[2]

There have been other pressures on companies as well. The past several decades brought major pressure to many corporations: downsizing; cost cutting; mergers; and partnerships, both domestic and foreign. Companies have restructured and reorganized divisions and departments. Because everyone wants to be efficient and competitive, these same pressures have affected the marketing and advertising operations. For example, a week after restructuring and eliminating almost four hundred corporate jobs, Wendy's again restructured its marketing group to better align departments and incorporate operations into the marketing unit. It merged the brand-management, media, and diversity-marketing teams, which earlier reported to the executive vice president–chief marketing officer, into a team led by the vice president–brand management. The company's press release indicated that "the move will facilitate greater alignment between media, message and creative as the company executes marketing initiatives."[3]

The advertising and marketing departments control the dollars and decide on the need for an advertising agency or, in some cases, multiple agencies for different products. At times, they may hire an agency to handle only creative or to place the advertisements in the media. They may choose to use freelancers or creative boutiques or to use a media-buying service or combine their media-buying strength for all their products with one agency. They may decide to staff an in-house agency to develop advertisements, as discussed in Chapter 5. It is their ball game. They call the shots.

Traditionally, all advertising functions are funneled through the advertising department, which is headed by an advertising manager or the director who operates under a marketing director. Broadly speaking, the advertising manager controls the entire advertising strategy and operation: budgeting, monitoring the creation and production of the advertising, research, planning the media schedule, and keeping expenditures in line. As the business grows and new lines of products are added, assistant advertising managers, usually known as product advertising *managers*, are appointed to handle the advertising for different brands of the company, working under the supervision of the advertising manager. Let's give you a little better perspective of the scope of brands to be managed by large marketers. Frito-Lay lists forty-five brands on its website, including Lay's Potato Chips, Smith's Crisps, Maui Style chips, Walker's potato chips, Grandma's brand cookies, Cracker Jack brand snacks, O'Kelly's Potato Skins, and Chester's corn snacks, in addition to the brands you normally associate with the company. In your spare time, take a look at the websites of Unilever (Knorr, Lipton, Dove, Pond's, etc.), Nestlé (Purina, Alpo, Stouffer's, Taster's Choice, Tidy Cats, etc.), and Kraft (Oreo, Jell-O, Maxwell House, Planters, Kool-Aid, Oscar Mayer, Breakstone's, Grape-Nuts, Chips Ahoy!, etc.) and look at the number of brands they market. In an effort to become more efficient, Procter & Gamble dismantled its Family and Health division in 2006, with brands moving to other divisions. They now operate three divisions: Beauty and Health, Household Care, and Gillette. Following is a sample list of products they sell, illustrating the complexity of their marketing.

P&G categories and representative product brands

Antiperspirants	Old Spice, Secret, Sure
Baby Care	Charmin, Children's Pepto, Dreft, Luvs, Pampers
Batteries	Duracell
Colognes	Old Spice
Cosmetics	CoverGirl, Max Factor
Dish Washing	Cascade, Dawn, Ivory, Joy
Feminine Care	Always, Tampax
Hair Care	Aussie, Head & Shoulders, Herbal Essences, Infusium 23, Pantene
Hair Color	Clairol
Health Care	Fibersure, Metamucil, Pepto-Bismol, Prilosec OTC, PUR, ThermaCare, Vicks
Household Cleaners	Bounty, Febreze Air Fresheners, Mr. Clean, Mr. Clean AutoDry Carwash, Swiffer
Laundry & Fabric Care	Bounce, Cheer, Downy, Dreft, Era, Febreze Air Fresheners, Gain, Ivory, Tide
Oral Care	Braun, Crest, Crest Glide Floss, Crest Whitestrips, Fixodent, Gleem, Scope, Oral-B
Paper Products	Bounty, Charmin, Puffs
Personal Cleansing	Camay, Clairol, Herbal Essences, Ivory, Noxzema, Olay, Old Spice, Safeguard, Zest
Pet Nutrition	Eukanuba, Iams
Prescription Drugs	Actonel, Asacol, Dantrium, Dantrium IV, Didronel, Macrobid, Macrodantin
Prestige Fragrances	Giorgio Beverly Hills, HUGO BOSS
Shaving	Braun, Gillette Fusion, Gillette M3Power, Gillette SatinCare, Gillette Venus
Snacks & Coffee	Folgers, Home Café, Millstone, Pringles
Special Fabric Care	Febreze

Obviously, it takes P&G a major effort to coordinate all the listed brands. Because companies vary in size and structure, it only makes sense that advertising and marketing staffs also differ from organization to organization. They may have a large department controlling all marketing activities, or they may have limited personnel in marketing, or they may rely on operation managers or the president to make the marketing decisions. Take The Coca-Cola Company, for example:

In 2005, The Coca-Cola Company named its first chief marketing officer (CMO), Mary Minnick, to manage all its brands.

More recently, it appointed a vice president–global marketing to coordinate and pull together the "Coke side of life" campaign in every market and across every channel. This global marketing position works with all of Coca-Cola's advertising and marketing agencies and will work on all Coca-Cola brands, overseeing the soft-drink giant's multibillion-dollar marketing budget.

EXHIBIT 6.1

Simple organization chart for advertising department.

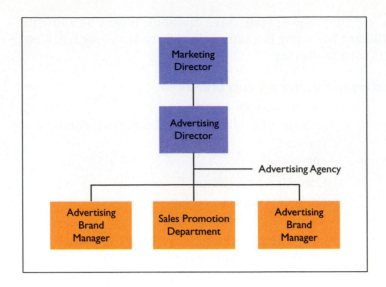

Companies are making changes to handle the changing consumer landscape and manage all the new technology options, especially large complex companies.

MARKETING SERVICES SYSTEM

With increasing structural and organizational changes in business, the results are being felt in the advertising and marketing function. The advertising department structure—the traditional system—worked well for most companies. Exhibit 6.1 illustrates this organizational structure. As companies such as Procter & Gamble grew with a multitude of brands, this structure needed to change.

Procter & Gamble (P&G) was founded by William Procter and James Gamble in 1837 as a maker of soap and candles. They formalize their business relationship by investing $3,596.47 apiece. Twenty-two years after the partnership was formed, P&G sales reached $1 million. P&G launched Tide in 1946 and won the American Dental Association's approval for Crest as an effective cavity fighter in 1960; Pampers, the first disposable diaper, was created in 1961. The first shampoo-conditioner was P&G's Pert Plus. P&G is known as a marketing innovator. It even invented the soap opera, a perfect consumer-sales vehicle. P&G has long been known as the world's finest marketing training ground. Remember that in Chapter 3 we talked about the pioneering and competitive stages. P&G is a master at marketing and product innovation. Recently, Tide Simple Pleasures, Gain Joyful Expressions, Febreze Noticeables, a variety of gadget Swiffer products, and Crest Pro Health toothpaste have been introduced.

In 1931, P&G developed a new organizational structure to solve its growing brands and marketing problems. The idea of brand management—setting up marketing teams for each brand and urging them to compete against each other—was the birth of the marketing services system. It became the model for handling brands. This concept has been widely adopted or modified, especially in the packaged goods fields and by a number of service-oriented companies. Under this concept, each brand manager is, in essence, president of his or her own corporation-within-the-corporation. The brand manager is charged with developing, manufacturing, marketing, promoting, integrating, and selling the brand.

The marketing services system has two parts (see Exhibit 6.2). One is the marketing activity, which begins with the **product manager** assigned to different brands. The other part is a structure of marketing services, which represents all the technical talent involved in implementing a marketing plan, including creative ser-

product manager
In package goods, the person responsible for the profitability of a product (brand) or product line, including advertising decisions. Also called a brand manager.

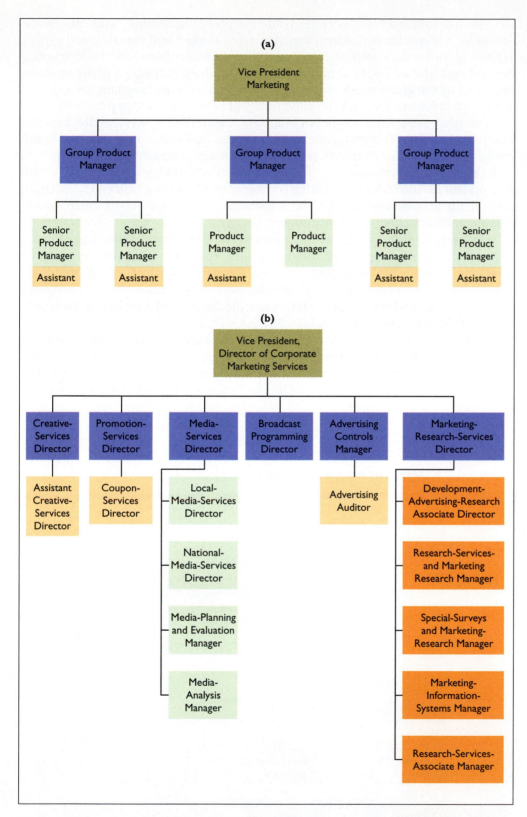

EXHIBIT 6.2

A large company with a marketing services division may be organized into (a) a marketing department; and (b) a marketing services department, where specialists in creative, media, and research advise product managers and consult with counterparts in the agency.

vices, promotion services, media services, advertising controls, and marketing research services. All of these services are available to the product manager, as is the help from the advertising agency assigned to that manager's brand. The product manager can bring together the agency personnel and his or her counterpart in the marketing services division, giving the company the benefit of the best thinking of both groups—internal and external. Each group has a group product manager who supervises the individual product managers.

The product manager is responsible for planning strategy and objectives, obtaining relevant brand information, managing budget and controls, and getting agency recommendations and is the primary liaison between the marketing department and all other departments. The product manager's plans must be approved by the group product manager, who then submits the plans for approval of the vice president for marketing and finally of the executive vice president.

The advertising department is a branch of the marketing services division. The vice president for advertising, responsible for the review and evaluation of brand media plans, attends all creative presentations to act as an adviser and consultant on all aspects of advertising. The vice president for advertising reports to the senior vice president, director of marketing (or the chief marketing officer, or CMO). In general, the average tenure of a CMO is less than 2 years, which isn't much time to create significant change or contribution.

Under this system, the advertising does not all come through one huge funnel, with one person in charge of all brands. The advantages to the corporation are that each brand gets the full marketing attention of its own group and that all brands get the full benefit of all the company's special marketing services and the accumulated corporate wisdom. The more important the decision, the higher up the ladder it goes for final approval (see Exhibit 6.3).

Large companies with many categories of products can have another layer of management called the **category manager**. All disciplines—research, manufacturing, engineering, sales, advertising, and so on—report to the category manager. The category manager follows the product line he or she is in charge of and decides how

category manager
A relatively new corporate position, this manager is responsible for all aspects of the brands in a specific product category for a company including research, manufacturing, sales, and advertising. Each product's advertising manager reports to the category manager. Example: Procter & Gamble's Tide and Cheer detergent advertising managers report to a single category manager.

EXHIBIT 6.3

The category manager is responsible for all aspects of the brands in his or her category. Each product's advertising manager reports to the category manager.

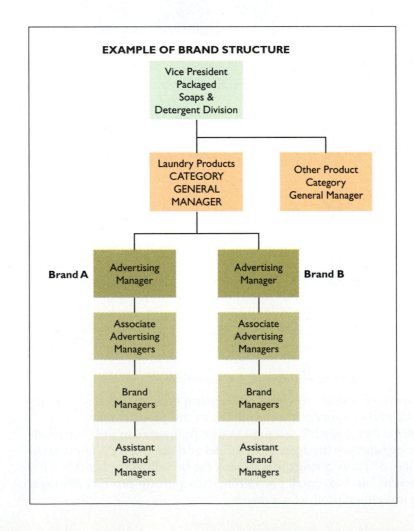

to coordinate each brand in that line. The category manager decides how to position brands in each category.

In 2003, Procter & Gamble restructured its 3,400 global marketers, restoring a level that had been eliminated a decade earlier. It reclassified about half of its global marketing directors to associate marketing directors. Brand managers report to either a marketing director or an associate director. Now senior brand managers who get promoted become associate directors instead of directors. These managers will stay in their position longer under the new system, giving them a broader experience with sales teams and research and development and other areas. Under the new system, a product's general manager is likely to remain in that position for 5 years. Brand managers' tenure in a position would be about 3 years, and assistant brand managers' jobs would last about 2 and 1/2 years. The P&G restructuring was an attempt to streamline the marketing organization.[4] A restructuring initiative, Organization 2005 & Beyond, was started in 1998 to accelerate the company's growth. It involved comprehensive changes in organizational structure, work processes, and culture to make employees stretch themselves and speed up innovation.

INTEGRATED MARKETING BRAND MANAGEMENT

Previously, we discussed integrated marketing, or one-voice marketing, from the agency perspective. There has been debate about whether agencies can effectively implement this concept because of their structure. One of the major problems is that agencies are set up as separate profit centers, which results in competition among their own units for a strong bottom-line showing.

Research involving marketing executives indicates that integration of advertising, promotion, public relations, and all other forms of marketing communications is the most important factor influencing how strategies will be set. Larry Light, the former chairman of the international division of Bates Worldwide, says, "The reason integrated marketing is important is consumers integrate your messages whether you like it or not. The messages cannot be kept separate. All marketing is integrated in the mind of consumers. Your only choice is how that message is integrated."[5]

An integrated marketing communication (IMC) study report found that "organizations are taking charge of the integration process themselves rather than looking to ad agencies or other suppliers to provide the integration."[6] Professor William Swain says, "While there is some agreement that corporations are better equipped than their agencies to oversee IMC, there is no universal agreement where within the organization IMC leadership does or should reside."[7] Most companies generally agree that traditional advertising agencies are not staffed or organized to efficiently manage integrated thinking. Another reason that agencies fail to properly provide integrated marketing services is that they primarily concern themselves with communicating to the end customer/consumer. They often omit nonadvertising marketing tactics (sales/training materials, incentive programs, etc.).

Integrated Functions

Integrated marketing communication can function in the marketing services system if there is management of this process among all the departments involved—advertising, sales promotion, public relations, and other existing departments. Some organizations call the process *integrated brand communication* (IBC). Radical organizational changes don't seem to work well with regard to implementation. Many organizations have found that integrated functions become evolutionary. However, there are marketers who feel that this kind of management isn't practical because the resistance to change by managers is just too great. Don Schultz, author of *Integrated Marketing Communications*, suggests that reengineering the communications function and structure within the company is sometimes necessary. He suggests the following functions:[8]

1. Start with the customer or prospect and work back toward the brand or organization. That's the outside-in approach. Most organizations are structured to deliver inside-out communications, which allows the budget cycle to dictate when communications can be delivered.

2. Good communications require knowledge of customers and prospects. Without specific customer information, the marketing organization will continue to send out the wrong message and information to the wrong people at the wrong time at an exorbitant cost.

3. A database is critical to carry out the IMC task.

4. Brand contacts—all the ways the customer comes in contact with the organization—are the proper way to think about communications programs. This goes beyond traditional media. It includes managing the impact and influence of packaging, employees, in-store displays, sales literature, and even the design of the product so that the brand clearly or concisely communicates with the right person, at the right time, in the right way, with the right message or incentive through the right delivery channel.

There are three forms of adaptation to integrated marketing within corporate structures:[9]

■ *Marcom (marketing communications) manager.* Adapting a business-to-business organizational structure called marcom management centralizes all the communication activities under one person or office (see Exhibit 6.4). Under this structure, all communication is centralized. Product managers request communication programs for their products through a marcom manager. The manager develops the strategy and then directs the communication programs either internally or externally.

■ *Restructured brand-management approach.* This approach reduces the layers previously involved in the process. All sales and marketing activities for the brand, category, or organization are reduced to three groups, all reporting to the CEO, and all are on the same organizational level. They are marketing services/communications (MSC), marketing operations, and sales. Marketing operations is responsible for

EXHIBIT 6.4

Marcom management centralizes all the communication activities under one person or office.

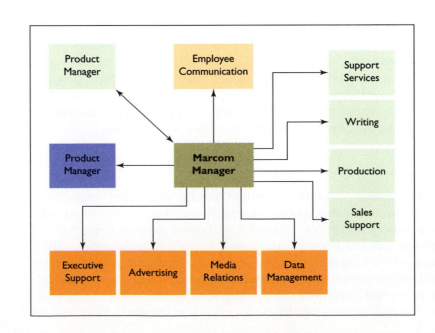

developing and delivering the product to MSC, which works with sales to develop and implement all sales and marketing programs (including advertising).

■ *Communications manager.* This approach names a communications manager who is responsible for approving or coordinating all communications programs for the entire organization. The various brands develop their own communications programs, as they have traditionally done. These plans go to the communications manager, who is responsible for coordinating, consolidating, and integrating the programs, messages, and media for the organization (see Exhibit 6.5).

IMC Focus

Using IMC to coordinate all messages a company communicates through advertising, direct marketing, public relations, promotion, and so on helps to create a unified image and support relationship building with customers. The key, however, is to determine exactly what your IMC strategy should achieve.

One of the first steps is to identify the specific target (such as users or influencers) and understand what each needs from your IMC campaign. To sharpen the focus, concentrate on one or two goals to avoid stretching the strategy or budget. Three such possible goals are the following:[10]

■ *Build brand equity.* By using IMC to reinforce your brand's unique value and identity, you increase awareness and encourage stronger preference among customers and prospects. The business-to-business advertisements for Scotchgard, the stain protector, are aimed at the textile and garment industry, for example, stating that the product keeps apparel in good shape by adding stain-shedding qualities.

■ *Provide information.* Business customers need a lot of information. Differentiate products or features if applicable.

■ *Communicate differentiation/positioning.* What does the product stand for and how is it better than the competitors' products? IMC helps convey your most significant points. For instance, a UPS advertisement stressed the range of guaranteed "urgent delivery" choices. These choices differentiated it from its competition while positioning it as being able to meet virtually any deadline.

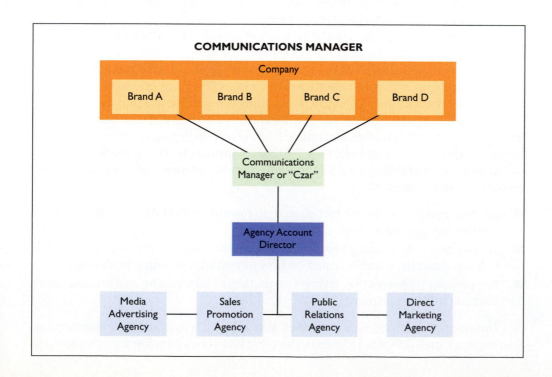

EXHIBIT 6.5

The communications manager approves or coordinates all communications programs for the entire organization.

Another View

Al Ries takes issue with the term *marcom*, saying, "The name encourages advertising people to go in the wrong direction. Advertising is not communication; advertising is positioning. What the best advertising does, however, is to establish and reinforce a position in the prospect's mind." That's the primary function of a marketing organization according to Ries. Of course, this thought is from one of the people who created the concept of positioning decades ago. He makes a point:[11]

> "Better ingredients, better pizza," says Papa John's.

> As a result of this positioning, Papa John's has become the third-largest pizza chain in America. Ries asks, "Do you know what the better ingredients are? Do you know that Papa John's uses fresh crushed tomatoes, real mozzarella cheese and distilled water in the preparation of its pizzas? Most people don't. Does it matter? Probably not. Better ingredients, better pizza is enough to position Papa John's a step above Pizza Hut and Domino's."

> Despite the structural quibbling among advertisers and agencies, in general, the concept of IMC itself has become a fundamental goal of most marketers and advertising agencies.

> Advertising agency TBWA also believed that integration is no longer enough to help companies compete. Its goal was not about taking one discipline and extending into other channels but about how to connect big ideas across all channels of communication.

Better Advertising Expenditure Expectations

John Wanamaker, founder of a department store in Philadelphia, is credited with saying decades ago, "I am certain that half the money I spend in advertising is wasted. The trouble is, I do not know which half." That uneasy sense of mystery has undergirded the growth of modern marketing according to consultants at Booz Allen Hamilton (who many times are in competition with advertising agencies). As a result, companies rely on imperfect metrics and anecdotes to guide their marketing programs to answer questions such as: What works best—sustained brand advertising or targeted retail promotion? Is likable media advertising a more effective vehicle than hard-sell direct marketing?

Companies can know how and where to apply marketing expenditures to achieve significant and lasting lifts in a product's or service's profitability. It is referred to as *return on investment (ROI) marketing*, which is the application of modern measurement technologies and contemporary organization design to understand, quantify, and optimize marketing spending. ROI marketing is not a fix but a philosophy.[12]

Recently, Briggs and Stuart studied some thirty *Fortune* 200 companies (including P&G, Johnson & Johnson, McDonald's, Unilever, Ford, etc.) to determine advertising effectiveness. They believe a "70/20/10 approach" could work in the new world order of marketing to guide marketers to better manage their investment resources. They suggest:[13]

- Seventy percent of the budget should go toward marketing strategies and tactics that are proven to work.
- Twenty percent should go for sustaining innovation—to provide a framework to force innovation and learning on how to optimize within a media type.
- Ten percent is speculative, trying new models of advertising and systematically learning from experiments.

Today, organizations view how they allocate and use marketing communication expenditures differently from in the past. Each tries to solve its interpretation of how to become more efficient and not waste half of its money, as Wanamaker (at the beginning of this section) was convinced was happening to his company.

SETTING THE BUDGET

Trying to get beyond Wanamaker's perception of what works and what doesn't, we generally agree that advertising is supposed to accomplish some objective. It is a business decision. The Folks advertisement (see Exhibit 6.6) is introducing the store into a new suburb and taking a little of the risk out of a consumer visit with a free appetizer. The store will be able to measure the effectiveness of the advertisement by the number of coupons redeemed. Advertisers expect a return for their investment despite the fact that they are totally different kinds of advertisers, each with a different reason for being.

What is an investment in an advertisement or campaign supposed to accomplish? Launch a new product? Increase a brand's awareness level? Neutralize the competition's advertising? Educate? Increase sales? A key question is, How much money will it take to accomplish the objective? Even if we have been successful with the product, do we know whether we are spending too much on advertising—or not enough? Despite all the technology available to help us to determine how much should be spent, the final decision is a judgment call by corporate management. Who the person is that is responsible for the budget decision varies across companies and according to objectives. Historically, the vice president of marketing and the vice president of advertising are the people most responsible for setting the advertising budget (see Exhibit 6.7). Two-thirds of advertising budgets are submitted for approval in September or October; almost 80 percent are approved during the period of September to November. As you might expect for such an important decision, most presidents or chief operating officers strongly influence the approval process.

Budgeting can be complex and may not be an exact science. Budgets are usually drawn up using one of four approaches: percentage of sales, payout plan, competitive budgeting, and the task method.

EXHIBIT 6.6

The opening of a new suburban store seeks to attract customers by making the product a strong value.

Courtesy of Lane Bevil+Partners and Folks.

Who Prepares Clients' Ad Budgets[a]		Who Approves Client's Ad Budgets[a]	
VP Marketing	63.2%	President or CEO	68.5%
VP Advertising	31.6	VP Marketing	37.3
Ad manager	22.2	Executive VP	20.9
Brand manager	16.3	Division manager	17.2
Ad agency	21.7	VP Advertising	14.4
Sales promotion	5.6	Treasurer or controller	8.6

[a]Totals more than 100% due to multiple responses.

Percentage of Sales

The percentage of sales method simply means the advertising budget is based on a percentage of the company's sales. For instance, a family restaurant chain might budget 5 percent of its sales for advertising. A company using this method to determine its advertising budget will not spend beyond its means because the advertising budget will increase only when sales increase. If sales decrease, so will the company's advertising; however, if competitive pressures are severe, the company may have to maintain or increase the budget to retain market share, even though there is no prospect of increased profit. This method can actually reverse the assumed cause-and-effect relationship between advertising and sales; that is, because the budgeting is based either on the previous year's sales—usually with some percentage of increase added—or next year's anticipated sales, then it can be said that the sales are causing the advertising rather than advertising causing the sales.

A Gallagher Report indicates that about 9 percent of companies surveyed take a percentage of last year's sales.[14] Roughly 35 percent use a percentage of anticipated sales, 30 percent combine needed tasks with a percentage of anticipated sales, 13 percent outline needed tasks and fund them, 13 percent set arbitrary amounts based on the general fiscal outlook of the company, and 9 percent calculate an average between last year's actual sales and anticipated sales for the coming year. In any method, a change in sales changes the amount of advertising expenditure.

A *BusinessWeek* study of start-up businesses' marketing budgets found that most followed the percentage-of-sales approach, devoting some percentage of their revenue to the marketing function. The amount they spent ranged from 1 percent on the low end to 12 percent or more on the high end. There's no magic to determining "how much," but there are rules of thumb. And you can find published norms for most industries. Determine whether the company will be margin-driven or volume-driven. Businesses such as supermarkets and hospitals are volume-driven and spend a very small percentage of sales on marketing because their sales are high and their margins are low. They may spend between 1 percent and 2 percent on marketing. By contrast, margin-driven companies like those in high tech and specialty retail have a smaller revenue base but more flexibility to build a higher percentage into their margins.[15]

Payout Plan

The payout plan looks at advertising as an investment rather than as an expenditure. It recognizes that it may take several years before the company can recover start-up costs and begin taking profits.

Exhibit 6.8 and Exhibit 6.9 are examples of typical payout plans. Let us go briefly through Exhibit 6.8, a payout plan for a new fast-food operation. In the first year of operation, the company spent the entire gross profits ($15,274,000) on advertising. In addition, the company invested $10,300,000 in store development for a first-year operating loss.

Systemwide Payout (Fiscal Years 1, 2, 3)

EXHIBIT **6.8**

New Fast-Food Company
Investment Payout Plan—
36-Month Payout

		Year 1		Year 2		Year 3
Sales		$84,854,000		$218,737,000		$356,248,000
Food cost	34%	28,850,000	34%	74,371,000	34%	121,124,000
Paper cost	5	4,245,000	5	10,937,000	5	17,812,000
Labor	22	18,668,000	20	43,747,000	20	71,250,000
Overhead	21	17,819,000	19	41,560,000	18	64,125,000
Total op. exp.	82	69,580,000	78	170,615,000	77	274,511,000
Gross profit	18	15,274,000	22	48,122,000	25	81,937,000
Advertising/Promo		$15,274,000		$48,122,000	13	$46,312,000
Store profit		0		0	10	35,625,000
Corp. invest.		10,300,000		0		0
Corp. profit		(10,300,000)		0		35,625,000
Cumulative		(10,300,000)		(10,300,000)		25,625,000

Investment Introduction—36 Month Payout

EXHIBIT **6.9**

Example of Package-Goods
Product-Payout Plan

	Year 1	Year 2	Year 3	3-Year Total	Year 4
Size of market (MM cases)	8	10	11		12
Share goal:					
Average	12%	25%	30%		30%
Year end	20	30	30		30
Consumer movement (MM Cases)	1.0	2.5	3.3	6.8	3.6
Pipeline (MM Cases)	.3	.2	.1	.6	—
Total shipments (MM Cases)	1.3	2.7	3.4	7.4	3.6
Factory income (@ $9)	$11.7	$24.3	$30.6	$66.6	$32.4
Less costs (@ $5)	6.5	13.5	17.0	37.0	18.0
Available P/A (@ $4)	$5.2	$10.8	$13.6	$29.6	$14.4
Spending (normal $2)	$12.8	$10.0	$6.8	$29.6	$7.2
Advertising	10.5	8.5	5.4	24.4	5.7
Promotion	2.3	1.5	1.4	5.2	1.5
Profit (Loss):					
Annual	($7.6)	$0.8	$6.8	—	$7.2
Cumulative	($7.6)	($6.8)	—	—	$7.2

In the second year, the company again invested gross profits ($48,122,000) in advertising and carried over the $10,300,000 debt from the first year. By the third year, sales had increased to the point where advertising as a percentage of gross sales had dropped to 13 percent, or $46,312,000, leaving a profit of $35,625,000. After covering the first-year debt of $10,300,000, the payout was $25,625,000.

If the company had demanded a 10 percent profit in the first year (0.10 × $84,854,000 = $8,485,400), it would have had to curtail advertising drastically, reduce corporate store investment, or do some combination of both. In that case, the company would have made a profit the first year but risked future profits and perhaps its own long-term survival.

Competitive Budgeting

Another approach to budgeting is to base it on the competitive spending environment. In competitive budgeting, the level of spending relates to the percentage of sales and other factors: whether the advertiser is on the offensive or defensive, media strategies chosen (for example, desire to dominate a medium), or answers to questions such as, Is it a new brand or an existing one? The problem here is that

ADVANTAGE POINT

Company Operating Philosophy and Profile
Chick-fil-A

Atlanta-based Chick-fil-A®, founded by entrepreneur and restaurateur S. Truett Cathy, has risen from rather humble beginnings to become America's second-largest quick-service chicken restaurant chain in the country.

Background

Cathy started in 1946 in the Atlanta suburb of Hapeville with a single location he named the Dwarf Grill. Cathy now presides over a chain of some 1,300 restaurants in thirty-seven states and Washington, D.C., generating annual sales of more than $2 billion.

The Chick-fil-A brand owes its success to three key factors:

- *Great food, consistently prepared.* Chick-fil-A uses only natural, all-white chicken breast meat, often considered the best part of the chicken. The signature Chick-fil-A sandwich is seasoned and breaded using a recipe that Cathy created in the early 1960s for his Dwarf House customers. Much as Cathy prepared his own menu items by hand, team members at Chick-fil-A restaurants across the country still bread chicken breasts by hand, squeeze lemons for Chick-fil-A lemonade, and hand-spin their milkshakes.

- *Adherence to sound, proven business principles.* Truett Cathy based his business on hard work, providing great food fast with a service-driven attitude that had customers returning as much for the hospitality as for the great food. As a chain, Chick-fil-A adheres to the basic biblical principles of fairness, honesty, and treating others how you would like to be treated. For example, every Chick-fil-A restaurant is closed on Sunday, allowing employees to spend time with friends and family and to worship if they choose. Other more secular business principles also have driven success at Chick-fil-A. For example, Chick-fil-A's franchise agreement with its restaurant Owner-Operators is unique to the industry. For a relatively small commitment fee, their unique Operator Agreement provides franchisees with an opportunity to sublease a Chick-fil-A chain restaurant, each month paying 15 percent of gross sales and 50 percent of net profits to Chick-fil-A, Inc., as a franchise fee. This profit-sharing system ensures that each Operator has the incentive to succeed—and Operators' success translates into success for the chain and the brand.

- *The creation and marketing of a memorable brand.* As the man who introduced the chicken sandwich to the quick-service industry, Cathy was determined to give his product (and later the chain that would bear his name) a meaningful—and memorable—name. The name "Chick-fil-A" was derived from the part of the chicken it was derived from: the breast fillet. Determined to give the name additional flair, Cathy added the "A" at the end, to reinforce top quality ("A-grade"). After the launch of the Chick-fil-A chain in 1967, the brand grew one restaurant at a time and one market at a time. Marketing efforts were public-relations-driven and locally focused, allowing restaurant franchisees (called Operators) and their employees—not to mention the food—to be the stars. As the brand grew beyond the southeastern and Sun Belt states in its bid to be a truly national brand, Chick-fil-A began to branch out, utilizing more aggressive marketing strategies, including event sponsorship, sports marketing, and advertising to supplement local initiatives. Most notable among these new marketing strategies—and the biggest contribution to the development of the Chick-fil-A brand next to Cathy himself—is the creation in 1995 of the chain's Eat Mor Chikin® Cow campaign.

History

Chick-fil-A did not actually start off as a restaurant chain; rather, it started as a simple chicken sandwich. Tinkering with a recipe for a boneless breast of chicken sandwich at his original Dwarf House restaurant, Cathy quickly realized he created a hit, as sales for the new chicken sandwich quickly began to outsell hamburgers (the former top seller). In 1963, Cathy decided to trademark his signature sandwich, branding it the "Chick-fil-A" sandwich.

In 1967, the first Chick-fil-A restaurant—a modest, 384-square-foot unit—opened in Atlanta's Greenbriar Shopping Center, the South's first enclosed shopping mall. Although small in stature, the restaurant represented a huge leap for the quick-service industry: the concept of mall-based dining (later to evolve into the modern food courts found in most malls today). At that time, mall managers were reluctant to allow dining concepts out of concerns about smoke and fumes. In addition to providing assurances about the impact on the mall's air quality, he stressed the potential economic impact of keeping mall shoppers in the mall during peak shopping times rather than losing them to nearby restaurants. With this sales pitch, Chick-fil-A quickly became synonymous with malls across America.

Over the next four decades, the physical aspects of the Chick-fil-A chain—number of locations, restaurant types, geographic reach, menu items, and the sheer size of the organization—continued to evolve. The 1970s saw the expansion of the Chick-fil-A concept throughout Georgia and into neighboring states (including North Carolina, Florida, South Carolina, and Texas). In 1986, the chain developed its first stand-alone Chick-fil-A restaurant. In 1996, Chick-fil-A introduced Truett's Grill—a 1950s diner-themed restaurant featuring retro décor and counter, table and drive-thru service—to commemorate Cathy's fifty years in the business. During that same period, the chain established its licensing program to enable food-service partners to operate Chick-fil-A restaurants in settings such as college campuses, hospitals, airports, and business and industry locations. Since 2000, the chain has concentrated on geographical expansion, moving into key regions in the Northeast and Midwest and on the West Coast.

Anchored by the signature Chick-fil-A Chicken Sandwich, the menu has maintained its focus on chicken as the anchor menu item, but the chain continues to develop new menu items and expand its menu offerings to appeal to its increasingly diverse customer base.

In Chapter 22, you'll see Chick-fil-A's marketing strategy and famous Cows advertising and integrated marketing examples. ■ ■ ■

competition dictates the spending allocation (and competing companies may have different marketing objectives). For example, one of Detroit's carmakers based its television budget solely upon what its competition was spending. As it turned out, the competitor was doing the exact same thing. Both were using bad logic as to any ROI.

The Task Method

The task method of budgeting is possibly the most difficult to implement, but it may also be the most logical budgeting method. The method calls for marketing and advertising managers to determine what task or objective the advertising will fulfill over the budgetary period and then calls for a determination of how much money will be needed to complete the task. Under this method, the company sets a specific sales target for a given time to attain a given goal. Then it decides to spend whatever money is necessary to meet that quota. The task method may be called the "let's spend all we can afford" approach, especially when launching a new product. Many big businesses today started that way. Many businesses that are not here today did too.

The approach can be complex. It involves several important considerations: brand loyalty factors, geographic factors, and product penetration. Advertisers who use this method need accurate and reliable research, experience, and models for setting goals and measuring results.

The task method is used most widely in a highly competitive environment. Budgets are under constant scrutiny in relation to sales and usually are formally reviewed every quarter. Moreover, they are subject to cancellation at any time (except for noncancelable commitments) because sales have not met a minimum quota, money is being shifted to a more promising brand, or management wants to hold back money to make a better showing on its next quarterly statement.

No one approach to budgeting is always best for all companies.

THE CHANGING MARKETING ENVIRONMENT

Marketers are in an irreversible restructuring in the way businesses operate—one that may require a major rethinking of the agency-client relationship in today's environment. The retail universe has consolidated, and the media universe has shattered. It is harder for an advertiser to reach mass numbers of consumers. In 1995, it took three television spots to reach 80 percent of the women in the United States. Five years later, it took ninety-seven spots to reach the same group. Some companies are calling for radical changes in the way they do business.

Coca-Cola is an American icon, yet it is slipping as consumers turn to coffees, juices, and teas—categories in which Coca-Cola has historically been weak. Recently, The Coca-Cola Company's new CMO Mary Minnick indicated that growth means more than simply boosting sales of Coca-Cola Classic. And innovation involves more than repackaging existing beverages in slightly different flavors. However, Coca-Cola did launch more than 1,000 new drinks or variations of existing brands worldwide in a year including the male-oriented diet drink Coca-Cola Zero and the coffee-flavored cola called Coca-Cola BlaK. Minnick is exploring new products in categories as far afield as beauty and health care. One of the first things she did as CMO was to fire Coca-Cola Classic's advertising agency.[16]

Companies, often using their advertising agencies, are creating their own movies, television shows, Internet sites, and online games, which they hope will be entertaining enough to endear viewers to the brands behind them.

Those marketers creating content haven't quit advertising. "We're continuing our traditional advertising—TV, radio, print, online—but we're adding content to that," said Vic Walia, the senior brand manager for Snickers, a Mars brand that created a mini television show called *Instant Def* that it posted online. "What we're trying to do is find new ways to continue to be relevant to teens and to young adults."[17] These views indicate that marketers are looking for new marketing and communication formulas. Today, the winning brand marketers are those learning to reconfigure their efforts in several ways:[18]

- Shift spending and management attention to digital media, and use those media to more effectively influence consumer purchase behavior.
- Develop formats to promote interactions with audiences, especially their most likely consumers.
- Create new research approaches and metrics that measure outcomes, not inputs.
- Combine "above-the-line" advertising (television, radio, and print) and "below-the-line" marketing (promotions, sponsorships, events, public relations) in new two-way, integrated campaigns.
- Create their own branded entertainment.
- "In-source" new skills and capabilities (new media, technology).

MANAGING BRANDS

Retailer Control

There is no doubt about who controls shelf space and entry into supermarkets, discounters, and mass merchandise stores today. It is the mass channel, not the mass media, that is demanding most of the marketing dollars. It is estimated that almost 60 percent of the manufacturers' marketing budgets goes to the retailer in the form of trade spending (advertisements in shoppers, displays, etc.). The anticipated adoption of product-tracking technology—radio frequency identification (RFID)—has the potential to allow manufacturers to track individual packages, not just stock keeping units; and some speculate that the technology might eventually give manufacturers more say about how and where their products are marketed. Says Peter Sealey, adjunct professor of marketing at the University of California at Berkeley, "I believe RFID will, unlike the Universal Product Code (UPC), shift power back to the manufacturer in some meaningful manner. The way we will know if this is happening will be the mix between advertising, consumer promotion, and trade incentives (now 25 percent, 25 percent, and 50 percent, respectively). Twenty years ago, the mix was 50 percent, 25 percent, and 25 percent. I believe the share of advertising will increase in the next five years, and if this happens, power will have shifted to manufacturers."[19] Today, the manufacturer is somewhat at the mercy of retailers like Wal-Mart, Target, Home Depot, Lowe's, Kohl's, Kroger, and others. Category managers must understand the needs of these retailers as well as they do the needs of consumers. They must be sure that their promotions are integrated into the retailer's total marketing program. Retailers like Wal-Mart favor strong consumer brands that are supported through consumer advertising.

Slotting Allowances

In a supermarket, every square foot costs money and needs to pay for itself by moving products and brands off the shelves quickly. There is only so much shelf space for the category manager to obtain from grocers. Slotting allowances began because manufacturers were creating more new products than the retailers' shelf space could accommodate, so to add a new product an old product had to be removed. Because grocers control the space, many charge slotting allowances for shelf space. This admission fee, which comes primarily from the marketer's trade promotion funds, ensures space for a period of about 3 to 6 months. Supermarkets use the slotting allowance to pay for slow-moving products and for administrative overhead for placing a new product into their system, including warehouse space, computer input, communications to individual stores about the product's availability, and the redesign of shelf space. The frozen-food section has only a finite amount of space and almost always demands slotting allowances. Fees are negotiated seperately for each item and can vary based on where in a store or on a shelf the new product is placed.

Message Experimentation

For 2007, marketers were spending 10 to 20 percent of their advertising budgets on what amounts to lab experiments as Briggs and Stuart suggested earlier in this chapter. They were trying to deal with new technologies and a fresh wave of creativity, which don't lend themselves to traditional interactive marketing. For example, in-game advertising is estimated to double each year until it reaches about $569 million by 2009; and casual games are simple and easy to learn and tend to be mainstream, older, more female, and highly engaged. Advertisers looking for technophiles are finding a home in Really Simple Syndication (RSS) feeds. Here, users subscribe to content from various sites, which is then "fed" to the users. OMD Digital's director says, "Clients are working to understand which media work, which platforms can scale, and which can achieve the objectives advertisers have in other media." He predicts that podcast advertising will be larger than blog advertising by 2010.[20]

Consumer Control: The Need to Manage Viral Technology

Neither corporations nor media control the communication revolution. At best, there is a dialogue. We'll take a shot at enriching your understanding of the implications to brands and the management of these new tools. Consumers talk on their blogs, podcasts, Moblogs, vBlogs (or vlogs) or chat rooms, and e-mails to friends about products and companies—the good and the bad, the truth and the lie. And, of course, there will always be something new—the digital and Internet communication devices and technologies will continue to be developed and used by consumers as part of their conversation. Obviously, brands can't control what consumers say. Many marketers do scan blogs for brand insights. Many companies are using technology to analyze all kinds of "consumer-generated media," including blogs, chat rooms, message boards, and forums. They monitor what is being said about their brands as an early warning system. The smart companies can influence the discussion, or open forum, and harnessing consumer trust. Business blogs can have conversations with consumers, employees, and media. Remember the value of integrated marketing communication (IMC). Folks restaurants use more than banner advertisements (see Exhibit 6.10). They use electronic coupons and e-mail newsletters (with consumer permission) and are experimenting with other nontraditional communication techniques.

■ *Business blogs.* There are several means of publishing blogs: free Web-based commercial services, subscription, hosted services, or software installed on your company server. Some smaller companies simply use TypePad or Blogger to give a custom look to their blogs. For companies that want to use a professional service, there is "server-side" software to be installed that gives you total control, good metrics, and your company domain name. However, it must be managed on your server. A number of blog search engines are available to aid

EXHIBIT 6.10

Folks uses more than banner advertisements to attract customers. It uses electronic coupons and newsletters, permission e-mails, and other nontraditional marketing techniques.

Courtesy of Lane Bevil+Partners and Folks.

in monitoring your brand category. A host of information is available, such as hits ranking or complex metrics tracking. For example, BlogPulse has a trend-graphing tool that allows you to track your brand against a competitive one. Blog-monitoring services charge big companies $30,000 to $100,000 a year. One such company, Umbria, uses its natural-language analysis to determine blogger demographics based on language, subject matter, and acronyms—for example, "fouled up beyond all recognition" (FUBAR), often used by male baby boomers, or "parent over shoulder" (POS), indicating a younger blogger. Sometimes, companies find conflicting insights about their products. An automobile company found that little kids love minivans but that teens want their parents to own SUVs.[21]

■ *Moblogs.* Blogs created by using mobile devices such as your camera phone or PDAs are called *moblogs.*

■ *Podcasting.* Podcasting is a method of downloading audio content to iPods or MP3 players. For example, Deloitte and subsidiaries offer clients a broad range of fully integrated services in areas that include accounting, assurance and advisory, risk, tax, management, financial, technology, and human capital consulting. At this writing, Deloitte's website featured Deloitte Insights listing thirteen categories of Podcasts; under consumer business, they listed five, including: "Getting ready for the aging consumers: What you need to know." The description read:

> In 2008, consumers within the 50–80 year old range will dominate the U.S. marketplace. With this demographic shift come multiple challenges and opportunities for Consumer Business companies. Is your business prepared to serve the aging consumer? Get tips and learn about four key areas every business will want to reconsider when developing strategies to serve this emerging market. Hear from Pat Conroy, National Managing Principal of Consumer Business, Deloitte & Touche USA LLP, how some innovative companies are "making time stand still" for older consumers. (18 minutes)[22]

- *Really Simple Syndication. Really Simple Syndication (RSS)* is a code that allows website or blog readers to subscribe to its services in order to automatically get updates. For example, cnn.com, NYT.com, and weather.com offer RSS so you can keep in the know.
- *Streaming video. Streaming video* describes playing an audio or video file directly from a website without downloading it first.
- *vBlog.* A *vBlog* or *vlog* is simply a video blog.
- *Wiki.* An open-end site on the Web where readers can edit and contribute is known as a *wiki.*

In Chapter 16, we talk about creating and writing for Web-related communications.

Today, marketers are forced to find the right formula and be innovative in marketing new and established products. "We believe in this age of increased clutter, the only risk is not to take a risk. If your gut doesn't bubble up with an instinct that isn't just right about an idea, then you should think about something else," says North America's BMW MINI brand marketing communications manager.[23]

The discussion of risk is not new with agency people. Years ago, Bill Borders of Borders, Perrin and Norrander said, "Risk taking is the lifeblood of an agency." However, a former director of creative at PepsiCo says, "The problem with most clients is that they are not willing to join the agency in the risk. Through the years Pepsi-Cola has told BBDO to take the risk. If you miss, we understand that not everything is going to be a home run. But it could be a single. Occasionally, we have burned the film knowing that we tried and it just didn't work."[24] Unfortunately, most clients can't find the courage to join PepsiCo in taking chances or risk to seek cutting-edge advertising.

Bob Moore, creative director of Fallon, Minneapolis, says, "I am a believer that you have to do strong ads that stand out. A lot of times that leads you to something that is different. By its very nature, different is going to lead you to something risky. What's risky gets people talking. You can do work that feels good, but no one notices it. It is like wallpaper. That's far riskier."[25]

Many clients are looking for advertising home runs to drive their brands from anyplace or media. But in many cases, a marketing executive is in power an average of 18 months on a brand (remember that the CMO averages 24 months). They only care about what's happening now, many critics say. The brand-management system attempts to prevent failure by relying strongly on research and testing. The brand managers are promoted if they don't make mistakes—as well as if they hit a home run. This creates brand managers who play it safe and won't take risks. Some companies are extending how long brand managers stay on a particular assignment. Advertising never pays for itself in the short term. Promotions always do. Yet, some marketers are calling for change and risk beyond the creative advertising idea (as did Coca-Cola's CMO mentioned earlier) in the way the industry looks at things. Mark Kaline, global media manager at Ford, says, "The most effective way to cope with change is to help create it. We cannot be afraid to take risk." He said, "We're willing to invest in the right ideas—from brand inspired merchandise to product tie-ins with movies to corporate sponsorships of landmark events or TV shows."[26]

Some advertisers are integrating technology into their strategy in nontraditional ways. TBWA\Chiat\Day and TEQUILA in Los Angeles used an old road-trip concept to align the redesigned Nissan Sentra with young urbanites and their 24-7 lifestyles by using Marc Horowitz's *Road Trip,* which created 168 hours of raw footage for the Web and other media vehicles. Marc's goal was to live in his car for 7 straight days as normally as possible while being filmed. He showered in public bathrooms, slept in his backseat, went on a date, and even entertained friends. But the footage captured Marc's lifestyle and the vehicle that complements it perfectly.

The lengthy raw footage was cut into numerous television spots, short films for blogs, and even a documentary. Marc's wild ride sparked a worldwide conversation and quantum-leaped the return you'd get from a standard media schedule.[27]

AGENCY-CLIENT RELATIONSHIPS

It has been said that agency-client relationships are much like interpersonal relationships: If you don't like each other, you move apart. If you like each other, you gravitate toward each other and great stuff gets produced. The agency should be trusted as an employee—it is in business with the client. The relationship between the agency and the client is a partnership. A self-promotion from Ames Scullin O'Haire agency said,

> There was a time when ad agencies were partners, not vendors. They were trusted, not suspected. They added value, not expenses. Then agencies got greedy. In pursuit of hefty fees, ad agencies began to pay more attention to their own business than their clients'. Merger mania began as conglomerates gobbled agencies like Pac Man with the munchies. Soon agencies became little more than order-takers. Ironically, today clients pay consultants tens of millions for marketing advice while beating up their ad agencies over courier charges. Where's the love, babe, where's the love? We're Ames Scullin O'Haire, an ad agency built around you.[28]

Some would say they are close to the heart of the problem.

Continental Consulting Group reported that many clients are not satisfied with their advertising agencies, claiming their shops are understaffed, overcompensated, and not as creative as agencies were two decades ago. The report also complained that there is less-experienced account management personnel and weak strategic thinking. Clients responded that the quality of agency staffers is less than it was 5 years ago, and more than half said the person heading their account is less experienced than an account manager would have been 5 or 10 years ago. Some 81 percent of those surveyed felt agency people are stretched too thin.

Nancy L. Salz Consulting, which since 1986 has sponsored what is known as the Salz Survey of Advertiser-Agency Relations, found in 2006 that when advertisers were asked to predict the effect on sales if their agencies were always able to do the best work possible, the respondents estimated an increase of 24.7 percent. By contrast, as recently as 2003, the response was as low as 20.8 percent.

Advertisers who were asked to assess the quality of the advertisements produced by their agencies gave the work a rating of 7.3 on a scale of 1 (terrible) to 10 (excellent). The survey average has been 7.2 and the highest response since 1998, when the figure reached 7.4. In response to another question about the tenseness of relationships with their agencies, the number who said the relationship grew more tense in the last year fell to 17 percent, a record low for the question. In 2005, the response was 41 percent. Advertisers are now saying, "No one knows the best way to use the Internet or how to get ads to people over their mobile devices." "And we're both in this together, facing a common challenge neither of us has a history with." "There's no business-as-usual, no been-there, done-that," Salz added. "This sort of thing turns people on."[29]

Agencies have always prided themselves on selling the creative product; however, many people feel today's agencies are not producing the strongest creative product. Some clients hire advertising agencies because they believe they can help them persuade customers to do or think something. Clients may select an agency based on the agency's ability to be persuasive. The real task for the agency is to become a persuasion partner.

Thomas N. Lentz

Vice President Advertising and Marketing Services, Broyhill Furniture Industries, Inc.

The Best of Both Worlds—An In-House Agency

I began my advertising career on a July morning in 1979 when I entered 380 Madison Avenue (Wow! Madison Avenue), stepped off the elevator on the 18th floor, and stared at "Ogilvy & Mather" in shiny chrome letters on a fire truck red wall (Wow! Ogilvy & Mather—home of the advertising industry's David). Here I was—a rookie assistant account executive at Ogilvy & Mather on the Owens-Corning Corporation account. I expected to continue my career as an agency "account management guy" for many years. However, after starting a family some nine years later, my wife and I realized the benefits of being closer to our families and out of the rigors of New York commuting. So I looked for advertising opportunities nearer our Carolina roots.

This search led me to Broyhill Furniture Industries, Inc., one of the world's largest manufacturers of residential furniture and one of the best known brands among consumers. The CEO interviewing me was looking for someone who knew nothing about furniture (he wanted fresh ideas) but had lots of experience with consumer marketing. My years on packaged goods accounts such as Procter & Gamble, Lever Brothers, Colgate-Palmolive, Bristol-Myers, and General Foods would come in handy. This seemed like the perfect fit for Broyhill and me.

Suddenly I'm The Client—no more agency guy for me. Now I would have an agency at my beck and call—or so I thought. Ironically, this former agency account manager does not use an agency for the advertising needs of Broyhill. In place of an advertising agency we have assembled a topnotch in-house agency staff. This staff handles all our agency needs from creative development to media negotiations/planning to public relations to production and traffic. Why? Because we have found that agencies do not make our lives easier—listen up all you potential agency folks.

Thomas N. Lentz

As a big New York agency account manager I was trained to be a strategic partner with our clients and to constantly bring "added value" to their business. Of course, my former agencies created, produced, and placed great advertising, but we understood the client's business so well we could make strategic recommendations, suggest new product ideas, or create innovative promotions all designed to grow their business and gain market share. The health of their business was paramount to the agency.

For Broyhill, agency relationships did not work. Agencies never really learned the nuances of the furniture business. They never understood the difference between branding and

When advertisers develop a new product or become disenchanted with their existing advertising, they will conduct advertising reviews in which their current agency and others can compete for the account. This review process may take several months. The advertiser will evaluate which agencies it wants to participate in the review. Keep in mind that there are agencies that specialize in certain types of accounts.

In moving from his role as president of Coca-Cola North America to chairman-CEO of Clorox Co., Donald R. Knauss was asked about his agency relationship philosophy. He responded, "First of all, my philosophy at agencies is that the people you work with over a long period of time are those who deliver great results. I'm not for the flavor-of-the-month club. I like to have long-standing relationships. And

retail advertising—and the fact that Broyhill needed to be both. How to represent furniture to the consumer is more important than how clever the headline needed to be. Agencies approached furniture advertising as if the consumer was bored with furniture and needed to be entertained by advertising. Quite the contrary, buying furniture and creating beautiful rooms is one category many consumers love. They are very similar to car consumers. They want to see lots of products and understand many of the features and benefits of these products. Consumers buy home shelter magazines to read the furniture ads just as women buy beauty magazines to peruse the beauty products advertised. There is even an entire cable network dedicated to the home, yet agencies think we need to be "creative." As a result, you could barely see the furniture in their ads.

Why have we chosen to go the in-house agency route? These regional agencies just didn't get it. The agencies did not study our business thoroughly enough to learn all the complexities of retail buyers, retail floor sales associates, distribution issues, and management idiosyncrasies. It seems that too many of today's agencies are staffed with account management types that do not know their client's business well enough to guide the creatives—people who often seem more interested in developing advertising they personally like and hope will win awards. Speaking of awards, in 1984 Benton & Bowles had a Clio-winning Scope mouthwash commercial in a test market. This award-winning commercial that everyone loved was tested against a "hidden-camera testimonial" campaign straight out of the sixties. Guess which campaign took Scope to #1 in the mouthwash category? The testimonial. We all wanted the clever, creative, award-winning campaign to be more effective, but consumers spoke with their pocketbooks.

An in-house agency staff often truly understands all the brand's marketplace dynamics better than an agency. With today's incredible computer technology and many young, creative people available, Broyhill has solved its advertising and marketing needs by building a small agency that lives and breathes furniture—and understands what the consumer wants in advertising. Our magazine advertising has consistently ranked #1 or #2 in Starch Readership research. Focus groups have given

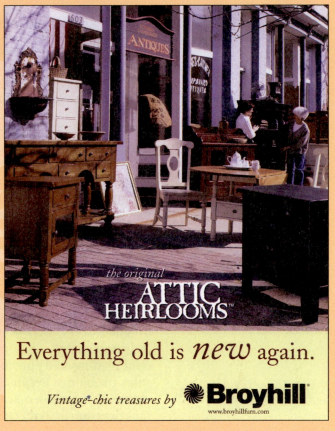

Everything old is new again.

our ads high marks in providing consumers the information they need. And as for awards—the ring of the cash register brings smiles and satisfaction to our marketing services staff.

An in-house advertising operation or an outside agency? To be successful both have to understand the client's business extremely well. But today I see more and more companies developing in-house agency capabilities. For many of us an in-house agency offers much of the same satisfaction as an advertising agency with the insight of the client. In many ways it's the best of both worlds—at least it has been for me.

Courtesy of Thomas N. Lentz, Vice President, Advertising and Marketing Services, Broyhill Furniture Industries, Inc. ■ ■ ■

certainly we had that approach at [Procter & Gamble Co., where Mr. Knauss began his career]. And it depends at Coke which categories you're talking about—we've had a similar approach as well.[30]

With competitive pressures mounting, companies are more enamored with brand strategies and solutions—whether they are "advertising" driven or not—than with creative work. As a result, companies seek solutions from a coterie of other advisers, not exclusively from advertising agencies. Today, agencies are again trying to find their place at the table. Many are changing their direction or focus: "Clients don't care where good ideas come from," says WPP Group Chief Executive Martin Sorrells.[31] Agencies seek to be full-service partners, as opposed to being vendors, where clients go for any and all business solutions.

Agency Search Consultants

A continuing trend is clients hiring consultants to help them seek out the best agency to handle their accounts (this is a similar process to companies hiring headhunters to find executives or other employees). It is the norm in account reviews for major advertisers to involve consultants, whose job is to do the initial screening, manage the search process, and in some cases negotiate compensation agreements. This may cost a client between $35,000 and $100,000. In the past, clients relied more heavily on their own marketing departments to conduct searches. Consultants have been hired more in recent years because fewer clients find they are qualified to do it themselves and because there have been so many changes in the agency landscape, according to an agency principal.[32] The consultant has been characterized as a "marriage broker" between client and agency.

There has been a continuing increase in clients reviewing their agencies. This is a natural result of the restructuring of businesses. When marketing departments get restructured and people change jobs, there is a tendency to start from scratch and this includes reviewing or changing advertising agencies. They send out a request for proposal (RFP) to potential agencies that asks a number of questions the client needs answered. One of the driving forces on account reviews is pressure on advertisers' marketing departments to sell more units and a fixation on quarterly financial results. That position deemphasizes the importance of long-standing relationships and puts the spotlight on how well agencies can deliver quick fixes to sales problems. Because marketers have already done as much downsizing as is practical, increases now have to be achieved through "real unit growth."[33] This creates pressure on both clients and agencies.

Selecting an Agency

Choosing an agency can be a complicated matter. Do you need a full-service agency, one with integrated services, one with strong media departments, or a specialized agency? After deciding whether you want a large, medium, or small; specialized or full-service; domestic or global agency, the following points may help you in evaluating specific agencies:

1. Determine what types of service you need from an agency and then list them in order of their importance to you—for instance, (a) marketing expertise in strategy, planning, and execution; (b) creative performance in television, print, radio, or outdoor; (c) media knowledge and clout, if media is part of the equation; (d) promotion and/or trade relations help; (e) public relations and corporate- or image-building ability; (f) market research strength; (g) fashion or beauty sense; (h) agency size; (i) location in relation to your office, or (j3) Web or new media capabilities. Your special needs will dictate others.

2. Establish a five-point scale to rate each agency's attributes. A typical five-point scale would be (1) outstanding, (2) very good, (3) good, (4) satisfactory, and (5) unsatisfactory. Of course, you should give different values or weights to the more important agency attributes.

3. Check published sources and select a group of agencies that seem to fit your requirements. Use your own knowledge or the knowledge of your industry peers to find agencies responsible for successful campaigns or products that have most impressed you. Published sources include the annual issue of *Advertising Age*, which lists agencies and their accounts by agency size, and the "Red Book" (*Standard Advertising Register*), which lists agencies and accounts both alphabetically and geographically. In case of further doubt, contact the American Association of Advertising Agencies, New York, for a roster of members. Of course, you can do this online.

4. Check whether there are any apparent conflicts with accounts already at the agency. When agencies consider a new account, that is the first question they ask (along with the amount of the potential billings).

5. Now start preliminary discussions with the agencies that rate best on your initial evaluation. This can be started with a letter asking if they are interested or a telephone call to set up an appointment for them to visit you or for you to visit the agency. Start at the top. Call the president or the operating head of the agency or office in your area, who will appoint someone to follow up on the opportunity you are offering.

6. Reduce your original list of potential agencies after the first contact. A manageable number is usually no more than three to five. Many can be eliminated by their RFP answers.

7. Again prepare an evaluation list for rating the agencies on the same five-point scale. This list will be a lot more specific. It should cover personnel. Who will supervise your account and how will the account be staffed? Who are the creative people who will work on your business? Similarly, who will service your Interactive, production (television), research, and promotion needs; and how will they do it? What is the agency's track record in getting and holding on to business and in keeping personnel teams together? What is the agency's record with vendors and media? Make sure again to assign a weighted value to each service aspect.

8. Discuss financial arrangements. Will your account be a straight 15 percent commission account, a fee account, a combination of both, or some performance formula? What services will the commission or fee cover, and what additional charges will the agency demand? How will new product work be handled from both a financial and an organizational point of view? What peripheral service does the agency offer, and for how much?

9. Do you feel comfortable with the agency?

10. If your company is a global one, can the agency handle all of your nondomestic business, and if so, how will they do it?

Client Requirements

The agency workload varies significantly for each client. Agencies may produce only a few advertisements for a client during a year, which isn't taxing on their creative and management abilities. At SLRS Advertising, only three trade print advertisements were created for Ideal Carpets during an entire year (see Exhibit 6.11). On the other hand, Ogilvy & Mather creates about 6,000 advertisements for IBM around the world requiring excellent creative and management skills.

Using Multiple Agencies

Many large clients may hire several agencies and give them different assignments for the same product or different brands. In some cases, this is changing the agency-client relationship by treating agencies as vendors and not as full marketing partners. One of the reasons for this change is that new marketing executives are under pressures from their CEOs. The message is, "I don't care about your situation. I need an idea and people who are passionate about my business."

In the 1950s, the agency-client relationship was defined in *The Encyclopedia of Advertising*:

> An advertising agency is an organization which provides advertising,
> merchandising and other services and counsel related to the sale of a
> client's goods or services. It is understood that the client agrees not to
> engage a second agency to handle part of the advertising of the product
> without the consent of the first agency.

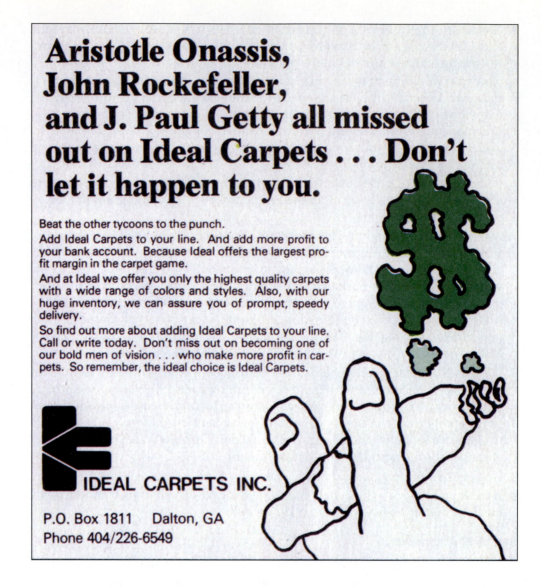

Traditionally, a marketer used one agency per brand. As companies got bigger and marketing more complex, this changed. For example, a number of years ago, Coca-Cola decided that its longtime agency wasn't creating enough big ideas. For additional creative ideas, it hired outside freelancers for a while and then hired about forty agencies and boutiques to create advertisements. Coca-Cola's contention was: *We know and understand our strategy better than our agencies do. So their job is to do the best execution of the strategy they can.*

Today, Coca-Cola has a number of different agencies working on its brands. It is not the only company to use multiple agencies. Many use a major global agency, plus a number of smaller creative shops. "The size of our business is such that it demands the expertise and attention of a number of agencies," said the national director of marketing communications at AT&T. "There are so many projects and assignments to be handled that one agency couldn't do it all. But using multiple agencies puts the onus on us to make sure all the messages are coordinated and represent one consistent voice coming from the company." These needs are different from a client having one agency partner to handle everything.[34]

The advertising business is famously cyclical, so it remains to be seen whether this multiple-agency trend is a permanent shift or a temporary blip. Right now, advertisers are looking for the best custom-made solutions to their marketing problems.

KLEPPNER VIEWPOINT 6.2

Tom Robinson

President, Robinson & Associates, Inc.
After All, They Did Buy Into the System!

*W*orking with franchises can be rewarding and challenging for the right advertising agencies, and a successful, long-term relationship with a franchise is as challenging as a successful marriage.

The reason that a franchisee "buys into a franchise" in the first place is because a system has been established that permits him/her greater opportunity for success and higher profitability versus a de novo entrepreneurial venture. After all, someone has taken some of the risk out of the venture and created a plan of action that has been proven to be successful in related markets with similar franchisees.

So where does the challenge come in? Many franchisees have contractual agreements with their franchiser to spend a preset percentage of sales on advertising and are encouraged to join an advertising cooperative for greater buying power and increased efficiency. The larger the advertising pool the greater the need for professional advertising and marketing—thus the agency relationship begins.

As group advertising begins where it has not been done before, sales generally increase significantly from the advertising and all goes well.

There are a few challenges. Consultants provided by the franchise monitor the franchisee/agency relationship and advise both on corporate recommendations and suggestions for marketing. After all, the franchiser has been successful and is marketing savvy. However, the franchisee's entrepreneurial spirit makes him feel he knows his local market better than anyone—after all he is paying the agency. Too, marketing is one of the few areas the franchisee feels autonomous.

Also, when the bloom wears off the new marketing effort, or a new competitor moves in, the "wow" sales increase dwindles and the question begins, "Is the agency really doing exactly what I need?"

Many large franchisers have a major voice in their franchisees' business. By contract, they grade their operations and marketing execution, award additional franchises on

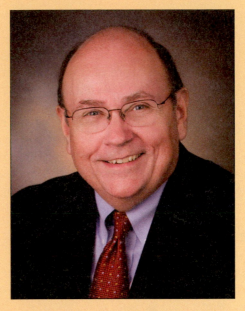

Tom Robinson

their perception of the success of the franchisee and provide a wealth of resources including a corporate marketing team that "assists" the agency in serving their client.

Working with franchisees is not for the faint of heart. Entrepreneurs are special or they would not be entrepreneurs. Treat them special. They have "bought in" to the system, but they tug at the reins every time they are pulled. Remember too, the franchiser brings a lot to the table, as do their representatives whose influence comes from the franchise and as well as their professional experience.

The relationship can be long, profitable and often challenging. Do your job. Remember your role. Be flexible. Remember who pays you—the franchisee. Yet, remember the company representative can be your greatest ally with the franchisee. Learn to listen. Learn to compromise. It will make your relationships with all your other clients even stronger. ∎∎∎

The Creative Digital Library

Global clients and major advertising agencies build creative digital libraries for agencies in different parts of the globe to use. For example, the McDonald's digital commercial archive holds commercials from the chain's advertising since 1967 that may be used by local co-ops and agencies. It is a password-only system, so consumers or competition can't access the files. Most archives include still graphic assets, such as logos, product shots, text custom advertisements, point-of-purchase displays, and other print material. Agencies like Euro RSCG MVBMS store digital commercials and print materials in its creative library, which is similar to the McDonald's library. It allows for integration of visuals to all agencies around the globe working on the account.

APPRAISING NATIONAL ADVERTISING

The big questions that national advertising and marketing management must answer are: How well is our advertising working? How well is our investment paying off? How do you measure national advertising, whose results cannot be traced as easily as those of direct-response and some Interactive advertising?

Advertising Goals Versus Marketing Goals

The answer is not simple. Much of the discussion on the subject centers around a report prepared for the Association of National Advertisers (ANA), which is the industry's premier trade association dedicated exclusively to marketing and brand building. The thesis of this study is that it is virtually impossible to measure the results of advertising unless and until the specific results sought by advertising have been defined. When asked exactly what their advertising is supposed to do, most companies have a ready answer: increase their dollar sales or increase their share of the market. However, these are not advertising goals, they are total **marketing goals** (see Exhibit 6.12).

National advertising alone cannot accomplish this task. It should be used as part of the total marketing effort. The first step in appraising the results of advertis-

marketing goals
The overall objectives that a company wishes to accomplish through its marketing program.

EXHIBIT 6.12

How would you define the goal for this ice cream advertisement?

Courtesy of The Johnson Group and Mayfield.

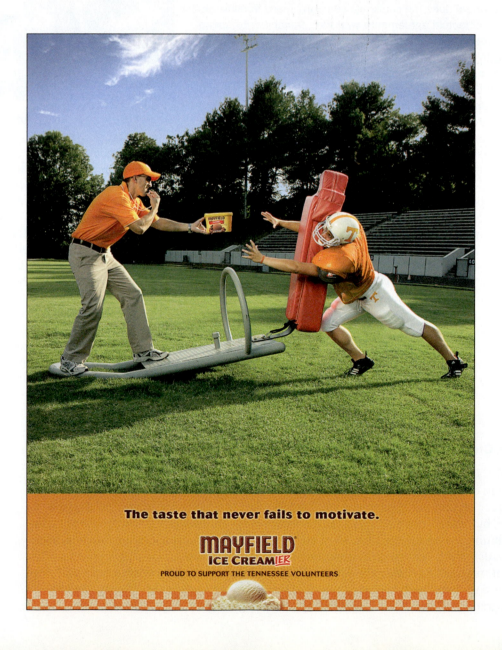

The taste that never fails to motivate.

MAYFIELD
ICE CREAM
PROUD TO SUPPORT THE TENNESSEE VOLUNTEERS

ing, therefore, is to define specifically what the company expects to accomplish through advertising. The ANA report defines an **advertising goal** as "a specific communications task, to be accomplished among a defined audience to a given degree in a given period of time."[35]

advertising goals
The communication objectives designed to accomplish certain tasks within the total marketing program.

As an example, let's look at a branded detergent. The marketing goal is to increase market share from 10 to 15 percent, and the advertising goal is set as increasing, among the 50 million housewives who own washing machines, the number who identify Brand X as a stain-removing detergent that gets clothes clean. This represents a specific communications task that can be performed by advertising independently of other marketing forces.

There may be a marketing-communication spectrum ranging from unawareness of the product to comprehension to conviction to action. According to this view, the way to appraise advertising is through its effectiveness in the communication spectrum, leading to sales.

From their research, Briggs and Stuart say Wanamaker was wrong—only 37 percent of advertising is wasted. The authors pin much of the blame on marketers' failure to even define success for campaigns at the outset—much less measure it properly on the back end. In the study, both P&G and Cingular have a clear definition of success for each marketing effort at the outset. In Briggs and Stuart's book *What Sticks*, they outline a program—Communication Optimization Process—to help the marketing team see what it might otherwise miss. The authors suggest that you go through the 4 M's—motivation, message, media mix, and maximization—to get everyone on the same page. Then link the gold-standard marketing effectiveness measurement of each M to the action plan. In other words, measure everything to see if it works.[36]

Researchers disagree on whether the effectiveness of national advertising—or, for that matter, of any advertising—should be judged by a communication yardstick rather than by sales. As a matter of fact, in Chapter 15 we discuss whether an advertisement's effectiveness should be measured by some research testing score.

CHANGES IN MARKETING

We remain in the midst of a revolution. This period of change has been compared to the French and Russian revolutions. The truth is that we are in the midst of several revolutions at once, including globalization, technology, management, uncertain economy, and consumers' controlling messages. We are in competition with everyone, everywhere in the world. Today's management buzzwords are *reengineering*, *downsizing*, and *eliminating hierarchy*. Small, flexible organizations have the advantage in today's world. Finally, we are undergoing a revolution in our business structure.

The Traditional Five P's of Marketing

The traditional five P's of marketing consist of the elements product, price, place, packaging, and promotion (which include positioning, advertising, sales promotion, public relations, and so forth). With a strategy in each of these areas, a person can put together an effective marketing plan. In the package-goods category, the general belief is that promotion accounts for about 90 percent of the marketing equation. Each product category may be different, as seen with automobiles, where price and product are key, with promotion being a small percentage. So the advertiser must understand what is important.

The New Five P's of Marketing

Longtime advertising executive Tom Patty says the old five P's served us well in a world dominated by stability and a growing economy with much less competitive pressures than we have today. Patty's new five P's are aimed at helping us succeed in a

Tim Mapes

Managing Director–Marketing, Delta Air Lines, Inc.
Agency Side or Client Side?

To be or not to be? Who knew Shakespeare's Hamlet was an ad major, soon to graduate, struggling with the decision to go client side or agency side?

Of course in today's business environment, you may be happy (and lucky) to find a job at either. But what draws people to one over the other? What enables success once there? And how, based on a bett3er understanding of life at each, might you make the best career decision and, in the process, improve the world of advertising management?

The Agency Side

Professional life on the agency side is frequently depicted in glamorous ways with stylish, fashionable people creating stylish, fashionable advertising for their clients. Agency offices are sleek and modern. The atmosphere electrically-charged with creativity as ad execs go about the sexy business that is advertising. "Power lunches" abound. This can in fact be accurate. But beneath the veneer Hollywood tends to apply to the ad agency business, life on the agency side goes far beyond the superficial. Ad agency staffers, particularly those in entry-level roles, deal with demanding clients, unreasonable deadlines, competitiveness from other staffers looking to make a name for themselves, and a host of other factors that can lead to a stressful work environment.

And that stress varies by the disciplines represented in each agency. Account management people work to stay out in front of brand strategy issues, overall process management and clients themselves. Creative people look to stay out in front of fashion and design trends, the latest production techniques, and ways to develop that next big idea. And media planners and buyers have to stay out in front of syndicated research, emerging media vehicles themselves, and measures of audience delivery. This collective effort to "stay out in front" drives a fast-paced, energetic organizational culture in agencies that is best suited for like-minded, resilient souls whom no one would ever describe as "wall flowers."

Creatively-driven agencies have been known to say, "it is all about the work" referring to the quality of their output as visible in the advertising and marketing communications activities they craft and churn out. Organizational emphasis is thus placed on the quality of the consumer insight and expression of the idea—and retention and advancement of people who can deliver either but better still both. The best, and most successful agencies, go well past concern for themselves (e.g., creative awards won) and focus instead on how their work as an agency directly or indirectly leads to success in their client's business. Agencies tend to be measured on the clients they keep and the work they do for them over time. Clients do not stay long at agencies who do not deliver desired business

Tim Mapes

results and agency staffers not seen by clients as key to their business depart even faster.

The Client Side

Staying within the Hollywood metaphor, client-side people are frequently depicted as mean-spirited, tyrants who boss agency personnel around without regard for the people involved nor respect for the process at hand. Clients are also often portrayed as overly-conservative oafs who fail to recognize, let alone act on, the agency's "big idea." Power-hungry boars whose self-regard displaces their understanding of the very customers they seek. This too can be regrettably based in fact. But life in client organizations tends to revolve around definitive business metrics like total sales made, revenue generated, costs avoided and other traditional definitions of market success. Staffers in client ad and marketing organizations deal with "the work" (advertising creative) but, like the best agencies, must see it in the broader context of delivering business success and not simply creative awards.

Life on the client side involves similarly long hours and the requisite "payment of dues" to move up. Paradoxically, clients can at times look to agencies for greater insight to their customers than they as clients have themselves. This is not always an abdication of responsibility. Client organizations can focus so much on "running the factory" that they lose touch with who is buying the product. But the best clients learn to function like agencies themselves in that they must have a commanding knowledge of consumer trends and research findings, brand strategy, media trends, production values and techniques, and estimate and billing processes—all the while leading their own organizations and being accessible to agency representatives and members of the media.

Perhaps of greatest value to those considering life on the client side is the ability to exert greater influence over advertising outcomes. Agencies can lead the client horse to the water but not make her or him drink. Thirsty clients get the best from their agencies by saying "yes" to the right recommendations and as an agency superior once told me, "clients get the advertising they deserve." Clients that contribute to, fight on behalf of, and say yes to the best agency ideas get more of them.

Requirements for Success at Either

So while there are clear differences in a day in your life as an ad person at an ad agency or a client organization, there are foundational elements in the work itself that can, and should, make the roles more alike than dissimilar. In fact, success on either the agency or client side requires the same 5 things.

Obsessive focus on the customer—It has been said that the business of selling begins with "no." As a form of selling, advertising and advertisers (at clients and agencies alike) have got to know everything possible about the prospective customer. Entire companies exist that conduct forms of "ethnographic" research by following targeted customers around to learn more about where they live, what they drive, how they dress, where they eat, what they read and all of the values and behaviors that drive purchase decisions. The closer to the customer you are, the more likely you are to know, and therefore meet, their needs.

Innate curiosity—While people tend to think of advertising as "art" it has components that are much more "science." Curiosity in what drives consumer behavior, why scientifically the eye is drawn to red faster than any other color, why black type on a white background is the most legible and a number of other otherwise seemingly disparate things can enable success. It never ceases to amaze me how something I read or heard related to a field that has nothing to do with my own actually applies if thought through more fully. In fact, some of the greatest advertising breakthroughs are driven off of "disruptions" to conventional wisdom. If you are not open to, nor curious about, these pieces of information, your ability to process them and contribute most fully can be limited.

Attention to detail—An early Account Supervisor of mine once told me, "the client never sleeps." Another at a different agency advised that when proof-reading a mechanical, "assume there is a mistake in it and that you have to be the one to find it no matter how many other signatures are already on the mechanical." There are rarely small mistakes in advertising—they go from big to bigger as campaigns run locally to globally. But attention to detail goes beyond the "downside" of mistakes to the "upside" of insights. Attention to detail can be the key to gaining a better consumer insight than your competitor and thus more likely market success. And in categories as competitive as colas, airlines and wireless communication, even the smallest of advantages can yield large scale benefits.

The ability to connect with people—Agencies tend to say that their greatest assets leave the company each night. It is no less true in client organizations. Inherently, advertising is a business that is about people. People as customers, people as colleagues. People as bosses and people as subordinates. People who devote themselves to serving clients as agency people and people who, if wise, do everything in their power to motivate their agencies as clients. It is a business, as Barbara Streisand sang of "people who need people" and those who can understand, empathize, connect with, and captivate others will succeed.

Those who do not rarely make it past an initial interview.

A "love of the game"—If you do not love, and I mean LOVE advertising, the question of agency or client side is irrelevant. Advertising inherently requires lots of time. Time spent in the office. Time spent in meetings. Time spent in focus groups and market research. Time spent traveling. And time spent with people you may not particularly care for! A love of the process (and of course the final output and resulting business success) is necessary to sustain you when things can become challenging or worse tedious.

One Person's View

For these and other reasons, in my personal view, the best clients are former agency people and, in turn, the best agency people are former clients. Stephen Covey suggests we "seek to understand before we seek to be understood." True understanding of what concerns or motivates your client is best developed by walking a mile (okay, miles!) in her or his shoes. Similarly, actual client experience seeing what has to go on in an agency to develop an idea in the first place, let alone transform it to an "ad-like object" or "comp" and finished, produced work appearing in the medium for which it was intended, can be an invaluable way of insuring that timelines are more reasonable and praise is forthcoming when great work appears.

Clients who "get" the demands of the agency business are more likely to show respect for processes employed and timelines required—and to recognize great teams and great work knowing just how challenging agency work can be. Similarly, agency professionals who know what it is like as a client to lose sleep at night because your pay check depends upon the success of a new product launch think more thoroughly about how to insure the benefits of that product's performance are clearly communicated in the advertising.

A former business-oriented yet creatively-minded boss of mine used to employ the phrase, "when you come to a fork in the road take it." Such guidance is brilliant on a number of levels but if for no other reason than that it challenges us to break with conventional wisdom.

If you happen to be facing a professional version of Hamlet's conundrum involving an opportunity at an agency or client, it might comfort you to know that in reality you will not make a bad decision—experience at one is invaluable to your success at the other should you ultimately ever wish to make a change. ■ ■ ■

world where chaos has replaced stability, where the fast-growing economy has slowed, and where global competition demands even greater levels of effectiveness and efficiency. The new five P's are more abstract and conceptual than the traditional ones. They include paradox, perspective, paradigm, persuasion, and passion.[37]

- *Paradox.* A paradox is a statement or proposition that, on the face of it, seems self-contradictory. Example: "All cars are the same; all cars are different." The paradox always contains within it an opportunity. An advertiser must exploit the differentiation. Miller used the paradox of "lite" beer to help focus on the dual benefits of the lite paradox, "Tastes Great, Less Filling." Everyone knows what a sports car is, but Nissan created a new category of sports cars in which it was first—the four-door sports car. To master the paradox, you first have to find or identify this opportunity and then exploit the changes. One way to create this unique identity is to be the first in something. For years, advertising told us that trucks are tough and rugged and durable, whereas cars are comfortable, luxurious, and safe. The new Dodge Ram exploits the paradox of combining many car-type features with the rugged look and performance of a Mack truck.

- *Perspective.* Perspective is the ability to see things in relationship to each other. The manufacturer's perspective isn't the proper perspective. Advertisers must look at every issue—whether it's a product issue, a pricing issue, or a distribution issue—from the consumer perspective. The only perspective is the consumer's perspective. Here, several questions need answers: What consumer need does my product or service satisfy? How does it satisfy this need differently and better than competitors? Similarly, as it relates to advertising, are we in the advertising business or are we in the persuasion business? We should be in the business of persuading consumers to think or to do something.

- *Paradigm.* Here we need a pattern example, a model way of doing things. We need to understand that we may not need to do business the "old" way. Certainly, the marketing bundle of Saturn reflects a new automotive paradigm. Instead of believing that product and price are the main ingredients of the marketing equation, Saturn believes that the major components are issues such as the experience of buying and owning a Saturn. They place much less emphasis on the product and much greater emphasis on the experiential component. There are also different advertising paradigms. In the model advertising paradigm, advertising has a simple task: "Show the product and communicate the product features and benefits." A very different paradigm is called the brand advertising paradigm, for which Saturn again is a good example. In this paradigm the task is to communicate who and what you are.

- *Persuasion.* Here we attempt to induce someone to do or think something. All marketing and sales jobs are in the business of persuasion. The advertising agency's role is to help the client persuade potential consumer audiences either to do or to think something. To be persuasive, you have to understand three essential components: the credibility of the speaker, the content of the message, and the involvement of the audience. Credibility and trust are emotional, not rational. You can't make someone trust you. You have to earn it over time. The Honda brand has credibility. Consequently, the advertising tends to be simple and sparse. For a brand with less credibility, you need to provide more content, more information to be persuasive. The content includes the position of the brand. It needs to address the consumer need or desire this product satisfies. Remember, consumers do not buy products; they buy solutions to their problems. They buy holes, not drill bits; they buy hope, not perfume. The third and final element in any attempt to persuade is that you must understand the motivation of your customers so you can create an emotional connection with them. You also need to select the right persuasion tool. For example, if the brand has a credibility problem, the most persuasive tool might be public relations, although it is more difficult to control the content of the message in public relations. In advertising, you get complete control of content.

■ *Passion.* Passion is an aim or object pursued with zeal or enthusiasm. We no longer have products for the masses. Instead, products are designed for specific needs and wants. Marketers are moving into a new paradigm in which advertising creates exciting, stimulating dialogues with consumers designed not just to make a sale but also to create a relationship. In this new marketing environment, you need passion.

SUMMARY ⬢

Procter & Gamble first developed the marketing service system. Today it has two parts: (1) brand management, under a brand manager, who is assigned a brand; and (2) marketing services, comprised of the technical talent involved in implementing the marketing plan, including creative services, promotion services, media services, advertising controls, and marketing research.

As companies consider implementing integrated marketing communications into their firms, there are three basic structures available: a centralized communication function under a marcom manager, a restructured brand manager approach, and the structure involving a communication manager who is responsible for approving and coordinating all communication programs.

Advertising budgets are usually drawn up using the task method, the payout plan, competitive budgeting, and the most commonly used percentage-of-sales method.

Advertisers are seeing the advantage of allowing their agencies more creative freedom and encouraging them to take more creative risk as long as it is on strategy. As Bill Borders said, "Risk taking is the lifeblood of an agency."

Agency search consultants are sometimes hired to help find the best agency for their company. The consultant has been characterized as a marriage broker between client and agency. Many clients hire several agencies for multiple products or for the same product. Many brand executives are in their positions an average of 18 months, and CMOs average little less than 2 years in their job.

The traditional five P's of marketing consist of product, price, place, packaging, and promotion. Tom Patty says the new five P's are paradox, perspective, paradigm, persuasion, and passion.

REVIEW ⬢

1. In how many product categories do Procter & Gamble products compete?
2. What is the marketing services system?
3. What is a category manager?
4. What are the major methods of developing an advertising budget?
5. Who in the corporation prepares most of the advertising budgets?
6. What is a slotting allowance?

PART FOUR

Media

CHAPTER 7

Media Strategy

The demand for efficiency, effectiveness, and creativity in the media-planning process has never been greater. The steady increase in the number of media and promotional options and unprecedented audience fragmentation have combined to create both excitement and uncertainty for advertisers and media executives. After reading this chapter, you will understand:

chapter objectives

1. the basic functions of the media planner
2. the role of media in the total advertising function
3. characteristics of the major media categories
4. relationships between media planning and target marketing

The media function, whether executed by an advertising agency, an independent media-buying and planning firm, an unbundled media shop, or a company's in-house media department, is becoming increasingly complex. Let's begin our discussion by examining the primary characteristics of the media function.

ORGANIZATION OF THE MEDIA FUNCTION

media planner
Responsible for the overall strategy of the media plan.

1. *Media planner.* The role of the **media planner** is to supervise all areas of the advertising campaign as it relates to the media function. Contemporary media planners have added the role of marketing specialist to their other duties. The media environment is changing so rapidly that it is part of the media planner's job to anticipate future trends in communications and keep agency management and clients abreast of major changes. In such an atmosphere, media planners have come to occupy a pivotal position in the advertising process.

2. *Media research.* The media research department coordinates both primary and secondary research data and functions as a support group for media planners. Often, the media research department is responsible for gauging and anticipating future trends in media. Sometimes the media research department is also responsible for estimating the likely audience for new magazines or television programs.

media buyers
Execute and monitor the media schedule developed by media planners.

3. *Media buying.* The media-buying department executes the overall media plan. **Media buyers** select and negotiate specific media placements, and they are responsible for monitoring postplacement executions. Depending on the size of a media unit, there may be separate buying groups for broadcast and print or even local and national broadcasts. Recently, some media departments have established units to research and buy Internet advertising or to construct client websites.

231

Few areas of marketing and advertising have experienced the change demonstrated by media planning in the last decade. The media function has been driven by changes in the number of media options as well as by the increasing expenditures in media and the financial risk associated with media-buying mistakes. When a medium-size company invests as much as $2.6 million in a single Super Bowl spot, careers may ride on the outcome!

In 2005, total advertising expenditures were over $271 billion, according to advertising forecasting expert Robert Coen of Universal McCann.[1] Projections for 2006 have advertising spending at over $286 billion.[2] The media planner of 2015 will be dealing with media outlets that probably don't exist today. Yet, these planners will have to provide clients with buying rationales, budget efficiencies, and measurable audience delivery in this unbelievably complicated environment.

THE NEW MEDIA FUNCTION

As the media adapt to new technology and methods of planning, there are a number of trends that set the tone for these changes and provide an assessment of the future of media planning and buying. Among the most important are convergence, interactivity, creativity, and engagement.

Convergence

convergence
The blending of various facets of marketing functions and communication technology to create more efficient and expanded synergies.

One of the primary trends of the next 5 years will be media **convergence**. Simply stated, convergence is the blending of distribution, content, and/or hardware from a number of media companies to create a new or significantly expanded communication system. Examples of convergence are numerous—cell phone companies offering Internet connections, newspaper companies creating websites, or NBC and Microsoft combining to create MSNBC. These types of collaborations are important for the businesses involved and may even expand promotional opportunities for advertisers. However, the audience is more interested in convergences such as WebTV, in which the home television becomes a computer link, or online selling that combines catalog merchandise, television-like product demonstrations, and immediate buying capabilities.

Consumers will continue to see numerous types of convergence. For example, when ESPN publishes a magazine or *ABC News* creates a popular website, the media that are created are the result of convergence. Most experts predict that marketing, media content, and technological convergences are in their embryonic stage. Although we are not certain where it will lead in the next 20 years, convergence is certainly a trend of the present and even more so of the future.

Interactivity

The future of advertising will be controlled to a great extent by the audience. Technology will allow consumers to deal directly with marketers for their entertainment, purchases, and other services, bypassing traditional media and marketing channels. The system will allow buyers and sellers to deal on a one-to-one basis with communication and products tailored to the interests of specific households and individuals.

In many cases, technological capabilities will probably outpace consumer utilization of these services. However, interactive media are dramatically changing marketing even in their infant stage.

Creativity

Interactivity not only will change the media function, but will most likely have dramatic effects on the creative process. For example, in an era of "permission marketing," the need for attention-getting creative techniques and interest-building advertising formats will be greatly diminished. When a person with an already determined product demand actively seeks out an advertiser, the dynamics of the relationship are dramatically different from mass advertising of past years.

Clients are demanding more creativity from their media planners. Media planners are being asked to think of and evaluate new and different media options to build additional exposure to consumers in effective and efficient ways. (See the accompanying Kleppner's Viewpoint 7.1, for example.) Media expertise is becoming increasingly important in developing and evaluating entertainment and experience marketing opportunities. Innovative uses of nontraditional media are generally designed to work with the more traditional media campaign for a brand. An interesting use of a new medium employed by Reebok to build on its television campaign was college students—or their foreheads, to be exact. Reebok hired 500 college students to wear temporary tattoos containing the Reebok logo and the slogan "The pain train is coming" on their foreheads. These students were strategically placed around the 26.2-mile course of the Boston Marathon in an attempt to take attention away from Adidas's sponsorship of the event. The students were paid between $20 and $30 each for 3 hours of work. Reebok also had four different brand messages illuminated on the sides of the Prudential Building in Boston during the race.[3]

Engagement

With the shrinking of television audiences and the proliferation of new media, advertisers and media planners are becoming more and more interested in the concept of **engagement**. The term *engagement* means slightly different things to different people, but it is commonly thought to take into account the ability of an advertising vehicle to deliver a receptive audience to the advertising in it. Joseph Plummer, Chief Research Officer of the Advertising Research Foundation, has said that engagement is turning on a prospect to a brand idea enhanced by the surrounding context. As put by media guru Erwin Ephron, engagement is the "hand-off of attentive consumers from media content to advertising."[4] Advertisers are interested in knowing which media make the advertising for their brand more effective.

engagement
The delivery of attentive consumers from a media vehicle to the advertising.

If there is a commonality in these trends, it is that they clearly demonstrate that media executives must be analytical, creative, and strategic in their approach to the media process. A knowledge of statistics, mathematical skills, and organized thinking are minimum requirements for media planners. For those people with the interest, imagination, and competency, media planning offers an extremely exciting, lucrative, creative, and challenging career in advertising.

MEDIA UNBUNDLING AND INDEPENDENT MEDIA-BUYING FIRMS

In a media environment characterized by convergence and creativity, one of the common approaches to the media function in recent years is known as *unbundling*. Basically, unbundling refers to the establishment of agency media departments as independent units apart from their traditional role as departments in full-service agencies.

Gilad Kat

Managing Director, Mediacom Tel Aviv
Media Creativity—Revenge of the Number Crunchers

Traditionally, creativity in advertising was predominately associated with the creation process of advertising messages, while the process of planning and buying media was many times treated merely as the delivery system. But that is no longer true. In the past several years media creativity has gained recognition and importance and is gradually taking the center stage when it comes to advertising creativity, to the extent that some are calling media the new creative.

This transformation is evident in the recent years' phenomena of having specific media categories added to most of the advertising industry's awards competitions, acknowledging creativity in media.

That being said, upon winning a Media Lions Grand Prix in Cannes last year, I still encountered a raised eyebrow here and there—"Media in Cannes?!?!?? What do all these number crunching, GRP driven geeks have to do with what is considered to be the most prestigious advertising festival in the world? What in the heck does media have to do with creative advertising?!"

So let's take a step back and look at what has happened, how this role transformation came about. . . .

It is probably difficult to separate the chicken from the egg (as always) . . ., in our case either new and innovative advancements in communication technology that lead to changes in media consumption or the other way around (changing communication needs that lead to the development of new technologies) but the result is quite clear—the fragmentation of audiences and of media, the rise of advertising clutter and increased consumer control over media content have created new challenges for the advertising industry with two main issues at stake—*access* to consumers (overcoming all barriers in order to reach people) and creating *engagement* defined by the ARF as "turning on a prospect to a brand idea." In other words, gone are the days where you could just flash a print ad or a TV commercial in front of your prospects and expect that to grab attention. It was suddenly up to us media people to leave our CPM state of mind, step up to the plate and come up with brilliant ideas.

At Mediacom we categorize media creativity into two realms:

1. *Creative use of media*—the use of existing classic media vehicles in creative, impactful and outstanding ways. For example when The Salvation Army in South

Gilad Kat

Africa wanted to collect clothes and blankets for the homeless, they brought down the temperature in movie theatres to a freezing 32°[F] accompanying this with a simple on screen message that said—"if you are this cold after 5 minutes, imagine how you would feel after a whole night . . ." and their donation boxes were *over filled*.

2. Innovative media—presenting a message in an unexpected environment and/or an unusual manner. For example when Adidas wanted to bring the Athens Olympic spirit to the far east (time zone differences meant that most of the exciting events occurred in the middle of night), they chose to hold the classic 100 meter dash in the heart of Tokyo's Shinjuku business district, only perpendicularly 33 floors up a high rise building, boasting their slogan "Impossible Is Nothing."

Given the above examples and many others, one can no longer say that media is not every bit as creative as rendering storyboards for print or TV ad campaigns. Big idea anyone?

Courtesy of Gilad Kat. ■ ■ ■

The idea of firms established solely to carry out the media function is not new. The first U.S. media-buying company, Time Buying Services, was founded in 1960. During the 1960s, a number of other media specialists opened for business, including Western International Media in 1966 and SFM Media in 1969. These early independents concentrated on television, which had the most negotiable rates and was the major medium for most national clients. The premise of these companies was that their media experts could obtain better commercial rates than could be obtained through full-service agencies, which often concentrated on creative services.

Although major advertising agencies took exception to this claim, the idea of breaking out the media function as a separate business has become an important reality in the last decade. With the new focus on the media function, there are two major areas of disagreement:

■ *Where media planning (as contrasted with media buying) should take place.* Some independent media firms have control of the overall media function including both planning and buying. In other cases, firms only execute the media plan provided by an agency or client. Some argue that by divorcing planning strategy from buying tactics you lose many of the efficiencies promised by the new emphasis on media.

■ *Degree of coordination between creative and media strategy.* Some agencies that have unbundled their media departments are now having second thoughts about this trend. According to Shelly Lazarus, CEO of Ogilvy & Mather, "I don't know how not to have a media person present in the room, given all the opportunites we have now. I would do everything right now to bring media closer in rather than further away."[5] This view is not shared by all. According to Jack Klues, the chairman of Publicis Groupe Media and one of the founders of Starcom MediaVest Group, an unbundled media operation, "I've lived for twentysomething years in a media environment where we were at the bottom of the agency food chain. I'm a better partner to my creative-agency brethren because I run my own business versus having to work my way through some agency food chain where I'm driving profits in and can't get money back to reinvest in my product. . . . I don't dismiss the benefits of physical proximity, but I would argue that your media director has the same access to resources, intellectual capital, financial capital, and can be as good as an outside strategic media partner. I would argue that just because he sits near you doesn't make him the peer of a more unbundled operation."[6] Some agencies that have unbundled their media departments are starting to bring media experts back in-house. According to *Adweek* magazine, each agency has begun to reintroduce media and creative in a different way. For example, Young & Rubicam (Y&R) hired a media strategist in its creative department in the role of director of communications planning and Euro RSCG has an executive creative director of media who is a liaison between the Havas shop and its media agencies.[7]

The concept of a totally unbundled media department is a core issue for many agencies. Historically, advertising agencies have promoted themselves to prospective clients on the basis of their being able to offer a complete menu of advertising services. Creative strategy and execution; account management and interface with a client's marketing department; and media research, planning, and placement could all be handled within a single agency. Up until the late 1980s, most agency reputations were determined by creative expertise and the number of award-winning advertisements and commercials they produced. Media departments (and the few independent media-buying firms that existed) were generally regarded as ancillary functions to the creative departments.

However, a number of factors changed the role of media and eventually led to the era of unbundling:

1. *Integrated marketing.* As clients began to view advertising as only one element in a complex marketing communication program, they began to see that advertising agencies were not the only source of communication expertise. To gain specialization in diverse areas, large companies often hired public relations firms, sales promotion agencies, and direct-response companies, in addition to their advertising agencies. As clients became comfortable dealing with a number of communication agencies, it was natural that they would look to specialization within the advertising function—such as unbundled media-buying companies.

2. *Cost factors.* As the cost of media time and space escalated, clients gave more attention to the media-buying function. Clients were demanding greater cost efficiencies, better identification of narrowly defined target markets, and accountability of media expenditures.

   The primary problem of achieving media cost efficiencies is that the goal of low cost is largely contradictory to the current move toward specialized media. Up until a few years ago, advertisers were faced with a limited number of media choices. In an environment controlled by a few mass circulation magazines, dominance by three major networks, and largely monopolistic daily newspapers, advertisers sought to reach as many people as possible, even when the strategy carried high waste circulation. In today's world of fragmented media with much smaller but homogeneous audiences, advertisers are routinely paying much more for each person reached than they did only a few years ago.

3. *Globalization.* As clients began to market throughout the world, the expertise and demands on agency media departments grew exponentially. Major clients recognized that without strategic media planning, global brands could not achieve worldwide recognition and dominance no matter how well the creative function was executed.

4. *Complexity of the media function.* Media planning has moved light-years away from the days of dominance by mass circulation media. Large corporations such as General Motors and Procter & Gamble have invested advertising dollars in a diversified media schedule including the Internet, numerous niche cable networks, and prototype interactive media on an experimental basis. In addition, companies are demanding that this advertising be monitored and coordinated with event marketing opportunities, sales promotion, and public relations. Often, there is a significant role for media planning in the execution of these programs. This type of expertise requires a much greater level of knowledge and specialization than can be provided by a traditional media department.

5. *Profitability.* In addition to the benefits that unbundling accrues to clients, it also has added a profit center for the agencies engaging in it. Now agencies can compete for clients' media accounts even when another agency handles the creative side. Unbundled companies such as Mediacom, Mediaedge:cia, Starcom MediaVest, and ZenithOptimedia are playing a significant role in the media plans of major advertisers (see Exhibit 7.1). Only a few years ago, the clients being served by these independent media buyers would have been handled by full-service agencies such as Young & Rubicam, Foote Cone & Belding, and Leo Burnett, all of which have unbundled their media departments.

Unbundling has given media executives a greater role in the overall planning of advertising strategy. It also has highlighted the importance of media as part of the advertising mix. It is obvious that, in a world of fragmented audiences and niche media, media decisions will continue to occupy a primary position in advertising planning. Advertisers increasingly realize the wasted effort and money in delivering even the most creative messages to the wrong audience.

Rank		Worldwide Billings (dollars in millions)	
2005	Media Specialist [Parent]	Headquarters	2005
1	OMD Woldwide 1 [Omnicom]	New York	$23,075
2	Starcom MediaVest Group 2 [Publicis]	Chicago	22,013
3	MindShare Worldwide [WPP]	London/New York	21,465
4	Carat 3 [Aegis]	New York	19,752
5	Mediaedge:cia [WPP]	London/New York	17,061
6	ZenithOptimedia [Publicis]	London	16,740
7	MediaCom [WPP]	New York	15,776
8	Universal McCann Worldwide [Interpublic]	New York	13,074
9	Initiative 4 [Interpublic]	New York	12,897
10	MPG [Havas]	Barcelona/New York	8,968

Rank		Recma's U.S. Billings (dollars in millions)	
2005	Media Specialist [Parent]	Headquarters	2005
1	OMD Woldwide [Omnicom]	New York	$10,365
2	MindShare Worldwide [WPP]	New York	10,185
3	Starcom USA [Publicis]	Chicago	8,495
4	Mediaedge:cia [WPP]	New York	7,795
5	Initiative [Interpublic]	New York	7,235
6	MediaCom [WPP]	New York	6,250
7	Carat Americas [Aegis]	New York	6,200
8	Zenith Media USA [Publicis]	New York	5,910
9	Universal McCann Worldwide [Interpublic]	New York	5,910
10	MediaVest [Publicis]	New York	5,665
11	PHD [Omnicom]	New York	4,335
12	MPG [Havas]	New York	2,250
13	Optimedia International U.S. [Publicis]	New York	2,185
14	Horizon Media	New York	1,445
15	Active International	Pearl River, N.Y.	879

EXHIBIT 7.1

World's Top Media Specialist Companies, Recma's Ranking by Worldwide Billings in 2005

Reprinted with permission from *Advertising Age*, April 2006, Vol. 12, pg. 2–12. Copyright © 2000 Crain Communication Inc.

BASIC MEDIA STRATEGY

Traditionally, media planners have used a *building block strategy* to develop a media schedule. Keeping in mind cost efficiencies, they started with the medium that reaches the most prospects and work down to those that reach the smallest portion of the audience. In the past, the first or second "blocks" were relatively easy to determine. Most national advertisers used network television or magazines as the dominant medium. The media planner then considered other vehicles to reach smaller audience segments.

As mentioned earlier, the media options available to supplement an advertiser's primary vehicles have grown dramatically. The introduction of vehicles such as the Internet, video games, and interactive television have brought major changes to the job of the media planner. These options also have created new ways to view the media function and media buying. Media planners are forced to go beyond costs in developing plans. When dealing with these specialized media, planners must consider factors such as additional weight against prime prospects, ability to deliver a communication message in a unique manner, and the prestige of a medium that may outweigh low audience delivery. More and more media planners are examining qualitative factors of the media such as the communication interactions between the audience and the individual media.

Historically, the advertising process began with development of broad marketing and advertising strategies, moved to creative execution, and finally to media

An Interview with Judy Franks

Executive Vice President, Director of Brand Behavior, Energy BBDO, Chicago

Judy Franks has had a highly successful media career. After graduating from Michigan State University, she worked in the Media Department of Leo Burnett for two years; Euro RSCG Tatham for twelve years, leaving as Senior Partner, Director of Media operations; and then for six years at Starcom Worldwide. She was Senior Vice President, Strategy Director at Starcom when she joined Energy BBDO in Chicago as Executive Vice President, Director of Brand Behavior in November 2005. Judy is also an instructor to the Wrigley Global Marketing College. In this role, Judy teaches integrated marketing communication to the Wrigley team around the world.

Judy Franks

Judy, before we discuss your position as Director of Brand Behavior at Energy BBDO, let me ask you this: Looking back on your media career, what is the most exciting effort in which you've participated? That is, what do you see as your "crowning achievement"? Please tell me about it.

That would have to be LEGO. While at Starcom, I was the Media Director whose team led the creation of the LEGO Star Wars Movie: *Revenge of the Brick*. This effort ultimately won a Bronze Clio Award for content/contact innovation. LEGO had a compelling, well-defined marketing problem. While LEGO has a highly successful Star Wars franchise, its relatively low marketing budget could be dwarfed by all the hype and commercial license clutter surrounding the release of the final Star Wars Movie: *Revenge of the Sith*. How could LEGO break through the clutter and engage both LEGO enthusiasts and Star Wars fans? We needed to find the connection solution.

To begin the process, we undertook "consumer insight immersion." There were no surveys or research instruments. We simply went to chat rooms and listened. We found that what Star Wars enthusiasts cared about most was *the story*. So, we listened. We convinced our client that instead of investing the entire Star Wars media budget behind traditional, :30 television commercials, we should create and air a LEGO Star Wars movie, instead! It was a scary moment, telling your client that outright selling of the toys wasn't as compelling as weaving the toys into a storyline! But, our LEGO clients are visionary marketers. They were willing to take an informed risk, and give kids what they want: the story! LEGO then shared this idea with Lucas to ensure that we had license approval, and that the storyline content was as authentic as possible. The folks at Lucas were heavily involved in the storyline development

and ultimate approval. We then worked with Treehouse Animation to bring the story to life. Imagine, a five-minute film with LEGO Star Wars product, telling a missing piece of the story that would soon unfold in theaters! We then had to find a "theater" to air our movie. We partnered with Cartoon Network who treated the film like a feature movie on-air: with teaser spots, tune-in reminders and a premiere airing on Mothers Day: Sunday May 8th, 2005. Now, all we could do was wait: how would the fans react?

We didn't have to wait long to feel the results of our efforts: we immediately spiked 500,000 visitors to LEGO.com! *The Revenge of the Brick* Movie was the #2 rated program on Cartoon Network for the entire day! LEGO had to add four additional servers to manage the Web traffic we created through ROTB. We saw over 525,000 references to the movie on Google the week after airing. And product sales exceeded plan by +100%. This experience held an invaluable lesson: give consumers compelling Brand Content and they will engage with you!

After experiencing that kind of excitement, that kind of success, why would you, a 20-year media veteran, leave media to assume a role at a Creative Agency as Director of Brand Behavior at Energy BBDO?

I was excited by the prospect of creating something new. The rules of [the] advertising game are changing. We can no longer build media connections and simply "fill" channels with "advertising." We need to create engaging Brand Experiences that leverage both the Brand Idea ("what" the Brand stands for) and the Brand Actions ("how" the Brand shows up in a consumer's world) into a single, spectacular outcome. This vision requires a high degree of collaboration. Not a structural "rebundling" of agency services, but an environment that truly embraced the power of Big Brand Ideas and collaborated with all kinds of talent to drive outcomes. I found a very special culture at Energy BBDO. I met with Tonise Paul (President and CEO of Energy BBDO) as well as the Head of Account Planning and the Head of Innovative Communications and, together, we created this position: Director of Brand Behavior. It took seven months to develop the position and, after a year of activation, it still isn't done. It may never be done!

What is your role as Director of Brand Behavior?

It is not enough for a Brand to creatively express its core meaning, the Brand must live what it says at every point of contact with the consumer. That's what Brand Behavior is all about. My job is to ensure that the brand lives what it says, because actions speak louder than words alone. Brand Experience is the sum total of "what" a brand stands for and "how" the brand presents itself in its relationship with consumers. Every point of contact offers an opportunity to drive both Importance and Meaning with consumers. In today's multi-channeled, highly fragmented media market place, the rogue brand experience can be quite difficult to manage!

What do you view to be your biggest challenge?

I have to balance three sides of a triangle. I work with our Creative teams to help them break the channel boundaries that have, historically, been imposed on their ideas. Our goal is to ensure that Big Brand Ideas can flow freely across communications channels. Some industry professionals call this "channel neutral" or "channel agnostic" thinking. I like to call it "Creative Freedom." In addition, I help the communications channel planners at our partner agencies understand the Brand Defining Idea, so they can build connections that will help to reinforce the Brand Idea. In today's media landscape, the medium is a critical part of the message. Channel Planners must be as invested in the Brand Idea as the Creatives who develop the content. Finally, I work with Clients to help them to realize the potential from leveraging the entire brand experience as part of a communications story. All points of contact create a "moment of truth," not just the advertising! But, maybe the biggest challenge of all is developing the mind-set that we have little control; the consumer is in control.

The need for integration makes so much sense, and it's easy to understand in concept, but I've found it difficult to translate into reality in the classroom. Can you help with that?

I just returned from teaching a five-day course at the Wrigley Global Marketing College in Munich. I was teaching Brand Managers about integration. Here's an assignment I gave them.

1. select a brand . . . any brand that interests you
2. buy a disposable camera
3. scout the brand for two weeks, take a picture whenever and wherever you see the brand. You may seek the brand out, that is, go to places you're sure you'll see it. But you may also see the brand in unexpected places, randomly about the world. Take a picture *every time*, at every touch point.
4. develop the pictures and carefully analyze what you see
5. arrive at a framework by answering the following three questions: What was expected? What was unexpected? What is missing?
6. finally, develop a more careful analysis of "what's going on with this brand?" What was your overall impression? Did you see a "Big Idea"? Was the Brand's "Behavior" consistent at every point of contact?

Let me give you an example of what you can learn from this assignment, because I did the homework too. For my brand, I selected a relatively new, upscale fashion line. It particularly interested me because I thought I'd see the line advertised in magazines, and I hadn't. So, I took my camera and went out into the world. The first place I saw the product was in a Saks Concept Store—a very pristine display in an unhurried shopping environment. During the next two weeks, I spotted the brand in a variety of locations. Once, I saw it in a discount fashion store. There, it was mixed with far less-expensive fare, tousled, and sometimes fallen off the rack. The next time I spotted the brand name, it was on an item from the fashion's clothing line, with the brand name stretched somewhat too tightly across the back side of a not-so-fit young woman. Finally, I found the brand at a bus shelter poster in Times Square. The Creative Content was a heavily tattooed and nearly naked male torso.

Very quickly, in analyzing my photos, I realized that the brand story here was in a state of confusion. The merchandising varied widely, the advertising creative content as well as its placement did not fit with my initial impression of the Brand. Of course, you can't control users of your brand, but you must be ready for the impact that users might have on the brand story. Brand Behavior had been mismanaged. I no longer believe this Brand can be relevant to me.

What do you do to fix Brand Behavior?

That depends upon "what's broken." Sometimes, it's a realignment of a single element of the Brand's marketing mix. Other times, it's an examination of several "missed

(continued)

opportunities" that result from vertical channel plans that don't relate well to each other. The solution to this often lies in a Big Brand Idea that is borne from an integrated planning approach. If all parties are aligned on a single outcome, and all Brand assets work together to drive the outcome the result will be a more consistent, and meaningful brand experience. Integrated planning requires collaboration. Collaboration is not a structural issue. It's a mind-set. The marketplace will mandate integration because the lines between what is content and what is the channel are becoming more blurred every day.

I've one last question. Again, collaboration makes sense, perfect sense. But I'm curious, in this collaborative environment, where do ideas come from?

Great ideas can come from anywhere: an idea can be borne from a highly creative solution to a business problem, an idea can stem from the core values of the brand, itself. Creative teams of copywriters and art directors often spark ideas that blossom into integrated, multi-platform campaigns. And, the media channels, themselves, are often great catalysts for compelling ideas. At Energy BBDO, we spend a lot of time and effort collaborating on ideas and nurturing the "sparks" that happen along the way so that we can create magic, Brand Energy per se. We call our process Total Work. In the end, it's not about "where" the idea started, or what form of advertising the idea will produce. Rather, it's about building enduring relationships between consumers and brands that will fuel growth. The creative output is taking on all types of exciting forms: documentary films, songs, interactive websites, virtual health institutes, and great television/magazine advertising as well! Its an exciting journey, and a great time to be in our business! ■ ■ ■

By Peggy Kreshel, Ph.D.
Associate Professor of Advertising
University of Georgia

placement, which was often viewed as nothing more than a channel for creative messages. Today, that notion is changing in some fundamental ways:

1. *Qualitative factors of media.* Media planners are increasingly working with the creative team to understand the qualitative core attributes of each medium to their target audience. These core values interact with advertising messages to enhance or diminish the advertising.

   For example, newspapers are about information, television scores better as an emotional medium, and direct mail is about personalization. The brand message is likely to work best when it is not in conflict with these qualitative factors.

   The experienced media buyer must be able to look beyond personal media preferences and determine the media vehicles that will best reach prospects. It may be that a network television spot is needed or the best ad placement may be a stock car carrying a sponsor's logo. In any case, media planners must be able to step away from their personal biases and put themselves in the place of a client's prime prospects.

2. *Fading distinctions among media.* Technology is changing the fundamental relationships among media, audiences, and advertisers and creating an environment where distinctions among media are fading. For example, is the delivery of newspaper content over a computer still a "print" medium? Likewise, are text messages available through television still "broadcast" signals?

   In this new environment, media planners must be creative in the utilization of media vehicles and look less at the distribution system and more at the audiences and communication effectiveness. Even the traditional organizations of agency media departments will have to be realigned to comply with changing media technology.

3. *Media accountability.* Changes in media buying and scheduling are putting pressure on media planners to become more knowledgeable in areas that were not part of their responsibility only a few years ago. In the near future, job functions such as media planner and media buyer may be replaced by more inclusive titles such as marketing communication specialist. The change in terminology is more than semantic; rather, it more accurately reflects both the job function and the expectations for the advertising media executive of the future.

Research has shown that networks also have distinctive brand identities that appeal to certain demographic and buyer categories. High brand identification for a network does not always translate into short-term viewership. For example, two "brands" among television networks are The Discovery Channel and The Weather Channel, but neither averages 1 percent of the viewing audience. However, it bodes well for these networks as audience fragmentation drives more and more viewers to niche vehicles.

Ultimately, advertising accountability means that businesses want to be able to link their advertising to specific sales of their brands. As noted earlier, it is difficult to determine exactly what contribution advertising makes to total sales, much less how it influences a single buyer or group of buyers. There are software programs available that try to make this link. Scanner data from the checkout counter are used to attempt to relate television viewing and purchase behavior to estimate the sales volume produced by viewers of specific shows.

4. *Value-added opportunities.* These are incentives offered by the media to advertisers to try to entice them to purchase more advertising time or space in their media vehicles. As a way of providing an extra benefit to advertisers, added value is a way to encourage advertisers to spend more money while providing them with things that have worth to the advertiser. These value-added opportunities can be anything from product placements, event sponsorships, or mixed-media promotions to tickets to sporting events or remote broadcasts. Here is an example provided by Chris Oberholtzer, a former Account Executive for Comcast. "For example, during recent reality television programming, advertisers such as Coke, Pizza Hut, Reebok, Pontiac and Visa all purchased inventory in the program. Then as an incentive to purchase advertising in every show once or twice, they were offered product placement within the actual program. So they were getting an added advertising message to drink Coke, eat Pizza Hut pizza, wear Reebok shoes, drive Pontiac automobiles, and use Visa credit cards in addition to the ads they were running in the commercial break. This is added value."[9]

Value-added opportunites are limited only by the collective imagination of the media planners and the media sales representatives.

The need to find ways to better link advertising and product sales becomes even more important as technology continues to change the nature of both mass media and advertising. Many advertisers predict that in the near future we will not be dealing with distinct media vehicles. Rather, through the use of in-home fiber optics, there will be a convergence of media into a single multimedia source in which telephones, interactive computers, movies on demand, and laser printers make obsolete the traditional media categories. Consumers will have much greater control over communication outlets, selecting only those entertainment, information, and advertising messages they want. Waste circulation will be limited because, by definition, self-selected communication will only go to prospects. The organizations we view as media today will be information sources, and the carriers of this information will be limited to a few cable outlets, telephone companies, or other common carriers.

Media Characteristics

Before a media strategy can be planned and implemented, we must have a basic knowledge of the characteristics and functions (both editorial and advertising) of the major media. Faced with a multitude of media choices, one of the most important attributes of a media planner is an open mind. From established message-delivery systems such as network television to the Internet and various nontraditional media, media planners must be able to sort out the media options that best fit the marketing and promotional goals of individual clients.

We must remember that advertising budgets are not growing as fast as the increase in media options, so hard budget choices are the rule of the day for agencies and their clients. "In broad terms, we cannot sell more cars, sneakers or boxes of cereal to . . . people as a result of new technology. To fund these new media efforts, marketing executives will need to take a fresh look at the macro-level allocation of budgets as new media forms begin to take on some of the blended attributes of traditional advertising media, promotion, and direct marketing."[10] Future chapters will discuss the various strengths and weaknesses of media vehicles from an advertising perspective.

PUTTING IT ALL TOGETHER: THE MEDIA PLAN

Knowing the characteristics of the various media is only a necessary first step. Not having a plan to organize media buys into a meaningful whole is analogous to trying to speak a language knowing many words but without grammar to make sense of it. Media planners must be able to use the distinctive attributes of each medium as part of a sophisticated analysis that leads to a complete media plan for an advertising campaign. Although there is no standard format, we offer a brief outline of a typical plan and then discuss in detail some of the most important elements:

A TYPICAL MEDIA PLAN

I. Marketing Analysis
   A. Fundamental marketing strategy: Sales, share of market, and profitability goals
      1. Demographics characteristics
      2. Lifestyle characteristics
      3. Geographic location
      4. Level of product usage
   B. Product benefits and differentiating characteristics
   C. Pricing strategy
   D. Competitive environment
      1. Number and competitive market share of product category firms
      2. Regulatory and economic situation facing product category

II. Advertising Analysis
   A. Fundamental advertising strategy
      1. Product awareness goals
      2. Target audience(s) advertising weight
   B. Budget
      1. Allocation to marketing communication mix
      2. Allocation by media category
      3. Allocation by media vehicle

III. Media Strategy
   A. Match media vehicles (*Time, Monday Night Football*, country music radio, etc.) with target audience media preferences

    B. Creative and communication considerations
       1. Need for product demonstration
       2. Need for complex message
       3. Daypart and/or seasonal requirements
       4. Media compatibility with message themes and competitive considerations
IV. Media Scheduling
    A. Print insertion dates and production requirements
    B. Broadcast allocations and availabilities
    C. Budget allocation each medium (magazines) and media vehicle (*Sports Illustrated*)
    D. CPM estimates (by total audience, prime prospects, etc.)
V. Justification and Summary
    A. Statement of advertising goals in terms of measurable results
    B. Research plan to measure achievement of advertising goals
    C. Contingencies for media schedule adjustments

No two media plans will have exactly the same components nor will they give the same weight to those media that they include. However, the following section discusses those elements that are found in virtually every plan.

Target Audience

As we have discovered, a **media plan** encompasses a number of factors involving both marketing strategy and advertising tactics. However, none is more crucial to the ultimate success of an advertising campaign than the proper identification of the prime target market(s) for a brand. If errors are made at this stage of the advertising process, it is virtually impossible for the advertising program to be successfully executed. The foundation of media planning is the identification of prime prospect segments within the audience of various media. More often than not, this process is aimed not only at finding demographic niches but also at identifying consumer needs and the product benefits that meet these needs.

Throughout the media-planning operation, buyers and planners must keep their focus on the total picture of consumer, product, and benefit rather than considering only reaching the target market at the lowest cost. In recent years, the process of evaluating media's contribution to the advertising message (in addition to the message itself) has become a major research track. Advertising researchers are constantly seeking more sophisticated tools to get a clear picture of consumers and the ways in which they interact with media and advertising messages.

In viewing these interactions, media planners are looking at cost efficiencies in more sophisticated ways than in previous years. At a minimum, this broader approach to cost efficiency requires that media plans maximize delivery of prospects as opposed to people or households. Until recently, media planners tended to concentrate on overall audience delivery by various media. The hope was that by reaching the greatest audience at the lowest cost, the media schedule would also reach a fair share of prospects. This strategy worked in a day of mass circulation magazines and network television domination of the airwaves. The most common measure of efficiency during that period was **cost per thousand (CPM)**. We offer a definition of CPM as we begin our discussion of the relationship between cost and targeting prospects. Cost per thousand is a means of comparing media costs among vehicles with different circulations. The formula is stated:

$$CPM = \frac{\text{Ad cost} \times 1,000}{\text{circulation}}$$

media plan
The complete analysis and execution of the media component of a campaign.

cost per thousand (CPM)
A method of comparing the cost for media of different circulations. Also, weighted or demographic cost per thousand calculates the CPM using only that portion of a medium's audience falling into a prime-prospect category.

If we assume that *People Weekly* magazine has a circulation of 3,823,600 and a four-color page rate of $198,500, then its CPM is calculated:

$$\textit{People Weekly CPM} = \frac{198{,}500 \times 1{,}000}{3{,}823{,}600} = \$51.91$$

Obviously, no medium provides an audience in which every member is of equal benefit to a specific advertiser, that is, with zero waste circulation. Also, keep in mind that there tend to be several readers per copy of every issue of a magazine. Let's assume that our client is a toy manufacturer and only wants to reach women with children 3 years old or younger. In order to measure *People Weekly*'s efficiency in reaching this audience, we might use some variation of the weighted or demographic CPM. Let's look at an example of the weighted CPM.

In this case, we find that from *People Weekly*'s 3,823,600 circulation, there are 1.5 million readers who have children under age 3. Now we calculate the CPM weighted to consider only our target audience rather than the total circulation of the magazine. Therefore:

$$\text{Weighted CPM} = \frac{198{,}500 \times 1{,}000}{1{,}500{,}000} = \$132.33$$

You will recall that in Chapter 4 we discussed a number of different means of identifying target markets. In the preceding weighted CPM example, a media planner can substitute any number of lifestyle, product user, or psychographic data for the demographic category we used in the *People Weekly* magazine example. It is important to note that CPM figures are important only as comparisons with those of other media. *People Weekly*'s weighted CPM of $132.33 is of interest only to the extent that it might be compared to another magazine with a CPM of $100.90.

Media planners are constantly attempting to fine-tune cost efficiencies against more useful and targeted client prospects. An important research focus of recent years involves adding a communication component to the CPM mix. Rather than just measuring the number of prospects who are potential readers or viewers of our advertising, we now add some measure of communication impact and audience awareness to the mix.

Among the primary communication considerations by media planners are the following:

1. *Creative predispositions of the audience.* For example, teens are predisposed to radio in a different way than to print.
2. *Qualitative environment for the message. Car and Driver* magazine reaches readers who are in the proper frame of mind for advertisements for automobiles and accessories.
3. *The synergistic effect.* Advertisers seek a combination of media, which results in a communicative effect that is greater than the sum of each one. For example, cell phone manufacturers use outdoor advertising to gain brand recognition, magazines for detailed product information, newspapers for dealer location and price, and television for demonstration and image. The net effect is greater than any single medium used alone.
4. *The creative approach.* Does the need for long copy or quality reproduction require print, even if other media might be more cost efficient?

Intuitively, we can understand that these and other communication components should not be ignored in developing a media plan. However, the conversion of intuition into hard data is not an easy process. In recent years, a great deal of attention has been given to quantifying the value of communication in the media plan. Without going into the complex methodology involved, let's examine a few of the possible weighted CPM adjustments that might be made to take into account communication factors:

■ *Probability of exposure to a medium.* Should a magazine reader and a person who passes an outdoor sign be given equal exposure weight?

■ *Advertising exposure weights to equalize the probability of an advertisement being seen.* Are the readers of *Time* more likely to see the average message for your product than the viewers of *ABC Evening News*?

■ *Communication weights to equalize the probability of an advertising message communicating.* What is the communication impact of a four-color magazine advertisement compared to a television commercial or a website banner?

■ *Frequency of exposure weights in the same medium.* Does the first exposure in a medium have the same or greater value than subsequent exposures?[11]

Research has shown that high levels of audience involvement with a medium are positively related to advertising response. These and other methods of audience communication weighting are attempts to address this relationship in the media-planning process as well as to give accurate estimates to the value of the audiences of various media.

Claritas' Potential Rating Index by ZIP Market (PRIZM)

A shortcoming of many audience analysis methods is that they consider only a single variable. In our earlier *People Weekly* example, we designated women with children under age 3 as our target market for toys. However, we know that within this broad category there are a number of differences. For example, a working woman might purchase toys from an Internet website. Some women may buy children's toys from a salesperson who comes to their homes to demonstrate them rather than watching television commercials for toys. Likewise, income, education, and other factors might change the purchase behavior of a woman in this general category. Media planners realize that a multivariable approach is often needed to correctly identify a particular target segment.

One of the most innovative methods of segmenting markets on a multivariable basis is the **Potential Rating Index by ZIP Market (PRIZM)** system developed by the Claritas Inc. PRIZM NE divides the population into fourteen social groups and further subdivides these large segments into sixty-six subcategories (see Exhibit 7.2 a & b). The primary variables for determining these social groups are lifestyle and income.

Potential Rating Index by ZIP Market (PRIZM)
A method of audience segmentation developed by Claritas Inc.

◄──────────────── LIFESTYLE ────────────────►			
URBAN Mega-Cities 18.7% US Population	**SUBURBAN** Cities and Big Towns 18.3% US Population	**SECOND CITY** Suburbs 21.4% US Population	**TOWN & COUNTRY** Exurbs and Towns 39.6% US Population
Urban Uptown	Elite Suburbs	Second City Society	Landed Gentry
	The Affuentials		Country Comfort
Midtown Mix		City Centers	
	Middle-burbs		Middle America
Urban Cares	Inner Suburbs	Micro-City Blues	Rustic Living

(INCOME on vertical axis, increasing upward)

EXHIBIT 7.2a
PRIZM Social Groups
Courtesy of http://www.claritas.com, 11 November 2006.

EXHIBIT **7.2b**

PRIZM NE Claritas Segmentation Groups

Courtesy of http://www.claritas.com, 11 November 2006.

Urban Uptown
04 Young Digerati
07 Money & Brains
16 Bohemian Mix
26 The Cosmopolitans
29 American Dreams

Midtown Mix
31 Urban Achievers
40 Close-in Couples
54 Multi-Culti Mosaic

Urban Cores
59 Urban Elders
61 City Roots
65 Big City Blues
66 Low-Rise Living

Elite Suburbs
01 Upper Crust
02 Blue Blood Estates
03 Movers & Shakers
06 Winners Circle

The Affluentials
08 Executive Suites
14 New Empty Nests
15 Pools & Patios
17 Beltway Boomers
18 Kids & Cul-de-Sacs
19 Home Sweet Home

Middle-burbs
21 Gray Power
22 Young Influentials
30 Suburban Sprawl
36 Blue-Chip Blues
39 Domestic Duos

Inner Suburbs
44 New Beginnings
46 Old Glories
49 American Classics
52 Suburban Pioneers

Second City Society
10 Second City Elite
12 Brite Lites, L'il City
13 Upward Bound

City Centers
24 Up-and-Comers
27 Middleburg Managers
34 White Picket Fences
35 Boomtown Singles
41 Sunset City Blues

Micro-City Blues
47 City Startups
53 Mobility Blues
60 Park Bench Seniors
62 Hometown Retired
63 Family Thrifts

Landed Gentry
05 Country Squires
09 Big Fish, Small Pond
11 God's Country
20 Fast-Track Families
25 Country Casuals

Country Comfort
23 Greenbelt Sports
28 Traditional Times
32 New Homesteaders
33 Big Sky Families
37 Mayberry-ville

Middle America
38 Simple Pleasures
42 Red, White & Blues
43 Heartlanders
45 Blue Highways
50 Kid Country, USA
51 Shotguns & Pickups

Rustic Living
48 Young & Rustic
55 Golden Ponds
56 Crossroads Villagers
57 Old Milltowns
58 Back Country Folks
64 Red Rock America

The PRIZM segments are arranged in descending order of affluence from the "Upper Crust," who reside in the Elite Suburbs social group, to "Low-Rise Living," whose residents live in the most urban and lowest socioeconomic areas of the country. The value of PRIZM groups is that these general segments can be matched with those products and media that members of a particular group are most likely to use. For example, inhabitants of the "Upper Crust" are older, have higher income, and are more highly educated. They are more likely to drive a luxury car, read *Architectural Digest,* and watch *Wall Street Week* on television. By identifying these groups geographically, companies can develop efficient marketing and advertising plans without the wasted circulation of a less targeted campaign.[12]

COMMUNICATION REQUIREMENTS AND CREATIVE ELEMENTS

As discussed earlier, media planners are interested increasingly in the differential value of various media and the value they add or subtract to specific advertising messages, that is, the engagement these media provide. Another dimension of this process is the manner in which art directors, copywriters, and media planners have begun to engage in the process at the strategic level rather than simply seeing their role as executing someone else's advertising plan.

There is growing recognition by both account supervisors and clients that the earlier in the process that media and creative functions are brought on board, the greater the opportunity for creative input into unique ways to position and advertise a brand. This early involvement also allows a more thoughtful approach to the various problems that will have to be addressed inevitably as the campaign goes from strategy to tactics to execution. Particularly now that **value-added opportunities** are usually an important part of the media buying and planning process, it is necessary for both the creative and media teams to know what opportunities are most desirable for a brand to pursue.

There is a wide gap between advertising exposure and advertising communication. The greater the input from the account team to both media and creative, the better the communication and coordination. Often, the creative and media teams must make compromises among those media with the best cost efficiencies and those with the best creative attributes to properly communicate the brand's core message. The earlier that these decisions can be made, the better it is for media buyers who must negotiate prices and determine availabilities of space and time.

In the past, a major criticism of advertising execution was that media and creative functions did not have enough knowledge of what each area was doing within the campaign strategy. The result, according to critics, was advertising that did not fully utilize the communicative strengths of the various media vehicles. As mentioned earlier in this chapter, the separation between the creative and media functions seems to have diminished in recent years. Among major advertising agencies, there seems to be a heightened sensitivity that creative/media cooperation is necessary for effective advertising.

In part, this cooperation has been necessitated by the convergence of media outlets, new media technology, and greater opportunities for interactive approaches to audiences. For example, when businesses experiment with Internet advertising, the integration of message, medium, and audience requires different approaches than in traditional media advertising. The process of planning advertising in new technologies and Interactive media demand that all the advertising functions work in concert to make the greatest impact with an audience that is very much in control of the communications process.

value-added opportunities
Extra things a medium will do for or provide to an advertiser that add value to the purchase of time or space in the medium.

GEOGRAPHY—WHERE IS THE PRODUCT DISTRIBUTED?

Geographical considerations are among the oldest factors in buying media. Long before advertisers were knowledgeable about the importance of demographics and target markets, they knew the areas in which their products were distributed and bought and those promotional vehicles that best reached those regions. Even in an era of narrowly defined audiences, geography remains a primary consideration of the planner.

Today, the geographic media-planning boundaries are often much smaller than in previous years. Instead of states or regions, the planner may be dealing in ZIP Codes and block units or even individuals, especially in direct mail and Internet advertising. Geographical considerations also are becoming more important as advertisers find that consumers in different parts of the country demonstrate markedly different attitudes and opinions concerning various product categories. Sometimes these geographic differences are obvious—food preferences in the South are distinctly different from those in the Northeast, just as the demand for snow tires is different in Orlando than in Chicago. Other reasons for differences in brand demand are less apparent.

Adding to the complexity of the media planner's job is the fact that media distribution demonstrates some of the same unpredictable distribution patterns as those of products. Some but not all of these differences can be explained when you look at the age or ethnic makeup of a particular market. For example, according to Nielsen data, Atlanta tends to have different television-viewing patterns than those in the country as a whole. The larger concentration of younger adults and African American viewers can account for some of the differences. These varying patterns of product usage and media preferences must be considered by planners as they develop a media schedule that will reach prime prospects. Planners must begin with the location of buyers and prospective buyers and their concentration in specific areas. Exhibit 7.3 demonstrates the dual nature of geographical areas and the concentration of prospects.

Obviously, Cell 1—with concentrated prospects in a local area—is the easiest to deal with. At the other extreme, an efficient plan for Cell 9 demands a great deal of creativity to appeal to prospects with special interests—say, antiques or fine jewelry—who are not concentrated in any geographical area. These dispersed groups might be reached through specialized magazines, direct mail, or the Internet.

Media planners not only need to know where prospects are located but also how consumers in different areas rate in terms of current and future sales potential. A common method of relating sales, advertising budgets, and geography is the **brand-development index (BDI)**. An example of the BDI is shown in Exhibit 7.4.

Regional differences in product usage require many firms to develop a secondary, localized media plan to supplement their national media schedule. National advertisers are increasingly using regional advertising options such as local cable and specialized product-specific publications such as restaurant guides. As research data that allow advertisers to define their markets and media technology more narrowly to reach these segments become more readily available, we will see an even greater use of localized media. In some cases, this localization will be a supplement to national campaigns; in other instances, we will see national brands adopt an area-by-area media schedule as their primary strategy.

brand-development index (BDI)
A method of allocating advertising budgets to those geographical areas that have the greatest sales potential.

EXHIBIT 7.3

Location and Concentration of Prime Prospects

Prime Prospects	Local	Regional	National
Concentrated	1	2	3
	4	5	6
Dispersed	7	8	9

ACME Appliance has a media budget of $2 million and sells in 20 markets. The media planner wants to allocate the budget in the 20 markets according to the sales potential of each market.

Market	Population (%)	ACME Sales (%)	Budget by Population (000)	BDI (Sales/ Population)	Budget by BDI
1	8	12	$ 160	150	$ 240,000
2	12	8	240	67	160,800
3	6	6	120	100	120,000
etc.					
20	100%	100%	$2,000		$2,000,000

Example: Market 2, based on its population, should have an advertising allocation of $240,000 (0.12 × $2,000,000). However, the sales potential of market 2 is only 67 percent as great as its population would indicate (sales/population or 8/12). Therefore, the media planner reduces the allocation to market 2 to $160,800 ($240,000 × 0.67) and reallocates funds to markets with greater potential such as market 1.

EXHIBIT **7.4**

The Brand Development Index Emphasizes Prime Sales Areas

MEDIA TACTICS: REACH, FREQUENCY, CONTINUITY, AND BUDGET

The media planner deals with four primary elements in developing the final media schedule:

1. *Reach (also called coverage).* Reach is the number of different people exposed to a single medium or, in the case of a multimedia campaign, the entire media schedule. It may be expressed as the number of prospects or as a percentage of the target audience; but in either case, it represents a nonduplicated audience. For example, if the target audience is 500,000 18- to 24-year-old males and 200,000 are exposed to the advertising, it may be expressed as a reach of 40 percent.

2. *Frequency.* **Frequency** is the number of times that each person in the audience is exposed to the media schedule. In our earlier example, if the 200,000 men reached in the campaign generated 1 million exposures, the frequency would be 5.0:

$$\frac{1,000,000}{200,000} = 5.0$$

frequency
In media exposure, the number of times an individual or household is exposed to an advertising vehicle for a specific brand within a given period of time.

3. *Continuity.* Continuity is the length of time over which a campaign will run or the length of time that reach and frequency will be measured. In other words, a 20 percent reach and 5.0 frequency might be accumulated over 1 week, 1 month (which is most typical), or 1 year. In evaluating reach and frequency, it is important that the continuity over which these elements are measured be clearly stated.

4. *Budget.* The budget is the major constraint of any advertising plan. The core consideration in all media planning is the budget. Although the relative weight given reach and frequency can be adjusted, the overriding constraint on the total weight of the advertising schedule is the budget.

As the media-planning process progresses, the planner moves from general strategy considerations to specific tactics. The planner must determine the most efficient and effective media to achieve already determined marketing and advertising objectives.

EXHIBIT **7.5**

Reach, Frequency, and Continuity Relationships with a Fixed Budget

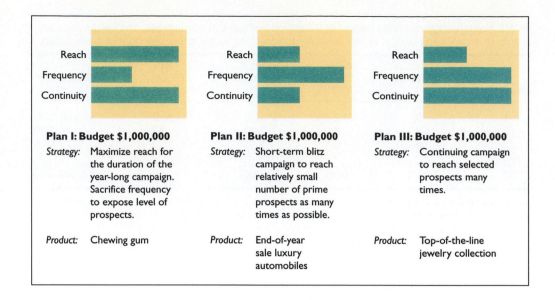

Plan I: Budget $1,000,000

Strategy: Maximize reach for the duration of the year-long campaign. Sacrifice frequency to expose level of prospects.

Product: Chewing gum

Plan II: Budget $1,000,000

Strategy: Short-term blitz campaign to reach relatively small number of prime prospects as many times as possible.

Product: End-of-year sale luxury automobiles

Plan III: Budget $1,000,000

Strategy: Continuing campaign to reach selected prospects many times.

Product: Top-of-the-line jewelry collection

The value of each media vehicle should be measured according to three criteria:

1. the cost of the vehicle
2. the number of target market members or the weighted target market quality of the audience reached by the vehicle
3. the effectiveness of the advertising exposures the vehicles deliver (e.g., the communications or qualitative component)

Reach, frequency, and continuity must be balanced against the demands of a fixed budget. From a practical standpoint, the media planner has control over reach and frequency. The budget is a strategic decision largely determined by the client. Likewise, the length of most campaigns is 1 year. The media planner must also consider the balance between the least-expensive media (efficiency) and those most able to communicate the core message and reach the best prospects (effectiveness). Exhibit 7.5 shows the relationship among the three elements in some typical media strategies.

The tactics associated with reach and frequency are a direct result of the previously agreed-upon marketing and advertising objectives and strategies. The decision to emphasize reach or frequency in the communication strategy will most definitely influence the media tactics. A number of tactics can be used when reach or frequency is desired:[13]

Reach Tactics

- Prime-time television reaches a large mass audience but is very expensive, so the budget may be quickly expended.
- Daily newspapers reach approximately 50 million homes and cover from 30 to 50 percent in many markets.
- Large circulation magazines such as *TV Guide* or *National Geographic* serve similar functions as network television but with smaller overall audiences.

Frequency Tactics

- Cable television, particularly specialized outlets such as The History Channel or The Discovery Channel, can be purchased at relatively low cost and tend to build frequency by reaching the same core viewers over a long period.
- Special interest magazines, as opposed to mass circulation publications, are able to reach the same audience over several issues.

■ Radio listeners tend to have one or two favorite stations and listen up to several hours daily.

Regardless of the specific techniques used by media planners to determine proper levels of reach and frequency, the overriding motive remains the same—to achieve cost efficiency with media dollars. However, a medium is not efficient if it is not first effective at communicating the message to the target audience. One of the most significant changes in media planning in recent years is a move from the goal of audience accumulation to one of measuring the effectiveness of the audience reached. In other words, advertisers realize that every member of a medium is not equal to every other member, even those with similar demographic characteristics.

The measurement of effective audiences takes various forms. Planners use a number of techniques to exclude waste circulation. For example, they develop estimates of communication impact versus exposure and they add qualitative variables such as media/message compatibility to their equations. Regardless of how they approach the issue, the overriding motive is to more precisely gauge the value of a particular prospect, medium, or message to the overall measure of advertising effectiveness.

THE MEDIA SCHEDULE

One of the final steps in the media-planning process is the development of a detailed **media schedule**. The media schedule is the calendar or blueprint for the media portion of the campaign. It also is the guide for media buyers to execute the media strategy developed by the planner. The schedule must offer in specific detail exactly what media will be bought, when they will be purchased, and how much time or space will be used for each advertisement or commercial. For example, if we decide to purchase *Sports Illustrated*, will we use four-color or black-and-white advertisements? Will we use the entire circulation of the publication or one of the numerous geographic editions offered? Which weekly editions will we buy?

The advertising schedule for a national brand may entail dozens or even hundreds of similar decisions. If local broadcast is a primary medium, there may be separate groups of media buyers who negotiate and purchase hundreds of radio and television stations. If cable or broadcast networks are a primary building block of the schedule, senior media executives with extensive television buying experience will negotiate buys that may run into the millions of dollars. Such advertising giants as General Motors and Procter & Gamble may spend an average of over $2.5 million daily on network television alone. Television media budgets at this level are executed in close coordination among senior marketing executives on the client side, their counterparts at agency or independent media-buying firms, and, of course, the networks.

Another concern at all levels of broadcast buys, but especially among networks and major affiliates, is time availability. As is discussed in Chapter 8, just because you want to buy spots on the *Super Bowl* or *CSI* doesn't mean they will be available. It is not unusual for a media-buying group to spend several days negotiating for time on a single network program.

The process of broadcast buying has improved in recent years through the introduction of electronic data interchange (EDI). Basically, EDI is a means of connecting the agencies, clients, and media involved in the buying process in a paperless system that allows the exchange of insertion orders and electronic invoicing. Not only is the system more efficient than former approaches to media buying, but it also significantly reduces errors by decreasing the number of people involved in the buying and billing process.

Another electronic media-buying process is available on the Internet. Several companies offer brokering services between advertisers and stations. These services not only list inventories of broadcast spots but also act as a central clearinghouse where media buyers can bid on available time. To this point, such services

media schedule
The detailed plan or calendar showing when advertisements and commercials will be distributed and in what media vehicles they will appear.

are a minor part of the total television time buying process, but they are becoming more important as the process of linking stations with agencies and clients becomes more complex.

Flighting

flighting
Flight is the length of time a broadcaster's campaign runs. Can be days, weeks, or months—but does not refer to a year. A flighting schedule alternates periods of activity with periods of inactivity.

One of the most used advertising scheduling techniques is **flighting**. Flighting consists of relatively short bursts of advertising followed by periods of total or relative inactivity. For example, a company might run a heavy schedule of advertising for 6 weeks and then run only an occasional advertisement to its best prospects over the next 6 weeks. The idea is to build audience perception for the product so that brand awareness carries over those periods of inactivity. Done correctly, the advertiser achieves the same brand awareness at a greatly reduced cost compared to a steady advertising schedule.

The concept is obviously appealing to advertisers that rarely think they have enough funds to reach all their prospects with a consistent advertising program. The problem facing the advertiser is that available research on flighting cannot predict precisely the awareness levels needed to achieve any particular flighting strategy. One thing is certain—advertisers must guard against significant erosion of brand awareness during breaks between flights. Exhibit 7.6 demonstrates the ideal outcome of a properly executed flighting strategy compared to a steady schedule with both using the same advertising budget.

In the steady schedule, audience awareness peaks fairly quickly (after about 20 weeks) and afterward shows little if any increase. The flighting schedule grows much more slowly, but because of budget savings it is able to reach more prospects and, therefore, actually achieve higher levels of brand awareness in the long term. As we cautioned earlier, an advertiser must be careful to consider the communication component of the media plan. Some media planners think that a flighting plan may sacrifice depth of communication even though minimal awareness may be achieved.

Regardless of the flighting schedule used, the following factors should be considered before using the strategy:

1. *Competitive spending.* How does your plan coincide with primary competitors? Are you vulnerable to competition between flights?
2. *Timing of flights.* Does the schedule go contrary to any seasonal features found in the product-purchase cycle?

EXHIBIT 7.6

Steady Versus Flighting Media Schedules

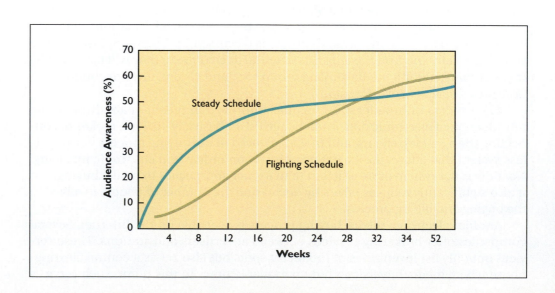

3. *Advertising decay.* Are you spending enough in peak periods to maintain awareness between flights?

4. *Secondary media.* Should secondary or trade media be used between flights to maintain minimal visibility?

A less extreme form of flighting is called *pulsing*. Pulsing schedules use advertising more or less continuously throughout the year but with peaks during certain periods. These peaks coincide with primary sales periods or a special promotion during contests or sweepstakes.

The Pressure of Competition

Advertising operates in a competitive environment, usually with a number of companies vying for the same consumers. Advertisers must be constantly aware of competitors' advertising strategy, product development, pricing tactics, and other marketing and promotional maneuvers. The media planner must not only develop an effective campaign for a product but also do so in a way that distinguishes his or her client's brand from the competition.

The media planner also must walk a tightrope between a healthy respect for competitors' actions and blindly reacting to every competitive twist and turn. Rather than operating from a defensive mentality, advertisers should take a practical stance in determining what their marketing and advertising plans can reasonably accomplish and how they meet the inroads of competing brands.

Many advertisers find it extremely difficult to analyze the market environment objectively. One of the primary functions of an advertising agency is to bring an objective voice to the table. Companies sometimes unrealistically judge the value and quality of their products. However, a key to successful marketing is an objective appraisal of both your products and those of the competition from the consumer's perspective.

For example, consumers who are aware of your brand but have never used it are probably satisfied with the product they are currently buying. Both the creative and media plans will have to work hard to give these consumers a reason to switch. In fact, we may have to recognize that some market segments cannot be captured regardless of the quality of our advertising. In such a case, brand switching would be an inappropriate strategy; instead, we might target another market segment with new advertising appeals, creatively positioned products, or both.

A competitive analysis must also consider various media alternatives and how they might be used to accomplish specific marketing goals. For example, a smaller company in a product category may find that television is impractical if it is dominated by advertisers with budgets that are beyond its reach. Likewise, we might find that certain media are so saturated with competitors' advertising that it will be difficult to gain attention for our message in the midst of high levels of competitive advertising. Media buyers must be aware of a number of marketing conditions in preparing the plan. The key point is that advertisers should undertake a thorough and candid appraisal of all aspects of the competitive situation. In doing so, a media buyer becomes an integral member of the campaign team.

The Budget

If there is any advertising axiom, it is that no budget is ever large enough to accomplish the task. With the spiraling cost of media over the last several years, media planners view the budget with a growing sense of frustration. In addition, media planners are constantly caught between large media (especially the major television networks) demanding higher and higher advertising rates while their audience sizes are declining and clients demanding more efficiency for their advertising dollars. Because the allocation of dollars to media is by far the largest portion of the advertising budget, it is the media planner who is expected to gain the greatest cost efficiencies.

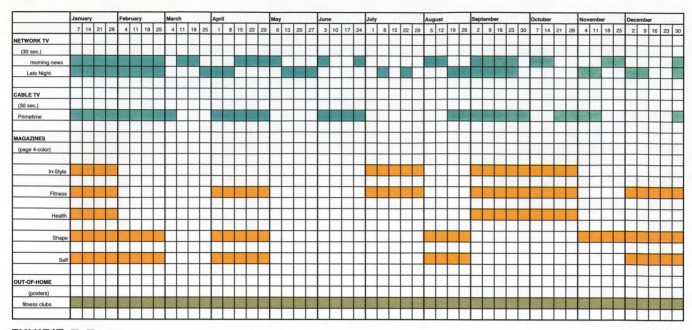

EXHIBIT 7.7

Media Flowchart 2007 Women's Athletic Shoe Brand

Advertisers and their agencies have reacted to this cost squeeze by instituting more stringent cost controls and accountability for their advertising dollars. In addition to these stricter controls on media costs, advertisers are constantly looking for alternative methods of promotion and advertising to hold down costs. Already, consumer sales promotion (sweepstakes, coupons, price-off sales, etc.) has passed advertising in terms of total share of promotional dollars. Advertisers also are using media such as cable and first-run syndicated programming to circumvent the high cost of network television. In addition, media planners and buyers will continue to put pressure on the media to provide them with a variety of value-added options. As media continue to fragment, we will see advertisers experiment with nontraditional media vehicles, some that did not exist only a few years ago.

In response to increases in advertising costs, advertisers are more precisely defining their prospects to cut down on waste circulation and are negotiating more aggressively with media for time and space. The fragmentation of media and audiences is driving up the CPM levels to a point that it is costing more and more to reach selected target audiences.

The media schedule is normally summarized in a flowchart that presents the overall media to be included as well as their audience estimates and costs. Exhibit 7.7 presents an example of a media schedule for a company that makes women's athletic shoes. The focus of this plan is largely on vehicles that reach young, active women.

SUMMARY ✹

The media function is undergoing rapid and significant changes at all levels. The competition for media dollars has never been greater, and the growing importance of new media technology promises to add even more options to the media mix. The trend toward localized media strategies, accompanied by the expansion of global markets, places even greater strains on the research, planning, and execution of media buys. As clients, agencies, and media attempt to make sense out of the mix of traditional and new media opportunities, the role of the media planner takes on even more importance.

While dealing in an unpredictable environment, a number of trends are certain to occupy the media community in coming years:

1. *Developing media/creative strategies to fully utilize interactive media.* After 200 years of the media controlling the communication process, advertisers must quickly adjust to greater audience feedback and control.
2. *Measuring media synergism.* Research technology must account for a complex mix of communication techniques vying for consumer time. The era of fiber optics, the Internet, and online versions of traditional media will require creative planning by media planners.
3. *Controlling media costs and accountability will become driving forces in the media process.* As the costs of reaching narrowly defined audience segments or even individual consumers increase, so does the demand for accountability from clients. What were acceptable levels of waste circulation in a period of mass media and low CPMs are no longer tolerable in a stage of individual marketing.
4. *Evaluating the value and impact of value-added options.* These have become more important in the media planning and buying process requiring planners to develop ways of evaluting the importance and effectiveness of the value-added options offered by the media.

These are only some of the many complex issues facing the media executive of tomorrow. Regardless of what the future brings, it is clear that the media-planning function will occupy an even more important role in an era of targeted advertising. The tension between increased media costs and a search for cost efficiencies by clients will result in planners becoming more willing to try new media or spin-offs of existing media. If there is one sure trend in an otherwise unpredictable area, it is that the advertising media function will continue to look for narrowly defined markets and, with few exceptions, disregard those media vehicles that promise substantial but largely undefined or unmeasured audiences.

REVIEW ⚙

1. How has the fragmentation of media audiences affected media planning?
2. In what significant ways has the responsibility of media planners changed during the last decade?
3. Briefly define reach, frequency, and continuity.
4. Discuss the applications of the brand-development index.
5. Discuss the role of value-added options in advertising planning.
6. What effect has unbundling of media departments had on the media planning process?
7. Discuss why media planning is becoming more creative.

TAKE IT TO THE WEB ⚙

Nielsen Media Research is a national ratings service for television and radio ratings. Review the data collection methods used by Nielsen as found at www.nielsenmedia.com. What are the strengths and weaknesses of this research approach? What kinds of improvements can be made?

The Television Bureau of Advertising (www.tvb.org) lists comparisons of the top U.S., Hispanic, and African American markets. Describe how this information might be of value to advertisers.

CHAPTER 8

Using Television

With ownership consolidations, blending of technology, and coproduced programming, television is truly a multidimensional medium. As the future penetration of digital television makes interactivity a reality, both advertisers and programmers will have to adapt to significant changes in the role of audiences with the medium. From a marketing standpoint, television is not a single medium; rather it is comprised of a number of related broadcast and cable entities that exhibit significant diversity as both advertising and programming sources. From large broadcast events such as the Super Bowl to local cable programming, each of the segments of the television industry has its special characteristics. After reading this chapter, you will understand:

chapter objectives

1. the diversified nature of the television industry
2. the multiple roles of television as an advertising medium
3. the changing position of network television
4. syndicated rating services and television research methodologies
5. the various segments of television viewing

Pros

1. Approximately 99 percent of all U.S. households have a television. Television viewing is particularly popular with many market segments that are primary target markets for advertisers.
2. Television's combination of color, sound, and motion offers creative flexibility for virtually any product message.
3. Despite recent audience declines, television remains extremely efficient for large advertisers needing to reach a mass audience. By utilizing selected cable outlets and local broadcast stations, advertisers are able to provide a local or regional component to national television schedules.
4. Government-mandated moves to digital television will open more opportunities for advertising and programming by early 2009.

Cons

1. The television message is short-lived and easily forgotten without expensive repetition.
2. The television audience is fragmented and skewed toward lower-income consumers. Daily viewing time declines significantly as income increases.
3. Shorter spots, some as short as 15 seconds, have contributed to confusing commercial clutter.
4. With remote control use, channel surfing by viewers, and the VCR and DVR (digital video recorder), the amount of time spent viewing commercials by the average television user has been greatly reduced.

Television, so ubiquitous and pervasive in our everyday lives, had very humble beginnings. In the 1920s when Philo Farnsworth, an Idaho teenager, envisioned the transmission of pictures over radio waves, he could not have imagined the medium that he was helping to launch. Unlike many scientists of the time who were experimenting with spinning disks similar to early film technology, Farnsworth was working on an all-electronic system. On September 7, 1927, Farnsworth and his team transmitted a line from one room to another. In his journal entry for the day, he stated:

> The received line picture was evident this time. Lines of various widths could be transmitted and any movement at right angles to the line was easily recognized. This was experiment #12.[1]

And so the age of television began.

In 2008, television will mark its sixtieth anniversary as a major advertising medium. However, at an age when most institutions are maturing, television continues to exhibit dramatic change and innovations. Television-viewing levels and advertising dollars have never been higher, and government-mandated introduction of digital technology by February 2009 will bring even more innovations in both advertising and programming. Because television has long been one of the most influential media for many people, even those who do not watch television are strongly influenced by it. Television news can set the political agenda, entertainment programming creates fads from hairstyles to putting new words and phrases into common use, and television advertising slogans become part of our everyday vocabulary.

In May 2004, 52.5 million people in the United States tuned into the final episode of *Friends*. Many of the viewers had come to identify with Rachel, Ross, Monica, Chandler, Joey, and Phoebe as their friends and wanted to see what the future held for the group. Such is the power of television. It is more than a simple channel of communication. In a real sense, it connects on an emotional basis with the viewing audiences and makes them part of the event they are watching.

The numbers for television are stunning. Approximately 99 percent of households have at least one television set, and average household viewing is more than 8 hours daily. In fact, Americans spend about twice as much time with television than with radio, the second most used medium, and about ten times more than with newspapers.[2] As impressive as the sheer numbers are, it is the qualitative dimensions of television as a source of news, entertainment, and advertising that are even more significant.

According to the Television Bureau of Advertising (TVB), television is regarded as the primary source of news by over 70 percent of respondents, with newspapers second at 12 percent. Obviously, advertisers want to be associated with a medium that not only reaches all segments of the population but also is highly regarded. TVB research found that television's credibility as a news source carries over to positive attitudes toward television advertising. For example, when asked about the image of media advertising, television ranked first as the most authoritative (51 percent), most exciting (76.5 percent), most influential (81.8 percent), and most persuasive (66.5 percent).[3]

Over the years, the complexion of television has changed dramatically. Television is moving from a mass medium to a niche medium similar in some respects to radio and magazines. Beginning with the VCR and moving toward the introduction of a number of interactive formats, audiences have become active participants in the communication process rather than passive receivers. A major catalyst for the introduction of two-way television communication is the Internet. With the growth in Internet use among consumers, it will be imperative for television to continue to move toward interactivity to combat the appeal of the Internet. Many television network executives and station managers have realized that the Internet presents opportunities—as well as challenges—for broadcasters to expand their audiences.

TELEVISION AS AN ADVERTISING MEDIUM

The business of television—and advertising is a major part of that business—is to function as an audience delivery system. Commercial television programming decisions are rarely made on the basis of aesthetics, entertainment value, or which news personality is most credible. Instead, "These are merely the vehicles for pricing and delivering the real product in the television business: eyeballs. . . . [T]elevision is a business for the mass manufacture, collection, and distribution of viewers to advertisers. . . . Not stars and stories, eyeballs and households."[4]

With an annual investment of more than $67.9 million in all forms of television advertising, it is difficult to imagine the medium without commercials.[5] However, in the earliest days of experimental television, commercials were actually illegal. It wasn't until May 2, 1941, that the **Federal Communications Commission (FCC)** granted ten commercial television licenses and allowed the sale of commercial time. The first commercial aired on July 1, 1941, during a Dodgers-Phillies baseball game. It was sponsored by Bulova watches and cost $4 for airtime and $5 for station charges. It is estimated that it was seen by 4,000 people.[6]

For a number of years, television has added program options at a growing rate. In the 1970s, a few independent stations offered sports and off-network reruns as an alternative to network affiliate programming. By the 1980s, cable was extending the number of stations available to the average household and a limited number of superstations such as TBS and WGN were accessible to most cable homes. However, although the number of channels increased, the variety of programming—most, network retreads—remained relatively stagnant except for sports, which proliferated at a quickening pace. However, by the 1990s, this situation took a dramatic turn as cable networks realized that in order to sustain their audiences and compete with the major broadcast networks for advertisers, they had to develop original programming.

Led by premium cable services such as Showtime and HBO, cable began to produce a number of original movies and even an occasional series. During the 1990s, the premium channels were joined by major cable outlets such as TNT and USA in producing a number of made-for-television films. In addition, basic cable networks were producing highly acclaimed programs such as A&E's *Biography*. More important, they were beginning to compete for the prime-time audience long dominated by the broadcast networks. Because both advertisers and audiences were attracted to these new programs, televison fragmentation accelerated and became the order of the day.

In about 25 years, television moved from basically three program and advertising options to a point where the average household received more than fifty channels. As Clarence Page, noted columnist and television commentator, stated,

Federal Communications Commission (FCC)
The federal authority empowered to license radio and television stations and to assign wavelengths to stations "in the public interest."

EXHIBIT 8.1

Television offers creative flexibility for product messages.

Courtesy © 2006, EPB.

 epb | GAS VS. ELECTRIC TV SPOT

MUSIC: SUSPENSEFUL MUSIC.

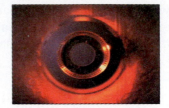

SFX: OMINOUS BLAST OF FURNACE STARTING UP

AS IF CUED BY THE THERMOSTAT, SMOKE BEGINS TO WAFT OUT OF THE WOMAN'S PURSE.

VO: If you've got gas heat, you're paying almost twice as much to heat your home as someone with a new electric heat pump.

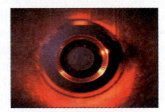

And gas prices keep going up.

SMOKE BEGINS BILLOWING OUT OF HER PURSE.

VO: So, maybe it's time to switch.

THE PURSE SPONTANEOUSLY BURSTS INTO FLAMES.

VO: Unless you've got money to burn.

EPB Electric Power. Affordable comfort.

"In my youth, Americans were united by watching the three network channels. Today, the audience is fragmented over dozens of channels and thousands of other new media choices, including video games, CD-ROMs, and the Internet. With broadcast audiences now fragmenting, we have to ask what happens to that common culture, those common reference points."[7]

With digital capabilities, networks can deliver a number of services to a household over the same conduit. Not only are there more options available but they can be tailored to the entertainment, news, and buying preferences of individual viewers on an interactive basis. In this interactive environment, viewers can participate in their favorite game shows and order merchandise directly from commercials. The vertical integration and capital resources of conglomerates, such as Disney and Time Warner, make this new interactive media landscape closer to a reality than many believe. It also will change the traditional relationships between the television industry and its advertisers.

While many of the technological changes are at least a few years in the future, television remains the primary medium for many advertisers. In addition to its high

EXHIBIT 8.1
Continued

 GAS VS. ELECTRIC TV SPOT

SFX: RUNNING WATER AND CLATTER OF DISHES.

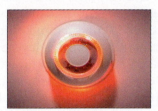
SFX: OMINOUS BLAST OF FURNACE STARTING UP.

AS IF CUED BY THE THERMOSTAT, SMOKE BEGINS WAFTING OUT OF THE MAN'S POCKET.

HE NOTICES SOMETHING IS AMISS.

VO: If you've got gas heat, you're paying almost twice as much to heat your home as someone with a new electric heat pump.

And gas prices just keep going up. So maybe it's time to switch.

THE WALLET SPONTANEOUSLY BURSTS INTO FLAMES.
VO: Unless you've got money to burn.

THE MAN FRANTICALLY WAVES AWAY THE SMOKE.

epb Electric Power
V/O: EPB Electric Power. Affordable comfort.

household penetration, television offers creative flexibility not found in any other medium. With its combination of sight, sound, color, and motion, television is equally adept at communicating humorous, serious, or tongue-in-cheek commercials. Television is a 24-hour medium with an ability to reach viewers of every lifestyle from homemakers to third-shift workers. Television also offers a number of advertising formats from the 10-second station ID to the 30-minute, program-length infomercial.

Limitations of Television

Cost Advertising and promotion, regardless of the medium or methods of distribution, are expensive. In recent years, there has been a great deal of publicity about the cost of television and commercials—especially those carried in blockbuster programs such as the *Super Bowl*, *American Idol*, or *Grey's Anatomy*. However, most people would be surprised to learn that even the most costly television commercials are much less expensive than print media on a cost-per-thousand (CPM) basis. For example, the average prime-time television commercial has a CPM of about $20 to $25 compared to a typical daily newspaper that delivers 1,000 readers for $65 to $70 or a national magazine's rate of $25 to $35.[8] Even with the highest-rated series charging over $500,000 for a 30-second spot, television is still cost-efficient for businesses needing to reach huge numbers of people.

As household viewing hours remain fairly constant, the growing number of options for television audiences has created an extremely fragmented audience and generally lower ratings for all segments of the industry. As discussed earlier, this trend and resulting CPM increases will probably accelerate in future years. Network advertisers, especially products depending on mass marketing such as package goods, automobiles, and fast-food franchises, are particularly concerned about these increases. They know that in spite of high CPM costs and continuing commercial rate increases, there is still no more efficient method of reaching a broadly based consumer market than through television.

However, with the competitive environment for viewers' time and attention, it also is imperative to make attention-getting commercials, which are often the most costly. Consequently, it is important to consider not only the cost of television time but also the production cost associated with commercials. Chapter 19 discusses in detail the process of commercial production. With some network television commercials budgeted for over $1 million, production expenses are another important cost consideration for any television advertiser.

clutter
Refers to a proliferation of commercials in a particular medium. This reduces the impact of any single message.

Clutter Television **clutter** is defined as any nonprogram material carried during or between shows. Commercials account for more than 80 percent of this material with the other time devoted to public service announcements and program promotional spots. In the last 2 years, the issue of television commercial clutter has become a major topic among advertisers and their agencies. As summarized by the director of communication insights at Omnicrom Group's OMD, "As ratings decline and demand for shows with higher ratings, in particular, remains strong, pressure is on networks to raise the number of ad minutes."[9]

According to WPP Group's MindShare media group, network television runs an average of about 15 minutes of nonprogram content per hour.[10] Advertisers are left to wonder if the commercials are as valuable now that there is so much clutter. Consumers may increase their avoidance of commercials if they are annoyed by all of the clutter. "Americans spend an average of four hours a day watching TV, an hour of that enduring commercials. That adds up to an astounding 10 percent of total leisure time; at current rates, a typical viewer fritters away three years of his life getting bombarded with commercials."[11]

Advertisers also point out that not only has the total nonprogram time increased, but the number of commercials has also grown with the use of shorter spots. In 1980, almost 95 percent of network television commercials were 30-second spots. By 2005, over 38 percent of commercial spots were 15 seconds or less.[12] Research has shown that the number of commercials contributes to the perception of clutter even when overall commercial time remains constant.

To try to combat this problem and break through the commercial clutter, some television networks have experimented with reducing the number of commercials and advertisers. They have allowed some advertisers to buy all of the commercial time within a particular program. "American Express Co., for example, sponsored an entire episode of *The West Wing* with a limited number of ads. Nissan North America and Time Warner Inc.'s Warner Brothers movie studio respectively sponsored debut episodes of *Heroes* on NBC and *Smith* on CBS—with limited ads."[13]

THE RATING-POINT SYSTEM

Television advertisers evaluate the medium according to the delivery of certain target audiences. In the case of networks and large affiliates, advertisers tend to look for exposure to fairly broad audience segments, such as women ages 18 to 49. Cable networks and some independent stations are evaluated by their ability to deliver more narrowly defined audiences that are both smaller in size and more expensive to reach on a CPM basis but that have less waste circulation.

The basic measure of television is the **rating point**. The rating, expressed as a percentage of some population (either television households or a specific demographic group such as women ages 18 to 49), gives the advertiser a measure of coverage based on the potential of the market. The rating is usually calculated as follows:

$$\text{Rating} = \frac{\text{program audience}}{\text{total TV households}}$$

When ratings are expressed as percentages of individuals, the same formula is used, but the population is some target segment rather than households. For example, if we are interested only in 18- to 34-year-old males, the formula would be:

$$\text{Rating} = \frac{18-34 \text{ males viewing program}}{\text{total } 18-34 \text{ males in population}}$$

A household rating of 12 for a program means that 12 percent of all households in a particular area that have a television set tuned their sets in to that station. Prime-time network programs usually achieve a rating of between 6 and 16, with the average being less than 9.

As we discuss later in this chapter, television advertising is rarely bought on a program-by-program basis. Instead, advertisers schedule a package of spots that is placed in a number of programs and dayparts. The weight of a schedule is measured in terms of the total ratings for all commercial spots bought—the **gross rating points (GRPs)**.

Gross rating points were calculated by multiplying the insertions by the rating. In the case of *All My Children*, the rating was 5.5×20 (the number of insertions) = 110 GRPs (see Exhibit 8.2).

Advertisers also use GRPs as the basis for examining the relationship between reach and frequency. These relationships can be expressed mathematically:

$$R \times F = GRP$$

$$\frac{GRP}{R} = F \text{ and } \frac{GRP}{F} = R$$

where R = reach, and F = frequency.

To use these relationships, you must know (or be able to estimate) the unduplicated audience. In the television schedule in Exhibit 8.1, we estimate that we reached about 50 percent of the entire target market and that the average number of times we reached each person in the audience was 5.5. We can check the formulas using the solutions previously calculated:

$$R \times F = GRP \text{ or}$$

$$\frac{GRP}{R} = F \text{ or } \frac{275}{5.5} = 50$$

$$\frac{GRP}{R} = F \text{ or } \frac{275}{50} = 5.5$$

One of the principal merits of the GRP system is that it provides a common base that proportionately accommodates markets of all sizes. One GRP in New York has exactly the same relative weight as one GRP in Salt Lake City. GRPs cannot be compared from one market to another unless the markets are of identical size. However, Exhibit 8.2 shows that the cost of television commercial time varies by city size.

rating point
The percentage of television households in a market a television station reaches with a program. The percentage varies with the time of day. A station may have a 10 rating between 6:00 and 6:30 p.m. and a 20 rating between 9:00 and 9:30 p.m.

gross rating points (GRPs)
Each rating point represents 1 percent of the universe being measured for the market. In television, it is 1 percent of the households having television sets in that area.

EXHIBIT **8.2**

GRPs measure weight of an advertising broadcast schedule.

Vehicle	Rating	Cost	Spots	GRPs
All My Children	5.5	$25,000	20	110.0
General Hospital	4.5	21,000	20	90.0
Guiding Light	3.3	19,000	11	33.0
One Life to Live	4.2	19,500	10	42.0
Total GRPs				275
Reach = 50.0				
Average Frequency = 5.5				

Here is an idea of the use of GRPs in two markets, Los Angeles and Boston: The advertiser has to decide how much weight (how many GRPs) to place in his or her markets and for how long a period. This is a matter of experience and of watching what the competition is doing. Suppose the advertiser selects 100 to 150 per week as the GRP figure. Within this figure, the advertiser has great discretion in each market. How shall the time be allocated? Put it all on one station? Divide it among all the stations? What yardstick should be used to decide? The answers depend on whether the goal is reach or frequency.

Look at the hypothetical pricing structure in Exhibit 8.3.

If we buy three prime-time spots in these markets, we would expect to receive 24 GRPs (3 spots × 8 average rating). However, it would be a serious mistake to equate a 24-GRP buy in Los Angeles with the same level in Boston. In Los Angeles, 24 GRPs would deliver 1,344,000 household impressions (0.24 × 5,600,000 HH [households]) at a cost of $75,300 (3 spots × $25,100 per spot). On the other hand, a 24-GRP buy in Boston would deliver 568,800 household impressions at a cost of $28,500. To estimate buys, advertisers often use the **cost per rating point (CPP)** calculation to estimate the cost of a particular schedule they are thinking of buying or a particular spot:

cost per rating point (CPP)

The cost per rating point is used to estimate the cost of television advertising on several shows.

$$CPP = \frac{\text{Cost of schedule or commercial}}{\text{GRPs}}$$

In this case:

Boston: $$CPP = \frac{28,500}{24} = \$1,187.50$$

Los Angeles: $$CPP = \frac{75,300}{24} = \$3,137.50$$

If we make the mistake of comparing GRPs from markets of different sizes, it would appear that a rating point costs more than 260 percent more in Los Angeles than in Boston. However, a rating point represents 56,000 households (1 percent of 5,600,000) in Los Angeles versus only 23,700 in Boston. A rating point in Boston costs $1,950 less than in Los Angeles. However, the advertiser is getting over 236 percent more households for a 264 percent higher cost in Los Angeles. This means that it is also costing more per person to advertise on television in Los Angeles.

In addition to the problem of intermarket comparisons, the GRP has other limitations. It does not tell us the number of *prospects* for the product who are being

EXHIBIT **8.3**

Television cost efficiency is measured on a cost-of-audience-delivered basis.

	TV Homes (000)	Average Cost per Spot	Average Prime-Time Rating
Los Angeles	5,600	$25,100	8
Boston	2,370	9,500	8

reached by a program. Still, the GRP concept does provide a unified dimension for making scheduling judgments.

It must also be remembered that GRPs alone cannot tell how effectively a broadcast schedule is performing. If an advertiser's target audience is women ages 18 to 49, for example, five household GRPs may deliver more women in that group than ten household GRPs will. This, as you would expect, is a function of where the GRPs are scheduled. Five GRPs during a Sunday night movie will almost always deliver many times more women ages 18 to 49 than will ten GRPs scheduled on a Saturday morning.

SHARE OF AUDIENCE

Although the rating is the basic audience-measurement statistic for television, another measure, the **share of audience** (or simply, share), is often used to determine the success of a show. The share is defined as the percentage of households using television that are watching a particular show. It is used by advertisers to determine how a show is doing against its direct competition.

Let us assume that the *Good Morning America* show has 5,000 households watching it in a market with 100,000 households. In this case, we know that the *rating* for *Good Morning America* would be 5.

$$\text{Rating} = \frac{Good\ Morning\ America\ \text{viewers}}{\text{total TV households}} \times 100 = \frac{5{,}000}{100{,}000} \times 100 = 5$$

The *share* calculates the percentage of *households using television (HUT)* that are tuned to the program. Let us assume that of the 100,000 households, 25,000 are watching television. In this case, the share for *Good Morning America* would be 25:

$$\text{Share} = \frac{Good\ Morning\ America\ \text{viewers}}{\text{HUT}} \times 100 = \frac{5{,}000}{25{,}000} \times 100 = 20$$

It is understood that both the rating and share of audience are expressed as percentages (hence, the factor of 100 in the equations). Therefore, we do not use decimal points to refer to the measures in the example as "5 percent" and "20 percent." Instead, we say that the rating is 5 and the share is 20.

THE MANY FACES OF TELEVISION

Although the average viewer probably makes little distinction among cable, premium cable, broadcast networks, syndicated programs, daytime, or any of the other permutations of television, they are in many respects unique marketing vehicles. Each of the various segments of the medium has its own advertising pricing structure, programming, target audience, and rating expectations. Exhibit 8.4 shows how advertising spending is distributed among the different types of television.

Except for the fact that they appear on the television screen, there is little similarity between The Travel Channel and the Cartoon Channel or between Home Shopping Network and MTV. Television has become primarily an individual-user medium with the majority of the audience viewing alone during most dayparts. The use of television as a personal medium is further demonstrated by the number of multiset households.

In the near term, as television technology continues to evolve, the medium will demonstrate even more diverse advertising opportunities. To some viewers, it will be primarily a source of immediate information such as stock quotes; for others, it will remain the primary entertainment outlet; and, as we enter a wireless society, for still others, it will be an out-of-home companion serving multiple purposes.

share of audience
The percentage of households using television tuned to a particular program.

EXHIBIT **8.4**

Advertising Spending by Types of Television in 2005 (in million $)

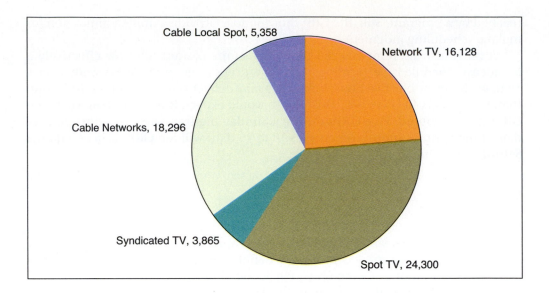

The process of media planning and buying of television has become extremely complex. Besides the proliferation of programming options, you may recall from Chapter 7 that there is often a variety of value-added options for agency media experts to consider. This section examines the many aspects of this extremely complex medium, which occupies so much of our time and advertisers' dollars.

NETWORK TELEVISION

In the 1987–88 television season, *The Cosby Show* was the top-rated program with an average audience share of 44. That same year, *Hunter*, a predictable police drama, had a respectable 19 rating with an average share of 34. Now fast-forward 10 years to the top-rated, award-winning *Seinfeld*, a show that many people would regard as a cult classic. In reality, *Seinfeld* finished behind the largely forgotten *Hunter* in average audience share for almost its entire run. Exhibit 8.5 shows the top network shows over the years. Note that the top-rated show in the 2005–2006 season, *American Idol*, had a rating that was less than half the rating size of *Gunsmoke*, the top-rated show in 1960, and less than a third as large as the top-rated show in 1950–51, *Texaco Star Theater*.

Although much has been written about the decline of network television numbers, why should anyone be surprised? Given the proliferation of television options, it would be an impossible task for **networks** to maintain earlier audience levels. As the television landscape is peppered with competition from The Discovery Channel to The Disney Channel, it is amazing that the Big Four (ABC, CBS, FOX, and NBC) have sustained the share levels they currently enjoy. This section discusses some of the key elements necessary to understand television networks as an advertising medium.

Clearance and Affiliate Compensation

Networks are comprised of local stations that contract to carry network programming. The exceptions are the so-called O&O (owned-and-operated) stations of the networks. These stations (e.g., KABC in Los Angeles and WNBC in New York City) are located in a few major markets and make up a small minority of any network's station lineup. The four major networks have affiliates in most television markets. The newest networks, WB and UPN, have affiliation agreements with smaller sta-

networks
Interconnecting stations for the simultaneous transmission of television or radio broadcasts.

Top-Ranked Regular Program Series Based on Household Ratings

Year	Program	Network	Rating (Hhld)	Share (Hhld)
1950–51	Texaco Star Theatre	NBC	61.6	81
1955–56	$64,000 Question	CBS	47.5	65
1960–61	Gunsmoke	CBS	37.3	62
1965–66	Bonanza	NBC	31.8	48
1970–71	Marcus Welby MD	ABC	29.6	52
1975–76	All in the Family	CBS	30.1	44
1980–81	Dallas	CBS	31.2	52
1985–86	The Cosby Show	NBC	33.8	51
1990–91	Cheers	NBC	21.6	34
1995–96	E.R.	NBC	22	36
2000–2001	Survivor	CBS	16.9	27
2005–2006	American Idol	FOX	17.7	*

* not available

EXHIBIT 8.5

Historical Ratings

Source: 1950–1996; *Nielsen 2000 Report on Television*; 2000–2001 Nielsen Media Research as found on www.chez.com/fbibler/tvstats/recent_data, 2002; 2005–2006 data: www.nielsenmedia.com, 5 January 2007.

tions in most markets. In fact, some of the CW affiliates (formerly WB and UPN) are secondary affiliates, which means they belong to another network and air CW shows on a delayed basis, often during non-prime-time hours.

Networks sell national advertising on the basis of station **clearance**. Network clearance is expressed as the percentage of the network's station lineup that has agreed to clear their schedules for network programming. In the case of the top four networks, clearances normally run close to 100 percent. The new networks often express their clearance rates as a percentage of the U.S. population that is potentially reached. Clearance rates are crucial to the economics of the smaller networks. For example, if a network fails to get clearance in New York City, it is shut out of 10 percent of the total national audience. Until a network reaches 70 percent potential coverage, it is usually not considered a national program by major advertisers.

Another primary factor in the relationship between networks and affiliates is station **compensation**. Compensation is a system whereby networks share advertising revenues with their affiliates in return for using local station time for their programs. At one time, station compensation was a major profit item for most stations. However, as the cost of network programming has increased and audience levels have fallen, the relationship between networks and stations over compensation has become contentious. Basically, networks have taken the position that the value of a station's local advertising spots is in large measure a result of the audience gained through popular network programming. Consequently, the networks are demanding that their affiliates share in the cost of this programming. For their part, the stations contend that without availability to stations, there would be no networks. In the future, stations may find that rather than being a source of profit, affiliation may be an expense. Regardless of the form the compensation debate takes, the root causes of costly programming and falling revenues will make compensation a continuing issue for discussion between networks and their affiliates.

clearance
The percentage of network affiliates that carry a particular network program.

compensation
The payment of clearance fees by a television network to local stations carrying its shows.

Network Ownership

Despite the fact that the major television networks are very large companies with revenues in the billions of dollars, each of them is a relatively small part of a major conglomerate. The network may not even be the most profitable media holding of the corporation. For example, The Walt Disney Company owns the ABC Television

Network and a number of local affiliated stations. It also owns, among many other holdings, ESPN's networks and its magazine; Lifetime and A&E networks; and, of course, The Disney Channel. In addition, the company owns theme parks, as well as Marimax, Touchstone, and Disney film studios and production facilities. A similar situation exists for each of the other networks.

The accelerated pace of acquisitions and mergers among media companies has raised some troubling questions in a number of quarters. For example, will the concentration of broadcast and cable ownership restrain the free flow of news and information, especially in the case of stories that relate to their parent companies? Will a lack of competition among media affect the economic marketplace in setting advertising rates? Will television content be restricted if networks are pressured to buy programming from production studios owned by the same parent company? Some have argued that Congress should prohibit companies from owning both the means of distribution (a station or network) and the production of content (a program production studio). It is unlikely to happen, but advertisers are very much concerned with the consequences of a marketing environment dominated by a few companies.

Network Commercial Pricing and Declining Audience Shares

As we noted earlier, television is in the business of delivering prospects to advertisers. The networks find themselves in the difficult position of encountering higher and higher program costs at a time when audience levels do not justify significant commercial price increases. Prime-time spots vary according to ratings and audience demographics, but an average 30-second commercial will cost approximately $150,000 on the four major networks.[14] At the high side, a spot on shows such as *Desperate Housewives* and *American Idol* will be over $550,000, while ABC's *Nightstalker* with its lower ratings will bring about $105,000.[15]

In the past few seasons, network advertising revenues have grown significantly. However, media buyers complain that these increases are a result of more commercials (the clutter problem) and unjustified rate increases that have resulted in higher CPMs. The networks are often in a dilemma, caught between advertisers clamoring for better cost efficiencies and stars of top-rated series demanding higher salaries. A further complication is that as popular shows age, there is an inevitable slippage in ratings. However, each year the stars earn higher salaries and networks are reluctant to cancel even their more expensive series, fearing that the odds are slim that potential replacements would fare as well.

Block Programming

Network executives not only have to choose programs that will appeal to a large segment of households and at least a handful of major advertisers, but their work is made even more difficult by the fickle television audience. Research has consistently shown that shows do not stand on their own but instead are greatly influenced by the programs directly before, called the *lead-in*, and the total daypart schedule, called a *block*.

The importance of lead-ins can be seen in the investment local stations make to schedule the most popular programming they can buy prior to their early evening news shows. The demand for strong news lead-ins is in large measure responsible for the enormous prices paid for off-network syndicated programs. The same principle is at work in building a network schedule. Programmers strive to make sure that individual programs will attain high ratings; but just as important, they want to ensure that the block will work together to attract consistently high audience levels.

Network programmers are very aware of the ebb and flow of audiences as they move from one program to another. The pricing of new network shows is dependent in large measure on their placement in the network schedule. Advertisers know that programs that follow proven hits have a high probability of success. An even better situation is the occasional new show that is scheduled between two popular returning programs. This is called a *hammock position*—the analogy being that the new program is placed between two trees (hit shows). Once a new show is on the air, it is judged by how it keeps the audience from its lead-in and sustains the strength of the block.

Network Television Advertising Criteria

Clients and their advertising agencies apply a variety of criteria in determining if, and to what extent, they will use network television spots. However, buying decisions are largely determined by three factors: demographics (demos), CPM, and demand.[16]

- *Demos.* Whereas at one time households were the unit of measure, today television advertisers place major emphasis on the demographics of television audiences. This change in criteria has altered the manner in which networks choose shows and the pricing structure for advertisers. For most advertisers, the makeup of the audience of potential network buys has become more important than the size of the audience. Of course, both advertisers and the networks demand that a show attain a certain minimum rating, but the price for shows with favorable demographics usually exceeds what their ratings alone would bring.

- *CPMs.* Although most advertisers are seeking favorable demographics and are willing to pay a premium to get them, other advertisers are driven primarily by cost considerations. Of course, no advertiser ignores the audience profile of its advertising buys. However, there are a number of advertisers who evaluate cost efficiencies and CPM levels on an equal basis with audience demographics. Advertisers of widely distributed package goods are more likely to take this approach than are advertisers for a product with more limited appeal. These companies take the position that, within certain broad audience criteria, they gain some benefit from virtually any audience because their product usage is so universal.

- *Demand.* The third criterion that determines the relationship between networks and advertisers is the demand for certain programs. Of course, demand is a function of both demographics and CPMs, but there are also qualitative factors—such as association with a special event such as the final episode of *American Idol* or with a star who has unique appeal to a particular target market such as Oprah Winfrey—that create a pricing structure over and above the objective numbers.

Avails Next Thanksgiving, begin to take note of the number of pages in your favorite magazines. Some November and December issues of popular publications swell to catalog size as advertisers compete for holiday sales. After the first of the year, these same publications will be very thin, with many advertisers standing on the sidelines after spending a sizable percentage of their budgets during the previous 2 months.

The broadcast media do not have the advantage of flexible advertising inventory. Every day, 365 days a year, each local station and network must sell more than four hundred 30-second spots. Television advertisers, like their print counterparts, want to heavy-up in peak buying seasons and on the most popular shows. Combined with the problem of high demand and finite network commercial time is the practical restraint that this amount of time cannot be sold on a spot-by-spot basis.

Networks must ration prime commercial spots among their major advertisers. The availability (called *avails* in network jargon) problem is solved, in part, by combining top-rated avails with less popular ones as advertisers buy packages of commercial time from each network. Whether an advertiser will gain availability to a top-rated show will depend largely on the company's total advertising investment on that network. Package plans allow the networks to work with agencies to place commercials across their entire schedule, with the understanding that each advertiser will have to accept some lower-rated (but demographically acceptable) spots in order to obtain some very desirable spots.

Up-Front and Scatter Buys Each May, major advertisers begin the negotiation process to buy commercials on the network prime-time lineup for the coming fall season. This is the so-called **up-front buying** season in which most prime-time spots are bought. In a period of less than a month, advertisers will purchase prime-time commercials worth several billion dollars. The up-front period opens with each network previewing its shows, followed by the actual negotiation for time. There is a separate negotiating period for cable. At one time, the up-front period consisted primarily of negotiation between major agencies and the three major networks. Today, the up-front buying process has become much more complex with a number of new players and different approaches by advertisers. Among the major up-front trends are:

1. *Greater demand for time.* In recent years, new categories of advertisers, telecommunication and prescription drug companies, have bought large amounts of television advertising as they have competed for consumer attention in a very competitive marketplace (see Exhibit 8.6).
2. *Globalization.* Agencies are having to position their U.S. up-front buys in a context of global media for their multinational clients.
3. *Special events.* The up-front market also is affected by time demands made by special events. For example, every 4 years, demand for political advertising by presidential candidates places an inordinate strain on an already tight commercial inventory. Likewise, when an election year coincides with a summer Olympics year, advertisers may be left scrambling for television time, especially during the third and fourth quarters.

up-front buying
Purchase of network television time by national advertisers during the first offering by networks. The most expensive network advertising.

EXHIBIT 8.6

Top Ten Network Television Advertisers, 2005 (in millions)

Reprinted with permission from *Advertising Age*.

NETWORK TV		Measured Ad Spending	
Rank	Marketer	2005	2004
1	Procter & Gamble Co.	$1,007.0	$1,197.2
2	General Motors Corp.	927.2	827.6
3	Johnson & Johnson	543.1	594.2
4	PepsiCo	510.2	438.2
5	Ford Motor Co.	496.6	507.3
6	Time Warner	486.9	481.2
7	GlaxoSmithKline	444.3	340.2
8	AT&T	424.1	539.3
9	Toyota Motor Corp.	385.8	344.5
10	Sprint Nextel Corp.	378.6	317.5

The up-front season is followed by a second phase known as **scatter plan** buys.[17] Scatter plans are usually bought on a quarterly basis throughout the year. They are designed for larger advertisers that want to take advantage of changing marketing conditions or, more often, for smaller advertisers that are shut out of up-front buys. Generally, scatter plans will sell at a higher CPM than up-front spots because there is less time inventory and smaller advertisers don't have the leverage to negotiate the CPM levels of huge network advertisers.

There also are up-front markets for other dayparts, children's programming, and prime-time cable. Early morning and midday programming each has its own up-front seasons, special advertising categories, and pricing structure. It is important to understand that network avails are often largely filled through the up-front seasons in each daypart.

Negotiation As mentioned in the last section, negotiation is the key to network buying. Because each advertising package is unique to a particular advertiser, there are no rate cards for network television advertising. Over the last several years, network rate negotiation has undergone a number of changes. First, the decline in network rating and share levels has created a more contentious atmosphere. But the fact is that network television, despite decreasing audiences, remains the best way to reach a mass market.

A second major change in the negotiation process is that advertisers are concurrently negotiating for time across a number of television options. As we mentioned, up-front negotiation still takes place among more or less discrete television formats (e.g., daytime, prime time, broadcast networks, cable networks). However, a number of media planners are looking to a diversity of options to reach a particular target market. As they negotiate network time, they are considering the cable, syndication, and even Internet markets that will be used as supplements to network or to keep overall costs down. With the billions of dollars at stake, agencies and their clients know that an extremely small difference in the cost of a rating point has great significance when a large national advertiser is involved.

Make-Goods One of the major elements of network negotiation concerns **make-goods**. As the name implies, make-goods are concessions to advertisers for a failure to achieve some guaranteed rating level. Make-goods are normally offered on the basis of total GRPs for an advertiser's television advertising schedule. That is, when the advertiser fails to achieve a certain agreed-on cost per point, the make-good provisions are initiated. At one time, make-goods were part of most advertising negotiations—they were always part of the up-front market. Make-goods usually take the form of future commercials to make up for a shortfall in ratings. Monetary refunds are virtually never given as part of a make-good plan.

It has only been in the last several years that make-goods have become a major point of contention between networks and agencies. Prior to that time, the networks were so dominant that it was rare for an advertiser to qualify for a make-good. Each network could reasonably expect to get a 25 to 35 share of the total prime-time schedule. Consequently, a make-good was a relatively risk-free incentive offered by networks to agencies and their clients.

The new competitive environment has changed the make-good situation dramatically. With several network shows achieving sub-10 ratings, the make-good has become a major negotiating point with agencies and a high-risk endeavor for networks. If a prime-time network schedule includes a number of low-rated or canceled shows, it may well mean the network will give up a significant portion of its inventory during the winter and spring to accommodate make-goods. In part because of make-goods, networks are very reluctant to support low-rated shows. Each season, there are a few shows that are canceled after one or two airings to prevent a significant demand for make-goods.

scatter plan
The use of announcements, over a variety of network programs and stations, to reach as many people as possible in a market.

make-goods
When a medium falls short of some audience guarantee, advertisers are provided concessions in the form of make-goods. Most commonly used in television and magazines.

SPOT TELEVISION

spot television
Purchasing of time from a local station, in contrast to purchasing from a network.

When national advertisers buy from local stations, the practice is known as **spot television** or spot buys. The term comes from the fact that advertisers are spotting their advertising in certain markets as contrasted to the blanket coverage offered by network schedules. The primary disadvantages of spot television are that it requires a great deal more planning and paperwork than network because each market must be bought on a one-to-one basis and it is more costly on a CPM basis than network buys.

Spot advertising is an extremely competitive market. Not only are more than 1,000 local stations competing for spot dollars, but the several thousand local cable outlets are becoming important players with many spot advertisers. In the future, broadcast stations will probably face a number of new competitive options from Internet services and other forms of local, interactive media. Largely as a result of this environment, increases in spot dollars are projected to remain relatively flat for broadcast stations as advertisers divert budgets to other forms of local television.

representative (rep)
An individual or organization representing a medium selling time or space outside the city or origin.

Today, most spot advertising is placed through station **representatives (reps)**. The rep is paid a commission by the station based on the time sold. The commission is negotiable, but it usually ranges from 5 to 10 percent depending on the size of the station. A good sales rep is both a salesperson and a marketing specialist for advertisers. The rep must be able to show a national advertiser how a schedule on WSB-TV in Atlanta or WCAX-TV in Burlington, Vermont, will meet a national company's advertising objectives.

Rep firms may have 100 or more station clients on a noncompetitive basis. Reps go to agencies and advertisers to convince them that the markets in which their client stations broadcast are prime sales areas for their brands. To make the purchase of spot buys more efficient, a rep will allow advertisers to buy all or any number of stations it represents. Because the idea is to provide one order and one invoice, it offers similar advantages to a network buy. However, the stations sold through a rep are not linked in any way other than being clients of a particular rep firm. These station groups are called **nonwired networks**. The commercials bought on a nonwired network, unlike a real network, are not necessarily broadcast at the same time or on the same programs. The nonwired concept is simply a means of providing buying efficiency and convenience for spot advertisers.

nonwired networks
Groups of radio and television stations whose advertising is sold simultaneously by station representatives.

As in the case of much of the television industry, the rep's role in the spot market will probably undergo significant changes as the move to consolidation in the television industry accelerates. For example, at one time, a single owner could only hold seven television licenses. In 2004, the rules changed to allow "a single entity to own any number of television stations on a nationwide basis as long as that station group collectively reached no more than 39 percent of the national TV audience."[18] Today, the rules allow a person or corporation to control stations with total television household coverage of up to 35 percent of the U.S. population. With this loosening of ownership rules, we have seen a significant growth in the number and size of station groups, some now owning dozens of stations. Some of these groups are large enough to support their own national sales force.

Regardless of changes in the manner in which spot advertising is bought and sold, the primary purposes for spot buys remain the same:

1. To allow network advertisers to provide additional GRPs in those markets with the greatest sales potential.
2. To provide businesses with less than national or uneven distribution a means of avoiding waste circulation incurred by network television.
3. To allow network advertisers to control for uneven network ratings on a market-by-market basis. For example, a network program with a 15 rating may demon-

Top Ten Primetime Broadcast TV Programs
For week of 11/07/05-11/13/05

Rank*	Program	Network	Household Rating**	Total Viewers***
1	CSI	CBS	18.2	29,546,000
2	Desperate Housewives	ABC	15.8	25,934,000
3	NFL Monday Night Football	ABC	14.3	21,860,000
4	Without a Trace	CBS	13.8	20,784,000
5	Grey's Anatomy	ABC	12.5	19,737,000
6	CSI: Miami	CBS	12.3	18,393,000
6	CSI: NY	CBS	12.3	19,225,000
8	Lost	ABC	12.0	20,012,000
9	Cold Case	CBS	11.1	17,424,000
10	NCIS	CBS	11.0	17,792,000
10	Survivor: Guatemala	CBS	11.0	18,981,000

*   Rank is based on U.S. Household Rating % from Nielsen Media Research's National People Meter Sample.
**   A household rating is the estimate of the size of a television audience relative to the total universe, expressed as a percentage. As of September 26, 2005, there are an estimated 110.2 million television households in the U.S. A single national household ratings point represents 1%, or 1,102,000 households.
*** Total viewers includes all persons over the age of two.

EXHIBIT 8.7

Television ratings vary by ethnic group.

Top Ten Primetime TV Programs Among African-Americans
For week of 11/07/05-11/13/05

Rank*	Program	Network	African-American Household Rating**	Total African-American Viewers***
1	Girlfriends	UPN	18.0	3,302,000
2	NFL Monday Night Football	ABC	17.8	3,146,000
3	Half and Half	UPN	15.9	2,884,000
4	All Of Us	UPN	15.6	2,953,000
5	CSI	CBS	15.1	2,888,000
5	Without a Trace	CBS	15.1	2,723,000
7	America's Nxt Top Model 5	UPN	14.4	2,505,000
8	Patti Labelle: Salute (S)	UPN	14.1	2,588,000
9	CSI: NY	CBS	14.0	2,537,000
10	Desperate Housewives	ABC	13.8	2,609,000

*   Rank is based on African-American Household Rating %.
**   The ratings above are a percent of the 13,170,000 African-American television households in the U.S.
*** Total viewers includes all African-American persons over the age of two.
(S)   Special
Updated every Wednesday

strate huge rating variances from one market to another. Ratings can vary widely due to demographic and viewing preferences of audiences within individual television markets. One reason that ratings can vary widely between markets is the viewing patterns of different racial and ethnic groups. Exhibit 8.7 shows the ratings for the top ten shows during a week in November. The first part of the chart shows the top ten shows among total television households. The bottom half of the chart shows the top ten shows during the same week among African American households. It is interesting to note that only half the shows appear on both lists.

4. National advertisers can use spot advertising to support retailers and provide localization for special marketing circumstances. Automobile companies are the leaders in spot advertising. As shown in Exhibit 8.8, the top five spot television advertisers are automobile companies. Automobile companies have extensive local dealer networks that are supported through spot television advertising.

EXHIBIT **8.8**

Top Ten Spot Television
Advertisers, 2005
(in millions)

Reprinted with permission from
Advertising Age.

SPOT TV		Measured Ad Spending	
Rank	Marketer	2005	2004
1	DiamlerChrysler	$528.0	$604.5
2	General Motors Corp.	341.3	444.6
3	Honda Motor Co.	338.8	384.1
4	Nissan Motor Co.	311.7	389.7
5	Ford Motor Co.	241.8	285.1
6	Yum Brands	213.2	209.7
7	Toyota Motor Corp.	179.8	236.2
8	Federated Department Stores	178.7	186.7
9	Verizon Communications	162.7	214.1
10	General Mills	155.2	213.2

Defining the Television Coverage Area

Before the advent of television, companies generally established sales and advertising territories by state boundaries and arbitrary geographical areas within them. However, television transmissions go in many directions for varying distances. Television research uses three levels of signal coverage to designate potential station coverage of a market area:

total survey area
The maximum coverage of a radio or television station's signal.

1. **Total survey area**. The largest area over which a station's coverage extends.
2. *Designated market area (DMA)*. A term used by the A. C. Nielsen Company to identify those counties in which home market stations receive a preponderance of viewers.
3. *Metro rating area*. An area that corresponds to the standard metropolitan area served by a station.

Local television stations also provide advertisers with signal coverage maps to show the potential audience reach of the station. The signal coverage designations have become less important in recent years as cable has greatly extended the area over which a television station can be viewed.

Local Television Advertising

Television advertising is increasingly purchased by local advertisers. Businesses as diverse as record stores and banks place advertising on local stations. However, a significant portion of the dollars invested in local television is placed by local franchise outlets of national companies. For example, McDonald's is a large local advertiser.

Buying and Scheduling Spot and Local Television Time Because advertisers have shifted more of their budgets to local markets, media buyers must be familiar with the specifics of buying spot and local television time.

The Television Day Spot and local television advertising is often purchased by daypart rather than by specific program. Each daypart varies by audience size and demographic profile. Media planners must be familiar with the audience makeup of various dayparts. Some typical daypart designations for East and West Coast time zones follow.

1. Morning: 7:00–9:00 a.m. Monday through Friday
2. Daytime: 9:00 a.m.–4:30 p.m. Monday through Friday
3. Early fringe: 4:30–7:30 p.m. Monday through Friday
4. Prime-time access: 7:30–8:00 p.m. Monday through Saturday

5. Prime time: 8:00–11:00 p.m. Monday through Saturday and 7:00–11:00 p.m. Sunday

6. Late news: 11:00–11:30 p.m. Monday through Friday

7. Late fringe: 11:30 p.m.–1:00 a.m. Monday through Friday

Preemption Rate A considerable portion of spot television advertising time is sold on a preemptible (lower-rate) basis, whereby the advertiser gives the station the right to sell a time slot to another advertiser that may pay a better rate for it or that has a package deal for which that particular spot is needed. Whereas some stations offer only two choices, nonpreemptible and preemptible advertising, others allow advertisers to choose between two kinds of preemptible rates. When the station has the right to sell a spot to another advertiser any time up until the time of the telecast, the rate is called the *immediately preemptible* (IP) rate (the lowest rate). When the station can preempt only if it gives the original advertiser 2 weeks' notice, the rate is designated *preemptible with 2 weeks' notice* and is sold at a higher rate. The highest rate is charged for a nonpreemptible time slot, the 2-week preemptible rate is the next highest, and the immediately preemptible rate is the lowest.

The following table is an excerpt from a rate card.

	I	II	III
Tues., 8–9 a.m.	$135	$125	$115

Column I is the nonpreemptible rate; column II is the rate for preemption with 2 weeks' notice; and column III is the rate for preemption without notice. Notice how the rate goes down.

Special Features News telecasts, weather reports, sports news and commentary, stock market reports, and similar programming are called *special features*. Time in connection with special features is sold at a premium price.

Run of Schedule (ROS) An advertiser can earn a lower rate by permitting a station to run commercials at its convenience whenever time is available rather than in a specified position. (This is comparable to run of paper in newspaper advertising; see Chapter 10.)

Package Rates Every station sets up its own assortment of time slots at different periods of the day, which it sells as a package. The station creates its own name for such packages and charges less for them than for the same slots sold individually. The package rate is one of the elements in negotiation for time.

Product Protection Every advertiser wants to keep the advertising of competitive products as far away from its commercials as possible. This brings up the concern about what protection against competition an advertisement will get. Although some stations say that they will try to keep competing commercials 5 to 10 minutes apart, most say that although they will do everything possible to separate competing advertisements, they guarantee only that they will not run them back to back or in the same pod or group of commercials in a break.

Scheduling Spot and Local Time *Rotation of a schedule* refers to the placement of commercials within a schedule to get the greatest possible showing. If you bought two spots a week for 4 weeks on a Monday-to-Friday basis, but all the spots were aired only on Monday and Tuesday, your rotation would be poor. You would miss all the people who turn to the station only on Wednesday, Thursday, or Friday.

Your horizontal rotation should be increased. Vertical rotation ensures there will be differences in the time at which a commercial is shown within the time bracket purchased. If you bought three spots on the *Tonight Show*, which runs from 11:30 p.m. to 12:30 a.m., but all your spots were shown at 12:15 a.m., you would be missing all the people who go to sleep earlier than that. To avoid this situation, you would schedule one spot in each half hour of the program, vertically rotating your commercial to reach the largest possible audience.

TELEVISION SYNDICATION

barter syndication
Station obtains a program at no charge. The program has presold national commercials, and time is available for local station spots.

Television syndication is the sale of television programming on a station-by-station, market-by-market basis. Syndication companies have programming to sell, and they seek to sell individual programs to at least one station in every market. Most major syndicated shows are sold on an advertiser-supported or barter basis. **Barter syndication** refers to the practice of offering the right to run a show to stations in return for a portion of the commercial time in the show, rather than selling the show to stations for cash. A majority of the commercial time on syndicated shows is packaged into national units and sold to national advertisers. The typical syndicated show comes with spots presold on a national basis, and the station sells the remaining time to local and spot advertisers.

Syndication began when producers sold their canceled network shows to stations for inexpensive "fillers" during late afternoon or other time periods not programmed by the networks. During the early days of syndication, no one thought that it was anything but a method for producers to pick up a few extra dollars by selling programs that had completed their network runs to local stations. During this period, syndication was a minor portion of television advertising.

Currently, syndication accounts for close to $4 billion in advertising revenues and major syndicated shows provide coverage comparable to the broadcast networks.[19] For example, leading syndicated shows such as *Wheel of Fortune* and *Everybody Loves Raymond* have potential coverage in excess of 90 percent of television households. Syndication is theoretically available in every television household, while cable programs can come only into less than 75 percent of homes wired for cable.

Like any television format, the key to syndication's success is quality programming. Syndicated programs are either *first-run* programs made for syndication, such as *Entertainment Tonight* and *The Oprah Winfrey Show*, or **off-network syndication** reruns such as *Friends* and *The X-Files*. Most long-running shows such as *Everybody Loves Raymond* and *Friends* entered the syndication market during their original network runs.

off-network syndication
Syndicated programs that have previously been aired by a major network.

Off-network shows have built-in audiences and reach predictable demographic segments. Advertisers also feel more comfortable with the known content of a high-quality rerun versus the less predictable talk and entertainment first-run product. In fact, advertisers are willing to pay a significant premium for most off-network syndicated programs compared to first-run shows with comparable ratings. In fact, a 30-second spot on *Friends* or *Seinfeld* in syndication can cost more than many prime-time network shows.

Syndication advertising costs vary much more than other types of television programming. Essentially, there is a three-tier pricing structure for the top fifty syndicated shows:

1. The top ten blockbusters include proven off-network reruns such as *CSI* and a handful of proven first-run winners such as *Entertainment Tonight* and *Wheel of Fortune*. These shows will have 30-second spot prices in the range of $65,000 to $215,000, with the network reruns invariably getting the top prices.

EXHIBIT **8.9**
New technology has made it possible for households to receive many more television stations than ever before. This has created the need for more program content such as syndicated programs.

2. The second tier includes a small number of shows that fall short of the top ten but still have a sizable, loyal audience. *Judge Judy* and *Dr. Phil* fall into this category and are priced in the $35,000 to $82,000 range for 30-second spots.
3. Finally, there are a number of talk shows and less popular reruns that will charge from $15,000 to $31,000.[20]

The demand for syndicated shows is driven by television's insatiable demand for programming—any programming. For local stations and cable networks with 24 hours to fill, there is simply not enough programming for the thousands of hours required to fill their schedules. In addition, as more and more cable networks are added, the demand continues to increase. Nickelodeon, Lifetime, TNT, The Family Channel, and a host of other cable networks are competing with local stations for off-network programs and driving up the price of those that remain in the syndication market. Adding to the demand for syndicated time are a number of national advertisers that use syndicated programming as a means of extending reach on a demographic and/or geographic basis. Generally, broadcast syndication will surpass cable networks in achieving significant levels of audience reach because the average over-the-air station has higher audience levels than cable networks.

The demand for syndicated programming has moved some stations to sign long-term contracts with program producers to guarantee continued access to certain shows. For example, in 1988, ABC Owned and Operated (O&O) stations contracted with *Jeopardy* and *Wheel of Fortune* through 2004 and other stations

EXHIBIT **8.10**

Top Ten Syndicated
Television Advertisers,
2005 (in millions)

Reprinted with permission from
Advertising Age.

SYNDICATED TV		Measured Ad Spending	
Rank	Marketer	2005	2004
1	Proctor & Gamble Co.	$322.6	$411.1
2	Johnson & Johnson	102.8	130.3
3	L'Oreal	102.0	72.1
4	GlaxoSmithKline	89.7	84.0
5	PeoplePC	87.2	17.0
6	Wyeth	84.5	71.0
7	Kellogg Co.	81.5	59.8
8	Time Warner	76.0	61.4
9	Vonage Holdings Corp.	69.6	0.9
10	Unilever	61.3	45.3

extended these contracts until 2005.[21] With the relatively few shows that can generate high audience levels, the stations had to make long-term commitments to ensure having them on their schedule in future seasons.

The Audience for Syndicated Television

Syndication has some of the same characteristics as cable. For example, although syndication generates high aggregate audience levels, it does so over multiple programs and showings rather than delivering a mass audience in a single showing as in the case of broadcast networks. In fact, syndicators sell programs on the basis of multiple airings known as *gross average audience* ratings. For example, let's assume that an airing of *CSI* on CBS has a local market affiliate rating of 15.0 and a *CSI* syndicated version has a rating of 5.0. If ACME, Inc., runs one spot on the network version and three spots on the syndicated version, the total rating points would be 15 for both shows. However, it's very difficult to compare the two because on network you're achieving your audience all at once. The network audience exposures are unduplicated exposure. In syndication, your ratings are based on spots running within a week.[22]

The future of syndication is extremely bright because local stations find it very lucrative. In the typical network show, stations may only be allowed to sell 1 minute of commercial time. In a syndicated show, the station can sell from 6 to 12 minutes of commercials depending on how the program was bartered to the station. Consequently, a syndicated program does not have to generate huge ratings to be a financial success for a station.

As shown in Exhibit 8.10, the top ten syndicated television advertisers include large package-goods companies such as Procter & Gamble and Johnson & Johnson as well as Time Warner and pharmaceutical giant GlaxoSmithKline.

Because local stations find syndication profitable and because the demand for new syndicated programming continues to grow, there is every reason to believe that syndication will be a major advertising vehicle for the foreseeable future. If anything, syndication will be an even stronger competitor to the traditional networks and the relationship between syndicators and stations may become more formal with long-term contracts and stations buying equity shares in syndicated programs to ensure continued access.

Stripping

stripping
Scheduling a syndicated
program on a 5-day-per-
week basis.

Most local stations schedule syndicated shows on a basis of five nights a week. That is, they will run *Jeopardy* or *Inside Edition* Monday through Friday in the same time slot. This practice is called **stripping** because the show is stripped across a time period. It is cost efficient to buy fewer shows for multishowings and allows a station to build a consistent audience for selling commercials to potential advertisers. Because most syndication is used as a lead-in either for early news or prime-time programs, stations don't want huge rating or audience composition swings from one day to another.

CABLE TELEVISION

Cable television has its roots in the small Pennsylvania town of Mahanoy City. In the 1940s, John Watson, an appliance store owner, was having difficulty selling television sets because of poor reception caused by a mountain range between Philadelphia stations and Mahanoy City. By placing an antenna on a surrounding peak combined with coaxial cable and amplifiers, cable television (then known as Community Antenna Television or CATV) had begun.

Soon cable systems were importing a variety of signals from different cities to rural households. By the 1970s, cable had become attractive to viewers throughout the country and it moved from remote areas to major cities. In 1972, pay television was launched when Home Box Office (HBO) began service. HBO initiated the era of original programming as opposed to simply extending the signals of over-the-air stations. Of equal importance, HBO's programming was delivered by satellite and provided universal availability for cable networks.[23]

From its humble beginnings, cable television has become a major medium in its own right with household penetration of more than 72 percent. In recent years, the cable advertising share of total dollars has shown double-digit increases. Both local and national cable advertising revenues continue to grow at a rate higher than many other forms of advertising.

The Contemporary Cable Television Industry

For the first two decades of its existence, cable customers were satisfied to get a wider option of over-the-air broadcast programs and cable operators were making satisfactory profits from cable subscription fees. However, cable industry executives realized that they were missing a major source of revenue by failing to open the medium to advertisers. For the last 25 years, cable has grown as it matured into a medium serving both viewers and advertisers.

The success of cable can be traced to two related elements:

1. Brand identification based on unique and selective networks and programs that appeal to targeted demographic audience segments
2. The investment by cable networks in first-run programming

Unlike broadcast networks that reach huge audiences for mass advertisers, cable provides advertisers with much smaller niche audiences that exhibit both common demographic characteristics and interests. Advertisers know that Lifetime, MTV, Cartoon Network, and The Discovery Channel will deliver predictable groups of viewers. Cable networks define their brands in the same way that product manufacturers do. For both, brand identification and awareness create a consistent environment for the users of these brands.

It is favorable brand recognition that provides the major impetus to cable success in bringing large national advertisers to the medium. As shown in Exhibit 8.11, with leading advertisers such as Procter & Gamble, General Motors, and Time Warner, cable is competing for the same advertisers as the broadcast networks.

Cable networks know that it is original programming that will bring both viewers and advertisers to a particular network. Only a few years ago, the majority of cable network programming consisted of off-network reruns and theatrical films that had usually been run several times on both broadcast networks and local stations. Today, cable networks annually invest billions of dollars in original programming, some of which is among the most popular on television. From ESPN's *Monday NFL* games to A&E's *Investigative Reports* and *Biography*, cable networks are appealing to a larger share of the total viewing audience.

cable television
Television signals that are carried to households by cable. Programs originate with cable operators through high antennas, satellite disks, or operator-initiated programming.

EXHIBIT **8.11**

Top Ten Cable Advertisers, 2005 (in millions)

Reprinted with permission from *Advertising Age*.

CABLE TV NETWORKS		Measured Ad Spending	
Rank	Marketer	2005	2004
1	Proctor & Gamble Co.	$828.8	$785.6
2	General Motors Corp.	322.1	303.9
3	Time Warner	282.0	210.7
4	GlaxoSmithKline	259.3	202.9
5	Altria Group	226.0	190.1
6	Walt Disney Co.	202.2	194.6
7	Johnson & Johnson	196.4	201.9
8	Sony Corp.	178.8	151.9
9	Petmeds Express	176.8	128.9
10	U.S. Government	175.3	134.8

The Future of Cable Advertising

A number of factors make cable television an attractive medium for advertisers:

1. *Ability to target audiences.* When advertisers consider cable television, its ability to reach specific demographic and lifestyle segments is almost always the prime consideration.

2. *Low cost.* The cable industry is faced with a competitive environment that prevents significant increases in CPMs. With an abundance of cable channels, many trying to prove themselves to advertisers, it is very unlikely that we will see the type of advertising increases that have been so prevalent among the major broadcast networks in recent years.

3. *A strong summer season.* In recent years, cable has counterprogrammed the networks by presenting some of their strongest programs opposite network summer reruns. Many advertisers have taken advantage of the audience shifts inherent in this strategy to move dollars into cable during what is typically a down viewing time for networks.

4. *Opportunity for local and spot cable advertising.* The majority of cable advertising dollars are spent at the network level. However, local cable advertising is growing at a rate significantly higher than network advertising. Local cable spending comes from national spot buyers looking to enhance advertising weight in specific markets and a wide variety of local firms such as restaurants, video stores, and small retailers. Because of cable's low advertising rates, these retailers now have a chance to use television.

One interesting trend of the last few years has been for cable networks to branch out and begin their own magazines. ESPN launched its highly successful *ESPN The Magazine* to sports fans in 1998. Nickelodeon has three successful spin-offs with *Nickelodeon, Nick Jr.,* and *Nick Jr. Family Magazine (NJFM)*. *NJFM*, geared to those families with children under age 12, has been named to *Adweek*'s magazine "hot" list several times in recent years.[24] Other magazines associated with cable networks have launched with less fanfare but with mixed success. A&E's *Biography* magazine, however, failed to make it as anything but a fan magazine.[25] These types of magazines offer advertisers the opportunity to negotiate cross-media deals to potentially have more impact on their target audiences.

In the future, cable advertisers will have at least three readily available advertising options. The first is traditional advertising spots carried on regular analog cable. A second option is targeted advertising using digital technology. For example, advertisers will be able to reach cable homes in specific ZIP Codes and neighborhoods or household members in specific demographic groups with tailored messages. A third option will be interactive advertising offered through special software

"RECIPE"
:30 TV Spot

Story Summary:
In the process of baking a cake, a woman tastes a bit of Mayfield milk that had spilled on her hand. Surprised by how good the milk tastes, she wants more. Looking around to make sure no one is watching, she picks up the measuring cup and then chugs the delicious Mayfield milk.

SCOTTIE V/O: One taste of Mayfield milk, and it hits you...

...all milks aren't the same.

Only Mayfield has the great taste...

...milk lovers can't resist.

Taste it and you'll see.

There's milk...then there's Mayfield.

EXHIBIT 8.12
Most local cable operators can insert commercials such as this one into their local systems.
Courtesy of the Johnson Group and Mayfield Dairies.

added to cable boxes on viewers' television sets. These interactive systems will allow consumers to shop directly from the screen during commercials. Two innovations in local cable advertising have greatly enhanced the importance of this segment—*cut-ins* and *interconnects*.

Although some cable advertising options are not readily available, current technology offers advertisers some sophisticated coverage alternatives. The first innovation is the use of *cut-ins* on network cable programs. Cable networks, like their broadcast counterparts, provide some advertising spots to local system operators to sell to local advertisers. Rather than having a spot appear on a largely unwatched local channel, commercials for the local pizza shop now can air on CNN's *Larry King Show* or ESPN's *Sports Center*.

A further strengthening of local cable advertising comes from the use of **interconnects**. "An interconnect exists where two or more cable systems [in the same market] link themselves together to distribute a commercial advertising schedule simultaneously."[26] In larger markets, an advertiser can simultaneously air several different commercials in various areas of the city. The agency gets a single bill from all the systems, which facilitates individual client billing. The use of interconnects has helped some national brands such as Guinness back up their national television plan in key markets. Interconnects have also been used with success by automotive dealers such as Ford to target spots to consumers in specific counties where various dealers do business.[27] The use of interconnects greatly enhances the prospects for bringing more spot advertisers to cable.

As cable has garnered more advertising dollars, research has improved to help advertisers measure the cable audience and plan the cable portions of their advertising campaign. In particular, Nielsen Media Research provides a number of services including overnight household ratings and local audience composition data. In addition, Mediamark Research Inc. (MRI) offers national product and cable media usage information. Advertisers also are able to obtain customized data for local market commercials and information about optimum local commercial efficiencies.

VIDEOCASSETTE RECORDERS AND DIGITAL VIDEO RECORDERS

Since its introduction in the 1970s, the *videocassette recorder (VCR)* has become as commonplace as television itself. Approximately 89 percent of American homes have a VCR and many households have multiple VCRs.[28] In some respects, the VCR is almost a medium in itself providing access to theatrical movies, made-for-VCR films, promotional and educational tapes, and, of course, providing the option of recording television shows for later viewing—called **time-shift viewing**.

At one time, it was anticipated that the primary usage of VCRs would be for off-air recording. In the early days of the VCR, advertisers thought that the VCR would be a method of increasing the audience of a show for those too busy to watch it during its originally scheduled time. However, studies show that more than half of recorded shows are never watched, the audiences for time-shift viewing tend to be demographically different than original audiences, and the VCR allows viewers to fast-forward through commercials—hardly an advantage for advertisers!

Many industry observers think the VCR will soon be an outdated relic, replaced by digital technology that allows much greater flexibility than the VCR. The *digital video recorder (DVR)* allows viewers to take control of their viewing in a manner never before possible.

The DVR digitizes all incoming signals and stores many more hours of programming than a VCR. The viewer can then pause in a program to answer the telephone, provide instant replay or slow motion on demand, and record for later viewing any program just as with a VCR; but it can be done much more quickly and easily, and it doesn't require a tape. It also allows advertisers to customize commercials for individual viewers. For example, let's say your favorite show is *Monday Night Football* but you are not a beer drinker. Therefore, instead of the network Coors commercial, you receive a commercial for Coca-Cola that is digitally stripped into the program. Furthermore, the commercial may be one that fits your age and interests, which are known to Coca-Cola from information you previously provided the cable provider.

Obviously, a number of issues among network advertisers, secondary advertisers, program providers, and the networks would have to be addressed before the technology could be used to refit commercials. Advertisers also worry that technol-

---

interconnects
A joint buying opportunity between two or more cable systems in the same market.

time-shift viewing
Recording programs on a VCR for viewing at a later time.

ogy, such as that of DVRs, makes skipping commercials very easy. According to a study conducted by Juniper Research, 53 percent of DVR subscribers skip at least some commercials.[29] This can allow them to watch a half-hour program in 23 minutes. However, one advantage of the system is that it can measure the households that are zapping commercials and measure actual commercial audience. This, in turn, brings up the issue of viewer privacy. Another concern of advertisers is that the technology may make pay-for-view movies a more viable option for viewers, which would further decrease commercial viewing.

DVRs did not take off quite as quickly as predicted in the first couple of years. One of the reasons was the high cost of a unit. However, some satellite and cable television companies began offering DVRs in their set-top boxes in order to lure subscribers. According to Mediamark Research, in 2006, DVR penetration of U.S. television households was estimated to be about 11 percent. They also reported that DVR households tend to be more upscale and are also more likely to be heavy users of magazines, newspapers, and the Internet.[30] The DVR provides technical convergence of computers, interactive communication, and multiple options for standard television. If DVRs achieve predicted levels of household penetration, advertisers will have to better target their commercials to audiences that are most likely to watch them and/or seek alternatives to the 30-second commercial.

BRAND INTEGRATION OR PRODUCT PLACEMENT

Product placement is when a real brand or product is included in a media vehicle (i.e., program, film, video game) in exchange for goods, services and/or money. The idea is that the brand is integrated into the programming such that it appears realistic to the viewer and may lead to a positive impression of the brand in the minds of the audience. Product placement is not new in television programs or movies, but more recently product placements have been showing up in songs, Broadway shows, and video games. According to marketing research firm PQ Media, "of the $3.5 billion product placement market, $1.88 billion was spent on television, $1.25 billion on movies and $325 million on other media."[31]

Fueled in part by advertisers' desire to increase the value of their television advertising and to recapture some of the audience lost to both network audience erosion and DVRs, advertisers have been more aggressive in seeking ways to integrate their brands into television programs. Brand integration can involve a range of activities from simply having the product appear in one episode of a television program to sponsorship of entire shows. The broadcast and cable networks have become very creative in the kinds of opportunities they offer advertisers. The following are some recent examples of successful brand integration:

- On an episode of *Rescue Me*, the main character, Tommy Gavin, gets a Cadillac Escalade from a gorgeous female admirer.[32]
- For the program *Extreme Makeover: Home Edition*, Sears products (furnishings, appliances, and other items) were featured as they were provided to families whose homes were being made over.[33]
- Florida Citrus worked with *Good Morning America* to sponsor a contest for Mother's Day called "Emeril's Breakfast in Bed."
- Coca-Cola is prominently featured on the judges' table in all episodes of *American Idol* while the host, Ryan Seacrest, urges viewers to call in on their Cingular Wireless phone to vote for their favorite contestant.

New technology is now making virtual product placements possible. This process uses digital editing to insert brand images in television programming and other video content that has already been filmed. This makes it possible to create new advertising inventory without giving up more programming time for commercials.[34]

The value of such integration is debated among advertisers. Most industry experts seem to feel that the value of the integration depends on how well the brand fits into the program and how well it is integrated into the campaign.[35] Traditional CPM comparisons do not provide an adequate assessment. Some measurement services are beginning to look at ways to measure the effectiveness of product placements. More value is placed on characters using the brand and/or saying the product name than on simply showing the product. Product placements are not seen as something that will replace commercials.

SYNDICATED RATING SERVICES

As mentioned earlier in this chapter, from an advertising perspective, television is simply an audience delivery system. Needless to say, it is crucial for advertisers and their agencies to have reliable data on which to make buying decisions and to determine if they are paying a fair price. The problems of accurately accounting for the increasingly fragmented television audience have become more and more difficult. At the same time, as audiences for each television outlet decrease, the magnitude of any error increases as a percentage of the total viewing audience. For example, a 1 rating-point error for a program with a 20 rating is 5 percent; the same error for a program with a 5 rating is 20 percent. Because advertising rates are determined directly by ratings, these errors are a cause for considerable concern among advertisers.

The Nielsen Ratings

People Meter
Device that measures television set usage by individuals rather than by households.

The primary supplier of syndicated television ratings is Nielsen Media Research.[36] The company was founded in 1923 by A. C. Nielsen to collect radio audience information, and it initiated television ratings in 1950. The Nielsen Television Index (NTI) provides network ratings on a national basis. Data are provided from 9,000 households. In these households, a **People Meter** is attached to each television set (see Exhibit 8.13 for an example of a People Meter). The People Meter has buttons assigned to each person living in the home and additional buttons for visitors.

Many advertisers are interested in local viewing levels, and Nielsen provides ratings for all markets through its Nielsen Station Index (NSI). In the fifty-six largest markets, Nielsen uses set meters (not People Meters) to measure household television set usage on a continuous basis. In each of the 210 television markets, Nielsen provides diaries in which individuals record their viewing habits. These diaries are administered four times a year during February, May, July, and November. These four periods are known as *sweeps*, and they are used to set the price of local commercials for the coming quarter.

In recent years, the ratings system has come under a great deal of scrutiny by both advertisers and broadcasters. Although a number of issues have been raised, we discuss three major areas of concern:

sweeps weeks
During these periods, ratings are taken for all television markets.

1. *Sweeps weeks.* In theory, **sweeps weeks** (or simply *sweeps*) are an efficient and relatively inexpensive means of estimating quarterly local market ratings. In fact, local market stations have sometimes used the period to artificially distort their ratings by airing sensational news exposés and special promotions and pressuring networks to program their best miniseries, movies, and specials to support their affiliates during sweeps.

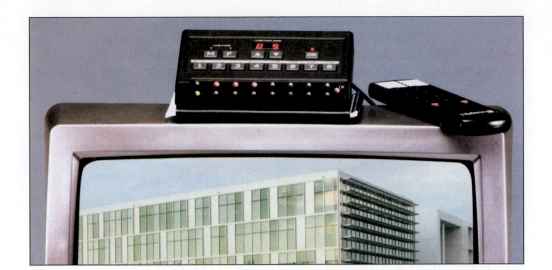

EXHIBIT 8.13
This People Meter device measures television set usage by individuals rather than by households.

The result is that the sweeps period ratings of local stations may have little relation to the 36 "unrated" weeks. Advertisers are extremely frustrated by what they see as inflated ratings and the accompanying higher commercial rates they pay for them. The alleged abuses of sweeps week programming have resulted in increasing calls for measuring of local audiences on a continuing basis.

2. *Diaries.* Everyone agrees that in an era of over-fifty-channel household reception and a trend toward individual viewing, the diary is an antiquated measurement tool. A number of major advertisers have called for People Meters in at least the top 125 markets, which would include approximately 75 percent of television households. It also would largely eliminate the current sweeps problem by providing ongoing audience measurements for most of the country. The major obstacle to implementing local People Meter ratings is cost. It is estimated that each metered market would require a minimum of 300 sampled households, or almost 40,000 homes, at a cost of several hundred million dollars—much more than either advertisers or broadcasters are currently willing to pay.

3. *Exposure value.* Another area of ratings that has generated great interest is estimating exposure levels for television commercials versus set usage. Advertisers want to know who is watching, who is paying attention, and what level of attention is being given any particular show. Nielsen is working on a method for making commercial ratings information available to advertisers.

Recently, Nielsen and Arbitron announced a joint research effort, Project Apollo, that holds promise in solving many of the problems facing broadcast audience measurement. They are engaged in a study using a Portable People Meter (PPM). As discussed in Chapter 9, the PPM is a device about the size of a pager that measures inaudible signals from the audio portion of television, radio, cable, and the Internet. It eliminates the nuisance of keeping a diary, and the PPM is particularly valuable in measuring the out-of-home audience of radio. This is being used in conjunction with ACNielsen's Homescan data, which allow consumers in the Nielsen panel the ability to record their consumer package-good purchases. This partnership between Arbitron and Nielsen holds promise for making more complete media exposure data and consumer purchase data available to advertisers. The major barrier to its use is the cost associated with its introduction.

Regardless of what form changes in syndicated ratings take in the future, it is clear that methods that served the television industry well in a period of three networks and a few stations in each market will not work in the fragmented landscape of the twenty-first century. A primary issue is how much the major players—stations, networks, and advertisers—are willing to pay to gather these elusive data.

Qualitative Ratings

As you will recall in our discussion of cable television, we commented on the need for cable networks to sell the quality and lifestyle of their audiences in contrast to the basic numbers reported by most major rating reports. Another type of qualitative audience measure seeks to offer insight into audience involvement or degree of preference for particular television shows or personalities. These measures can be used to determine if a person can be successfully used as a testimonial spokesperson or to see if a popular show is beginning to wear out.

The best-known qualitative research service is Marketing Evaluations, which compiles a number of "popularity" surveys called "Q" reports. The most familiar of these are **TVQ** and Performer Q.

Let us assume that a television show, *Lost,* is familiar to 50 percent of the population and that 30 percent of the people rank it as one of their favorite shows. The Q score would be calculated as follows:

$$Q = \frac{FAV}{FAM} \text{ or } \frac{30}{50} = 60$$

Interestingly enough, the fragmentation of television has taken its toll not only on average program ratings but also on the TVQ scores. Because the number of people watching any particular show is so much lower now than in past years, the general recognition level of television personalities has fallen significantly in recent years. A generation ago, Lucille Ball and Jackie Gleason were as well known as the president. Today, many television stars have a loyal following among their fans but are not necessarily household names.

TVQ
A service of Marketing Evaluations that measures the popularity (opinion of audience rather than size of audience) of shows and personalities.

SUMMARY ✸

In the near future, television will become more than a medium of information, entertainment, and advertising. Television, in its various permutations, will be an interactive system that will allow viewers to pay bills, make airline reservations, receive pay-per-view programming on demand, and even play computer games with other viewers. How long it will be before these systems are generally available and what their final form will take are still very much in question. However, programmers, advertisers, and the general public will all be dealing with a dramatically changed television medium in the not too distant future.

In addition to its functional options, television is becoming a gateway to a world of communication never before imagined. Every aspect of the medium from audience research to news must be reevaluated in terms of viewer control and a changing economic base. Throughout most of the last century, it was understood that American mass media would be largely financed by advertisers using a business plan of reaching the largest audience possible at the lowest cost per person. The fragmentation of the television audience has changed programming, financing, and the criteria of what constitutes a "mass" medium.

Although television advertising faces an uncertain future, it is an uncertainty filled with opportunities for those who have the creativity and insight to operate in an era of an audience-driven medium. Nowhere will the customer-oriented notion of the marketing concept be more apparent than in interactive television. It appears certain that both advertisers and viewers will soon pay a higher price for access to the numerous options offered by television. In return, astute advertisers will be reaching customers and prospects on a one-to-one basis with some form of permission marketing being the rule rather than the exception.

REVIEW

1. Discuss major changes in network television advertising during the last 20 years.
2. Define the following terms:
   a. rating
   b. share of audience
   c. people ratings
   d. TVQ ratings
   e. clutter
3. Compare and contrast syndication and spot television buying.
4. Discuss the relationship between networks and their affiliates.
5. Describe the up-front television buying market for prime time.
6. Compare and contrast cable networks with broadcast networks.

TAKE IT TO THE WEB

The Television Bureau of Advertising (TVB) is a nonprofit trade association of the broadcast television industry in America. The TVB website provides valuable information about audience analysis, television ratings, advertising revenue figures, and more. Visit www.tvb.org and compare weekly and monthly rating trends for both broadcast and cable.

Public information about the cable industry, including the history, research in the field, and technological developments of cable television, is provided by the Cable Center. Visit the website at www.cablecenter.org and review the history of cable television. Make predictions on what you think will be the next big thing for cable.

The mission of the Cable Television Advertising Bureau is to supply information to advertisers to assist in media planning. Visit www.cabletvadbureau.com and list three reasons why advertisers would choose to include cable in their media mix. While you are there, check out the special case study section profiling national companies that have chosen cable as a medium in which to advertise.

CHAPTER 9

Using Radio

With a host of formats and numerous stations in even the smallest towns, radio provides advertisers with options to reach very narrowly defined niche prospects. Radio also is among the most popular media with high levels of listenership throughout the day. Radio offers the opportunity for advertisers to reach some audiences, such as teenagers, working women, and light television viewers, that are sometimes hard to reach with other media. After reading this chapter, you will understand:

chapter objectives

1. the role of radio as a selective medium
2. radio's strength as a secondary medium
3. radio's ability to reach audiences at a low cost
4. attempts to overcome radio's lack of a visual dimension
5. different roles of AM and FM radio
6. the rating systems used in radio

Pros

1. Radio is a primary medium for targeting narrow audience segments, many of whom are not heavy users of other media.
2. Radio is a mobile medium going with listeners into the marketplace and giving advertisers proximity to the sale.
3. Radio, with its relatively low production costs and immediacy, can react quickly to changing market conditions.
4. Radio has a personal relationship with its audience unmatched by other media. This affinity with listeners carries over to the credibility it offers many of the products advertised on radio.
5. Radio, with its low cost and targeted formats, is an excellent supplemental medium for secondary building blocks to increase reach and frequency to specific target markets.

Cons

1. Without a visual component, radio often lacks the impact of other media. Also, many listeners use radio as "background" rather than giving it their full attention.
2. The small audiences of most radio stations require numerous buys to achieve acceptable reach and frequency.
3. Adequate audience research is not always available, especially among many small market stations.

During the week of March 6, 1949, the top-rated radio show was the *Lux Radio Theater*, which reached almost 30 percent of American households.[1] By contrast, the most popular television show of the 2006 season, *American Idol*, received a household rating over 17.7 on its highest rated night.[2] Until the 1950s when television became the major broadcast medium, radio was the primary national medium for both advertisers and audiences.

Radio was the most prestigious of the national media from 1926, when the first network (The National Broadcasting Company) was formed, until the mid-1950s. During those golden years of radio, the family gathered around the living room radio set to listen to Jack Benny, Fred Allen, and Bob Hope entertain them while news personalities such as Edward R. Murrow enlightened them. All of this programming was brought to the audience by the major advertisers of the day. The advent of coast-to-coast television broadcasts and the introduction of instant hits such as *I Love Lucy* and *The $64,000 Question* during the early 1950s accelerated radio's decline as a national medium.

Despite its minor position on the national scene, as a local medium, radio advertising revenues are over $18 billion and the medium demonstrates impressive reach (see Exhibit 9.1). Each week, radio reaches about 94 percent of all adults and 93 percent of teenagers.[3] By reaching prospects with targeted formats from urban to all-talk, radio commercials can create an intimate, one-to-one relationship with prospects. In addition, radio can achieve effective creative effects at a lower production cost than virtually any other media.

In the early days, radio listening was often a group activity.

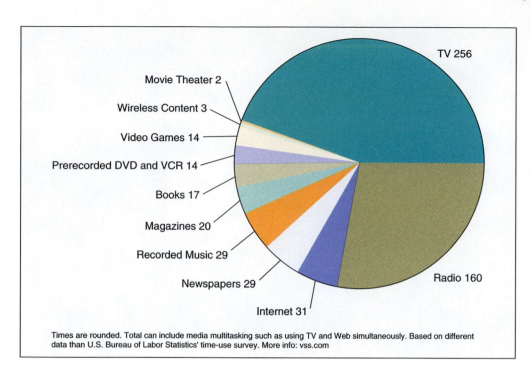

TV 256

Movie Theater 2

Wireless Content 3

Video Games 14

Prerecorded DVD and VCR 14

Books 17

Magazines 20

Recorded Music 29

Newspapers 29

Internet 31

Radio 160

Times are rounded. Total can include media multitasking such as using TV and Web simultaneously. Based on different data than U.S. Bureau of Labor Statistics' time-use survey. More info: vss.com

EXHIBIT **9.1**

Average Daily Share of Time Spent with Each Medium

The average consumer will spend 9 hours 35 minutes a day using media in 2006 (time in minutes).

Source: *Advertising Age*, 2 Jan. 2006. Copyright © 2006 Crain Communications, Inc. Used with permission.

THE CONTEMPORARY RADIO INDUSTRY

Like most media, radio is having to adapt to a new competitive environment and a very different economic structure. Only a few years ago, the Federal Communications Commission (FCC) limited ownership of radio stations to seven FM and seven AM stations with only one of each in a single market. However, the FCC gradually loosened ownership restrictions and the Telecommunications Act of 1996 allowed corporations or individuals to control as much as 35 percent of the U.S. market (with other rules governing local station ownership determined by the size of a market). The new ownership rules changed the radio industry from one of numerous small groups to one comprised of a few huge conglomerates.

Led by companies such as Clear Channel with over 1,200 stations and Infinity Broadcasting with over 180 stations, more and more radio stations belong to these mega-owners. Many radio stations are owned by large media companies that also own television stations or newspapers. Accompanying this new movement to large group ownership is a revival of radio as a preferred advertising medium for a number of major businesses. As many advertisers seek to reach more narrowly defined targets, radio offers them the opportunity to more efficiently reach a niche market.

Radio and New Technology

Some observers think that the audio platform of the next decade will be computers and satellites, not a radio dial. More and more radio executives see the future of radio as an Internet business with numerous options for reaching niche audiences and eventually individuals with tailored programming, music, and advertising. Websites have become the new business model for radio. Broadcasters are facing new copyright regulations regarding the performance fees they must pay for streaming their on-air programming over the Internet. Despite these challenges, Internet radio listening is continuing to grow.

HD Radio and **satellite radio** also pose challenges for traditional broadcast radio. Satellite radio is available by subscription and contains few if any commercials. It

HD Radio
Offers terrestrial radio stations the ability to deliver additional programming on the same amount of bandwidth with higher-quality sound. It requires a special receiver.

satellite radio
Available by subscription and contains few if any commercials. It requires a special receiver but offers near-CD-quality sound.

Satellite radio currently reaches an upscale audience.

requires a special receiver but offers near-CD-quality sound. Penetration of satellite radio is growing but is still small and has tended to attract largely an upscale audience.[4] HD Radio offers terrestrial radio stations the ability to deliver additional programming on the same bandwidth with higher-quality sound. Some say that this could help revitalize AM stations. While HD Radio also requires a special receiver, there is no subscription fee for consumers.

To predict precisely the future of radio, even in the near term, is difficult. However, we can examine some of the major trends that will drive the medium during the coming years.

1. The size of the audience listening to radio stations over the Internet is growing rapidly. In 2000, 11 percent of Americans said that they had listened to radio stations over the Internet. By June 2005, over 40 percent said they had listened (see Exhibit 9.2).

2. More listeners to Internet radio are becoming habitual listeners. As of June 2005, over 20 percent of Americans age 12 and older said they listened to radio stations online in the past month. About 6 percent said they listened to radio stations over the Internet in the past week.

EXHIBIT 9.2

Two in Five Americans Have Listened to Radio Stations Online

Courtesy: Arbitron Radio Today 2003.

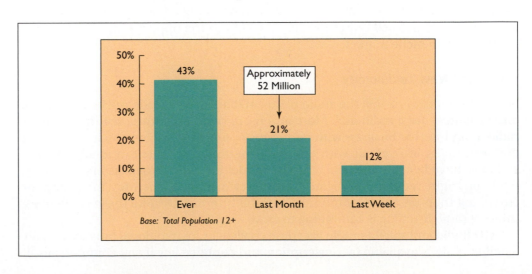

3. Young audiences are more likely to prefer to listen to the radio via the Internet. According to a survey of 12- to 24-year-olds conducted by the University of Southern California Media Lab, 54 percent of respondents said they preferred the Internet while 30 percent preferred radio when given a choice between listening to music over the Internet or on traditional stations.[5]

The future of radio as a medium for the delivery of more specialized and personalized programming is very bright. However, the form that this transmission will take, whether local stations can survive satellite and Internet systems, and how advertisers will utilize the new technological options fully are very much up in the air.

FEATURES AND ADVANTAGES OF RADIO

Radio is an ideal medium for the segmented marketing of the twenty-first century. In many respects, radio was the forerunner of many of the localized marketing and advertising strategies so much in use today. As the **Radio Advertising Bureau (RAB)** points out, "Radio gives you the opportunity to take advantage of the most powerful form of communication—the human voice. The right combination of words, voices, music, and effects on radio can help you establish a unique 'one-on-one' connection with your prospects that lets you grab their attention, evoke their emotions, and persuade them to respond. All this at a fraction of the production cost of other broadcast media."[6]

According to the Radio Marketing Bureau, radio offers a number of advantages not found in most other media. Some of the primary elements of interest to advertisers are the following:

1. *Radio targets.* One of the greatest strengths of radio is its ability to deliver advertising to a very selective audience. It would be difficult to find a market segment whose needs, tastes, and preferences are not reached by some station's programming.

   Radio's combination of high overall reach and ability to provide numerous formats makes it a multifaceted medium. In some sense, each programming category, whether country, classical, all-talk, or rhythm and blues, can be treated as a distinct medium for marketing purposes. From a marketing perspective, radio has the ability to reach prospects by sex, age, race, or interest with a format that adds an even greater dimension to its already strong personal communication environment. For example, Exhibit 9.3 shows the age, education, race, and gender of the audience for four popular radio formats.

2. *Radio reaches a majority of the population several hours per day.* Radio can even deliver higher-income and educational segments that are of prime importance to many advertisers (see Exhibit 9.4).

3. *Radio advertising influences consumers closest to the time of purchase.* No major medium can compete with radio as a means of reaching prospects as they approach a purchase decision. Although both outdoor and point-of-purchase advertisements also reach consumers in the marketplace, neither can deliver a sales message the way radio can.

4. *Radio reaches light users of other media.* Light viewers of television spend more time with radio than they do with television. In addition, radio can fill in gaps in both newspaper and magazine coverage of prime audiences.

5. *Radio works well with other media.* Radio can reach light users of other media and fill in gaps in a media schedule. For many years, a fundamental marketing strategy for radio has been to promote its ability to successfully work with other media to increase reach and frequency or to reach nonusers or light users of other media. The radio industry realizes that the majority of its revenues comes

Radio Advertising Bureau (RAB)
Association to promote the use of radio as an advertising medium.

EXHIBIT **9.3**

There is a radio format for everyone.

Courtesy: Arbitron's *Radio Today 2006 Edition*.

	Alternative	Contemporary Hits/Pop	Adult Contemporary	Urban Contemporary
Sex (persons 18+)				
Women (18+)	32.6%	62.3%	65.6%	53.5%
Men (18+)	67.4%	37.7%	34.4%	46.5%
Education (persons 18+)				
<12th Grade	7.4%	9.2%	6.3%	13.9%
HS Grad	26.0%	30.0%	28.3%	36.0%
Some College	39.2%	39.9%	38.6%	36.8%
College Grad	27.3%	20.9%	26.7%	13.3%
Age				
12–17	14.6%	24.5%	3.0%	19.8%
18–34	26.1%	24.9%	7.7%	24.2%
25–34	30.6%	23.1%	14.4%	23.8%
35–44	18.3%	15.8%	22.0%	16.7%
45–54	8.0%	8.2%	13.0%	8.7%
55–64	1.6%	2.2%	16.0%	3.6%
65+	.7%	1.2%	11.6%	2.8%
Race				
Black	2.8%	10.8%	11.1%	77.5%
Hispanic	13.5%	17.0%	13.1%	8.2%
Other	83.7%	72.2%	75.8%	14.3%

from advertisers that use radio as a secondary medium. Radio provides affordable repetition that delivers high levels of awareness—a key component in gaining market share.

6. *Much of radio listening takes place on an out-of-home basis.* This means that radio can reach consumers where they are and where other media are sometimes not readily available (see Exhibit 9.5).

7. *Radio delivers consistent listening patterns.* Unlike television, radio offers year-round coverage with little or no summer audience drop-off. Likewise, radio maintains high audience levels throughout the day.

8. *Radio delivers its messages at a very low CPM level.* Advertisers are increasingly giving more attention to cost efficiencies. Radio delivers its audience at a CPM level below that of virtually any other medium. Not only are the CPM levels low, but radio's recent increases also have been below that of major competitors.

9. *Radio provides advertisers with both immediacy and flexibility.* Radio advertising has the ability to react quickly to changing market conditions. With relatively short production deadlines and inexpensive creative techniques, radio is an excellent medium to take advantage of fast-breaking opportunities.

EXHIBIT **9.4**

Radio Reaches Upscale Consumers

Courtesy: RAB Market Fact Book for Advertisers 2002–2003.

	Weekly Reach	Average Listening Time per Day
Adults with Incomes of $50,000+	94.9%	3:34 hours/minutes
College Graduates	94.8%	3:13 hours/minutes

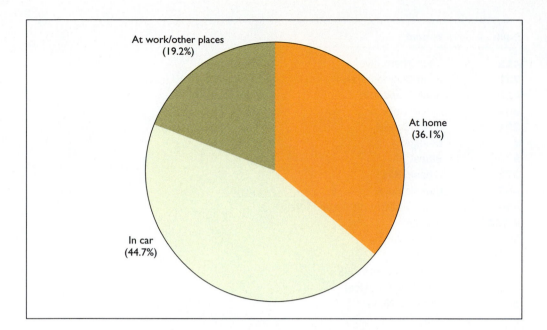

EXHIBIT **9.5**
Radio Reaches Customers Everywhere
Compiled by RAB from RADAR 85, June 2005, © Copyright Arbitron based on adult weekly cume, Monday–Sunday 24 hours.

The ability to anticipate or react to changing conditions cannot be underestimated. For example, when the Indianapolis 500 ends on Memorial Day afternoon, radio commercials touting the winner's tire and oil brands begin running that evening. The simplicity of radio can be a major advantage in making tactical marketing decisions. Radio's sense of immediacy and flexibility, all at a cost within the budget of even the smallest advertiser, has made it an important part of the advertising strategy of many advertisers.

LIMITATIONS AND CHALLENGES OF RADIO

No medium is suited for every marketing and advertising situation. Like all media, radio has special strengths and weaknesses that must be considered by advertisers considering placing radio in their media schedule. Radio has a number of characteristics that make it an ideal vehicle for numerous advertisers as either a primary or secondary medium. By the same token, advertisers need to be aware of some of the major disadvantages that must be considered before scheduling a radio buy. Four of the major problems facing advertisers using radio are (1) the sheer number of stations, which creates a very fragmented environment especially for those advertisers needing to reach a general audience; (2) clutter; (3) the medium's lack of a visual element; and (4) increased use of MP3 players and digital radio.

Audience Fragmentation

One of the great strengths of radio is its ability to reach narrowly defined audience niches with formats of particular interest to specific listeners. However, some advertisers wonder if the extent of segmentation has resulted in an overly fragmented medium with audience levels for most stations so small that it is difficult to reach a brand's core prospects. For those product categories with broad appeal, **audience fragmentation** has made it difficult to gain effective reach and frequency without buying several radio stations or networks. Radio executives respond that although there are a few major markets in which competition has forced stations into continually narrowing their program formats, for the most part, radio remains among the most effective means of achieving the target marketing desired by the majority of advertisers. However, to put the situation in perspective, in 2005, there were 10,600 commercial radio stations on the air in the United States. Exhibit 9.6 shows a breakdown of these stations by format.

audience fragmentation
The segmenting of mass-media audiences into smaller groups because of diversity of media outlets.

EXHIBIT **9.6**

Radio Format Analysis

Source: M Street Corp., © 2006.
Obtained from
http://www.newsgeneration.com/
radio_resources/stats.htm.

Rank	Format
411	Adult Alternative
721	Adult Contemporary
417	Adult Standards
307	Album Rock
291	Black Gospel
6	Bluegrass
9	Blues
277	Classic Hits
465	Classic Rock
536	Contemporary Hit Radio (Top-40)
2,054	Country
31	Easy Listening
144	Ethnic
13	Farm News and Talk
182	Fine Arts/Classical
30	Financial News
5	Folk
391	Hot Adult Contemporary or "Adult CHR"
156	Jazz
22	Modern Adult Contemporary
716	New stations (no designated formats yet)
205	New Rock - Modern Rock
1,021	News/News - Talk
778	Oldies
58	Pre-teen
229	R & B - Urban
4	Reading Service
1,183	Religion
838	Religious - Contemporary
71	Religious - Gospel
316	Soft Adult Contemporary
205	Soft Urban Contemporary
361	Southern Gospel
916	Spanish
531	Sports
900	Talk
8	Travel Info
665	Variety
37	Weather/Traffic

Clutter

As discussed in Chapter 8, clutter is a major concern to advertisers. The more commercials and other nonprogram content, the less likely it is that listeners will recall any particular advertising message. The number of radio commercials has always been significantly greater than in television. However, with deregulation, the time devoted to commercials has steadily increased. Some radio stations are running over 30 percent advertising during peak listening periods.

This increased clutter seems to impact young audiences the most. A recent study by Arbitron of radio listeners found that "the lowest rated minute during an average

A look inside a radio studio.

commercial break is 92 percent of the size of the audience before the spots began." However, "younger audiences were more likely to tune out than older listeners."[7]

Lack of a Visual Element

A fundamental problem for advertisers is radio's lack of a visual component. At a time when advertisers are attempting to enhance brand image and build consumer awareness, many advertisers find radio's lack of visuals a difficult problem to overcome. With the growth of self-service retailing and competitive brand promotions, package identification is crucial for many advertisers.

Radio has long used a number of creative techniques to substitute the ear for the eye and to attempt to overcome the lack of visuals. Sound effects, jingles, short and choppy copy, and vivid descriptions attempt to create a mental picture. In recent years, radio has attempted to show that images familiar to consumers from television commercials can be transferred to consumers through radio.

Increased Use of MP3 Players

There has been a dramatic increase in the use of MP3 players and prerecorded music, particularly among younger audiences. According to a study conducted by the University of Southern California Media Lab, 85 percent of 12- to 24-year-olds say that they would choose their MP3 players over broadcast radio as their preferred music source.[8]

TECHNICAL ASPECTS OF RADIO

The Signal

The electrical impulses that are broadcast by radio are called the *signal*. If a certain station has a good signal in a given territory, its programs and commercials come over clearly in that area.

EXHIBIT 9.7

In amplitude modulation (a), waves vary in height (amplitude): frequency constant. Frequency modulation (b) varies the frequency but keeps the height constant. These drawings, however, are not made to scale, which would reveal that width is the significant difference between AM and FM. The FM wave is twenty times wider than the AM wave. This fact helps to explain how FM captures its fine tones.

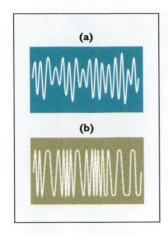

amplitude modulation (AM)

Method of transmitting electromagnetic signals by varying the amplitude (size) of the electromagnetic wave, in contrast to varying its frequency. Quality is not as good as frequency modulation but can be heard farther, especially at night.

frequency modulation (FM)

A radio transmission wave that transmits by the variation in the frequency of its wave rather than by its size (as in amplitude modulation [AM]). An FM wave is twenty times the width of an AM wave, which is the source of its fine tone. To transmit such a wave, it has to be placed high on the electromagnetic spectrum, far from AM waves with their interference and static, hence its outstanding tone.

Frequency

All signals are transmitted by electromagnetic waves, sometimes called *radio waves*. These waves differ from one another in frequency (the number of waves that pass a given point in a given period of time). Frequencies for AM stations are measured in kilohertz or kHz and FM stations' frequencies are measured in megahertz or MHz. The FCC has assigned the following frequencies to all radio stations:

AM: 540 to 1,700 kHz

FM: 88.1 to 107.9 MHz

Amplitude

All electromagnetic waves have height, spoken of as *amplitude*, whose range resembles the difference between an ocean wave and a ripple in a pond; and speed, measured by the frequency with which a succession of waves passes a given point per minute. If, for example, a radio station operates on a frequency of 1,580 kHz, this means that 1,580,000 of its waves pass a given point per second.

On the basis of these two dimensions—amplitude and frequency—two separate systems have been developed for carrying radio waves. The first system carries the variations in a sound wave by corresponding variations in its amplitude; the frequency remains constant. This is the principle of **amplitude modulation (AM)**. The second system carries the variation in a sound wave by corresponding variations in its frequency; the amplitude remains constant. This is the principle of **frequency modulation (FM)** (see Exhibit 9.7a & b).

The technical structure of AM and FM radio has created, in effect, two distinct media, each offering different values to the listener and the advertiser. AM signals carry farther but are susceptible to interference. FM has a fine tonal quality, but its signal distances are limited. A particular station's quality of reception also is determined by atmospheric conditions and station power (broadcast frequency).

SELLING RADIO COMMERCIAL TIME

Radio advertising dollars are very much concentrated at the local level. Despite significant growth in both radio network and spot advertising, local advertising continues to dominate industry revenues.

Buying radio can be a difficult task because of the number of stations and formats available to advertisers. For example, there are over 850 stations in Texas alone. Even the most sparsely populated state, Wyoming, has over 150 commercial stations. In addition, there are dozens of distinct formats throughout the country from which to choose, including over 700 Latin/Hispanic format stations.[9]

Recent consolidation of radio ownership offers the potential for major changes in the radio rate structure and the way radio time is bought. From the outset of the move to group ownership, major radio group executives promised advertisers better service and more efficient buying procedures. Rather than dealing with many individual stations or independent rep companies, a media buyer in a streamlined environment could negotiate time availability and rates for hundreds of stations while dealing with a single person and submitting one insertion order.

Although ownership consolidation may have the potential to drive up local radio rates and give stations more leverage with advertisers, it does not eliminate the fierce competition that radio faces for local advertising dollars. Radio advertising continues to operate in a challenging environment as it competes for local advertisers. Radio must compete with traditional selective media, such as newspapers, Yellow Pages, and direct response, that also reach targeted audiences. In addition, radio is competing with newer media such as the Internet and both broadcast and cable television, which see local advertising as major profit centers.

Network Radio

The demise of network radio as a major national medium and the beginning of local radio began in 1948 with the introduction of television. Average ratings for Bob Hope's radio show dropped from 23.8 in 1948 to 5.4 in 1953. Soap operas left radio for television throughout the 1950s until *Ma Perkins*, the last survivor, went off the air in 1960. The last major radio dramas, *Suspense* and *Have Gun Will Travel*, ended in 1962 and the era of network radio was essentially over. For the next decade, network programs were largely confined to news and occasional short features.

Network radio, while still a minor source of advertising dollars, has remained relatively stable in the last few years. Media planners continue to look to network radio as a means of extending reach to working women and light users of other media and building greater brand awareness through inexpensive additional frequency to prime target segments. Network radio advertising only accounts for $814 million of the over $19.6 billion spent annually in radio.[10] Leading advertisers on network radio include national retail chains, pharmaceutical companies, and package-goods advertisers.

Radio networks are much different from those in television as is the relationship between radio networks and their affiliates. Radio networks are basically program providers; but unlike television, a single radio station may belong to several radio networks simultaneously. For example, a station might get sports reports from one network, personality profiles and news from another, and entertainment fare from yet another. Whereas in television local stations sell advertising time on the basis of the strength of the network programming, in radio the networks must depend on local ratings to garner national advertising support.

In contrast to television in which each network such as NBC provides a single broadcast service (we will not consider cable-distributed services such as MSNBC or CNBC) and has a permanent lineup of affiliates, ABC Radio provides a number of targeted networks. For example, ABC has several full-service networks including the Prime Network directed at adults ages 25 to 54 with a news/talk format and Galaxy Networks with a number of 24-hour music formats for various demographic markets. In addition, ABC also provides individual programs and news breaks that are broadcast daily throughout the day.

Regardless of the way a radio station uses network programming and the many differences with television, radio networks do offer some of the same advantages as

Network radio was
huge in the late 1940s.

their television counterparts. For example, an advertiser prepares one insertion order for multiple stations, pays one invoice, and is guaranteed uniform production quality for the commercials scheduled on all stations. Radio networks also provide economical reach and, like all radio, target special audience segments who often are light users of other media.

Radio networks have benefited from the use of satellite technology. The availability of satellite links for national radio programmers offers a number of advantages for their local station affiliates:

1. Stations are guaranteed quality programming based on the latest audience research for a particular format.
2. Radio networks bring celebrities to the medium that local stations could not afford.
3. Even the smallest stations can obtain national advertising dollars as part of a network. Stations that would not be considered by national advertisers as part of a local spot buy may now be included in a network radio schedule.
4. The cost efficiencies of sharing programming with several hundred other affiliates keep both personnel and programming costs to a minimum.

Network radio will never return to its former status as a primary medium for national advertisers. However, as a source of program services, with its ability to target narrow audience segments, it will continue to play an important role for a number of national advertisers.

Spot Radio

spot radio
Buying radio time on local stations on a market-by-market basis by national advertisers.

As you will recall from our discussion in Chapter 8, *spot advertising* is the buying of local stations by national advertisers. Advertisers spend approximately $3.5 billion in **spot radio** advertising each year.[11] It is almost always a second medium for national companies to build added reach and frequency against selected target mar-

RADIO

Rank	Marketer	2005	2004
1	AT&T	$204.6	$275.7
2	Verizon Communications	195.5	210.5
3	News Corp.	156.8	147.0
4	Walt Disney Co.	155.9	142.3
5	Time Warner	147.4	191.4
6	General Electric Co.	135.9	120.2
7	Home Depot	132.9	151.7
8	General Motors Corp.	124.5	106.8
9	Safeway	121.4	114.5
10	Berkshire Hathaway	120.9	81.3

EXHIBIT 9.8

Top U.S. Advertisers in Radio

Source: Top U.S Advertisers in 10 MediaAd Spending Totals by Media, *Advertising Age*, June 26, 2006, pg. S-11. Copyright © 2006 Crain Communications, Inc. Used with permission.

kets. Spot radio offers these advertisers an opportunity to react quickly to changing competitive challenges and hit narrowly segmented markets with little waste circulation. As shown in Exhibit 9.8, for example, Verizon Communications ranks among the top users of radio with expenditures of $195 million.[12] However, this expenditure represents less than 8 percent of the company's annual advertising budget.

Despite the relatively low percentage of total advertising dollars, spot radio serves important functions for a number of advertisers. To those companies with a national presence that have widely differentiated market potential, spot radio can provide added weight in selected regions or individual markets. A second group of heavy spot radio users are national companies with extensive retail outlets. Spot radio commercials allow these companies to build on their national brand awareness with localized spots directed at the local community. For example, Home Depot and Burger King are advertisers that depend on spot radio to augment their national advertising. As is the case in other categories of the medium, advertisers take advantage of the flexibility and low cost offered by spot radio.

Just as with television, most spot radio broadcast purchases are made through reps. In principle, radio reps serve the same function as those in television. The best reps are those who serve as marketing consultants for their client stations. They work with agencies to match target audiences with the appropriate stations on their client list. Sometimes this is done on a market-by-market basis. In other cases,

Satellite technology has helped radio networks become popular again.

buys are made through nonwired networks in the same manner as they are made through television nonwired networks, which we discussed in Chapter 8. It remains to be seen what effect consolidation within the radio industry will have on the relationship between reps and stations. As more and more local stations are bought by major groups, it may mean that a significant amount of spot advertising will be sold directly by group salespersons bypassing rep firms and that reps will be left primarily to sell smaller market stations through their nonwired networks. The rep/station relationship is just one more area of potential change in an industry where reorganization has become the rule.

AM Versus FM as an Advertising Medium

FM dominates the overall listening audience and is the clear leader in most formats. With the exception of several major all-talk stations, most AM stations are far down the list of stations in terms of ratings and audience share. In fact, AM stations tend to reach an older audience with talk, news, and specialty formats such as gospel and nostalgia.

The growth of FM radio audiences and advertising revenues during the last 30 years is one of the most important trends in the industry. FM technology was adapted for radio shortly before World War II. During the war, all broadcast station construction was halted, but a few stations that had gone on the air prior to the start of the war continued to operate. For almost three decades after the close of the war, FM was largely confined to noncommercial and classical stations with few listeners and little or no advertising. The exceptions were the jointly owned AM/FM stations, which usually duplicated programming on both stations. Because AM and FM radio sets were sold separately and there was little original programming, few incentives existed for listeners to purchase the more expensive FM sets.

In 1975, FM independent stations (those without an AM partner) reported a combined loss of almost $10 million. Just 3 years later, these same stations had profits of slightly less than $25 million. Obviously, this type of economic turnaround did not happen by accident. A number of factors contributed to the vitality of FM with both advertisers and audiences. Among the major elements are the following:

1. In 1972, the Federal Communications Commission ruled that owners of both AM and FM stations in the same market had to program different formats. This ruling opened the way for FM as a separate medium.
2. The sound quality of FM is markedly better than that of AM. Because music formats dominate radio, FM steadily gained audience share at the expense of AM.
3. The decline in the cost of FM sets coincided with the popularity of the medium. Thirty years ago, radio sets with an FM band were much more expensive than AM-only sets. Also, few cars were equipped with an FM radio. Currently, about nine out of ten car radios are AM/FM and virtually all radio sets are equipped with both AM and FM bands.
4. As radio audiences turned to FM for the most popular music formats, AM was left with an audience skewed to older listeners, a less than prime market segment for most advertisers. Therefore, the switch to FM by audiences was followed quickly by an increase in advertising dollars.

FM is likely to continue to be the dominant radio medium as AM stations search for those formats that will attract niche audiences. In fact, many observers say that it was only the popularity of talk radio in the last 20 years that saved AM from economic disaster. HD Radio may make it possible for AM stations to see a resurgence in listenership with its promise of high-quality sound.

Types of Programming   As we previously discussed, radio is a medium constantly searching for targeted audiences to deliver to advertisers. It also is a medium over-

A typical "on air" sign at a radio station announces that the station is broadcasting a transmission.

whelmingly devoted to music. The typical radio station depends on a music format and unique talent to appeal to the largest audience in a particular listener demographic. Unlike television, where viewers tune to a certain program for a half-hour or hour and then move to another station for another show, radio audiences tend to demonstrate loyalty to a station because of the type of music, sports, or information it programs.

For a number of years, the "country" format has been carried by more stations than any other. Approximately 2,000 stations report that they program some form of country music as their primary format. The number of country music stations can be attributed, in part, to the large quantity of small stations in rural and small-market areas where country music is most popular. Although many of the newer country styles have brought country into the mainstream and larger markets, it has its roots in small town America.

To advertisers, it is often the quality of the audience as much as its size that is of most importance. For example, those relatively few stations with "children," "public affairs," or "agriculture and farm" formats might be exactly the advertising vehicle for particular advertisers seeking to reach small but (for them) profitable prospects.

One of the problems for radio stations is that they function in an environment of economic Darwinism in which only the strongest survive. Although every station would like to be the leader in a popular format, radio executives know that it is extremely difficult for more than one or two stations in a market to be financially successful in any particular format. Why would an advertiser buy a market's third- or fourth-rated country station?

Consequently, second- and third-tier stations are constantly searching for niche formats that will allow them to be the leader among some audience segment that is of value to advertisers. Specialty formats, such as classical or jazz, usually depend on an upscale audience that is difficult for advertisers to reach in other media. However, with as many as fifty stations in most large markets, developing niche formats is not only cutthroat but also often gets a little silly. For instance, stations without impressive total numbers may resort to calling themselves the number-one station in a particular daypart (e.g., midnight–6 a.m.) or developing subcategories of a format to differentiate themselves from other stations (easy listening country).

Radio should be considered a quasi-mass medium. Despite its high aggregate audiences, the number of people listening to any particular station at a given time is very small. Even the top stations in a market will be lucky to achieve ratings of 6 or 7, and a rating of 1 to 3 is more common. Consequently, an audience increase that would be insignificant in other media might make a major difference in the financial health of a radio station. For example, a change of one rating point for a station with an average rating of 3 is an increase of 33 percent, a figure that often will move a station significantly up the rankings among stations in a market.

RADIO RATINGS SERVICES

As discussed in Chapter 8, the growth of television has created some significant problems in determining accurate audience-rating data. However, the problems in television research pale in comparison to those facing radio. Not only are there more than ten times the number of radio stations compared to television, but also the lack of specific programming on most stations makes respondent recall much more difficult than in television. As we have discussed, television recall is not a problem for the majority of viewers where meters are used. In addition, much of the radio audience listens out-of-home where it is impractical to keep a diary or reach respondents by telephone.

Dozens of companies provide research services for radio. However, most of these firms are engaged in program consulting or custom research for individual stations and advertisers. The major source of local syndicated radio ratings and the dominant company in radio research is **Arbitron Inc.**, which provides audience data through its Arbitron Radio division.

Arbitron measures radio audiences in over 280 local markets through the use of listener diaries. All members of sampled households over the age of 12 have a personal diary in which they record listening behavior over a 7-day period. Rating periods in a specific market last for 12 weeks. The number of weeks that a market is sampled is determined by its size, with over ninety-five of the largest metropolitan areas sampled on a continuous basis throughout the year. The smallest markets are sampled for only one 12-week period, and the ratings are published in a condensed version of the larger ratings books. Overall, Arbitron mails out more than 2.6 million diaries each year.[13]

In 1998, Arbitron began a service to collect webcast audience information. The service measures the audience of specific broadcast station websites. With this service, Arbitron passively and continuously measures online usage of a panel of consumers who have agreed to be monitored. Arbitron estimates that over one in five U.S. consumers age 12 and above have tuned to an Internet broadcast of an AM/FM station they listen to.[14]

Because of the local nature of radio, station ratings are much more critical to most advertisers than those for networks. However, as we have discussed earlier, network radio is important to a number of national advertisers. As major businesses move into network radio advertising, the demand for accurate ratings will become even more important. The primary source of radio national network ratings is the **Radio's All-Dimension Audience Research (RADAR)** reports, also a service of Arbitron. Research data for RADAR reports are collected through 7-day listening diaries kept by consumers.[15]

Because much of radio listening occurs outside of the home, and advertisers and radio stations are interested in capturing data on radio listening throughout the day, Arbitron has developed a Portable People Meter (PPM). It expects to have panels of PPM users in ten markets by 2008. The PPM can track what consumers listen to on the radio, watch on television, stream on the Internet, or hear in stores. This small mobile device is worn by Arbitron panel members and detects identification codes that can be embedded in the signal transmission. This signal is collected automatically by the device and sent daily to Arbitron for analysis.[16] The hope is that this device will eventually eliminate the need for diaries and permit more accurate data collection that is less intrusive for the respondents.

An overriding problem in dealing with radio ratings is money. The funds available to solve an advertising research problem are directly related to the level of advertising expenditures by major advertisers. For example, when General Motors

---

Arbitron Inc.
Syndicated radio ratings company.

Radio's All-Dimension Audience Research (RADAR)
Service of Statistical Research, Inc., that is the primary source of network radio ratings.

Out-of-home radio listening poses measurement challenges. The Portable People Meter was developed to help minimize this problem.
Courtesy of Ron Komball Photography, http://www.ronkimballstock.com.

and Procter & Gamble invest over $15 billion annually in television, there is a major incentive to invest millions of dollars in research.[17] On the other hand, even though the problems may be more difficult in media such as radio and outdoor, the overall advertising investment will simply not support a research expenditure comparable to that of television.

BUYING RADIO

Radio demonstrates a number of characteristics as an advertising medium:

■ Advertising inventory is perishable, and when a spot goes unsold, revenue is permanently lost.

■ Radio is normally used as a supplement to other media. Therefore, coordination with the total advertising plan is crucial for most radio sales.

■ Every radio buy is unique. Almost all radio advertising is sold in packages of spots that are tailored, to some degree, to each advertiser.

■ Because of the unique nature of each buy, a fixed rate card rarely exists for radio advertising. Pricing is largely the result of negotiation between media buyers and radio salespersons.

Despite the complexity of buying radio advertising, the fundamentals of buying radio are very similar to those of other media. For example, as with most advertising plans, we must examine a number of elements before we proceed to an advertising execution:

1. Review product characteristics and benefits and decide whether these benefits can be effectively communicated through radio.

2. Who is the target market and can they be reached effectively with radio and, if so, what formats, what dayparts? For example, Hispanic audiences are more likely to spend time listening to radio—particularly to one of several Spanish radio formats—than are non-Hispanic audiences.[18] According to Arbitron reports, African American audiences are more likely to spend their radio listening with urban adult contemporary, urban rhythmic contemporary hit, or religious radio formats.[19] The ability to reach audience segments with this type of pinpoint precision remains radio's major strength.

3. Who is our competition? How are they using radio and other media? Will radio provide a unique differentiation for our product or will we be up against strong competing messages?

4. What is our basic advertising and marketing strategy and can it be effectively carried out with radio?

In virtually all advertising situations, we start with a clear delineation of our target market. This audience definition is particularly important in buying radio because of the narrowly defined formats that are offered by the medium. We then must look at the cost of alternative radio outlets and must compare the options available against the CPM/prospects or CPP. Radio, from both a marketing and creative standpoint, must be considered in terms of the advertising objectives we have set out for our advertising. For example, radio in general or a specific station may meet our objectives for reach and cost but fail in terms of the creative strategy. Because radio advertising is often used as a secondary medium, it may be the case that we will evaluate radio in terms of how it complements other more primary media in our advertising schedule and what proportion of our budget should be devoted to radio in this complementary role.

Once we have decided that radio can play a role in our advertising plan, we must begin the task of selecting particular stations that both reach our target audience and provide a program environment that fits our product image. As we have discussed, the number of radio stations provide advertisers, particularly those with national distribution, with many options from which to choose. For some advertisers, network radio is a better option—in terms of cost and guaranteed quality of editorial—than a spot or local schedule. Nevertheless, radio is one of the most challenging aspects of media planning.

The final step in radio buying is the actual scheduling of the spots. Because most advertisers use a great number of spots to achieve reach and/or frequency, the scheduling process can be difficult. Although radio spots are often 60 seconds, some advertisers use shorter messages to gain frequency while a few opt for longer-form commercials to achieve greater impact. In addition, decisions such as whether to use specific dayparts or use a combination of time periods and, in a few instances, whether to take advantage of program sponsorship or on-site event promotions must be considered. Regardless of the final determinations of these and other questions, radio can provide great flexibility and fit into the plans of virtually every advertiser.

Because of the complicated nature of radio, buyers must often rely on the expertise of radio sales personnel—at the station, network, or rep level. Given the nature of radio buys, it is imperative that both buyers and sellers understand the relationship involved in the process. This starts with credibility. One of the primary ways a radio salesperson gains trust is to position radio as a part of the marketing plan. This entails walking a fine line between aggressively selling the medium and your station and at the same time acknowledging the strengths and contributions of other media.

Rather than trying to convince heavy newspaper advertisers to move out of the medium, it is more reasonable to show how radio can make newspaper advertising more effective. The key to successful selling is identifying with the problems of the clients. To do this, the salesperson needs to show advertisers that radio can solve their specific marketing problem. Remember, advertisers are not interested in buy-

EXHIBIT 9.9

Radio Dayparts

Morning Drivetime	6:00 A.M. to 10:00 A.M.
Midday	10:00 A.M. to 3:00 P.M.
Afternoon Drivetime	3:00 P.M. to 7:00 P.M.
Evening	7:00 P.M. to 12:00 A.M.
Overnight	12:00 A.M. to 6:00 A.M.

ing time—they are interested in finding prospects and demonstrating major product benefits to these prospects.

One aspect of using spot radio for national advertisers was recently made easier. In October 2003, the radio industry announced the industry's first national system for electronic invoicing and commercial verification. This system, called RadioExchange, is designed to improve the speed and accuracy of spot radio buys.

USING RADIO RATINGS

We defined both television ratings and share of audience in Chapter 8. Radio ratings and share figures are calculated in the same way. However, the size of the radio audience and the highly fragmented nature of programming and formats have created a system in which ratings are used differently than in television. This section discusses some uses of ratings that are unique to radio.

Among the primary differences between the use of ratings in television and their use in radio are the following:

1. Radio advertisers are interested in broad formats rather than programs or more narrowly defined television scatter plans.
2. Radio ratings tend to measure audience accumulation over relatively long periods of time or several dayparts. Most television ratings are calculated for individual programs.
3. The audiences for individual radio stations are much smaller than those for television, making radio ratings less reliable.
4. Because most radio stations reach only a small segment of the market at a given time, there is a need for much higher levels of advertising frequency in order to increase reach compared to other media. Consequently, it is extremely difficult to track ratings information accurately for national radio plans that include a large number of stations.

Let's begin our discussion by examining several definitions used in radio-rating analyses.

Geographic Patterns of Radio Ratings

Radio audience ratings use two geographic boundaries to report audiences: Metro Survey Area (MSA) and Total Survey Area (TSA). Typically the majority of a station's audience comes from within the MSA.

- *Metro Survey Area.* An MSA always includes a city or cities whose population is specified as that of the central city together with the county (or counties) in which it is located.
- *Total Survey Area.* The TSA is a geographic area that encompasses the MSA and certain counties located outside the MSA that meet certain minimum listening criteria.

Definitions of the Radio Audience

The basic audience measures for television are the rating and share of audience for a particular show. It would be a serious mistake to buy radio and television on the same basis without considering major differences in the way audience figures are considered between the two media. In radio, audience estimates are usually presented as either **Average Quarter-Hour (AQH)** audiences or the cumulative or unduplicated audience (Cume) listening to a station over several quarter hours or dayparts.

Average Quarter-Hour (AQH)
Manner in which radio ratings are presented. Estimates (AQHE) include average number of people listening (AQHP), Rating (AQHR), and Share (AQHS) of audience. The Metro Survey Area (MSA) population can be used to determine Share.

Average Quarter-Hour Estimates (AQHE)

1. *Average Quarter-Hour Persons.* The AQH Persons are the estimated number of people listening to a station for at least 5 minutes during a 15-minute period.
2. *Average Quarter-Hour Rating.* Here, we calculate the AQH Persons as a percentage of the population being measured:

(AQH Persons/population) × 100 = AQH Rating

3. *Average Quarter-Hour Share.* The AQH Share determines what portion of the average radio audience is listening to our station:

(AQH Persons to a station/AQH Persons to all stations) × 100 = AQH Share

Cume Estimates Cume estimates are used to determine the number or percentage of different people who listen to a station during several quarter-hours or dayparts.

1. *Cume persons.* The number of different people who tuned to a radio station for at least 5 minutes.
2. *Cume rating.* The percentage of different people listening to a station during several quarter-hours or dayparts.

(Cume persons/population) × 100 = Cume rating

Let's look at a typical station's audience and calculate these formulas.

Station XYYY, Friday 10 a.m.–3 p.m., Adults 12+

AQH Persons = 20,000

Cume persons = 60,000

Metro Survey Area population = 500,000

Metro Survey Area AQH Persons = 200,000

For station XYYY:

AQH Rating = (20,000/500,000) × 100 = 4

Cume rating = (60,000/500,000) × 100 = 12

MSA AQH Share = (20,000/200,000) × 100 = 10

Using our XYYY example, we can also calculate the following:

1. Gross Impressions (GI) = AQH Persons × number of commercials
   If we buy six commercials on XYYY, we have purchased 120,000 impressions:

   20,000 AQH Persons × 6 spots = 120,000 GI

   Remember, these are impressions, not people.

2. Gross Rating Points = AQH Rating × number of commercials
   Again, six commercials would deliver 24 GRPs (4 AQH Rating × 6 spots).

   The media planner must be able to manipulate the various radio data to develop a plan most suited to a particular client. Although the computer makes these manipulations quickly, it doesn't substitute for a basic understanding of the process. The same budget, and even the same number of spots, used in different dayparts and across multiple stations, can deliver vastly different levels of cumes, reach, frequency, and demographics.

SUMMARY ✺

Every day more Americans use radio than any other medium. With thousands of stations, multiple formats, inexpensive production, and low commercial cost, it can provide effective reach and frequency for a number of product categories.

Technology is taking the immediacy and person-to-person nature of radio to another level. With satellite transmission and out-of-home capability, radio can reach individual customers with programs and commercials tailored to their demographics and lifestyle. New audience-measurement technology holds the promise of being able to track some of this out-of-home audience enjoyed by radio.

Radio has a significant advantage in achieving high penetration among light users or nonusers of other media. Given the current demand by advertisers for narrowly defined audience segments, radio is increasingly becoming at least a secondary option in more and more media plans.

Despite the opportunities for radio to become more important in the advertising plans of both large and small advertisers, the medium faces four major problems. First, the audience delivered by radio is very fragmented. It is better at delivering frequency than reach. Second, commercial clutter is a problem. A third major problem with radio is the lack of a visual element. Many advertisers think that without strong visual brand identification the medium can play little or no role in their advertising plans. The industry has sponsored a number of research studies to show that radio can work effectively with television to remind consumers of the commercials they have seen previously. Probably the biggest problem currently facing radio, however, is the increased use of the Internet and MP3 players, which threatens to diminish the size of the radio audience.

REVIEW ✺

1. Define the following:
   a. drivetime
   b. satellite radio
   c. HD Radio
2. What is the major disadvantage of radio for most advertisers?
3. What are the primary advantages of radio to advertisers?
4. What is spot radio?
5. What is the role of radio networks?
6. Who are the listeners of AM radio? What do they listen to?
7. Where do most advertisers obtain radio audience information?
8. What is the difference between an AQH Rating and a Cume rating?

TAKE IT TO THE WEB ✺

At www.arbitron.com, learn how the Portable People Meter (PPM) device is used to measure media statistics such as traditional radio and television, Internet radio, and digital television. What benefits does the PPM have over the traditional practice of manual measurement?

How does the Radio Advertising Bureau (www.rab.com) work to promote radio as the best alternative for advertisers?

Arbitron Internet Broadcast Service (www.arbitron.com) measures ratings for radio and video on the Internet. What are the key issues advertisers will need to address as Web Radio gains popularity?

CHAPTER 10

Daily News • Post • Citizen • Times • Sun

Morning News • Banner Herald • Daily Post

Observer • Times-Recorder • Journal

Sentinel • Gazette • Constitution • Herald

Using Newspapers

ewspapers are the leaders in terms of local advertising revenue and trail only television in terms of total advertising revenue. Each day approximately 53.5 million newspapers are distributed, providing a large segment of the population with news, entertainment, and advertising.[1] Newspapers also enjoy a reputation for credibility that creates a positive advertising environment. After reading this chapter, you will understand:

chapter objectives

1. the changing character and role of newspapers in the marketing mix
2. challenges to newspaper advertising from other media
3. the marketing of newspapers to readers and advertisers
4. the many categories of newspaper advertising
5. the newspaper advertising planning and buying process
6. the role of weeklies and ethnic-oriented newspapers

Pros

1. Newspapers appeal primarily to an upscale audience, especially those adults age 35 and older.
2. Newspaper advertising is flexible with opportunities for color, large- and small-space advertisements, timely insertion schedules, coupons, and some selectivity through special sections and targeted editions.
3. With coupons and sophisticated tracking techniques, it is much easier to measure newspaper response rates than response rates of many other media.
4. Newspapers have high credibility with their readers, which creates a positive environment for advertisers.

Cons

1. Many newspapers have about 60 percent advertising content. This high ratio of advertising, combined with average reading time of less than 30 minutes, means few advertisements are read.
2. Overall newspaper circulation has fallen far behind population and household growth. Readership among a number of key demographics such as teens and young adults has not kept pace with population growth.
3. Advertising costs have risen much more sharply than circulation in recent years.

On an average weekday, newspapers are read by over 50 percent of the adult population and by an even greater percentage of readers from households with higher-than-average income and education levels. Annual advertising revenues in these newspapers are almost $50 billion with approximately 84 percent coming from local advertisers.[2] In addition, national advertisers are looking increasingly to local and regional advertising strategies to communicate with target consumers in the most effective manner.

Newspaper advertising offers a number of advantages to businesses from large national corporations to the smallest retailer. Among the most important features of newspaper advertising are the following:

- Newspapers offer significant flexibility of advertising formats and audience coverage. Advertisers can buy space ranging from a full-page, four-color advertisement to a small classified notice. In addition, virtually every newspaper offers a variety of specialized advertising plans, including online options, to allow advertisers to reach selected portions of the newspaper's total circulation.

- Newspapers are especially useful in reaching upscale households and opinion leaders. However, compared to most other media, newspapers have significant reach in many major demographic segments.

- Newspapers offer advertisers a number of creative options including preprinted inserts, advertising in their Internet editions, and the ability to deliver product samples.

- Finally, newspapers provide an environment of credibility and immediacy unmatched by most media. A number of surveys have shown that consumers regard newspaper advertising as an important and reliable source of both information and advertising—just the type of medium with which advertisers want to be associated.

So, why is the newspaper industry so concerned about its future? The fact of the matter is that a number of trends pose challenges for newspaper publishers.

1. *Circulation.* According to the Newspaper Association of America, in 1976, newspaper circulation was 77 million; as already mentioned, by 2005, this figure was approximately 53.5 million in spite of significant increases in both population and households during that period.[3] Throughout the 1990s, newspaper circulation dropped about 1 percent each year.

   The reasons given for the decline in newspaper circulation vary from not enough time in single-parent and two-income families to devote to newspaper reading, to younger demographic segments that don't like to read or that never developed the habit of reading newspapers, to other media, especially television and the Internet, that have encroached on the newspaper's position as the preferred method of getting news and information. All of these factors have probably played a role in the decline of newspaper readership.

   Different newspapers have attacked the readership problem with diverse approaches. In some cases, newspapers engage in aggressive subscription sales campaigns including setting up booths in grocery stores or on college campuses (see Exhibit 10.1, for example). Others have set up programs to provide newspapers to middle and high schools in an attempt to give young readers experience with the medium. Still other newspapers such as the *New York Times* have accepted the inevitability of circulation decreases but point to their upscale readership. For example, a *New York Times* executive said, "The quality of our journalism demands a premium price from readers. That, in turn, attracts the kind of audience that is very, very appealing to advertisers."[4] Of course, a formula that works for the *New York Times* is transferrable to few other papers.

EXHIBIT 10.1
Some newspapers are trying to increase their readership among college students.
Courtesy of Karen W. King.

2. *Advertising revenues.* Obviously, the advertising community has not ignored newspaper circulation problems. As recently as 1980, newspapers' share of total advertising revenue was 28 percent. Currently, the figure is about 18 percent including online revenue.[5]

   Several problems have beleaguered newspapers in maintaining their share of advertising dollars. A number of retail chains have turned to direct mail and inserts to reach customers. Even the inserts that are distributed through newspapers provide lower profits for newspapers than traditional advertising. Second, newspapers have been unable to increase support from national advertisers. Although many national advertisers look to regional and local strategies, newspapers have had a difficult time gaining significant support from major national advertisers. Despite a number of newspaper initiatives to overcome national advertisers' reluctance to use the medium, dollars in the sector remain small.

   Although newspapers have never enjoyed a large amount of revenue from national advertisers, currently their franchise with local advertisers is being threatened from a number of quarters. Local television; local cable cut-ins; free niche advertising books featuring real estate, automobiles, and so forth; regional and city editions of magazines; and, of course, radio continue to fight for local advertising dollars that 30 years ago would have gone automatically to newspapers. Later in this chapter, we discuss some of the ways that newspapers are countering these problems.

3. *Changing technology.* Newspapers, like all media, face challenges from new media technology. In fact, many believe that the newspaper as we know it will be dramatically changed by this technology—not the many functions it serves but the method of distribution. The argument is that the cost of paper, ink, postage, and physical distribution is simply not going to be viable in a world of electronic communication. Going back no further than 1990, virtually no one outside the scientific community had ever heard of the Internet.

   In light of the foothold enjoyed by the Internet, with continued improvements in instantaneous delivery, clarity and reliability of content, and portability of technology over the next 20 years—it is hard to imagine thick wads of paper being thrown in the driveways of the 2025 household! This gloomy prediction for newspapers does not mean the functions of newspapers will be dead or even that the companies that provide these services will be gone. It certainly does not mean that there will not be reporters, advertising salespeople, and most of all businesses with dollars to spend to reach a literate audience. It does mean that the methods of reaching these customers and "readers" will change dramatically.

Currently, many newspapers provide websites for their readers and/or advertisers. But as we discuss later in this chapter, the immediacy of newspapers is being replaced by electronic formats—many developed by newspapers themselves. In addition, newspaper classified advertising, which provides about 35 percent of total revenues for the newspaper industry, is being challenged by dozens of online websites such as Craig's list seeking a share of the classified market.[6]

The continuing challenge for both newspaper publishers and newspaper advertising executives is to provide the audience with readers to look to the daily paper as a primary source of information, advertising, and entertainment. The task is becoming more difficult as newspapers try to serve a diverse audience of readers who are young or old, readers who are affluent or middle class, and readers of numerous ethnic cultures. It is clear that newspapers will face growing competition from other media and information sources as they attempt to retain their position as a leading medium. The newspaper industry faces both problems and opportunities. However, it is obvious that long-term trends will continue to endanger the basic foundation of newspaper readership and advertising. In the meantime, newspapers, despite declines in readership, remain one of the most effective means of reaching a broad, heterogeneous audience.

As can be seen throughout the remainder of this chapter, newspapers need innovative initiatives to function successfully in this competitive environment. As we discuss major aspects of contemporary newspaper advertising, we must keep in mind the evolving and dynamic nature of the industry.

THE NATIONAL NEWSPAPER

Historically, the United States, unlike most other developed countries, did not have a national newspaper. When the first newspapers were founded, distances were too great and unique regional concerns made nationally distributed newspapers impractical. However, a number of newspapers now have national circulation, national stature, or both.

TNS Media Intelligence, a company that compiles data on advertising expenditures, defines a national newspaper as having the following characteristics:

- It publishes at least 5 days per week.
- It has printed copies that are sold, distributed and available nationwide.

Based on these criteria, there are three national newspapers: the *Wall Street Journal, USA Today,* and the *New York Times.* The *Wall Street Journal* is an upscale, specialized paper with an emphasis on financial news but with great influence in politics and public policy issues. With a circulation of more than 1.7 million, it is the second-highest-circulation newspaper in the country. It also is among the most respected newspapers in the world, and it reaches readers with the most elite audience demographics of any U.S. newspapers.

All three of the leading national publications have extensive websites. However, not all newspaper websites are profitable. The *Wall Street Journal* has a profitable

Rank	Publication	Average Daily Circulation
1	USA Today*	2,199,052
2	Wall Street Journal	2,070,498
3	New York Times	1,136,433
4	Los Angeles Times (a)	907,997
5	Washington Post	751,871
6	New York Daily News	735,536
7	New York Post	678,086
8	Chicago Tribune (b)	574,754
9	Houston Chronicle (a)	527,744
10	San Francisco Chronicle (a) (b)	468,739
11	Arizona Republic (a)	452,016
12	Boston Globe	434,330
13	Newark Star-Ledger	394,767
14	Atlanta Journal Constitution (b)	381,373
15	Minneapolis-St. Paul Star Tribune (a)	378,316
16	Philadelphia Inquirer (a)	364,974
17	Cleveland Plain Dealer	348,759
18	Detroit Free Press (c)	347,447
19	St. Petersburg Times (a)	337,515
20	Portland Oregonian	335,980

* USA Today's Friday circulation is listed in the Sunday column.

EXHIBIT 10.2

Top Twenty U.S. Daily Newspapers by Circulation

Source: Audit Bureau of Circulations, Editor and Publisher; Mediainfocenter.org.

website largely because of its reputation and specialized business content; it is able to charge an annual subscription fee of $99 (or $49 if a person subscribes to the print edition). By comparison, many other newspaper sites are free, advertising supported, and only marginally profitable.

In 1982, the Gannett Company made a commitment to develop *USA Today* as a general-readership national newspaper. While newspaper purists often criticized the paper's lack of depth, *USA Today* was popular with readers from the beginning with a mix of bright colors, short articles, and extensive business and sports coverage. The paper now has a circulation of almost 2.2 million. Exhibit 10.2 shows the largest U.S. newspapers.

The problem facing all newspapers that aspire to national circulation is finding a profitable advertising niche. A national newspaper is a hybrid vehicle for most advertisers. Unlike other newspapers, national papers are unlikely to gain advertising from grocery stores, department stores, and other local product categories that have been traditionally major profit centers for newspapers. Instead, *USA Today* and other national newspapers depend on national automotive, computer, and communication companies and financial services for much of their revenue.

While the *New York Times* is now classified as a national newspaper, most large metropolitan newspapers such as the *Washington Post* and the *Chicago Tribune* are considered regional advertising media. They are bought much like spot broadcast to reach specific high-potential markets as a supplement to other primary media. Despite attempts by some newspapers to broaden their coverage, most advertisers classify all newspapers other than the *Wall Street Journal*, the *New York Times*, and *USA Today* as regional.

Newspapers will probably continue to have a difficult time reaching out to national advertising as a primary medium. Newspapers have a long tradition as a local vehicle, which is a difficult perception to change. The key to a move toward national newspapers is not how papers define themselves but how they are defined by readers and advertisers. Until a number of newspapers achieve widely dispersed, upscale audiences (not likely for any but a handful of papers), advertisers will continue to regard the medium as a local vehicle with occasional national advertising opportunities. The Internet now offers newspaper publishers an opportunity to reach a national and even an international audience.

MARKETING THE NEWSPAPER

It is obvious from our discussion thus far that newspapers are a product in need of extensive marketing to both readers and advertisers. Like any product with declining sales, newspapers must make a number of strategic and tactical decisions to reverse the trends they are seeing. Despite being the second leading source of advertising dollars, the traditional retail base of newspaper revenues is being challenged by a number of new and traditional media competitors. At the same time, newspapers are finding it more difficult to maintain the broad base of readership that has made them such a powerful medium for more than 200 years.

A positive trend among newspapers is the quality, as contrasted to the quantity, of readership enjoyed by newspapers. Newspapers are strong among college graduates and households with incomes in excess of $100,000. Unfortunately, newspaper circulation also skews toward the oldest portion of the population. Newspaper readership is inversely related to age with those in the 18 to 34 age group (prime prospects for the majority of advertisers) the least likely to read newspapers on a regular basis.

Newspapers have taken a number of steps to identify their customers and advertisers, as well as the preferences of both. This process starts with marketing research. It is rare for any newspaper not to conduct at least one readership or market survey each year. Large newspapers annually sponsor several studies of their markets. A number of concerns have become apparent as a result of these studies.

Among the most important of these concerns is the fact that readers are obtaining their information from a number of sources including television and the Internet. They no longer see the newspaper as an indispensable source of information. Although many advertisers regard newspapers as the most economical means of reaching a mass audience, especially at the local level, many are adopting strategies that replace newspaper advertising with direct mail and other forms of promotion such as product sampling. On the plus side, these same studies demonstrate that newspapers maintain their reputation for integrity and prestige as sources of both advertising and editorial information.

Although newspapers face some formidable challenges, there is no question that they will remain a major advertising medium in the foreseeable future as newspapers continue to offer unique advantages to both readers and advertisers. However, because newspapers dominated the local market for so long, they did not develop a marketing mentality. Unfortunately, the industry is now playing catch-up with its more aggressive media competitors. The next sections discuss how newspaper publishers are marketing the medium to both readers and advertisers. We examine some of the approaches that newspaper publishers are using to protect and extend their franchise with both readers and advertisers.

Marketing to Readers

Newspapers are fully aware that they cannot reverse the decline in advertising share unless they first address the problem of falling readership. Advertisers will only buy newspaper space when they are convinced that the medium will deliver prospects for their brands. Some elite newspapers may be able to survive decreasing readership by marketing the quality of their audience. However, most newspapers will continue to depend on a broadly based audience and high household penetration for their financial success.

Because the current problems facing newspaper advertising are caused by a number of factors, publishers must address several issues if they are to compete with other media in the future. Among the primary steps that newspapers should take are the following:[7]

1. Maintaining good circulation numbers should be a high priority. Newspapers should continue to emphasize getting newspapers into the

hands of younger readers. Many newspapers have put in place programs that provide newspapers to grade schools and make it easy for college students to get newspapers.

2. Editors and reporters should be free of control by marketing departments. The news staff should understand that the newspaper is a business enterprise and that even they can make use of market research in the development of a more reader-friendly newspaper, but this does not mean that the editorial product should be directed by advertising or business concerns. To do so will undermine the newspaper's editorial credibility, which is one of its major strengths.

3. Go after the opportunities in national advertising. Newspapers should move aggressively to gain new national advertising dollars. Newspaper advertising departments must continue to explore creative approaches to demonstrate that newspapers can provide national advertisers with desirable audiences that cannot be reached effectively with other media.

4. More newspapers should follow the lead of some innovative newspapers and consider their websites as a distinctive product rather than a mere spin-off from the printed paper. The Internet can offer profitable opportunities to exploit a fuller range of information than what is printed in the newspaper. The Internet can reach specific readers (and nonnewspaper readers) with selective news, digital content, and advertising and—properly marketed—make a newspaper's website a profit center rather than merely a value added to both readers and possible advertisers.

5. Give readers a choice and market to new audience segments. For example, several newspapers have developed youth-oriented sections within the general newspaper. The marginal costs are often worth the expense, even if only a relatively few new readers are added. In addition, newspapers will need to find ways to appeal to an increasingly diverse population.

6. Invest in research and explore ways to make their Internet site complement the information provided in the newspaper. This will allow the newspaper to remain competitive over the long term even though it may not contribute to short-term profits.

Despite the medium's many strengths, newspapers will continue to see a need to aggressively market themselves to readers. Most newspaper readers and potential readers see the value of a newspaper in local news and sports and other information with relevance to their lives. Readers want information about things to do and places to go, self-help articles, local news of personal interest, and national and international news that has an effect on their lives. In a diverse, multicultural society, appealing to diverse reader interests is extremely difficult. But newspapers will have to find ways to address this heterogeneous population if they are to maintain their position as a primary source of news and advertising.

Marketing to Advertisers

Advertising constitutes more than 70 percent of all newspaper revenues, and more than 50 percent of total newspaper space is devoted to advertising. Clearly, newspapers must continue to attract a number of business categories if they are to remain financially viable. In a fragmented media market, newspapers are finding it more difficult to maintain their share of advertising. As shown in Exhibit 10.3, leading advertisers in newspapers include department stores and communication and entertainment companies.

One of the problems facing newspapers is the dramatic increase in advertising rates and CPM caused by rising fixed costs. Obviously, other media have had significant advertising cost increases, but few were higher on a percentage basis than newspapers.

EXHIBIT **10.3**

Top Ten Advertisers in Newspapers

Ranked by measured spending in 2005.

Source: Robert Coen's Media Analysis at Universal McCann, "Top U.S Advertisers in 10 MediaAd Spending Totals by Media," *Advertising Age*, 26 June 2006, S-11.

NEWSPAPER

Rank	Marketer	2005	2004
1	Federated Department Stores	$831.6	$907.4
2	AT&T	643.0	831.5
3	Verizon Communications	625.7	650.2
4	General Motors Corp.	583.9	461.8
5	Sprint Nextel Corp.	546.9	605.2
6	Time Warner	358.9	368.2
7	Sears Holdings Corp.	234.3	206.2
8	DaimlerChrysler	225.9	166.8
9	Walt Disney Co.	218.2	258.2
10	General Electric Co.	210.5	180.3

In order to justify this growth, it is imperative that newspapers continue to convince advertisers that they are an efficient means of meeting a variety of marketing and advertising objectives. In order to accomplish this goal, newspapers must develop a plan that shows a diverse group of current and potential advertisers that newspapers should be a part of their media plans.

The marketing task for newspapers is a twofold undertaking: (1) to deliver the audience and (2) to compete for advertisers. Research by the newspaper industry has shown that newspaper advertising is considered high on believability and trustworthiness relative to other major media types (see Exhibit 10.4).

The newspaper industry must convince advertisers that it represents the best local medium and at the same time demonstrate to national advertisers that it should constitute an important element of their advertising strategy. To accomplish these goals, newspapers must retain local retailers that have traditionally comprised the bulk of newspaper revenues and must gain more support from national advertisers that have not used newspapers to any great extent. In the current media climate, neither job will be easy. However, newspapers have an advantage in providing readers with localized, in-depth information concerning products and services in their community.

Newspapers have taken a number of steps to position themselves more favorably to advertisers. One approach has been to provide readership as well as paid circulation data. Virtually all media report readership or total viewers, whereas newspapers have traditionally reported only the number of newspapers distrib-

EXHIBIT **10.4**

Most Believable and Trustworthy Advertising

Source: NAA, 2007. From Attitudes Toward Media Advertising 2006, NAA; How America Shops & Spends 2006, NAA. Prepared by MORI Research. Used with permission.

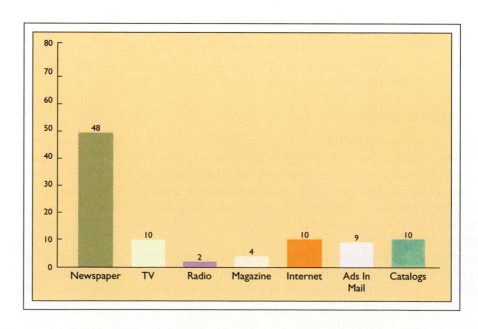

uted. Obviously, this difference in reporting standards relative to other media places newspapers at a significant disadvantage. As mentioned earlier, in 2005, daily newspaper circulation was approximately 53.5 million. However, when including pass-along readers, the newspaper audience is likely more than twice that number. Newspaper executives have long advocated readership as the circulation standard of the medium.[8]

Newspapers are finding that their marketing efforts are most successful when they develop a client-oriented perspective with their advertisers. Rather than attempting to sell an array of advertising options to their clients, many newspapers are training their salespeople in consumer relationship management, which is also known as **relationship marketing**. According to Brenda White, vice president and director of Print Investment at media agency giant Starcom, "They [sic newspapers] need to talk to us about marketing solutions, about what's important to my brand and how our brands can work together versus here's our rate card, mechanical specs, and this is the deadline." She encourages them to embrace digital technology that can be offered from their websites. "It's a liquid world out there and they need to expand their brands across multiple media platforms," she said.[9]

This concept, which has its roots in direct-response advertising, attempts to develop a team approach between the newspaper and its advertisers to work together as partners to solve problems rather than operating on a salesperson/customer basis. Newspapers are approaching major advertising agency media buyers on a personal basis to demonstrate the utility of newspaper advertising in national media schedules.

Many of the past complaints of media buyers centered around the difficulty of making multipaper buys across a number of markets. This is a particular problem for media buyers who are accustomed to the relative ease of buying national broadcast spots and magazines. To address the buying problem, newspapers developed information centers to make it easier for national and regional advertisers to know what services and products are available for advertisers. The **Newspaper Association of America (NAA)**, in cooperation with *Editor & Publisher* magazine, provides advertisers with a database of which newspapers provide special editions, targeted inserts, and other advertising options to make it easier to plan multinewspaper media buys.

As we discuss in later sections, newspapers are developing advertising strategies that try to meet the demands of the smallest retailer as well as the largest national firms.

relationship marketing
A strategy that develops marketing plans from a consumer perspective.

Newspaper Association of America (NAA)
The marketing and trade organization for the newspaper industry.

NEWSPAPER INSERTS, ZONING, AND TOTAL MARKET COVERAGE

Newspaper advertising executives must provide service to a number of advertisers, many with distinctly different marketing and advertising problems. Although there are a number of variations of newspaper advertising strategy, we discuss four approaches here:

1. *Full coverage of a newspaper's circulation.* In the past, most newspapers simply sold advertising space in their pages and advertisers received whatever circulation the paper provided. Large department stores, grocery stores with a number of locations, and national businesses with widely distributed products could take advantage of the majority of a newspaper's readers while other advertisers had to accept some level of waste circulation.

2. *Zoned preprints.* By the early 1980s, targeted direct mail began to offer advertisers a viable alternative to newspaper advertising without its inherent waste circulation. Newspapers countered by offering advertisers the opportunity to have advertising circulars and preprinted inserts delivered with the paper. The first

businesses to make significant use of inserts were grocery stores and major retailers. In recent years, newspaper preprints have become the major vehicle for the distribution of coupons for businesses such as fast-food franchises.

The next step in the evolution of newspaper preprints, again in reaction to direct-mail competition, was the zoned distribution preprints. Rather than simply being inserted in every issue of the newspaper, zoned preprints could be delivered to specific ZIP Codes within a metropolitan area. Initially, most papers offered these so-called zoned preprints only in upscale ZIP Codes; but in recent years, advertisers have been able to buy any ZIP Code within a newspaper's primary circulation area. In some instances, newspapers have begun to distribute preprints to even smaller, sub-ZIP-Code circulation clusters called *microzones*.

Preprints have become so popular that they have replaced traditional advertising as the primary revenue source for newspapers. (See Exhibit 10.5 for an example

EXHIBIT 10.5

Preprinted inserts are popular with many large advertisers.

Courtesy of Homer TLC, Inc. Copyright 2006.

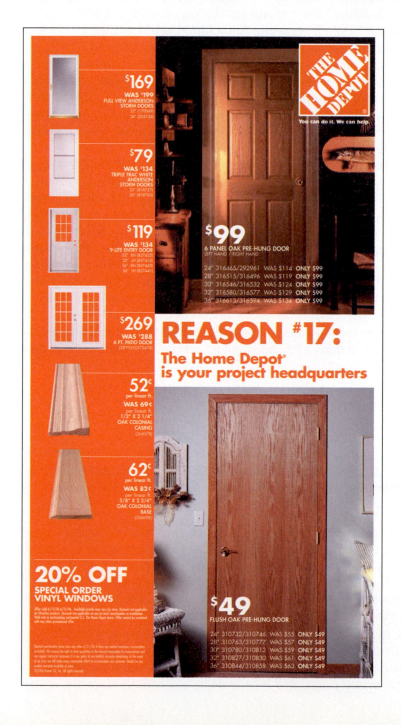

FSI Rank	Marketer	2005	2004
1	Procter & Gamble Co.	$168.9	$135.7
2	General Mills	51.2	57.3
3	SC Johnson	42.7	42.2
4	Reckitt Benckiser	39.1	29.3
5	Unilever	37.1	36.3
6	Altria Group	34.8	36.4
7	L'Oreal	31.8	30.9
8	Colgate-Palmolive Co.	27.0	28.4
9	Johnson & Johnson	26.6	25.5
10	Bradford Exchange	25.8	18.2

EXHIBIT 10.6

Top Ten Advertisers in FSIs

Ranked by measured spending in 2005.

Source: Robert Coen's Media Analysis at Universal McCann, "Top U.S Advertisers in 10 Media Ad Spending Totals by Media," *Advertising Age*, June 26, 2006, pg. S-11.

of a preprinted insert.) In 1997, preprinted freestanding inserts surpassed traditional newspaper advertising, or run-of-paper (ROP), for the first time. The growth of revenue produced by inserts continues to outstrip the growth in revenue provided by ROP. Today, the majority of newspapers provide ZIP-Code zoning for advertising inserts. As you can see in Exhibit 10.6, the largest advertisers in freestanding inserts tend to be consumer package goods such as Procter & Gamble and General Mills.

Although preprinted inserts allow newspapers to compete with direct mail, they also create problems for the newspaper industry. Among the major issues are the following:

- Inserts are less profitable than ROP advertising.
- Although surveys show that newspaper inserts attain higher reach and are preferable to direct mail, the newspaper is no more than an advertising delivery system for these inserts.
- As ROP advertising decreases, the space for news and editorial matter (the so-called *news hole*) shrinks and, ultimately, it may change the character of newspapers as both an advertising and information medium.

Despite any associated problems, **zoning** has offered newspapers a compelling weapon against direct mail and other forms of targeted media. It also holds the potential for bringing an increased number of national advertisers to newspapers:

zoning
Newspaper practice of offering advertisers partial coverage of a market, often accomplished with weekly inserts distributed to certain sections of that market.

1. *The zoned newspaper.* In addition to preprint zoning, many metropolitan newspapers are providing suburban weekly or even daily sections in the newspaper to serve both the reader and advertiser demand for information about particular suburbs of a city. In the past, many newspapers devoted limited resources to these sections. Today, most newspapers are making meaningful investments in their zoned editions and, in many cities, publishers have been rewarded with significant readership and advertising increases.

     The zoned newspaper has major advantages for both advertisers and publishers. Advertisers can gain the advantages of zoning but still run ROP advertising, which has greater prestige and credibility. The zoned newspaper also overcomes the problem of insert clutter. Some major newspapers, especially their Sunday editions, carry dozens of inserts, which drastically decreases their readership and impact.

2. *Total market coverage.* Ironically, while newspapers seek to serve those advertisers that are interested in a narrowly defined group of readers, they also find that a number of advertisers are seeking total penetration of a market. Because no newspaper has complete coverage of its market (in many markets, it is as low as 30 percent), other means must be used to augment regular circulation

total market coverage (TMC)
Newspapers augment their circulation with direct mail or shoppers to deliver all households in a market.

and achieve **total market coverage (TMC)**. Total market coverage may be accomplished in a number of ways:

- Weekly delivery of a nonsubscriber supplement carrying mostly advertisements
- Using newspaper-supported direct mail to nonsubscribers
- Delivering the newspaper free to all households once a week

Regardless of the method used to achieve total market coverage, the aim is the same, that is, to reach all the households in a market whether or not they are newspaper subscribers. The objective is to combine the regular daily paper with a supplemental TMC product and, thus, allow advertisers to reach virtually 100 percent of the households in a market.

CATEGORIES OF NEWSPAPER ADVERTISING

Newspapers provide a number of categories and subcategories of advertising. This section discusses some of the primary types of newspaper advertising.

All newspaper advertising is divided into two categories: *display* and *classified*. **Classified advertising**, which is carried in a special section, is comprised of a variety of advertisements from a small notice announcing a yard sale to those for the largest automobile dealers and real estate firms. **Display** is all the nonclassified advertising in a newspaper. Within the display category, advertising is considered either *local* (also called *retail*) or *national*. According to the Newspaper Association of America, newspaper advertising revenues amount to more than $49 billion and come from the following sources:[10]

classified advertising
Found in columns so labeled, published in sections of a newspaper or magazine that are set aside for certain classes of goods or services—for example, help wanted positions.

display
Newspaper ads other than those text-only ads in the classified columns. Display ads are generally larger and can include color, photos or artwork to attract reader attention to the product.

	Percentage of Total
Classified	35.0
Local	44.9
National	16.0
Online	4.1

As we mentioned earlier, marketing research is an important element of newspaper advertising. Newspaper executives have sponsored a number of research studies showing that newspapers are equal to or better than their media competitors on a number of measures. Much of this research has been oriented toward audience delivery data, demonstrating the quality and/or the size of newspaper readership.

Classified Advertising

Classified advertising (the common "want ads") is often ignored unless you are looking for a car, house, or job. Newspapers also carry advertisements with illustrations in the classified section. These are known as *classified display* advertisements and normally are run in the automotive and real estate sections. All these notices are included under the heading of *classified advertising*, which has its own rate card and is usually operated as a separate department within the newspaper. Classified revenues account for almost $16 billion annually, and the classified department is the most profitable department of most newspapers.

Competition for classified advertising constitutes one of the most serious financial threats to the newspaper industry. To understand the problem facing newspapers, we have to examine a number of factors that are rapidly changing the face of classified advertising. First, the classified advertising sector is very concentrated in three areas: employment, real estate, and automotive. These three categories account for about 80 percent of all classified dollars. This concentration among so few advertisers has allowed specialized online services to gain a foothold in competition with newspapers' more broadly defined classified sections. That is, a person wanting a car can look at websites that are dedicated to only automobiles.

The initial competition for newspaper classified advertising came from online services that introduced two concepts to the world of classifieds: *aggregation* and *vertical sites*. Newspapers regarded classified as local advertising and catered more or less exclusively to the local employment and real estate markets and so forth. However, new Web competitors offered vertical services, that is, a single category of classified advertising such as jobs; and, perhaps more important, they compiled (or aggregated) classified advertising from across the country. Prospective job seekers, particularly those looking to relocate from other areas, now could look at a single site and see employment opportunities anywhere in the country (or even internationally) without going to the trouble of subscribing to a number of out-of-town newspapers.

Newspapers have countered these incursions from independent online classified sites in two ways. First, the vast majority of newspapers have created their own websites, most with classified sections. Second, newspapers have established a number of aggregate sites such as www.CareerBuilder.com, which is a consortium of newspapers that handles job listings and related information. Founded in 2002, CareerBuilder.com has a presence in more than 200 markets around the country.[11]

Newspaper advertising executives know that significant dollars are going to be shifted to online classified services. For them, the key is to use their strong franchise in the classified market to capture the lion's share of the dollars being diverted from print classified advertising.

It is important to emphasize that despite the recent challenges to newspaper classified advertising, newspapers remain the most used source of such notices. Nevertheless, in only a few years time the Internet has brought dramatic changes to classified advertising. Some predict that in the near future—and we are already seeing this on a limited basis—print classified advertising will be devoted largely to a directory of websites, a starting place for further shopping and gathering detailed information. Regardless of where classified advertising moves, it seems that newspapers will need to continue to position themselves to take advantage of future changes.

Display Advertising

Virtually all nonclassified newspaper advertising falls into the category of display advertising. The general segment of display advertising is divided into two subgroups: local and national.

Local Advertising   Newspaper advertising has an overwhelming local focus. The financial structure of the newspaper industry is built on retailer support; and, by any measure, newspapers are the most popular local advertising medium with both readers and advertisers. Local advertising refers to all nonclassified advertising placed by local businesses, organizations, and individuals. Traditionally, newspaper advertising revenues have been provided by major retailers and that continues to this day. See Exhibit 10.7 for an example of a local display advertisement.

Because of their dependence on retail advertising, newspapers are acutely aware of any changes in the local advertising landscape that might impact advertising dollars. Some of the major retailing trends and the potential impact on newspaper advertising are the following:

■ Consolidation of general merchandising and discount retailers will continue to reduce the number of retail advertisers, and it has the potential to reduce the amount of total retail advertising dollars. In recent years, mergers and acquisitions have resulted in a greater concentration of sales among leading retailers.

EXHIBIT **10.7**

A local display
advertisement.

Courtesy of Lane Bevil + Partners.

Fewer retail outlets present two problems for newspapers. First, consolidation of retail ownership can result in a decrease in total retail advertising dollars. Second, because each of these retail conglomerates accounts for a greater share of dollars, the risk associated with the loss of any account is much greater than in past years when the number of retailers spread total newspaper advertising revenues among numerous businesses.

- In addition to a concentration of traditional retail outlets, they also have created a concentration of services not usually associated with these type of outlets. For example, rather than having separate outlets for automotive repairs, banking, home decorating, and eye care, many of the new mega-stores are housing all these services under one roof.

- Retailers are moving to promote their store names as brands. Because price has traditionally been a key ingredient in newspaper advertising, this shift may have a significant effect on newspapers. As image—rather than price— becomes a core retail strategy for many of these chain retailers, we may see a diversion of dollars from newspapers to television or even upscale magazines.

- Retailers will continue to add shopping options to cater to the changing preferences of consumers. Catalogs, online marketing, and other options will augment in-store selling and may result in a shift of advertising dollars to other media.

- As retailers move to promote themselves as brands, we will see more emphasis on store brand and private-label merchandising. Traditionally, a private-brand marketing strategy has resulted in a reduction in advertising budgets; and newspapers fear that this might happen if there is significant movement to house brands among national retailers.

Although predicting the future of retail advertising is difficult, newspaper advertising directors can anticipate continuing changes in the near term. Nowhere in advertising and marketing is the concept of relationship marketing more important than in the alliance between newspapers and their retail advertising customers.

National Advertising One of the recent success stories in newspaper advertising is the increase in national advertising. Despite these increases, national newspaper advertising remains a relatively small contributor to overall revenues. In 2005, national advertising represented approximately 16 percent of all newspaper advertising revenue.

Two elements have contributed to growth in national newspaper dollars. First, many national advertisers, particularly newer categories such as Internet services and telecommunications, are relying on newspapers to target high-potential markets. Many of these high-tech companies also see newspapers as a highly credible source, just the environment needed for a new business with little consumer brand recognition.

A second factor in the growth of national newspaper advertising is the success of the Newspaper National Network (NNN). The NNN was formed in 1994 when twenty-three major U.S. newspaper chains gave funds to the NAA to provide an avenue for national advertisers to gain easy access to national newspaper buys. The NNN provides a network of participating newspapers, which could be bought using one insertion order and one invoice. The intent of the NNN was to duplicate for national media buyers the convenience they experience in buying network television.

Many national advertisers do not consider newspapers equal to other media. When they think of national media, media planners often think of network and cable television and magazines. If the NNN and other industrywide efforts do no more than create a higher profile and greater consideration of newspapers among national advertisers, they will have served an important purpose.

The NNN also provides national advertisers with **Standard Advertising Units (SAUs)** from one newspaper to another (see Exhibit 10.8). Standardization allows national advertisers to purchase space in virtually every major U.S. newspaper and prepare one advertisement that will be accepted by all of them. As you can see, NNN formats are flexible enough to provide virtually every advertiser a design that will fit any creative execution.

Overcoming some of the more cumbersome buying procedures has helped newspapers to market the medium more effectively on a national basis. However, these procedural changes have not addressed one of the most serious points of disagreement between national advertisers and newspapers—the continuing debate over the so-called local/national rate differential. Most newspapers charge a substantial premium to national advertisers. This differential generally ranges from 40 to 60 percent. Newspapers defend the difference on the basis that they must pay an agency commission for national advertising and many of these advertisers are only occasional users of their papers, unlike retailers from whom they enjoy continuing support.

In summary, newspapers must overcome several obstacles if they are to increase their national advertising share. Given the tight retail market and the potential for growth in the national sector, newspapers must continue to make it easier for national advertisers to buy the medium. An effective system of national newspaper advertising will take time. In addition, it seems clear that some accommodation must be made concerning the national/local rate issue. Perhaps the

Standard Advertising Unit (SAU)
Allows national advertisers to purchase newspaper advertising in standard units from one paper to another.

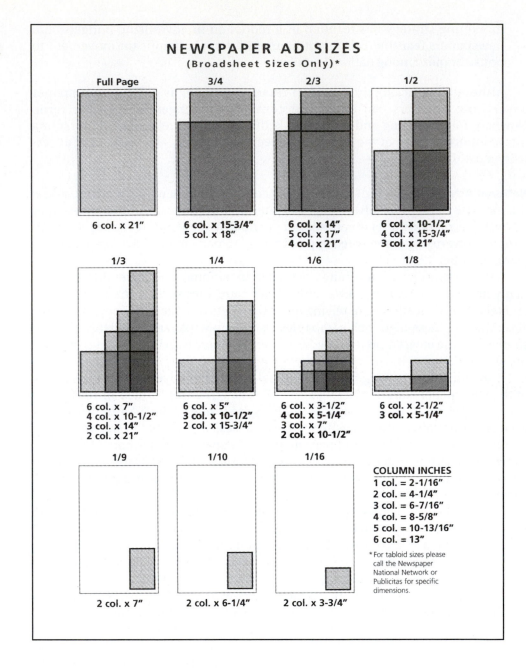

NEWSPAPER AD SIZES
(Broadsheet Sizes Only)*

Full Page
6 col. x 21"

3/4
6 col. x 15-3/4"
5 col. x 18"

2/3
6 col. x 14"
5 col. x 17"
4 col. x 21"

1/2
6 col. x 10-1/2"
4 col. x 15-3/4"
3 col. x 21"

1/3
6 col. x 7"
4 col. x 10-1/2"
3 col. x 14"
2 col. x 21"

1/4
6 col. x 5"
3 col. x 10-1/2"
2 col. x 15-3/4"

1/6
6 col. x 3-1/2"
4 col. x 5-1/4"
3 col. x 7"
2 col. x 10-1/2"

1/8
6 col. x 2-1/2"
3 col. x 5-1/4"

1/9
2 col. x 7"

1/10
2 col. x 6-1/4"

1/16
2 col. x 3-3/4"

COLUMN INCHES
1 col. = 2-1/16"
2 col. = 4-1/4"
3 col. = 6-7/16"
4 col. = 8-5/8"
5 col. = 10-13/16"
6 col. = 13"

* For tabloid sizes please call the Newspaper National Network or Publicitas for specific dimensions.

ultimate catalyst for finding solutions to the problems of national advertisers will be the mutual self-interest of both groups.

Cooperative Advertising

One of the historical outgrowths of the newspaper local/national rate differential was the development of a relationship between national advertisers and their retail distributors called **cooperative (co-op) advertising**. We discuss cooperative advertising more fully in Chapter 14, but it is such an important part of newspaper advertising that we need to mention it here.

    Co-op advertising is placed by a local advertiser but paid for, all or in part, by a national advertiser. The national manufacturer usually provides the advertisements, allowing space for each participating retailer's logo. The original reason for the development of co-op advertising was that it allowed national advertisers to place advertisements at local rates.

cooperative (co-op) advertising
Joint promotion of a national advertiser (manufacturer) and a local retail outlet on behalf of the manufacturer's product on sale in the retail store.

Today, co-op is a huge source of advertising funds. Co-op also is a source of building goodwill with distributors and retailers and exercising some creative control over local advertising, as well as saving money for national advertisers.

Because national advertisers pay anywhere from 50 to 100 percent of the cost of locally placed co-op, it extends the budgets of local advertisers as it saves money for national firms. It is ironic that a system that was developed largely to circumvent the national/local newspaper rate differential is strongly supported by the newspaper industry. Because newspapers receive over half of all co-op dollars placed, their sales staffs are extremely aggressive in helping retail accounts find and use co-op money.

The Rate Structure

The local advertiser, dealing with one or two newspapers, has a fairly easy job buying newspaper space. The rate structure and discounts for any one newspaper are usually straightforward. However, as we have seen, the national advertiser has a much more difficult time. An advertiser buying space in a number of newspapers confronts an unlimited set of options and price structures, including discounts, premium charges for color, special sections, preferred positions, and zoned editions. In the following discussion, we look at some of the primary options and rate decisions that an advertiser must make.

Discounts Newspapers are divided into two categories: those with a uniform **flat rate** offering no discounts and those with an **open rate** providing some discount structure. The open rate also refers to the highest rate against which all discounts are applied. The most common discounts are based on *frequency* or *bulk* purchases of space. A bulk discount means there is a sliding scale so that the advertiser is charged proportionally less as more advertising is purchased. A frequency discount usually requires some unit or pattern of purchase in addition to total amount of space.

flat rate
A uniform charge for space in a medium, without regard to the amount of space used or the frequency of insertion. When flat rates do not prevail, time discounts or quantity discounts are offered.

open rate
In print, the highest advertising rate at which all discounts are placed.

Frequency Within 52-Week Contract Period Full-Page Contract		Bulk Within 52-Week Contract Period	
Open Rate	**$2.50/Column Inch**	**No. of Column Inches**	**Rate**
10 insertions	2.30	500	2.40
15 insertions	2.20	1,500	2.30
20 insertions	2.10	3,000	2.20
30 insertions	2.00	5,000	2.10
40 insertions	1.90	10,000	2.00
50 insertions	1.80	15,000	1.90

ROP and Preferred-Position Rates The basic rates quoted by a newspaper entitle the advertisement to a run-of-paper (ROP) position anywhere in the paper that the publisher chooses to place it, although the paper will be mindful of the advertiser's request and interest in getting a good position. An advertiser may buy a choice position by paying a higher, preferred-position rate, which is similar to paying for a box seat in a stadium instead of general admission. An athletic shoe advertiser, for example, may elect to pay a preferred-position rate to ensure getting on the sports page. A cosmetic advertiser may buy a preferred position on the women's page. There are also preferred positions on individual pages. An advertiser may pay for the top of a column or the top of a column next to news reading matter (called *full position*).

Each newspaper specifies its preferred-position rates; there is no consistency in this practice. Preferred-position rates are not as common as they once were. Now many papers simply attempt to accommodate advertisers that request a position.

Combination Rates A number of combinations are available to advertisers. What they all have in common is the advantage of greatly reduced rates for purchasing several papers as a group. The most frequently seen combination rate occurs when the same publisher issues both a morning and an evening paper. By buying both papers, the advertiser can pay as little as one-third to one-half for the second paper. This type of combination may involve as few as two papers in a single metropolitan market or many papers bought on a national basis. In either case, the advertiser has to deal with only one group and pays a single bill.

The Rate Card

For most media, the advertising rate card, if it exists at all, is simply a starting point for negotiation. As discussed earlier, most radio and television stations don't publish formal rate cards because rates are determined by negotiated scatter plans that are unique to each advertiser. During the 1980s, many consumer magazines also initiated a system of rate negotiation. Today, newspapers are one of the few media to generally maintain rate integrity by offering all advertisers the same rates and discounts. Many newpapers do offer frequent advertisers value-added options such as featured positions on their websites.

Unlike broadcast media with their fixed time inventory and magazines with their lengthy advertising production cycles, newspapers can adjust quickly to whatever advertising space is needed. We only have to look at the typical newspaper's bulky Sunday and Wednesday (best grocery day) editions compared to the lightweight Saturday edition to see the flexibility enjoyed by newspapers.

Despite a traditional rate card, we should not leave the impression that newspapers do not accommodate advertisers with flexible rates in the face of competitive pressure. For example, the following options are available:

- *Multiple rate cards.* Many newspapers offer a number of rate cards for different categories of advertisers. For example, package goods, travel, business, and retail stores may all qualify for different rates. Some advertisers think that the array of different rates makes the buying process unnecessarily complex; and, for national advertisers and other multiple-paper advertisers, it has the same effect as individual rate negotiation. Newspapers see the process as a type of yield management in which a premium is charged for high-demand space.

- *Newspaper merchandising programs.* Many newspapers, while refusing to negotiate rates directly, are willing to make other types of merchandising concessions. These programs, also known as value-added programs, may include sharing of detailed audience research and providing free creative or copy assistance to advertisers.

- *Offer pickup rates.* An advertiser that agrees to rerun an advertisement may receive a lower rate. This encourages return business and passes along some of the savings that the newspaper enjoys from not having to deal with the production process involved with a new advertisement.

Comparing Newspaper Advertising Costs

National advertisers, many of whom consider hundreds of newspapers in a single media plan, want to make cost comparisons among their potential newspaper buys. Advertisers use CPM for the purpose of making comparisons between advertising cost and audience delivery.

Using the CPM for newspaper rate comparisons has two advantages:

1. It reflects the move to page and fractional-page space buys. Media planners are much more comfortable using the standardized space units of the NNN than lines or column inches in space buys.

2. Comparisons among media are more easily calculated using a standard bench-mark such as the CPM. Although qualitative differences among newspapers and other media must still be considered, the CPM does offer a consistent means of comparison:

Newspaper	Open-Rate Page Cost	Circulation	CPM
A	$5,400	165,000	$32.72
B	3,300	116,000	28.45

Example: $\dfrac{\$5,400 \times 1,000}{165,000} = \$32.72$

The Space Contract, the Short Rate

If a paper has a flat rate, obviously there is no problem with calculating costs—all space is billed at the same price regardless of how much is used. However, space contracts in open-rate papers must have flexibility to allow advertisers to use more or less space than originally contracted. Normally, an advertiser will sign a space contract estimating the amount of space to be used during the next 12 months. Such a space contract is not a guarantee of the amount of space an advertiser will run but rather an agreement on the rate the advertiser will pay for any space run during the year in question.

The space contract involves two steps: First, advertisers estimate the amount of space they think they will run and agree with the newspaper on how to handle any rate adjustments needed at the end of the year; they are then billed during the year at the selected rate. Second, at the end of the year, the total linage is added. If advertisers ran the amount of space they had estimated, no adjustment is necessary; but if they failed to run enough space to earn that rate, they have to pay at the higher rate charged for the number of lines they actually ran. That amount is called the **short rate**.

As an example, let us assume that a national advertiser plans to run advertising in a paper with the following rates:

- Open rate, $5.00 per column inch
- 1,000 column inches, $4.50/column inch
- 5,000 column inches, $4.00/column inch
- 10,000 column inches, $3.50/column inch

The advertiser expects to run at least 5,000 column inches and signs the contract at the $4.00 (5,000-column-inch) rate (subject to end-of-year adjustment). At the end of 12 months, however, only 4,100 column inches have been run; therefore, the bill at the end of the contract year is as follows:

Earned rate: 4,100 column inches @ $4.50 per column inch = $18,450

Paid rate: 4,100 column inches @ $4.00 per column inch = $16,400

Short rate due = $ 2,050

or

Column inches run × difference in earned and billed rates

= 54,100 column inches × .50

= $2,050

short rate
The balance advertisers have to pay if they estimated that they would run more advertisements in a year than they did and entered a contract to pay at a favorable rate. The short rate is figured at the end of the year or sooner if advertisers fall behind schedule. It is calculated at a higher rate for the fewer insertions.

rebate
The amount owed to an advertiser by a medium when the advertiser qualifies for a higher space discount.

If the space purchased had qualified for the 10,000-column-inch rate ($3.50), the advertiser would have received a **rebate** of $5,000. The calculation then would be:

Paid rate: 10,000 column inches @ $4.00 per column inch = $40,000

Earned rate: 10,000 column inches @ $3.50 per column inch = $35,000

Rebate due = $ 5,000

Newspapers will credit a rebate against future advertising rather than actually paying the advertiser. Some papers charge the full rate and allow credit for a better rate when earned.

CIRCULATION ANALYSIS

The Audit Bureau of Circulations

Audit Bureau of Circulations (ABC)
The organization sponsored by publishers, agencies, and advertisers for securing accurate circulation statements.

Prior to the founding of the **Audit Bureau of Circulations (ABC)** in 1914, those newspaper publishers that bothered at all provided advertisers with self-reported circulation figures. Obviously, many publishers grossly inflated their circulation and created an adversarial relationship among newspapers, advertising agencies, and clients.[12]

The ABC serves advertisers, agencies, and publishers. It is a self-regulating and self-supporting cooperative body. Revenues for the ABC come from annual dues paid by all members and auditing fees paid by publishers. Exhibit 10.9 shows a portion of an ABC audit report. It should be noted that the information in ABC reports is constantly changing in response to subscribers' needs.

The ABC report includes the following primary information:

1. Total paid circulation
2. Amount of circulation in the city zone, retail trading zone, and all other areas (*Note:* The *city zone* is a market made up of the city of publication and contiguous built-up areas similar in character to the central city. The *retail trading zone* is a market area outside the city zone whose residents regularly trade with merchants doing business within the city zone.)
3. The number of papers sold at newsstands

The ABC reports have nothing to do with a newspaper's rates. They deal with circulation statistics only. Publishers have always been glad to supply demographic data on their readers, but the ABC now has its own division for gathering demographic data for many of the markets in the United States. All data are computerized and quickly available.

Although the verification of newspaper circulation seems to be a relatively straightforward process, it has been surrounded by controversy in recent years. In particular, two areas are of primary concern to the newspaper industry:

1. *Discounted circulation and bulk sales.* ABC rules require that to qualify as paid circulation, copies must be sold for 50 percent or more of the standard subscription price. The rule was initiated to prevent newspapers from simply giving away unsold papers and counting them as normal circulation in determining advertising rates.

   Newspaper publishers, while admitting that strict controls must be applied to deep-discounted or free circulation, argue for greater flexibility. They point out that newspapers delivered free to rooms in upscale hotels, made available on airplanes or at special events such as trade shows, or sold at greatly discounted prices to college students are reaching prime advertising prospects.

W:\dcp2\PROTOTYP\NEWS2005\NwspStmt.fm

Audit Bureau
of Circulations

**Newspaper
Publisher's
Statement**

Subject to Audit

For six months ended September 30, 2006

Publication Name

Anytown (Blue County), Illinois

www.l

This publication also participates in the ABC Reader Profile Study:	Estimated Average Issue Adult Readers	Morning (Mon. to Fri.)	Sunday
	The Newspaper Name	93,800	108,500
Month Day - Month Day, Year	Subscriber Readers	84,200	85,800
	Single Copy Readers	8,000	20,700
Latest Data Available	Pass-Along/Other Readers	1,600	2,000
(See Separate Report for Details)	Reach (18+)	31%	36%
	Average Frequency	3.4	3.4
	Gross Rating Points (GRPs)	155.8	144.1
	Readers Per Copy (RPC)	2.8	2.9

		Sun	Cmbd Avg (Mon.-Fri.)	Mon	Tue	Wed	Thu	Fri	Evening Sat
						Morning			
1.	**TOTAL AVERAGE PAID CIRCULATION**	**36,571**	**31,514**	**29,619**	**32,309**	**32,119**	**30,809**	**31,019**	**31,059**
	Core Newspaper with replica electronic	*36,400*	*31,400*	*29,500*	*32,200*	*32,100*	*30,700*	*30,900*	*30,900*
	Core Newspaper	36,386	31,329	29,434	32,124	31,934	30,624	30,834	30,874
	Electronic Editions (See Par. 6B & SDR) *(when applicable)*	125	125	125	125	125	125	125	125
	Other Unique Editions (See Par. 6B & SDR) *(when applicable)*	60	60	60	60	60	60	60	60
	Total Average Paid Circulation	**36,571**	**31,514**	**29,619**	**32,309**	**32,119**	**30,809**	**31,019**	**31,059**
1A.	**AVERAGE PAID CIRCULATION - Core Newspaper**								
	Paid for by Individual Recipients (≥50% of basic)								
	Home Delivery and Mail	23,020	19,815	19,020	20,010	18,520	19,010	20,020	20,510
	Single Copy Sales	11,500	9,000	7,500	9,500	10,000	9,500	8,500	8,300
	Subtotal	**34,520**	**28,815**	**26,520**	**29,510**	**29,520**	**28,510**	**28,520**	**28,810**
	Paid for by Individual Recipients (≥25%, <50% of basic)								
	Home Delivery and Mail	180	180	180	30	180	30	180	30
	Single Copy Sales	0	0	0	0	0	0	0	0
	Subtotal	**180**	**180**	**180**	**30**	**180**	**30**	**180**	**30**
	Total Average Paid by Individual Recipient Circulation -								
	Core Newspaper	**34,700**	**28,995**	**26,700**	**29,540**	**29,700**	**28,540**	**28,700**	**28,840**
	Other Paid Circulation: (See Par. 6A)								
	Single Copy Sales	115	115	115	115	115	115	115	115
	Educational Programs	590	890	1,390	1,140	890	640	790	590
	Employee/Independent Contractor	220	220	220	220	220	220	220	220
	Third Party Sales	361	359	359	359	359	359	359	359
	Third Party Sales - Payment made with barter (See Par. 6B)	400	750	650	750	650	750	650	750
	Subtotal	**1,686**	**2,334**	**2,734**	**2,584**	**2,234**	**2,084**	**2,134**	**2,034**
	Total Average Paid Circulation - Core Newspaper	36,386	32,329	29,434	32,124	31,934	30,624	30,834	30,874
	Total Paid Circulation - Electronic Editions	125	125	125	125	125	125	125	125
	Total Paid Circulation - Other Unique Editions	60	60	60	60	60	60	60	60
	TOTAL AVERAGE PAID CIRCULATION	**36,571**	**31,514**	**29,619**	**32,309**	**32,119**	**30,809**	**31,019**	**31,059**
	Other Audited Distribution (Optional)	0	0	0	0	0	0	0	0
	Total Distribution (Optional)	0	0	0	0	0	0	0	0
	Days Omitted from Averages (See Par. 6B)	3	None	1	None	None	None	None	None

Definitions:
Core Newspaper: all editions that maintain the same basic identity, contain articles of interest to the general public, appear in the same format and language, and include full ROP advertising.
Electronic Edition Replica: all digital editions that maintain the same basic identity and content as the core newspaper, including all authorized ROP advertising.
Electronic Edition Non-Replica: all digital editions that maintain the same basic identity of the core newspaper but with content that may differ.
Unique Editions: all editions that maintain the same basic identity as the core newspaper; contain articles for specific audience segments, may appear in a different format or language, and may contain ROP advertising.
SDR: Supplemental Data Report, when included, provides enhanced data for this reporting category.

	This publication also has Web Site Activity audited by ABCi. See Par. 6B		Total	Daily	Mon. to Fri.	Sat. & Sun.
Audit Bureau of Circulations **ABCinteractive**	**Month day - day, year** Latest Data Available	Page Impressions	4,723,001	157,434	178,245	100,201
		Unique Users	250,550	8,948	40,741	6,540

01-0000-0

900 N. Meacham Road • Schaumburg, IL 60173-4968   T: 847.605.0909 • F: 847.605.0483   www.accessabc.com

Many advertisers take the position that the liberal interpretation of circulation advocated by some publishers would take the industry back to pre-ABC days when newspapers counted any distribution as quality circulation.

Ultimately, the debate will be settled by advertisers, not newspaper publishers. The basic ABC auditing process is the standard by which most media buyers judge newspapers. Advertisers may accept some changes in the requirements for audited circulation. However, it is doubtful that they will agree to the most liberal changes in bulk and discount circulation advocated by some in the industry.

2. *Readership versus paid circulation.* Newspapers are at a significant disadvantage in that they measure audiences by circulation or newspapers distributed rather than the total readers of these newspapers. Most large- and mid-size papers routinely commission readership and market research from a number of companies. Again, whether readership replaces or supplements circulation will be up to advertisers. Given the long history of circulation as the norm for measuring newspaper audiences, it may be a hard sell.

The ongoing debate over circulation simply emphasizes the competitive environment in which newspapers are operating. Regardless of how these issues are settled, the decline in paid circulation, the loss of household penetration, and the decrease in newspapers' share of total advertising dollars are all concerns that must be addressed by the industry.

Technology and the Future of Newspapers

As we discussed in an earlier section, the Internet has the potential to significantly change the way in which readers search and respond to classified advertising. Although we are still some years away from the fulfillment of the most optimistic predictions of the electronic superhighway, it is clear that new technology must be a factor in the marketing plans of any media company.

Newspaper executives are beginning to view themselves as information providers, not newspaper editors and publishers. This distinction is not one of simple semantics. Rather, it allows people to think beyond the newspaper as a print-on-paper product and consider alternative delivery systems as well as the type of information that is provided. Hundreds of daily newspapers have websites. The need to have an effective Web presence may be underscored by the fact that young adults are spending far less time than older adults with the printed newspaper (see Exhibit 10.10).

EXHIBIT 10.10

Newspaper advertisements can be a good way to deliver an advertiser's Web address to the target audience.

Courtesy of Lane Bevil + Partners.

Despite its potential threat, the daily printed newspaper has advantages to the Internet including convenience and portability. With the increased use and access consumers have to the Web via their cell phones and other mobile devices, these and other forms of new media will likely become a decided threat to traditional newspapers. The fact that newspapers are moving aggressively into the world of new media is testimony to the changing world of both advertising and communication.

NEWSPAPER-DISTRIBUTED MAGAZINE SUPPLEMENTS

One of the most enduring newspaper traditions is the Sunday magazine supplement. For years, most major dailies published a Sunday magazine with features on gardening, local lifestyles and fashion, and personalities. Today, only a few survive. Most of these are concentrated in major newspaper markets where they attract national advertisers and the newspapers are large enough to invest millions of dollars annually in these upscale publications. From a marketing perspective, national supplements appeal to advertisers that gain network buying efficiency, a broad-based newspaper circulation, a magazine format, consistent quality reproduction, and a CPM lower than both newspapers and most magazines.

Individual newspapers view the expense of production combined with declining advertising support as the primary reasons to move to syndicated national publications. The two leaders in the category are *USA Today* and *Parade*. Both magazines deliver huge readership (at a cost to both newspapers and advertisers that is less than most independent supplements). *Parade* tends to be more popular at larger newspapers with a circulation of 32.7 million in 340 papers. In fact, *Parade* is the largest circulation consumer magazine by a wide margin. *USA Today* is distributed by more than 612 newspapers but has a lower circulation of 23.4 million. As is the case with most consumer magazines, both publications offer numerous opportunities for regional buys. Although several advertisers such as the Franklin Mint advertise on a national basis, some form of less-than-full-run buy is very common in Sunday supplements.

A number of other supplements reach ethnic markets in newspapers directed toward these readers. Among the most well known is *Vista*, a magazine carried in over thirty newspapers with large Hispanic audiences. It is published on a monthly basis and has a rate base of 1 million.

Comics

Any discussion of newspaper special features would have to include a mention of the comics. The newspaper comic traces its origins to 1889 when the *New York World* used newly installed color presses to build circulation with a comic section. The importance of comic strips became obvious in 1895 when two titans of journalism, Joseph Pulitzer and William Randolph Hearst, waged a fierce battle over ownership of the most popular cartoon of the day, *The Yellow Kid*.

In 1897, *The Katzenjammer Kids* was introduced as the first modern comic strip with separate panels and speech balloons. In 1912, Hearst's *New York Evening Journal* published the first full page of comics. From the 1920s on, comics became a major source of readership with the introduction of *Blondie*, *The Phantom*, *Beetle Bailey*, and *Peanuts*.

Although not a major advertising vehicle, comics are used by a number of advertisers to reach millions of readers. Editors constantly evaluate comics as they choose among the hundreds of available strips. For those advertisers that want to use the comic sections, there are networks that sell the comic sections in a variety of combinations so that advertisers can place an advertisement simultaneously in a number of papers.

THE ETHNIC AND FOREIGN LANGUAGE PRESS

With the changing multicultural environment in the United States, it is not surprising that a number of media are being introduced to reach these audiences with information, entertainment, and advertising. The role played by newspapers varies among the major ethnic markets. The largest and fastest-growing group of ethnic newspapers is Spanish-language newspapers. This growth coincides with a Hispanic population that is outpacing all other segments in the United States. Hundreds of Hispanic newspapers are available in the United States. Unlike other members of the ethnic press, many successful Hispanic-oriented newspapers are dailies. The best evidence of the importance of the Hispanic press is the support and investment in these publications by major newspaper companies (see Exhibit 10.11).

EXHIBIT 10.11

There are hundreds of Spanish-language newspapers in the United States.

Source: © 2006, *La Voz.*

Despite healthy circulation growth, Hispanic newspapers face a number of problems reaching a very fragmented Spanish-language population with roots in a number of countries with different cultures and product preferences. In addition, surveys show a wide disparity in language preferences. Some would like their information in Spanish, some prefer English, and still others prefer a bilingual publication. Despite these problems, the Hispanic press is among the fastest-growing sectors of the newspaper industry in both readers and advertising revenues.

The African American press has not shown the same economic vitality as its Hispanic counterpart. The African American press was at its height from the 1930s to the early 1960s with almost 300 papers and total circulation of 4 million. These newspapers were sources of news, political action, and advertising. They contributed to much of the social progress made during this period. Among their significant legacies was the drive for passage of the Voting Rights Act and other civil rights legislation during the term of President Lyndon Johnson.

Ironically, the African American press has suffered financially as opportunities have opened to African American citizens. During the 1960s and 1970s, the majority press began to incorporate coverage of African American readers into its papers. As time went on, it was less important to have separate newspapers to cover news of African American readers.

Mergers and consolidations, so common in the media industry, have also influenced the African American press. For example, in 2000, PublicMedia Works, Inc., an African American owned multimedia group, bought Sengstacke Enterprises, which published the *Chicago Defender*, the *Michigan Courier*, the *New Pittsburgh Courier*, and the *Memphis Tri-State Defender*. With stronger financial backing and synergism from a more broadly based media company, it may be that these African American newspapers can be restored to their former vigor.

A continuing problem for traditionally African American newspapers is the preference among the African American population for television and a few selected magazines. Given this trend, it is not surprising that advertisers, particularly major national companies, have shifted significant dollars from newspapers to television, radio, and magazines with high African American audiences.

The Asian press faces many of the same problems of both the Hispanic and African American press—only more so. Like the Hispanic population, the Asian population comes from dozens of different cultures and languages from Chinese to Indian. Lumping Asian consumers into a single category makes the same mistake as considering all Hispanic consumers to be alike. Added to the problem is that the Asian population is not nearly as large as the Hispanic population so the large population centers to support a national Asian press system are not as readily available.

Still, a number of newspapers serve the Asian population. New York City's Chinese-language *Brooklyn Chinese Monthly* and Japanese-language the *Rafu Shimpo* and San Jose's *Viet Mercury* all have circulations of from 20,000 to 50,000. Interestingly enough, the foreign language press in the United States is not a new phenomenon. Beginning in 1732 when Benjamin Franklin published *Philadelphische Zeitung (Philadelphia Newspaper)*, the foreign language press has played a major role in this country. The increasingly multicultural nature of the United States is reflected in a growing number of newspapers available in more than forty languages. Virtually every language is represented by at least one newspaper. From French, Italian, and German to Vietnamese, Chinese, and Arabic, every part of the world is represented by a publication unique to an ethnic group.

Ultimately, the success of the ethnic press is largely determined by the same formula used by mainstream media—advertising support. As population diversity increases along with growing economic power among these groups, we should expect to see growth in advertising-supported media directed at these cultural and ethnic members. The degree to which newspapers will fill this communication gap remains to be seen.

WEEKLY NEWSPAPERS

Weekly newspapers fall into a number of categories: suburban papers covering events within some portion of a larger metropolitan area, traditional rural weeklies providing local coverage, specialty weeklies covering politics or the arts, and free shoppers with little editorial content. According to the NAA, there are almost 6,700 weekly newspapers in the United States with a total circulation over 50 million.[13] During the last 30 years, the complexion of the weekly newspaper field has changed dramatically. Far from its rural, small-town roots, the typical weekly is more likely to be located in a growing suburb and, rather than covering weddings and family reunions, its major topics are probably zoning disputes, overcrowded schools, crime, and how to control future growth while increasing the county's tax base.

As important as their content is the marketing strategy employed by many weeklies. More and more weeklies are part of networks. These networks are sometimes owned by a single company, including the major local daily newspaper, or they may be independent weeklies that joined a consortium to sell their space through a single rep. These groups recognize that the core city trade zone is no longer as economically viable as in previous years. Today, many cities exist only as suburban clusters with one or two large malls anchoring the advertising base. Retailers in these malls depend on a narrowly defined suburban area or neighborhood for their customers rather than on an entire metropolitan area. In some cases, these suburban newspaper groups exist as a supplement to the daily metropolitan newspaper.

From an advertising standpoint, the strength of suburban weekly newspaper networks is that they can serve equally well small, local advertisers that may buy a single member of the group and national advertisers or major retailers that want high penetration into most of the suburban market. Weekly growth will be concentrated in suburban and urban areas for the foreseeable future. Weeklies, once rarely considered by large metropolitan retailers or national advertisers, now play a more important role in the localized marketing strategies of many advertisers.

SUMMARY ⬤

With almost $50 billion in annual advertising revenues, about 53.5 million daily circulation, it is hard to view the future of newspapers as anything but bright. However, newspaper publishers recognize that they face a number of challenges if they are to maintain their historical position as a major source of news and advertising.

As newspapers attempt to increase national advertising, their local advertising franchise is coming under increasing attack from a number of quarters. For example, local cable companies provide advertisers opportunities to cut in to major cable networks that provide targeted opportunities to reach viewers interested in news, music, or sports, often at a CPM less than that of the newspaper. Metropolitan newspapers are competing with suburban weeklies and shoppers intent on exploiting the move to the suburbs by both consumers and retailers.

Added to the traditional advertising competitors is the potential for Internet and other new digital-based media formats to take away both readers and the lucrative classified advertising market. Finally, newspapers are continuing to deal with a declining reader base as younger market segments are increasingly finding alternative sources for information and entertainment.

Newspapers have a major advantage over most of their competitors in that they are perceived as among the most believable and trustworthy mass communication vehicles. They have an established brand that most competitors look upon with envy. As we discussed in this chapter, newspapers must continue to experiment with alternative methods of reaching audiences to prepare for the new moble and digital formats for delivering news. Larger newspapers have already made a number of strides in the area of technology. However, the major challenge for the future is how to make these alternative delivery systems widely accepted and profitable.

REVIEW ⚙

1. What are some of the factors that have eroded the local newspaper advertising base?
2. What are the primary advantages of newspaper magazine supplements?
3. Many newspapers are offering "value-added" merchandising to advertisers. Explain.
4. What does the term *relationship marketing* mean in newspaper advertising?
5. Contrast zoned editions and total market coverage programs.
6. What are three major categories of newspaper advertising and how much advertising revenue does each account for?
7. What are the two major problems in newspapers gaining national advertising?
8. In what area have newspapers been most successful in achieving standardization?
9. What is the difference between short rate and rebate?

TAKE IT TO THE WEB ⚙

The Political Newspaper Advertising website (www.naa.org/political/ads) produced by the Newspaper Association of America attempts to inform the political consulting community about the benefits of newspaper advertising. List three possible advantages of newspaper advertising for political campaigns.

The *New York Times* (www.nytimes.com) and the *Washington Post* (www.washingtonpost.com) both offer electronic editions of their newspapers. Compare "front-page" coverage of national issues. Decide which edition would fit your needs and why.

The *Amarillo Globe News* online edition has a variety of online advertisements for viewing at www.amarillo.com/ads. Check out a few of the advertisements to get an idea of the different types of advertisements that can be created.

CHAPTER 11

Using Magazines

Most magazines today appeal to niche readers, particularly those in categories with special value to advertisers. Virtually all magazines are targeted to the special interests, businesses, demographics, or lifestyles of their readers. Magazines have adopted Internet technology to provide Web versions of their publications as a way to reach new readers, to increase loyalty among their readers, and to generate advertising revenue. After reading this chapter, you will understand:

chapter objectives

1. the history and development of the American magazine
2. how magazine space is sold to advertisers
3. the characteristics of consumer and trade publications
4. the role of magazines as a targeted advertising medium
5. the usefulness of magazines in national media plans
6. the effect of new communications technology on magazines

Pros

1. The number and range of specialized magazines provide advertisers with an opportunity to reach narrowly targeted audiences that are otherwise hard to reach.
2. Magazines provide strong visuals to enhance brand awareness, and they have the ability to deliver a memorable message to their niche audiences.
3. Most magazines offer some form of regional and/or demographic editions to provide even greater targeting and opportunities for less-than-national advertisers to use magazines.
4. Magazines are portable, they have a long life, and they are often passed along to several readers. Business publications are especially useful as reference tools, and leading publications within various industries offer advertisers an important forum for their messages.

Cons

1. In recent years, magazine audience growth has not kept up with increases in advertising rates. Magazines are among the most expensive media per prospect. The growth in advertising rates has exceeded growth in audience size.
2. Advertising clutter has become a concern of many magazine advertisers. Many magazines approach 50 percent advertising content; consequently, time spent with any single advertisement is often minimal.

3. Most magazines have relatively long advertising deadlines creating a lack of immediacy of the message. This long lead time can reduce flexibility and the ability of advertisers to react to fast-changing market conditions. In the age of the Internet during which consumers are used to getting up-to-date information on demand, this poses a problem for some advertisers.

4. Despite the obvious advantages of magazine specialization, it means that a single magazine rarely reaches the majority of a market segment. Therefore, several magazines must be used or alternative media must supplement magazine buys. With thousands of consumer magazines from which to choose, advertisers often have difficulty in choosing the correct vehicle.

ADVERTISING AND CONSUMER MAGAZINES

In 2005, approximately 4.7 percent of U.S. advertising dollars were spent in magazines. The top ten advertisers in magazines include package-goods companies, automobile manufacturers, pharmaceutical companies, and a media company (see Exhibit 11.1).

With the introduction of television as a national advertising medium in the 1950s, magazines began to market themselves as a specialized medium to reach targeted prospects within the more general population. Unable to duplicate the huge numbers that the three television networks at the time could deliver, magazines based their economic future on the quality of audience they could deliver rather than the quantity. The modern niche magazine evolved in much the same way as narrowly formatted radio stations, and both did so as a reaction to the ultimate mass appeal of television.[1]

Magazines today find that they must continue to change and adapt to a marketplace that exhibits both competitive and economic pressures. The magazine industry is undergoing changes in all aspects of the way it does business. In fact, there is little in the way of magazine production, distribution, circulation, or advertising that is not undergoing some type of transition.

The contemporary magazine faces many opportunities and challenges in the twenty-first century. Some of these problems are also concerns in both the radio and newspaper industries. The segmented and fragmented nature of magazine publishing means that publications are constantly seeking to define their audiences in narrower ways. Like the radio industry, magazines find that marketers invest an overwhelming percentage of their advertising dollars in the two or three leaders in a category, leaving a small share of advertising dollars to the others. This has led magazines to attempt to create editorial differentiation directed to interest groups that are often too small to support them financially. More than two-thirds of magazine titles have a circulation of less than 500,000 readers.

EXHIBIT 11.1

Top Ten Magazine Advertisers Ranked by Measured Spending in 2005

Source: Robert Coen's Media Analysis at Universal McCann, "Top U.S. advertisers in 10 MediaAd spending totals by media," *Advertising Age*, 26 June 2006, S-11.

MAGAZINE			
Rank	**Marketer**	**2005**	**2004**
1	Procter & Gamble Co.	$826.1	$758.2
2	Altria Group	543.3	439.7
3	General Motors Corp.	497.8	502.3
4	Johnson & Johnson	410.3	349.5
5	Time Warner	352.9	346.4
6	L'Oreal	344.1	336.5
7	Ford Motor Co.	339.0	386.6
8	DaimlerChrysler	312.2	368.1
9	GlaxoSmithKline	265.3	187.6
10	Unilever	248.9	146.0

Just as magazines are similar in some respects to radio, they also have characteristics in common with newspapers. The costs of paper, delivery, and marketing to readers and advertisers are creating profitability problems even as gross revenues increase. The *National Directory of Magazines* reports that there are over 6,300 consumer magazines in the United States.[2] Many of these have very small circulations. In such a competitive marketplace, gaining and maintaining readership are constant headaches for publishers. One only has to look at the number of discounted subscriptions for even the most popular magazines to see the extent of the problem.

Five or more magazines are introduced each week covering topics as diverse as shopping, aviation, and competitive swimming. Although consumer magazines have a number of attributes in common, in many respects each magazine or category of magazines has unique problems and opportunities. In this atmosphere, simultaneous successes and failures exist among different categories of publications. Women's service magazines, long a leading consumer magazine category, have experienced a number of significant changes in recent years in an attempt to fend off competition from women's lifestyle magazines such as *O, The Oprah Winfrey Magazine*, and *Real Simple*.[3]

In order to understand the contemporary consumer magazine industry, we have to examine two primary factors: (1) selectivity and (2) cost versus revenue considerations.

Selectivity

Although magazines represent an eclectic continuum of titles and interests, the success stories are almost universally confined to narrow editorial interests and audience segments. A sampling of some of the top magazines in terms of advertising revenues and advertising pages demonstrates this range of interests. For example, *Real Simple, New York, Dwell*, and *In Touch Weekly* are among the leaders in advertising revenue growth in recent years.[4] Virtually the only thing these publications have in common is that they have been able to find a distinctive niche among both readers and advertisers.

Magazines are searching for the right editorial formula in a market that is increasingly fragmented (see Exhibit 11.2). Although there are very few large homogeneous groups, there are homogeneous segments within more general groups. For example, publishers have long tried to effectively reach the valuable teen market. However, they find that no market as such exists. Boys and girls differ markedly not only in what they read but also in the amount of reading they do, with teen girls reading significantly more than boys.

The Evolution of the Modern Magazine Although selectivity is one of the keys to contemporary magazine success, audience and editorial selectivity is actually rooted in the historical development of magazines. The magazines of the mid-nineteenth century were targeted to audiences of special interests, were sold at a high cost, and carried little advertising. Most magazines were literary, political, or religious in content and depended on readers or special interest groups to provide most of their financial support.

In the latter years of the nineteenth century, a rising middle class, mass production, and national transportation combined to provide the opportunity for nationally distributed branded goods. The opportunities offered by national brands could be exploited only with the efficiencies of mass promotion. During the 1890s, a number of publishers provided the foundation for today's advertising-supported, mass circulation magazine. Frank Munsey (*Munsey's*) and S. S. McClure (*McClure's*) were among the most successful publishers of the period. However, it was Cyrus H. Curtis who "developed the magical possibilities of national advertising, and demonstrated more clearly than anyone else that you could lose millions of dollars

READ ABOUT WHERE ALL YOUR LAWYER PALS ARE GOING. BESIDES HELL, OF COURSE.

No one keeps better tabs on movement within our industry than we do. But now you can turn to us for expanded coverage of transactional law, general business and coming soon, a new leisure section. There's never been a better time to subscribe, so call 404-521-1227. **THE FULL STORY.**

on your circulation by selling at a low price yet make more millions out of your advertising. . . ."[5] The formula was so successful that by 1900 his *Ladies' Home Journal*, under the editorship of Edward Bok, was the first magazine to achieve a circulation of 1 million.

Until the advent of radio in the 1920s, magazines remained the only national advertising medium. With the introduction of radio, magazines had to share the national advertising dollar. Still, magazines were the only visual medium available to national manufacturers. However, when television came on the scene in the 1950s, people's reading habits became viewing habits, and national magazines had to change to survive.

The change from a mass to a class medium, which began in the competitive turmoil of the 1950s, continues up to the present. Perhaps the most dramatic indication of this change was the March 2000 demise of the monthly version of *Life* after 64 years of publication. This was followed by the failure of the much-hyped *Talk* magazine in 2002.

Today, even the largest circulation publications tend to appeal to a fairly narrowly defined market segment. For example, *Sports Illustrated, Time, Better Homes and Gardens,* and *Modern Maturity*—all among the circulation leaders—would not be classified as general editorial magazines. Only newspaper-distributed *Parade* and *USA Weekend* have both large circulations and general appeal. However, as discussed in Chapter 10, they are hybrid publications that many advertisers consider more as newspapers than as magazines.

Costs and Revenues

Consumer magazine revenues are huge, and publications are largely dependent on advertising for their existence. Typical consumer magazine content consists of just about 47 percent advertising pages.[6] While the advertising industry as a whole was hit hard by advertising cancellations following the September 11, 2001, tragedy, many publications were dealt a further blow when tobacco advertisers substantially curtailed or eliminated their advertising in magazines. Publishers are increasingly concerned about profitability.

Magazine cost concerns can be summarized largely in four primary categories:

1. *Marketing costs.* With the number of publications and a sometimes fickle readership, publishers are seeing significant increases in the cost of gaining and maintaining readers. Currently, approximately 70 percent of consumer magazine revenue is from subscriptions as opposed to newsstand sales. Consequently, it is imperative for publishers to invest huge sums of money in gaining new readers and keeping current ones. Likewise, escalating printing and postage costs have made direct-mail campaigns increasingly expensive. The competitive environment of magazine publishing prevents many publishers from raising the cost of subscriptions to cover higher expenses. About 55 percent of magazine revenue comes from advertising.[7]

2. *Postage and distribution costs.* Since 1995, the U.S. Postal Service (USPS) has imposed several rate increases on magazine publishers. These increases have been far greater than the rate of inflation, and they have caused a major rift between publishers and the USPS.

   At the same time that publishers are facing hefty increases in postal charges, they are witnessing similar boosts in the cost of newsstand distribution. Consolidation at both the retail and wholesale levels has created a more streamlined—and limited—distribution channel. Retailers, concerned with profit margins, are insisting that wholesalers limit the number of titles sent to them. "As a result, magazines seem to be losing the distribution levels they once took for granted. More outlets are being controlled by a smaller group of companies, making it harder for new titles to get to the newsstand."[8] The result has been an even greater reliance on subscription sales and a continuing upward cost spiral for publishers. Wal-Mart, which accounts for 15 percent of all single-copy magazine sales, for example, chose a few years ago not to carry several men's magazines such as *Maxim, Stuff,* and *FHM*. Wal-Mart executives reported that they received many complaints about the suggestive nature of the covers on these so-called "laddie" magazines.[9]

3. *Concentration of advertisers.* Although a primary strength of magazines is their selectivity, it works against them in terms of broadly based advertising appeal. Magazines receive a disproportionate percentage of their advertising revenues from a very few product categories. Twelve categories account for 87 percent of all magazine advertising (see Exhibit 11.3). Just ten companies provide almost one-third of all consumer magazine revenues. In fact, Procter & Gamble, the top magazine advertiser in 2005, accounted for about 6 percent of total advertising revenue in consumer magazines.[10]

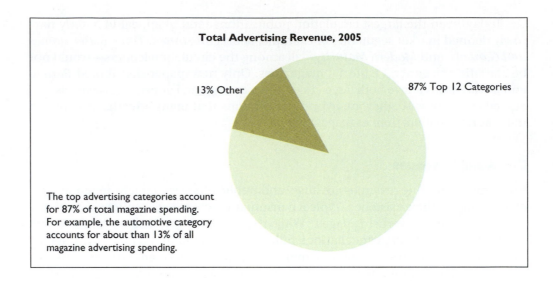

Total Advertising Revenue, 2005

13% Other

87% Top 12 Categories

The top advertising categories account for 87% of total magazine spending. For example, the automotive category accounts for about than 13% of all magazine advertising spending.

If even one of these major advertisers decreases its magazine spending, it can have a significant impact on a number of publications. Advertising cutbacks are even more damaging to magazines geared to a very narrow interest such as computing or golf. In these cases, a magazine has few practical alternatives to make up for the loss of even one large advertising client.

Over the past 20 years, magazines have tried to insulate themselves from their dependence on advertising by shifting a disproportionate percentage of the cost of magazines to readers.

4. *Increases in discounting.* Growth in the amount magazines charge advertisers has slowed with the slowing of the economy. Many magazines are offering large discounts off of their regular rate card to regular advertisers. As advertisers push for more efficiencies in their media plans, magazines have been pushed to provide a wider array of discounts and value-added opportunities.

Cross-Media Buys

There are few magazine, television, or newspaper companies in the United States today. They have been replaced by multimedia companies with interests in all traditional media as well as the Internet, interactive media, and various forms of direct response. Magazines are major players in many of these huge conglomerates, and they form a symbiotic relationship with their media partners. From an advertising standpoint, it can be of great benefit for a magazine to be sold as part of a multimedia package—known as a **cross-media buy**.

cross-media buy
Several media or vehicles that are packaged to be sold to advertisers to gain a synergistic communication effect and efficiencies in purchasing time or space.

Because magazines reach niche audiences, they can often reach prime prospects who are light users of other media. Companies such as Time Warner and Disney can offer advertisers hundreds of options for their advertising messages—often at a significant discount compared to buying the same properties on an individual basis. One of the most creative cross-media sellers is Disney. In the sports arena, for example, Disney can offer package deals with ABC, ESPN, *ESPN The Magazine*, and ESPN radio programming.

In another example of cross-media planning opportunities, in 2006, the Meredith Corporation created a new video unit to leverage content from its magazine titles and television stations. This unit creates video media programming based on content from Meredith Corporation's magazines such as *American Baby* and *Better Homes and Gardens*. This gives advertisers the option of reaching their target audiences across multiple platforms including the Internet, cable, and network and syndicated television.[11]

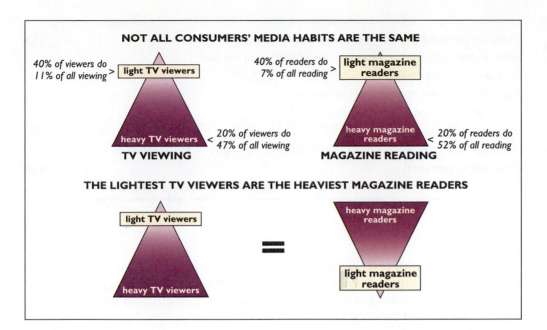

EXHIBIT **11.4**
Magazines' Role in the Media Mix
Source: MRI Quintiles. Courtesy of Magazine Publishers of America.

One of the appealing features of cross-media buys for national advertisers is the complementary nature of magazines and television in reaching different segments of the general population. As Exhibit 11.4 demonstrates, television simply does not reach those prospects who are the heaviest users of magazines. There is such a strong inverse relationship between magazine readership and television viewing that mass advertisers are almost compelled to use both media. Not only does the combination of magazines and television extend reach, but it also provides a welcome diversity of advertising themes and creative executions.

Despite some obvious advantages to advertisers in terms of lower media costs, advertisers should be careful in analyzing cross-media buys. Marketers have to realize that a package of media owned by a single company is not necessarily the best choice in each category. For instance, even though we buy spots on *Monday Night Football* (*MNF*), are we sure that *ESPN The Magazine* is a better fit for our target audience than *Sports Illustrated*, or is ESPN.com a better Web choice than CNN/SI.com? There is nothing inherently wrong with cross-media buys as long as advertisers realize that they are put together largely for the benefit of the media companies. As single media companies come to control more and more media properties, the possibilities of building tailored media packages for individual advertisers increase.

MAGAZINES AS A NATIONAL ADVERTISING MEDIUM

Advantages of Magazine Advertising

Depending on the product and advertising objectives, magazines may offer a number of advantages as primary or secondary media vehicles. This section examines the primary considerations that determine whether or not magazines in general—or a particular title—will be included in a media plan.

1. *Does it work?* An advertiser is interested in the various advantages and characteristics of a medium only to the extent that these elements allow the medium to contribute to sales and profits. In recent years, Magazine Publishers of America (MPA) has commissioned a series of studies conducted by independent research firms to determine the value of magazines as an advertising tool.

   In one study, results showed that over half of magazine readers said they took or plan to take action as a result of exposure to magazine advertisements.

EXHIBIT **11.5**

Actions Readers Took or Plan to Take as a Result of Exposure to Specific Magazine Ads

Source: MRI Quintiles. Courtesy of Magazine Publishers of America.

Consider purchasing the advertised product or service	19%
Gather more information about advertised product or service	11
Visit the advertiser's website	10
Purchase the advertised product or service	8
Visit a store, dealer or other location	7
Save the ad for future reference	6
Recommended the product or service to a friend, colleague or family member	5
Took any action (net)	**51%**

Base "Actions Taken" based on respondents recalling specific ads

Almost one-fifth of magazine readers said they had considered purchasing the advertised product or service, and about 11 percent said they gathered more information about the product or service. Ten percent said they visited the advertiser's website (see Exhibit 11.5).[12]

2. *Audience selectivity.* Assuming that magazines can accomplish the required communication task, the next question is whether they can reach a specific target market. It is here that magazines excel. There is a magazine targeted to virtually every market segment and almost everyone reads a magazine during a given month. There are magazines for almost every demographic and interest group (see Exhibit 11.6). With magazines, total readership is often a secondary advertising consideration to how the magazines reach target audiences. Approximately 70 percent of all consumer magazines have a circulation of less than 500,000.

3. *Long life and creative options.* Unlike a short-lived broadcast message or the daily newspaper, many magazines are kept and referred to over a long period of time, while some are passed along to other readers. In addition, magazines are portable with over three-fourths of magazine readers saying they sometimes read magazines in such places as doctors' offices, someone else's home, or at work.[13] In this disposable media world, magazines are almost alone as a long-term medium. Magazines are often used as reference sources—articles are clipped, back issues are filed, and readers may go back to a favorite magazine numerous times before finally discarding it. Advertisers potentially benefit from each of these exposures.

   The magazine is also a visual medium with a number of creative options. Magazines offer advertisers a wide range of flexible formats such as double-page spreads, bright colors, and even product sampling. Magazines are particularly well suited to long copy. Discussions of detailed product attributes for automobiles and consumer electronics as well as advertising for financial services lend themselves to magazines (see Exhibit 11.7).

4. *Availability of demographic and geographic editions.* In Chapter 10, we discussed newspaper zoning as a reaction to advertiser demand for selected segments of a publication's circulation. On a national scale, magazine demographic and geographic editions meet the same demands of large advertisers. It is very rare that a national magazine does not offer some type of regional or demographic breakout of its total circulation. These special editions are called **partial runs** and are so common and important to magazine advertising that they are discussed separately in a later section of this chapter.

5. *Qualitative factors and engagement.* Advertisers are interested in the demographics of the audience, but they are also interested in how audience members think of themselves when they read a particular publication. The *Playboy* man

partial runs
When magazines offer less than their entire circulation to advertisers. Partial runs include demographic, geographic, and split-run editions.

and the *Cosmopolitan* woman are as much a matter of readers' perception as a reality. Unlike many other media, magazines offer advertisers relatively high levels of audience involvement or engagement. Consequently, magazine advertisers are more apt to use understated creative approaches as contrasted to the hard-sell advertising found in so many other media. Few media connect with their audiences to the degree that magazines do. According to a recent Roper Public Affairs study, almost half of all consumers say that advertising adds to the enjoyment of reading a magazine (see Exhibit 11.8).

In Chapter 7, we discussed the PRIZM system of categorizing people by their lifestyle characteristics. Increasingly, magazines use psychographic and lifestyle research to sell advertisers on the qualitative aspects of their audiences. Take a moment to review the various PRIZM categories in Exhibit 7.2a and try to match these audiences with the primary readers of some major magazines. Research indicates that magazines are preferred by a wide margin as a source of ideas and information on topics as diverse as automobiles, fashion, and fitness. This editorial connection with readers should carry over to a connection between readers and

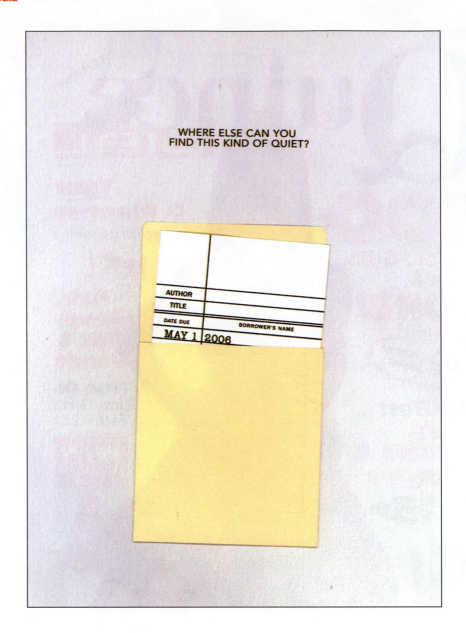

advertisers. When readers pick up *Parents*, *Money*, *Quarter Horse News*, or *PC Computing*, there is little doubt about their interests. These same readers also watch prime-time television, listen to the radio on the way home from work, and see numerous billboards each day. However, it is difficult to anticipate what they are thinking about at these moments. On the other hand, specialized magazines can practically guarantee a synergism between the reader and editorial content, which in many cases will carry over to advertising content.

Results of a study released by Knowledge Networks in June 2003 provide evidence that reader involvement is linked to advertising recall. Knowledge Networks created an index of reader involvement that is calculated using reading frequency, amount of time spent reading, and preference for the magazine as measured by Mediamark Research Inc. (MRI). Based on interviews with over 1,000 readers of five, large-circulation magazines (*Better Homes & Gardens*, *National Geographic*, *People*, *Reader's Digest*, and *TV Guide*), the results suggested that readers who are highly involved with a magazine are more likely to recall advertising in that magazine than are low-involvement readers.[14]

Despite the recent attention given to the qualitative nature of magazines, the ultimate measure of magazines as an advertising vehicle will be determined by

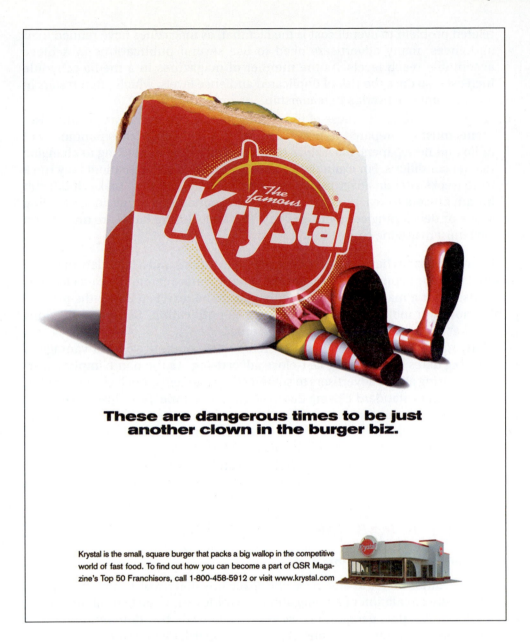

their ability to deliver prime prospects at a competitive cost. Media planners will continue to judge magazines on a cost-efficiency basis using criteria such as CPMs, reach, and frequency. The final evaluation of magazines, as with any medium, is whether they can deliver the right audience, at the right price, and in the right environment to help contribute to the achievement of the communication objectives.

Disadvantages of Magazine Advertising

Despite the many advantages that magazines offer advertisers, there are some important considerations for advertisers contemplating buying magazines.

1. *High cost.* As we have discussed, magazines generally are the most expensive medium on a CPM basis. It is not unusual for specialized magazines to have CPM levels of over $100 compared to $15 to $25 on average for prime-time shows. However, in an era of niche marketing, the CPM is important only in relation to the prospects reached and the waste circulation of a medium. A

related problem to overall cost is the fact that, as magazines have refined their audiences, many advertisers need to use several publications to achieve acceptable reach levels. As the number of magazines in a media schedule increases, so does the risk of duplicated audience levels, which often results in an unacceptable overlap in readership.

closing date
The date when all advertising material must be submitted to a publication.

2. *Long* **closing dates**. Because of the printing process, most magazine advertisements must be prepared well ahead of publication. Unlike the spontaneity of radio and newspapers, magazines tend to be inflexible in reacting to changing market conditions. For example, a monthly magazine advertisement may run 8 to 10 weeks after an advertiser submits it. This long lead time makes it difficult for advertisers to react to current marketing conditions either in scheduling space or developing competitive copy. The long closing dates are one reason why most magazine copy is very general.

Many magazines have one date for space reservations and a later date for when material must be submitted. Normally, the space contract cannot be canceled. It is not unusual for a magazine to require that space be reserved 2 months prior to publication and material sent 6 weeks before publication. Some publications require that material be submitted with the order.

fast-close advertising
Some magazines offer short-notice advertising deadlines, sometimes at a premium cost.

Many magazines have sought to overcome the competitive disadvantage of long closing dates by providing **fast-close advertising**. As the name implies, fast-close advertising allows advertisers to submit advertisements much closer to publication dates than standard closing dates allow. At one time, fast-close advertising was very expensive, carrying a significant premium compared to other advertising. However, competitive pressure and improvements in print technology have seen many publications offer fast-close advertising at little or no extra expense.

The remaining sections of this chapter examine some specific features and techniques involved in buying advertising in magazines.

FEATURES OF MAGAZINE ADVERTISING

Partial-Run Magazine Editions

Partial-run editions refer to any magazine space buy that involves purchasing less than the entire circulation of a publication. The oldest and most common partial-run edition is the geographic edition, followed by demographic and vocational/special interest editions. Basically, the partial-run edition allows relatively large-circulation magazines to compete with smaller niche publications for specialized advertisers.

As advertiser demand for more and more narrowly defined audiences has increased in recent years, magazines with fairly small circulations and/or specialized editorial formats have begun to offer some form of partial-run edition. Again, the smaller the circulation and the more specialized the content of a magazine, the more likely it is that the geographic edition will be the only partial run offered.

Some magazines that offer partial-run editions offer only geographic ones. On the other hand, major publications, especially large-circulation weeklies such as *Time*, *Newsweek*, and *People*, offer dozens of options to advertisers. These publications combine both geographic and demographic editions so that an advertiser can reach *Time* readers who occupy positions in top management throughout the country or in selected locations. *Time*, for example, offers hundreds of ways to buy advertising in the magazine, including both demographic and regional editions.

As advertisers continue to demand that all media deliver narrowly targeted audiences and the techniques honed by direct mail and other direct-marketing media become more prevalent, we will see the majority of magazines offering some form of partial-run circulation. Computer technology and advances in high-speed printing also are allowing magazines to meet these advertiser requirements.

Split-Run Editions A special form of the partial-run edition is the split run. Whereas most partial-run editions are intended to meet special marketing requirements of advertisers, split-run editions normally are used by both advertisers and publishers for testing purposes. The simplest form of split-run test is when an advertiser buys a regional edition (a full run is usually not bought because of the expense) and runs different advertisements in every other issue.

Each advertisement is the same size and runs in the same position in the publication. The only difference between the advertisements is the element being tested. It may be a different headline, illustration, product benefit, or even price. A coupon is normally included; and the advertiser, based on coupon response, can then determine the most productive version of the advertisement. This split-run technique is called an *A/B split*. Half of the audience gets version A and half version B.

As the competition for readers has grown, so has the use of split-run tests by magazines themselves. Magazines occasionally experiment with different covers for the same issue—either for testing purposes or to take advantage of some story of regional interest. The split-run technique has been instrumental in providing both publishers and advertisers with insight into how magazine advertising can be most effective. Partial-run and split-run editions offer a number of benefits to advertisers (and, in some cases, publishers):

1. Geographic editions allow advertisers to offer products only in areas in which they are sold. For example, snow tires can be promoted in one area, regular tires in another (see Exhibit 11.9).
2. Partial runs can localize advertising and support dealers or special offers from one region to another. As advertisers increasingly adopt local and regional strategies, the partial-run advantages will become even more apparent.
3. Split-run advertising allows advertisers to test various elements of a campaign in a realistic environment before embarking on a national rollout.
4. Regional editions allow national advertisers to develop closer ties with their retailers by listing regional outlets. This strategy also provides helpful information to consumers for products that lack widespread distribution.

Partial-run editions also have some disadvantages that make them less than ideal for all advertising situations:

1. CPM levels are usually much higher than full-run advertising in the same publication, and close dates can be as much as a month earlier than other advertising.
2. In the case of demographic editions, the lack of newsstand distribution for these advertisements can be a major disadvantage if single-copy sales are significant for the publication.
3. Some publications bank their partial-run advertising in a special section set aside for such material. There also may be special restrictions placed on partial-run advertising. For example, such advertising often must be full page and only four-color advertising is accepted by some publications.

Selective Binding **Selective binding** makes the customization of partial-run editions even more sophisticated. Although the concept of selective binding is essentially the same as that of partial-run advertising, it refers to different editorial material or large advertising sections that are placed in less than the full run of a publication. Using computer technology and sophisticated printing techniques,

selective binding
Binding different material directed to various reader segments in a single issue of a magazine.

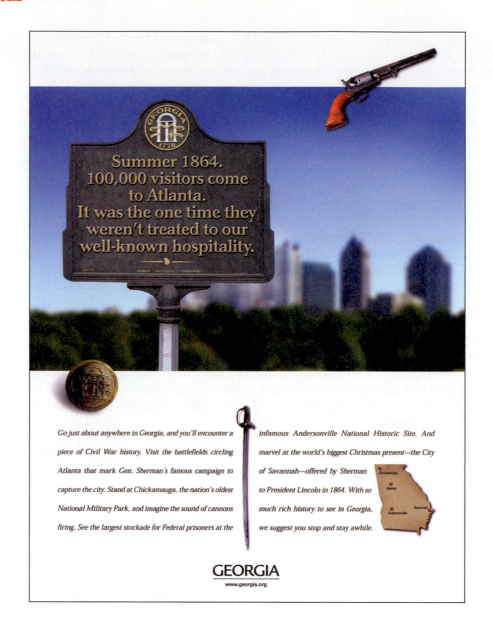

advertisers and publishers can develop advertising and editorial material specifically for one group or even for individual readers.

Selective binding first gained popularity among major farm publications in the early 1980s. Articles and advertisements were published only in editions delivered to farmers who raised certain types of crops or livestock. In recent years, selective binding has been offered to advertisers by consumer magazines on a limited basis.

Selective binding is most useful when there are significant subcategories of larger target markets within a publication's audience. Occasionally, a magazine will offer selective binding that is fully integrated into the editorial format of a magazine. More commonly, the technique is used with multipage advertising inserts distributed to a select audience segment identified by age, income, and so forth.

Selective binding is an example of a technology that, in order for it to be successful, must be advertiser driven. That is, advertisers must be convinced that it offers enough value to justify the additional expense. Many advertising executives think that the practical applications of selective binding are more apparent for business and farm publications than for consumer magazines, which have a number of selective publications.

Obviously, the widespread use of selective binding has major implications for direct mail. If the technique becomes widely used, advertisers could combine the individual characteristics of direct mail with the high-prestige environment of the magazine. Just as important, selective binding costs the advertiser about double what a normal magazine advertisement costs, but direct-mail CPMs generally run five times that of consumer magazines. Like most partial-run techniques, a major drawback of selective binding is that it can only be used for subscribers.

Because selective binding adopts some of the techniques of direct response, it also raises the same questions of readers' concerns with invasion of privacy. If subscribers are targeted by anything more than name and address, they may regard selective binding as inappropriate, with negative consequences to both the advertiser and magazine. Still, the idea that each reader can have a custom-made magazine, including both editorial and advertising material of specific interest to that individual, is an intriguing concept.

City Magazines Magazines directed to readers within a particular city are not a new idea. *Town Topics* was published in New York City in the late nineteenth century, but most observers credit *San Diego Magazine*, first published in the 1940s, as the forerunner of the modern city magazine. Today, city magazines are available in virtually every major city—and most of the largest cities have several.

At one time, city magazines were often regarded as nothing more than booster publications for a city. Many of them were published by a local business or tourism organization and they offered little in terms of hard news or in-depth reporting. Although most city magazines continue to feature lifestyle and entertainment stories, a growing number of publications report on local business, technology, and medical issues. Many publishers are combining the traditional strengths of the city magazines with specialized publication content and initiating such titles as *Chicago Bride*; *Atlanta Business Chronicle*; or the *Fulton County Reporter*, a publication devoted to the Atlanta legal scene.

Because of the generally upscale readership of city magazines, they are popular with upscale local and regional firms and even some national advertisers that want to target individual markets. Advertising revenues are very cyclical. A soft economy often leads to a decrease in advertisement pages because of the downturn in retailing and automobile sales, two prime categories of city magazine advertising. In addition, city magazines are normally a supplement to mainline advertising for many of these magazines' clients. Consequently, when the advertising market goes soft, they are often among the first media to be dropped. Whereas the city magazine was formerly a domain of large metropolitan centers, we now find successful publications in cities with populations of less than 100,000 (e.g., Macon, Georgia; see Exhibit 11.10).

City publications are in some ways a hybrid between small-circulation specialty publications and the partial-run editions of national magazines. However, they have an advantage over both in reaching upscale local audiences with editorial and advertising content specifically directed to the special, local interests of their prime prospects. Approximately ninety city and regional magazines have come together to sell their space to advertisers as a magazine network. Advertisers can buy space in groups of these magazines with one single insertion order at a cheaper price than if they were buying space in each separately. This allows the magazines to compete more effectively with national magazines.[15]

Custom Publishing

Another growing and specialized area of magazine publishing is custom publishing. It is one of the fastest-growing sectors of the magazine business and consists of

advertiser-produced publications intended to reach prospects or current customers in a communication environment totally controlled by the marketer. These publications are a cross between direct mail and traditional magazine publishing.

Custom publishing is not a new concept. In 1949, General Motors commissioned its agency, Campbell-Ewald, to publish *Friends*, a magazine sent to Chevrolet car and truck owners. However, since those early days, custom magazines account for expenditures of several hundreds of millions of dollars with more and more companies seeing them as an extension of their direct-response marketing. Most mainline magazine publishers such as Time Inc., Meredith, and Hearst have customized publishing divisions. Many of these publishers offer custom publishing services to their advertisers. For example, Hearst offers advertisers writers, editors, and designers as well as production services for developing custom content. This content can be used in custom magazines and can also be used in such media as CD-ROMs, books, and/or newsletters.[16]

The objectives of custom publishing vary from company to company. For Lincoln, *CitySource* was a way of introducing its Lincoln LS sport sedan. Sabre Group uses *VirtuallyThere* as a value-added guidebook for customers booking trips through its affiliated travel agencies. The U.S. Postal Service uses *deliver* magazine to keep marketers informed about the benefits and uses of direct mail in marketing campaigns.

Regardless of the specific use of custom publishing, to be successful it needs to function as part of a planned and integrated marketing program. Custom magazines can be a valuable tool for companies to speak directly to their customers and prospects. The current status of custom publishing is made possible through market research. "People and their buying patterns have never been segmented so precisely before. Most marketers today know a lot about the individual man, woman, or child buying their products, and custom media is considered the best way to talk to them."[17]

Some custom-published magazines are evolving to look much like traditional publications. One of the most obvious features of this transition is the acceptance of outside (albeit noncompetitive) advertising by some publications. It is sometimes hard to tell them from other magazines on the magazine racks. Some of these magazines are less expensive than other magazines in their category. For example, Walgreens and Wal-Mart both create and sell their own lower-priced magazines to their customers.

MAGAZINE ELEMENTS

Once an advertiser has made the hard choice of which magazine to select among the hundreds of options, the job is not over. Now the media planner must decide the size, color, placement, and format that will best serve the advertiser's marketing goals and the creative message.

Size

The page size of a magazine is the type area, not the size of the actual page. For convenience, the size of most magazines is characterized as standard size (about 8 by 10 inches, like *Time*) or small (about 4 3/8 by 6 1/2 inches, like *Reader's Digest*). There also are a few oversized publications such as *Rolling Stone*, but they are the exception. When you are ready to order advertising space and send creative materials to a publication, you must get the exact sizes from the publication because sizes may have changed.

Position, Color, and Size of Magazine Advertising

Space in magazines is generally sold in terms of full pages and fractions thereof (half pages, quarter pages, three columns, or one column; see Exhibit 11.11). The small advertisements in the classified pages of many magazines are generally sold by the line. Magazine covers are the most expensive positions in most magazines, although some magazines offer deep discounts for large advertisers. The front cover of a magazine is called the first cover, which is seldom, if ever, sold in American consumer magazines (although it is sold in business publications). The inside of the front cover is called the second cover, the inside of the back cover is the third cover, and the back cover is the fourth cover.

Advertisers are trying constantly to determine the optimum combination of color, size, and placement that will achieve the highest readership. Exhibit 11.12 shows twelve different combinations of elements and the effect that they have on recall compared to a standard four-color advertisement. These findings are consistent with most research, which has determined that four-color advertising is worth the additional cost in terms of added attention and readership. By the same token, this same research indicates that a two-color advertisement fails to add to reader attention levels and is usually not worth the additional expense.

Another concern of many advertisers is the placement of an advertisement within a magazine. Traditionally, many advertisers have regarded right-hand pages

EXHIBIT **11.11**

Various Ways of Using Magazine Space

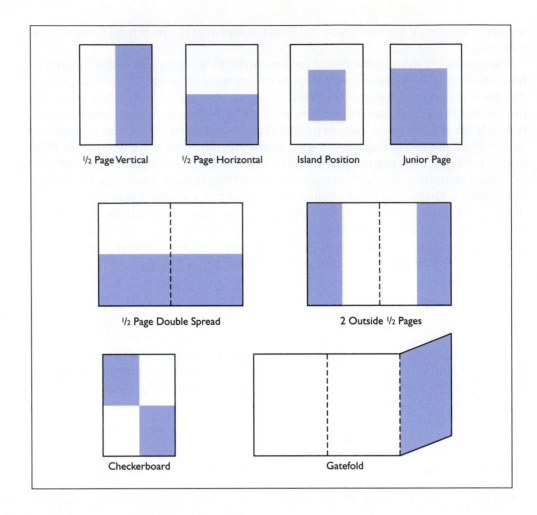

½ Page Vertical   ½ Page Horizontal   Island Position   Junior Page

½ Page Double Spread

2 Outside ½ Pages

Checkerboard

Gatefold

at the front of the book, preferably near related editorial matter, as the ideal advertising placement. "FFRHPOE" or "far forward, right-hand page opposite editorial" is routinely stamped on many insertion orders delivered to magazines in spite of no evidence that these positions add any value to an advertisement.

As the size of an advertisement increases, the audience does not grow proportionately (nor does the cost). For example, in Exhibit 11.11, note that an advertisement that is less than a full page achieves 81 percent of the impact of a full-page unit. If we run a two-page spread, we increase readership by 12 percent (even though we have increased the space by 100 percent). The reason, of course, is that

EXHIBIT **11.12**

Readership of Advertising by Type of Unit, Color, and Position

Courtesy of Magazine Publishers of America.

Ad Type	Recall Index
Full page*	100
Inside front cover	112
Inside back cover	100
Back cover	115
Multi-page units	117
Two-page spread	112
Less than full page	81
Four color	100
Spot color(s)	92
Black and white	87
First half of the issue	100
Second half of the issue	98

*Four color, two color and black and white

as size increases there are not enough nonexposed readers remaining to continue to increase readership at the same rate.

Although the increase in audience exposures is not proportionate to increases in magazine advertisement size, larger space allows more creative flexibility. Advertising objectives that require long copy can be much more effectively presented in a larger space. Larger advertisements have greater impact and recall over time, even though in the short term they don't score significantly higher than smaller space advertisements. It is important to remember that these studies held creative content constant while in reality the quality of the message is perhaps the most important variable in advertising readership and recall. These findings point out again that the specific objectives and creative approach must be considered in designing magazine advertising.

Bleed Pages

Magazine advertising is able to use a number of formats and designs unavailable or impractical in other media. A common technique is bleed advertising in which the advertisement runs all the way to the edge of the page with no border. **Bleed** advertisements are used to gain attention and use all the space available. Without a border, the advertisement does not have the appearance of being confined to a particular space (see Exhibit 11.13). Typically, bleed advertising will be seen by 10 to 15 percent more readers than nonbleed advertising.

There is no standardization for premium charges for bleed advertising. In the competitive marketplace for magazine advertising, a number of publications offer bleed advertising at no charge as a value-added or extra incentive for advertisers. Even when a magazine has a standard charge for bleed advertising,

bleed
Printed matter that runs over the edges of an outdoor board or of a page, leaving no margin.

EXHIBIT 11.13
Two-Page Spread Bleed Advertisement
Courtesy of Blattner Brunner and Hardie Canyon.

large advertisers often make these charges a point of negotiation with publishers. With modern printing equipment, most advertisers contend that bleed charges are an unjustified anachronism and many resent even minimal charges for bleed.

Inserts and Multiple-Page Units

Multiple-page advertising covers a broad spectrum of insertions. The most common form of multipage advertising is a facing, two-page spread. Among the most frequent users of multipage inserts and spreads are automobile manufacturers. They face an extremely competitive environment; they need to show their cars in the most favorable, bigger-than-life fashion; and they often have an in-depth story to tell about the features of their brands—all reasons to use large space advertising. A spread increases the impact of the message and eliminates any competition for the consumer's attention. Gatefold spreads come off the front cover and normally are either two or three pages.

Cost is a major consideration when planning inserts. Although the insert will be less expensive per page than run-of-publication advertising, the advertiser is still concentrating significant dollars in the publications that carry the inserts. This expense will reduce the number of media vehicles that can be included in a media schedule. Because an advertiser is putting a disproportionate share of advertising into one or a few vehicles, the likely result is a reduction in reach and frequency compared to a more traditional media plan.

Finally, one of the problems with the growing use of multiple-page advertising is that it has lost much of its novelty to consumers. When a reader can turn to practically any consumer magazine and find numerous examples of such advertising, they come to be taken for granted, even by serious prospects. It is important to work closely with the creative team to make sure that such expensive space is going to be fully utilized with a meaningful message. The most effective multiple-page units are for advertisers with an interesting product, a new story to tell, and an interested and involved group of prospects.

HOW SPACE IS SOLD

Advertising Rates, Negotiation, and Merchandising

In the competitive world of magazine advertising, it is not surprising that publishers are constantly seeking merchandising and value-added programs to differentiate their titles from others in a particular category. Unfortunately, many publishers find themselves in a situation in which advertising rates are the primary consideration for most advertisers.

Scheduling and buying full-run magazine advertising was at one time the easiest function for a media planner. Clients usually bought full-page advertisements, circulations were audited, discounts for frequent usage were obtainable from straightforward rate cards, and rates were consistent for every advertiser that qualified for available discounts. In addition, most advertisers would buy only a few high-circulation publications.

The rate situation underwent fundamental changes when magazine advertising experienced a downturn in revenues during the 1980s. Faced with flat advertising revenues and new publications continually coming into the market, magazines began to negotiate with individual advertisers for special rates. This practice of one-to-one negotiation is called *going off the card*. Starting as a short-term fix during a period of weak advertising spending, negotiation has become a common practice among magazines with many advertisers regarding the rate card as simply a point at which to start negotiation.

EXHIBIT **11.14**
Good Housekeeping
Seal is one of the
oldest magazine
merchandising tools.

Obviously, publishers would like to maintain rate integrity and attempt to do so with a number of merchandising and value-added plans. One of the most common means of magazine merchandising is through brand extensions. The Good Housekeeping Seal (see Exhibit 11.14) is one of the oldest and most recognized merchandising tools. The publication sponsors research laboratories through which products are reviewed or evaluated. Only advertisements for products that pass the evaluations conducted by the Good Housekeeping Research Institute are accepted by the publication. Readers are offered a money-back guarantee if the product is found to be defective within 2 years of purchase.[18] The program is almost 100 years old and still going strong.

Magazine merchandising services take numerous forms, and they are used by virtually every major magazine. *Better Homes & Gardens* produces greeting cards, provides real estate services, and franchises garden centers. Meanwhile, consumers can buy *Family Circle* classical CDs, *Field & Stream* bass lures, and *Popular Mechanics* work boots. In order to promote its *Parenting* magazine, Time Inc. bought a product-sampling company, First Moments, that delivers products to new mothers in hospitals. Ownership of First Moments allows the delivery of *Parenting* magazine, subscription offers, and related samples to build relationships with both readers and advertisers.[19]

The key to merchandising programs is to coordinate a magazine's reputation and expertise with marketing techniques that help advertisers sell their products. Among the more traditional merchandising programs are trade shows, conferences, newsletters, database services, and copromotions such as point-of-purchase displays that highlight certain advertisers that are using a publication. For example, *Cooking Light* (Exhibit 11.15) sponsored a series of *Cooking Light* Supper Club dinners around the country to demonstrate the products of its advertisers. Attendees were charged between $49 and $59 for a value of $100 or more. Each dinner was attended by as many as 250 people who were given door prizes and goody bags full of merchandise and information from advertisers as well as their *Cooking Light* meal.[20] All of these techniques allow advertisers to extend the message of their advertising into related areas and provide an added value to their magazine advertising buy.

Magazines and the Internet

Magazines were among the earliest media to utilize the Internet as part of their overall marketing and merchandising plans, and they remain heavily involved in online endeavors. The most common use of the Internet by publishers is the online version of print publications. Hundreds of publications offer full or edited online versions of their magazines. They are often designed to help build brand loyalty among readers. These online vehicles may be advertiser supported, used as a value added for advertisers, and/or intended to extend the audience reach of the core magazine to online users. Smart publishers have recognized the opportunity that the Internet offers to enhance the value of their titles. Robin Steinberg, SVP and Director of Print Investment at MediaVest, offers this advice to publishers, "Readers 'love and trust magazines. Those emotional ties must be tapped and publishers should encourage a dialog between readers and the publication via digital media. . . . Build an online

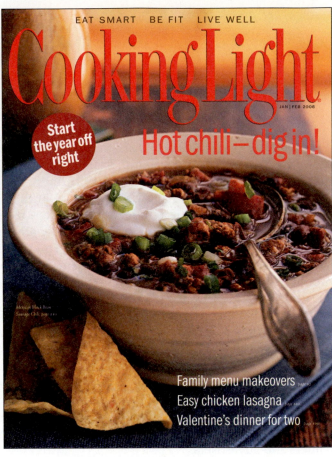

EXHIBIT 11.15

Cooking Light Magazine sponsors supper clubs for its readers.

Courtesy of Southern Progress Corporation, a subsidiary of Time Inc.

community where the common thread is your brand.'"[21] Both magazines and advertisers can benefit from this multiplatform tie-in. Some magazines have even launched their websites before the first issue hit the stands.[22]

Magazines also have entered into numerous joint ventures with other businesses for various online objectives. Many of the online sites are established as part of cross-media programs as in the CNN/SI mentioned earlier. In other cases, magazines have coventured with established sites to create a synergy between the expertise of an online company and the visibility of a magazine. Hearst's purchase of an interest in iVillage.com allowed the company to promote its women's books (e.g., *Redbook, Country Living,* and *Good Housekeeping*) in a compatible environment. Interestingly, the relationship between magazines and online interests has moved in both directions. For example, Krause Publications published *eBay Magazine* and Ziff-Davis introduced *Yahoo! Internet Life* magazine.

In addition, a number of titles have begun to use the Internet as a traditional e-commerce business. For example, Meredith offers its *Better Homes & Gardens* books and a select group of other products on its website. Regardless of the objectives of a magazine's online presence, the selective, targeted audiences of magazines offer an ideal marriage for the one-to-one marketing of the Internet.

Magazine Rate Structure

In the examples that follow, we assume the advertiser is making a full-run magazine buy. That is, the entire circulation of the publication is being purchased. An advertiser buying a partial-run edition will consider a number of other options. A typical rate card for a monthly publication might look like this:

Vogue's Color Rates (four-color)

Space	1 ti	3 ti	6 ti	12 ti
1 page	115,200	111,744	109,440	105,984
2/3 page	87,545	84,919	83,168	80,541
1/2 page	77,760	75,427	73,872	71,539
1/3 page	51,840	50,285	49,248	47,693

An advertiser buying this publication will pay $115,200 for a one-time, four-color, full-page insertion. The advertiser that buys at least twelve four-color full-page insertions in the publication will pay only $105,984 per advertisement for the same space.

Before placing a magazine on its advertising schedule, the advertiser will compute the cost efficiency of that publication against others being considered. Let's assume that *Vogue* has an average paid circulation of 1,293,185. Using the CPM formula discussed earlier, we can calculate the efficiency of the publication as follows:

$$\text{CPM} = \frac{\text{Cost per page}}{\text{Circulation}} \times 1,000 = \frac{115,200}{1,293,185} \times 1,000 = \$89.08$$

Discounts

Frequency and Volume Discounts The one-time, full-page rate of a publication is referred to as its basic, or open rate. In the case of *Vogue*, its open rate is $115,200. All discounts are computed from that rate. Most publications present their discounts on a per-page basis in which rates vary according to frequency of insertion during a 12-month period, as we have done here. However, some publications use either **frequency** or volume discounts based on the number of pages run. For instance, frequency discounts offered by a magazine might look like this:

Frequency	Discount %
3 times to 5 times	4
6 times to 8 times	6
9 times to 11 times	9
12 times to 17 times	12

frequency
In media exposure, the number of times an individual or household is exposed to a medium within a given period of time.

In a similar fashion, the volume discount gives a larger percentage discount based on the total dollar volume spent for advertising during a year. The volume discount is convenient for advertisers that are combining a number of insertions of different space units or that are using a number of partial-run insertions. Volume discounts offered by *People* magazine might look like this:

Volume, $	Discount Percentage
2,700,000 or more	10
2,100,000–2,699,999	8
1,500,000–2,099,999	6
800,000–1,499,999	4

Other Discounts In addition to discounts for volume and frequency, individual magazines offer a number of specialized discounts, usually for their largest advertisers. Among the more common discounts in this category is a lower per-page price for advertisers that combine buys with other publications or media owned by the same magazine group. We previously discussed these arrangements in the section on cross-media buys. As media companies become larger, the opportunities for these buys will be more numerous. Cross-media discounts operate similarly to volume discounts except advertisers accumulate credit across a number of media vehicles.

The Magazine Short Rate

As we have seen, most magazine discounts are based on the amount of space bought within a year. However, the publisher normally requires that payment be made within 30 days of billing. Therefore, an advertiser and a publisher sign a space contract at the beginning of the year and agree to make adjustments at the end of the year if the space usage estimates are incorrect. If the advertiser uses less space than estimated, the publisher adjusts using a higher-than-contracted rate. If more space is used, the publisher adjusts using a lower rate.

Let's look at a typical short rate, using the rate card for *Vogue*. Beauty hair care products contracted with *Vogue* to run six pages of advertising during the coming year. At the end of the year, Beauty had only run five pages. Therefore, it was short the rate for which it had contracted and an adjustment had to be made, as follows:

Ran five times. Paid the six-time rate of $109,440 per page = $(5 \times 109,440)$
$$= \$547,200$$

Earned only the three-time rate of $111,744 per page = $(5 \times 111,744)$
$$= \$558,720$$

Short rate due $(\$558,720 - \$547,200) = \$11,520$

Some publishers charge the top (basic) rate throughout the year but state in the contract "rate credit when earned." If the advertiser earns a better rate, the publisher gives a refund. If the publisher sees that an advertiser is not running sufficient pages during the year to earn the low rate on which the contract was based, the publisher sends a bill at the short rate for space already used and bills further advertisements at the higher rate earned. Failure to keep short rates in mind when you are reducing your original schedule can lead to unwelcome surprises.

Magazine Dates

There are three sets of dates to be aware of in planning and buying magazine space:

1. *Cover date.* The date appearing on the cover
2. *On-sale date.* The date on which the magazine is issued (the January issue of a magazine may come out on December 5, which is important to know if you are planning a Christmas advertisement)
3. *Closing date.* The date when the print or plates needed to print the advertisement must be in the publisher's hands in order to make a particular issue

For example:

***In-Style* (published monthly)**
- March issue
- On sale February 24
- Closes December 19

***People* (published weekly)**
- March 5 issue
- On sale February 23
- Closes January 15

Magazine Networks

The term *network*, of course, comes from broadcast when affiliated stations cooperated to bring audiences national programming as early as the 1920s. In recent years, a special adaptation of the network concept has been employed by virtually every medium as a means of offering advertisers a convenient and efficient means of buying multiple vehicles. There are newspaper networks, outdoor networks, and even networks for direct-mail inserts and comic strips. Magazines are no exception.

As we mentioned earlier, one of the problems of the growing specialization in magazines is that advertisers increasingly need to buy a number of titles to achieve reach and frequency goals. Another consequence of smaller circulations is that magazine CPM levels have increased. Many large national advertisers have complained about both the difficulty of buying numerous magazines and the higher CPMs. In order to accommodate these advertisers, a number of publishers have established **magazine networks**. As with networks in other media, their intent is to make it possible for an advertiser to purchase several publications simultaneously with one insertion order, one bill, and often significant savings compared to buying the same magazines individually.

magazine networks
Groups of magazines that can be purchased together using one insertion order and paying a single invoice.

Currently, there are dozens of magazine networks, some representing dozens of different titles. The network concept allows several magazines to compete for advertisers by offering lower CPMs and delivering a larger audience than any single publication. Networks must be carefully tailored to reach a particular audience segment with as little waste circulation or audience duplication as possible. Although there are a number of magazine networks, they generally fall into two categories:

1. *Single publisher networks.* Here a network is offered by a single publisher that owns several magazines and will allow advertisers to buy all or any number of these publications as a group. For example, Hearst Magazine Group publishes over twenty magazines and allows advertisers that use multiple titles to build network discounts.

   The publisher network can be especially effective in encouraging a media buyer to choose among similar magazines. For example, let's assume a media buyer has decided to purchase space in *Cosmopolitan* and *Town and Country*, both Hearst magazines. A third option is to purchase either *Redbook*, another Hearst magazine, or *Family Circle*. Assuming that both magazines meet the advertising criteria of a particular client, the discounts available from buying *Redbook* as part of the Hearst network may well sway the media buyer in that direction.

   To a degree, the single publisher network is being replaced by cross-media buying. As more and more magazines become part of media conglomerates, they no longer confine a "network" buy to magazines but broaden the concept to all media vehicles owned by a particular company.

2. *Independent networks.* The second type of magazine network is made up of different publishers that market magazines with similar audience appeals. A rep firm that contracts individually with each publisher and then sells advertising for magazines within the group usually offers these networks. The concept is similar to the space wholesaling that George Rowell began in the 1850s. Media Networks, Inc., the largest independent network firm, offers several networks, each geared to a specific audience. For example, the Media Networks Executive Network consists of seven magazines including *Fortune* and *Business Week* (see Exhibit 11.16). Even though different publishers own these magazines, they know that there are advantages to cooperating in selling space to large advertisers.

MAGAZINE CIRCULATION

As with any medium, accurate magazine readership measurement is extremely important to advertisers. Media planners don't buy magazines, television spots, or outdoor signs—they buy audiences. More specifically, they buy certain groups of people who are customers or prospects for their products. In the magazine industry, there are two distinct methods of determining audiences: *paid circulation* and *the rate base*.

The more commonly used and reliable method of audience measurement is paid circulation. Most major consumer magazines have their circulations audited by an outside company. Magazine rates are based on the circulation that a publisher promises to deliver to advertisers, referred to as the *guaranteed circulation*. Because the guaranteed circulation is the number of readers advertisers purchase, it also is referred to as the **rate base**, or the circulation on which advertising rates for a specific magazine are based.

rate base
The circulation level on which advertising rates are based.

You will recall from our earlier discussion that magazine publishers are finding it increasingly expensive to maintain high readership levels. As circulation for a magazine rises, the increases are sometimes created by marginally interested readers who subscribed because of special introductory deals, among other things. Publishers usually find it very expensive to keep these fringe readers when it is time to renew subscriptions. Added to the problem is the fact that major auditing organizations, such as the Audit Bureau of Circulations (ABC), require that a subscriber must pay at least 50 percent of the full subscription price to be counted as a reader. Consequently, magazines are limited in the marketing promotions they can use and still count readers as paid for auditing purposes.

In the last few years, a number of major magazines have lowered their rate bases substantially. Rate base management is fundamentally a financial consideration. As circulation rises, advertising rates also will increase. However, if publishers are spending more on marketing to keep circulation figures artificially higher than they can gain in increased advertising revenue, it doesn't make economic sense to continue to do it.

Magazine circulation figures can vary a great deal from month to month largely due to newsstand sales. In the past, many publishers have averaged their circulation over a 6- or 12-month period. According to the *Wall Street Journal*, "... magazines can finesse their monthly circulation figures to make it appear as though they are consistently delivering the rate base advertisers expect. Whether or not this fudging is deliberate, the monthly information provided by publishers—which is widely used to judge a magazine's success—is often inaccurate."[23] Many publishers argue that they should be judged by ABC on an average monthly circulation basis rather than on the circulation of individual issues.

It is clear that advertisers would rather buy space in magazines with a quality readership, that is, those readers who are interested in both the magazine and its advertising. By the same token, advertisers generally will gravitate to those publications with the largest number of readers within their target audience. Common sense tells us that publishers, particularly of second-tier magazines, will continue to explore whatever steps necessary to keep circulation levels as high as possible within their profit constraints.

A magazine does not necessarily offer a guaranteed rate base to advertisers. In fact, a number of audited publications do not make a specific guaranteed circulation claim. These publishers provide advertisers with accurate circulation for past issues, but they don't take any risk for circulation shortfalls in the future. In the volatile world of magazine advertising, many smaller magazines do not want to deal with the financial problems of make-goods related to audience decreases.

Readership

In magazine terminology, *readership* usually combines paid circulation (subscribers and newsstand purchasers) with pass-along readers. For example, according to ABC, *Newsweek* has a paid circulation of 3.1 million. According to Mediamark Research Inc., *Newsweek* has 18.9 million readers. This means that there are approximately 6.1 readers per copy (RPC).[24] The more general the publication's editorial, the more likely it is to have significant pass-along readership.

Many advertisers and even magazine publishers are concerned about the use of readership as a substitute for paid circulation. Historically, the use of readership is rooted in the magazine industry's competition with television. As we discussed in the last section, magazines are retrenching somewhat from a "numbers at any cost" circulation mentality and again selling quality of readership. Nevertheless, publishers want to keep readership surveys to take into account fairly their total readers.

It would seem that total readership, accurately measured, would be a reasonable approach to measuring magazine audiences. The problem arises from the fact that many media buyers regard pass-along readers of consumer magazines as inherently inferior to paid circulation. Between those advertisers that see no value in readership and those that view it as equal to paid circulation, there is probably a middle ground. As in most marketing and advertising questions, the real answer is determined by the specific objectives of the publication and its readers. However, regardless of the value that one places on readership, most acknowledge that it is different from paid circulation.

MEASURING MAGAZINE AUDIENCES

We now turn to the issue of how publishers verify the circulation and readership of their magazines. Advertisers normally will not purchase a magazine unless its publisher can provide independent verification of the magazine's readership. In magazine terminology, readership has two distinct meanings. One refers to the time spent with a publication. The other, and the one we discuss here, includes all readers of a magazine as contrasted to only those who buy a publication.

The Audit Bureau of Circulations

The Audit Bureau of Circulations (ABC) is the largest of several auditing organizations that verify magazine circulation. The ABC provides two basic services: the Publisher's Statements or "pink sheets" (because of their color), which report 6-month periods ending June 30 and December 31; and the ABC Audits, or "white sheets," which annually audit the data provided in the Publisher's Statements. The ABC reports total circulation, as well as circulation figures by state, by county size, and per issue during each 6-month period. ABC reports also state the manner in which circulation was obtained—for example, by subscription or by newsstand sales—and any discounts or premiums provided to subscribers. Exhibit 11.17 is a sample of the ABC Publisher's Statement.

The ABC reports are matter-of-fact documents that deal only with primary readers. They do not offer information about product usage, demographic characteristics of readers, or pass-along readership. As we discussed in the previous section, the ABC continues to be embroiled in the debate over how to define paid cir-

EXHIBIT 11.17

ABC offers circulation analysis for publications.

Courtesy of Audit Bureau of Circulations.

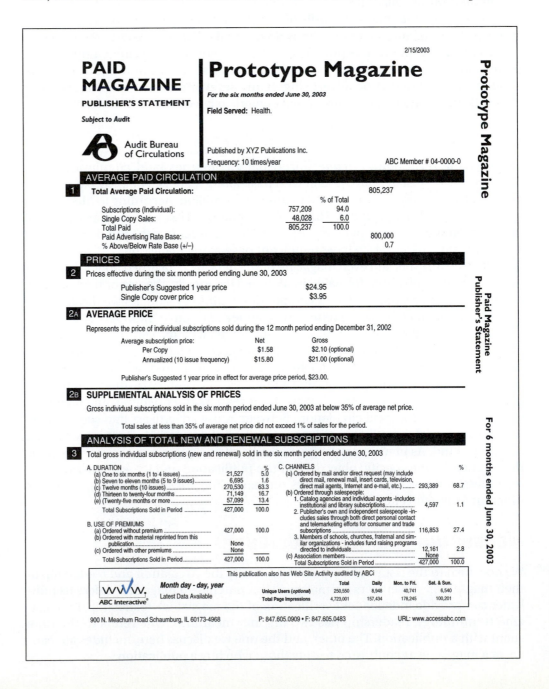

culation. The controversy is yet another indication of the importance that both publishers and advertisers place on the accuracy of audience data.

Syndicated Magazine Readership Research

Advertisers are, of course, interested in the primary readers of magazines. But they are also interested in who these readers are and what they buy, as well as pass-along readers who are given the publications. Currently, there are two principal sources of syndicated magazine readership research: **Simmons Market Research Bureau (SMRB)** and **Mediamark Research Inc. (MRI)**.

Mediamark Research Inc. (www.mediamark.com) methodology consists of selecting a sample of over 26,000 people and eliciting media usage, demographic characteristics, lifestyle, and product-purchase information. Using a combination of personal interviews and self-administered questionnaires, respondents report on magazine readership and product usage. Simmons Market Research Bureau (www.smrb.com) has a sample of over 25,000 adults including over 7,500 Hispanic/Latino adults. The data are collected via mailed questionnaires and measure media usage, including data on several hundred magazines, with an emphasis on audience and product-usage information.

Simmons Market Research Bureau (SMRB) and Mediamark Research, Inc. (MRI)
Two competing firms that provide audience data for several media. Best known for magazine research.

THE BUSINESS PRESS AND BUSINESS-TO-BUSINESS ADVERTISING

Professional Candy Buyer, American Cemetery, The Science Teacher, Mediaweek, and *Journal of Athletic Training* are only a handful of the more than 10,000 publications that make up the business press. Business-to-business (B2B) communication is a marketplace where million-dollar deals are commonplace and the methods for sales, marketing, and advertising are markedly different from those in consumer advertising. A number of media and promotions are used to reach business buyers. We discuss them in this chapter because traditionally business magazines have constituted the primary source of B2B expenditures.

Prospects for most business advertisers are fewer and more concentrated; audiences tend to be experts concerning the products they purchase; and audience selectivity is much more important than the CPMs or reach measures used in consumer media. Another feature of business publications is their efficient reach of major decision makers (see Exhibit 11.18). Given the specialized audience of these

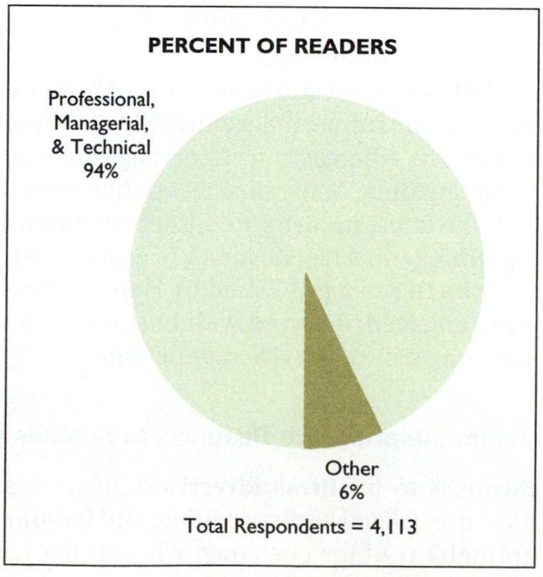

PERCENT OF READERS

Professional, Managerial, & Technical 94%

Other 6%

Total Respondents = 4,113

EXHIBIT 11.18
Occupation of Readers of Specialized Business Magazines
Source: Cahners Advertising Research Report, www.cahnerscarr.com, 18 September 2006.

KLEPPNER VIEWPOINT 11.1

Mary Beth Burner

Business Development Director, Southern Progress Corporation, a Subsidiary of Time Inc.
Research

The mere word systematically invokes an immediate thought of pocket protectors, horn-rimmed glasses and calculators. Bookish individuals who spend hours studying every minute detail of inner-workings then report these analyses in reams of charts, graphs, and tables of data. Well, you're right. As a director of consumer magazine Advertising Research, I'm guilty as charged (minus the pocket protector). But there are countless more descriptors that should also be part of the stereotype for media researchers: strategist, creative mind, marketer, psychologist, brand developer, and armed competitor.

Magazine Advertising Researchers use strategic skills and creative analysis of data to prove that a magazine is the most efficient buy, has the most compatible editorial for a product's message, or can provide the best reach of a target market. Magazine selling in the ad industry is akin to brand marketing within the consumer marketplace. A sales representative from a consumer magazine seeks to sell his product (the magazine ad space) into the agency's media plan, above other competitors considered. An integral part of the magazine selling process, research data is the "currency" with which comparisons of magazines are made. Who reads the magazine? What are the demographics of readers? How much time do they spend reading the magazine? How much do they spend on your product? What are desirable positions within the magazine editorial to place a particular ad? Did readers notice and absorb the advertisement after placement in an issue?

Mary Beth Burner

All of these questions can be answered with research: "Magazine X" has 15 million devoted readers nationwide—an educated, affluent, youthful readership that bought 21 million packages of your product in the last six months, purportedly after noticing your ad next to their favorite column in the magazine, with which they loyally spend an average of 90 minutes reading each month.

publications combined with moderate cost, the business magazine continues to be a cost-efficient medium.

Both the tone and advertising of business publications differ significantly from those of consumer magazines. The business press is a medium of reference and commerce, whereas consumer magazines are vehicles of entertainment, news, and leisure reading. Many business publications are used on a regular basis to keep up with the latest industry trends, competitive activity, and product category marketing strategy. In a recent survey of executives from companies with $5 million dollars or more in sales published by Harris Interactive, "executives reported they were more engaged/involved with business to business media than with general business magazines, television or newspapers."[25]

business-to-business advertisers
Advertisers that promote goods through trade and industrial journals that are used in the manufacturing, distributing, or marketing of goods to the public.

Communicating the Business-to-Business Message

Business-to-business advertisers must consider a number of factors in addressing their specialized audiences. First and foremost, the message must be directed at the profitability of the customer. Whereas few consumer advertisements contain tech-

Prove it, you say? A plethora of research data reports all of these things and much, much more. Studies are conducted daily by magazines, by media research firms, or by magazine organizations like MPA. A variety of research exists for marketing purposes: focus groups, online polls, reader panel surveys, advertising response measurement, third party syndicated surveys (i.e., Mediamark Research Inc.), magazine subscriber surveys, editorial readership surveys, ScanTron product purchase data, coupon redemption tracking, and circulation data, to name a few. Yet, all of this data is meaningless if you don't bring it to life using a little creativity in developing your "unique selling proposition" and strategy. This is where psychology, creativity and brand marketing all play a key role in advertising research.

Consider this: an agency representing an athletic footwear client decides to run print advertising in consumer magazines, and the women's fitness magazine category is a top consideration. The agency, under heavy budget constraint, decides to put the majority of print budget in one key fitness magazine to emphasize frequency. You must aid your sales rep in putting your magazine's best foot forward to prove why you are the athletic footwear client's ideal advertising and marketing partner. As Magazine X, your key competitor in this category is Magazine Y, another reputable fitness magazine. After running the numbers based on the footwear account target audience of "Women who purchased any athletic shoes in the last year," the data shows this:

	Page Rate	Audience	Composition	Index (US = 100)	CPM
Magazine X	$100,000	10,200,000	68%	144	$9.80
Magazine Y	$140,000	11,800,000	65%	141	$11.86

At a glance, it seems your competitor, Magazine Y, reaches more of the target audience and might be the better option. But consider that the agency's priority is frequency and readers' likelihood to purchase shoes. Magazine X's strengths are cost efficiency (lower CPM), and a higher reader affinity (44% more likely than the average American to buy athletic shoes). Surely this will help your sales rep in negotiating against the competitor, but it's also important to bring it to life. It might sound impressive to say "over 10 million of Magazine X readers bought shoes in the last year" but without comparative data, how does that differentiate your magazine? If you did a little further digging to learn that your readers purchase an average of 2 pairs of athletic shoes a year, multiplied by 10.2 million, then extrapolate the data to something visible and tangible to bring it to life. For instance, "if you were to line up toe-to-heel all of the shoes that Magazine X readers bought in the last year, it would cover the distance from Portland, Maine, to Los Angeles, California, *twice*." Or, "The number of Magazine X readers who bought athletic shoes in the last year outnumber the population of the *largest* city in the US—our group of 10.2 million readers sporting new shoes is larger than all of the residents of New York City combined." Statements such as these illustrate just how viable a media partner your magazine can be for this athletic footwear company wishing to reach shoe fanatics. . . .

Magazine Researchers *are* guilty-as-charged with calculators and infinite graphs—necessary tools to depict data—but also wear the hats of *Psychologist* for logic and reasoning, *Creative Mind* to illustrate findings, *Strategist* to discern the most competitive angle, and *Brand Developer* to uniquely market the magazine's identity. Next time you spot an ad for a product in your favorite magazine, know how much magazine researchers and sales reps reasoned and fought to get it there. ■ ■ ■

nical product specifications and details about equipment compatibility and delivery terms, these are the types of information commonly contained in business publications.

In communicating with the business community, there are a number of considerations:

1. Appeal to prospects in terms of specific job interests and demands. The advertisement should address how a product or service can increase the productivity and enhance the job performance of a particular function.

2. Sell the benefits to the buyer, not the features of the product. Again, these benefits need to be couched in terms of sales and productivity.

3. The job of business advertising, particularly for high-end products, is to support and facilitate the sales function. Business transactions, unlike their consumer counterparts, are rarely completed with a single advertisement or even solely through advertising. Most business advertising is a means of moving prospects into the personal sales channel or to seek more information. That is, advertising should function to make the job of personal selling or prospect follow-up easier.

4. Avoid product puffery. Remember, the readers of your advertising are trained professionals with high levels of expertise in their fields. They expect to see product information, often with detailed diagrams, charts, and technical specifications. The type of appeals common in consumer media will not work in the business and trade press.

5. Business advertising, just like consumer advertising, needs to have clear objectives that are measurable in terms of specific target publics.

6. Pass-Along Readership. A significant number of business publication readers receive their magazines on a pass-along basis. We noted earlier that such readership among consumer magazines is generally regarded as inferior to paid circulation. However, one of the notable differences between business and consumer publications is the way advertisers view pass-along readership. The typical consumer medium has a relatively short life and low pass-along readership. Occasionally, a recipe will be clipped or a magazine will be passed on to a neighbor, but consumer magazines are read largely for pleasure and tossed aside. In any case, advertisers view pass-along readership of consumer magazines as vastly inferior to primary readership.

Business publication advertisers, in contrast, view pass-along readership as quite valuable. For one thing, readers don't normally browse through *The Journal of Cell Biology* or *Plastics Engineering*; they pay close attention to the copy. For another, some business publications limit their circulation in a way that forces pass-along readership.

Corporate Branding

Although business-to-business selling is about buying products, it also is about buying the reputation of the companies with which other companies do business. A general consumer may take a chance with an unknown company for a product costing even several hundred dollars. The same is rarely true in the world of business marketing wherein the future of a business can be at stake when major purchases are made.

In recent years, more and more emphasis has been placed on corporate branding by companies. As companies grow and become more complex in terms of different divisions, products, and distribution channels, it becomes difficult to approach customers with a single message. Corporate branding attempts to integrate a company's total image through a coordinated marketing communications process.

Ideally, corporate branding allows a company to speak with its various customers through advertising, public relations, the Internet, and even product design and other identity programs such as logos and product trademarks. Effective corporate branding allows a company to establish its reputation and set brands apart from the competition. It also allows a company to provide a consistent message to prospects, customers, stockholders, and employees.[26]

The remainder of this section examines some of the special features of the business-to-business sector and the differences and similarities with consumer advertising.

Audiences of the Business Press

There are both important qualitative and quantitative differences between readers of business publications and the typical audiences of consumer magazines. Most important, trade publications are part of the job for most readers. They are not read for entertainment but rather will be judged on the basis of how well they improve the readers' ability to do their jobs, market their products, and improve their profits. Consequently, business magazines must develop a depth of understanding of their readers that typically is not required in the consumer press.

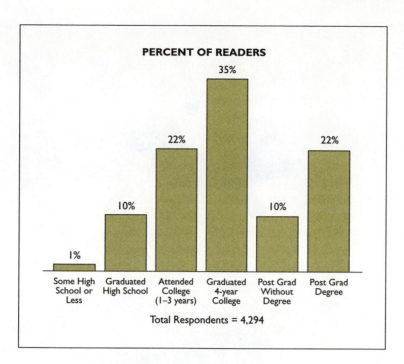

EXHIBIT **11.19**

The Maximum Level of Education Attained by Readers of Specialized Business Magazines

Over two-thirds of the readers have completed 16 to 20 years of schooling. Twenty-four percent of the general national population has 4 or more years of college and beyond.

Source: Cahners Advertising Research Report, www.cahnerscarr.com.

In addition to the approach that readers take to the business press, there also are significant differences in the audience composition of business versus consumer magazines. In terms of age, income, job categories, education (see Exhibit 11.19), and other basic demographic data, business publications skew far higher than typical consumer magazines. Basically, the tone of a business magazine, both in editorial and advertising, is one of a problem solver. There is a special relationship between business magazines and the industries they serve.

Competition for Business-to-Business Advertising

Television, newspapers, radio, and consumer magazines are the core of consumer advertising. On a national basis, television is in fierce competition for consumer dollars, whereas radio and newspapers serve local retailers in reaching these same buyers. However, business selling and marketing have devoted most of their dollars to personal sales, trade and business publications, and direct mail.

As discussed earlier, for most major accounts, marketing communication is used as a means of providing entry for personal selling. Studies show that, by an overwhelming margin, executives with purchasing authority will not make appointments with salespersons unless they have a thorough knowledge of the companies and products they represent (see Exhibit 11.20). In many respects, the environment of business marketing was unchanged for the 50 years from the end of World War II to the mid-1990s. Then—you guessed it—the Internet became a major force in business marketing.

The Internet and Business-to-Business Marketing

The Internet gained acceptance faster in B2B marketing than in consumer marketing. For one thing, businesses were mostly computer savvy long before the Internet came along, so it represented just another phase in the development of computer integration into the business world. The Internet also was more functional for B2B marketing because the number of customers was infinitesimal compared to most consumer products. Both customers and their e-mail addresses could be identified

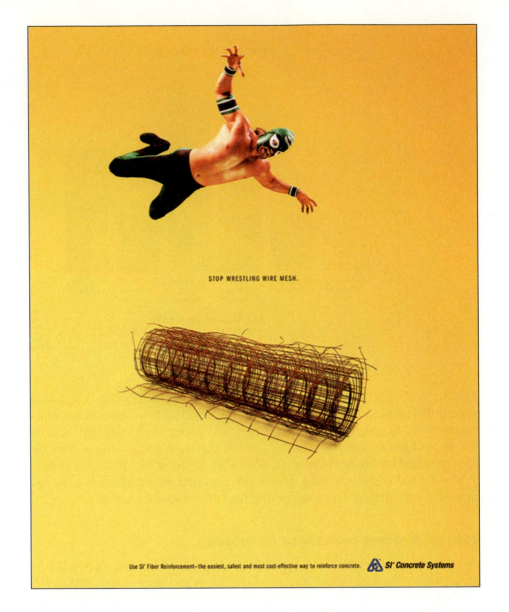

STOP WRESTLING WIRE MESH.

Use SI° Fiber Reinforcement—the easiest, safest and most cost-effective way to reinforce concrete. 🔺 *SI° Concrete Systems*

easily, and the Internet quickly became part of the integrated marketing communication plans of most companies.

Despite the greater utility of Internet B2B marketing, it was used in relatively traditional ways of reaching customers and providing websites with product information; and for less expensive products or regular customers, it provided a method of order taking. However, the use of the Internet in B2B marketing and potentially the practices of business selling changed dramatically in the late 1990s with the introduction of the Internet auction.

The Internet Auction and Business-to-Business Marketing

When Ford Motor Company wants to purchase several million dollars' worth of rubber hoses or General Mills wants to buy 10 million cereal boxes, the procedure has been to send out product specifications to a network of suppliers or their wholesalers and typically, after a round of questions and negotiations, accept bids from qualified companies. In this process, however, sometimes suppliers got the word about a buy, and purchasing agents were never sure that they were getting the best deal.

The coming of the Internet auction has promised to change many of the methods of marketing and selling goods in the business-to-business world. Basically, it allows buyers and sellers to make a connection, bid on parts and supplies, and make the final deal through a direct-marketing channel between buyer and seller. This process has even greater potential for change given the emphasis placed on price in the business-to-business environment. Once a supplier meets buyer specifications for steel, packaging cartons, or electrical wiring, it becomes a generic commodity.

The Internet is a marketplace that closely resembles those envisioned in many economic models in which advertising, brand reputation, and company name have little relevance to how a product is purchased. These Internet auctions also provide a true global economy to the process. Sellers from around the world—even in auctions in which buyers and sellers have never heard of each other—theoretically have an equal chance to make a sale if the price is right.

Although a change of this magnitude in the business marketplace is no doubt interesting, why should advertisers care? If manufacturers have immediate and full communication with all potential suppliers and products become generic commodities with sales almost totally dependent on price, what role is there for advertising and promotion? If we review the section on corporate branding, we see that many of the advantages of such promotions assume the need for enhanced company reputation and product identity—roles largely unnecessary in a virtual auction marketplace.

Whether it is a household buying an airplane ticket from expedia.com or a large corporation buying a million dollars' worth of industrial paper products from www.ipproducts.com, the concept is the same: Price, not advertising and promotion, sells. According to Jim Casella, CEO of Reed Business Information, "There are many more options for B2B advertisers today. For example, 5 years ago they would spend their marcom [marketing communication] dollars 90 percent on print and 10 percent on exhibitions or events. Today they split their marcom dollar along the following lines: 60–70 percent online, including key words and 10 percent for events."[27]

Business Publication Expansion of Services

You will recall that we discussed the fact that many consumer magazines have introduced a number of merchandising and ancillary services. Because of the specialized nature of business-to-business publications, they are even better positioned to engage in ancillary services than their consumer counterparts. As the competition for B2B advertising and promotional dollars increases, business publications have increasingly engaged in a number of ventures to reach their core readers and at the same time increase the profitability of their companies:

1. *Subscriber list rentals.* Major business publications find that their subscriber list is one of the most valuable commodities they own. In fact, depending on the degree of specialization and the industry they service, business publications make as much as 10 percent of their total revenue from list rentals.

2. *Event-related publications.* Golf tournaments, car shows, and conventions from religious denominations to service organizations often provide an advertiser-supported program with the schedule of the event as well as information about the group. These publications are usually published by an independent trade publisher.

3. *Custom publications.* As we discussed in an earlier section, custom publishing is a very lucrative business. These custom magazines are a major source of revenue for many trade publishers.

4. *Trade shows.* In Chapter 14, we discuss the role of trade shows in the marketing channel. Major trade shows bring buyers and sellers from an entire industry together to view new products and methods of doing business. In some cases, business publications organize and sell sponsorship to these shows usually

under the name of the publication. A named trade show demonstrates leadership in the field and can also be a profitable enterprise for the publication.

Entry into ancillary services usually is more successful for established magazines than for their smaller competitors that are less well known. Magazines provide credibility and high visibility to these ancillary events, which would be lacking without the tie-in to a major publication. Seeing the growth of promotional techniques in business-to-business advertising, many magazine publishers employ ancillary vehicles to add to their overall profitability and decrease their dependence on advertising from their publications.

Regardless of their format, ancillary activities offer a number of advantages to a publisher. First, they utilize the publisher's knowledge of a particular industry to help clients develop a coordinated promotional and advertising campaign. Second, they gain revenue from companies that do not use advertising as a primary business-to-business marketing tool. Finally, they increase a magazine's credibility by demonstrating far-reaching expertise in a number of promotional areas. In the future, we will see publishers developing a variety of information services and promotional techniques in addition to their basic magazines.

Business publications are different from consumer magazines in several ways. This section briefly discusses the more important ones.

Types of Business-to-Business Publications

Despite the wide array of business publications, they can generally be placed in one of four categories:

- Distributive trades (trade)
- Manufacturers and builders (industrial)
- Top officers of other corporations (management)
- Physicians, dentists, architects, and other professional people (professional)

trade paper
A business publication directed to those who buy products for resale (wholesalers, jobbers, retailers).

Trade Papers Because most nationally advertised products depend on dealers for their sales, we discuss advertising in **trade papers** first. Usually, this advertising is prepared by the agency that handles the consumer advertising, and in any new campaign both are prepared at the same time. The term *trade papers* is applied particularly to business publications directed at those who buy products for resale, such as wholesalers, jobbers, and retailers. Typical trade papers are *Supermarket News*, *Chain Store Age*, *Hardware Retailer*, *Women's Wear Daily*, and *Home Furnishings Retailer*.

Almost every business engaged in distributing goods has a trade paper to discuss its problems. Trade papers are a great medium for reporting merchandising news about the products, packaging, prices, deals, and promotions of the manufacturers that cater to the particular industry. The chain-store field alone has more than twenty such publications. Druggists have a choice of over thirty, and more than sixty different publications are issued for grocers. There are many localized journals, such as *Texas Retailer*, *Michigan Food News*, *Southern Jewelry News*, and *California Apparel News*.

Industrial Publications As we move into the world in which a company in one industry sells its materials, machinery, tools, parts, and equipment to another company for use in making a product or conducting operations, we are in an altogether different ballpark—the industrial marketing arena.

There are fewer customers in this arena than in the consumer market, and they can be more easily identified. The amount of money involved in a sale may be large—hundreds of thousands of dollars, perhaps even millions—and nothing is bought on impulse. Many knowledgeable executives with technical skills often share in the buy-

EXHIBIT 11.21

Some of the Many Business Publications Read by Advertising Media Planners

Reprinted with permission. Copyright Crain Communications and © VNU Business Media, Inc. Reprinted with permission.

ing decision. The sales representative has to have a high degree of professional competence to deal with the industrial market, in which personal selling is the biggest factor in making a sale. Advertising is only a collateral aid used to pave the way for or to support the salesperson; hence, it receives a smaller share of the marketplace budget.

Advertising addressed to people responsible for buying goods needed to make products is called industrial advertising. It is designed to reach purchasing agents, plant managers, engineers, controllers, and others who have a voice in spending the firm's money.

Management Publications   The most difficult group for a publication to reach is managers. After all, even the largest companies have only a relatively few decision makers. When these decision makers are widely dispersed across a number of industries and job descriptions, publications find they must be extremely creative to reach them.

The management category is one that straddles a gray area between consumer and business-to-business publications. Magazines such as *Business Week*, *Fortune*, and *Nation's Business* have characteristics that would place them in either the business or the consumer category. Even magazines such as *Time* have at least some of their partial-run editions listed in the *Business Publications SRDS*.

Professional Publications The *Standard Rate and Data Service* (**SRDS**), in its special business publication edition, includes journals addressed to physicians, surgeons, dentists, lawyers, architects, and other professionals who depend on these publications to keep abreast of their professions. The editorial content of such journals ranges from reports about new technical developments to discussions on how to meet client or patient problems better and how to manage offices more efficiently and profitably. Professional people often recommend or specify the products their patients or clients should order. Therefore, much advertising of a highly technical caliber is addressed to them.

Controlled Circulation Magazines are sometimes distributed free to selective readers. Free circulation is known as **controlled circulation**. The term *controlled* refers to the fact that publishers distribute only to a carefully selected list of people who are influential in making purchase decisions for their organization. They use the same database techniques that direct mailers use in building their mailing lists. Controlled circulation makes sense when dealing with an easily defined audience of decision makers. To some media planners, the logic of controlled circulation is not very different from that of direct mail except that the advertising is delivered in an editorial environment. Despite the fact that controlled circulation is widely used in the trade press, it is not universally embraced. In the past, most research has indicated that a high percentage of both clients and media directors prefer the reader commitment inherent in paid circulation.

The number of controlled publications in the business field plays a major role in their share of advertising-to-circulation revenues compared to consumer magazines. On average, approximately two-thirds of trade publication circulation is controlled. A number of publications use a mix of controlled and paid circulations in which qualified readers receive the magazine free and others can buy it if they wish.

Controlled circulation creates a significant dependence on advertising support. Unlike consumer magazines, business publications have been largely unsuccessful in shifting to a reader-driven revenue stream. This dependency on advertising is another reason why business publications suffer so much during economic downturns.

Vertical and Horizontal Publications Industrial publications are usually considered to be either horizontal or vertical. A **vertical publication** is one that covers an entire industry. An example is *Snack Food & Wholesale Bakery*, which contains information concerning research and development, manufacturing, product quality, marketing, warehousing, and distribution.

A **horizontal publication** is edited for people who are engaged in a single function that cuts across many industries. An example is *Purchasing Magazine*, which is circulated to purchasing managers. It discusses trends and forecasts applicable to all industries.

Circulation Audits

Business-to-business advertisers are keenly interested in the circulation of the publications in which they advertise. In some respects, the readership numbers are

---

Standard Rate and Data Service (SRDS)
SRDS publishes a number of directories giving media and production information.

controlled circulation
Sent without cost to people responsible for making buying decisions. To get on such lists, people must state their positions in companies; to stay on it, they must request it annually. Also known as qualified-circulation publications.

vertical publication
Business publications dealing with the problems of a specific industry: for example, *Chain Store Age*, *National Petroleum News*, *Textile World*.

horizontal publication
Business publications for people engaged in a single job function regardless of the industry: for example, *Purchasing Magazine*.

(a)

(b)

EXHIBIT **11.22**

Two Major Magazine Auditing Services

(a) Courtesy of Audit Bureau of Circulations.

(b) Courtesy of Verified Audit Circulation.

more important than those in general consumer magazines. The total audience is smaller, the CPM for most publications is significantly higher than consumer magazines, and the competition makes it imperative that business-to-business marketers reach their target audience in a timely fashion.

Because of the number and diversity of audiences contacted by the trade and business press, a number of auditing organizations are used by business publishers and advertisers. More than 500 trade and industrial magazines are audited by the Business Publications Audit (BPA) of Circulation International, the leading business auditor. Because many business publications are circulated to a general business audience, the ABC is used for publications such as *Business Week*, and a few publications use both auditing firms.

A third auditing organization is the Verified Audit Circulation (VAC). Founded in 1951, VAC provides circulation audits for a wide variety of newspapers, shoppers, magazines, and even Yellow Pages directories. There are a number of publications in the business area that are not audited. Although an unaudited publication can survive, there are a number of business-to-business advertisers and agencies that, as a matter of policy, will not consider an unaudited publication (see Exhibit 11.22).

AGRIBUSINESS ADVERTISING

At one time, farm media, both print and broadcast, were geared largely to the millions of families who lived and worked on small farms. In recent years, the farm press has had to adapt to dramatic changes in the way agriculture is conducted in this country. Between 1940 and 1991, the number of farm workers declined by almost 70 percent. During that same period, the number of farm residents dropped from 31 million to 5 million.[28] These numbers have continued to decline in the last 15 years.

Contemporary agribusiness media and advertisers are tailoring their messages to a concentrated industry of huge farm cooperatives and farm managers with income and educational levels that rival those of the CEOs of any major business. Although weather and crop prices are still major topics of the farm press, these publications are likely to be discussing the weather in Russia and price controls and export policies as opposed to what is happening in a local community.

The farm press is facing many of the problems of the business press. A number of media competitors have come on the scene in recent years to take advertising dollars from the print media. Unlike business-to-business advertising in which television and radio have only recently been used by advertisers, farm broadcasting has a long history of serving the farm community.

There are a number of local and regional farm broadcasters, but on a national level the primary sources of agribusiness news and advertising are those that follow:

- *AgDay*, a daily syndicated television show, reaches an average of 260,000 households each morning and is carried by about 160 stations (www.agday.com).
- The weekly *U.S. Farm Report*, which is syndicated to about 97 percent of the nation's television households, is the nation's longest-running agricultural news program (www.farmjournalmedia.com).
- *National Farm Report* is syndicated to some 240 radio stations (www.tribuneradio.com).
- *The Agri-Voice Network* is a network of fifty smaller midwestern radio stations broadcasting daily farm reports (www.tribuneradio.com).

In addition, a number of websites have been established by the farm media and agribusiness advertisers.

Advertising products to the agribusiness community uses many of the same techniques demonstrated by other sectors of business marketing. However, agribusiness promotional techniques are even more specialized than those of traditional business-to-business selling. The relatively small agribusiness population makes sophisticated information readily available. Agribusiness advertising can target audiences and deliver a message that solves specific problems of the farm industry.

The business of farming has been hit hard during recent years with an uncertain farm economy, high prices for feed and other supplies, and unpredictable weather. These factors have combined to make it very difficult for farm magazines and agribusiness advertising in general. A continuing consolidation of farms has reduced the number of farmers and companies involved in agribusiness. This trend toward consolidation has been reflected in the farm press by lower circulation and fewer advertising dollars during the last two decades.

Ironically, as the number of farms and major agribusiness suppliers has decreased, the number and diversity of media competing for advertising dollars in the sector have grown dramatically. In order to compete in this environment, farm publications have utilized many of the techniques of the business press in expanding the means they use to reach their audiences. For example, these magazines have accumulated sophisticated databases to develop subscriber list rentals, do their own direct mail to nonsubscribers, and publish special catalogs and other material. Like the business press, farm magazines will probably see more revenue coming from nonpublishing sources as they become more successful in promoting these ventures. (See Exhibit 11.23 for examples of farm publications.)

The Organization of the Farm Press

Farm magazines fall into three classifications: general farm magazines, regional farm magazines, and vocational farm magazines.

General Farm Magazines The three major publications in this category are *Farm Journal, Successful Farming*, and *Progressive Farmer*. In recent years, each of these publications has experienced circulation decreases reflecting the consolidation of the farming industry. The general farm publications are designed to address all aspects of farm life but with a clear emphasis on business.

Regional Farm Magazines A number of farm publications are directed to farmers in a particular region. These publications tend to be general in nature, but they contain little of the family-oriented topics found in the large-circulation farm magazines. They address issues of crops, livestock, and government farm policy unique

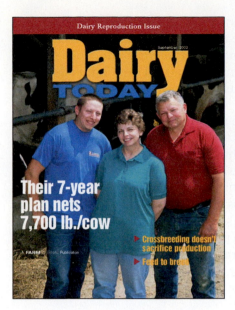

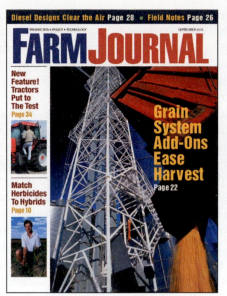

to a particular region. Among the publications in this category are the *Prairie Farmer*, the majority of whose readers live in Indiana and Illinois; the *Oregon Farmer-Stockman*; and the *Nebraska Farmer*.

Vocational Farm Magazines The last category of farm publications comprises those devoted to certain types of farming or livestock raising. Typical of these publications are *The Corn and Soybean Digest*, *The Dairyman*, *American Fruit Grower*, and *The Tomato Magazine*. Many of the vocational magazines combine elements of both regional and vocational publications—for instance, *The Kansas Stockman* and *Missouri Pork Producer*.

Whatever farmers' interests may be, a number of publications are edited to cater to them. Many farm homes take several publications.

SUMMARY

The challenges and opportunities facing consumer magazines cover a wide range of concerns. From practical considerations of cost management in distribution and printing to the ways in which the Internet can be integrated into traditional magazine practices, publishers must deal with an ever-changing marketplace.

In spite of these challenges, magazines are well positioned to deal with communication issues in the future. Magazine readers are among the most upscale of any media audience. Ironically, they show great strength among Internet users that, combined with the selective nature of most publications, may offer a profitable convergence for many publishers. New technology aside, magazines are well positioned as a major marketing and advertising tool.

Magazines can play a role as either the primary medium for a national advertiser or as a niche medium to reach prime prospects. Magazines will continue to be a major source of news, information, and entertainment for millions of prime prospects. It is this combination of prestige and segmentation that gives magazines a major qualitative advantage over most other media. The fact that magazines are asking readers to carry a major share of the financial support of magazines also has enhanced their value to advertisers.

The combination of upscale readers, opportunities for targeted advertising, editorial involvement, and both reach and frequency among a number of qualitative and quantitative audience segments of importance to advertisers will work to the advantage of magazines in the future. Despite these positive characteristics, magazines will continue to face a number of economic problems. Some, like postage increases and newsstand distribution concerns, are beyond their immediate control. In the long term, it may be that financial elements will determine the future of the medium as much as readership.

Business-to-business publications are facing a number of challenges now and in the future. Among the most obvious is the consolidation of many industries into fewer and fewer firms. This merging of firms has resulted in a decrease in both the number of potential advertisers to support the business press and in the number of companies that are being reached with advertising.

A second major trend in the business press has been the growth of competition for advertising dollars. At one time, trade and business publications had a virtual monopoly in the business sector and the farm press had only radio as a major competitor. Today, that situation has changed dramatically. Business advertisers are putting their marketing communication dollars in numerous vehicles as well as the Internet and utilizing sophisticated database technology to demand immediate and measurable results from their advertising.

Because of the relatively low price of trade magazine advertising, it is possible to appeal to specialized job interests with different messages in a variety of publications. The messages of these publications are also specialized. Factual copy with product information is presented to a knowledgeable audience in a manner that would be impractical in most consumer magazines.

Business-to-business publications are an ideal medium for reaching the targeted audience segments that advertisers seek in an environment suited to the mood of that audience. Business magazines also provide audience involvement to a degree impossible in most other media formats and the affinity for these magazines carries over to the advertising messages.

With the ability of computers to track employment demographics and new technology to reach readers through partial-run editions and selected binding, business magazines can compete in an increasingly competitive media environment. On the negative side, business magazines face the same problems of rising postage, printing, and marketing costs as their consumer counterparts. Quality, credibility, believability, and audience selectivity are the elements that will continue to make the business press a primary choice of business-to-business advertisers.

REVIEW ⊛

1. Two of the major concerns of the magazine industry are costs and selectivity. Explain.
2. Why would an advertiser want to use both television and magazines?
3. What are some qualitative features of importance to magazine advertisers?
4. Contrast full-run and partial-run magazine editions.
5. What is selective binding?
6. What is the role of negotiation in setting magazine advertising rates?
7. Contrast circulation and readership in magazines.
8. What are the major competitors for business magazines?
9. What has been a primary method for business magazines to extend their services and increase profits?
10. What are vertical and horizontal publications?

TAKE IT TO THE WEB ✺

Several magazines have online extensions on the Web. Mediaweek.com (www.mediaweek.com) is the online version of *Mediaweek* magazine, which provides media professionals with the latest marketing profiles and indicators, directories for traditional media and national networks, and more. Visit Mediaweek.com as an example of an online magazine and discuss the advantages and disadvantages of having an online edition versus having a print edition only.

Visit either the online edition of *Lucky* magazine (www.luckymag.com) or the online edition of *Sports Illustrated* (www.si.com) and list ways in which the website encourages visitors to subscribe to the print version of the magazine. Were the tactics employed by the websites able to convince you to subscribe?

The Magazine Publishers of America (MPA) is the industry association for consumer magazines. Government Action is one of several topics addressed on the MPA website (www.magazine.org). Review the MPA's position on the topics addressed under this heading including marketing to children and the marketing of weight-loss products and pharmaceuticals through direct-to-consumer advertising. What other issues facing the magazine industry will likely fall under government regulation?

CHAPTER 12

Out-of-Home Advertising

*O*utdoor advertising is an attention-getting medium without equal. With the current move to targeted formats in most advertising vehicles, outdoor is fast becoming the last of the truly mass media. In recent years, there has been a dramatic change in the definition of out-of-home media as the standard highway billboard is being joined by many innovative out-of-home approaches. After reading this chapter, you will understand:

chapter objectives

1. basic marketing strategy of out-of-home advertising
2. the various types of out-of-home media
3. the legislative environment of outdoor advertising
4. out-of-home advertising's role in brand building
5. the complementary function of out-of-home media
6. measurement of the outdoor audience

Pros

1. Outdoor can provide advertising exposure to virtually every adult in a geographic market with high frequency and at a very low cost per exposure.
2. With 24-hour exposure, outdoor is an excellent means of supplementing other media advertising for product introduction or building brand-name recognition.
3. With the use of color and lighting, outdoor is a medium that gains immediate audience attention and can provide reminder messages in proximity to retail outlets such as fast-food franchises.
4. The outdoor industry has diversified the product categories using out-of-home in an attempt to lose its image as a "beer and cigarette" medium.

Cons

1. With a typical audience of high-speed drivers, outdoor is unable to communicate detailed sales messages. Copy is usually limited to headline length—seven to ten words.
2. Outdoor advertising is extremely difficult to measure, making audience comparisons with other media almost impossible.
3. Outdoor has been attacked in many communities as a visual pollutant, which has made it the topic of some controversy. It also faces a number of additional legal restrictions in selected jurisdictions. In a few states (e.g., Alaska, Hawaii, and Vermont), some local governments have banned the medium altogether. This negative image may discourage some advertisers from using outdoor.

Outdoor is the oldest form of promotion. Evidence of outdoor messages can be found in prehistoric carvings on bronze and stone tablets in the Middle East. In ancient Egypt, outdoor was a popular means of posting public notices as well as sales messages. Placed on well-traveled roads, they became the forerunner of the modern highway billboard. Painted advertising dates to Pompeii where elaborately decorated walls promoted local businesses.

In this country, outdoor "broadsides" announced the Boston Tea Party and reported the Boston Massacre, and posters publicized the presidential campaign of Andrew Jackson. The first American commercial billboard was a poster by Jared Bell for the 1835 circus season. Throughout the 1800s, posters promoted a number of products and political causes. In 1850, signs were first used on streetcars in major cities and by 1870 some 300 bill-posting firms served advertisers throughout the East and Midwest.

In 1900, the first standardized outdoor sign format was introduced, and national advertisers such as Kellogg's and Coca-Cola began to share the outdoor market with local advertisers. The modern era of outdoor advertising was introduced when the automobile created a mobile society early in the twentieth century. In addition to a population on the move, outdoor benefited from new printing techniques and a growing advertising industry that was always looking for effective means of reaching prospective customers. During this period, the industry adopted standardized signs; formed the forerunner of its national trade association, the **Outdoor Advertising Association of America (OAAA)**; established what is now the **Traffic Audit Bureau for Media Measurement (TAB)** to authenticate audience data; and initiated a national marketing organization, OAAA Marketing.[1]

Use of outdoor advertising by major advertisers is increasing. Fueled by advertisers' need to gain brand awareness and a number of new outdoor formats, the industry is growing at a rate surpassed by only cable television and Internet advertising (see Exhibit 12.1). The variety of outdoor advertising vehicles has even resulted in the term *out-of-home advertising* replacing the more familiar term

Outdoor Advertising Association of America (OAAA)
Primary trade and lobbying organization for the outdoor industry.

Traffic Audit Bureau for Media Measurement (TAB)
An organization designed to investigate how many people pass and may see a given outdoor sign, to establish a method of evaluating traffic measuring a market.

EXHIBIT **12.1**

Outdoor Advertising Revenue Growth

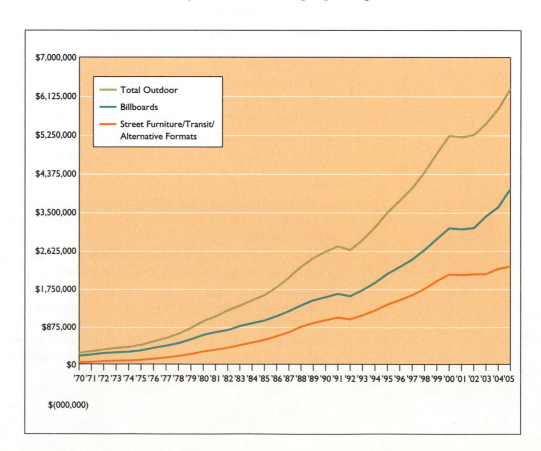

$(000,000)

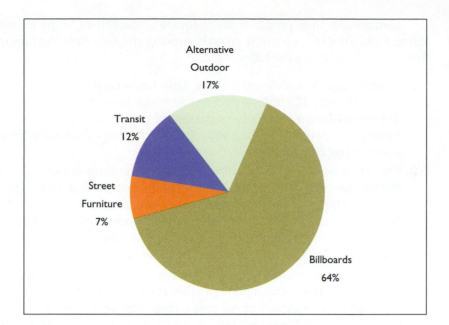

EXHIBIT **12.2**
Categories of Out-of-Home Advertising 2005
Source: © OAAA, 2005.

outdoor advertising in recent years to more fully reflect the scope of this industry. Today, *outdoor* normally has a more narrow meaning, referring only to highway posters and large signs. The change is more than just semantic because it reflects the diversity of the industry and its marketing strategy.

Although traditional billboards are still the primary source of industry revenues, they constitute only 64 percent of the industry's total income (see Exhibit 12.2).

The growth of alternative advertising options offered by out-of-home is a major reason for the growth of the industry. Overall, the OAAA estimates that there are more than thirty types of out-of-home media, including everything from the largest outdoor signs to airport and shopping mall kiosks, stadium signs, and airplanes towing banners (see Exhibit 12.3).

EXHIBIT **12.3**
Types of Out-of-Home Media
Courtesy of Outdoor Advertising Association of America,
http://www.oaaa.org.

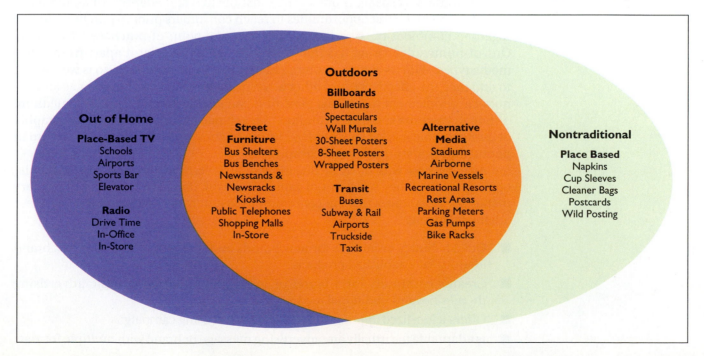

Media executives predict that the future of the out-of-home industry will continue to be one of consistent growth. Among the contributing factors to out-of-home's popularity are the following:

1. *An increasingly mobile population.* Americans rarely stay in one place for long. Approximately 125 million people commute to work each day, placing them in the out-of-home market for a variety of messages. Consumers are spending more time traveling to their jobs. In 2003, average commute times were estimated to be 24.3 minutes.[2]

2. *Cost of out-of-home advertising.* No major medium comes close to matching the inexpensive CPM levels of out-of-home advertising. The relatively low cost of out-of-home means that advertisers can generate extremely high levels of both reach and frequency at inexpensive prices. These affordable CPM figures mean that out-of-home can be an ideal medium to fill in gaps among target segments missed or underexposed by other media.

3. *Media fragmentation.* Outdoor advertising is benefiting from the growing audience fragmentation witnessed in other media. In the last 35 years, the dramatic increase in the number of television channels per household and the number of magazines and radio stations during the same period has resulted in a more fragmented audience for most media. Although the ability to target prospects is a major benefit for many advertisers, widely distributed package goods and other mass-appeal brands need high levels of exposure to virtually everyone. Outdoor can inexpensively deliver massive audience exposures.

4. *Advertiser diversification.* Once heavily used by tobacco and alcohol beverage companies, the outdoor industry now appeals to a more diversified roster of advertisers. As shown in Exhibit 12.4, beer and wine didn't even show up as one of the top ten categories of outdoor advertising in 2005. Companies such as McDonald's, Verizon, General Motors, Nextel, and Coca-Cola all have made major investments in outdoor. The result has been increased revenues and an improved public image for the outdoor industry.

STRATEGIC ADVERTISING AND OUT-OF-HOME

Out-of-home advertising is one of the most flexible and adaptive of all media. It provides one of the last opportunities to reach consumers prior to purchase. In this regard, it combines the best features of radio and point-of-purchase advertising. Out-of-home advertising has many characteristics that set it apart from other media types. With its ability to command attention, out-of-home also is well suited to enhance the effectiveness of other advertising media. It can function as an economical supplement to a media plan, or it can stand alone as a primary medium. Although there are some opportunities to reach particular portions of a geographic or demographic market with outdoor, its major strength is its ability to reach broad population centers quickly and cheaply.

As is the case with other media, individual advertisers have specific marketing objectives when they select out-of-home. However, there are a number of primary marketing advantages that are common to most out-of-home buys. Among these are the following:

- Quickly builds awareness for new brands and maintains and reinforces brand identity for established products
- Creates continuity for a brand or message by extending basic advertising themes beyond traditional media
- Offers a localized approach for national advertising campaigns
- Is adaptable to virtually any advertising message or brand with multiple formats

Top 10 Outdoor Advertising Categories (based on 2005 year-end outdoor expenditures)

1. Local Services and Amusements
2. Media and Advertising
3. Retail
4. Insurance and Real Estate
5. Public Trans., Hotels and Resorts
6. Financial
7. Restaurants
8. Communications
9. Automotive Dealers and Services
10. Automotive, Auto Access and Equipment

Top 20 Outdoor Brands (based on 2005 year-end outdoor expenditures)

1. McDonald's Restaurants
2. Cingular Wireless Services
3. Verizon Long Distance Business and Res.
4. General Motors Corp. Var. Auto and Trk.
5. Anheuser-Busch Beers
6. Nextel Wireless Services
7. Warner Brothers Movies
8. Coca-Cola Soft Drinks
9. Verizon Wireless Service
10. Miller Beers
11. Cracker Barrel Old Country
12. State Farm Insurance
13. Geico Auto Insurance
14. Citibank Consumer Services
15. Apple Computers
16. DiageoBeverages
17. Sony Movies
18. Coors Light Beer
19. Starbucks Coffee Store
20. Paramount Movies

EXHIBIT 12.4

Top Outdoor Advertisers

Courtesy of Outdoor Advertising Association of America, http://www.oaaa.org.

- Provides local support by offering directions to retail outlets
- Serves as a point-of-purchase reminder to customers in the shopping and buying process
- Can enhance direct-response offers by providing Web addresses and telephone numbers (see Exhibit 12.5 for example)

Despite the fact that a number of high-profile national advertisers are using out-of-home currently, the medium remains an essentially local vehicle. The majority of outdoor advertising revenue comes from local advertisers. However, in

EXHIBIT 12.5

Outdoor advertising can enhance direct response from consumers by providing websites.

Courtesy of The Johnson Group.

INSURING 15 MILLION AMERICANS.

ChattanoogaCanDo.com

recent years, a number of changes in the out-of-home industry have taken place that make it likely that more national advertisers will consider out-of-home as part of their future advertising schedule. For example:

1. *Consolidation of ownership.* Only a few years ago, the outdoor business was made up primarily of local companies that provided little audience research, had no national force, or had limited funds to upgrade their facilities. Today, the industry is dominated by large conglomerates that control hundreds of sites throughout the country. These companies are in a position to deal effectively with large national and regional advertisers to gain a larger share of their advertising budgets.

2. *Research.* National advertisers routinely expect sophisticated audience and creative effectiveness research to justify their expenditures. In past years, out-of-home research fell far short of other major media. Even basic demographic data were unavailable in some markets. In recent years, the out-of-home industry has made major strides in providing meaningful research to prospective advertisers. As we discuss later in this chapter, the industry provides audited audience information as well as eye movement research and demographic segmentation information in areas as small as ZIP Codes. Obviously, the outdoor research investment does not compare to that of media with ten times its advertising revenues, but marketers are being given reasonable information on which to base their media decisions.

3. *Increased and improved creative opportunities.* The quantity and quality of out-of-home production and options have improved dramatically in the last decade. Rather than simply printed or painted signs, advertisers have the choice of options such as back-lit dioramas, vinyl surfaces for outdoor and transit, a number of building-size signs, and interactive and digital mobile media.

4. *Terminology.* Over the years, outdoor developed a terminology that was unique to the industry. Not only did media buyers feel uncomfortable dealing in a "foreign" language when buying outdoor, but also, more important, the terminology made intermedia comparisons difficult. With the adoption of the gross rating point (GRP) as the basic measure of outdoor audience reach, the industry has taken steps to address this issue.[3]

Although outdoor can achieve a number of advertising goals, it is not suitable for every advertiser or every advertising or marketing situation. Like other advertising media, outdoor is most successful when it is used in accordance with narrowly defined marketing objectives that utilize the strengths of the medium. In some respects, outdoor presents special challenges because in almost every case it is used as a supplemental medium in a more general campaign (see Exhibit 12.6).

EXHIBIT 12.6

Outdoor advertising is most effective when the message takes advantage of the strengths of the medium.

Courtesy of Huey + Partners and The Daily Report.

Because out-of-home is rarely a primary campaign building block, it must be coordinated, both creatively and in terms of audience reach, with other media. It is important that the main advertising themes be translated properly to outdoor, so that the target audience is exposed to a seamless message. Outdoor is rarely effective as a stand-alone medium. Its major strength is the extension and reinforcement of the more detailed advertising messages carried in other media.

Of course, no amount of planning can overcome some of the inherent weaknesses in a medium. While analyzing the strengths of out-of-home, advertisers also must consider its shortcomings and how these may influence a particular marketing, media, or creative strategy. Because exposure to outdoor is both involuntary and brief, there is little depth of communication, even among a product's most loyal customers. It is estimated that the average person sees most signs for less than 10 seconds.

In addition, most out-of-home vehicles provide little audience selectivity. The major advantage of most out-of-home advertising is that it is more a shotgun than a rifle. Even though advertisers can tailor their messages to reach specific audiences by pinpointing certain neighborhoods or specific streets, such as roads that lead to stadiums or shopping malls, targeting specific audiences is not considered a primary attribute of the medium.

Finally, as the popularity of out-of-home advertising has grown, it has encountered availability problems. In major markets, demand for premium outdoor sites means some advertisers cannot have access to choice locations. Despite these disadvantages, properly executed outdoor advertising can be an inexpensive method of gaining immediate product visibility.

OUTDOOR REGULATION AND PUBLIC OPINION

Outdoor advertising's major advantage—its size—is also a significant public relations problem. For years, environmentalists and public activists have argued for strict limits or complete removal of all outdoor signs. However, a number of research studies conducted suggest that many consumers see value in outdoor advertising and think that its positive aspects outweigh the negatives. Given the controversies that surround outdoor, it may be well to examine some of the primary areas of criticisms and the reaction of the outdoor industry to them.

Federal Legislation

The most comprehensive attempt at regulating outdoor advertising dates to the **Highway Beautification Act of 1965** (known as the "Lady Bird Bill" because Mrs. Lyndon Johnson lobbied for the legislation). The Act restricted the placement of outdoor signs along interstate highways and provided stiff penalties for states that failed to control signs within 660 feet of interstates. Since passage of the legislation, the number of signs has been reduced from 1.2 million to less than 400,000. Most of the remaining signs are concentrated in commercially zoned areas. Exhibit 12.7 outlines some of the major provisions of the Act.

Highway Beautification Act of 1965
Federal law that controls outdoor signs in noncommercial, nonindustrial areas.

Tobacco Advertising

Historically, one of the most criticized aspects of outdoor advertising was the promotion of tobacco. Critics charged that the uncontrolled exposure of cigarette messages encouraged usage by underage smokers. In April 1999, the issue became moot when outdoor advertising of tobacco was banned as part of an agreement with forty-six state attorneys general and the major tobacco companies.

In the 1980s, one-third of all billboards promoted tobacco products. This concentration of dollars not only made the outdoor industry too dependent on one

EXHIBIT **12.7**

Federal and State Controls

Source: The Highway Beautification Act of 1965 (23 U.S.C. 131).

Summary of Existing Outdoor Advertising Control Programs

■ Billboards are allowed, by statute, in commercial and industrial areas consistent with size, lighting, and spacing provisions as agreed to by the state and federal governments.

■ Billboard controls apply to Federal-Aid Primaries (FAPs) as of June 1, 1991; interstates, and other highways that are part of the National Highway System (NHS). The FAP routes were highways noted by state DOTs to be of significant service value and importance. Approximately 260,800 FAP Miles existed as of June 1, 1991 (226,440 rural miles and 34,360 urban miles). These roads have full HBA protections and controls are very important. Maps can be obtained from your state DOT or FHWA Division office or from the OAAA in Washington, D.C.

■ States have the discretion to remove legal nonconforming signs along highways; however, the payment of just (monetary) compensation is required for the removal of any lawfully erected billboard along the Federal-Aid Primary, interstate, and other National Highway System roads.

■ States not complying with the provisions of the HBA are subject to a 10 percent reduction in their highway allocations.

■ States and localities may enact stricter laws than stipulated in the HBA.

■ No new signs can be erected along the scenic portions of state-designated scenic byways of the interstate and federal-aid primary highways.

product category, but the controversy surrounding outdoor also discouraged other product categories from buying the medium. "Conventional wisdom once dictated that the outdoor industry couldn't survive without the . . . dollars from U.S. tobacco marketers. Now it seems not only can the industry survive the loss of that revenue, it can thrive in a nicotine-free world . . . outdoor's day of reckoning is fast becoming its day in the sun."[4]

The OAAA Code of Industry Principles

The industry has moved on a number of fronts to improve its image and create positive public relations in the communities it serves. One step to counteract negative publicity toward the industry has been the enactment of a voluntary *Code of Industry Principles* by the OAAA. As part of this code, outdoor companies are asked to limit the number of billboards in a market that carry messages about products that cannot be sold to minors. Specifically, the code asks that member companies establish "**exclusionary zones** that prohibit advertisements of all products illegal for sale to minors that are either intended to be read from, or within 500 feet of, established places of worship, primary and secondary schools and hospitals."[5]

Outdoor Industry Public Service

Each year, the outdoor industry contributes hundreds of millions of dollars worth of donated space to a number of charities and public service campaigns. Many of these messages are posted in connection with local service projects. However, the OAAA has formed a number of partnerships to coordinate national projects with organizations such as the Advertising Council and the National Center for Missing and Exploited Children. The outdoor industry donates over $400 million worth of outdoor space and production each year to nonprofit organizations.

exclusionary zones (outdoor)

Industry code of conduct that prohibits the advertising within 500 feet of churches, schools, or hospitals of any products that cannot be used legally by children.

The Outdoor Advertising Plan

Successful outdoor advertising depends on both a strategic marketing plan and effective execution of the creative, media, and research elements of this strategy. A number of strategic issues should be considered before we move ahead with the creation of outdoor messages. Among the most important are the following:

1. *Clearly stated objectives.* As we discussed earlier, most outdoor advertising is used as either an introduction for a new product or event (such as a sale) or as a reminder to keep consumers continually aware of a brand. With its headline format, outdoor is rarely suited to offer a complete sales message. Furthermore, national advertisers do not usually use outdoor as their primary medium. Consequently, it is extremely important to plan the outdoor portion of the total advertising campaign in a manner that will ensure maximum efficiency and support to other advertising and promotional vehicles.

2. *Define the target market.* Generally, outdoor media has broad coverage throughout a market. However, outdoor does offer some opportunities for geographic targeting (see Exhibit 12.8). "Most products and brands have distinct regional and local-market purchase patterns. It is common to find that a large group of local markets [or areas within a single market] will index at or above 130 in per-capita brand purchases. Geo-targeting with outdoor is a fine complement to demo-targeting with television or print."[6] It is also a great way to put special emphasis in areas of cities or neighborhoods that contain a large number of residents who belong to specific ethnic groups that may be important to a brand.

3. *Specify measurable goals.* An outdoor plan needs to specify what objectives it hopes to accomplish and how these goals will be measured. For example, do we want outdoor to contribute to increases in brand awareness, increases in sales, or higher market share? Finally, what research methodology will be used to determine if these goals were met and what was the contribution of outdoor?

EXHIBIT 12.8

Outdoor can help regional brands such as this one achieve broad reach in specific geographic markets.

Courtesy of The Johnson Group and Mayfield Dairies.

plant
In outdoor advertising, the local company that arranges to lease, erect, and maintain the outdoor sign and to sell the advertising space on it.

4. *Coordinating the buy.* Outdoor advertising is purchased from local outdoor companies known as **plants**. Increasingly, most local plants are part of large national outdoor companies that provide network buying options to national and regional advertisers. With today's tight marketplace, it is more important than ever for agencies and advertisers to work with plants well ahead of the starting date for a campaign. Ideally, space should be purchased at least 4 months in advance; some markets require even more time. Like spot television and radio, out-of-home is a supply-and-demand business with site availability a recurring problem.

5. *Postbuy inspection (called riding the boards).* After the posters are up, an in-market check of poster locations should be made. This inspection determines that proper locations were used and that the signs were posted or painted properly. It also helps ensure that billboards containing the client's message are not obstructed by such things as trees or poles.

All this only emphasizes that successful outdoor advertising demands the use of the same fundamental principles of advertising planning that apply to other media. In some respects, planning in outdoor is even more complex than in other media. Media planners must make certain that the characteristics and objectives of outdoor mesh properly with those of more dominant media. The complementary nature of outdoor is an overriding concern in most outdoor schedules. The planner must be certain that outdoor can, in fact, reinforce the media schedule in a cost-efficient manner.

FORMS OF OUTDOOR ADVERTISING

As we mentioned at the outset of this chapter, outdoor is only one of several categories of out-of-home advertising. However, in terms of revenues, public familiarity, and long-term usage, the two basic forms of outdoor are posters and painted bulletins (see Exhibit 12.9). In either case, the message is designed by the advertising agency. The creative design is then reproduced on paper or vinyl and posted on panels. The larger painted bulletins are prepared by outdoor company artists either in a studio or on site. Even large posters that once were painted are now being reproduced in vinyl.

EXHIBIT 12.9

Posters and bulletins make up the standardized outdoor industry.

Courtesy of Outdoor Advertising Association of America, http://www.oaaa.org.

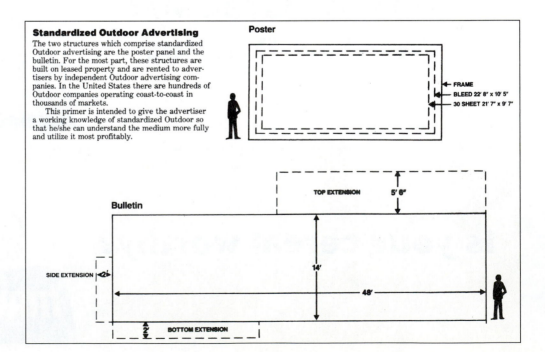

Standardized Outdoor Advertising
The two structures which comprise standardized Outdoor advertising are the poster panel and the bulletin. For the most part, these structures are built on leased property and are rented to advertisers by independent Outdoor advertising companies. In the United States there are hundreds of Outdoor companies operating coast-to-coast in thousands of markets.

This primer is intended to give the advertiser a working knowledge of standardized Outdoor so that he/she can understand the medium more fully and utilize it most profitably.

Poster Panels

The thirty-sheet poster is the most widely used form of outdoor advertising. The most common type of poster is really two posters in one. Bleed and thirty-sheet posters, which use the same frame, constitute the typical highway billboard with which we are so familiar. Poster buys can be made for a single location or for total national coverage.

The primary use of most posters is to reach the majority of a market quickly and inexpensively. However, with geomarketing, posters also can be used to reach more targeted prospects. For example, posters placed in financial districts or on routes to the airport reach more affluent customers and business travelers.

The standard poster panel measures 12 feet by 25 feet. The bleed poster either prints to the edge of the frame or uses blanking paper matching the background of the poster. The term *bleed* is, of course, borrowed from the bleed magazine advertisement that has no border. The term *sheet* originated in the days when presses were much smaller and it took many sheets to cover a poster panel.

Today, posters are often printed on vinyl instead of paper. The vinyl-wrapped poster uses the standard thirty-sheet board, but by "wrapping" or covering the entire board, it expands the coverage area. Wrapped posters are usually available at any thirty-sheet location. Although it lasts longer and retains color better than paper, vinyl is more expensive to produce so it is used at high-traffic locations and for longer contract periods than paper posters.

Poster displays are sold on the basis of *illuminated* and *nonilluminated* panels. Normally, poster contracts are for 30 days with discounts for longer periods. Those panels in locations with high-traffic volume are illuminated normally for 24-hour exposure. A typical poster showing will consist of 70 to 80 percent **illuminated posters**, but major advertisers often request full-illuminated postings. When buying an outdoor showing, the advertiser is provided information about the number of displays, the number that are illuminated and nonilluminated, the monthly and per-panel cost, and total circulation or exposure.

The Eight-Sheet Poster

Another important type of outdoor advertising is the eight-sheet poster. **Eight-sheet posters** measure 5 feet by 11 feet, slightly less than one-third the size of thirty-sheet posters. Eight-sheet posters are bought by small, local businesses as well as by national companies. Often they are placed immediately adjacent to the point of sale as the last customer contact before a purchase decision. These compact posters add enormous reach and frequency to advertising plans at a modest cost.

Eight-sheet posters rapidly build brand awareness, announce new products and services, and provide reminder messages for a brand. In addition, eight-sheet

illuminated posters
Seventy to eighty percent of all outdoor posters are illuminated for 24-hour exposure.

eight-sheet poster
Outdoor poster used in urban areas, about one-fourth the size of the standard thirty-sheet poster. Also called *junior poster*.

EXHIBIT 12.10

Poster panels such as this one can quickly attract attention.

Courtesy of The Johnson Group and Ski.

space costs are much lower than traditional billboards and, because of their smaller size, production costs are significantly lower as well. The average CPM of eight-sheet posters is approximately half that of thirty-sheet posters.

In most markets, zoning regulations are more favorable for the smaller eight-sheet posters than for traditional billboards. Therefore, they can be used in a cost-effective way to reach various target audiences without expensive waste circulation. Like billboards, eight-sheet posters generally are bought to support a larger advertising campaign. Eight-sheet posters can enhance television by adding frequency and recall, and they add a visual element to radio messages. They also can offer reminder messages to print media. Eight-sheet posters are handled by special poster plants but frequently appear concurrently with thirty-sheet showings in a market.

Painted Bulletins

rotary bulletin (outdoor)
Movable painted bulletins that are moved from one fixed location to another in the market at regular intervals. The locations are viewed and approved in advance by the advertiser.

Painted bulletins are the largest and most prominent type of outdoor advertising. Painted bulletins are of two types: *permanent* and the more popular *rotary*. The permanent bulletin remains at a fixed location and can vary in size because it is never moved. The **rotary bulletin (outdoor)** is a standardized sign that is three times larger (14 feet by 48 feet) than the standard poster, and it is placed at high-traffic locations for maximum visibility. Rotary bulletins can be moved from site to site to ensure maximum coverage of a market over a period of months. Both types of bulletins are almost always illuminated.

Bulletins as shown in Exhibit 12.12 are approximately four times more expensive than posters. In recent years, the basic bulletin has been augmented with special embellishments, such as cutouts, freestanding letters, special lighting effects, fiber optics, and inflatables. Painted bulletin contracts usually are for a minimum of 1 year; however, short-term contracts are available at a higher monthly rate.

Rotary bulletins offer advertisers the advantages of the greater impact of the painted bulletin combined with more coverage and penetration than a single site could deliver. A rotary bulletin can be moved every 30, 60, or 90 days, so that during a 12-month period consumers throughout the market will have seen the advertiser's message.

Spectaculars

As the name implies, outdoor spectaculars are large, one-of-a-kind displays designed for maximum attention in urban centers. They may consist of special lighting or other types of ingenious material and innovations. In some cases, they utilize a building as the canvas for the message. Spectaculars are very expensive, and both production and space rentals are negotiated normally on a one-time basis with the minimum contract for most spectaculars being a year.

With the advent of new technology in outdoor advertising, what was once a spectacular may soon be the norm. Currently, the outdoor industry is using a variety of digital and laser technology for computerized painting/printing systems. More and more outdoor is being printed on flexible vinyl, which provides consistent, magazine-quality reproduction in all markets. In the future, outdoor planners envision the ability to provide satellite-distributed video images similar to giant television screens on which computerized messages can be changed immediately. Regardless of what new technology comes to outdoor, it is obvious that the traditional paper poster soon may be history.

A growing segment of the spectacular category is the *wall mural* (also called *wallscapes*). Actually, it was ancient Roman wall paintings that gave outdoor advertising its start. Wall murals, done properly and in selected areas, can add a sense of urban art to an area. Many building surfaces will not hold paint well and, from a practical standpoint, most building owners will not allow someone to paint their building.[7]

THE ELEMENTS OF OUTDOOR

Outdoor advertising is a visual medium with creative elements playing a much greater role than in most other advertising vehicles. The creative options available for outdoor and out-of-home advertisers are almost limitless with dozens of shapes and sizes offered to carry persuasive messages. As the OAAA points out, "Designing outdoor advertising is visual storytelling. The expression of an idea can surprise viewers with words or excite them with pictures . . . designing for the outdoor medium is a challenging communication task that requires the expression of a concept with clarity and austere focus."[8]

Outdoor Design

Designing an outdoor display is among the most difficult tasks for a creative team. Creating a picture and a few words to be seen by fast-moving traffic at distances of up to 500 feet is hard enough—to do so in a manner that moves customers to buy a product adds an obstacle not found in other media. However, outdoor also is one of the most enjoyable media to work with from a creative standpoint. Its size and color allow maximum creativity without the space constraints of other advertising vehicles. For example, in Tokyo, TBWA Worldwide took advantage of the unique qualities of billboards when it created human billboards for Adidas. These boards, designed to promote the beginning of soccer season, had a ball and two players suspended at a 90-degree angle on a giant vertical soccer field. The humans played 10- to 15-minute games five times per day attracting sizable audiences.[9]

Copy   Outdoor only allows a headline, usually no more than seven words. Unlike copy in traditional media, there is no theme development and copy amplification. Conciseness is not only a virtue but also a necessity. Advertisers have learned to work with these constraints to provide not only interesting but also motivating sales messages.

Color   Color is one of the primary advantages of outdoor. However, colors must be chosen carefully to ensure readability. Outdoor designers use those colors that create high contrast in both hue (red, green, etc.) and value (a measure of lightness or darkness). For example, Exhibit 12.11 demonstrates eighteen combinations of colors with one being the most visible and eighteen the least visible.

Outdoor Advertising and Digital Technologies

One of the difficulties facing outdoor advertising is developing a way to have clients visualize creative concepts in a realistic environment. Most other media can demonstrate how an advertisement or commercial will look or sound in finished form. Translating an 8½" × 11" piece of paper to a 300-square-foot billboard is more difficult. However, a growing number of outdoor plants are providing Internet systems that allow advertisers and media planners to see how their posters will appear in actual locations. The systems offer a driver's view of a poster location. Through computer scanning, any creative execution can be superimposed on the board. The system can also be used to make riding the boards a thing of the past as advertisers can now view posters from their office computers.

Computer technology also offers the potential for a number of creative innovations in outdoor. Computers for some time have directed the design and painting

EXHIBIT **12.11**

Some color
combinations are much
more effective than
others for outdoor
advertising.

Courtesy of Outdoor Advertising
Association of America,
http://www.oaaa.org.

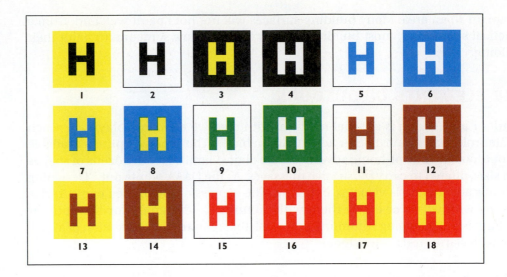

process on vinyl, which is used in most of the larger bulletin displays. In addition, individual advertisers and plants are beginning to use digital technology on billboards that offer changing messages such as days-to-Christmas and other current text. As we mentioned earlier, some outdoor executives envision a day when most high-traffic signs will consist of digital displays that are similar to large television screens and programmed from a central location.

BUYING OUTDOOR

Both the methods and terminology used in buying outdoor advertising are different in a number of ways from those used in other media. Poster advertising is purchased on the basis of *gross rating points* (*GRPs*). You will recall from our earlier discussion of television that 1 GRP is equal to 1 percent of the population. Similarly, GRPs normally are bought in units of 50 or 100 and measure the duplicated audience reached by a poster allotment. An allotment is the number of posters used in an individual buy. To achieve a showing of 50 GRPs in a market means that an advertiser will have daily exposures to outdoor messages equivalent to 50 percent of the adult population of the market.

The audience for outdoor is called the *daily effective circulation* (*DEC*) and is calculated by using the following formula:

24-hour traffic count = 36,000

For nonilluminated posters, the traffic count is multiplied by 0.45; therefore,

$0.45 \times 36,000 = 16,200$ adult DEC

For illuminated posters, the traffic count is multiplied by 0.64; therefore,

$0.65 \times 36,000 = 23,040$

Let's examine a market and work through these calculations:

Market: Anytown

Population: 800,000

Audience level purchased: 50 GRPs

Allotment: Twenty-six posters (twenty illuminated, six nonilluminated)

Explanation: Our twenty-poster allotment generated a DEC of 400,000. We calculate this by the following formula:

$$\text{GRPS} = \frac{\text{Daily effective circulation}}{\text{Market population}}$$

$$50 \text{ GRPS} = \frac{400,000}{800,000}$$

You may not compare GRP levels in markets of different size, except as a measure of advertising weight and intensity. For example, 50 GRPs might require an allotment of 50 or 100 posters in a large market, whereas in a very small market 50 GRPs might be achieved with one or two posters. By the same token, in a market of 2 million population, a 50 GRP buy would generate a DEC of 1 million, whereas the same weight in a market of 50,000 would show a DEC of only 25,000.

VERIFYING

The success of outdoor advertising is dependent on providing advertisers and agencies with reliable research data on which they can base their media-buying decisions. The outdoor industry, dealing with an audience that is entirely out-of-home and on the move, faces significant challenges in developing audience research.

The Traffic Audit Bureau for Media Measurement (TAB)

The primary source of out-of-home audience information is the Traffic Audit Bureau for Media Measurement (TAB). Founded in 1933, the nonprofit organization audits the circulation of thirty-sheet posters; bulletins; eight-sheet posters; shelter advertising displays; and, most recently, truck advertising. The TAB provides market-based traffic data on a designated marketing area (DMA) by designated marketing area basis. These data give advertisers audited traffic counts to give them an idea of the numbers of people in a market who pass their displays. The TAB updates data annually and checks visibility of signs as well as traffic flow.[10]

Nielsen and Arbitron have both been working on new ratings systems for outdoor that can provide some of the demographic audience data desired by advertisers. In 2005, Nielsen began collecting outdoor ratings data in Chicago using a passive Portable People Meter and personal Global Postioning System (GPS) device, such as the one being tested for television and radio, to track outdoor audiences. In 2006, Nielsen expanded the program to include Los Angeles as well. Expansion of this system could potentially allow the tracking of outdoor exposure in an affordable way.[11]

Communication Effectiveness

In addition to traffic audits, which are primarily measures of potential audiences, advertisers are interested in the communication effectiveness of outdoor advertising. In order to address this issue, Perception Research Services (PRS) was engaged by the OAAA to conduct eye-tracking studies to determine the levels of outdoor visibility and the impact of this visibility. Using a technique that recorded drivers' and passengers' eye movements, PRS found that 74 percent of subjects noticed outdoor signs and 73 percent of those read the copy. Results also showed that the size of boards and creative enhancements such as three-dimensional figures and board extensions increased attention levels. Overall, the study showed that outdoor can be effective in building brand recognition and it is able to draw attention from all target groups (see Exhibit 12.12).

Another approach to measuring outdoor communication uses personal computers to measure the potential audience exposed to an outdoor campaign. This

EXHIBIT 12.12

Outdoor is becoming a popular choice among advertisers who want to increase brand awareness.

Courtesy of Chick-fil-A.

system combines cost and audience information in order to determine if specific campaign objectives have been met with a particular outdoor campaign.

Marketing and Rate Data

■ The Simmons Market Research Bureau (SMRB) conducts an annual national consumer study with over 25,000 respondents. SMRB reports the reach of target audiences, media usage habits, and outdoor delivery for over 8,000 consumer products and services.[12]

■ The *Buyer's Guide to Outdoor Advertising* contains rate guides for thirty- and eight-sheet posters and bulletins. The *Buyer's Guide* provides information concerning costs, number of panels in a showing, and market population.

As the outdoor industry has sought to encourage more advertising from package-goods and retail advertisers, it has adopted many of the buying practices used by other media. One of the potential benefits of consolidation within the outdoor industry is a movement toward more industrywide support for a number of research and audience measurement studies. As outdoor continues to appeal to major national advertisers, it will become necessary to provide standardized audience data and research.

Trends in Outdoor Advertising

Out-of-home advertising is becoming a popular choice with a number of advertisers seeking increased brand awareness and a means of differentiating themselves from traditional media messages. In an environment in which people are bombarded by hundreds of messages every day, outdoor is a means of gaining high attention levels to a mass audience.

Outdoor complements and enhances other media advertising by providing high levels of reach and frequency at a lower cost than most other media. Research shows that outdoor can create a synergistic effect when combined with other media. In particular, out-of-home offers advertisers a last chance to create brand awareness among potential prospects. The influx of product categories such as package goods, cellular companies, retailers, and high-profile fashion brands has given the outdoor industry much needed diversification.

Research and reliable audience measurements continue to be a challenge to the industry. In recent years, outdoor has sponsored a number of new and innovative approaches to verifying the reach and communication effectiveness of the medium. Computer technology has permitted researchers to undertake a number of studies that would have been impossible only a few years ago.

Finally, the industry is able to provide even better creative approaches for advertisers. The use of computer design, vinyl and other new materials, online visualization of final creative products, and new digital technologies combine to make outdoor even more appealing to advertisers. The many formats of out-of-home are motivating a number of advertisers to use the medium—even those who resist traditional outdoor posters. The remainder of this chapter discusses some of the out-of-home formats beyond billboards.

TRANSIT ADVERTISING

Transit advertising is designed to accomplish many of the same tasks as traditional outdoor messages. It builds brand awareness and provides reminder messages to a mobile population. Transit provides extensive reach and high repetition at a fraction of the cost of other media. Because transit audiences demonstrate repetitive travel patterns, transit advertising provides extremely high levels of frequency and consistent reach year-round. Transit is one of the fastest-growing segments of out-of-home advertising. It accounts for almost 20 percent of outdoor advertising revenue.

The transit advertising category is defined by the OAAA as "advertising displays affixed to moving vehicles or positioned in the common areas of transit stations, terminals and airports."[13] The basic marketing strategy of transit advertising is that it reaches a mobile urban population on an out-of-home basis. Unlike billboards, exposure often takes place in an environment where there is more time to read a message and, in the case of interior displays, where the audience is exposed over a relatively long period of time during the average commute. An advertiser can either get broad or very targeted reach depending on its needs.

Exterior Displays

Exterior displays provide the largest revenue source in transit advertising. These messages are carried on the outside of buses; subway cars; taxis; and, increasingly, on the sides of trucks (see Exhibits 12.13 and 12.14).

Whereas exterior signs are generally available on all sides of a bus, the basic units are the king-size bus posters and the queen-size posters. King-size posters are carried on both the curb and street sides of buses, whereas queen-size posters are displayed on the curb (see Exhibit 12.15). A more recent innovation is the full-bus or subway wrap in which an entire vehicle is covered by a single advertising display. Material is used to cover the windows so that passengers can see from the inside, but it maintains a continuous design when viewed from the outside (see Exhibit 12.16). All exterior signs are printed on vinyl and either placed in frames or, more often, affixed with adhesive. In most markets, advertisers can choose from a number of bus routes to create all or only a portion of a market. The intent of exterior signs is to reach both pedestrian and vehicular traffic primarily during daylight hours.

EXHIBIT 12.13

Exterior displays provide exposure to both pedestrians and vehicular traffic.

Courtesy of Chick-fil-A.

EXHIBIT 12.14

Taxi toppers can be seen in many large metro areas.

Source: Copyright James Estrin/The New York Times.

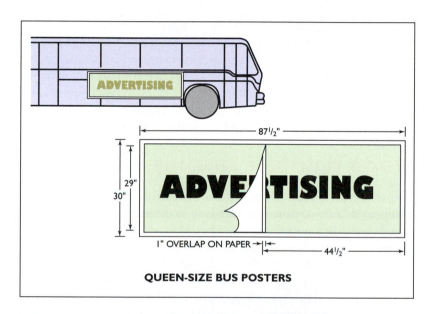

EXHIBIT 12.15
Two of the Most Popular Exterior Transit Formats

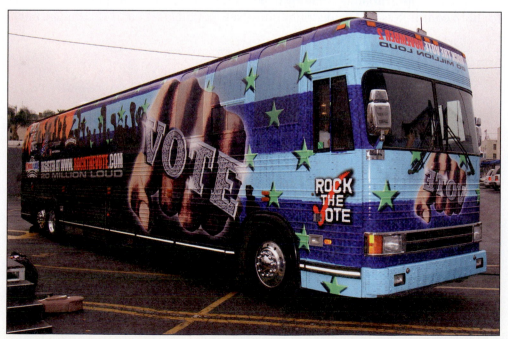

EXHIBIT 12.16
Bus wraps turn the entire bus into a single advertising display.
Source: AP Wide World Photos.

Interior Displays

Interior signs, often referred to as *car cards*, come in a number of sizes and they are fitted into racks inside buses and subway cars. The advantage of interior signs is that they can be seen over a relatively long period of time, especially compared to most other forms of outdoor. Interior signs are ideal for building high levels of frequency because most commuters travel the same routes on a daily basis. Occasionally, interior signs include cards or tear-off slips that can be taken by riders—thus combining features of both transit and direct-response advertising. Interior displays can also be found in some taxis.

Some major transit systems in the United States have been experimenting with the use of transit television in their fleets. The Milwaukee bus transit system has also tested the use of location-based text messaging services. Riders on the Milwaukee system were prompted via in-bus advertising to send a text message for a chance to win a $500 shopping spree to the grocery chain, Sentry Foods. The company estimated it would reach its goal of 50,000 contest entries.[14]

Airport Displays

There are many different options available for airport displays. Among familiar formats are back-lit panels, courtesy phone centers, wall wraps, baggage carousels, baggage carts, airport bus shelters, and kiosks in terminals and at the gates. Regardless of the specific format, airport displays are intended to reach pedestrian traffic in a captive environment. This medium's ability to generate significant audience levels and reach an upscale audience has resulted in a number of advertisers moving into the medium.

STREET FURNITURE ADVERTISING

A specialized sector of the outdoor medium is street furniture advertising. This category of out-of-home advertising is defined as "advertising displays, many of which provide a public amenity, positioned at close proximity to pedestrians and shoppers for eye-level viewing, or at curbside to influence vehicular traffic."[15] In this category of out-of-home advertising are such options as bus benches, in-store displays, shopping mall displays, kiosks, bicycle racks, and bus shelter panels.

Shelter posters are a fast-growing medium in major metropolitan areas. Shelter displays are approximately 4 feet by 6 feet and provide attention-getting messages for both commuters and pedestrian traffic (see Exhibits 12.17 and 12.18). The back-

EXHIBIT 12.17
A Typical Station Poster

Viewing Area:
44" H × 28" W

One Sheet
Poster Size:
45" H × 30" W

ONE SHEET POSTERS

EXHIBIT 12.18
Shelter advertising is used to promote a variety of products.
Source: Copyright © Andrew Hetherington.

lit panels provide 24-hour exposure with no clutter from competing media. Shelter operators offer full market coverage or geographic targeting in selected sections of a metropolitan area.

Like station posters and interior transit, shelter advertising generates extremely high frequency among commuters. The cost of individual panels varies with the population, the number of displays purchased, and the length of contracts (space contracts run from 1 to 12 months). The CPM for shelter is comparable to other forms of transit with CPMs running at only a few cents. Even though the posters are small by outdoor standards, ". . . when you take into account that they're seen at eye level, they have every bit as much . . . impact as the big boards which obviously are viewed from a much greater distance."[16]

Shelter advertising is a large medium within the street furniture category. It is used by a number of major advertisers, and it has been a leader in developing the type of diverse advertising support sought by other forms of out-of-home. Shelter advertising, although accounting for a small portion of total advertising, will continue to grow at a faster rate than overall advertising expenditures. Finally, rather than facing the regulatory problems of outdoor, the revenues generated by shelter posters are often shared with municipal transit companies, making the medium a welcome revenue producer to many cities facing tight budgets.

ALTERNATIVE OUT-OF-HOME ADVERTISING

Alternative out-of-home advertising includes a variety of formats that reach audiences when they are engaged in specialized activities. This is the broadest form of out-of-home advertising and includes everything from parking meters, cinema, and stadium advertising to trash bins, health clubs, and subway tunnels. It also includes shopping bags, roadside logos, beach sand impressions, and commercial restrooms.

There are many opportunities for advertisers within some of these alternative options. For example, cinema advertising can include advertisements in a slideshow or 1- to 2-minute commercials run before the movie, interactive kiosks, or posters in the theaters. Stadium advertising can include scoreboard, restroom, trash can, or concession stand signage. Fitness club advertising permits access to an active hard-to-reach target through flat panel posters in gyms, through full-video opportunities, and through health club sampling networks with relatively low CPMs. Estimated CPMs for standard panels in gyms are $2.00, and video network CPMs are about $24.00.[17]

Many of the most creative and innovative media plans in recent years have made use of alternative out-of-home advertising options, and some of the media in the out-of-home category are more similar to promotions than to traditional advertising. These less-traditional media types sometimes offer the best opportunity for reaching hard-to-reach target audiences. See Case 12.1, for example. The case describes the media plan put together by MediaCom-Israel for Procter & Gamble's Biomat laundry detergent. This plan, which won the coveted Media Grand Prix Lion at the Cannes International Advertising Festival in 2005, did not use any traditional media. According to Doug Checkeris, CEO of The Media Company in Toronto and the Canadian representative on the media jury of the festival, "As technology provides consumers with ever-increasing control of the advertising messages they receive, access to consumers, so long taken for granted, can no longer be assumed. No matter how good the message is, if consumers do not receive it, the creative genius is wasted."[18]

In another example, Procter & Gamble (P&G) had the "Pottypolooza" created to bring to events such as festivals and fairs where consumers might be in need of a restroom. The Pottypolooza is a truck painted with signage for Charmin toilet tissue inside and out. It contains several extremely clean flush toilets and is stocked with Charmin, Safeguard soap, Pampers changing tables, and Bounty paper towels. It has been very popular with consumers. During the holiday shopping period in 2006, P&G brought a Wall-Street-themed mobile public bathroom truck to Times Square. It was a big hit with holiday shoppers.[19]

Some of the newer forms of alternative out-of-home media involve putting advertising messages in places where we aren't used to seeing them. LCD screens mounted in elevators play commercials. Garbage trucks have carried advertisements for Glad trash bags.[20] Dry cleaning bags carried advertisements for *Desperate Housewives*.[21] Even eggs have been used to carry stickers promoting things such as CBS programming.[22]

Another form of alternative out-of-home advertising is interactive outdoor media. Interactive outdoor advertising is a fast-growing segment of the alternative outdoor media segment in large part due to its ability to engage the consumer. According to the OAAA, three interactive technologies that are receiving a lot of attention are short message service or multimedia messaging service (SMS/MMS), Bluetooth and WiFi. Content can be delivered in text form with images and audio-clips as well as with Web-based content. Several different types of devices can receive these messages including computers, mobile phones, personal digital assistants (PDAs), and some portable game consoles. Even some static billboards are becoming interactive. According to *Advertising Age*, "With more cellphones equipped with Bluetooth, consumers can request more information or download music, while 'digital ink' lets marketers change their messages and video screens respond to touch."[23]

SUMMARY ⚙

Out-of-home advertising is fast becoming part of mainstream media. Although it currently comprises a small but growing percentage of total advertising revenues, it is likely to continue to grow in the next decade. Outdoor offers an opportunity for advertisers to provide brand reminders to current customers and introduce brands to prospective customers at a cost of less than virtually any other medium.

In many respects, out-of-home can function in the same way as point-of-purchase advertising to reach consumers immediately before purchase. With the many options available in out-of-home, there is a format for almost every advertising objective. As traditional media become more fragmented, outdoor remains a medium that can provide both reach and frequency to a mass audience. At a time when outdoor is appealing to national advertisers, industry consolidation is creating efficient means of buying multiple markets. Many advertisers are finding the new interactive out-of-home media options to be particularly appealing.

Out-of-home media also are enjoying the benefits of more sophisticated research addressing both audience measurement and communication effects of the medium. As more national advertisers begin to consider out-of-home advertising, it will be necessary for the industry to provide research similar to what is available from other media competitors.

REVIEW ⚙

1. Why is a diversity of product categories important to the outdoor industry?
2. Why has the term *out-of-home* partially replaced *outdoor*?
3. What are the primary categories of out-of-home advertising?
4. What is the function of the Traffic Audit Bureau for Media Measurement (TAB)?
5. Why has transit advertising grown significantly in recent years?
6. What are the primary uses of outdoor for most advertisers?
7. What are the major advantages of the eight-sheet posters?
8. What are the major disadvantages of outdoor posters?

TAKE IT TO THE WEB ⚙

The Outdoor Advertising Association of America (OAAA) is a trade association that represents the outdoor advertising industry. Visit its website (www.oaaa.org) and create a list of all the different kinds of creative outdoor advertising opportunities you see listed.

Lamar Advertising handles traditional billboard advertising as well as placement of advertisements on transit shelters, benches, and transit buses. View Lamar's product gallery on the Lamar website (www.lamar.com) and list the advantages and disadvantages of these alternate forms of advertising.

The John W. Hartman Center for Sales, Advertising, and Marketing History is part of the Rare Book, Manuscript, and Special Collections Library at Duke University. Check out the Outdoor Advertising Archives (http://scriptorium.lib.duke.edu/hartman/oa/outdoor.html) and compare some of the earlier billboards with what you see on the roads today.

CASE HISTORY

Communication Goals

P&G was relaunching Biomat, a low-priced clothes washing powder, specifically targeting the Jewish Orthodox sector (15% of population). The Orthodox are almost unreachable via traditional media: for religious reasons, they do not own TVs or radios, and have limited suitable print publications. They also have negative attitudes towards "classic" persuasive advertising. Despite obstacles, the goal was to create a "big-bank" effect, suitable for a brand relaunch.

Innovative Media Strategy

The Orthodox have a well-accepted belief (and religious commandment) of aiding the weak. Our idea was to connect this belief to Biomat: Biomat helps you help the needy. The mechanism of the promotion was simple: bring your used/unneeded clothes to us, we will wash them (with Biomat, of course) and distribute them to the needy. The main feature was a Biomat-branded truck with a giant washing machine in the back. Wherever the truck stopped (in Orthodox town centers), people gathered with their sacks of clothing and were able to see how their clothes donations were washed with Biomat.

Engaging Creativity

We appealed to the target by engaging their core beliefs, and we overcame the media access limitations of the target by focusing on out-of-home activity. An alliance with a non-profit organization ensured the believability of the campaign, especially important for this target group. Equally important was that Biomat and its superior cleaning properties were clearly and successfully communicated in all materials, including PR.

Encompassing the Audience

The Biomat-branded truck and events were supported by wild street postings detailing the activity and the dates. The in-street communication was also supplemented with insertions in traditional Orthodox print publications, through in-store shelf communication, as well as through huge PR coverage and free publicity.

Effectiveness

Biomat's shares in the Orthodox sector have grown by almost 50% since the activity began. The campaign was a huge success and the client (P&G) is planning to do it again in the upcoming fiscal year.
Courtesy Gilad Kat, Managing Director, MediaCom Tel-Aviv, and Procter & Gamble.

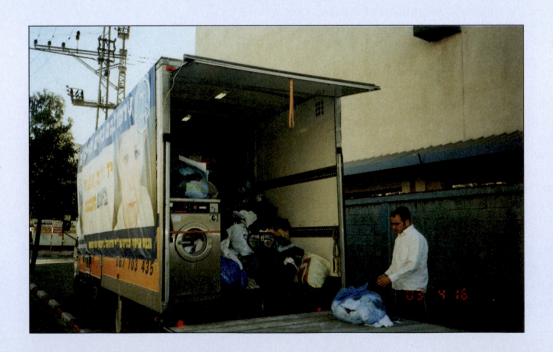

הלבן של ביומט

עושה לך נחת כל פעם מחדש.

"יש רגעים שהם אושר צרוף ונחת אמיתית בכל פעם מחדש. כשאת מבקרת עם משפחתך את הוריך, אבא שלך מחבק בברכות את "הבן יקיר" שלך ושואל אותו על פרשת השבוע. גם הפעם הקטנצ'יק שולך בזריזות תשובה קולעת... וכמו תמיד, את נוצרת בליבך את הרגע המתוק הזה, עד הפעם הבאה..."

כשמדובר בכביסה של המשפחה שלך את יודעת שעם ביומט הכביסה שלך תצא בדיוק כמו שאת רוצה - החולצות לבנות ובוהקות והבגדים ללא רבב. ביומט מותאמת במיוחד עבור צורכי המשפחה החרדית והיא תמיד הבחירה החכמה. דור אחר דור, משפחתך נשארת נאמנה לביומט, שמוכיחה שוב ושוב כי הנאמנות משתלמת.

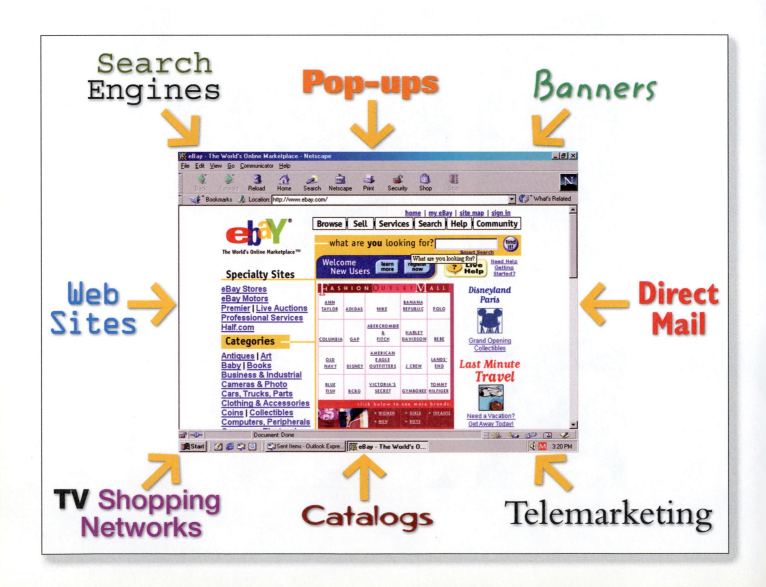

CHAPTER 13

Internet and Direct-Response Advertising

*S*ince the mid-1990s, every aspect of direct response from selling techniques to consumer information acquisition has undergone dramatic change. Today, virtually every advertiser is using the techniques of direct response as a key ingredient of marketing strategies. The Internet is often, but certainly not always, used by advertisers as a form of direct-response advertising. You have seen the Internet discussed in Chapter 7 through Chapter 12 as it has implications and is being used in various ways by all of the traditional media. In the discussion of the Internet, this chapter will principally focus on the uses not previously discussed. After reading this chapter, you will understand:

chapter objectives

1. **effects of new technology on direct-response advertising**
2. **the future growth of the Internet and direct response**
3. **planning for marketing on the Internet**
4. **the concept of consumer relationship management**
5. **the principles of integrated marketing and direct response**
6. **major components of direct-response marketing**

The Internet—Pros

1. The Internet offers a relatively inexpensive, quick, and easily available interactive medium especially among niche markets such as the business-to-business market.
2. The Internet provides advertisers with a combination of interactive audio and video capabilities that can engage the consumer.
3. The Internet is among the most flexible media with an ability to change messages immediately in reaction to market and competitive conditions.

The Internet—Cons

1. To this point, the Internet is just beginning to perform for advertisers. Early failures made some advertisers cautious about exploring the unique possibilities offered by this medium.
2. Despite the growing popularity of the Internet as a means of informal communication, some consumers are still reluctant to use the service for purchasing products and services. In particular, consumers are reluctant to give their credit card numbers over the Internet even though secure sites are available.

3. The sheer number of commercial and noncommercial websites makes it difficult for consumers to know what is available or, once known, to have much time to spend with any single site.

Direct Response—Pros

1. Direct response has the potential to reach virtually any prospect on a geographical, product usage, or demographic basis.

2. Direct response is a measurable medium with opportunities for short-term, sales-related response.

3. Direct response allows advertisers to personalize their messages and build an ongoing relationship with prime target audiences that is often impossible in traditional mass media vehicles.

Direct Response—Cons

1. High cost per contact is a major problem with many forms of direct response, especially direct mail. Expenses for printing, production, and postage have all increased significantly in recent years.

2. To keep up with an increasingly mobile population, prospect lists must be updated constantly at considerable expense to advertisers.

3. Public and government concerns with privacy issues have become a major problem for the direct-response industry. Internet marketers, in particular, are facing restrictive legislation and regulations at both the state and federal levels that have limited their ability to reach new prospects through certain types of contacts.

There is nothing new about the concept of selling directly to consumers. Benjamin Franklin sold scientific books by mail in the 1740s; and more than 100 years ago, Montgomery Ward had a thriving mail-order business through its catalog (see Exhibit 13.1). For the last 25 years, marketers have moved toward a more personal relationship with their customers. They have progressed steadily:

- From mass marketing wherein prospects were reached relatively indiscriminately at the lowest possible cost per impression
- To category marketing wherein prospects who belong to some broad demographic category such as women ages 18 to 34 were targeted
- To niche marketing wherein these broad categories were more narrowly defined (e.g., women ages 18 to 34 with children)
- To group (or community) marketing wherein prospects who regard themselves as part of a group with common interests (e.g., tennis players, opera lovers, antique collectors) are reached with messages and product benefits that acknowledge these interests
- To one-to-one marketing wherein products and messages are tailored to the expressed interest of the individual

From the first direct-mail research of the 1920s to computer-driven technology of the Internet, direct-response marketers have been able to refine their identification and outreach more precisely to various customer groups. It was not that many years ago that people were amazed when direct-mail offers addressed customers by name in the body of letters. Now, almost all of them are individually addressed.

At the same time this technological renaissance was taking place, the competitive environment was lessening the distinction among brands, resulting in (1) price competition with shrinking profit margins for sellers and/or (2) a reliance on trusted brands to provide customers with a perception of consistent quality. For example, the local Ford dealer faced with an informed customer armed with the latest dealer invoice information from edmunds.com is faced with a choice of lowering the profit margin or increasing after-sale service. In fact, the dealer probably will have to do

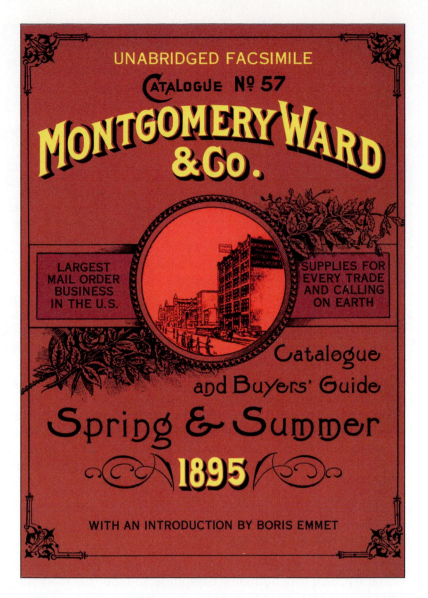

EXHIBIT 13.1

Mail-order catalogs have been thriving for more than one hundred years.

Courtesy of *Montgomery Ward & Co. Catalogue* (1895) 1969. Reprint, New York: Dover.

some of both because a large percentage of car buyers are using the Internet as an information source. According to research conducted by the Polk Center for Automotive Studies, over one-third of first-time car buyers listed the Internet as their most important informational tool compared to 8.2 percent for television, 4.4 percent for magazines, 3.6 percent for newspapers, and 1.1 percent for radio.[1]

Marketers are increasingly asking their marketing communication programs to blend old and new communication strategies. On the one hand, television commercials and other traditional media messages are establishing or maintaining brand visibility and positioning. On the other hand, high brand identity makes contact through e-mail and websites much more effective. Although new technology can reach consumers with interactive media at a time of the prospect's choosing and with messages crafted to meet the needs of each individual, alone it can be difficult to create brand image.[2]

DIRECT RESPONSE AND THE INTERNET

Throughout this text, we offer examples of ways in which the Internet has dramatically changed the way marketers and the media do business. In this section, we discuss other advertising opportunities on the Internet including a look at ways it is being

INTERNET

Rank	Marketer	2005	2004
1	Vonage Holdings Corp.	$275.7	$58.7
2	GUS	166.1	86.5
3	Time Warner	166.1	141.7
4	Dell	156.6	119.5
5	United Online	150.7	82.6
6	Verizon Communications	144.0	124.7
7	Netflix.Com	136.8	170.3
8	TD Ameritrade Holding Corp.	113.8	76.2
9	General Motors Corp.	110.5	66.1
10	Hewlett-Packard Co.	108.0	139.2

used by direct-response firms to promote products and services. We also examine some of the primary concerns facing direct response and its use of new technology.

It is estimated that in 2006 almost 70 percent of U.S. households paid for Internet access.[3] With over 210 million users in the United States, it is not surprising that advertisers are continuing to look for new and better ways to use the medium.[4] As you can see in Exhibit 13.2, the list of the largest Internet advertisers includes online marketers, large corporations such as General Motors, and media conglomerates such as Time Warner. According to a recent research study on advertising industry trends conducted by the American Advertising Federation, more than half of the agency respondents said that they expect to shift at least 20 percent of their television budgets into online video by 2010.[5] Seeing the potential of the Internet as an advertising medium, large advertisers such as McDonald's, Estée Lauder, and General Motors have all used the Internet for branding campaigns as well as for a direct-marketing tool.[6] Online advertising in 2006 was estimated at $16.4 billion and is estimated to grow to $36.5 billion by 2011.[7]

Customer Relationship Management

customer relationship marketing (CRM)
A management concept that organizes a business according to the needs of the consumer.

Customer relationship management or **customer relationship marketing (CRM)** is a core principle of both direct-response and Internet marketing. The concept of CRM should be viewed from both the customer and marketer perspective. From the standpoint of the consumer, it is clear that the audience feels empowered by interactive media and they use this empowerment in a proactive manner. From a lifestyle standpoint, research shows that online audience members use some traditional media less than they did before gaining Internet capability and less than those who are not online. In addition, some audiences, particularly teens and young adults, use the Internet at the same time they are using traditional media.

In addition to media usage, consumers also are embracing online couponing, entering sweepstakes online, and participating in other targeted sales promotion activities. It is not surprising that consumers would respond to targeted promotions tailored to their interests. Likewise, businesses are happy to avoid the expense of waste circulation by reaching this selective audience.

The CRM concept offers several other advantages to businesses. Although sacrificing some control to consumers, marketers are dealing with a much higher percentage of prospects than in mass advertising or even in the direct-response methods used only a few years ago. For example, the combination of sophisticated software and the Internet allows companies to achieve the following:[8]

- More effective cross-selling and upselling from current customers
- Higher customer retention and loyalty
- Higher customer profitability

- Higher response to marketing campaigns
- More effective investment of resources

None of these benefits should be surprising. As a company develops a closer relationship with each of its customers, we would expect that it would use the greater understanding to approach consumers with offers that fit their interests and tastes. The use of interactive technology allows businesses to deal with the unique purchasing, lifestyle, and behavioral histories of each customer. Rather than dealing with statistical aggregations of groups of customer data, a business now has the capability of one-to-one marketing. Communication and product offers can be based on predetermined consumer needs and can be differentiated from similar competitive offers. The end results are that the consumer gains better value and the company engenders continued customer loyalty.[9]

THE INTERNET AND MARKETING RESEARCH

Clearly one of the primary benefits of Internet marketing is the ability to gain information about individual buying habits and product preferences. These data are, of course, collected as part of the consumer transaction process. However, one of the emerging advantages of Internet technology is the ability to collect market research quickly and inexpensively from a larger respondent base than might be possible with conventional research methodology. The Internet allows marketers to reach samples of specific consumers to determine a number of product, marketing, or advertising responses. Instead of being confined to a few locales, a marketer can now sample on a global basis. Even something as relatively simple as getting response data back from product testing is faster and demonstrates higher levels of cooperation than other methods.

The dangers of online testing involve a possible loss of competitive advantage by testing on the Web. In addition, there are questions about samples and perceptions in online testing. An important concern is that online respondents may be different than the general public. There are also troubling questions about whether concepts are graded differently during online surveys. As online transactions become more common and Internet household penetration continues to increase, the differences between online and offline testing will likely diminish.

Privacy Concerns

The same technology that allows marketers to reach consumers on a one-to-one basis is creating major public-relations problems over privacy concerns about the collection and use of personal information. The problem is so great that many observers think that the potential of new technology and online direct response will not be fulfilled until consumers are satisfied about the use and security of personal data.

Marketers are facing a number of concerns about how and under what circumstances they can contact a person online. The debate has created a new vocabulary for online marketers:

- **Spam** refers to unsolicited and usually unwanted online advertisements or promotional messages. *Spammers* are those companies that send these messages.
- **Opt-in** is a form of permission marketing in which online customers are sent messages only after they have established a relationship with a company. The customer may have purchased a product previously from the company or signed up on a company website giving the firm permission to send product announcements or promotional material. Ford Motor Company has an opt-in program known as "The Connection." The online system offers various promotions and discounts to Ford owners. However, only customers who have

spam
Online advertising messages that are usually unsolicited by the recipient.

opt-in
A form of permission marketing in which online customers are sent messages only after they have established a relationship with a company. Only consumers who have granted permission are contacted.

opt-outs
Procedures that recipients
use to notify advertisers
that they no longer wish to
receive advertising
messages. A term usually
associated with online
promotions.

granted permission are contacted and Ford assures them that no information is shared with other companies.

■ **Opt-out** is a mechanism by which customers can notify online promoters that they do not want to receive spam.

A study reported by *Advertising Age* in 2003 showed that 40 percent of online users say that they are angry about e-mail spam and another 58 percent are furious.[10] This number is undoubtedly greater today as spammers have become more clever at fooling spam filters. Congress has considered and passed legislation to limit the use of spam. The direct-marketing industry has come out strongly against e-mail spam. According to H. Robert Wientzen, president and CEO of the Direct Marketing Association (DMA), "It recently occurred to me that spammers are to e-mail users what weeds are to gardeners."[11] In October 2003, the American Association of Advertising Agencies (AAAA), the Association of National Advertisers (ANA), and the DMA worked together to establish a set of nine self-regulatory guidelines to help protect the use of legitimate e-mail marketing. These guidelines encourage members to: [12]

1. Use an honest subject line.
2. Include a valid return e-mail address as well as a physical address for those who wish to contact the company.
3. Clearly identify the subject and the sender at the beginning of the e-mail.
4. Provide a clear and conspicuous e-mail option for consumers to remove themselves from the list.
5. Ensure that electronic name-removal features are prompt and reliable.
6. Offer options for removal of consumers from commercial e-mail lists for each brand or product featured.
7. Not acquire e-mail address through automated systems (i.e., spiders and robots) without the consent of the consumer.
8. Not provide e-mail lists to unrelated third parties for their use.
9. Provide the sender's privacy policy in the body of the e-mail or via a link.

The idea of spam, opt-in, and opt-out seems relatively straightforward. However, specific implementation can be very difficult. For example, the first message in an online promotion is spam—it was unsolicited. Marketers, even the most ethical ones, are pushing to continue to allow mass online messages with the proviso that consumers can then opt out of future communication. (For more Internet and interactive advertising terms, visit the Interactive Advertising Bureau website at www.iab. net/resources/glossary.asp.) Any regulation requiring that consumers give prior permission for every online promotional message could effectively kill many direct-response campaigns. It also is argued that stringent opt-in requirements would work against small companies and new brands by making it more difficult to get their messages to the public. However, consumers are often receptive to e-mail messages when they have opted in to an e-mail list. A survey conducted by the e-mail firm Bigfoot Interactive found that when consumers have opted in to receive regular e-mail from a business, they derive more satisfaction from the relationship than those consumers who did not choose to receive the messages.[13]

In response to growing public concerns, the FTC has launched a number of inquiries about online policies and practices. The FTC advocates four elements for online privacy policies:

1. Disclosure of what information is collected
2. Choice for customers to opt-out

3. Access by consumers to their personal information

4. Security standards for information use and access

Consumers are likely to feel more comfortable doing business with companies that have good consumer privacy policies.

Online as a Complement to Other Media

As discussed in the previous media chapters, for most media categories, including other direct-response media, online seems to serve a complementary rather than competitive role. As evidence of this, next time you flip through a magazine, take note of the number of advertisements that send readers to a company's website for more information or to place an order. (See Exhibit 13.3 for example.)

Television seems to work well with online messages. The medium's high credibility can build brand equity among large groups of prospects very quickly. Television reaches a mass audience in a typical advertising environment of formal

EXHIBIT 13.3

A magazine advertisement can drive customer traffic to a website for more information.

Courtesy of Huey+Partners and Atlanta History Center.

STORM CORPS: Alternative Spring Break 2006
Made Possible by a Grant from
Rebuilding Hope & Homes

THE HOME DEPOT
FOUNDATION
Building Affordable Healthy Homes

EXHIBIT 13.4

Banner advertisements on the Internet must gain attention quickly.

Courtesy of The Home Depot Foundation.

programming interspersed with 30-second commercials. During the same time that a person is viewing a television show, a typical Internet user may have visited five or six websites and the advertising they were exposed to may have been more like outdoor than traditional print or broadcast. Research suggests that many television audience members are surfing the Web at the same time they are "watching" television. This is particularly true of young adult and youth audiences.

Television networks are getting more creative in their use of the Internet and cross-media deals to attract advertisers. In 2006, for example, NBC began an online-only series called *StarTomorrow*. The online audience could view, on demand, episodes of bands trying out to win a record deal with a successful producer. In the style of *American Idol*, viewers cast votes for the people they would like to see move on to the next round. NBC ran a prime-time special on its television network before the show started to promote it to viewers. Nissan signed on as a title sponsor and received a 15-second spot on each Internet video and a prominent placement of its logo on the stage where bands performed. Nissan had banner and display advertisements on the website and a marker on the homepage as well as exposure and product placements on the NBC network in promotion spots.[14]

In 2007, CBS invested in and hired virtual world content developer Electric Sheep Company, the developer of *Second Life* virtual world (www.secondlife.com). CBS filmed a commercial promoting one of its television network shows in *Second Life* and plans to develop several other virtual projects with the company including a *Star Trek*–themed area for CBS inside *Second Life*. CBS Interactive President Quincy Smith said, "We believe that all these virtual worlds represent next generation communications platforms."[15]

Many online promotions must deal with three groups of prospects. The first, and by far the larger, group for most sites consists of surfers and casual users. For these consumers, Web advertising must gain attention quickly if the consumers are going to click a banner or spend time with a commercial message (see Exhibit 13.4). The second group is the entertainment/information-oriented regular users of a site. This group of users is looking for an interactive activity and will return to a website often if it provides them with the entertainment and information they seek. The other group of users consists of those who are actively in the market for a product or service. They are information seekers who may have seen the website in a media advertisement, run across the site on a search engine, or actively sought out a specific site because of familiarity with a brand. In any case, the site should provide relevant, up-to-date product information including price, purchase instructions, warranties, and so forth. If you think about it, the process is much the same for media advertising in which advertisements and commercials first gain awareness and attention for a brand and retailers close the sale. The media-Internet relationship is, in some respects, the same as that of the media and retailers.

Some research has shown that the average online user will not wait very long for a connection before moving to another site. The sheer number of online options has created a level of impatience unseen in other communication technology. The effect of this impatience is a heightened need by companies for brand awareness. Branding accomplishes two goals in the online world:

1. It gains awareness for the website itself. In the early years of online commerce, the Super Bowl might well have been named the "**dot-com**" Bowl given the number of commercials bought during the game by online companies. Some products such as prescription drugs send consumers to their websites to read a full disclosure of the possible negative side effects of their products in order to satisfy FDA requirements.

2. Branding is important for the companies that want high visibility on the Web. Online consumers, like their offline counterparts, will gravitate to companies, products, and brands with which they are familiar. The difference is that the online attention span makes branding more important than ever before.

A number of companies have found that traditional advertising works better than online messages to encourage website visits. As long as this is the case, the complementary relationship between online and traditional media will continue. As one leading online executive pointed out, "At the end of the day, [interactive advertising] is just one more way to communicate with the consumer. It needs to be integrated in everything that an agency does for a brand or a business because treating it as a separate part of the mix ultimately doesn't work."[16]

dot-coms
A generic designation that refers to companies engaged in some type of online commerce.

Global Communication and Branding

The Internet is instant, intrusive, and international. It is a medium with no boundaries; consequently, it presents a challenge to international advertisers. As we discuss in Chapter 23, global companies realize they must adapt to local market conditions, but at the same time it is important for them to maintain a consistent presence and identification if they are to be truly worldwide companies.

Although the Internet presents problems for multinational companies attempting to execute localized strategies on a global basis, it does offer a number of major advantages to them. For example, companies can provide information about their products as well as receive orders from consumers in other countries without incurring additional expense. An example of a service that has benefited from being able to communicate to a broader international audience is higher education. Most colleges and universities in the United States provide information about themselves to an international audience on the Internet. In addition, most of these academic institutions put application materials and forms online, which saves them a great deal of money in materials and mailing costs.

Companies can advertise on search engines such as as Google and Yahoo!, and/or they can pay to receive favorable placement on search engines. Consumers are much more likely to click on the first websites that come up when they do a search than they are to click on the later ones. This can be a great way for smaller companies to get the attention of consumers who are in the market for their particular product or service.

Youth Audiences

The amount of time the Internet is used by audiences varies by age. Teens and young adult audiences who have grown up with the Internet—sometimes referred to as the Internet generation—report spending more time using the Internet than watching television. According to research conducted by Harris Interactive and Teenage Research Unlimited, 13- to 24-year-olds spend 16.7 hours per week online (excluding e-mail) and 13.6 hours watching television. By contrast, they spend only about 12 hours per week listening to the radio, less than 7 hours talking on the phone, and 6 hours reading either books or magazines that are not related to their studies.[17]

Youth audiences report that the control over the content offered by the Internet is the primary reason that they prefer to use the Internet. Teens and young adults are better able than other demographic groups to use more than one form of media at a time, and they often surf the Web while they are watching television.[18] As pointed out by Wendy Harris Millard, chief sales officer for Yahoo!, "Our industry needs to evaluate and change our communications approach to successfully reach this key target market. This generation is a revolutionary consumer group, actively in control and entrenched in their media experience, and their patterns will influence the future of media spending."[19]

Internet Dayparts

As with radio and television, there appear to be distinctive daypart usage patterns on the Internet. According to a study conducted by the Online Publishers Association, there are five distinct Internet dayparts:

1. Early morning (M–F, 6 a.m.–8 a.m.)
2. Daytime (M–F, 8 a.m.–5 p.m.)
3. Evening (M–F, 5 p.m.–11 p.m.)
4. Late night (M–F, 11 p.m.–6 a.m.)
5. Weekends (Sat–Sun, all day)

Although search engines and e-mail appear to have little variation in usage by time of day, content sites experience distinct differences in usage by daypart. Early morning and daytime dayparts have a larger concentration on news and information sites relative to other dayparts. Evening and weekend dayparts show an increased concentration in entertainment and sports sites relative to daytime. In contrast to television, Nielsen//NetRatings reports that daytime has the largest audience in terms of size and number of minutes of usage. However, evening and weekend dayparts are a better time to reach those under the age of 18. Usage of the Internet at work peaks between 10:00 a.m. and noon. At-home usage is the highest between 5:00 p.m. and 9:00 p.m.[20]

EXHIBIT 13.5

Unlike television, Internet usage is highest in the daytime.

Courtesy of Hyunjae Yu.

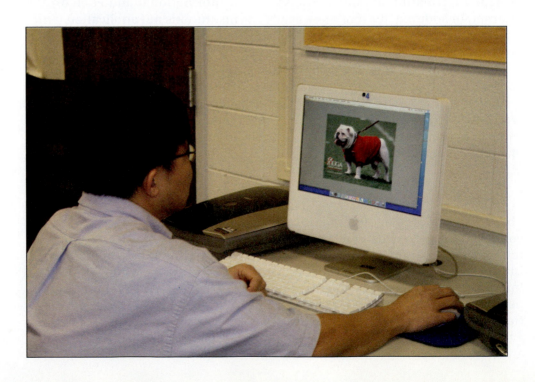

THE WIRELESS AND BROADBAND REVOLUTION

As exciting as the last decade's technological developments have been, most experts think that we have only scratched the surface of the potential for new communication systems. Their optimism is grounded in the possibilities afforded by wireless and broadband technology. Wireless technology allows interactive communication without being wired to a computer. The first phase of the wireless revolution was the cell phone. Today, with Bluetooth technology, a variety of electronic devices including such things as cell phones, computers, PDAs, and game consoles can communicate without being connected with wires. While still in its infancy, the technology is in place that makes the delivery of advertising messages from one Bluetooth device to another. Rather than checking for the nearest Starbucks or a stock quote, we will be able to use a handheld device to receive text messages, redeem coupons, make purchases, and comparison shop.

Cell phones are fast becoming an information tool with access to the Internet. Consumers can check the weather, find movie schedules, locate various retail categories in a particular location, and receive preprogrammed information. For example, if a particular stock drops to a certain level, you can be alerted automatically so that you can place a sale order with your broker—all from a fishing dock in the Bahamas!

As pointed out by Assistant Media Director Sunayana Sarkar of Starcom MediaVest in Kleppner Viewpoint 13.2, understanding and embracing these changes in the media landscape are essential for those who want to work in advertising.

THE ROLE OF THE INTERNET IN ADVERTISING AND MARKETING

From an advertising and marketing perspective, there are a number of uses for the Internet and commercial websites:

1. *As a source of direct sales.* Internet direct sales may be accomplished as stand-alone e-businesses, such as Amazon.com, or as an ancillary to an established business, such as cataloger Crate and Barrel (www.crateandbarrel.com), or as a traditional retailer, such as Home Depot, which augments walk-in traffic with a merchandising website.

2. *As a source of advertising-supported communication.* Virtually every magazine, newspaper, and major broadcast outlet has some Internet presence. Often newspapers or television news programs give their website address at the end of news stories so that interested readers can obtain more in-depth information about a specific story. There also are a number of Internet-only media, such as Salon, that have only Internet audiences. Most of these communication outlets have attempted to be advertising supported, but few have been able to turn a profit from their Internet-only services.

3. *As a source of marketing and promotion information.* Thousands of businesses large and small have established websites to provide product information, enhance stockholder relations, and report current company news. Advertising agencies have scrambled to find a way to service clients' Internet demands effectively. Many major agencies such as Leo Burnett have established separate interactive divisions to offer interactive marketing to clients. Other agencies have integrated online and offline advertising strategies within the traditional advertising agency account team, but this is becoming more rare.

4. *As builders of consumer engagement.* Increasingly, advertisers are finding ways to engage consumers when they visit their websites in attempts to help build

KLEPPNER VIEWPOINT 13.1

Hugh J. Martin, Ph.D.

Associate Professor, Grady College of Journalism & Mass Communication, University of Georgia

Of Search Engines, Ad Prices, and Blind Sales

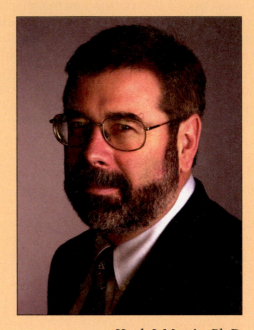

Hugh J. Martin, Ph.D.

A report that Google and Yahoo! are losing ad sales to an upstart might, at first glance, raise doubts about the search giants' understanding of the advertising business. However, a closer look suggests the famously smart people at Google and Yahoo! know exactly what they are doing.

The article in *The New York Times*[*] reports a new company, Quigo Technologies, convinced Fox, ESPN, and Cox Enterprises to abandon the search giants as providers of text advertising. These ads appear beside your search results in response to the words you are searching for.

Quigo, unlike Yahoo! and Google, tells advertisers where ads appear on the Web and allows advertisers to buy ads on specific sites, *The Times* reports.

It may seem odd for search giants to conceal this information because advertisers target people likely to buy their products. So most advertisers want to appear on websites with content that attracts large numbers of people potentially interested in their products—if you sell sporting goods, you want to be on the big sports sites.

How Search Advertising Works

According to *Advertising Age*,[†] the search giants make most of their money from these text ads.

Advertisers buy key words, and their ad appears when those words are typed in a search engine. The advertiser only pays if someone clicks on an ad. Advertisers bid a certain amount for each click, and that determines how often and where their ads appear.

The search giants display the ads on their pages and on innumerable other websites participating in their advertis-

brand connections and to encourage consumers to regularly visit the site. Some products such as the BMW Mini Cooper (www.miniusa.com) have included video games or contests while others have social networks or blogs set up for consumers to interact with each other or with company personnel.

CONSUMER-CONTROLLED ONLINE COMMUNICATION

The big news for advertisers in 2006 was consumer-created content. *Advertising Age*, for the first time, picked the consumer as the advertising agency of the year.[21] Consumers contributed text content on blogs, created videos such as the much-cited "Diet Coke and Mentos Experiment," and spread the word online about this content creating a viral buzz. Advertisers are finding ways to join the trend. The Internet makes it possible for advertisers to run edgier and more consumer-produced content than they would be able to run in the broadcast media. According to advertising guru Stuart Elliot, "Major marketers believe they can take greater risks online because users tend to be younger and more accustomed to irreverent humor. Procter has underwritten

ing programs. The advertiser knows how many clicks it paid for, but not where the clicks came from.

If advertisers knew ads were appearing on sites they want to target, wouldn't they buy even more ads? So why is this information concealed?

Concealing Information Increases Ad Revenues

I am indebted to Roy W. Kenney and Benjamin Klein, authors of a 1983 article in the *Journal of Law and Economics*,§ for this explanation:

Advertisers consider some websites to be better than others. They may be attracted by the large number of sites available through Google and Yahoo, but most advertisers would probably like to select some sites and ignore the rest.

But advertisers cannot select sites, so they must instead estimate the average value of a click from all sites, desired or not. Many people who click on an ad will not buy anything. And sites with small amounts of traffic probably have smaller proportions of buyers among those who do click on ads.

So the best sites will generate large numbers of clicks and many more likely buyers. Another way to think of this is that average sales per click will be much higher on the desirable sites.

If advertisers could identify the desirable sites they would bid more for those, and advertising would be concentrated there. But Google and Yahoo! would be forced to sell ads for much less on the undesirable sites, and their total advertising revenue would decline.

Two Alternatives

What if Google and Yahoo! instead offered to sell advertisers websites in groups—or bundles—and included some less desirable sites in each bundle? Buyers would look for bundles they considered bargains, and only bid for those.

The search giants would be forced to sell ads on the remaining bundles for less than buyers would pay if they did not know what bundle they were getting.

Another alternative would allow buyers to experiment, buying ads on a variety of sites to see which sites produced the best results. Advertisers would make adjustments after their initial purchase, asking the search giants to redirect ads to sites generating the most sales. But this would be costly for the search giants. It would also have the same effects on ad prices and revenues as the other alternatives.

A Change Is (Probably) Gonna Come

The existing arrangements also make it possible for Google and Yahoo! to distribute ads differently than expected. For example, an ad on 1,000 blogs might generate 1,000 clicks, but few buyers. The same ad on a few big news sites might generate the same 1,000 clicks and deliver far more potential buyers. Google and Yahoo! are asking buyers to trust that this is not happening.

The *Times* article also reports some buyers are worried about click fraud. This happens when people click on ads just to generate revenue for the sites where they appear (Google and Yahoo! share some of the revenue with the site).

The article says Google is planning to give advertisers more information about where ads appear. The search giant is feeling competitive heat from companies like Quigo. It will be interesting to see what happens next.

*Louise Story, "An ad upstart forces Google to open up a little," *New York Times*, 26 February 2007, C1.
†Advertising Age, *Search Marketing Fact Pack 2006* (New York: Crain Communications, 2006); available from http://adage.com/images/random/searchfactpack2006.pdf, accessed 4 March 2007.
§Roy W. Kenney and Benjamin Klein, "The economics of block booking," *Journal of Law & Economics* 26, no. 3 (October 1983): 497–540.

viral campaigns for mainstream brands such as Folgers coffee, Crest toothpaste, Febreze fabric spray and ThermaCare heat wraps."[22] Anheuser-Busch created BudTV (www.budtv.com) to provide entertainment content that engages the consumer. One of the first shows, *Finish Our Film*, invited consumers to create the middle story content for a program. The beginning and ending of the program, produced by Matt Damon and Ben Affleck's production company, were posted online.[23]

Many Internet users, particularly teens and young adults, are spending a great deal of time socializing online. What began as e-mails and instant messaging between friends is becoming much bigger with blogging, podcasting, wikis, and the creation of such sites as MySpace, Facebook and YouTube. Investment firm Piper Jaffray has dubbed this type of Internet content consumption "communitainment."[24] Advertisers are taking note of this trend and are trying to find ways to become part of these sites. This must be done in such a way as to engage consumers rather than making them feel as though the advertiser is invading their personal space. In 2006, for example, Nike teamed up with Google to launch a social networking site, http://Joga.com, to help them keep in touch with their young adult consumers.[25] The possibilities for this type of advertising are just beginning to be tapped.

Sunayana Sarkar

Assistant Media Director, Starcom MediaVest Group, New York

Five Tips to Help You Survive Your First Year in a Media Agency

Sunayana Sarkar

1. **Excel in Excel.** Knowledge of MS Excel—knowing how to toggle through a pivot table, import external data or filter through 1000s of rows of data—is critical. It will not only increase your efficiency by reducing the working time on a project, but help you survive when you have to crunch numbers at record speed to answer those urgent questions from your client and supervisors.

   Ability to use MS PowerPoint to create an effective presentation goes a long way too. Always remember that your presentation slides need not have every single sentence outlined. The presentation should be the visual that brings your ideas to life and highlights the key points that you would want your client to take away. Remember that a good presentation can make or break an idea—however good your ideas are, if your client can't visualize them you stand a chance of losing out on a brilliant strategy.

2. **Be a Trend Expert.** While developing target profiles, agencies rely on syndicated research data for demographics and psychographics. But often our own social observations can help in understanding the consumers and developing key targeting insights. For example, it could be as simple as watching teenagers in a mall: how are they dressed, what brands they are buying, what beverages are they drinking, what CDs are they browsing in a music store? Keeping up with the latest news, watching TV, reading magazines and browsing the Internet also help in understanding social phenomena and consumer trends!

3. **Embrace the Changing Media Landscape.** Technology has revolutionized the media landscape. About two decades ago, there were three major television networks, 7000+ radio stations, 2000+ print vehicles. Today the choices are endless and consumers have control—Television offers 7 networks, more than 50 cable networks, 500 channels, digital cable, satellite TV, high definition and Interactive TV. Television is now portable on your mobile phone, I-Pod and is available "on demand" through devices like Digital-Video-Recorder, Video-On-Demand and webcast on your computer. Radio has leapt forward as well—online streaming, Podcasting and Satellite Radio, etc. There are more than 12,000 print vehicles that can be accessed online and even on your mobile phone. The mobile phone is the new powerful medium—a medium in your pocket. It is making possible interactivity that is exponential in comparison with television. Gaming has also emerged in recent years as new media for marketers to reach a captivated audience through in-gaming placement and brand integration. With the increasing household penetration of broadband Internet, consumers will have even more control and user generated content like Blogging, Chats and Social Networking represents a growing opportunity for marketers.

4. **Think Beyond Traditional Flowcharts.** Traditional Media Planning often speaks in terms of "number of on-air-weeks on TV," "reach," "frequency" and "impressions." While these are still a very integral part of any media plan, the focus has moved away from "exposures" to "engagement." The key is to create a strategy that makes an emotional connection with the consumer, captures their attention in a more engaging manner and evokes consumer participation. With the many media choices, consumers are media multi-tasking and marketers have to compete even harder for their attention—requiring them to find creative solutions by creating an engaging experience for the target.

5. **Find a Mentor.** A few agencies proactively assign mentors for recent college graduates who join the company. It is smart to find a mentor at the beginning of your career. It could be someone at work whom you respect and would like to follow in his/her footsteps—someone who has been in the company/industry for some time. Make an appointment with that person, introduce yourself (if they don't know you well), and let him/her know your career goals. Mentors can make a big difference by helping you identify your next steps, giving you an experienced perspective on the important career decisions. ■■■

DIRECT-RESPONSE MARKETING: AN OVERVIEW

Although direct-response marketing has embraced many of the techniques and technologies of interactive media, it would be a mistake to think that traditional means of direct response from direct mail to infomercials are going away in the near future. Direct marketing and advertising will continue to use a number of options to reach consumers and prospects. The next section discusses some of the primary areas of direct response.

Objectives of Direct Response

Most direct-response campaigns have at least one of the following objectives:[26]

1. *Direct orders.* Include all direct-response advertising that is designed to solicit and close a sale. All the information necessary for the prospective buyer to make a decision and complete a transaction is provided in the offer.
2. *Lead generation.* Includes all direct-response advertising that is designed to generate interest in a product and provide the prospective buyer with a means to request additional information about the item or qualify as a sales lead for future follow-up.
3. *Traffic generation.* Includes all direct-response advertising conducted to motivate buyers to visit a business to make a purchase. The advertisement provides detailed information about the product but usually no order form.

Traditional advertising often works in concert with direct response. For example, direct-response advertisements and commercials offering a number of products and services are a major source of revenue for virtually every medium. In addition, direct-response offers, whether by mail or other media, are enhanced by brand advertising that gives consumers confidence to order goods directly.

Major Advantages of Direct Response

Regardless of the means of reaching consumers with direct-response offers, there are a number of characteristics that these approaches have in common:

1. *Direct response is targeted communication.* With the exception of mass media direct response, the advertiser determines exactly who will be reached by the sales message. The copy can be tailored to the demographic, psychographic, and consumption profile of the audience. In addition, both the timing and production of advertising are totally under the control of the advertiser.
2. *Direct response is measurable.* One of the disadvantages of most traditional advertising is that only the results can be estimated. However, in many forms of direct response the results can be computed to the penny. Furthermore, the advertiser is able to measure precisely various messages and other creative alternatives.
3. *The message of direct response is personal.* Whether by mail, media, or computer, the direct-response marketer is able to identify consumers more than ever and reach them with targeted, personalized messages. Many in the direct-response industry think it is only a matter of time before one-to-one advertising will be commonplace.

In part, the growth of direct response is directly attributable to a changing marketplace. We have moved from a manufacturer-driven economy to one that is dominated by huge retailers. In the twenty-first century, we are finding that consumers are increasingly in charge. Home computers and high-speed connectivity are making it practical for consumers to avoid traditional media and

EXHIBIT 13.6
Teens and young adults now spend more time on the Internet than with other media.

Courtesy of Tommy King.

make purchasing decisions on a one-to-one basis with sellers. Soon consumers will no longer be limited by traditional market channels; rather, whether they live in a major city or a remote village, they will have immediate availability to goods and services. This is a marketing environment in which direct response will prosper.

In an environment of increasing accountability for marketing and advertising dollars, direct response can provide measured results. However, because of the expense of much direct response, it is imperative for most direct-response offers to reach a narrowly targeted audience. Many direct-response formats (e.g., mail catalogs, mail-distributed product samples, etc.) can be extremely expensive if directed at nonprospects. On a CPM basis, any type of direct-mail solicitation is much more costly than traditional media exposure. However, a properly executed direct-response campaign will reach a significantly higher percentage of prospects with much less waste circulation than mass advertising. In addition, a major portion of the investment in direct response is intended to create an immediate sale whereas advertising investment is usually only one step in a process of building awareness and brand equity with the hope of leading to a sale sometime in the future.

As we see in this chapter, direct-response advertising takes many forms and is expected to accomplish a number of marketing objectives.

DATABASE MARKETING

The key to successful direct response is a thorough knowledge of each business's customers. This information includes not only consumers' demographic characteristics but also their purchase behavior and their interests and lifestyles. Not long ago, a consumer database consisted largely of basic information about the person, perhaps some information about recent purchases, and a lot of guesswork about what product might be bought next.

Businesses are looking for methods of combining personal information with purchase behavior to predict future purchases and the type of offers and advertising messages that will move an individual to a future purchase. Seeking this information has required marketers to undertake much more sophisticated research and data cross-checking than in previous years. Many refer to this process as *data mining.* Using computer technology, businesses are sorting through large amounts of data to look for new consumer insights, market segments, and patterns of behavior. Data mining attempts to find those characteristics of current customers that relate most meaningfully to prospects. It allows companies to enhance profitability by examining how they have been successful in the past and apply those lessons in the future.

The primary consideration of database marketing is how to use information to predict future purchases. A number of predictive models are being used by businesses. These models are referred to as *behavior maps*, and they allow marketers to combine recent purchasing activity and consumer profiling to offer a relatively accurate picture of what will be purchased in the future and what offers will move that customer to make a purchase. For example, it is senseless for the local video store to offer a "Fifth Movie Free" promotion to a customer who usually rents five movies at a time. "When marketers understand individual purchase patterns, they learn what circumstances, if any, are necessary to spur sales. They also find out which offers may be exercises in futility—before they waste lots of time and money in the discovery process."[27]

In order to accomplish behavior mapping and other sophisticated consumer purchasing identification methods, consumer data must be managed centrally. This need for data management has led to the development of *data warehouses*, which are centralized companywide data storage and retrieval systems.

The ACME Catalog Company has the following information on a customer:

Jane I. Buyer, married, 39, two children: boy 7, girl 9

Lives in an affluent ZIP Code

Address: 677 Brookhaven Dr., Evanston—June 1998–present

101 Sunny Lane, Chicago—April 1994–June 1998

44 Olive Blvd., Miami—May 1991–March 1994

777 Main St., St. Louis—Sept. 1989–May 1991

Purchases from ACME:	Crystal glasses	$210	5/12/01
	Man's leather jacket	340	9/22/01
	Woman's sweater	99	4/11/00
	Snow skis	233	3/25/00
	Desk set	49	12/10/99
	Dress	98	12/10/99
	Perfume	124	10/4/98
	Diamond bracelet	750	8/3/98

From this very simple database example, you can tell several things about the customer. She comes from an upwardly mobile household and, judging by the items she purchases, she has reasonably high levels of discretionary income. From a marketing standpoint, she does not purchase children's items from ACME. (Is she a potential customer for these items?) The most troubling part of the data is that she has not made a purchase for some time. Should ACME make a special offer to renew the relationship or contact her by phone or by e-mail? We know that keeping her as a customer will be much less expensive than gaining a new customer with her profit potential.

The key to CRM and the benefits of database marketing is to provide information that allows a company to maintain the loyalty (and profitability) of its customers. The primary element in data mining is that the end result is a relationship that is beneficial to both the company and the consumer.

THE DIRECT-RESPONSE INDUSTRY

The direct-response advertising industry has grown dramatically in the last 20 years, and this growth is likely to continue. This growth was fueled in part by Internet advertising; however, there are many other forms of direct response including catalogs, inserts, coupons, direct television and radio, and direct mail. This section reviews some of the key forms of direct response and discusses some of the opportunities and challenges they present.

Television and Direct-Response Marketing

Like all television advertising, direct response has the advantage of sight, sound, and motion, coupled with toll-free 800 numbers and/or Internet ordering capability to make it a seamless sales process. Television direct response also has benefited from the growth of cable outlets, which offer firms a number of additional options to use the medium for direct selling.

Direct-response television (DRTV) comes in a variety of formats, but the most familiar are the short-form spot (30 seconds to 2 minutes) and the program-length infomercial. With the linkage of traditional television and the Internet or toll-free calling, television is becoming more and more a primary direct-response medium. The convergence of the Internet and television is moving us one step closer to interactive television, as discussed in Chapter 8. DRTV marketers are designing their messages with a twofold purpose: (1) immediate sales response and (2) bringing prospects to a company's website in order to have them bookmark the site and become regular customers. The most used forms of DRTV are the following:

- *The traditional 30-second format with a tagline allowing consumers to order merchandise.* With DRTV being combined with Internet selling, this format is becoming increasingly popular, especially with well-known products and brands with established demand. This traditional advertising commercial format can be fairly expensive relative to the number of sales leads it generates.
- *The 2- or 3-minute commercial.* This longer spot usually has problems gaining clearance during peak periods and, consequently, most often is scheduled in fringe-time programming such as late-night movies. The format has the advantage of allowing more sales time and an opportunity for information about ordering the product.

infomercial
Long-form television advertising that promotes products within the context of a program-length commercial.

- *The infomercial.* In the last decade, the **infomercial** has become a multibillion-dollar advertising format. Utilizing well-known personalities, slick production techniques, and blanket coverage during certain dayparts, the infomercial has created a number of legendary product success stories. However, with the advent of various forms of interactive and convergent technology, it remains to be seen whether infomercials will continue to be as prevalent in the future.

Regardless of its format, DRTV has certain inherent advantages as an advertising tool:[28]

1. It shows the product in use and provides opportunities for product demonstrations in realistic circumstances.
2. DRTV can create excitement for a product. For example, *Sports Illustrated* has used sports clips for what would otherwise be an advertisement for a static magazine.
3. DRTV offers immediate results. Within 15 minutes of a commercial spot, a company will receive 75 percent of its orders.
4. Because most DRTV spots are not time sensitive, they can be scheduled in fringe dayparts for significant discounts. In addition, production costs of most DRTV are less than traditional television commercials.

5. DRTV complements retail sales. For generally distributed products, businesses find that they sell as many as eight units at retail for every one ordered through direct response.

6. DRTV is a great technique for testing various product benefits and measuring sales response.

Direct-response advertising is sold both on a paid and **per inquiry (PI)** basis. In fact, with the competitive environment so prevalent in the broadcast area, PI is relatively common in television, especially in fringe time. Basically, PI advertisers share their risk with a television station or cable channel. There are no initial costs for time, but the television outlet will divide the profits (if any) when the orders come in. PI advertising can be very beneficial, especially to companies with good products but little capital.

per inquiry (PI)
Advertising time or space for which medium is paid on a per-response-received basis.

Television Shopping Networks

The logical extension of long-form infomercials is an entire network devoted to selling. Home shopping channels have been a major source of product sales for the past decade. It is not unusual to see name-brand merchandise being sold on QVC or the Home Shopping Network and a diverse group of celebrities appearing to sell products such as dolls, sports memorabilia, and jewelry. A number of major retailers and designers use home shopping networks to sell their products to this niche consumer market.

Although home shopping has grown significantly in recent years, the executives involved in these ventures see the full potential for home shopping being in interactive systems. The most optimistic proponents of shopping networks predict that they will change retailing fundamentally in the next two decades. Some experts estimate that sometime in the next 20 years traditional retailing will all but be replaced by interactive home shopping. Of course, we have seen similar predictions for the Internet in recent years. Nevertheless, there is little question that these networks will continue to grow and occupy a larger place in general retailing.

Radio and Direct Response

Radio, despite its targeted audiences and niche programming, has not been a major player in direct-response marketing. Traditional radio has suffered from its lack of visualization. Radio is deficient in many of the elements so familiar to direct response in other media. Radio cannot show a product, no coupons can be provided, and a toll-free number cannot be flashed on a screen.

As discussed in Chapter 9, all of this may change with the growth of streaming audio. With the introduction of computer-based audio programming, an advertiser can incorporate all the missing elements of traditional radio in this new convergent medium. As in the case with interactive television, electronic coupons can pop on the screen; offers can not only be seen along with the music but also downloaded at the request of the listener; and, with database technology, listeners can be prompted about products that fit their consumer profiles.

While the economic promise of "visual" radio is in the near future, for the present, radio can serve as a valuable supplement for a variety of direct-response marketers. The combination of low commercial rates and tightly targeted audience composition makes possible high frequency to saturate prime prospects. Even with the competition from other forms of direct response, radio can continue as a niche medium for direct-response marketing. For example, it can be fairly effective at delivering 800 numbers and Web addresses to potential customers.

Per inquiry also makes radio a bargain for many direct-response advertisers. Radio stations often find that PI advertising is a means of moving unsold commercial inventory. With the number of stations and commercial spots available, it is almost impossible for even the most prosperous stations to sell all of their time. Unsold inventory can be especially acute during certain months such as the after-Christmas period. Rather than using this time for public service announcements or station promotions, the sales manager may be willing to run PI spots at significant discounts.

Magazines and Direct Response

Magazines provide a targeted medium for a number of direct-response advertisers. As discussed in Chapter 11, the success of most magazines depends on their ability to reach a targeted group of readers with common interests, demographics, or vocations. It is in the area of business and trade publications that direct response is especially important. Magazines with editorial objectives geared specifically toward some particular business or profession can be extremely beneficial for direct-response marketers. In the business press, the majority of direct-response messages are attempting to gain leads for personal salespersons and telemarketers or are being used as a means of follow-up.

Despite the importance placed on business-to-business magazine direct response, consumer magazines also can provide an important means of reaching prospects. You only have to look in the back of many major publications to find lengthy classified sections offering a number of direct-response products. In addition, the majority of regular magazine advertisements carry some form of direct response either to provide additional information to consumers or to provide opportunities for direct orders.

Many of the magazine characteristics we discussed in Chapter 11 are of primary importance to direct-response advertisers. Audience selectivity, combined with high reach among prospects who are not heavy users of other media (especially television), makes magazines ideal for many direct marketers. Magazines also appeal to a number of major advertisers because of the prestige associated with national publications. Magazine direct response provides the intimacy of direct response with the traditional advertising virtues of magazines.

Catalogs

One of the oldest and most popular forms of direct-response selling is the catalog. The use of catalogs dates at least to 1498 when Aldus Manutius published his book catalog containing fifteen titles. Since its humble beginnings, the catalog has become a keystone of direct marketing. As early as 1830, New England companies were selling fishing and camping supplies by mail. By the end of the 1800s, both Sears, Roebuck and Co. and Montgomery Ward brought retail merchandise to every household in the country through their catalogs. By 1904, Montgomery Ward was mailing more than 3 million catalogs to potential customers in the United States. Consumers could even buy homes through catalogs. Sears, Roebuck and Company sold more than 100,000 homes by catalog from 1908 to 1940.[29]

Today, the catalog industry is facing many of the uncertainties and challenges of other forms of marketing and advertising. The role of the Internet has huge potential for the industry, and many in the industry see the need to make important long-term decisions regarding how interactive media will fit into their future. Whether the Internet is a curse or an opportunity is in the eye of the beholder.

The role of the Internet is a major question for catalogers that mail billions of catalogs each year. However, it is only one of the several challenges facing traditional catalog sales companies. Another challenge is presented by the

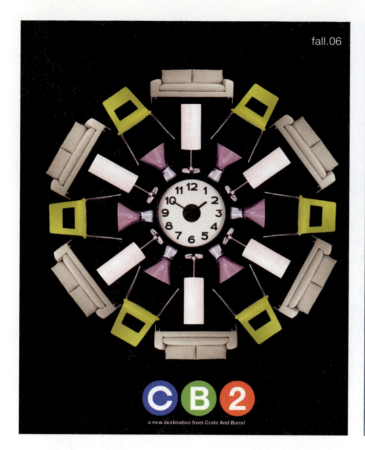

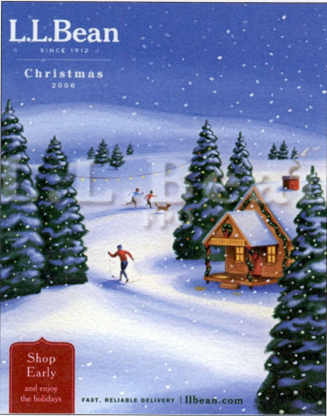

increasing number of companies, including mainline retailers such as Nordstrom and Gap, that are going into either catalog sales or Internet sales or, in many cases, both. The growing number of catalogs has significantly increased the players in an already crowded field. Some—like L.L. Bean, the longtime marketer of outdoor gear and clothing—have reacted to competition from mainline retailers by opening new retail stores themselves. Since 1998, Bean has expanded from one headquarters outlet in Freeport, Maine, to a number of retail sites.

At the same time, virtually every cataloger has gone into Internet selling. Many traditional catalogers such as Lands' End see a number of benefits in e-commerce. Online systems are able to adjust to changing trends in merchandising or weather. For example, if a particular winter proves milder than usual, a company may change its focus to lightweight outerwear. The Internet may offer catalog companies relief from catalog-related production and postage costs that account for a large percentage of their total operating costs. Catalog companies realize that the Internet, traditional brand advertising, and the core catalog are all part of multiple channels that must work together to reach consumers. Different customers prefer different channels, and the same customers will use various channels at different times. Earlier, we discussed data warehouses. Catalogers must embrace the concept of the data warehouse as they integrate information into a single transaction history regardless of what channels a customer uses.

As catalogers move into online options, they are finding that their basic marketing techniques must adapt to these new channels. One of the primary challenges is to deal with the customer-controlled online environment and to find ways to encourage prospect visits to a cataloger's website. Catalog companies find that there are fundamental differences between online and offline selling. For example, "Paper catalogs are intrusive by nature, online catalogs are passive by nature. Once businesses understand this fundamental limitation of e-cataloging, they can become creative in the ways that generate more traffic and, importantly, more sales, through the Web."[30]

Regardless of the channel(s) used by a catalog seller to reach prospects and customers, there are a number of keys to the successful process of moving a person from a prospect to a buyer:

1. *The right product.* As with any product or service, the selling process must begin with merchandise that appeals to consumers. Quality, price, consumer benefits, and range of merchandise are all elements in successful selling. However, catalogers often find that an added consideration is uniqueness of products. Generally, catalog sellers have a difficult time moving merchandise that is easily obtainable at retail outlets. Product differentiation is always important, but doubly so for catalog products.

2. *Exciting creative execution.* Remember that the customer can't try on clothes, handle camping gear, or sample a food item. The sales story has to be conveyed in attention-getting messages that grab the imagination of the reader.

3. *Reach a targeted group of prospects.* No element of direct selling is more important than the prospect list. Waste circulation is even more expensive in direct marketing than in other forms of promotion, and every effort has to be made to keep it to a minimum.

4. *Fulfillment and customer service.* Nothing will kill a catalog company faster than a reputation for faulty customer service. The process begins with knowledgeable customer representatives; then the right merchandise must be shipped promptly; and finally, when mistakes are made, they need to be dealt with fairly and quickly.

5. *The process of successful selling doesn't end with a single purchase.* Catalogers must establish a means of database management that will allow product inventory management as well as a means of determining the quality of customers on a lifetime value basis.

DIRECT-MAIL ADVERTISING

Despite recent competition from e-mail, telemarketing, and other direct-marketing options, direct mail remains a primary advertising vehicle. More than $55 billion is spent on direct-mail advertising, which represents about 20 percent of estimated advertising expenditures in the United States.[31] Because of the rising expenses associated with direct mail, it is anticipated that direct mail's share of direct-response advertising will decrease in the future. However, it remains an important direct-response advertising tool.

One of the problems facing direct mail is that the sheer volume of mail coming to households makes gaining a competitive advantage very difficult. Clearly, the number of mailing pieces combined with the "junk mail" perception held by many people is a challenge for direct mailers. This challenge is all the more reason that direct mailers must take steps to reach targeted prospects with an interesting message and a worthwhile product (see Exhibit 13.8). Assuming that a business has a quality product and a competitive offer, the success of direct mail usually hinges on the mailing list.

In direct mail, the advertiser determines the circulation. The list is the media plan of direct mail. Just as the media planner must carefully analyze the audiences

EXHIBIT **13.8**

It is important to get direct-mail pieces into the hands of real prospects.

Courtesy of Georgia Higher Education Savings Plan.

of the various vehicles that will make up the final media schedule, the advertiser must carefully choose the list(s) that will provide the greatest number of prospects at the lowest cost. Most lists are compiled lists; that is, they are developed from a number of existing sources. The problem for the direct-mail advertiser is developing these names into a single list and then fine-tuning it for accuracy, nonduplication, and so forth.

There are a number of organizations that are involved in the direct-mail list process:

- *List brokers.* Some of the key figures in direct mail are **list brokers**. Brokers function as liaisons between mailers who need lists of particular target prospects and those with lists to rent. The primary functions of list brokers include determining the availability of appropriate lists, negotiating with list owners on behalf of their clients, and offering general marketing advice. The list broker is generally paid a commission of approximately 20 percent by list owners.
- *List compilers.* The list compiler is usually a broker who obtains a number of lists from published sources and combines them into a single list and then

list broker
In direct-mail advertising, an agent who rents the prospect lists of one advertiser to another advertiser. The broker receives a commission from the seller for this service.

rents them to advertisers. The first format list compiler is considered to be Charles Groves, superintendent of Michigan City schools. In the late 1800s, he compiled lists of teachers by writing to other school superintendents around the country. He then sold the lists to textbook publishers and other companies wanting to reach teachers.[32] Compilers tend to specialize in either consumer or business lists, although a few do both.

list manager
Promotes client's lists to potential renters and buyers.

■ *List managers.* The **list manager** represents the list owner just as the broker is the agency for the mailer. The primary job of the list manager is to maximize income for the list owner by promoting the list to as many advertisers as possible. List managers are usually outside consultants, but some large companies have in-house list managers. Most national magazines, DVD clubs, and other direct marketers offer their lists for rent. These lists are ideal direct-response vehicles because most have been accumulated through sales to narrowly defined, specialized audiences. They also have the benefit of providing prospects who are proven direct-mail buyers.

merge/purge
A system used to eliminate duplication by direct-response advertisers who use different mailing lists for the same mailing. Mailing lists are sent to a central merge/purge office that electronically picks out duplicate names. Saves mailing costs, especially important to firms that send out a million pieces in one mailing. Also avoids damage to the goodwill of the public.

■ *Service bureaus.* Service bureaus engage in a number of functions. One of the primary jobs of the service bureau is to improve the quality of lists. This function is called list enhancement, which includes a number of steps. One of the most important is known as **merge/purge**. Basically, merge/purge systems eliminate duplicate names from a list. Such duplication is costly to the advertiser and annoying to the customer. For example, duplicate mailings offset any personal contact with the customer by portraying the message as a mass mailing—and one done with little care. Merge/purge is accomplished by computers that are so sophisticated that names are cross-checked against the same addresses and similar spellings.

lettershop
A firm that not only addresses the mailing envelope but also is mechanically equipped to insert material, seal and stamp envelopes, and deliver them to the post office according to mailing requirements.

■ *Lettershop.* The **lettershop** is in reality a mailing house. These companies coordinate the job of mailing millions of pieces of mail, from printing labels to keeping abreast of the latest postal regulations. Large lettershops even have a representative of the U.S. Postal Service on the premises to work with every aspect of the delivery of mail in a timely fashion.

response lists
Prospects who have previously responded to direct-mail offers.

■ *Response lists.* The majority of mailings are sent to people on existing lists. However, a number of mailing-list houses sell or rent lists of people who have responded previously to a direct-mail offer or demonstrated some interest in doing so. People on **response lists** are those who are prone to order by mail; therefore, these lists are more productive than compiled lists and the rental charges are higher than for compiled lists. By combining response and compiled lists, a mailer can reach both previous customers and a larger pool of prospective customers.

Response lists are often obtained from previous customers of a company (see Exhibit 13.9). These are called *house lists* and are among the most valuable commodities of a direct mailer. Owners of house lists rent their lists to non-competing companies, and they are often a major source of revenue. Advertisers can find an endless number of response lists of people who have gone on cruises, hunted specific animals, or have bought books on psycho-analysis in the past 6 months.

List Protection

Because mailing lists are so valuable, companies go to great lengths to protect them from misuse. The most common list abuse is multiple mailings beyond an agreed-upon limit. For example, one direct mailer reported that a company rented its list on a one-time basis and used it thirteen times.

EXHIBIT 13.9

Retailers can use direct mail to help bring customers to their stores.

Copyright of Homer TLC, Inc.

The traditional protection for such misuse is to include a number of fictitious names so that the list owner can trace the number of mailings. This is known as *list decoying*. In addition to protecting the list itself, list renters should also ask for a sample of the mailing material. Occasionally, a mailing may be in bad taste or contain a deceptive offer. However, the much greater problem is that the mailing offer may be too closely competitive with the list owner's products. Renting a list should provide additional profit, not additional competition!

Testing Direct-Mail Advertising

In 1926, Claude Hopkins published *Scientific Advertising*, which many advertisers credit with providing the foundation of formal advertising research. Hopkins based his findings on the results of direct-mail and direct-response offers, and testing and research remain a core element of modern direct-mail advertising. The key elements in testing direct mail are the list, the offer (or featured consumer benefit), and the creative presentation.

Let's look at some examples of the type of elements most commonly tested in direct mail:

1. *List tests:*
   Various list sources including response lists
   Demographic segments
   Geographic segments
2. *Offer tests:*
   Guarantee wording
   Free-trial, send-no-money-now offers
   Use of incentives
3. *Format tests:*
   Single mailing versus series
   Window versus closed envelope
   Live postage versus meter
   Envelope size
4. *Copy tests:*
   Personalization
   Letter length
   Use of testimonial
   Various opening paragraphs
5. *Layout and design tests:*
   Photographs versus line art
   Four color versus one or two color
   Type size and font
   Product alone or with models

Direct-mail testing can be expensive so it is important to concentrate on major elements that normally determine the success or failure of a mail campaign (see Exhibit 13.10). It is extremely crucial to research validity to test only one element at a time. Too many mailers try to cut corners by testing several items in a single mailing. Obviously, if you change the format, the mailing list, and the offer, it is impossible to determine what factor created any changes in test results.

Other Direct-Mail Techniques

Because of the expense of stand-alone direct mail, many advertisers are looking at alternative means of distribution of their sales pieces. Some of the primary print alternatives are the following:

- *Package inserts.* A number of companies will allow the insertion of sales messages when they ship merchandise. These messages, called *bounce-back circulars*, are delivered to customers who are proven direct-marketing users. In addition, the cost is much less than solo mailings because the sales message is being delivered as part of another package. Generally, package inserts are limited to five offers.

EXHIBIT 13.10
Photos and artwork in direct-mail pieces can be tested.
Courtesy of McRae Communications, AAA Atlanta Council, and Creativity Atlanta.

■ *Ride-alongs.* A form of package inserts is the ride-along, which is included in a company's own packages. **Ride-alongs** have many of the same advantages of package inserts except they are going to a company's loyal customers with whom a company has a proven and recent sales relationship. Depending on the product, ride-alongs can be extremely profitable because the overhead is so low.

■ *Statement stuffers.* Few companies miss an opportunity to include a message with your monthly bill. The idea behind statement stuffers is the same as ride-alongs, and they have several advantages. First, they cost nothing to deliver because the mailing expense is going to be incurred in any case. Second, they are at least seen, because everyone eventually gets around to opening their bills. Finally, most recipients are credit qualified and have already dealt with the company before or they would not be getting a statement.

■ *Ticket jackets.* A popular form of ride-along is promotions on airline, bus line, or train ticket jackets. Companies such as car rental firms find that ticket jackets are an ideal way to reach their prime target audiences.

■ *Cooperative (joint) mail advertising.* With the cost of postage continuing to increase, direct mailers often attempt to share expenses through cooperative mailings. A number of firms specialize in joint mailings. These mailings may include as many as twenty different advertising offers in one envelope. Each

ride-alongs
Direct mail pieces that are sent with other mailings, such as bills.

advertiser provides a coupon or other short message, and the joint mailer handles the mailing and divides the cost among the advertisers.

Cooperative mailings have two major drawbacks. First, they are extremely impersonal because each advertiser's message must be very short. Second, it is difficult to reach specific customers through joint mailings with the same precision that marketers would have with their own lists. The dilemma of joint mailings is that as the number of participating advertisers increases, the cost per advertiser goes down, but, likewise, the unique feature of the mailing decreases.

The use of inserts is big business and is growing as the cost of postage increases. It is estimated that as many as 25 billion inserts are distributed in various venues. The insert's position as an alternative "medium" can be demonstrated in the number of sources that are seeking to track the advertising options available to advertisers. For example, both SRDS and the DMA's Alternative Response Media Council have devoted resources to tracking the choices open to advertisers in placing inserts.

SUMMARY ✿

Direct-response marketing is targeted, personal, and measurable. In an era of increasing accountability, these traits have moved it center stage as a means of reaching and selling to a diverse universe of consumers. In terms of sales produced and expenditures, it represents more dollars than all other forms of advertising combined. It is rare for a company not to include direct marketing and direct-response advertising as major elements in its marketing mix. Companies have come to realize that the ability to combine personal messages with highly selective audience segmentation gives direct response advantages seen in few other media. The tremendous strides in computer technology have made the future of direct response both exciting and uncertain.

While not all forms of Internet advertising are direct response, the emergence of the Internet has given a new focus to many of the practices of direct marketing. The Internet and other forms of interactive media are changing the landscape of marketing dramatically. The challenge is to make the obvious advantages of e-commerce profitable for general selling and take advantage of the ability of this interactive medium to engage the consumer.

Regardless of the channel that direct response uses, its flexibility makes it practical for virtually every advertiser. In addition, the ability to test and verify direct marketing is vitally important in the current era of accountability and measured results. Not only does measurement of direct response provide a major advantage to advertisers, but it also creates the type of audience databases so valuable to companies in all their advertising, marketing, and promotion endeavors.

There is little question that direct advertising will continue to outpace most other forms of media advertising. Not only will direct response become more important in the marketing plans of many companies, but also because of its influence even more sophisticated forms of audience segmentation will emerge in the future. History will probably mark the 1990s as the end of the era of mass media and mass audience delivery. In the future, even the one-to-one communication of today will slowly give way to some form of interactive media. There is little question that direct response will play a major role in this transition.

In addition to the technological advances of direct-response advertising, societal changes also are working in its favor. For example, the two-income family, working mothers, an aging population, and less leisure time are only a few of the factors leading people to favor in-home buying. Greater demand and customer acceptability of direct response are pushing more companies to enter the field.

Perhaps the greatest challenge facing direct marketing is public skepticism, especially concerns over privacy issues. However, industrywide efforts sponsored by the Direct Marketing Association and other organizations have made great strides in improving the industry's image. The fact that most *Fortune* 500 companies routinely include some form of direct marketing in their promotional plans is testimony to its growing respectability among advertisers and improved credibility among consumers. Nevertheless, the industry is aware that legislation affecting its operation is constantly being introduced and presents a threat to future growth.

REVIEW ⚙

1. What have been some of the major factors causing the growth of direct-response advertising?
2. What is direct marketing?
3. What steps have been taken to improve the image of direct-response advertising?
4. What role does database marketing play in direct-response advertising?
5. What is the key element in direct mail?
6. What is the function of a list compiler?
7. What is the fulfillment function?
8. What is the difference between a list broker and a list manager?

TAKE IT TO THE WEB ⚙

Would you feel comfortable using your credit card to make an online purchase? Visit Amazon.com (www.amazon.com) and Barnes & Noble (www.bn.com) and review their privacy policies and terms-of-use agreements.

The J. Crew clothing company has traditionally been known for catalog sales. Visit the website (www.jcrew.com) to see how J. Crew has adapted to encourage online sales.

Almost every business you can think of has an Internet address. Visit Target at www.target.com and, from the generic to specific, list the benefits of an online store. Are there items you would never order online?

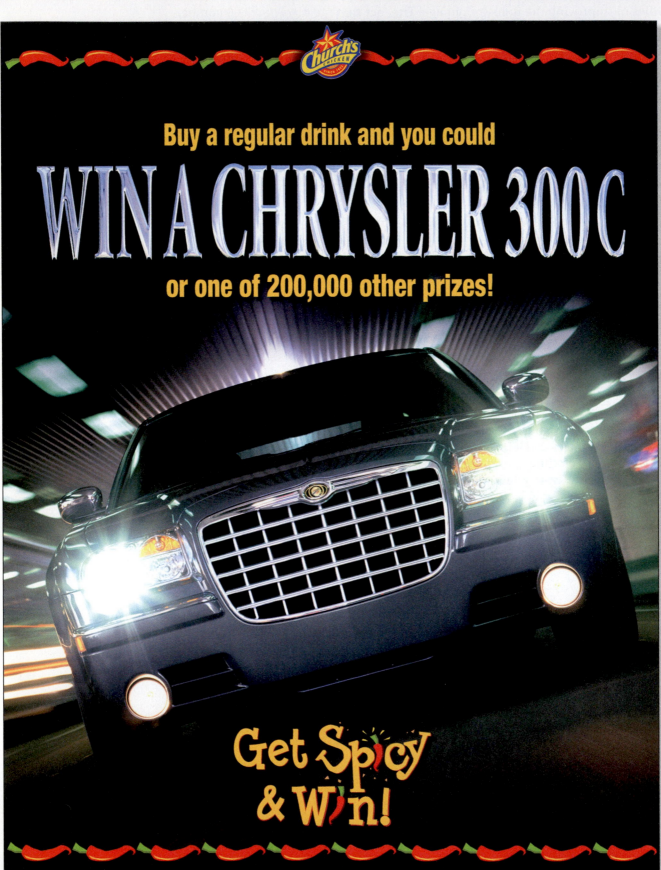

CHAPTER 14

Sales Promotion

Today's promotions are crafted toward achieving a specific result within the overall marketing of a product or service. In other words, to achieve successful promotions you must know the desired result *and* understand the marketing context within which this goal is being sought.

In this chapter, you will explore the most common goals used within the promotion industry to achieve promotion excellence. After reading this chapter, you will understand:

chapter objectives

1. the complementary roles of sales promotion and advertising
2. the various formats and executions of sales promotion
3. uses of sales promotion as consumer and trade incentives
4. current trends in sales promotion
5. the major reasons for the growth of sales promotion

Pros

1. Sales promotion provides a means of encouraging consumer sales response.
2. Sales promotion is extremely flexible with a number of techniques to reach consumers across demographic and lifestyle categories. There are few product categories that cannot benefit from some form of sales promotion.
3. Sales promotion functions at both the consumer and trade levels to encourage high levels of distribution and goodwill with the distribution channel.

Cons

1. If not executed properly, sales promotion can damage brand equity by replacing the image of a product with price competition.
2. Because of the variety of formats and techniques of promotion, care must be taken to coordinate the various messages of advertising and sales promotion. High levels of promotion demand some form of integrated marketing communication if the company is to speak with a single "voice."
3. Some forms of promotion such as couponing have become so prevalent that they no longer provide a competitive differentiation for a brand and, in fact, may become a consumer expectation rather than a temporary sales boost.

Traditional sales promotion has been considered an activity that offers customers, salespeople, or resellers a direct inducement for purchasing a product. And it still does. However, promotion may be more than a sales inducement today. As marketing communicators' tools have changed and the goal of integrated communications has evolved, the definition has broadened. Momentum, a global promotion company, says it moves "brand-in-mind" to "brand-in-hand" by using core disciplines such as event marketing, promotional and retail marketing, and sponsorships. WPP Group's classification of services lumps "direct, promotional and relationship marketing" together. Other companies also talk about adding brand value through promotion—about creating communications with a compelling sales stimulus and building promotional campaigns that build market share and executions that increase brand value. These ideas aren't really in conflict. They are actually holistic because integrated marketing is concerned with—to use Ogilvy's 360-degree branding model—every point of contact building the brand—including promotion. New technology is changing marketers' ability to communicate—from using in-store television networks to text messaging. We've talked about many of these technologies in the media chapters.

TRANSACTIONAL AND RELATIONAL PROMOTION

High-profile marketer Craig McAnsh believes experience has shown that promotion is primarily used to accomplish results across two main categories: *transactional* and *relationship*. As the names imply, *transactional* promotional tactics are associated with the actual purchase of a product or service or a visit to a distributor/retailer, whereas *relationship* tactics are focused on the customer's relationship with the product, service, or distributor/retailer. Understanding the differences between these two strategic uses of promotion is significant as we work toward identifying what makes a promotion excellent.

Transactional Promotion

Loss leaders, money-off coupons, and price rollbacks are all effective ways to execute a discount promotion. These tactics become excellent when their implementation is well branded and simple and meets the right customer motivation thresholds.

Value-added promotional tactics include (among many other tactics) gift with purchase, two for one, percentage more free, free delivery, and toys in cereal boxes. Because even getting the *chance* to receive something free is an added value, sweepstakes and contests fall into this category as well. Promotion excellence occurs when the presentation of the value being added is simple, fits the brand image and target audience, and is the *perfect* amount to drive the sale without impacting long-term profitability of the business. If the promotion tactic helps redefine an entire industry, that's good, too.

The Church's Kids' Meal is an example of a value-added promotion in which the promotion became the product. The Kids' Meal—and the free toy inside cereal boxes—has become one of the most iconic examples of value-added promotion (see Exhibit 14.1).

One of the primary reasons for the consistent and pervasive use of discounting and value-added tactics is that their success or failure is immediate and measurable. Old-school marketers still feel that direct and immediate results are the only reasons to use promotions. Savvy marketing professionals utilize innovative promotional strategies to achieve a variety of results beyond transactions.

Relational Promotion

Relationship-building promotions are becoming more popular because traditional (i.e., one-way) communication has reached the point of oversaturation. Traditional

EXHIBIT **14.1**

The free four collectable Icky Stickies are a Kids' Meal promotion.

Courtesy of The Botsford Group and Church's.

marketing messaging has been applied to every possible media vehicle from television to fruit to bathroom walls. The Internet has been firing messages at consumers in all sorts of creative ways—e-mail spamming, adver-gaming, pop-up windows, banners, links, chat room infiltration, search engine optimization, and literally hundreds of other variations.

Connecting with the consumer is the goal of relationship promotional strategies. There are four stages of connection within relationship-building promotional strategies. Each of these relationship stages is important at some point in the life cycle of a brand (remember our discussion in Chapter 3).

Introductions are the first stage in building a relationship. This is when promotion is used to develop awareness for a product, service, or distributor/retailer. First impressions are very important in establishing company-to-consumer relationships because you don't often get a second chance. These promotional introductions should be infused with your product or service brand personality. Publicity, street marketing, and even cross-promotion are very simple promotional tactics employed to make introductions that are direct and personal.

We all come into contact with numerous examples of **sales promotion** each day. The various forms of sales promotion remind us of brands and persuade us to make purchases in subtle ways that often make little or no conscious impression. When you turn the page on the Chick-fil-A calendar, not only do you see their name but you have the opportunity to take advantge of the value coupons (see Exhibit 14.2). When technical support managers tee up their golf balls given to them by their computer vendor, they are reminded of the vendor's services. And when doctors write prescriptions with the pen left behind by the pharmaceutical rep, a particular drug is being promoted. All of these items and thousands more are examples of sales promotion.

sales promotion
(1) Sales activities that supplement both personal selling and marketing, coordinate the two, and help to make them effective. For example, displays are sales promotions. (2) More loosely, the combination of personal selling, advertising, and all supplementary selling activities.

EXHIBIT **14.2**

The Chick-fil-A calendar offers more than just a calendar and coupons.

Courtesy of Chick-fil-A.

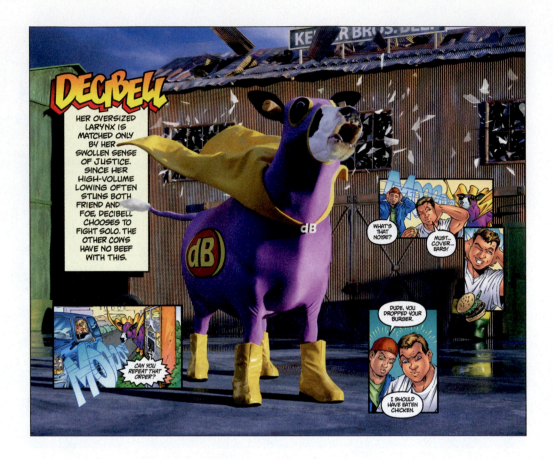

A LITTLE BACKGROUND

Before we talk about promotion tactics, let's review where we came from. Many sales promotion techniques were well established by 1900, but they often consisted of gimmicks and trinket give-aways rather than the well-planned promotional campaigns we see today. However, many modern methods of sales promotion were initiated by retailers and manufacturers of the nineteenth century. In 1895, both Asa Candler and C. W. Post were offering coupons for free Coca-Colas and reduced prices on boxes of Grape-Nuts cereal. At the same time, Adolphus Busch was promoting his beer with free samples; lithographs of "Custer's Last Stand"; and red, blue, and gold pocket knives. By 1912, Kellogg's was including rag dolls, cartoons, and spoons in its cereal boxes.

These and the other forerunners of modern sales promotion recognized that brands need attention and differentiation to gain sales and that customers react positively to extra incentives when making purchase decisions. Sales promotion provided both. What most sales promotion of the period failed to do was complement a company's overall marketing program and provide long-term strategies for brand building. In fact, on occasion the give-aways and promotions overshadowed the product. A classic example is Topps bubble gum baseball cards. After years of promoting the cards as an incentive to buy gum, in 1990 the company dropped the gum and simply began marketing the baseball cards as collectibles.

By the 1960s, promotion firms were offering marketing advice to complement their promotional programs. Promotion firms, in response to client demand, were transformed from companies developing stand-alone incentive programs to full-service marketing consultants. They began to offer expertise in consumer marketing, merchandising, and branding. During this period, the full-service promotion shop took root and integration with advertising and marketing became the norm.[1]

Today, in order to provide better balance between advertising and sales promotion we are finding that a number of companies are consolidating overall responsibility for both under a single corporate executive. Despite the fact that advertising and sales promotion are different in many respects, coordination between them is imperative. More and more sales promotion and advertising agencies are consolidating, or at the very least coordinating their efforts to retain clients who demand a synergistic approach to their total advertising and promotional programs. "Ad agencies, promo shops, and even premium suppliers are feverishly buying or cultivating disciplines to complement their core expertise. Promo execs sitting at the pitch table with their sister ad agencies find themselves more central to the conversation as ad shops turn to promo types for their expertise at retail."[2]

Despite the merging of advertising and sales promotion in terms of both management responsibility and creative execution, we should be aware that they differ in both execution and objectives. Yet, it is impossible to be successful as an advertiser, marketing executive, or promotion manager without a knowledge of the broad concepts involved in the total system of **marketing communication**.

This chapter discusses the primary types of sales promotion and how they complement media advertising. As with advertising, the opportunities for successful execution of sales promotion programs depend on an understanding of the marketing objectives of a particular firm or individual brand. Both advertising and sales promotion failures are most often a direct result of poor planning and a lack of integration with the elements of the marketing mix.[3]

marketing communication
The communication components of marketing, which include public relations, advertising, personal selling, and sales promotion.

PROMOTION AND ADVERTISING

Effective sales promotion has two basic functions: (1) to inform and (2) to motivate. Normally, sales promotion is most effective when its message is closely related to advertising themes. Point-of-sale displays may feature a testimonial spokesperson who is simultaneously appearing in television commercials; counter displays often use the same headlines and copy style as print advertisements; and product sampling will offer miniature packages to enhance brand identification promoted in the company's advertising. Although the means of communication may be different than in advertising, consistent information and formats are key ingredients in successful promotions.

The second aspect of promotions—motivation—differs in some major respects from advertising. Motivation, in a marketing sense, is the means used to move a customer to purchase a brand. This process usually moves across a continuum from awareness (initially hearing about a product) to purchase. In Exhibit 14.3, we can see that advertising and sales promotion have markedly different responsibilities in the communication and purchase process.

The key to successful marketing communication is determining the purposes and objectives of advertising, sales promotion, and other components and how best to coordinate and integrate these objectives. In the past, a major distinction between advertising and sales promotion was that sales promotion was viewed as a short-term sales incentive and advertising was intended to build brand equity over time. Today, most marketers recognize that it is counterproductive for sales promotion to gain short-term sales at the expense of long-term brand equity. One only has to look at a number of package-goods categories that have used coupons and other price-oriented deals to realize that consumers see little inherent value in the brands and simply purchase the one with the lowest cost at any given moment. In

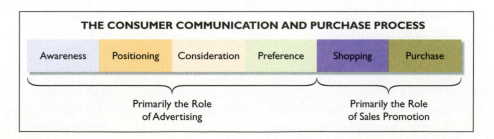

THE CONSUMER COMMUNICATION AND PURCHASE PROCESS

| Awareness | Positioning | Consideration | Preference | Shopping | Purchase |

Primarily the Role of Advertising

Primarily the Role of Sales Promotion

EXHIBIT 14.3
Advertising and sales promotion should function in a complementary fashion.

this environment where promotion must work with advertising and contribute to the overall marketing goals, objectives for promotion might include the following:[4]

- To gain trial among nonusers of a brand or service
- To increase repeat purchase and/or multiple purchases
- To expand brand usage by encouraging product uses in addition to usual use
- To defend share against competitors
- To support and reinforce an advertising campaign/theme or specific image
- To increase distribution and/or retailer/dealer cooperation

Note that none of these objectives advocates short-term sales increases except when these sales are part of a larger marketing strategy. For example, when we encourage product trial by nonusers or expansion of uses by present customers, the implication is that these trials will lead to long-term consumer relationships. In turn, consumer relationships, initially gained through promotion, will be reinforced over time by advertising.

Promotion Strategy

An analysis of a product's performance takes into account both surface indications and underlying problems facing the brand. In-depth situation analyses and strategy development can help determine the incentive needed, the type of promotion likely to have the greatest appeal, and the media required to reach the desired audience. Partners & Levit suggests what to consider in establishing strategy:[5]

1. *Customer attitudes and buying behaviors.* Determine who your customers are demographically and psychographically. Establish what about your brand attracts them and how they make their buying decisions.
2. *Brand strategy.* Consider your level of dominance in the product category. How will sales promotion factor into performance? What are the strengths and time period before returns are realized?
3. *Competitive strategy.* Evaluate past performance, both yours and your competitors', and determine what activities, levels of spending, and time periods produced the best results.
4. *Advertising strategy.* How do you currently promote your product in your existing markets? Which media best suit your needs?
5. *Trade environment.* What are your distributors' attitudes toward the brand? What are your competitors' attitudes?
6. *Other external factors.* What resources are available and what unpredictable factors may influence a product's availability or pricing (e.g., weather, raw materials)?

Promotional expenditures are directed at a wide range of programs. *PROMO* magazine lists some of the major categories of trade and sales promotions and the investment in each:[6]

Event marketing	$171 billion
Premiums and incentives	$46.5 billion
Direct NO!marketing	$49.5 billion
Product sampling	$1.8 billion
Point-of-sale displays	$17.5 billion
Sponsorships	$13.9 billion
Licensing	$5.9 billion
Fulfillment	$3.6 billion
Sweepstakes, games, contests	$1.8 billion
In-store promotion	$925 million

Total promotion budgets are generally divided into three categories: consumer advertising, consumer promotion (usually referred to as either sales promotion or simply promotion), and trade promotion (known as dealer promotion or merchandising). Whereas coordination among these promotional classifications is important, they each serve a distinct purpose. Let's examine the role of each in the marketing mix and the share of promotional budgets spent in these promotional categories.

1. **Consumer advertising**. The role of measured media advertising is to build long-term brand equity and promote basic product attributes, location of dealers, and/or comparisons with other products. The percentage of total promotional budgets spent on advertising has declined steadily over the last decade. Approximately 25 percent of promotional dollars are currently spent in advertising. Church's (see Exhibit 14.4) uses traditional advertising to promote awareness for its "Grand Opening."

2. *Consumer sales promotion*. These are sales promotional incentives directed to the consumer. Cents-off coupons are the most common consumer promotion, but premiums, rebates, and sweepstakes also are frequently used. Driven primarily by a decrease in the use of coupons, consumer sales promotion has fallen slightly to 25 percent of spending.

3. *Trade promotions*. Accounting for about half of the promotional budget, trade incentives are designed to encourage a company's sales force or retail outlets to push their products more aggressively. These are the most expensive types of promotion on a per-person basis. Winning dealers or retailers may get a trip to Hawaii, a new car, or a cash bonus. Behind the significant increase in trade promotions is the fact that companies think they get more immediate payout for their spending in this sector and that they have more control over expenditures than in other forms of promotion.

Despite some movement of dollars among the three categories, the long-term trend seems to be a ratio of 75 percent of promotional dollars in trade and sales promotion and 25 percent in advertising. The relatively low figure for advertising might be even further depressed if we had an accurate measure of the advertising dollars that are allocated to support major promotions such as sweepstakes, rebates, or sales. For example, it is estimated that as much as 20 percent of total advertising expenditures are devoted to supporting some form of promotion. Most marketing executives predict minimal future increases in advertising's share of total promotion budgets.

consumer advertising
Directed to people who will use the product themselves, in contrast to trade advertising, industrial advertising, or professional advertising.

EXHIBIT 14.4

Church's uses outdoor advertising to promote its "Grand opening."

Courtesy of The Botsford Group and Church's.

FORMS OF SALES PROMOTION

The remainder of this chapter discusses the primary types of sales promotion. Priority is given to those techniques most associated with advertising, especially at the consumer level. However, we also briefly discuss trade-oriented promotions. In all cases, we need to keep in mind the complementary purposes of advertising and promotion. The most frequently used forms of sales promotion are:

- Event marketing
- Premiums and incentives
- Point-of-sale displays
- Sponsorships
- Licensing
- Sweepstakes, games, and contests
- Product sampling
- In-store promotions
- Cooperative advertising
- Trade shows and exhibits
- Directories and Yellow Pages
- Trade incentives

Event Marketing

Event marketing spending reached $171 billion in 2005. The average event-marketing budget was estimated to be about $800,000. Some 96 percent of national marketing executives say they use events in their marketing mix. To give you an idea of how much they spend on events, note that budgets vary significantly: about a third of marketers spend less than $50,000 a year on events; some 20 percent spend $100,000 to $500,000; and roughly 25 percent spend over $500,000.

How do marketers know if they are getting their money's worth from a marketing event? A *PROMO* survey indicated about half of marketers measure event results by sales volume, and others track headcount. They also measure purchase intent, and some count Internet hits after an event. The push for higher return on investment (ROI) has marketers cutting street-team budgets.

Most brands rely on buzz marketing to drive event traffic; that's likely to grow as marketers co-op pop culture (think film screenings and concerts) and recruit brand ambassadors. There's so much competition for mind share—podcasts, social networking, socialized content via new media. "Some events evolve through cell phones and social networking. Verizon Wireless gave away 10,000 tickets to its Grammy-week Fugees concert via street teams and text messages: subscribers who responded quickest got a "ticket" via MMS, then showed the bar code on their phone screens to get into the show. The Chiquita brand uses local grassroots marketing to gain attention (Exhibit 14.5).

What do Tide detergent, Home Depot, Hot Wheels, Coca-Cola, Viagra, and DuPont have in common? Besides being among the largest and most sophisticated brands in the world, they are primary sponsors of NASCAR racing teams. Corporations spend more than $1 billion a year for NASCAR sponsorships and promotions. Annual sales of NASCAR-licensed merchandise is now over $2 billion. It is estimated that there are 75 million NASCAR fans, with more than half being hard core.

Benefit by Association One of the oldest types of advertising is the testimonial by which a brand gains from an association with a celebrity through a product endorsement. The idea, of course, is that the star power of famous sports or enter-

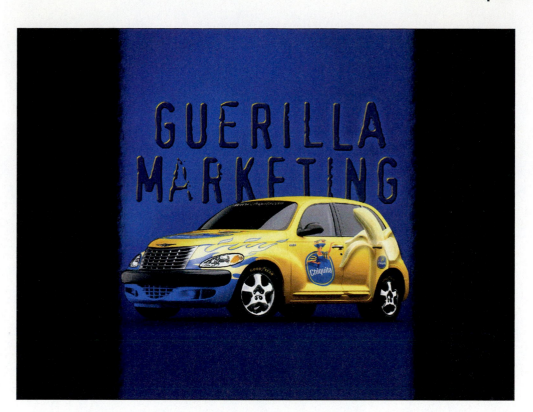

EXHIBIT 14.5
The Chiquita brand uses local grassroots marketing to gain attention.
Courtesy of The Botsford Group and Chiquita.

tainment figures will rub off on the brand. It is this idea of benefit by association that has driven event-marketing and product-licensing deals to multibillion-dollar levels.

There are three basic approaches to product association and tie-ins:

1. *Event marketing.* There is hardly a sporting event, musical concert, or art exhibit that does not enjoy some form of corporate sponsorship. From sponsored scoreboards at football stadiums to the Nike swoosh on players' uniforms, every aspect of public events is open to purchase by a business. We have even divided up parts of events for sponsorship. The Olympics is among the most high-profile event-marketing venues with companies making multimillion-dollar investments in return for being named an official sponsor.

   Advertisers understand that sports fans and patrons of the arts are extremely loyal to their special favorites. Sponsors hope that an association with these events will increase brand visibility and foster goodwill for their products. Event marketing is most effective when it involves a long-term relationship that offers advertisers a chance to develop a continuing connection with a loyal audience.

2. *Staged promotions.* A staged promotional event differs from event marketing in that the sponsor not only sponsors an event but also initiates it. Among the most sponsored events of this type are concerts. Each summer, companies with youth-oriented brands such as Coca-Cola, PepsiCo, and Levi Strauss hit the road with the band du jour for a cross-country tour. These events combine product sampling, couponing, interviews with local media, and in-store publicity to maximize brand identification with the band.

3. *Product licensing.* Related to event marketing is the concept of commercial relationships with movies, television shows, cartoon characters, and so forth to gain recognition for a brand. Examples of licensing agreements cover numerous opportunities. Sometimes it involves product placement in a film.

   Movie licensing often involves a marketing tie-in between a fast-food company and a toy manufacturer or some other children-related item. It is common for fast-food companies to join with movies, television shows, or networks, using the popularity to bring customers into their restaurants for toys, books, cups, or so forth.

The biggest beneficiaries of licensing agreements are toy manufacturers. It is estimated that nearly half of toy revenues come from licensed figures. They include movie personalities, children's television characters, and so on. Action toys have become a core income source for most toy manufacturers. These companies invest millions in these agreements, and their success is largely dependent on the popularity of a particular entertainment project. Not all licensing agreements involve entertainment, and some involve cross-licensing contracts between two brands. For example, the Lincoln Town Car Cartier model combined two prestigious brands and offers a number of cross-promotions.

In 2005, retail sales for licensed goods totaled almost $107 billion. Entertainment and character licensing accounted for about $47 billion in sales, with licensing revenue at $5.85 billion.

As you can see from our discussion, the opportunities for event sponsorship and licensing agreements are endless. However, their success depends on a positive connection with a brand's target market. In order to accomplish this goal, it is imperative that the image of the event and that of the product are compatible and that there is a logical relationship between the product and the event.

Virtual Advertising

Throughout the text, we have discussed advertising and marketing via Internet and computer-based technology. Among the most interesting are the so-called virtual advertisements. Computer-generated advertisements, logos, and products are superimposed on a live video feed or inserted into a completed movie or television show. These computer-inserted brand messages are not seen and, in fact, don't exist at the actual event. By utilizing technology and creativity, it is now possible to seamlessly integrate an image into a live event or program after filming has taken place with the ability to target a specific demographic in any given market. You may have seen the yellow first-down markers on your television screen or the advertisements behind home plate that change. The fans at the games don't see these advertisements because they are electronic. And during the last summer Olympics, NBC virtually placed the national flags of swimmers into each lane—at the bottom of the pool.

The technique has been adapted for product placement in movies and television shows. Producers will be able to insert local or regional brands in films and television shows. As you might imagine, purists are not particularly happy about the intrusion of product promotions into entertainment content, but virtual advertising does open up interesting possibilities to reach target audiences. There are also potential legal ramifications to the use of this technique.

Deals

Deals are a catch-all category of promotional techniques designed to save the customer money. The most common deal is a temporary price reduction or "sale." The cents-off coupon is also a consumer deal because it lowers the price during some limited period. A deal also may involve merchandising. For example, a manufacturer may offer three bars of soap wrapped together and sold at a reduced price. Another deal possibility is attaching a new product to a package of another established product at little or no extra cost—an effective way of new-product sampling. Among the most familiar deals are rebates toward the purchase of a product. Mail-in rebates are among the most common deals offered by manufacturers. Here consumers purchase a product and send away in order to receive the reward. Premium offers are offers of free or discounted merchandise used as an incentive for the customer to purchase more.

The downside of offering frequent deals is that a promotion may start off as a temporary incentive and become, to some buyers, an expectation. Deals can be extremely effective in building sales at the trade level. Trade deals offered to retailers and wholesalers and others in the trade channel are discussed later in the chapter as a type of trade incentive.

Sponsorships

Some people include sponsorships under event marketing, but companies like *PROMO* magazine review it as a separate item. For clarity, we'll briefly mention some aspects. Sponsorship spending is on the rise—U.S. marketers spent about $13.9 billion in 2006. In 2005, Anheuser-Busch was the leader in sponsorship spending, forking out $310 million. Other top spenders for the category have been PepsiCo, Inc.; General Motors Corp.; The Coca-Cola Co.; Nike, Inc. ($205 million); Miller Brewing Co.; DaimlerChrysler Corp.; and Ford Motor Co. Combined, these companies spent almost $2 billion. A few examples of their sponsorships include the Super Bowl half-time show, NASCAR racing events, golf tournaments, and tennis tournaments. There are also sponsorships of entertainment tours and attractions, cause-related activities, festivals, fairs, and the arts.[7]

Research shows that "true" online sponsorshiip programs generate significantly better results for marketers in terms of intent to purchase, brand recognition, and ROI than traditional advertisements. In separate programs, Sony and Intel sponsored online courses teaching people how to be better digital photographers. In both cases, for every dollar spent on the promotion, the marketer received $50 in retail spending. ROI for traditional media advertisements is roughly two to one.[8]

Point-of-Purchase Advertising

The retail industry is slowly changing the way it reports some promotional activities. All in-store marketing services are now referred to as *retail marketing services*. Retail marketing—which includes **point-of-purchase** (P-O-P), retail merchandising, and in-store services—is estimated to be about $20 billion. Quick-service restaurants like Church's often uses in-store merchandising to promote specific products. Exhibit 14.6 illustrates a special price promotion taking the risk out of the consumer's sampling by offering a special deal. The biggest portion of retail spending, P-O-P, is estimated to be $17.5 billion. "Marketing-mix modeling still reinforces that trade spending has the highest level of return on investment and then within consumer support . . . those [efforts] closer to the point of consumption and point-of-sale tend to have the higher return," Rick Lenny, Hershey Co. CEO, said. In general, he said, Hershey uses advertising to create awareness for new brands and new platforms but views in-store support—whether through sampling or through activities tied in with retailers' own strategies—as the best way to capitalize on those high-return investments.

In-store services hit almost $925 million, as retailers expand in-store television and brands elbow for attention on-shelf. In-store television continues to gain through expansion of Wal-Mart and Target's in-store television networks. P.O.P. Broadcasting Co. brings advertisements on-shelf with motion-sensitive ShelfAds that play advertisements and track traffic and sales.

P-O-P is tailor-made for a retail environment in which almost 60 percent of consumer purchases are unplanned. In recent years, the industry has sponsored a number of studies to help retailers and manufacturers better utilize P-O-P. Findings of these studies demonstrate that P-O-P has several primary advantages as a sales promotion technique:

point-of-purchase
Displays prepared by the manufacturer for use where the product is sold.

EXHIBIT 14.6

This poster promotes a deal that reduces the consumer's risk to try the product.

Courtesy of The Botsford Group and Church's Chicken.

TRY THE BEST SPICY CHICKEN IN TOWN!

50¢ Per piece

Limit 2 Pieces (Legs & Thighs only)

1. *Motivates unplanned shopping.* One major study indicated that displays at the end of aisles and at the checkout counter were most conducive to promoting sales. The same study also found that factors such as the age of the shopper, predilection to influence by in-store deals, and time pressure all played a role in the influence of P-O-P. It also showed that retailers could influence impulse buying by encouraging shoppers to go down as many aisles as possible.[9]

2. *Offers brand and product reminders.* One of the major roles of P-O-P is to remind consumers about product categories and brands that they might overlook. The P-O-P industry is upgrading the creative options available for in-store selling. In addition to the familiar cardboard signage, more and more displays are utilizing computer technology to change messages electronically and target selective demographic shopper segments.

3. *Influences brand switching.* Consumers show remarkably low levels of brand loyalty in food categories. In a study by the Meyers Research Center, "more than half of grocery shoppers would switch brands if their preferred items were not available, compared to only a third of shoppers who would do the same if their favorite non-food items were unavailable."[10]

This research not only shows the need for P-O-P but also indicates that the use of such displays will be an ongoing necessity to motivate unpredictable consumers.

The major industry trade association, Point of Purchase Advertising International (POPAI), in cooperation with the Advertising Research Foundation (ARF), has been engaged in a multiyear study to provide reliable audience measures and place P-O-P on a level with other measured media such as print and broadcast. According to POPAI, the study seeks to measure:

1. *The amount of P-O-P advertising erected in stores.* The industry knows that all the signage that is purchased and distributed is not displayed.
2. *The estimated number of consumer impressions generated.* The study seeks to gather data concerning reach, frequency, and CPM in order to allow intermedia comparisons.
3. *The effectiveness of P-O-P advertising.* Ultimately, the industry hopes to provide information on sales increases that are attributable to P-O-P.

One of the historical problems facing P-O-P advertising has been guaranteeing that the displays were properly displayed or even displayed at all. In the past, manufacturers' salespersons were largely responsible for maintaining in-store displays. Particularly among small companies, signs were simply placed by manufacturers' reps in those stores that would give them space. Now, marketing in-store displays is a much more sophisticated process and is highly coordinated at both the local and national levels. For huge retailers such as Home Depot and Wal-Mart, some P-O-P signs are made exclusively for their outlets.

To ensure better usage of in-store displays, a number of companies have hired independent firms called retail merchandising service companies to work with retailers to gain maximum P-O-P coverage on an outsourcing basis. Many companies find that "hiring merchandising companies may mean extra costs, but the expense is offset by the fact that crack sales forces don't need to waste valuable selling time setting up displays, doing store sets and out-of-stock correction, or updating merchandise."[11]

In the future, we will see even more innovations in the uses of P-O-P and retail services. The in-store industry will provide better research as well as utilize a number of electronic, interactive, and broadcast media.

Increasingly, P-O-P will be dominated by retailers and manufacturers will be required to meet rigid requirements to gain retail shelf and floor space. Retail space is the most valuable commodity that local merchants have, and they will allocate P-O-P spots only to those companies and brands that provide the highest-quality displays, greatest merchandising and advertising support, and, most importantly, the most significant profit potential.

Not only are these innovations in in-store retailing interesting in themselves, but also they point out once again that advertising, promotion, and marketing are increasingly becoming interrelated to the point that it is difficult to tell when one stops and the other begins. Rather than trying to decide in what category a promotion element belongs, managers are becoming more concerned with using whatever techniques work.

Premiums and Incentives

Premiums are items given to customers in exchange for a purchase or some other action such as a store visit or test drive. In other words, they are rewards given with strings attached. Premiums and incentives are among the most common sales incentives with spending about $46 billion. Church's chicken uses 3-D glasses and promotion in both English and Spanish to attract customers to the "kids' meal." "Get a SPY Kids 3-D Spy Guide with 3-D Glasses in each Church's® Kids' Meal while supply lasts. Now Available on DVD and Video." See Exhibit 14.7.

premium
An item other than the product itself given to purchasers of a product as an inducement to buy. Can be free with a purchase (for example, on the package, in the package, or the container itself) or available upon proof of purchase and a payment (self-liquidating premium).

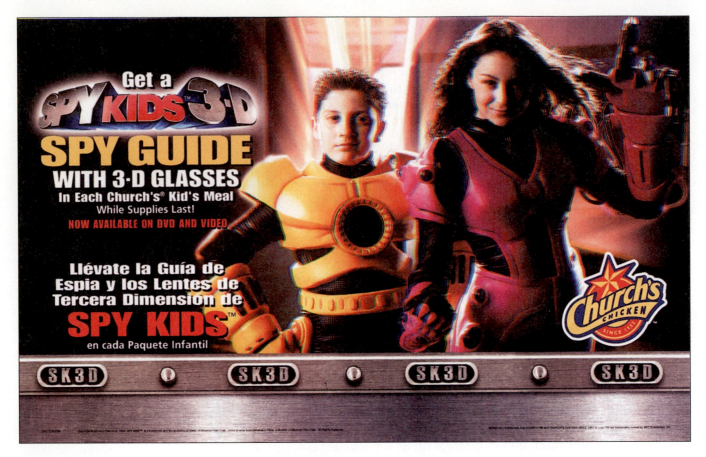

EXHIBIT 14.7

This promotion promotes the "Kids' Meal" with Spy Guide and 3-D glasses and the DVD and video. It is promoted in English and Spanish.

Courtesy of The Botsford Group and Church's.

Premiums are not only one of the largest categories of sales promotion, but they also are among the oldest. Premiums date to the mid-1700s when calendars, wooden specialty items, and other promotional products were quite common. According to the industry's major trade association, Promotional Products Association International (PPAI), by the 1850s specialty printers had established a relatively formal business for premium items.

Premiums are comprised of a number of types of merchandise, with writing instruments, calendars, and clothing being the most popular. The key to successful premium promotions is that the merchandise has some logical connection to the product and the target market. Remember that premiums are not traditional gifts; they are marketing gifts. Premium offers are generally categorized by either the purpose or the method of distribution. Among the major sectors of the premium industry are the following:

traffic-building premium
A sales incentive to encourage customers to come to a store where a sale can be closed.

1. **Traffic-building premiums.** Most premiums are offered at the time of purchase. However, other premiums, particularly those associated with high-cost products and services, are given for merely visiting a retailer, real estate development, or automobile dealer.

2. *Continuity premiums.* Continuity premiums build in value as a consumer continues to buy a product. The key to successful continuity premiums is that "programs shouldn't neglect the brand. Frequent flyers or rewards cards for restaurants, or points to redeem gifts for credit card purchases, etc., are a great chance to build brand image by getting consumers actively involved with them for months, or even years. If prizes, too, are related to the brand, so much the better."[12]

In recent years, continuity premium programs have been widely adopted by e-commerce companies. Various incentive websites use continuity programs to encourage return visits and brand awareness. Consumers who visit these sites are offered points toward rewards for clicking on sponsoring merchant sites, searching for information, or making purchases.

3. *In- or on-pack premiums.* Also called **direct premiums**, these are among the most popular items with both advertisers and customers because they offer an immediate incentive and instant reward in return for a purchase. The direct premium has become so popular that advertisers are constantly searching for ways to differentiate their offers.

    Many direct premiums are offered as a copromotion so that compatible brands can cooperate and extend promotional opportunities while at the same time reducing costs to the participating companies. Diet Coke packages carried samples of excerpts from upcoming novels by major publishers such as Doubleday. The Diet Coke Story promotion was in response to research that showed Diet Coke drinkers were greater-than-average book readers.[13]

4. **Self-liquidating premiums.** Regardless of the method of distributing the premium, the most popular type of premium is the self-liquidating offer (SLO). As the name implies, these premiums are designed to require that customers pay all or a major portion of their cost. On average, customers are required to pay approximately 75 percent of the premium. It is not surprising in this era of tight budgets that self-liquidating premiums are the most popular and the fastest-growing category. During the last decade, self-liquidating offers have increased by more than 30 percent and the average cost to consumers has risen sharply.

At one time, it was thought that SLOs could only be marketed successfully for low-end merchandise, usually under 5 dollars. However, marketers are finding that consumers will pay considerably more for items that have high perceived value or interest.

In some cases, the premiums have become so popular that they have actually become major profit centers for a company. Coca-Cola and Harley-Davidson are but two of the many examples in which branded merchandise is so popular that it is sold as "stand-alone" stock. This merchandise is no longer a premium, but it shows the popularity that some brands (and their premiums) have achieved.

With the thousands of available items for premium markets, it is extremely important that great care be given to the selection of this merchandise. The primary concern is that any premium promotion is complementary to the overall marketing goals of a firm and that the relatively high investment in such an endeavor can be justified.

Loyalty Incentives Loyalty has become the mantra of marketers, moving strategies far beyond the one-time purchase, the sample, or the sweeps. It's all about getting to know those customers, earning and keeping their business, and staying in touch. The Coca-Cola North America's "My Coke Rewards" is Coca-Cola's largest reward program. A Spanish-language version marks the company's first fully bilingual, Internet-based initiative. The program plays on a tactic Coca-Cola uses in some of its most successful promotions, hiding a code under the cap. Players then register online to redeem rewards.

    Loyalty "programs" have even begun to creep into the corporate world as employee incentives. Just like a frequent flyer can build points to redeem for merchandise or an airline flight, employees can now earn points based on a variety of job performance criteria to redeem for lifestyle experiences, gift cards, or merchandise. The programs keep employees engaged, focused on performance, and dedicated, hopefully for the long haul, says Karen Renk, the executive director of the Incentive Marketing Association.[14]

Interactive and Digital

A *PROMO* 2006 Industry Trends Report indicated that some 49 percent of major marketers used some form of interactive or digital promotion. Take podcasts, for

direct premium
A sales incentive given to customers at the time of purchase.

self-liquidating premium
A premium offered to consumers for a fee that covers its cost plus handling.

KLEPPNER VIEWPOINT 14.1

David Botsford
CEO, The Botsford Group
Getting the Retail Support You Want

No matter how much time and money a packaged goods manufacturer pours into its brands, what happens—or doesn't happen—on the sales floor can quickly turn dreams into nightmares on the market share front.

With 70 percent of all brand purchase decisions made at retail, according to the Point-of-Purchase Advertising Institute, the store is more than just a place to win a battle. It's an opportunity to win the war.

Increased display activity, more in-store merchandising, and additional retail ad support are three major avenues for influencing these purchase decisions.

Of course, the importance of your category to the retailer, as well as your brand's position in the category, determines the degree of retailer support possible. I've never met a manufacturer, however, whose retail support couldn't be increased. It comes down to three things: Motivate retailers to authorize incremental support for your brand; ensure the support you get builds the brand (all support is not created equal), and get the support promised implemented at the store level (which only happens 40 percent of the time).

The good news is you don't need a SWAT team to get this done. Just follow the five rules listed here and you'll see measurable results every time.

Rule 1: Collaborate. If you don't help the retailer build his business, he isn't going to be motivated to build yours. Don't take programs to your retailers that simply induce brand switching. Develop ideas that expand the category or increase profitability—or both if you can pull it off. Start by becoming familiar with each retailer's distinct needs, wants, and rules. Ditto for the retailer's brand personality and merchandising style.

Integrate with the retailer's brand and you'll earn the opportunity to talk about yours (don't, however, leave cre-

David Botsford

ative development in the retailer's hands!). Additionally, factor store employees, the gatekeepers of implementation, into your program. If your field force or agency doesn't know the lay of the land at the store level, get educated quickly. Talk to a representative sampling of key employees (two or three people per chain). Most appreciate being asked, plus you'll learn something.

Rule 2: Differentiate. Retailers don't want the same program you gave their competitor down the street. They need promotions that set them apart from rivals. Differentiation doesn't have to be a budget buster. Lightly customized creative is one way to accomplish this in a cost-effective manner. For example, by using different photography for competing retailers in overlapping markets we were able to

example, a tool being tested and tweaked that may have found its niche as a customer loyalty builder rather than a vehicle for advertisements, says Matt MacQueen, experience planning director for Arc Worldwide, Chicago. Purina offered audio podcasts of its *Animal Advice* radio program topics including animal training, pet care, pet insurance, and behavioral theories. The audiocasts were followed later by video podcasts of Purina's Incredible Dog Challenge. Purina divided the program into free 5-minute downloadable segments on iTunes and Purina.com. Good podcasting should support a marketer's objectives, strategy, and message, and it should build its consumer relationship. According to the report, marketers used interactive channels to build brand loy-

increase retailer support of a recent outdoor campaign. The return on investment for comarketing can also be very high, especially if you focus on high-volume retailers. We've seen clients use this avenue to achieve double-digit volume lifts, increases that resulted in the program paying for itself many times.

Rule 3: Motivate. Even though some retailers will tell you it isn't necessary, find ways to tie store-level incentives to in-store implementation—it can make you look like a hero. Make sure the programs are flexible enough to meet retailer guidelines. For retailers that don't allow direct employee rewards, consider staging special events for top-performing associates, awarding the store's own gift certificates, or offering store-specific promotions (it's hard for a chain's headquarters to argue with this one).

Rule 4: Communicate. About a week before a program starts, make sure to check in with the folks who are physically responsible for getting displays and merchandising out of the back room and into the store. Clearly mark shipping containers with the program name, start date, and exact store location desired. Do the same thing with merchandising materials.

Rule 5: Participate. Let the retailer become part of your account-specific planning without relinquishing control of your creative, brand positioning, and marketing strategies. Most retailers not only have fun doing so, but also they'll be flattered at the offer and will begin to view you as a partner, not just a vendor.

At the close of a recent meeting of our agency and a client with marketers at one of the top ten U.S. food chains, the retailer thanked us profusely for including it in the process, adding: "I wish other manufacturers approached account specific marketing this way."

That's a wake-up call to manufacturers and agencies if I've ever heard one.

Courtesy of David Botsford and The Botsford Group. ■ ■ ■

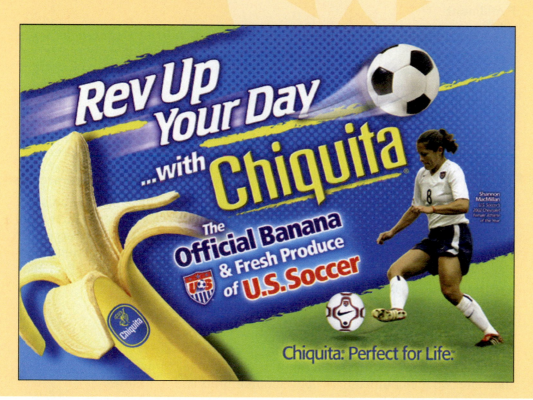

Chiquita: The Official Banana of U.S. Soccer.
Courtesy of the Botsford Group and Chiquita.

alty, prompt a sale, drive consumers to websites, collect personal data, and offer incentives.[15]

Marketers have had mixed experiences on the social networking sites. Consumers have not been happy with those on YouTube, for example, that hide the fact that they are promoting something. So marketers must be careful how they promote on new technology sites, or risk a backlash.

Anheuser-Busch launched a new marketing venture, a Web-based television network, after the 2007 Super Bowl called Bud TV. The 24/7 "network," featuring both live and on-demand programming, was carried on up to seven channels. It used branded content for A-B products—but also independent offerings, such as

Webisodes, celebrity interviews, comedy, short films, and consumer-generated content, even sports events. The channels also were dedicated to specific genres, while music downloads were also available.[16]

At a pre–Super Bowl event, Sprint conducted an on-stage event during the NFL Experience in which twenty-four NFL players greeted fans and sent the messages over handsets provided by Sprint over a 6-hour period. The goal was to expose consumers to the Sprint brand, while they had fun with NFL players, said Dawn Ridley, senior vice president for Players, Inc., the licensing and marketing subsidiary of the NFL Players Association, which arranged the event.[17]

Consumer-generated advertisement-making contests have been successful. A Chipotle winner was posted on YouTube. "Dady" stars a bald-headed father who is presented with a hand-made drawing from his young son, only to criticize the tyke for not doing justice to the shape of his head or even spelling his name correctly. The kicker? Chipotle customers don't settle for anything but the best. "Dady" (catch the clip on YouTube to understand the intentional misspelling) amassed 2.25 million views on YouTube only 2 weeks after its initial posting.[18]

Fulfillment

fulfillment firm
Company that handles the couponing process including receiving, verification, and payment. It also handles contest and sweepstakes responses.

The physical work of handling, organizing, and responding to requests for merchandise is normally managed by **fulfillment firms**. The fulfillment of marketing offers has become a two-sided coin in recent years, as traditional, "analog" order completion has been supplemented by virtual delivery of digital incentives and premiums. In all cases, customer satisfaction and efficiency remain top priorities for brands and their fulfillment shops. Marketers' fulfillment budgets have been static for the past several years. As a result, fulfillment houses are trying to play more roles for each brand client. For example, marketing and fulfillment services agency The JAY Group provides its pharmaceutical industry clients with warehousing, real-time order processing, inventory control, and distribution systems to enable timely delivery to end users.[19] Fulfillment firms usually operate on a fee basis according to the number of requests. Their work is crucial to the success of any promotion. Sloppy fulfillment services can virtually guarantee an unsuccessful promotion as well as long-term damage to customer goodwill. Fulfillment is an extension of customer service and it is your company, not the fulfillment firm, that will be blamed if something goes wrong.

Specialty Advertising

The same items used in premium promotions—clothing, writing instruments, calendars—are among the most popular with specialty advertisers.[20] However, there are two major differences between premiums and specialties:

1. Advertising specialties are imprinted with the advertiser's name, logo, or short advertising message. Premiums are not normally imprinted because the customer is being given a reward for purchasing a product.
2. Unlike premiums, specialties are given with no obligation on the part of the recipient.

The uses and formats of advertising specialties are almost limitless with more than 15,000 items available to carry out virtually any marketing objective. Specialties also complement other media and can be targeted to prime prospects with little waste circulation. The ideal specialty is one that is used on a regular basis, thereby creating continuing frequency with no additional cost.

The disadvantages of specialties include their significant expense on a CPM basis and, like outdoor, the fact that they offer little opportunity for a sales message.

In addition, there is no natural distribution system for specialties and, depending on the item selected, production time may take up to 6 weeks.

Specialty advertising has experienced significant growth in recent years as businesses have attempted to establish brand identities in an increasingly competitive environment. Like so many areas of advertising, specialties have been influenced by e-commerce and the Internet. The Web also has the potential to change many traditional sales approaches within the industry. Instead of using expensive catalogs, reps show an array of targeted merchandise using portable computers.

Because a major role of specialty advertising is to provide long-term brand awareness, it is not surprising to find the heaviest users in markets with little perceived product differentiation and a number of competitive brands. Financial institutions, such as banks and stockbrokers, hospitals and health-care providers, and telecommunication and Internet companies are examples of categories that spend heavily on specialty advertising.

Specialty advertising, like all forms of promotion, should be planned in terms of specific marketing goals and objectives. One survey of advertisers found some of the primary reasons for using specialties:[21]

1. To promote customer retention and appreciation
2. To use in connection with trade shows
3. To build goodwill and enhance company image
4. To create awareness for new products and services
5. To generate sales leads and responses

In choosing a specialty item, it is important to determine that the item has some logical relationship to both the target market and the product or service being promoted. The item needs to have some useful function if the specialty is going to be kept as a reminder of a brand. Because the advertising message can be no more than a few words, a specialty needs to adapt the theme of a company's overall advertising campaign to offer an integrated communications approach to consumers.

Coupons

Coupon promotions are among the oldest forms of sales promotion, and they are without question the most pervasive category within the promotion industry. Marketers spent $7.23 billion on couponing in 2005. Marketers distributed 323 billion coupons in 2005, up 10 percent; consumers redeemed 3 billion, a 0.93 percent redemption rate, per coupon. **Free-standing inserts (FSIs)** accounted for 88 percent of coupon distribution. Expiration dates stay steady, averaging 3 months.

There are two basic approaches to coupon marketing and distribution. Traditionally, the primary marketing objectives for distributing coupons are to encourage product trial by prospective customers and to combat competitive encroachments against present customers. Both of these goals were normally addressed through mass coupon distribution. By far the most preferred method of coupon distribution is the free-standing insert (FSI) usually included in Sunday newspapers. FSIs are responsible for more than 86 percent of total coupon distribution, while handout co-op, handout off-store location, in-ad, in-pack, in-pack cross ruff, instant redeemable, Internet, and Sunday supplement coupons have also increased. Electronic distribution accounted for 8.8 percent of total redemption, whereas Internet coupons measured 0.2 percent of total redemption. Folks Southern Kitchen uses FSIs to distribute coupons on a quarterly basis (see Exhibit 14.8). This promotion attempts to sell a number of options—platters; All-You-Can-Eat BBQ Ribs; and five coupon options, hopefully to bring customers back at least five times.

One of the recurring complaints about the number of coupon promotions is that they create price competition at the expense of building brand loyalty. In

specialty advertising
A gift given to a consumer to encourage a purchase.

coupon
Most popular type of sales-promotion technique.

free-standing inserts (FSIs)
Preprinted inserts distributed to newspaper publishers, where they are inserted and delivered with the newspaper.

EXHIBIT 14.8

The FSI promotes an "All-You-Can-Eat BBQ Ribs" deal, "Pick 2 Pick 3," and five coupon deals to drive repeat business.

Courtesy of Folk's and Lane Bevil+Partners.

recent years, a number of major advertisers have taken steps to include coupon promotions within a traditional advertising environment. Such an approach serves to encourage product trial and build brand equity.

In addition to FSI and other blanket coupon distribution methods, we are starting to see a number of more targeted efforts. These more narrowly defined approaches to coupon promotions have one of two goals:

1. To reach targeted prospects based on lifestyle and demographic information
2. To build loyalty among current customers

In both cases, scanning checkout data and information from other computer-based, data-retrieval systems gives manufacturers insight into past purchase behavior of individual buyers. Using this information, retailers and manufacturers can provide offers that reflect specific consumer behavior and brand preferences.

Internet and Mobile Coupons

Despite low numbers of coupons obtained online, the combination of consumer convenience and manufacturers' ability to build customer databases makes the growth of Web couponing inevitable. Procter & Gamble's website typically tells consumers, "Don't forget to look for the P&G brandSAVER coupon insert in your home-delivered paper on Sunday—you could save more than $30 on some of your favorite P&G brands!" Online services such as Catalina Marketing's valupage.com and Val Pak Direct Marketing's valpak.com offer coupons in exchange for some consumer information. As online services continue to develop consumer databases, we will see a number providing services such as e-mail offers tailored to a person's past buying behavior. Although Internet-distributed coupons constitute a small percentage of total coupons, the increasing household Internet penetration and online couponing offer significant potential for inexpensive, targeted coupon promotions.

Same-day coupons are getting a little exposure. For example, Yahoo! offered coupons for a free Baskin-Robbins ice cream cone; and Toys "R" Us ran a series of same-day offers via e-mail and on coolsavings.com for its "12 Deals of Christmas" campaign.

In a mobile coupon experiment, Motorola Corporation rolled out M-Wallet, in which consumers loaded credit or debit card information into their cell phones, then swiped phones at the checkout to pay. M-Wallet or a similar service could become a platform for targeted coupon distribution, with offers pegged to the user's purchase history.

same-day coupons
Coupons that are designed to be used almost instantly, or same day.

Coupon Redemption Fraud

When we redeem our 50-cent coupons, we give little thought to the significant investment for manufacturers offering them. Unfortunately, those interested in defrauding manufacturers through the illegal redemption of coupons are very much aware of their value. The most common type of fraud occurs when a person sends in coupons for which no product purchase has been made. There have been instances in which criminals have obtained thousands of coupons and sent them to manufacturers using the name of supermarkets and other retailers. In some cases, manufacturers have spent millions of dollars on redemptions for fraudulent claims.

The industry is working with bar code technology and other techniques to address the problem. However, regardless of the distribution method, coupon fraud and misredemption remain problems.

Sampling

We have emphasized throughout the text that regardless of the quality of the advertising and promotion, ultimately the product must sell itself. This is the philosophy behind product **sampling**. Sampling is the free distribution of a product to a prospect. In recent years, product sampling has grown significantly and in many cases has replaced coupons as a manufacturer's primary method of gaining product trial. The sampling expenditure by marketers is estimated at $1.8 billion. Experts say sampling's growth will continue, fueled by its measurability.

One million consumers got a surprise in late 2005 when they opened their doors to the Domino's pizza delivery guy. He brought their pizza and a complimentary 20-ounce bottle of Coca-Cola Zero, and a coupon toward the purchase of a pizza and Coke Zero.

sampling
The method of introducing and promoting merchandise by distributing a miniature or full-size trial package of the product free or at a reduced price.

experiential sampling
A companies use of specialty vehicles to engage consumers and give them samples to enhance the contact experience.

Sampling has always been a successful tactic for trial and conversion. The tactical side of sampling has changed as companies move from goody boxes to **experiential sampling**, meaning that there are tours with big trucks to get consumers into the whole experience. Mobile sampling events seem less sterile (and goodies raise consumers' participation). For example, Hershey's used its KISSMOBILE—a 26-foot-long, 12-foot-tall specialty vehicle to introduce its ICE BREAKERS Fruit Sours. The vehicle has served up more than 4 million Hershey's samples since 1997.[22]

Direct mail is the most popular method of sample distribution, but it is not as strong today as in the past. Advertisers are increasingly utilizing creative approaches to get samples into the hands of prospective buyers. One of the significant changes in sampling is the move away from mass distribution campaigns and toward narrowly targeted dissemination. Targeting of prospects allows manufacturers to drastically decrease waste and obtain more accurate results from sampling tests. Some of the growing areas of sampling include the following:

1. *Newspaper distribution.* As newspapers define their delivery areas in smaller geographic areas (e.g., ZIP Codes and block units), the medium has gained a share of sampling expenditures.
2. *Event/venues marketing.* Because events such as rock concerts and sporting events tend to appeal to specific demographic and/or lifestyle segments, they offer ideal venues for sampling. In many cases, venue sampling—for example, suntan lotion at the beach—gives an immediate opportunity for product usage.
3. *In-store sampling.* Usually, in-store sampling is combined with a coupon incentive to encourage immediate purchase of the product. It is rare that a trip to the grocery store doesn't include at least one opportunity to sample some food product and receive a coupon.
4. *In-pack/co-op programs.* On-pack and in-pack distribution is popular when one product has a natural affinity to another. Washing machines often are delivered with a box of detergent, or shaving cream might come with a razor attached. In other cases, a multibrand manufacturer might want customers to inexpensively sample a new product by including it with one of its established brands.
5. *Internet sampling.* Many of the same characteristics that offer substantial advantages for Internet coupon distribution apply to sampling over the Internet. Samples woo consumers online, too, where they swap data for products. One study indicated that 70 percent of consumers have completed a survey to get a sample. A major advantage of this approach is that by sending samples only on request, manufacturers drastically decrease waste distribution.

Sweepstakes and Contests

The primary goal of most promotions is to gain immediate sales and consumer involvement. The "Church's for Churches" promotion encourages groups of people (from churches or other religious or civic groups) to register for the good of their group (see Exhibit 14.9). In the past couple of years, the need to keep consumers engaged fueled technology gains as a prime tool for games, contests, and sweepstakes. Whether it's a text-messaging campaign, online sweepstakes, or an interactive game, the Internet continues to dominate the field. Marketers prefer cyberspace largely for its cost efficiency, immediate data-collection capabilities, and ability to keep consumers engaged. Some 34 percent of brands use interactive promotions—including games, contests, and sweepstakes—according to *PROMO*'s 2006 Industry Trends Report. In 2005, just 12.8 percent of marketers listed offline games, contests, and sweepstakes in their top three spending tiers.[23]

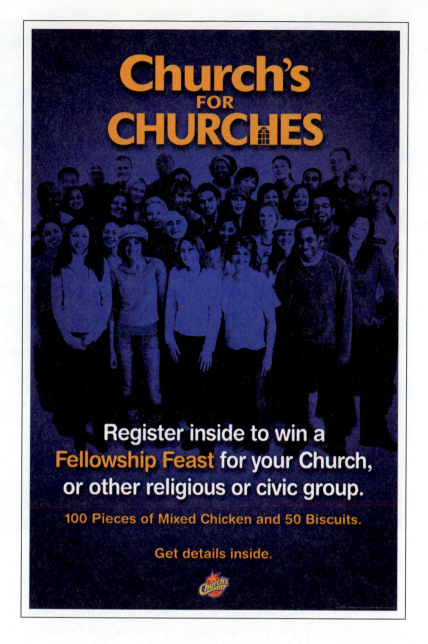

Church's
FOR
CHURCHES

Register inside to win a
Fellowship Feast for your Church,
or other religious or civic group.

100 Pieces of Mixed Chicken and 50 Biscuits.

Get details inside.

EXHIBIT 14.9

Here's a chance to win 100 pieces of chicken for your church or religious group or civic club.

Courtesy of Church's and The Botsford Group.

There is movement away from the standard program in which consumers figuratively drop their names in a hat toward an experience in which consumers have more of an opportunity to interact with a brand. The methods in which games, contests, and sweepstakes are deployed are changing to ensure a more engaging consumer experience across multiple touch points, says a representative of Archway Marketing.[24] In addition, the level of interactivity has increased and prizes are not only bigger but also more customized and lifestyle based. Church's "Get Spicy & Win" promotion could win a customer an automobile or one of 100,000 prizes (Exhibit 14.10 shows a game piece).

Annual expenditures for **sweepstakes** and **contests** are approximately $1.8 billion. Each year, more than 70 percent of American businesses sponsor a game of some kind and it is estimated that almost 30 percent of the population will enter a commercially sponsored contest or sweepstakes. The major marketers of these games are soft drink companies, fast-food franchises, and movie studios. Exhibit 14.11 shows a promotion for Church's in conjunction with a Metro-Goldwyn-Mayer Pictures' Queen Latifah. Participants gained game pieces in stores in addition to major prizes. Obviously, an objective was to drive traffic to the store. A contest or sweepstakes is an ideal marketing strategy for these companies.

sweepstakes
A promotion in which prize winners are determined on the basis of chance alone. Not legal if purchaser must risk money to enter.

contest
A promotion in which consumers compete for prizes and the winners are selected strictly on the basis of skill.

EXHIBIT **14.10**

Peel to Win

The game piece could make a customer a winner of an automobile.

Courtesy of The Botsford Group and Church's.

Because contests call for some element of skill, there must be a plan for judging and making certain that all legal requirements have been met. The typical contest is much more expensive than a sweepstakes. When millions of entries are anticipated, even the smallest overlooked detail can be a nightmare for the contest sponsor. It is estimated that almost 30 percent of the public enter either a sweepstakes or contest each year. A major contest can place a tremendous burden on a company to properly administer and judge. Most games are handled by outside firms specializing in these promotions.

Another limitation of contests is the time (and skill) required of participants. The majority of consumers are not going to devote the time necessary to complete a contest. Therefore, if the intent of the promotion is to gain maximum interest and participation, a sweepstakes will probably be better suited to the objective. On the other hand, a cleverly devised contest that complements the product and appeals to the skills of prime prospects can be extremely beneficial and encourage greater involvement than a sweepstakes.

The Deceptive Mail Prevention and Enforcement Act Sweepstakes that require a purchase (known as *consideration*) by an entrant are considered lotteries and, with the exception of state-sponsored lotteries, are usually illegal. The next time you receive a sweepstakes offer, notice that there is some language indicating that no purchase is necessary to enter. Despite these disclaimers, it has been alleged that a number of people, especially the elderly, have assumed that a purchase

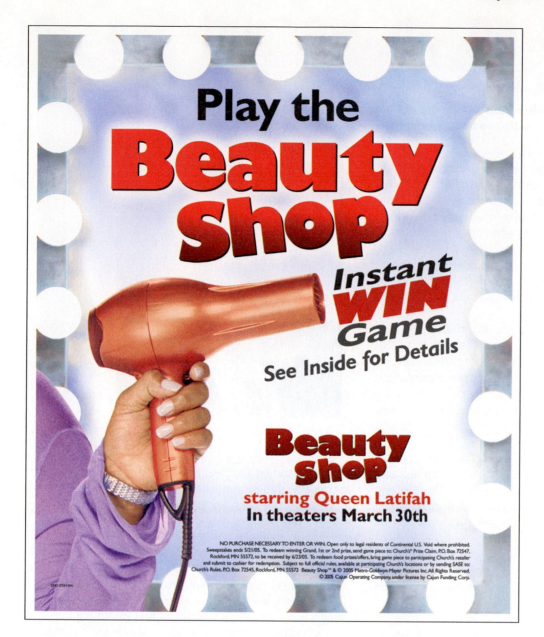

EXHIBIT 14.11
An example of a contest cross-promotion between the food store and a new movie.
Courtesy of The Botsford Group.

would enhance their chances of winning. In some cases, people bought thousands of dollars worth of merchandise as they entered one sweepstakes after another.

In 1999, Congress passed the Deceptive Mail Prevention and Enforcement Act, which addressed a number of these issues. Industry criticism of the bill has been directed largely at the provision for a national opt-out list in which recipients can remove their name from all sweepstakes solicitations. As one promotion executive commented, "It [the legislation] will have a chilling effect. . . . Some marketers who make occasional use of sweepstakes may not use them. I don't think you will see marketers abandoning sweepstakes, but they may proceed more cautiously."[25]

Cooperative Advertising

Historically, co-op advertising was initiated primarily as a means of overcoming the significant rate premiums charged to national advertisers by newspapers. Although that is still a purpose of co-op, it also has become a major category of trade promotion with annual expenditures of more than $30 billion. The marketing goals and

Charles H. Van Rysselberge, Cce

President and CEO, Charleston Metro Chamber of Commerce
Chambers of Commerce Use 360 Degree IMC Communications

Chambers of commerce are misunderstood creatures in society. Even though they have had that name for over 500 years, chambers are constantly challenged to effectively reveal their full-self as to what they really do and their relevancy!

The first known use of the term chamber of commerce was established in Marseilles, France, in 1500. In America, many chambers began as a board of trade but soon adopted the term chamber of commerce.

Charleston, South Carolina, is the oldest local chamber of commerce in America, whose origin dates back to 1773.

The first half of the 1900s, chambers developed an image as primarily one of boosterism and trade promotion. In the 1950s, chambers were frequently considered as a location to obtain a city map and not much thought was given as to what else they were providing to members and the public.

By the 1960s, when issues of education, racial unrest, growth, environmental concerns, etc., began to surface, chambers had to confront social issues of the day and develop programs of greater substance. The need to fix and improve the product (city/region) became as important as promoting it!

I frequently tell people that the fact that the Charleston Metro Chamber of Commerce has a staff of 42 people is a pretty good indication that we do a lot more than just provide city maps!

In July 2006, the Charleston Metro Chamber of Commerce launched an image campaign for the purpose of better positioning and increasing awareness of the Chamber's program of work and successes. We must constantly reinvent ourselves to ensure our relevancy!

Charles H. Van Rysselberge

In preparation for that, we had to identify primary and secondary goals. We conducted research with focus groups, membership surveys and one-on-one interviews with non and dropped members to see how the image campaign could motivate and get people involved.

We also focused on brand positioning with the who, what, how and why of the Chamber. Of course, identifying our eight different target audiences was also very important.

In addition, we had to consider our value proposition as being a smart business investment and identifying our challenges and threats, as well as our approach and timeline.

The image campaign is trying to demonstrate that the Charleston Metro Chamber of Commerce is focused on the everyday pocketbook issues of business. Examples include:

objectives differ from one manufacturer or retailer to another, but some of the primary purposes of co-op include the following:

1. It benefits retailers by allowing them to stretch their advertising budgets. Most co-op is offered on a 50 percent basis; that is, the national firm pays half of the local advertising costs. However, a number of co-op plans will reimburse retailers at a rate of 100 percent. In other cases, a manufacturer will place some limit on the amount of reimbursement according to a formula based on sales of the product by the retailer. Federal law requires that regardless of the formula of reimbursement, manufacturers must treat all retailers proportionately the same.

2. National manufacturers build goodwill with retailers; encourage local support of their brands; and, by having the retailer place the advertising, qualify for lower local rates, especially in newspapers. Manufacturers also gain a positive

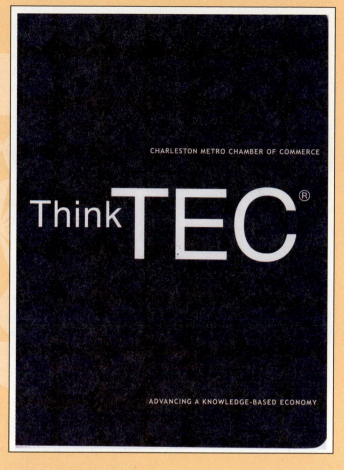

- raising the money and managing a half-cent sales tax campaign to provide $1.3 billion of funding for transportation infrastructure issues along with greenspace and mass transit
- military base retention due to BRAC 2005
- attracting discount airline service
- K–12 education issues
- high school dropout issue
- environmental and urban sprawl issues
- pro-business legislation at the local, state and federal level
- creation of higher wage paying jobs through innovation/technology initiatives
- business retention and expansion
- business research
- in addition to the numerous seminars and networking events
- as well as the numerous products and services we provide to members

It is too early in the process to evaluate our success with the image campaign, but so far, we have had a lot of positive feedback.

As a journalism student in the Advertising/Public Relations Department, I was so extremely fortunate to discover the chamber of commerce profession as a career for my communication background. When I completed graduate school, my course was set on the chamber as a career, and I have never looked back!

I found that a city is more interesting to promote than a traditional consumer product. It has more character and is in a constant state of change, which makes it fascinating and unable to ever completely conquer, which is the endless challenge of it all! ■ ■ ■

association between local retailers and their products, thus enhancing the brand equity among customers of specific retailers. Many co-op advertisements are prepared by national advertisers and require only that retailers add their logo.

3. The media are among the strongest supporters of co-op. Co-op allows current advertisers to place more advertising and at the same time brings new advertisers into the marketplace. Because co-op involves local advertising, it is not surprising that the majority of co-op dollars is spent in newspapers. However, in recent years, co-op has reflected the diversity of local media. About 60 percent of co-op budgets are spent in newspapers, followed by direct mail, television, and radio, each with approximately 10 percent. In the future, we will see significant dollars going into local cable co-op programs and this will increase the share of television co-op.

One of the surprising aspects of co-op advertising is the amount of money that is available but goes unspent. It is estimated that as much as one-fourth of co-op dollars goes unspent. The main reason for the failure to fully use co-op is primarily a result of a lack of knowledge on the part of retailers as to how to use co-op dollars or an unwillingness to meet the restrictions placed on their expenditure by manufacturers.

Vendor Programs A special form of co-op normally used by large retailers is the **vendor program**. The primary difference between vendor programs and other forms of co-op is that they are initiated by retailers. Vendor programs are custom programs designed by retailers (often in cooperation with local media). In vendor programs, manufacturers are approached by retailers to pay all or a share of the program.

For example, a department store might plan a summer "Beach Party" promotion. The store would then approach manufacturers of swim wear, sunglasses, suntan preparations, and so forth and request funds to support the advertising and promotion of the event. Often, manufacturers fund vendor programs from their unspent co-op money.

Ingredient Manufacturer Co-Op Most co-op programs are set up between manufacturers and retailers. However, as discussed in Chapter 2, many companies make ingredients that they sell to other manufacturers for inclusion in finished products. The strategy of advertising for both the ingredient and the final product is called end-product advertising (for example, Intel computer chips: Intel doesn't make computers) and represents another opportunity for co-op. Often, the ingredient manufacturer will contract with finished product manufacturers to co-op with retail outlets or even to co-op in the manufacturer's national advertising to promote the ingredient.

Manufacturer-to-Wholesaler Co-Op Occasionally, distribution in an industry is dominated by a relatively few wholesale outlets and manufacturers have little direct relationship with retailers. In this situation, it often is worthwhile for manufacturers to allocate co-op dollars to wholesalers that then make co-op arrangements with individual retailers. Most manufacturers avoid going through wholesalers because they lose both the goodwill and control achieved by direct allocation of co-op dollars by the national company.

Controlling Co-Op Dollars Retailers are paid for advertising when they submit documentation or proof of performance. The advertisements or proof can be matched with the media invoice. For radio and television cooperative advertisements, the Association of National Advertisers, the RAB, and the TvB developed an affidavit of performance that documents in detail the content, cost, and timing of commercials. The adoption of stricter controls in broadcast co-op has been a contributing factor in the growth of co-op dollars for both radio and television. Stations provide manufacturers with the actual on-air commercial and the context in which it ran online.

Despite attempts to improve the process, expenditures of co-op dollars still are allocated improperly out of neglect or inexperience by retailers. In a few cases, there is evidence of outright fraud. Co-op fraud usually takes one of two forms. In the first, retailers bill manufacturers for advertisements that never ran, using fake invoices and tear sheets. The second type of fraud, called double billing, occurs when manufacturers are overcharged for the cost of advertising. Basically, retailers pay one price to the medium and bill the manufacturer for a higher price by using a phony (double) bill. It should be noted that double billing is regarded as an unethical (in most circumstances, illegal) practice, and only a small minority of retailers and media engage in it.

Trade Shows and Exhibits

It is estimated that over 100 million people will attend more than 5,000 trade and consumer shows this year. Products as diverse as boats and cosmetics will

---

vendor program
Special form of co-op advertising in which a retailer designs the program and approaches advertisers for support.

be promoted through these shows. In some cases, a show will be open to both the trade and the public and might be visited by 100,000 prospects. In other cases, the shows are extremely selective and open by invitation only to a few dozen prospects.

Trade shows are one of the best examples of integrated promotion. They combine a number of media and other forms of marketing communication. Trade show sponsorship is almost never used as a stand-alone marketing tool. A trade show can fulfill a number of objectives including product introduction, lead getting, and direct selling. Research shows that trade shows are most successful for those sponsors with high brand recognition. The use of trade magazines and other forms of promotion and communication, including e-commerce, work both before and after the show to encourage the final sale.

The higher the level of brand recognition created before a show, the less time sales reps have to spend creating a product image and the more time they can devote to selling. By the same token, trade shows create opportunities for on-site market research as well as follow-up by personal or online selling.

Overall, trade shows are a major component in the marketing strategy of many firms. However, trade shows are normally only one piece in a total marketing program rather than an end in themselves. Trade shows provide a number of advantages for both buyers and sellers. They allow face-to-face selling at a cost much lower than traditional personal sales calls. In addition, trade shows are a self-selecting process with only serious prospects attending. Although some sales take place at these exhibits, they are more likely to provide leads for future sales calls or introduce new product lines to prospective customers.

Directories and Yellow Pages

Today, the Yellow Pages is being attacked on all sides by the explosion of Web-based information and directories. Google, Craig's List, or local sites offer advertisers a lot of directory choices. It isn't as simple as it was when the Yellow Pages basically dominated a market. However, it is still an important advertising vehicle for local businesses. Directories are a cost-efficient medium that reaches serious prospects who are in the mood to purchase. It is estimated that there are more than 10,000 printed directories aimed at both consumers and trade buyers (and many of these are also online). Because directory advertising is available when the purchase decision is being made, there are few companies that do not include at least some directory advertising in their marketing plans. Many retailers, particularly service businesses such as plumbers, rely on directories as their only type of promotion.

According to Knowledge Networks/SRI (formerly Statistical Research, Inc.), 76 percent of all U.S. adults refer to the Yellow Pages monthly, and 88 percent of those who use the Yellow Pages ultimately make or are likely to make a purchase.[26] Research also shows the average Yellow Pages user looks at more than five advertisements when scanning the directory, so it's even more important to make your brand stand out.

The evolution of the marketplace can be witnessed through Yellow Pages subject headings that trace changes in consumer lifestyles. For instance, the increases in listings for day care centers, elder care, divorce lawyers, moving companies, and truck rentals indicate a society that is increasingly mobile while pursuing careers and ending marriages.

Directory advertising has many of the characteristics of the more expensive direct-response media but with none of their intrusiveness. It also offers advertisers a continuing presence and high frequency without continuing advertising expenditures. Specialized directories are a major medium for business-to-business advertising and frequent reference sources for business buyers.

Directories, printed or online, are an important complement to other forms of advertising and promotion. In many cases, the medium is the last chance to reach the prospect at the time a purchase decision is being made. More than half of users have not made a purchase decision when they turn to the directory. Directories can offer marketers an opportunity to reach people seeking information.

Trade Incentives

Although the average consumer is not familiar with trade promotions, businesses will spend some $25 billion in promotions to reach wholesalers, retailers, and company sales personnel. These promotions are referred to as sales incentives or simply **incentives**. Incentives include everything from cash bonuses to travel, with various types of merchandise (clothing leads the list) being the most popular type of incentive.

incentives
Sales promotion directed at wholesalers, retailers, or a company's sales force.

Sales promotions directed to the trade channel are called incentives. There are two types of incentives: *dealer incentives*, which are directed to retailers and wholesalers, and *sales incentives*, which are directed to a company's sales force. Almost 80 percent of incentives are offered to direct salespeople. The most common incentives to wholesalers or retailers are price reductions in the form of promotional allowances. In effect, these incentives are comparable to cents-off promotions at the consumer level. In addition, sweepstakes, contests, and continuity promotions (some with prize catalogs) based on sales volume are all used at the trade level.

Employee motivation remains the backbone of the industry, and employers have broadened programs to recognize key personnel beyond the top sales earners. "We're seeing a higher proportion of incentive items that cost less than $100," says Mike Hadlow, president of USMotivation, Atlanta. "Managers are saying, 'OK, we've recognized the top 20 percent of our company, now what are we doing to motivate the middle 60 percent?' The types of incentives are changing as well. There is a rise in products that enhance life at home, like big-screen TVs and electronic equipment. In 2003, there was a strong desire for 'lifestyle' programs and more programs that recognize the sacrifices of the family when it comes to work. Online fulfillment has created programs that are cheaper, faster and more efficient than distributing printed catalogs. Many companies are moving their incentive program online, enabling employees to check their status and the types of products to choose from."[27]

Regardless of the type of incentive used, primary objectives are to motivate either members of the distribution channel or company reps to achieve higher sales and profitability. Dealer and trade incentives are becoming more and more crucial as retailers take greater control of the distribution channel. Most dealers have the option of selling a number of brands from different manufacturers. Manufacturers have to compete for retail distribution and, once achieved, for dealer support for their brand (e.g., premium shelf space, co-op advertising agreements, and in-store recommendations to customers). As one incentive consultant pointed out, the relationship between a manufacturer and a dealer is similar to that of a tenant and a landlord. "The dealer actually owns the distribution channel. The manufacturer is really just a tenant in the channel. Just like anything else in life, the power lies with the owner."[28]

The key to successful incentive programs is to have them complement overall business strategy. The goals that the incentive programs are intended to address should be very specific. For example, a company may use incentives to gain support for a new product line, to motivate salespersons to increase sales to current retailers, or to expand distribution to new retailers or in new territories.

There is no question that trade incentives can be extremely effective in increasing sales, productivity, and morale. However, increasingly, regulatory agencies are questioning the ethics of some trade incentives that do not provide full disclosure to customers. For example, in a retail store, consumers may seek objective information from a salesperson about one brand over another. How objective can retailers be if they are receiving significant rewards for promoting a particular brand? Currently, there is no effective system of providing consumer disclosure for trade incentives. However, as competition in many industries grows more intense and the financial value of incentives increases, we may see both state and federal regulators take a new look at the entire system of trade incentives.

Cause Marketing

Another is a recent trend toward cause marketing. Much love can be generated by companies that are able to tap into the growth in "doing good" for others. Nickelodeon's "Big Help" promotion has been an excellent relationship-building program and allows fans to get involved in something they believe in. The Home Depot Foundation helps promote National NeighborWoods Month, a program to encourage more trees in neighborhoods (see Exhibit 14.12).

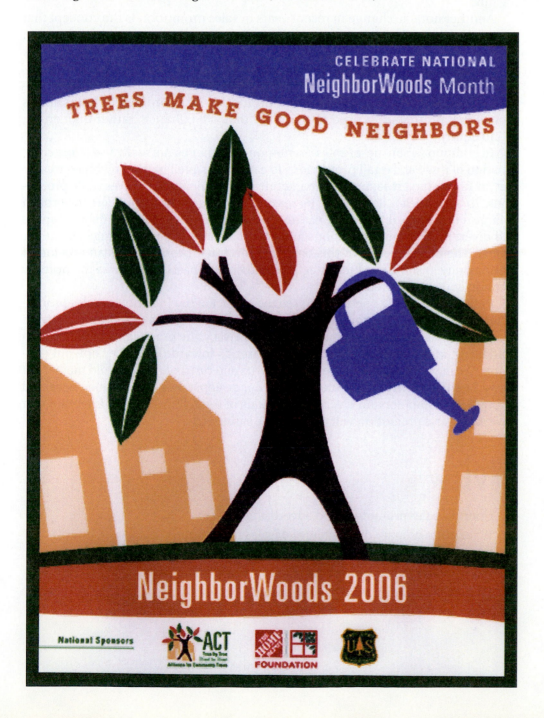

EXHIBIT 14.12

Home Depot Foundation is also a "cause" promoter.

Courtesy of Idea Engineering and The Home Depot Foundation.

SUMMARY ⚙

It is clear that distinctions among the various elements of marketing communication are becoming less clear and less important to both marketers and their customers. Businesses are increasingly demanding accountability for the dollars invested in promotion. Whether a customer is reached through traditional media, e-commerce, or one-to-one selling is less important than the contribution to profits that these elements contribute.

Remember that promotion is a powerful and versatile weapon in the marketing arsenal. Promotions can be successfully implemented to achieve both transactional and relationship goals. By understanding this and identifying the life-cycle stage through which a brand is passing (remember the spiral in Chapter 3), skillful marketers will maximize the effectiveness of promotions within the overall marketing mix.

Another notable change in recent years in sales promotion is the concept that promotion, like advertising, must contribute to brand image and brand equity. Astute marketers reject the idea that sales promotion is intended only for a quick fix or immediate sale at any cost. Today, promotion and advertising have a complementary relationship that works to develop a seamless relationship with consumers. Not only must advertising and promotion be coordinated, but it also is crucial that promotion is used in a manner that will enhance, rather than erode, brand equity.

In addition to consumer sales promotion, companies normally use some combination of trade and retail promotions to carry out overall marketing objectives. In fact, by far the largest segment of marketing communication involves trade promotions. To a significant degree, the increase in trade promotions reflects the growth of large retail chains that require national manufacturers to compete for shelf space and divert funds from promotions and advertisements that encourage consumer loyalty. The consequence of this emphasis on trade promotion is an erosion of brand equity in some product categories and an emphasis on price as the primary factor in consumer purchases.

Finally, we are only beginning to see the impact of the Internet on sales promotion. Technological convergence has created new ways to reach and cultivate prospects. It also has created concerns about privacy, the practicality of permission marketing, and how to deal with growing trends toward consumer opt-out programs. We may not be able to predict the twists and turns of new and old media, but as we see the growth in online couponing, sweepstakes, and games accessed through the computer and electronic versions of the Yellow Pages, it is certain that advertising and promotion will never be the same.

REVIEW ⚙

1. Contrast sales promotion and advertising.
2. What is the primary disadvantage of sales promotion?
3. What are the major advantages and disadvantages of event marketing?
4. What are the primary purposes of co-op advertising?
5. What is the primary regulation of co-op?
6. Why is point-of-purchase advertising so important to many advertisers?

TAKE IT TO THE WEB 🔶

In 1944, Chiquita (www.chiquita.com) became the first company to brand a banana. Take a look at the distinctive stickers that have been used over the years to market Chiquita bananas. What are some advantages to having such a unique label?

LidRock, created by the Convex Group, has turned an ordinary fountain drink lid into a way to deliver mini CDs and DVDs to consumers anywhere fountain drinks are sold. How can LidRock (www.lidrock.com) change the ways in which music and movies are previewed? What are some of the advantages and disadvantages of this approach?

PART FIVE

Creating the Advertising

CHAPTER 15

Research in Advertising

Advertisers must understand what motivates consumers in the marketplace in order to create effective advertising. Research is a critical information tool that can help advertisers understand how consumers react to their messages and why they react that way. After reading this chapter, you will understand:

chapter objectives

1. how advertisers use research
2. the role of the account planner
3. anthropology, sociology, and psychology, in relation to advertising
4. values, lifestyle, and life-stage research
5. research steps in advertising
6. types of advertising research

As we discussed in earlier chapters, there are many questions to be answered before the advertising is developed. What consumer need does our product or service satisfy? How does it satisfy differently and/or better than competitors' product or service? How can we reach consumers? In this chapter, we look at various types of research available—product, market, consumer, advertising strategy, and message research—to answer the advertiser's questions. We also examine ways to judge whether an advertisement will communicate effectively before we spend the money to run it in the media.

You cannot build strong campaigns without knowing and understanding the motivations, attitudes, and perceptions behind consumers' choices. Failure to understand the consumer will likely result in failure for the product or service. If it were easy to be successful, new products wouldn't have such a high failure rate, and established brands might not get into trouble. Advertisers would simply plug in the magic formulas. But there are no formulas to guarantee success. Was the failure of the many upstart dot-coms a lack of money or strategy, or was it a lack of understanding of how consumers used (or would use) the Internet at that time? Or was the medium so new that even consumers didn't understand it? What role, if any, did the advertising play in the success or failure of these brands?

Think about how you buy products or services. Why do you choose your toothpaste or laundry detergent brands? Why do you buy the products you put in your shopping cart—either in the store or online? Is it the brand? Is it the price? Quality? Package? Do you really know? Do you buy them because you have studied their ingredients so you feel they are superior or do you buy them because these are the brands your mother used to buy? It is not always rational. Could you explain the reasons for your preferences to a marketing researcher? Do you apply the same thought pattern to items you buy at the supermarket or drugstore? For that matter, why do you choose the supermarket where you usually shop? Location? Image?

Layout of the store? Prices? Service? Fresh vegetables? Chances are you may consider as many as three brand options. Those options make up your competitive set. These brands immediately come to mind when you think about buying a product or service. How did they get to be the top-of-mind brands in your brain? Marketing guru Sergio Zyman says, "In marketing, understanding the why is the crucial step, because when you understand why, it's a lot easier to figure out how to produce what you want."[1]

What kind of advertising motivates you to buy something? As a marketer, how do I reach you? What was the last advertisement that made you go out and buy anything? And what message do consumers take away from viewing, hearing, or reading an advertising message (see Exhibit 15.1)?

RESEARCH IS AN INFORMATIONAL TOOL

Research is and should be used to help improve an advertiser's effectiveness and profitability by staying in touch with the consumer. More specifically, research is used most often in the following ways:

- to help identify consumers
- to help look for new ideas in products or services
- to help improve what is offered in products or services
- to help pinpoint causes of possible problems
- to monitor activities
- to help in communications development
- to study promotional tools

THE RIGHT KIND OF RESEARCH

The kind of research and how much research is needed are always legitimate questions. And there are dangers. Former chairman of Roper Starch Worldwide's Roper division commented on a classic failure—Ford's Edsel—and the misuse of research. In the case of the Edsel automobile, the research was used to make people believe something that wasn't true, not to design a product to meet consumers' tastes. Ford designed a powerful, flashy car with a horse-collar grille before doing any consumer research. After the car was designed, research found consumers wanted a quietly styled, conservative, American-made, Mercedes-Benz-like vehicle. Ford then tried to make consumers fit the car by marketing Edsel as a conservatively styled automobile. It generated interest, but when consumers saw the car they were disappointed.

On the other hand, Roper cited the launch of new Coca-Cola in the 1980s as an example of research overreliance and overkill. In several taste tests, new Coca-Cola beat Pepsi, but other studies showed that sweeter products often are preferred initially. In-house and outside research for Coca-Cola failed because it didn't run normal usage taste tests on consumers. If the researchers had given consumers a case of new Coca-Cola and asked them what they thought 2 or 3 weeks later, more accurate responses would have been generated. Roper concluded that people shouldn't always follow the findings of a research study, whether it be a consumer products study or a political campaign. There are dangers despite the potential rewards.

PUBLIC ATTITUDE TOWARD SURVEY RESEARCH

Research shows that refusals to cooperate in survey research are on the rise as are negative attitudes toward survey research. The Council for Marketing and Opinion Research (CMOR) Respondent Cooperative Study conducted in 2003 showed that

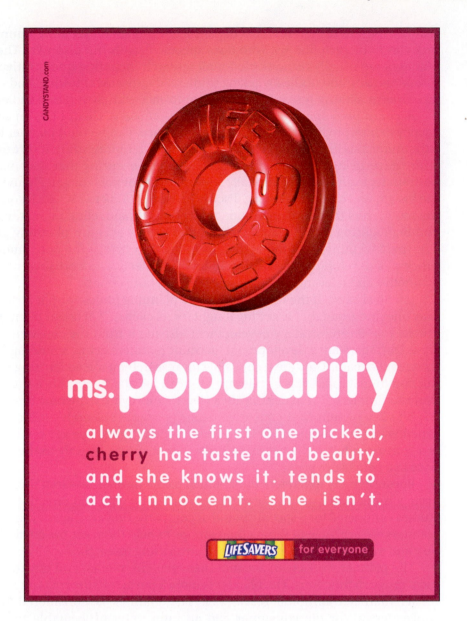

EXHIBIT 15.1

For this LifeSavers campaign, research provided insight into the way people eat, share, and enjoy them.

LifeSavers® is a registered trademark of KF Holdings, Inc., and is used with permission. Courtesy of Foote Cone & Belding, New York.

surveys are receiving record high refusal rates. The CMOR attributes this trend in part to the growth in answering machine ownership and call-screening devices used by consumers. Perhaps even more troublesome is the fact that fewer respondents see the value of participating in survey research. The study confirmed that shorter interviews can help increase the response rate.[2]

If consumers refuse to participate in consumer survey research, it will become more difficult for advertisers to gauge consumer attitudes and opinions. Refusal rates are often higher among African American and Hispanic populations, making it even more difficult to assess attitudes and opinions among these important segments of the population.

ACCOUNT/BRAND PLANNERS AND CONSUMER INSIGHTS

A British concept of research has become fundamental for many worldwide agencies. In the 1980s, some U.S. agencies moved toward copying the British restructuring of the research department. British agencies found clients doing much of their own research, yet the agency research function remained necessary to understand the information on consumers and the marketplace. The agencies restructured or

account planner
An outgrowth of British agency structure in which a planner initiates and reviews research and participates in the creative process. In some agencies, the planner is considered a spokesperson for the consumer.

reduced the size of their research departments and added **account planners**. Their task was to discern not just who buys specific brands but also why. The account planners are usually responsible for all research including quantitative research (usage and attitude studies, tracking studies, advertisement testing, and sales data) as well as qualitative research (talking face-to-face with their target audiences).

Account planning is based on a simple premise. A client hires an advertising agency to interpret its brand to its target audience. The account planner is charged with understanding the target audience and then representing it throughout the entire advertising development process, thereby ensuring that the advertising is both strategically and executionally relevant to the defined target. Planners provide the insight and clarity that move discussion from *I think* to *I know*. It sorts through the multilayers that develop around marketing a brand, eliminating the irrelevant and highlighting the relevant. According to British account planning guru Chris Crowpe, "Account Planning is the discipline that brings the consumer into the process of developing advertising. To be truly effective, advertising must be both distinctive and relevant, *and* planning helps on both counts."[3]

Jon Steel says, "If the agency has a true planning philosophy, it is interested in only one thing, and that is getting it right for its clients."[4] Account planning plays a crucial role during strategy development, driving it from the consumer's point of view. During creative development, account planners act as sounding boards for the creative team. They are responsible for researching the advertising before production to make sure it is as relevant as it can be; and finally, once the work runs, they monitor its effect in depth with a view to improving it the next time around.

The key benefit to the creative teams is usable research—information that explains and communicates, giving them useful insights. The key benefit to clients is a consumer-focused advertising strategy that speaks directly to the target audience in a persuasive way.

Because many marketers direct much of the needed research themselves, the agency is not necessarily a partner in planning the type and direction of research studies conducted for a specific brand or company. However, agency researchers or planners are available to the account groups to help them get the needed information and may be involved in all kinds of advertising research.

The planner works with account management, media, and creative, covering most research functions. The planner is more a partner to the account and creative teams than a traditional researcher. The planner is considered the team's spokesperson for the consumer and an interpreter of available research (see Exhibit 15.2). To work, advertising must deeply understand, empathize with, and speak the same language as the consumer.

WHAT KIND OF RESEARCH IS NEEDED?

Now that we have a better understanding of the research structure, let us look at the kinds of research available and some specific examples. Keep in mind that marketing has become far more complex than in the past because of the tremendous increase in new products, the high cost of shelf space, the expansion of retailer control over the distribution system, changing media habits, overload of information, and the bewildering array of communication choices.

Marketing research—up-front research—tells us about the product, the market, the consumer, and the competition. There are four basic considerations in any market research undertaking: (1) maintaining a consumer-behavior perspective; (2) being sure the right questions are being asked; (3) using appropriate research techniques and controls; and (4) presenting the research findings in a clear, comprehensible format that leads to action. After completing market research, we do advertising research—principally pretesting of advertisements and campaign evaluation—to get the data we need to develop and refine an advertising strategy and message.

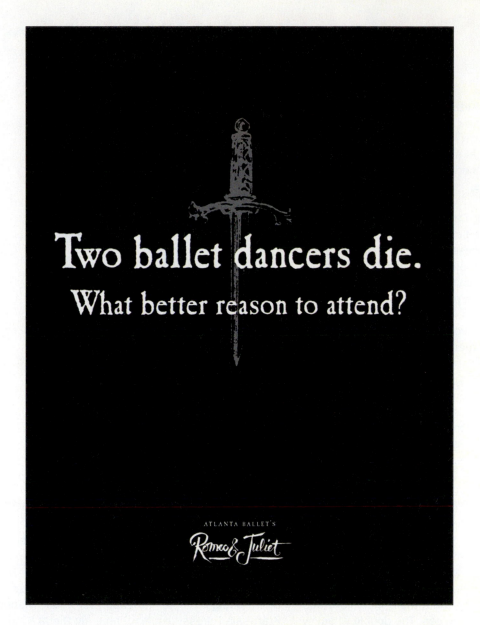

EXHIBIT 15.2
Whom do you think is the target audience for this message?
Courtesy of Blattner Brunner and the Atlanta Ballet.

The behavioral sciences—anthropology, sociology, and psychology—have had a strong influence on up-front research.

Anthropology and Advertising

Today, marketers employ anthropologists and ethnographers who use direct observation to understand consumer behavior. They study the emotional connection between products and consumer values. When Warner-Lambert wanted to find out what consumers thought of Fresh Burst Listerine, a mint-flavored product designed to compete with Scope, they paid families to set up cameras in their bathrooms and film their routines around the sink. Users of both brands said they used mouthwash to make their breath smell good, but they treated their products differently. Users of Scope typically swished and spat it out. Devotees of the new Listerine felt obliged to keep the mouthwash in their mouths longer; one went so far as to keep it in his mouth until he got to his car. (See "Kleppner's Viewpoint 15.1" for another example of observing consumers.)

Ogilvy & Mather's Discovery Group has used cameras. It sends researchers into homes with handheld cameras to get up-close pictures of how people behave in various aspects of their lives. Hours of footage then are condensed into a documentarylike 30-minute video that gives marketers and agency staff the chance to see

Brad Majors

Former CEO, SOCOH Marketing LLC, and Senior Vice President, Lintas Worldwide
Lessons in Brand Loyalty at the Point of Sale

I confess—I'm a stalker. Not the kind that makes women nervous. The kind that bothers store managers.

I stalk people shopping for goods and services. And when watching them doesn't answer my questions about their purchase decision process, I ask questions. Generally speaking, I only question friends and acquaintances, so don't worry about being accosted in a store when all you want to do is buy shampoo in peace.

Are people brand loyal and if so, why? How much more will they pay for a brand before they select another? What would make them try another brand? Unfortunately, we marketers are learning that buyers are much less loyal than we would like.

Here's an example. Traditional marketing wisdom holds that brand preferences are formed early in life, when consumers are young and willing to experiment. As consumers age, they become more loyal to brands that perform according to expectation. Thus, if anyone in a brand's franchise is loyal, it's seniors.

The Roper Report's Public Pulse (April 2002) explored "The Myth of Brand Loyalty and the Reality." Roper looked for loyalty patterns among categories and age groups and found some behavior worth noting. One of their key findings was that "categories themselves drive brand loyalty a lot more than age does." In fact, Roper makes the point that older consumers have a certain savvy gained by their many life experiences, making them more inquisitive and adventurous regarding brand choices. The double whammy is that many seniors now have enormous disposable income. Losing them when they have all that money to spend hurts twice as much.

That brings me to Gloria, my neighbor. She's a senior and as savvy as the Roper folks say she is. We went shopping together Friday night, as we do from time to time. As I pushed my cart around the store to cover my stalking behavior, I watched different people read packaging copy, examine in-store displays and make their brand choices. I kept an eye on Gloria as she considered the various brands of ice cream, studying flavors and ingredient information on the package. After she made her decision, I asked what had influenced her choice. "Well, I knew I wanted peach ice cream and usually get Breyers," she said. "But I've heard that Mayfield was very good and wanted to try their peach flavor." Sorry, Breyers, but don't

Brad Majors

take Gloria and her money for granted. She's enjoyed your product for years, but not without a regular assessment of its value.

In addition to that new brand trial, the Raspberry Vinaigrette flavor offered by Ken's Steakhouse intrigued Gloria enough for her to ignore her usual Wishbone and Kraft salad dressings. And, recently Gloria tried an alternative cleaning product, OxiClean, because of its multi-purpose flexibility and its advertised stain-removing claims. This is particularly interesting since Roper says that household cleaning products have traditionally had high brand loyalty among seniors. Well, they better not depend on Gloria to stick with those brands when something new just might work better.

Quantitative studies can tell us a lot about brand loyalty. They're a valuable tool for marketers. However, nothing beats observing real shoppers in the selling environment. This adds a human face to the insights of that research. You can take this a step further—instead of critiquing the ads you see on TV or in magazines, try withholding your own assessment and, instead, just watch the reactions of others as they review the advertisement. You might be surprised at what you see and hear. ■■■

how people really communicate and interact in certain situations. The videos may give marketers a clearer sense of how people use their products and their motivation, which can influence marketing decisions and help craft creative strategy.[5]

Several years ago, Whirlpool appliances enlisted an anthropologist to tap into consumers' feelings about and interactions with their appliances. They visited people's homes to observe how they used their appliances and talked to all the household members. Usage patterns and behavior emerged that helped Whirlpool gain insight into the flow of household activities and how tasks got accomplished. For instance, after finding that in busy families women aren't the only ones doing the laundry, Whirlpool came up with color-coded laundry controls that children and husbands can understand.[6]

Anthropologists have found that certain needs and activities are common to people the world over. Body adornment, cooking, courtship, food taboos, gift giving, language, marriage, status, sex, and superstition are present in all societies, although each society attaches its own values and traditions to them. Anthropologists see the United States as a pluralistic society made up of an array of subcultures. In each subculture lives a different group of people who share its values, customs, and traditions. Think about the cultural differences among Italian, Polish, African American, and Hispanic populations as a starting point.

We are all aware of regional differences in the American language. For example, a sandwich made of several ingredients in a small loaf of bread is a "poor boy" in New Orleans, a "submarine" in Boston, a "hoagie" in Philadelphia, and a "grinder" in upstate New York. Geomarketing allows advertisers to use these cultural differences in food preferences, terminology, and subgroup identities when they advertise their products.

Sociology and Advertising

Sociology examines the structure and function of organized behavior systems. The sociologist studies groups and their influence on and interaction with the individual. Advertisers recognize group influences on the adoption of new ideas, media use, and consumer purchase behavior. They use sociological research to predict the profitability of a product purchase by various consumer groups.

Social Class and Stratification We are a society that is clustered into classes determined by such criteria as wealth, income, occupation, education, achievement, and seniority. We sense where we fit into this pattern. We identify with others in our class ("these are my kind of people"), and we generally conform to the standards of our class. Experienced advertisers have recognized that people's aspirations usually take on the flavor of the social class immediately above their own.

Social-class structure helps explain why demographic categories sometimes fail to provide helpful information about consumers. A professional person and a factory worker may have the same income, but that doesn't mean their interests in products will coincide. In today's marketing environment, research has shown that no single variable, such as age, income, or sex, will accurately predict consumer purchases. We have discovered that using several variables gives a more accurate prediction of consumer behavior. Think of the differences between homemakers and working women of the same age, income, and education in their food preferences for themselves and their families, usage of convenience goods, child care, and media habits.

Trend Watching Quantitative research is as important as ever, but there seems to be a premium on nuggets of more attitudinal, psychographic market smarts with which marketers hope to base the creative approach to their communication.

Trends come from all forms of media and advertising. They come from music, from politics, from travel, and from the Internet. They develop everywhere. Fads, on the other hand, are like crushes; they burn fast and hot but die quickly and often leave a bitter taste. Pokemon cards, the Macarena and Beanie Babies came and went quickly. Trends are a product of society. They reflect our changing attitudes, behaviors, and values. They are the most obvious and most concrete signs of the times. Trends can be two sizes: macro and micro.

Macro trends are about the "big issues"—our definitions of happiness, success, fulfillment. Macro trends come from the way people think. They emerge when people feel a dissatisfaction with the status quo in their own lives and in society. They announce our new definitions of happiness. Some of the neotraditionalism is reflected in the return to traditions—people setting new priorities in the balance among work, family, and friends.

Micro trends are the details in the bigger picture. They are the tangible manifestations of the macro trends in fashion, music, and sports activities. For example, the macro trend of neotraditionalism will foster micro trends such as cooking schools cropping up as members of the microwave generation try to behave like their grandparents and throw dinner parties. In 2001, retro nostalgia was big. Chrysler's PT Cruiser became *Motor Trend*'s Car of the Year replacing the Lincoln LS.

Generally, young people set trends, but not every young person is a trendsetter. Those most comfortable on the cutting edge are the ones called *early adopters, alphas, trendsetters, leading edgers,* and *innovators,* and all these terms mean the same thing. These are the people who are willing to experiment. Not all trends will work for a brand. Yet, look at what Mountain Dew did by using extreme sports and over-the-top imagery to become the extreme brand despite being around for over 30 years. Many companies spend a lot of money trying to track trends. Coffeehouses and teahouses—are they fads or trends?

Cohort Analysis Using a research technique called cohort analysis, marketers can assess consumers' lifelong values and preferences and develop strategies now for products they will use later in life. Cohorts are generations of people with the same birth years and core values. According to advertising executive Natalie Perkins, these values are formed by significant events between the ages of 13 and 20 and endure throughout one's life. For example, such events as the Great Depression, the Korean War, McCarthyism, the Vietnam War, the sexual revolution, the Gulf War, and the War in Iraq or the influence of Martin Luther King Jr., television, computers, divorced and single families, and environmental crisis can form a value system.

Generally, we study consumers using demographics, psychographics, lifestyles, and behaviors. Cohort analysis combines these data and adds to the consumer profile by examining the past as well as the present. By identifying a generation's collective hot buttons, mores, and memories, advertisers can hone messages and create persuasive icons to better attract that generation.[7] This kind of research can aid in developing a product marketing plan that follows the lifetime of a consumer.

Life-Stage Research Advertisers have traditionally considered the family as the basic unit of buying behavior. Most traditional households pass through an orderly progression of stages, and each stage has special significance for buying behavior.

family life cycle
Concept that demonstrates changing purchasing behavior as a person or a family matures.

Knowledge of the **family life cycle** allows a company to segment the market and the advertising appeal according to specific consumption patterns and groups. Of course, the concept of the family has significantly changed over the past decades. Yet, there are still crucial points in the lives of consumers—they leave home, get married or stay unmarried, bear children, raise children, and send adult children into lives of their own. As a result of these life transitions, people suddenly or gradually go from one stage of life to another.

According to census data, the nature of the traditional family life cycle has changed in the past 30 years. For example, people are waiting longer to get married, women are postponing childbearing, the incidence of divorce has almost tripled,

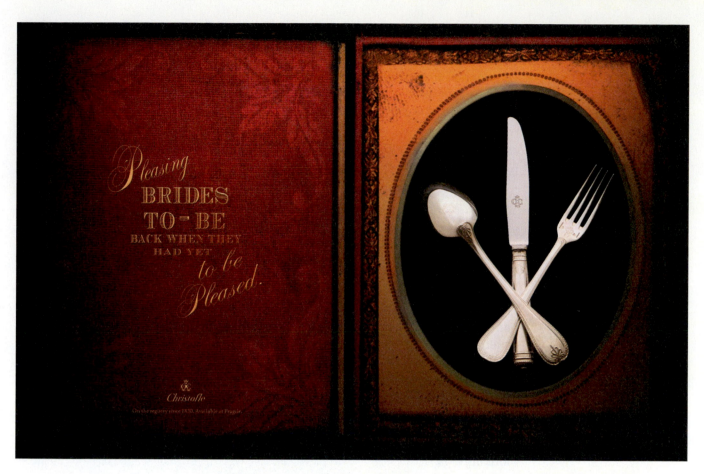

EXHIBIT 15.3
An advertiser may test the power of this lifestyle appeal.
Courtesy of Blattner Brunner.

the proportion of single-parent households has significantly increased, and more young adults are living with their parents than in the past. As a result, some advertisers have reevaluated the way they look at the family life cycle. By examining these segments' subgroups, advertisers begin to get a clearer picture of buying behavior and lifestyles. Researchers refer to these subgroup studies as *life-stage research*. As with the family life cycle, life-stage research looks at the crucial points in consumers' lives. Advertisers can find syndicated research services that analyze young singles, newlyweds, young couples, mature couples, and teenage households. Advertisers need knowledge of the life stages to help them develop and understand the changes taking place today in the twenty-first century so they can create more effective integrated marketing communications (see Exhibit 15.3).

Consumption Research Advertisers often find it useful to study consumers' consumption patterns to help them learn more about their target audience. Recently, politicians have also studied these personal buying habits in an effort to determine where they can find higher concentrations of likely supporters. This can give them insight into where to focus their advertising efforts. According to the *International Herald Tribune*, some political strategists, including those working for President George Bush and California Governor Arnold Schwarzenegger, believe that this type of research can tell more than their party label about a voter's political views. "In simplest terms: A homeowner who drives a Volvo, reads the *New Yorker* and shops at Whole Foods Market is likely to lean Democratic. A pickup driver with a hunting and fishing license who reads *Time* magazine probably leans to the right."[8]

Research has also looked at consumption patterns of some consumer groups based on their stage of acculturation. For example, Spectra Marketing has developed a consumption-driven model called the Culture Point Model™ to identify three consumer segments in the U.S. Hispanic population. These three groups are called: Least Acculturated, Most Acculturated, and Bi-Cultural. Using a combination of demographic variables including income, age, and language preference, marketers can explore variation in consumption patterns between these groups to help identify message strategies for each group.[9]

Psychology and Advertising

Psychology is the study of human behavior and its causes. Three psychological concepts of importance to consumer behavior are motivation, cognition, and learning. *Motivation* refers to the drives, urges, wishes, or desires that initiate the sequence of events known as "behavior." *Cognition* is the area in which all the mental phenomena (perception, memory, judging, thinking, and so on) are grouped. *Learning* refers to those changes in behavior relative to external stimulus conditions that occur over time.[10] These three factors, working within the framework of the societal environment, create the psychological basis for consumer behavior. Advertising research is interested in cognitive elements to learn how consumers react to different stimuli, and research finds learning especially important in determining factors such as advertising frequency. However, in recent years, the major application of psychology to advertising has been the attempt to understand the underlying motives that initiate consumer behavior. Companies are also interested in studying emotions. For example, Kellogg hired a cognitive psychologist to explore women's feelings about food. As a result of insights gained, Special K was not pitched as simply a low-fat breakfast food. Advertisements for Special K were developed that featured average women caught between polar passions for doughnuts and great-looking legs.[11]

Values and Lifestyles The research company that popularized psychographic segmentation developed Values and Life Style (VALS™). SRI Consulting Business Intelligence's VALS is designed to predict consumer behavior by profiling the psychology and demographics of U.S. consumers. It segments respondents into eight clusters of consumers, each with distinct behavioral and decision-making patterns that reflect different primary motivations and available psychological and material resources (see Exhibit 15.4).

VALS classifies consumers along two key dimensions: primary motivation (what in particular about the person or the world governs his or her actions and activities) and resources (the range of psychological and material resources available to sustain that self-concept).[12]

This classification takes into account an individual's primary motivation such as ideals, achievement, or self-expression. Resources, on the other hand, include both material and acquired attributes (e.g., money, position, education) and psychological qualities (e.g., inventiveness, interpersonal skills, intelligence, energy).

According to VALS, an individual purchases certain products and services because he or she is a specific type of person. VALS is a network of interconnected segments. Neighboring types have similar characteristics and can be combined in varying ways to suit particular marketing purposes.

Advertisers can use the VALS typology to segment particular markets, develop marketing strategies, refine product concepts, position products and services, develop advertising and media campaigns, and guide long-range planning.

Yankelovich's MindBase, a segmenting tool, identified eight major consumer groups with shared life attitudes and motivations and an understanding of consumers' generational cohort. These eight groups are each divided into three subgroups that reflect distinctions in how they react in the marketplace and to marketers' efforts. Here are the eight major MindBase segments:[13]

EXHIBIT 15.4
VALS Lifestyle Categories
Courtesy of SRI Business
Intelligence.

VALS™ Groups

Most Resources

INNOVATORS

Exhibit each of the three motivations. Successful, sophisticated, have abundant resources, receptive to new products

Ideals	Achievement	Self-Expression
THINKERS	**ACHIEVERS**	**EXPERIENCERS**
Motivated by ideals, satisfied with life, mature, well informed, open to new ideas, conservative, practical	Motivated by achievement, deep commitment to career and family, favor established, prestige products and time-saving devices	Motivated by self-expression, enthusiastic, impulsive, seek variety and excitement, avid consumers who want to look good and have cool stuff
BELIEVERS	**STRIVERS**	**MAKERS**
Motivated by ideals, conservative, deep-rooted family values, religious, and loyal to community, will buy American	Motivated by achievement, trendy and fun-loving, limited financial resources, need approval from others, active consumers	Motivated by self-expression, practical, self-sufficient, prefer value and durability to luxury

Least Resources

SURVIVORS

Narrowly focused lives, dreams limited by resources, conservative, cautious consumers, brand loyal

- I am Expressive.
- I am Driven.
- I am At Capacity.
- I am Rock Steady.
- I am Down to Earth.
- I am Sophisticated.
- I Measure Twice.
- I am Devoted.

Neuromarketing Research

Marketers are exploring the use of brain wave research to try to better understand consumers. Although this research may sound Orwellian at first blush, according to Harvard Professor Gerald Zaltman, brain wave research is trying to understand consumer motivation, not "insert ideas into people's thinking."[14] The theory behind this type of research is that it can provide marketers with an honest consumer reaction to a product or an advertisement.

With the help of neuroscientists, marketers can use a functional magnetic resonance imaging (fMRI) scanner to determine how much oxygen different parts of the brain are using when a person is exposed to an advertisement or a product. Different colors show up on the scan depending on which part of the brain is stimulated with thought. Electroencephalograms (EEGs) are also used by some marketers to monitor consumers' brain activity while viewing advertisements. Through a special cap worn by subjects, the EEGs measure electrical impulses produced by the brain. They can be used to assess reactions to all or parts of a commercial message because different parts of the brain show attraction, revulsion, recall, and level of attention, for instance. However, it can be difficult to interpret what this activity means.[15]

These kinds of tests can be very costly. According to Akshay Rao, professor of marketing at Minnesota's Carlson School of Management, renting an fMRI scanner and testing twenty subjects costs about $15,000.[16] EEGs are comparatively less expensive. According to Caroline Winnett, vice president of marketing for NeuroFocus, a company that conducts advertising research, these tests are less expensive than fMRIs and cost about the same as a typical focus group.[17]

Marketing Environment

Companies and agencies want to accumulate as much information about their markets as possible before making crucial integrated marketing decisions. Technology has been assisting marketers in getting more information faster.

Universal Product Code Universal Product Code (UPC) information has greatly enhanced the process of tracking product sales. When the grocer scans a price into the register at the checkout, that information is instantly available to the retailer. Scanner reporting systems have allowed marketers to track their performance quickly—rather than monthly or bimonthly—and at local levels. UPC information allows marketers to determine what their share of market is, if one kind of packaging or in-store advertising sells better, and which retailers sell the most units. Cash-checking cards can be scanned into the system to keep a record of what kind of products consumers buy. This offers the retailer and manufacturer the opportunity to target promotions directly to people who have used the product in the past. This information can contribute to any database marketing effort by the retailer.

Single-Source Data For single-source data, retail tracking scanner data are integrated with household panel data on purchase patterns and advertisement exposure. The information comes from one supplier and is extracted from a single group of consumers. These data can be combined with other research sources to supply micromarketers with a wealth of information on who, what, and how. Despite these new micromarketing capabilities, research firms are far more adept at generating data than most clients are at using the information.

Database Marketers Database marketers use sweepstakes entries, rebate information, merchandise orders, free-product offers, requests for new-product information, and purchase information to build consumer databases telling them a great deal about how consumers live. This information offers many opportunities for database marketing (see Exhibit 15.5).

Internet Data Many major advertisers and research companies have embraced the Internet for online focus groups, surveys, and other marketing research, despite the Internet's flaws and problems (e.g., how representative Web users are of the overall

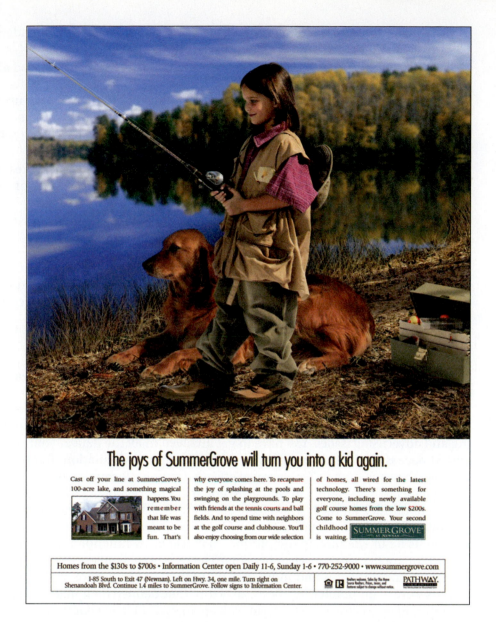

EXHIBIT 15.5
One way to test the
success of this
advertisement is by the
number of calls to the
phone number provided.
Courtesy of McRae
Communications and Pathway
Communities.

population). Online research shouldn't replace traditional marketing research, but harnessing the Internet improves the research process. Web-based research should be part of the mix.

General Motors Corporation created real-time, online clinics to gather consumer reaction to upcoming products. Mark Hogan, president of GM's e-commerce unit, said, "The days (of bringing) 1,000 people over a weekend to look at our products will soon be a thing of the past." Nissan's development of the Xterra sport utility vehicle stemmed partly from cybersurfer input. After winning *Motor Trend* magazine's SUV of the year (1999), Nissan sent 1,500 e-mails to targeted buyers to find out the credibility of the awards among consumers.[18]

THE SERIES OF RESEARCH STEPS IN ADVERTISING

The term *advertising research* is broadly defined as including research that contributes to all four stages of the advertising process:

1. *Advertising strategy development.* Research tries to answer many questions: Who is the market and what does it want? What is the competition we are specifying?

What communication do we want our selected market to get from our advertising? How will we reach the persons selected as our market?

2. *Advertising execution development.* There are two kinds of research used at the execution stage of advertising. The first is exploratory research to stimulate the creative people and to help them know and understand the language used by consumers. The other is research to study proposed creative concepts, ideas, roughs, visuals, headlines, words, presenters, and so forth to see whether it can do what the creative strategy expects of it.

3. *Evaluating pretesting executions.* Pretesting is the stage of advertising research at which advertising ideas are tested. Partly because of the finality of much pretesting, it is the most controversial kind of advertising research.

4. *Campaign evaluation.* Campaign evaluation usually involves a tracking study to measure the performance of a campaign.

The primary goal of advertising research is to help in the process of creative development. Before we examine the research process advertisers would use in developing advertising strategy for campaigns, let us get a better perspective on using research information.

Translating Information into Strategy

Information isn't enough by itself to answer marketing problems. A few years ago, the brilliant McCann Erickson researcher, Jack Dempsey, said, "By itself information has no value." It acquires value only when the strategist takes "a point of view" about what the information means—a point of view that is relevant to the marketing and advertising issues. You have to get involved in all the data at your disposal and, if necessary, fill in some gaps by acquiring more information. But then you have to step back from it. The secret of effective strategy formation lies in deciding which data are important and which are not. It is a process of organizing simplicity out of complexity, for the best strategic insights are usually the very simple ones.

Take the consumer's point of view. Ask yourself what the consumer is really buying. Is he or she buying the product because of its functional benefits? How important are the psychological benefits? The corporate landscape is littered with examples of companies and industries that failed to appreciate what their consumers were really purchasing. Because of this, they defined their markets inappropriately and often disastrously. Begin with an analysis of how people behave rather than an analysis of how they feel or what they believe. You will probably get into these issues, but behavior is the foundation from which you build. And above all, try to see the world with the consumers' eyes.

Think about the question, "How many pairs of shoes do you buy in a year?" Now, if you disregard such factors as style and fashion, the number of shoes bought in a year depends largely on how much walking is done, not on age, sex, or social class. These may be associated variables but less determinant than the amount of walking the individual does. You see, information by itself has no value.

Market, Product, Competitive, and Consumer Research

Basic information is gathered and analyzed to determine the marketing strategy for a product or service, projected sales, the source of business, pricing and distribution factors, geographic information, and how to develop data to identify the size and nature of the product category. This kind of research includes data on competitors, sales trends, packaging, advertising expenditures, and future trends. Situation analysis helps to define clearly the market in which the product or service competes (see Exhibit 15.6).

Prospect research is critical to define clearly who is expected to buy the product or service. Studies may identify users, attitudes, lifestyles, and consumption patterns—all of which identify the prime prospect.

EXHIBIT **15.6**
Situation Analysis

The amounts and kinds of information required will vary according to the product category and marketing situation. Exhibit 15.7 outlines strategy choices indicated by different levels of brand trial and awareness. It is difficult to talk about strategy until you have information on awareness levels for each brand in the market. "Brand trial" will occur if what consumers know about the brand fits in with their needs and is sufficiently important or motivating. The relationship between a brand's level of awareness and its trials may be expressed as a ratio. A high ratio will suggest one strategy option, a low ratio another. For example, ratio of high awareness to low trial (lower-left-hand box of Exhibit 15.7) clearly indicates that what people know about the brand is not sufficiently motivating or relevant, and the brand may need repositioning.

Research does not always tell us what we want to hear, which can create problems if we think an advertising idea is really strong. Take the classic "Avis. We try harder" campaign. It tested poorly in research. Consumers said the "We're number two" concept meant Avis was second rate. Research was against running it, but creative genius Bill Bernbach fervently believed in the idea and convinced Avis to take a chance with it. Today, the Avis campaign is considered one of the most powerful and most memorable advertising campaigns in history.

Advertising Strategy or Message Research

Most products have a number of positive appeals that could be successfully promoted, so how do we go about making the decision as to which direction to go with

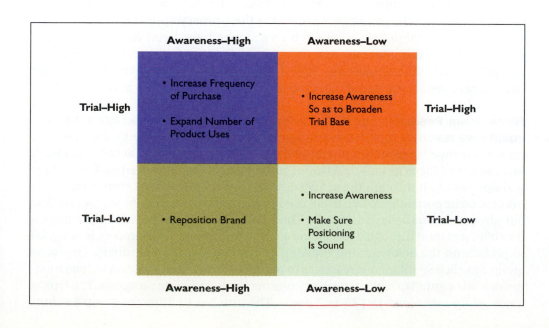

EXHIBIT **15.7**

Brand Trial/Awareness Ratios: Strategic Options

Greg Nyilasy, Ph. D.

Senior Research Account Executive, Hall & Partners New York
www.hall-and-partners.com
How I've Learned to Love Research

*W*as it love at first sight? I wouldn't exactly say that. . . .

Picture this. Really junior copywriter comes up with great brand name for swanky new alcoholic beverage ad agency is pitching. Really cool beverage, for cool people, cool package design and . . . even cooler brand name! What's more, the client likes it at the presentation. Agency Executive Creative Director shaking hands, personnel congratulating in droves, general manager buying frames to put layouts on wall. Claps, confetti, champagne. Cut to two weeks later. Copytesting results in. Name "too cool." Older target doesn't like it. Younger target likes it too much. Isn't it polarizing? Too edgy? We've got to be serious here, this is alcohol. Can't we have something safer? Oh, the other agency has it. Never mind. Pitch over. Agency offices quiet. Nobody plays office basketball for at least two days straight. Confetti vacuumed.

Copywriter thinking, research: not cool.

Well, the thing is, I was wrong.

The first realization came a good two years later when I read Alan Hegdes' *Testing to Destruction* (and by the way, I enrolled in my PhD in mass communication research). It was somewhat of a revelation that advertising research,

Greg Nyilasy, Ph. D.

albeit often misused, doesn't necessarily have to suck. It doesn't necessarily lead to mediocre creative, it doesn't have to be unimaginative and it isn't after all the work of the devil.

The second revelation came, when I joined Hall & Partners NY. I had to come to the conclusion that research

an advertisement or appeal? The idea is to choose the one that is most important to the majority of our target. Because selecting the primary appeal is the key to any advertising campaign, many research techniques have been developed to find which appeal to use. Message research is used to identify the most relevant and competitive advertising sales message. It may take many forms, but focus groups and concept testing are frequently used to evaluate creative ideas and strategies.

focus group
A qualitative research interviewing method using in-depth interviews with a group rather than with an individual.

qualitative research
This involves finding out what people say they think or feel. It is usually exploratory or diagnostic in nature.

Focus Group Research **Focus groups** became fashionable in the late 1960s as a **qualitative research** tool that was often used to provide a more in-depth way to explore creative ideas than through rigid quantitative tests. Later account planners saw the use of focus groups as a way of getting early consumer feedback to an idea without putting it through the artificiality of a formal test. Focus groups have also become an important qualitative tool used by marketers and account planners to find out why consumers behave as they do. The focus group offers a means of obtaining in-depth information through a discussion-group atmosphere. This process is designed to probe into the behavior and thinking of individual group members. The focus group can elicit spontaneous reactions to products or advertisements. A trained moderator leads a group of eight to twelve consumers, usually prime prospects. The typical focus group interviews last 1½ to 2 hours. The number of different group sessions

at its best was the highest-grade fuel for brand building imagination, it could add enormously to the creative product itself, and it was the greatest tool to break through the subjectivity of any one decision maker and enter the consumer's mind, the most important one in the whole marketing communications game.

So how do you go about executing a communications research program that doesn't suck? What are some of the principles of good research? Here are some thoughts:

- Advertising-only communication projects are things of the past, so should be advertising-only research projects—In today's fragmented media space, few brands can afford not to have feedback on all Integrated Marketing Communications touchpoints.
- You have to be smart about integration, however. Not all communication disciplines work the same way. And they don't all work as advertising does—Product placements, sponsorships, direct marketing, public relations, etc. generate communication response in different ways. Good research acknowledges that and offers a true understanding how each individual communication discipline works.
- Even within a single communication discipline there are different ways to build a brand—Involvement, persuasion, salience or behavioral stimulation are all possible avenues to brand commitment. Research has to measure effectiveness against what route the communication was supposed to be taken, not a scorecard of uniform norms.
- True integration is speaking with a single voice through all brand touchpoints. As a result it is also much more than the sum of its parts—Good research should be able to account for this amplification effect.

- Brand response is more important than communication response—Communication is not an end in itself, it's a tool to strengthen brand relationships. Sounds simple, yeah? Still many advertisers look for single magic scores of advertising awareness.
- The more you customize research, the better it will fit with your brand—There are no two identical brands, market situations or communication efforts, so why should their research be standardized? The more you tailor your research tools, the more insightful and specific the results are going to be. Research heaven, only for you.
- Advertising is both art and science: so research should be both creative and disciplined—You cannot expect imaginative insights from an unimaginative study design. You cannot expect anything other than mere opinion from an analysis that's not scientifically disciplined.
- Communications pretesting is both about maximization and minimization—maximization of creative potential, and minimization of financial risk. The best strategy is to test early concepts diagnostically with qualitative methods and final executions predictively with quantitative methods.
- Communications tracking should be forward- and not backward-looking—Following the effectiveness of campaigns and relating it to your brand's health is not an exercise in building historical backlogs. Tracking is not about the past, it is about offering guidance how to strengthen brand relationships in the future.

These are just a few ideas to jumpstart your thinking how to look at research in a different way. Look for research that's sensitive, innovative, imaginative and offers insights for nurturing brand relationships. It's difficult to find it but once you do, you can't help falling in love with it. . . . ■ ■ ■

varies from advertiser to advertiser based somewhat on expense, topic being discussed, and time considerations. The client usually watches the interview from behind a one-way mirror so as not to disrupt the normal function of the group.

An example of a client for whom focus groups provided much needed insight is Nikon. Nikon has long been considered the brand of choice of professional photographers and serious hobbyists. However, the company found a need to expand its message to consumers who shop at places such as Best Buy and Circuit City to capture the average picture taker. In focus groups, Nikon heard things like, "Nikon is too much camera for me. I just need to take pictures of my kids." A new effort was aimed to broaden the consumer base, according to McCann-Erickson's creative director Pete Jones, and give consumers the confidence to take a great picture.[19]

As we indicated earlier, researchers are using more online focus groups to gather consumers' responses to questions and products.

Videoconferencing links, television monitors, remote-control cameras, and digital-transmission technology allow focus group research to be accomplished over long-distance lines. Many advertising agencies believe videoconferencing enriches the creative process because it gives more people input. This technique allows more agency and client people to watch groups from all over the country without having to travel.

There are critics of the overemphasis on focus groups. They point to the fact that many good ideas—whether a 30-second commercial or a new product or concept—often get killed prematurely because they did not do well with a focus group. One increasing criticism is the growing number of "professional" respondents who are savvy enough to go from focus group to focus group, speaking the marketers' language and picking up an easy $50 or $75 each time. Most account planners agree that focus groups should never be used as a replacement for quantitative research. But these groups are useful to determine consumer reaction to certain language in a television commercial or in the development process for creative.

concept testing

The target audience evaluation of (alternative) creative strategey. Testing attempts to separate good and bad ideas and provide insight into factors motivating acceptance or rejection.

Concept Testing Concept testing is a method to determine the best of a number of possible appeals to use in your advertising. A *creative concept* is defined as a simple explanation or description of the advertising idea behind the product.

A tourism association developed several appeals that might motivate prime prospects to drive 2 hours to the mountains from a large metro area in another state:

1. Only 2 hours to relaxation
2. Mountain fun in your own backyard
3. The family playground in the mountains
4. Escape to white-water rafting, fishing, and the great outdoors
5. Weekend vacation-planner package

By using cards with the theme statement and/or rough layouts, the advertiser tries to obtain a rank order of consumer appeal of the various concepts and diagnostic data explaining why the concepts were ranked as they were. The tourism group found that targets had not realized they were so close to these mountain areas. As a result, mountain areas had not been considered in their vacation or recreation plans. In the case of a car rental company, a test of vacation travelers found that one benefit stood out: the lowest-priced full-size car. The second most important benefit was no hidden extras.

One drawback of concept testing is that consumers can react only to the themes presented to them. You may find that they have chosen the best of several bad concepts.

Pretest Research The client wants assurances that the advertising proposed will be effective. In pretesting, a particular advertisement passes or fails or is selected as being better than all the others. The only alternative is for the client to depend solely on the judgment of the agency or its own personnel.

In general, there are two levels of research aimed at helping advertisers determine how well an advertisement will perform. **Copy testing** is done in two stages:

copy testing

Measuring the effectiveness of advertisements.

1. Rough copy research is needed to determine if the copy is effectively achieving its goals in terms of both message communication and attitude effects.
2. Finished copy research is done on the final form of the copy to evaluate how well the production process has achieved communication and attitude effects (see Exhibit 15.8).

Pretesting is the stage of advertising research in which a complete advertisement or commercial is tested. It is important that the objectives of pretesting research relate back to the agreed-upon advertising strategy. It would be wasted effort to test for some characteristic not related to the goal of the advertising.

A number of variables can be evaluated in pretesting, including the ability of the advertisement to attract attention, comprehension by the reader/viewer, playback of copy points (recall), persuasion (the probability that the consumer will buy the brand), attitude toward the brand, credibility, and irritation level.

Response Criterion	Measurement
Cognitive (Think)	
Attention	Eye camera
Awareness	Day-after recall
Affective (Feel)	
Attitude	Persuasion
Feelings	Physiological response
Conative (Do)	
Purchase intent	Simulated shopping
Sales	Split cable/scanner

EXHIBIT 15.8

Effectiveness Measures by Type of Consumer Response for Copy Research

Source: Adopted from John D. Leckenby and Joseph T. Plummer, "Advertising stimulus measurement and assessment research: A review of advertising testing methods," *Current Issues and Research in Advertising*, 1983, 155.

Pretests should be used as guides and not as absolute predictors of winners or losers. In copy testing, a higher score for one advertisement over another does not guarantee a better advertisement. As Bill Bernbach once said, "Research is very important, but I think it is the beginning of the ad." Norm Grey, former creative director and now head of the Creative Circus, once commented on creative testing, "If you don't like the score an ad gets, demand another test. The only thing that's certain is that you'll get another score." These comments do not imply that creative testing is bad. They simply point to the fact that it is controversial and simply another tool for the advertiser.

There have been arguments about the value of testing advertisments for years. In general, clients demand them and agency creatives are suspect of the process. Australian social researcher Hugh Mackay says, "The best advertising research never, at any stage, mentions advertising. The pre-testing [sic] of rough executions puts a fence around what you can talk about with consumers. The real challenge is to establish what concepts exist in the consumer's mind."[20] Ed McCabe of McCabe & Company makes a distinction between research and testing: "Without great research, you can't make great advertising. However, testing is the idiocy that keeps greatness from happening. Testing is a crutch the one-eyed use to beat up the blind." He points to his Hebrew National hot dog campaign in which an actor portraying Uncle Sam is brought up short by the company's insistence on exceeding federal regulations because its products are kosher and must "answer to a higher authority." The advertisements did not test well, and the client was reluctant to run them. After much discussion, the advertisements ran. Some 20 years later, the advertisements were still running. The point is that testing can be useful, but it is not a foolproof science. If you were spending millions of dollars on a creative idea, wouldn't you do everything possible to reduce the risk or, to put it another way, "to better guarantee" a chance for success?

Campaign Evaluation Research In evaluating advertising within the total marketing effort, an advertiser should analyze the market and competitive activity and look at advertising as a campaign—not as individual advertisements. This information can help determine whether changes in the advertising strategy are needed to accomplish the objectives established for the campaign or to deal with a changed situation (see Exhibit 15.8).

Advertisers frequently conduct tracking studies to measure trends, brand awareness, and interest in purchasing, as well as advertising factors. The research at the end of one campaign becomes part of the background research for selecting the next campaign strategy.

TESTING CREATIVE RESEARCH

Creative research takes place within the context of the preceding research stages. This kind of research aids in the development of what to say to the target audience and how to say it. Copy-development research attempts to help advertisers decide how to execute approaches and elements. Copy testing is undertaken to aid them in determining whether to run the advertising in the marketplace.

1. A good copy-testing system provides measurements that are relevant to the objectives of the advertising. Of course, different advertisements have different objectives (for example, encouraging trial of a product).

2. A primary purpose of copy testing is to help advertisers decide whether to run the advertising in the marketplace. A useful approach is to specify action standards before the results are in. Examples of action standards are the following:

   ■ Significantly improves perceptions of the brands as measured by _____.

   ■ Achieves an attention level no lower than _____ percent as measured by _____.

EXHIBIT 15.9

Research can test the power of this visual.

Courtesy of Blattner Brunner and Zippo.

3. A good copy-testing system is based on the following model of human response to communications: the reception of a stimulus, the comprehension of the stimulus, and the response to the stimulus. In short, to succeed, an advertisement must have an effect:

■ On the eye and the ear—that is, it must be received (reception)

■ On the mind—that is, it must be understood (comprehension)

■ On the heart—that is, it must make an impression (response)

4. Experience has shown that test results often vary according to how complete a test is. Thus, careful judgment should be exercised when using a less-than-finished version of a test. Sometimes what is lost is inconsequential; at other times, it is critical.[21]

Forms of Testing

Each advertiser and agency use similar but modified steps in the testing of creative research. The following are examples of this process.

Concept Testing As mentioned earlier, concept testing may be an integral part of creative planning and is undertaken for most clients as a matter of course. Creative concept testing can be defined as the target audience evaluation of (alternative) creative strategy. Specifically, concept testing attempts to separate the "good" ideas from the "bad," to indicate differing degrees of acceptance, and to provide insight into factors motivating acceptance or rejection.

There are a number of possible concept tests:

1. *Card concept test.* Creative strategies are presented to respondents in the form of a headline followed by a paragraph of body copy on a plain white card. Each concept is on a separate card. Some concepts cannot be tested in card form (for example, those requiring a high degree of mood, such as concepts based on humor or personalities).

2. *Poster test.* This is similar to a card test except that small posters containing simplified illustrations and short copy are used rather than plain cards without illustrations.

3. *Layout test.* A layout test involves showing a rough copy of a print advertisement (or artwork of a television commercial with accompanying copy) to respondents. Layout tests are more finished than poster tests in that they use the total copy and illustration as they will appear in the finished advertisement. Additionally, whereas a card or poster test measures the appeal of the basic concept, the purpose of the layout test may be to measure more subtle effects such as communication, understanding, and clarity.

Finished Print Tests This testing procedure can take many forms of measuring the finished advertisement as it would appear in print. One such testing procedure used for finished print advertisements goes something like this: Test advertisements, finished or unfinished, are inserted into a twenty-page magazine in a folder containing both editorial and control advertisements. Prospects preview the magazine in one-on-one interviews in high-traffic malls. Respondents are questioned regarding unaided, aided, and related recall of the test advertisement. Next they are asked to focus on the test advertisement only and are probed for reactions. Agencies are furnished with diagnostic data to improve the advertisement. The advertisements are measured for stopping power, communication, relevance, and persuasion. Likes and dislikes about the advertisement are also provided (see Exhibit 15.10).

EXHIBIT 15.10

We can use research to measure what benefits this advertisement communicates to the target.

Courtesy of the Johnson Group and Litespeed Lunaris.

Testing Unfinished Commercials Generally, commercial testing on film or videotape falls into one of four categories:

1. *Animatics.* This is artwork, either cartoons or realistic drawings that are computer generated or hand drawn. Some animatics show limited movement; those that do not are usually called video storyboards.
2. *Photomatics.* These are photographs shot in sequence on film. The photos may be stock (from a photo library) or shot on location.
3. *Liveamatics.* This involves filming or taping live talent and is very close to the finished commercial.
4. *Ripamatics.* The commercial is made of footage from other commercials, often taken from advertising agency promotion reels. Ripamatics are used many times for experimentation on visual techniques.

Finished Commercial Testing Television testing techniques can generally be classified into two categories:

1. Those that attempt to evaluate a commercial's effectiveness in terms of viewers' recall of a certain aspect of the commercial
2. Those that attempt to evaluate a commercial's effectiveness in terms of what it motivates a viewer to say or do

Recent advances in production technology are helping the testing process. The more closely the test spot resembles the finished commercial, the more accurate the test results will be. Computer animation has become less expensive, so there is more computer-generated artwork in commercial testing.

Readership

Advertisers face mounting competition both in the market and on the printed page. It is important to have the ability to determine if an advertisement is being seen. One such readership service that supplies this kind of information is the Starch Readership Service from Roper Starch.

The Starch Readership Service is designed to measure the extent to which advertisements are being seen and read and the level of interest they arouse. Starch interviews more than 75,000 consumers each year to determine their responses to more than 50,000 print advertisements. Starch uses the recognition method of interviewing. With the publication open, the respondent explains the extent to which he or she has read each advertisement prior to the interview. For each advertisement, respondents are asked, "Did you see or read any part of this advertisement?" If yes, a prescribed questioning procedure is followed to determine the observation and reading of each component part of each advertisement—illustration, headline, signature, and copy blocks. After these questions are asked, each respondent is classified as follows:

- *Noted reader.* A person who remembers having previously seen the advertisement in the issue being studied.
- *Associated reader.* A reader who not only noted the advertisement but also saw or read some part of it that clearly indicated the brand or advertiser.
- *Read most.* A person who read half or more of the written material in the advertisement.

Clients receive Adnorm data with the Starch Readership Reports. Adnorms enable advertisers to compare readership data of their advertisement in a given magazine issue to the norm for advertisements of the same size and color in the same product category. These data can help advertisers identify the types of layouts that attract and retain the highest readership. They can also compare current advertisements against those of competitors, compare the current campaign against previous campaigns, compare the current campaign against a competitor's previous campaign, and compare current advertisements against the Adnorm tables.

Criticisms of Copy Testing Research

Standard copy testing techniques have long been criticized by advertising agency personnel. They see many of these techniques as giving an unfair advantage to boring and/or irritating advertisements while penalizing more innovative approaches. According to John Kastenholz, vice president of consumer and market insights at Unilever, "There is a feeling, particularly among creative directors, that copy testing can undermine the ability to produce breakthrough creative ideas."[22] Many marketers and advertising agency executives recognize that most of the commonly used techniques do not adequately assess consumers' emotional response to advertising, and they don't feel as though there have been adequate advances in the methods used. The former executive vice president director of research and insight for Interpublic Group of Companies, Joe Plummer, says that "there's been no fundamental advance in copy testing since the early 1980s. So much new information is available today on how the mind works and processes emotional responses to stories, metaphors and symbols."[23] Several companies have new techniques under development that hold promise for future copy testing research.

SUMMARY ✺

Advertising is a people business. Successful advertisers know who their prospects are and—to whatever extent is practical—their needs and motives, which result in the purchase of one product or service and the rejection of another. Consumer behavior is usually the result of a complex network of influences based on the psychological, sociological, and anthropological makeup of the individual.

Advertising rarely, if ever, changes these influences but rather channels needs and wants of consumers toward specific products and brands. Advertising is a mirror of society. The advertiser influences people by offering solutions to their needs and problems, not by creating these needs. The role of the advertiser is to act as a monitor of the changing face of society.

Advertisers pay special attention to what we call up-front research or market research that reflects the market, the consumer, and the competition. Such information as cohort analysis, VALS, and MindBase can help us understand consumer lifestyles and values, which aids in developing strategies.

Once all of this information is digested, it is used in the four stages of advertising development: strategy development, execution development, pretesting of executions, and campaign evaluation. By itself, information has no value. It acquires value only when we take a point of view about what the information means.

There are a number of stages of testing available in creative research ranging from concept testing and commercial testing techniques to finished print and commercial tests. It is much less expensive to test concepts and advertisements prior to buying expensive media schedules.

REVIEW ✺

1. Why are sociology, psychology, and anthropology important to advertising?
2. What kind of research is used in advertising execution development?
3. What is the role of the animatic commercial?
4. What is neuromarketing and how is it used by some advertisers in advertising development?
5. How are focus groups used in advertising research?

TAKE IT TO THE WEB ❀

Greenfield Online (www.greenfieldonline.com) is a survey center that gathers personal information about you in exchange for possible cash prizes and other rewards. How has the Internet changed the process of taking surveys? Are you more willing or less willing to participate in an online survey than a telephone or face-to-face interaction?

Advertising for Oreo cookies has tended to emphasize the emotional connection consumers have with the brand. Visit www.nabiscoworld.com/oreo/memories to see how the "Moments of Oreos and Milk" section of the website makes use of this emotional connection.

How does Pepsi (www.pepsi.com) use Pepsi promotions to attract consumers to its website? How could Pepsi use its website to gain both demographic and psychographic information about consumers?

To get a more complete look at the eight Yankelovich MindBase segments, check out www.yankelovich.com/products/MindBase.PS.pdf.

Creating the Message

*E*arlier, we discussed developing integrated marketing communication strategy. It has been said that strategy is everything. "Sometimes creative leads, sometimes strategy leads," says British creative director Tony Cox, "but both have to remain close in harmony for a great ending." Great advertising copy is essential to great advertising no matter what the medium. Understanding consumers and what appeals to them is part of the developmental process needed to create great copy. Here we talk about print and online game plans. After reading this chapter, you will understand:

chapter objectives

1. the nature and the use of appeals
2. the creative work plan
3. elements of a print advertisement
4. structure of a print advertisement
5. copy styles
6. slogans
7. new format and content messages

"At the heart of an effective creative philosophy is the belief that nothing is so powerful as an insight into human nature, what compulsions drive a person, what instincts dominate their action, even though his or her language so often can camouflage what really motivates them."

—Bill Bernbach

In IMC, we talk about message integration and reinforcement across the many touchpoints consumers encounter, whether in a print advertisement, on the Web, or on television—every medium. This consistency in tone, messaging, and visual appearance is called *touchpoint integration*. The Folks coupon advertisement (see Exhibit 16.1) looks like a regular print advertisement. However, it is an advertisement on a radio program website, not the Folks site. So the Web advertisement offered a reduced price and tried to drive traffic to the Folks website. It is one of its integrated messages. This kind of touchpoint integration is the hallmark of brands such as Starbucks, McDonald's, Nike, and many others. This is true, but there is more to the equation. "The creative people who can get into the heart—not just the brain—and make people cry or laugh or silently say, 'yeah, that's how I really feel' will be the superstars," says Lou Centlivre, formerly of Foote Cone & Belding. John Pepper, former CEO of Procter & Gamble, notes, "I have seen through 25 years that the correlation between profitable business growth on our brands and having great copy on our brands isn't 25 percent, it's not 50 percent. It is 100 percent. I have not

seen a single P&G brand sustain profitable volume growth for more than a couple of years without having great advertising."[1]

Because everything in the marketplace (and the world) appears to be changing, are there new rules for developing advertisements? Of course. The game has indeed changed. Earlier we said the long-held tenets sometimes distort our view of what might be and what should be. It has been asked, "What is going to replace the old rules? Anarchy?" In some ways, new rules haven't been written, especially in new technology communication. There is more scope for intuitive thinking, for experimentation, for innovation. Oh, once again I forgot to tell you, there are no rules. There have never been "rules." That said, we need to understand there are nonrules or guidelines that are generally accepted and sometimes draw on years of research results or accumulated wisdom of creative communicators. You might say they are similar to fashion rules—some things just work better. And it's your job to figure out which. This probably sounds like a contradiction, but it really isn't.

In this chapter we'll discuss "how to . . ." and the words will form what appear to be rules. It is a means of sharing and analyzing. Ken Roman, former CEO of Ogilvy & Mather Worldwide, says, "Recipes don't work for a very simple reason: This is a business of ideas. Ideas don't derive from rules; they derive from principles."[2] The real challenge is to use this knowledge in the context of your specific communication problem. Remember that earlier in this text we talked about creative risk. Look at taking smart risks, where you know what the norm of thinking is, and go from there—with caution. The goal is to communicate.

CREATIVE RISK TAKING

As media and advertising businesses move through this period of transformation, marketers want insights to tap into their consumers' emotional connections. They want to narrow the field and move away from the traditional mass audience quantifications of reach and frequency. They want to build relationships.[3] Many of the fundamental beliefs are under siege; but certain rules, beliefs, and methodologies have served the business well, and restraint is called for. At the same time, agencies owe their clients effective advertising and must find ways to accomplish this. "An idea that hasn't been done before might, on the surface, look really risky," argues Bob Isherwood of Saatchi & Saatchi. "It's an area where no one has gone before. There is no precedent. But usually the biggest risk lies in ideas that are predictable." Ideas that are predictable don't get noticed. As Oscar Wilde once said, *an idea that does not involve risk does not deserve to be an idea.* David Jones, CEO of global agency network Euro RSCG Worldwide, says rather than talking about how to redefine creativity in a fast-changing world, "[w]e should just get on and do it."[4] Some of the most well-liked advertisements were based upon a creative director's gut instinct of what consumers would like. Jones cites Procter & Gamble's effort for the Charmin toilet tissue creation that plays off the many euphemisms for elimination. He also says creatives should "trust your gut." Advertising is changing fast, and to not take a risk is risky—even though it's scary to do so. Risk is about breaking rules or guidelines.

"A lot of creative people think creative risk taking means doing ads that scare the life out of you," says Singapore creative director Garry Abbott. "Good ads don't rely on borrowed ideas. Risk is about *freshness*." Finding out from consumers what it really is like being them so that ads can respond to their needs is a risk many don't take. According to Hugh Mackay, one way to accomplish this is to "take a set of familiar elements and rearrange them in an unfamiliar way so that the reader recognizes both the familiar and the unfamiliar. In other words, present something the readers recognize as themselves, their lives, their dreams, but with a twist, so they're a bit startled by it, or get an extra insight from it."[5] Is this a rule? No. It is a way of thinking about how to solve a problem. The *Daily Report* is a legal newspaper and Huey+Partners appeal to the athlete and wannabes in this creative use of type and visual (see Exhibit 16.2).

All creatives have a responsibility. Erik Veruroegen, executive creative director, TBWA Paris, says: "I am against advertising where people just show crap and say 'but it works.' We have a mission to stop that. The consumer does not like advertising at all. It interrupts. It is pretentious to believe that the consumer will give you a chance just because you're there. Advertising must earn the right to be paid attention to, but you can't be different for the sake of being different."[6]

A CHALLENGE AND CREATIVE VISION

Before we get to details about developing advertisements, let us put today's and tomorrow's advertising in perspective. Let us see what challenge lies ahead for us in creating effective concepts and advertisements.

We know we are living in an explosive information age. It is also true to say that knowledge is power, and the speed with which marketers utilize that knowledge in the future will determine success or failure. Because advertising is, in its most basic form, a conveyor of information, it will be at the center of this revolution. But there are a number of factors working against that happening.

EXHIBIT 16.2

A modern sports look and youthful copy appeal take aim at the target.

Courtesy of Huey+Partners and Russell.

According to global creative director John Hegarty, we are already having to deal with a major communication problem. It's called *time famine*. How do consumers assimilate this ever-growing mass of messages that is being directed at them? How do they cope with the volume of traffic going through their brains? How do they process this valuable information as opposed to allowing it to pass straight through unnoticed? Another related issue that has been debated for years is media clutter. Are consumers reaching the point of "overchoice," as futurist Alvin Toffler predicted? "We are racing against overchoice—the point at which the advantages of choice and individualization are canceled by the complexity of the buyer's decision-making process."[7]

Yet another issue is our audience's ability to turn us off. Advertisers interrupt viewing and listening, or we sit alongside printed material shouting for attention. As electronic media take a greater hold on the distribution of information, our audience will have great control over turning us off, unless we are compelling and necessary. This is totally true with the Internet or TiVo—the user controls the information. Unless we recognize the change in the balance of power and take into account our consumers' aspirations, we will be cut out of the loop and become irrelevant. What can we do as communicators?

Strategy and Great Writing

Don't forget the importance of strategy as you read about how to create. Often there are dangers in our decision process. Frederick Smith, founder of Federal Express, said, "We thought we were selling the transportation of goods; in fact, we were selling peace of mind. When we finally figured that out, we pursued our goal with vengeance."[8] A few years ago, The Ritz-Carlton found its traditional market suddenly getting younger and looking at the hotel as old-fashioned. Their agency helped the hotel change its focus to the next generation by telling its brand story in a more relevant and contemporary way meshing strategy and strong creative.

Another brilliantly simple idea was created for *The Economist*. The typical advertisement for *The Economist* (a British publication read in more than 140 countries) has been three columns of copy. The advertisements talked about the benefits of reading the publication—much information aimed at a sophisticated, well-educated target. Yet, a simple poster says,

I've never read *The Economist*.

SIGNED, MANAGEMENT TRAINEE. AGE 42.

The concept was even integrated in a longer T-shirt message:

My dad reads *The Economist* and all I got was this lousy tee shirt, a penthouse apartment in New York, two Ferraris, an eighty foot yacht, my own private jet, and an island retreat in the Caribbean.

There is a valuable message in these examples for those creating advertising: The faster ideas get across, the more powerful they become. As you reduce the idea down, as you hone it to its essential structure, its power increases. The faster it penetrates the mind, the longer it stays there. You aren't trying to buy newspaper, magazine, or Web space or time in a commercial break. The space you are trying to buy is in the consumer's head. That is the most valuable space. That is what you are trying to influence. Ogilvy & Mather Singapore carried *The Economist* a step further. The head read "Money back guarantee." That was the advertisement. Their simplistic advertisements have become so famous as a technique that some advertisers mock them. Wonderbra copied the layout and the copy read:

"I never read *The Economist*."

LINDA FOSTER, CEO. AGE 29.

WONDERBRA

Luke Sullivan, long-time executive creative director at a number of hot agencies, speaking of creating advertising ideas, says it is simple: simplicity, simplicity, simplicity. Tony Cox says, "Inside every fat ad is a thinner and better one trying to get out." Maurice Saatchi on simplicity says: "Simplicity is all. Simple logic, simple arguments, simple visual images. If you can't reduce your arguments to a few crisp words and phrases, there's something wrong with your argument."[9]

Fallon Worldwide's self-promotion says, "The crucial part of the creative process is what we call relentless reductionism. It means having the discipline and will to drive for focus. A focus that results in a single-mindedly compelling idea. Then Fallon expands the idea. This is where creativity takes over, as we take this single-minded idea and apply it to every step of the consumer's path to purchase." You're getting the idea.

Was it Oscar Wilde—it doesn't really matter—who understood that an idea got better as it got faster? How do we do that? The brilliance of our craft is to reduce, to distill messages down, not to elongate. Remember Abraham Lincoln's quote, "You can fool all the people some of the time, and some of the people all the time, but you cannot fool all the people all of the time." He captured the essence of modern politics in one sentence, and most of us remember it. Great writing is about using fewer words to be more compelling. When you do that, you liberate your ideas to become more powerful, more involving, and hopefully more memorable. Brevity not only allows us to become more powerful, it allows us to become more stimulating. If you are more stimulating, there is a good chance you are becoming more relevant. We have to change because our audience is demanding it.

The Greeks said that information is taken through the heart. As we have moved from the unique selling proposition (USP) to the *emotional selling proposition*, we need to understand that the way we talk to consumers must also change. Advertising still needs to be based on the foundation of product or corporate attributes. But we must remember that it may no longer be unique nor will it necessarily be obvious.

Creative Vision

Creativity isn't just about putting a strategy down on a piece of paper. It is also about capturing the essence of that strategy and giving it a creative vision that is both compelling and competitive. What worked yesterday isn't necessarily going to work today or tomorrow. The consumer has not only less time to listen to us but also less inclination.

HOW DO WE CREATE GREAT ADVERTISING?

Saatchi & Saatchi's Kevin Roberts has said: "Do you really want a great ad? If you want a quiet life—no highs, no lows, no struggle, no passion—forget great ads." The opposite of a great ad is not a bad ad but an average one. The response to good ads? "Let's analyze." The response to great ads? "I want more."

We've already heard this, but we need to hear another viewpoint. Ron Huey, award-winning creative director of Huey+Partners, says, "Simplicity is the key to great advertising. Take the single most salient feature of your product or service and communicate that in a simple, thought provoking or entertaining way. Good copy speaks to the common man. It should be smart, entertaining and conversational, not fancy or frilly. Today's best creative people are resilient. Great ideas are killed every day for sometimes stupid reasons. The best creatives accept that and come back with something even better." Huey's thoughts on advertising through the years: "The great ads from Bernbach in the '60s, Fallon McElligott in the '80s, Wieden [Wieden & Kennedy], Goodby [Goodby, Silverstein & Partners] and The Martin Agency today, all have a common thread—The headline, visual and logo communicate the idea immediately." He also believes, "Three quarters of today's best ads use humor. But it's wry humor. Not a bathroom joke or humor that's intended to shock people."[10] Huey says, "One path we always investigate when concepting print is a 'visual solution.' By that, I mean an ad where the idea is really imbedded in the visual and usually communicates 90% of what you're trying to say. In this approach, the headline is more of straight payoff to complete, or bullet-proof, the communication."

THE NATURE AND USE OF APPEALS

appeal
The motive to which an advertisement is directed; it is designed to stir a person toward a goal the advertiser has set.

Advertising motivates people by appealing to their problems, desires, and goals, and by offering a means of solving their problems. Let us look at the value of using a psychological **appeal** in advertising. David Martin, founder of The Martin Agency, points to decades of research indicating the relative strengths of motives and appeals in advertising. He believes human desires are woven into our basic nature. They do not change with lifestyles or external environmental stimuli. Consumers will always have a desire for food and drink; for rest, comfort, and security; and for a sense of social worth, independence, power, and success. Parental feelings to protect and provide are basic. Human nature is a constant. Humans are born with certain instincts: fear (self-preservation), hunger (need for food and drink), sex (love), and rage (anger). People also have five senses: sight, touch, smell, hearing, and taste. The instincts and senses are often a starting point for advertising appeals.[11]

Ron Huey

President/Executive Creative Director, Huey+Partners, Atlanta
Getting Your Message Through? It's Simple.

The average person is blindsided by over 3,000 messages a day. Not just television commercials, magazine and newspaper ads, but also outdoor boards, radio spots, Internet pop-ups, signs on trucks, signs on trees, signs on just about anything that will stand still. It's a deafening roar for the consumer's attention to say the least. So how do you create communication that can actually communicate in this environment? The key, for me at least, has always been simplicity. Make a simple point in a very compelling and simple way and, chances are, people may actually pay attention. The tendency, however, is to try and say everything. Put forth every conceivable product benefit. That's okay, it's a natural inclination. After all, they're probably all things worth saying. It's a fast car, a luxurious car, a safe car, a well-engineered car, a stylish car, a car that fits your needs. The problem is that now no one knows what kind of car you're offering. You've made a lot of pertinent points, but no one point has penetrated with any meaning. So the first step is to put a single strategic stake in the ground. Stand for something rather than trying to stand for everything. Now you must bring your simple strategy to creative life in an arresting, impactful way. Remember, consumers aren't eagerly awaiting the next advertisement from you or from anyone else, for that matter. (They've already been hit by 3,000 today.) In fact, you will be an uninvited guest, you will be interrupting their day. So it's important that you intrigue them and invite them in. Make your point and do so in a way that entertains them and rewards for spending time with your message. It's that simple.

Ron Huey

Courtesy of Huey+Partners ■ ■ ■

The creative genius of the late 1960s, the late Bill Bernbach, put it this way:

There may be changes in our society. But learning about those changes is not the answer. For you are not appealing to society. You are appealing to individuals, each with an ego, each with the dignity of his or her being, each like no one else in the world, each a separate miracle. The societal appeals are merely fashionable, current, cultural appeals, which make nice garments for the real motivations that stem from the unchanging instincts and emotions of people—from nature's indomitable programming in their genes. It is the unchanging person that is the proper study of the communicator.[12]

John Hegarty says, "There was always one word that came through [when defining great advertising]: irreverence. Because what you are doing is changing the rules. You are trying to do something in an incredibly different way which captures the imagination." Jeff Goodby of Goodby, Silverstein & Partners adds, "Great advertising scrabbles logic a little bit, it jumps beyond that by being likable and watchable and captivating. It surprises you." Someone once said that great advertising is great ideas simply executed.[13]

Most products have a number of positive appeals that could be successfully promoted, so how do we go about making the decision as to which direction to go with an advertisement or appeal? The idea is to choose the one that is most important to the majority of our target members. Because selecting the primary appeal is the key to any advertising campaign, many research techniques have been developed to find which appeal to use, as discussed in Chapter 15.

Whether created by research or in other ways, the appeal provides the basis of the advertising structure. This appeal can be expressed in many ways. Here, we discuss how to make use of words, called *copy*, in presenting the appeal.[14]

GREAT ADVERTISING ELEMENTS

The Creative Council of Ogilvy & Mather Worldwide found that examples of great advertising have certain elements in common (the same fundamental principles apply to direct-response and sales promotion):[15]

- *Potent strategy.* The strategy is the heart of advertising. It is impossible to do great advertising if the strategy is weak or does not exist at all.
- *Strong selling idea.* Great advertising promises a benefit to the consumer. The idea must be simple, and it must be clear. The brand must be integrated into the selling idea.
- *Stands out.* A great advertisement is memorable, even when competing for attention with news and entertainment.
- *Always relevant.* Prospects can easily relate the advertising to their experience and to the role of the product in their lives.
- *Can be built into campaigns.* No matter how clever one idea may be, if you cannot make it into a campaign, it is not a great idea.

STRUCTURE OF AN ADVERTISEMENT

In some instances, the promise is the whole advertisement. Usually, however, a fuller exposition is required, in which case the promise can act as the headline—the first step in the structure of the advertisement. Most advertisements are presented in this order:

- Promise of benefit (the headline)
- Spelling out of promise (the subheadline, optional)
- Amplification of story (as needed)
- Proof of claim (as needed)
- Action to take (if not obvious)

Nobody reads body copy in an advertisement. "Lies, lies, and more lies," say Steve Lance and Jeff Woll. Long copy isn't needed when a picture can tell a thousand words. Borrow a page from your Internet site. If you're giving people a benefit and relevant information, long copy can work. But you have to work hard to make it work.[16] People tend to scan print advertisements in the following manner: illustration first, followed by the headline, first line of the body copy, and then the logo. If they are still interested, they will go back and read the rest of the copy. Yes, you can get people to read the copy, but the first sentence and first paragraph are extremely important in keeping readers. As a matter of fact, the drop-off rate of readers is pretty significant during the first fifty words, but not so great between fifty and 500 words.

The Headline

The headline is the most important part of a print advertisement. It is the first thing read, and it should arouse interest so the consumer wants to keep on reading and get to know more about the product being sold. If the headline does not excite the interest of the particular group of prime prospects the advertiser wants to reach, the rest of the advertisement will probably go unread.

Get prospects' attention by telling them what they want to know immediately. Don't make them guess the brand's benefit. You certainly should consider using a benefit in the headline. Ask yourself, "What's our promise and what's our proof?" Why do so many advertisements get it wrong, when it isn't that hard to get it right? Figure out why people would really benefit from your brand or service. Then tell 'em. Make it interesting. Make it readable.[17]

No formula can be given for writing a good headline. However, several factors should be considered in evaluating an effective headline:

- It should use short, simple words, usually no more than ten.
- It should include an invitation to the prospect, primary product benefits, name of the brand, and an interest-provoking idea to gain readership of the rest of the advertisement.
- The words should be selective, appealing only to prime prospects.
- It should contain an action verb.
- It should give enough information so that the consumer who reads only the headline learns something about the product and its benefit.

Not every headline is going to adhere to these guidelines. However, when you write a headline that excludes any of these points, ask yourself: Would this headline be more effective if it did adhere to the guidelines? You want to be sure you have thought through the process.

Many headlines fall into one of four categories:

1. *Headlines that present a new benefit.* The moment of peak interest in a product is when it offers a new benefit. That is why, in our innovative society, you often see headlines such as these:

    Your second cup of coffee is back.

    FOLGERS SIMPLY SMOOTH

    Introducing Gillette Fusion. Breakthrough technology on the front and back.

    GILLETTE FUSION

    Introducing a high performance tampon with Sport Level Protection.

    PLAYTEX SPORT

    When mucus causes your child's chest congestion, try new Children's Mucinex Mini-Melts and send mucus on its way.

    MUCINEX MINI

    Now calcium can change the way you look at water.

    PROPEL

    Introducing the first in-ear headphones from Bose.

    BOSE

    Discover a whole new way to relieve stress.

    AVEENO

2. *Headlines that directly promise an existing benefit.* Products cannot be offering new benefits all the time, of course, so headlines often remind consumers of a product's existing features:

    Tell hunger to get lost.

    PRIA POWERBAR

Flavor can change how you look at water.

PROPEL

Great things happen when 362 robots put their microchips together.

HYUNDAI

A lightbulb that uses 75% less energy. Your planet will thank you.

GE ENERGY SMART BULB

Cure winter skin and winter blues with Curel.

CUREL ULTRA HEALING

In just 4 weeks, see even the deepest wrinkles start to fill in.

NEUTROGENA INTENSIVE

Cheerios can lower cholesterol 4% in 6 weeks.

CHEERIOS

3. *Curiosity-invoking and provocative headlines.* By invoking curiosity, an advertiser may grab attention from an otherwise disinterested audience by challenging the curiosity of the readers, thereby prompting them to read further and leading them into the key message. David Ogilvy warned against using heads that don't communicate the benefits because of the large numbers of readers that don't read the body copy. It can work, but the writer must be careful to

The joys of SummerGrove will turn you into a kid again.

Get the life you've always dreamed of living in a spectacular SummerGrove custom home. Enjoy special extras, such as fine brick and stone exteriors,

outside living areas, and professional landscaping. Plus use your creativity to add custom touches and upgrades inside and out. You'll have your choice of premium, wooded homesites offering incredible lakefront and golf course living. Not to mention all the excitement

of three great amenity areas, including swimming, tennis, a clubhouse, parks, and a lazy river. Come create your very own SummerGrove custom home. And experience the joy of getting exactly what you want.

Homes from the $130s to $700s • Information Center open Daily 11-6, Sunday 1-6 • 770-252-9000 • www.summergrove.com

I-85 South to Exit 47 (Newnan). Left on Hwy. 34, one mile. Turn right on Shenandoah Blvd. Continue 1.4 miles to SummerGrove. Follow signs to Information Center.

MMRG New Homes.pdf 1   10/23/06 10:28:12 AM

EXHIBIT 16.3
Copywriter Amy Lokken uses a little curiosity to draw readers into the ad's many benefits.
Courtesy of Pathway Communities and McRae Communications.

build a strong relationship between the curiosity point and the brand. "The joys of SummerGrove will turn you into a kid again," is a good introduction to get readers of the publication to "want" information. There is too much information to include in a headline, so creating a little curiosity helps readership (see Exhibit 16.3).

We all have something in common.

STARBUCKS

Mom, I hate vegetables.

CAMPBELLS

Every night you see a dirty film & don't even know it.

OLAY FACIAL EXPRESS

Live fast, die a senior citizen.

ROLLING STONE

The ceasefire of the sexes.

SONY BRAVIA

Does travel seem to magnify your pain?

THERMACARE

I'm thinking of a number from one to ten.

PILLSBURY DINNER ROLLS

The question headline that works best is the kind that arouses curiosity so the reader will read the body copy to find the answer. Readers do not like being tricked. They want a strong relationship between the curiosity and the product.

4. *Selective headlines.* Readers looking through a magazine or newspaper are more likely to read an advertisement they think concerns them personally than one that talks to a broad audience. The selective headline aimed at a particular prime prospect who would be more interested in the product is often used. If the head says, "condominium owners," and you don't own a condominium, you probably won't pay attention; conversely, if you do own a condominium, you might read it. A Pampers advertisement head reads, "Babies absorb everything around them. Wetness doesn't have to be one of them." Obviously, if you don't have a baby in your life, you probably aren't going to read this advertisement. However, if you do have a baby, you may be attracted to the copy. Four such headlines that specifically reach out to special groups are the following:

- To All Men and Women
- To All Young Men and Women
- To All College Men and Women
- To All College Seniors

The first headline is addressed to the greatest number of readers, but it would be of the least interest to any one of them. Each succeeding headline reduces the size of the audience it addresses and improves the chances of attracting that particular group. What about "All College Seniors Who Need Jobs"? You get the idea!

Besides addressing a particular group directly, headlines can appeal to people by mentioning a problem they have in common:

New GoodNite's Underpants control odor. And build confidence.

GOODNITE'S

Tell your sore throat to just chill.

VICKS 44 SORE THROAT

Most baby bottoms stink. (And their tops aren't great, either.)

HEALTHTEX

The new TD Ameritrade. An investor's company, not an investment company.

TD AMERITRADE

Another vital quality in headlines is specificity. Remember, consumers are more interested in the specific than the general. Therefore, the more specific you can be in the headline, the better: "A Peppermint Peroxide Toothpaste That Will Help Kill Bacteria and Keep Tartar from Your Teeth" is better than "A Nice-Tasting Toothpaste That Cleans Your Teeth."

A headline must say something important to the reader. The actual number of words is not the deciding factor; long or short headlines may work well. But say what you need to say in as few words as possible. Remember, simple is better, but it can be more than one sentence.

A Priceless Moment at Carolina Herrera

NO: $0

NO: $0

NO: $0

NO: $0

NO: $0

NO: $0

The perfect dress: $5,990.

MASTERCARD

The Subheadline

If the message is long, it can be conveyed with a main headline (with large type) and a subheadline (with smaller type but larger than the body copy). The subheadline can spell out the promise presented in the headline. It can be longer than the headline, it can invite further reading, and it serves as a transition to the opening paragraph of the copy. Heil uses the head as part of the visual (see Exhibit 16.4).

Headline: **HolyCow**
Subhead: **It's startling how Heil parts extend the life of your truck.**

HEIL

Headline: **Get healthy skin for life.**
Subhead: **AVEENO Daily Moisturizing Lotion is clinically proven to actually improve the health of your dry skin.**

AVEENO

Amplification

The headline and, if used, the subheadline are followed by the body copy of the advertisement. It is here that you present your case for the product and explain how the promise in the headline will be fulfilled. In other words, the body copy amplifies what was announced in the headline or subheadline. What you say and how deep you go depend on the amount of information your prime prospect needs at this point in the buying process. A high-cost plasma television screen probably calls for more explanation than a low-cost product, such as a barbecue sauce with a new flavor. If a product has many technical advances, there probably is not sufficient room to detail all the features. In this case, the objective is to create enough interest to get the prime prospect to the store for a demonstration and more information. "Discover a clinically proven way to treat cold sore symptoms up to 3 1/2 days faster," is a clear benefit.

Amplification should emphasize those product or service features that are of primary importance but cannot be included in the headline. Take, for example, the FiberMesh trade advertisement (see Exhibit 16.5).

Concrete That's Tougher Than You Think.

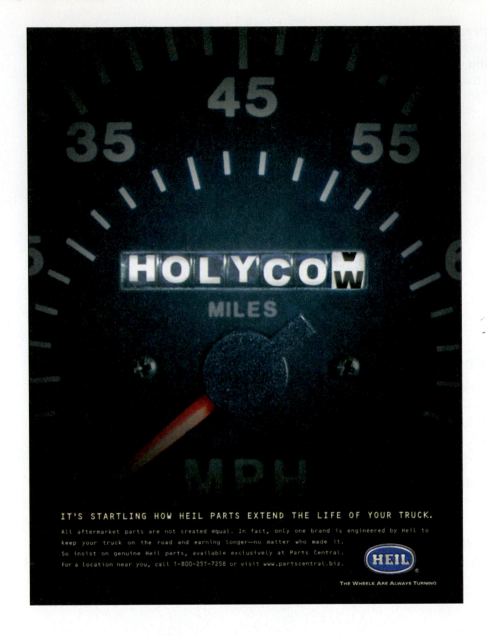

And then the amplification:

If you're not specifying FiberMesh fiber reinforcement for your concrete applications, consider this: nothing can reduce shrinkage cracks, resist impact shattering and abrasion or reduce water migration like FiberMesh. With twenty billion
square feet of concrete in every conceivable application, you can be sure our
fiber will work for whatever you're working on. (plus an 800 phone number and a
Web address)

Proof

The body copy does amplify what the headline promised. At times the process acts
to reassure the consumer that the product will perform as promised. Consumers
may look for proof in an advertisement, and proof is particularly important for
high-priced products, health, and new products with special features. Here are a
few ways in which proof can be offered to the reader.

CONCRETE THAT'S TOUGHER THAN YOU THINK.

If you're not specifying FiberMesh® fiber reinforcement for your concrete applications, consider this: nothing can reduce shrinkage cracks, resist impact shattering and abrasion or reduce water migration like FiberMesh. With 20 billion square feet of concrete in every conceivable application, you can be sure our fiber will work for whatever you're working on.

800.635.2308 | www.fibermesh.com

EXHIBIT 16.5

Body copy can explain the details of a product or service features that cannot be explained in the headline.

Courtesy of FiberMesh and The Johnson Group.

Seals of Approval Seals of approval from such accredited sources as *Good Housekeeping* and *Parents* magazines, the American Dental Association, the American Medical Association, the American Heart Association, and Underwriters Laboratories allay consumers' fears about product quality. Such endorsements distinguish a product, and a seal of approval can give a new product an edge of credibility in the market place. Samsung Blood Pressure Monitors have the Good Housekeeping Seal. The Seal protects consumers for up to 2 years; Good Housekeeping will replace the product or refund the purchase price.

Guarantees Zippo lighters uses its guarantee as a major selling point in print advertisements (see Exhibit 16.6). Wendy's, Arby's, and Mrs. Winner's have offered consumers money-back guarantees for trying specific products to reduce the risk and get trial by consumers. Manufacturers of Silent Floor systems guarantee their floors will be free from warping or defects. "Crest Whitestrips and Crest Whitestrips Premium provide you with a beautiful, visibly whiter smile—guaranteed. If you are not satisfied with your results, Crest Whitestrips will refund your purchase. Simply return your receipt and package UPC within 60 days of purchase. Call 1-800-395-8423 for more information."

Trial Offers and Samples BMG Music offers any eight CDs for the price of one with its 10-day risk-free trial. Procter & Gamble offered free industrial-strength Spic and Span liquid samples to consumers who called a toll-free telephone number to reduce the risk and to get trial. Similar offers are made at www.pg.com. Infomercials often have low-risk trials.

Warranties Pacific Coast Down Comforters also has a "100% allergy-free warranty." Sherwin-Williams SuperPaint is advertised with a 20-year warranty against peeling.

EXHIBIT 16.6

Zippo features its guarantee.

Courtesy of Blattner Brunner.

James Hardie Building Products touts a 50-year warranty for its siding. Lees Carpets has "a stain resistance technology that will repel most liquids, including juice, coffee and other spills, four times longer than other carpets . . . guaranteed. Plus, we back it with an industry leading 25-year no exclusions warranty."

Reputation Copy for V8 juice touts its American Heart Association approval. Or, as Spring Air mattress says, "The award winning mattress more people prefer for 5 straight years" (and also has the Good Housekeeping Seal).

Demonstrations "Before" and "after" demonstrations are used to show how a product works. Starch Research says showing models to demonstrate cosmetic products is powerful. In one advertisement, Almay showed a supermodel from the neck up, making it easy to see her facial imperfections—or lack thereof—after using Almay's line of hypoallergenic cosmetics. Find a way to tell consumers a benefit, and you will do well; find a way to show them, and you will fare even better.

Testimonials The ability to attract attention to advertisements and offer a credible source has made testimonials a popular device. Testimonials should come from persons viewed by consumers as competent to make judgments on the products they are endorsing. BB&T bank (headquartered in Winston-Salem, North Carolina) used a campaign of business customers' stories to attract more business customers. One advertisement read: "As far as I'm concerned, if your word's no good, nothing else about you is good. . . . They're in the bank ready to answer our needs. That sets them apart."

With its "My Life. My Card," advertisements starring Robert DeNiro, Tiger Woods, Ellen DeGeneres, and big-wave surfer Laird Hamilton, American Express created an image of high-end exclusivity. John Hayes, chief marketing officer for American Express, admits the glut of celebrity advertisements "makes it tougher than ever" to stand out. But American Express's history of tastefully portraying the rich and famous gives it an edge at landing A-list talent.[18]

Dean Rieck, president of Direct Creative, promotes the use of testimonials and suggests that companies actively collect testimonials and success stories. He says they support advertisers' claims and build confidence. He also suggets:[19]

- Use testimonials from people who are similar and relevant to prospects. A teacher will believe other teachers; a business owner will believe other business owners; seniors will believe seniors. Testimonials are more effective if they are from experts or people with relevant experience.

- Don't try to rewrite or fabricate testimonials. The real words of real people are always more believable than anything a writer can come up with. Besides, making them up isn't ethical.

- Testimonials are a form of proof, so increase the credibility of that proof whenever you have a chance. Use full names when possible. Appropriate titles may be an indication of a person's experience or expertise.

COPY STYLE

As with a novel or a play, good advertising copy has a beginning, a middle, and an ending. And, like a novel, the transition must be smooth from one part to another. Up to this point, we have discussed how the building blocks of copy are put together. Now we need to think about what it takes to create special attention and persuasion. It takes style—the ability to create fresh, charming, witty, human advertising that compels people to read. Remember what Ron Huey said: "Take the single most salient feature of your product or service and communicate it in a simple, thought-provoking or entertaining way." See the product in a fresh way, explore its possible effects on the reader, or explain the product's advantages in a manner that causes the reader to view the product with a new understanding and appreciation.

Most advertisements end with a close by asking or suggesting that the reader buy the product. The difference between a lively advertisement and a dull one lies in the approach to the message at the outset.

The lens through which a writer sees a product may be the magnifying glass of the technician, who perceives every nut and bolt and can explain why each is important; or it may be the rose-colored glasses of the romanticist, who sees how a person's life may be affected by the product. That is why we speak of **copy approaches** rather than types of advertisements. The chief approaches in describing a product are the factual, the imaginative, and the emotional.

copy approach
The method of opening the text of an advertisement. The chief forms are the factual approach, the imaginative approach, and the emotional approach.

Factual Approach

In the factual approach, we deal with reality—that which actually exists. We talk about the product or service—what it is, how it is made, and what it does. Focusing

KLEPPNER VIEWPOINT 16.2

Amy Lokken
Senior Writer, McRae Communications, Atlanta

Think out of the box. Break through the clutter. Engage the consumer. Phrases like these are bandied about in meetings all the time. Clients recite them. Marketing directors latch on to them like rallying cries. But if you translate this marketing-speak, all it really means is: "We want something different. Something good. But we have no idea what it is."

This isn't anything new. Companies have always wanted to set themselves and their products apart. The challenge for the creative team is finding new ways to do this. Coming up with creative solutions that are unexpected—attention grabbing—while still supporting the brand.

An example from my own experience jumps to mind. About a year ago, one of our clients in the building products industry introduced a new housewrap called RainDrop. (In case you don't spend your free hours on a construction site, I can tell you that housewrap is simply a moisture-resistant material that's wrapped around a house before the siding goes on to keep water out of the walls.) They had tried the traditional catalog and product sheet write-ups, but sales were lagging. No one was getting the message that this new product—the first ever housewrap with drainage channels—was indeed a revolution in the building world.

So the client asked for something "out of the box." Something to reinvigorate their sales force, and also use as a tool for selling to customers. We proposed delivering the information in an unusual way—a comic book. This format would allow us to entertain our target audience and make our product seem exciting, even heroic, while showing off the needed attributes. The book would feature the adventures of a new superhero, RainDrop Man, whose mission was to save the world from inferior housewraps and bad building practices. We gave him a secret identity and a dastardly villain to fight, and we created the first book.

Now imagine you're walking the aisles at a typical building product trade show. You're seeing all of the basic demonstrations. Salesmen are rambling about their products. People are handing you the usual brochures. Then you turn the corner, and a guy in a green spandex suit with a cowl and a cape hands you a comic book and asks you to join the fight against the evils of mold, moisture, and rot. That's unexpected. And from all the positive feedback our client received, it worked wonders with their sales force and their customers. So much so that we just published our second issue with even more villains and bigger action.

There's no telling how far RainDrop Man will go. (We're thinking action figures and lunch boxes.) And there's no telling how far your creative ideas can take you and your clients. So be willing to think in new ways. To try something different. Even if it involves putting a fairly large man in a pretty tight spandex suit. ■■■

Amy Lokken

on the facts about the product that are most important to the reader, we explain the product's advantages.

One of the interesting things about a fact, however, is that it can be interpreted in different ways, each accurate but each launching different lines of thinking. Remember the classic example of an 8-ounce glass holding 4 ounces of water, of which can be said: "This glass is half full" or "This glass is half empty." As you know, both are correct and factual. The difference is in the interpretation of reality, as the Mitsui O.S.K. advertisement headline for shipping seafood says, "We cater to the best schools." Their copy talks facts: "MOL takes a great deal of pride in catering to the needs of the world's most discriminating shippers. Salmon, shrimp, crabs, mussels and other gourmet seafood, for example, are delivered in 409-high-cube reefer containers so that they arrive fresh and delectable in Asian and American markets." Skill in presenting a fact consists of projecting it in a way that means the most to the reader.

The factual approach can be used to sell more than products or services. Facts about ideas, places—anything for which an advertisement can be written—can be presented with a fresh point of view.

Imaginative Approach

There is nothing wrong with presenting a fact imaginatively. The art of creating copy lies in saying a familiar thing in an unexpected way. The Johnson Group took herbs from Kettleby Herb Farms and made them interesting. Their curiosity approach just makes you want to find the answers (see Exhibit 16.7). The headline reads, "Quite possibly the most delicious toilet bowl cleanser you've ever put in your mouth." Part of the body copy answers questions and puts the benefit in place, "Rosemary. For centuries it's been one of the world's most popular herbs in the kitchen and bathroom. Chefs praise its singular ability to liven any meat dish, particularly lamb and pork roast. And while less well known, boiling a handful of rosemary in two cups of water makes a powerful antiseptic cleaning solution. . . ."

Emotional Approach

Emotion can be a powerful communicator. The feelings about your product or company can be an important plus or minus. Copy using psychological appeals to love, hate, or fear has great impact. "When other hospitals told Dawn Buxbaum her unborn baby would not survive, our doctors said he could be saved. Talk about a second opinion." The illustration and headline in Exhibit 16.8 bring out not only warmth and maternal instincts but also emotion—every parent can identify with the photo. "Life's biggest events are necessarily the ones seen on the nightly news." Often the copy will continue the emotional appeal, although at times it will take a factual direction to inform the reader about specific features of the product to convince the reader of its value.

Research indicates that emotion can create positive feelings, such as warmth, happiness, and delight, which work best for low-involvement goods. For higher-involvement, higher-ticket items, such as CD players or automobiles, emotions must be unique and mesh with the brand. Kodak has produced advertisements that are so emotional they bring tears to your eyes.

What science can tell us about the brain and about "emotion" has grown exponentially over the last 20 years. Kevin Roberts, CEO Worldwide of Saatchi & Saatchi, talks about the use of emotion. Research tells us that human beings *think* with feeling and emotion. We just can't help it. Emotion is the *key* to every decision we make, every thought we have, whether it's to click on an attached file or reach for our usual brand of soap powder. Human beings tend to take everything personally and respond with feeling. Joseph Ledoux, one of the world's leading researchers

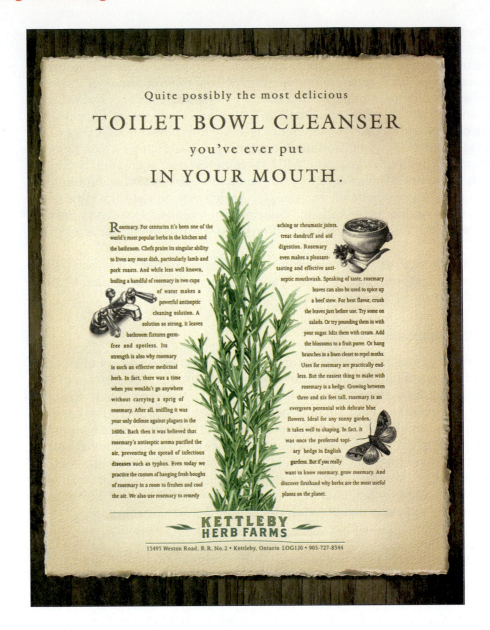

into the emotional brain, had this to say: "Emotions are mostly processes at an unconscious level."

They are quick and focused on what really matters. They acknowledge that intuition, loyalty, and emotion can't be quantified, and then move on.

All the stuff we've been told about "think before you act" and "think it through" is rubbish. It doesn't happen. Rational man is a myth. Women, of course, have always been too smart to have gotten into the rationality arena because in reality it doesn't work. Humans have the ability to focus. People focus on new events, on changes in their environment. They disregard the everyday and the routine. They pay attention until a need is satisfied and then they move on. How do we attract attention? Kevin Roberts believes we can only do this with emotion.

"Put emotion first. Pull them with emotion, touch them with emotion, compel them with emotion. It may make them laugh, make them cry, make them jump."[20]

However, using mixed emotions may have dangers. According to Williams and Aaker, our ability to assimilate mixed emotions is, to some extent, a function of age and culture. Older adults are more at ease with complex emotional issues. Cultural influences make an even larger difference. Americans are quite happy with mixed messages (such as images and word play), so long as they're not about emotions. In

Life's biggest events aren't necessarily

the ones seen on the nightly news.

carter's
celebrating childhood

EXHIBIT 16.8
Every parent can identify
with the emotional pull.
Courtesy of Carter's.

contrast, Asian cultures tend to be more comfortable with mixed emotions. Williams and Aaker found that Asian Americans were more at ease with appeals based on mixed emotions.

The Center for Emotional Marketing research shows that advertising that provokes a strong emotional response without providing sufficient product information often breaks through the clutter but is unlikely to change behavior and increase market share. Such advertising connects with consumers but then fails to make use of that connection with the credible information needed to change people's minds. This is "emotional undersell"—a situation in which advertising captures consumers' attention and engages them emotionally but fails to close the deal.[21]

COMPARATIVE ADVERTISING

Comparing your product directly with one or more competitors is called **comparative advertising**. It is actually encouraged by the Federal Trade Commission, but it has risks:[22]

> *Commission policy in the area of comparative advertising encourages the naming of, or reference to competitors, but requires clarity, and, if necessary, disclosure to avoid deception of the consumer. Additionally, the use of truthful comparative advertising should not be restrained by broadcasters or self-regulation entities.* The Commission has supported the use of brand comparisons where the bases of comparison are clearly identified. Comparative advertising, when truthful and nondeceptive, is a source of

**comparative
advertising**
It directly contrasts an
advertiser's product with
other named or identified
products.

important information to consumers and assists them in making rational purchase decisions. Comparative advertising encourages product improvement and innovation, and can lead to lower prices in the marketplace.

Some advertisers think it isn't smart to spend money to publicize your competition. Others think it creates a bad atmosphere for the company that demeans all advertising. Pepsi has frequently run advertisements in *Nation's Restaurant News* featuring "Coke and Pepsi View Your Business Two Different Ways," and the copy talks about how they do business differently. Apple has taken on the generic PC in a number of advertisements promoting the benefits of Apple.

Despite each comparative advertisement being different, there are certain rules of thumb that can be applied: (1) The leader in the field never starts a comparative campaign. (2) The most successful comparison advertisements are those comparing the product with products identical in every respect except for the special differential featured in the advertisement. The stronger the proof that the products are identical, the better. (3) The different features should be of importance to the consumer.

SLOGANS

Originally derived from the Gaelic *slugh gairm*, meaning "battle cry," the word *slogan* has an appropriate background. A slogan sums up the theme for a product's benefits to deliver an easily remembered message in a few words—"It's the Real Thing."

There have been many very memorable slogans in advertising over the years; for example: "Just Do It" (Nike); "Tastes Great, Less Filling" (Miller Lite); "Good to the Last Drop" (Maxwell House); "Does She . . . Or Doesn't She?" (Clairol); "When It Rains It Pours" (Morton Salt); "We Try Harder" (Avis). Even though not all effective slogans are etched in every consumer's mind, many slogans do help communicate the essence of the product position: for example, "Pawleys Island. Arrogantly Shabby."

Used even more often on television and radio than in print, slogans may be combined with a catchy tune to make a jingle. Slogans are broadly classified as either institutional or hard sell.

Institutional Slogans

Institutional slogans are created to establish a prestigious image for a company. Relying on this image to enhance their products and services, many firms insist that their slogans appear in all of their advertising and on their letterheads. An entire advertisement may feature the slogan. Some institutional slogans are familiar:

Think in Ideas

ISHARES

Higher Standards

BANK OF AMERICA

Advance

ACURA

You're in good hands with Allstate.

ALLSTATE INSURANCE

Sense and Simplicity

PHILLIPS

The Document Company

XEROX

Hard-Sell Slogans

These capsules of advertising change with campaigns. Hard-sell slogans epitomize the special or significant features of the product or service being advertised, and their claims are strongly competitive.

M&M's. The Milk Chocolate Melts in Your Mouth—Not in Your Hands.

M&M'S

Is it in you?

GATORADE

Get Met. It Pays.

METLIFE

We'll Pick You Up.

ENTERPRISE CAR RENTAL

General Electric (GE) purged its 24-year-old slogan "We Bring Good Things to Life" for "Imagination at Work." It is difficult to change a slogan in which you have invested millions of dollars for one that isn't proven. The reason for the change was the old slogan no longer represented where the corporation was heading. Research about "Good Things" brought surprises. "Nearly everybody said it meant only two things: lighting and appliances," says GE's Judy Hu, general manager for corporate advertising and marketing communications. The company ranks as one of the world's largest and most diversified technology and service companies. Its holdings range from aircraft engines and power generators to financial services and a television network.

The U.S. Army took a risk and dropped its 20-year-old slogan, "Be All You Can Be," in favor of "An Army of One." The change brought about cries from critics and Army traditionalists.

"Most companies want a really great tagline that can crystallize the brand across different audiences," says Tracey Riese, president of branding consulting firm TG Riese.[23]

Some marketing gurus argue that large marketers, such as Anheuser-Busch and Coca-Cola, should forget one-size-fits-all themes and come up with different slogans to reach different audiences. Most marketers haven't bought into this theory.

Slogans are widely used to advertise groceries, drugs, beauty aids, and liquor. These are products that are bought repeatedly at a comparatively low price. They are sold to consumers in direct competition on the shelves of supermarkets, drugstores, and department stores. If a slogan can remind a shopper in one of those stores of a special feature of the product, it certainly has served its purpose. Slogans can also remind shoppers of the name of a product from a company they respect. Not all advertising needs slogans. One-shot announcements—sale advertisements for which price is the overriding consideration—usually do not use slogans. Creating a slogan is one of the fine arts of copywriting.

Elements of a Good Slogan

A slogan differs from most other forms of writing because it is designed to be remembered and repeated word for word to impress a brand and its message on the consumer. Ideally, the slogan should be short, clear, and easy to remember.

Advanced Medicine for Pain

ADVIL

Nationwide Is On Your Side

NATIONWIDE INSURANCE

Where Shopping Is a Pleasure

PUBLIX MARKETS

Can You Hear Me Now?

VERIZON

Zoom-Zoom

MAZDA

You can do it. We can help.

HOME DEPOT

Aptness helps:

Love the skin you're in

OLAY

Trusted by More Women Than Any Other Brand

MASSENGILL

A Diamond Is Forever

DE BEERS CONSOLIDATED MINES

It is an advantage to have the name of the product in the slogan:

Kroger. For Goodness Sake.

KROGER

Nationwide Is On Your Side

NATIONWIDE INSURANCE

It pays to Discover.

DISCOVER CARD

THE CREATIVE WORK PLAN

Before most agencies start creating an advertisement, they develop a creative work plan to guide them in the right direction. The brief is the starting point for the creative process. You will recall from Chapter 3 that the creative brief consists of the following elements:

- Key observation
- Communication objective
- Consumer insight
- Promise
- Support
- Audience
- Mandatories

What does a brief accomplish? In simple factual terms, a good brief should accomplish three main objectives. First, it should give the creative team a realistic view of what the advertising really needs to do and is likely to achieve. Second, it should provide a clear understanding of the people that the advertising must address; and finally, it needs to give clear direction on the message to which the target audience seems most likely to be susceptible. In some agencies, there is a creative briefing in which an account planner will outline the nature of the advertising problem for the creative team and suggest ways of solving it.[24]

CREATIVE WORK PLAN

PRODUCT: **NEW ORLEANS**

KEY FACT

Bevil Foods is a 30-year-old New Orleans– based frozen food company. In 1993, Bevil Foods will introduce a new line of premium frozen entreés to be distributed nationally.

PROBLEM THE ADVERTISING MUST SOLVE

Currently there is **NO awareness** of the New OrLeans product among potential consumers.

ADVERTISING OBJECTIVE

To achieve 70% awareness of the product at end of year 1. To communicate the taste and low-calorie/low-fat benefits of the product.

CREATIVE STRATEGY

PROSPECT DEFINITION

1. Women 25–54, professional/managerial, with household incomes of $25,000 plus.
2. Adults 25+ professional/managerial, with household incomes of $25,000 plus.

   Psychographically, these people tend to be active, concerned with their health, and "on the go" a lot.

PRINCIPAL COMPETITION

Lean Cuisine, Weight Watchers, Healthy Choice.

KEY PROMISE

New Orleans are lite entreés with the great taste of New Orleans.

REASON WHY

Less than 300 calories; low fat, great tasting, original New Orleans recipes, served in fine restaurants for 30 years.

MANDATORIES

Must use logo, calorie and fat information, and original New Orleans recipes in each ad.

EXHIBIT 16.9

A Creative Work Plan

The purpose of the work plan is to provide proper direction for the creative team prior to developing ideas, heads, and copy. Exhibit 16.9 shows a work plan format originally developed by Young & Rubicam that is widely used by a number of agencies. Note that the work plan emphasizes factual information and research data. The creative process is not a "shot in the dark" but rather, depends on knowing as much as possible about the product, the consumer, and the expected benefits. The advertising professional is able to channel objective information into a creative and attention-getting sales message. Many agencies and clients have their own format and style for specific information they think necessary for creative strategy development.

TESTED GUIDELINES FOR CREATING AN ADVERTISEMENT

Philip W. Sawyer, editor, *Starch Tested Copy*, after years of studying Starch Advertisement Readership Studies, shares his findings with you. Following are some specific rules and thoughts on developing effective advertising:[25]

What follows are 10 guidelines that we believe advertisers should keep in mind whenever they sit down to create an ad. As we offer these, we are well aware that any number of ads ignore these guidelines yet are very successful. That's fine. Mark Twain broke almost every rule of grammar when he wrote *The Adventures of Huckleberry Finn*. But he had to know the rules before he could break them effectively.

1. *Keep it simple, stupid.* The KISS principle, as this is called, has no better application than in advertising, yet it is probably the most abused principle of all. Here is the best argument for simplicity: A great many magazine readers do not

read magazines to look at the ads. Therefore, advertising needs to catch the eye quickly, deliver its message quickly, and allow the reader to leave as quickly as possible. Ads that clutter the page with multiple illustrations and varied sizes and styles of type offer no central focus for the eye, no resting place. Because of these visual disincentives for staying with "busy" ads, readers naturally move on, having spent little or no time with them.

2. *You're not selling the product; you're selling the benefits of the product.* An old *New Yorker* cartoon depicts a pompous-looking young man at a party, talking to a young woman. "Well, that's enough about me," he says. "Now, what do you think about me?" Most advertisements suffer from the same kind of egotism. They assume that the reader is as interested in the product as is the advertiser. In reality, most readers do not enter the advertiser's realm readily. They do so only when convinced that the product will do something for them. If an advertiser does not answer the reader's implicit question—What's in it for me?—the ad is unlikely to attract any real interest.

   Most ads are simply descriptive; they explain what the product or service is. The worst ads give you a long history about the company, its values, commitments, and size—as if anyone really cares. But the best ads directly address the problems that the product or service solves and suggest how that solution makes life better for the potential consumer.

3. *When appropriate, spice it up with sex.* Psychologist Joyce Brothers once predicted that "the days of sexy advertising are numbered. The reason is that within five years, the number of marriageable women will be greater than the number of marriageable men. This will be the beginning of the 'she' generation, which will be a generation unimpressed with sex as a selling point."

   Dr. Brothers makes the common (and, it could be argued, sexist) mistake of assuming that men are interested in sex and women are not. In truth, the publications that carry the sexiest advertising today are women's publications. And that kind of advertising attracts considerable notice and readership and will continue to do so until human beings reproduce exclusively by parthenogenesis.

   At the same time, it should be emphasized that sexy ads tend to be simple ads—perfectly reasonable because clutter and salaciousness are not really compatible. The best ads of this type may feature nudity but are not explicitly erotic. To the politically correct, we say: Sex sells. Get used to it.

4. *Use celebrities.* Opinion surveys indicate that Americans do not believe an ad simply because it features a well-known person hawking the product. However, according to our data, ads with celebrities earn "noted" scores that are 13 percent higher than average. They are particularly effective with women readers, scoring 15 percent higher than average, compared with 10 percent higher for men. Overall, ads with testimonials from celebrities score 11 percent above the average, whereas testimonials from noncelebrities actually earn below-average scores. Celebrities may not be believable, but they are very effective at attracting reader attention, which is the first job of any advertisement.

5. *Exploit the potential of color.* Print advertising has the potential to contend with television. The moving image is a profoundly effective means of communication, and anyone who has ever tried to amuse a baby knows that the eye has an inherent attraction to motion. At the same time, the eye is also attracted to bold, bright, and beautiful color. Our data indicate that one-page color ads earn "noted" scores that are 45 percent higher on average than comparable black-and-white ads; two-page color ads earn scores that are 53 percent higher than similar black-and-white ads. Generally, the more colorful, the better (as long as the advertiser keeps in mind the other nine principles).

Television has a lock on the moving image, but print's ability to generate astonishing, eye-catching colors is substantial, and publications should do everything possible to stay current with new advances in color technology.

6. *Go with the flow.* Every ad has flow to it, and the flow is determined by the positioning of the various creative elements. Ads with good flow send the reader's eye around the page to take in all the important elements: the illustration, headline, body copy, and brand name. Ads with bad flow may attract a fair amount of attention at first, but send the reader off the page. For example, a number of advertisers make the mistake of placing a flashy illustration toward the bottom of the page and the copy and headline at the top. In such cases, the most powerful element of an ad can turn out to be the most detrimental, because that alluring illustration steals attention away from the copy.

   For another example, consider the automobile industry and the way some advertisers position the automobile on the page. The eye, our data indicate, tends to follow the car from back to front. Thus, if the car is facing to the right on the page and is positioned above the body copy, the eye, moving back to front, ends up over the beginning of the copy, exactly the right place if you want to have your copy read. But consider how many advertisers position their cars facing left to right, thus "leading" the reader to the right side of the page, the point at which the reader is most likely to continue on to the next page without studying the rest of the ad.

7. *Avoid ambiguity.* Although it appears that Europeans accept, if not welcome, ambiguous themes and symbols, we have found that Americans have little tolerance for advertising that does not offer a clear and distinct message. Several years ago, Benson & Hedges attracted a great deal of attention with an ad featuring a man clad only in pajama bottoms and a bewildered expression, standing in a dining room in the middle of what appears to be a brunch party. The trade press evidently was far more attracted to the ad than were readers, who, our data indicated, were as nonplused by the ad as its star was by his predicament, and reacted with considerable hostility to the advertiser who dared to confuse them.

   Americans like it straight. They choose not to spend a great deal of time thinking about the messages in their advertising. If the point of the ad is not clear, the typical American reader will move on to the next page.

8. *Heighten the contrast.* We live in a visual culture, and one thing that delights the eye is contrast. So advertisers would do well to employ what might be called "visual irony" in their advertising. One suggestion is to contrast the content of the ads.

   American Express produced one of the best ads of 1988 by featuring the diminutive Willie Shoemaker standing back to back with the altitudinous Wilt Chamberlain. The contrast was humorous and eye-catching. Another way to fulfill this principle is to contrast the elements constituting the form of the ad— color, for example. Our data indicate that using black as a background makes elements in the foreground pop off the page. Stolichnaya earned average scores with a horizontal shot of the product against a white background. When the same layout was produced with a change only in the background, from white to black, the scores increased by 50 percent on average.

9. *Use children and animals.* Almost any advertising can succeed with an appeal to the emotions, and children and animals appeal to all but the most hardhearted. It is logical, of course, to use a close-up of a child when selling toys. (Yet flip through an issue of a magazine for parents and notice how many products for children's clothing, for example, do not use children—a missed opportunity if there ever was one.) And pets, of course, are naturals for pet food.

The trick is to find an excuse to use a child or furry little beast when your product is not even remotely connected to those models. Hewlett-Packard pulled this off beautifully by featuring a Dalmatian and the headline, "Now the HP LaserJet IIP is even more irresistible." The ad won the highest scores in the computer and data equipment product category for a Starch Readership Award. Hitachi has used the double lure of celebrity Jamie Lee Curtis and various animals—cats and parrots primarily—to hawk the company's televisions in a campaign that has consistently garnered the highest "noted" scores for the category.

10. *When an ad has a good deal of copy, make it as inviting as possible.* A source of never-ending astonishment to us is the advertiser that insists on shrinking and squeezing copy into a tight corner of an ad in order to maximize "white space"— a triumph of style over common sense. Others present copy over a mottled background, making it almost impossible to read easily. Two other common problems are reverse print over a light background, offering too little contrast, and centered copy (i.e., unjustified right and left margins), which forces the reader to work too hard to find the beginning of each line. An advertiser that includes a fair amount of copy obviously hopes that it will be read. Relatively few readers choose to spend the time to read most of the copy of any advertisement; if you get 20 percent of magazine readers to delve into your copy, you are doing very well. So the challenge is to make the whole process as easy for the reader as possible. Good content alone will not attract readers. The best-written, wittiest, and most powerful copy will be overlooked unless it is well spaced and sufficiently large and clear to invite the reader.

OUTDOOR MESSAGES

The new production technologies offer the opportunity to create something bigger than life. Here you can create disruption from the ordinary. A giant peach sitting in a field will attract attention because it is a thousand times larger than a peach should be. The Richards Group in Dallas created an outdoor poster that had a cow on a billboard threatening to jump (Exhibit 16.10). We all know that cows don't climb up on billboards or jump off, yet we look.

EXHIBIT 16.10

Chick-fil-A's cows attract attention. The visual disruption of seeing climbing cows and the spelling make us look.

Courtesy of Chick-fil-A.

Scott Scaggs

Creative Director, Trone, High Point, North Carolina
The Implicit Message Says More than Your Headline

You're driving home from the beach and you see two signs. They both say "Fresh Fruit Ahead." As an advertising junkie you say to yourself, "what a weak headline," but as a consumer you think, "I could always eat a little something."

The first sign is hand-painted on a few weathered planks that must have been a fruit crate at one time. The red paint spells out "Ed's Fruit Stand" in an odd combination of lower case and capital letters and an unidentifiable drawing of fruit-like objects adorns the top of the sign.

The second sign has been professionally printed in color (although it's a little sun-faded) and includes clip art showing an arrangement of fruit. There's a Fruitco company logo proudly displayed at the bottom.

So how do you decide which fruit stand to visit? The explicit message (the words and the subject matter of the visual) is exactly the same. But the implicit message could not be more different. I would bet that you already know which fruit stand would draw your business.

The same dynamic exists for every piece of marketing communication. The takeaway message is a combination of the explicit and the implicit. In fact, I would argue that the audience is more influenced by what they read between the lines than by reading the actual lines.

Has a friend ever tried to tell you about a really cool commercial? His retelling will almost always fail to make you feel the way he did when he saw it. Even if he could recite the copy from the spot verbatim, you would still be missing whatever was so captivating about the way it was shot, cast, edited, scored, or directed. The empty look on your face would probably be followed by his comment, "I guess you had to see it." What he really means is that you had to experience the crafted combination of the explicit and implicit communication in the spot to fully appreciate its message. Hopefully no one would actually say that.

Credibility is greatly enhanced by supporting the explicit with the implicit. That means if you're creating a brochure for a premium quality brand, you'd better support that position with the execution of the idea. Think about heavy paper stock versus something flimsy. Are you using high-end, stylized photography or images shot by the client's cousin who shoots weddings on the side? There are hundreds—if not thousands—of decisions that

Scott Scaggs

affect the way the piece will be received. Just remember that those decisions need to support the idea expressed by the words on the page.

The unfortunate reality is that many clients are not sensitive to the power of the implicit message. As an example, they may ask the agency to add the word "sophisticated" to the headline and ask for the logo to be 150% bigger. "And bump up the point size of the copy while you're at it." You know it doesn't look quite right after fulfilling those requests, but you're afraid it's just a difference of opinion on a subjective matter.

As an expert in marketing communication, you should stand your ground on these points. An incongruous implicit message negates the explicit message and confuses the audience. It's like delivering serious news with a goofy grin. It is our job as advertising professionals to help clients understand that there should be no random decisions in our craft. All aspects of creating communication for their brands must be thought through so that every layer of the message is right.

As for the fruit stand, I would have to visit Ed's because I can't support a company that uses clip art. But maybe that's just me. ■ ■ ■

Just a few thoughts on outdoor. First, you have a responsibility to create something wonderful because most people dislike ads cluttering up the environment. You should ask, as with any medium, how the ad will be integrated into the other kinds of communications. In Chapter 12, an overview of creative was given. Generally, there should be no more than seven words in the main head. No, we're not saying it won't communicate with more than seven; but the more you have, the harder it is to grasp quickly. This is truly a medium in which simple is better. Reduce all the elements, if possible. If you have a bottle of Sobe energy drink as your illustration, do you need to also have a logo? Maybe, but if the bottle is large enough, you'll easily see the logo on it. The point is to reduce the visual and verbal elements down to their simplest form.

TODAY'S MESSAGE TOOLS

Today's advertising tools offer advertisers many ways to attract attention and hopefully communicate with people who want the message. And they are changing every day. Did iPhone from Apple change the way we think of phones? Certainly, iPod changed the way we listened to music. Let's take a look at a few of these.

Start with the Consumer Across Channels

The world's largest sport shoemaker, Nike, controls about 20 percent of the U.S. market. Nike has maintained a consistent brand image across various channels, making sure that what consumers experience in stores carries over seamlessly to the Web. Nike has an integrated marketing model that involves all elements of the marketing mix from digital to sports marketing, from event marketing to advertising to entertainment, all sitting at the table driving ideas.

"We create demand for our brand by being flexible about how we tell the story," says Nike's Trevor Edwards, vice president, global brand and category management. "We do not rigidly stay with one approach. We do not start with the medium," Mr. Edwards says. "We always start with the consumer and then look for the best ways to connect with them."[26]

Views of Viral Rules

Rich Silverstein, a founder of Goodby Silverstein & Partners, the San Francisco-based agency famed for the "Got milk?" campaign, says his agency has yet to actually pay to post a video on YouTube. It's far better, he says, to turn these people into your distributors by making advertisements so great that consumers pass them around and upload them to such sites. The trouble with this guessing what works from purely an advertiser's standpoint is that it's like pop music: How many people have ever been able to figure out the formula for a Top 40 hit? Silverstein, for instance, points to two short Web films his firm made for Specialized Bikes. One of them, a faux news report about a biker who outraces a police car, was viewed 82,000 times on YouTube. The other, a clever cartoon about a hapless mountain biker who ignores a danger sign and is clawed by a bear, gnawed by piranhas, struck by lighting, and chopped by a woodsman's axe, has been viewed 5,000 times. Kevin Roddy, former executive creative director of Bartle Bogle Hegarty, says, "I believe if you want to be successful in the world of viral, you need to play by the rules of entertainment, not the rules of selling. A lot of brands might have difficulty with that. But as soon as you [sell], people say, 'Well, I'm not going to do your work for you.'"[27]

Here are a couple of definitions of tools used by creative people in the changing world of marketing technology:

Webisodes: A series of mini-movies created for the Web. In 2001, Fallon advertising revolutionized the Internet with the BMW film series, *The Hire.* Five years later, they were back with a low-interest commodity Brawny Paper Towels film series. The theme was lack of performance—about how women are basically disappointed in their husbands. Each 10- to 12-minute reality episode was compelling and full of laughs. For example, "Lay [sic] around the house," is perceived as a universal problem.[28]

Rich media: This method of communication that incorporates animation, sound, video and/or interactivity is going to overtake search marketing as the dominant form of Web advertising by the end of the decade. In general, consumers will click on a rich media ad five times to a single banner ad.

Sales Mission

Maxine Clark, founder and CEO of Build-A-Bear-Workshop says, "Selling on the Internet shouldn't be your priority. Instead, focus on building an online community that enhances your ability to communicate with customers. Unless you have only an online presence, the number one goal of your site should be to drive business to your physical locations, where you can deliver on your brand promise."[29] Folks restaurants, naturally, have a website for store locations and menu information. They also offer products to consumers on the Internet. Exhibit 16.11 is an example of Folks' electronic newsletter to people who want to be on the list.

Developing Games

The marketing community is fixed on games' product-integration potential. Burger King has had success when critics laughed. Here are a few thoughts on creating games from the creators of "The Getaway: Black Monday" (a Playstation game). The size of the team varies in the development process and gets bigger as it nears completion. The creative team consisted of fifteen programmers, ten animators/cinematic artists, and around twenty other production staff including sound designers, musicians and composers, and a performance director. The team had a ninety-page screenplay, which was broken into scenes and storyboards for production. Actors rehearsed for a month for the real-life elements of the film so that the entire performance could be shot in one take. The console writing is just like film and theater writing and requires its own set of rules and limitations. Game writers have to work within the boundaries of what can be done successfully in a game. It is very important to have a background in game production. A good writer needs to be asking: How can we shorten this? (Gamers have a short attention span.) How much animation/modeling/FX/programming time is this going to require? And how are we going to communicate the story in gameplay? One of the greatest challenges is being silent yet entertaining—guiding a player without being overt.[30]

EXHIBIT **16.11**

Folks' E-Mailed eNewsletter

Courtesy of Folks and Lane Bevil+Partners

WHAT'S COOKING AT FOLKS!

FOLKSKITCHEN.COM — FALL 2006

NEW Gift Cards!

The new Gift Cards are here! They are like a plastic credit card, and you can add any amount to the card (min. is $10). Keep them in mind for Stocking Stuffers for the upcoming Holiday season.

Call Ahead Seating

Just call ahead to your favorite Folks and give your name & time you want to dine. When you arrive, you get the next available table.

Lunch Punch Cards   *Coming Soon*

Folks has Lunch Combos for only $7.29, drink included. Become a frequent Good to Go® luncher at Folks, and you can earn a FREE lunch (to-go only)! After 8 visits, you'll receive a FREE lunch (up to $10 value). Who said there's no such thing as a FREE lunch?!

Great South Catering

Folks has been catering for over 25 years. Choose from our Catering menu or we can customize a menu for your event. Pick-up from your local Folks or delivery available from our Catering Center (set up & serve is available, too). Call the Catering Experts at 404-874-5555.

Email Sign-up

Sign up to receive this newsletter and coupons each month via email. Simply fill out the sign-up slip & turn it in or register online.

Starter + Entree+ Dessert= $7.99/$8.99

Our Start to Finish 3-Course meal has gotten even better. You have even more choices from two price points ($7.99 & $8.99). Plus, now you have Soup of the Day as a Starter option and NEW Bread Pudding as a Dessert option.

NEW Food!

We've added some Fall meals such as Chicken Pot Pie, Double-Barrel Pork Chops, Blackjack Mountain Meatlaof & Baked Half-Chicken. We also added some Southern regional favorites such as Louisiana Chicken and Southwest Chicken. All these NEW entree are available as part of Start to Finish promotion (Starter + Entree + Dessert = $7.99/$8.99).

Open Thanksgiving

Like last year, Folks will be OPEN on Thanksgiving Day serving food from 11am to 7pm in the dining room and offering carryout services from 10am until 7pm. We'll also offer our special Thanksgiving Complete Meal that includes all the fixins for only $9.99 per person (Sliced oven-roasted Turkey, gravy, cornbread dressing, your choice of two veggies, bread and a slice of Pecan Pie or cup of Cobbler of the Day). Comeand visit us and let us take care of your meal for the day while you just relax.

Thanksgiving Ham and Turkey Breast

 Let us help with your Thanksgiving meal that you will serve at home, so you can relax and enjoy your day. Folks will be selling a Brown Sugar Spiral Sliced Ham (9 lbs) and Turkey Breast Slices for only $7.99/lb. as well as traditional sides and desserts. Let *us* do the cooking! Simply fill out an order form provided at the tables with all your information and turn it in to your server. Then, pick it up at your specified date and time and ENJOY!

#6494

$3 Off Two Meals

Purchase any two entrees from our regularly-priced menu and receive $3 off the total check. Offer expires 12/31/06. Limit one coupon per party per visit.

Folks Southern Kitchen SINCE 1978

Offer valid for dine-in or take-out. Please present coupon before ordering. Not valid on children's menu, All-You-Can-Eat, "Start to Finish" or with any other special or promotion.

Buford
Hwy. 20 & PIB
770-945-7514

Conyers
1081 Iris Dr.
770-922-2830

Cumming
Hwy. 20 @ GA 400
770-844-9633

Douglasville
Hwy. 5 @ I-20
770-949-8400

Gainesville
1500 Browns
Bridge Rd.
770-534-1300

Hiram
5096 Jimmy Lee
Smith Pkwy.
770-943-5447

Jonesboro
6564 Tara Blvd.
770-968-8965

Lawrenceville
450 Hurricane Shoals
770-963-0666

Marietta
Sandy Plains
@ Canton Hwy.
770-425-2322

Peachtree Corners
7075 Jimmy Carter Blvd.
@ Holcomb Bridge
770-416-1143

Roswell
925 Holcomb
Bridge Rd.
770-998-2100

Smyrna
2590 Spring Rd.
770-432-7333

Stockbridge
Hwy. 138
@ Hannover Pkwy.
770-474-6668

Tucker
LaVista Rd. @
Northlake Pkwy.
770-493-6925

Windy Hill
Cobb Pkwy.
@ Windy Hill
770-952-5111

Woodstock
Hwy. 92 @ I-575
770-516-0308

SUMMARY ✿

With all the advertising formats and tools, simplicity is the key to great advertising. Good copy speaks to all people. The great creative shops of today have a common thread running through their advertising—the headline, the visual, and the logo communicate the idea immediately.

Advertising motivates people by appealing to their problems, desires, and goals and by offering them a solution to their problems, satisfactions of their desires, and a means of achieving their goals.

In general, advertisements have a definite structure consisting of a promise of benefit in the headline (and maybe the spelling out of the promise in a subheadline), amplification of the story or facts, proof of claim, and action to take. Effective heads can be long or short, but they need to clearly communicate the message. The subheadline can expand on the promise presented in the headline and can provide transition between the headline and the first sentence of the body copy. The body copy is where you build your case with consumers for the product and support the promise in the head or subhead. The details about the product or service are presented here, along with support for your claim.

The creative essence of copywriting is to see a product in a fresh, unique way. The chief approaches used to describe products are factual, imaginative, and emotional. A slogan sums up the theme for a product's benefits. It needs to be a memorable message with few words.

Slogans can be developed from several points of view; the institutional and hard-sell viewpoints are the most common.

The place to start planning an advertisement is the creative work plan or the creative brief for any advertising format. If written properly, the creative work plan will tell you what the message should be in the advertisement and what the advertisement is to accomplish. It tells you the advertisement's specific purpose. However, no work plan will tell you how to execute the copy—that's part of the creative process.

REVIEW ✿

1. What is time famine?
2. How can advertisers use psychological appeals?
3. What are Ogilvy's great advertising elements?
4. What's the purpose of the headline?
5. What is the purpose of amplification?
6. What is meant by "copy style"?
7. What are the characteristics of an effective slogan?
8. What is the key to developing outdoor?

The Total Concept: Words and Visuals

*I*deas and advertisements. How does a creative team get from an idea to a finished advertisement? What kinds of visuals are best? How do we generate fresh ideas? After reading this chapter, you will understand:

chapter objectives

1. concepts and executional ideas
2. left- and right-brain ideas
3. how a creative team works
4. visualizing the idea
5. principles of design
6. kinds of visuals

"Advertising is not art. It is a business masquerading as art," claims John Butler, creative director of Butler, Shine, Stern & Partners. He has told this to many good art directors and writers when they balked at a layout comment or an editorial mandate and refused to budge. He suggests they can go to a craft store and buy a canvas and some oils, because this is advertising, and "it is not a spectator sport."[1] More and more clients are realizing that creative advertisements work better, are more memorable, and make their point more effectively in the marketplace. You can run a good creative ad fewer times. People can remember it after seeing it three times rather than thirty times. Any unique selling proposition (USP) advantage is gone in 15 minutes if you don't create an emotional bond with consumers. Grey Worldwide's chief creative officer says, "You should bring together art and commerce. But you can do some of the most engaging, funny work in the world and if it doesn't motivate the consumer to do something or stimulate some part of their brain, then it doesn't work."[2] So again we find that there isn't a simple set of rules that works for creating strong advertisements or other marketing communications. But all agree that strategic concepts, insights, and ideas are the foundation.

CREATE RELEVANT IDEAS

All advertising, irrespective of where and how it appears, can only be successful if it has an impact on the audience it is addressing. And the only way you can be sure of achieving this is if the content (idea) is so compelling that it creates a desire among those exposed to want more information—to want to know more.[3]

What are some of the great ads you remember from your growing-up years? Why do you remember them? There probably was an idea that was relevant or entertaining to you. Our minds work in mysterious ways. We have to learn to take the reader or viewer beyond the strategy. We also need to go beyond style into a magical dimension. You probably remember, "Just Do It." It helped define a company. "I can't believe I ate the whole thing," is another classic for those that are old enough to remember or fortunate enough to have seen it as part of advertising history. Brylcreem's Greasy Kid's Stuff; Avis's When You're Only No. 2, You Try Harder; Volkswagen's Lemon; Wendy's Where's the Beef?; and AT&T's Reach Out and Touch Someone were all memorable campaigns. Before we can create this kind of advertising, we have to learn to develop the idea behind the strategy.

George Lois, the outrageous art director, was once asked, "What is advertising?" He answered, "Advertising is poison gas. It should bring tears to your eyes, and it should unhinge your nervous system. It should knock you out." He admitted that his description is probably excessive but regards it as a forgivable hyperbole because it certainly describes the powerful possibilities of advertising. Great advertising should have the impact of a punch in the mouth. Great advertising should ask, without asking literally, "Do you get the message?" And the reader (viewer) should answer, without literally answering, "Yeah, I got it!" Lois says all of this can be accomplished with the "big idea." Scott's Miracle Grow delivers its message (see Exhibit 17.1).

EXHIBIT 17.1

Scott's Miracle Grow developed its product idea and message.

Courtesy of Scott's Miracle Grow.

And today, that Big Idea may be aimed at consumers in television, magazines, mobile, short-content films, or any other medium. Ideas are an obsession at Crispin Porter + Bogusky (CP+B). Jeff Benjamin, the agency's interactive director, is one of its idea stars. He developed the Web element that would go along with a series of television spots for the Subservient Chicken campaign. "Even if another agency had thought to bring back the 'Have It Your Way' slogan, it probably would have just replayed the original Burger King song from 30 years ago and shot some spots around that," says Pete Favat, executive creative director for Boston-based advertising shop Arnold Worldwide. "They are like pitbulls when it comes to finding creative ways to deliver a message." The BK site attracted over 460 million in 2 years to the site.[4] Obviously, that was a Big Idea.

The creative process can be broken down into four basic areas: concepts, words, pictures, and the medium or vehicle used to present them. The dictionary defines a *concept* as a general notion or idea, an idea of something formed by mentally combining all its characteristics or particulars. In advertising, the total concept is a fresh way of looking at something—a novel way of talking about a product or service, a dramatic new dimension that gives the observer a new perspective. A concept is an idea. Many in advertising, including Lois, call it the big idea—one that is expressed clearly and combines words and visuals. The words describe what the basic idea is, and the visuals repeat what the words say or, even better, reinforce what the words say or provide a setting that makes the words more powerful.

Your creative concept must not only grab attention, it must also get across the main selling point and the brand name. How often has someone seen a compelling advertisement only to later say, "I don't remember the brand name or product."

IDEAS COME FROM THE LEFT AND RIGHT BRAIN

The left hemisphere of the brain provides reasoning, controls verbal skills, and processes information (characteristics of copywriters). The right side provides intuition, processes information, controls the creative process, thinks nonverbally, responds to color, and is artistic (characteristics of art directors). So we are talking about a left-brain person and a right-brain person working together to develop a concept. Each comes to the table with a different point of view.

Bill Backer created a host of memorable campaigns—"Millertime," "Soup Is Good Food," "Things Go Better with Coke," "Tastes Great, Less Filling"—and in his book, *The Care and Feeding of Ideas*, he defines a *basic idea* or *concept* as an abstract answer to a perceived desire or need. An **executional idea** is a rendering in words, symbols, sounds, colors, shapes, forms, or any combination thereof of an abstract answer to a perceived desire or need. We use the word *execute* in advertisement development. It is a schizophrenic verb. It means to complete or put into effect or to use according to a pattern—as a work of art. Of course, it also means "to put to death."

It is the idea that drives things. John Hegarty has a quote blown up on his wall from a dictionary and it says, "An idea is a thought or plan formed by mental effort." In other words, the color blue is not an idea. It's a means of making your idea more profound. Brett Compton of Blattner Brunner decided to get a little offbeat for the American Red Cross, "Officials warn no beer till February," in what appears to be a news article (see Exhibit 17.2). Instead, below the photograph the caption says "If running out of beer outrages you, why doesn't running out of blood? The American Red Cross is critically low on blood every holiday season. To learn how you can help, visit givebloodredcross.org or call 800-GIVE-LIFE."

executional idea
A rendering in words, symbols, shapes, forms, or any combination thereof of an abstract answer to a perceived desire or need.

Officials warn no beer till February

Bi-beaked beetles infest American barley.

By BRETT COMPTON
Staff Writer

This year's football season will end entirely different than years past. That's because America is within a week, maybe a few days, of completely running out of beer. So all that celebrating and nail biting in the stands will be done while every fan is stone cold sober.

Ironically, the culprit is one that is hardly visible to the naked eye. The bi-beaked beetle, barely the size of the period at the end of this sentence, was accidentally imported into the U.S. some ten years ago in a load of mangos. Once this beetle got a taste of American barley it couldn't

be stopped.

Now America's barley supply has been completely decimated. Beer producers thought there was enough barley in reserves to get through the shortage without needing to inform consumers, but it now seems demand has drastically outpaced supply.

Iowa barley grower, Richard Bryson says, "the problem will be under control by Spring. We've got a pesticide coming that will wipe the [beetles] out." Will the beer-loving American public be able to wait that long? Looks like we'll all just have to wait and see. But it's safe to say wine and football probably don't have much of a future together.

If running out of beer outrages you, why doesn't running out of blood? The American Red Cross is critically low on blood every holiday season. To learn how you can help, visit givebloodredcross.org or call1-800-GIVE-LIFE.

THE CREATIVE TEAM

In general, the responsibility for the visual, layout, and graphics is that of the art director. The copywriter has the job of creating the words for the advertisement and maybe the advertising concept. We say "maybe" because when creative teams are used it is the responsibility of the team to develop a concept. The copywriter needs to understand art direction, and the art director needs to appreciate the impact of words. Together they need to have a rapport to be successful. Both are concept thinkers. Both think in terms of words and pictures, after team members arm themselves with all the information they need. When they have settled on a target audience and a creative strategy, these left- and right-brain people begin to create.

This relationship between copywriter and art director is almost like a marriage. You spend an average of 8 hours a day with your partner—that's 40 hours a week, or 2,080 hours a year. The truth is that better teams feed off each other. Each has its own method of developing big ideas. But there probably isn't a single method. Dick Lord, creative legend, says, "I get my biggest drawing pad and I'll draw little thumbnails and I'll just do headlines or visual ideas. I'll brainstorm myself. I'll sit by myself and do 60, 70—I don't edit them. And then you go over them a little later and you find maybe 10 or 12 that you could look at again. Then, you get with your art director partner, and say, 'Well, what have you got? I have this.'" Some art directors and copywriters like to work by themselves first.

THE IDEA

Strong ideas may be difficult to develop but are worth fighting for when you find one. Strong ideas are simple ideas (see Exhibit 17.3). People do not remember details as clearly as they recall concepts. In advertising, simple concepts become

EXHIBIT 17.3

The Botsford Group created a stunning promotion for Chiquita based upon a simple idea.

Courtesy of Chiquita and The Botsford Group.

KLEPPNER VIEWPOINT 17.1

Megan Jean Sovern
Copywriter, Leo Burnett, Chicago
Can Art Exist in Advertising?

Only if you sneak it in while no one's looking.

My sophomore year in college I did what no parent wants their child to do. I became a Poetry major. My mother disowned me, my father turned to the bottle and then I made a compromise. I declared advertising as my second major and convinced myself I could be a poet in copywriter clothing. And now as a copywriter at Leo Burnett Chicago, I'm still hoping no one finds me out. I keep my poetry books hidden between advertising annuals in my office. And I only wear my beret and drink lattes in the safety of my own home. Is it hard living a double life? Sometimes. But I'm not alone. There are other writers, painters, musicians and filmmakers doing the same thing. Here's how we (and maybe one day, you) can bring art into advertising.

1. **Know when the time is right OR ELSE.** Not every assignment is an opportunity to "change the world." For example if you try to introduce poetry into a [W]eb banner for a financial institution, the conversation will go something like this. Poetry will say, "Hello, I'm poetry and I want to make you beautiful." And the [W]eb banner will say, "Shut the hell up. Just tell me if we have free checking." You will be

Megan Jean Sovern

humiliated. And your creative director will tell you not to come out of your office until you've thought about what you've done. BUT. If you're given the

great advertisements through attention to detail—the words, type style, photography, and layout. A great advertising concept might survive poor execution, but the better crafted the advertisement, the better the chances that prospects will become customers.

We are not necessarily talking about hitting home runs with breakthrough advertising. We are not talking about Nike, Coca-Cola, or Pepsi, or glamorous products. We are talking about ideas that solve problems and communicate to consumers. Ogilvy & Mather took the declining Lever Brothers' Surf detergent brand and increased its sales by more than 20 percent by telling it like it is—doing laundry is a drag and there's no point in trying to deny it. Research showed that 45 percent of all laundry-doers do laundry only as a last resort. Lever's even has a name for them—the un-laundry people. The campaign's idea was to accentuate the negative by playing up the drudgery of doing laundry in a lighthearted way.

A few years ago, BBDO presented a concept to KFC based on the old joke about the chicken crossing the road to illustrate customers' preference for KFC. But, in 1989, KFC had used a "Cross the Road" campaign from Young & Rubicam that franchises disliked. Also, rival Wendy's International was using a "Why People Cross the Road" campaign for chicken nuggets.[5] This is one of the reasons advertisers must do research and both agencies and clients maintain libraries of their work (and research the history of the category). At times, using an old idea may work but it

540

chance to create a new campaign for a candy company founded on puns and smart characters with smart dialogue, then by all means get on with your bad artistic self.

2. **Know your audience and hug them 'til it hurts.** Men looking for a beer that's great tasting and less filling are not receptive to poetry. Well, maybe some are, but they're very secretive about it. But don't let that discourage you. Audiences far and wide are looking to connect with something. And they least expect it to be an ad.

Nike brought aspiring athletes a hero by sculpting Michael Jordan into a modern day David. His voice stands as strong as his figure and people chant his name not just in worship, but in hope that one day a crowd will chant their own. And they aren't the only ones. Housewives needing appreciation, environmentalists searching for progress, college students looking to lead the culture of cool. They all need voices and we represent them.

Yes, we sell stuff, but we also have a social responsibility. You're given 30 seconds and an 8 1/2 X 11 sheet of paper, to make an impact, not just on sales numbers but on your audience. Will they remember your work? Will they feverishly tear out your ad and tape it to a wall? Will they love your work so much they want to become involved in the brand? I hope so, because when this happens art has collided with advertising and there's no turning back.

3. **To make artful ads, you must fill the well with art, not ads.** Ad people make the fatal mistake of looking at ads to find inspiration. DO NOT DO THIS. Ad annuals are great for seeing what else is out there. And they make incredible bookends. But they don't hold the answers you're looking for when beginning an assignment. If anything, they will just piss you off. If you need help getting started, go to the movies. Pay attention to where people laugh, gasp or cry. Also mind the parts where they get up and go to the bathroom. Read a book, magazine or bathroom stall. A professor told me once to read the *New York Times* every Sunday and I try. And if I don't, I leave it on my coffee table so I look incredibly smart when guests are over. You should do the same.

If you're an artist, look to other artists to elevate your thinking. I read more than I write and I'm a stronger writer for it. Because by studying how other writers use their voices, I've learned how to raise my own.

You're carving out a style, a niche, a something no one else can replace or copy. You're weaving your art into your career and people will want to marry you because you're smart and original and rich. Trust me.

And well I guess if I have any other advice, it's to not get too caught up in this great big ad world. Art isn't created under the pressure of deadlines and creative directors. It surfaces when you least expect it. So don't stare at a screen for hours on end. Start with a canvas, a blank page, a note or a scene. Then open your secret drawer, get out that beret and create something that will scare your parents. Because it's really about freaking your parents out. Ultimately it always is.

■ ■ ■

could have risks. You could argue whether or not there are original ideas, but certainly we seek fresh executions.

In an ideal world, the idea needs to come alive, leap off the page, or grab your senses while you watch television. In addition, creative ideas do two important things: (1) They make the prime prospect consider your product first. (2) They implant your brand name indelibly in the prospect's mind and connect it to the positive attributes of your products.

Visualizing the Idea

It is time to execute the big idea. At this stage of the process, the creative team forms mental pictures of how the basic appeal can be translated into a selling message. Just as a good novel has various subplots that are brought together in a creative and interesting, cohesive story line, a good advertisement has a well-coordinated layout that flows freely to create a compelling message about the product and its benefits.[6] You might visualize a sports car as speeding on a mountain road and around hairpin curves. You might see a sedan of understated luxury in front of a country club. Or you might simply see a close-up of the grill.

These mental pictures can be shown in words or in the crudest form. The crucial thing is to imagine the kind of mental picture that best expresses your idea.

While thinking in the visual form (remember, a picture is worth a thousand words), find the words that work with the visual for the most powerful effect. Show, if you can. Make as many versions of the basic idea as you can. Tweak or stretch your idea to the limit. Remember, Dick Lord said he sketched seventy rough ideas with heads. And, yes, they could be done on the computer, but Fallon's Tom Lichtenheld believes sketching on paper and tweaking on his Mac work best for him. There is no magic number of sketches. Try every possibility, but remember that your end result must deliver the basic message and the brand name. Do the illustration and copy deliver the creative work plan promise?

Marketing Approach to Visualization

We know that advertisements are not created for the sake of creativity. Each advertisement is created for a specific marketing purpose. All advertisements for a product should conform to the same set of objectives, even though some advertisements may not appear to be related; and usually, they use the same theme or slogan in each advertisement.

Using all the information you have about the product or service, write a statement of the one thing you need to say about the product to the prime prospect. This is your promise or the basic theme. A family restaurant might shift to low-fat menu items and promise, "We offer you all the things you like about family-style restaurants—convenience, great-tasting foods, and reasonable prices, with the added benefit of fitting into your lifestyle since you want food that is nutritious and good for you." The illustrations must reflect these marketing concepts.

The promise is a consumer benefit statement that tells the prospects what the product will do for them.

THE CREATIVE LEAP

Are we about ready to begin to create an advertisement? Yes, if we have done our homework. Joseph Wallas, a creative theorist, said creativity is the product of four developmental stages: preparation, incubation, illumination, and verification or evaluation. A Leo Burnett creative director has said, "The best creative comes from an understanding of what people are thinking and feeling. Creativity is a sensitivity to human nature and the ability to communicate it." Starch Research suggests that we have to evaluate the consumer, address the consumer's needs, and suggest the clear benefit of using the product: "Tell her how her life will change for the better if she uses the product, and she'll pay close attention."

Where does the inspiration come from? Some think brainstorming or free association is the answer to creative inspiration, but others say very few ideas come from these techniques. A crazy idea may be the spark for a great campaign. The idea usually comes when you are not looking.

Former Creative Director Jim Aitchison gives a few suggestions for the source of inspiration for an idea:[7]

- Is there an idea in the packaging—shape, color, label, or material the product is made of?
- How is the product made? Where is it made?
- How about the product's history?
- Can you show what happens with the product?
- Any new ideas from the product's old advertising?

The process is one part reason, one part heart, and one big part simple intuition, say others. So the creative leap is not necessarily the same for everyone. There may be truth that you spend more time on the logical process, and then the emo-

EXHIBIT 17.4

The images, headline, and logo must work as one to be effective.

Courtesy of AppleGrove Restaurants, an Applebee's® franchise company, and McRae Communications.

tional part comes more easily. Once you get the idea—the concept and visual and words that work together—you've made the creative leap. Leonard Monahan developed a visual idea for North protective work gloves that got right to the point of product advantage by using a wet sponge cut out in the shape of a hand as the illustration. The headline read, "This is what your hand looks like to most toxic chemicals." The headline and visual spoke to the reader as one. A mundane product became the most talked-about advertisement in its industry.

Layout

The creative leap is only the first step in advertisement making. The advertisement itself has a variety of elements: headlines, illustration, copy, logotype, maybe a subheadline, several other illustrations of varying importance, a coupon—the number of components varies tremendously from advertisement to advertisement. Putting them all together in an orderly form is called *making up the layout of the advertisement*. **Layout** is another of those advertising terms that is used in two senses: It means the total appearance of the advertisement—its overall design and the composition of its elements; it also means the physical rendering of the design of the advertisement—a blueprint for production purposes. You will hear some say: "Here's the layout," while handing another person a typed or keyboarded copy and a drawing. Right now, we are talking about the layout as the overall design of the advertisement. The same principles apply to outdoor. The Applebee's headline, "Driving is so much easier than cooking," is difficult because these elements must work together (see Exhibit 17.4). The images and the copy must function as one. How did the creative team decide to present the "idea" in this manner?

Layout Person as Editor

Although the person who creates the visual idea may be the same person who makes the layout, the two functions are different. The visualizer translates an idea into visual form; a layout person uses that illustration and all the other elements to make an orderly, attractive arrangement.

Before putting pencil to paper, however, the layout person—usually an art director—and the writer review all of the elements. The first task is to decide what is

layout
A working drawing (may be computer developed) showing how an advertisement is to look. A printer's layout is a set of instructions accompanying a piece of copy showing how it is to be set up. There are also rough layouts, finished layouts, and mechanical layouts, representing various degrees of finish. The term *layout* is used also for the total design of an advertisement.

most important. Is it the headline? The picture? The copy? How important is the package? Should the product itself be shown, and if so, should it be shown in some special environment or in use? Is this advertisement to tell a fast story with a picture and headline, or is it a long-copy advertisement in which illustration is only an incidental feature? The importance of the element determines its size and placement within the advertisement.

The Need to Attract Attention

Disruption. Attracting attention. Getting noticed. High visibility. No matter how you say it, this is the primary creative objective of an advertisement. Today's advertising has to work very hard to get noticed. You cannot rely on strategy alone—the positioning, the product appeals, the demographic and psychographic data that tell you what wavelength the consumer is on—to sell the consumer. Obvious as it sounds, you cannot sell people until you attract their attention. Put another way, people are not going to read the advertisement if they do not see it. Remember, your advertisement is competing with all the advertising clutter and editorial matter in a publication. Unfortunately, most advertisements in most publications are invisible.

All the creative elements—the visual, the headline, the copy—must be strongly executed if the advertisement is to succeed. John Hegarty says, "You're using words and pictures. What you don't want to do is make the pictures do what the words are doing, and the words do what the picture is doing. So you've got to decide which is leading, which is taking you forward, and if it's the picture then you almost certainly will want a very simple headline. Or it's the other way around—a simple picture and an intriguing headline. So there is a kind of juxtaposition."[8] If the idea is being carried by the headline, it will have a twist, a turn, maybe shock—or some sort of disruption. The visual will play a straight role. And vice versa if the message is being carried by the picture. Research cannot tell us which creative techniques will work best because creative is not that scientific. Research generally tells us what has been successful, but there are no yardsticks to measure breakthrough advertising ideas. The basic guidelines for writing and designing advertisements are helpful, but there are not really any rules. How do you get an advertisement to stand out? The illustration is usually the key. Either an advertisement grabs people or it does not, and most often it is the illustration that gets them. Of course, many illustrations cannot tell the story alone—they require a headline to complete the communication. So the headline is extremely important to keep people's interest. If you are interested in furniture, you identify with the Broyhill illustration (see Exhibit 17.5).

There are three basic means of attracting attention:

1. Using the visual alone
2. Using the headline alone
3. Using a combination of the visual and headline

Do not assume that because we listed the visual first that the art director is more important than the copywriter. Remember, they are a team working together on both visual and language ideas.

Basic Design Principles

There are some general principles that guide the design of advertising and promotional layouts. Some art directors may use different terminology from that used here, but the basic assumptions are the same.

The following design principles, properly employed, will attract the reader and enhance the chances that the message is read.

EXHIBIT 17.5
This advertisement depends on the power of the picture.
Courtesy of Broyhill Industries.

Unity All creative advertising has a unified design. The layout must be conceived in its entirety, with all its parts (copy, art, head, logo, and so forth) related to one another to give one overall, unified effect. If the advertisement does not have unity, it falls apart and becomes visual confusion. Perhaps unity is the most important design principle, but they are all necessary for an effective advertisement.

Harmony Closely related to unity is the idea that all elements of the layout must be compatible. The art director achieves harmony by choosing elements that go together. This process is similar to dressing in the morning. Some items of clothing go together better than others—for example, stripes, plaids, or paisleys with solid colors. The layout needs harmonious elements to be effective; there should not be too many different typefaces or sizes, illustrations, and so on.

Sequence The advertisement should be arranged in an orderly manner so it can be read from left to right and top to bottom. The sequence of elements can help direct the eye in a structural or gaze motion. Place the elements so that the eye starts where you want it to start and travels a desired path throughout the advertisement; Z and S arrangements are common.

Emphasis Emphasis is accenting or focusing on an element (or group of elements) to make it stand out. Decide whether you want to stress the illustration, the headline, the logo, or the copy. If you give all of these elements equal emphasis, your advertisement will end up with no emphasis at all.

Contrast You need differences in sizes, shapes, and tones to add sparkle so the advertisement will not be visually dull. Altering type to bold or italic or using extended typefaces brings attention to a word or phrase and creates contrast between type elements. Contrast makes the layout more interesting.

Balance By balance, we mean controlling the size, tone, weight, and position of the elements in the advertisement. Balanced elements look secure and natural to the eye. You test for balance by examining the relationship between the right and left halves of the advertisement. There are basically two forms of balance: formal and informal.

Formal Balance The Chick-fil-A calendar layout (see Exhibit 17.6) has elements of equal weight, size, and shape on the left and right sides of an imaginary vertical line drawn down the center of the advertisement. Such symmetrical advertisements give an impression of stability and conservatism. Keep in mind that not all formal layouts will have exactly equal weight. For instance, a logo may be on the lower right-hand corner and not have an equal element on the opposite side, but if all other elements are symmetrical, we would consider it a formal layout.

EXHIBIT 17.6

Formal Balance

If we draw a line down the center, you have basically equal weight on both sides.

Courtesy of Chick-fil-A.

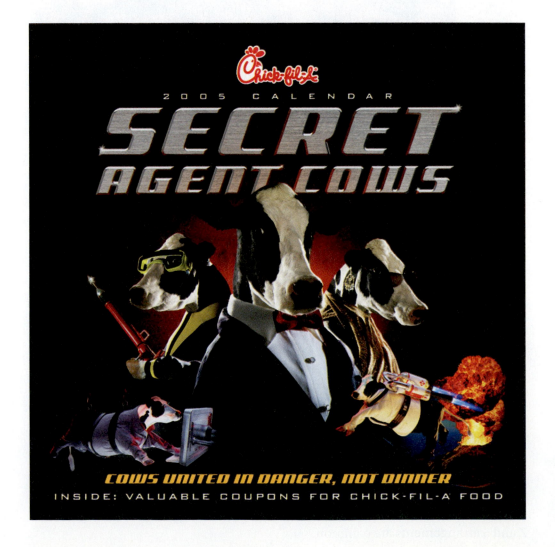

Informal Balance The optical center of a page, measured from top to bottom, is five-eighths of the way up the page; thus, it differs from the mathematical center. (To test this, take a blank piece of paper, close your eyes, then open them, and quickly place a dot at what you think is the center of the page. The chances are that it will be above the mathematical center.) Imagine that a seesaw is balanced on the optical center. We know that a lighter weight on the seesaw can easily balance a heavier one by being farther away from the fulcrum. (The "weight" of an element in an advertisement may be gauged by its size, its degree of blackness, its color, or its shape.) In informal balance, objects are placed seemingly at random on the page but in such relation to one another that the page as a whole seems in balance. This type of layout arrangement requires more thought than the simple bisymmetric formal balance, but the effects can be imaginative and distinctive, as illustrated by Exhibit 17.6.

Other Composing Elements

Color One of the most versatile elements of an advertisement is color. It can attract attention and help create a mood.

Psychology of Color

Your personal and cultural associations affect your experience of color. We see colors as warm or cool mainly because of long-held (and often universal) associations. Yellow, orange, and red are associated with the heat of sun and fire; blue, green, and violet with the coolness of leaves, sea, and the sky. Warm colors seem closer to the viewer than cool colors, but vivid cool colors can overwhelm light and subtle warm colors. Using warm colors for foreground and cool colors for background enhances the perception of depth.

Although red, yellow, and orange are in general considered high-arousal colors and blue, green, and most violets are low-arousal hues, the brilliance, darkness, and lightness of a color can alter the psychological message. While a light blue-green appears to be tranquil, wet, and cool, a brilliant turquoise, often associated with a lush tropical ocean setting, will be more exciting to the eye. The psychological association of a color is often more meaningful than the visual experience.[9]

Depending on the product and the advertising appeal, color can be used for a number of reasons:

- It is an attention-getting device. With few exceptions, people notice a color advertisement more readily than one in black and white. Roper Starch research studies indicated color newspaper advertisements were read 61 percent more often than black-and-white advertisements.

- Some products can be presented realistically only in color. Household furnishings, food, many clothing and fashion accessories, and cosmetics would lose most of their appeal if advertised in black and white. Studies are done to find the best consumer colors and to spot color trends. For instance, the Pantone Color Institute asked consumers to select their current and future color preferences in specific product categories. In addition, a questionnaire collected data on demographics and placed the respondents into five lifestyle categories: prudent, impulsive, pessimistic, traditional, and confident.

- Color can highlight specific elements within an advertisement but should be carefully built into the advertisement. Occasionally, an advertiser will use spot color for a product in an otherwise black-and-white advertisement. Any color needs to be an intregal part of the advertisement and not an afterthought. We discuss the technique of color production in Chapter 18 and packaging in Chapter 21.

KLEPPNER VIEWPOINT 17.2

Jeanne Spencer

Partner, Idea Engineering, Inc., Santa Barbara, California

Good Design = Better Communication

How do you evaluate a creative portfolio when selecting an agency or design team? How do you evaluate the work that is developed for you? And why does it matter? Research has shown evidence that the benefits of graphic design include both long and short term effects on consumers' psychological influences and buying trends. Effective graphic design aids in memory retention, particularly in the case of qualitative attributes. Good design creates a visual identity that aids in rapid recognition. Structured effectively, graphic design helps to organize information for easy interpretation and understanding of the message. How well your message performs is ultimately decided by the marketplace. However, there are some basic questions you can keep in mind to most effectively evaluate creative work, whatever the medium.

Jeanne Spencer

1. **Is it engaging?** In the context that it will be seen, will it catch your audience's attention and persuade them to pause and learn more? If it's a trade show booth, will it stand out in the convention center? If it's a magazine ad, will someone stop and read it?

    Usually the most successful creative is engaging because it connects with your audience's emotions in some way.

    Does what initially attracts attention relate to its overall purpose and message? An ad with a shocking photograph causes us to pause and engages our emotion, but if the message of the ad is that this is the healthiest breakfast cereal available, the disconnect will make us feel unnecessarily manipulated. Similarly, music or a popup ad on a website can attract attention, but they can also annoy.

    Overall, the creative needs to be appropriate to its context, while distinct from what surrounds it and relevant to the message. A compelling message and idea is the most important thing. Design choices that help create that distinction are color, scale, and the selection and treatment of images.

2. **Is it legible?** If your audience can't read it, they're not going to get your message. At first glance, if the headline is in a display font that takes too long to decipher, they won't bother. If your audience is seniors, is the type large enough for them to comfortably read it? There are governmental guidelines for designing everything from websites to signage for visually impaired audiences. But in general, legibility tends to be affected by things like type that is not distinct enough from a background color or image, or that is too small or too crowded. Similarly, images can be evaluated in terms of legibility. Does the diagram clearly communicate its information? Is this photo cropped or colorized in a way that is engaging or simply confusing?

    When reviewing a logo design, consider if it will be legible when reproduced at a small size or in a single color.

3. **Does it have the appropriate hierarchy of information?** When you look at a brochure or ad, is your eye attracted to the most important thing first? Then the next most important? Then the next? This is at the heart of good graphic design—being able to arrange

Nuprin, formerly a prescription anti-inflammatory medication, was reclassified for over-the-counter sales in 1984. It increased its share of the ibuprofen market by using a superficial product difference—the yellow tablet. Nuprin's advertisements that simply said research showed two Nuprins gave more headache relief than Extra Strength Tylenol did not advance its share. A Grey

the elements of communication (words, images, choice of materials) to appropriately tell a story. The story starts at the beginning (the image or headline that first catches your eye) then may immediately go to the end (the call to action) or there may be 30 pages that build and support the story in between. But the story is always best told when it follows a planned sequence, and creating a sequence is not possible if everything has the same level of importance. Not every bit of information on a page can be the biggest, brightest, and most eye-catching. Not if you want your audience to focus on a specific message.

4. Is it consistent with your brand identity? If not, why not? We've been assuming that before you started developing ads or brochures that your basics are in place, including your brand's personality and positioning vis-a-vis your competition. We've also assumed that the visual side of your brand identity is clear: the logo, colors, fonts and image treatment that are consistently used to create brand recognition. So when you look at a new creative piece in development, besides making sure that it's on target in carrying the personality and core messages of your brand, also look at the visual consistency.

If it's part of a series, inconsistency can be confusing. If it's reaching out to a new audience, stretching the brand's visual identity could be appropriate. If a new product line is being launched, a variation on the main brand will probably be helpful, both internally and for your audience in differentiating from the other product lines.

Consistency is not a holy grail, but brand identities are frequently diffused over time by too many variations. This limits the impact that consistent usage can give, as well as the increase in legibility that comes from familiarity with consistent usage.

5. Can any of these areas be improved? Can it be more engaging? More legible? Have better hierarchy? Be more consistent with the brand? You don't need to tell your creative team how to accomplish these things, but these are useful ways of describing areas that do need improvement.

A Few Don'ts

Some things that can seem like good ideas just don't maximize your results in creative development.

Don't limit design options before discussing with your creative team: Take advantage of their experience and familiarity with creative options. If you know that you want to reach a specific audience and have determined that direct mail is the best method, design considerations can help determine things like: (1) Size: should it be bigger or unusually shaped for more distinctiveness? At what points does it affect cost of production or mailing? (2) Whether it should be a self-mailer or what options for packaging would help it stand out more. (3) What unusual paper or printing process might enhance the impact. (4) Whether your audience dislikes seeing wasted paper and would respond more favorably to a postcard with a link to a website for more information.

Don't crowd in too much information: If you've heard the term "white space," it's not referring to the value of the color white, but to the principle that having some clear space on a page can both help visually balance it and help draw your eye to what is most important. It can be tempting due to limited budgets or a desire to communicate as much as possible to keep adding more, but it does start to reduce the impact of what is there. It's back to legibility and hierarchy and being engaging.

Don't prioritize your personal preferences . . . unless you are the target audience. Otherwise, the fact that you don't like yellow just doesn't matter. What does matter is if yellow helps your material be more eye-catching in its context.

Don't have too many people making final creative decisions: Feedback is great. You don't want to miss something obvious because the schedule was too tight to get key people to review information or buy in to a concept. But the more people involved in creative evaluation, the more likely it is that someone will be involved who doesn't fully understand the marketing goals or how to evaluate creative work. Then things get modified based on personal preference.

Identify whoever is ultimately responsible for decision making. That person needs to be involved and reviewing at all key points in the process. Keep the group small.

Great creative is dependent on great ideas that tell a message in compelling and engaging ways. Beyond that, the talent, technical skills and experience that graphic designers bring to the process does make a big difference in how that idea takes form. Knowing how to evaluate creative—and not limit it—can help you find the best team to work with and help you get the most successful results.

Our shared goal is communication, and great design helps you communicate better. ▪ ▪ ▪

Advertising creative director said, "You have to convince consumers that your product is different before they will believe the product is better." The color idea happened when Grey Advertising's group creative director emptied a whole bunch of pain relievers on his desk and found Nuprin was the only yellow tablet there. Color was a way to dramatically and graphically show that

Nuprin was different. Thus, the yellow-tablet campaign was born, showing a black-and-white photo of hands holding two yellow tablets. More recently, AstraZeneca's Nexium, a prescription pill that stops the stomach's acid-producing mechanism, is known as the "little purple pill." Advertisements showed the purple pill, and the copy said, "Get a free trial certificate and ask your doctor about the Purple Pill called NEXIUM." The advertisements sold $2.8 billion of the little purple things in 2002. In 2003, Bristol Meyers sold the product to CVS drug stores as their exclusive brand.

Color can be extremely important in everything from advertising layouts, products, and packaging to the psychological messages consumers perceive. Starch Advertisement Readership Service also has consistently found that bold colors and contrast increase an advertisement's pulling power.

■ In creating for the Web, designers must deal with a smaller color palette than what is available in print. Advertisers are using bright colors to grab attention on the screen that they would never use in print. This use is making brighter hues more acceptable in our daily lives.

Predicting Popular Colors

The Pantone Color Institute conducts color research on color psychology, preferences, and professional color applications. Another organization that predicts colors is the Color Association of America, which forecasts color trends for products and fashion. Another group, the Color Marketing Group (CMG), is a not-for-profit association of some 1,500 designers that forecasts trends 1 to 3 years in advance for all industries, manufactured products, and services. The Color Association of the United States forecasts are released 20 months in advance. Obviously, these predictions have an impact on advertisers. Usually color trends are evolutionary, but that has changed somewhat since 9/11. The stresses that beset our society are having a direct influence on the direction of the color palette. Leatrice Eiseman of the Pantone Color Institute indicates that this continuing quest for harmony means colors should be pleasing and not disturbing. Margaret Walsh, director of the Color Association, sees soft, colorful hues coming to the rescue in an age of high anxiety. And for Color Marketing Group's Melanie Wood, today's consumer wants to feel safe and tranquil in an otherwise crazy world. Colors that refresh and rejuvenate will lead the way with innocent tones giving us a sense of freshness and a promise of tomorrow. Recently, the Color Marketing Group predicted, interior/environmental design colors would consist of soft, colorful hues would come to the rescue in their annual color study. They concluded the influence of global warming on colors for the home is very much about the red family but receives an unexpected bolt of electric blue, which is so much different from what was seen in the past. Obviously, as the mood changes the colors change.[10]

Most brands are so connected to one or two colors that the brand is evoked just by looking at two swatches side by side. Purple and orange? FedEx, of course. What about Home Depot? What delivery company used "brown" as identification? You get the idea. Would you brand a financial company with a pink and purple color scheme? These colors certainly have their place in communications but in this case probably would not create an image of a solid, savvy investment company.

Color Globalization and Regionalization

With the global aspects of today's business and design environment, color is crossing borders and boundaries. Still, strong regional and cultural preferences remain. For example, the bright and sunny colors of tropical areas such as Costa Rica

EXHIBIT 17.7
In some instances, art director's feel that color aids in the feel and look of the message. In this case, Tropicana thought the orange-sunburst background would be more effective than white space in communicating Tropicana Essentials Fiber is orange juice plus.

Courtesy of Tropicana.

appear out of place and out of context when applied to a setting like New York City; and in Seattle where the weather is primarily gray all winter, people choose brighter colors such as yellow. Many of the same factors affecting the concerns and moods of Americans appear on a global basis, which is unusual.

White Space Some layout people and designers become so preoccupied with the illustration that they forget that white space, or blank space, is a very significant design tool. The basic rule for using white space is to keep it to the outside of the advertisement (see Exhibit 17.7). Too much white space in the middle of an advertisement can destroy unity by pushing the eye in several directions and confusing the reader.

Preparing the Layout

The layout is the orderly arrangement of all the copy elements in a print advertisement. It is basically a blueprint that the production people will follow to complete the finished advertisement. An advertisement may go through different levels of roughness as it is developed. These different types of layouts represent different stages of conventional (not electronic) development of the advertisement.

- *Thumbnail sketches:* Miniature drawings trying out different arrangements of the layout elements. The best of these will be selected for the next step.
- *Rough layouts:* Drawings that are equivalent to the actual size of the advertisement. All elements are presented more clearly to simulate the way the advertisement is to look. The best of these will be chosen for the next step. Usually, a computer rough and a computer comprehensive will look very close to the finished piece (if there aren't any changes). You probably couldn't tell which was finished first. However, many times the rough is used for discussions and then any graphic or text changes are made.
- *The* **comprehensive**, *or mechanical, layout* (*often just called the* comp *or the* mechanical): All the type set and placed exactly as it is to appear in the printed advertisement. Illustrations are drawn or scanned into position. Most comps are computer comps but could be illustrated. Computer comps look very much like finished advertisements and are used for client approval.

comprehensive
A layout accurate in size, color, scheme, and other necessary details to show how a final advertisement will look; for presentation only, never for reproduction.

Once the basic advertisement for a campaign has been approved, layouts for subsequent advertisements usually consist of just a rough and finished layout.

Computer Design

Generally, most agency layouts are created in-house by their digital artists. However, there are independent graphic houses or freelance artists who may have a particular expertise in developing designs or illustrations or a particular computer expertise. In some cases, these freelancers simply work as the marketer's design department.

You know all about being able to do layouts and design on computers. However, let's be sure we're on the same page of information. We define *computer graphics* as the ability to draw or display visual information on a video terminal. Raster scan graphics are the most common computer display. Each spot on the screen, called a **pixel**, represents a location in the computer's memory. The number of individual pixels will determine the resolution of the image—this is the difference between poor-quality, computer-set type or visuals and good, reproduction-quality images. The more pixels, the higher the resolution and the smoother the image. The resolution of a screen controls its clarity and sharpness. This is probably more than you wanted to know.

pixel
The smallest element of a computer image that can be separately addressed. It is an individual picture element.

In the past, the creation and production processes have been separate. However, with the simplicity of today's computer software, it is possible for one person to do both layout and production, although software expertise may continue to keep these functions specialized. Today, mastery of layout demands a keen knowledge of art, type, design, and also photography, computers, and electronic imaging.

Type Management

Type may be one of your most valuable assets, and yet it is tricky to manage. You need to understand how your particular computer stores fonts beyond its basic operating system.

Open Type is a font format (you'll learn more about type in the next chapter) jointly developed by Adobe and Microsoft. This font format is superior to *Type 1* and *TrueType* formats, because it gives designers more typographic control. It has a greatly expanded character set, which can include thousands; Type 1 and TrueType are limited to 256. A single-font Open Type font provides for many nonstandard characters: true-drawn small caps, extended ligatures sets, swash and alternative characters, dingbats, and symbols, as well as extensive foreign language support in a single font.[11]

Sheri Bevil

Senior Partner, Sheri Bevil Design and Lane Bevil+Partners
Visual Disruption Can Aid in Attracting Readers

There are those who say the advertising strategy of "disruption" is dead, because of new media—and the fact that consumers are in control. But that isn't quite the story of the word. Let's give a simplistic definition of "disruption" as being something that is not suppose to be there. There is disruption when a TV spot shows up in the middle of your favorite program. I'm not talking about media disruption, I'm talking creative disruption.

In new media and old media we must attract attention. It may be telling a "relevant" story about the product or service or solving a problem of some sort. Disruption may simply be placing an elephant in a cornfield. We are not accustom to seeing an elephant in a corn field. It is "disruption" of what is normal. In this case, it is "visual disruption." No matter the message, we often need a treatment that attracts attention. Not a gimmick, but something that relates in some way.

Visually we may be thinking about something simple like the Chick-fil-A cows on top a billboard (or doing something usual in a TV commercial—cows on top of a car). We normally don't see cows in this manner. Cows are suppose to be in fields. Their creators, The Richard Group found that their cow idea was fresh, adaptive to all media, and would attract attention. They didn't have the money to spend on marketing like a McDonald's. They had to be smarter to be competitive.

To stand out, consider disrupting the way people see things or think, by giving them a new approach. Something

Sheri Bevil

that is different from the norm in how messages are presented. Maybe, push consumer's comfort zone. The concept of "ad disruption" can be positive and can be applied to many ad platforms—new and old. So the next time you're looking to connect, stand out, find your elephant in a cornfield. ■■■

Complicating the management of type fonts is the fact that they come in a number of formats that have evolved over the years.

PostScript Type 1. An earlier bitmap file that handled on-screen displays, a corresponding PostScript file took care of reproduction. Today's font-management utilities track the pairs when you activate them.

TrueType. Apple developed a system to incorporate the two aspects of PostScript into one file. There are actually two TrueType formats, Mac and Windows, but Mac OS X supports both. Windows TrueType font names end in ttf or ttc.

OpenType. This font also stores all information in one file. It incudes either PostScript or TrueType information running on either Mac or Windows and supporting advanced attributes including advanced character sets.

Dfont. Apple introduced the Mac-only format in the Mac OS X operating system, which is essentially TrueType that plays well with its internal UNIX subsystem.

EXHIBIT **17.8**

Percentage of Top-
Scoring Ads

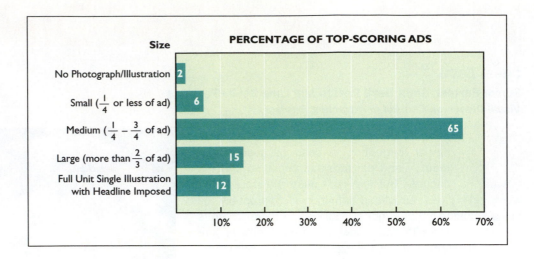

The Visual

Research indicates that 98 percent of the top-scoring advertisements contain a photograph or illustration, proving that human beings are highly visual creatures, according to Cahners Advertising Performance Studies.[12] In most advertisements, the photograph or illustration takes between 25 and 67 percent of the layout space (see Exhibit 17.8).

Art Directing and Photography

Art directing and photography are twin disciplines—each, in theory, raises the other up a notch. Having a great photo in the wrong layout makes for bad advertising. Betsy Zimmerman, art director at Goodby, Silverstein & Partners, says, "The layout's gotta come first. It might look great as a photo, but once you put it in its environment, it is totally different." Jeff Weiss, a noted creative director, says every advertisement contains two things: what you want to say and how you want to say it. What art directing can do is deliver things emotionally, not intellectually. Great art direction takes the selling idea and furthers it without you even knowing it. Take Saks, for example. Its advertisements cannot just say that Saks is glamorous in words—they have to feel glamorous and sophisticated.[13]

Photography can be very expensive. A photo for use in an advertisement may cost between $700 and $10,000, depending on the photographer's reputation and the advertiser's willingness to pay. It costs money to go on location to take photos (see Exhibit 17.9).

The Artist's Medium

The tool or material used to render an illustration is called the artist's medium, the term *medium* being used in a different sense than it is in the phrase *advertising medium* (for example, television or magazines). The most popular artist's medium in advertising is photography. Britain's award-winning art director Neil Godfrey says, "I like to use something people can believe in. I rarely use illustration. Nine-tenths of the time, it just doesn't have the impact of photography." Tom Lichtenheld adds, "Even though people are savvy to retouching, they still believe that photographs don't lie." But sometimes there is the cost factor. "Photography, to be any good these days, costs the earth," says writer Malcolm Pryce, "but you can get brilliant illustration comparatively cheaply."[14] A simple product shot such as the one shown in Exhibit 17.10 can take many hours to shoot the needed images. Other popular tools are pen and ink, pencil, and crayon. Perhaps a photograph will be

EXHIBIT 17.9
Shooting photographs
on location can be
expensive.
Courtesy of Lane Bevil+Partners.

used as the main illustration for an advertisement, but pen and ink will be used for
the smaller, secondary illustration. The choice of the artist's medium depends on
the effect desired, the paper on which the advertisement is to be printed, the printing process to be used, and, most important, the availability of an artist who is
effective in the desired medium. Exhibit 17.11 shows specialized art that requires a
special illustration expertise.

EXHIBIT 17.10
The shooting of some
products requires
specialty photographers
and sometimes food-
preparation people.
Courtesy of Chick-fil-A.

EXHIBIT 17.11

This art requires an illustrator who specializes in a specific style.

Courtesy of Chick-fil-A.

Trade Practice in Buying Commercial Art

Creating an advertisement usually requires two types of artistic talent: the imaginative person, who thinks up the visual idea with a copywriter or alone and makes the master layout, and an artist, who does the finished art of the illustrations. Large agencies have staff art directors and layout people to visualize and create original layouts, as well as studios and artists to handle routine work.

In the largest advertising centers, a host of freelance artists and photographers specialize in certain fields for preparing the final art. In fact, agencies in some cities go to one of the major art centers to buy their graphic artwork for special assignments.

There are two important points to observe in buying artwork, especially photographs. First, you must have written permission or a legal release (see Exhibit 17.12) from anyone whose picture you will use, whether you took the picture or got it from a publication or an art file. (In the case of a child's picture, you must obtain a release from the parent or guardian.) Second, you should arrange all terms in advance. A photographer may take a number of pictures, from which you select one. What will be the price if you wish to use more than one shot? What will be the price if you use the picture in several publications?

Freelance artists' and photographers' charges vary greatly, depending on their reputation, the nature of the work, in what medium the work is being used, and whether the advertisement is to run locally, regionally, or nationally. An art illustration for a magazine may cost $200 if by an unknown artist and up to about $5,000 if

EXHIBIT **17.12**

Typical Model Release

SLRS Advertising   MODEL/PERFORMANCE RELEASE

For value received and without further consideration, I HEREBY CONSENT that all pictures/photographs taken of me and/or recording made of my voice or musical or video performances, may be used for advertising purposes, by SLRS Advertising, Inc., and by advertisers SLRS Advertising, Inc., may authorize or represent, in any manner. I understand that illustrations/performances may be edited, changed or reproduced in any manner without my approval. I agree that all reproductions thereof and plates, films, and tapes shall remain the property of SLRS Advertising, Inc., or of advertisers represented by SLRS Advertising, Inc.

WITNESS_____   SIGNED_____

SOC. SEC. NO._____

IF SUBJECT IS A MINOR UNDER LAWS OF STATE OF PERFORMANCE

GUARDIAN_____

WITNESS_____   DATE_____

SLRS COMMUNICATIONS, INC./P.O. BOX 5488/ATHENS, GA 30604-5488/(706) 549-2665)

by an established artist. A photography session may cost $200 a day for an unknown photographer to about $2,500 for an established photographer. People charge what they think the art or photography is worth or what the client can or is willing to pay. As a result, the better the reputation of the artist or photographer, the more expensive the final product will likely be. The Folks advertisement in Exhibit 17.13 used different photos of food items and china placements, and the different photos were combined into one illustration on the computer.

EXHIBIT **17.13**

This advertisement used multiple photos of food items and china placements, and the different photos were combined into one illustration on the computer.

Courtesy of Lane Bevil+Partners.

Other Sources of Art and Photography

Clients will not always be able to afford the money or time for original advertising art or photography. There are three basic sources of ready-made images: clip art, computer clip art, and stock photos.

Royalty-Free Stock Illustrations These illustrations are available from a multitude of services. The art may be available on CD-ROM (or on the Web), in which case the illustrations are ready to use. All you have to do is download to your computer. Almost any kind of image is available: families, men, women, children, business scenes, locations (e.g., farm, beach), and special events. The disadvantage to using these illustrations is that you have to match your idea to available images, and many of the illustrations are rather average. The advantages are the very reasonable costs and extensive choice of images. Some art services offer a monthly computer disc (or online service) with a wide variety of images; others offer specialized volumes—restaurant art, supermarket art, or medical art, for example. Once you purchase the service, the art is yours to use as you see fit.

Stock Photos There are hundreds of stock-photo libraries available to art directors and advertisers. Each maintains thousands of photographs classified according to the subject categories, including children, animals, lifestyle situations, city landscapes, sports, and models. A photographer submits photos to the stock company, which will publish some photos in its catalog, on a CD-ROM, or on their website. The photographer pays for the space occupied by the photos. Clients then browse through the stock company's offerings to research its files for a suitable photo. The art director or advertiser then leases or contracts for use of the selected photo to feature in an advertisement. The fee is based on the intended use of the photo. Some of these are royalty free.

More than 80 percent of graphic design professionals use stock imagery in their work when the situation calls for it. *Graphic Design: USA* found a number of reasons for deciding to use stock images:[15]

- *Time pressure:* Deadlines and fast turnarounds
- *Budget restraints:* Stock is less expensive than assignment photography offering clients cost savings.
- *Quality, choice, variety:* Stock collections have grown in quality, sophistication, and quantity.
- *Ease of accessibility:* Lots of resources, royalty-free options, digital delivery, and e-commerce sites for easy access

SuperStock.com has over a million stock images. Another company, Comstock's online access service allows you to buy single images, discs, or a subscription. It has 100,000-plus royalty-free images and premium (requires usage fee). Comstock says, "Stock photo pricing isn't based on the known cost of producing the photo: It's based on exactly how you will use it. The more modest your project, the less an image will cost." Its online service offers, "Your selection, hand picked from our library of more than 5 million images for download." The agency can select images and then instantly download low-resolution thumbnail images for inspection. The image may also be marketed and delivered by means of CD-ROM. Images are scanned, stored, digitized, and reproduced on a CD-ROM. Gettyimages.com sells photographs, art and film images. Google can also provide hundreds of international companies supplying all three types of visual images.

SUMMARY ✸

We have now made the transition from thinking of ideas to making advertisements. We have started with the primary consumer benefit, the most important thing we can say about the product.

In advertising, the total concept is a fresh way of looking at something. A concept is an idea. A big idea is one that expresses the message clearly and combines words and visuals. Another way of looking at it is that a basic idea is an abstract answer to a perceived desire or need.

The creative team consisting of an art director and a copywriter next develops the best approach to presenting the executional idea—a rendering in words, symbols, sounds, shapes, and so forth of an abstract answer to a perceived desire or need. Then comes layout preparation (usually done by an art director), in which the various elements of the advertisement are composed into a unified whole. Creating an advertisement that will attract attention is one of the art director's primary concerns. When arranging the elements of an advertisement, the layout artist has to consider the principles of design: unity, harmony, sequence, emphasis, contrast, and balance.

Advertisements usually begin as thumbnail sketches. Subsequent steps are rough layout, the finished layout, and the comps. The computer simplifies this process: In computer design, the roughs are no longer rough, and the comprehensives are better because the layout and typography are exact.

In most cases, art and photography are original executions of the art director's ideas, illustrated or shot according to his or her specifications by freelance artists or photographers. When time or money is short, clip-art or computer-art services or stock photography may be used.

REVIEW ✸

1. What is the big idea?
2. What is the executional idea?
3. What do art directors and copywriters do?
4. What are the basic means of attracting attention?
5. What is a comp?
6. What are stock photos?

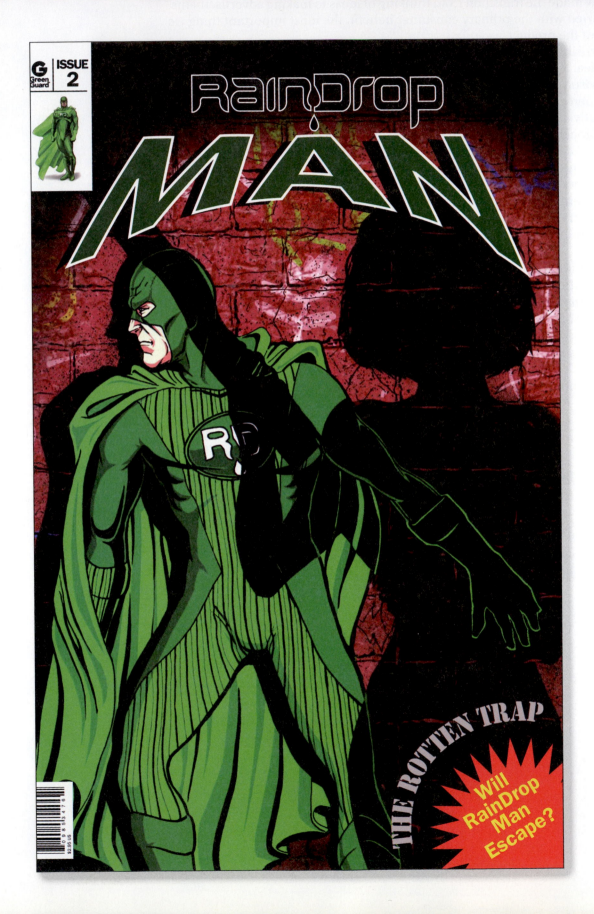

CHAPTER 18

Print Production

Over the past 15 years, computer-to-plate (CTP) and direct-to-press digital printing began to alter the print and publishing industries' production. Since then, the majority of printers and publishers have successfully completed the transition from film to digital file exchange. Advertisers were forced to join this journey. After reading this chapter, you will understand:

chapter objectives

1. production departments
2. digital and traditional production processes
3. mechanicals and artwork
4. proofing

Our ideas have been developed and the client has approved everything. It is now time for the print production people to take these ideas and create a finished advertisement for publication. Because the production process can be complicated and involves quality, time, and cost factors, it is helpful if all advertising and marketing people have some working knowledge of the basics of the production processes. What do we need to send to the publication so it can print the piece? What are the preparation steps and printing procedures for the brochure or insert? How long will this take?

This conversion process, going from the original layout to the finished piece, is the responsibility of the advertiser or agency and is called *print production*. Production requirements differ from advertisement to advertisement. The staff may be producing magazine or newspaper advertisements; collateral brochures; or direct-response, outdoor, or transit advertisements. They need a working knowledge of all these production processes, as well as publication mechanical specifications. The planning process may involve a great deal of money and people. Before we get into the organization, let us look at some important issues.

Keep in mind that in most cases digital is only part of the process. Digital presses have limitations for large runs (printing millions of pieces). Printers have millions of dollars in presses that work fine and will only change when there is a clear quality and economic advantage. But it is changing. In late 2006, Canon had a four-page advertisement in the *Wall Street Journal*: "What's next for color starts with what's next from Canon." Finally, someone has the courage to call its copier a press. The second head said, "Finally. A digital press innovative enough to come from Canon." The copy claims, "Introducing the Canon imagePRESS C7000VP. For a totally new kind of digital production printing that rivals offset quality." This is capable of handling some marketer's small printing jobs. Its paper size is small compared to regular offset presses that take paper sizes three and four times larger than Canon's 11" × 17". You're not going to print your twelve-page promotion piece or 700,000 advertising inserts on this machine. But we talk later in this chapter about the basic printing processes.

PRODUCTION DATA

Production people need to be well versed in the technical aspects of art and type processes, printing methods, and duplicate plates, which we discuss later in the chapter. Let us look first at sources of information for print media. As you would expect, most publications have a production or advertising specification link on their website. Some have PDF downloads for display, classified, and special sections, which include all production specifications.

The Standard Rate and Data Service (SRDS) production source—SRDS Print Media Production Data—provides complete data on all critical advertising production specifications for most business and consumer magazines and newspapers. Production, traffic, and graphic design personnel use this resource to confirm essential production information, so they can control production deadlines and budgets. Of course, each publication determines its own advertising due dates and mechanical specifications based on printing requirements. Exhibit 18.1 shows some of the digital advertising specifications for a typical publication.

EXHIBIT 18.1

2008 Mechanical Digital Requirements

2008 MAGAZINE DIGITAL ADVERTISING SPECIFICATIONS

Desktop File Format

Quark XPress saved as Postscript (print to disk). Instructions for creating these files consistent with vendor specifications can be obtained from our production department or online. High-end File Format

TIFF/IT-PI (CT, LW/NLW, and/or HC and FP files required for each page. Do not rename TIFF/IT/PI files once they are created.) CT Resolution 254 dpi (RES 10) or 304.8 dpi (RES 12). LW Resolution 2400 dpi. Supply one composite CT/LW, NLW per page. No offsets applied. Black text should be merged with LW/NLW file.

Media

- 100 or 250 MB Zip Disk
- ISO9660 CD-ROM
- Macintosh or Scitex formatted 5.25" 650 MB or 1.2 GB Optical Disks, (512 Bytes/sector). For Scitex disks, format must be RMX or UFS 2.0. Use native or extended handshake only.

Media Label Requirements

- Publication Name, Issue and Date
- Agency Name and Phone Number
- Contact Person and Phone Number
- Advertiser
- Vendor Name
- File Name/Number
- Print window of the directories on media

Electronic Transfer

Internet/FTP, WAM!NET, WAM!GATE, and Modem (e-mail not acceptable for transfer of ads). Instructions for electronic transfer are available from our production department.

Document Construction

- Build pages to trim and extend bleed 1/8" beyond page edge.
- All high-resolution images, artwork, and fonts must be included when the postscript file is written.
- Use only Type 1 fonts. Use stylized fonts only; DO NOT apply style attributes to fonts.
- All colors must be CMYK unless color will be printing as a spot color. Total area density should not exceed 300%. No RGB images allowed.
- DO NOT nest EPS files within other EPS files.
- All elements must be placed at 100% size. DO NOT rotate or crop images within Quark. This must be done in original application, i.e. Illustrator, Photoshop, etc., prior to placing.
- Place 6mm 5%, 25%, 50%, 75%, 100% CMYK patch strip on left side of document plate.
- Registration offset must be set to 30 pts.
- Bleed must be set to 0.125".
- Required trapping must be included in file.

(continued)

EXHIBIT 18.1 Continued

Proofs

All off-press proofs must include a SWOP (Specifications for Web Offset Publications) approved color bar to be considered acceptable SWOP proofs. Proofs made using digital proofing systems should use a digital control bar having similar content to the hard-dot film control bar. Type of proof/manufacturer must be identified on proof.

This color control bar should have the following characteristics: Screened areas with rulings of 133 lines per inch with tint values of 25%, 50%, and 75% of each of the primary colors in physical proximity to a solid patch.

Two-color overprints of the same 25%, 50%, 75% and solids are also recommended. Additional areas such as 1%, 2%, 3%, 5%, and 95%, 97%, 98%, 99%, may be useful, especially for digital output. A gray balance bar must be included on the proof, designed to match the neutral appearance and weight of black tints of three different values, under standard viewing conditions.

The three-color gray balance portion of the color bar should have the values below:

Black	Cyan	Magenta	Yellow
75%	75%	63%	63%
50%	50%	40%	40%
25%	25%	16%	16%

This color bar could take the form of a manufacturer's color control guide, a GCA/GATF Proof Comparator or a GATF/SWOP Proofing Bar or their digital equivalents. An exposure control element may also be included where appropriate.

A Digital Proofing Control Bar, provided by the manufacturer, obtained from SWOP, Inc. or created in-house, must be included on all proofs, in order for them to be considered acceptable SWOP proofs. This bar should contain all the elements as described above. Gray balance should appear neutral and similar to that of a SWOP press proof and the substrate should appear similar in hue and brightness to Textweb Proofing Paper.

Digital color bars should meet all requirements for color bars continued herein.
Supply a digital proof calibrated to SWOP specifications that represents the final digital file at 100%.

The following proofs are acceptable:

- Kodak Approval Digital Color
- Polaroid Pola-Proof
- Screen TrueRite
- Optronics Intelliproof
- Matchprint

Required SWOP color bars available as a free download at www.swop.org/downloads.html. Failure to provide proper SWOP proof will result in publisher pulling proper proof at advertiser's expense of $100. Should you have difficulty supplying a SWOP proof, please contact our production department.

PRODUCTION PLANNING AND SCHEDULING

To ensure that the creative and production work moves along with the necessary precision, a time schedule is planned at the outset. The closing date is the date or time when all material must arrive at the publication. Once this is known, the advertiser works backward along the calendar to determine when work must begin to meet the date.

Now that we better understand the production environment, let us take a look at the key considerations in a number of production steps.

Digital Studios

Prior to computer-generated layouts for advertisements or promotional printed materials, most art directors only had to design, create accurate mechanicals, and specify color breaks or other information on paper tissues. The production managers were responsible for the remaining production steps and procedures. Today, many art directors and/or studio designers working on their computers perform many production steps.

Some agencies call their computer area an image studio or digital imaging studio, where art directors work on computers to develop the visuals and layout. In some agencies (especially in small- or medium-size shops), the agency art directors take on part of production. They design, typeset, do layouts, create tints, scan, separate, produce final film, and in some cases transmit the job directly to the press or service bureau. In general, many production jobs will require the services of outside vendors or service providers. Many agencies rely on outside services for image setting, high-resolution scanning, and printing. Then there are electronic prepress shops that offer image-setting verification for computer-generated files, which may be required by some publications. If asked to do so, they will use their expertise in taking care of trapping and other operations necessary to prepare the files for film output. Suppliers can be found for almost every stage of the prepress operation.

DIGITAL PRODUCTION

Despite creating advertisements on a computer, much of the production still involves converting the advertisement from the computer screen to film for the publication or printer according to specifications. To some extent, the advertising person controls only a portion of the advertisement's production efforts. If you have a print advertisement going into a publication, the publication sets its own specifications standards of how advertisements are to be produced and presented. Traditional production requires converting all of the advertising elements to film and then to plates for printing. Total digital production is converting the computer images directly to plates, bypassing any film. The advertisement created digitally on your computer may still have to be converted to a piece of film so that printing plates can be made. You have to understand the requirements.

The creation of an advertisement is primarily digital. A printer's or publication's prepress operation is a digital process. Once the press has a plate made from either traditional or digital technology, the printing process is generally traditional but changing. However, the actual printing changes are moving at a much slower pace than the prepress changes that we've seen over the past decade.

Technical Considerations

Problems with digital advertising are often attributed to technology issues, and there can be many of these. Not only must the printer be computer proficient, but also the computer artist must be knowledgeable in preparing files so they can output properly. The computer artist must have font and photo files in the proper resolution.

Compatibility Even today, file compatibility can also be an issue. The files should be saved in a version common to all parties involved in the process. Today's computer artists, writers, prepress service providers, and publishers work in a variety of computer environments that can lead to file compatibility problems. Often, agencies will send a test file to determine whether or not their electronic files can be read correctly. This may avoid unnecessary lost time, frustration, and film costs. Some of the issues: On which types of digital files should the print workflow be based? Who should be responsible for creating these final exchange formats—the agency, a prepress vendor or service bureau, or the printer? And what tools and best practices should be put in place to ensure file integrity and a job's success? Software developers have created many of the sophisticated tools needed to verify digital file integrity regardless of the format.

Industry Standards There are several printing industry organizations that work together to improve quality and technology. They set guidelines for production: SWOP (Specifications Web Offset Publications) and GRACoL (General Requirements for Applications in Commercial Offset Lithography). They promote better communication between print buyers (advertisers and agencies) and print suppliers to improve processes to maintain printing as a competitive force in the communications marketplace. Most publications follow their guidelines.

These organizations have accredited file format standards such as PDF/X-1a and TIFF/IT-P1; industrywide adoption has been slow. Many believe that the real issues aren't technological but instead are financial. The investment can be huge. Printers continue to accept, and even request, everything from native application files to nonstandard Adobe PDF (portable document format) files to CT/LWs. CT/LWs are RIPped files. Once a CT/LW is generated, depending on the components of your file, it may consist of two files (NLW and CT, or LW and CT) or one file (NLW or LW). All files must be present. All images and fonts are embedded in the files and do not need to accompany the CT/LW. Yes, we said it could be complex.

It is the production director's job to understand what form or format(s) must be submitted.

Preflighting The term *preflight* has been adopted by the graphic arts community to generically refer to file verification at any stage in the print or multimedia work flow. The term was borrowed from the checklist procedures airplane pilots use before taking off. In print production, it is used to make sure digital files will image correctly. But in today's digital work flow, it's common knowledge that the process of controlling digital content file quality occurs at various stages in the production chain. Some production people split the definition of file verification. They define preflighting as the process that happens at the creative stage during document creation in a native application file. This process thoroughly analyzes a design or electronic mechanical for output readiness, regardless of the intended output device. It is a way to discover incomplete or missing digital files or fonts.

Postflighting The term *postflighting* is defined as the verification that takes place at the prepress phase, when the final file format is created and used to drive digital contract proofing, platesetting, or digital printing. So just because you produce an advertisement or collateral material using accepted software, the process of verification of those images is still complex.

On any given job, agency production managers have to check who is responsible for preflighting, the prepress service provider/printer or the agency.

Color Calibration This is another issue of concern to everyone in the process. All monitors, proofing devices, and printers must be calibrated so that images and hard copy look the same no matter where the files are viewed. Otherwise, a client may output a digital proof on the other side of the country that doesn't match what the prepress or printer is producing.

Bidding When the advertiser or agency is producing collateral material, it must find a printer that can efficiently produce the job at a reasonable price. There are online services, such as printbid.com, that assist in getting the best cost. It should be remembered that not every printer can efficiently produce every job—or at the same quality. It becomes the production manager's job to ensure that the "right" printer is chosen. Usually, the advertiser or agency requests three bids from comparable printers.

PREPRESS PROCESS

What has to be done to the layout design before it can be printed involves the preparation for the act of printing. The Broyhill page shown in Exhibit 18.2 is actually a comp used for discussion of concept, copy, layout, and illustration in

Broyhill's in-house agency. Then come executions and production. Here we outline the major steps for the traditional and digital methods:

Traditional: Advertisement concept: copy, layout, and approvals
                 Typesetting
                 Electronic color separations
                 Layout
                 Film preparation
                 Platemaking
                 Printing
Digital: Advertisement concept: copy, layout, and approvals
                 Scanning
                 Layout
                 Proofing
                 Preflight
                 Proofing
                 Film preparation (if not CTP)
                 Platemaking
                 Printing

EXHIBIT 18.2

This comp is a discussion piece for concept, layout, and copy before the final layout and production begin.

Courtesy of Broyhill Furniture Industries.

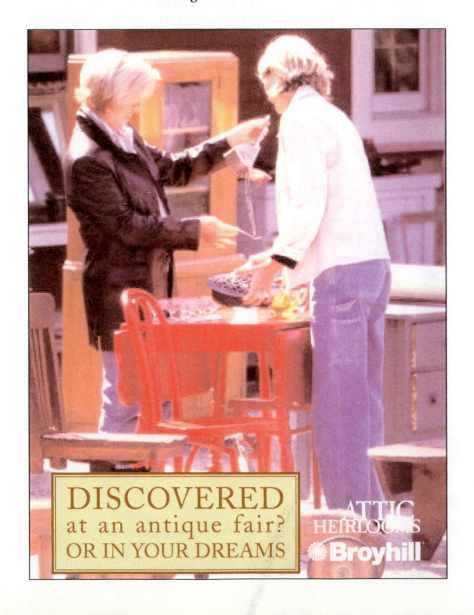

DISCOVERED
at an antique fair?
OR IN YOUR DREAMS

ATTIC HEIRLOOMS
Broyhill

PRINT PRODUCTION

The agency's print production group performs the transformation process from the original creative concept to the client's printed communication. This may include magazines, newspapers, outdoor and transit, point of purchase, collateral brochures (see Exhibit 18.3), and direct response. This group must have a working knowledge of all these production processes, as well as publication mechanical specifications, budgetary considerations, and quality requirements. Last but not least, the group must understand the time span available for the execution. All of these factors may be interrelated in a complicated manner.

Print production people are not merely technical people who are knowledgeable. They are also graphic arts consultants, production planners, and production liaison people. They function both internally, with the creative, traffic, media, and account management areas, and externally, with graphic arts vendors and the print media.

The size of a print production group is related to the billing size of the agency. A very small agency may employ a single print production expert. In a very large agency, the print production staff, headed by a print production manager, may consist of a considerable number of people with very specialized expertise.

EXHIBIT 18.3

RainDrop Man produced a 12-page comic for promotion of GreenGuard Moisture Management systems on gloss paper. The need for such collateral material is typical of most marketers.

Courtesy of McRae Communications and PACTIV.

The print operations area encompasses the following:

- Illustration buyers are versed in various forms of photographic and illustrative techniques. They know the available talent and make all contracts with photographers, illustrators, digital artists, and others in coordination with art directors (see Exhibit 18.4).

- Typography experts are trained in the creative as well as technical aspects of typography. They select and specify type, working with the art directors. Of course, in some agencies, the art director may create the final type on his or her computer. Or the type director may send the disc to a supplier for final output.

- Print producers coordinate all print production activities with the traffic, account management, and creative groups.

- Printing buyers specialize in the production planning and buying of outdoor and transit advertising and newspaper and magazine inserts, as well as collateral printed material from brochures to elaborately die-cut direct-mail pieces. A printing buyer's knowledge reaches into properties of paper and ink and into the capabilities of printing, binding, and finishing equipment.

In addition to those functions already mentioned, a large production department may include estimators and proofreaders. Generally, clients require an agency to submit a production budget on work to be done. As a rule, a total yearly campaign production budget is estimated to give the client an understanding of approximately how much advertisements and/or collateral will cost to produce. Clients must sign off on each project's production cost in advance of the work being prepared. It is important for the production department to supply accurate production cost estimates.

The production department works closely with the traffic department, which sets and monitors schedules of the operation from creative through final production.

EXHIBIT 18.4

Robert Willett is a PhotoShop specialist who sometimes incorporates photos, type, and design elements into special graphics.

Courtesy of Robert Willett Design.

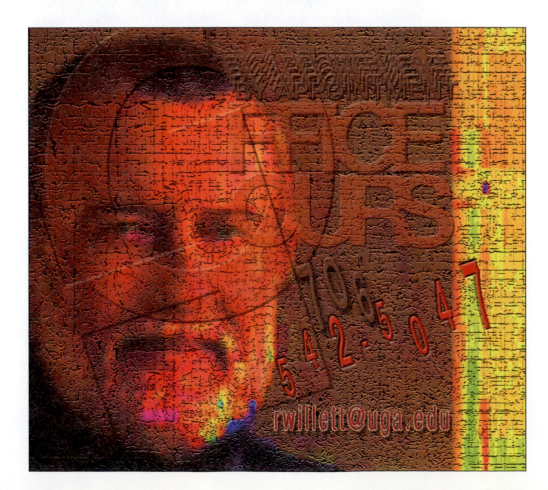

KLEPPNER VIEWPOINT 18.1

Sheri Bevil

Senior Partner, Sheri Bevil Design and Lane Bevil+Partners

"Huge File, Just Upload and Send"

Most agencies send ads, art work, layouts and other electronic image files to printers, media and clients almost daily. However, some of those files can be extremely large, if not simply huge, and not suitable for most email systems. There are a number of upload services that can compress huge files so that email systems can handle them. Some printers, service bureaus have their own upload systems, that makes it easy to send. And all an advertiser, agency, designer has to do is upload the files into their system according to the directions.

Sheri Bevil

- To eliminate font issues, always "select all" the type in Illustrator and "create outlines." All your fonts become "art" and the receiver of the file (whether for print production or viewing) will see what you created with the same fonts WITHOUT having to send the fonts with the file.
- When sending files to printers for print production via email or Internet (FTP sites), it's best to "stuff" or "zip" your files to protect them before their trip through cyber space. There are several great software programs for this. Always check with the receiver of the files to make sure that they can "unstuff" or "unzip" the files once they have received them.
- There are several FREE services to use for uploading files that are too big to email (for example: www.yousendit.com and www.mailbigfile.com). Depending on the service, you can upload files from 100 to 512 mb. They are very simple to use. Simply type in the email address of the recipient, then there will be a place to click and "browse" the files on your computer.

Locate the appropriate file and click. Now, it's in the drop down window as the file to send. Then, click "send file." The time it takes to upload depends on the size of the file. You will have to wait for the "your file has been sent successfully" message. Then, the service emails the recipient to let them know that there is a file ready for them to download. The recipient simply clicks on the link to go to that file and then will be able to download the file to their computer. Most services leave this file available for downloading for 7 to 14 days.

Courtesy of Lane Bevil+Partners. ■ ■ ■

Computer to Plate

As the printing industry moves from film to CTP (computer to plate), it means the production specifications are also changing. There has been a growing use of computer-to-plate printing, which eliminates the film traditionally required to make plates for the press. Now it is typical for the agency to give high-resolution PDF files to the printer. It may mean JPEGs can be used. But it should be remembered that the advertiser or agency doesn't control the specifications for publication. If it is an advertisement for a magazine, the magazine controls how the publication will be printed—digital or traditional or a mix. However, digital design is controlled by the agency. If the agency is producing collateral material (brochures, inserts, etc.), the agency controls more of the process. The agency selects the printers and can use those that match its production preferences.

Producing plates directly from computer files rather than film has its advantages. It may provide better registration and a crisper dot, which result in a sharper image on press. The digital work flow cuts both design and printing schedules.

Another advantage of computer-to-plate technology is the proofing and approval process. In traditional printing, if a problem was detected on the job, it could take as long as 16 hours to make corrections, shoot and strip new film, remake plates, and restart the presses. Digital technology allows a printer to pull the plate, correct the digital files, prepare a new plate, and mount the plate in approximately 30 minutes. Now let's look at the printing options.

SELECTING THE PRINTING PROCESS

In most cases, the printing process used depends on the medium in which the advertisement is running, not on the advertiser or the agency. However, in some areas, such as sales promotion, advertising inserts, direct mail, and point of sale, the advertiser must make the final decision regarding print production. To deal effectively with printers, the advertiser must have some knowledge of the basic production techniques and which one is the most appropriate for the job at hand.

If the printing process is not predetermined, the first step in production is to decide which process is most suitable. There are three major printing processes:

- Letterpress printing (from a raised surface)
- Offset lithography (from a flat surface)
- Rotogravure (from an etched surface)

Each of these printing processes has certain advantages and disadvantages, and one process may be more efficient than another for a particular job. Once the printing process has been established, the production process has been dictated, for all production work depends on the type of printing used.

As we have indicated, the prepress operation is in transition from traditional to digital operations. Once the advertisement, collateral advertising, or promotion has been created and converted to a printing plate, the printing process is very similar to what it has been for many decades. The presses are more efficient now than ever before, but the printing concept is not new.

Letterpress Printing

letterpress
Printing from a relief, or raised, surface. The raised surface is inked and comes in direct contact with the paper, like a rubber stamp.

Letterpress printing isn't as popular as it once was in printing publications; however, advertisers have many uses for this printing process, and you should know the basics. In its simplest form, think of the concept of **letterpress** as follows: If you have ever used a rubber ink stamp (with name, address, etc.), you've applied the principle of letterpress printing. You press the rubber stamp against an ink pad. Then, as you press the stamp against paper, the ink is transferred from the stamp to the paper, and the message is reproduced.

In letterpress printing, the area to be printed is raised and inked. The inked plate is pressed against the paper, and the result is a printed impression (see Exhibit 18.5).

Your artwork, photographs, type, and so forth must be converted to a photoengraving (a process of making the plate a raised surface) before printing can occur. The advertiser or agency must supply the photoengraving or duplicates of such plates to the newspaper, magazine, or letterpress printer. In general, this process doesn't reproduce photos as well as offset or gravure. Each of the printing processes has advantages and disadvantages that the advertising person needs to learn over time. There are several types of letterpress presses. The "job press" platen can print many forms, but it can also die cut (cut shapes in paper), emboss (raise images on paper), perforate, and score (which creases so thicker paper can be folded).

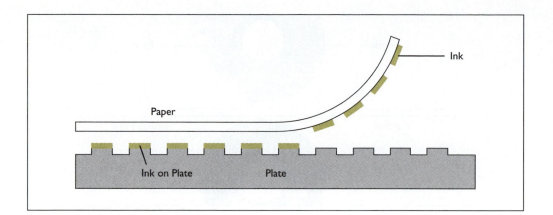

EXHIBIT 18.5
Letterpress Printing
The letterpress printing
process involves a plate
with a raised surface.

Offset Lithography

In its basic description, **offset lithography** is a photochemical process based on the principle that grease and water will not mix. In theory, offset can print anything that can be photographed. In reality, although there are some things that will not print very well by offset, it is the preferred process for most jobs, accounting for 80 to 90 percent of all printing jobs.

Offset lithography is a planographic (flat-surface) process using a thin, flat aluminum plate that is wrapped around a cylinder on a rotary press. The plate is coated with a continuous flow of liquid solution from dampening rollers that repel ink. The inked plate comes in contact with a rubber blanket on another cylinder. The inked impression goes from the plate to the rubber blanket. The inked blanket then transfers or offsets the inked image to the paper, which is on a delivery cylinder. The plate does not come in direct contact with the paper (see Exhibit 18.6).

Because offset is a photographic process, it is very efficient and is the most popular printing process in this country. It is used to reproduce books (including this text), catalogs, periodicals, direct-mail pieces, outdoor and transit posters, point-of-sale displays, and most newspapers.

Advertisers or their agencies must supply the artwork and electronic mechanicals or films from which offset plates can be made.

Rotogravure

The image in **rotogravure** printing is etched below the surface of the copper printing plate—the direct opposite from letterpress printing—creating tiny ink wells (tiny depressed printing areas made by means of a screen). The gravure plate is inked on the press and wiped so that only the tiny ink wells contain ink. The plate is

offset lithography
Lithography is a printing process by which originally an image was formed on special stone by a greasy material, the design then being transferred to the printing paper. Today, the more frequently used process is offset lithography, in which a thin and flexible metal sheet replaces the stone. In this process, the design is "offset" from the metal sheet to a rubber blanket, which then transfers the image to the printing paper.

rotogravure
The method of printing in which the impression is produced by chemically etched cylinders and run on a rotary press; useful in long runs of pictorial effects.

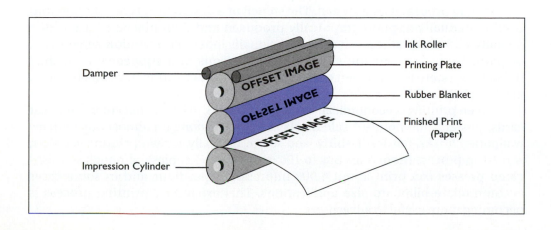

EXHIBIT 18.6
Offset printing press system, showing image coming off plate, onto rubber blanket, and offsetting to paper.

EXHIBIT 18.7

Rotogravure

In the rotogravure process, ink wells fill with ink.

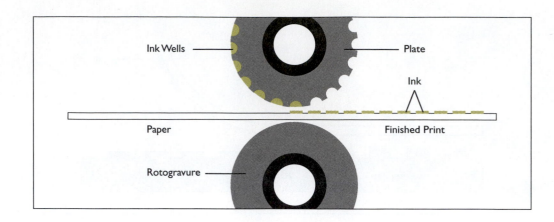

then pressed against the paper, causing suction that pulls the ink out of the wells and onto the paper (see Exhibit 18.7).

Gravure is used to print all or parts of many publications, including national and local Sunday newspaper supplements, mail-order catalogs, packaging, newspaper inserts, and large-run magazines, for example, *National Geographic*. The gravure plate is capable of printing millions of copies very efficiently; however, it is not economical for short-run printing. Rotogravure becomes competitive with offset when printing exceeds 100,000 copies. When printing exceeds a million copies, gravure tends to be more efficient than offset. Rotogravure prints excellent color quality on relatively inexpensive paper, but the preparatory costs are comparatively high, and it is expensive to make major corrections on the press.

Sheet-Fed Versus Web-Fed Presses

Letterpress, offset, and gravure printing processes can all utilize sheet-fed or web-fed presses:

- Sheet-fed presses feed sheets of paper through the press one at a time. The conventional sheet-fed press prints about 6,000 to 7,000 "sheets" per hour.
- Web-fed presses feed paper from a continuous roll, and the printing is rapid—about 1,000 feet per minute. Most major promotional printing utilizes web-fed presses.

Screen Printing

screen printing

A simple printing process that uses a stencil. It is economical but is limited in reproduction quality.

Another printing process, **screen printing**, which is based on a different principle than letterpress, offset, and rotogravure, is especially good for short runs. This simple process uses a stencil. The stencil of a design (art, type, photograph) can be manually or photographically produced and then placed over a textile (usually silk) or metallic mesh screen (it actually looks like a window screen). Ink or paint is spread over the stencil and, by means of a squeegee, is pushed through the stencil and screen onto the paper (or other surface), as illustrated in Exhibit 18.8.

Screen printing is economical, especially for work in broad, flat colors, as in car cards, posters, and point-of-sale displays. It can be done on almost any surface: wallpaper, bricks, bottles, T-shirts, and so on. Basically, screen printing is a slow, short-run process (from one copy to 100 or 1,000 or so copies), although sophisticated presses can print about 6,000 impressions per hour and in some cases accommodate billboard-size applications. This expanding printing process is becoming more useful to advertisers.

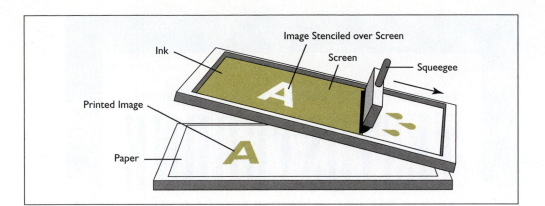

EXHIBIT **18.8**
Screen Printing

UNDERSTANDING TYPOGRAPHY

Type has always been an important part of advertisement design. It creates moods, enhances or retards readability, and gives your communication an image. Type inspires passion. Hermann Zapt's favorite typeface is Optima. George Bernard Shaw insisted all his works be set in Caslon.[1] Type is powerful. It is one of the most important design tools. Type creates communication that is friendly and inviting. It keenly focuses attention. It organizes the complex and creates a mood.

It is now more important than ever before for advertising people to understand how to use type because so much of it is being created in-house on the agency or client computer. Before the computer explosion, art directors would use specialists—typesetters or typographers—for type. Most agree that few art directors or designers have as good an understanding of type use as typesetters or typographers. Getting type up on the screen does not mean that it is typeset effectively. We talk about this again after we learn some of the fundamentals.

The art of using type effectively is called **typography**. It entails a number of issues: choosing the typeface and size of type; deciding on the amount of space between letters, words, and lines; determining hyphenation use; and preparing type specifications for all the advertisement copy. The Howard Merrell & Partners' advertisement for the Museum of the Mountain Man (see Exhibit 18.9) uses type that reflects the mood of the product and design. The treatment of the body copy also reflects the mood of the design.

typography
The art of using type effectively.

TYPE AND READING

The objective of text typography is to provide quick and easy communication. Display headlines are supposed to attract the reader's attention and encourage reading of the body copy. Using uppercase typography does not generally accomplish these objectives. Notice the difference in the typefaces in Exhibit 18.10. Which of these would not be good for body copy in a magazine?

More than 95 percent of text is set in lowercase letters. Research has shown that readers are more comfortable reading lowercase letters than all caps. Studies have also proved that the varying heights of lowercase letters forming words create an outline shape that is stored in the reader's mind, which aids in recalling the words when they are seen. Words comprised of lowercase characters can be read faster than words set in all caps.

The ideal reading process occurs when the eye is able to scan across a line of copy, grasp groups of three or four words at a time, and then jump to another set of words, then another. The separate stops, or fixational pauses, take about one-quarter of a second each. Words in lowercase letters allow this process to take place. On the other hand, words set in all caps force the reader to read individual letters and

EXHIBIT 18.9

This type is appropriate for the mood of the product (Mountain Man Museum) and design.

Courtesy of Howard, Merrell & Partners.

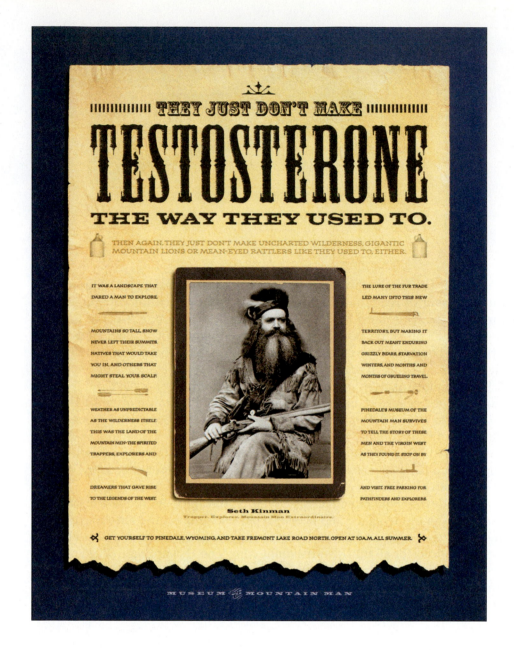

EXHIBIT 18.10

Examples of different typefaces, each representing a different mood or feeling. Each are the same size text.

Futura

Zapfino

Big Caslon

Chalkboard

Arial Black

Optima ExtraBlack

COPPERPLATE GOTHIC BOLD

mentally combine the letters into words, and the words into phrases and sentences. The result is a 10 to 25 percent slowdown in reading speed and comprehension.

There are times when all-cap headlines or subheadlines are, graphically, the right thing to use. Design may take precedence over the "rules of communication," or you may not be able to convince a client or art director that lowercase is a better idea. In these instances, words and lines should be held to a minimum. More than four or five words on a line and more than a couple of lines of all caps become difficult to read.[2]

TYPEFACES

The typeface selected for a particular advertisement is very important. Exhibit 18.11 illustrates the major classifications of type: text, old Roman, modern Roman, square serif, sans serif, and decorative.

TYPE FONTS AND FAMILIES

A type font is all the lowercase and capital characters, numbers, and punctuation marks in one size and face (see Exhibit 18.12). A font may be roman or italic. Roman (with a lowercase *r*) type refers to the upright letter form, as distinguished from the italic form, which is oblique. Roman (capital *R*) denotes a group of serifed typeface styles.

Type family is the name given to two or more series of types that are variants of one design (see Exhibit 18.13). Each one, however, retains the essential characteristics of the basic letter form. The series may include italic, thin, light, semibold, bold, medium, condensed, extended, outline, and so forth. Some type families have only a few of these options, whereas others offer a number of styles. The family of type may provide a harmonious variety of typefaces for use within an advertisement.

Measurement of Type

Typographers have unique units of measurement. It is essential to learn the fundamental units of measure if you are going to interact with production

Text   Old English
Old Roman   Garamond
Modern Roman   Century
Square Serif   Lubalin
Sans Serif   Avant Garde
Decorative   Ransom

EXHIBIT 18.11

Examples of Families of Type

EXHIBIT 18.12

Examples of Two Optima Type Fonts, Regular and ExtraBlack

Optima
Abcdefghijklmnopqrstuvwxyz
ABCDEFGHIJKLMNOPQRSTU
1234567890(&?!%',;)* VWXYZ

Optima ExtraBlack
abcdefghijklmnopqrstuvwxyz
ABCDEFGHIJKLMNOPQRSTU
1234567890$(&?!%',;)* VWXYZ

EXHIBIT 18.13

A family of type retains its basic letter form and style characteristics through all its variations. Some type families consist of only roman, italic, and bold versions. Others, such as the popular Helvetica family, have many variations and different stroke thicknesses.

Helvetica Thin
Helvetica Light
Helvetica Light Italic
Helvetica
Helvetica Italic
Helvetica Italic Outline
Helvetica Regular Condensed
Helvetica Regular Extended
Helvetica Medium
Helvetica Medium Italic
Helvetica Medium Outline
Helvetica Bold
Helvetica Bold Compact Italic
Helvetica Bold Outline
Helvetica Bold Condensed
Helvetica Bold Condensed Outline
Helvetica Bold Extended
Helvetica Extrabold Condensed
Helvetica Extrabold Condensed Outline
Helvetica Extrabold Ext.
Helvetica Compressed
Helvetica Extra Compressed
Helvetica Ultra Compressed

people. The *point* and the *pica* are two units of measure used in print production in all English-speaking countries. Let us take a closer look at these two units of measure.

Point A **point (pt)** is used to measure the size of type (heights of letters). There are 72 points to an inch. It is useful to know that 36-point type is about one-half inch high and 18-point type is about one-fourth inch high. Exhibit 18.14 illustrates the major terms used in discussing the height of type. Type can be set from about 6 points to 120 points. Body copy is generally in the range of 6 to 14 points; most publications use type of 9, 10, or 11 points. Type sizes above 14 points are referred to as display or headline type. However, these ranges are simply labels—in many newspaper advertisements, the body copy is 18 points or so, and there have been advertisements in which the headline was in the body-copy size range. Exhibit 18.15 provides a visual perspective on basic type sizes.

Points also are used to measure the height of space between lines, rules, and borders, as well as the height of the type.

Pica A **pica** is a linear unit of measure. A pica equals 12 points of space, and there are 6 picas to an inch. Picas are used to indicate width or depth and length of line.

Agate Line Most newspapers (and some small magazines) sell advertising space in column inches or by the *agate line*, a measure of the depth of space. There are 14 agate lines to a column inch, regardless of the width of the column. Newspaper space is referred to by depth (agate lines) and width (number of columns); for "100 × 2," read "one hundred lines deep by two columns wide."

point (pt)
The unit of measurement of type, about 1/72 inch in depth. Type is specified by its point size, as 8 pt., 12 pt., 24 pt., 48 pt. The unit for measuring thickness of paper, 0.001 inch.

pica
The unit for measuring width in printing. There are 6 picas to an inch. A page of type 24 picas wide is 4 inches wide.

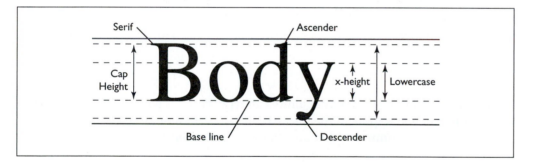

EXHIBIT 18.14

Major Terms for Type Height

EXHIBIT 18.15

A Visual Perspective of Type Sizes

8 point Baskerville Semibold Advertising Production
10 point Baskerville Semibold Advertising Production
14 point Baskerville Semibold Advertising Production
18 point Baskerville Semibold Advertising
36 point Baskerville
48 point Baskervill

EXHIBIT 18.16

This Wild Things outdoor advertisement type appears as white ink. It isn't—it is reverse type (white or light type on a dark background).

Courtesy of Blattner Brunner, Pittsburgh, Atlanta, Washington.

Line Spacing Also called *leading*, line spacing is the vertical space between lines of type and is measured in points from baseline to baseline of type. Lines are said to be set solid when no additional line spacing has been added. Space is added to make type more readable. The rule of thumb is that the extra space should be no more than 20 percent of the type size. Thus, if you are using 10-point type, the maximum extra space between the lines is 2 points, for a 12-point leading.

Type specifications are usually determined by art directors, print production personnel, or specialized type directors. The following may be involved in the final decision:

- Type set in lowercase letters is read 13.4 percent faster than type set in all caps.
- Reverse copy—white or light type on a dark background—is read more slowly than black on white. As a result, you should be extra careful in choosing type size and a readable typeface when a reverse is desired. Exhibit 18.16 shows a reverse copy treatment.

TYPESETTING

Earlier in this chapter, we said that almost all typesetting is performed on a desktop computer. The typographer of the future is an art director or designer—maybe even a copywriter—for whom type is more a means than an end.

Guides for Using Type

- Use only original type. Don't assume the prepress service bureau or printer has the exact same font.
- Remember that as a buyer of a type package you only license the usage rights. You have to acquire a multilicense if the font is to be used on more than one computer.
- Computer artists need to keep a running list of both screen fonts and printer fonts (screen fonts are used by the computer for display on the screen; printer fonts are downloaded to the printer for output).
- Talk to your prepress service provider or printer about fonts being used in electronic mechanicals; otherwise, the advertisement or collateral piece may not look as intended.
- Avoid type smaller than 6 points, especially in serif typefaces (letters having "feet," such as Bodoni). The thin parts of small type characters can disappear when output is of high resolution, making text difficult to read.
- When using reverse type, avoid type that is too small (6 points) or delicate. Sans serif and bold typefaces are better choices. Large blocks of reverse type are difficult to read.

■ When possible, convert type to a graphic (vector objects) in EPS (Encapsulated PostScript) files. Common problems for prepress service providers are font substitutions or PostScript errors caused by type in imported EPS graphics.

ELECTRONIC MECHANICAL AND ARTWORK

After the copy has been approved and placed in the advertisement on the desktop system with the rest of the advertisement's material (e.g., illustrations, logos), the advertiser will approve the electronic comp or rough. After approval, the digital file is sent to prepress.

Art for Prepress Services

Discuss the types of art being used—transparencies (like 35-mm slides, reflective art), line drawings or illustrations, digital photography—with the prepress service or printer. Agency production people need to ask (or check publication mechanical requirements—see Exhibit 18.17 a & b) about what kind of electronic files are preferred. You get the picture—the right files, fonts, and technical requirements are necessary for prepress production to run smoothly. You cannot assume the prepress service, printer, or publication can run your material just because it looks good on your computer. For example, in Exhibit 18.17 a, a simple printed napkin band has exact specifications. And to cut a printed piece into shapes requires a die cut (Exhibit 18.17 b).

There are several types of art that production people have to deal with, including line art and halftones in both black and white and color.

Line Art

Any art, type, or image that is made up of a solid color (and has no tonal value) is called *line art*. If you set type on your computer, it is line art (if it is in solid form). Artwork drawn in pen and ink is line art because the ink has no tonal value. Generally, such art is drawn larger than needed for the mechanical so as to minimize the art's imperfections when it is reduced and printed.

Line Tint You can give line art some variation in shades by breaking up the solid color with screen tints or benday screens. Exhibit 18.18 uses a screen tint to give the illusion of gray and contrast. This may be done on the computer layout, or the platemaker adds the screens during the film-stripping stage just prior to platemaking.

Line Color Artwork does not need to be in color to produce line plates in two, three, or more flat colors. It can be added or changed on the computer. Remember, each color may require a separate plate. Line color provides a comparatively inexpensive method of printing in color with effective results. For example, Exhibit 18.19 uses a black plate and another for the spot color red—one plate for each color.

A solid color (flat or match color) is printed with the actual color. The color is specified with a Pantone Matching System (PMS) color reference number, and the printer mixes an ink that is literally that color. It is like going into a paint store, choosing a color swatch, and having the clerk mix the paint to match your color. The ink is applied to the paper through printing, and the specified color is obtained.

Halftones

At the end of this chapter, we discuss some of the new production technology (including stochastic screening), which may eventually change the way photos are reproduced.

If you look at black-and-white photographs, you will recognize that they are different from line art—they have tonal value. Such photos have a range of tonal value between pure blacks and pure whites and are called **continuous-tone** artwork.

continuous tone
An unscreened photographic picture or image, on paper or film, that contains all gradations of tonal values from white to black.

EXHIBIT **18.17**

(a) The mechanical requirements for a printed napkin band.

Courtesy of Lane Bevil+Partners.

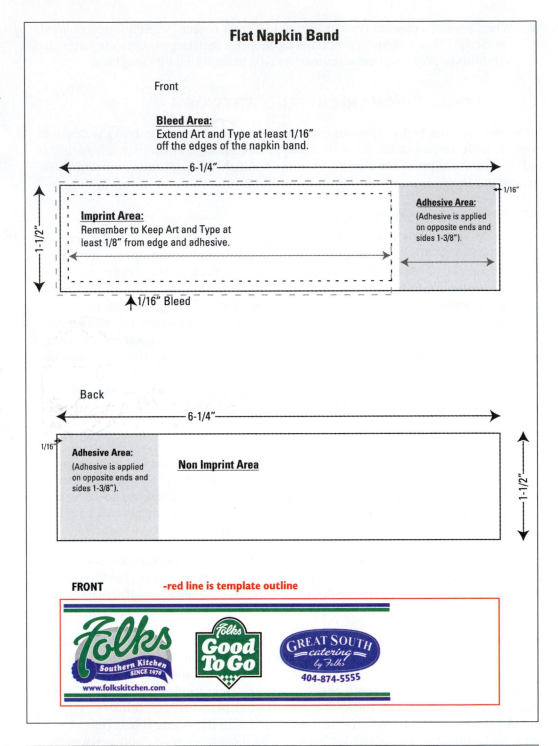

Flat Napkin Band

Front

Bleed Area:
Extend Art and Type at least 1/16″ off the edges of the napkin band.

6-1/4″

1-1/2″

1/16″

Imprint Area:
Remember to Keep Art and Type at least 1/8″ from edge and adhesive.

Adhesive Area:
(Adhesive is applied on opposite ends and sides 1-3/8″).

1/16″ Bleed

Back

6-1/4″

1/16″

Adhesive Area:
(Adhesive is applied on opposite ends and sides 1-3/8″).

Non Imprint Area

1-1/2″

FRONT   -red line is template outline

(b) A die cut is a printed piece that is cut out into a shape or has a cut-out circle or logo, for example.

Courtesy of The Johnson Group.

Advertising Production
Advertising Production
Advertising Production

To reproduce the range of tones in continuous-tone art, the art (photo) must be broken up into dots or lines. The art is then called a halftone. Halftones may be reproduced either with a printer's camera (rarely, these days) or digitally; either way breaks the image into dots. Remember that black ink is black ink and not shades of gray, so the production process must create an optical illusion by converting the tonal areas to different-size halftone dots on the printed paper that the eye perceives as gray. If you look at the printed halftone gray areas with a magnifying glass, you will see little black dots. The more dots per inch, the greater the quality of detail

Valentine's Special

February 9 - 14, 2006

Dinner for 2

$19.99
Includes:
• One Fried Green Tomatoes Appetizer
• TWO - Pick 2 Platters
• One Slice of Caramel Cake

Pick 2 Platter
Create your own special platter by picking two of the following:

Calabash Shrimp
Catfish Fillets
Fried Chicken
Gulf Shrimp
White Fish

Livers or Gizzards
Grilled Sirloin Tips
Country Fried Steak
St. Louis BBQ Ribs
Smothered Chopped Steak

www.folkskitchen.com

Douglasville
Hwy 5 Near I-20
770-949-8400

Folks®
Southern Kitchen SINCE 1976

Call ahead for take-out.

reproduced from the original. The quality of the paper must also increase to accommodate the higher dot levels, which drives up paper costs. Again, you may need to check the printer/publisher's specifications on the number of dots or resolution that is required.

The Halftone Finish If you want to make a halftone of a photograph, the computer artist or the platemaker can treat the background in a number of ways; that treatment is called its *finish*. Several techniques that can be applied to halftones include the following:

- *Square halftone.* The halftone's background has been retained.
- *Silhouette.* The background in the photograph has been removed by the photo platemaker or the computer operator.
- *Surprint.* This is a combination plate made by exposing line and halftone negatives in succession on the same plate.
- *Mortise.* An area of a halftone is cut out to permit the insertion of type or other matter.

Line Conversion A line conversion transforms a continuous-tone original into a high-contrast image of only black-and-white tones similar to line art. The conversion transfers the image into a pattern of some kind: mezzotint, wavy line, straight line, or concentric circle. Most design software programs offer a number of line conversion choices.

Two-Color Halftone Plates A two-color reproduction can be made from monochrome artwork in two ways. A screen tint in a second color can be printed over (or under) a black halftone. Or the artwork can be photographed twice, changing the screen angle the second time so that the dots of the second color plate fall between those of the first plate. This is called a *duotone*. It produces contrast in both colors of the one-color original halftone.

Four-Color Process Printing Another printing system is needed when the job requires the reproduction of color photos. This system is called a **four-color process**. The four colors are cyan (blue), magenta (red), yellow, and black. (*C, M, Y,* and *K* are the letters used to indicate these colors.) These are the least number of colors that can adequately reproduce the full spectrum of natural colors inherent in photography. The first three—cyan, magenta, and yellow—provide the range of colors; the black provides definition and contrast in the image.

Full-color or process color requires photographic or electronic scanner separation of the color in the photographs (or other continuous-tone copy) into four negatives, one for each of the process colors. This process of preparing plates of the various colors and black is called *color separation* (see Exhibit 18.20). If you examine any of the color advertisements in this text (or any other publication) with a magnifying glass, you will find the halftone dots in four colors.

Digital Scanners Transforming a photograph into a digital file is done by using a *scanner*. There are two basic types: flatbed and drum scanners. You probably have used a flatbed scanner. These require little training and their quality varies. Printers or agencies use professional scanners that are capable of creating high-quality images. In general, a drum scanner, in which the original photo or image wraps around a drum that rotates next to a light source, is capable of producing very high-quality results. It is the most expensive image-capturing device on the market. These machines digitally scan the photos to be used in advertisements. They create the dot pattern used in making a halftone by the traditional method. The important thing to remember is that photographs (whether color or black and white) must be broken up into a dot pattern to print.

four-color process
The process for reproducing color illustrations by a set of plates, one that prints all the yellows, another the blues, a third the reds, and the fourth the blacks (sequence variable). The plates are referred to as process plates.

EXHIBIT **18.20**

Four-color process printing involves combining four plates— blue (cyan), red (magenta), yellow, and black—to produce the desired colors and contrasts.

Courtesy of Sheri Bevil Design.

Color Proofing

Achieving color reproduction that satisfies advertising agencies and advertisers is one of the most crucial roles of the magazine production manager. Agencies generally demand to see a proof before the job is printed. In today's electronic color production, traditional proofing systems seem to have taken a backseat to digital color proofers, color printers, networked color copiers, and short-run color production devices.

For the most accurate contact proofs—those requiring the best match to jobs printed by conventional offset lithography—nothing beats a film-based laminated, or single-sheet, off-press proof. An off-press proof ensures that color separations have been made according to customer expectations.[3]

Press Proofs

For years, press proofs, or progressives, usually made on special proofing presses, were the standard proofs sent to agencies for checking. Prior to the development of off-press proofs, color separators used press proofs. Making a press proof involved stripping the separations on film, making plates, mounting the plates on a proof press, and printing the desired number of proofs. Press proofs are made with ink on paper—often the same paper that will be used for the job—rather than with a photographic simulation process of off-press systems. Today press proofs are still used by many advertising agencies that are willing to pay the steep price for what they believe is the most accurate proof. In theory, press proofs provide a virtually exact representation of the final project.

Progressive Proofs (Progs) These proofs give the advertiser a separate proof for each color (red, yellow, blue, and black), as indicated in Exhibit 18.21, as well as a proof for each color combination (red and yellow, red and blue, blue and yellow)— seven printings in all. After approval by the advertiser and agency, the proofs are sent to the printer to use as guides in duplicating the densities for each color.

Off-Press Proofs

These proofs are made from film negatives generated from the electronic file. The same films will be used to make printing plates. These proofs are less expensive and faster than press proofs, and they are adequate in most cases. Off-press proofs are the typical color proof today. No plate or printing is involved. There are numerous types of off-press (prepress) proofing systems. The most popular are overlay and adhesive proofs.

Overlay Proofs The development of overlay proofing enabled color proofs to be made from film without using a proof press. The overlay proofs consist of four

EXHIBIT 18.21

This advertisement needed to be sent to numerous publications. The production people had to send an electronic file to each publication (or as specified by the publication).

Courtesy of Charleston Regional Development Alliance.

MatchPrint

A high-quality color proof used for approvals prior to printing. Similar to a Signature print.

exposed sheets containing the cyan (blue), magenta (red), yellow, and black process colors overlaid on a backing sheet. The four overlays (yellow, red, blue, and black) are then stacked to produce a composite image. Because they use multiple, separate, plastic layers, overlay proofs cannot be expected to accurately predict color on press, but they are still used today for checking color break or general color appearance and position.

Adhesive or Laminate Proof In 1972, DuPont introduced the first off-press proofing system that closely resembled printed images, known as the Cromalin system. Cromalin is a laminated or single-sheet proof in which four (or more) layers are exposed separately and laminated together to reproduce the image of cyan, magenta, yellow, and black separations. Cromalins use dry pigments to produce images on photosensitive adhesive polymers or pretreated carrier sheets. Cromalin is generally considered the superior adhesive process. The proofs are keyed to SWOP (Specifications for Web Offset Publications)/GAA (Gravure Association of America) guidelines, which set standards for inks, density of tones, reverses, and other technical matters. Among the highest-fidelity four-color proofs are the **MatchPrint** and the Signature proof, both very similar but from different suppliers.

There are digital hard and soft copy systems that eliminate film to produce continuous-tone proofs. The soft proofing systems allow production and design people to call up a digitized color image and evaluate it before separations are made for an intermediate or position proof. The interactive proofing system gives the agency more flexibility with deadlines and saves time and money for clients.

Types of Proofs The choices of types of proof are numerous. Production managers need to decide how accurate a proof is needed or, to put it another way, how much quality they need to pay for. Obviously, they don't want expensive proofs if they are not needed. Here are a number of proof types:

Proof Type	Color Accuracy	Cost
Black-and-white laser	Prints can show color breaks but no color. 300–600 dpi.	Inexpensive
Bluelines	Proofs made from exposing film to light-sensitive paper. They show only a single-color image. Uses halftone film.	Inexpensive
Velox	Simple black-and white proofs made from film on photographic paper. Uses halftone film.	Moderate
Digital high end	Proofs made from an electronic file. Made by Kodak, 3M, among others. Several processes all meet industry standards. 1800 dpi and higher. Cannot proof actual film.	Moderate
Desktop digital	Usually uses ink jet or thermal wax and gives fairly accurate approximation of color. 300 dpi. Needs color management system to give close approximation of color.	Inexpensive
Laminate/adhesive	Composite proofs are created by exposing the color separations in contact to proofing film and laminating the results. Uses halftone film. Very accurate in color match.	Moderate
Overlay	Made up of layers of acetate attached to a backing substrate. Each overlay film has an image from each separation color. Colors indicate color breaks; not very accurate. Uses halftone film.	Moderate
Press	Proof run on printing press. Uses halftone film. Uses actual printing inks to give most accurate proof.	Expensive

DUPLICATE ADVERTISEMENTS

Can we get this Charleston advertisement (see Exhibit 18.21) out of our computer to ten publications? Ten uploads? Ten CDs? Maybe. Most print advertisements run in more than one publication. Frequently, advertisers have different publications on their schedules, or they need to issue reprints of their advertisements or send material to dealers for cooperative advertising. There are various means of producing duplicate material of magazine or newspaper advertisements. The most common means of sending advertisements to more than one publication is simply sending a digital file to the publication.

OTHER PRODUCTION ADVANCES

The changes in technology over the past decade have changed the prepress and printing processes. Future production managers and art directors will continue to have many new options for handling their projects. These new techniques will range from color separation, color management, proofing, and platemaking to printing. The following techniques are of particular interest.

Stochastic Screening and Color Separations

Stochastic screening, or frequency modulation screening, is a process for producing incredible tone and detail that approximates photographic quality. With conventional screens, the dots are spaced equally on a grid (e.g., 110 or 133 lines per inch) and the tonal value is achieved by increasing or decreasing the size of the dots. On the other hand, stochastic screening has very tiny dots all of the same size, and their numbers vary according to the tonal value. Used by a quality printer, the image appears to be continuous-tone or photographic quality and much better than any traditional process. At this time, few companies produce this process. These companies offer an advertiser the ability to produce higher-quality color separations, which in turn allows them to print sharper color advertisements.

HiFi Color High-fidelity color is expanding what we know and can do with print reproduction techniques and processes. HiFi color was born out of the limitations of the conventional color printing gamut, which is only a fraction of what the human visual system can see. It is a group of emerging technologies that will expand this printing gamut and extend control by improving and increasing tone, dynamic range, detail, spatial frequency modulation, and other appearance factors of print and other visual media.

HiFi color comprises the technologies of stochastic, or frequency modulation screening; four-plus color process and waterless printing methods; specialty papers, films, coatings, and laminates; and proofing systems, color management systems, software, and hardware.

Color Management Systems (CMS) The ideal—and we have not yet gotten to this point in technology—is seeing an image on a screen and getting an exact printed image, or, as it is touted, what you see is what you get. This is very important in terms of quality control and design. As images go through the production process, the information is transformed in different ways—for example, as photographic data in the original; as pixels of red, green, and blue on the computer screen; or as dots of cyan, magenta, yellow, and black on paper. Software color management systems can bring more consistency to this process, but designers need to know what they can and cannot control. It can be complex even with a color management system.

Waterless Printing The new technology of waterless printing is losing popularity. Most offset presses use a dampening system of water to cover the plate. Offset is based on the fact that water and grease (ink) don't mix. In waterless printing, a silicone-coated plate is used that rejects ink in the nonimage areas. The result is spectacular detail, high-line screens, richer densities, and consistent quality throughout the press run: in short, great quality. However, according to Doug Koke, principal of IP/Koke printing, "Waterless has not been widely accepted. The plates are far too sensitive, scratch easily, and are temperature sensitive."[4] Offset dominates printing today.

Digital Printing Today, digital printing accounts for less than 2 percent globally of the $500 billion printing industry. It is an offshoot of offset technology. Indigo Press, the first digital printing system, was created in the Netherlands in 1993. Presently, the resolutions and finish of the Indigo Press's digitally printed materials rival offset. It requires a minimum of preflight production tweaking. However, the page size is relatively small to be competitive. Recently, the Indigo company merged into Hewlett-Packard. In direct-digital printing, workstations send files to the press. Film is not used, and in some cases neither are plates. Today there are several digital printing systems. Basically, information is transferred onto electrophotographic cylinders, instead of plates, and these cylinders use toner to print process color instead of printing ink. There are also other presses that digitize pages onto special plates and are used for short printing runs. It is predicted that digital printing will eventually revolutionize the printing press. There is change in the air.

The computer and digitization are spawning most of this advancement in printing and production technology. The day is not far off when the printing and production industry will have a completely filmless, digital process.

The student of advertising production will have to learn these advances in the field, many of which will be both revolutionary and evolutionary, complicating the decision as to which system to use.

SUMMARY

All advertising people need to understand the basics of production. The production terms, concepts, and processes are not easy to learn but are essential to know because they affect budgets, time, and efficiency issues.

Publishers set mechanical requirements for their publications. Advertising production people need to be familiar with sources of information pertaining to print production requirements.

Today most advertisements are created on the computer (digital). The comps presented to clients appear to be computer finished. The process from the computer screen to a finished advertisement in a publication may be completed digitally or by using a mix of traditional processes. The future will involve more computer-to-plate digital production.

There are three basic kinds of printing processes: letterpress (printing from a raised surface), offset lithography (printing from a flat surface), and gravure (printing from a depressed surface). In addition, silk screen or screen printing offers advertisers additional production applications. The form of printing may affect the type of material sent to the publication to reproduce the advertisement.

Advertisers may use new prepress digital technology or traditional means to prepare advertisements for production. The publication tells the advertiser what type of material is required or accepted. Each method of prepress has advantages and disadvantages, depending on the degree of quality desired. Typography concerns the style (or face) of type and the way the copy is set. Typefaces come in styles called families. The size is specified in points (72 points per inch). The width of typeset lines is measured in picas (6 picas to an inch). The depth of newspaper space is measured in lines. The space between the lines of type is called leading or line spacing.

The graphics and production processes can be complex because what you see isn't always what really is. Continuous-tone art (a photograph) must be converted into halftone dots (may be scanned or use traditional printer's darkroom procedure) so that the tonal values of the original can be reproduced. Line art has no tonal value; it is drawn in black ink on white paper using lines and solid black areas.

Production technology is constantly changing to produce printed materials faster, more cheaply, and more efficiently. Achieving color reproduction that satisfies advertising agencies and advertisers is one of the most crucial roles of the magazine production manager. There are a multitude of proofs for the production manager to choose from dictated by the need to match colors exactly and the expense involved. "How much quality do we need?" is an often-asked question in terms of which proof to use. Color management systems help advertisers get what you see.

REVIEW

1. Differentiate among the three basic printing processes.
2. What is a digital file?
3. What is continuous-tone copy?
4. What is line art?
5. What are color separations?
6. What colors are used in four-color printing?
7. When is a laminate/adhesive proof used?

CHAPTER 19

The Television Commercial

The trade headlines yell, "The 30-second spot is dead," and book titles lament, *Life After the 30-Second Spot*. The reason is more audience and cost efficiency, not the impact upon those actually watching. Despite TiVo, audience fragmentation, new media, new screens, and the decline of traditional networks' influence, television commercials remain a powerful medium. It is complicated by a number of factors, including the battle for eyeballs by other screens. This creates a challenge for advertisers. After reading this chapter, you will understand:

chapter objectives

1. copy development
2. creating the commercial
3. producing the commercial
4. controlling the cost
5. the short film

Maybe this chapter should be called the "short film" to include all video advertising as was mentioned in Chapter 16. Much of the same thinking applies to all forms of video. Take the big idea; blend sight, sound, motion, and technology; and add the ability to impact emotions, build in entertainment, and you have a very powerful advertising tool. Television still reaches multitudes of potential consumers with great impact. And this is still a time of experimenting with all the new marketing tools. According to MediaPost's David Goetzl, Converse athletic shoes couldn't resist the mass-appeal pitch for their Chuck Taylor's. "At some level, Converse decided niche campaigns are good, but reaching the 16 million viewers on NBC's *Deal or No Deal,* a show designed to appeal to a broad group, is better. No need to experiment (which Converse has) with viral marketing or blogs or YouTube or instant messenger when millions can be reached in a mere 30 seconds. (Assuming, of course, few of those millions are zapping the ads with DVRs.) And while you're at it, don't just buy the 30s, weave your brand into the stage or story line for a tidy premium."[1] Television still has power.

THE POWER OF THE TELEVISION IDEA

Here are a few convincing examples of television's marketing and communication power.

As the last century ended, Subway found its sales to be flat promoting low-fat benefits. In January 2000 its agency developed two television spots featuring Jared Fogle (you've probably seen recent commercials featuring him), who lost 245 pounds on a strictly Subway diet, and Tae Bo master Billy Blanks. "We've been doing low-fat for 3 1/2 years and did well generating about 5 percent sales increases, but using those two spots drove the business 15 to 20 percent," said

Chris Carroll, director of marketing. With this new approach some stores' sales were up as much as 40 percent. Initially, the client rejected the agency's commercial idea three times.[2] More recently, in 2007, Subway used Jared to attack its competitor's products for the amount of meat and calories.

Whereas most top-tier banks sell products, BB&T preempts respect for the individual in its advertising. Consumer brand-switching intentions increased 300 percent after exposure to BB&T advertising. In one commercial, a lady says, "I'm a great grandmother. Seventy-one and counting. I've danced to the swing. I've danced to the tango. I've seen money wasted. Thrown away. I've seen it used . . . to accomplish things . . . I never dreamed possible. I will teach my great grandchildren . . . to know the difference." The last frame says, "BB&T. You can tell we want your business."

The Johnson Group positioned their wireless client Cricket as the wireless phone that is replacing land lines and emphasized the value proposition, "Why pay for two?" Exhibit 19.1 shows a spot where in a darkened room, a conventional phone moves off the table and across the floor, seemingly under its own power. On the exterior of the house, we see the phone moving down the steps to join other phones on the sidewalk. A close-up reveals each phone being carried by a team of crickets. There is now a parade of phones moving down the street. The crickets are carrying the hordes of phones to a cliff and tossing them over. The crickets cheer as the phones crash. Cut to a mnemonic device: A home phone and a Cricket phone on a tabletop. Suddenly, the home phone is jerked out of the shot by its cord, leaving only the cricket phone. The commercial voiceover says,

> Everywhere you look home phones are being replaced by Cricket. Cricket service works just like your home phone, with all local calls you want for one low, predictable price. Plus, plenty of free long distance. So when one phone does more and costs less—why pay for two? Cricket. It could be your only phone.

Some of the characteristics of good television advertising cut through clutter, appealing to consumers with humor, intelligence, charm, and emotion. Good ads are like good people. They're smart, funny, and engaging. You tend to remember them long after they're gone. You shouldn't even think about getting into consumers' wallets unless you first get into their lives. If you knew how to do this, you wouldn't have to read the rest of this chapter. On the other hand, many people who are supposed to know this don't practice it.

Media-buying agency Starcom Media Services says television advertising drives advertising awareness among viewers. Apparently, the main problem with a television spot is that often nonrelevant ads are shown. So the discussion is not about interruption but rather about relevance of the commercial content.[3]

THE PROBLEMS OF TELEVISION

The medium poses some problems discussed in earlier chapters: commercial clutter that leaves viewers confused about advertisers, loss of audiences, high production costs, zapping, TiVo, and fewer eyeballs. For example, according to Roper Reports, 38 percent of viewers say they often switch to another channel when ads come on, up 24 percent from 1985.[4] These problems are constant reminders to advertisers of the need to plan their messages very carefully. But it is precisely this adversity that breeds creative innovation. Roper finds 31 percent of viewers say they are often amused by funny or clever commercials (up 5 percent from 1993); and about 70 percent agree that advertising is often fun or interesting to watch.

The 30-second spot is priced on the potential to get in front of a lot of eyeballs.

cricket
Comfortable Wireless®
REPOSITIONING | "CRICKET THIEVES"
:30 TV SPOT

The Johnson Group created 30-second TV spots that positioned Cricket as the wireless
phone that is replacing land lines and emphasized the value proposition —"Why pay
for two?"

IN A DARKENED HOME, A TELEPHONE MOVES
OFF OF THE TABLE AND ACROSS THE FLOOR,
SEEMINGLY UNDER ITS OWN POWER.

CUT TO THE EXTERIOR OF THE HOUSE.
PHONES ARE MOVING OUT OF THE HOUSE AND
DOWN THE EXTERIOR STEPS.

THEY ARE JOINED ON THE SIDEWALK BY OTHER
PHONES.

V/O: Everywhere you look, home phones are
being replaced...

CLOSE-UP REVEALS THAT EACH PHONE IS BEING
CARRIED BY A TEAM OF CRICKETS.

V/O: ...by Cricket.

THERE'S NOW A PARADE OF TELEPHONES
MOVING DOWN THE STREET.

V/O: Cricket service works just like your home
phone, with all the local calls...

CUT TO SCENE AT THE TOP OF A CLIFF. HORDES
OF TELEPHONES ARE BEING CARRIED TO THE
BRINK THEN TOSSED OVER.

V/O: ...you want for one low, predictable price.

SFX: SOUND OF CRICKETS CHEERING AND
PHONES CRASHING.

V/O: Plus, plenty of free long distance.

CUT TO MNEMONIC DEVICE: A HOME PHONE
AND A CRICKET PHONE ON A TABLETOP.
SUDDENLY, THE HOME PHONE IS JERKED OUT
OF THE SHOT BY ITS CORD, LEAVING ONLY THE
CRICKET PHONE.

V/O: So when one phone does more and costs
less—why pay for two?

V/O: Cricket. It could be your only phone.

EXHIBIT 19.1
Cricket Thieves
A big idea of dropping
your home phone—
"Why pay for two?"—
emphasizes the value of
using Cricket wireless
in a dramatic and
interesting way.
Courtesy of The Johnson Group.

Artistic Fads

The creative teams are constantly looking for new ways to grab a viewer's attention.
However, many of these techniques become popular and then soon fade from the
scene. Remember the shaky camera, claymation, morphing one object into
another object, and using the oldies film footage? There is a continuing search for
some new way to wake up and shake up an audience. Simply having a sound strategy isn't enough to make a viewer watch. There must be a sound strategy wrapped

in a strong creative idea. We're back to the big idea concept. We take the big idea and blend visuals, words, motion, and technology to create emotional reactions—done properly, this is what makes television the most powerful advertising medium.

Advertising to male football fans has given us a number of tasteless commercials that fall under the category of frat-house humor. A few years ago a Miller Lite commercial showed two attractive young women, sitting in an outdoor café, begin to argue about the merits of Miller Lite beer. It escalates into a hair-pulling, clothes-ripping brawl. The naughty male fantasy concludes with one saying to the other, "Let's make out!" Not so long ago, commercials tailored to guys pushed a few predictable buttons—sex, but also a kind of aggressive and crude frat-house humor. Bud Light—to pick another prominent marketer to the football-watching demographic—ran a series of commercials during a Super Bowl that featured a dog that bit a man's crotch, a monkey that propositioned a woman, and a horse that passed gas in a couple's face. The prevailing theme of commercials airing during Sunday afternoon football is men as the butt of the joke—men acting silly or men humiliating themselves or being humiliated by others.[5] This too will change.

It is all about targeting.

COPY DEVELOPMENT AND PRODUCTION TIMETABLE

The creative process is difficult to predict. It isn't always easy to develop new breakthrough copy within the planned timetable or guess the client's reaction to the copy. The agency may love it; the client may hate it. It may take time to develop the right ideas. However, it is important to develop a reasonable timetable for copy development and production. A typical copy development timetable sequence might include the following:

- Copy exploratory
- Present ideas to client
- Revisions to client for approval to produce
- Circulate copy for clearance (legal, R&D, management)
- On-air clearance (network/local stations)
- Prebid meeting (specifications/sets)
- Bid review/award job
- Preproduction meeting
- Shoot
- Postproduction
- Rough cut to client for approval
- Revisions
- Final to client
- Ship date

The advertising agency and the client share responsibility for such a timetable. How long does it take for a one- to five-day shoot with 2 to 10 actors to clear this process? Anywhere from 11 to 43 days. This range illustrates the complexity of the process. It isn't easy to generalize.

CREATING THE COMMERCIAL

Many creative people believe it is easier to create a good television commercial than it is to create a good print ad. After all, the television creative person has motion to command more attention, sound, professional actors, producers, directors, and editors. They should be able to communicate with all that support if there is a grain of an idea.

The television commercial has two basic segments: the video (the sight or visual part) and the audio (spoken words, music, or other sounds). The creation process begins with the video because television is generally better at showing than telling; however, the impact of the words and sounds must be considered. Can you visualize this part of a FedExKinko's spot:

(open on a meeting in the lobby of a small business)

Boss: OK, the presentation's tomorrow, so let's make sure we all know our usual responsibilities . . . Jeff, you keep feeding me old information.

(Jeff nods)

Boss: Dean, I need you to continue not living up to your résumé.

(Dean nods)

Boss: Sue, you're in charge of waffling.

Sue: Are you sure?

Boss: Jerome, you'll talk a big game, then do nothing.

Jerome: Let's do it.

Boss: Rick, can you fold under pressure for me?

Rick: Like a lawn chair.

Visual Techniques

There are a number of visual tools for the creative team to use in constructing the spot.

Testimonials Testimonials can be delivered by known or unknown individuals. Viewers are fascinated with celebrities. Some celebrities (for example, Cindy Crawford) have staying power for years and years in their ability to grab a viewer's attention. And Tiger Woods keeps on successfully pitching for Buick. He's also pitched for American Express, Accenture, EA Sports, Nike, Rolex, Tag Heuer, and Titleist. About 20 percent of all TV commercials feature a celebrity.[6] And former Bears player, coach, and sports commentator Mike Ditka pitched for Levitra. In 2006, Peyton Manning pitched for Reebok and Sony, the latter alongside golf prodigy Michelle Wie. In 2005, Manning landed $10.5 million in endorsements according to *Sports Illustrated*, amongst the highest of any athlete.[7]

There is always a risk with some celebrities of getting into trouble or publicly saying the wrong thing or supporting the wrong cause, but it is worth it because of all the attention they get and the impact they have, claims a vice president for Total Research Corp.[8] It costs an advertiser about $20,000 to research a celebrity to get diagnostic information of not only the personality but also whether the personality fits its product or service. For credibility, Slim-Fast has used satisfied customers to show how much weight they have lost.

Serials Serials are commercials created in a series in which each commercial continues the previous story. The technique was made popular more than a decade ago by the Taster's Choice couple. Several beer companies have also tried the serial approach, as have Pacific Bell telephone, Ragu spaghetti sauce, and Energizer batteries.

Oldies Footage Classic television and film sequences are now easily manipulated to create ads that target media-savvy viewers. Audiences have seen John Wayne selling Coors beer, Ed Sullivan introducing the Mercedes M-class sport-utility vehicle, Fred Astaire sweeping with a Dirt Devil, and Lucy Ricardo and Fred Mertz pushing tickets for the California lottery. PacificCare used original source footage from an *I Love Lucy* episode and made Fred and Ethel talk about PacificCare services.[9]

Spokesperson Often this technique features a "presenter" who stands in front of the camera and delivers the copy directly to the viewer. The spokesperson may display and perhaps demonstrate the product. He or she may be in a set (a living room, kitchen, factory, office, or outside) appropriate to the product and product story or in limbo (plain background with no set). The product should be the hero. The spokesperson should be someone who is likable and believable but not so powerful as to overwhelm the product. In some cases, this is presented with humor.

Demonstration This technique is considered old television. However, creative thinking can make this a modern technique. Product demonstrations have long been a mainstay of advertising, none perhaps better known than the series of torture tests for Timex watches, which carried the triumphant theme "It takes a licking and keeps on ticking." It is popular for some types of products because television is the ideal medium for demonstrating to the consumer how the product works: how a bug spray kills, how to apply eye makeup in gorgeous colors, or how easy it is to be in an accident with VW's Jetta, or plug your guitar into a VW car's stereo. These commercials had lots of impact by demonstrating in an interesting manner. When making a demonstration commercial, use close shots so the viewer can see clearly what is happening. Try to make it unexpected, if possible. You may choose a subjective camera view (which shows a procedure as if the viewer were actually doing whatever the product does), using the camera as the viewer's eyes. Make the demonstration relevant and as involving as possible. Do not try to fool the viewer for two important reasons: (1) Your message must be believable; and (2) legally, the demonstration must correspond to actual usage—most agencies make participants in the commercial production sign affidavits signifying that the events took place as they appeared on the TV screen.

As good as the 30-second commercial can be, it isn't as good as the video-based demonstration. For example, *Drivers Talk* radio host, Rick Titus demonstrated a Ford F-150 pickup truck Web video. The immersion rate was tremendous and voluntary. Those viewers staying with the entire competitive demonstration probably were a good indication of people with an intent to buy.[10]

Close-Ups Television is basically a medium of close-ups. The largest TV screen is too small for extraneous details in the scenes of a commercial. A fast-food chain may use close-ups to show hamburgers cooking or the appetizing finished product ready to be consumed. With this technique, the audio is generally delivered off-screen (the voiceover costs less than a presentation by someone onscreen).

Story Line The story-line technique is similar to making a miniature movie (with a definite beginning, middle, and end in 30 seconds), except that the narration is done offscreen. A typical scene may show a family trying to paint their large house with a typical paint and brush. The camera shifts to the house next door, where a teenage female is easily spray-painting the house, the garage, and the fence in rapid fashion. During the scenes, the announcer explains the advantages of the spray

EXHIBIT 19.2

"Freezer" Spot

This Mayfield ice cream commercial uses a story inside of a supermarket to make a point about its creamier ice cream.

Courtesy of Mayfield and The Johnson Group.

"FREEZER"
:30 TV Spot

Story Summary:
As a dad and his daughter walk through the freezer aisle in the grocery store, they notice the Mayfield ice cream freezer floating in mid air, tethered only by the case's electric plug. Amazed, they look through the glass to see that all of the Mayfield cartons are floating to the top of the freezer. As dad cautiously opens the door to select a flavor, the cartons begin to "escape," rising up toward the ceiling.

GIRL: Hey dad. What kind of ice cream is that?

DAD: Oh, that's... Wow!

GIRL: Can we get some?

DAD: You bet.

GIRL: Cool!

SCOTTIE V/O: Looks like the cream really does rise to the top.

And you can't get creamier ice cream than Mayfield.

Like new Mayfield Cookies & Cream.

It's just not ice cream.

It's ice creamier.

GIRL: What flavor do you want?

DAD: All of 'em!

painter. In a Mayfield ice cream ad (see Exhibit 19.2), a dad and daughter are walking through the freezer aisle in the supermarket. They notice the Mayfield ice cream freezer floating in the air, tethered only by its electric cord. Amazed, they look through the glass to see that all the Mayfield ice cream cartons are floating to the top of the freezer. As the dad cautiously opens the door to select a flavor, the cartons begin to escape, rising up toward the ceiling. The voiceover says: "Looks like the cream really does come to the top. And you can't get creamier ice cream than Mayfield."

Comparisons Their soft drink has sodium. Our brand is sodium free. Their beer is loaded with carbs. Our beer has next to none. Our sandwich has more meat and less calories. Comparing one product with another can answer questions for the viewer. Usually, the comparison is against the leader in the product category. You could do a user lifestyle comparison between your brand and a competitive brand. In direct product comparisons, you must be prepared to prove in court that your product is significantly superior, as stated, and you must be credible in the way you make your claim, or the commercial may induce sympathy for the competitor.

Still Photographs and Artwork By using still photographs and/or artwork, including cartoon drawings and lettering, you can structure a well-placed commercial. The required material may already exist, to be supplied at modest cost, or it can be photographed or drawn specifically for your use. Skillful use of the television camera can give static visual material a surprising amount of movement. Zoom lenses provide an inward or outward motion, and panning the camera across the photographs or artwork can give the commercial motion (*panning* means changing the viewpoint of the camera without moving the dolly it stands on).

Slice-of-Life Slice-of-life is a dramatic technique in which actors tell a story in an attempt to involve people with the brand. It is a short miniplay in which the brand is the hero. Most slice-of-life commercials open with a problem, and the brand becomes the solution.

The viewer must see the problem as real, and the reward must fit the problem. Because problem solving is a useful format in almost any commercial, slice-of-life is widely used. Brands selling largely emotional benefits (jeans, soft drinks, beer, greeting cards, athletic gear) have employed the format in great numbers.

Customer Interview Most people who appear in television commercials are professional actors, but customer interviews involve nonprofessionals. An interviewer or offscreen voice may ask a housewife, who is usually identified by name, to compare the advertised kitchen cleanser with her own brand by removing two identical spots in her sink. She finds that the advertised product does a better job.

Vignettes and Situations Advertisers of soft drinks, beer, candy, and other widely consumed products find this technique useful in creating excitement and motivation. The commercial usually consists of a series of fast-paced scenes showing people enjoying the product as they enjoy life. The audio over these scenes is often a jingle or song with lyrics based on the situation we see and the satisfaction the product offers. In many cases, it is the music that holds it all together. It can be used effectively to update a brand or sell a lifestyle. It is a challenge to link with the brand and can be costly to produce since you have to shoot 15 or so vignettes.

Humor Humor has long been a popular technique with both copywriters and consumers because it makes the commercial more interesting. The dangers are that the humorous aspects of the commercial will get in the way of the sell and that the viewer will remember the humor rather than the product or the benefit. The challenge is to make the humorous copy relevant to the product or benefit. Do you remember the Jones Soda three-legged dog begging for scraps from a skateboarder? The dog ends up with the bottle as a leg, all in humor.

animation
Making inanimate objects appear alive and moving by setting them before an animation camera and filming one frame at a time.

Animation Originally, **animation** consisted of artists' inanimate drawings, which were photographed on motion-picture film one frame at a time and brought to life with movement as the film is projected. Historically, the most common form of animation was the cartoon. Certainly a favorite among children but also popular with all ages, the cartoon is capable of creating a warm, friendly atmosphere both for the product and for the message. Today, computer graphics can be extremely realistic and have changed the nature of animation. The cost of animation depends on its style: With limited movement, few characters, and few or no backgrounds, the price can be low. Many traditional animators have been replaced with digital artists.

Stop Motion When a package or other object is photographed in a series of different positions, movement can be simulated as the single frames are projected in sequence. Stop motion is similar to artwork photographed in animation. With it, the package can "walk," "dance," and move as if it had come to life.

Rotoscope In the rotoscope technique, animated and live-action sequences are produced separately and then optically combined. A live boy may be eating breakfast food while a cartoon animal trademark character jumps up and down on his shoulder and speaks to him.

Problem Solution This technique has been around since the beginning of television. The purpose of many products is to solve the prime prospect's problem—a headache, poor communication, or plaque. You get the idea. The product is selling the solution. Problem solution is similar to slice-of-life but lacks the depth of story line or plot development. Be sure to let the visuals tell the story. Solve the problem with visuals.

Mood Imagery This technique is expensive and difficult. It often combines several techniques. The main objective is to set a certain mood and image for the product you are trying to sell. Strong imagery can sell ideas (see Exhibit 19.3). Zippo creates mood, mystery and surprise as a figure moves up metal stairs to music and SFX and then a flash from a Zippo and the torch of the Statue of Liberty lights. The copy reads, "ZIPPO. Use it to start something."

EXHIBIT 19.3

Zippo

Some ideas naturally lend themselves to mood imagery. Zippo uses a little suspense with sound effects and stark lighting to add mystery.

Courtesy of Blattner Brunner.

Split and Bookend Spots A variation on the serial commercial is the split spot: Two related (usually 15-second) spots run with a completely unrelated spot between them. For example, Post Grape-Nuts ran a split spot in which a woman asks a man how long the cereal stays crunchy in milk. The man does not want to find out, but she insists, and viewers are left hanging. Next is an unrelated 30-second commercial for another product. The couple then comes back, and she says, "After all this time it's still crunchy." The theory behind split and bookend commercials is that breaking out of the expected format will get your product remembered.

Infomercials As discussed in Chapter 8, the infomercial is a commercial that looks like a program. These commercials sell everything from woks to make-a-million-in-real-estate programs, and usually run for 30 minutes. The National Infomercial Marketing Association recommends that every infomercial begin and end with a "paid advertisement" announcement so that consumers understand what they are watching. The obvious advantage is that the advertiser has an entire program about its product.

Combination Most commercials combine techniques. A speaker may begin and conclude the message, but there will be close-ups in between. Every commercial should contain at least one or two close-ups to show the package and logo. Humor is adaptable to most techniques. Animation and live action make an effective mixture in many commercials, and side-by-side comparisons may be combined with almost any other technique.

Visual Vicissitudes Commercials that weave together a string of apparently nonstory-driven scenes, full of talking heads, lush landscapes, or crisp graphic shots. Music and sound can help to serve as a pacing guide.

Bug Place a "bug" in the lower right-hand corner of the commercial. That's the thing the networks often use that let's you know what network you're watching. And always end your commercial with your brand name prominently on the screen.[11]

Video Influence

Many visual techniques used in commercials have evolved from the music video industry. These include hyperkinetic imagery, visual speed, and sophistication; ironic, wise-guy attitudes; unexpected humor; quick, suggestive cuts rather than slow segues; narrative implications rather than whole stories; attitudes, not explanations; tightly cropped, partial images instead of whole ones; mixtures of live action, newsreel footage, animation, typography, film speeds, and film quality; and unexpected soundtrack/audio relationships to video.

Which Technique?

Over the years there have been a number of studies to help advertisers make up their minds as to what kind of commercials to run. However, none provide all the answers. Ogilvy & Mather found that people who liked a commercial were twice as likely to be persuaded by it compared to people who felt neutral toward the advertising. Perhaps the single most striking finding was the fact that commercial liking went far beyond mere entertainment. People like commercials they feel are relevant and worth remembering, which could have an impact on greater persuasion. Original or novel approaches alone seem to have little to do with how well a commercial is liked. Ogilvy & Mather also found that liking was a function of product category. A lively, energetic execution also contributed to liking but was less important than relevance. In other research findings, Video Storyboard tests reinforce that consumers like commercials with celebrities. Consumer preference for this type of commercial has risen in the past 10 years. Such commercials are more persuasive than slice-of-life vignettes or product demonstrations; celebrities are bested only by humor and kids as executional elements that characterize persuasive commercials.

Ideas generate production techniques and sometimes thinking of the technique choices generates "ideas." The technology allows you to create almost anything you can visualize. These are your communication tools.

Planning the Commercial

Let us review some of the basic principles of writing the commercial script. In planning the commercial, there are many considerations: cost, medium (videotape or film), casting of talent, use of music, special techniques, time, location, and the big idea and its relationship to the advertising and marketing objectives and to the entire campaign.

■ You are dealing with sight, sound, and motion. Each of these elements has its own requirements and uses. There should be a relationship among them so that the viewer perceives the desired message. Make certain that when you are demonstrating a sales feature, the audio is talking about that same feature.

■ Your audio should be relevant to your video, but there is no need to describe what is obvious in the picture. When possible, you should see that the words interpret the picture and advance the thought.

■ Television generally is more effective at showing than telling; therefore, more than half of the success burden rests on the ability of the video to communicate.

■ The number of scenes should be planned carefully. You do not want too many scenes (unless you are simply trying to give an overall impression) because this tends to confuse the viewer. Yet you do not want scenes to become static (unless planned so for a reason). Remember, always know your target, younger audiences digest more scenes quickly than older audiences. Study TV commercials and time the scene changes to determine what you personally find effective. If you do this, you will discover the importance of pacing the message—if a scene is too long, you will find yourself impatiently waiting for the next one.

■ It is important to conceive the commercial as a flowing progression so that the viewer will be able to follow it easily. You do not have time for a three-act play whose unrelated acts can be tied together at the end. A viewer who cannot follow your thought may well tune you out. The proper use of opticals or transitions can add motion and smoothness to scene transitions.

■ Television is basically a medium of close-ups. The largest TV screen is too small for extraneous detail in the scenes of a commercial. Long shots can be effective in establishing a setting but not for showing product features.

■ The action of the commercial takes more time than a straight announcer's reading of copy. A good rule is to purposely time the commercial a second or two short. Generally, the action will eat up this time, so do not just read your script. Act it out.

■ You will want to consider the use of *supers* (words on the screen) of the basic theme so that the viewer can see, as well as hear, the important sales feature. Many times, the last scene will feature product identification and the theme line.

■ If possible, show the brand name. If it is prominent, give a shot of the package; otherwise, flash its logo. It is vital to establish brand identification.

■ Generally, try to communicate one basic idea; avoid running in fringe benefits. Be certain that your words as well as your pictures emphasize your promise. State it, support it, and, if possible, demonstrate it. Repeat your basic promise near the end of the commercial; that is the story you want viewers to carry away with them.

■ Read the audio aloud to catch tongue twisters.

■ As in most other advertising writing, the sentences should usually be short and their structure uncomplicated. Use everyday words. It is not necessary to have something said every second. The copy should round out the thought conveyed by the picture.

- In writing your video description, describe the scene and action as completely as possible: "Open on husband and wife in living room" is not enough. Indicate where each is placed, whether they are standing or sitting, and generally how the room is furnished.

Writing the Script

Writing a TV commercial is very different from writing print advertising. First, you must use simple, easy-to-pronounce, easy-to-remember words. And you must be brief. The 30-second commercial has only 28 seconds of audio. In 28 seconds, you must solve your prime prospect's problems by demonstrating your product's superiority. If the product is too big to show in use, be certain to show the logo or company name at least twice during the commercial. Think of words and pictures simultaneously. You usually divide your script paper into two columns. On the left, you describe the video action, and on the right you write the audio portion, including sound effects and music. Corresponding video and audio elements go right next to each other, panel by panel (see Exhibit 19.4).

EXHIBIT 19.4

A Television Script with Storyboard

TV SCRIPT: Pawleys "Leave Us Alone"

VIDEO		AUDIO
1. MS: BEACH SCENE PEOPLE IN CHAIRS OUTSIDE OF HOUSE		MUSIC: IN AND UNDER (George Winston quiet jazz) ANNCR:Pawleys is a great
2. CU: CHILD DIGGING IN SAND WITH OCEAN BACKGROUND		family resort.
3. MS: PEOPLE WALKING ON ALMOST EMPTY BEACH		It is nature at its best....
4. LS: LADY ALONE WALKING INLET		a beautiful pristine...beach
5. WIDE SHOT OF EMPTY BEACH, FEW HOUSES		Don't come, we're having fun.
6. END FRAME	 Pawleys *Don't Disturb Us!*	Pawleys is OUR beach.

(continued)

EXHIBIT 19.4
Continued

VIDEO	AUDIO
	MUSIC: IN AND UNDER (George Winston quiet jazz)
1. MS:BEACHSCENE 3 PEOPLE IN CHAIRS SITTING OUTSIDE OF BEACH HOUSE. BEACH BLANKET IN SAND.	ANNCR: Pawleys is a great
2. CU: CHILD DIGGING IN SAND WITH OCEAN BACKGROUND.	family resort.
3. MS: PEOPLE WALKING ON ALMOST EMPTY BEACH. A FEW HOUSES ARE IN THE BACKGROUND.	It is nature at its best. . .
4. LS: LADY ALONE WALKING INLET WITH DISTANT HOUSE OR TWO.	a beautiful . . . pristine beach
5. WIDE SHOT OF EMPTY BEACH, FEW HOUSES.	Don't come, we're having fun.
6. END FRAME.	
	Pawleys is OUR beach.

Write copy in a friendly, conversational style. If you use an off-camera announcer, make certain that his or her dialogue is keyed to the scenes in your video portion. Although it is not always possible, matching the audio with the video makes a commercial cohesive and more effective. The audio—words, sound effects, or music—in a script is as important as the video portion. They must work together to bring the viewer the message. You need strong copy and sound and strong visuals. All are vital for an effective commercial.

Some agencies add visuals to their scripts. They use specially designed sheets of paper, usually 8 inches by 11 inches, with boxes down the center for rough sketches of the video portion (see Exhibit 19.4) called photoscripts. For presentations, most agencies use full-size television storyboards.

Developing the Storyboard

Once the creative art and copy team has developed a script, the next step is to create a **storyboard**, which consists of a series of sketches showing key scenes developed in the script. It is a helpful tool for discussing the concept with other agency or client personnel, who may not know the background or who may not be able to visualize a script accurately. Without a storyboard, each individual may interpret the script's visuals differently.

Storyboard Versus Finished Look It is extremely difficult, if not impossible, to visualize the look of a finished commercial from the storyboard. Most clients are very literal minded and don't visualize storyboards very well. Storyboards should stimulate the imagination of someone's vision prior to shooting. The quality of the storyboards varies from virtual stick figures in limbo to full-color drawings or photos. Keep in mind, using this limited medium, it is a difficult task to show all the details that are necessary to understand for production purposes.

Storyboards consist of two frames for each scene. The top frame represents the TV screen (visual). The bottom frame carries a description of the video (as per script) and the audio for that sequence (some storyboards carry only the audio

storyboard
Series of drawings used to present a proposed commercial. Consists of illustrations of key action (video), accompanied by the audio part. Used for getting advertiser approval and as a production guide.

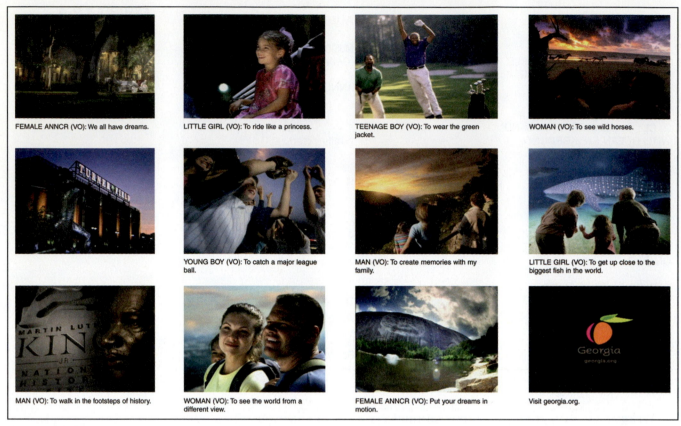

FEMALE ANNCR (VO): We all have dreams.

LITTLE GIRL (VO): To ride like a princess.

TEENAGE BOY (VO): To wear the green jacket.

WOMAN (VO): To see wild horses.

YOUNG BOY (VO): To catch a major league ball.

MAN (VO): To create memories with my family.

LITTLE GIRL (VO): To get up close to the biggest fish in the world.

MAN (VO): To walk in the footsteps of history.

WOMAN (VO): To see the world from a different view.

FEMALE ANNCR (VO): Put your dreams in motion.

Visit georgia.org.

EXHIBIT 19.5

A Photoboard

Courtesy of the State of Georgia and McRae Communications.

portion). The number of sets of frames varies from commercial to commercial and is not necessarily dictated by the length of the commercial. There may be 4 to 12 or more sets of frames, depending on the nature of the commercial and the demands of the client for detail.

The ratio of width to depth on the TV screen is 4 by 3. There is no standard-size storyboard frame, although a common size is 4 inches by 3 inches.

The storyboard is a practical step between the raw script and actual production. It gives the agency, client, and production house personnel a common visual starting point for their discussion. Upon client approval, the storyboard goes into production.

Assessing the storyboard requires answering a number of questions: Is there a campaign idea? Is it on strategy? Is the campaign idea meaningful? Credible? Provocative? Does the execution showcase the campaign idea? Is the benefit visualized? Does it tell a picture story? Is it clear, credible, and compelling? Does the board represent a commercial or a campaign? Are the ideas communicated clearly in visual-audio elements? Does it sell versus tell?

Exhibit 19.5 is an example of a photoboard. The photoboard is similar to the storyboard but shows the actual frames (photos) that were shot. It is frequently used by companies as a sales tool to show merchants and dealers exactly what kind of advertising support they will be given.

Other Elements of the Commercial

opticals
Visual effects that are put on a TV film in a laboratory, in contrast to those that are included as part of the original photography.

Opticals Most commercials contain more than a single scene. Optical devices or effects between scenes are necessary to provide smooth visual continuity from scene to scene. They are inserted during the final editing stage. The actual **opticals** may be one of the director's functions. However, these are used to aid in the transition of getting from one scene to the next scene or establishing a visual. Sometimes which technique depends on the importance of a particular scene or the detail that

ECU - An Extreme Close Up shows, for example, person's lips, nose, eyes.

CU - The Close Up is a tight shot, but showing face on entire package for emphasis.

MCU - The Medium Close Up cuts to person about chest, usually showing some background.

MS - The Medium Shot shows the person from the waist up. Commonly used shot. Shows much more detail of setting or background than MCU.

LS - The Long Shot shows the scene from a distance. Used to establish location.

EXHIBIT **19.6**

Examples of Camera Directions

needs to be seen. Exhibit 19.6 illustrates some basic optical decisions. Among the most common are the following:

- *Cut.* One scene simply cuts into the next. It is the fastest scene change because it indicates no time lapse whatsoever. A cut is used to indicate simultaneous action, to speed up action, and for variety. It keeps one scene from appearing on the screen too long.

- *Dissolve.* An overlapping effect in which one scene fades out while the following scene simultaneously fades in. Dissolves are slower than cuts. There are fast dissolves and slow dissolves. Dissolves are used to indicate a short lapse of time in a given scene, or to move from one scene to another where the action is either simultaneous with the action in the first scene or occurring very soon after the preceding action.

- *Fade-in.* An effect in which the scene actually "fades" into vision from total black (black screen).

- *Fade-out.* This is opposite of a fade-in. The scene "fades" into total black. If days, months, or years elapse between one sequence of action and the next, indicate "fade out . . . fade in."

■ *Matte.* Part of one scene is placed over another so that the same narrator, for example, is shown in front of different backgrounds.

■ *Super.* The superimposition of one scene or object over another. The title or product can be "supered" over the scene.

■ *Wipe.* The new scene "wipes" off the previous scene from top or bottom or side to side with a geometric pattern (see Exhibit 19.7). A wipe is faster than a dissolve but not as fast as a cut. A wipe does not usually connote lapse of time, as a dissolve or fade-out does. There are several types of wipes: flip (the entire scene turns over like the front and back of a postcard), horizontal (left to right or right to left), vertical (top to bottom or bottom to top), diagonal, closing door (in from both sides), bombshell (a burst into the next scene), iris (a circle that grows bigger is an iris out), fan (fans out from center screen), circular (sweeps around the screen—also called clock wipe). Wipes are most effective when a rapid succession of short or quick scenes is desired or to separate impressionistic shots when these are grouped together to produce a montage effect.

■ *Zoom.* A smooth, sometimes rapid move from a long shot to a close-up or from a close-up to a long shot.

Sound Track The audio portion of the commercial may be recorded either during the film or videotape shooting or at an earlier or later time in a recording studio. When the sound track is recorded during the shooting, the actual voices of the people speaking on camera are used in the commercial. If the sound track is recorded in advance, the film or videotape scenes can be shot to fit the copy points as they occur; or if music is part of the track, visual action can be matched to a specific beat. If shooting and editing take place before the sound track is recorded, the track can be tailored to synchronize with the various scenes.

Music Not all commercials need music. But think about it early in the process. Music has the ability to communicate feelings and moods in a unique way. As a

EXHIBIT **19.7**

Example of a Wipe

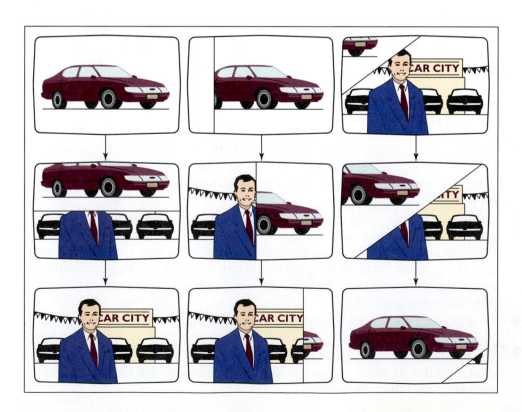

result, the use of music can make or break a television commercial. In some commercials, it is every bit as important as the copy or visuals. It is often used as background to the announcer's copy or as a song or jingle that is integral to the ad.

Some examples of popular music used by commercials:

Allstate used "Never My Love" by the Associations

Best Buy used "Wait a Minute" by the Pussycat Dolls

Geico's "Caveman in the Airport" commercial used "Remind Me" by Royksopp

Diet Coke's "Loft" commercial used "I Like the Way" by the BodyRockers

Nike's "Warming up" used "Rock and Roll Ain't Noise Pollution" by AC/DC

Talbot's used "You're a Wonderful One" by Marvin Gay

Target used "Shape of Things to Come" by Mac Frost and the Troopers

Here are some ways you can put music to work:[12]

- *Backgrounds.* In many commercials, background music is used primarily to contribute to the mood. Appropriate music can establish the setting; then it can fade and become soft in the background.
- *Transitions.* Music can be an effective transition device to carry viewers from one setting to another. For example, the music may start out being sedate as the scene is peaceful. As it switches to the product being used, the music changes to rock and the tempo builds, marking the transition from place to place.
- *Movement.* Sound effects (SFX), natural sounds, and music can contribute to movement. Music that moves up the scale, or down, supports something or someone moving up or down.
- *Accents.* Music can punctuate points or actions. The "beat" of the music and visuals can match to hold viewers' attention and drive the commercial. Musical sounds—as little as a single note—can attract attention.

New or Old Music As mentioned earlier, some advertisers pay big money to professional musicians to develop a special tune or lyrics for a commercial or campaign. The previous wisdom was that original tunes could be cheaper. The cost of an original track ranges from $10,000 to $50,000 not factoring in residuals to singers and musicians. Licensing a hit song from an established act can range from $250,000 to more than $1 million. The superexpensive buys are what people talk about: Celine Dion's $14 million Chrysler deal, the $5 million "Start Me Up" for Microsoft, Bob Seger's "Like a Rock" for Chevy, Sting for Jaguar, or the Led Zeppelin association with Cadillac. These deals raise the bar in costs. However, there are countless smaller acts available for much less. "You have to have guts to buy songs no one has ever heard before," says Eric Hirschberg at Deutsch.[13]

Music can set the mood for a commercial. General Mills introduced Berry Burst Cheerios centered on the 1970 pop tune by the Partridge Family, "I Think I Love You." The song set the mood for the humorous television commercials.

Licensed music gains instant access to the listener's subconscious. It lets a brand such as Buick communicate trust and reliability with its use of "Stand by Me" by Ben E. King, which also worked the same way for Citibank. Or it lets McDonald's promote a folksiness with Randy Newman's "You've Got a Friend in Me," only months after it had gained fame in the popular family hit movie *Toy Story*.[14] Gap's khaki love fest, set to the tune of "Mellow Yellow" by Donovan unites baby boomers and Generation Xers in a nirvana of perceived coolness.

Whether you're using country, rock, or Latin, the tone of the music can help transfer drama, love, happiness, or other feelings to the viewer. It is a tool to cue the viewer's feelings. Original music can be written and scored for the commercial, or licensing of old or popular songs can be obtained, which can be very expensive. The least expensive music is stock music sold by stock music companies. It is cheap because it is not exclusive.

PRODUCING THE TELEVISION COMMERCIAL

The job of converting the approved storyboard is done by television production. There are three distinct stages to this process:

1. Preproduction includes casting, wardrobing, designing sets or building props, finding a location or studio, and meeting with agency, client, and production house personnel.

2. Shooting encompasses the work of filming or videotaping (although some digital cameras bypass tape) all scenes in the commercial. Several takes are made of each scene.

3. Postproduction, also known as editing, completion, or finishing, includes selecting scenes from among those shots, arranging them in the proper order, inserting transitional effects, adding titles, combining sound with picture, and delivering the finished commercial. Exhibit 19.8 shows a photoboard with the finished commercial.

In charge of production is the producer, who combines the talents of coordinator, diplomat, watchdog, and businessperson. Some producers are on the staffs of large agencies or advertisers. Many work on a freelance basis. The work of a producer is so all-embracing that the best way to describe it is to live through the entire production process. Let us do that first and pick up the details of the producer's job in the section headed "Role of the Producer."

Let us begin with the problems of shooting the spot, for which a producer appoints a director.

The Director's Function

As the key person in the shooting, the director takes part in casting and directing the talent, directs the cameraperson in composing each picture, assumes responsibility for the setting, and puts the whole show together. A director of a regional commercial will earn about $7,500 per day, and national commercial directors average about $13,000 per commercial; however, better-known directors may demand $25,000 to $35,000 per spot. The Source Maythenyi, an advertising and production database service, recently estimated that there are 4,000 specialized commercial directors and that doesn't include a growing number of feature film directors.[15]

The Bidding Process

There is only one way to provide specifications for a commercial shoot when you are seeking bids from production companies, and that is in writing. There is an industry-accepted form (AICP Bid and Specification Form). The agency and client provide information for this form. The use of this form ensures that all production companies are provided with identical job specifications for estimating production costs. It ensures that all bids are based on the same information.

The Preproduction Process

A preproduction meeting must be held prior to every production. The agency producer is expected to chair this meeting. The following agency, client, and production company personnel usually attend:

Brach's | "SINGING SMILES"
:30 TV SPOT

The Johnson Group created a 30-second TV spot for Brach's that introduced their "smile" packaging, showcased the variety of candies available, and reminded viewers of the company's history.

SPOT OPENS ON A WOMAN PUSHING A SHOPPING CART BY A DISPLAY OF BRACH'S CANDY BAGS. SEVERAL OF THE BAGS BURST INTO THE SONG, "When You're Smiling."

BAGS: *When you're smiling, when you're smiling...*

THE ENTIRE DISPLAY OF BAGS JOINS IN, AS THE WOMAN LAUGHS.

BAGS: *...the whole world smiles with you!*

A WOMAN CARRYING A BAG OF CANDY WALKS IN FRONT OF THE CAMERA.

GUMMI BAG: *When you're laughing...*

CUT TO TIGHT SHOT OF BIN OF CANDY SINGING, THEN THE ENTIRE DISPLAY JOINS IN.

BIN: *...when you're laughing.*

ALL BINS: *The sun comes shining through!*

CUT TO TWO BAGS IN A SHOPPING CART.

BAGS: *So keep on smiling...*

THE BAGS ARE PUT ONTO A CHECKOUT CONVEYOR BELT, AND THE BAG BOY PICKS ONE UP.

BAGS: *'Cause when you're smiling, baby...*

THE BAG BOY DROPS THE BAG OF CANDY INTO A GROCERY BAG.

MAPLE NUT BAG: *The whole world...*

THE CAMERA WHIPS UP TO AN UPSIDE DOWN BAG. THEN, PULLS OUT TO REVEAL A WOMAN POURING CANDY INTO HER MOUTH AND SMILING.

DOUBLE DIPPERS BAG: *Smiles with you!*

CUT TO END FRAME.

V/O: Brach's. Making smiles since 1904.

EXHIBIT 19.8

The Johnson Group introduced Brach's "smile" package. It also showcased the variety of candies available and reminded viewers of the company's history. The end frame says "Brach's. Making smiles since 1904."

Courtesy of The Johnson Group.

Agency: producer, creative team, account supervisor

Client: brand manager or advertising manager

Production company: director, producer, others as needed

The following points should be covered at every preproduction meeting: direction, casting, locations and/or sets, wardrobe and props, product, special requirements, final script, legal claims/contingencies, and timetable update.

In addition to covering the points just listed, the creative team and the director will likely present shooting boards and the production thinking behind the commercial. The shooting boards should be used for the following purposes:

- to determine camera angles
- to determine best product angles
- to project camera and cast movement and help determine talent status (extra versus principal)
- to determine number of scenes to shoot
- to determine timing of each scene

ROLE OF THE PRODUCER

Agency Producer

The producer's role begins before the approval of the storyboard. Conferring with the copywriter and/or art director, the producer becomes thoroughly familiar with every frame of the storyboard.

1. The producer prepares the "specs," or specifications—the physical production requirements of the commercial—to provide the production studios with the precise information they require to compute realistic bids. Every agency prepares its own estimate form. In addition, many advertisers request a further breakdown of the cost of items such as preproduction, shooting, crew, labor, studio, location travel and expenses, equipment, film, props and wardrobe, payroll taxes, studio makeup, direction, insurance, and editing.

2. The producer contacts the studios that have been invited to submit bids based on their specialties, experience, and reputation; meets with them either separately or in one common "bid session"; and explains the storyboard and the specs in detail.

3. The production house estimates expenses after studying specs, production timetable, and storyboard. Generally, a 35 percent markup is added to the estimated out-of-pocket expenses to cover overhead and studio profit. Usually, the production company adds a 10 percent contingency fee to the bid for unforeseen problems. The bids are submitted. The producer analyzes the bids and recommends the studio to the client.

4. The producer arranges for equipment. The studio may own equipment, such as cameras and lights, but more often it rents all equipment for a job. The crew is also freelance, hired by the day. Although the studio's primary job is to shoot the commercial, it can also take responsibility for editorial work. For videotape, a few studios own their own cameras and production units; others rent these facilities.

5. Working through a talent agency, the producer arranges, or has the production company arrange, auditions. Associates also attend auditions, at which they and the director make their final choices of performers. The client may also be asked to pass on the final selection.

6. The producer then participates in the preproduction meeting. At this meeting, the producer, creative associates, account executive, and client, together with studio representatives and the director, lay out final plans for production.

7. During the shooting, the producer usually represents both the agency and the client as the communicator with the director. On the set or location, the creative people and client channel any comments and suggestions through the producer to avoid confusion.

8. It is the producer's responsibility to arrange for the recording session. Either before or after shooting and editing, he or she arranges for the soundtrack, which may call for an announcer, actors, singers, and musicians. If music is to be recorded, the producer will have had preliminary meetings with the music contractor.

9. The producer participates in the editing along with the creative team. Editing begins after viewing the dailies and selecting the best takes.

10. The producer arranges screenings for agency associates and clients to view and approve the commercials at various editing stages and after completion of the answer print.

11. Finally, the producer handles the billings and approves studio and other invoices for shooting, editing, and payment to talent.

The "Outside" Producer

An **outside producer** is the person representing a production company whose entire business is filmmaking. The agency producer hires him or her to create the TV commercial according to agency specifications.

outside producer
The production company person who is hired by the agency to create the commercial according to agency specifications.

Shooting

Most productions consist of the following steps:

1. *Prelight.* This is simply the day (or days) used to set the lighting for specific scenes. To do this exclusively on shoot days would tie up the entire crew.

2. *Shooting.* This phase of the production process is the filming (or taping) of the approved scenes for the commercial. These scenes are then "screened" the next day (dailies) to ensure that the scene was captured as planned.

3. *Wrap.* This signals the completion of production. It is at this stage that most of the crew is released.

4. *Editing.* This takes place after the completion of the shoot. Scenes are screened and selected for use in the commercial. The scenes are then merged with a sound track, titles, and opticals, composing a completed or finished commercial.

The role of the client and account service at the shoot is one of advisor. It is really the creative's day, and it is their responsibility to deliver the spot. In situations in which the client needs to provide input on the set, the prime contact is the account representative or agency producer. The producer is generally the liaison between the agency and the director. This chain of command is simple and direct and eliminates confusion on the set, which is an absolute necessity when shooting.

Postproduction Process

Postproduction begins after a production company exposes the film in the camera at the shoot. The film that comes out of the camera must be developed and then printed onto a new strip of positive film called the *dailies*. The editor then screens these dailies and selects the good takes from the day's shooting.

The editor then physically splices the takes selected from each scene together with the next to create a *rough cut*, which is a rough rendition of the finished commercial. Once the editor has cut this film and the agency and client approve the cut, the editor takes the original film that was shot and developed and pulls the takes from that film that match the selected workprint takes.

Today, virtually all final edits, effects, and opticals are done on videotape using computers. The original camera film takes (35 mm motion-picture film) are transferred electronically to 1-inch videotape. During this transfer of film to videotape, the color is corrected.

The editor then takes this material into a video edit, in which each take is run on videotape and the *cut-in* through *cut-out* points for each take are laid down in sequence, from the first frame of the first scene to the end frame of that scene (to match the workprint), until the entire commercial is laid down from the color-corrected videotape matter (called the *unedited tape master*). Titles and other special effects are added during this final unedited-tape-to-edited-tape session. The sound (which the editor and agency had worked on along with the picture) is then electronically relayed onto the video-edited master, and the spot is finished. Sound complicated? It is. Just think of the steps involved in Exhibit 19.9. This was a unique way to create interest in the ballet. A shot of two unlikely ballet participants sitting watching television, cut to a close up of the guys' faces like a light is going off in their heads. Zoom back to see both standing in a semi-karate stance. And a fight-ballet begins—from shots of close ups to action shots simulating almost ballet form, which is a difficult thing to accomplish—until the end frame, "Atlanta Ballet."

Postdirectors are independent contractors in the production mix. They are in the business of cutting film and creatively supervising videotape transfers from

EXHIBIT 19.9

This spot has many shots and angles. In the editing, someone had to decide which part of each shot to use and what transition would take the viewer from one shot to the next. The flow of the fight had to come across as a simulated fight ballet.

Courtesy of Blattner Brunner.

film; supervising video edits and special effects; recording narration, sound, music, and sound effects; mixing these sounds together; relaying them onto the picture; and delivering a finished product to the agency.

Computer Postproduction Technology

The computer has revolutionized some aspects of print production and prepress activities and is also active in revolutionizing television postproduction. Advances in hardware and software are continuing to change the creation and production of television commercials. Names such as Silicon Graphics, Avid, Inferno, Flame, and Quantel's Henry and Harry have been mainstays for a number of years. Terms such as *3-D animation, compositing, morphing, 2-D animation, nonlinear editing, live-action compositing,* and *real time* are common among the professionals who generate visual images and special effects. The systems used for many special effects are still expensive. With any Mac, producers can develop many of the same video effects at a lower cost but usually at a slower speed. When discussing computer hardware and software, each system has a plus and a minus. However, the availability offers creative and production people more options to create unique visuals and commercials.

It is safe to say that today's **computer-generated imagery (CGI)** offers creative minds great new opportunities in production and postproduction. This technology allows creative people to squash, squeeze, stretch, and morph objects in less time than ever before. Computers are turning live action into cartoon action. At production facilities, creative talents can use digital-graphics/animation-compositing systems to top four or five layers of live action with five or six layers of graphics, all simultaneously, allowing the finished visual composite to be seen as it develops. A Motorola Razr phone spot opens with an attractive woman sitting in her stylishly spare home. It's clear she misses her boyfriend as she watches a TV displaying images of the couple. A moment later, she coolly smiles as an idea pops into her head. The woman closes her laptop and then everything around her magically starts to fold up and disappear. Finally, the floor beneath her folds away and transforms into a Razr that she picks up to her ear. Thinking this is pretty easy. The first thing the CGI people did was get "folding" defined. The effects process basically required reconstructing the entire spot in 3D so that it could be dismantled and then "transformed" into the Razr. The original footage was shot in Brazil.[16]

CGI Wizardry   Remember the Diet Pepsi cans having a wild party in a convenience store fridge while all the other drinks, including unmistakable cans of Diet Coke, complain about the noise? Or, the Budweiser Clydesdale who held the pigskin for the point-after attempt in the Super Bowl? Or the beer-slurpin' frogs? These are largely computer-generated (CG) or a mix of special techniques. The ability of animators and software engineers to imbue their characters with a greater sense of charm and warmth has made skeptics become computer converts. Now we have the ability to make photorealistic animals or monsters, for example. They look real, for the most part, only now they can do things no animal (or monster, for that matter) could be trained to do.

CGI and cel animation both play big roles in television commercial production. Costs of both are dropping, software is improving, and the proliferation of CGI has created a growing reservoir of artists, techniques, and trends. The classic Coca-Cola polar bears could exist only in CGI. Cost, however, is still a major factor in using CGI and is considerably higher than live-action budgets. "National spots are rarely budgeted below $250,000 for a 30-second commercial; they can easily reach $1 to $2 million on the high end for clients like Coca-Cola, auto companies, and other large corporations," says executive producer Paul Golubovich.[17]

computer-generated imagery (CGI) Technology allowing computer operators to create multitudes of electronic effects for TV—to squash, stretch, or squeeze objects—much more quickly than earlier tools could. It can add layers of visuals simultaneously.

Recently, we have seen in television production an awareness that CGI can be used to help create things that couldn't otherwise be created. Taking different techniques and marrying them into one cohesive unit is difficult, but with developing software, and more skilled people, the process becomes easier and more creative.

The combination of elements from two or more photographic sources often produces a striking effect. With the advent of computers, the process of combining different layers became much easier, but at the same time it is more complex because the variety of combinations is now seemingly limitless. You may have heard of some of the following electronic production tools and techniques:

- *Compositing.* In the digital realm, *compositing* is the umbrella term for many processes required to technically accomplish image combination in the computer.

- *Matte.* Essentially a silhouette in black and white matte is the necessary signal for the computer to cut out the part of the image intended to be visible. It can also exist in many other physical forms, such as a painting on glass or a masked-off camera composition.

- *Keying.* Keying is electronically composing one picture over another. The two types of keying are luminance and chroma-keying. This term came from the word *keyhole* and is interpreted by the computer as a signal enabling a hole to be cut in a clip layer.

- *Chroma-keying.* This is another matte derivation method in which the computer sources a specific color (usually green, blue, or red) to create a key signal. This is a way of performing automatic matte extraction, using the colored background. In a weather program that has a map and the weatherperson in front of the map, the map is an electronic image chroma-keyed off of a green screen. The weatherperson can't actually see the map without looking at a monitor. All that is actually behind them is a color screen. The computer interprets it as a hole and replaces the hole with the layer behind it, in this case a map.

- *Keyer.* A keyer is simply an electronic composer.

- *Morphing.* **Morphing** is an industry term for metamorphosing, which means transforming from one object to another. For example, in a Schick shaving spot, a man's head turns into a 3-D cube, and for Exxon a car turns into a tiger. This CG technique allows its operator to move between the real world and CG by electronically layering visual transitions between live action.

  The cost of morphs varies. They can range from $5,000 for a "garage" job using a PC up to $70,000, depending on the complexity. But meticulous advance planning remains the key to a successful job. A Schick shaving heads commercial, which morphed a series of six talking shaving heads and upper torsos, required a two-day blue-screen shoot, composited over a bathroom background.[18]

- *Harry.* The Quantel Henry/Harry online system is an editing device with an optical device tied to it. It allows computer composites to mix with live video. Ninety percent of Harry work can now be created on a Macintosh. The Harry is faster and much more expensive, but the Mac appears to be closing the gap.

- *Flame.* On the other hand, Flame is an optical device with an editing device tied to it. It functions as a high-capacity, random-access, multilayer compositing system, with video editing, effects, and digital-audio capacity. So you can see that you have to have the right technology for the right job. And, yes, it can be confusing to the nonproduction person in the advertising industry. A Visa "super heroes" spot featured a damsel-in-distress scenario. Thor wields his lightning-charged hammer through the sky. The Flame artist had to create the sky and Thor so it looked like it was going to rain, not storm.

morphing
An electronic technique that allows you to transform one object into another object.

eph | GAS VS. ELECTRIC TV SPOT

SFX: RUNNING WATER AND CLATTER OF DISHES.

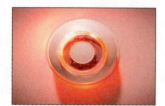

SFX: OMINOUS BLAST OF FURNACE STARTING UP.

AS IF CUED BY THE THERMOSTAT, SMOKE BEGINS WAFTING OUT OF THE MAN'S POCKET.

HE NOTICES SOMETHING IS AMISS.

VO: If you've got gas heat, you're paying almost twice as much to heat your home as someone with a new electric heat pump.

And gas prices just keep going up. So maybe it's time to switch.

THE WALLET SPONTANEOUSLY BURSTS INTO FLAMES.

VO: Unless you've got money to burn.

THE MAN FRANTICALLY WAVES AWAY THE SMOKE.

V/O: EPB Electric Power. Affordable comfort.

EXHIBIT 19.10

This spot has a special effect of smoke coming out of a man's back pocket because his wallet is on fire.

Courtesy of The Johnson Group.

- *In-house desktop.* Some agencies use computers to interface with video composers. This has made video editing, long the domain of highly trained specialists, a viable in-house option. This has allowed agency personnel to cut and paste video images just as desktop computers cut-and-paste print graphics. The quality isn't quite the level of the production houses' hardware and software, but it is getting closer and allows agencies to cut costs and use them for producing the storyboard, the animatic for testing, and rough cuts. It is uploaded or sent by DVD to the production company, where the spot is polished into a final commercial of broadcast quality. Those clients that do not need top-quality images can complete the entire commercial postproduction process on the system.

In this EPB Electric power commercial (see Exhibit 19.10), they had smoke coming out of the man's wallet in his back pocket. A simple request by the creative team, but what technique would you have used to get this special effect?

CONTROLLING THE COST OF COMMERCIAL PRODUCTION

The cost of producing a TV commercial is of deep concern to both the agency and the advertiser. The chief reason that money is wasted in commercials is inadequate preplanning. In production, the two major cost items are labor and equipment. Labor—the production crew, director, and performers—is hired by the day, and equipment is rented by the day. If a particular demonstration was improperly rehearsed, if a particular prop was not delivered, or if the location site was not scouted ahead of time, the shooting planned for one day may be forced into expensive overtime or into a second day. These costly mistakes can be avoided by careful planning.

Small Budget Spots

Bart Cleveland, a well-respected creative director and partner of McKee Wallwork Cleveland in Albuquerque, talks about creating quality commercials on a shoestring budget. Many clients' budgets don't live up to the size of national players. Here are a few of his thoughts.

> Great ideas don't have to cost a lot if you know what ideas cost to produce. Teach your creative people what production costs. If they understand the basic costs of production, they know their scope of possibilities within a budget. They won't waste time on ideas with large casts or incredible special effects. I've learned the hard way that an idea beyond its budget is a bad idea. It's just a brilliant thought lost to bad production quality. Few clients know how good quality happens but they can recognize the difference between good and bad. They will think their agency doesn't know what it's doing when they get bad quality and they will be right."[19]

Cost Relationship

Several areas that can have a dramatic impact on television production costs are the following:

- *Location or studio.* Is the commercial planned for studio or location? Location shoots, outside geographic zones, mean travel time and overnight accommodations for the crew, adding a minimum average cost of $7,500 per away day.
- *Talent.* The number of principals on the storyboard is important and can be expensive. The more people on camera in your commercials, the higher the talent residual bill. The rates for talent are based on the Screen Actors Guild (SAG) union contract. For national commercials, you can roughly estimate your talent cost per on-camera principal as .0015 percent of your media budget for the spot, that is, $15,000 per person per $10 million in exposure. If 20 on-camera people are involved in your spot, expect a $300,000 bill. That chunk of your budget may exceed the entire net cost of production. So it is important to discuss how many on-camera principals are planned for the spot and how many are absolutely necessary.
- *Residuals.* Another major expense is the residual, or reuse fee, paid to performers—announcers, narrators, actors, and singers—in addition to their initial session fees. Under union rules, performers are paid every time the commercial is aired on the networks, the amount of the fee depending on their scale and the number of cities involved. If a commercial is aired with great frequency, a national advertiser may end up paying more in residuals than for the production of the commercial itself. This problem is less severe for the local advertiser because local rates are cheaper than national rates. The moral is: Cast only the number of performers necessary to the commercial and not one performer more.

- *Special effects.* If the board indicated the use of special effects or animation (either CGI or cel), ask how the special effect will be achieved. It is not unusual for complicated CG effects to cost $6,000 to $12,000 per second and more! To prevent surprises, ask questions. What may appear to be a simple execution on the surface may contain extremely expensive elements. Neither the agency nor client should be satisfied until everyone understands the project. Anything short of this can result in surprise creative expenditures.

- *High Definition shooting.* Shooting in HD could increase costs by $10,000.

- *Estimate costs.* Given the potential complexity of shooting commercials due to a wide range of factors (location, special rigs, special effects, talent, set construction), it is not uncommon to believe a relatively "simple" looking spot presented in storyboard form will be "relatively" inexpensive. This is simply not the case. Both the client and the agency must always, always require a rough cost for each spot recommended. The number provided will help put the project into focus relative to the planned media support for the commercials. Generally, it is not uncommon for clients to spend 10 percent of their planned media budget in production. As this percentage escalates, the production decision becomes more difficult, particularly in today's economic climate.

- *Editorial fee cost.* There is a creative labor fee for the editor's service. This charge is for the editor's and assistant editor's time. Depending on the editor and the difficulty of the edit, a creative fee can range from $400 to $500 (to supervise sound only, for example, on a single-scene commercial) to more than $9,000 to cut a multi-image, complex spot with special effects manipulations and music.

- *The cost of film transfer and videotape conform or edit and finishing.* This cost can range from about $1,000 for this work, including tape stock and finished materials, to $7,500 for expensive and difficult treatments.

- *Special effects and titling.* This cost can range from $100 to make a title art card and include it in the edit session to $10,000 to $30,000 for heavy design, frame-by-frame, picture manipulations.

- *Recording and mixing.* The cost of recording and mixing a voiceover, music, and sound effects together can range from $450 to $4,000 or more.

If you total all these possibilities, from the combined lowest to the combined highest, the cost can be $2,136 to $67,100 to edit a 30-second commercial!

Unions and Cost

The last approved contract was in 2003. It was a three-year contract; however, it was extended until 2008. The Joint National Boards of SAG and the American Federation of Television and Radio Artists (AFTRA) approved the contract negotiated with the Joint Policy Committee on Broadcast Talent Union Relations (JPC) of the Association of National Advertisers (ANA) and the American Association of Advertising Agencies (AAAA), was ratified by the unions' 140,000 members. The contract was to expire on October 29, 2006, but it was extended for two years. It amounted to an up-front 5.5 percent increase in the industry's overall payment of wages and residuals, plus a 1 percent increase in employer contributions to the SAG and AFTRA pension and health plans. We mention this because the agreement affects production, residual payments, and total costs. It is also very complex and complicated. For example, the main session rate for on-camera principals is $535.00, the rate for on-camera groups of three to five is $391.65, and the rate for off camera groups is $226.90. Here is a snapshot of some of the areas covered, with rates and specifics:[20]

Program Class A Second Use for on-camera principals is $122.70, on-camera groups (three to five) is $113.70, and off-camera groups (three to five) is $226.90. The Third Use for on-camera principals is $97.35.

Program Class B/with New York market is $1,501.80 for on-camera principal, $644.70 for the three to five on-camera groups. However, without New York, on-camera principals are paid $825.60. If it is a Spanish language program, the on-camera principal rate is $1,932.00. The contract covers Stunt Adjustments, Ad LIB, and Hazard payments. It also states rates for casting and auditions, principals, general extras, hand models, body makeup/oil, costume fitting, interviews, location meal allowance, mileage allowances, meal period violations, travel time to and from the location. There are also mileage fees based upon the vehicle: auto, trailer, motorcycle. It also includes skates, skateboard, bicycle, moped. It specifies wet, snow, smoke, dust work extra compensation. And the advertiser also has to pay an additional 14.3 percent toward health and retirement contributions.

As you can see, the union negotiated just about everything. Exhibit 19.11 shows a spot featuring a dancing chimp as talent. They could have used stock film footage or the zoo's chimp. The contract covers animal use and payments. It is

EXHIBIT 19.11

Real Party features a dancing chimp. The cost and use of animals are not forgotten in the union pricing.

Courtesy of The Johnson Group.

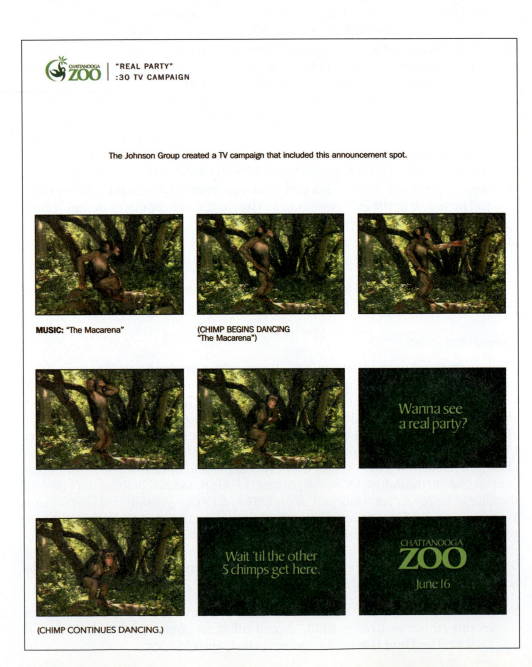

CHATTANOOGA ZOO | "REAL PARTY" :30 TV CAMPAIGN

The Johnson Group created a TV campaign that included this announcement spot.

MUSIC: "The Macarena"

(CHIMP BEGINS DANCING "The Macarena")

Wanna see a real party?

Wait 'til the other 5 chimps get here.

CHATTANOOGA ZOO June 16

(CHIMP CONTINUES DANCING.)

one of the reasons that it is sometimes cheaper to shoot commercials in other countries. Because almost all the professional talent in this country are members of one of the appropriate unions, an advertiser or agency must abide by these contracts or be blacklisted from all the available talent.

AFTRA represents actors, other professional performers, and broadcasters in television, radio, sound recordings, nonbroadcast/industrial programming, and new technologies, such as interactive programming and CD-ROMs.

A few other union advertisers are involved in one fashion or the other in the United States and Canada:

ACTRA—Alliance of Canadian Television and Radio Artists. A national organization of Canadian performers working in film, television, video, and all other recorded media.

AFM—American Federation of Musicians. The largest union in the world representing the professional interests of musicians.

DGA—Director's Guild of America. Represents members in theatrical, industrial, educational, and documentary films, as well as live television, filmed and taped radio, videos, and commercials.

There is a host of other nonunion organizations that may be involved in creating and producing commercials.

ASCAP—American Society of Composers, Authors and Publishers. Allows creators and publishers to receive payment for the use of their musical property and provides users of that music with easy and inexpensive legal access to the world's largest and most varied catalog of copyrighted music.

BMI. Source for the song titles, writers, and publishers of the world's most popular music—the BMI repertoire—in a searchable database of millions of items, updated weekly, together with the Web's most complete fund of information for and about songwriting and music licensing.

Television Production Cost Averages

The average cost to produce national television commercials in 2000 declined 3 percent for 30-second spots and 1 percent for commercials regardless of length, according to the AAAA's Television Production Cost Survey. Only two times in the 14-year history of the annual report, in 1995 and 1997, was a decrease reported. In actual dollars, the 3 percent decrease represented $11,000—the difference between the national thirty average cost of $332,000 reported in 2000 and $343,000 reported in 1999. For national commercials of all lengths, production cost decreased to $306,000 in 2000.[21]

Lower Production Company Costs/Directors' Fees and the Rise in Studio Shoots

The survey showed that, among other factors related to decreased costs, the average total production company net cost was $228,000 in 2000.

Directors' fees per 30-second commercial averaged $21,000 in 2000. In 1999, they climbed 16 percent. Shooting commercials in the studio increased to 19 percent, while combination (in studio and location) shoots decreased to 17 percent when compared to the previous study. When shot in a studio, a national thirty took an average of 13 hours, compared to 14 hours when filmed on location. An average of 18 hours was required to shoot a 30-second commercial shot both in the studio and on location.

In 2007, advertisers urged everyone from agencies and production companies to find ways of cutting production cost. Commercial production shooting days in Los Angeles generally range from about 5,650 to a little over 6,500 per year. The Entertainment Industry Development Corporation (EIDC) tracks this shooting day information.

DROP IN POSTPRODUCTION FEES

The 2001 survey found the average cost to edit and finish an original 30 decreased 2 percent to $42,000.

Creative/labor fees decreased by 8 percent, and music costs posted a 3 percent drop compared to a 35 percent increase in 1999. Video finishing remained the same whereas sound recording and mixing increased by 20 percent.[22]

Postproduction Management

Although the camera crew may be shooting in another country, your agency head-quarters may be on the opposite coast from the production company, and creative directors may be in transit, everyone needs to look at and approve the latest work (whether location, imagery, schedules, or treatments). There are several technology systems to allow consultation. For example, IOWA's WireDrive is used by many production companies/agencies to better manage projects online with all the cast of characters. It allows sharing of computer files and feedback of the commercial via a Web-based interface. Some of the production companies will put up location photos and storyboards as soon as they get a new job so clients and agency personnel can get involved from other locations. Clients only see their projects. Whenever new still images, QuickTime clips, or other materials are ready to be reviewed, a notification e-mail goes out. Since no one wants to download 10Mbs worth of data, people can view thumbnails, quickly accessible from any Internet dial-up or high-speed connection, and then click their computer for full details.[23] Clearly, times have changed as advertisers, production companies, directors, and agencies are all using different forms of digital links in the production process that save time, money, and travel.

ANA Guidelines for Achieving Cost Efficiencies in Television Production

Clients have their say in the television production cost issue. The 340 members of the Association of National Advertisers (ANA) represent more than 8,000 brands that collectively spend over $100 billion in marketing communications and advertising. "Producing effective television commercials is one of the most important—and expensive—parts of the marketing process," said Production Management Committee Chair and Manager, Advertising Production, Soni Styrlund, from General Mills, Inc. The ANA issues guidelines to its member companies for achieving cost efficiencies in television commercial production. The ANA's Production Management Committee created 15 guidelines covering a wide range of issues: For example, preproduction planning, bidding procedures, location shooting, rights negotiations, digital asset storage, and talent reuse considerations.[24] Highlights of the guidelines include the following:

1. *Formalize television production guidelines.* Prepare comprehensive guidelines that institutionalize best practices and establish expectations for all involved parties.

2. *Use a production expert.* Whether internal or external, project related, or ongoing, tap the know-how of an experienced production person.

3. *Set production budgets prior to creative development.* Establish up-front budget parameters for producing commercials as well as for testing them. Don't discourage the agency from presenting ideas that exceed the parameters, but insist on options that stay within the budget estimate.

4. *Set a realistic time line prior to creative development.* Clarify the airdate at the start of creative development so that a realistic time line can be prepared.

5. *Determine whether multiple bidding or single bidding is more advantageous.* Potential cost considerations need to be balanced against deadline constraints, time input, and overall process efficiency.

6. *Consider building individual spots into pools.* Pooling the production of similar ads can reduce shooting days, resulting in significant cost savings.

7. *Consider shooting in secondary U.S. markets as well as off-shore.* Cities outside the major U.S. markets can provide a wealth of professional talent as well as other untapped resources.

8. *Evaluate the number of shoot days required.* Consider shaving a production day and extending overtime and/or using a prelight day for product shots.

9. *Use cost-plus on specific categories.* Within a firm bid, convert certain expenses (e.g., crew, film, pension, and welfare, and location) to a cost-plus basis.

10. *Break out color-corrected packaging for hero product.* Use your design resource or internal capabilities to produce color-corrected packaging and mock-ups rather than paying agency or production company markups.

11. *Leverage the overall buying power of your company and your agency/holding company.* Use your clout to negotiate reduced rates for such services as talent payment, commercial distribution, element storage, and insurance.

12. *Manage roles and responsibilities during the process.* Limit the number of people involved in the production process. Empower one key decision maker to call the shots during prep and production.

13. *Establish a digital asset library to reuse and repurpose existing footage.* Create a centralized, Web-based storage facility for video, audio and logo assets. Before production begins, check this library to see what might be usable.

14. *Set up a profit center for music.* Actively claim and collect royalties for original music created for advertising. Be sure to negotiate retention of publishing royalties up front.

15. *Revisit talent payments and reuse often.* Considerable savings are possible via careful attention to talent use and rotation scheduling.

The Short Film

According to research companies, billions of videos are being streamed in the United States, but highly concentrated on a few large sites. It is clear that videos are changing Web advertising. It offers advertisers creative ways of reaching consumers using all the knowledge of television production, but without the limitations. On the other hand, just as television had to learn what worked, online films are still in a learning and experimentation curve.

Research indicates shorter ads (:7 to :10) that are designed specifically for online video opportunities create a better user experience and are driving publishers to continue to add in-stream advertising to their video content en masse.

New technologies and formats are developing (e.g., video chats with ads included, online games with video ads before and between scenes). And for advertisers lacking

ADVANTAGE POINT

Production Schedule

A typical complex production schedule for a finished computer commercial can cost more than $1.5 million and take 6 months to complete.

Production Schedule

Bidding Studio	Stage or Location Shoot without Special Effects	Special Effects Shoot
Includes:	2–3 Weeks	3–6 Weeks
• Screening directors' reels		
• Sending job specification		
• Bids (AICP form) returned		
• Bid comparison by agency		
• Estimating supplemental costs (music, travel, etc.)		
Preproduction	Stage or Location Shoot without Special Effects	Special Effects Shoot
Includes:	2–3 Weeks	3–6 Weeks
• Casting		
• Location search		
• Set design		
• Wardrobe fittings		
Shoot	Stage or Location Shoot without Special Effects	Special Effects Shoot
Roll camera	1–7 Days	1–7 Days
Postproduction	Stage or Location Shoot without Special Effects	Special Effects Shoot
Includes:	2–3 Weeks	4–10 Weeks
• Edit film		
• Film color correction		
• Post–special effects		
• Casting voiceover talent		
• Recording voiceover talent		
• Demo music		
• Music recording		
• Final audio mix and masters		

video assets, there are still ways to take advantage, including building Flash ads to play in video spots.[25]

SUMMARY ⚙

Television remains the most powerful advertising medium because of its ability to blend sight, sound, and motion to create emotional reactions. The time to communicate is very short—usually 15 seconds to 30 seconds—and creates a challenge for communicating the product story or position.

There are numerous creative techniques available to the creative team: testimonials, demonstrations, slice-of-life, interviews, humor, animation, serials, infomercials, and so forth. Research can aid the creative decision process in terms of which technique is appropriate for the strategy.

Storyboards are usually created to help communicate the idea to the advertiser and the production company. It is important that everyone clearly visualizes the same commercial before time and money are invested in the idea.

Developing commercials requires some understanding of production terminology such as wipes, dissolves, and close-ups that help communicate the nature of a particular visual or transition from one scene to the next. Writing and visualizing the commercial in simple and easy-to-understand terms are essential to success—it is, after all, a visual medium. Because bad production can destroy a good idea, producing the finished commercial is just as important as conceiving the big idea.

Producing the commercial involves three distinct stages: preproduction, shooting, and postproduction. CGI allows creative people to do almost anything they can imagine—but the cost may be high.

REVIEW ⚙

1. What is a bookend commercial?
2. What cost-relationship factors are involved in the making of a TV commercial?
3. What is the purpose of a storyboard?
4. Who attends the preproduction meeting?
5. What is a Harry?

CHAPTER 20

The Radio Commercial

n print and television, visuals are an integral part of communication. Radio is a different medium, one for ears alone. After reading this chapter, you will understand:

chapter objectives

1. the nature of the medium
2. how to create from a strategy
3. structuring the commercial
4. writing the commercial
5. musical commercials
6. producing radio commercials
7. unions and talent

Writing radio advertising should be easy. All you have to do is talk to someone about the product. Right? Well, maybe. Stan Freberg—comic, adman, great radio creator—was one of the pioneers of creative radio who created spots for the Radio Advertising Bureau: ". . . okay people, now when I give you the cue, I want the 700-foot mountain of whipped cream to roll into Lake Michigan, which has been drained and filled with hot chocolate. Then the Royal Canadian Air Force will fly overhead towing a 10-ton maraschino cherry." We'll leave the rest to your imagination, or you can hear the rest at http://radiohof.org/comedy/stanfreberg.html. Great radio advertising like this is actually very difficult. You need to awaken images in the listener's mind by using sound, music, and voices. Some do this simply by talking to the listener.

Nobody talks one-to-one better than Tom Bodett in commercial after commercial. Bodett's voice is the voice of Motel 6. He was a regular commentator on National Public Radio's popular news program in the 1980s, *All Things Considered.* Someone at The Richards Group ad agency heard Bodett and asked him if he'd be willing to use his voice talents as a deadpan radio bullfrog to market a national chain of economy motels. He agreed. Ad-libbing the tag line, "We'll Leave the Light on for You," in the very first commercial session gained success for the chain and for Bodett. He remains the spokesperson for Motel 6 after more than 15 years. And the tag remains the same. The campaign is one of the longest-running advertising campaigns and continues to win awards for its creativity and effectiveness in the lodging industry. One of his commercials, "Business Talk," makes fun of today's business language. It is written by Christopher Smith and speaks to the business traveler:

> Hi. I'm Tom Bodett for Motel 6, with a word for business travelers. Seems business has its own language these days. Full of buzzwords, Like buzzwords. Or Net Net.

The commercial goes on to name a multitude of business speak sayings: *outsource your accommodation needs, deliverables, matrix* of *actionable* items, *cost-effective,* and so on.

You'll get clean, comfortable rooms at the lowest price, Net Net, of any national chain. . . .

Then he puts an unusual twist on the traditional Motel 6 ending, "*We'll leave the light on for you.*"

I'm Tom Bodett for Motel 6. We'll maintain the lighting device in its current state of illumination.

The agency uses a little "disruption of the norm" to hold your attention despite a formula that has worked and is not tired. The concept is simple. The strategy and execution are superb.

THE NATURE OF THE MEDIUM

Despite media going through a revolution of sorts, radio has the power to achieve sales results and market impressions at a significant savings in cost. Satellite radio and podcasting are making finding an audience as tough as cable TV.[1] Radio gives you the time to tell a story. In print and television advertising, visual images can be powerful in attracting attention and full of emotion. Radio is different. There is no visual image or color to attract people to the message. Yet, sound messages can be powerful. Remember Freberg's maraschino cherry awakening images in the listener's mind. Some would argue that radio is the most visual medium, if you do your job right.

"In radio there's no place to hide anything. No place for mistakes, poor judgment, or weakness. Everything is right there in front of you for 30 or 60 seconds. Everything must be good for the spot to be good. The concept, copy, casting, acting, production—everything. One of them goes wrong, sorry, but it's tune-out time,"[2] says Copywriter Tom Monahan. Let us take a closer look at the nature of the medium.

Phil Cuttino, radio advertising expert, often refers to "watching radio—the most misunderstood medium." Before the beginning of widespread viewing of television in the mid-1950s, families used to "watch" the radio. We have all heard excerpts from radio's **theater of the mind**—*Superman, The Lone Ranger, Bulldog Drummon, Inner Sanctum,* and Orson Welles's fabulous spoof, *War of the Worlds.* People watched the radio because the mental imagery that came with every episode was breathtaking or scary or beautiful or just plain funny. However, television's combination of audio and visuals was very compelling and certainly effective as a storyteller and theater. Television also was, and is, a dynamic advertising medium. Unfortunately, radio was subordinated to the position of music, talk, and other audio-oriented programming.

theater of the mind
In radio, a writer paints pictures in the mind of the listener through the use of sound.

ANNCR:	Due to the highly technical nature of Hangers new dry cleaning process, the following commercial message is being translated.
KIRK:	Hi, I'm Kirk Kinsell, president and CEO of Hangers Cleaners.
ANNCR:	I'm Kirk and I'm da man at Hangers.
KIRK:	At Hangers, we've revolutionized dry cleaning by using liquid carbon dioxide instead of harsh chemicals.
ANNCR:	We've plowed a boatload of money into R&D so your clothes won't stink.
KIRK:	It's the same carbon dioxide that puts bubbles in soft drinks. Only now, we're using it to clean clothes.
ANNCR:	Our new dry cleaning process is kickin'.
KIRK:	Given the molecular properties of CO_2, only 74 BTUs are required to vaporize one pound of liquid.
ANNCR:	I don't have the foggiest idea what he just said.

KIRK: As a result, there's no need to worry about heat-set stains, fading colors, or shrinkage.

ANNCR: You'll look good. Really good.

KIRK: Bring your dry cleaning to Hangers. We'll keep your clothes looking, smelling, and feeling like new.

ANNCR: We can't wait to clean your clothes.

TAG Morrisville up to 5/6:   Join us Saturday, May 6, for our Grand Opening in Morrisville. Cary Parkway and Highway Fifty-four.

Lower Priority Among Creatives

Despite being attacked as dead, the 30-second television spot remains key in developing impact in many ad campaigns. The short film on the Web may be gaining favor, but the fastest way for a creative team to get noticed is probably to create a highly noticed television spot. In major publications, there are commentaries on television commercials, as well as objective and subjective ratings. Television is the closest way that ad people come to "show biz." Another contributing factor to radio's lowly position in the creative pecking order is the fact that most creative teams consist of art directors, designers, and copywriters. Because radio has no material visuals, the visual arts people are out of business when it comes to radio. This tends to lead the creative team to print, television, or interactive media.

Over time, a new type of radio commercial has emerged, which Cuttino calls "print radio." When radio is needed, some copywriters, who are experienced in print advertising but know little about radio, tend to fall back on a familiar copy format. As a result, we hear "print radio" all the time. There is a headline, a subhead, body copy, a logo, and a slogan—an audio newspaper ad.

To understand the importance of radio, you need to understand the cynical nature of the American consumer.

No one believes anyone anymore. American consumers are searching for an excuse to disbelieve what you are saying. All they need is a cue that you are trying to sell them something and they will blank you out mentally. They may not change the dial, but this is a case of "the lights are on, but nobody's home." Before you can tell consumers your story, you must disarm them, entertain them, amuse them, and get them on your side.

Radio, like magazines, is a very personal medium. Almost everyone has a favorite radio station. Many consumers listen to Net radio online where some stations use broadband and streaming video content. Consumers get to know the radio personalities; they attend events sponsored by their radio station. It is this kind of listener allegiance, this nonhostile environment, that makes it easier for marketers to approach the listenership. Remember, consumers are not waiting to hear your commercial. They are listening to the radio for entertainment, so entertain them and then sell them. Entertainment is your admission ticket to their consciousness.

The future is uncertain for traditional radio. The Internet has challenged traditional radio in the home and office, but radio has maintained its dominance in the car. Digital satellite radio brings more challenges to local radio and advertisers.[3]

FLEXIBILITY, MARKETABILITY, AND PROMOTIONABILITY

Radio offers more than other advertising media. It has the flexibility, the marketability, the promotionability, and the price to fit advertisers' needs to reach their targets—if they choose the right stations and use the right message.

- You have 60 seconds all to yourself. Print ads have to fight for attention with other ads on the page. Television has to contend with channel surfers because viewers have favorite television programs, whereas radio listeners have favorite radio stations. In the time span of a 60-second radio commercial, no other advertising can interfere with your message. The main equalizer in radio is the ability of a locally produced radio spot to be on a level playing field with any national spot. The power of a radio commercial is the idea, the imagery. Unlike television, national-quality production can be easily created for a reasonable cost. Your advertiser can be as big as any other marketer for 60 seconds.

- Radio has the most captive audience of any media. The advent of mass transit has not changed the fact that in most cities, to get from point A to point B, you still have to get in your car and drive. The heaviest radio listenership occurs in the morning and afternoon drive times. During that time, listeners cannot go to the kitchen for a beer, answer the door, or pick up a magazine. They are trapped in their cars, listening to the traffic report, the news, and your radio commercial.

- Listeners and advertisers have many programming formats to choose from: country, adult contemporary, news/talk/sports/business, oldies, top 40, religion, classic rock, urban rhythm and blues, easy listening, alternative rock, variety, ethnic, classical, gospel, jazz, new age, and preteen. This makes radio a highly selective medium for the advertiser. Reflecting the ethnic multinational nature of our society, there also are foreign-language stations in many markets available to advertisers.

CREATING THE COMMERCIAL

Radio commercials are developed through a thought process similar to that used in other media despite requiring a different style of advertising. As with any advertising, you have to understand your target. As Tom Little, award-winning creative director, once said, "People don't buy products. They buy solutions to problems." Last year people bought about 350,000 quarter-inch drill bits in this country. People didn't want quarter-inch drill bits. They wanted quarter-inch holes.

The radio creative writer has to refer back to the objectives and strategy and describe the target in both demographic and psychographic terms before beginning the creative process. The writer needs to be sure the message is going to be believed—that it says the right things to the right people—and needs to ask if the copy strengthens the brand position, the place the advertiser wants to occupy in the consumer's mind. Is it credible? Does the writer have all the copy points that research indicates is needed? Is it human? Is it believable communication? Do people really talk like that? Or is it simply copy lingo? These are some of the things the radio copywriter must think about when sitting down to the blank page or the computer screen.

The writer for radio has the opportunity to develop an entire commercial alone (although in some agencies a creative team may work on a project). That means writing the script, picking the talent, and producing the commercial. In radio, the copywriter enjoys the freedom to create scenes in the theater of the listener's imagination by painting pictures in sound—a car starting or stopping, a phone ringing, water running, ice cubes falling into a glass, crowds roaring, a camera clicking. Remember, sound alone has an extraordinary ability to enter people's minds.

Here, Steven Lang, creative director, former agency copywriter, radio producer, and voice talent, uses imagination to sell antiques:

Steven H. Lang

Creative Director *Southern Broadcasting*

Steven H. Lang

*W*hat makes a good radio commercial? It produces the desired results for the client. That is the only true measure of success. Not awards or compliments. Just results. Anything else is a failure. So how do you create a successful radio commercial? You observe the following methods as a template and build the rest of the ad around them.

Listening to people talk only about themselves can be extremely tedious. You try to get away as quickly as possible, don't you? So why do most radio commercials center on the client rather than on the listener? Radio can be such an engaging medium, yet most clients want to turn it into a brag fest. "We have the biggest this!!! We have the most that!!! We're number one in blah blah!!!" Yawn. Click. So what should you do? Change your focus.

Instead of making the client the subject of the ad, make the listener, or how the listener can benefit, the subject of the commercial. People, by nature, are self-interested. So by speaking about subjects of interest and importance to them, they'll naturally pay more attention. Talking to someone is always better than trying to talk at everyone. This doesn't mean just using the word *you* all the time but also fashioning a commercial the listener can identify with by showing both a problem and a solution. However, in our overcommunicated world, just getting the listener's attention and holding it can be an arduous task. So take them to the theater.

A runaway asteroid in deep space. High noon on the streets of the Old West. On a street corner during rush hour. With a few sound effects and a couple minutes in a studio, you can create any environment of sounds from the past, present, or future. Then you sit back and wait for your listeners' imagination to fill in the pictures. By using theater of the mind to involve the listeners in your commercial, they are more apt to follow your message and relate to your product or offer. Video and computer animation can also create these types of environments, but you lose the process of engaging the imagination, and it is much more expensive and time consuming. However, it takes more than just theater of the mind to get your message across.

You must also be sure that they'll hear it again and again and again.

Repetition plays a huge part in the success of a radio commercial. Even a poorly written ad can increase effectiveness to some degree by increasing repetition. Why? "Because sound is intrusive," says Roy H. Williams, a sales and marketing consultant. He notes, "While driving, how many times have you turned down the radio while trying to find a street or turn? How many songs do you know by heart, though you've never set out to learn them?" The intrusive nature of radio, combined with repetition, makes an extremely effective method of getting your message across.

With proper subject focus, theater of the mind, and sufficient repetition, you can stand out from the clutter with radio commercials that get results. As radio programming and sales legend Dan O'Day noted, radio is mass salesmanship.

Courtesy of Steven H. Lang, Creative Director, and Southern Broadcasting.

Forum Antiques 60

Descending drum roll followed by symbol.
A dirty white snowball full of fangs and claws rolls down the steps and splatters against the wall into three white tiger cubs; two brothers, Keno and Kibo and a sister, Kari.

Turn of the century music
Keno and Kebo reform into a smaller snowball and roll off down the hall, while Kari strolls into the dining room containing a cherry corner cupboard. Already over fifty years old, it's still in perfect condition. Kari ambles over, sniffs around the base, raises up her front legs, and extends her soon to be fearsome claws. Down the corner cupboard she drags them, with little cherry shavings curling to the floor. A knock at the door distracts her, and as she ambles into the kitchen a man named Mister Ringling is walking out the door with Keno and Kebo under his arms. Kari runs after them only to be cut off by a slamming screen door.
(slam) Followed by mournful Fiddle
So she simply stands there and mews ferociously.
No one will ever know what became of that rare white tiger cub but the claw marks she left remain on that beautiful eighteen thirties cherry corner cabinet. See them for yourself at Forum Antiques, seven sixty north chase street. Two floors and who knows how many stories.

Let us look at the three elements the copywriter uses to create mental pictures, memorability, and emotion: words, sound, and music and jingles.

Words

Words are the basic building blocks of effective radio commercials. They are used to describe the product, grab attention, create interest, build desire, and evoke a response from the listener. As with the success of Motel 6, the warmth of the human voice may be all that is needed to communicate your message.

Here, Dow's Great Stuff tongue-in-cheek football commercial says:

ANNC:	(tongue-in-cheek delivery, background music) Every autumn Nate Turner embarks on a mission to explain football to women. Patiently he tries to clarify the West Coast offense. And why it is normal for one man to pat another's fanny. Maybe this year he'll break through.
YOUNGER GUY:	(more serious) Think that's a waste of energy? You should see what your home is doing! Get Great Stuff insulating foam sealant. It fills the cracks where heat and cold air escape. Look for Great Stuff in the red and yellow can anywhere home improvement products are sold.

Sound

Used properly, sound can unlock the listener's imagination and create feelings. Any sound effect used should be necessary and recognizable; you should never have to explain it for the audience.

The sound has to convey a special message or purpose; it has to attract attention and complement the words. Sound can underscore a point; create feelings of suspense, excitement, or anger; and invoke almost any mood you desire.

There are three basic sources of sound effects: manual, recorded, and electronic. Manual effects are those that are produced live, either with live subjects or with studio props; opening doors, footsteps, and blowing horns are examples. Recorded effects are available from records, tapes, or professional sound libraries. They offer the copywriter almost every conceivable sound—dogs barking, cats meowing, leaves blowing, thunder crashing, cars racing. Electronic effects are sounds that are produced electronically on special studio equipment. Any sound created by using a device that generates an electrical impulse or other electronic sound is an electronic effect.

Music and Jingles

Music can be very powerful in catching the listener's attention and evoking feelings. Thus, music has been called the "universal language." Different kinds of music appeal to different emotions: A minor key is sadder than a major key; an increased tempo creates a sense of anticipation. We'll talk more about music a little later.

Commercials are often set to music especially composed for them or adapted from a familiar song. A few bars of distinctive music played often enough may serve to identify the product instantly. Such a musical logotype usually lasts from 4 to 10 seconds. **Jingles** have been a popular means of making a slogan memorable—think of the music for Coca-Cola, Pepsi, Chevrolet, and McDonald's over the years—but are not as popular at this moment.

When Bob Garfield, the editor-at-large for *Advertising Age*, talks about old advertising jingles, it's not long before he breaks into song. "Oh, I wish I were an Oscar Mayer wiener," he sings, not entirely out of tune. "I remember that stupid jingle," he says. "But I don't remember what I had for breakfast, where my car keys are and what my kids' names are." That's the power of the jingle, feels Garfield. Just mention Oscar Mayer and suddenly there's a relentless tune—at once pleasing and irritating—crossing the lips, if only silently.

Despite that potency, though, ad jingles are on the wane, overtaken by pleasingly familiar commercial standbys like the Rolling Stones's "Start Me Up," which Microsoft enlisted to sell Windows. Advertisers say they're totally out, gone the way of Atari 2600s, indoor smoking, and Libyan bellicosity. The jingle, however, may be poised for a comeback, say some advertisers, agencies and pop-culture watchers. Why? Well, for one thing, no one can deny its power.[4]

Plop plop, fizz fizz—oh, what a relief it is!

Folk's Southern Cooking Cous Cous jingle version says:

> Now hold the capers and the sun dried tomatoes
> Hold the Cous Cous and those tarragon potatoes
> When I'm in the mood for some comfort food
> Nobody knows me like my Folks.

Madison Avenue is turning to music stars to pen original ditties for commercials. When Ford executives looked to launch its "Bold Moves," including licensing an old hit for their spring 2006 campaign, they explored many musical options, listening to demo tapes of unreleased songs. Ford selected an unreleased song, "Go," cowritten by the first *American Idol* winner, Kelly Clarkson, because it fit the mood and tempo the automaker wanted. To date, Clarkson's fans could only download it legally from a Ford-sponsored website, addictedtokelly.com.

Collaborative Music Alliances

Alternative rock band *They Might Be Giants* is behind catchy songs in Dunkin' Donuts ads. Country singer Toby Keith has just composed a new song for Ford's pickup truck. And hip-hop artist Jadakiss has written raps for sneaker-maker Reebok International Ltd.[5]

Advertisers are using this music trend to try to reach the 18-to-25 market because people this age make brand choices that can influence their buying decisions for life. This group doesn't want in-your-face sales pitches, industry observers said; it wants fresh music.

Ad agency Leo Burnett invited country music star Jo Dee Messina to its offices as part of its "Artist in Residence" program, in the hopes of using her songs in ads. The program was started in 2005, and has welcomed artists from the entire music spectrum.

jingle
A commercial or part of a commercial set to music, usually carrying the slogan or theme line of a campaign. May make a brand name and slogan more easily remembered.

Gone are the days when signing over song rights to marketers was looked down upon by artists and fans alike. "Advertising is the new radio," says Rob Swartyz, executive creative director at TBWA\Chiat\Day, in a sentiment echoed around the ad music industry. This new collaborative environment means that the music industry may no longer charge astronomical fees (which ranged from $10,000 into the millions for a popular song), especially if the marketer is willing to work with the artist in many venues, including concert promotion.[6]

Create from Strategy

The Charleston Metro Chamber of Commerce used a strategic creative idea in print, television, and radio. It was the meeting "name tag." The message (reasons to join) was written on the tag along with the name. Exhibit 20.1 shows the print. But the radio copy included the same message. "Judith. I joined the chamber for lots of reasons. But the one that really attracted me was their Center for Business Research. It provides me with info that I could never afford to track down on my own. Like current economic trends. Economic forecasts. It let me know what's happening and what's about to happen. That helps me make good decisions. Like a magic eight ball that really works. Charleston Metro Chamber of Commerce." A simple integrated idea with big results.

Recently, the Slinky coil toy brought the Slinky jingle heard on television since 1963 to radio. The new campaign introduced a different version of the jingle. It begins in the traditional, sing-song manner, but then it shifts into a faster rock-like rendition. The lyrics remain basically the same, just shifted around a bit. In an attempt to integrate the brand, the Slinky website (poof-slinky.com), had downloadable wallpapers and information on the jingle, as well as its advertising and history. Despite limited media exposure, there was an attempt to integrate the brand. The newer version of the Slinky jingle maintains the core feeling of the original. Mom will recognize it from the past, but it is a little more modern so today's kids can better relate to the radio commercial.[7] Below is the new version of the 30-second radio lyrics:

EXHIBIT 20.1

"Hello, My Name is Judith"

An integrated message for radio, TV, and print.

Courtesy of Charleston Metro Chamber of Commerce.

What walks downstairs
Alone or in pairs
And makes the happiest sound?
Everyone knows it's Slinky
It's Slinky, it's Slinky
For fun, it's a wonderful toy
It's Slinky, it's Slinky
It's fun for a girl and a boy
A spring, a spring, a marvelous thing
It makes a 'slinkity' sound
Everyone knows it's Slinky

DEVELOPING THE RADIO SCRIPT

You will find some differences in the formats used in the script examples in this chapter. This is because most agencies have their own format sheets for copywriters. Formats also vary according to how the script will be used: If you are going to be in the studio with the producers and talents, you can verbally explain how the script is to be read or answer any questions that come up. If, however, you are going to mail the script to DJs to be read live, you need to be certain that anyone reading it will understand exactly what you want. The guidelines shown in Exhibit 20.2 illustrate explicit script directions.

Radio, Theater of the Mind

One of the biggest mistakes you can make in creating radio is the failure to recognize the fact that everyone has mental images of sounds that they hear. When no material images exist, sound creates an image in the mind's eye. It is the duty of the radio writer/producer to take control of the listener's imagery and guide it to a positive reaction that seeds the memory with the targeted message and leads to the proper response. For instance, a writer creates a commercial featuring a car dealer who is screaming about a sale, assuming that the tactic will get the listener's attention and will

EXHIBIT 20.2

Example of Radio Form Directions

Length: 60	
Job No. 3364	
LEFT SECTION OF PAGE IS FOR INFORMATION RELATING TO VOICES, ANNOUNCER, MUSIC, SOUND, USUALLY IN CAPS.	The right section of the script consists of copy and directions. It should be typed double-spaced. Pause is indicated by dots (...) or double dash (— —). <u>Underline</u> or use CAPS for emphasis.
MUSIC:	Music is usually indicated by all caps. WILLIAM TELL OVERTURE ESTABLISH AND FADE UNDER. In some cases, music is underlined. Directions may be indicated by parentheses ( ).
VOICE #1:	(LAUGHING LOUDLY) Excuse me sir...
OLD MAN:	Yes... (RAISING VOICE) What do you want?
SFX:	SUPERMARKET NOISES, CRASHING NOISES AS SHOPPING CARTS CRASH. Sound effects indicated by SFX: (:08) BUZZER
SINGERS:	He's bright-eyed and bushy-tailed...
ANNCR:	This indicates announcer talking.
VO:	Voice Over

EXHIBIT 20.3

Peterman Painting

This commercial is simply focused on professional painters, with a little alliteration. Playing with Ps for fun and attention.

Courtesy of Steven Lang of Southern Broadcasting Companies and VoiceUnders.com.

*Peterman Painting : 30

*   Steve Lang

Pondering the possibility of painting? Then perhaps you should pick Peterman Painting. The people of Peterman Painting are painting professionals. Perpetrating perpetual painting perfection has allowed Peterman Painting to proper and profit. Possibly paintable property includes homes, businesses, and rental property. Peterman Painting also pleases its patrons' purses. Pick the professional painters particularly prestigious people prefer to pick–Peterman Painting on the Newton Bridge Road.

eventually lead the consumer to the dealership because of the "incredible savings." Unfortunately, the mind's eye of the listener doesn't see a sleek new car or the money saved; the listener sees a middle-aged man in a garish plaid suit yelling. In communications, it is important to be concerned about how people feel about your advertisement.

The late creative director Tom Little used to brag about radio's ability to paint pictures in the mind, "I had to spend $40,000 to build an airline set for our television ads, but I could build that same set in the minds of radio listeners for almost nothing."

The Elements of a Good Radio Commercial

- *Be single-minded, focused.* Don't ask the consumer to take in too much information at one time. Prioritize your copy points. Think of your commercial as a model of our solar system. The major copy point is the sun and all the other copy points are planets of varying degrees of importance, but they all revolve around and support the central idea (see Exhibit 20.3).

- *Research your product or service.* Many clients keep tabs on their competition, but they rarely relate their features and benefits to factual data. Meaningful statistics can give substantial support to your message.

- *Relate to the consumer.* When you tell consumers your story, always relate the brand to their wants and needs. Do not assume they will come to the right conclusion. At the Retreat it is your house and your rules (see Exhibit 20.4).

- *Generate extension.* You can multiply the effect of your commercial many times over by achieving extension—consumers picking up phrases from the spot and using them. A clever phrase or execution can have consumers asking other people if they have heard the spot, people requesting the spot to be played on the radio, and even DJs mentioning the spot.

- *Produce an immediate physical, emotional, or mental response.* Laughter, a tug on the heartstrings, or mental exercises of a consumer during a radio spot help seed the memory and aid message retention.

EXHIBIT 20.4

Retreat/Synovus Mortgage Company

Courtesy of Steven Lang of Southern Broadcasting Companies and VoiceUnders.com.

*The Retreat : 30

*   Steve Lang

Barking/shushing sfx
Female This is Kelly and Scooby. Kelly is trying to sneak Scooby into her new apartment that doesn't allow pets. Too bad Kelly didn't move into The Retreat most talked about student community. At the Retreat, indoor pets are welcomed in the craftsman style cottages. And with private yards, Kelly wouldn't have to worry about where Scooby does what <u>Scooby</u> will do. The Retreat. Your house. Your rules. Male: Learn more at retreat dot com. Brought to you in part by Synovus Mortgage Company, Equal Housing Lender and a Georgia Residential Mortgage Licensee.

■ *Use plain, conversational English.* Be a clear communicator. Don't force your characters to make unnatural statements. This is not the boardroom—no "execubabble," just clear, plain, and simple English.

WRITING THE COMMERCIAL

Some agencies have a special creative director in charge of radio advertising. For years, the feeling has been that agencies have assigned junior talent to write radio commercials. It is now hoped that having a specific person in charge of radio will generate enthusiasm for doing great radio. Some agencies have special units that focus only on radio, such as Hill Holiday Radio, a division of Hill Holiday Advertising.

There are radio boutiques that have been used for many years by clients and agencies to help create and produce radio commercials. Some of the most popular boutiques include World Wide Wadio, Radioland, Right Brain Visions, and Funny Farm Radio Hollywood. Funny Farm Radio says, "We encode your existing audio/video, or create and produce with you, create a custom branded MiniRemote to your specs, and stream it on your website or send it to your (clients') customers in emails. And make you look good to gadzillions."

The radio commercial, like the TV commercial, has as its basic ingredient the promise of a significant and distinctive benefit or position. Once the promise has been determined, you are ready to use the arsenal of words and sounds to communicate your product. Ways to vitalize the copy include the following:

■ *Simplicity.* The key to producing a good radio commercial is to build around one central idea. Avoid confusing the listener with too many copy points. Use known words, short phrases, and simple sentence structure. Keep in mind that the copy needs to be conversational. Write for the ear, not the eye. Get in the habit of reading your copy out loud.

■ *Clarity.* Keep the train of thought on one straight track. Avoid side issues. Delete unnecessary words. (Test: Would the commercial be hurt if the words were deleted? If not, take them out.) Write from draft to draft until your script becomes unmistakably clear and concise. At the end of the commercial, your audience should understand exactly what you have tried to say. Despite having several facts in your commercial, make sure you have the big idea.

■ *Coherence.* Be certain that your message flows in logical sequence from first word to last, using smooth transitional words and phrases for easier listening.

■ *Rapport.* Remember, as far as your listeners are concerned, you are speaking only to them. Try to use a warm, personal tone, as if you were talking to one or two people. Make frequent use of the word *you.* Address the listeners in terms they would use themselves.

■ *Pleasantness.* It is not necessary to entertain simply for the sake of entertaining, but there is no point in being dull or obnoxious. Strike a happy medium; talk as one friend to another about the product or service.

■ *Believability.* Every product has its good points. Tell the truth about it. Avoid overstatements and obvious exaggerations; they are quickly spotted and defeat the whole purpose of the commercial. Be straightforward; you want to convey the impression of being a trusted friend.

■ *Interest.* Nothing makes listeners indifferent faster than a boring commercial. Products and services are not fascinating in themselves; the way you present them makes them interesting. Try to give your customer some useful information as a reward for listening.

■ *Distinctiveness.* Sound different from other commercials and set your product apart. Use every possible technique—a fresh approach, a musical phrase, a particular voice quality or sound effect—to give your commercial a distinct character.

ADVANTAGE POINT

The Sound Production Company

Here are three excerpts from sound production companies' Web sites appealing to advertisers and agencies. They discuss their capabilities in terms of studio equipment and writing, voice talent, directing, production, etc.

STUDIO CENTER

Established in 1966, Studio Center was one of the first production companies to specialize in broadcast advertising. It has eighteen studios in Los Angeles, Las Vegas, Virginia Beach/Norfolk, and Memphis. Each production studio is equipped with Pro Tools and either Yamaha O2R, Soundcraft, or Mackie boards. It matches talent with microphone, choosing from tube-type Neumann U-67s and U-87s; TLM-103s, 170s, and 193s; Rode NT2s; Sennheiser shotguns; and Audio-Technica 4060s.

Their Digital Network

Studio Center has taken the potential of ISDN technology to the limit. With WorldNet Tokyo Enhanced APT-X, WorldNet APT-X 100s, Telos XStreams, Telos Zephyrs and Musicam codecs, it can connect with virtually any studio in the world. Audio sessions are routinely conducted with talent located at multiple Studio Center locations at no additional cost to advertisers or agencies.

Studio Center has more than 150 nonunion talent under exclusive contract. Plus, it has hundreds of specialty performers, access to worldwide talent, union voices, and production for full signatory compliance. Studio Center produces more than 14,000 audio projects every year.

FAMOUS RADIO RANCH

So you gave birth to a great radio script—at least it sure looks like it on paper. Now you need experienced creative sharpshooters whose aim will be amazingly on target for great production. Well, dude or dudess, you've come to the right place.

Spanish Language Services

Amidst the ever-increasing din of English and Spanish-language radio and television advertising, an artfully crafted humorous or dramatic radio spot becomes a breath of fresh air. Following the same "reach-out" guidelines that the Famous Radio Ranch has established over the years for English language advertising audiences, it is now successfully reaching the Spanish language market.

KAMEN ENTERTAINMENT

Studio A is the flagship of Kamen Entertainment's five state-of-the-art recording studios. The recording booth is specially designed for recording both individual voice-overs and singers to large ensembles and bands. The control room is large enough to sit ten people, very comfortably. It has armed Studio A with a 64-track Pro Tools digital audio workstation (loc to pix) loaded with plenty of computing power and a dazzling selection of effects and digital signal processing. To control this production powerhouse, it has installed a 32 fader, fully automated, digital ProControl console to make mixing a breeze. Extra amenities include an iMac with a high-speed T1 Internet connection and wireless internet (Wi-Fi) for its producers' laptops. And don't forget, it has the biggest lava lamps you've ever seen! ■ ■ ■

Some Techniques

Basically a medium of words, radio—more than any other medium—relies heavily on the art of writing strong copy. However, just as print ads and TV commercials include pictures and graphics to add impact to the copy, radio creates mental pictures with other techniques. Radio copywriters can choose among many proven techniques to give more meaning to the copy, to help gain the attention of the busy target audience, and to hold that attention for the duration of the commercial. Some of these techniques parallel those used in television.

- *Humor.* Humor is an excellent technique for service and retail businesses. Consumers never relate an ad to the advertising agency that produced it; they only relate the spot to the advertiser. Therefore, humor can portray a company as friendly, likable, and easy when negotiating a sale. The Hangers Cleaners spot was not intended to break you up laughing. But each uses subtle "disruption" to raise a chuckle and make the commercial(s) memorable.

  Many award-winning radio spots use humor. Tom Little said humorous spots often won awards because they stood out from the hundreds that he had to listen to. If that's true, then the same probably works for consumers. Humor may be part of any writing technique we have discussed. Humor is often appropriate for low-priced packaged products, products people buy for fun, products whose primary appeal is taste, or products or services in need of change-of-pace advertising because of strong competition. Be very careful about making fun of the product or the user or treating too lightly a situation that is not normally funny.

- *Emotion.* This is an effective method to use when the topic is emotional. Family, health care, donations, mental care, security, and similar products and services use emotion to stimulate the targeted response.

- *Music and sound effects.* Music creates the mood, and sound effects create the imagery in the consumer's mind. Jingles can be very memorable and effective when they relate directly to the product or service.

- *White space.* This is a term used in print advertising. However, white space in radio can be extremely compelling. A 60-second spot may start with music or sound effects with no copy for 45 seconds, bringing the consumers' curiosity into play and leaving them wide open to accept a provocative message.

- *Dialogue.* This is a great technique to use in many situations. Dialogue doesn't confront the consumer; it allows the listener to eavesdrop on the conversation. Dialogue is also very successful when the advertiser has a product that appeals to men and women. Dialogue between a man and a woman allows the commercial to play to both targets. Loco's casual restaurant plays with the name of a product and dialogue to generate interest and name recognition (see Exhibit 20.5).

- *Sex.* It can sell very well.

- *Straight announcer.* Sometimes the simplest approach works best. In this commonly used and most direct of all techniques, an announcer or personality delivers the entire script. Success depends both on the copy and on the warmth and believability of the person performing the commercial. Tom Bodett for Motel 6 is all these things and one of the reasons the commercials are still so popular. This approach also works particularly well when a positive image has previously been established and a specific event is being promoted, such as a sale.

- *Combination.* Radio techniques may be mixed in countless ways combining music, sound effects, an announcer, and a person. You might notice that the advertisement uses the name of the product five times in interesting ways to gain brand recognition. To select the right technique for a particular assignment, follow the guidelines discussed in Chapter 19 for selecting television techniques.

*Loco's : 30

*　　　　　Steve Lang

Voice 1: Welcome to Loco's Deli and Pub
Voice 2: Give me the biggest thing you've got.
Voice 1: Ok. Coming right up.
Voice 2: So what is it?
Voice 1: The Biggest Thing We've Got is a half pound of roast beef, ham, turkey, American cheese and fixings.
Voice 2: What's it called?
Voice 1: The Biggest Thing We've Got.
Voice 2: Yes.
Voice 1: That's it's name.
Voice 2: Yes is it's name?
Voice 1: No, The Biggest Thing We've Got is.
Voice 2: All I want is . . . oh nevermind! Just give me grilled reuben, chips, salsa, and a drink and tell me what the damage is.
Voice 1: That's a totally different sandwich and totally different commercial. For The Biggest Thing We've Got, Reuben, the Damage, pool, darts, and drink specials, come to Loco's on Baxter, East and Westside.

TIMING OF COMMERCIALS

Time is the major constraint in producing a radio commercial. Most radio stations accept these maximum word lengths for live commercial scripts:

- 10 seconds, 25 words
- 20 seconds, 45 words

In prerecorded commercials, you may use any number of words you can fit within the time limit. However, if you use more than 125 words for a 60-second commercial, the commercial will have to be read so rapidly that it may sound unnatural or even unintelligible. Remember, if you insert sound effects, that will probably cut down on the number of words you can use. If you have footsteps running for 5 seconds, you are going to have to cut 10 to 12 words. You need to time the musical intros and endings or sound effects because each will affect the number of words allowable. It is not unusual to go into the recording studio with a script that is a couple of seconds short because the extra time allows the talents to sound more natural. Actors need some breathing room to sound sincere.

MUSICAL COMMERCIALS

Music can be a powerful tool for getting your product remembered. As musical writer Steve Karman has said, "People don't hum the announcer."[8]

In writing musical commercials, you have to start with an earthquake, then build to something really big. In other words, there is no room for subtlety. The thought process and strategy are different from those in regular songwriting.

There are three main elements to writing commercial music:

1. *Intro:* The beginning of the song. The tempo and lyrics may be established here.
2. *Verse:* The middle of the song. This is where the message is developed. There may be several verses.
3. *Theme or chorus:* May be the conclusion of the song.

Often you begin with the chorus to establish your theme, or you may repeat the theme throughout. The theme is what listeners remember. Some musical forms, such as blues, can be thought of as both verse and chorus. A theme may serve as a musical logotype for a product, lasting about 4 seconds to 10 seconds.

Sheri Bevil of Lane Bevil+Partners says, "Folks restaurants hired Jack Turner to do an original score and lyrics for a number of jingles. Usually the radio opens with one of the jingles. Then the promotional message goes over the bed of music (usually an announcer). Then it ends with another jingle. The jingle takes up 28 to 30 seconds leaving another 30 seconds for the specific message." In some cases, Bevil says, "The spot would also end with a 5- to 10-second tag."

Southern Boy Version: Folks Southern Kitchen
I've been a southern boy all my life
Got a Southern drawl and a Southern wife
When I'm in the mood for some comfort food
Nobody knows me like my Folks.

Many commercials are composed especially for the advertiser or product. Others are simply adapted from a familiar song. A melody is in the public domain, available for use by anyone without cost, after its copyright has expired. Many old favorites and classics are in the public domain and have been used as advertising themes. That is one of their detriments: They may have been used by many others.

Popular tunes that are still protected by copyright are available only by (often costly) agreement with the copyright owner. An advertiser can also commission a composer to create an original tune, which becomes the advertiser's property and gives the product its own musical personality.

Do you have the talent to write a jingle? Does the typical copywriter have the ability to do so? In general, the job of writing such copy is left to the music experts.

Audio Technology

As you use your iPod, you are aware of the radical change in the way music and sound are recorded and downloaded. A little more than a decade ago, the world of high-fidelity multitrack recording (and sync-to-picture for television) belonged solely to record companies, postproduction houses, and commercial ventures.

In the early 1990s, software was created for the Macintosh that allowed true four-track recording and simultaneous musical instrument digital interface (MIDI) file playback. The simple interface was based on the integrated portable studio metaphor and required no sophisticated knowledge of the software. It looked and functioned like a four-track mixer/recorder, but it turned any Macintosh into a CD-quality production environment. You know what's happened since then. You can now purchase software for $300 that will give you the professional studio sound. And many bands and companies use even less expensive software that works on any computer.

It is easy to record your basic ideas digitally from the very beginning, and add and edit digital audio tracks to your composition. You can then use the software to transfer the master digitally to a digital audiotape (DAT) or CD. Today, every step in the multitrack production of digital audio is in the hands of the individual. For example, here are some of the technology options offered by Studio Center:

Choose from real-time delivery via ISDN, distribution with DGS, digital delivery as a .wav, .aiff, or .mp3 file via e-mail or ftp posting. Digitally, we can send your audio via the internet as an .aiff file, .wav file, or .mp3 file. We can also upload your files to our ftp site for you to retrieve at your convenience. Fully produced spots may be transmitted for electronic distribution to radio stations via DGS. You have a format choice of audio CD, CD-ROM, DAT, Zip Disc, Beta, Reel or Cassette.

METHODS OF DELIVERY

There are three ways a radio commercial can be delivered: live, by station announcer, and prerecorded.

The Live Commercial

A live commercial is delivered in person by the studio announcer, disc jockey, newscaster, or other station personality, or perhaps by a sports reporter from another location. Although generally read from a script prepared by the advertiser, the commercial is sometimes revised to complement the announcer's style. If time allows, the revised script should be approved in advance by the advertiser. Ad-libbing (extemporizing) from a fact sheet should be discouraged because the announcer may inadvertently omit key selling phrases or, in the case of regulated products such as drugs, fail to include certain mandatory phrases.

Some commercials are delivered partly live and partly prerecorded. The prerecorded jingle, for example, can be played over and over with live-announcer copy added. Sometimes the live part (the dealer "tie-up") is left open for the tie-in ad of the local distributor.

One advantage of the live commercial is that the announcer may have a popular following, and listeners tend to accept advice from someone they like. For example, *The Steve and Vikki Morning Show* is the top-rated morning show in Atlanta. Vikki does endorsement commercials for Intimacy. "I'm Vikki Locke. Like most women I spent years wearing the wrong bra size until one day a friend told me about Intimacy. . . ." Steve McCoy talks about how his family breathes better because he installed a Pureatech air treatment system for his home. They both have a big following and bring credibility to their spots. Generally, the other big advantage is cost: Station announcers usually do your commercials free of extra talent costs, although some announcers may demand higher rates.

Word of Mouth: Live Radio Endorsements A new approach of audio product placement is alive and well in radio and gets high marks for effectiveness. The thought is that polished or scripted commercials don't penetrate the consumer's psyche. Let's look at an example:

> At Star 94-FM in Atlanta, Steve and Vickie gab on-air about a comedian. Out of the blue, Steve says, "Maybe you can suggest she could use a Swiffer WetJet at home. Vickie responds by telling the audience how she sponged up spilled soy sauce last night. With the Swiffer WetJet," she sings songs, "it was so easy and fast to clean." For 2 1/2 minutes, which included an amusing debate on how long dropped food can linger on the floor before it becomes inedible, they name the product a combined eight times. The WetJet paid the station for a 60-second commercial and compensated the disc jockeys. But they got 90 seconds of freebies.

The media ad placement company, Varson Group, specializes in "word-of-mouth" endorsements. The DJs are provided with talking points (copy guide) with facts and tidbits about the product. Three on-air mentions by name per segment are encouraged. Exaggeration—this shampoo has changed my life—is not as effective with other kinds of product placement, and this technique is not without criticism. However, Vickie Locke of Star 94 says she declines numerous offers, and her rule of thumb is: "If I don't use it, or don't like it, I don't do it." Steve McCoy agrees, and adds "The beauty of live endorsements is that at times they fit right into the show."[9]

Station Announcer

For a campaign dealing with a retail offer that will change frequently, advertisers often use a station announcer reading copy written by the agency. This is recorded at the station at no charge to the client—sometimes even with the client's musical theme in the background. This type of delivery allows for frequent changes in copy at no cost.

The Prerecorded Commercial

Advertisers undertaking a regional or national campaign will not know local announcers' capabilities. In any case, it would be impractical to write a separate script to fit each one's particular style. Commercials for these campaigns are, therefore, usually prerecorded. Not only does this assure advertisers that the commercial will be identical each time it is aired, but it also allows them to take advantage of techniques that would be impractical in a live commercial. (Actually, in many instances, "live" commercials are recorded by the station so that they can run even when the announcer is not on duty.)

Talent and Unions

As with television, the use of and payment to performers appearing in radio commercials are dictated by the American Federation of Television and Radio Artists (AFTRA) commercial contract. Talent is paid a session fee when the commercial is recorded. Other requirements for payment based on usage include spot, network, dealer, demo, copy testing, and foreign use. It is another cost the advertiser must consider.

The complexity of the 2003 to 2006 (extended until 2008) union contract can be seen in the following list or in its entirety at AFTRA.org. For example, minimum session fees are as follows:

Actor, announcer, sole, duo is	$235.40
Group singer/speaker	173.40
Then there are the use fees:	13 weeks
Network program commercial	$1,029.30
Regional network program	770.75
Outside New York, Chicago, or Los Angeles	235.40
New York alone	350.40
Chicago or Los Angeles alone	319.60
Any two of the above	429.80
Demo/copy test	162.20
Additional hour	40.55

PRODUCING THE RADIO COMMERCIAL

Although there are certain broad similarities, producing radio commercials is far simpler and less costly than producing TV commercials. First, the agency or advertiser appoints a radio producer, who converts the script into a recording ready to go on the air. After preparing the cost estimate and getting budget approval, the producer selects a recording studio and a casting director, if necessary. If music is called for, the producer calls a music "house" that usually composes, arranges, and takes all steps necessary to get the finished music. If the music is not a big-budget item, the producer may call for "stock" music (prerecorded and used on a rental basis).

After the cast has been selected, it rehearses in a recording studio, which can be hired by the hour. However, because most commercials are made in short "takes" that are later joined in editing, a formal rehearsal is usually unnecessary. When the producer feels the cast is ready, the commercial is acted out and recorded on tape. Music and sound are taped separately and then mixed with the vocal tape by the sound-recording studio. By double- and triple-tracking music and singers' voices, modern recording equipment can build small sounds into big ones. However, union rules require that musicians and singers be paid extra fees when their music is mechanically added to their original recording. After the last mix, the master tape of the commercial is prepared. When final approval has been obtained, duplicates are made for release to the list of stations.

Steven Lang uses VoiceUnders.com, which is an online audio resource, to get voices from coast to coast and even across the "pond," from the United Kingdom. He sends them a script and they send him an MP3 in return. If necessary, they talk and redo. It is pretty simple.

Things to Remember During Production

Often the account executive or client will be at the recording session; however, Phil Cuttino has a bias against having either of them at a recording session. He feels their presence creates too many problems, which can inhibit great production. Among these are the talent and engineer tighten up, and everyone is concerned about time instead of producing an effective spot. He suggests that you use a phone patch from the studio to play the spot for the account executive first. Then, with his or her blessing, call the client for the final approval. The engineer and talent should remain in the studio until the final approval is achieved. Some other production thoughts:

- *Call ahead.* Have the studio pull the music and sound effects selections.
- *Studio.* Find a studio that has several talented engineers who will quickly learn your style. Make sure the studio has a good SFX and music library and the latest technology.
- *Brain power.* During production, use everyone's brain to make the spot better. Ask for input from your engineer and voice talent. Remember, they probably have been involved in more spots in a week than you have in months.
- *Take your time.* Don't push the talent or engineer. Lead them to what you want.
- *Keep up with the technology.* New technology will always broaden your creative envelope.
- *Casting.* Acting professionals usually have the best and most believable voices because they are visualizing the scene. This is particularly true with dialogue or group scenes. Go to plays often to find new talent. Do not look at the people who are auditioning for a part in the spot. They will try to sell you with facial expression, body language, and hand motions—all worthless on radio. At first, allow talent to give you their own interpretation of the scene. You may be inspired by their rendition.

EXHIBIT 20.6

Georgia Mountain Fair

Courtesy of Steven Lang of Southern Broadcasting Companies and VoiceUnders.com.

---

*60ca
*Steven Lang

The morning sun sparkles off Lake Chatuge as you stand gazing over the threshold of history—ready to take a step back over a hundred years; into the pioneer village of the forty-eighth annual Georgia Mountain Fair. As you stroll down the paths, you see folks quilting, squeezing cider, blacksmithing, and even making moonshine. You walk past the old school house and log cabin wondering what it was like to live back then. Suddenly you're snapped back to the present as the sounds from the children's midway fill your ears, and you begin browsing the Georgia Mountain Fair's crafts and exhibits, marveling at the skill and patience it takes to create such works of art. As you come to the Anderson music hall, you wonder what kind of shows are on tap today—fiddlin', a pageant, clogging, gospel music, or maybe a country music legend. Heading out the gate, you take a minute to watch the sun sink below the mountains and pack away the memories of a relaxing day away from it all at the Georgia Mountain Fair, August fifth through the sixteenth at the Georgia Mountain Fairgrounds in Hiawasse. Learn how to get away for a day, call seven zero six eight nine six forty-one ninety-one.

Steps in Radio Production

We may summarize the steps in producing a commercial as follows:

1. An agency or advertiser appoints a producer.
2. The producer prepares cost estimates.
3. The producer selects a recording studio.
4. With the aid of the casting director, if one is needed, the producer casts the commercial.
5. If music is to be included, the producer selects a musical director and chooses the music or selects stock music.
6. If necessary, a rehearsal is held.
7. The studio tapes music and sound separately.
8. The studio mixes music and sound with voices.
9. The producer sees that the master is prepared for distribution on appropriate medium and sent to stations.

You are on the air!

SUMMARY ✹

Radio can be visual, despite its lack of visuals. It paints a picture in the listener's imagination and truly becomes a theater of the mind. Words, sound effects, and music are the tools of the radio copywriter. The biggest limitation is that the radio copywriter is always working against the clock.

It is the duty of the radio writer and producer to take control of the listener's imagery and guide it to a positive reaction that seeds the listener's memory with the targeted message and leads to the proper response. The power of a radio commercial is the idea imagery.

When developing a commercial, it is important to keep it simple and concentrate on one main idea. Repetition of the main selling ideas is considered necessary, but the main thing is to get the listeners to remember the brand and message. Some of the writing techniques and formats include straight announcer, slice-of-life, jingle-announcer, customer interview, and humor.

As with television, all performers appearing in national commercials are subject to union compensation agreements.

REVIEW ✹

1. Why is radio called the theater of the mind?
2. Briefly summarize the elements of good radio commercials.
3. What is white space in radio?
4. Name four radio station programming formats.
5. What are the three main elements to writing commercial music?
6. What are the steps in radio production?

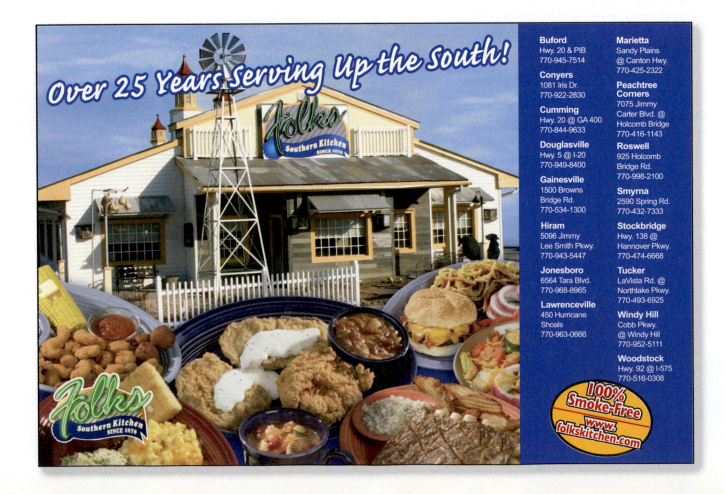

Trademarks and Packaging

Brand names and naming are not something to take lightly. Product names and trademarks are very important to brand equity, brand identity, and the marketing process. In today's market, advertising and packaging must support each other. After reading this chapter, you will understand:

chapter objectives

1. what a trademark is
2. protecting the trademark
3. forms of trademarks
4. general trademark rules
5. the process for developing memorable names
6. packaging and marketing
7. packaging and research

The brand name is one of the most important assets of a company, and the trademark is the brand's asset. A name communicates the essence of a company, product, or service, forming the foundation of any brand. It creates the images and associations in a consumer's mind. Today, naming presents a formidable challenge because legally available names that are clear, distinct, and memorable are in short supply. There are millions of registered trademarks in the United States alone. If you attempt to come up with a corporate or product name, you may decide there are no appropriate new names left to claim. The wrong choice may lead to charges of trademark infringement if you pick a name owned by someone else. Once you have the right name, you must protect it.

THE INVESTMENT IN A NAME

Consider the financial investment in a name. In 2007, AT&T merged and changed the name of BellSouth (a huge former Ma Bell company) and Cingular (the 6-year-old wireless leader) brands into the AT&T brand. The newspaper announcement read: "BellSouth, Cingular, AT&T. Joining together for the way you live." The body copy read, "The dependable services of BellSouth, the wireless coverage of Cingular and the global reach of AT&T are coming together to bring you America's most complete and secure network. TV, broadband, phone and wireless—all working together for the way you live and work." It took over $4 billion to make Cingular the largest wireless company. What will it take to make Cingular's customer think positive of AT&T (an old brand) in the same way? Or, the BellSouth customer? Or, do they care as long as their services work?

Let's look at it in longer terms. Consider the trademark of Coca-Cola, a brand invented in 1886. Think of the corporate and financial loss if Coca-Cola lost the exclusive right to its trademark. It is not impossible for companies to lose that right. It is for this reason that they go to great lengths to protect their trademark with a special staff who monitor all use of the brand(s) to protect their investment. Companies such as Coca-Cola have become so concerned about their brand image, use, and reputation on the Web that they have taken steps to prevent, or at least monitor, what's going on in cyberspace. Coke has brand cop lawyers. Some spend their time surfing the Web, tracking repeat offenders, and writing cease and desist letters centered on Coke brand abuses, online and off line. Many of these cases are first investigated by Coke's trade research department. The nature of such infractions is studied to determine the need for legal action by the corporate legal department. They ask interlopers to stop using the Coke brand or trademark. Among the most common types of online brand abuses are the following:[1]

- Unauthorized use of logos and images
- Use of a company's name on a competitor's site
- Unauthorized framing, in which a website appears within another site
- Domain abuse and parody sites
- Unauthorized use of a company's name or product in metatags
- Diverting users away from a website by hiding key words in background text

All companies face the same threat to their brand and trademark, which we will talk about later in this chapter.

AN OVERVIEW

Today, a brand name not only has to be memorable, distinctive, easy to pronounce, and durable, but it also has to work globally. That takes more than a large vocabulary and a thesaurus. There are actually naming specialists who make a science of knowing the origin and esoteric meaning of words. In some cases, they also study the emotional reaction to certain sounds. They study naming trends and clichés, spelling and pronunciation ambiguities, and know expedient ways to conduct legal searches and acquire trademark protection. If it is to be a global name, they look at potential foreign language problems. Graphic experts may participate in the naming process because the graphic expression of the name often determines its success or failure in the marketplace. Although the ultimate reason for settling on a certain name may be purely subjective, it's usually tested to see the reactions of the target or users.

From Corporate Identity to Brand Identity

The first book dedicated to trademarks was published in 1924. A trademark established the character of a company and influenced the appearance of a product. Gordon Lippincott, founder of Lippincott & Margulies (now called Lippincott Mercer), coined the term *corporate identity* in 1943 to encompass all the ways a company identifies itself, from a new corporate name and logo to the color of its buildings. Today, the corporate mark is still the cornerstone of an identity program, but it involves much more. Partially due to technology and expanding avenues of communication, corporate identity has become an all-encompassing discipline that embodies the corporate personality, history, reputation, and vision. The best corporate programs closely associate the logo with what a company stands for. The Islas Secas Resort in Panama logo reflects the corporate brand identity and brand image (see Exhibit 21.1).

Most people associate Volvo with safety, even though nothing in the logo or name (which means "rolling") directly conveys that attribute. A few years ago, research indicated that consumers thought Volvo cars were too boxy and staid. As a result, Volvo began to migrate its branded image by making sleeker cars and adding attributes such as high performance to safety. But the logo hasn't changed.

EXHIBIT 21.1
The Islas Secas Resort in Panama trademark reflects the corporate brand identity and brand image.
Courtesy of Idea Engineering, Inc. & Islas Secas Resort.

Although a logo can connect a company to its attributes and positioning in the marketplace, it can't do the job alone. A brand identity system can. The visual identity is the better known part of the brand identity system. It uses the elements of the corporate identity system but is wider and deeper. The building blocks of the system include a company's name, trademarks, tagline, and logo. It also focuses on the elements that come together in almost any communication: imagery, typography, design, color, and consistent message. It may include a system that maps different communication vehicles (e.g., brochure, Web site, direct mail, and CD-ROM) to audience content and production values. Education and training may play a part in the system.[2] Without a consistent and cohesive approach to brand identity, a company's communications may not generate the desired results.

There are also digital issues. Lippincott Mercer, a brand-consultant company that currently helps manage identity (including Advanta, Nissan, Samsung, McDonald's, Borders, Citibank, Fresca, Medco, Olive Garden, Coca-Cola, and Ameriprise Financial), believes that globalization and consolidation will continue as major business trends for many years to come. As a result, advanced communications and information technologies, such as the Internet, and company intranets, will provide firms with bold new avenues for delineating and projecting their corporate and brand identities.[3]

A LITTLE HISTORY OF TRADEMARKS

Lanham Act

There were few trademarks used on general merchandise prior to the Civil War. In 1870, the rapid growth in trade identity gave rise to the first federal trademark law. Lacking sufficient legislative safeguards, concerned manufacturers met in 1878 and founded the United States Trademark Association. Its name was changed to the International Trademark Association (INTA) in 1993. This organization promoted the enactment of the Trade-Mark Act of 1881 and revisions in 1905 and 1920. In 1946, Congress passed the Lanham Act. It defined a trademark and expanded the concept of infringement, permitted the registration of service marks, provided incontestability status for marks in continuous use for five years, and provided that federal registration of a trademark would constitute "constructive notice of the registrant's claim of ownership thereof."

In 1996, President Clinton signed the Federal Trademark Dilution Act passed by Congress. It provided owners of famous trademarks with a federal cause of action against those who lessened the distinctiveness of such marks by the use of the same or similar trademarks on similar or dissimilar products or services. Unlike trademark infringement, a dilution action does not require proof or likelihood of consumer confusion. An amendment was added later that year in the form of the Anticounterfeiting Consumer Protection Act of 1996.[4]

Patent and Trademark Office and Technology

In 2000, the agency once known as the Patent and Trademark Office was renamed the United States Patent and Trademark Office (USPTO). The USPTO reviews all trademark applications for federal registration and determines whether an applicant meets the requirements for federal registration. Owning a federal trademark registration on the Principal Register provides several advantages, for example:

- Constructive notice to the public of the registrant's claim of ownership of the mark
- A legal presumption of the registrant's ownership of the mark and the registrant's exclusive right to use the mark nationwide on or in connection with the goods and services listed in the registration
- The ability to bring an action concerning the mark in federal court
- The use of U.S. registration as a basis to obtain registration in foreign countries
- The ability to file the U.S. registration with the U.S. Customs Service to prevent importation of infringing foreign goods

WHAT IS A TRADEMARK?

trademark
Any device or word that identifies the origin of a product, telling who made it or who sold it. Not to be confused with a trade name.

logotype, or **logo**
A trademark or trade name embodied in the form of a distinctive lettering or design. Famous example: Coca-Cola.

We have said that brands are among the most valuable assets a marketer has. When a product is manufactured and a brand is created, it must be distinctive from the competition. There are several types of company and product identifications. The **trademark**, also called a brand name, is the name by which people can speak of the product. Very often a trademark will include some pictorial or design element. If it does, the combination is called a **logotype** (or simply a **logo**). Exhibit 21.2 shows the Folks logo.

Trademarks are proper terms that identify the products and services of a business and distinguish them from the products and services of others. Specifically, a trademark is a word, design, or combination used by a company to identify its brand and to distinguish it from others, and it may be registered and protected by law. Trademark formats can include letters, numbers, slogans, geometric shapes, pictures, labels, color combinations, product and container shapes, vehicles, clothing, and even sound.

Trademarks can also be termed *service marks* when used to identify a service. In general, a trademark for goods appears on the product or its packaging, and a service mark is used in advertising to identify the services.

The logo design is an extremely important element in the successful marketing of a product. It is difficult to sell a product until a reasonable level of name recognition

EXHIBIT 21.2
This is the current design scheme used by Folks.
Courtesy of Lane Bevil+Partners.

is achieved among consumers. The creation of a logo is so important that a number of firms have been established whose primary function is the design of logos, packages, and corporate identity. Most designers attempt to forge a compatible relationship among the package design, logo, and advertising for the product. A strong logo on the package and in product advertising creates an environment of recognition. Folks wanted a Folks ToGo logo to be used for more than take out. It would be used on products to buy from their stores or on the Web including such items as: salad dressings, BBQ sauce, fried green tomato kits, etc. One idea for the Web was to have the ToGo logo on a truck that would drive across the screen to create movement and on shipping boxes, etc. Exhibit 21.3 shows the evolution of the design process for that design.

Logo designs come in several basic forms including abstract symbols (the apple used by Apple Computer) or logotypes, a stylized rendition of a company's name. You can also use a combination of both. Promoting an abstract symbol can prove very costly and isn't recommended for a small budget. Such logos are also harder to remember. Logotypes or word marks are generally easier to recall. If you use an abstract symbol, it should be used in connection with the business name. Some advertising agencies design logos for clients themselves. Some of the mega-agencies may have sister companies that specialize in this area of brand development. In many cases, the corporation takes responsibility for the process. Professional design firms will charge anywhere from $4,000 to $15,000 for a logo alone. Research and development of corporate identity programs may cost as much as $150,000. Keep in mind that there are thousands of independent designers around who charge from $20 to $150 per hour, based on their experience. As a rule of thumb, a good logo should last at least 10 years. If you look at the amortization of that cost over a 10-year period, it doesn't seem so bad.

Every successful organization tries to develop an intriguing logotype. Sansum Clinic's logo (see Exhibit 21.4) was a challenge to Idea Engineering. What we mean is a logo that is distinctive enough to project the visual personality of the organization. A Sansum Clinic isn't a bottle of BBQ sauce. Its goals are different. The logo must be applicable to all Sansum communications—letterheads, envelopes, brochures, Websites (sansumclinic.org), newsletters, etc. It must work in all integrated marketing formats.

EXHIBIT **21.3**

The evolution of the ToGo design. There are slight changes in each of these designs.

Courtesy of Lane Bevil+Partners.

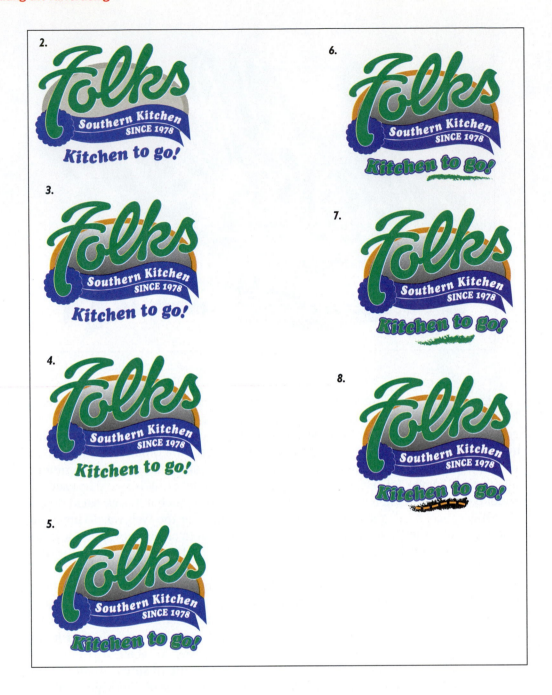

Trademarks should not be confused with trade names, which are corporate or business names. General Motors, for example, is the trade name of a company making automobiles whose trademark (not trade name) is Buick. The terms *trademark* and *trade name* are often confused. **Trade names** are proper nouns. Trade names can be used in the possessive form and do not require a generic form. Many companies, however, use their trade names as trademarks. For example, Reebok International Ltd. is the corporate name, and Reebok may be used as a trade name, as "Reebok's newest line of athletic shoes is for children." Reebok also is used as a trademark: "Are you wearing Reebok athletic shoes or another brand?"

If you're confused, think of yourself as a new product. Your surname is your trade name (e.g., Lane, Smith, Bevil). Your gender is the product classification (Female Lane, Female Smith, or Female Bevil). Your given name then is the brand

trade name

A name that applies to a business as a whole, not to an individual product.

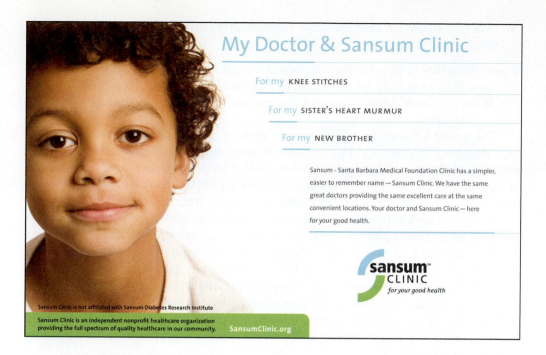

EXHIBIT 21.4
This logo has to work in all communication formats. Check out sansumclinic.org which shows television commercials.

Courtesy of Idea Engineering, Santa Barbara.

(Lois Lane, Judy Smith, Sheri Bevil) because it distinguishes you from other family members (like Sarah Bevil).

Some personal names (as with product names) may sound the same but may have different spellings—Sherry, Sherri, or Sheri, or even Cheri (Kwik-Draw, Quick-Draw, Kwic, Kwik, Quick). Or they may simply be very familiar names— Jennifer, Jane, Jessica, Sarah, Hanna, Emily (or Jeff, Steven, Robert, Tom, Wade, Greg)—or clearly distinctive, like Ruhanna (or unusual like Hudson or McCall). Yet, distinctive names may appear difficult to read or pronounce. Companies and products have a similar problem. They want names that can easily become familiar to consumers, yet be easy to read, easy to pronounce, and easy to remember.

General Electric's Naming Process

"You don't walk away from a tag line on a whim," Beth Comstock, former corporate vice president and chief marketing officer of General Electric (GE), spoke of the trademark "We bring good things to life." "We now have six different businesses ranging from health sciences to consumer finance to entertainment and needed a vision statement that encapsulated everything we do." Comstock and BBDO developed "What we can imagine we can make happen." They then took the phrase and told its story in a format that everyone at GE around the world could relate to, "Imagination at Work."[5]

General Electric (GE) has a simple procedure for developing trademarks for its brands. GE's branding strategy has a number of steps:[6]

1. *Pick a name.* General Electric, for example.
2. *Create a memorable trademark.* The GE monogram is recognized the world over.
3. *Make a promise.* For 60 years, GE promised better living through electricity, which became better living through technology, for the past 30 years.
4. *Effectively communicate the promise.* GE has always had highly imaginative and memorable work produced by its agencies.
5. *Be consistent.* Even as GE grows and modifies its business, it carefully manages the use of its identity worldwide.

6. *Don't get bored.* GE kept the same strategic promise for 30 years before recently changing to "Imagination at Work."

If you follow this basic strategy, your brand should thrive.

For a firm to qualify for an exclusive trademark, several requirements must be met. If these criteria are not satisfied, the trademark is not legally protected and will be lost to the firm.

The use of a design in an ad does not make it a trademark, nor does having it on a flag over the factory. The trademark must be used in connection with an actual product. It must be applied to the product itself or be on a label or container of that product. If that is not feasible, it must be affixed to the container or dispenser of the product, as on a gas pump at a service station.

The trademark must not be confusingly similar to trademarks on comparable goods. It must not be likely to cause buyers to be confused, mistaken, or deceived as to whose product they are purchasing. The trademark must be dissimilar in appearance, sound, and significance from others for similar goods. In disputes, it is up to a court to decide these issues. The products involved do not need to be identical. For example, Air-O was held in conflict with Arrow shirts. The marks will be held in conflict if the products are sold through the same trade channels or if the public might assume that a product made by a second company is a new product line of the first company.

Trademarks must not be deceptive—that is, they must not indicate a quality the product does not possess. For instance, the word *Lemon* was barred from soap that contained no lemon, as was the word *Nylodon* for sleeping bags that contained no nylon.

Trademarks must not be merely descriptive. For example, when people ask for fresh bread, we cannot trademark our bread Fresh. When people ask for fresh bread, they are describing the kind of bread they want, not specifying the bread made by a particular baker. To prevent such misleading usage, the law does not protect trademarks that are merely descriptive and, thus, applicable to many other products.

Trademark Protection

Because a trademark is so valuable, companies go to great lengths to protect their brand names. In recent years, there have been a number of court cases involving allegations that one company has infringed on the trademark of another.

In deciding whether trademark infringement has taken place, several factors are considered by the courts:

1. distinctiveness of the complainant's mark,

2. similarity of the marks,

3. proximity of the parties' products,

4. likelihood of the complainant's bridging the gap between noncompeting products,

5. similarity of the parties' trade channels and advertising methods,

6. quality of the alleged infringer's products, and

7. sophistication of the particular customers.

Recently, a federal judge ruled that an Ohio-based Internet company infringed on copyrights held by BellSouth Corp. (now AT&T). The judge held that the RealPages website owned by Don Madey did not have the right to use RealPages as its identification or as part of its Internet address. BellSouth has held a trademark on the phrase "Real Yellow Pages" since 1984. The Web site also used the phrase "let your mouse do the walking" but agreed to stop using that phrase. BellSouth also owns the copyright to the phrase "let your fingers do the walking." Bellsouth said it had no choice but to protect its marks, and it filed suit only after trying to discuss the issue with the website company.[7]

Beware if your trademark is based on a common word. It will be considered legally weak and difficult to protect. Monitor the use of your trademark vigorously, and don't let any competitor use your mark even briefly. If you want to start a trademark infringement suit, don't do it unless you have detailed records and can document lost profits accurately.

Trademark Loss

In short, if you don't use a trademark properly, you can lose the rights to it. What would happen to Coca-Cola if the courts ruled you or anyone could call a soft drink Coke? You could then make your brew in your bathtub and sell it. Some companies have seen the untimely demise of a trademark. That's right—untimely demise. Many familiar words today were once valid trademarks:

aspirin	cornflakes
yo-yo	nylon
escalator	thermos
lanolin	raisin bran
cellophane	linoleum

To protect a trademark, advertisers must use it with a generic classification so the trademark does not become the name of the product. Originally, Thermos was the trademark owned by the Aladdin Company, which introduced vacuum bottles. In time, people began asking, "What brand of thermos bottle do you carry?" The word *thermos* had come to represent all vacuum bottles, not just those made by Aladdin. The courts held that *Thermos* had become a descriptive word that any manufacturer of vacuum bottles could use because *thermos* (with a lowercase *t*) was no longer the exclusive trademark of the originator. This could be very scary to any brand.

Name Change Risks

When America Online announced that it was officially changing its name to AOL, the news caused barely a ripple. The pioneering Internet company unofficially had been known as AOL for years. Most cyberspace brands have yet to generate the kind of emotional bond that many consumers feel for brick-and-mortar establishments, such as Marshall Field's or Rich's whose monikers were switched to Macy's with grumblings from consumers. Federated Department Stores Inc. decided to rechristen a number of other regional department store brands with the Macy's brand. The move helps Federated expand Macy's into a national brand and, in the process, help reduce national advertising costs. But when a change sparks vehement objections from longtime customers, it serves as a reminder to marketers that when you rename a company, you might be toying with customer loyalty. The dropping of the wireless category leader Cingular name brought criticism from the marketing community when it was merged with the new AT&T. Many thought that Cingular's brand image was more modern and exciting than the old stodgy AT&T image. However, it is too early to report any consumer concerns, if any. Most companies that serve the business community can adopt a new name with minimal fanfare because, unlike consumer companies, they rarely encounter customers who feel personally betrayed by the brand change. It also is easier for business-to-business firms to communicate the name change to their customers because their target markets tend to be smaller than those of a consumer company. About 90 percent of the name changers nationwide in 2005 were in the business-to-business arena. Technology companies lead the pack partly because they are in a young industry with enterprises that sometimes change their focus to keep pace with new technologies. "There is a certain amount of equity that comes with a brand name or company name. In most cases you don't want to risk losing customers who have come to know and trust that name," said Teena Massingill, manager of corporate public affairs for Safeway Stores based in Pleasanton, California.[8]

Selecting Brand Names

Think about all the possible associations of Mountain Dew. On the one hand, there's the serene, relaxing scenario of a quiet mountain trail or lake. But that wasn't what the folks at Mountain Dew wanted for the brand. They wanted to associate the brand with aggressive, incredibly cool, extreme-sports type activity. The brand is for people who push themselves and consider the outdoors an adventure waiting to happen. The product as both words and as a brand has been defined as anything but a serene experience. They managed the brand name. Another challenge in naming is that no word or name exists without both positive and negative connotations. However, a brand can redefine a word. A brand name will be accepted in its ultimate context, if you control the context.[9] A strong brand name will aid branding objectives by helping create and support the brand image. There are several considerations in the brand name selection.[10]

■ The name should differentiate the product from the competition. In some product categories, there is a limit to how different brand images can be. In fragrances there has traditionally been one basic image—romance. There is great similarity among the brand names: Caleche, Cacharel, and Chantilly. Consider more distinctive names such as Obsession, RED, Passion, Romance, Eternity, Fracas, and Tiffany. In either direction, creation and support of the brand image—abstract promise rather than actual benefit—are the dominant factors in name selection.

■ The name should describe the product, if possible. Brand names such as Post-it, Pudding Pops, Eraser Mate, and lastminutetravel.com are very descriptive. They communicate to consumers exactly what to expect.

■ The product should be compatible with the brand name. In other words, do not name a sleeping tablet "Awake."

■ The name should be memorable and easy to pronounce. One-word, one-syllable brand names are often considered ideal—Fab, Tide, Dash, Bold, Surf, Coke, and Tab. Even though short names may be more memorable, they may be limiting in identifying the type of product or its use.

Al and Laura Ries, brand consultants, recommend the following considerations in naming a brand:[11]

■ The name should be short, for instance, Jell-O, Nilla, TheraFlu. Shortness is an attribute that is even more important for an Internet brand.

■ The name should be simple. Simple is not the same as short. A simple word uses only a few letters of the alphabet and arranges them in combinations that repeat themselves. Many viral-related names are not simple, but many are distinctive: Flickr, Frappr. ThermaCare is simple and descriptive. Schwab is a short name but not simple because it uses six letters of the alphabet.

ADVANTAGE POINT

Naming a Chicken Sandwich

Atlanta-based Chick-fil-A® was founded by entrepreneur and restaurateur S. Truett Cathy. His chain has some 1,300 restaurants in 37 states and Washington, D.C., generating annual sales of more than $2 billion. Naming a chicken sandwich seems easy, but not so if you invented it. However, the development of the brand name—Chick-fil-A—is a prime example of how much thought and care Chick-fil-A founder Cathy put into developing the brand even before the first restaurant opened in 1967.

Having introduced the concept of the chicken sandwich to the restaurant industry, Cathy didn't have much of a point of reference for naming his new product. Originally wanting to trademark the sandwich itself, Cathy initially chose the name "Chicken Steak Sandwich," then "Chicken Steak Burger." Cathy was informed by a patent attorney that he would need to take a "dictionary word" and misspell it, "turn it upside down," to make it unique enough to be registered for a trademark.

Undaunted, Cathy began brainstorming. For him, the chicken fillet was representative of the best part of the chicken and the part he used in his chicken sandwich. Playing with that concept, Truett eventually settled on "Chick-fil-A." Even the capital "A" at the end of the word had significance for Cathy, for to him, it represented top quality, sanitary conditions, and excellent service. ▪ ▪ ▪

Coca-Cola is both a short and simple name. Autobytel.com suffers from being too complicated.

■ The name should be unique. Unique is a key characteristic that makes a name memorable. No name is totally unique unless you create it from scratch, such as Acura, Lexus, or Kodak. Remember, a common or generic name is not unique.

■ The name should be alliterative. If you want people to remember something, rhyme it for them. Alliteration is another way to improve your brand's memorability: Bed Bath & Beyond, Blockbuster, Volvo, and Weight Watchers.

■ The name should be speakable. Try Abercrombie & Fitch and Concierge.com.

The Sansum-Santa Barbara Medical Foundation Clinic was shortened to Sansum Clinic. Exhibit 21.5 shows a before and after design.

EXHIBIT 21.5

Before and after logos of the Sansum Clinic as designed by Idea Engineering.

Courtesy of Sansum Clinic and Idea Engineering Inc.

Forms of Trademarks

Branding experts agree that although still very relevant, the overall value of a company's name has diminished. Convergence, globalization, and the dot-com influx have caused a shift in the branding strategy. The vast majority of the words in the *Oxford English Dictionary* have been registered and trademarked. A recent Interbrand corporate study revealed that 80 percent of the naming projects lasted three months or less. According to projected naming trends, 19 percent of those surveyed thought "coined" or fabricated names will remain popular because there are not many good dictionary names left; 9 percent of respondents saw a trend toward adopting names that had been part of company heritage (e.g., a founder's name); and 57 percent saw a trend toward more "real" names—either a single or compound word (e.g., Apple, JetBlue, BlackBerry, Tide).[12] The following are examples of traditional trademark forms.

Dictionary Words Many trademarks consist of familiar dictionary words used in an arbitrary, innovative, or fanciful manner. Many common words have already been used, causing the advertiser to seek other methods to name a product: Apple computers, Verbatim data disks, Deer Park spring water, Nature Made vitamins, Ivory soap, Dial soap, Equal sweetener, Whopper burgers, Glad plastic bags, Coach leather, Target, Folks restaurant, and Pert shampoo. This type of trademark must be used in a merely descriptive sense to describe the nature, use, or virtue of the product: Look at the word *natural* and related names such as Natural Blend, Natural Brand, Natural Impressions, Natural Light, Natural Man, Natural Silk, Natural Smoothe, Natural Stretch, Natural Suede, Natural Sun, Natural Touch, Natural Woman, and Natural Wonder; or the prefix *opti* as used in Opti Fonts, Opti Free, Opti-Fry, Opti-Grip, Opti Heat, Opti Pure, Opti-Ray, Opti-Tears, and Opti Twist. A few years ago, OrangeGlo International created a new kind of cleaner using an oxygen booster to remove stains and odors and get laundry whiter. It was called OxiClean. In the beginning it was sold primarily on television directly to consumers, then in specialty stores like Bed Bath & Beyond, and later on grocery shelves. As it began moving more into the mainstream and taking away from established products, competitive products were introduced with their versions of "OXI" or "OXY" products.

The possible advantage of using dictionary words is that consumers will easily recognize them. The task is to get people to associate the word(s) with the product. Just think what the following real product names using dictionary words are about: Healthy Choice, Oracle, Skin Bracer, Budget Rent-A-Car, Wonder Bra, Computer Associates, Big Mac, Action Plus, Hotmail, and AquaFresh.

At times, a name can be somewhat limiting. For instance, when Burger King moved into a breakfast menu, its name was a limitation because people do not think of burgers as breakfast.

Coined Words When we run out of dictionary options, we sometimes make up words, such as Google, Avaya, FedEx, Ticketron, Advil, Infiniti, Primerica, Kleenex, Xerox, NYNEX, UNUM, Norelco, Exxon, Delco, Keds, Kodak, Mazola, TransAir, Häagen-Dazs, Chick-fil-A (see Exhibit 21.6) and Tab. **Coined words** are made up of a new combination of consonants and vowels. The advantage of a coined word is that it is new, and it can be made phonetically pleasing, pronounceable, and short. Coined words have a good chance of being legally protectable. The challenge is to create a trademark that is distinctive. Ocean Spray took the ingredients of cranberries and apples and created the name Cranapple, which is distinctive, descriptive, and relatively easy to pronounce. There is, however, a Cranberry Apple herbal tea. Is this confusing? Probably not.

The simpler coined words are one syllable. It is common to coin trademark words that have a vowel next to a hard consonant or a vowel between two hard consonants, such as Keds. This structure can be expanded—Kodak, Crisco, or Tab.

coined word
An original and arbitrary combination of syllables forming a word. Extensively used for trademarks, such as PoFolks, Mazola, Gro-Pup, Zerone. (Opposite of a dictionary word.)

EXHIBIT 21.6
Chick-fil-A Logo
Courtesy of Chick-fil-A.

Personal Names These may be the names of real people, such as Calvin Klein, Liz Claiborne, Anne Klein, Estée Lauder, Tommy Hilfiger, Perry Ellis, Pierre Cardin, Alexander Julian, Ralph Lauren, L.L.Bean, Jenny Craig, Forbes, and Sara Lee; fictional characters, such as Betty Crocker; historical characters, such as Lincoln cars; or mythological characters, such as Ajax cleanser. A surname alone is not valuable as a new trademark; others of that name may use it. Names such as Ford automobiles, Lipton teas, Heinz foods, and Campbell's soups have been in use for so long, however, that they have acquired what the law calls a "secondary" meaning—that is, through usage the public has recognized them as representing the product of one company only. However, a new trademark has no such secondary meaning.

There are a lot of names that use Mrs.—Mrs. Fields, Mrs. Winner's, Mrs. Richardson's, Mrs. Allison's, Mrs. Smith's, Mrs. Dash, Mrs. Baird's, Mrs. Butterworth's, Mrs. Lane's, and Mrs. Paul's.

Foreign names have been successfully used to endow a product with an exotic quality. Because the market is now global, they are more common. The argument against creating foreign names may be the problem of pronunciation or remembering. However, foreign names are part of the global landscape: Toyota, Feni, Gianfranco Ferre, Corneliani, Lubiam, Bertolucci, Giorgia Brutini, Shiseido, Gucci, Volkswagen, Fila, Ferrari, and L'Aimant.

Geographical Names A geographical name is really a place name: Nashua blankets, Utica sheets, Pittsburgh paints, and Newport cigarettes. These names are old trademarks and have acquired secondary meaning. Often the word *brand* is offered after the geographical name. The law does not look with favor on giving one person or company the exclusive right to use a geographical name in connection with a new product, excluding others making similar goods in that area. However, if the name was chosen because of a fanciful connotation of a geographical setting rather than to suggest that the product was made there, it may be eligible for protection, as with Bali bras and Klondike ice cream bars.

Geographical names can be combined with dictionary words to create trademark names such as Maryland Club coffee and Carolina Treat barbecue sauce. The options are many: Georgia Coffee, Texas Instruments, Texas Trails, New York Woman, Florida Queen, Newport Harbor, Georgia-Pacific, and Atlanta Bread. Think of the number of businesses in your community using the city, county, or state name or a geographical region: mountains, coastal, piedmont, tidewater, lake, and so on—Piedmont Hospital, Mountain Man Museum, and Great South Catering (see Exhibit 21.7).

EXHIBIT **21.7**
Great South Catering
Courtesy of Lane Bevil+Partners.

Initials and Numbers Many fortunes and years have been spent in establishing trademarks such as IBM, IKEA furniture, RCA, GE, AC spark plugs, A&W root beer, J&B whiskey, A.1. steak sauce, and V8 vegetable juice. Hence, these are familiar. In general, however, initials and numbers are the most difficult form of trademark to remember and the easiest to confuse and imitate. How many of these sound familiar: STP, DKNY, S.O.S., AMF, SK, M.O.M.S., S.A.V.E., A.S.A., A&P, 6–12, or 666? There are also combinations of initials and numbers: WD-40 lubricant; numbers and words: 9-Lives cat food, 4 in 1, Formula 44, Formula 109, Formula 28, Formula 36, 4 Most; or dictionary words and initials: LA Gear. In 1949, Mr. Kihachiro Onitsuka began his athletic footwear company (Onitsuka Co., Ltd.) by manufacturing basketball shoes out of his living room in Kobe, Japan. He chose the name ASICS for his company in 1977, based on a famous Latin phrase *Anima Sana in Corpore Sano*, which when translated expresses the ancient ideal of "A Sound Mind in a Sound Body." Taking the acronym of this phrase, ASICS was founded on the belief that the best way to create a healthy and happy lifestyle is to promote total health and fitness.

Pictorial Many advertisers use some artistic device, such as a distinctive lettering style or a design, insignia, or picture. The combination, as mentioned before, is called a logotype or logo. As you can see, names can be categorized into a number of different types and functions. Some branding and naming experts include a few other categories and examples:

Connotative: Duracell

Bridge: DaimlerChrysler, Westin

Arbitrary: Apple, Yahoo!

Descriptive: Pizza Hut, General Motors

The Successful Trademark

Whatever the form of a specific trademark, it will be successful only if it is distinctive and complements the manufacturer's product and image. As we mentioned earlier in this chapter, the trademark cannot be considered an isolated creative unit. In most cases, it must be adaptable to a package and certainly to other branding communications. It must also be adaptable to many different advertising campaigns, often over a period of many years. The longer a trademark is associated with a brand, the more people recognize it and the greater its value. People are familiar with the Home Depot trademark, but how many are familiar with the The Home Depot Foundation, which is a distinctive extension of the corporate brand (see Exhibit 21.8)?

Global Trademarks

The federal registration of trademarks with the USPTO is not valid outside the United States. However, if you are a qualified owner of a trademark application pending before the USPTO or of a registration issued by the USPTO, you may

EXHIBIT **21.8**

Home Depot Foundation Logo

Courtesy of Idea Engineering Inc.

seek registration in any of the countries that have joined the Madrid Protocol by filing a single application, called an "international application," with the International Bureau of the World Property Intellectual Organization, through the USPTO. Also, certain countries recognize a U.S. registration as the basis for filing an application to register a mark in those countries under international treaties.

General Trademark Rules

Putting a lock on the ownership of a trademark requires taking the following steps:

1. Always be sure the trademark word is capitalized or set off in distinctive type. KLEENEX, *Kleenex*, **Kleenex**.
2. Always follow the trademark with the generic name of the product, or by using the word *brand* after the mark: Glad disposable trash bags, Kleenex tissues, Apple computers, Tabasco brand pepper sauce.
3. Do not speak of the trademark word in the plural, as "three Kleenexes," but rather, "three Kleenex tissues."
4. Do not use the trademark name in a possessive form, unless the trademark itself is possessive, such as Levi's jeans (not "Kleenex's new features," but "the new features of Kleenex tissues"), or as a verb (not "Kleenex your eyeglasses," but "Wipe your eyeglasses with Kleenex tissues").

It is the advertising person's responsibility to carry out these legal strictures in the ads, although most large advertisers will have each ad checked for legal requirements including trademark protection.

Companies should control how the trademark is used in writing ads and so forth. Many companies provide departments and units with written guidelines instructing the use of trademarks. For example, Kodak has a ten-page document for proper use, with examples of incorrect usage, of its trademarks. This document includes trademark printing instructions for black-and-white and color usage. Blockbuster Corporation warns its employees, "Always use the exact registration or trademark form." You should never change the word or design; never change the upper and lowercase letters; never change the colors; never change the plural or singular form; never add the word *the* to the word or design; never add a design to the word or vice versa; and never make the mark a possessive noun.

DuPont promotes the correct use of its Teflon trademark (see Exhibit 21.9). "Protecting the Teflon trademark is critical to the successful management of a very valuable asset. Improper use of the trademark, or allowing others to use it improperly, lowers its value and can ultimately turn a respected trademark into a common generic term."

Registration Notice

Legal departments at some companies go to great lengths to protect their valuable trademarks. Some common ways of indicating trademark registration follow:

- The "®" symbol after the trademark as a superscript. Example: Mrs. Winner's®
- A footnote referenced by an asterisk in the text.
    Example: McDonald's*
    *A registered trademark of McDonald's Corporation.
    or
    *Reg. U.S. Pat. Tm. Off.
    or
    Registered in the U.S. Patent and Trademark Office.

EXHIBIT **21.9**

Guidelines on the use of the Teflon trademark.

Courtesy of DuPont.

Rule 1: Show Registration.

Show registration status, by using the symbol "®" each and every time the trademark appears.

If there is no ® on a keyboard, as in some electronic mail systems, use parenthesis "R" parenthesis: (R). For countries where the registration symbol is not recognized, use an asterisk (*).

Acceptable	Unacceptable
Teflon® resin	No designation of registration status
Teflon(R) resin	
*Teflon** resin	Teflon resin

IMPORTANT: Regardless of whether "®", (R), or (*) is used, a footnote must be used at least once in each document. Examples of acceptable footnotes:

* *Teflon* is a registered trademark of DuPont.

Teflon® is a registered trademark of DuPont for its fluoropolymer resins.

Rule 2: Be Distinctive.

Make the trademark distinctive from the surrounding text each and every time.

Acceptable	Unacceptable
Initial Cap: Teflon® resin	Any instance where the trademark is not distinguished from surrounding text, such as: "gaskets with teflon"
All Caps: TEFLON® resin	
Bold: **Teflon**® resin	
Italics: *Teflon*® resin	
Color: Teflon® resin	

Rule 3: Use Correct Generics.

Use the correct generic (common name) for the trademark at least once per package. Generic is the term for the class of goods for which the mark is registered.

Acceptable	Unacceptable
Teflon® resins	*Teflon*® president, *Teflon*® gasket, *Teflon*® cookware, *Teflon*® business
Other acceptable generics: films, fibers, finishes, fabric protector, fluoropolymer, fluoroadditive, micropowder, coating solutions, PTFE, PFA, FEP, ETFE	

NOTE: Although not generics, it is acceptable to refer to the *Teflon*® trademark and the *Teflon*® brand.

Rule 3: Use Correct Generics.

The trademark is the trademark. Don't embellish upon it!

Acceptable	Unacceptable
	Possessives: *Teflon*®'s wear resistance
Wear resistance of *Teflon*®	
Coatings of *Teflon*®	**Hyphens:** *Teflon*®-coated
Fabrics using *Teflon*® wear longer	**Line Breaks** Fabrics using *Teflon*® wear longer
Coat pans with *Teflon*®	**Verbs:** Teflon® your pans
Teflon®	**Coined Words:** *Teflon*® ized

■ A notation of the registration in the text or as a footnote on the same page.

■ If a trademark is repeated frequently in an ad, some firms require the registration notice only on the first use.

Most companies require notice of unregistered but claimed words and/or symbols as their trademark by using the "TM" symbol. The football sporting event named "Chick-fil-A Bowl" uses the "TM" symbol (see Exhibit 21.10).

EXHIBIT 21.10

The Chick-fil-A Bowl Game logo uses the "TM" symbol.

Courtesy of The Chick-fil-A Bowl.

HOUSE MARKS

house mark
A primary mark of a business concern, usually used with the trademark of its products. General Mills is a house mark; Betty Crocker is a trademark; DuPont is a house mark; Teflon II is a trademark.

As mentioned earlier in this chapter, trademarks are used to identify specific products. However, many companies sell a number of products under several different trademarks. These companies often identify themselves with a **house mark** to denote the firm that produces these products. Kraft is a house mark, and its brand Miracle Whip is a trademark.

SERVICE MARKS, CERTIFICATION MARKS

service mark
A word or name used in the sale of services to identify the services of a firm and distinguish them from those of others, for example, Hertz Drive Yourself Service, Weight Watchers Diet Course. Comparable to trademarks for products.

A company that renders services, such as an insurance company, an airline, or even a weight-loss center, can protect its identification mark by registering it in Washington as a **service mark**. It is also possible to register certification marks, whereby a firm certifies that a user of its identifying device is doing so properly. Teflon is a material sold by DuPont to kitchenware makers for use in lining their pots and pans. Teflon is DuPont's registered trademark for its nonstick finish; Teflon II is DuPont's certification mark for cookware coated with Teflon that meets DuPont's standards. Advertisers of such products may use that mark. The Woolmark symbol (see Exhibit 21.11) is a registered trademark owned by The

EXHIBIT 21.11

Certification Mark

Reproduced with the permission of The Woolmark Company.

ADVANTAGE POINT

A Few Words from USPTO's Website

*A*ny time you claim rights in a mark, you may use the "TM" (trademark) or "SM" (service mark) designation to alert the public to your claim, regardless of whether you have filed an application with the USPTO. However, you may use the federal registration symbol "®" *only* after the USPTO actually *registers a mark* and *not* while an application is pending. Also, you may use the registration symbol with the mark only on or in connection with the goods and services listed in the federal trademark registration.

WHAT IS A TRADEMARK OR SERVICE MARK?

- A *trademark* is a word, phrase, symbol, or design, or a combination of words, phrases, symbols, or designs, that identifies and distinguishes the source of the goods of one party from those of others.
- A *service mark* is the same as a trademark, except that it identifies and distinguishes the source of a service rather than a product. Throughout this booklet, the terms *trademark* and *mark* refer to both trademarks and service marks.

DO TRADEMARKS, COPYRIGHTS, AND PATENTS PROTECT THE SAME THINGS?

No: Trademarks, copyrights, and patents all differ. A copyright protects an original artistic or literary work; a patent protects an invention. For copyright information, go to http://lcweb.loc.gov/copyright. The United States Patent and Trademark Office (USPTO) reviews trademark applications for federal registration and determines whether an applicant meets the requirements for federal registration. The office does not decide whether you have the right to *use* a mark (which differs from the right to register). Even without a registration, you may still *use* any mark adopted to identify the source of your goods or services. Once a registration is issued, it is up to the owner of a mark to enforce its rights in the mark based on ownership of a federal registration.

FORM FOR FILING A TRADEMARK APPLICATION

Using the Trademark Electronic Application System (TEAS) available at www.uspto.gov/teas/index.html, you can file your application directly over the Internet. Features of electronic filing include:

- *Online help.* Hyperlinks provide help sections for each of the application fields.
- *Validation function.* Helps avoid the possible omission of important information.
- *Immediate reply.* The USPTO immediately issues an initial filing receipt via e-mail containing the assigned application serial number and a summary of the submission.
- *24-Hour availability.* TEAS is available 24 hours a day, seven days a week (except 11 PM Saturday to 6 AM Sunday), so receipt of a filing date is possible up until midnight EST.

If you do not have Internet access, you can access TEAS at any Patent and Trademark Depository Library (PTDL) throughout the United States. Many public libraries also provide Internet access.

USPTO prefers you to file online but you may either mail or hand deliver a paper application to the USPTO. You can call the USPTO's automated telephone line at (703) 308–9000 or (800) 786–9199 to obtain a printed form. *You may Not submit an application by facsimile.* ■ ■ ■

Woolmark Company. The Woolmark Company controls the use of its trademark by licensing manufacturers who are able to meet the strict performance criteria of the Woolmark program. The Woolmark is a symbol of quality which denotes that the products concerned meet the specifications laid down by The Woolmark Company and will give the consumer satisfaction for the life of the product, given average wear and usage conditions.

COMPANY AND PRODUCT NAMES

Corporate Name Changes

Over the years, thousands of companies have undergone corporate name and identity changes. Corporations can spend millions of dollars to complete the process. Costs include hiring consultants, advertising, and changing logos and designs on such items as stationery, uniforms, trucks, and planes.

In 2001, Accenture spent $175 million to introduce its new name. It was formerly known as Anderson Consulting, a global management and technology consulting company. It hired Landor, a brand identity company owned by Young & Rubicam, to develop a name. They sifted through 5,500 potential options. The original list was pared down to 550, then to 50, and then to 10 names. The name didn't actually originate with the brand identity company. An employee from Oslo, Norway, combined *accent* and *future*. It also contains a "greater than" sign (>) hanging over the *t* like an accent mark, but the consonant isn't pronounced differently.[13]

Miles Laboratories ran an ad stating, "After all these years, we think it's time you call us by our first name: Bayer. Today Miles becomes Bayer." The copy started: "You know us as Miles, one of America's largest companies. But in nearly 150 countries, our name is Bayer. Bayer is one of the biggest health care, chemical and imaging technology companies in the world. . . . You already know Bayer for aspirin."

The Process for Developing Memorable Names

There probably isn't a single procedure everyone accepts for selecting names. Ruffell Meyer of Landor Associates says, "The misconception is that you have a couple of people sitting around over a pizza lunch. The first step is to meet with senior management to talk about the direction of the company, its values and image. Does it want to be known for speedy service? Later employees and customers may be included in the discussion."[14]

Once the information is gathered, the brand identity staff begins the name-generation and image-making processes. The tools are likely to include software packages that can morph word combinations. Landor has a database with more than 50,000 names. A typical list of possibilities can exceed a thousand names. Cingular, the result of the merger of SBC Communications and BellSouth Mobility (now part of AT&T), was created from a list of 6,000 names.

A basic legal search should be made of each name to see if someone else owns the rights to it. Before investing too much time and energy in developing a total identity program around a name, find out if anyone else owns it. Naming consultants can refer you to patent attorneys who can conduct a preliminary screening of names registered in the United States. The cost is usually less than $100 per name. A more comprehensive U.S. trademark search typically costs more than $1,000 per name, so you may want to narrow your choice down to a couple of finalists before proceeding to that level.

Private trademark search firms will conduct searches for a fee. The USPTO cannot aid in the selection of a search firm. Search firms are often listed in the Yellow Pages section of telephone directories under the heading "Trademark Search Services" or "Patent and Trademark Search Services." This process reduces the possibilities by about 80 percent. You again analyze the remaining names against the objective and reduce them to a list of about a dozen or so. At this point, you would probably perform a linguistic analysis to determine what happens when the name is translated into foreign languages. Then you might test the names on consumers. You get the idea. Correctly done, the result is a memorable name that is adaptable to a number of advertising formats. Now let us look at the specific steps. First, pull together the basic information:

- *Describe what you are naming.* In your description, include key features and characteristics, competitive advantages, and anything else that differentiates your company, product, or service from the rest of the field.
- *Summarize what you want your name to do.* Should it suggest an important product characteristic (e.g., Blokrot for treated lumber) or convey a particular image (e.g., Pandora's Secrets for an expensive perfume)? Write down the characteristics and images you want your name to convey.
- *Describe whom you are targeting with the name.* Identify your targets and their demographic and lifestyle characteristics. Would they react more positively to a traditional, conservative name or to a liberal, flashy one? List the name qualities you think would appeal to them (name length, sound, and image).
- *List names that you like and dislike.* Try to come up with a few dozen current names in both categories (include your competitors' names). Note words and roots that might work for your new name and jot them down.
- *Build a list of new name ideas.* Start with the list of names that you like and add to it by pulling ideas from a good thesaurus (e.g., *The Synonym Finder* by Jerome Rodale), a book of names (e.g., *The Trademark Register of the United States*), relevant trade journals, a book of root words (e.g., *Dictionary of English Word Roots* by Robert Smith), or other sources.
- *Combine name parts and words.* Take words, syllables, and existing name parts and recombine them to form new names.
- *Pick your favorites.* Select several names that meet all your criteria (just in case your top choice is unavailable or tests poorly).

Next, verify the name's availability and test your favorites:

- *Conduct a trademark search.* As mentioned previously, before investing too much time and energy in developing a total identity program around a name, find out if anyone else owns it.
- *Test your name before using it.* Regardless of how fond you are of the new name, others may have different opinions. Solicit reactions to your name from prospective customers, stockholders, and industry experts.

Name Ownership Conducting a trademark search wasn't enough to prevent problems for Cola-Cola. They ran into a controversy with Fruitopia's name. Students at Miami University in Ohio came up with a total marketing plan, which included a product name, for a sparkling water and juice drink in development for the Minute Maid brand at Coca-Cola Foods Canada. When they presented it to Coca-Cola, Coca-Cola thought the name Fruitopia was very "iffy." The product rolled out in the United States in 1994 with the Fruitopia name; although there was no question about the legal rights of ownership—Coca-Cola had paid the university a fee for all the students' work—there was a question of who developed the name. Coca-Cola said that a marketing group, working independently with its advertising agency, came up with the name. This is a reason most companies don't take unsolicited proposals for new products, ads, or product names. If Coca-Cola had not paid for the rights to the students' work, there could have been a legal battle for the name Fruitopia.

Name Assistance The naming of products may be developed by the advertiser or the advertising agency, working independently or together. There are companies and consultants that specialize in helping companies and agencies develop memorable names. Namestormers uses software to help develop product and company names such as CarMax (used-car dealer network), Pyramis (medical systems), AutoSource (auto parts network), Spider's Silk (lingerie), CareStream (health care company), and Wavemaker (notebook computer). Goldman & Young uses linguistic architecture to define image strategy and positioning, then creates names such as Polaroid Captiva, Nissan Pathfinder, Audi Avant, Clairol Whipsical, Honda Fourtrax ATV, Pep Boys PartsUSA, Pizza Hut QuickStix, Bristol-Myers Squibb Excedrin Migraine, Pfizer Zoloft, and GMC Yukon. Namelab, another company that develops names, used constructional linguistics to create the names Acura, Compaq, Geo, Lumina, and Zapmail. Then there are the large global brand identity companies that also develop names (Landor Associates, Interbrand, Lippincott Mercer, Identica, FutureBrand, etc.). Keep in mind that anyone in the process can create a name.

PACKAGING

Fully leveraging the power of company brands is contingent on the establishment of meaningful dialogue with the customer. Solidifying customer relationships takes time and true marketing strategy. Clear, concise brand communications are an important part of this strategy, and should be carefully designed into every product and every product's packaging.

Packaging presents an integral part of every company's brand communications to the customer. Since virtually every product and service in the marketplace is packaged, it is absolutely crucial that companies "get it right." Nothing communicates the brand and its values like packaging. At a time when products enjoy widespread distribution in multiple channels, packaging goes a long way to selling the product.[15]

Product packaging is the most important point-of-sale merchandising tool. The average package on the supermarket shelf has only about one-seventeenth of a second to attract our attention. After that, the design, color, words, and . . . oh yes . . . the product itself have to interest us enough to put it in our cart and take it home. With the thousands of food products on the shelves, products need to get noticed or else they become just another fallen casualty in the fickle supermarket arena. The design of Doc Jack's Grillin' Soss—a prescription for barbeque bliss—helps attract the consumer to this original formula. Exhibit 21.12A, B, and C shows package designs for different types of products.

How many times have you bought or almost bought a product simply because you liked the packaging? Some people will only buy milk in the clear plastic jugs instead of the opaque paper containers, even though the paper reduces the damage of nutrients from light. Packaging doesn't just focus on functional aspects such as versatility and food safety anymore. A great deal of the emphasis is directed purely to aesthetics. Revamping new products can be risky. If a product looks too different from before, companies may alienate loyal customers. For example, when Nestlé decided to change the packaging of KitKat candy from foil wrap to plastic, emotionally attached consumers protested the change, even though the new package would keep the product fresh three times longer.

Holistic Approach

According to designer Wendy Jedlicka, package design should be a holistic endeavor that requires looking at the entire environment the packaging is working within—the product's durability; manuals, instructions, and other printed materials that are stuffed into a package; and the package's ability to communicate on a retail shelf.[16]

EXHIBIT 21.12

Doc Jack's label and container are designed to attract attention on the shelf. American Clay projects the product's function. And GoToMyPC reflects a modern business influence.

Courtesy of Idea Engineering Inc.

The product package is much more than a container. The package must be designed to take several factors into account. First, it must protect the package contents (see Exhibit 21.13); every other consideration is secondary to the function of the package as a utilitarian container. Second, the package must meet reasonable cost standards. Because the product package is a major expense for most firms, steps must be taken to hold down costs as much as possible.

Once these two requirements of package protection and cost are satisfied, we move to the marketing issues involved in packaging. These include adopting a

EXHIBIT **21.13**

The TV commercial touts the milk jug's value of protecting flavor and vitamins.

Courtesy of Howard, Merrell & Partners.

package that is conducive to getting shelf space at the retail level. A unique package with strange dimensions, protruding extensions, or nonflat surfaces is going to be rejected by many retailers. A package must be easy to handle, store, and stack. It should not take up more shelf room than any other product in that section, as a pyramid-shaped bottle might. Odd shapes are suspect: Will they break easily? Tall packages are suspect: Will they keep falling over? The package should be soil resistant. Does it have ample and convenient space for marking? The product should come in the full range of sizes and packaging common to the field.

For products bought upon inspection, such as men's shirts, the package needs transparent facing. The package can make the difference in whether a store stocks the item.

Small items are expected to be mounted on cards under plastic domes, called blister cards, to provide ease of handling and to prevent pilferage. Often these cards are mounted on a large board that can be hung on a wall, making profitable use of that space. Remember, the buyer working for the store judges how a product display will help the store, not the manufacturer.

Once we have considered the requirements of the retail trade, we can turn our attention to designing a container that is both practical and eye-catching. The package is, after all, the last chance to sell to the consumer and the most practical form of point-of-purchase advertising. Therefore, it should be designed to achieve a maximum impact on the store shelf. Striving for distinctiveness is particularly critical in retail establishments such as grocery stores, where the consumer is choosing from hundreds of competing brands.

Changing Package Design and Marketing Strategies

Design firms redesign packages to suit changing market strategies for existing consumer products and develop new packaging concepts for product introduc-

EXHIBIT 21.14

"Packaging for products must stand out on the store shelf to be effective."

Courtesy of the Procter & Gamble Company. Used by permission.

tions. In 1998, the Swiffer revolution began. Swiffer conveys speed and ease of cleaning, which translates into the same meaning around the globe. Today there are numerous Swiffer products: Swiffer Wet, WetJet, Max, and Dusters. Procter & Gamble took great care in designing the packaging. The packaging had to attract attention and hold the different content items (see Exhibit 21.14). Several trends in package design can be cited. One is the increasing tendency to use packaging to shore up store brands. Another is the use of sophisticated design approaches or unique packaging to establish a high quality for upscale, private-label brands. There has also been a shift from packaging that suits the convenience of the manufacturer to packaging that is "consumer friendly" in terms of opening, using, and reclosing. In short, package design is responding to a more sophisticated, discerning consumer.

Problem-Solving Designs: Old Spice Red Zone

Issue Old Spice was ready to introduce a new, superior antiperspirant technology and needed a subbrand that embraced the positioning of "unapologetic masculinity."

Brand Response Interbrand researched the target audience and competing products to understand how to clearly communicate the concepts of premium and masculine to men. Additionally, it examined language, color, and texture of traditional products purchased by men to create a visual vocabulary. Old Spice Red Zone is for guys who push limits. The strong, silver logotype includes a gauge built into the *o* of *Zone*. The background texture is reminiscent of texture found on power tools, and the metallic feel of the whole package communicates a masculine and premium message to men.

Most brand identity firms not only assist in product or company names but also are product design and packaging experts.

Packaging and Marketing

At one time, the role of product packages was generally confined to protecting the product. Only the package label was linked with promotional activities. The Uneeda Biscuit package introduced in 1899 is generally considered to be the first that was utilized for promotion. However, few companies followed Uneeda's lead.

During the depression of the 1930s, the role of packaging as a promotional tool changed dramatically. Most companies had limited advertising funds during this period so they resorted to using the package as an in-store means of promotion. So successful were their efforts that the role of packaging in the marketing mix became routinely accepted by manufacturers.

The package design for most products is developed in much the same way as an advertising campaign. Although each package is developed, designed, and promoted in a unique fashion, there are some common approaches to the successful use of packaging as a marketing tool.

1. *The type of product and function of the package.* Is the product extremely fragile? Do consumers use the product directly from the package? Are there special storage or shipping problems associated with the product?

2. *The type of marketing channels to be used for the product.* If the product is sold in a variety of outlets, will this require some special packaging considerations? Will the package be displayed in some special way at the retail level? Are there special point-of-purchase opportunities for the product?

3. *The prime prospects for the product.* Are adults, children, upper-income families, or young singles most likely to buy the product? What package style would be most appealing to the target market?

4. *Promotion and advertising for the product and its package.* Will the package be used to complement other promotional efforts? Are on-pack coupons or premiums being considered? Can standard package-design ideas be adapted to any special promotional efforts being considered?

5. *The relationship to other packages in a product line.* Will the product be sold in different sizes? Is the product part of a product line that is promoted together? Does the product line use the same brand name and packaging style?

6. *The typical consumer use of the product.* Will the package be stored for long periods in the home? Does the product require refrigeration or freezing? Are only portions of the product from the package used?

The answers to these and other questions can be obtained only through careful research. The package designer must strive for a balance between creativity and function.

Packaging and Color

Advertisers are very much aware that colors work on people's subconscious mind and that each color produces a psychological reaction. Reactions to color can be pleasant or unpleasant. Color can inform consumers about the type of product inside the package and influence their perceptions of quality, value, and purity. Thus, color in packaging is an important tool in marketing communications. The Johnson Group designed a series of packaging for a new Breakfast in a Bag (see Exhibit 21.15).

What kind of consumer perceptions would you encounter if you brewed the same coffee in a blue coffeepot, a yellow pot, a brown pot, and a red pot? Would the perceptions of the coffee be the same? Probably not. Studies indicate that coffee from the blue pot would be perceived as having a mild aroma, coffee from the yellow pot would be thought of as a weaker blend, the brown pot's coffee would be judged too strong, and the red pot's coffee would be perceived as rich and full-bodied.

Kodak is yellow. Fuji is green. United Parcel Service is brown. Home Depot is orange. Color has strong influence and should be considered carefully. Color is one of the main tools that package designers use to influence buying decisions.

EXHIBIT 21.15
The line of breakfast in a bag products use color to help distinguish one product from another.
Courtesy of The Johnson Group.

Consumer reactions to colors are emotional rather than intellectual. Because about 80 percent of consumer choices are made in stores and 60 percent of those are impulse purchases, marketers must consider that package colors can play a major role in the success or failure of a product.

On your next shopping trip, see if you react the way most shoppers do to packages that use these colors:

- Red packaging (or a brand name that is bold and large) makes our hearts beat faster and increases our adrenalin flow. The color communicates power and vitality and stimulates a desire to conquer. Red also conveys a sense of structure, sensibility, practicality, and dependability. By retaining the red roof as an identifying symbol, Landor, branding consultants, helped reinforce the perception of Pizza Hut as a destination. To further differentiate the brand, a freehand typography was used along with an entire palette of icons that symbolized the freshness of its ingredients and ultimately provided Pizza Hut with the brand relevance it desired. It followed through on all the boxes and promotional material.

- Yellow is the most visible of all colors (which is why it is used on road signs) and makes packages look larger. Kodak is yellow. Yellow is also used to convey a cut-rate price image and, if not used properly, can detract from the perceived quality of the product.

- Blue implies cleanliness and purity and induces thoughts of sky and water. Often it conveys feelings of serenity, prestige, confidence, knowledge, and credibility. Think of how Tiffany's blue box has been burned into the consumer's mind. Repositioning Pepsi's brand identity worldwide in 1998, designers used blue as a conceptual platform and differentiating color to create distinctive new packaging. Pepsi moved toward a distinctively blue look to better compete against Coke's dominant red. The scope of the project included new designs for cans, bottles, vending machines, soda fountains, and vehicles which, in turn, also triggered the need for graphic changes in collateral and signs. Pepsi changed to a heavier reliance on blue than in the past. The design supports this in several ways: the italicized logo, the use of a background with lots of depth and two blues, and an abstract ice background for the Pepsi logo that gives a "visceral representation of refreshment."

- White makes us feel fresh and light and is often used on lower-fat and diet foods. It is associated with dairy products (milk) and, hence, implies the ultimate in freshness and purity. In Germany, white suggests premium quality, but in England, white suggests budget quality.

- Black is always elegant and sophisticated, and manufacturers use this color to imply a sense of class and quality for their products.

Package Research

Extensive research should be done before packaging is developed to uncover the brand's chief assets. While some assets are overt, others might be dormant, or remain uncovered. Consumer-based research into the brand experiences that impact their perception and decision-making should then be assessed. The ensuing package design solution can then honestly and directly communicate brand values and, hopefully, create an emotional connection with the consumer.

Effective packaging is a vital part of marketing a product today. The only absolute in testing a package design is to sell it in a test-market setting. There are several aspects of assessing a package design, including recognition, imagery, structure, and behavior.

- *Recognition.* A package must attract attention to itself so that the consumer can easily identify it in the retail environment. The recognition properties of a package can be measured. Research can determine how long it takes a consumer to recognize the package and what elements are most memorable.

- *Imagery.* Although the package must be easily recognized, it must also project a brand image compatible with the corporate brand-imagery objectives. A package can reinforce advertising or it can negate it.

- *Structure.* The objective is to determine any structural problems consumers pinpoint that may inhibit repeat purchases. Is the package easy to open? Is it easy to close? Is it easy to handle? Is it easy to use?

- *Behavior.* This can be the most expensive means of researching packages. Often this approach presents simulated shelf settings to groups of people and monitors whether they pick up or purchase a product.

Package Differentiation

Twelve suburban women sit around a focus group table, psyching themselves up to talk about cat food for two hours. Through the course of the evening, only two things really perk them up: the chance to describe their cats and a vacuum-packed foil bag of cat food.

Even before they have examined the nuggets of cat food, most have said they would buy it, intrigued by the high-tech, bricklike bag they have come to expect to see in the coffee aisle, certainly, but never spotted before among the cans, boxes, and bags of pet food.

It is a point increasingly driven home to marketers of food, health and beauty product lines, and over-the-counter drugs: The package is the brand.

Marketers are paying more attention to package design because products are so much more at parity these days. When differentiation through taste, color, and other product elements has reached parity, packaging makes a critical difference.[17] A case in point is Pepsi-Cola's changing can designs to attract attention. In 2007, Pepsi decided to take a risk with its Pepsi can design. For 109 years, it fiercely guarded the packaging of Pepsi, but decided to create new can designs every 3 to 4 weeks. The new graphics are part of a broader new thematic campaign for Pepsi-Cola that emphasizes the brand's "fun, optimistic, and youthful spirit." Experts say they may risk confusing or alienating consumers who rely on visual cues to find the brand.[18]

Brand Identity

Brand identity is a specific combination of visual and verbal elements that helps achieve the following attributes of a successful brand: create recognition; provide differentiation; shape the brand's imagery; link all brand communications to the brand; and—very important—be the proprietary, legal property of the company that owns the brand.

There are surprisingly few components that make up a brand identity. These include name logos, which are the designed versions of a name; symbols; other graphic devices; color; package configuration and permanent support messages—slogans and jingles. Brand identity companies work with an agency, a corporation, or both in developing packaging and may be involved with the total design concept of a corporation or a brand. For example, when you think of McDonald's Corporation—the hamburger people—what comes to mind? Golden arches? Employee uniforms? Cup designs? Paper or box designs? Logo? Paper bags? Premiums? Letterheads? Publications? There are many elements that help identify McDonald's, and every element has its name or logo for starters. The corporate design people help the marketer and sometimes the agency develop strong corporate visual communications.

Package Design

A product's package is more than a necessary production expense. Therefore, much care needs to be given to the role of packaging in integrated marketing, relationship marketing with its emphasis on quality, and interactive media. In its promotional function, the package does everything a medium should. At the point of purchase, it alone informs, attracts, and reminds the consumer. At the point of use, it reinforces the purchase decision. Quality and value are viewed as relatively new marketing concepts, yet some 18 years ago the Design and Market Research Laboratory showed that quality perception was one of the key criteria for packaging assessment. But quality and value have always been part of the marketing and packaging equation.

Because packaging is such an important weapon in the marketing arsenal, it should be approached as other marketing elements with marketing research, specifically user research with target consumers. Blattner and Brunner's client Zippo has many quality products. The product design is very much part of the package (see Exhibit 21.16).

Frank Tobolski, president of JTF Marketing/Studios, says research techniques measure the communication strengths and weaknesses of package graphics. They answer such questions as: Do the graphics communicate well? Do the graphics reinforce and enhance the image positioning? Do the products and package sell? He reports on a case in which a toy company developed new packaging for a line of products. Perceptual and imagery evaluation in diagnostic laboratory tests was performed, indicating some problems and potential negative sales effects. To obtain behavioral sales data, test quantities of packages were produced for a balanced store test. For 6 weeks during the Christmas season, eighteen stores stocked the new test design, and eighteen stocked the existing control design. Toy specialty, discount, department store, and mass

EXHIBIT 21.16

The product design can be a very important part of the package equation.

Courtesy of Blattner Brunner.

merchandiser stores were used for the matched store pairings. The bottom line after 6 weeks found the existing control packages sold 63 percent more units than the test packages. Even after adjusting the test stores, the new designs sold 35 percent less.[19] A major loss in sales was diverted by testing. Imagine the loss if there had been a full new-package rollout.

Today's packaged-goods marketing managers constantly face the critical task of justifying expenditures in terms of the potential return on investment (ROI). Although most can instantly give you current sales figures, few know the yield on their latest shelf media or, specifically, packaging design.

Why? There is growing evidence that packaging design has a much stronger impact on sales than is realized.

As any brand manager will tell you, packaging represents a substantial portion of brand equity. When the word *Coke* is uttered, it is more than likely that an image of the trademarked, hourglass-shaped bottle comes to mind.

A Package Value survey suggests that marketers should benchmark new packaging proposals against their own brand equity. The study interviewed a total of 251 men and women, all primary grocery shoppers. Those polled were shown a card with a brand name printed on it and asked to rate the brand on a scale of 1 (agree strongly) to 5 (disagree strongly). Using "top box" methodology, only respondents who said they "agreed strongly" with all statements were included in the final results.

The subjects were then shown photos of actual packaging. The difference between the scores recorded when people were supplied with a brand name and when they were influenced by actual packaging is what makes the study intriguing. For example, when asked to rate the quality of Procter & Gamble's Tide, both the brand name and the packaging got scores of 61.[20]

Special Market Packaging

In the never-ending search for relevance and credibility with 13- to 26-year-old Millennials, many brand marketers are seeking the expertise of progressive multidisciplinary artists and agencies, rather than conventional branding firms, to create brand and marketing communications that break through, connect, and resonate with these savvy, discriminating, and hard-to-reach Millennials. Over 100 million strong, they are the largest and most techno-savvy generation in

American history. There is little doubt technology has democratized the market-place, shifting the power to consumers. In our on-demand world of 24-7 media, Millennials have mastered the art of selective hearing, purposely choosing to whom and to what they will listen.

Millennials represent a complex marketing challenge. Some brands are commissioning up-and-coming artists to consult on brand strategy and product design, packaging, retail environments, branded entertainment, motion graphics, and advertising. The idea is simple: Use the expertise and credibility of today's best contemporary artists and the power of art to connect with discriminating Millennials who are immune to conventional brand strategies or tactics.

For example, Coca-Cola launched The Club Coca-Cola project at Studio One in Cape Town as part of a global campaign that introduced a limited edition, contour shaped aluminum Coca-Cola bottle in nightclubs. Each bottle is branded with contemporary graphics designed by some of the most progressive creative firms in the world, including U.S.-based MK12 and Designers Republic in Europe. Printed in ultraviolet ink, each bottle design has a common graphical theme of "optimism" and "a better world," key to the Coca-Cola brand identity.[21]

Future Predictions   Although predictions are just that, one can usually make an intelligent and reasoned guess about the future by relying largely on the past and current trends that are evolving. With that caveat, Landor's brand identity expert, Allen Adamson, predicts five directions that may influence the future of branding.[22]

1. There may have been a time when the marketer called the shots, but that is certainly not true today. Consumer perception of a product's performance controls its success. Since a brand is a promise, one must ensure that the promise is fulfilled at each and every point of contact.

2. Customers interact with brands everywhere. 360-degree branding is here to stay. Purchase decisions are not made only at the point-of-sale so it is critical that you be in your customer's face with a consistent and coordinated expression of identity as often as is feasible.

3. Overextending your brand is not much different. Brands can stretch too far and the result can be jarring: erosion of brand equity. Most brands can probably be stretched into a plethora of categories. But often, brands become stronger when their scope is narrowed. Crest's line extension whiteners come in many shapes and forms, but distinctive names and packaging keep them straight in the consumer's mind (see Exhibit 21.17).

4. Most brand alliances that are formed are driven more by short-term promotional tactics than by long-term strategy. All marketing tactics should be undertaken within the context of a brand being a long-term asset. Partnering with competitors of nontraditional companies or products may enhance the brand's value, but choosing the wrong partner can cause substantial damage. Like people, brands are judged by the company they keep.[23]

5. Branding is not solely the purview of the marketing organization. The brand is the soul of the organization, and understanding its core values becomes the responsibility of everyone within the organization. Every point of contact (not just advertising and promotion) must be on-brand, and every individual within the organization should be charged with the responsibility of knowing exactly what that means.

Once a trend has been assimilated into the culture, it no longer is a trend.

Brands are long-term assets. As such, they need to be managed that way. Considering the future, looking at trends that are currently evolving can help better position brands over the long term. Creating value in tomorrow's brands requires a look at what is changing today.

Change is often subtle. It is rarely an all-of-a-sudden epiphany. Brand stewards must respond as they see trends evolving; they must be cognizant of changes in consumer thinking and observant to even slight changes in consumer behavior because even small changes, over time, can accumulate to become major trends. The challenge is in identifying the change as it is happening and adjusting your branding in concert with that change.

SUMMARY

Packaging is a very important part of the brand equity equation. It has been labeled as the only true method of international branding.

A product's trademark is like a person's name. It gives a product an identity and allows customers to be sure they are getting the same quality each time they purchase it. In addition, the trademark makes advertising and promotion activities possible. For established products, the trademark is one of the company's most valuable assets. It would be very difficult to estimate the value of trademarks such as Coca-Cola, Pepsi-Cola, IBM, and Mercedes. That is why companies take such pains to protect their trademarks.

The trademark can take the form of a word, a design, or a combination of both. Their formats can include letters, numbers, slogans, geometric shapes, color combinations, and so forth. When a trademark is a picture or other design, it is called a logotype. The same principle of trademark protection applies to logos as it does to brand names. Successful trademarks may take many forms; however, they should be easy to pronounce, have something in common with the product, and lend themselves to a variety of advertising and design formats.

The package design is developed in much the same way as an advertising campaign. Package research can help in assessing a number of factors, including recognition, imagery, structure, and behavior. Packaging is an important marketing tool and should be researched with target groups. Brand identity continues to be an important issue.

REVIEW ✸

1. What is a trademark?
2. What is a service mark?
3. How can you lose a trademark?
4. What are the steps to putting a lock on the ownership of a trademark?
5. Name several marketing issues involved in packaging.

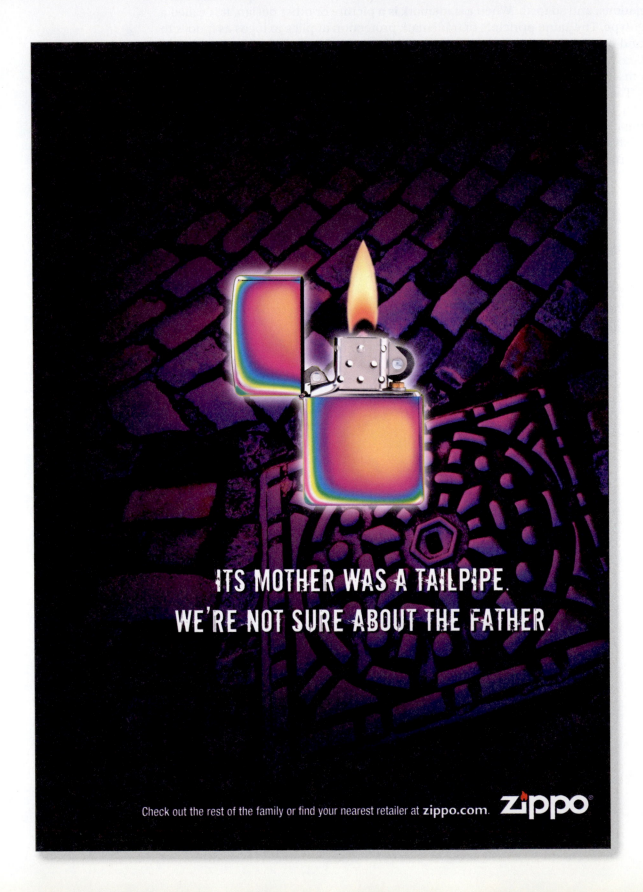

CHAPTER 22

The Complete Campaign

oday's advertisers usually create campaigns that fit into their integrated marketing communication program. They don't create just an ad by itself. After reading this chapter, you will understand:

chapter objectives

1. situation analysis
2. creative objectives and strategy
3. media objectives and strategy
4. sales promotion plans
5. research posttests

In Chapter 3, we focused on the premise that a brand is a living entity that is created through communication. It carries a history, which represents its accumulated capital, but it must continue to build new communication by asserting its presence, its sovereignty, and its territory. In doing so it must maintain a consistent identity. The four components (see Exhibit 22.1 as a refresher) are synthesized into an action plan for developing all communications for a brand (integrated marketing), including advertising, promotion, public relations, direct marketing, Internet, mobile, package design, buzz, etc. There are a lot of options. Today, most advertisers and agencies view their marketing communications as "media neutral," meaning there won't be a bias toward using advertising or any other specific discipline as the main communication tool in order to receive a maximum return on investment. In some situations, traditional advertising may not be needed in the plan, or, at least it is not what drives the plan. Advertisers' main concern is reaching every consumer's "touch point."

BRANDS ARE NOT BUILT OVER NIGHT

Every marketer should understand brands are rarely built overnight. Success may be measured in years or decades. Coca-Cola wasn't built in a year. BMW has been the ultimate driving machine for 30 years. We can't get there with a single ad. Maybe we start or continue the process with a strong campaign where all the integrated communications from the company or brand dovetail all other messages or impressions about the brand.

In this chapter, we discuss how to specifically build advertising campaigns—*campaign*, as defined by Webster, being a "series of planned actions."

You've learned about the important components of the advertising process—development of strategy, media, research, print ads, and broadcast—all of which are extremely important. We don't generally think in terms of individual ads because most brand advertising depends on a series of ads run over a period of time—in other words, a campaign.

EXHIBIT 22.1

A planning process for building a strong brand equity in marketing communications plans.

4.
Creative
Brief

3.
Brand Equity
Probe

2.
Strategic Options
and Recommended Plan

1.
Brand Equity Audit

A CAMPAIGN VERSUS ADS

There is no magic timeframe for a campaign. Yet, as a general rule, campaigns are designed to run over a longer period of time than an individual ad, although there are exceptions. The average length of a regional or national campaign is about 17 months, although it is not uncommon for a campaign to last 3 or 4 years, and a few campaigns have lasted much longer.

For example, in 1929 DuPont started using the campaign theme "Better Things for Better Living Through Chemistry." Fifty-five years later it was changed— "Through Chemistry" was dropped. That is building a lot of brand equity. Basically, the messages remained true to its original campaign premise. On the other hand, some campaigns need to change. In 2001, Ford Truck Division dropped its year-old "Ford Country" for a back-to-basics return to its reliable "Built Ford Tough." The automaker's truck division decided that "Built Ford Tough" carried a punch similar to Chevy's "Like a Rock," that "Ford Country" hadn't been able to deliver. Ford hadn't totally stopped using "Tough," but it had faded somewhat during the "Ford Country" effort. The point is that advertisers must understand their product and consumers in a changing marketplace. There is no reason to change an advertising campaign for the sake of change. Many marketing experts believe many advertisers give up on many campaigns too quickly.

CHANGING CAMPAIGNS RISK

There is never a guarantee that the next campaign will be as strong, let alone stronger, than the original. And some companies grope for a better campaign over and over again with little success. For example, in the mid-1970s, Burger King had perhaps its most famous campaign, "Have It Your Way," but decided it was time to change. So it followed with 16 or more different campaigns, looking for success, from "Aren't You Hungry for Burger King Now?" to "We Do It Like You Do It When We Do It at Burger King" to "Get Your Burger's Worth." In 2004, Burger King looked to the marketing—built around a revival of the chain's venerable "Have It Your Way" slogan—and a menu of new products for a much-needed turnaround. Russ Klein, Burger King CMO, says Burger King is no longer flipping marketing strategies as often as burgers—having had new marketing executives and campaigns almost annually for the past 8 years. He says, "This team is absolutely committed to the 'Have it Your Way' brand position and campaign."[1]

Ken Roman, former CEO of Ogilvy & Mather Worldwide, suggests that even the most successful campaigns need refreshing over time. People change, products change, markets change. There are times when campaigns simply wear out because market or competitive changes require a new message.[2]

Pepsi-Cola has been known for advertising to the "Pepsi Generation," but in the process different ad campaigns have been used to generate interest and success. Some are significantly different from previous ones, whereas others are simply tweaks in message or strategy:

Pepsi Generation Advertising Themes

1979 Catch the Pepsi Spirit

1982 Pepsi's Got Your Taste for Life

1984 Pepsi. The Choice of a New Generation

1989 A Generation Ahead

1995 Nothing Else Is Pepsi

1997 GeneratioNext

1999 The Joy of Cola

2000 The Joy of Pepsi

2003 Pepsi. It's the Cola

2007 It's the Cola

Remember in the advertising spiral in Chapter 3 we said that sometimes companies will try to expand targets with different kinds of promotional efforts. Snickers moved their campaign strategy from "hunger" to "satisfaction" because it is broader. The "Most Satisfying" campaign included television, viral, and outdoor. The television featured a troubadour with an acoustic guitar who sang a Snickers ballad in a dead-pan manner. He was featured in the viral effort. The Web was used as a conduit for devotees to create their own messages and write songs.[3]

Adding online advertising to a television campaign boosts brand awareness, but the inclusion does little to impact sales, according to a study by Dynamic Logic. Although broadcast ads upped the linking of a brand to a message or value proposition by nearly 13 points, the Web added 7 points. Television spots increased the ability to influence purchase decisions by nearly 6 points, whereas the Web only contributed a mere 0.4 point incremental boost. The Web was stronger at raising awareness and association than influencing purchase decisions.[4]

CAMPAIGN DIVERSITY

How would you as an advertiser handle diversity issues in a campaign? Separate campaigns for African Americans? Hispanics? Asians? What about for global products? This could become an issue.

In Chapter 4, we discussed targeting to different groups of people. In the 1980s and 1990s, advertisers began to be very conscious of using multiracial faces

KLEPPNER VIEWPOINT 22.1

Steven Guyer

Account Executive, G2 Direct & Digital–New York

Agencies: The Next Level of Continuing Education

For many of you in college, this spring means that you will prepare responses to new business pitches in your capstone course (we affectionately referred to it as the "campaigns" class). It's an opportunity to show your professors and peers how you think and work in a group. During the process, you apply the fundamentals of advertising and demonstrate how research, strategy, media, and creative have to work together. But the learning and competition doesn't end at graduation. At around the same time, real-world agencies with real-world clients will conduct similar competitions that foster talent through the process, and you'll need the experience from college to prepare you for your next step into an agency.

Just after completing my "campaigns" class and graduating college, the New York office of G2 Direct & Digital challenged me and other new, young ad professionals in *Direct Marketing Training* to apply what we learned in college to respond to a new business proposal.

During this 4-month program, G2 Direct & Digital's industry experts guided us through advertising best practices during weekly seminars and one-on-one follow-ups. We were divided into preselected teams and given the freedom to create our own "agencies" with billings, staffing plans, titles, and agency cultures. Several months of work was distilled into a final one-hour presentation where our ideas were judged and a winning agency was chosen (just as in the "campaigns" class). The presentation was scored based on our research, consumer insights, strategic planning, media, and even team chemistry. Yet there's one major difference that takes the competition beyond a college course—the clients considered for these competitions are often considered for future pitches.

Steven Guyer

So all your preparation in your college "campaigns" classes actually does relate to the real world. And sooner than you might think.

The G2 Direct & Digital *Direct Marketing Training* program gives you, as a young ad professional, a chance to showcase talent, learn the roles and responsibilities of each department in the agency, and apply what you know. These programs are more than an exercise; they provide you the kick-start skills needed to prepare you as the next generation of advertising professionals. ■ ■ ■

in their ads, if not targeting exclusively to a specific group—Asian, African American, Hispanic, and so on. Benetton, a global clothing chain, ads had a path-breaking campaign in the 1980s highlighting models of many races, each one very distinct. Today, there are over 7 million Americans who identify themselves as members of more than one race—the look of America has changed. Recently, the *New York Times* reported that among art directors and casting agents, there is a growing sense that the demand is weakening for traditional blond-haired, blue-eyed models. Many campaigns have purposely highlighted models with racially indeterminate features. The *New York Times* calls this "Generation E.A.: Ethnically Ambiguous." Ron Berger, the chief executive of Euro RSCG MVBMS Partners, says, "Today what's ethnically neutral, diverse or ambiguous has tremendous appeal." Any campaign needs to bring together all the advertising elements we have discussed into a unified campaign. This calls for an advertising plan. As we have emphasized, good advertising starts with a clear understanding of both short- and long-term marketing goals. These goals are often expressed as sales or share-of-market objectives to be accomplished for a given budget and over a specific time period.

With our marketing goals in mind, we begin to build the advertising plan with a situation analysis.

SITUATION ANALYSIS

To plan and create future advertising, we need to establish a current benchmark or starting point—this is the role of the situation analysis. It has two time orientations: the past and the present. In other words, it asks two basic questions: Where are we today, and how did we get here? The rest of the advertising plan asks the third basic question: Where are we going in the future?

The situation analysis is the first step in developing a campaign. Exhibit 22.2 reminds us of the planning process discussed earlier in Chapter 3. There are strategic steps that must be taken in the planning process. Campaigns are planned; they don't just happen.

The Product

Successful advertising and marketing begin with a good product. At this point, we need to analyze our product's strengths and weaknesses objectively. Most product failures stem from an overly optimistic appraisal of a product. Among the questions usually asked are the following:

1. What are the unique consumer benefits the product will deliver?
2. What is the value of the product relative to the proposed price?
3. Are adequate distribution channels available?
4. Can quality control be maintained?

The Charleston Convention Bureau represents area restaurants, hotels, retailing, and tourist sites to name a few. Each of their ads have the look of a campaign no matter which local aspect they are selling. Take a look at these two ads in Exhibit 22.3.

Prime-Prospect Identification

The next step is to identify our prime prospects and determine if there are enough of them to market the product profitably. As discussed in Chapter 4, there are a number of ways to identify the primary consumers of our product.

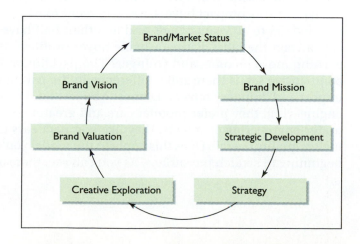

EXHIBIT 22.2

Planning Cycle

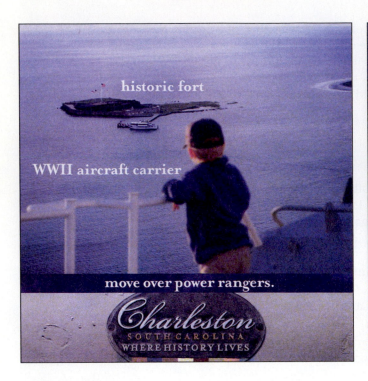

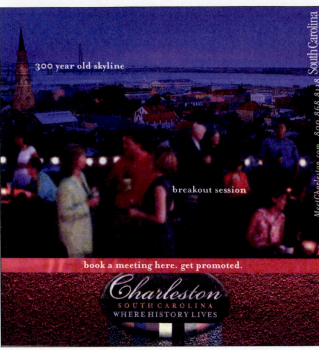

EXHIBIT 22.3

These two ads create different reasons for coming to Charleston, but they maintain the essence of the campaign.

Courtesy of the Charleston Convention Bureau.

Who buys our product and what are their significant demographic and psychographic characteristics? Can we get a mental picture of the average consumer? Who are the heavy users of the product—the prime prospects? Remember the 80/20 rule; do we need to find those market segments that consume a disproportionate share of our product and determine what distinguishes them from the general population? Finally, we need to examine the prime-prospects' problem. What are their needs and wants in the product or product type?

Competitive Atmosphere and Marketing Climate

We carefully review every aspect of the competition, including direct and indirect competitors. Which specific brand and products compete with our brand, and in what product categories or subcategories do they belong? Is Mountain Dew's competition 7-Up or Sprite, Sun Drop or Crush, or does it extend to colas, iced teas, and milk? If so, to what extent in each case?

What cars will the anticipated subcompact Ford Blue Oval, designed by Mazda, directly compete? Indirectly? It's competitive set will probably include the Toyota Yaris, Nissan Versa, Honda Fit, Scion xA, Kia Rio, Chevrolet Aveo, and the Hyndai Accent. When we examine the demographic competitive set, we find the typical subcompact buyers are 50 percent to 55 percent female, over half are married, 35 to 40 years of age, and less than half have a college degree. Which cars attract the most distinguishable buyer profiles—typically better educated, earning more income, and younger? The psychographic profile gives you the competitive set. Is there still a difference in the psychographic profiles between import and domestic buyers? Domestic buyers tend to be motivated by style over engineering; they prefer roomier cars and greater performance. Import buyers prefer engineering over style; they like compact cars and believe imports offer higher quality overall. Does this apply to the model you're advertising? Now we're beginning to scratch the surface. As you can see, there are numerous factors.

CREATIVE OBJECTIVES AND STRATEGY

At this point, we begin to select those advertising themes and selling appeals that are most likely to move our prime prospects to action. As discussed in Chapter 16, advertising motivates people by appealing to their problems, desires, and goals—it is not creative if it does not sell. Once we establish the overall objectives of the copy, we are ready to implement the copy strategy by outlining how this creative plan will contribute to accomplishing our predetermined marketing goals:

1. Determine the specific claim that will be used in advertising copy. If there is more than one, the claims should be listed in order of priority.
2. Consider various advertising executions.
3. In the final stage of the creative process, develop the copy and production of advertising.

Creative Criteria for Campaigns

Most advertising experts agree on the need for similarity between one advertisement and another in developing successful advertising campaigns. Another term, *continuity*, is used to describe the relationship of one ad to another ad throughout a campaign. This similarity or continuity may be visual, verbal, aural, or attitudinal.[5]

Visual Similarity All print ads in a campaign should use the same typeface or virtually the same layout format so that consumers will learn to recognize the advertiser just by glancing at the ads. This may entail making illustrations about the same size in ad after ad and/or the headline about the same length in each ad. A number of ads in campaigns have appeared throughout this book (e.g., Zippo, Mayfield, SummerGrove, Charleston Metro Chamber of Commerce, and Charleston Regional Development Alliance, etc.). Each illustration in the Tropicana campaign (see Exhibit 22.4) ads is

EXHIBIT 22.4

You can visually tell that these ads are part of the same campaign.

Courtesy of Tropicana.

EXHIBIT 22.5

These Reid & Barton ads have similar layouts, but are not the same.

Courtesy of Blattner Brunner.

visually treated in the same manner, and there is a similar feel with the photographs and similar location. For a different kind of client and reader (see Exhibit 22.5), ads may use similar styles, but there is still definite continuity. We have the same visual feel from ad to ad. We stress visual continuity—not sameness. These examples pertain to print, but the look could easily be carried over to television or direct marketing (see Exhibit 22.6). Strong continuity from medium to medium can strengthen the communication. This also applies to all the elements of integrated communications (promotions, Web, etc.).

Another device is for all ads in a campaign to use the same spokesperson or continuing character in ad after ad. Still another way to achieve visual continuity is to use the same demonstration in ad after ad from one medium to the other. Mayfield has used the same yellow in the background for outdoor and print to add a little visual continuity.

Verbal Similarity It is not unusual for a campaign to use certain words or phrases in each ad to sum up the product's benefits. It is more than a catchy phrase. The proper objective is a set of words that illuminates the advertising and encapsulates the promise that can be associated with one brand only.

Here are a few campaign phrases that have worked:

Mmm mm good.

CAMPBELL'S SOUP

The ultimate driving machine.

BMW

We'll leave a light on for you.

MOTEL 6

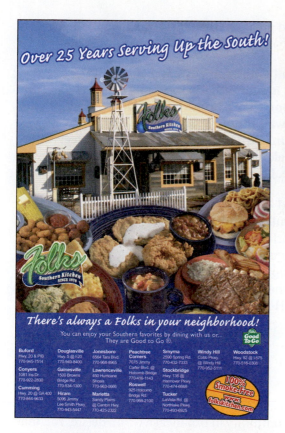

EXHIBIT 22.6

Folks branding, price ads, FSIs, and outdoor ads are driven by a similar design. Yet, the objectives are too different to simply plug in a single design.

Courtesy of Folks and Lane Bevil+Partners.

No, but I did stay at a Holiday Inn Express last night.

HOLIDAY INN EXPRESS

Good to the last drop.

MAXWELL HOUSE

Imagination at work.

GE

Pepsi used the words "You're in the Pepsi Generation" to help position it among a younger audience and make Coca-Cola appear to be an old-fashioned brand. But it didn't limit all the upbeat, self-assuring benefits of membership of being part of the Pepsi Generation to people between 13 and 24 years of age; it opened it up to everybody—everybody wanted to be in the Pepsi Generation. It wasn't a point of time in years, it was a point of view. No matter what your age, you could be part of the Pepsi Generation. Great words and great strategy make great campaigns. Here are a few other words and classic campaign strategies:

> **Aren't you glad you use Dial? Don't you wish everybody did?**
> **You're in good hands with Allstate.**
> **American Express. Don't leave home without it.**
> **Have it your way at Burger King.**
> **Is it true blondes have more fun? Be a Lady Clairol blonde and see!**
> **You deserve a break today, at McDonald's.**
> **Nike. Just do it.**

Repeating the benefits, theme, and key copy points in ad after ad bestows continuity across all media and helps to build brand personality.

We have shown a number of Charleston Regional Development Alliance ads earlier in this text to give you a real taste of its campaign. These ads use visual, verbal, and attitudinal similarity (see Exhibit 22.7 A, B, and C).

Campaigns need to be flexible so they can carry from ad to ad. Baby Gap used a verbal concept that could be endless. Here are a few examples:

Baby Gap is gift.
Baby Gap is newborn. A, B, C
Baby Gap is spring.
Baby Gap is jeans.

Aural Similarity You can create aural continuity in broadcast, if you desire. You may use the same music or jingle in commercial after commercial. Using the same announcer's voice in each ad also helps build continuity—a classic is "This is Tom Bodett for Motel 6." The same sound effect can make a campaign very distinctive. Avon used the sound of a doorbell for many years in its "Avon Calling" advertising. Maxwell House used the perking sound for its Master Blend commercials, giving an audible campaign signal.

Attitudinal Similarity Some campaigns have no theme line that continues from ad to ad. What they do have is an attitude that continues from ad to ad. Each ad expresses a consistent attitude toward the product and the people using it. The commercial's attitude is an expression of brand personality. The "Pepsi Generation" campaign was more than words. It communicated an attitude to younger consumers and older consumers. We cannot leave out the Nike shoe campaign, that said, "Just Do It"—or its swoosh campaign.

Everyone agrees that Nike is one of the strongest brand names in the world and not just because it sells great products. Its presence and identity are so strong that many people want to connect with the brand. It signifies status, glamour, competitive edge, and the myriad intricacies of cool. It is this description that is communicated in every message, no matter to whom it is directed. Nike's secret of success resides along a delicate and emotionally charged progression that connects the company, the consumers, and the abiding fantasies that are tethered to sports.[6] In true integrated marketing fashion, its personality is communicated to all—from employees, to stockholders, to consumers. It is conveyed through its corporate culture, as well as through its advertising.

Defining an attitude doesn't have to exclude visual or verbal continuity. The Charleston Regional Development Alliance campaign has visual continuity (see Exhibit 22.7).

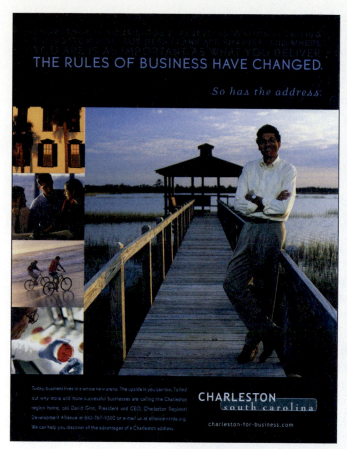

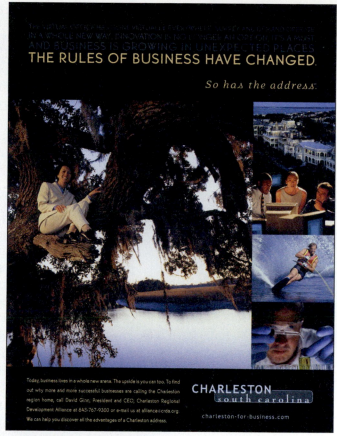

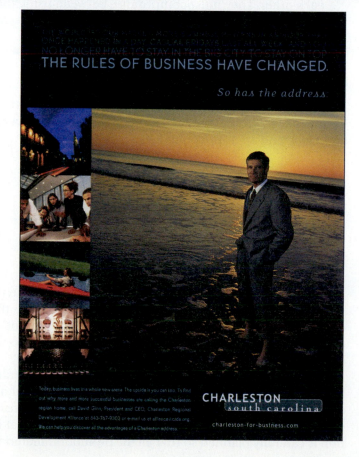

EXHIBIT 22.7

Charleston Regional Development Alliance ads use visual, verbal, and attitudinal similarity.

Courtesy of the Charleston Regional Development Alliance.

MEDIA OBJECTIVES

Although we have chosen to discuss creative strategy before media objectives, both functions are considered simultaneously in an advertising campaign. Creative planning and media planning has the same foundations—marketing strategy and prospect identification—and they cannot be isolated from each other. The media plan involves three primary areas.

Media Strategy

At the initial stages of media planning, the general approach and role of media in the finished campaign are determined:

1. *Prospect identification.* The prime prospect is of major importance in both the media and the creative strategy. However, the media planner has the additional burden of identifying prospects. The media strategy must match prospects for a product with users of specific media. This requires that prospects be identified in terms that are compatible with traditional media audience breakdowns. You will recall that this need for standardization has resulted in the 4A's standard demographic categories discussed in Chapter 4.

2. *Timing.* All media, with the possible exception of direct mail, operate on their own schedule, not that of advertisers. The media planner must consider many aspects of timing, including media closing dates, production time required for ads and commercials, campaign length, and the number of exposures desired during the product-purchase cycle.

3. *Creative considerations.* The media and creative teams must accommodate each other. They must compromise between using those media that allow the most creative execution and those that are most efficient in reaching prospects.

Media Tactics

At this point, the media planner decides on media vehicles and the advertising weight each is to receive. The question of reach versus frequency must be addressed and appropriate budget allocations made.

Media Scheduling

Finally, an actual media schedule and justification are developed, as described in the example in Chapter 7.

The Promotion Plan

As with any integrated communications planning, the promotion plan for consumers is discussed very early, and its relationship to the advertising plan (and other communications activities) is determined. Promotion activities may involve dealer displays, in-store promotions, premiums, cooperative advertising, and coupon offers.

Once a theme for communications has been established, creative work is begun on the promotion material, which is presented along with the consumer advertising material for final approval. Naturally, advertising and promotion materials reinforce each other. Once the promotion material is approved, the production is carefully planned so that all the promotion material will be ready before the consumer advertising breaks.

OTHER INTEGRATED ELEMENTS

Don't forget the importance of every aspect of your integrated marketing communication (IMC) functioning as one voice. You need to keep focused on the brand or positioning throughout the marketing mix. Toyota introduced its Yaris to 18 to 34 year olds through a lot of platforms hoping 30 percent of the buyers will be under 30. To reach the younger audience, the marketer has to make sure the Yaris was everywhere they spend time. Instead of portraying who would be driving it, the communications always featured the car front and center. The media plan was basically a screen-based plan. They launched over-mobile phone service with 26-episodes of *Prison Break* available to Sprint customers; with each 2-minute "mobisode" preceded by a 10-second ad; later they appeared on the Web, a contest sponsorship of consumer-generated commercials, a profile on MySpace.com, a custom community on Facebook.com, video games, and integration of the product into Fox's comedy show *MadTV* through a series of sketches. The target does consume mass media, they just don't consume it in a broad-scale sense.[7] This was a creative media plan as well as a series of integrated messages.

"Mountain Dew is all about exhilaration and energy, and you see that in all that we do," says Scott Moffitt, director of marketing for Mountain Dew. "Whether it is advertising, events, endorsements, or simply premiums, conveying the 'Dew-x-perience' is paramount."[8] Not only does Mountain Dew have strong advertising, but it has grassroots marketing programs and a sports-minded focus. So the range of IMC is endless and should be seamless. With packaging, remember Tiffany's blue box—a symbol of luxury. As mentioned in the last chapter, Pepsi has only permanently changed its label or logo ten times since the drink was invented in 1898. In 2007, Pepsi created thirty-five new designs for the year for its cans and were to duplicate this in 2008. They also involved consumers by asking them to design a billboard for Times Square, and they could contribute to an evolving billboard canvas on the Web. It is the latest attempt by companies trying to connect with the short attention spans of teens and young adults. And even characters may become brand icons: Ronald McDonald, Wendy, the Exxon Tiger, Jack of Jack-in-the-Box, the Pillsbury Doughboy, and AFLAC's duck. Don't forget endorsers or spokespersons. You can even use color as *the purple pill* did. Every piece of marketing communication can be integrated including every piece of your Web effort.

GETTING THE CAMPAIGN APPROVED

We now have a complete campaign: the ads, the media schedule, sales promotion material, and costs for everything spelled out, ready for management's final approval. For that approval, it is wise to present a statement of the company's marketing goals. The objectives may be to launch a new product, to increase sales by *x* percent, to raise the firm's share of the market by *z* percent, or to promote a specific service of a firm. Next, the philosophy and strategy of the advertising are described, together with the reasons for believing that the proposed plan will help attain those objectives. Not until then are the ads or the commercials presented, along with the media proposal and the plans for coordinating the entire effort with that of the sales department.

What are the reasons for each recommendation in the program? On what basis were these dollar figures calculated? On what research were any decisions based? What were the results of preliminary tests, if any? What is the competition doing? What alternatives were considered? What is the total cost? Finally, how may the entire program contribute to the company's return on its investment? Those people who control the corporate purse strings like to have definite answers to such questions before they approve a total advertising program.

RESEARCH—POSTTESTS

The final part of the campaign entails testing its success. Posttesting falls into two related stages. In the first, the expected results are defined in specific and measurable terms. What do we expect the advertising campaign to accomplish? Typical goals of a campaign are to increase brand awareness by 10 percent or improve advertising recall by 25 percent.

In the second stage, the actual research is conducted to see if these goals were met. Regardless of what research technique is used (e.g., test markets, consumer panels, etc.), the problem is separating the results of the advertising campaign from consumer behavior that would have occurred in any case. That is, if we find that 20 percent of the population recognizes our brand at the end of a campaign, the question arises as to what the recognition level would have been if no advertising took place. To answer this question, a research design is often used as a pretest. The pretest is intended not only to provide a benchmark for the campaign but also to determine reasonable goals for future advertising.

A 10-year study by Information Resources Inc.'s BehaviorScan showed that advertising produces long-term growth even after a campaign ends. The study emphasized television campaigns and concluded the following:

■ Increased ad weight alone will not boost sales.

■ Typically, advertising for new brands, line extensions, or little-known brands produced the best incremental sales results.

■ Campaigns in which the "message in the copy is new" or the media strategy had changed also produced good sales results.

■ Results of copy recall and persuasion tests were unlikely to predict sales reliably.

The study also suggested that discounting results in "training customers to buy only on a deal," and the trade promotion actually worked against television advertising. However, coupons often helped a brand message and spurred a sale.

The test was conducted in 10 markets with household panels of 3,000 respondents in each market. The commercials were transmitted to two equal groups of homes. This study compared purchase information obtained through scanners and a card encoded with demographic and other information that was presented at supermarket checkout stands.[9]

Campaign Portfolio

Pathway Communities Throughout the book you have seen examples from SummerGrove. These particular ads have used the same headline and almost identical layout format, which make for easy consumer identification. Each copy sells the benefits of their amenities. Exhibit 22.8 shows three of the campaign ads.

Tennessee Aquarium The Tennessee Aquarium not only used advertising, but a little guerilla effort to hit people on the street (see Exhibit 22.9).

Mayfield This dairy has long used Scottie Mayfield as their spokesperson, usually in a humorous and entertaining manner (see Exhibit 22.10). The ice cream television and print reinforces each other and the creative concept.

Georgia 529 Plan It is difficult to make people believe they really need to start saving money for college. It is somewhat confusing and very competitive. As with any financial advertising, there are regulations which regulate what can and cannot be said. The Georgia 529 Plan uses a strong media mix including Internet and direct mail. Here are a few examples (see Exhibit 22.11).

The joys of SummerGrove will turn you into a kid again.

Get the life you've always dreamed of living in a spectacular SummerGrove custom home. Enjoy special extras, such as fine brick and stone exteriors, outside living areas, and professional landscaping. Plus use your creativity to add custom touches and upgrades inside and out. You'll have your choice of premium, wooded homesites offering incredible lakefront and golf course living. Not to mention all the excitement of three great amenity areas, including swimming, tennis, a clubhouse, parks, and a lazy river. Come create your very own SummerGrove custom home. And experience the joy of getting exactly what you want. SUMMERGROVE

Homes from the $130s to $700s • Information Center open Daily 11-6, Sunday 1-6 • 770-252-9000 • www.summergrove.com

I-85 South to Exit 47 (Newnan). Left on Hwy. 34, one mile. Turn right on Shenandoah Blvd. Continue 1.4 miles to SummerGrove. Follow signs to Information Center. PATHWAY

The joys of SummerGrove will turn you into a kid again.

Cast off your line at SummerGrove's 100-acre lake, and something magical happens. You remember that life was meant to be fun. That's why everyone comes here. To recapture the joy of splashing at the pools and swinging on the playgrounds. To play with friends at the tennis courts and ball fields. And to spend time with neighbors at the golf course and clubhouse. You'll also enjoy choosing from our wide selection of homes, all wired for the latest technology. There's something for everyone, including newly available golf course homes from the low $200s. Come to SummerGrove. Your second childhood is waiting. SUMMERGROVE

Homes from the $130s to $700s • Information Center open Daily 11-6, Sunday 1-6 • 770-252-9000 • www.summergrove.com

I-85 South to Exit 47 (Newnan). Left on Hwy. 34, one mile. Turn right on Shenandoah Blvd. Continue 1.4 miles to SummerGrove. Follow signs to Information Center. PATHWAY

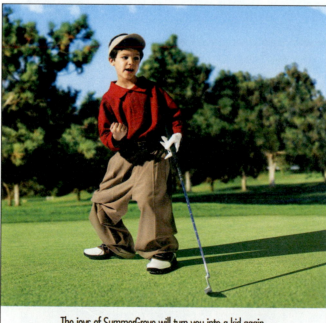

The joys of SummerGrove will turn you into a kid again.

All it takes is one swing on the 18-hole golf course. You'll forget the busy life you lead and remember how much fun it is to have, well, fun. And it won't stop there. You'll play at the pools and tennis courts. Go boating on the 100-acre lake. Then remember the simple pleasures of a day at the park or a trip down the lazy river. You'll also experience the joy of finding just the right home. We've got a variety of styles to choose from by some of the area's best builders. Including golf course homes from the low $200s and custom lake homes from the $300s. Come to SummerGrove. Your second childhood is waiting. SUMMERGROVE

Homes from the $130s to $700s • Information Center open Daily 11-6, Sunday 1-6 • 770-252-9000 • www.summergrove.com

I-85 South to Exit 47 (Newnan). Left on Hwy. 34, one mile. Turn right on Shenandoah Blvd. Continue 1.4 miles to SummerGrove. Follow signs to Information Center. PATHWAY

EXHIBIT 22.8

These SummerGrove development ads are clearly different but have a similar look and feel. Notice each uses the same headline.

Courtesy of McRae Communications and Pathway Communities.

EXHIBIT 22.9

The Tennessee Aquarium outdoor and guerrilla efforts carry the same theme. Other ads promote specifics like the otters.

Courtesy of The Johnson Group.

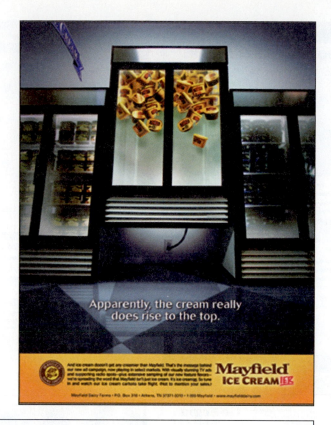

EXHIBIT 22.10

Mayfield Ice Cream's television and print ads promote the same images and the creamier concept.

Courtesy of The Johnson Group.

"FREEZER"
:30 TV Spot

Story Summary:
As a dad and his daughter walk through the freezer aisle in the grocery store, they notice the Mayfield ice cream freezer floating in mid air, tethered only by the case's electric plug. Amazed, they look through the glass to see that all of the Mayfield cartons are floating to the top of the freezer. As dad cautiously opens the door to select a flavor, the cartons begin to "escape," rising up toward the ceiling.

GIRL: Hey dad. What kind of ice cream is that?

DAD: Oh, that's... Wow!

GIRL: Can we get some?

DAD: You bet.

GIRL: Cool!

SCOTTIE V/O: Looks like the cream really does rise to the top.

And you can't get creamier ice cream than Mayfield.

Like new Mayfield Cookies & Cream.

It's just not ice cream.

It's ice creamier.

GIRL: What flavor do you want?

DAD: All of 'em!

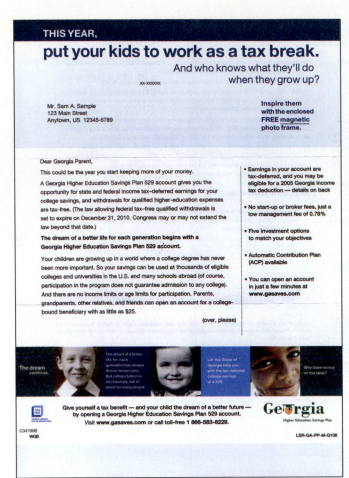

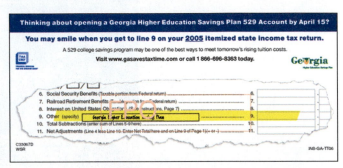

EXHIBIT 22.11

The Georgia 529 Plan uses these Internet and direct mail communications to reach their target.

Courtesy of Georgia Higher Education Savings Plan.

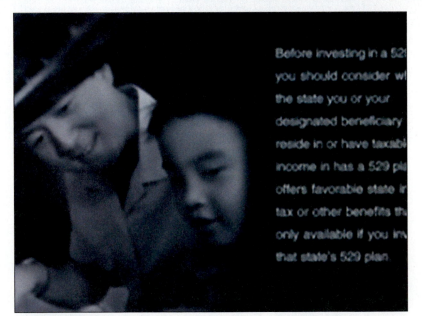

CASE HISTORY

In Chapter 5, Chick-fil-A's operating philosophy was discussed. Here, we want to share one of the world's great integrated marketing campaigns.

Background

Atlanta-based Chick-fil-A®, founded by entrepreneur and restaurateur S. Truett Cathy has risen from rather humble beginnings to become America's second-largest quick-service chicken restaurant chain in the country.

Cathy started in 1946 in the Atlanta suburb of Hapeville with a single location he named the Dwarf Grill. Cathy now presides over a chain of some 1,300 restaurants in 37 states and Washington, D.C., generating annual sales of more than $2 billion.

Marketing

Chick-fil-A's marketing strategy throughout the chain's history can be summed up in two words: maximizing resources. From the beginning, the Chick-fil-A's brand was built on people, product, and purpose.

People: Truett Cathy was an important person to leverage, but so, too, were the growing number of franchise operators who represented the Chick-fil-A brand in their own community.

Product: Armed with a great tasting product, the chain recognized that its main challenge was merely to get people to try it.

Purpose: Honoring Cathy's desire to run the business on Biblical principals, restaurant operators provided customers with a unique quick-service dining experience, highlighted by a friendly, service-oriented atmosphere.

Necessitated by limited marketing budgets, Chick-fil-A's early marketing efforts were locally focused. One early marketing program that Cathy adopted that still is employed today is product sampling. Leveraging their location within malls, Chick-fil-A operator and team members frequently offer free product samples of the Chick-fil-A Chicken Sandwich (and later other products, such as Chick-fil-A Nuggets, Chick-fil-A Chick-n-Strips, etc.). In those early days, the chain's marketing slogan was: "Taste It! You'll Love It For Good." Even as the chain grew, expanding into a regional—and eventually, a national—brand, Chick-fil-A maintained a local focus for its marketing efforts. Restaurant openings highlighted the marketing calendar, and Cathy personally attended every new mall opening.

In 1981, Steve Robinson—a former marketing executive with Six Flags—joined Chick-fil-A as its director of marketing (currently, he serves as senior vice president of marketing), and was charged with developing the company's overall marketing strategy. Realizing that the brand's strength was in its local store's efforts, and recognizing that the chain's marketing budgets were limited relative to other quick-service brands, Robinson created a marketing strategy that turned convention on its head—literally.

While most quick-service chains focused most of their marketing spending on national programs and allotted proportionally smaller amounts to regional (and even smaller amounts to local) efforts, Robinson proposed the opposite. He knew he did not have the advertising dollars to compete with other brands on a national level so he focused those dollars in the cities and the immediate market areas where the restaurants could be found.

Chick-fil-A initiated a field marketing strategy that leveraged this model. At the store level, unit marketing directors (UMDs) were hired, who were responsible for all marketing activities within a three- to five-mile radius of their restaurant. For larger markets with multiple restaurants (e.g., Atlanta, Dallas, Orlando, etc.), Robinson recommended hiring area marketing directors (AMDs). An AMD would report directly to the group of operators in their market, and their duties would include marketwide sponsorships, partnerships, events, promotions, and public relations.

On a national level, Chick-fil-A focused the remainder of its marketing dollars on systemwide promotions and sports sponsorships (which today includes the *Chick-fil-A Bowl*, as well as sponsorship of Southeastern Conference, Atlantic Coast Conference, and Big 12 Conference championship events). At all levels, Chick-fil-A relied heavily on public relations as a cost-effective means to support the brand locally, regionally, and nationally.

In terms of advertising dollars, Chick-fil-A typically focused locally. Point-of-purchase materials and local print and radio ads made up the bulk of the chain's advertising arsenal for many years. But as the chain grew—both geographically and in terms of sales—the need to support the brand with a memorable campaign grew as well.

In 1995, Chick-fil-A brought in a new advertising agency—Dallas-based The Richards Group. Stan Richards, the agency's founder and chief creative officer, recommended a unique approach to advertising for Chick-fil-A that would not work for just any company: concentrate on billboards. Given its limited budgets, Chick-fil-A could not make much of an impact in television advertising (national or local), radio, or even print. But billboards were a truly local advertising medium, and the exposure to local traffic was just what the chain needed to drive customers to their restaurants. And the price was right to allow Chick-fil-A to "own" billboards.

The now-famous "Cow" billboard (featuring two, three-dimensional cows perched atop a billboard, painting the words: "Eat Mor Chikin") was not the first "edgy" billboard concept developed, but it certainly was the campaign that stuck. With the cows, Chick-fil-A had an irreverent, humorous, and extremely memorable campaign with creative messages that helped cut through the clutter and maximize the chain's use of outdoor advertising. It did not take long for the "Cow" campaign to extend far beyond billboards and into every aspect of Chick-fil-A's marketing efforts, including:

- Point-of-purchase materials
- Print advertising
- Radio advertising
- Television advertising (local and in support of national sponsorships)
- Merchandise sales
- Event support
- Its popular *Cow Calendar*. Now the number one selling calendar in the nation.

Leveraging such a memorable campaign, Chick-fil-A has been able to generate impact in all advertising media without having to commit huge advertising budgets to generate exposure through repetition. The campaign also has won several awards since its inception, including the 1996 OBIE award for outstanding outdoor advertising; the 1998 Silver Effie award, presented by the New York American Marketing Association; the 1997 Silver Lion presented at the Cannes International Advertising Festival; and most recently was named to the OBIE Outdoor Hall of Fame.

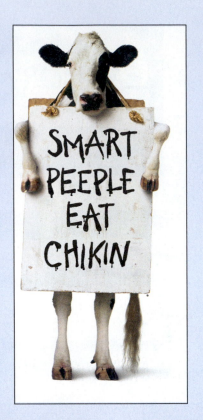

CASE HISTORY

Background

Folks Restaurant Management Group (FRMG) operates twenty-plus restaurants in northern Georgia—primarily metropolitan Atlanta—known as Folks. The restaurant was reborn out of another restaurant concept in 1996 that featured fried foods. The new restaurant started as a "casual family" restaurant—with a Southern flavor. As with other retail or restaurants service companies, their marketing adjusts almost daily to sales and customer traffic. Its biggest sales day of the year is Mother's Day.

Competition

The fast-growing Atlanta market is one of the most competitive restaurant markets in the country so their competition is broad-based. Near every Folks restaurant, new concepts open almost weekly, keeping the competition fierce. National chains like Chili's, Longhorn's, Applebee's, etc., are generally near each of the Folks locations. There are also a number of "grazing" restaurants that attract many of the same people.

Target

Historically, each store pulls a slightly different mix of consumers—some a little older, a little better educated, more ethnic, and so forth. Dinner attracts families—from young families to grandparents in the middle-income range. Research indicated the need to better target women 25 to 49 years of age.

Media

Folks primarily uses radio, FSIs, direct marketing, newspaper, outdoor, Web advertising and promotion, and cable television. Television and radio have been used primarily for brand recognition and a large part of the budget directed at seasonal promotion. The Folks share of voice is low because of its small budget in comparison to Outback and other national chains. It is a marketing challenge.

Creative

Folks creates more than ads and promotions. The restaurant business demands a multitude of marketing communications including in-store material, table tents, menu designs, kids' coloring pieces, kids' menus, take-out menus, employee motivational programs, Web site promotions, and public relations activities in addition to advertising. One plus is that the restaurant is positioned as a "Southern Kitchen," with the menu featuring many southern foods and vegetables. This is also problematic because the market migration is toward Hispanics and non-Southerners. Reaching consumers is a daily challenge against larger national competition.

Results

The restaurant continues to keep its core customer and is aggressively seeking a broader customer base. Despite the increase in competition, Folks continues to steadily grow.

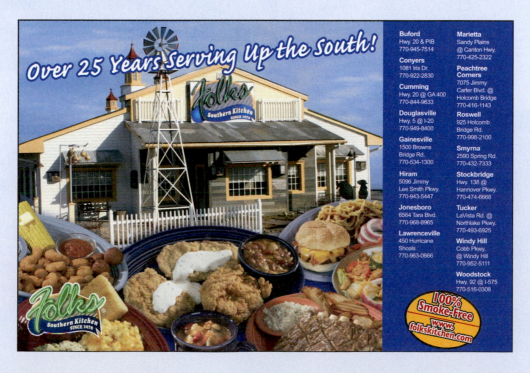

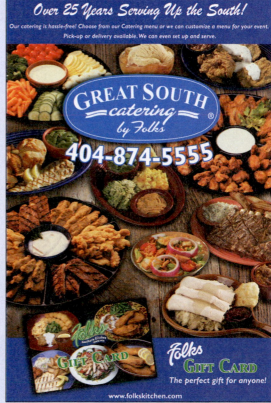

Seafood Bayou Platter
$10.99
Stuffed Crab • White Fish • Clam Strips • Gulf Shrimp

Friday Catfish Fry
$7.99
Served with fries and slaw.

Pecan Crusted Trout
NEW Only $9.99

All-You-Can-Eat Mix & Match
Choose 1, 2 or all 3!
• Blue Ribbon Fried Chicken
• Classic Country Fried Steak
• Hand-breaded Catfish Fillets
$9.99
No sharing and no doggie bags, please.

$3 Off Two Meals
Limit one coupon per party per visit.

$5.99 2 pc. (all dark) "Atlanta's Best" Fried Chicken
Limit one coupon per party per visit.

$5.99 Classic Country Fried Steak (single serving)
Limit one coupon per party per visit.

$5 OFF Any Size Party Platter (each platter)

FREE Kid's Meal
Limit one coupon per party per visit.

FREE Fried Green Tomatoes or Cobbler of the Day!
Limit one coupon per party per visit.

$25 OFF! Catering Orders over $250

$3.00 Off!
• 8 or 16 pc. Mixed Chicken Picnic
• Combo Picnic - 8 pc. Mixed Chicken & 4 pc. Country Fried Steak

Good To Go

Open Thanksgiving Day

There's a lot going on at your Folks

Friday Catfish Fry
$7.99

The complete Folks Holiday Feast
$9.99
Available November 21 – January 1
Feast includes Oven-roasted turkey breast slices with cornbread dressing and gravy, your choice of two veggies, bread and our famous iced Tea. Plus, your choice of Cobbler or Pecan Pie for dessert.

$5 Off Any Size Party Platter (each platter)

$3 Off Two Meals

FREE Kid's Meal

The Folks Garden Patch
Buffet includes Salad Fixins, Fresh Soup of the Day, & bread. All-You-Can-Eat.
Add the Garden Patch to any entree on the menu. FREE
Garden Patch Buffet only available in Snellville!
2277 East Main St. • 770-972-3060

Open Thanksgiving Day

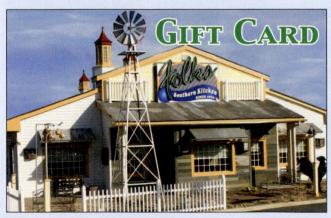

GIFT CARD

Fisherman's Feast
Folks SEAFOOD

RAINBOW TROUT
SHRIMP SKEWERS
GUMBO Great as a starter or one of your sides.
SHRIMP TRIO
COCONUT SHRIMP
SHORE PLATTER
BAYOU PLATTER
FISH CAMP PLATTER

For a change of pace, try our Strawberry Lemonade!

Dive right in! Fisherman's Feasts are served with your choice of two sides and bread.

SHORE PLATTER $8.99
Gulf Shrimp, One Crab Cake and White Fish (grilled or fried).

FISH CAMP PLATTER $9.99
Catfish Fillets, One Crab Cake and Calabash Shrimp.

BAYOU PLATTER $10.99
Gulf Shrimp, One Crab Cake, Clams and White Fish (grilled or fried).

RAINBOW TROUT $8.99
Grilled with herb, lemon pepper or Cajun seasonings or golden-fried.

CRAB CAKE DINNER $7.99
Two delicious golden Crab Cakes.

COCONUT SHRIMP (12) $7.99
Served with Orange Sesame Ginger Dipping Sauce.

SHRIMP SKEWERS $9.99
Count them – you get 3 full skewers of sizzlin' grilled shrimp served over rice pilaf.

SHRIMP TRIO $9.99
If you love Shrimp, this will be your pick – one Shrimp Skewer over rice pilaf, Gulf Shrimp and Coconut Shrimp.

NEW SIDES
• Rice Pilaf
• Steamed Mixed Veggies
• Gumbo
• Fruit Cup

Fisherman's Feast
Folks SEAFOOD

RAINBOW TROUT
SHRIMP SKEWERS
SHRIMP TRIO
COCONUT SHRIMP
SHORE PLATTER
BAYOU PLATTER
FISH CAMP PLATTER

$3 Off Two Meals
Purchase any 2 entrees from our regularly-priced menu and receive $3 off the total check. Offer expires 6/19/06.
Limit one coupon per party per visit.

FREE Kid's Meal
Enjoy one FREE Kid's Meal from the $2.69 Kid's Menu with an adult meal purchased from our regular menu. Offer expires 6/19/06.
Limit one coupon per party per visit.

FREE Fried Green Tomatoes or Cobbler of the Day!
Purchase any meal from our regular menu & receive a FREE Fried Green Tomatoes appetizer or Cobbler of the Day. Offer expires 6/19/06.
Limit one coupon per party per visit.

$3.00 Off!
Choose from:
• 8 or 16 pc. Mixed Chicken Picnic
• Combo Picnic with 8 pc. Mixed Chicken & 4 pc. Country Fried Steak

Good To Go

Buford Hwy. 20 near PIB 770-945-7514

Cumming Hwy. 20 at GA 400 770-844-9633

SUMMARY ⊛

The steps in preparing a national campaign for a consumer product are the following:

1. Situation analysis
   a. Product analysis
   b. Prime-prospect identification
   c. Prime-prospects' problem analysis
   d. Competitive atmosphere and market climate
2. Creative objectives and strategy
   a. Determination of specific copy claims
   b. Consideration of various advertising executions
   c. Creation of ads and commercials (and other integrated communications)
3. Media objectives
   a. Media strategy—includes prospect identification, timing, and creative considerations
   b. Media tactics
   c. Media scheduling
4. Promotion plan (and/or other integrated programs)
5. Campaign approval
6. Research posttests

In general, advertising campaigns need to have similarity from ad to ad. It may be visual, verbal, aural, or attitudinal. Campaigns should be designed to last and not be changed simply because you are bored with them.

REVIEW ⊛

1. What is the basic purpose of an ad campaign?
2. What is ad continuity?
3. What is involved in the situation analysis?
4. What are some of the means of guaranteeing continuity in a campaign?

PART SIX

Other Environments of Advertising

International Advertising

*A*t one time, U.S. firms considered their international marketing operations separately from domestic sales and promotion. However, in an environment with a Nissan automotive plant in Tennessee; Hondas rolling off an Ohio assembly line; and Mercedes and BMW making luxury cars in the Deep South, the global village is in our own backyard. Globalization is much more than just doing business abroad. Multinational firms operate in an atmosphere of converging cultural, political, communication, and business issues where companies battle head-to-head for local buyers in what is often worldwide competition. In this chapter, we will examine the challenges facing companies that must increasingly compete for customers on a global scale. After reading this chapter, you will understand:

chapter objectives

1. the evolving nature of the global market
2. the role of advertising and advertising agencies in international marketing
3. changes in U.S. advertising and marketing practices as a result of global competition
4. cultural and political considerations in international marketing
5. organizing advertising management to compete in the global marketplace
6. effects of a diverse U.S. population on domestic advertising and media

The purchase of goods from abroad is so entrenched in the American economy that we often forget that the global market is a phenomenon of relatively recent vintage. For example, the first Toyota automobile, the Toyopet Crown, was not introduced in the United States until 1957. After selling only 288 cars in the first 14 months, Toyota withdrew from the U.S. market in 1961. In 1965, Toyota launched the Corona with a design more suited to American drivers. By 1972, Toyota reached $1 million annual sales and today is challenging General Motors to become the world's largest car manufacturer.[1]

The changing complexion of global advertising and marketing is readily apparent from an examination of how American businesses and advertising agencies are now competing with multinational companies from developed countries throughout the world. For example, a recent gobal survey of teens asked them what brands they found most "likeable." The top three brands were Sony (Japan), Nokia (Finland), and Adidas (Germany)—Coca Cola, in eighth place, was the highest-ranked American brand, although it rated number one in familiarity.[2] As reflected in the current trade imbalance in the United States, American consumers prefer foreign-made goods in a number of major product categories.

Economies are growing at rates much higher than those found in either North America or Europe providing lucrative areas for expansion. In 1950, New York and London ranked first and second respectively among the world's thirty largest cities. In the coming decade, New York will fall to seventh and London will drop off the list altogether. Overall, Asia will be the home of seven of the top ten cities, led by Tokyo with a population of 27 million. Of the top thirty largest cities, North America and Europe will include only two—New York and Paris.[3] A significant percentage of future growth in marketing and advertising will be more concentrated in the Far East, Middle East, and Latin America as sellers seek new customers for their goods and services. This trend has been ongoing for some time as a number of major U.S. companies are spending more than 50 percent of their advertising budgets abroad.

Recognizing that global markets offer promise for new customers is one issue, but being able to effectively enter these markets is a much more difficult problem. For example, one of Procter & Gamble's most popular products, the Swiffer Wet Mop, was such a flop in Italy that it was taken off the market. While American consumers embraced the time-saving features of the mop, which eliminates the need for a water bucket, Italian buyers take pride in spending considerable time on cleaning chores. For example, Italians spend 21 hours per week on household chores other than cooking compared to just 4 hours for U.S. families.[4] In another case, Folgers coffee was introduced in China in metal cans only to find that most Chinese households don't have can openers. As one marketing researcher pointed out, "It's important that companies understand the local context and connect with local players. Products have to be developed with them. It's no use designing a product in the West and taking it over to consumers. It's crucial to find out what's right with these economies."[5]

In Chapter 1, we discussed how early advertising in the United States grew as a result of a number of economic, social, and cultural factors. In many respects, today's world marketplace demonstrates many of the same characteristics. Only by understanding these broader issues can we tell the full story of the global economic expansion. It can be argued that the global business revolution of the last decade is fundamentally a communication revolution that, in country after country, has resulted in demands for more open political systems, which inevitably leads to demands for more economic choice. Without an expansion of communication, it is doubtful that the current political and economic environment would exist.

No where is the expansion of global marketing more apparent than in the increase in international advertising spending levels. Rather than the U.S. domination of past years, current spending shows that less than half (twelve of twenty-five) of the top one hundred global advertisers are headquartered in the United States (see Exhibit 23.1). While the United States is still dominant in terms of advertising spending with 48.8 percent of the total, it is far outpaced by China's 84.7 percent annual increase in growth rate.[6] The expansion of international marketing and advertising is occurring during a period of significant change in global relationships. These alliances cover a continuum from broadly based country and continental connections to aspirations of individual consumers for a better standard of living. Global marketers are faced with the dilemma of dealing with wide-ranging differences among global consumers and at the same time finding some commonality among diverse markets on which to base brand messages. For example, marketers find that while urban Chinese teenagers are a huge potential market, they

EXHIBIT **23.1**

Top 25 Global Marketers

Ranked by measured media spending in the 77 countries.

Adapted from *Advertising Age*.

Rank 2004	Rank 2003	Advertiser	Headquarters	Measured Media Ad Spending 2004	2003	% Chg
1	1	Procter & Gamble Co.	Cincinnati	$7,922	$6,734	17.6
2	3	General Motors Corp.	Detroit	3,918	3,293	19.0
3	2	Unilever	London/Rotterdam	3,462	3,395	2.0
4	5	Ford Motor Co.	Dearborn, Mich.	2,798	2,434	15.0
5	7	L'Oreal	Paris	2,646	2,284	15.8
6	4	Toyota Motor Corp.	Toyota City, Japan	2,608	2,475	5.4
7	6	Time Warner	New York	2,495	2,301	8.4
8	8	DaimlerChrysler	Auburn Hills, Mich./ Stuttgart, Germany	2,371	2,081	14.0
9	11	Johnson & Johnson	New Brunswick, N.J.	1,922	1,700	13.0
10	9	Nestle	Vevey, Switzerland	1,899	1,848	2.8
11	10	Walt Disney Co.	Burbank, Calif.	1,895	1,795	5.6
12	12	Nissan Motor Co.	Tokyo	1,812	1,630	11.1
13	13	Altria Group	New York	1,645	1,504	9.4
14	15	Honda Motor Co.	Tokyo	1,642	1,462	12.3
15	20	Coca-Cola Co.	Atlanta	1,507	1,284	17.4
16	14	Sony Corp.	Tokyo	1,480	1,496	−1.0
17	16	Volkswagen	Wolfsburg, Germany	1,455	1,364	6.7
18	17	McDonald's Corp.	Oak Brook, Ill.	1,442	1,329	8.5
19	18	Pfizer	New York	1,349	1,288	4.7
20	21	GlaxoSmithKline	Greenford, Middlesex, U.K.	1,303	1,173	11.1
21	19	PepsiCo	Purchase, N.Y.	1,286	1,287	−0.1
22	24	Reckitt Benckiser	Windsor, Berkshire, U.K.	1,278	967	32.2
23	22	Danone Group	Paris	1,278	1,035	23.5
24	31	Deutsche Telekom	Bonn, Germany	1,097	794	38.1
25	25	General Electric Co.	Fairfield, Conn.	1,043	934	11.7

are conflicted about many of the changes in that country. "This generation has more choices than at any other time in China's history, but they're not entirely comfortable with these choices. They want to express themselves, but only in a safe, socially acceptable context."[7]

As we will discuss throughout this chapter, American companies face another set of obstacles in competing for global sales. Among the major challenges is overcoming significant anti-American opinions abroad. The roots of these attitudes are varied, but many are related to the marketing of American products. For example:

- *Exploitation*—the feeling that American companies take more than they give.
- *Corrupting influence*—the view that American brands enhance thinking and behavior that clash with local customs and debases cultural or religious norms.
- *Gross insensitivity and arrogance*—in many cultures there is a perception that Americans believe everyone wants to be like them.
- *Hyper-consumerism*—As we will see in this chapter, a continuing challenge for multinational marketers and their agencies is to find those shared feelings and attitudes that are consistent from country to country to give their brand messages continuity. At the same time, it is imperative that these companies are sensitive to the distinct differences and pride that consumers feel toward their national and cultural heritages.

THE MULTINATIONAL CORPORATION

An expected consequence of the global economy is the creation of the multinational corporation. Operating in hundreds of countries and selling billions of dollars worth of goods and services, these giant enterprises rival many small countries in terms of economic output. They occupy a place beyond that of a simple seller of merchandise. The CEOs of these firms function as quasi-political and cultural leaders with a scope of influence unknown in earlier times. However, regardless of their influence, the basic motivation of these multinationals is the same as that of the corner pizza shop—to make a profit and expand their customer base.

The fundamental economic model remains the same regardless of the company's size. As companies reach a saturation point within existing markets, they seek new buyers to continue to increase both sales and profitability. It so happens that as the United States and other prosperous countries reached a level of market satiation, the technological means of instant communication and rapid transportation made global trade possible. At the end of World War II, American businesses were at the vanguard of the rebuilding process, first in Western Europe and later in Asia. During these early years of global expansion, multinational marketing was largely confined to U.S. companies, with few competitors headquartered outside the United States. However, since the 1970s, U.S. business has had to share the world market with a number of companies headquartered abroad. In many product categories, such as textiles and electronics, there is virtually no U.S. manufacturing remaining. In other industries, such as automobiles, the U.S. market share has shrunk by more than half in the last two decades. Likewise, advertising, long considered a U.S. invention, is truly a global enterprise with many of the icons of U.S. advertising, such as J. Walter Thompson, now controlled by foreign holding companies.

In an ironic twist, the emerging foreign markets that at one time were viewed only as a means of new sales and profits for U.S. and European companies have increasingly become sources of intense competition. Much to the dismay of some major companies, some of this competition comes in the form of products almost identical to those of the originating company. For example, the Chinese Shuanghuan Laibao SRV is virtually the same as the Honda CR-V and, at a 2005 car show, Chinese automaker Red Flag showed a concept car that looked much like the Rolls-Royce Phantom—for half the price. "While Western car makers may be horrified by China's blatant commandeering of their ideas, they are also understandably wary of making enemies in the world's fastest growing car market. Every major car company is desperate to get a slice of the Chinese sales boom. To do this the Chinese government usually requires them to form an alliance with a Chinese company and, although the communist regime may be embracing capitalism, all large investments have to be cleared by the authorities."[8]

As disconcerting as China's alleged "reverse engineering" of automobiles is to automakers, most consumers are astute enough to know that a half-price Rolls-Royce is unlikely to deliver comparable value. However, in a more general arena, the Chinese are proving themselves to be worthy competitors for the global consumer's dollar. For example, in the 2005 Industrial Design Excellence Awards (IDEA) competition, six Chinese companies entered the contest, and Lenovo, a Chinese company that recently acquired IBM's personal computer unit, won a major award. Even more impressive, Samsung, the Korean electronics company, has won more IDEAs than any other corporation in the world; this year it tied with Japan for first place in number of awards.[9] It is clear that manufacturers, marketers, and advertisers are adapting to a new and very competitive global marketplace where no company can be complacent regardless of how commanding its market position might be.

Another significant feature of global marketing and advertising is the paradox of a greater ability to communicate across international borders accompanied by growing nationalism and suspicion of outside influences in many countries. Clearly, communication technology, open trade movements, and improved transportation are making international marketing and advertising more efficient. On the other hand, a growing sense of nationalism and increasing protectionism are impeding foreign expansion into many markets. Perhaps people are reacting to a communication revolution that threatens to merge and blur the differences in cultures.

Whatever the reason, a growing sense of isolationism is a factor that international marketers must weigh with great care.

In some cases, isolationism can be resolved in part by greater sensitivity to other cultures, a willingness to learn local customs, and an openness to new ideas. In an attempt to deal with local culture and at the same time enjoy the advantages and efficiencies of global marketing, many companies have adopted the concept of *glocalization*. The term was popularized by British sociologist Roland Robertson in the 1990s and seeks to combine the twin aims of globalization and localization. The terms usually denote one or both of the following:

1. The creation or distribution of products or services intended for a global or transregional market but customized to suit local laws or customs.
2. Using electronic communication technologies, such as the Internet, to provide local messages on a global or transregional basis.[10]

Glocalization seeks to emphasize the belief that international sales of a product are more likely to succeed when companies adapt the product and/or promotion specifically to a particular locale. For example, the increasing presence of McDonald's restaurants throughout the world is an example of globalization; at the same time, the menu adaptations and even its architecture on a market-by-market basis is an attempt to appeal to local culture is an example of glocalization. For promotions in France, McDonald's substituted "Asterix the Gaul" for its familiar Ronald McDonald mascot.[11] The process of glocalization is more a concept than a concrete strategy. However, it reminds us that localized market strategies are both good business and good corporate citizenship.

A greater sense of local country traditions may be more important than business expertise and even the most astute marketers sometimes misunderstand local customs. For example, Wal-Mart has found that its formula of one-stop discount selling, which is so successful in the United States, does not always translate abroad. In 2006, Wal-Mart withdrew from both Germany and South Korea. The reasons for these failures were numerous, but the core reason was a failure to adapt to local culture. For example, German customers were uncomfortable by checkout clerks smiling at them—a practice insisted on by Wal-Mart. In addition, German shoppers are more likely to go to a number of stores looking for the best quality and price on individual items rather than making a majority of their purchases at a single store. On the other hand, Korean customers view service as more important than low price, and stores resemble small department stores rather than warehouses.[12] In the global arena, it is important to view differences in lifestyle and traditions, as well as consumer behavior, objectively rather than making judgments about customs or cultures in other parts of the world. Despite setbacks, the global economy will continue to grow, fueled by the emergence of middle-class societies in an increasing number of countries. In addition, communication technology is permitting advertisers to reach prospective buyers never before available to them. A growing global demand and a rising standard of living will combine to make advertising even more prevalent throughout the world.

THE INTERNET AND INTERNATIONAL COMMUNICATION

While a number of factors has fueled international marketing, a necessary element in the expansion of global business activity has been the growth of communication technology, particularly in developing regions. "People in the Third World aspire to First World living standards. They develop that aspiration through watching television, seeing advertisements for First World consumer products sold in their counties, and observing First World visitors to their countries. Even in the most remote villages and refugee camps today, people know about the outside world."[13]

Beginning in the 1960s, both print and broadcast media expanded in overseas markets. Sometimes these media were locally produced and, in other cases, U.S. publishers of news magazines such as *Time* and *Newsweek* and business publishers like the *Wall Street Journal* offered international editions. However, these media were available only in economically developed countries and, even then, only where a free press was established. It wasn't until the introduction of satellite communication that the potential for truly global communication became a reality.

In 1962, NASA engineers transmitted a fuzzy picture over the Telstar satellite to a receiving station in England. Barely 20 years later, in 1976, Home Box Office (HBO) initiated satellite delivery of television programming followed by Ted Turner's TBS Superstation, which opened the potential for commercial satellite television on a regular basis. Today, viewers throughout the world are able to receive signals via direct broadcast satellite or satellite ground stations owned by a number of cable operators. Since 1975, India has experimented with satellite communication to reach rural areas, and China also has embarked on an ambitious program of reaching rural communities. The predominant worldwide satellite system is Rupert Murdoch's STAR-TV, which reaches more than fifty countries and potentially half the world's population.[14]

The introduction of satellite television brought the possibility of reaching the majority of the world's population with information, entertainment, and advertising. It permitted businesses to expand into a number of countries much faster and efficiently than could have been dreamed of 20 years before. However, as impressive as the promise of satellite is, it pales in comparison to the distribution and usage of Internet technology. No communication technology has ever grown at the rate of the Internet. The latest figures indicate that Internet usage has reached 800 million people and will soon pass the one billion mark. The penetration of Internet communication is growing in every sector of the globe with only Latin America lagging average usage rates (see Exhibit 23.2). In addition, the potential for future growth is clearly outside the United States and Europe. For example, although China ranks second in the world in total numbers of usage, less than 8 percent of the population is on the Internet compared to almost 75 percent in the United States. Similar growth potential exists in India, Russia, Brazil, and Mexico, all with Internet usage below 20 percent, but there are rapid increases in households with computer capability.

EXHIBIT 23.2

Internet World Users by Language

Adapted from
www.InternetWorldStats.com.

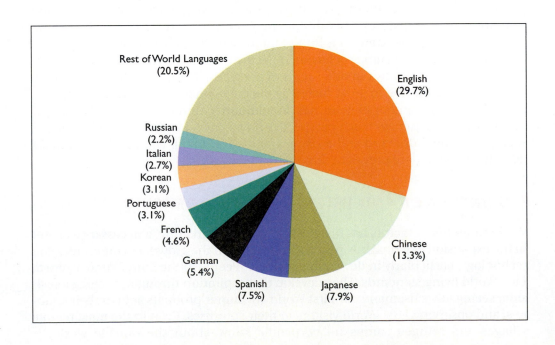

The Internet offers marketers immediate access to customers in areas of the world where traditional communication would have been totally impractical. "The interactive and dynamic nature of the Web makes it a powerful tool for marketing. . . . The wonderful thing about Web marketing is that it is right for all types of products and provides a level of interaction with customers that is on a par with personal sales visits."[15] Today, the technological problems of global communications have been largely overcome. However, the challenge facing both Internet and satellite communication is utilizing the technology in a diverse world community. ". . . despite all the apparent benefits of global Internet marketing, marketers cannot take other countries and their populations for granted. The European countries are a good example. Europeans live on a single continent, have open borders, trade freely, and are moving to a unified economy. Yet each country retains its distinct personality and its own language. And, in the case of marketing, individuals in each country will likely react differently to promotions."[16]

As we will discuss later in this chapter, the key to successful global marketing is finding those common appeals that will work on a universal basis (e.g., a mother's concern for her child's well-being). At the same time, marketers must understand the inherent differences in how these broad appeals may have to be adapted to various markets.

Unlike print or even traditional television advertising, the Internet, at a relatively low cost, can reach international market segments with messages adapted to both the language and local culture. A so-called "cultural Internet" is being developed in which a basic Web site may provide information and advertising in Spanish to a worldwide Hispanic market. However, within this larger service, there will be numerous opportunities for targeting with nuances of the language or specific brand appeals. In this country, a number of mainstream business sectors, such as banks and automobile dealers, have offered for some time Spanish-language versions of their Web sites.

In addition to basic differences in consumer language and cultures, multinational marketers also face the problem of country-by-country variances in matters such as privacy and legal and regulatory standards. In South Korea, advertisers can be fined more than $800,000 for failing to identify their messages as promotions and allowing recipients to opt out of future communication. Malaysia has no specific laws regulating e-mail promotions; Germany demands that such promotions be clearly identified as such; and in Spain promotional e-mails are strictly forbidden unless prior consent is obtained from recipients—and even then they must be identified as "publicity." Online marketers must be aware that regulations differ widely by country. Internet promotions sent to an international audience should at a minimum include the following elements:

1. Provide opportunities to opt in or opt out of future communication
2. Give honest and credible information
3. Prohibit the use of randomly generated addresses
4. Set standards to prevent relaying e-mail from computers with authorization.[17]

The advantage of communication without borders can be a major problem when offers or advertising themes that are illegal in some countries are widely disseminated. Often, advertisers will carry a statement on their website that promotions are specific to a particular country or offers that are not permitted in particular countries should be considered void. In themselves, these steps may not eliminate the problem, but, at a minimum, they may show good faith on the part of the company and at least lessen any potential legal or regulatory problems. Although the Internet and satellite transmission can provide businesses with instantaneous worldwide communication, there are numerous problems yet to be solved.

THE DEVELOPMENT OF GLOBAL MARKETING AND ADVERTISING

As discussed earlier, during the years shortly after World War II, international business meant American products, marketing, and advertising carried abroad. American companies exported a variety of goods as most of the world began the difficult recovery from the war. Today, America no longer dominates global commerce, and advertising and marketing are truly worldwide. As multinational companies compete on an international stage, we see the effects through the development of universal brands and even a similarity of products and advertising among people in diverse cultures and societies. Many American consumers, like their foreign counterparts, do not know or care whether a brand is made by an overseas company. When American consumers drink a cup of Lipton tea, wash with Dove soap, or make a sandwich with Hellman's mayonnaise, few give a thought to them being products made by a Dutch company, Unilever. Luckily for the American economy, overseas customers of Procter & Gamble's Tide, Pampers, and Charmin feel the same way about these brands.

At one time, whether or not to enter the international market was a major strategic decision for many American businesses. Today, becoming a player on the international scene is a given for most companies, and the only decision is how to best compete in the global arena. Not only is the success of American businesses more dependent on exporting products abroad, but even American companies that sell only domestically are finding major competition from imported goods in virtually every product category. Firms comtemplating entering foreign markets face a number of decisions concerning both the advisability of such a move and the strategy and tactics involved in its execution:

1. Is the company organized from a marketing, production, and financial perspective to successfully compete in international markets?

2. What specific markets offer the greatest chance for success, lowest risk, and highest profit potential?

3. How can the firm best enter the global market? Companies use one of three basic means of market entry:
   a. Export goods to independent wholesalers and retailers in host countries. This strategy involves the least risk and, depending on local country contacts, may be the quickest means of gaining entry. However, it usually offers the lowest profit potential and often relinquishes control over marketing strategy including pricing, promotion, and consumer research. Normally, it is a strategy used by smaller companies with limited product lines or investment.
   b. Joint venturing with established local businesses. This approach offers more control over marketing strategy and offers insights into best businesses practices from in-country partners. In a number of countries, joint venturing is the only legal means of establishing a major product presence since some nations will not allow majority ownership of businesses by foreigners.
   c. Totally owned enterprises. Some companies establish totally owned subsidiaries in overseas markets includng manufacturing plants, distribution systems and control over promotion and advertising. This approach has the advantage of being able to fully manage the marketing and production process, but is the slowest and most expensive means of establishing a presence. Often companies will undertake direct investment only after demonstrating a successful track record in the market. For example, Toyota, Honda, and Nissan imported cars to the United States for many years before building American automotive plants.

4. What is the most efficient marketing program and organization? Can a global theme be imported to local consumers or should localized messages and marketing techniques be used? Should local advertising and promotion agencies be used or should a company develop a coordinated advertising plan across international boundaries?

It is difficult to develop rigid guidelines for global commerce because each company faces unique issues and deals with them in a variety of ways. Traditionally, a major failing of American companies going abroad, especially those with little multinational experience, has been treating a foreign market as if consumers were homogeneous in terms of demography and product preference. Companies accept without question that domestic American markets demonstrate wide variance among different market segments and geographic areas. Yet, they sometimes don't translate this concept to foreign markets. To a degree, this mindset is based on a lack of research, but more often it shows an appalling ignorance of local cultures and traditions.

International marketing involves many elements from organizational management to advertising execution. However, a common characteristic is the search for efficiencies when doing business on a worldwide basis. As we examine the leading multinational marketers in various countries, many of the same companies and brands—Ford, Sony, Nestlé, Unilever, Coca-Cola—appear again and again. Even though a one-size-fits-all strategy for international marketing will rarely work, significant economies of scale do exist for these companies.

GLOBAL MARKETING AND ADVERTISING

The term **global marketing** was popularized in a classic article by Harvard professor Theodore Levitt entitled "The Globalization of Markets." At the heart of the concept is the assumption that consumer needs are basically alike all over the world and consumers will respond to similar appeals regardless of cultural differences. Among other things, Levitt argued that advances in communication technology and marketing efficiencies were making it possible to achieve unprecedented economies of scale by developing and marketing global brands. A fairer reading of Levitt would suggest that he advocated a global approach when it was appropriate, and he encouraged companies to look for such opportunities whenever possible.

Global marketing is a balancing act between keeping costs low through advertising efficiency and communicating effectively with local buyers. In an ideal situation, companies would be able to adopt a single advertising and marketing strategy throughout the world. Product development, advertising themes and media, distribution channels, and target marketing would be identical from one country to another. Such an approach would save large multinational marketers millions of dollars in creative production costs alone. A one-size-fits-all approach is rarely practical. For example, both fast-food franchises and soft drink companies have found that products must be significantly changed to fit the customs and tastes of various cultures.

Italians drink more bottled water than any country in the world—almost three times as much as Americans. However, most Italians think that it is bad manners to eat or drink anywhere but at the table. It is even illegal to sell food or drink at places such as newsstands. Nestlé is attempting to change ingrained habits about out-of-home food consumption, but it is facing major challenges. When asked about the idea of eating on the go, one Italian lawyer said, "It gives me goose bumps to even think about it."[18] During the Muslim holy month of Ramadan, the faithful fast during the day and spend time feasting with family starting at sundown. During the iftar, or evening breaking of the fast, television viewing is a central part of the celebration and ratings remain high well into the night. Many Middle-Eastern marketers

global marketing
Term that denotes the use of advertising and marketing strategies on an international basis.

spend more than half their annual advertising budget during Ramadan, and in Egypt 30-second spots sell for as much as $7,000, double their normal rate.[19]

These and many other examples from around the world point out the difficulty of adopting a true global marketing plan. However, there are times when circumstances dictate a global marketing strategy. For example, in 2006, World Cup soccer matches were broadcast to 189 countries—a rare opportunity for multinational firms to reach a global audience with highly rated programming. Companies such as Anheuser-Busch and MasterCard International adopted television advertising that emphasized brand identification and simple messages that cut across cultural divides. For example, MasterCard's commercials had cheering fans from thirty different countries and a tagline "Football fever. Priceless"—as the account executive explained, its universal appeal worked in any language.[20] Wal-Mart, in an attempt to appeal to Hispanic customers in the United States, and expand its sales overseas, developed a number of World Cup-related marketing strategies selling a number of country-specific goods related to the competition.[21] World Cup marketing is an example of using a central theme but adapting it to the interests of customers in diverse markets.

The problems encountered by regional free trade agreements are prime examples of the difficulties inherent in global marketing. The most publicized effort is the **European Union (EU)**, which promised to create a pan-European market that would rival the United States in terms of consumer expenditures and total value of goods. Despite a number of significant steps including introducing the euro in 1998 as a common currency, full implementation of the EU has not been easy. Countries that have been political and economic rivals for centuries are being asked to set aside their differences and make significant compromises for the common good. The EU experienced a setback on May 29, 2005, when almost 55 percent of French voters rejected the EU's proposed constitution and three days later the Dutch followed suit in a nonbinding referendum with 62 percent voting no. Similar problems have emerged in trade agreements around the globe. In our own country, the Central America Free Trade Agreement (CAFTA) and the **North American Free Trade Agreement (NAFTA)**, which seek to open borders between the United States and various regions of North and South America, are being condemned in some quarters as antienvironmental and exploitative of workers and small farmers. Likewise, attempts at free trade agreements in the Far East have run afoul of lingering suspicions among long-time political rivals. Whether trying to implement a large-scale program such as free trade or simply introducing a new product abroad, growing nationalistic agendas in many countries make it more imperative than ever to fully understand the global customer.

In developing a successful multinational marketing organization a number of areas must be addressed.

Management

Regardless of a firm's specific marketing strategy, it is invariably coordinated by top management. However, management coordination does not preclude significant latitude for decision making at lower levels. It is unrealistic to think a multinational company, such as Nestlé, can fully manage as many as 7,000 worldwide and local brands, including such disparate products as Polo clothing and Carnation milk, from its Vevey, Switzerland, headquarters. However, Nestlé can create and maintain very sophisticated control centers to market its products according to consistent standards for product quality, advertising and promotion, and distribution. A commonly used management approach by multinational companies is to consolidate strategic management decisions at corporate headquarters and give local managers flexibility to develop specific tactics within these general principles.

European Union (EU)
The developing economic integration of Europe. Potentially a single market of some 380 million consumers in 2005.

North American Free Trade Agreement (NAFTA)
A treaty designed to eliminate trade barriers among the United States, Mexico, and Canada.

One of the major management challenges for multinational corporations is developing a strategic plan for branding and advertising themes that can be easily adapted globally. One approach to this problem is looking at major brands as an umbrella under which a number of related products can be marketed rather than treating each brand as a unique product. For example, Procter & Gamble is beginning to turn its Pampers diaper brand into a baby health-care line; SK-II, a dominant Procter & Gamble brand of skin care products in Asia, is being introduced in the United States as a holistic skin care line to be used for virtually any skin problem faced by women; and the company is testing Mr. Clean AutoDry and Mr. Clean Magic Eraser extending the brand to additional consumer markets.[22] Savvy marketers such as Procter & Gamble know that they must offer products that meet unique needs in different cultures. However, global brand building allows advertising and promotion to support a number of product adaptations under a central brand and, in many cases, use a focused theme, such as McDonald's "i'm lovin' it" campaign (see Exhibit 23.3).

Ironically, marketing concentration, which once featured a consolidation of advertising agencies to service global accounts, is being decentralized among a number of firms. At one time, the trend was for even the largest companies to have no more than four agencies, and this is still the case in many instances. However, other multinational marketers have moved to engaging more local agencies to take advantage of local nuances that cannot be effectively addressed by global agencies operating at some distance from local markets. The execution of international marketing and advertising is divided into two camps. On the one hand, agencies are willing to tolerate the added expense and management headaches to deal with a number of local agencies. The contrasting view is that efficiencies of centralized control employing a few agencies are worth the potential loss of a local character in their advertising. Few companies totally employ either strategy; rather they develop a management style with aspects of both approaches.

Varieties in different languages

Title	Language	Literal meaning	Used in
i'm lovin' it	English	"I am loving it."	Austria, Australia, Belarus, Belgium, Bulgaria, Canada, Czech Republic, Denmark, Finland, Greece, Hong Kong, Hungary, India, Indonesia, Republic of Ireland, Israel, Italy, Japan, South Korea, Macau, Malaysia, Malta, Netherlands, Netherlands Antilles, Aruba, Suriname, New Zealand, Norway, Poland, Portugal, Puerto Rico, Romania, Serbia, Singapore, Slovak Republic, Slovenia, South Africa, Sweden, Switzerland, United Kingdom, United States and Lithuania.
ich liebe es	German	"I love it."	Germany, Estonia
أنا أحبّه (ana uḥibbuhu) as well as أكيد بحبّه (akid behibuhu)	Arabic	"I love it."	Arabic-speaking countries in the Middle East
我就喜欢 (我就喜歡) (Pinyin: Wǒ jiù xǐhuān)	Chinese	"I just like (it)."	Mainland China, Taiwan
c'est tout ce que j'aime	French	"It's everything (that) I love."	France, French-speaking countries in West Africa
c'est ça que j'm	Canadian French	"That's what I love." (j'm = j'aime)	Canada
love ko 'to	Filipino	"I love this."	Philippines
me encanta	Spanish	"I love it." (lit. It enchants me)	Most Spanish-speaking countries in Latin America and United States, Puerto Rico
me encanta todo eso	Spanish	"I love all that." (lit. All that enchants me.)	Chile, Argentina
amo muito tudo isso	Portuguese	"I really love all of this."	Brazil
işte bunu seviyorum	Turkish	"This is what I love."	Turkey
вот что я люблю	Russian	"that is what I love."	Russia
я це люблю	Ukrainian	"I love it."	Ukraine
man tas patīk	Latvian	"I like it."	Latvia (though the English-language version is still common)
Ja' tyck' om ä'	Swedish	"I like it."	Sweden (Norrland)
Jeg elsker det	Danish	"I love it."	Denmark

EXHIBIT 23.3

Some international companies such as McDonald's have successfully adopted global themes.

Courtesy of Wikipedia.

Advertising Execution

Regardless of the organizational configuration, a company's international advertising and marketing strategy must adapt in some way to almost every country it enters. However, there are some fundamental decision points that are common to many of these activities. The three problem areas most frequently encountered by multinational firms are:

1. *Language differences.* Language differences present the most obvious starting point for developing global advertising, and it also is the one with some major pitfalls. There are a number of legendary instances when advertising translations resulted in embarrassment for a brand. Today, major international advertisers use translation firms that go beyond simply word substitution and use experienced in-country language experts who look for language nuances—a process called *language localization* rather than simply translation.

2. *Media research and usage.* In many countries, media research is nonexistent or based on unreliable data. In addition, media usage in many parts of the world is much different than in the United States. For example, cinema advertising is extremely popular in parts of Europe, and India's newspaper readership is much higher than in the United States. Likewise, daily television household viewership averages approximately 8 hours in Japan and only 3 hours in Great Britain.

3. *Cultural considerations.* Perhaps the most difficult area of international advertising is dealing with the many cultural components firms attempt to communicate with potential buyers. Advertising needs to demonstrate how products and services solve problems and provide consumer benefits in a context that is comfortable and understandable to consumers in each country. A growing sense of nationalism in many countries is making consumers wary of products that fail to present a localized position in terms of their marketing and communication programs. It is gaining an understanding of these cultural and nationalistic elements that often require multinational companies to engage in joint venturing or, at the very least, making use of local employees in each host country.

Technology and more efficient transportation are becoming more readily available to make the *idea* of international advertising and global marketing a reality. However, it is rarely possible to accommodate all the cultural and national differences in any single marketing strategy. Global marketing is such an appealing concept from a cost and efficiency standpoint that companies are tempted to adopt it even with its obvious pitfalls. It can be argued that the misapplication of global marketing places the well-being of the firm ahead of the consumer. Exhibit 23.4 demonstrates the continuum of a one-strategy, one-execution global marketing approach versus a consumer-oriented marketing concept with a different-strategy, different-execution approach in each country.

EXHIBIT 23.4

Multinational firms usually develop marketing plans that represent a compromise between the needs of consumers and the firm.

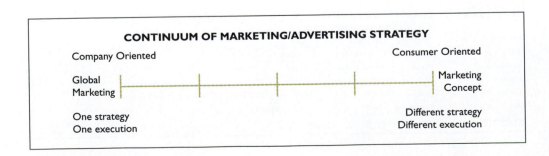

As shown in Exhibit 23.4, global marketing is rarely an either/or decision. Rather it is a continuum involving a number of steps requiring decisions about both products and marketing strategy that must complement each other.

For example:

1. *Export both the product and the advertising to other countries.* This approach is the strictest interpretation of global marketing. In this situation, the product (including name and logo) and marketing strategy would be identical in every country. Starbucks is an example of a company that comes close to this model. With 11,000 stores in 37 countries, it has kept the basic "coffee house" image that has worked so well in the United States.[23] However, only a few companies are as fortunate as Starbucks to have a product that lends itself to this approach. Nevertheless, the advantages in efficiency and cost savings for such a strategy are so obvious that some form of global marketing is the goal that most firms seek and rarely find.

2. *Adapt a product and marketing plan exclusively for the international market or large geographical areas.* It is common for companies to develop specific products, brands, and advertising strategies for regions of the world such as Europe or Asia. This approach is closely related to global marketing, but recognizes that even broadly marketed products need some localization.

3. *Export the product, but change the name.* Unilever markets its premium-quality detergent under a number of brand names including Wisk in the United States, Skip in parts of Europe, and Omo in its other global markets. While devising a global campaign for the product, the company and its agency, Lowe & Partners, kept the established brand identities but developed a consistent campaign for them using the theme "Dirt is good." Advertising executions emphasized that part of being a child is getting dirty and that rather than having parents worry about it, they should use Unilever detergents to solve the problem. The commercials showed the fun that children have getting dirty and played up the fact that "Kids think differently about getting their clothes dirty" and invited parents to do the same.[24]

4. *Keep the brand name and advertising strategy, but adapt the product country by country.* Australia's Jacob's Creek Wines sells Semillon Chardonnay in Belgium, but it is not available in Brazil. Likewise, Merlot is sold in Canada, but not in either Belgium or Brazil. However, the company uses the same brand and packaging globally, changing only the flavor of its wines on a country-by-country basis.

5. *Keep the brand name and product, but adapt the advertising to each country.* This is one of the more common strategies used by multinational firms. While it is expensive to adopt this plan, it is much less costly than changing the basic product, packaging, and brand name for each country. This approach also allows a company to emphasize differences in usage and positioning. That is, while coffee is a universal drink, the level of consumption, habits of drinking (dinner versus breakfast), and age of heavy users all demonstrate vast differences from one country to another, differences that can be accommodated in advertising without changing the basic brand or product.

6. *Adapt both the product and the advertising to each country.* This is the most expensive plan, but one that fulfills consumer demand for localization of promotions and products. Few companies can afford to fully adopt this approach, and few products would demand such an extreme approach.

There are numerous variations on each of these designs. The important point is that no idea will work for every brand or product category in every country. Even themes that would seem to be universal, demonstrate wide variations of adoption and acceptability from one country to another.

Sensitivity

One of the positive aspects of multinational business is that it is bringing people to a greater awareness and understanding of diverse cultures. However, consumer behavior and the aspirations this behavior demonstrates involve fundamental core values of a culture. In recent years, multinational businesses have had to deal with numerous complaints about their operations in developing countries. Even the corporations acknowledge that there is a fine line between opening new markets for their products and exploitation. The problem is not a new one. In 1621, the charter of the Dutch West India Company outlined its responsibility thusly, ". . . for the preservation of the places, keeping good order, police and justice." Few companies are burdened with that level of accountability. However, a primary consideration of globalization and effective management is the development of a sensitivity to the host countries in which they operate. A strict adherence to centralized management makes it difficult for decision makers to effectively manage diverse markets with the same foresight as local executives who share a common culture and perspective with their customers. In recent years, there has been a heightened sensitivity to the responsibilities of companies conducting business as guests in host countries.

To some extent, a divide exists among almost all nations at some level. Witness the ongoing problems concerning tariffs, defense, etc., between Canada and the United States, two countries linked by many common goals for almost 200 years. However, the problems are even greater among long-established economies of Europe and North America and their emerging trade partners. "The ideological differences between the developed Western nations and the newly developed and developing nations of the East are manifested in a variety of ways. The role of entrepreneurship, business customs, work practices, consumer expectations, organizational structures, attitudes to foreign investment, business/government relations, and the time horizon of decision making, are just a few of the culturally related factors which affect the competitiveness of a nation. While these factors are not new in the world economy, what is, perhaps, new is the extent to which, and the form in which, different cultures are interacting with each other."[25]

Many of the problems in international marketing and business relationships are a matter of a failure to understand how consumers in significantly different cultures will view communication and other activities. It is mandatory that messages be reviewed not just for accuracy, but, equally important, for cultural appropriateness. For example, a major international company wanted to recognize and honor the twenty-four countries participating in a recent World Cup soccer event. The company distributed promotional displays with flags of each nation. One of the flags was that of Saudi Arabia, which contains a passage about Allah. The display insulted a number of Islamic followers since they feared that the display would eventually be placed in the trash, thus, insulting their religion. Commenting on the flap, one executive commented, "In today's competitive business environment, your company cannot afford to operate with a domestic approach in a global economy. The ability to communicate across cultural borders is a necessity for anyone reaching out to markets made up of different ethnicities."[26] Marketing sensitivity embraces a range of considerations, and more companies are demonstrating that they understand that there is an important balance to be reached between maximizing sales and profits and being a responsible marketer. Clearly, the notion of global marketing has ethical and philosophical elements that cannot be ignored.

THE MULTINATIONAL ADVERTISING AGENCY

As American business moved into the global marketplace after World War II, their agencies soon followed. In these early years, the basic organization and practice for global agencies was similar to the model developed over a century in this country.

That is, they tended to be full-service agencies executing all aspects of advertising on a country-by-country basis as needed by their clients. The contemporary international agency is much different than those in the pioneering years of the 1940s and 1950s when McCann Erickson and J. Walter Thompson led American agencies into the worldwide arena. They usually started foreign branches on a country-by-country basis with local branch agencies typically responsible for the advertising of a few large U.S. clients in a limited number of countries.

This approach to international advertising was extremely expensive and did not guarantee that the foreign branches would adequately service and coordinate the international marketing needs of their clients. During the 1970s, most U.S. agencies moved from full ownership of foreign offices to some form of joint venture or minority ownership of existing foreign agencies. This plan overcame the long start-up time involved in beginning a new agency and provided advertising plans that reflected local business practices and culture. Joint ventures also recognized the growing expertise of local advertising talent and the fact that around the world many overseas agencies were providing client services on a par with major American agencies. However, up until the 1990s, agencies were still responsible for the advertising of their clients, and business was conducted internationally similar to that for domestic clients.

In the last 20 years, there have been a number of significant changes in international advertising on the agency side. Perhaps the most noteworthy is the growing trend for clients to take much of the marketing communication function in-house. This functional change is apparent in the titles found among many corporations. Now the international marketing plans are conducted by executives with such titles as *global brand manager* or *global marketing officer*. In many cases, the agency-client relationship has changed from one of long-term partner to specialist for specific creative or media buying functions. "The separation of planning from creative and the development of in-house strategic capabilities by clients—who, thanks to database technologies, now know far more about their customers' actual behaviors than any outside partner can tell them—gives marketers the freedom to shop around for creative services."[27] The most significant result of this change is that multinational companies are now calling on small agencies for creative work. In the past, these agencies would have been out of the mix since they are not staffed up to handle a full-service account.

Let's examine some of the major areas of global advertising from the agency-client perspective.

Growth of Major Advertising Centers Outside the United States

Advertising revenues in the United States account for approximately 48 percent of the world's total. However, much of this advertising is placed by foreign-owned agencies. American dominance of advertising was changed forever on June 26, 1987, when Martin Sorrell bought J. Walter Thompson and placed it under his London-based WPP group. Over the next 20 years, he would acquire other American advertising icons such as Ogilvy & Mather, Young and Rubicam, and Grey Global Group.[28] Other long-time U.S. agencies, such as Leo Burnett, also have been bought by overseas holding companies. In addition to these acquisitions, the changing landscape of global advertising can be seen in the list of the largest worldwide marketing organizations (see Exhibit 23.5). Only three of the top ten businesses are headquartered in the United States.

Among these huge enterprises, worldwide revenues often comprise less than half of company totals. More significant is the fact that among the top ten firms revenue growth is greater outside the United States. As we discussed earlier, the primary motivation for marketers to go abroad is the potential for higher revenues and profits. Likewise, advertising agencies and marketing firms are finding that

Rank 2004	Rank 2003	Marketing Organization	Headquarters	Worldwide Revenue 2004	Worldwide Revenue 2003	Worldwide Revenue % Chg	U.S. Revenue 2004	U.S. Revenue 2003	U.S. Revenue % Chg	Revenue Outside the U.S. 2004	Revenue Outside the U.S. 2003	Revenue Outside the U.S. % Chg
1	1	Omnicom Group	New York	$9,747.2	$8,621.4	13.1	$5,223.4	$4,720.9	10.6	$4,523.8	$3,900.5	16.0
2	2	WPP Group[1]*	London	9,370.1	8,062.5	16.2	3,552.1	3,347.5	6.1	5,717.9	4,715.0	21.3
3	3	Interpublic Group of Cos.	New York	6,200.6	5,863.4	5.8	3,436.5	3,284.2	4.6	2,764.1	2,579.2	7.2
4	4	Publicis Groupe	Paris	4,777.3	4,408.9	8.4	2,039.6	1,982.5	2.9	2,802.8	2,344.2	19.6
5	5	Dentsu*	Tokyo	2,851.0	2,393.0	19.1	48.2	48.8	–1.2	2,802.8	2,344.2	19.6
6	6	Havas	Suresnes, France	1,866.0	1,877.5	–0.6	730.7	789.8	–7.5	1,135.3	1,087.7	4.4
7	8	Aegis Group	London	1,373.6	1,067.4	28.7	427.9	383.4	11.6	945.8	684.0	38.3
8	7	Hakuhodo DY Holdings*	Tokyo	1,372.1	1,178.8	16.4	0.0	0.0	NA	1,372.4	1,178.8	16.4
9	9	Asatsu-DK	Tokyo	473.3	413.9	14.3	2.6	4.3	–38.1	470.6	409.6	14.9
10	10	Carlson Marketing Group	Minneapolis	346.9	322.4	7.6	246.5	234.0	5.3	100.4	88.4	13.6
11	11	MDC Partners	Toronto/New York	316.8	278.8	13.6	215.9	175.3	23.2	100.9	103.5	–2.5
12	12	Incepta Group	London	279.8	254.1	10.1	69.0	71.6	–3.7	210.8	182.5	15.5
13	13	Monster Worldwide	New York	251.6	241.5	4.2	163.8	149.7	9.4	87.8	91.7	–4.3
14	15	Digitas	Boston	251.6	209.5	20.1	251.6	209.5	20.1	0.0	0.0	NA
15	14	HealthSTAR Communications	Woodbridge, N.J.	203.0	233.0	–12.9	203.0	233.0	–12.9	0.0	0.0	NA
16	16	Alloy	New York	194.1	182.6	6.3	194.1	182.6	6.3	0.0	0.0	NA
17	18	Cheil Communications	Seoul	185.9	173.0	7.4	14.4	10.2	40.2	171.5	162.8	5.4
18	23	Aspen Marketing Services	West Chicago, Ill.	180.0	134.0	34.3	180.0	134.0	34.3	0.0	0.0	NA
18	NA	G2R[2]*	Seoul	180.0	NA	NA	0.0	NA	NA	180.0	NA	NA
20	17	Tokyu Agency	Tokyo	176.0	182.0	–3.3	0.0	0.0	NA	176.0	182.0	–3.3
21	19	George P. Johnson Co.	Auburn Hills, Mich.	172.9	150.0	15.3	133.5	117.9	13.3	39.4	32.1	22.7
22	49	aQuantive	Seattle	157.9	NA	NA	157.9	NA	NA	0.0	0.0	NA
23	22	Doner	Southfield, Mich.	155.7	137.0	13.7	141.3	122.7	15.2	14.4	14.3	0.7
24	25	Clemenger Communications	Melbourne	147.4	118.6	24.3	0.0	0.0	NA	147.4	118.6	24.3
25	24	Select Communications	Koblenz, Germany	145.0	120.0	20.8	60.0	48.5	23.7	85.0	71.5	18.9

Notes: Figures are in millions of U.S. dollars. Revenue figures are supplied by companies via *Ad Age* questionnaire or taken from public documents. An asterisk (*) indicates figures are *Ad Age* estimates. WPP and Havas totals for U.S. are actually for North America. [1]WPP Group figures include estimates for Grey Global Group. [2]G2R is a holding company for LG Ad and Wunderman Korea. Rankings for 2003 are based on data compiled in 2005. Major currencies converted at average annual exchange rates: $1.248975 per euro, $1.838858 per British pound, $0.009307 per yen, and $.000879 per SK won in 2004 versus $1.141325 per euro, $1.645217 per British pound, $0.008566 per yen, and $.000839 per SK won in 2003. To purchase profiles of the world's top 50 marketing organizations in pdf format, go to **AdAge.com, QwikFIND aaq51m**

EXHIBIT 23.5

World's Top 25 Marketing Organizations

Ranked by worldwide revenue in 2004.

Courtesy of *Advertising Age.*

emerging markets in a number of regions offer more growth potential than the more mature U.S. and Western European economies. It is difficult to predict precise trends among multinational markets. However, it is a certainty that developing regions of the world will continue to offer significant growth potential over the next two decades and beyond.

Effects of Integrated Marketing Communication on Worldwide Agencies

As you will recall, in Chapter 2 we introduced the notion of *integrated marketing communication*. We noted that marketers are much more interested in reaching consumers by the most effective venue rather than pigeonholing their marketing communication into artificial categories of advertising, promotion, etc. This approach is even more apparent in global marketing where the preferred means of commercial messages covers a wide range of avenues including out-of-home, product placement, cell phones, and other new technologies as well as traditional advertising media. To serve their clients, advertising agencies have had to remake themselves into marketing communication organizations to serve the diverse needs of multinational clients.

The major advertising holding companies passed a watershed in 2001 when the so-called "big three" (Interpublic Group of Companies, Omnicom Group, and WPP Group) derived less than half their gross income from advertising services. The remaining income came from public relations, sales promotion, specialty shops, and research services. Exhibit 23.6 shows the diverse sources of income derived by three of the largest holding companies. Similar results can be seen across a variety of marketing firms. For example, in the future many of these companies will derive significant income from developing Internet and other specialized communication campaigns using video games and other interactive media.

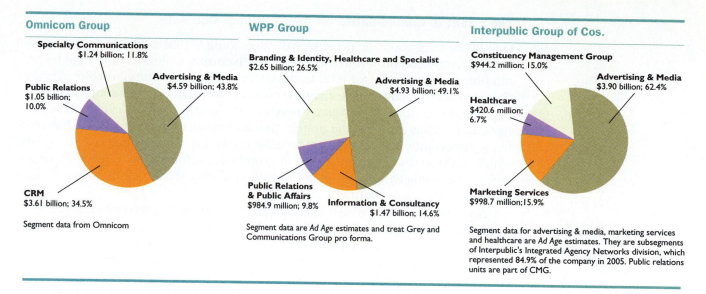

Omnicom Group

Specialty Communications
$1.24 billion; 11.8%

Public Relations
$1.05 billion;
10.0%

Advertising & Media
$4.59 billion; 43.8%

CRM
$3.61 billion; 34.5%

Segment data from Omnicom

WPP Group

Branding & Identity, Healthcare and Specialist
$2.65 billion; 26.5%

Advertising & Media
$4.93 billion; 49.1%

Public Relations
& Public Affairs
$984.9 million; 9.8%

Information & Consultancy
$1.47 billion; 14.6%

Segment data are *Ad Age* estimates and treat Grey and
Communications Group pro forma.

Interpublic Group of Cos.

Constituency Management Group
$944.2 million; 15.0%

Advertising & Media
$3.90 billion; 62.4%

Healthcare
$420.6 million;
6.7%

Marketing Services
$998.7 million; 15.9%

Segment data for advertising & media, marketing services
and healthcare are *Ad Age* estimates. They are subsegments
of Interpublic's Integrated Agency Networks division, which
represented 84.9% of the company in 2005. Public relations
units are part of CMG.

EXHIBIT 23.6

**Worldwide 2005 Revenue
by Discipline**

Source: Advertising Age,
May 1, 2006.

The development of the diversified agency is largely in response to clients' shifting dollars from traditional advertising into other areas of marketing communication. While the share of nonadvertising promotional dollars has grown significantly in the United States, these increases are even more apparent in foreign markets where reaching consumers often demands a greater use of nontraditional communication channels than in the United States. Clients are increasingly demanding that their agencies be able to coordinate all phases of their marketing communication programs.

Although the move to provide clients with an array of communication services is understandable, the changes have had a number of ramifications for agencies. For example, the need to provide more services has led to numerous mergers of advertising, public relations, and sales promotion agencies under a single management umbrella. However, the business model used in public relations and sales promotions is very different from advertising, and agencies have often demonstrated significant internal conflicts as they attempt to coordinate these functions. In addition, many agencies find that keeping consistent quality control across several promotional and marketing subsidiaries is a challenge, particularly on a worldwide basis.

While the last 20 years has largely been a period of growth and diversification by international agencies, a countertrend toward decentralization has been evident in recent years. A number of major multinational marketers have opted for using a number of smaller agencies rather than one or two mega-shops for their global brands. This approach is most evident on the creative side. As companies have brought overall advertising strategy in-house and selected independent media buying organizations to handle global media placement, they have hired a number of agencies to gain creative alternatives for their global brands. Rather than creative ideas being dictated from a single global agency, clients are looking for ideas from a number of shops. In some cases, small agencies are developing themes for a particular country, but, in a number of instances, these smaller agencies have created advertising executions that have been adopted on a global basis. Motorola, Sony and Disney all took the decentralized route despite once embracing the single lead-agency concept. These clients appear to prefer choice and a bit of interagency competition to the relative ease of one-stop shopping.[29] The downside of using a multi-agency approach is the problem of keeping the brand image and positioning consistent as well as potential difficulties of management control of diverse voices. From a practical standpoint, the major advertising holding companies, after building huge global organizations, find that they may be competing with regional competitors that they never considered rivals before.

The Effect of Consolidation on Agency-Client Conflicts

One of the long-standing principles of advertising is that agencies do not accept clients that market brands in competition with current clients. It would not be permissible for the agency for Ford to simultaneously handle the Chevrolet account. Certainly, the noncompete principle is common sense for a number of reasons.

First, to be effective, an agency needs to be a partner with its clients. This partnership involves not only the preparation and execution of advertising but also, more importantly, a collaboration on basic marketing strategy and business goals, which includes sharing a great deal of proprietary information. Clients are reluctant to share this type of information with an agency that is simultaneously handling a competing account.

Noncompete clauses also have pragmatic considerations. For example, if an agency is servicing two competing brands, which brand is assigned to the more senior copywriter and art director? Which media planner handles which client? When media avails are scarce, which client has first priority on prime media spots? For a number of reasons, both agencies and clients have, from the beginning of the agency-client relationship, agreed that the client conflicts should be avoided.

The noncompete system worked well when there were hundreds of independent agencies and clients had little trouble finding an agency to handle their advertising. However, with the consolidation of both businesses and agencies, the fundamentals of the advertising relationship have changed dramatically over the last 25 years. Only a limited number of agencies have the resources to handle a top 50 multinational advertising account (or, more likely, a diversified marketing communication program).

In recent years, two major changes have taken place on the agency and client side to reflect the new reality of how agency conflicts might be handled. First, clients such as Procter & Gamble and Colgate-Palmolive have agreed that they will normally define agency clients by product category rather than on a corporate basis. That is, although an agency could not have Crest and Colgate toothpaste as clients, a single agency might handle the Bounty paper towel account for Procter & Gamble and the Colgate toothpaste account for Colgate-Palmolive. The logic is sound because the marketing strategy, brand managers, and even the target markets are much different for the two brands, even though they are owned by competing corporations. That concession by major clients has alleviated many potential conflicts.

On the agency side, advertising holding companies have been established to create so-called *fire walls* among the agencies they own. The term indicates that there will be no cross-sharing of sensitive client information among agencies owned by the same corporate entity. In theory, this allows different agencies under the McCann Erickson Worldwide umbrella to simultaneously service accounts from competitors such as Johnson & Johnson, L'Oréal, and Unilever. For the clients, it gives them access to the best agencies to handle their globally distributed brands. The system is not perfect, and there are still instances when even the best fire walls don't overcome client apprehensions. However, the combination of a liberalized view of what constitutes a product conflict on the client side with the emergence of the holding company concept by agencies addresses a serious issue in both domestic and international advertising.

Research and the Multinational Consumer

Nowhere is the changing relationship between international agencies and clients more apparent than in market research. Marketers have long known that understanding the global consumers of a brand presents unique challenges. Multinational research, especially studies attempting to discern common purchase behavior involving a number of countries, deals with issues that domestic marketing research rarely faces. Because of the unique problems involved, over the last decade more multinational marketers are taking primary responsibility for consumer research. Research for multinational brands is one of the primary areas in which centralization works far better than the locally oriented approach found in many creative or media executions and offers efficiencies in both cost and reliability.

Without centralized planning, research will not be comparable from country to country, making global strategy decisions all but impossible. As global marketing becomes more complex, there will be increasing reliance on research data gathered by clients and given to agencies on a project-by-project basis. Unilever's "Dirt is good" campaign, which we discussed earlier, was approved only after research showed that a unifying theme would work across a number of brands and in various international markets. Consumer research demonstrated that a standard approach could work despite many differences in particular markets. The campaign was successful in shifting ". . . the focus from tedious stains to the freedom to explore life and grow through activities like playing, sports, and art that create a need for Omo, Persil, Via, Ala, and Unilever's other dirt-magnet brands."[30] The theme allows a number of creative executions of children playing in dirt, kicking a soccer ball on a muddy field, or finger painting. However, the company would never have taken the risk of a single theme without reliable research to back up the decision.

The same research also addressed the problem of packaging. With 249 separate package designs, the company needed to present a single face at the store level and yet keep the unique character of its diverse brands. The firm is using what it calls a spat—a happy-looking icon with an orange center and five rounded pink spokes. The company uses the design on packaging and in-store promotions throughout the world. The Unilever example underscores the fact that centralized, corporate research is often needed since this type of corporate level, strategic research decisions would rarely come from an advertising agency—especially one with less than global brand responsibility.

Coca-Cola is another multinational company that recently established an internal account planning and research group. The intent of the office is to facilitate global consumer insights by centralizing the planning and research function. This level of centralization will allow Coca-Cola to have a better understanding of how consumers in different countries relate to its various brands and the communication that will resonate within numerous countries. This organization will allow the company to understand ". . . consumer behavior and consumer insights through data not available to agencies. . . . Marketing is much more the domain of clients and communications is much more the domain of agencies. . . . We [Coke] are looking to have fewer ideas work across the geography."[31] As a major multinational agency CEO commented, "I see more and more businesses asking for a global view of their customers' assets. When you are dealing with Ford Motor Company and IBM Corporation, you cannot have a country or region doing data on their side the way they want . . . [it requires] one person sitting on top of it aligning all the processes and tools."[32]

Although the reliability of global research data has improved immensely in recent years, it is the interpretation of the research that creates the major problems for international marketers. Even developing a logo that is both understood and effective across a number of countries can present major obstacles. At the heart of the research process is finding a means to effectively translate key advertising and marketing information into global advertising executions. Although traditional language translation is important, translation must also include an understanding of the subtle nuances of culture and traditions within a country.

In this sense, **marketing translation** refers to the execution of the basic marketing plan to a number of countries. This translation involves not only language

marketing translation
The process of adapting a general marketing plan to multinational environments.

and numerous shades of meaning but also accounting for differences in media usage and availability, legal restrictions on various types of promotion, and basic advertising practices. It is the unusual advertising plan that can be introduced worldwide without numerous adaptations.

A vital element in the translation process is the brand audit. Brand audits are designed to gain consumer perspectives about a specific brand. The brand audit attempts to define what a brand means to consumers worldwide and then develop market strategies that will enhance the brand's future sales potential. Often a brand audit demonstrates that the general perceptions that a company has of its brands don't match those of its customers in specific countries. For example, Tide detergent found that "whiteness" was a common consumer touch point in choosing a cleaning product. Using the whiteness as a product benefit, Procter & Gamble used this across a number of cultures and advertising translations. Similarly, Procter & Gamble has created a multinational campaign for Head & Shoulders around the theme of a dandruff treatment that is kind to your hair (see Exhibit 23.7).

Regardless of the function—creative, media, or research—agencies face two major problems in meeting the demands of clients:

1. First, they must accommodate the organizational structure of their clients. An agency with several multinational accounts often finds that the specific needs for account management will differ from one client to the other. In effect, some agencies find that they need different management organizations for each client.

2. The second major problem faced by multinational agencies is how to manage centrally and communicate locally. The adage "think globally, act locally" is a dilemma for every agency. Agencies must translate broad client marketing strategies to the level of the individual customer in each country they serve.

THE MULTINATIONAL ADVERTISING PLAN

As we have seen, international advertising involves much more than simply transporting advertising abroad. It requires a broad range of experience and an ability to deal with subtle nuances. In many cases, advertising decision making in an international environment must be executed with more instinct and less reliable research than in U.S. marketing. Despite these differences, the basic function of advertising remains the same regardless of the arena. All advertising begins with sound planning and an adherence to basic marketing strategy. Although consumer preferences may be more difficult to determine in overseas marketing, differentiated brand benefits still must constitute the central theme of most advertising messages. And like their domestic counterparts, all forms of marketing communication should be coordinated and integrated rather than presented as a series of unrelated advertising and sales promotion messages.

Although advertising basics may be consistent, international advertisers deal with special problems in execution and practices from country to country. The multinational marketer will find that the use and receptivity of advertising as well as its objectives and basic goals demonstrate extraordinary diversity. As firms introduce products on a worldwide basis, problems range from something as familiar as product category competition to the much more difficult problem of convincing buyers to change established habits or overcoming previously held cultural prohibitions concerning the use of a product.

Regardless of the objective of a particular international campaign, advertisers must deal with a host of situations unique to each country. In this section, we will discuss two areas of primary concern to international agencies and their clients: (1) creative and cultural considerations and (2) media planning and buying procedures, including legal restrictions and regulations.

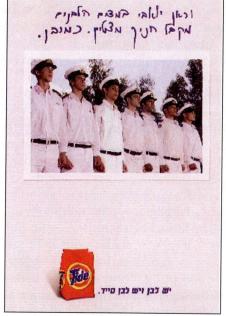

EXHIBIT 23.7

Procter & Gamble has developed global themes for a number of its core brands.

(a) and (e) Courtesy of Geller Nessis Leo Burnett Israel and Procter & Gamble; (b) (c) and (d) Courtesy of Trio Advertising; (f) Courtesy of Bauman Ber Rivnei Saatchi-Saatchi Israel.

Creative and Cultural Considerations

International advertising messages involve much more than simply selling products. While sales and profits remain the primary objective of any promotional message, the creative function for multinational advertisers has changed dramatically in recent years. Multinational marketers increasingly realize that there is a social, cultural, and, in some cases, a political component to their advertising. The proliferation of foreign-based products, especially in developing countries has led to charges of exploitation and insensitivity to local cultures by international companies. It is no longer sufficient for advertisers to simply introduce new products and depend on latent demand for sales and profits. There is a growing sense of worldwide nationalism where advertising must communicate interesting messages in a vernacular acceptable to local consumers. Advertising is at the forefront of presenting communication that can either dissuade or heighten these concerns among local buyers.

Advertising inadvertently functions on a number of social and cultural levels in addition to selling products and services. "Advertising exerts a formative influence whose character is both persuasive and pervasive. . . . Even where adapted to local scenarios and role models, those shown often come from sectors of society, such as the upwardly mobile urban middle class, which embrace or are receptive to Western values and mores. . . . At the same time, international advertising also acts as an integrating force across national boundaries. It disseminates messages using universal symbols and slogans, and establishes a common mode of communication among target audiences in different parts of the world. . . . Consequently, international advertising can be viewed as a force integrating societies and establishing common bonds, universal symbols, and models of communication among peoples in different parts of the globe."[33]

The failure of advertising to account for local culture can lead to serious problems that may linger for years in the attitude of local consumers toward a brand. A major problem in exporting U.S. advertising is that Americans, as consumers, tend to be accepting of satire, humor, metaphors, and figures of speech that are viewed with disfavor in other parts of the world. For example, a Nike commercial broadcast in China depicted NBA star LeBron James defeating a cartoon kung fu and a pair of dragons. A number of viewers complained that the commercial showed the Chinese to be weak and incapable of defending themselves. The government's State Administration for Radio, Film and Television banned the ad saying that "all advertisements must uphold national dignity and interest, and respect the motherland's culture."[34] Earlier, Toyota ran afoul of the same authority by placing print advertisements in Chinese publications that showed stone lions, traditional symbols of Chinese power, bowing to a Toyota Land Cruiser PRADO.

It is impossible to curtail all cultural missteps in international advertising. However, multinational advertisers are much more aware of the potential pitfalls than in earlier years and are taking steps to prevent them. Many agencies are hiring specialists, such as cultural anthropologists, and making greater use of in-country research and consultants to more fully understand the consumption habits of buyers. Successful creative executions begin with an in-depth awareness of a country's culture, customs, and buying habits. Sometimes this analysis is as simple as being aware of local holidays, how they are celebrated, and if commercial tie-ins are appropriate. From worldwide holidays, such as Rosh Hashanah to country-specific celebrations, such as German Unity Day and Health and Sports Day in Japan, advertisers need to know the local customs surrounding these events and whether their commercialization is appropriate.

As we have seen, advertising creativity is no longer an American monopoly. Both agencies and clients are open to ideas from around the world. Whereas at one time creative strategy was normally generated in the United States and adapted abroad, we are routinely seeing ideas and advertising executions originating in a foreign market and adopted for global use. The advertising sophistication of overseas markets is increasingly recognized and the idea of U.S. dictated advertising programs is being quickly replaced by a partnership that acknowledges both the talent level of overseas advertisers and the contribution they can make to a greater understanding of international communication. We are seeing a maturation process that has evolved over the last 30 years in which multinational companies have moved through three basic phases:

1. *Moving into foreign markets.* The first phase involved the decision by companies to move into international markets. Although many large companies had a limited international presence prior to World War II, in the last half of the twentieth century companies began to routinely market their products on a worldwide basis.

2. *Local emphasis in marketing strategy.* Beginning in the 1980s, companies developed more pragmatic, locally oriented marketing and advertising plans. Companies realized that a one-plan-fits-all strategy would not work and began to view markets on a more individualized basis. Unfortunately, these efforts at localization were often based on little solid information and were too often more stereotypical than factual.

3. *Research-supported localization and segmentation.* Currently, we are seeing in many markets the implementation of consumer-based marketing guided by many of the same conceptual foundations found in the United States and other developed advertising economies. While it may be many years before the majority of countries reach the level of research complexity and consumer understanding enjoyed in this country, the very fact that marketers sense the need to respect the needs and aspirations of these consumers is a major step in the right direction.

Media Planning: A Global Perspective

Historically, the media function has suffered from three primary problems in international advertising:

1. *Media availability and or/usage levels.* Even with the introduction of satellite television, higher worldwide household set penetration, and the distribution of a number of television networks on a global basis, media planning is still a complex problem for multinational companies. However, services such as CNN International, Disney Channels operating in more than sixty countries, and ESPN operating a number of international outlets have made uniform communication much easier for global marketers. However, some countries, notably China, which has tremendously high levels of household television penetration, do not allow foreign programming. The state controlled CCTV network does allow advertising from overseas companies and receives about 90 percent of its total revenue from advertising, much of it coming from global companies such as Procter & Gamble.[35]

    International services such as these can be combined with local and regional stations and networks to offer advertisers a choice of general channels for global brands and more specialized coverage for brands unique to a single country or region. In addition, the introduction of global television opportunities allows similar brand-building strategies as those used in campaigns originating in more developed countries. Although satellite television adds an important option for media planners, numerous print vehicles, particularly news and business journals such as *Time* and the *Wall Street Journal*, have well-established international editions to reach targeted, upscale consumers.

    The growing availability of international vehicles should not ignore the fact that media usage varies greatly on a country-by-country basis. For example, cinema advertising, regarded as a very minor medium in America, is a primary vehicle in Asia and parts of Europe. Out-of-home and radio advertising also are extremely important in many countries.

2. *Legal prohibitions.* In every country that allows advertising, there is some form of regulation. The degree and type of regulation is usually a function of two issues:

a. The length of time that advertising has existed and the degree of sophistication that it has attained.

b. The degree of freedom that business and the press enjoy. The extent of advertising control is directly correlated with a country's level of press freedom.

Despite differences in advertising regulation and control, there is a good deal of consistency among developed countries in terms of the prevalent types of advertising restraints. In most major advertising markets, advertising is controlled through a combination of self-regulation and legislation. This process is similar to what is found in this country with the Federal Trade Commission and a number of trade and business organizations such as the Council of Better Business Bureaus. For example, in Great Britain the primary self-regulatory entity is the Advertising Standards Authority, which receives complaints about misleading advertising and recommends various voluntary remedies to advertisers. A similar organization, the European Advertising Standards Alliance (EASA), coordinates the efforts of twenty-eight self-regulatory bodies across the continent. Underscoring the importance of self-regulation on a worldwide basis, the International Chamber of Commerce announced a revision of its basic code, which was first drafted in 1937. The 2006 version, which is used as the basis of self-regulation in many countries, seeks to define marketing and advertising taking into account new technology and the means of communication.[36]

In addition to formal legal restrictions and broad self-regulatory agencies, there are a number of industry-specific self-regulatory bodies throughout the world similar to those found in the United States. For example, the Union of European Beverage Associations announced a wide-ranging program to limit vending machine sales of soft drinks in primary schools, and a number of other marketing groups adopted similar steps in the face of criticism of targeting children under 12 for the sale of high sugar drinks. In addition, a consortium of food marketers committed to a program to promote "... health, diet, and physical activity."[37] One result of global marketing is that the legal and self-regulatory system founded in the United States has spread to a number of countries as consumers become more sophisticated and empowered to monitor the effects of advertising.

Many of international advertising's limitations are similar to those in this country. For example, alcohol and tobacco products as well as other categories may be limited or excluded from all or certain media. In addition, international media planning must be closely coordinated with creative executions because there are a number of restrictions concerning the type of messages that can be used in various media from country to country. While space does not allow us to discuss the many advertising restrictions that are imposed by various countries, we can highlight some of the more general restrictions common to advertising regulators throughout the world.

■ *Comparative advertising.* In the United States, advertisers name competitors in their advertising. However, the practice of comparison advertising is strictly regulated or banned outright in numerous other countries where it is considered a form of unfair competition. The prevalence of prohibitions concerning comparative advertising makes it ill-advised as a technique in most international advertising campaigns.

■ *Advertising to children.* Again, the United States is among the most permissive countries in the world in terms of children's advertising. Many countries ban any advertising to children and exclude all advertising in children's programming. In other cases, the hours permitted for advertising to children are very limited. The prohibitions against advertising to children cover a wide range of issues. Sweden and Norway ban all television advertising aimed at children. In Holland no celebrity endorsers can be used in broadcast commercials directed at children, and Spain outlaws the use of fictional characters in television food advertising. Outside the United States, a single campaign directed to children using U.S. standards would be very difficult to execute.[38]

■ *Internet advertising.* As more businesses turn to the Internet as a means of product information, promotion, and customer research, it becomes difficult to stay within the rules of international commerce. Because the Internet does not allow a marketer to limit geographic coverage, many advertisers include a statement that all product claims meet U.S. (or whatever countries the promotion is intended for) legal and regulatory standards and are intended for persons residing in those countries. This does not provide a foolproof solution for future liability, but it does provide companies with a defense if challenges are made in foreign jurisdictions. At this point, legal scholars are debating the degree of accountability incurred by Internet marketing. "When a marketer places advertising . . . on a server in Chicago, Boston, or New York that advertising . . . offer may be accessed throughout the world. From a legal perspective, the question is whether countries other than the United States can exert jurisdiction over advertising . . . material that is deemed unlawful by that foreign country."[39]

■ *Standards of truth.* In the United States and much of Western Europe, humor, exaggeration, and hyperbole are accepted formats for advertising. The majority of consumers and regulators alike take the view that creativity can sometimes stray from literal product facts to gain an audience's interest. However, multinational advertisers should err on the side of being extremely conservative in making product claims. Claims touting amazing, stupendous, or marvelous product benefits may be accepted as tolerable puffery in the United States, but can end up costing a company dearly abroad.

3. *The lack of reliable audience research.* Like all advertising executives, media planners must take a multinational perspective as clients and media move across borders to add market share and audiences. During the last two decades, the international media buying function has changed dramatically. Searching for cost efficiencies and recognizing the unique problems of international media buying, multinational clients have demanded special expertise from their agencies. In this environment, the demands for cross-cultural media research have become crucial.

Outside of a few major advertising markets, media research has traditionally been either nonexistent or the data were notoriously unreliable. Even basic information such as paid circulation for print media is often unavailable or, if numbers exist, they are unaudited. For example, an executive for a major agency doing business in China, commenting on media circulation figures, said, "There is gross exaggeration to a point that would be criminal in any other country."[40] In addition to fundamental media research, media planners also often lack basic information about target audiences including data about their purchase and media usage habits.

While a lack of audience and market data is a continuing concern to multinational marketers, the problems associated with media planning have improved dramatically in the last decade. For example, in recent years availability of television ratings have expanded to include countries throughout the world including Kenya, Uganda, Kuwait, Thailand, and even Iran. Although global media planning still presents major challenges, two factors have dramatically improved the ability of advertisers to reach target prospects:

1. *The rapid expansion of efficient global communication.* Cable and satellite television channels, combined with global distribution of movies and the introduction of the Internet, have created practical opportunities for millions of worldwide exposures.

2. *The expansion of global retailers.* As we discussed earlier in the case of Wal-Mart, customers do not always embrace a standard pattern of merchandising and

shopping experiences. However, in the long term, global buyers are likely to become more accustomed to similar goods and merchandise with both media and creative strategy becoming more standardized as a result.

In addition to specific executions of media objectives, media planners must also deal with the special problems of developing and executing a strategic plan on an international basis. Media buying is so complex for large multinational advertisers that the media function is increasingly concentrated in huge multinational media planning companies or brokers that buy for a number of agencies. These media specialists, such as London-based Zenith Optimedia Group, can afford to hire highly trained personnel, conduct multinational audience research, and establish data-bases that would be beyond the financial reach of most individual advertising agencies. Planners within these organizations also can gain significant media discounts by buying for groups of clients instead of on the basis of single companies or brands.

ADVERTISING AND ETHNIC DIVERSITY IN THE UNITED STATES

As we have discussed, global marketing has become a central strategy for many U.S. companies. However, American firms do not have to go abroad to deal with the challenges of multicultural marketing. Recent data from the U.S. Census Bureau indicated that more than 25 percent of the residents of California (42 percent), New Mexico (36 percent), Texas (33 percent), New York (28 percent), and Arizona (27 percent) prefer a language other than English at home.[41] While we tend to emphasize the marketing practices of a relatively few global companies, in our own country even the smallest retailers are facing challenges in reaching out to a diverse population and, to a degree, dealing with many of the marketing and promotion problems of companies operating on a worldwide stage. The three major ethnic minorities in the United States are Hispanics, Asian Americans, and African Americans with Native Americans comprising slightly less than 1 percent of the population.

In the last decade, and looking forward over the next 25 years or more, the complexities of ethnic marketing will grow as well as the opportunities offered to those companies that successfully connect with these growing populations. However, the task of marketing to a diverse population is made difficult by three trends:

1. *Majority-minority transition.* The marketplace is changing more quickly than many companies can adapt. Non-Hispanic whites account for less than half the population in Texas, California, New Mexico, and Hawaii. Nine other states including major regions such as New York and Florida will soon follow.

2. *Race is more difficult to determine.* In the 2000 Census, almost seven million respondents listed more than one racial background. This figure included 4 percent of all children. Traditional designations of ethnicity will be significantly less relevant in the future.

3. *Citizens of the world.* Through the Internet and other technology, immigrants more easily stay connected to family and homeland and, consequently, assimilation and acculturation can be a longer process.[42]

At both the national and local levels, marketers cannot ignore the growing importance of a diverse population. For example, the Hispanic and African American share of the total U.S. population is about 19 percent and 15 percent, respectively. The Hispanic population passed the African American segment in 2001, and it will continue to outpace the population growth of all other ethnic groups in coming decades. Four percent of the U.S. population is Asian American, a group that increased by 30 percent during the decade of the 1990s. It is estimated that by 2050 slightly more than 50 percent of the U.S. population will be comprised of these groups with Hispanics making up as much as one-third of the total.

Traditionally, the U.S. ethnic population has been concentrated in a few regions and urban centers of the United States. For example, eight counties in Texas have a Hispanic population of at least 90 percent, while 51 percent of Asian Americans live in just three states (California, New York, and Hawaii). Major American companies are aggressively courting Hispanic buyers both in this country and abroad (see Exhibit 23.8). However, during the last decade significant

EXHIBIT 23.8

Reaching out to new markets both at home and abroad.

Courtesy of Homer TLC Inc.

growth in the ethnic population has taken place in a number of different places. For example, the three fastest growing states in terms of Hispanic populations are North Carolina, Georgia, and Arkansas, with some counties in those states demonstrating increases of 500 percent or more from the 1990 to 2000 Census. As shown in Exhibit 23.9, the ethnic population is skewed toward younger age groups accentuating the rapid future increase in the Hispanic population. The rise in multicultural consumers combined with their significant increase in buying power is perhaps the major development in marketing in recent years.

Marketers in a number of product categories are taking note of the growing importance of these consumers. Not only is the multicultural market expanding faster than the general population, but its buying power is also increasing at a greater rate. In a special report, the *Wall Street Journal* explored the challenges and opportunities of diversity. As the report pointed out, "If companies are going to sell products and services globally, they will need a rich mix of employees with varied perspectives and experiences. They will need top executives who understand different countries and cultures."[43] The report went on to explore how Harley-Davidson during the last decade has successfully expanded its customer base from almost exclusively white males to women and people of color. In order to market to these groups, the company increased its vice presidents and managers from 5 percent a decade ago to 25 percent today and its senior managers from 15 percent to 25 percent during the same period. As the company stated, it needed a management and marketing team that more closely reflected the customer base it wanted to attract.

Companies are coming to realize that it is not enough to simply identify ethnic market segments. Advertisers know that they have to develop both products and messages that realistically meet their special needs and are presented in a communication environment that speaks to them in a credible manner. Companies also realize that the market is so large and growing at such a rapid pace that it has to be a major part of virtually any company's future plans. The Hispanic market alone will grow by as much as one-third by 2010 according to the U.S. Census Office. For a number of years, progressive companies such as Bank of America and Burger King have provided an array of services to their Latino customers, such as Spanish-language voice mail, Spanish-fluent employees, and bilingual menus. Today, most major companies are becoming more proactive in their advertising and marketing plans to ethnic customers. For example, a survey by the Association of National Advertisers found that slightly more than half of responding firms had created separate units to handle multicultural marketing with almost one-third of these having autonomous budget responsibility. As the author of the report concluded, "Having a stand-alone department with profit-and-loss objectives was a key factor to organizations really driving their multicultural success."[44]

Companies generally give greater attention to the Hispanic market than either the African American or Asian American market for two reasons. First, the rate of assimilation and acculturation is much higher among Asian Americans and African Americans than among Hispanics. While there are pockets of high Asian American populations, their relatively low percentage of the general population has forced them to assimilate into U.S. society more rapidly than Hispanics. Statistics such as completion of high school and college, income, and English fluency indicate that Asian Americans are in many ways part of the cultural mainstream. Even though they demonstrate unique product preferences, the overall market size of the Asian American population means that much less market support will be directed toward them. Likewise, the African American population data shows that in many respects they are remarkably similar to the general population. A number of studies have shown that when income is held constant, buying behavior among African Americans and Caucasians is very similar. Notwithstanding these similarities, research reveals that all ethnic minorities tend to respond favorably to companies and brands that direct marketing and advertising messages to their individual

How population LifeCycles add up to an increasingly diverse America.

EXHIBIT **23.9**

LifeCycles: The American Consumer 2006

Courtesy of *Advertising Age*

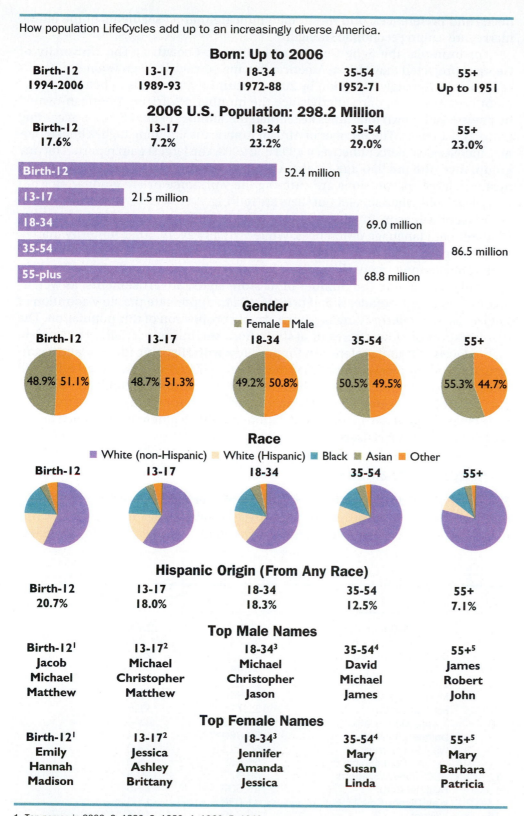

Born: Up to 2006

Birth-12	13-17	18-34	35-54	55+
1994-2006	1989-93	1972-88	1952-71	Up to 1951

2006 U.S. Population: 298.2 Million

Birth-12	13-17	18-34	35-54	55+
17.6%	7.2%	23.2%	29.0%	23.0%

Birth-12   52.4 million
13-17   21.5 million
18-34   69.0 million
35-54   86.5 million
55-plus   68.8 million

Gender
Female   Male

Birth-12	13-17	18-34	35-54	55+
48.9% 51.1%	48.7% 51.3%	49.2% 50.8%	50.5% 49.5%	55.3% 44.7%

Race
White (non-Hispanic)   White (Hispanic)   Black   Asian   Other

Birth-12   13-17   18-34   35-54   55+

Hispanic Origin (From Any Race)

Birth-12	13-17	18-34	35-54	55+
20.7%	18.0%	18.3%	12.5%	7.1%

Top Male Names

Birth-12[1]	13-17[2]	18-34[3]	35-54[4]	55+[5]
Jacob	Michael	Michael	David	James
Michael	Christopher	Christopher	Michael	Robert
Matthew	Matthew	Jason	James	John

Top Female Names

Birth-12[1]	13-17[2]	18-34[3]	35-54[4]	55+[5]
Emily	Jessica	Jennifer	Mary	Mary
Hannah	Ashley	Amanda	Susan	Barbara
Madison	Brittany	Jessica	Linda	Patricia

1. Top names in 2000. 2. 1990. 3. 1980. 4. 1960. 5. 1940
Population numbers rounded. More info: census.gov; ssa.gov. Sources: Census Bureau population projections for 2006; Social Security Administration (names)

needs and preferences, and recent data indicate that all segments of the ethnic market are gaining economic strength.

For example, the Selig Center for Economic Growth at The University of Georgia, projected that African American buying power would grow almost 25 percent to approximately $1 trillion by 2010. It attributed the gains to better employment opportunities, particularly since the number of African American-owned businesses has grown four times faster than the number of all U.S. firms according to the U.S. Census. The number of African Americans attaining high school diplomas increased 10 percent between 1993 and 2003, the largest gain reported for any group. Also, the median age for the African American population is 30.2 years, meaning larger proportions are entering the workforce or are graduating from entry-level jobs while smaller numbers are retiring.[45]

A second reason for the greater marketing efforts expended in reaching Hispanics are language differences. While virtually every other minority market adopts English very quickly (certainly within one generation), Spanish remains a preference among many Hispanics even when they become fluent in English. One only has to note the number of in-store signs, advertisements, as well as Spanish-language broadcast and print media to appreciate the slow adoption of English as the preferred language for a sizable proportion of this population. The combination of slower rates of assimilation, including partiality to Spanish, higher levels of brand preferences for products with Hispanic themes, and a continually growing market to see that the move to Hispanic-based marketing will increase at a rate much greater than the general economy. Exhibit 23.10 shows that the major marketers to the Hispanic market are, for the most part, the same as to buyers in general—another indication that this segment is very much on the radar of primary advertisers.

Diversity and U.S. Advertising

How advertisers deal with U.S. diversity is a matter of both sensitivity and profitability. At one time advertisers thought that a certain percentage of their advertising placed in foreign language or ethnic-oriented media would provide a sufficient

EXHIBIT 23.10

Top 20 Hispanic Marketers

Network TV easily dwarfs other media spending.

Courtesy of *Advertising Age*, January 30, 2006, p. 5-6.

Rank	Company	Jan.– Nov. 2005	Chng vs. '04
1	Procter & Gamble Co.	$148,210	2.7%
2	General Motors Corp.	106,748	8.6
3	Sears Holdings Corp.	69,915	−26.2
4	PepsiCo	68,443	4.4
5	Johnson & Johnson	67,251	8.2
6	McDonald's Corp.	65,996	7.1
7	Ford Motor Co.	61,771	11.5
8	Toyota Motor Corp.	56,966	41.6
9	DaimlerChrysler	56,860	−10.4
10	Wal-Mart Stores	56,223	13.3
11	Verizon Communications	51,536	5.3
12	SBC Communications	49,977	−9.8
13	Hyundai Corp.	45,507	16.5
14	Walt Disney Co.	41,038	15.3
15	L'Oreal	36,745	10.4
16	Home Depot	36,560	36.1
17	Altria Group	36,409	−3.1
18	SABmiller	36,109	65.6
19	U.S. government	32,258	−12.1
20	Yum Brands	30,936	7.2

Notes: TV and print spending in thousands of dollars. Percentage changes are vs. first 11 months of 2004. Source: TNS Media Intelligence

accommodation to this market. However, language or media is no longer the defining force in ethnic marketing. Today, it is more important to deal with the texture of cultural differences—differences that cut across age, geography, and language. According to the Pew Hispanic Center, 72 percent of first-generation Hispanic immigrants are Spanish-language dominant, 47 percent of the second generation are bilingual, and 78 percent of third-generation Hispanics are English dominant.[46] However, as companies are quickly finding out, language does not define how a person regards his or her cultural roots. Even among Hispanics who are English dominant or who speak no Spanish, they are as likely to have strong values in the Hispanic community as those who speak Spanish.

The emergence of a value-driven, as contrasted to a language-driven, marketing strategy is a primary change in the strategy and execution of ethnic marketing. The debate has shifted from language as a barometer of assimilation to one of self-concept among ethnic populations. As one marketing executive indicated, "The reality that Hispanics have not assimilated and will not assimilate like previous immigrant groups gives rise to a new marketing imperative. Simple translations are no longer acceptable to this increasingly savvy consumer group. Nor is featuring Hispanic faces in general-market advertising effective on its own. Marketing to U.S. Hispanics requires greater consumer insight and cultural and linguistic skills than ever before."[47]

Marketers are facing an interesting dilemma in attempting to reach the U.S. ethnic market. On the one hand, firms know that they have to acknowledge the growing diversity of their buyers to profitably market their products. On the other hand, there is a growing acceptance of diverse cultures among all segments of the population—especially teens—that suggests the future will be one of constant borrowing from a number of cultural identities. According to Stephen Palacios, *intra-culturalism,* that is, the tendency for American youth to adopt traditions and attitudes of cultures other than its own, is becoming the norm. Another marketing executive points out, ". . . the days of marketing according to vertical lines of ethnicity are fading" and they are being replaced by an appeal to aspirations and lifestyle that can cut across numerous cultural characteristics.[48] For example, Exhibit 23.11 shows how diverse music categories are popular across all ethnic groups.

Each of the major ethnic groups present special problems and opportunities for marketing and advertising. As we will discuss later in this chapter, there are many subcultures within each group. For example, an Asian American of Japanese

NeoPets, in its fifth annual Youth Study for *Ad Age,* reveals the diverse interest of kids (7 and under) and tweens (8–12) among all ethnic/racial groups. Music is a good place to start: **"I LOVE . . .**

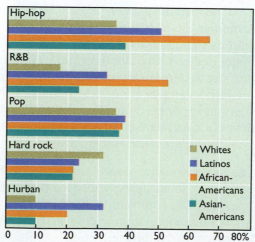

EXHIBIT 23.11

Musing about Music

From Tiffany Meyers, "Culture Mosaic," *Advertising Age,* March 13, 2006, p. 5-2.

Source: NeoPets Youth Study 2006.

EXHIBIT **23.12**

Steady Growth on the Horizon

Courtesy of *Advertising Age*, January 31, 2005, p. 5-2.

Hispanic media forecasts (dollars in millions)

	2003	2004*	2005*	2006*
TV	$1,774	$1,990	$2,169	$2,429
Radio	628	664	738	804
Print	310	360	404	460
Outdoor	74	76	82	91
Internet	45	75	113	163
Total Hispanic	2,831	3,166	3,505	3,947

Percentage growth

	2003	2004*	2005*	2006*
TV	17%	12%	9%	12%
Radio	7	6	11	9
Print	8	16	12	14
Outdoor	10	3	8	10
Internet	350	67	50	45
Total Hispanic	14	12	11	13

Source: HispanTelligence, Bureau of Labor Statistics, Census Bureau and MediaMark Research Inc.'s 2004 database.
* Years are estimates.

heritage may have much different product preferences than a person with a Korean or Vietnamese heritage. In the following section, we will discuss some of the primary elements in marketing to various groups.

Media To a degree, the growth of the ethnic market as well as the degree of its assimilation can be gauged by growth of the ethnic press. The number of foreign-language and ethnic-oriented media outlets demonstrates both the size of these populations and also their potential for marketers. Because of the relatively low-cost entry into the market, ethnic newspapers are the largest medium in terms of number of vehicles (although they are far surpassed by the audiences of ethnic-oriented television). Exhibit 23.12 offers an overview of the Hispanic media, by far the largest category of the ethnic press. Every Hispanic medium is growing at a rate far greater than mainstream journalism. In many cases, major publishers and networks have taken full or partial ownership of media within these groups to insure a means of reaching this lucrative advertising market. The print sector provides a huge range of circulation, editorial quality, and advertising sophistication. Ethnic newspapers provide niches for reaching every imaginable target segment.

One can find newspapers aimed at Russian, Chinese, Korean, Filipino, Armenian, and African American readers, to name only a few. They include publications that are issued on a sporadic basis with circulations of a few hundred to major dailies with more than 100,000 readers. Most of the ethnic-targeted publications have demonstrated significant circulation and advertising increases during the last decade. The one exception is the African American press. With few exceptions, newspapers directed to the African American community have shown severe drops in circulation compared to their peak during the 1940s.

The decline of the African American press can be attributed to two primary causes:

1. The civil rights movement of the 1960s and 1970s pushed mainstream media, led by local newspapers, to begin more balanced coverage of the African American community. As major newspapers began to gain African American readers, circulation and advertising revenue shifted from the African American press to traditional publications. For example, the century-old *Chicago*

Defender, one of the historic luminaries of the African American press, currently has a circulation of 15,000 compared to a peak of 250,000 in the 1960s.[49]

2. Another factor in the decline of the African American press was the fact that it was much easier for major newspapers to assimilate African American readers compared to other ethnic populations. There is no language barrier in reaching the African American community so advertisers don't have to make decisions concerning English versus indigenous languages. Although there are differences of media and product preferences among African Americans, just as among the white majority, they represent a much more homogeneous market than either Asian American or Hispanic American consumers.

In the past, most ethnic newspapers were owned by small, independent publishers. However, major newspaper chains are aggressively marketing ethnic publications especially to the Hispanic market. Led by *El Nuevo Herald* in Miami, *La Opinion* in Los Angeles, and *Hoy* in both New York and Chicago, these newspapers provide both readers and advertisers with information about news and products directed to the Hispanic market (see Exhibit 23.13). Hispanic-oriented magazines also have been extremely popular with this market. With a fashion, glamour, and celebrity emphasis, the major publications in this segment have been extremely profitable in recent years (see Exhibit 23.14). It is interesting that the majority of the most popular Hispanic publications are owned by mainstream publishers, demonstrating again the importance of this market to both general advertisers and the general press.

Although print media have had success in reaching the ethnic market, it is television that has attracted the majority of ethnic advertising dollars in the last decade. Reaching the ethnic market is not a new strategy. For almost three decades, syndicated television shows such as *Soul Train* have targeted African American audiences. Until the 1990s, ethnic programming was largely confined to syndicated

Rank	Newspaper	2005 Ad Revenue	% Chg
1	El Nuevo Herald (Miami)	$72,620.6	11.5
2	La Opinion (Los Angeles)	51,417.7	4.4
3	El Diario (Ciudad Juarez, Mexico)	30,571.2	24.1
4	El Diario La Prensa (New York)	24,005.2	−1.0
5	Hoy (New York)	12,289.0	−39.1
6	La Raza (Chicago)	12,037.3	19.8
7	Hoy (Chicago)	11,105.9	−48.1
8	Hoy (Los Angeles)	8,725.6	4.5
9	El Norte (El Paso, Texas)	8,688.9	10.5
10	Washington Hispanic	8,485.3	68.5
11	La Voz de Phoeniz	7,519.9	72.7
12	Al Dia (Dallas)	7,120.2	33.4
13	TV y Mas (Phoenix)	7,032.9	−4.4
14	El Sentinel (Miami-Ft. Lauderdale)	6,312.0	−10.5
15	Diario Las Americas (Miami)	6,244.6	4.9
16	Diario La Estrella (Dallas)	6,017.8	20.5
17	Nuevo Mundo (San Jose, Calif.)	4,913.5	−30.3
18	Prensa Hispana (Phoenix)	4,735.1	9.9
19	El Latino (San Diego)	4,652.4	13.8
20	Lawndale News (Chicago)	4,572.0	−13.6
21	Al Dia (Philadelphia)	4,336.2	21.0
22	El Especial (New York)	3,189.4	−2.2
23	La Voz de Houston	3,180.9	14.2
24	Mundo L.A. (Los Angeles)	3,121.7	1.5
25	Vida en el Valle (Fresno, Calif.)	2,814.5	4.5

EXHIBIT 23.13

Top 25 Hispanic Newspapers

By measured advertising revenue.

Courtesy of *Advertising Age*.

Dollars are in thousands. Measured newspaper ad spending from TNS Media Intelligence. Percent change is computed from figures for 2004.

EXHIBIT 23.14

Top 25 Hispanic Magazines

By measured advertising revenue.

Courtesy of *Advertising Age*.

Rank	Magazine	2005 Ad Revenue	% Chg
1	People en Español	$38,651.5	12.8
2	Latina	29,497.9	20.9
3	Reader's Digest Selecciones	14,811.3	−1.1
4	TV y Novelas Estados Unidos	10,852.3	57.8
5	Vanidades	10,126.1	23.9
6	Hispanic Business	8,312.9	−7.1
7	Healthy Kids en Español	6,932.9	213.6
8	Ser Padres	6,787.3	−2.1
9	Hispanic Magazine	6,507.5	−14.1
10	Vista	5,625.1	8.2
11	Mira!	5,177.9	107.1
12	Futbol Mundial	4,923.9	28.1
13	Cosmopolitan en Español	4,369.8	46.9
14	Cristina La Revista**	3,280.6	−1.8
15	Selecta	3,180.5	−2.7
16	TV Notas	3,023.5	37.1
17	Shape en Español	2,925.9	−7.4
18	Ocean Drive en Español	2,825.0	21.5
19	Siempre Mujer*	2,813.7	NA
20	Sports Illustrated Latino*	2,505.9	NA
21	AARP Segunda Juventud	2,226.7	317.5
22	Nuestra Gente**	2,025.1	−57.4
23	Espera	1,886.1	−5.5
24	Estylo	1,870.5	0.8
25	Sobre Ruedas	1,778.7	−12.6

Dollars are in thousands. Measured magazine ad spending from Media Economics Group's HispanicMagazineMonitor. *Launched in 2006. **Ceased publication.

shows and a few locally produced programs in major markets. However, cable brought opportunities to reach segmented audiences that had never been possible through broadcast television. Just as cable made it possible for history buffs, golfers, and chefs to have channels directed to their interests, likewise, it made narrowly focused ethnic programming practical. The introduction of channels such as Black Entertainment Network (BET) furnished entertainment and information for the African American audience that were not provided by mainstream networks.

The same model is now working for the Hispanic market. The Latino television market is dominated by Univision and Telemundo, a division of NBC Universal. Rather than being niche players among larger television rivals, they have become dominant competitors for younger viewers regardless of language and have won the ratings battle on some occasions. This popularity has not been lost on mainstream broadcasters who have taken a number of steps to compete for the Hispanic audience. For example, ABC decided in 2005 to make its entire primetime lineup bilingual. At considerable expense, the network now subtitles all its shows and dubs four of its highest profile programs including *Desperate Housewives* and *Lost*.[50]

The growth and influence of Hispanic television also is apparent in program development at the major networks. Shows such as *George Lopez* obviously have great appeal to Hispanic audiences, but networks are also going a step further to design shows modeled after popular Spanish-language soap operas. Typically, these soaps, unlike the American format that may run for decades, are short form stories or "telenovelas" that run for 13 weeks and wrap up to a conclusion. In developing these shows, the networks hope to attract younger female viewers of all backgrounds. However, they also acknowledge that it is a way to connect with the growing Hispanic viewership and to compete with Spanish-language broadcasters. The networks' interest was no doubt heightened by Univision's *Contra Viento Y Marea* (*Against All Odds*), which was broadcast in December

2005 and ranked first in its time slot among young adults regardless of language.[51]

Language continues to be a major obstacle in reaching the multinational audience. Despite the success of Spanish-language media, we are seeing more English-language programming and advertising directed to the bilingual or English-dominant market. For example, there are two English-language cable outlets for the Hispanic market, SiTV and Mun2. SiTV was launched in 2004 with an all-English format. The objective of SiTV is to reach young Latinos who primarily speak English and secondarily to create cross-over appeal to African Americans, Asian Americans, and others who are fans of Latino pop culture but do not speak Spanish.[52] Mun2 (pronounced *mundos* or "two worlds") is a sister outlet to NBC's Telemundo aimed at the Latino youth market with a predominance of English-language programming.

The Asian American market is even more difficult to come to grips with because of the diversity of languages within a relatively small market. Presently, there are two Asian-language networks, ImaginAsian TV and AZN Television. Both are available in limited markets, but the high levels of income and education of the Asian American market make them popular with advertisers attempting to reach this market. A popular strategy for most advertisers is to place advertising in mainstream media but on programs that have high levels of ethnic viewers, listeners, or readers. For example, *Monday Night Football* has high viewership among African Americans and young Hispanic men while shows such as *Desperate Housewives* and *Lost* have a huge following among Hispanic women. Regardless of the advertising plan of a particular advertiser, it is clear that the ethnic market is a fundamental part of the marketing strategy for virtually every major company.

The Message It is important to emphasize that whether advertisers are using English-language or foreign-language media, marketers must be sensitive to the messages and cultural connotations they communicate. Sometimes these problems are as basic as problems in adapting well-known slogans to diverse markets. For example, Taco Bell's tagline, "Think Outside the Bun," designed to lure consumers away from traditional fast-food chains translated "man does not live by bread alone."[53] It is obvious that advertisers are trying a number of approaches to address the problems inherent in reaching these audiences, and they are demonstrating a level of sensitivity that, unfortunately, was missing in earlier years. As we have seen, advertisers are now able to communicate with ethnic buyers through a number of media outlets. However, reaching the U.S. ethnic markets presents challenges similar to the ones multinational advertisers have found overseas. Advertisers must develop messages that are both sensitive to specific ethnic cultures and, at the same time, provide an effective sales message. Attempts by mainstream advertisers to develop campaigns to reach these markets have resulted in a huge growth in advertising agencies concentrated in ethnic marketing.

Major advertisers such as Target, Sears, and JCPenney are producing Spanish-language advertising circulars, in-store signage, and some, such as Wal-Mart, even offer Spanish-language magazines distributed free in stores with high levels of Hispanic patronage. Wal-Mart also is using its highly sophisticated inventory tracking system to coordinate merchandising and advertising between its stores in Mexico and those in the United States. For example, Wal-Mart saw the success that its Mexican stores achieved by devoting significant space to baby and children's clothing and stocking a large selection of items with cartoon characters. Based on Mexican sales, the company tweaked its inventory in U.S. stores catering to a Hispanic population. These and other efforts are paying off as a recent survey showed that 36 percent of Hispanic shoppers rated Wal-Mart as their favorite store with no other retailer named by more than 4 percent.[54]

Despite the many positive strides taken by firms over the last 20 years, problems still plague outreach efforts to the ethnic market. As one Hispanic marketing executive said, "Advertisers and their marketing departments are looking at the Hispanic community as a group when in fact there are many factors that make up this 'Group' and they must take into account the diversity which includes the country of origin, whether they are the first or second generation here in the U.S., and their general location . . . a second generation Latino living in Texas would react differently to an ad that is geared toward a second generation Latino living in New York or a second generation Latino living in Miami, Florida."[55] For example, General Motors ran a Saturn commercial in Miami showing a woman in a Mexican dress in front of the Alamo. Unfortunately for GM, the overwhelming majority of the Miami Hispanic community is Cuban American, and the commercial had little or no relevance to them.[56]

While major marketers continue to reach ethnic markets in niche media with messages directed at specific target segments, they also are aware of the growing acculturation of ethnic products, entertainment, and messages into mainstream American cultural and media. Major network portrayals of the ethnic population still lag behind reality, but, nevertheless, we are seeing entertainment and advertising themes that highlight ethnic subjects. In 2005, for the fiftieth anniversary of Crest toothpaste, Procter & Gamble decided to bring back the "Crest Kid" campaign. It was last used in 1960 and featured children crying "Look Mom—no cavities." In the new version, the advertising featured Cuban-born Enya Martinez who was chosen from 3,000 candidates for her white smile (see Exhibit 23.15).

Over the last several years, a number of major marketers have changed their product images to reflect a changing population. "In 1989, Aunt Jemima, the matriarch of the pancake-and-syrup products from PepsiCo's Quaker Oats, had her headband removed, got a new hairstyle and was outfitted with a lace collar and pearl earrings. With heightened recognition of the buying power of Latinos, African-Americans and other demographic groups, many advertisers want to make sure their brand accoutrements—slogans, logos, and spokespersons—match the tenor of the day."[57] The trend toward both ethnic specific marketing and cultural assimilation into mainstream advertising will continue as these markets continue to grow in both population and purchasing power.

Marketers are often creative in conveying cultural diversity to their promotional mix. For example, brands as diverse as McDonald's, Chrysler, and Jose Cuervo tequila have initiated promotions celebrating Cinco de Mayo, a minor Mexican holiday commemorating a Mexican militia victory over the French army in 1862. "Savvy marketers with an eye for the burgeoning Hispanic market—and, even more, the cross-ethnicity appeal of Hispanic culture—have caught on. Homemade Mexican food, mariachis and sombreros have in the past five years given way to McDonald's-sponsored street festivals, giant Jose Cuervo margaritas and a 900-pound piñata in the shape of a Chrysler car."[58] More than any particular promotion, events such as Cinco de Mayo underscore the fact that assimilation is not a one-way street. Just as immigrants to this country adopt many U.S. products and customers, American consumers embrace everything from salsa to Chinese food, and these products become part of the total fabric of the "melting pot." This assimilation can be traced in the prediction that close to half of third-generation Latinos marry non-Latinos, which may have major implications for future marketing strategy.

The Product For many years, virtually all multicultural marketing programs consisted of the development of products and brands specifically for various segments of the ethnic market. However, as this population has grown we are seeing a significant number of brands being introduced from abroad—either by American-based multinational corporations or foreign-based companies exporting popular brands to the U.S. expatriate market. Alen, a major Mexican manufacturer of household

EXHIBIT 23.15

The new Crest campaign demonstrates the changing demographics of the American Market.

Courtesy of Procter & Gamble.

cleaning products, exports a number of its brands to the United States. The company believes that there is a ready-made U.S. market of Mexican immigrants who are already familiar with the brand. Likewise, companies such as PepsiCo and Colgate-Palmolive, with strong Mexican subsidiaries, have imported some of their products to the United States. For example, PepsiCo has introduced chili-flavored lollipops with a mango-gum center, and Colgate-Palmolive has imported two of its most popular brands—Suavitel, a fabric softener and Fabuloso, a liquid cleaner. These companies have a dual strategy of primarily appealing to the Hispanic market and at the same time building future sales through cross-over purchases by the general population.

While these brands have the advantage of having been "test marketed" in other countries, there are still challenges to successful importation. Perhaps the biggest hurdle is realizing that even though the brands are the same, the consumers are not. These differences must be reflected in advertising and promotion. As one Hispanic advertising executive commented, importing advertising along with a product is a perfect way to throw away money. "We [immigrants] live a different reality. We're in a foreign land, don't have family around and everything is in a different language. The people get acculturated and have different tastes.

Someone may be watching a telenovela but be completely American."[59] Regardless of how a product comes to the U.S. market, the landscape shows numerous examples of how companies are adapting their product offerings to the ethnic markets.

Success in the ethnic market is based on relevant communication, delivered through credible media, and backed with products that meet the needs of specific market segments. In other words, profits in the ethnic marketplace are generated according to the same formula found in any other sector. Success is also based on planning using insightful research. In the next section, we will discuss how marketers are trying to put the research part of the multicultural puzzle together.

Research For many years, marketers either ignored the ethnic market or based decisions on invalid research or stereotypes. The lack of reliable research was based on a number of factors including:

- Often researchers had little or no experience in ethnic marketing.
- Respondents sometimes were uncooperative with researchers because of language barriers and a lack of full explanations of the research's aims.
- There was an unavailability of ethnic-oriented syndicated research studies.
- The weighting of research samples often did not fully take into account the ethnic population especially in some major markets.

Regardless of the reasons, the result was a scarcity of information concerning the multicultural market. Today, that situation is changing, driven primarily by the growth in sales and profitability and the significant investments that are being made in marketing efforts to tap this segment. Research dollars, as is the case with any business expenditure, are driven by the potential return on investment. In the case of advertising research, dollars invested in research are directly correlated with the increasing expenditures in advertising dollars allotted to ethnic audiences. When advertising budgets were relatively small, companies were willing to make advertising decisions more on intuition than hard data. However, firms spending millions of dollars to reach the multicultural market can't risk flawed decision making concerning their advertising investments. The combination of overall population increases and higher levels of buying power continues to make the ethnic market one that is hard to ignore.

Improved research in the ethnic markets also has resulted in a more realistic view of the significant differences exhibited within these groups, and it has avoided potentially disastrous stereotypes that often create ill-will among the very markets a firm is trying to cultivate. Like any market research, the primary objective should be to better serve the needs of a target segment by providing products and advertising messages that most appropriately address their needs. In a major study of Hispanic consumers, *People en Espanol* found significant differences between Hispanic buyers and the general population.[60] Some of these findings include:

1. Hispanics are much more likely to go shopping, with 56 percent agreeing with the statement "I love to shop" compared to 39 percent of the general population.
2. Hispanics are much more influenced by advertising than the general population. They are likely to purchase products because of brand image or a perception that a brand is new and trendy.
3. They are more likely to pay with cash, with only 15 percent using credit cards compared to 40 percent of the general market.

4. Hispanics are almost 40 percent more likely to download music than the general population. However, overall Internet usage shows little usage (11 percent) among the Spanish-dominant population.

5. Perhaps most significant was the finding that there is a retro acculturation taking place. Even English-dominant Hispanics are turning back to their Latin roots in terms of language and media preference.

The latter finding has major implications for the way a company markets to Hispanics. In terms of products, media, and language there needs to be a significant sensitivity to the way in which this market is approached. From the research, it is clear that the Hispanic population takes increasing pride in their heritage—regardless of their language preference, a fact that needs to be closely watched as advertising executions are developed.

For the past 30 years, social scientists attempted to determine the degree to which immigrants have been assimilated into American society. Assimilation of the Hispanic population is taking place at a slower rate than other ethnic groups have demonstrated in the past for a number of reasons:

1. The geographic proximity of Latin America makes travel and interaction with one's native country relatively easy.

2. The constant flow of Hispanic immigrants refreshes the number of predominately Spanish speakers.

3. The growth of Spanish language media in the United States has contributed to a relatively slow rate of assimilation.

While knowledge of language usage and rates of assimilation have implications across the marketing spectrum, nowhere is the value of such research more apparent than at the retail level. The technology of product scanning and permission marketing, so prevalent in mainstream market research, is being efficiently utilized to identify and research the ethnic market. Major retailers, such as Home Depot, Circuit City, and IKEA, are using census data and targeting software to identify prime markets for Hispanic shoppers and react accordingly with products and promotions. CVS pharmacies classified all its drugstores into one of four categories according to the level of Hispanic customers. These different levels are used to determine the degree of Spanish-language in-store signage and the degree of Spanish-oriented promotions it will use. These research studies are helpful in communicating with an individual store's customer base, but it also can contribute to profitability. As a Circuit City executive commented, "If you're looking at return on investment, you're not going to go to the expense of redoing signage for 2% to 3% of the population."[61]

One of the best indicators of the importance of ethnic research is the money invested by both advertisers and media. Nielsen Media Research provides national television ratings through its National Hispanic People Meter sample, and the company also measures local Hispanic television audiences in nineteen of the largest Hispanic markets. Likewise, the Arbitron Hispanic Market Service provides radio ratings for twenty-four of the largest Hispanic markets. Similar services are available from both rating services for African American broadcast audiences. On the print side, most of the major ethnic print publications are audited by one of the several services that provide guaranteed circulation figures. Multicultural research is underscoring the fact that multicultural consumers have traditional purchase habits and customs that must be reflected in advertising and promotion. However, research shows that when a brand gains acceptance in the minority community, there is a significant level of brand and company loyalty that makes the effort extremely profitable.

SUMMARY ⊛

It is clear that both at home and abroad global and multinational advertising has moved from special niches to an integral part of the promotion plans of the majority of companies. In this country, even the smallest retailer engages in some form of international marketing—either in the goods it sells or those it buys. As more countries improve both their economic situation and their openness to trade with other nations, we will see even more business conducted on an international basis.

While multinational marketing has many unique features, contribution to profitability is the primary objective of all promotional endeavors. The driving force behind multinational marketing is the search for new markets by the countries from the mature economies of the United States, Japan, and Europe to the emerging industrial powers of China and India. In many respects, the search for overseas markets has been the motivation for foreign trade since the days of the early Dutch, English, and Spanish traders in the fifteenth and sixteenth centuries—and, for that matter, the Phoenicians of prehistoric times. When countries can no longer sustain economic growth within their own borders, they look to cross-border commerce for trading partners. Although the scope of contemporary international marketing is being conducted on an unprecedented scale, the basic impetus has remained the same for more than a thousand years.

Many of the recent innovations in international advertising have been driven by the introduction of new forms of communication technology. In the 1970s, major U.S. publications began worldwide distribution of foreign-language editions. Print was followed by satellite transmissions of television signals and, more recently, the emergence of the Internet. Each has contributed to a faster pace of advertising and marketing on a worldwide basis.

The potential rewards of marketing in emerging countries can be substantially greater than the same effort invested in domestic marketing. However, multinational companies have learned that overseas marketing and advertising are very different from traditional American advertising. Although the basic functions may be the same, the complexities of dealing in a global economy are testing the planning, research, and managerial abilities of both companies and their advertising agencies. The internal difficulties experienced by the European Union, a developed region with one of the highest standards of living in the world, reinforce the problems companies face as they introduce their products in emerging nations.

One thing is certain, advertising will play a major role as companies move into more overseas markets. The most successful brands usually will be those that establish the first beachhead in emerging markets by taking pioneering risks. The common criteria for U.S. advertising—CPMs, cost-per-point, audited circulation and verified ratings, and even short-term return-on-investment—are often not applicable in many foreign markets. Instead, experience, judgment, and calculated risk-taking must be used to deal with the intricacies of international marketing.

Moreover, even those U.S. businesses that do not participate in multinational advertising will be faced with the challenges of ethnic diversity in this country. The growth in size and buying power of the African American, Hispanic, and Asian American markets will increasingly require the creative use of media, promotion, and sales messages to reach this eclectic marketplace. Not just business expertise but also sensitivity to the culture, language, and values of other people will be a requirement in this new environment. However, for those willing to devote the time to learn how to operate in this diverse market, the rewards will be great. Clearly, multicultural advertising will continue to undergo a period of dramatic change throughout this decade.

REVIEW ✹

1. What are some of the advantages and disadvantages of the Internet in international marketing?
2. How do legal restrictions effect the execution of multinational marketing?
3. Discuss the marketing concept in terms of global marketing.
4. What are some of the potential advantages and disadvantages of free trade agreements?
5. Discuss the importance of cultural considerations in executing international advertising.
6. Discuss some of the primary means of entering foreign markets by U.S. firms.
7. Discuss the role of product development in meeting the demands of both international marketing and the U.S. ethnic population.
8. What effect has cultural assimilation had on American marketing?
9. Discuss advertising research as a tool for overcoming ethnic stereotyping.

CHAPTER 24

Economic, Social, and Legal Effects of Advertising

*M*arketing communication is the face of your company and your brands. Advertising messages give the impressions that create, in part, the customers' perceptions of a company's brand. Because advertising is such a prevalent element of business, it often comes under greater scrutiny than other elements of the marketing mix. The assessment of advertising is ongoing, and it is conducted in both formal and informal settings. From government regulators and the courts to irate consumers writing letters to complain about a television commercial, companies know that the messages they communicate can have significant consequences—both positive and negative. However, it is the public's trust in its honesty and fairness that ultimately determines advertising's effectiveness as a sales tool. Because it is so pervasive, advertising has a special responsibility to adhere to high ethical and honest business standards as it serves to create economic expansion.

The basic goals of advertising have changed little over the last 150 years. Most advertising introduces consumers to products and brands and, once this is accomplished, creates brand loyalty and repeat purchases by establishing a unique brand position in consumers' minds. Advertising can also advocate social causes, to sway public opinion concerning controversial issues, or underscore a firm's corporate citizenship. This chapter will examine the diverse methods that advertisers employ as both economic and social communication tools and the constraints under which advertisers work. After reading this chapter, you will understand:

chapter objectives

1. the societal and economic dimensions of advertising
2. cause-related marketing as a sales tool
3. distinctions between legal and responsible advertising
4. the Federal Trade Commission's role in advertising regulation
5. First Amendment status of advertising messages
6. corporate citizenship and advertising self-regulation
7. the Advertising Council's role as a social institution

ADVERTISING CRITICISM: A HISTORICAL PERSPECTIVE

Advertising criticism is not a new phenomenon, but the public's perception of advertising and its expectations have changed markedly over the last 130 years. Before discussing some contemporary areas of advertising evaluation, let's begin by tracing the history of advertising criticism:

1. *The Era of Exaggerated Claims, l865–1900.* During this period most people accepted advertising as "buyer beware" communication in which virtually any claim for a product was allowed. Some advertising claims during this period, especially for patent medicine, were so outlandish that one wonders how anyone could have possibly believed them.

2. *The Era of Public Awareness, 1900–1965.* It was during this period that both the public and government regulators began to reject the notion of a laissez-faire, unregulated economic system. By the turn of the century, legislation such as the Pure Food and Drug Act of 1906 demonstrated Congress's recognition that the public was demanding protection from monopolies as well as the prevailing untruthful portrayal of products and services. Many responsible advertisers feared for the very existence of the industry as deceptive advertisements became more prevalent during the closing years of the nineteenth century. It was during this period that both enlightened media executives and advertisers realized that there were real opportunities to provide consumers with helpful information that would enhance both their public image and profitability (see Exhibit 24.1).

3. *The Era of Social Responsibility, l965–present.* During the last 40 years, advertisers have come to realize that truth alone is not sufficient to meet the demands of ethical advertising. Companies acknowledge that they must meet a higher standard of social responsibility than simply providing literally truthful advertising. Critics of advertising and, for that matter, advertisers deal with a delicate philosophical balancing act. Without totally rejecting the classical economic concept of the rational buyer, both critics and enlightened marketers agree that some level of consumer protection is needed. The concept of consumer protection spawned the consumer movement of the l960s, oversight of environmental safety, and a heightened awareness of various claims featured in modern advertising.

The Role of Corporate Responsibility

During much of the last century there has been a move toward corporations taking more responsibility for noneconomic endeavors from supporting humanitarian causes, being environmentally responsive, and supporting numerous social issues. In the opinion of some economists, the notion of the corporation as a social organization runs counter to its primary goal as a profit-making institution. They would argue that, rather than being indifferent to an improved society, diverting resources from business to society in the long run harms both. More than 200 years ago in his classic book *The Wealth of Nations*, Adam Smith popularized the notion that individuals should pursue a selfish course and, in return, society as a whole would be the better for it. The book explored the intellectual framework that explained the benefit of a free market. Smith is most often recognized for the expression "the invisible hand," a term which he coined to demonstrate how self-interest guides the most efficient use of resources in a nation's economy, with public welfare coming as a by-product. To underscore his laissez-faire convictions, Smith argued that state and personal efforts to promote social good are ineffectual compared to unbridled market forces."[1] Smith explained his philosophy, "Every individual is continually exerting himself to find out the most advantageous employment for

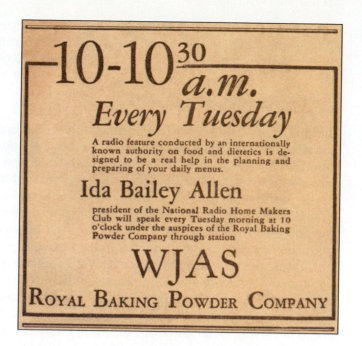

whatever capital he can command. It is his own advantage, indeed, and not that of the society, which he has in view. But the study of his own advantage naturally, or rather necessarily, leads him to prefer that employment which is most advantageous to the society."[2]

In today's global business environment, the ideas of Adam Smith are not as easily adaptable to a complex business climate. There is no easy answer to the question of the proper role of companies as members of society. One critic of corporate responsibility wrote, "The 20th century proved [Adam Smith to be correct]: Profit seeking corporations, constrained and buttressed by moderate government regulation and spending, did far more to increase the welfare of the world than a proliferation of 'socially responsible' governments. And the 21st century is proving it yet again: China's embrace of Adam Smith has yielded the greatest alleviation of poverty in history."[3]

Ilyse Hogue of the Rainforest Action Network expressed a contrary view, "Increasingly, citizens and progressive businesses are recognizing the false divide that the modern-day economic system is struggling to overcome. Should we have to choose between higher quarterly returns or assuring the health of our children's future? More people are saying no. There has to be a way to do both."[4] Clearly, there are no definite answers to the many questions raised by the sometimes conflicting social responsibilities that the public places on businesses. Likewise, advertising, as the communicator of corporate philosophy, often finds itself the focal point of much of this debate.

ADVERTISING AS AN ECONOMIC AND SOCIAL INSTITUTION

Despite the ongoing debate about the proper social role of business, the majority of both consumers and marketers agree that the social and economic components of advertising are not mutually exclusive. Marketing executives are part of society and benefit from environmental awareness, better education, and other societal issues that are brought to the public's attention through advertising. A number of studies indicate that buyers support those companies and brands that have gained a reputation for being good citizens and actively promote their good works. By the same token, to the extent that advertising contributes to a stronger economy, advertisers and the public gain a higher standard of living.

The Economic Role of Advertising

There is little debate that the primary role of advertising is communication. However, there is a major dispute over whether this information is helpful to consumers. On the one hand, advertising advocates view advertising as providing necessary information to allow consumers to make informed decisions about new products and choose the best brands to solve a problem. The contrary view by those critical of advertising is that it provides consumers with little useful information and advertisers are much more interested in persuading prospects to buy products they don't need at inflated prices than offering useful information. The "persuasion versus information" debate is one that will never be resolved because it is a function of two forces: (1) the biases of the proadvertising and antiadvertising camps and (2) the fact that advertising does function in both roles.

We would be extremely naive to think that advertising (or any marketing sales tool) is not trying to influence our behavior. Firms are in business to sell goods and services and to present their products in the most favorable light possible. As long as the message is truthful and accurate, advertising is serving a function that both buyer and seller understand. By the same token, we would expect that the best persuasion is based on solid information about the benefits offered by a particular brand. Another aspect of the information-persuasion debate focuses on the brevity of advertising. That is, a slogan, billboard, or headline—no matter how creatively written—impart little or no information. Advertisers would argue that their messages need to be considered over the long term, not on an ad by ad basis. Brands such as Coca-Cola, Tide, Sony, and Toyota have established such a high degree of familiarity with consumers that much of their advertising is devoted to maintaining top-of-mind awareness as contrasted to selling in a traditional sense.

Some economists expand the criticism of advertising as persuasion to one of "advertising as a detriment to market entry." That is, advertising, by providing little information, works to the detriment of new products entering the market. They see the role of advertising as being one of encouraging brand switching among established products rather than allowing consumers to make informed decisions about new products coming into the marketplace. Within these extreme positions are many specific pros and cons about the economic value of advertising. Let's review some of the major arguments for and against the economic role of advertising.

The Economic Arguments in Favor of Advertising

1. Advertising provides consumers with information to make informed decisions about new products, availability of products, price, and product benefits. "Brands and advertising are things people can see, touch, and feel, and they know if a company's ads and brands are reliable and can be counted on as is often said, the fastest way to kill a bad product is to advertise it—because consumers will try it and find out firsthand how bad it really is."[5]

2. Advertising supports largely unrestricted media that disseminate news and entertainment. In addition to the social benefits of an independent press, advertising provides employment for the thousands of editorial, production, and administrative workers in these media.

3. By promoting product differentiation, advertising encourages continuing product improvements and the introduction of new and innovative goods and services (see Exhibit 24.2). Competing brands are forced to enhance the benefits of their products to maintain market share.

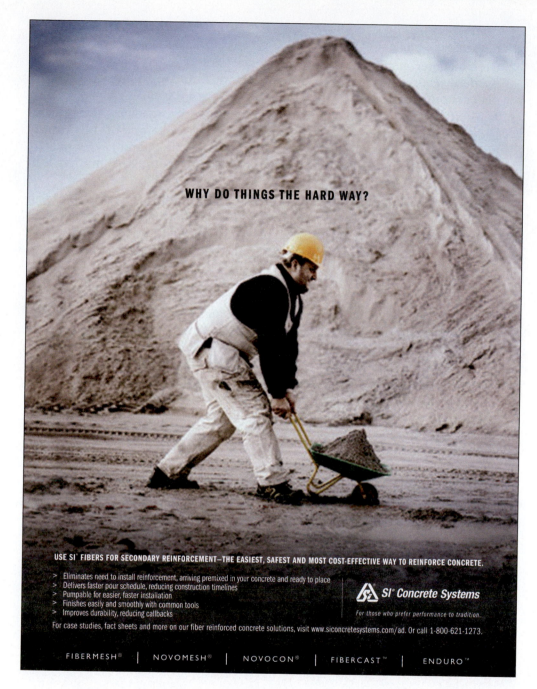

4. Mass advertising permits companies to achieve economies of scale in production that more than offset the per unit cost of advertising and, combined with competition among opposing brands, results in lower prices.

5. Advertising contributes to increases in the overall economy by increasing generic as well as brand consumption. For example, faced with a steady decline in consumption of cold cereals, a consortium of the big four cereal makers (i.e., Kellogg's, General Mills, Post, and Quaker Foods) devised "The better breakfast" generic campaign to promote the nutrition and convenience of cereals.[6]

The Economic Arguments Against Advertising

1. The intent of advertising is to persuade, not inform. Critics dismiss the notion that advertising distributes information on which consumers can base informed decisions. They contend that advertising communicates extravagant

product claims and, at best, is guilty of sins of omissions by providing only positive information about a brand.

2. On a macroeconomic basis, advertising spending is largely wasted because it primarily causes consumers to switch from one brand to another without any net economic gain to society.

3. Many economists challenge the notion that advertising lowers the price of products and services. To the contrary, they charge that one of the primary goals of advertising is to insulate a brand from price competition by emphasizing emotional appeals so that price comparisons become less important in purchase decisions.

4. The high rate of advertising expenditures in many product categories makes it difficult, if not impossible, for new products to enter the market. For example, in product categories such as cigarettes, beer, and laundry products in which two or three firms dominate each category, product introductions by other companies are extremely rare.

What conclusions can we draw after reviewing the pros and cons of these arguments concerning the economic role of advertising? The fact is that there is evidence to support each of these claims and counterclaims for advertising. One can find cases in which advertising *was* the catalyst for the introduction of a new and profitable brand or product category. On the other hand, there are numerous examples of product categories in which the objective of advertising is to maintain market share and encourage consumers to substitute one brand for another.

Even in product categories that seem to demonstrate evidence for one side or the other, there is often a middle ground. For instance, there is no question that market share in a number of food and household product segments is dominated by a handful of companies. However, although a few national firms hold dominant market share among these national brands, the emergence of store brands in outlets such as Wal-Mart and Kroger offer consumers many low-price options in products as varied as disposable diapers, batteries, garbage bags, and soft drinks.

It is difficult to deal in generalities when evaluating the economic value of advertising. Advertising's contribution to product sales depends on a host of circumstances unique to each product. The utility of advertising in a market for a relatively new product category, such as satellite radio, is much different than for beer or cigarettes, which are characterized by flat sales and brand switching. However, if sophisticated, multinational companies are spending billions of dollars on advertising, it is obvious that advertising must be contributing to their profitability.

THE SOCIAL ROLE OF ADVERTISING

While it is generally agreed that advertising bonds with consumers on both an economic and cultural basis, in recent years it is the effect of advertising on society that has drawn the most attention and controversy to the industry. Perhaps the fundamental question raised in the social context of advertising criticism is whether advertising shapes and defines culture or simply mirrors an evolving society. As we will see, the answer is some of both. Certainly the study and criticism of advertising as a social force has been an ongoing topic of discussion for more than 50 years. A half century ago, David Potter contrasted the economic and cultural roles of advertising:

> The most important effects of this powerful institution are not upon the economics of our distribution system; they are upon the values of our society. If the economic effect is to make the purchaser like what he buys, the social effect is, in a parallel but broader sense, to make the individual like what he gets—to enforce already existing attitudes, to diminish the

range and variety of choices, and in terms of abundance, to exalt the materialistic virtues of consumption.[7]

During the last two decades, many researchers have significantly changed their approach to the study of culture and advertising. At one time, there was a clear dichotomy between the two major types of cultural effects of advertising on the audience:

1. *Advertising's inadvertent social role.* Those advertising scholars interested in inadvertent social effects often studied advertising from the viewpoint that the ubiquitous, redundant messages presented by advertising through the mass media created various changes in the way the audience responded to their environment. This perspective assumed that advertising conveys largely unintended messages that, nevertheless, impart information about society in general or some segment of the public. By the sheer weight of exposure, advertising sets a social agenda of what is expected, what is fashionable, and what is tasteful for a significant number of people. These influences are particularly true for the young, the undereducated, and the impressionable. More often than not researchers in the so-called "critical-cultural" mode regard these consequences of advertising on society as decidedly negative.

2. *Advertising's overt social role.* A second, less studied area of advertising's social and cultural role deals with the role of advertising as an agent of social change. That is, those campaigns whose primary objective is the promoting of a social agenda. Every day we encounter advertising messages promoting safe driving, adult literacy, environmental causes, and a host of other forms of social activism (see Exhibit 24.3). Given the efficiencies of advertising in selling products, it is not surprising that more special interest groups have recognized the value and effectiveness of advertising.

In the last decade, we have seen a movement to a different view of advertising and cultural effects. A new school of researchers is studying the trend toward advertising adopting techniques which at one time were inadvertent effects, as an integral part of their advertising strategy. In this view, advertising's cultural dimension is not separated from its economic dimension. In this point of view, consumption cannot be understood outside the societal and group implications in which it is undertaken. Furthermore, advertisers simultaneously incorporate cultural icons in their advertising and, at the same time, use advertising to create new ones. ". . . culture is the accumulation of shared meanings, rituals, norms, and traditions among the members of an organization or society. Consumption choices simply cannot be understood without considering the cultural context in which they are made: culture is the lens through which people view products."[8]

This school of research assumes that advertising is no longer promoting products, but, rather, brands are positioned as another part of a person's cultural experience. Products are now bought less for function than as a statement about how people see themselves. In this approach, brands still function as a form of differentiation, but they are used more as audience segmentation strategies than to highlight product distinctions. In this perspective, companies are ". . . no longer simply branding their own products, but branding the outside culture as well—by sponsoring cultural events, they [can] go out into the world and claim bits of it as brand-name outposts."[9]

Sophisticated research techniques increasingly allow marketers to understand why consumers purchase particular brands by moving beyond the functional benefits of a product and concentrating more on the symbolic meaning that brands convey to particular buyers or market segments. By doing so, advertisers can create both products and, some would argue, images that closely match the world view of potential buyers. "Good advertisers know how to analyze which properties of a specific product or service will resonate best with consumers. To do this,

EXHIBIT 24.3

Social causes are
adopting basic
marketing and
advertising techniques.

Courtesy of National Association of
State Foresters.

advertisers must develop a deep understanding of the meanings that are resident
in each consumer's culturally constituted world."[10]

Advertising is quickly moving to a point where so-called secondary or inadvertent effects of advertising are becoming part of the primary theme of many advertisers. As products become homogenized, sellers look to advertising and brand
image as the principal difference among competing products. As we discussed earlier, differentiation is not found in the product itself but in the mind of the consumer. More importantly, once a brand achieves a dominant position based on
image and cultural associations, it is much more difficult for competitors to match
than real product differences.

While the debate continues about the role of advertising and culture, there is
no question that advertisers know that effective advertising must mirror the social
and cultural values by channeling the predispositions of consumers into purchases
of particular brands. Advertisers realize that people react in a positive or negative
way to the total environment in which a product is presented—including media,
message, and presentation—and advertisers must be sensitive to both the intended
and inadvertent cues they impart in their marketing.

Some Specific Social Criticisms of Advertising

Since the late 1880s, advertising has been the focus of numerous examples of criticism from a host of sources. In recent years, social criticism of advertising has taken precedent over its economic effects. The range of criticism involves advertising strategies, advertising's execution, the audience targeted, and even those groups making use of it. Everyone and everything in advertising's social realm are fair game. Some representative examples of social criticisms of advertising include:

■ *Privacy concerns.* In recent years, consumers have become increasingly concerned about privacy issues. This heightened awareness is in large part due to the development of sophisticated communication technology. The intrusion of spam, other types of unsolicited e-mail, and tracking devices such as radio frequency identification (RFID) tags have made consumers aware of the numerous techniques used by marketers and others to follow their behavior. The Do Not Call Registry legislation to limit telemarketing is the clearest evidence that both the public and legislative bodies are taking public fears about privacy and intrusiveness issues seriously. In a letter to the Federal Trade Commission, the American Advertising Federation affirmed its support of privacy legislation. "The goal of this principle is that personal information should not be used in a way that goes beyond an individual's understanding and consent. If the manner of use of the information is not foreseen, then the consumer has not provided implicit consent."[11]

■ *Product placement.* Product placement is not a new technique. Gordon's Gin is said to have had Katharine Hepburn toss its product overboard in *The African Queen*. The technique gained popularity with the sales success of Reese's Pieces after being seen in *ET*.[12] However, as the public has become more resistant to traditional media advertising, advertisers are using various placement techniques as part of their core marketing strategy rather than as a minor component of a marketing plan. Reality shows such as *The Apprentice* build their scripts around featured products. While many audience members don't seem to be concerned about these activities, critics question the ethics involved. "Product placements are inherently deceptive, because many people do not realize that they are, in fact, advertisements. We're [Commercial Alert] running a campaign to require disclosure of product placement in all media, including TV, movies, videos, video games, books and 'adversongs.'"[13]

■ *Advertising's role in obesity.* A number of lawsuits have been filed against fast-food chains charging that their promotions of high-calorie, fatty menu items have led to various health problems. The suits are particularly critical of the chains' longtime emphasis on promotions to children.

Specific Areas of Social Criticism of Advertising

Space doesn't allow us to fully deal with the uses and criticism of social aspects of advertising. However, companies are being held accountable for both the products and services they provide and the advertising and promotion that support them. Although there are unique features to each of the social criticisms we have analyzed, they tend to focus on four areas:

1. *Advertising content.* By far the most criticized area of advertising is the content of specific advertisements and commercials. Critics point to a spectrum of alleged abuses including the use of sexual themes, exaggerated product claims, debasement of language, the creation of stereotypes, and manipulating children with unrealistic promises. In 1957, Vance Packard's *The Hidden Persuaders* set forth the idea that advertisers were secretly manipulating consumers through "subliminal perception." Using motivational research techniques,

Packard alleged that advertising used hidden messages or flashed icons in television shows and movies that operated below the level of conscious perception, but, nevertheless, changed the audience's purchase behavior. While most psychologists agree that Packard greatly overstated the use and value of motivational research, the book did put even greater public scrutiny on advertising. For example, even though there was no evidence that the media were involved in the practice, the major networks issued statements that they would not allow the practice.[14]

The majority of these objections are directed at alleged exaggerated claims in advertising. Many critics charge that advertising is more likely to provide misinformation, negative content, and in some cases, outright falsehoods rather than useful consumer information. As we will discuss later in this chapter, there are few business enterprises that undergo more governmental and regulatory scrutiny in advertising. But apart from these formal constraints, advertisers know that it is counterproductive to mislead consumers. Although false or misleading advertising may influence a consumer to make an initial purchase, it is rare that an unsatisfied consumer will return.

One of the long-standing areas of advertising criticism is the portrayal of various segments of society. Many observers claim that advertising deals in objectionable stereotypes in its treatment of the elderly, women, and minorities. In recent years, even advertising's harshest critics agree that most mainstream marketers have made noteworthy strides in portraying these groups in a more realistic and favorable light. However, there are those who see that the advertising has significant room for improvement. "Three decades after the women's movement offered women greater equality and expanded roles, a small chorus of media critics laments what it sees as a one-dimensional portrayal of women by Madison Avenue, characterized by nudity, extreme thinness, sensuality, even bondage. With their dual emphasis on physical perfection and sexuality, such ads, these critics say, can create body dissatisfaction, fuel addictions, and subtly legitimize violence and bondage."[15]

Ironically, one of the audience segments that seems to have lost ground in the struggle for advertising realism is men. In recent years, a number of voices have been raised about the representation of the "bumbling male" in numerous advertisements and commercials. For example, the theme of many ads is that the simplest household chore, particularly those involving child care, are beyond the capacity of any male. In one commercial, the mother must take care of the family's children (with the appropriate brand of decongestant) after her dim-witted husband allowed them to play in the snow wearing only T-shirts. In other cases, men are portrayed as so hormonally challenged that the very sight of an attractive woman sends them into a state of involuntary lust and ineptitude. Recently, J. Walter Thompson, one of the world's largest agencies addressed the problem: "Men have faded into a collective boob-dom, a sort of Jackass meets *The Man Show* meets *The Simpsons*. As result, the way we approach the men's market is ripe for reinvention."[16]

Beyond simple fairness in the treatment of various segments of the population, there is a growing awareness that advertising should present a more realistic image of reality. For example, in recent months, advertisers as diverse as Nike and Dove soap have launched campaigns that have moved away from the traditional view of women as wafer-thin models in size one dresses. Critics have long attacked advertising and the media in general for presenting unattainable images of women that contribute to low self-esteem and even eating disorders. Many observers give credit to Dove's "Campaign for Real Beauty" effort, which featured women in all shapes and sizes. As the publisher of *Glamour* magazine commented, "There's a definite trend going on in society and the marketplace of self-acceptance and being comfortable in your own skin."[17] While, as critics are quick to point out, there is much yet to do in fairly and accurately depicting society, there is growing evidence that the industry is aware of the problem, and it is moving to correct many of the ills of the past.

Despite the real and widespread concerns about stereotyping of various segments of the population, most of the complaints about advertising concern executions in specific advertisements and commercials. In recent years, numerous advertising messages have come under attack for their insensitivity to some group or another. For example, in a commercial for Nissan Titan trucks, the theme from the film *The Bridge on the River Kwai* was used—a film that depicted a ruthless Japanese World War II prison camp. Many viewers thought that using the theme for a Japanese company was insensitive, and the company quickly changed the music. Likewise, the National Football League refused to renew its agreement with erectile-dysfunction remedies because the league thought that the commercials had become increasingly risqué. As a league executive commented, "When we began [sponsorship in] the category it was a man's health issue. The marketing and advertising took a different direction in the entire category."[18] The league went on to emphasize that it was the advertising content, not the product, that led to rejection of the advertising.

It is clear that advertisers must be extremely careful how they promote their products. In an environment of greater consumer understanding and awareness of advertising, marketers must be extremely sensitive to a range of subjects that might have potential for upsetting a portion of the audience. The use of inappropriate humor, messages in poor taste (particularly sexual themes), violent content, and stereotyping should be carefully considered in creating advertising messages. At a time when advertisers are acutely aware of these issues, it is paradoxical that the fragmentation of the media and the numerous options for reaching an audience have made content that would be ill-advised in general circulation media acceptable in some narrowly focused venues, such as the Internet.

2. *Advertising of certain product categories.* As we discussed previously, the most frequent criticism of advertising concerns the themes and appeals used in specific advertisements and commercials. However, there are a few product categories that some critics think should not be advertised regardless of how well the ads and commercials are executed. In general, the trend is toward a more liberal stance by both advertisers and media in terms of acceptability of advertising. Now that tobacco advertising is virtually nonexistent in mainstream media, some of the remaining products and product categories that garner the most controversy are:

- Distilled spirits (as contrasted to beer and wine). One of the long-standing, self-imposed taboos of advertsing was that hard liquor would not be promoted on broadcast media. Up until the mid-1990s liquor advertising was largely confined to magazine ads and outdoor ads. However, the industry was finally able to gain access to cable television and, in a few instances, radio and local television. In 2004, NASCAR agreed for the first time to allow car sponsorship by liquor companies. Since the cars will be featured on television broadcasts of races, many see this as a backdoor method of gaining entry to general television advertising. Nevertheless, there is danger attendant to the NASCAR relationship. "While spirits marketers see opportunity, there's risk as well. Seeing a whiskey-themed car zipping around the track at 180 mph could raise objections. Also, NASCAR attracts thousands of viewers too young to drink."[19] In the case of tobacco, alcohol, and, more recently, food products with high fat and sugar content, the debate is not so much concerned with advertising executions as it is with the appropriateness of the products themselves. For example, one study indicated that 74 percent of respondents thought that television liquor advertising would encourage teenagers to drink liquor.[20] If an individual or group sees a product category as detrimental to consumers, the evaluation of the advertising for a particular brand is moot.

■ Condoms. For the past two decades, health professionals have advocated widespread promotion of condoms in the battle against sexually transmitted diseases. However, even in light of the AIDS epidemic, most television outlets prohibit the advertising of condoms, a position that many in the public health community think is indefensible. The major networks have been fearful of criticism from conservative media watchdogs and various religious groups. During the 1990s, condom advertising was accepted for some late-night television spots. However, in 2005, led by NBC, advertising for Trojan condoms was accepted for primetime, but the commercials were required to emphasize the health benefits of the product.

■ Advertising to children. A special category of advertising criticism is promotional messages to children. There are a number of products such as soft drinks, fast foods, and cereals that are deemed acceptable for general advertising but not in programs directed toward children. Since the audiences of virtually every program have a significant group of youngsters watching, it is very difficult for even the most conscientious advertiser to avoid reaching a sizeable number of children. However, the growing commercial outreach in venues produced solely for a children's market, including online games and videos as well as traditional television shows, is a source of vehement debate among many opponents of children's marketing.

3. *Excessive advertising.* Most of the criticism in this category is directed toward television because print ads are easily ignored by simply turning the page. Approximately 25 percent of television network time is devoted to commercials with higher percentages on local stations and during late-night and daytime periods. Both direct mail and telemarketing have for some time fought critics who wish to impose legal restrictions on them. More recently, Internet spam has come under legislative scrutiny and may soon join telemarketing as an "invitation only" medium. In addition to the nuisance of unwanted and intrusive advertising, new technology, accompanied by sophisticated databases, has increased consumer concerns over privacy issues.

In addition to the public policy concerns of excessive advertising, there are many within the advertising industry who see it as having the potential to dilute their ROI. Communication research confirms that the number of messages and the order of messages (i.e., first, middle, last) in a commercial block will affect the recall and impact of advertising. In response to advertisers' criticism of excessive clutter, Clear Channel, the country's largest station owner, announced that it was cutting the amount of commercial time on its stations. Early results showed an increase in time spent listening—it remains to be seen if the experiment will be financially viable in the long term.[21] Regardless, it does demonstrate that excessive advertising is a concern of both the audience and the advertising industry.

4. *Advertising's unwanted influences on society.* The harshest critics of advertising are those that think the very existence of persuasive advertising content is contrary to the best interest of consumers. Criticism in this category covers a litany of alleged abuses. Among the major theses of this school of thought is that advertising *makes* people buy things they don't want or need, lowers morals, and generally exploits the most susceptible segments of society. However, most research shows that mass communication, especially overtly persuasive communication such as advertising, has a very difficult time making even small changes in behavioral intentions or attitudes. The idea that consumers will take some action solely because of advertising is contrary to virtually every theory of communication.

ADVERTISING AND SOCIAL CAUSES— THE ADVERTISING COUNCIL

The most organized effort of social advocacy is the Advertising Council, which has for many years marshaled the advertising industry to support a number of causes. From its World War II beginnings as the War Advertising Council, the Advertising Council recently celebrated its sixtieth anniversary. During those six decades, the council has sponsored some of the most well-known public service campaigns and undertaken a number of projects—addressing issues such as racial tolerance, equal rights, job and fair housing opportunities, health awareness, and education (see Exhibit 24.4).

The Ad Council continues to be a major means of disseminating social messages because evidence shows that its efforts work to improve society in a number of significant ways. The Council's success stories include:

- Applications for Big Brothers and Big Sisters mentors soared from 90,000 a year to 620,000 in nine months, a sevenfold increase in the number of inquiries to Big Brothers and Big Sisters agencies.

- Ready.gov received more than 18 million unique visitors within the first 10 months of the launch of the Department of Homeland Security's preparedness campaign.

- Sixty-eight percent of Americans say that they have personally stopped someone who had been drinking from driving. The old saying "One more for the Road," has been replaced with "Friends Don't Let Friends Drive Drunk."

- Safety belt usage is up from 14 percent to 79 percent since the Safety Belt campaign launched in 1985—saving an estimated 85,000 lives and $3.2 billion in costs to society.

EXHIBIT 24.4

A wide array of organizations use the services of the Advertising Council.

Courtesy © 2006 United Negro College Fund/Advertising Council, Inc. Used with permission.

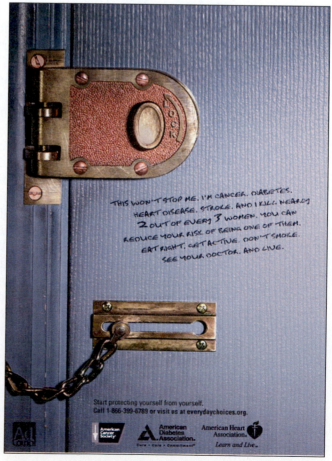

- Since 1972, The United Negro College Fund campaign has helped the organization raise more than $2.2 billion to graduate 350,000 minority students from college with the help of the "A Mind Is a Terrible Thing to Waste" slogan.
- Some 6,000 children were paired with a mentor in just the first 18 months of the Ad Council's mentoring campaign.
- Destruction of our forests by wildfires has been reduced from 22 million acres to less than 8.4 million acres per year, since the Forest Fire Prevention campaign began.
- The amount of total waste recycled increased 24.4 percent from 1995 to 2000, and 385.4 percent from the 1980s after the launch of the Environmental Defense campaign.[22]

The council depends on volunteers from across the advertising spectrum. Major agencies produce most of the advertising on a pro bono basis, and the media donate time and space to carry these advertisements and commercials. It is difficult to estimate the equivalent of paid advertising that the Council has enjoyed since its founding, but it would certainly be in the billions of dollars.

At one time, the council was the unchallenged organization for idea or public service advertising. However, based largely on its record of success, a number of other organizations have begun to use advertising as a primary tool to deliver social messages. For the last 30 years, a number of organizations including the National Organization for Women (NOW), Mothers Against Drunk Drivers (MADD), and Planned Parenthood have all mounted campaigns that have competed with the Advertising Council for creative services and donated time and space. These private organizations have been joined by a number of companies placing paid advertising promoting some cause related to product marketing. We will discuss these marketing promotions in the next section, but they offer another type of alternative to Ad Council public service announcements.

A second challenge for the Council is finding the type of galvanizing topics that were so prevalent in its early years. When the War Advertising Council was conceived, the war effort offered a number of campaigns that the public embraced without question. No one had to convince the public that it was a good idea to conserve tin and fat or not to discuss information about ship movements or factory output. Even after the war, campaigns directed at preventing forest fires and protecting the environment were overwhelmingly accepted by the majority of the public. Unlike the wartime efforts of the War Advertising Council and the early campaigns of the Ad Council, more recent campaigns dealing with the environment, capitalism, the role of the family, the fight against AIDS, and even the proper approach to the "war on terrorism" and support for our troops are topics that engender significant controversy.

Even seemingly inoffensive campaigns such as a recent one to educate parents about the V-chip capability to block unwanted television programming has provoked complaints from child advocates as not going far enough and civil libertarians as a first step toward media censorship. However, despite these problems, the Advertising Council continues to select, define, and address some of the nation's most pressing problems. Council programs will result in the donation of more than $1.5 billion in time and space this year. In many respects, the Council created a new role for advertising in the promotion of ideas and opinions. Although some people have reservations about the role of advertising in promoting social institutions and issues, proponents argue that there is no more effective or inexpensive means of getting their messages to the public.

Advertising and Cause-Related Marketing

In 1983, American Express sponsored a campaign promising to make a donation to the renovation of the Statue of Liberty each time someone used his or her American

Express credit card. This initiative is generally considered to be the introduction of *cause-related marketing* (also called *social marketing*). The days of companies supporting a number of charities with a check and a photo opportunity are nearly over. Today, large corporations are engaging in *strategic philanthropy* in which they market their good deeds in the same way they market their products. As one advertising executive said, ". . . corporate-social-responsibility initiatives . . . serve as forms of advertising and brand building . . . customers get impressions about products from hundreds of sources, but when they believe a company is a good citizen, they feel more positive about a brand."[23] In 2005, cause-related marketing expenditures accounted for more than $1.2 billion and is growing at a rate of approximately 8 percent annually with more major companies engaging in socially related campaigns (see Exhibit 24.5).

Companies also are using strategic planning in their philanthropy. "Corporations are focusing their efforts. Instead of volunteering across the spectrum, they're targeting their efforts toward causes that make sense for the vision of the company and the needs of their employees. Companies are looking for high-impact projects where they can really make a difference."[24]

Most research in cause-related marketing indicates that consumers rarely make purchase decisions solely because a company is supporting some favored cause.

EXHIBIT 24.5

The Home Depot Foundation is one of the many corporate-supported nonprofit organizations.

Courtesy of The Home Depot Foundation.

However, studies do show that such support can be a deciding factor in making choices among similar brands. That is, it becomes another source of product differentiation.

Companies engaging in cause-related marketing strategically plan these campaigns around several concepts:

■ UPS focuses its philanthropy on literacy, hunger, and employee volunteerism. In 2005, 43,000 UPS workers engaged in more than 460,000 hours of volunteer projects. The company emphasizes grassroots endeavors to show that it is part of the local community.

■ McDonald's long association with children makes the support of Ronald McDonald Houses for the families of ill children an excellent fit.

■ The Home Depot underscores its home-building products with volunteer efforts and financial support for play spaces, affordable housing, and disaster relief.

■ Avon, like many cause-related efforts, has linked its brand with core concerns of its primary target market through its efforts in the fight against breast cancer.

In the past, some companies have refrained from cause-related marketing efforts because they feared that consumers would view their efforts as exploitative. However, a number of research studies indicate that consumers welcome the opportunity to be part of a worthy cause with their purchases, and they reward companies for their efforts. Exhibit 24.6 shows that many consumers indicate a willingness to reward those companies with their loyalty, even to the point of switching brands to show their support.

EXHIBIT 24.6

Do-Gooding Done Right

Source: *Advertising Age*, June 13, 2005, p. 31.

Top ways Americans say a company's commitment to good corporate citizenship would influence their opinion of, relationship with or behavior toward that company.

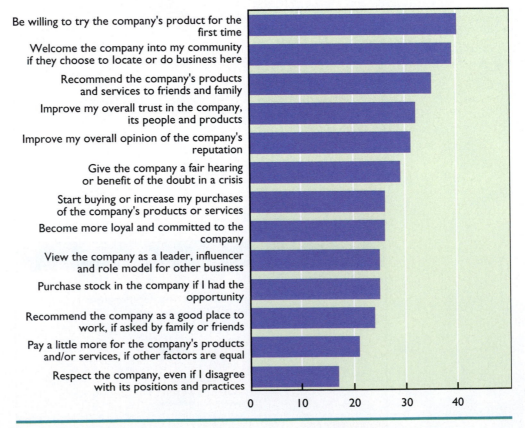

KLEPPNER VIEWPOINT 24.1

Kelly Caffarelli

Executive Director of The Home Depot Foundation
Using Philanthropy to Achieve Social and Corporate Goals

"Doing well by doing good" is a frequently used phrase to explain why businesses give back to their communities. Companies talk about being a good corporate citizen and being a neighbor of choice. One can question, though, whether philanthropy is the business of business, as Nobel Prize winner Milton Friedman did in his influential article "The Social Responsibility of Business Is to Increase Profits."[1] I think that philanthropy conducted in a strategic way, aligning with the strengths and reputation of a company while engaging a variety of stakeholders, offers a multitude of benefits to corporations.

To be effective in the first instance, the area in which a philanthropic organization focuses must be aligned with the relevant business. Societal efforts must fit with strengths of the for-profit endeavor in order to achieve credibility. To dispute opinions such as Friedman's, the program focus should also directly benefit the corporation. For example, it is easily understandable that The Home Depot Foundation focuses its work on building affordable housing. It makes sense that a company whose business is home improvement should work to help those of modest means achieve the dream of homeownership. The efforts in the community provide an opportunity for the company to put its talents to work for the public good. Moreover, more homeowners mean more customers and higher revenues.

Equally important is for the philanthropic efforts to be focused. Making grants in a scattershot way or merely in response to requests is an ineffective method of impacting a community for the better. Moreover, it makes it very difficult for an organization to articulate how it has given back to a community and to create awareness of its philanthropic achievements. In order to be focused, the organization must (a) clearly define a specific unmet need, (b) envision a means of addressing the need, (c) identify the necessary resources and put them to work effectively, and (d) establish the desired outcomes.[2] Only by working through these criteria can an organization say with any confidence that their social investments are actually having an impact. The fact that the issues typically being addressed often require a long-term view makes articulating tangible steps and goals all the more important.

While it makes sense for The Home Depot Foundation to work in housing, to be focused it needed to narrow its work to create homes that are not only affordable, but also "green." The unmet need is available housing units that are affordable for low- to middle-income households to purchase and live in, a well-documented societal need. A means of addressing that need was to increase the production of homes that are moderately priced, are energy and resource efficient, reduce material waste, use durable materials, and provide good indoor air

Kelly Caffarelli

quality. The resources available are funding, volunteer time, training, and technical assistance for those building homes. By partnering with successful nonprofit organizations, the Foundation is able to leverage its resources and ensure that the work is completed effectively. The desired outcome is to have a sufficient number of housing units that are affordable, not only to purchase, but also to live in and which offer a healthy and sustainable environment for the residents.

The ultimate issue is, of course, the bottom line. Strategic philanthropic investments that create bonds with important stakeholders—shareholders, suppliers, customers, employees, community leaders—can create financial opportunity, as well as reputational benefits, for a company. More and more, investors are using a social and environmental filter to select mutual funds. For example, in 2005, over $179 billion in assets were held by such funds.[3] As markets become more global, and therefore more competitive, and the need to attract, motivate, and retain talented employees increases, corporate reputation becomes all the more important. Studies demonstrate that both customers and employees say that they would "recommend" a company for its products and services, or as a place to work, because of good corporate citizenship.[4]

[1]Milton Friedman, "The social responsibility of business is to increase its profits," *New York Times Magazine*, 13 September 1970.
[2]Richard Mittenthal, "Effective philanthropy: The importance of focus," *Briefing*, The Conservation Company, 2002, 2.
[3]Joshua Humphreys, Research Director, "2005 Report on Socially Responsible Investing Trends in the United States," Social Investment Forum, January 24, 2006, p. iv.
[4]Golin Harris Study, "Doing Well by Doing Good." ■ ■ ■

Cause marketing generally falls into one of the following tactical categories:[25]

1. *Transactional programs* in which a company contributes to a cause based on consumer purchase of a brand. Mars M&Ms gave 50 cents to the Special Olympics for every specially marked wrapper mailed to the company.

2. *Message promotions* link a brand with information about some cause such as preventing skin cancer. Crest toothpaste supports dental hygiene programs through the Boys and Girls Clubs of America with its "Healthy Smiles 2010" campaign.

3. *Licensing programs* permit companies to use charities' logos in their advertising. For example, ConAgra Foods and America's Second Harvest partnered to focus on the "Feeding Children Better" campaign in many of the companies' promotions.

Regardless of how cause-related marketing is executed, the public should view it as a more legitimate means of helping accomplish some social need rather than as simply an extension of a firm's marketing program. "When it comes to cause marketing, businesses walk a fine line between doing the right thing for the right reasons and doing the expected thing to create the right appearance. Marketers that don't get the difference risk breeding cynicism, but many that build social responsibility into their corporate DNA are reaping multilayered benefits."[26]

Advertising Influence on Editorial Decisions

There are a number of options available to provide financial support for a media system—the government and political parties, church-affiliated organizations, other special interest groups such as labor unions, full payment by the audience, and advertising. Historically, each of these options has been used to support a press system. In the United States, a combination of advertising and subscription charges has been deemed the best approach. The theory behind the adoption of advertising as a primary source of media funding is that, by having economic support spread out over numerous advertisers, it assures that no one entity can exercise undue influence over editorial content.

It would be naive to think that this wall between advertising and editorial has never breached but, nevertheless, that was the guiding principle. During the modern period of advertising, the first major change in the concept came in the early days of radio, and later in television, when sponsors produced and owned the shows carried by networks and local stations. Most of the audience considered this an acceptable arrangement because the shows were entertainment rather than news and information. However, by the 1970s, it had become prohibitively expensive for single advertisers to bear the total cost of producing a show. This marked the end of "fully sponsored" shows. Programs such as *The Firestone Hour, The United States Steel Hour,* and *The Kraft Music Hall* were replaced by network-controlled programs in which advertisers participated by buying individual spots, but, in theory at least, they had no control over program decisions. The move from single sponsorship to participating commercial buys also was motivated by quiz show scandals during the 1950s in which contestants had been given answers ahead of time. Congress and the public demanded that the networks take more control of content. Today, we are seeing a limited return to advertiser control of programming. For example, the CNBC series *dLife* is a program targeted to diabetes sufferers where an independent producer buys a half-hour slot and then resells time in the form of program participation, segment sponsorship, and on-screen logos. The show is promoted as a combination of medical information, entertainment, and education.[27] Some observers think that such long-form, targeted programming, with its educational component, may replace traditional advertising spots, promoting direct-to-consumer drugs, which have come under heavy criticism.

A number of research studies indicate that a large majority of the public believes that editorial content is being influenced by advertisers. The American Society of Newspaper Editors (ASNE) and the Radio-Television News Directors Association (RTNDA) recently surveyed thousands of citizens and journalists. What they found was disturbing:

- 79 percent of the American public believe that "it's pretty easy for special interest groups to manipulate the press," according to ASNE (55 percent of newspaper journalists agree).
- 84 percent of Americans say "news reporting on local TV is improperly influenced by advertisers often (51 percent) or sometimes (33 percent)," according to the RTNDA (43 percent of TV news directors agree).[28]

As many observers point out, when the media lose credibility with their audience, it harms both themselves and the advertisers that use them. Unfortunately, there are a number of examples of gray areas between editorial and advertising content. Let's look at some of the ways in which relationships between advertisers and the media are changing:

1. *Withholding advertising as an attempt to control editorial decisions.* One of the most common attempts to control editorial independence is the threat by an advertiser that it will withhold advertising dollars unless a medium makes editorial decisions favorable to a company. In some cases, an advertiser may want favorable coverage of a firm, and in other instances a company demands a medium kill a story critical of a company. In either case, such a demand can involve major ethical as well as financial decisions on the part of the media. In an unusual and highly publicized 2005 case, General Motors pulled all its advertising from the *Los Angeles Times* over what the company characterized as "factual errors and misrepresentations in the editorial coverage" of the company. The company later relented and began placing advertising with the publication. This type of public hostility between a medium and a major advertiser is rare. However, in recent years some companies have asked for prior notification of news stories that concern companies with advertising scheduled in the publication or program. Both BP (formerly British Petroleum) and Morgan Stanley demanded that media notify the companies if negative editorial coverage was planned so that advertising could be withdrawn. As one former editor pointed out, the plan ". . . raises ethical issues. It can have a chilling effect on editors' judgment and their willingness to do certain stories if they know . . . that ads might be pulled."[29] That is often the intention of the advertisers asking for such concessions.

2. *Advertiser-financed productions.* Withholding advertising is an example of an adversarial relationship between the media and advertisers—a situation which is to no one's benefit. In recent years, a number of advertisers have worked with local and network television outlets to jointly produce programming. One of the formal examples of such advertiser involvement is the Family Friendly Forum, a consortium of major advertisers, which underwrites the development of family-oriented network television shows. According to the mission statement of the Forum, it seeks ". . . to support and promote the development of 'family friendly' television across all programming genres between the hours of 8 and 10 p.m., when adults and children are most likely to watch television together." The Family Friendly Programming Forum has initiated a number of different initiatives to carry out this mission:
   - Script Development Fund to help fund family-friendly scripts
   - Scholarship Program for students who work on family-friendly projects

- Annual Symposium to engage and educate the networks, writers, producers, and press
- Annual Family Television Awards, which recognize outstanding family television[30]

Although few people question the motives of these companies to bring family entertainment to television, many critics see any involvement between advertising and programming as cause for concern.

The one area of television that has been considered off-limits to product placement has traditionally been news programming. However, in recent years the barriers that shielded news programming from placement deals are falling in the face of competitive pressure for traditional advertising dollars. "Product placement, media and branded entertainment agencies say they are increasingly being pitched opportunities from local stations to integrate their clients' products into news programming in exchange for media buys or integration fees. . . . Radio-Television News Directors Assn. president Barbara Cochran warned that integrating advertisers into news programming could backfire, costing local stations viewers instead of having the intended effect of increasing ad sales. 'You're selling the credibility of the news, and if viewers start thinking your news is for sale, then the credibility of your news is lost and your audience is lost,' she said."[31] While stations are required to disclose that segments are paid for by advertisers, critics worry that busy viewers don't really pay attention to such disclaimers and regard the programs as news and information rather than promotions.

In a similar situation, the *Today* show on NBC was criticized for not revealing that some of the product experts appearing on the show were being paid by the companies whose brands they recommended. In one of the strongest statements about the trend toward nondisclosure of promotional information within a news format, *Advertising Age* editorialized, "It's despicable for journalists to take money to hawk products on TV news and talk shows. Journalists who do so should be fired. And TV stations and networks must disclose to viewers if the TV outlet, staffers, or on-air guests have been paid to make product endorsements."[32]

Some media watchdogs and media trade associations are sufficiently worried about the problem of editorial dilution that they have issued guidelines to stem the expansion of this type of programming and advertising integration in the editorial process. A typical example of these guidelines was developed by the Poynter Institute:

> News operations should use press releases and video news releases very selectively and only when journalistically justified. Journalists should clearly inform viewers/listeners when corporations, public relations agencies, news release services, advertisers or others who are not journalists provide any material you [a medium] are using in a news story. Viewers and listeners should know when a politician, political party, movie studio, theme park or other group or individual pays for satellite, fiber connection or studio time that the journalist uses for presenting a story.[33]

The FCC also has joined the chorus advocating full disclosure. In April, 2005, the FCC insisted that broadcasters offer disclaimers when broadcasting so-called video news releases (VNR). While the directive was directed specifically at VNRs, there is no question that the spirit of the edict would require disclosure of any third-party, commercial participation in a news show.

3. *Product placement.* In the last decade, the most prevalent type of editorial-promotion alliance is product placement. At one time, product placement was confined to the inclusion of a particular product in a television show or movie.

Usually, the placements were no more intrusive than the occasional Coke machine in the background of a scene. However, with the growing antipathy toward advertising by viewers and the glut of commercials vying for prospects, product placement techniques have become more prominent and the relationship to programming more formal. For example, the soap opera *All My Children* worked Enchantment Perfume into a hospital scene on the show while *General Hospital's* Jack and Phyllis discussed how GM's OnStar service could get help during a snowstorm.

In the past, product placements were largely confined to movies and television shows. However, in the last few years there are a growing number of instances of print media providing promotional opportunities within editorial content. Sometimes the association is overt—the *New York Times* announced plans to superimpose "branded watermarks" over certain editorial content such as stock listings. In other cases, publishers and editors have worked with advertisers to have their products given some exposure such as using a certain brand of appliance in a kitchen scene or a specific make of car in the background of a fashion shot. In rare cases, magazines have provided story lines and product recommendations in exchange for participation fees or advertising. Many publications are feeling pressure from advertisers who are offered numerous opportunities for such placements in television and want the same consideration from major magazines.

Regardless of the demands from advertisers for print placement, support for such a trend is decidedly negative among editorial staffers. For example, the American Society of Magazine Editors (ASME) has gone on record strongly opposing any ties between advertising and editorial. As the president of ASME said, "Trends in advertising are going to come and go. The one thing that's going to keep you [magazines] in business is your relationship with your readers, and if you jeopardize that, then you jeopardize the franchise."[34] Given the financial struggles faced by many publications, it will be interesting to see if magazines can withstand the temptation to accept this new revenue stream.

The movement to product placement is not confined to traditional media. The popularity of video games has provided a ready-made market for the placement of numerous products, especially those directed toward a young, male audience. Like their television counterparts, video game makers are increasingly weaving product placements into story lines. Marketers such as Jeep, Puma, and Motorola are only a few of the major advertisers using video game placements. The growth of video game placements has been phenomenal, rising from $34 million in 2004 to an estimated $562 million by 2009.[35] The latest category of video game advertising is the "advergames" where a video game is created solely to promote a product. These are often offered online in connection with a promotional offer through a fast-food outlet or some children- or teen-oriented product.

We will no doubt see more examples of product placement in the future. With the introduction of digital technology, producers are able to place products in programs at any time. They can change brands for regional buyers, and they can add a product to a program long after the original production of that show. For example, reruns of *Andy of Mayberry* might someday show the Taylor family sitting down to a meal with a box of Kellogg's Corn Flakes or a bottle of Heinz 57 Sauce on the table.

4. *The advertorial.* For many years, business firms and other organizations have used advertising to express their views about some issue or public policy concern, negotiations with labor unions, even potential legal problems faced by a company. These paid advertising messages promoting an opinion rather than a product are known as **advertorials**, that is, a combination of an advertisement and an editorial viewpoint. The expressions, when clearly identified as

advertorial
The use of advertising to promote an idea rather than a product or service.

advertising, are an entirely acceptable means of expressing an opinion and gaining public support.

However, since the early 1980s, the use of the advertorial has changed dramatically and its critics would say for the worse. Today, many advertorials are designed to look very much like editorial matter or television programming. Sometimes the advertorials are extended length sections of several pages liberally sprinkled with advertisements giving the section the look of the general publication. Advertising copywriters or public relation specialists produce advertorial sections rather than the editorial staff. The "editorial" matter is an extension of the advertising message, and it is dictated by a sponsor.

The relationship between advertisers and the media they support is often an uneasy truce. Critics point out that with 50 percent to 75 percent of the print media's revenues and virtually 100 percent of broadcast support coming from advertisers, it is unreasonable to expect that at least some publishers and station owners will not be influenced by those who pay the bills. The editorial and programming side wants total control over content with the ability to explore controversial and unpopular topics. Advertisers view the media as a means of reaching their target markets and, not unexpectedly, they often shy away from association with content they think will cause negative connections to their brands.

ADVERTISING'S LEGAL AND REGULATORY ENVIRONMENT

Successful advertisers know that they depend on consumer trust for their long-term success. To a significant degree, honest and truthful advertising is part of building this consumer trust. Despite philosophical disagreements that we discussed earlier in this chapter, most advertisers are well aware of the ethical dimensions of their messages and strive to act in a principled manner. However, for the last 50 years, a number of governmental, industry, and consumer advocacy groups have monitored and regulated advertising. Today, advertising operates in an environment of regulation and public scrutiny unprecedented in earlier times. Studies indicate that the majority of the public agrees that government has a legitimate role in ensuring accurate product information because trustworthy advertising is an important ingredient in a free market economy. When untrue or misleading advertising is disseminated, the implied relationship between the consumer and the advertiser is violated, creating *market failure*.

Today, not only the public, but the advertising industry itself, agrees that those companies that use illegal or unethical advertising tactics should be dealt with severely. Not only is deceptive advertising wrong, but it also creates a lack of trust in all advertising, making it more difficult for honest businesses to effectively promote their products and services. There are three basic constraints on advertising:

1. Laws and regulations of legally constituted bodies such as Congress and the Federal Trade Commission.
2. Control by the media through advertising acceptability guidelines.
3. Self-regulation by advertisers and agencies using various trade practice recommendations and codes of conduct.

caveat emptor
Latin for "Let the buyer beware," represents the notion that there should be no government interference in the marketplace.

During the early days of exchange, businesses operated under the libertarian notion of **caveat emptor**, "let the buyer beware." This concept was based on the classical economic concept of a free marketplace of ideas and assumed perfect knowledge on the part of the participants in that marketplace. That is, buyers and sellers were presumed to have equal information, and it was assumed that both groups, being rational, would make correct economic choices without government interference.

In this century, the complexities of the marketplace have led to the rejection of many of the principles of caveat emptor. Rather, both businesses and the public realize that buyers have far less information than sellers, and they must be protected by legal guarantees of the authenticity of advertising claims. To shield the public from false and misleading advertising, numerous laws have been passed. Chief among these is the Federal Trade Commission Act, which we discuss first.

THE FEDERAL TRADE COMMISSION (FTC)

As we briefly discussed in Chapter 1, the Federal Trade Act was passed in 1914 in reaction to public and congressional concerns over large firms driving out small competitors in a number of industries. Oil, railroads, steel, shipping, and several other core businesses were increasingly dominated by one or two companies. These huge corporations often introduced business practices that today would be considered restraint of trade but were often legal at the time.

The Federal Trade Commission Act declared that "unfair methods of competition are hereby declared unlawful." In its early years, Congress regarded unfair methods of competition as those involving business-to-business transactions, and it did not give the FTC jurisdiction over consumer advertising and other consumer-related activities. The primary mission of the FTC during this period was to protect local retailers from unfair pricing practices by large national chains.

It was not until 1922, in *FTC v. Winsted Hosiery Company,* that the Supreme Court held that false advertising was an unfair trade practice. Then, in 1938, passage of the **Wheeler-Lea Amendments** broadened this mandate to include the principle that the FTC could protect consumers as well as businesses from deceptive advertising. Today, the FTC has sweeping power over advertising for virtually all products sold or advertised in interstate commerce.

Wheeler-Lea Amendments
Broadened the scope of the FTC to include consumer advertising.

The Role of the FTC in Regulating Deceptive Advertising

Among the several objectives of the FTC is to create a free marketplace based on dissemination of complete, truthful, and nondeceptive advertising. In addition to advertising concerns, the FTC also investigates various sales practices and illegal pricing activities. One of the primary concerns of the FTC is to ensure that consumers are protected from deceptive advertising. At the heart of FTC enforcement is the notion that advertisers must be able to **substantiate** their claims. Failure to provide substantiation is the key finding when advertising claims are judged to be deceptive. According to the FTC, the commission uses a three-part test to determine if an advertisement is deceptive or untruthful:

substantiate
The key to FTC enforcement is that advertisers must be able to prove the claims made in their advertising.

1. *There must be a representation, omission, or practice that is likely to mislead the consumer.* A statement does not have to be untrue to be deceptive. Sometimes advertisers will make a claim that is literally true, but the total impression of the ad is misleading.

2. *The act or practice must be considered from the perspective of a consumer who is acting reasonably.* In other words, the advertiser is not responsible for every possible interpretation, no matter how unreasonable, that might be made by a consumer.

3. *The representation, omission, or practice must be material.* In other words, the claim, even if it is not true, must be judged to have had some influence over a consumer's decision. For example, the courts have ruled that using plastic ice cubes in a soft drink commercial is not deceptive because no claims are being made about the ice cubes.

In most cases, when the FTC challenges an advertising claim, the company being investigated either provides substantiation or agrees to discontinue the advertising claim in question. For example, the FTC accused the maker of Wonder

Bread of unsubstantiated claims that the bread not only built healthy bones but also helped children's memories because it contains extra calcium. The FTC challenged the claims, saying that they had no scientific support. The company, without admitting wrongdoing, agreed to stop the advertising.[36]

Methods of FTC Enforcement

The FTC has a number of means of addressing deceptive advertising. Unless there is evidence of fraud, the first step is for the FTC to work with advertisers to validate a claim or to have advertisers end deceptive practices. In the majority of cases, an advertiser and the FTC will reach a compromise concerning the advertising claims under review, and the investigation will end. However, if an advertiser refuses to discontinue its alleged deceptive practices, there is further recourse for both parties. The following steps outline a typical model for FTC intervention in alleged deception:

1. *The first step in the process is a claim of deceptive practices to the FTC.* The complaint can come from the general public, special interest groups, competitors (by far the major source of complaints), or the FTC staff.

2. *The FTC begins its investigation with a request for substantiation from the advertiser.* At this point, many advertisers, rather than providing substantiation, voluntarily agree to delete the challenged claim from future advertising. However, if substantiation is provided and the advertising continues, the FTC moves to the next step of evaluating the claims.

3. *If the FTC finds the practice to be unsubstantiated and, therefore, deceptive, a complaint is issued.* At this point, the advertiser is asked to sign a **consent decree** in which the firm agrees to end the deceptive practice or advertising. Most complaints are settled in this manner. An advertiser that continues the practice after signing a consent decree is liable for a fine of $10,000 per day.

4. *If an advertiser refuses to sign a consent decree, the FTC issues a* **cease and desist order**. Before such an order can become final, a hearing is held before an administrative law judge. The judge can dismiss the case and negate the cease and desist order. If it is upheld, the company may appeal the decision to the full commission.

5. *Even if an advertiser agrees to abide by a cease and desist order, the FTC may find that simply stopping a particular practice does not repair past damage to consumers.* To counteract the residual effects of deceptive advertising, the FTC may require a firm to run **corrective advertisements** that are designed to "dissipate the effects of that deception." Orders for corrective advertising are not limited to the FTC. In August, 2006, U.S. Judge Gladys Kessler directed the four largest tobacco companies to air spots, run newspapers ads, and produce packaging and in-store signage to counter earlier tobacco advertising that hid the dangers of smoking.[37]

6. *If a company cannot reach agreement with the FTC, its next recourse is the federal courts*—first, to the Federal Court of Appeals and, finally, to the Supreme Court.

It is extremely rare that a case goes beyond the cease and desist stage. Companies know that they will incur significant legal costs even if they eventually prevail in the courts. More importantly, most companies don't want the continuing unfavorable publicity that invariably results from extensive disputes with the FTC. Because brand equity and brand reputation are so important to most firms, the threat of public embarrassment is a primary concern when an advertisement or sale is challenged.

consent decree
Issued by the FTC. An advertiser signs the decree, stops the practice under investigation, but admits no guilt.

cease and desist orders
If an advertiser refuses to sign a consent decree, the FTC may issue a cease and desist order that can carry a $10,000-per-day fine.

corrective advertising
To counteract the past residual effect of previous deceptive advertising, the FTC may require the advertiser to devote future space and time to disclosure of previous deception. Began around the late 1960s.

FTC Rules and Guidelines

The FTC's major responsibility is to protect consumers from deceptive advertising, promotions, and sales techniques. As part of this mission, the FTC engages in a broad program of education for both businesses and consumers to inform them of their rights and, in the case of businesses, to offer advice concerning specific implementation of the FTC's regulations and other legislation that might affect them. Basically, the FTC is responsible for enforcement and education in three areas:

1. *Federal laws passed by Congress.* Dating to the late 1800s, Congress has passed a number of laws concerning fair trade, business practices, and consumer protection. As these laws are enacted, some agency must be given primary responsibility for enforcement. Increasingly, this task has fallen to the FTC. For example, the FTC has established a major program to administer the "Fair Debt Collection Practices Act," which provides a number of rights to the public when dealing with debt collectors. These include issues such as the times when calls are permitted (8 AM to 9 PM), under what circumstances a person can be contacted at work, etc.

2. *Formal FTC Industry Rules.* The areas of FTC enforcement are extremely broad. However, no agency can provide complete oversight over all the consumer advertising and trade practices in the marketplace. Consequently, the FTC tends to concentrate its efforts on those areas that affect the most consumers and have demonstrated the highest percentage of buyer complaints. Part of this effort is to issue rules that offer guidance to both consumers and businesses within certain high-profile industries. Some examples of areas where these rules have been issued include:

   - *The Telemarketing Sales Rule.* The FTC is responsible for both the "National Do Not Call Registry" and the "Telemarketing and Consumer Fraud and Abuse Prevention Act." Among the several provisions of the Act, callers are required to provide caller ID information, there is demand disclosure of certain information about callers and their companies, and it prohibits unauthorized billing. Modeled after several state laws, the registry went into effect in October 2003 and provided for fines of up to $11,000 per unauthorized call. Telemarketers who run afoul of the FTC can find that it can be a very expensive misstep. For example, in 2005, DIRECTV was fined $5.3 million by the FTC for making thousands of calls to households that had been placed on the Do Not Call Registry.[38]

   - *The Used Car Rule.* Over the years, used car sales have been one of the areas that have generated numerous complaints from consumers. According to the FTC, the Used Car Rule is intended to prevent oral misrepresentations and unfair omissions of material facts by used car dealers concerning warranty coverage.

   - *The Contact Lens Rule.* The rules issued by the FTC cover many industries that we would not necessarily think would require this degree of special attention. However, the primary criterion for issuing a rule is the number of complaints from the public and the seriousness with which the FTC regards the problem in terms of consumer safeguards. In the case of the Contact Lens Rule, one of the major problems addressed was patients not being able to get a copy of their prescriptions. Among other provisions of the rule, the FTC made the right to obtain such a prescription mandatory.

The commission is constantly monitoring consumer complaints and takes a proactive stance in communicating its expectations and interpretations to the business community and the public. Although there is certainly a punitive dimension to the rules, one of the goals of the FTC is to offer assistance and advice concerning FTC regulations and enforcement criteria before advertisers inadvertently violate FTC rules.

The FTC rules normally apply to a single industry, but the FTC also continually reviews general advertising and marketing practices. As in the case of industry-specific rules, the FTC considers those practices that are most likely to create confusion among consumers as well as those that are clearly deceptive. These general regulations are normally referred to as guidelines as contrasted to the more formal, industry-centric rules. Among the most common areas of FTC inquiry for which guidelines have been issued are:[39]

Environmental Claims In recent years, a number of companies have made claims about the environmental benefits of their products. The FTC requires that environmentally related claims be qualified and, when such claims are made, the specific nature of the benefits be made clear. For example, a trash bag may be labeled "recyclable." However, since trash bags are not separated from other trash, it is unlikely that the recyclable bag is of any environment benefit.

The Term *Free* in Advertising The use of offers such as "buy one, get one free" or "two for one sale" has become so prevalent and abuses so widespread that the FTC issued a four-page guide for nondeceptive usage of the term *free*. The guide emphasizes that when the word *free* is used, a consumer has the right to believe that the merchant will not recoup any cost associated with the purchase of another item. A "two for one" deal requires that the first item is sold at regular price or the lowest price offered within the last 30 days. The commission also requires that any disclosure about the offer price must be made in a conspicuous manner in close conjunction with the offer. In other words, a fine print footnote in an advertisement is not acceptable disclosure.[40]

Made in the U.S.A. FTC Guidelines require that a product has to be "all or virtually all made in the United States" for it to be advertised or labeled as "Made in the U.S.A." This rule excludes products where contents or parts are imported and the product is simply assembled in the United States from carrying the "Made in the U.S.A." designation.

Advertising as a Contract One of the many gray areas of advertising is the degree to which an advertisement constitutes a binding, contractual agreement with consumers. For the most part, the courts and the FTC have ruled that it is unreasonable to expect an advertisement or commercial to contain all the details expected in a formal contract. The commission assumes that contractual details will be part of the final sales negotiation whereas advertising is normally the first step in the transaction. To this end, the courts have been lenient on pricing errors in ads where no deception is intended. For example, a newspaper misprint offering a car for $2,000 would not place the dealer under a legal mandate to sell cars for that price. The courts have held that no reasonable buyer would expect that a sale would be made under those conditions.

However, under certain circumstances advertisements have been regarded as constituting binding offers. For example, when there is a specific commitment, no error in the ad, and the defendant has some control over potential liability, a court may find an obligation to provide a product or service at an advertised price. For example, retailers have been found liable for advertising claims when they offer a product at a certain price but have no intention of selling the product for that price. Instead sellers attempt to move potential buyers into a more expensive alternative. These so-called "bait-and-switch" tactics have been consistently held to be deceptive, and heavy fines and other penalties have been levied against businesses found guilty of using such tactics. In general, advertisers would be well-advised to treat specific advertising claims as if they had the force of a contract.

Fact Versus Puffery "Puffery consists of exaggerated opinions, usually at the highest degree of exaggeration, which means superlatives, such as 'the best' or 'superior.' You puff your product. . . . It can be the best tasting, best looking, best lasting . . . or just plain the best."[41] The use and boundaries of puffery are extremely controversial. Some critics categorize any statement that is not literally true as deceptive. However, the legal definition of **puffery** is that it is "an exaggeration or overstatement expressed in broad, vague, and commendatory language, and is *distinguishable* from misdescriptions or false representations of specific character-istics of a product and, as such, is not actionable." Advertisers must be wary of pushing the boundaries of puffery. For example, it is easy to cross the line between humor or hyperbole and misleading claims.

puffery
Advertiser's opinion of a product that is considered a legitimate expression of biased opinion.

Testimonials A long-held concept in both communication theory and advertising research is that people like to identify with role models and celebrities. This belief is at the heart of testimonial advertising, which seeks to enhance a brand's reputation by having a sports star, entertainment personality, or acknowledged expert endorse a brand. At one time testimonial advertising, especially celebrity endorsements, were viewed very liberally by regulators. However, in recent years, the FTC has taken a much more literal approach to the role of product endorsements. Specifically the FTC has ruled that:

- Endorsements must always reflect the honest opinions, findings, beliefs, or experience of the endorser.
- In particular, when the advertisement represents that the endorser uses the endorsed product, then the endorser must have been a bona fide user of it at the time the endorsement was given.[42]

The FTC and the courts have held that endorsers who willfully engage in decep-tion can be held liable along with the advertiser for damages. This ruling gives many would-be endorsers pause before they jump into a commercial. In recent years, a number of celebrities have introduced their own lines of cosmetics, fragrances, and clothing in concert with major manufacturers. Besides the obvious marketing advantages of name recognition and celebrity appeal of the brands, it removes any potential problems involved with third-party endorsements of the products.

Warranties and Guarantees The FTC demands that warranty information be avail-able before purchase for consumer products that cost more than $15. The concern with warranties is so great that, even though it is an area of interest across product categories and industries, the FTC has seen fit to issue a rule for the "Pre-Sale Availability of Written Warranty Terms." The guideline also demands that advertis-ing phrases such as "satisfaction guaranteed" or "money-back guarantee" be backed up with written terms of these assurances.

The Robinson-Patman Act and Cooperative Advertising

The FTC, through its antitrust division, has responsibility for enforcing another law affecting marketing and advertising, the **Robinson-Patman Act**. The Robinson-Patman Act is part of a three-law "package" that evolved over a period of almost 50 years. These laws and their purposes are:

1. *1890 Federal Sherman Antitrust Act.* It was designed to prevent alliances of firms conceived to restrict competition.
2. *1914 Clayton Antitrust Act.* This act amended the Sherman Act. It eliminated preferential price treatment when manufacturers sold merchandise to retailers.
3. *1936 Robinson-Patman Act.* In turn, this law amended the Clayton Act. It pre-vents manufacturers from providing a "promotional allowance" to one retailer

Robinson-Patman Act
A federal law, enforced by the FTC. Requires a manufacturer to give proportionate discounts and advertising allowances to all competing dealers in a market. Purpose: To protect smaller merchants from unfair competition of larger buyers.

or wholesaler unless it is also offered to competitors on a proportionally equal basis. Prior to Robinson-Patman, some manufacturers were using a loophole in the Clayton Act to give money back to their bigger customers in the form of promotional allowances. For example, large retailers might be given co-op advertising allowances that were unavailable to small retailers that, in effect, lowered the price of the goods sold to favored customers. Thus, the promotional allowance was a device for under-the-table rebates.

The regulation of co-op allowances has evolved as the media environment has become more complex and the relationships between retailers and manufacturers have changed. At the time Robinson-Patman was passed, the vast majority of retail advertising dollars were placed in newspapers. Today, with a growing number of local advertising options, the FTC requires that retailers must be able to choose from various media and promotional alternatives. For example, a manufacturer may not limit co-op dollars to television, knowing that many retailers in smaller markets might not have practical access to television advertising. Such an offer is known as an *improperly structured program.*

The evolving relationship between retailers and manufacturers is another aspect of Robinson-Patman that has changed since the act was passed. As in the case of the FTC itself, the primary intent of the act was to protect retailers from manufacturers. Today, many regulators are concerned with the leverage that is wielded by huge retail chains against these same manufacturers. For example, most large retailers charge **slotting fees**, which are payments to retailers by manufacturers to gain shelf space. Retailers argue that prime shelf space is their "product" and stores should receive payments to make this space available.

slotting fees
Payments to retailers by manufacturers to gain shelf space.

The FTC has a continuing review of the role of slotting fees since it fears that they have the potential to prevent marketplace entry of new brands or prevent small retailers from gaining access to established brands because of disproportionately high slotting fees. Again, slotting fees, as in the case of other promotional payments, are only illegal if they are administered with the intent to limit competition.

THE FEDERAL FOOD, DRUG, AND COSMETIC ACT

Because of a public outcry over shocking disclosures of unsanitary conditions in meat packing plants and the use of dangerous additives in food as well as continuing scandals concerning patent medicines, the original Food and Drugs Act was passed by Congress on June 30, 1906, and signed by President Theodore Roosevelt. It prohibits interstate commerce in misbranded and adulterated foods, drinks, and drugs. In 1938, Congress passed the Federal Food, Drug, and Cosmetic Act, which established the Food and Drug Administration (FDA). It superseded the original legislation and gave the FDA responsibility for

- Extending control to cosmetics and therapeutic devices.
- Requiring new drugs to be shown safe before marketing—starting a new system of drug regulation.
- Eliminating the Sherley Amendment requirement to prove intent to defraud in drug misbranding cases.
- Providing that safe tolerances be set for unavoidable poisonous substances.
- Authorizing standards of identity, quality, and fill-of-container for foods.
- Authorizing factory inspections.
- Adding the remedy of court injunctions to the previous penalties of seizures and prosecutions.

One of the most active and controversial areas of FDA regulation is consumer prescription drug advertising. Until 1997, pharmaceutical companies could advertise prescription drugs only to doctors. Then, consumer advertising was permitted. By 1999, drug companies were spending more than $1 billion on direct-to-consumer (DTC) prescription drug advertising. By 2005, that figure had grown to $4 billion and many consumer advocates as well as doctors feared that many of the claims did not meet FDC guidelines for such advertising. The FDA has begun an aggressive campaign of enforcing promotional regulations, often sending formal letters of warning to drug companies. Some drug companies have sharply reduced their advertising budgets and criticized the agency for overzealous enforcement of a program that it initiated. A spokesman for the FDA defended its position, "This [the current enforcement campaign] is not a crackdown, it is an enforcement. We're continuing our close monitoring . . . we're prepared to take whatever action necessary to stop misleading promotion."[43]

The jurisdiction of the FDA to control and regulate labeling was enhanced when Congress passed the Nutritional Labeling and Education Act of 1990. Beginning on January 1, 2006, the agency was given greater enforcement authority over labeling, and labeling information was enhanced to include data about trans fat, allergen groups, and whole grain ingredients. Consumer protection groups applauded the new enforcement activity as a step toward more fully informing consumers about food ingredients. With its new authority, the FDA may become much more aggressive in the enforcement of regulations dealing with health claims on labels and packaging, sometimes borrowing strategies from the FTC.

The United States Postal Service

Benjamin Franklin created the forerunner of the United States Postal Service (USPS) in 1772. At the end of the Civil War there was a major outbreak of mail swindles, and in 1872 Congress passed the Mail Fraud Statute, the nation's oldest federal consumer protection statute. Mail fraud is any scheme in which the USPS is used to obtain money by offering a deceptive product, service, or investment opportunity. To obtain a conviction, postal inspectors must prove (1) the offer was intentionally misrepresented and (2) the U.S. mail was used to carry out the fraud. Postal inspectors investigate a number of criminal activities. In particular, the inspectors protect postal customers from mail advertising and promotion schemes involving the elderly and other susceptible groups.

For a number of years, the USPS has been empowered to obtain a mail stop order against a company sending false advertising. However, until recently there was no penalty attached to the stop order. In 1999, the Deceptive Mail Prevention and Enforcement Act (DMPEA) gave the USPS significantly more power to deal with mail fraud. The primary change brought about by DMPEA is that the USPS can impose civil penalties of up to $1 million for the first offense depending on the volume of mail involved.[44]

ADVERTISING AND THE FIRST AMENDMENT

The wording of the First Amendment makes no distinction between advertising or commercial speech and other forms of expression. However, until the 1970s the courts consistently ruled that advertising had virtually none of the rights guaranteed to other types of speech. The open "marketplace of ideas" was never considered a privilege of advertising, and it was held to a much stricter standard than other forms of expression.

In addition to a variety of limitations, advertisers have been frustrated by what they regarded as changing and often contradictory decisions by the Court concerning commercial speech. Although advertising continues to function under regulations that would be unacceptable if applied to other speech, the trend of the last 60 years has been toward giving commercial speech greater constitutional protections. Nevertheless, despite a more open environment for commercial messages, judicial opinions supporting commercial speech still deny full First Amendment protection to advertising. In order to understand the legal protections afforded commercial speech, let's outline the major court opinions involving advertising.[45]

1942 The Supreme Court ruled that advertising was not entitled to First Amendment protection. The Court ruled that there were *no* restraints on government's right to prohibit commercial speech.

1964 The Court decided that advertising that expressed an opinion on a *public issue* was protected by the First Amendment, but only because it did not contain commercial speech.

1975 The Court gave advertising its first constitutional protection when it overturned a Virginia law making it a criminal offense to advertise out-of-state abortion clinics in Virginia newspapers. However, the ruling left open the question of protection for purely commercial speech that did not deal with opinions or controversial public issues.

1976 In what many advertisers regard as the major breakthrough for commercially protected speech, the Court held in the case of *Virginia State Board of Pharmacy v. Virginia Citizens Consumer Council* that the state of Virginia could not prohibit the advertising of prescription drug prices. It said, in effect, that society benefits from a free flow of commercial information just as it benefits from a free exchange of political ideas.

1979 Advertisers' optimism that they had finally achieved full constitutional protection was short-lived. In the case of *Friedman v. Rogers* the Court upheld the right of the state of Texas to prevent an optometrist from using an "assumed name, corporate name, trade name or any other than the name under which he is licensed to practice optometry in Texas." In its decision, the Court said that First Amendment protection for commercial speech is not absolute and that regulation of commercial speech can be allowed even when the restrictions would be unconstitutional "in the realm of noncommercial expression."

1980 Prior to this year, the Court seemingly ruled on each case involving commercial speech on a purely ad hoc basis. Even as cases were settled, advertisers were left with little if any guidance or precedents. However, in 1980 the Court articulated a set of guidelines concerning the constitutional protection that would be afforded commercial speech. These guidelines were set forth in the case of *Central Hudson Gas & Electric v. Public Service Commission of New York*.

This case concerned a prohibition by the New York Public Service Commission against utility advertising. The state's rationale was that the ban was compatible with public concerns over energy conservation. In overturning the prohibition, the Court established a four-part test to determine when commercial speech is constitutionally protected and when regulation is permissible. These guidelines known as the *Central Hudson Four-Part Test* are:

1. *Is the commercial expression eligible for First Amendment protection?* That is, is it neither deceptive nor promoting an illegal activity? No constitutional protection can be provided for commercial speech that fails this test.

2. *Is the government interest asserted in regulating the expression substantial?* This test requires that the stated reason for regulating the advertisement must be of primary interest to the state rather than of a trivial, arbitrary, or capricious nature.

3. *If the first two tests are met, the Court then considers if the regulation of advertising imposed advances the cause of the governmental interest asserted.* That is, if we assume that an activity is of legitimate government concern, will the prohibition of commercial speech further the government's goals?

4. *If the first three tests are met, the Court must finally decide if the regulation is more extensive than necessary to serve the government's interest.* That is, is there a less severe restriction having accomplished the same goals?

In the *Central Hudson* case, the Court ruled that although the case met the first three guidelines, a total prohibition of utility advertising was more extensive than necessary. Thus, it failed the fourth part of the test and was ruled unconstitutional. The *Central Hudson* guidelines remain the foundation on which most commercial speech cases are considered.

1986 Most advertisers thought that *Central Hudson* had provided significant protection in limiting the right of states to ban legitimate advertising. However, in the case of *Posadas de Puerto Rico Associates v. Tourism Company of Puerto Rico* the Court seemed to once again strengthen the ability of states to regulate advertising. This case involved a Puerto Rican law banning advertising of gambling casinos to residents of Puerto Rico even though casino gambling is legal there and the casinos were permitted to advertise outside of Puerto Rico. In a five to four decision, the Court ruled that the ban met all four standards of the *Central Hudson Four-Part Test.*

1988 Many legal scholars see this year as marking a significant change in the Court's attitude toward advertising and, just as importantly, a change in its interpretation of *Central Hudson. Board of Trustees of the State University of New York v. Fox* dealt with a college regulation that restricted "private commercial enterprises" on campus. Students challenged the regulation, arguing that at events such as "Tupperware parties" noncommercial subjects were discussed. Because the regulation had the effect of prohibiting both noncommercial and commercial speech, it was too broad and, therefore, did not meet the fourth part of the *Central Hudson* test.

Unfortunately for advocates of commercial speech, the Court upheld the college's regulation. The Court ruled that regulations must be "narrowly tailored," but not necessarily the "least restrictive" option available. Critics of the decision point out that the term "narrowly tailored" is vague and may risk weakening the protections of *Central Hudson.*

1993 In *City of Cincinnati v. Discovery Network,* the Court seemed to offer a clear victory for proponents of First Amendment protection of commercial speech. In a six to three decision, the Court held that the Cincinnati City Council violated the First Amendment by banning newsracks for free promotional publications but allowing them for traditional newspapers. The Court ruled that because the ban was based solely on the content of the publications in the racks, it did not meet the "narrowly tailored" test. The case was widely seen as a victory for commercial speech.

1996 Legal scholars predict that two cases heard in this year may provide a significant step in affording more complete constitutional protection to commercial speech. In *44 Liquormart, Inc. v. Rhode Island,* the Court ruled that a Rhode Island ban on price advertising for alcoholic beverages was unconstitutional. The Court referred to the *Central Hudson* case and ruled that the Rhode Island law failed to prove that the ban on price promotions advanced the state's interest in promoting temperance (that is, it failed the third test of *Central Hudson*). Furthermore, the legislation was more extensive than necessary to accomplish the goals of the state (here, it failed the fourth test of *Central Hudson*).

Writing for the majority of the Court, Justice John Paul Stevens said, "Bans that target truthful, nonmisleading commercial messages rarely protect consumers from such harms. Instead, such bans often serve only to obscure an 'underlying governmental policy' that could be implemented without regulating speech."[46] Commenting for the advertising industry, Wally Snyder, president of the American Advertising Federation, noted, "The Supreme Court ruling represented the strongest opinion to date protecting truthful advertising from government censorship."[47]

In a subsequent case that year, the Court underscored the *Rhode Island* decision by returning to the Fourth Circuit U.S. Court of Appeals case involving a Baltimore ban on alcoholic billboard advertising. In *Anheuser-Busch, Inc. v. Schmoke,* the beer maker challenged the city ordinance on constitutional grounds of denial of First Amendment right to free speech. However, demonstrating the unpredictability of cases dealing with advertising, the appeals court upheld its original verdict, ruling that because alcoholic beverage companies had other avenues for their advertising, the ban was not as broad as the Rhode Island law and, therefore, constitutional.

1999 The Greater New Orleans Broadcasters Association sought to overturn a ban on broadcast advertising for gambling enterprises that dated to the Communications Act of 1934. Advocates of the ban argued that the government had a legitimate interest in protecting compulsive gamblers from the temptation that casino gambling fostered. In upholding the ban, the Fifth Circuit Court of Appeals commented that the restriction was appropriate because of the "powerful sensory appeal of gambling conveyed by television and radio."[48]

In June 1999, when the case reached the Supreme Court, the lower court decisions were overturned using the earlier *Central Hudson* guidelines. According to *Central Hudson,* any government restrictions on truthful commercial speech had to be shown to advance some government interest and be no more extensive than necessary. The Court ruled that the casino advertising ban did not sufficiently advance the government's stated interest to protect compulsive gamblers and did not do so in the least intrusive way.[49]

Some advertisers were encouraged that the *New Orleans Broadcasters* case might mean greater First Amendment protection for advertising, perhaps even lifting the prohibition against broadcast tobacco advertising. However, the Court was careful to write its decision narrowly. It "focused on the irrationality of making distinctions among advertisers, while at the same time suggesting that a more uniform and coherent policy of advertising restrictions might well have been upheld. . . . [It] left the door open for the Court to uphold, in future cases, restrictions on the advertising of other lawful products."[50]

Advertising and the First Amendment in the Twenty-First Century During the early years of this century, there have been a number of cases dealing with advertising and commercial speech. None appear to have the importance of previous decisions, such as Central Hudson, and they appear to continue the trend of unpredictability of decisions dealing with commercial speech. The primary decisions include:

1. *Lorillard Tobacco Co. v. Reilly.* In 2000, the attorney general of Massachusetts issued a number of restrictions on tobacco advertising in the state—including banning all outdoor advertising within 1,000 feet of elementary or secondary schools and playgrounds and placed limitations on advertising in retail stores. Several tobacco companies appealed the regulations on the basis that they violated their rights to free speech. The limitations were upheld at the appellate level, but in 2001 the Supreme Court overturned the state regulations on the basis that they "violated tobacco companies' right to free speech."

2. *FDA's role in tobacco marketing.* The Supreme Court ruled in 2002 that the FDA's authority over the marketing communication of drugs and related products must meet certain First Amendment guidelines. Specifically, the Court ruled that the FDA did not have the authority to impose rules on tobacco marketers that would have prevented the use of certain types of imagery and colors in advertising and point-of-purchase material. The decision was applauded by the advertising industry as a strong statement that regulatory requirement must consider First Amendment implications. However, at this writing, a Democratic Congress has explored legislation which would grant greater authority to the FDA in regards to tobacco control.

3. *Kasky v. Nike.* In the case of *Kasky v. Nike*, the California Supreme Court and the Supreme Court seemed to send mixed signals for First Amendment protection of commercial speech. For a number of years, detractors charged Nike with tolerating poor working conditions in its overseas plants. In an effort to rebut its critics, Nike sent the news media information offering its side of the debate. Marc Kasky brought suit alleging that the comments were commercial speech and, therefore, did not have full First Amendment protection afforded political discourse and could be challenged on a similar basis to advertising product claims. In 2002, the California Court agreed, ruling four to three that the comments by Nike constituted advertising and, therefore, the company was ordered to establish the truthfulness of its claims under the state unfair practices act. In June 2003, the Supreme Court returned the case to the California Court without comment. In September 2003, Nike and Kasky reached an out-of-court settlement, thereby leaving the legal position of corporate speech and related advertising in limbo.

4. *Kellogg's and the Center for Science in the Public Interest (CSPI).* Potential litigation with far-reaching impact on the First Amendment rights of advertisers is the threat by the CSPI and other consumer advocates to file a $2 billion lawsuit against Kellogg's for marketing, what they regard as unhealthy food, to children. A number of marketing and advertising groups sharply criticized the action, many on First Amendment grounds. A 4A's spokesperson was quoted as saying, "This action is breathtaking in its willful disregard for the First Amendment protections guaranteed to us all." Meanwhile, a representative of the Association of National Advertisers said the suit was "an extraordinarily radical misconstruction of the First Amendment."[51]

5. *United States et al. v. United Foods, Inc.* Most court cases deal with issues concerning restricting communication from a company or individual. *United States v. United Foods* dealt with the question of whether or not the government can compel an entity to engage in some speech. In 1990, Congress authorized the Secretary of Agriculture to establish a Mushroom Council. The Council was allowed to collect a mandatory assessment from mushroom growers. The funds were primarily used for generic advertising to promote mushroom sales. United Foods argued that their mushrooms were of higher quality than competitors, and it did not want to participate in the Mushroom Council's generic program. The Court ruled that ". . . the mandated support is contrary to the First Amendment principles set forth in cases involving expression by groups which include persons who object to the speech, but who, nevertheless, must remain members of the group by law or necessity."[52]

Because of the unique nature of communication, it may be that the Supreme Court will never be able to issue a totally definitive decision that will cover every instance of commercial speech. Instead, most of the decisions considered by the courts involve narrowly defined issues that often pertain to messages dealing with a single industry or product category. These decisions underscore the fact that each case has distinctive elements that don't necessarily provide precedents in other circumstances. Still, there is little question that the Supreme Court will continue to demand that the government meets a high standard of public interest before agreeing to any prohibition of commercial speech.

Corporate Speech and Advertising

In recent years, we have seen a tremendous growth in corporate advertising espousing some idea or corporate philosophy as contrasted to selling a product or service. Like all other forms of commercial speech, corporate advertising falls into a gray area. Similar to its decisions regarding commercial speech, the Supreme Court has ruled that corporate advertising is protected under certain circumstances. In *First National Bank of Boston v. Bellotti,* the Court overturned a state law that prohibited national banks from using corporate funds to advocate voting against a state constitutional amendment that would allow the legislature to impose a graduated income tax.

Over the years the Court has delineated several legal principles concerning corporate speech:

1. Spending money to speak does not, in itself, result in the loss of First Amendment rights.
2. Speaking on commercial subjects does not entail loss of First Amendment rights.
3. Speaking for economic interests does not entail loss of First Amendment rights.[53]

We should note that the Court is saying that a commercial aspect to speech does not *necessarily* remove that speech from the rights granted by the First Amendment. However, the converse of this view does not automatically grant these rights to either advertising or corporate speech.

Advertising and the Right of Publicity

A private individual is protected by the right of privacy from having his or her likeness used in an advertisement without permission. Laws vary from state to state, but every state has some legislation that addresses the right of privacy of an individual. In many jurisdictions, the use of a name or picture of a person without prior consent is a misdemeanor. However, civil liability, potentially involving significant monetary judgments, is a much greater concern to advertisers.

Generally, the courts have ruled that public figures including celebrities have far less protection than the general public in terms of their right of privacy. However, in recent years the courts have made it clear that this distinction of public versus private persons is related to news, not advertising or other commercial use. Legal precedent makes it clear that public figures are protected from commercial use of their name or likeness by a doctrine of the right of *publicity* (as contrasted with a right of *privacy*).

In the past, most issues of privacy dealt only with living personalities. However, in recent years some states, notably California, have addressed the issue of deceased celebrities. John Wayne, Humphrey Bogart, and other stars from the past have been used in a number of commercials with the permission of their estates. Because state laws vary widely, advertisers should be extremely prudent in using a personality's name or likeness. The normal course of action is that an advertiser or agency will never use a model, personality, or likeness without legal permission. For example, the courts have ruled against a number of advertisers that used impersonators in commercials without permission.

ADVERTISING OF PROFESSIONAL SERVICES

One of the most controversial areas of commercial speech involves advertising by professionals, especially attorneys and health-care providers. Until the mid-1970s, virtually all forms of professional advertising were banned, often by trade associations such as state medical groups or bar associations. Critics of restrictions on professional advertising claim that one of the overriding concerns of trade associations supporting these bans was to limit competition for established professionals and, in fact, constituted restraint of trade.

Supporting this claim, research indicates that among doctors, those most likely to use advertising are physicians who have been in practice the least time, those who have smaller practices, and females.[54] Due in part to concerns that the bans constituted barriers to market entry, absolute prohibition of attorney (and by extension most other professions) advertising was lifted in 1977 in the case of *Bates v. State Bar of Arizona*. The Supreme Court ruled that state laws forbidding advertising by attorneys were unconstitutional on First Amendment grounds. The fourth test of the *Central Hudson* case, not an issue in 1977, seems to reinforce the *Bates* decision. That is, most legal scholars think that the total prohibition of a class of advertising will generally not meet the fourth test because any such total ban will be considered broader than necessary. Professional associations still have the right to enforce some regulations over issues such as accuracy and presentation, but they cannot prohibit their members from advertising.

In 1988, the Supreme Court extended the right of attorneys to advertise professional services. A Kentucky lawyer, Richard Shapero, was cited for violating a Kentucky law prohibiting targeted mail solicitations to people who were facing foreclosure. The Court ruled that although personal contact by an attorney could be prohibited, a letter posed no threat of pressure to consumers who are under threat of legal action. The *Shapero* case had the immediate effect of lifting the ban on targeted letters in the twenty-five states that had previously prohibited them.

In 1993, the Court made an interesting distinction among various types of professional solicitations. The Florida board of accountancy banned personal solicitations for clients, either in person or by telephone. In *Edenfield v. Fane*, the Court overturned the ban and, in doing so, made a clear distinction between lawyers and accountants. The Court held that, unlike lawyers, CPAs are not trained in the art of persuasion, they are dealing with clients who probably have had a previous professional relationship with an accountant, and the client of a CPA is probably not under the stress that a lawyer's potential client might be. The court found that it was unlikely that the potential clients of a CPA would be subject to "uninformed acquiescence" which might be the case with a lawyer's client.

A 1995 case demonstrated that the courts consider a number of circumstances in ruling on professional solicitations and they are not prepared to issue blanket denials of most state regulations. The Court upheld a Florida Bar Association rule prohibiting lawyers from sending direct mail to accident victims. The Court took the position that an accident victim is in a more vulnerable state of mind than a person facing foreclosure—the circumstance of those solicited by Shapero. Again, referring to the *Central Hudson* guideline, "The state had a substantial interest in protecting the integrity of its legal system."[55]

Taking note of the growing use of the Internet for commercial purposes, Congress passed the Controlling the Assault of Non-Solicited Pornography and Marketing Act (CAN-SPAM) Act of 2003, which establishes requirements for those who send commercial e-mail, spells out penalties for spammers and companies whose products are advertised in spam if they violate the law, and gives consumers the right to ask e-mailers to stop spamming them.

The law, which became effective January 1, 2004, covers e-mail whose primary purpose is advertising or promoting a commercial product or service, including content on a Web site. A "transactional or relationship message"—e-mail that facilitates an agreed-upon transaction or updates a customer in an existing business relationship—may not contain false or misleading routing information, but otherwise is exempt from most provisions of the CAN-SPAM Act.

The FTC enforces the CAN-SPAM Act. CAN-SPAM also gives the Department of Justice (DOJ) the authority to enforce its criminal sanctions. Other federal and state agencies can enforce the law against organizations under their jurisdiction, and companies that provide Internet access may sue violators, as well. Among the major provisions of the Act are:

- *It bans false or misleading header information.* Your e-mail's "From," "To," and routing information—including the originating domain name and e-mail address—must be accurate and identify the person who initiated the e-mail.
- *It prohibits deceptive subject lines.* The subject line cannot mislead the recipient about the contents or subject matter of the message.
- *It requires that your e-mail give recipients an opt-out method.* You must provide a return e-mail address or another Internet-based response mechanism that allows a recipient to ask you not to send future e-mail messages to that e-mail address, and you must honor the requests.
- *It requires that commercial e-mail be identified as an advertisement and include the sender's valid physical postal address.* Your message must contain clear and conspicuous notice that the message is an advertisement or solicitation and that the recipient can opt out of receiving more commercial e-mail from you. It also must include your valid physical postal address.[56]

The regulations concerning spam underscore a central theme of all First Amendment and commercial speech limitations. That is, that under no circumstances will the courts offer any level of protection to speech that is untrue or misleading. The advertising industry expects no such exceptions, but it does assume that in the future truthful advertising will be given full protection of the law.

STATE AND LOCAL LAWS RELATING TO ADVERTISING

Disputes between major corporations and federal agencies such as the FTC garner most of the headlines in the area of advertising regulation. However, most companies are small firms dealing in a local or regional market and, due to limited resources, fly below the radar of federal regulatory bodies. Most federal control of advertising and marketing practices is specifically directed toward intrastate regulation. During the early 1900s, major advertisers realized that something had to be done to thwart the charlatans and frauds that were preying on an unsuspecting public and causing widespread mistrust of all advertising. However, most of their efforts were directed at the national level with local advertising abuses largely ignored. *Printers' Ink,* a leading trade magazine of the time, proposed state and local advertising regulations to address the growing problem of false advertising (see Exhibit 24.7). Basically, it sought to regulate "untrue, deceptive, or misleading advertising." However, it has only been in the last decade that enforcement at the local level has become a major force in advertising regulation. Primary local advertising regulation has been undertaken by the National Association of Attorneys General (NAAG), which has become very aggressive in addressing a number of national trade issues including advertising as they impact local consumers.

For example, most people probably believe that multibillion-dollar sanctions against major tobacco companies were the result of actions by the federal government. In reality, the 1998 Master Settlement Agreement (MSA) was crafted by a consortium of forty-six states and five territories. The MSA, much of which addressed the manner in which tobacco could be advertised and pro-

THE *PRINTERS' INK* MODEL STATUTE FOR STATE LEGISLATION AGAINST FRAUDULENT ADVERTISING

Any person, firm, corporation, or association, who with intent to sell or in any wise dispose of merchandise, securities, service, or anything offered by such person, firm, corporation, or association, directly or indirectly to the public for sale or distribution, or with the intent to increase the consumption thereof, or to induce the public in any manner to enter into any obligation relating thereto, or to acquire title thereto, or an interest therein, makes, publishes, disseminates, circulates, or places before the public, or causes, directly or indirectly, to be made, published, disseminated, circulated, or placed before the public, in this state, in a newspaper or other publication, or in the form of a book, notice, handbill, poster, bill, circular, pamphlet, or letter, or in any other way, an advertisement of any sort regarding merchandise, securities, service, or anything so offered to the public, which advertisement contains assertions, representation, or statement of fact which is untrue, deceptive, or misleading shall be guilty of a misdemeanor.

EXHIBIT 24.7

Printers' Ink Was an Early Leader in the Fight for Truthful Advertising

moted, was the most high-profile case brought by members of the NAAG. However, it is only one of a number of suits involving national companies that have been brought by state attorneys general. For example, attorneys general have negotiated a $100 million agreement with a major brokerage house concerning actions by some of its brokers, investigated pharmaceutical industry pricing tactics, and brought suit against major telecommunication companies and health insurance firms.

Today, the NAAG continues to undertake a number of initiatives on a state level as well as frequently having members testify before Congress to offer suggestions for new legislation or to support pending national laws. Among the topics under consideration by the NAAG that have implications for advertising and marketing are:

1. Internet and telecom privacy issues
2. Moving company practices
3. Predatory lending concerns
4. Automotive and tire safety
5. Telemarketing fraud

In 2005, Blockbuster settled claims initiated through the NAAG for $630,000. State attorney generals alleged that Blockbuster's "No late fees" campaign did not fully communicate with consumers concerning potential penalties for late or nonreturn of rentals. As part of the settlement with forty-seven states and the District of Columbia, Blockbuster agreed to reimburse consumers who were charged fees if they did not understand company policies.[57]

On the face of it, no one would question that companies and advertisers should be held accountable for their actions regardless of whether the oversight is conducted by state, local, or national authorities. However, many advertisers have raised questions about the extent that states will be allowed to go beyond or contradict national legislation. Formerly, it appeared the lines between state and federal enforcement were relatively clear. However, in the last decade there has been an obvious shift toward more state control, which creates potential problems for national advertising if it has to meet an array of local standards. On the other hand, the NAAG argues that by the cooperative efforts of the various state attorney generals, it is moving to provide standardized regulation across a number of concerns at the state level, but it still leaves potential problems of uneven enforcement from state to state. . . .

COMPARISON ADVERTISING

One of the most controversial areas of advertising is the comparison of one brand with one or more of its competitors. J. Sterling Getchell is generally credited with the first major use of comparison advertising when the Getchell Agency introduced the Chrysler car in the 1930s by inviting customers to "Try all three."

Comparison advertising began to be widely used after the FTC pushed for more comparative advertising in 1972. The commission urged ABC and CBS to allow commercials that named competitors. Until then, only NBC had permitted such messages, whereas ABC and CBS would allow only "Brand X" comparisons in which competitors were implied but not directly named. The FTC continues to foster comparative advertising, even going so far as to warn trade associations against industry codes that prohibit such comparisons.

Despite the continuing use of the technique, many marketers are concerned that comparison advertising has a number of pitfalls for those using it. The three primary problems often cited in comparison advertising are:

- Comparative advertising runs the risk of inadvertently promoting competitive brands and/or appearing to offer credibility to them by including their names. Logic tells us that only those brands that offer genuine competition will be named in a comparison campaign.
- Some comparison advertising techniques may appear unfair to consumers and damage not only the reputation of the brand using it but advertising in general.
- Firms often fear that comparative advertising claims will precipitate lawsuits by companies that think their brands have been unfairly disparaged. The majority of complaints and lawsuits are brought by competitors who think that a company's comparative claims are deception or untrue. When comparison advertising is used, it increases the chances of such objections.

The financial and public relations fallout from such litigation can be extremely serious. For example, as a result of a lawsuit brought by H&R Block in federal court, Intuit, maker of tax-preparation software, TurboTax, agreed to change statements in its advertising. The advertisements claimed that "more returns were prepared with TurboTax last year than at all the H&R Block stores combined." A U.S. District Court upheld H&R Block's complaint, and, while Intuit disputed the findings, it agreed to delete the claims.[58] Comparison advertising may result in legal action even when a competitor is not named directly. For example, in June, 2005, a federal judge ordered Gillette to stop advertising claims that its vibrating M3Power razor can raise consumers' hairs so they can be sliced off more cleanly than with other razors. Connecticut U.S. District Court Judge Janet C. Hall granted a preliminary injunction sought by rival razor maker Energizer Holdings Inc., manufacturer of Schick brand razors. Specifically, Judge Hall barred Gillette's claims that the M3Power could "change the angle of hair in relation to the skin" or "extend or lengthen hair" in a significant way.[59] Even though Schick razors were not named in the advertising, as the second largest maker in the category, Schick thought that the ads disparaged its products. As we noted earlier in this chapter, product substantiation is important in any advertising, but particularly in comparison advertising where, in effect, advertisers must substantiate both the qualities of their brand as well as those of any other brands to which they are making comparisons.

THE ADVERTISING CLEARANCE PROCESS

While advertisers operate in an environment of extensive regulation at both the state and federal level, some of the most effective advertising evaluations are conducted by the industry itself. The vast majority of advertisers not only want to produce truthful advertising, but they also are interested in making sure that their peers do likewise. Advertising self-regulation is both philosophical and pragmatic. On the one hand, when consumers are misled by dishonest advertising, all advertisers pay a price in a loss of trust. Just as importantly, if consumers believe deceptive claims for a brand, they can hurt sales and profits of competitors. Advertisers, advertising agencies, and the media that carry their advertising all play a part in the process of ensuring that advertising serves the public interest.

The media are a major element in the **advertising clearance process** because they represent an independent reviewer of advertising messages. There are numerous examples of general media prohibitions of specific product categories such as NC-17 movie advertisements, alcohol, and certain types of sexually oriented product categories. In other cases, individual advertisements are refused because they appear to be fraudulent or they may demean a competitor. It is important to remember that in general the media review process is voluntary, and it is up to each medium to set its own standards—the scope and diligence exercised by the various media vary a great deal.

Advertising trade associations, individual media, and media groups often establish their own codes of ethics. Some newspapers and magazines, in varying degree, investigate the reliability of advertisers before accepting their copy. Some publishers have strict rules about acceptable advertising executions to prevent the publication of false or exaggerated claims and to preserve the aesthetic tone of their publications. Most publications clearly label advertisements that might be confused with editorial content.

Radio and television stations generally try to investigate a company and its product before broadcasting advertising messages that might be misleading or controversial. For example, the networks and the National Association of Broadcasters (NAB) have established codes regulating the advertising of medical products and contests, premiums, and other offers. All the networks maintain so-called acceptance departments, which screen both commercial and noncommercial scripts, either rejecting or challenging for substantiation any questionable material.

The American Advertising Federation, an organization of leading national advertisers, has long campaigned for "truth in advertising." Other organizations that promote ethical standards are the American Association of Advertising Agencies and the Association of National Advertisers. The Institute of Outdoor Advertising encourages its members to improve the design of their advertising posters and signs and, more importantly, to make sure they do not erect advertising billboards in locations where they will mar the landscape or otherwise offend the public.[60]

Sometimes it is difficult to predict when a commercial will be turned down. In one case, a network reportedly rejected a commercial because models were not wearing wedding rings even though it was obvious from the context of the commercial that they were living together. In another case, CBS and NBC stopped running commercials for Miller Brewing, which they thought unduly disparaged Anheuser-Busch Budweiser and Bud Light brands.[61] The major television networks

advertising clearance process
The internal process of clearing ads for publication and broadcast, conducted primarily by ad agencies and clients.

are particularly vigilant concerning commercials directed to children. For example, toys are one of the most scrutinized advertising categories. The networks take pains to ensure that young children can tell the difference between commercials and programming by limiting advertising time by limiting commercials during preschool blocks to the top and bottom end of programs rather than in the middle. Basic guidelines for toy commercials include:

- Toys must be presented literally and realistically.
- Animation is limited to about 10 seconds a spot.
- Copy must clearly disclose if parts are sold separately and if batteries are not included.[62]

While many media do a good job of ad screening, the proliferation of media outlets and the resulting competitive pressure for advertising dollars have led to a lowering of review standards on the part of some media. The importance of the media screening process was emphasized in 1998 when the FTC issued a *Guide for the Media*, which stressed the importance of the media in stopping dishonest advertising. In the prologue to the guidelines, the FTC wrote, "Government agencies and self-regulatory groups can step in once the law has been violated, but only the media can stop false ads before they are disseminated."[63]

Lax enforcement of media guidelines or ignoring obviously deceptive and misleading advertising can have significant implications for the media. Media should carefully review advertising they accept as a matter of public trust, but careless acceptance of advertising also can carry legal liability for a medium. If a statement in an advertisement or commercial is false or defamatory, the media can be sued along with the advertiser. This notion was underscored in 2002 when then FTC Chairman Timothy Muris introduced the idea that those media that ran clearly misleading advertising were leaving themselves open to legal action. In response, a number of media trade organizations complained that the threatened action was unconstitutional under free speech protections. However, Chairman Muris responded that "there is no constitutional right to run false advertising."[64]

A primary emphasis of the FTC has been those media carrying fraudulent diet and weight loss ads, which were blatantly false. The "get tough" approach to media indifference obviously worked. In a survey conducted by the FTC, the Commission found that so-called "red flag" weight loss ads (those with obviously false claims) dropped from 50 percent of total ads in January 2005 to 15 percent in May of that year. Commenting on the results of the survey, FTC Chairwoman Deborah Majoras said, ". . . our overweight population is a societal problem that requires personal responsibility, governmental responsibility, and corporate responsibility."[65]

In 2005, the government demonstrated how serious it is about regulating false advertising when the DOJ launched the latest salvo in its ongoing effort to eliminate online gambling activity in the United States by announcing a $7.2 million settlement with *The Sporting News* in connection with that company's acceptance of advertisements for offshore gambling sites on its Web site, in its publications, and on its radio stations. The DOJ has long taken the position that offshore gambling sites are illegal in the United States and, further, that entities that aid and abet the offshore sites in targeting U.S. consumers—including media outlets that accept ads for such sites—are equally liable for the gambling law violations. *The Sporting News* settlement is the latest development in this investigation. *The Sporting News*, while not admitting any liability or violation of law, agreed to pay $7.2 million—a $4.2 million fine and $3 million in corrective advertising in the form of public service ads designed to discourage online gambling activity. The settlement amount reflected the profits that *The Sporting News* reportedly received from Spring 2000 through the end of 2003 from the acceptance of Internet gambling ads.[66]

Despite threats of formal legal action, from a practical standpoint, unless a medium knowingly accepts deceptive or libelous advertising, its chances of liability are not great. However, a more practical concern for the media is the loss of goodwill with their audiences if a deceptive ad is cleared for publication or broadcast. No responsible agency or medium would argue that deceptive advertising should be created or run.

SELF-REGULATION BY INDUSTRYWIDE GROUPS

Self-regulation by the advertising industry is not new, but it has become much more evident and effective in the last 25 years. Today, there are a number of initiatives to ensure that advertising is truthful. Some of these efforts are undertaken by groups within specific industries, and others are intended to review more general advertising. Industry self-regulation serves two important purposes beyond ensuring more informative and truthful advertising. First, it seeks to overcome the relatively poor public perception of advertising by showing that there is a concerted attempt within the industry to foster responsible advertising. Second, strong self-regulation may ward off even stricter government control. For example, two of the most aggressive industry self-regulation initiatives have involved the pharmacy and beverage industries—both under scrutiny by both regulators and consumer protection groups.

The Pharmaceutical Research and Manufacturers of America (PhRMA) instigated a far-reaching code of conduct to address concerns about direct-to-consumer advertising. The code called for prior review by the FDA of all advertising, a discussion of both the risks and benefits of a drug, and the health conditions for which a drug is intended to be clearly spelled out. Some observers saw the code as a negotiating tool as the FDA begins discussions of drug advertising regulations. "The long-awaited code of conduct issued . . . by a pharmaceutical industry looking to head off government-imposed regulation of direct-to-consumer drug advertising is seen by many as wishy-washy by design, and a mere starting point to bargain for bigger chips."[67] Whether this cynical view of the industry's motives is correct or not, it does point out the benefit of implementing such industry codes at a time when it is not in a crisis mode.

Similarly, beverage companies are facing numerous regulations calling for restrictions or bans on the sale of soft drinks in schools. In addition, there have been calls for government-mandated health warnings on soft drink labels. In the face of this criticism, the American Beverage Association and high-profile members such as Coca-Cola and PepsiCo enacted a voluntary policy to head off stricter legislation. The association spent millions of dollars promoting the voluntary guidelines, which limited the sale of carbonated soft drinks, especially in elementary and middle schools.[68]

We should not suggest that codes of advertising are only enacted by industries in peril. Most major trade associations have guidelines about the marketing and advertising of their products. The advertising industry itself has a long history of promoting truthful advertising (see Exhibit 24.8). These efforts offer the public, competitors, and other interested parties a voluntary forum for negotiation without resorting to a formal legal or regulatory body for the adjudication of disagreements. One of the ways in which the business promotes better advertising is through various guidelines and codes of practice promoted by advertising agency groups and media associations as well as trade and professional associations. One of the leading advertising groups promoting truthful and ethical advertising is the American Advertising Federation (AAF). A primary

KLEPPNER VIEWPOINT 24.2

Dr. Peter Cressy
President/CEO of the Distilled Spirits Council

Corporate Social Responsibility in Advertising: A Road Well Paved by the Distilled Spirits Industry

In an era of corporate mistrust and a growing emphasis on social responsibility, the Distilled Spirits Council (DISCUS) has carved a path to good corporate citizenship through its *Code of Responsible Practices for Beverage Alcohol Advertising and Marketing*. Advertising for many products has come under increased scrutiny by public officials, regulators, and third-party advocacy groups. The distilled spirits industry, on the other hand, has been at the forefront of forging good advertising practices and has been repeatedly cited as a model for effective self-regulation of advertising.

For over 70 years, distilled spirits companies have abided by the DISCUS *Code*, a voluntary set of guidelines issued by the spirits industry trade association for the responsible content and placement of spirits advertising and marketing. These *Code* guidelines have been revised throughout the decades as social mores, the marketplace, and technology have changed.

Throughout its history, the core principle of the *Code* has been and remains to market beverage alcohol products to adults in a responsible and appropriate manner. As an industry, distillers are committed to adhering to a tough advertising and marketing code and holding ourselves to a standard higher than mandated by any law or regulation. Self-regulation is flexible, responsive, and particularly suitable in light of the First Amendment issues

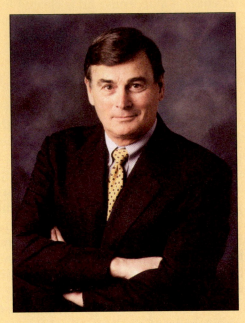

Dr. Peter Cressy

that otherwise would be raised by government regulation of advertising.

Unique among other industries, the spirits industry *Code* historically has provided for a Code Review Board, composed of senior member company representatives, which is charged with reviewing complaints about advertising and marketing materials. After receiving a complaint,

---

aim of the AAF is to foster truthful and fair advertising through local advertising clubs.

Despite the best efforts of federal regulatory agencies, the media, and individual advertisers, the opinion persists among a large group of consumers that advertising is either basically deceptive or does not provide sufficient information. Given the investment that companies are making in advertising, this perception is a major problem and one that all honest businesses need to address on a united front. As we will see in the next section, the advertising industry is making substantial investments in moving against deceptive advertising.

Better Business Bureaus

One of the best-known, aggressive, and successful organizations in the fight for honest and truthful advertising is the national network of Better Business Bureaus (BBBs) coordinated by the Council of Better Business Bureaus, Inc.

the Board determines whether the advertisement is consistent or inconsistent with the provisions of the *Code*. The Board relays its decision to the advertiser and, if a provision of the *Code* has been violated, urges that the advertisement be revised or withdrawn. For DISCUS member company advertisements, the time between receipt of a complaint and Code Review Board action often is a matter of days. There has been 100 percent compliance by DISCUS members with Board decisions and a high level of compliance by non-DISCUS members.

For decades the distilled spirits industry has effectively addressed complaints about spirits advertising, but until recently the decisions of the Code Review Board were not made public. As a consequence, the rigor of the Board's review process and company adherence to the Board's decisions were not widely recognized. To make the industry's review process more transparent and understandable to the public, in 2005 DISCUS began publishing semiannual public reports detailing complaints against specific spirits advertisements, decisions of the Code Review Board, and the responsive actions taken by each advertiser. By providing for a public report about complaint decisions, the operation of the distillers' advertising code also significantly differs from other industry codes. To the best of our knowledge, DISCUS is the first trade group representing American businesses to issue a public report regarding the proceedings of how an industry regulates itself according to its own internal code. This new transparency provision allows the public at large to better evaluate and appreciate the DISCUS *Code* review process, which the FTC—the lead federal agency with advertising oversight—has repeatedly pointed to as a model of self-regulation and a step above and beyond what others are doing.

Incorporating transparency into the DISCUS *Code* review process has had an immediate and positive impact. Our members continue to achieve full compliance, and we are experiencing a quicker response time and an increased compliance rate among nonmembers. We believe the *Semi-Annual Report* is an important element of our longstanding corporate responsibility efforts, and the distillers' transparent reporting system also has been recognized as a model for other industries by regulators and industry critics, and now is receiving acclaim by the business community.

In June 2006, the *Semi-Annual Report* was the recipient of the best "Business Ethics Communications" award by PR News Corporate Social Responsibility (CSR) Awards. The CSR Awards honor corporations and their partners that have implemented and executed highly successful CSR campaigns in the last 12 months. PR News calls the CSR Awards "the gold standard in corporate citizenship and communications worldwide." DISCUS also was named a finalist in the American Business Awards[SM] "Best Corporate Social Responsibility Program" category for our public reporting system.

Publishers and other media executives also have responded to the distillers' tough voluntary advertising standards. Under a new provision added to the distillers' *Code* in 2003, beverage alcohol advertising and marketing should be placed only in a medium where at least 70 percent of the audience is reasonably expected to be 21 years of age or older. Several trend-setting magazines have established subscription-only editions in response to the distillers' move to a 70 percent adult demographic, which ensure that spirits companies can reasonably expect to meet this standard.

We believe that these efforts have implications beyond the beverage alcohol industry. The distillers' advertising *Code*, with its transparent complaint review process, is a dynamic example of how an industry can effectively regulate itself, promote corporate social responsibility, and raise public confidence. Dr. Peter Cressy is the President/CEO of the Distilled Spirits Council. He is the former Chancellor of the University of Massachusetts Dartmouth and former President of the Massachusetts Maritime Academy. He is a retired Navy Rear Admiral. ■■■

(CBBB). The forerunners of the modern BBBs date to 1905, when various local advertising clubs formed a national association that today is known as the National Advertising Federation. In 1911, this association launched a campaign for truth in advertising coordinated by local vigilance committees. In 1916, these local committees adopted the name Better Business Bureaus, and they became autonomous in 1926. Today, there are approximately 120 local bureaus in the United States and Canada.

In many respects, the work of the CBBB mirrors that of the FTC—without the attending force of law. Some of the key areas of concern for the CBBB and its affiliates are: Internet shopping, warranties and guarantees, comparative price claims, testimonials, and credit fraud. The efforts of the organization are primarily educational with its two-volume *Do's and Don'ts in Advertising* providing the foundation for its efforts. The volumes offer advertisers advice covering most of the basic questions encountered by companies. The "Basic Principles" offers the following overview of the BBBs' philosophy of self-regulation:

Creative Code of the American Association of Advertising Agencies

ADOPTED APRIL 26, 1962

The members of the American Association of Advertising Agencies recognize:

1. That advertising bears a dual responsibility in the American economic system and way of life.

To the public it is a primary way of knowing about the goods and services that are the products of American free enterprise—goods and services that can be freely chosen to suit the desires and needs of the individual. The public is entitled to expect that advertising will be reliable in content and honest in presentation.

To the advertiser it is a primary way of persuading people to buy his goods or services, within the framework of a highly competitive economic system. He is entitled to regard advertising as a dynamic means of building his business and his profits.

2. That advertising enjoys a particularly intimate relationship to the American family.

It enters the home as an integral part of television and radio programs, to speak to the individual and often to the entire family. It shares the pages of favorite newspapers and magazines. It presents itself to travelers and to readers of the daily mails. In all these forms, it bears a special responsibility to respect the tastes and self-interest of the public.

3. That advertising is directed to sizable groups or to the public at large, which is made up of many interests and many tastes.

As is the case with all public enterprises, ranging from sports to education and even to religion, it is almost impossible to speak without finding someone in disagreement. Nonetheless, advertising people recognize their obligation to operate within the traditional American limitations: to serve the interests of the majority and to respect the rights of the minority.

Therefore we, the members of the American Association of Advertising Agencies, in addition to supporting and obeying the laws and legal regulations pertaining to advertising, undertake to extend and broaden the application of high ethical standards. Specifically, we will not knowingly produce advertising that contains:

    a. False or misleading statements or exaggerations, visual or verbal.

    b. Testimonials that do not reflect the real choice of a competent witness.

    c. Price claims that are misleading.

    d. Comparisons that unfairly disparage a competitive product or service.

    e. Claims insufficiently supported, or which distort the true meaning or practicable application of statements made by professional or scientific authority.

    f. Statements, suggestions, or pictures offensive to public decency.

We recognize that there are areas subject to honestly different interpretations and judgment. Taste is subjective and may even vary from time to time as well as from individual to individual. Frequency of seeing or hearing advertising messages will necessarily vary greatly from person to person.

However, we agree not to recommend to an advertiser the use of advertising that is in poor or questionable taste or is deliberately irritating through content, presentation, or excessive repetition.

Clear and willful violations of this Code shall be referred to the Board of Directors of the American Association of Advertising Agencies for appropriate action, including possible annulment of membership as provided in Article IV, Section 5, of the Constitution and By-Laws.

Conscientious adherence to the letter and the spirit of this Code will strengthen advertising and the free enterprise system of which it is a part.

- Primary responsibility for truthful and nondeceptive advertising rests with the advertiser. Advertisers should be prepared to substantiate any claims or offers made before publication or broadcast and, upon request, present such substantiation promptly to the advertising medium or the Better Business Bureau.

- Advertisements that are untrue, misleading, deceptive, fraudulent, falsely disparaging of competitors, or insincere offers to sell shall not be used.

- An advertisement as a whole may be misleading although every sentence separately considered is literally true. Misrepresentation may result not only from direct statements but also by omitting or obscuring a material fact.[69]

Although the BBBs have no legal authority, they are a major influence on truth and accuracy in advertising. The BBBs are able to exert both the force of public opinion and peer pressure to set up voluntary efforts to address examples of potentially misleading or deceptive advertising.

THE NARC SELF-REGULATION PROGRAM

The National Advertising Review Council (NARC) was founded in 1971, in response to the many different consumer movements pushing for more stringent government regulation of advertising and concerns among major advertisers that advertising honesty was not being given enough attention within the industry. The major advertising organizations—the American Advertising Federation, the American Association of Advertising Agencies, and the Association of National Advertisers—approached the CBBB and together formed the National Advertising Review Council (NARC). NARC's primary purpose was to "develop a structure which would effectively apply the persuasive capacities of peers to seek the voluntary elimination of national advertising which professionals would consider deceptive." Its objective was to sustain high standards of truth and accuracy in national advertising through voluntary self-regulation. At the outset, consumers and consumer advocates submitted a number of complaints concerning deceptive advertising. However, in a short time, advertisers became the major watchdog lodging the majority of complaints against their competitors—a situation that continues today. "The NARC works because it is tough enough to satisfy consumer advocates, business-minded enough to respect advertising's role in the marketing process and effective enough to keep the Federal Trade Commission off the industry's back."[70]

NARC established a number of units that are administered by the CBBB (see Exhibit 24.9). The primary investigative unit is the **National Advertising Division (NAD)** of the Council of Better Business Bureaus. The NAD is staffed by full-time lawyers who respond to complaints from competitors and consumers and to referrals from local BBBs. They also monitor national advertising. The National Advertising Review Board (NARB) provides an advertiser with a jury of peers if it chooses to appeal a NAD decision. In 1974, the Children's Advertising Review Unit (CARU) was established to review the special advertising concerns of advertising directed to children. We will discuss the CARU in detail later in this section. These units "review only national advertisements—those ads disseminated on a nationwide or broadly regional basis. . . . Product performance claims, superiority claims against competitive products and all kinds of scientific and technical claims in national advertising are the types of cases accepted by the NAD. NAD is *not* the appropriate forum to address concerns about the 'good taste' of ads, moral questions about products that are offered for sale or political or issue advertising."[71]

After a complaint is received, the NAD determines the issues, collects and evaluates data, and makes an initial decision on whether the claims are substantiated. If the NAD finds that substantiation is satisfactory, it announces that fact. If the NAD finds that the substantiation is not adequate, it will recommend that the advertiser modify or discontinue the offending claims. If the advertiser does not agree, it may appeal to the NARB. NAD decisions are released to the press and also are published in its monthly publication *NAD Case Reports*.

The NARB is composed of seventy members—forty representing advertisers, twenty representing advertising agencies, and ten from the public sector. Five members, in the same proportion, are assigned to hear an appeal. If the panel determines the NAD's decision is justified but the advertiser still refuses to correct the deceptive element, the NARB may refer the advertising to the appropriate

National Advertising Division (NAD)
The primary investigative unit of the NARC self-regulation program.

THE NATIONAL ADVERTISING REVIEW COUNCIL

The Council of Better Business Bureaus

Directors of the National Advertising Review Council

Administration and Funding

National Advertising Review Council

Advertising Self-Regulation Policy

National Advertising Division

National Advertising Review Board

Children's Advertising Review Unit

EXHIBIT 24.9

The NARC review process is established to ensure fairness and provide an objective examination of advertising.

Reprinted with permission of the Council of Better Business Bureaus, Inc., copyright 2003. Council of Better Business Bureaus, Inc., 4200 Wilson Blvd., Arlington, VA 22203. World Wide Web: http://www.bbb.org.

government agency. Underscoring the competitive nature of advertising claims, competitor challenges are by far the largest source of NAD cases. According to the NAD, there are six primary areas that provide most of the challenges brought to the organization:

1. Product testing
2. Consumer perception studies
3. Taste/sensory claims
4. Pricing
5. Testimonial/anecdotal evidences
6. Demonstrations

In a number of cases, complaints involve comparative advertising. For example, a challenge is often made when product testing or product demonstrations involve other brands' alleged deficiencies. In terms of complaints, the largest product category is health and health aids, followed by food and beverage. It is no coincidence that these are two of the most competitive product categories.

In our examination of the NAD/NARB process, we should understand that it cannot

- Order an advertiser to stop an ad
- Impose a fine
- Bar anyone from advertising
- Boycott an advertiser or a product

What it can do is bring to bear the judgment of an advertiser's peers that a company has produced advertising that is not truthful and is harmful to the industry, to the public, and to the offender. This opinion has great moral weight. It is reinforced by the knowledge that, if the results of an appeal to the NARB are not accepted, the whole matter will be referred to the appropriate government agency and at the same time will be released to the public. This step, unique in business self-regulation machinery, avoids any problem of violating antitrust laws, presents the entire matter to public view, and still leaves the advertiser subject to an FTC ruling on the advertising.

The Children's Advertising Unit of the NAD

Children's Advertising Review Unit (CARU)
The CARU functions much as the NAD to review complaints about advertising to children.

Both consumer groups and advertisers have long recognized that children's advertising is fundamentally different from commercial messages directed to adults. Because of the special circumstances involved with advertising to children, the NAD, in cooperation with the advertising community, founded the **Children's Advertising Review Unit (CARU)** in 1974. The CARU's work primarily deals with the following areas:

- Product presentations and claims
- Sales pressure
- Disclosures and disclaimers
- Comparative claims
- Endorsements and promotions by program or editorial characters
- Premiums, promotions, and sweepstakes
- Safety
- Interactive electronic media

During the last few years, two of the major areas of concern to children's advocates have been food advertising and the growing use of the Internet as a sales tool to reach children. Effective in April, 2000, the Children's Online Privacy Protection Act (COPPA) sought to protect the privacy of children under the age of 13 by requiring parental consent for the collection or use of any personal information by marketers. Among the several provisions of the act, it requires that advertisers include a privacy policy, parental notification of information collected concerning their children, and a requirement that information collected be confidential and secure. The FTC has the primary oversight for COPPA. FTC enforcement and advertisers' adherence to provisions of the act have been so satisfactory that CARU has not become involved as a key player in the enforcement process.

A second major area of concern, food advertising and its alleged contribution to childhood obesity, demonstrates many similarities with the battle over tobacco advertising in the 1990s. The importance of the topic can be seen in the 2005 issuance by CARU of a ninety-two-page white paper entitled "Guidance for Food Advertising Self-Regulation." The food industry is coming under blistering attacks by Congress, consumer advocates, medical and scientific groups and lawyers threatening legal action akin to that faced by tobacco companies in the past. It is in this environment that the CARU is attempting to mediate between the food industry and critics to develop advertising best practices acceptable to both groups.

Two of the most vocal detractors of food marketing are Senator Tom Harkin of Iowa and the Institute of Medicine (IOM), an associated organization of the National Academy of Science. Senator Harkin has been specifically critical of the CARU for not having done enough to put teeth in the self-regulatory process. In what was characterized by *Advertising Age* as potentially the "end of kids ads as we know them," the IOM report entitled, *Food Marketing to Children and Youth: Threat or Opportunity?* gained wide publicity and gave critics of food advertisers ammunition for future action. The report reviewed how marketing influences children and youth and provided comprehensive reviews of the scientific evidence on the influence of food marketing on diets and diet-related health of children and youth. The study was requested by Congress and sponsored by the U.S. Centers for Disease Control and Prevention (CDC). The researchers concluded that current food and beverage marketing practices put children's long-term health at risk. If America's children and youth are to develop eating habits that help them avoid early onset of diet-related chronic diseases, they have to reduce their intake of high-calorie, low-nutrient snacks, fast foods, and sweetened drinks, which make up a high proportion of the products marketed to them.[72]

Not only was the CARU criticized by healthy-eating advocates, but also by some within the food industry itself. CARU's board has come under criticism from those in the food industry that think some of the tougher self-regulatory stances have gone too far. As the CARU undertakes a review of its guidelines, it is ". . . expected to take food companies to task over the truthfulness and fairness of its claims and insure good advertising practices toward kids, and by doing so, help fend off increasingly vocal public ad political critics and show that the food business is capable of self-regulation."[73] A spokesperson for Kraft Foods, one of the major supporters of the CARU, commented that the new rules on children's food advertising were "regrettable."

In general, the CARU's mission is similar to that of the NAD except it considers the special circumstances of the younger audience reached by children-oriented advertising. As the current controversy surrounding food advertising demonstrates, questions concerning children's advertising have few easy answers. To the critics that think that no advertising should be directed to children, even the strictest advertising guidelines are unsatisfactory. However, given the economic support of the media through advertising, it is unlikely that any such ban will ever be invoked. It is imperative that all parties involved (media, advertisers, parents, special interest groups, and government) work to ensure that children's advertising is appropriate for the audience to which it is intended. With public opinion running against them, advertisers must be extremely cautious about the content of all advertising messages directed to children.

SUMMARY ❂

In this chapter, we have discussed the many restraints on the practice of advertising. These include legal, ethical, social, and economic considerations. It is obvious that legal and regulatory bodies are devoting increasing resources to review dishonest and misleading advertising. However, it is important to remember that the ethical and honest practice of advertising is rarely the result of threats of legislation or punishment. Rather, advertisers, their agencies, and the mainstream media know that attention to the ethical and social problems of content, presentation, and the acceptability of a host of product categories, claims, and advertising practices is good business as well as responsible corporate citizenship. Although legal restraints on advertising are an important part of the advertising environment, it is unusual for major advertisers to develop advertising strategy solely because of governmental regulations.

As we discussed in the beginning of this chapter, advertisers are adopting a much more sensitive perception of their audiences and customers than their counterparts of 25 years ago. The diversity of the marketplace, growing fragmentation of the media, and concerns with public policy issues such as the demand for consumer privacy are topics rarely considered by advertisers only a few years ago. Those advertisers who fail to take account of the current sensitivity of consumers toward social issues run the risk of inadvertently initiating major public relations problems for themselves.

We cannot be certain what the future of advertising holds in terms of social and cultural issues, but we do know that it will be a time of change and adaptation. The public interest will be an increasingly important part of the modern advertiser's agenda—much more important than formal legal restrictions. It is a given that the public will not tolerate untruthful, misleading, and deceptive advertising. But more than simply being truthful, contemporary advertising must incorporate the idea of social responsibility as routinely as it depends on a well thought out marketing plan. As part of this social responsibility, advertising will be used more extensively as a tool for change in society. Rather than confined to selling products and services, advertising will play a larger role in presenting ideas and opinions concerning a host of social issues.

Among major advertisers, there is no disagreement that advertising should be fair and truthful and follow both the letter and the spirit of the law. Advertisers are among the most aggressive groups in weeding out the charlatans who make it difficult for all advertisers by eroding public confidence. For the foreseeable future, it is clear that advertisers will have to contend with numerous, sometimes conflicting, and constantly changing advertising regulations.

REVIEW ✸

1. Compare and contrast the social and economic issues involved in the practice of advertising.
2. Discuss two arguments for and against advertising.
3. Discuss the difference between inadvertent and intended social roles of advertising.
4. What is the role of the Advertising Council in encouraging social advertising?
5. Why is substantiation considered the foundation of FTC enforcement?
6. What is the importance of cease and desist orders in FTC enforcement?
7. Briefly discuss the *Central Hudson Four-Part Test.*
8. What role does advertising puffery play in enforcing advertising regulations?
9. What are some of the pitfalls of comparison advertising from both a legal and practical perspective?
10. Discuss the role of the media clearance process and advertising self-regulation.
11. What is the primary role of the NARB, NARC, and the CARU in supporting advertising self-regulation?

GLOSSARY

A

account planner An outgrowth of British agency structure in which a planner initiates and reviews research and participates in the creative process. In some agencies, the planner is considered a spokesperson for the consumer.

advertising Advertising consists of paid notices from identified sponsors normally offered through communication media.

advertising clearance process The internal process of clearing ads for publication and broadcast, conducted primarily by ad agencies and clients.

Advertising Council A nonprofit network of agencies, media, and advertisers dedicated to promoting social programs through advertising.

advertising goals The communication objectives designed to accomplish certain tasks within the total marketing program.

advertorial The use of advertising to promote an idea rather than a product or service.

American Association of Advertising Agencies (AAAA, 4As) The national organization of advertising agencies.

amplitude modulation (AM) Method of transmitting electromagnetic signals by varying the amplitude (size) of the electromagnetic wave, in contrast to varying its frequency. Quality is not as good as frequency modulation but can be heard farther, especially at night.

animation Making inanimate objects appear alive and moving by setting them before an animation camera and filming one frame at a time.

appeal The motive to which an advertisement is directed; it is designed to stir a person toward a goal the advertiser has set.

Arbitron Inc. Syndicated radio ratings company.

audience fragmentation The segmenting of mass-media audiences into smaller groups because of diversity of media outlets.

Audit Bureau of Circulations (ABC) The organization sponsored by publishers, agencies, and advertisers for securing accurate circulation statements.

Average Quarter-Hour (AQH) Manner in which radio ratings are presented. Estimates (AQHE) include average number of people listening (AQHP), Rating (AQHR), and Share (AQHS) of audience. The Metro Survey Area (MSA) population can be used to determine Share.

B

barter Acquisition of broadcast time by an advertiser or an agency in exchange for operating capital or merchandise. No cash is involved.

barter syndication Station obtains a program at no charge. The program has presold national commercials, and time is available for local station spots.

behavioral research Market research that attempts to determine the underlying nature of purchase behavior.

bleed Printed matter that runs over the edges of an outdoor board or of a page, leaving no margin.

brand A name, term, sign, design, or a unifying combination of them, intended to identify and distinguish the product or service from competing products or services.

brand-development index (BDI) A method of allocating advertising budgets to those geographical areas that have the greatest sales potential.

brand equity The value of how such people as consumers, distributors, and salespeople think and feel about a brand relative to its competition over a period of time.

brand extension These are new product introductions under an existing brand to take advantage of existing brand equity.

brand name The written or spoken part of a trademark, in contrast to the pictorial mark; a trademark word.

business-to-business advertisers Advertisers that promote goods through trade and industrial journals that are used in the manufacturing, distributing, or marketing of goods to the public.

C

cable television Television signals that are carried to households by cable. Programs originate with cable operators through high antennas, satellite disks, or operator-initiated programming.

category manager A relatively new corporate position, this manager is responsible for all aspects of the brands in a specific product category for a company including research, manufacturing, sales, and advertising. Each product's advertising manager reports to the category manager. Example: Procter & Gamble's Tide and Cheer detergent advertising managers report to a single category manager.

caveat emptor Latin for "Let the buyer beware," represents the notion that there should be no government interference in the marketplace.

cease and desist orders If an advertiser refuses to sign a consent decree, the FTC may issue a cease and desist order that can carry a $10,000-per-day fine.

centralized exchange A system of trade and marketing through specialized intermediaries rather than direct exchange of goods between buyers and producers.

Children's Advertising Review Unit (CARU) The CARU functions much as the NAD to review complaints about advertising to children.

classified advertising Found in columns so labeled, published in sections of a newspaper or magazine that are set aside for certain classes of goods or services—for example, help wanted positions.

clearance The percentage of network affiliates that carry a particular network program.

closing date The date when all advertising material must be submitted to a publication.

clutter Refers to a proliferation of commercials in a particular medium. This reduces the impact of any single message.

coined word An original and arbitrary combination of syllables forming a word. Extensively used for trademarks, such as PoFolks, Mazola, Gro-Pup, Zerone. (Opposite of a dictionary word.)

comparative advertising It directly contrasts an advertiser's product with other named or identified products.

compensation The payment of clearance fees by a television network to local stations carrying its shows.

competitive stage The advertising stage a product reaches when its general usefulness is recognized but its superiority over similar brands has to be established in order to gain preference. See pioneering stage, retentive stage.

comprehensive A layout accurate in size, color, scheme, and other necessary details to show how a final advertisement will look; for presentation only, never for reproduction.

computer-generated imagery (CGI) Technology allowing computer operators to create multitudes of electronic effects for TV to squash, stretch, or squeeze objects much more quickly than earlier tools could. It can add layers of visuals simultaneously.

concept testing The target audience evaluation of (alternative) creative strategy. Testing attempts to separate good and bad ideas and provide insight into factors motivating acceptance or rejection.

799

conjoint analysis A research technique designed to determine what consumers perceive as a product's most important benefits.

consent decree Issued by the FTC. An advertiser signs the decree, stops the practice under investigation, but admits no guilt.

consumer advertising Directed to people who will use the product themselves, in contrast to trade advertising, industrial advertising, or professional advertising.

contest A promotion in which consumers compete for prizes and the winners are selected strictly on the basis of skill.

continuous tone An unscreened photographic picture or image, on paper or film, that contains all gradations of tonal values from white to black.

controlled circulation Magazines sent without cost to people responsible for making buying decisions. To get on such lists, people must state their positions in companies; to stay on it, they must request it annually. Also known as qualified-circulation publications.

convergence The blending of various facets of marketing functions and communication technology to create more efficient and expanded synergies.

cooperative (co-op) advertising Joint promotion of a national advertiser (manufacturer) and a local retail outlet on behalf of the manufacturer's product on sale in the retail store.

copy approach The method of opening the text of an advertisement. The chief forms are the factual approach, the imaginative approach, and the emotional approach.

copy testing Measuring the effectiveness of advertisements.

corrective advertising To counteract the past residual effect of previous deceptive advertising, the FTC may require the advertiser to devote future space and time to disclosure of previous deception. Began around the late 1960s.

cost per rating point (CPP) The cost per rating point is used to estimate the cost of television advertising on several shows.

cost per thousand (CPM) A method of comparing the cost for media of different circulations. Also, weighted or demographic cost per thousand calculates the CPM using only that portion of a medium's audience falling into a prime-prospect category.

Council of Better Business Bureaus National organization that coordinates a number of local and national initiatives to protect consumers.

coupon Most popular type of sales-promotion technique.

cross-media buy Several media or vehicles that are packaged to be sold to advertisers to gain a synergistic communication effect and efficiencies in purchasing time or space.

customer relationship marketing (CRM) A management concept that organizes a business according to the needs of the consumer.

D

direct premium A sales incentive given to customers at the time of purchase.

direct-response advertising Any form of advertising done in direct marketing. Uses all types of media: direct mail, television, magazines, newspapers, radio. Term replaces mail-order advertising. See direct marketing.

display Newspaper ads other than those text-only ads in the classified columns. Display ads are generally larger and can include color, photos or artwork to attract reader attention to the product.

distribution channel The various intermediaries, such as retailers, that control the flow of goods from manufacturers to consumers.

dot-coms A generic designation that refers to companies engaged in some type of online commerce.

E

eight-sheet poster Outdoor poster used in urban areas, about one-fourth the size of the standard thirty-sheet poster. Also called *junior poster*.

end-product advertising Building consumer demand by promoting ingredients in a product, for example, Teflon and Nutrasweet.

engagement The delivery of attentive consumers from a media vehicle to the advertising.

European Union (EU) The developing economic integration of Europe. Potentially a single market of some 380 million consumers in 2005.

exclusionary zones (outdoor) Industry code of conduct that prohibits the advertising within 500 feet of churches, schools, or hospitals of any products that cannot be used legally by children.

executional idea A rendering in words, symbols, shapes, forms, or any combination thereof of an abstract answer to a perceived desire or need.

experiential sampling A companies use of specialty vehicles to engage consumers and give them samples to enhance the contact experience.

F

family life cycle Concept that demonstrates changing purchasing behavior as a person or a family matures.

fast-close advertising Some magazines offer short-notice advertising deadlines, sometimes at a premium cost.

Federal Communications Commission (FCC) The federal authority empowered to license radio and television stations and to assign wavelengths to stations "in the public interest."

Federal Trade Commission (FTC) The agency of the federal government empowered to prevent unfair competition and to prevent fraudulent, misleading, or deceptive advertising in interstate commerce.

flat rate A uniform charge for space in a medium, without regard to the amount of space used or the frequency of insertion. When flat rates do not prevail, time discounts or quantity discounts are offered.

flighting Flight is the length of time a broadcaster's campaign runs. Can be days, weeks, or months—but does not refer to a year. A flighting schedule alternates periods of activity with periods of inactivity.

focus group A qualitative research interviewing method using in-depth interviews with a group rather than with an individual.

four-color process The process for reproducing color illustrations by a set of plates, one that prints all the yellows, another the blues, a third the reds, and the fourth the blacks (sequence variable). The plates are referred to as process plates.

free-standing inserts (FSIs) Preprinted inserts distributed to newspaper publishers, where they are inserted and delivered with the newspaper.

frequency modulation (FM) A radio transmission wave that transmits by the variation in the frequency of its wave rather than by its size (as in amplitude modulation [AM]). An FM wave is twenty times the width of an AM wave, which is the source of its fine tone. To transmit such a wave, it has to be placed high on the electromagnetic spectrum, far from AM waves with their interference and static, hence its outstanding tone.

frequency In media exposure, the number of times an individual or household is exposed to an advertising vehicle for a specific brand within a given period of time.

frequency In media exposure, the number of times an individual or household is exposed to a medium within a given period of time.

fulfillment firm Company that handles the couponing process including receiving, verification, and payment. It also handles contest and sweepstakes responses.

full-service agency An agency that handles planning, creation, production, and placement of advertising for advertising clients. May also handle sales promotion and other related services as needed by client.

G

global marketing Term that denotes the use of advertising and marketing strategies on an international basis.

gross rating points (GRPs) Each rating point represents 1 percent of the universe being measured for the market. In television, it is 1 percent of the households having television sets in that area.

H

HD Radio Offers terrestrial radio stations the ability to deliver additional programming on the same amount of bandwidth with higher-quality sound. It requires a special receiver.

Highway Beautification Act of 1965 Federal law that controls outdoor signs in noncommercial, nonindustrial areas.

hoarding First printed outdoor signs—the forerunner of modern outdoor advertising.

horizontal publication Business publications for people engaged in a single job function regardless of the industry: for example, *Purchasing Magazine*.

house mark A primary mark of a business concern, usually used with the trademark of its products. General Mills is a house mark; Betty Crocker is a trademark; DuPont is a house mark; Teflon II is a trademark.

I

idea advertising Advertising used to promote an idea or cause rather than to sell a product or service.

illuminated posters Seventy to eighty percent of all outdoor posters are illuminated for 24-hour exposure.

incentives Sales promotion directed at wholesalers, retailers, or a company's sales force.

industrial advertising Advertising addressed to manufacturers who buy machinery, equipment, raw materials, and the components needed to produce goods they sell.

infomercial Long-form television advertising that promotes products within the context of a program-length commercial.

in-house agency An arrangement whereby the advertiser handles the total agency function by buying individually, on a fee basis, the needed services (for example, creative, media services, and placement) under the direction of an assigned advertising director.

institutional advertising Advertising done by an organization speaking of its work views, and problems as a whole, to gain public goodwill and support rather than to sell a specific product. Sometimes called public-relations advertising.

integrated marketing communication (IMC) The joint planning, execution, and coordination of all areas of marketing communication.

interactive era Communication will increasingly be controlled by consumers who will determine when and where they can be reached with promotional messages.

interconnects A joint buying opportunity between two or more cable systems in the same market.

J

jingle A commercial or part of a commercial set to music, usually carrying the slogan or theme line of a campaign. May make a brand name and slogan more easily remembered.

L

layout A working drawing (may be computer developed) showing how an advertisement is to look. A printer's layout is a set of instructions accompanying a piece of copy showing how it is to be set up. There are also rough layouts, finished layouts, and mechanical layouts, representing various degrees of finish. The term *layout* is used also for the total design of an advertisement.

letterpress Printing from a relief, or raised, surface. The raised surface is inked and comes in direct contact with the paper, like a rubber stamp.

lettershop A firm that not only addresses the mailing envelope but also is mechanically equipped to insert material, seal and stamp envelopes, and deliver them to the post office according to mailing requirements.

lifestyle segmentation Identifying consumers by combining several demographics and lifestyles.

list broker In direct-mail advertising, an agent who rents the prospect lists of one advertiser to another advertiser. The broker receives a commission from the seller for this service.

list manager Promotes client's lists to potential renters and buyers.

logotype, or logo A trademark or trade name embodied in the form of a distinctive lettering or design. Famous example: Coca-Cola.

M

magazine networks Groups of magazines that can be purchased together using one insertion order and paying a single invoice.

make-goods When a medium falls short of some audience guarantee, advertisers are provided concessions in the form of make-goods. Most commonly used in television and magazines.

market A group of people who can be identified by some common characteristic, interest, or problem; use a certain product to advantage; afford to buy it; and be reached through some medium.

marketing communication The communication components of marketing, which include public relations, advertising, personal selling, and sales promotion.

marketing concept A management orientation that views the needs of consumers as primary to the success of a firm.

marketing goals The overall objectives that a company wishes to accomplish through its marketing program.

marketing mix Combination of marketing functions, including advertising, used to sell a product.

market profile A demographic and psychographic description of the people or the households of a product's market. It may also include economic and retailing information about a territory.

market segmentation The division of an entire market of consumers into groups whose similarity makes them a market for products serving their special needs.

marketing translation The process of adapting a general marketing plan to multinational environments.

mass communication era From the 1700s to the early decades of the last century, advertisers were able to reach large segments of the population through the mass media.

mass production A manufacturing technique utilizing specialization and interchangeable parts to achieve production efficiencies.

MatchPrint A high-quality color proof used for approvals prior to printing. Similar to a Signature print.

media buyers Execute and monitor the media schedule developed by media planners.

media plan The complete analysis and execution of the media component of a campaign.

media planner Responsible for the overall strategy of the media plan.

media schedule The detailed plan or calendar showing when advertisements and commercials will be distributed and in what media vehicles they will appear.

merge/purge A system used to eliminate duplication by direct-response advertisers who use different mailing lists for the same mailing. Mailing lists are sent to a central merge/purge office that electronically picks out duplicate names. Saves mailing costs, especially important to firms that send out a million pieces in one mailing. Also avoids damage to the goodwill of the public.

morphing An electronic technique that allows you to transform one object into another object.

N

National Advertising Division (NAD) The primary investigative unit of the NARC self-regulation program.

national advertising Advertising by a marketer of a trademarked product or service sold through different outlets, in contrast to local advertising.

networks Interconnecting stations for the simultaneous transmission of television or radio broadcasts.

Newspaper Association of America (NAA) The marketing and trade organization for the newspaper industry.

niche marketing A combination of product and target market strategy. It is a flanking strategy that focuses on niches or comparatively narrow windows of opportunity within a broad product market or industry. Its guiding principle is to pit your strength against their weakness.

nonwired networks Groups of radio and television stations whose advertising is sold simultaneously by station representatives.

North American Free Trade Agreement (NAFTA) A treaty designed to eliminate trade barriers among the United States, Mexico, and Canada.

O

off-network syndication Syndicated programs that have previously been aired by a major network.

offset lithography Lithography is a printing process by which originally an image was formed on special stone by a greasy material, the design then being transferred to the printing paper. Today, the more frequently used process is offset lithography, in which a thin and flexible metal sheet replaces the stone. In this process, the design is "offset" from the metal sheet to a rubber blanket, which then transfers the image to the printing paper.

open rate In print, the highest advertising rate at which all discounts are placed.

opticals Visual effects that are put on a TV film in a laboratory, in contrast to those that are included as part of the original photography.

opt-in A form of permission marketing in which online customers are sent messages only after they have established a relationship with a company. Only consumers who have granted permission are contacted.

opt-outs Procedures that recipients use to notify advertisers that they no longer wish to receive advertising messages. A term usually associated with online promotions.

Outdoor Advertising Association of America (OAAA) Primary trade and lobbying organization for the outdoor industry.

outside producer The production company person who is hired by the agency to create the commercial according to agency specifications.

P

partial runs When magazines offer less than their entire circulation to advertisers. Partial runs include demographic, geographic, and split-run editions.

penny press Forerunner of the mass newspaper in the United States that first appeared in the 1830s.

People Meter Device that measures television set usage by individuals rather than by households.

per inquiry (PI) Advertising time or space for which medium is paid on a per-response-received basis.

pica The unit for measuring width in printing. There are 6 picas to an inch. A page of type 24 picas wide is 4 inches wide.

pioneering stage The advertising stage of a product in which the need for such a product is not recognized and must be established or in which the need has been established but the success of a commodity in filling that need has to be established. See competitive stage, retentive stage.

pixel The smallest element of a computer image that can be separately addressed. It is an individual picture element.

plant In outdoor advertising, the local company that arranges to lease, erect, and maintain the outdoor sign and to sell the advertising space on it.

point (pt) The unit of measurement of type, about 1/72 inch in depth. Type is specified by its point size, as 8 pt., 12 pt., 24 pt., 48 pt. The unit for measuring thickness of paper, 0.001 inch.

point-of-purchase Displays prepared by the manufacturer for use where the product is sold.

positioning Segmenting a market by creating a product to meet the needs of a select group or by using a distinctive advertising appeal to meet the needs of a specialized group, without making changes in the physical product.

Potential Rating Index by ZIP Market (PRIZM) A method of audience segmentation developed by Claritas Inc.

premarketing era The period from prehistoric times to the eighteenth century. During this time, buyers and sellers communicated in very primitive ways.

premium An item other than the product itself given to purchasers of a product as an inducement to buy. Can be free with a purchase (for example, on the package, in the package, or the container itself) or available upon proof of purchase and a payment (self-liquidating premium).

Printers' Ink Model Statute (1911) The Act directed at fraudulent advertising, prepared and sponsored by *Printers' Ink*, which was the pioneer advertising magazine.

product differentiation Unique product attributes that set off one brand from another.

product life cycle The process of a brand moving from introductions to maturity and, eventually, to either adaptation or demise.

product manager In package goods, the person responsible for the profitability of a product (brand) or product line, including advertising decisions. Also called a brand manager.

product-user segmentation Identifying consumers by the amount of product usage.

professional advertising Advertising directed at those in professions such as medicine, law, or architecture who are in a position to recommend the use of a particular product or service to their clients.

psychographics A description of a market based on factors such as attitudes, opinions, interests, perceptions, and lifestyles of consumers comprising that market.

public relations Communication with various internal and external publics to create an image for a product or corporation.

puffery Advertiser's opinion of a product that is considered a legitimate expression of biased opinion.

Pure Food and Drug Act Passed in 1906 by legislation, it was one of the earliest attempts by the federal government to protect consumers.

Q

qualitative research This involves finding out what people say they think or feel. It is usually exploratory or diagnostic in nature.

R

Radio Advertising Bureau (RAB) Association to promote the use of radio as an advertising medium.

Radio's All-Dimension Audience Research (RADAR) Service of Statistical Research, Inc., that is the primary source of network radio ratings.

rate base The circulation level on which advertising rates are based.

rating point The percentage of television households in a market a television station reaches with a program. The percentage varies with the time of day. A station may have a 10 rating between 6:00 and 6:30 p.m. and a 20 rating between 9:00 and 9:30 p.m.

rebate The amount owed to an advertiser by a medium when the advertiser qualifies for a higher space discount.

relationship marketing A strategy that develops marketing plans from a consumer perspective.

representative (rep) An individual or organization representing a medium selling time or space outside the city or origin.

research era In recent years, advertisers increasingly have been able to identify narrowly defined audience segments through sophisticated research methods.

response lists Prospects who have previously responded to direct-mail offers.

retail advertising Advertising by a merchant who sells directly to the consumer.

retentive stage The third advertising stage of a product, reached when its general usefulness is widely known, its individual qualities are thoroughly appreciated, and it is satisfied to retain its patronage merely on the strength of its past reputation. See pioneering stage, competitive stage.

return-on-investment (ROI) One measure of the efficiency of a company is the rate of return (profits) achieved by a certain level of investment on various business functions including advertising.

ride-alongs Direct mail pieces that are sent with other mailings, such as bills.

Robinson-Patman Act A federal law, enforced by the FTC. Requires a manufacturer to give proportionate discounts and advertising allowances to all competing dealers in a market. Purpose: To protect smaller merchants from unfair competition of larger buyers.

rotary bulletin (outdoor) Movable painted bulletins that are moved from one fixed location to another in the market at regular intervals. The locations are viewed and approved in advance by the advertiser.

rotogravure The method of printing in which the impression is produced by chemically etched cylinders and run on a rotary press; useful in long runs of pictorial effects.

S

sales promotion (1) Sales activities that supplement both personal selling and marketing, coordinate the two, and help to make them effective. For example, displays are sales promotions. (2) More loosely, the combination of personal selling, advertising, and all supplementary selling activities.

same-day coupons Coupons that are designed to be used almost instantly, or same day.

sampling The method of introducing and promoting merchandise by distributing a miniature or full-size trial package of the product free or at a reduced price.

satellite radio Available by subscription and contains few if any commercials. It requires a special receiver but offers near-CD-quality sound.

scatter plan The use of announcements, over a variety of network programs and stations, to reach as many people as possible in a market.

screen printing A simple printing process that uses a stencil. It is economical but is limited in reproduction quality.

selective binding Binding different material directed to various reader segments in a single issue of a magazine.

self-liquidating premium A premium offered to consumers for a fee that covers its cost plus handling.

service advertising Advertising that promotes a service rather than a product.

service mark A word or name used in the sale of services, to identify the services of a firm and distinguish them from those of others, for example, Hertz Drive Yourself Service, Weight Watchers Diet Course. Comparable to trademarks for products.

share of audience The percentage of households using television tuned to a particular program.

short rate The balance advertisers have to pay if they estimated that they would run more advertisements in a year than they did and entered a contract to pay at a favorable rate. The short rate is figured at the end of the year or sooner if advertisers fall behind schedule. It is calculated at a higher rate for the fewer insertions.

Simmons Market Research Bureau (SMRB) and Mediamark Research, Inc. (MRI) Two competing firms that provide audience data for several media. Best known for magazine research.

siquis Handwritten posters in sixteenth- and seventeenth-century England—forerunners of modern advertising.

situation analysis The part of the advertising plan that answers the questions: Where are we today and how did we get here? It deals with the past and present.

slotting fees Payments to retailers by manufacturers to gain shelf space.

spam Online advertising messages that are usually unsolicited by the recipient.

specialty advertising A gift given to a consumer to encourage a purchase.

spot radio Buying radio time on local stations on a market-by-market basis by national advertisers.

spot television Purchasing of time from a local station, in contrast to purchasing from a network.

Standard Advertising Unit (SAU) Allows national advertisers to purchase newspaper advertising in standard units from one paper to another.

Standard Rate and Data Service (SRDS) *SRDS* publishes a number of directories giving media and production information.

storyboard Series of drawings used to present a proposed commercial. Consists of illustrations of key action (video), accompanied by the audio part. Used for getting advertiser approval and as a production guide.

stripping Scheduling a syndicated program on a 5-day-per-week basis.

substantiation The key to FTC enforcement is that advertisers must be able to prove the claims made in their advertising.

sweeps weeks During these periods, ratings are taken for all television markets.

sweepstakes A promotion in which prize winners are determined on the basis of chance alone. Not legal if purchaser must risk money to enter.

T

target audience That group that composes the present and potential prospects for a product or service.

target marketing Identifying and communicating with groups of prime prospects.

theater of the mind In radio, a writer paints pictures in the mind of the listener through the use of sound.

time-shift viewing Recording programs on a VCR for viewing at a later time.

total market coverage (TMC) Newspapers augment their circulation with direct mail or shoppers to deliver all households in a market.

total survey area The maximum coverage of a radio or television station's signal.

trade advertising Advertising directed to the wholesale or retail merchants or sales agencies through whom the product is sold.

trade name A name that applies to a business as a whole, not to an individual product.

trade paper A business publication directed to those who buy products for resale (wholesalers, jobbers, retailers).

trademark Any device or word that identifies the origin of a product, telling who made it or who sold it. Not to be confused with a trade name.

Traffic Audit Bureau for Media Measurement (TAB) An organization designed to investigate how many people pass and may see a given outdoor sign, to establish a method of evaluating traffic measuring a market.

traffic-building premium A sales incentive to encourage customers to come to a store where a sale can be closed.

TVQ A service of Marketing Evaluations that measures the popularity (opinion of audience rather than size of audience) of shows and personalities.

typography The art of using type effectively.

U

up-front buying Purchase of network television time by national advertisers during the first offering by networks. The most expensive network advertising.

V

value gap The perceived difference between the price of a product and the value ascribed to it by consumers.

value-added opportunities Extra things a medium will do for or provide to an advertiser that add value to the purchase of time or space in the medium.

Values and Lifestyle System (VALS) Developed by SRI International to cluster consumers according to several variables in order to predict consumer behavior.

vendor program Special form of co-op advertising in which a retailer designs the program and approaches advertisers for support.

vertical publication Business publications dealing with the problems of a specific industry: for example, *Chain Store Age*, *National Petroleum News*, *Textile World*.

W

War Advertising Council Founded in 1942 to promote World War II mobilization, it later evolved into the Advertising Council.

Wheeler-Lea Amendments Broadened the scope of the FTC to include consumer advertising.

Y

yield management A product pricing strategy to control supply and demand.

Z

zoning Newspaper practice of offering advertisers partial coverage of a market, often accomplished with weekly inserts distributed to certain sections of that market.

ENDNOTES

Chapter 1

p. 3   Courtesy of Shutterstock

p. 4   Courtesy of John W. Hartman Center for Sales, Advertising & Marketing History; Duke University. http://library.duke.edu/specialcollections/hartman/index.html

1. J. Robert Moskin, *The Case for Advertising* (New York: American Association of Advertising Agencies, 1973), 7.
2. Roland Marchand, *Advertising the American Dream* (Berkeley: University of California Press, 1985), 76.
3. Kris Oser, "Package goods' online spending to jump $80M," *Advertising Age*, 30 January 2006, 26.
4. Randall Rothenberg, "The advertising century," *Advertising Age: Special Issue*, 1999, 12.
5. George Burton Hotchkiss, *An Outline of Advertising* (New York: Macmillan, 1957), 10.
6. James Playsted Wood, *Magazines in the United States* (New York: The Ronald Press, 1949), 99.
7. "The Industrial Revolution," www.4.ncsu.edu, 23 August 2005.
8. "An opportunity for publishers," *Advertising Age*, 12 September 2005, 22.
9. John McDonough, "From a birth in lower Manhattan to an unmatched global reach," *Advertising Age*, 18 March 2002, C8.
10. Frank Deford, *The Old Ball Game* (New York: Atlantic Monthly Press, 2005), 91, 95.
11. Cynthia Crossen, "Fraudulent claims led U.S. to take on drug makers in 1900s," *Wall Street Journal*, 6 October 2005, B1.
12. James Harvey Young, "The story of the laws behind the labels," www.cfsan.fda.gov, 3–4.
13. From the Federal Trade Commission Mission Statement.
14. Ralph M. Hower, *The History of an Advertising Agency* (Cambridge, MA: Harvard University Press, 1949), 180.
15. Edward Robinson, "Businessman of the century," *Fortune*, 6 September 1999, 227.
16. "Radio captivates a nation," *Advertising Age*, 28 March 2005, 34.
17. Louis Vloedbeld, "The rise of the Bakelite and Catalin radio in the U.S. during the 1930s," www.2.let.uu.nl, 5 January 2006.
18. Lydia Boyd, "Brief history of the radio industry," John W. Hartman Center, Duke University, www.scriptorium.lib.duke.edu/radio, 2.
19. "Brief history of World War Two advertising campaigns: Conservation," John W. Hartman Center for Sales, Advertising and Marketing History, Duke University Library, http://scriptorium.l.b.duke.edu/adaccess/.
20. John McDonough, "Ad Council at 60—Facing a crossroads," *Advertising Age*, 29 April 2002, C–4.
21. Herbert Zeltner, "Proliferation, localization, specialization mark media trends in past fifty years," *Advertising Age*, 30 April 1980, 148.
22. "TV turns on America," *Advertising Age*, 28 March 2005, 44.
23. This section is adapted from Cait Murphy, "Introduction: Wal-Mart rules," *Fortune*, 15 April 2002, www.fortune.com.
24. Cait Murphy, "Introduction: Wal-Mart rules," www.fortune.com, 15 April 2002.
25. Alice Z. Cuneo, "Marketers get serious about the 'third screen'," *Advertising Age*, 11 July 2005, 6.
26. "Madison & Vine and ROI," *Advertising Age*, 28 March 2005, 6 2.
27. Bob Garfield, "The chaos scenario," *Advertising Age*, 4 April 2005, 1.

Chapter 2

p. 36   Jumbo

1. Brain Steinberg and Suzanne Vranica, "The ad world's message for 2005: Stealth," *Wall Street Journal*, 30 December 2004, B1.
2. Brain Steinberg, "TV on-demand may make ads more targeted," *Wall Street Journal*, 9 November 2005, B1.
3. Noreen O'Leary, "They want the world, and they want it now," *Adweek.com*, 20 December 2005.
4. Kevin Maney, "A very different future is calling—on billions of cell phones," *USA Today*, 27 July 2005, 3B.
5. Adapted from David W. Schropher, *What Every Account Executive Should Know About a Marketing Plan* (New York: American Association of Advertising Agencies, 1990).
6. Rance Crane, "Emirates' lead agency: A network of partners," *Advertising Age*, 3 April 2006, 14.
7. Mathew Creamer, "Engaged: Ad groups take on ROI," *Advertising Age*, 25 July 2005, 4.
8. Abbey Klaassen, "Is Court TV guarantee birth of new ROI trend?" *Advertising Age*, 13 June 2005, 46.
9. Jack Neff, "ROI: The marketer's obsession," *Advertising Age*, 20 June 2005, S-1.
10. A term coined in the early 1930s by Professor Neil H. Borden of the Harvard Business School to include in the marketing process such factors as distribution, advertising, personal selling, and pricing.
11. Rich Thomaselli, "Selling drugs: Glaxo's crafty plan," *Advertising Age*, 20 February 2006, 1.
12. Jonah Bloom, "Agencies that attempt to reinvent via half measures are set up to fail," *Advertising Age*, 27 February 2006, 32.
13. Scott Davis, "Fixing brand bloat: Put focus on consumer-centric portfolio strategy," *Point*, July 2005, 5.
14. Jim Lentz, "Marketing isn't one-size-fits all," *Advertising Age*, 21 February 2005, 22.
15. Matthew Creamer, "Ogilvy looks to the power of one," *Advertising Age*, 31 October 2005, 8.
16. Rance Crain, "Marketers look at new ideas, and PR becomes the closer," *Advertising Age*, 29 July 2002, 15.
17. "The times of our lives: Temporalities of social institutions," www.trinity.edu, 17 January 2006.
18. James W. Carey, "Advertising: An institutional approach," in C. H. Sandage and Vernon Fryburger, *The Role of Advertising* (Homewood, IL: Richard D. Irwin, 1960), 4.
19. David Futrelle, "Are your kids normal about money?" *Money*, December 2005, 55.
20. Susan Linn, "Marketing blitz out of control," *Atlanta Journal-Constitution*, 28 February 2005, A9.
21. "Ford realizes customer is job 1," *Advertising Age*, 30 January 2006, 12.
22. Kenneth E. Clow and Donald Baack, *Integrated Advertising, Promotion, and Marketing Communication* (Upper Saddle River, NJ: Prentice Hall, 2004), 80.
23. Michael R. Solomon, *Consumer Behavior* (Upper Saddle River, NJ: Prentice Hall, 2004), 230.
24. Geoffrey A. Fowler, "Buying spree by China firms is a bet on value of U.S. brands," *Wall Street Journal*, 23 June 2005, B1.
25. Scott Leith, "New sodas flood market," *Atlanta Journal-Constitution*, 6 September 2002, F-1.
26. Viewpoint, "No shame in KFC's real name," *Advertising Age*, 2 May 2005, 26.

27. Rich Thomaselli, "Nike finds a way to go to Wal-Mart," *Advertising Age*, 3 March 2005, 1.
28. Harper W. Boyd Jr., Orville C. Walker Jr., John W. Mullins, and Jean-Claude Larreche, *Marketing Management* (New York: McGraw-Hill/Irwin, 2002), 267.
29. Mya Frazier, "Big Lots makes big money as land of marketers' misfit ploys," *Advertising Age*, 30 May 2005, 49.
30. Clayton M. Christensen, Scott Cook, and Taddy Hall, "It's the purpose brand, Stupid," *Wall Street Journal*, 29 November 2005, B2.
31. William M. Bulkeley, "Kodak sharpens digital focus on its best customers: Women," *Wall Street Journal*, 16 July 2005, 1A.
32. Jessica E. Vascellaro, "The times they are a-changin'," *Wall Street Journal*, 18 January 2006, D1.
33. "Listening to customers in the electronic age," *Fortune*, 1 May 2000, 318.
34. Steven Gray, "Will Starbucks's embrace of drive-through service undercut its hipster image?" *Wall Street Journal*, 6 January 2006, A9.
35. Gina Chon, "Mercedes seeks to recapture luxury rankings," *Wall Street Journal*, 30 January 2006, B4.
36. "Question of the day," *Wall Street Journal*, 10 January 2006, D6.
37. David J. Pike, "Product by design," *American Demographics*, February 2001, 38.
38. Jack Neff, "P&G kisses up to the boss: Consumers," *Advertising Age*, 2 May 2005, 18.
39. Mya Frazier, "CMO takes center stage in JCPenney cultural, strategic shift," *Advertising Age*, 25 April 2005, 14.
40. Ann Zimmerman, "Wal-Mart sets out to prove it's in vogue," *Wall Street Journal*, 25 August 2005, B1.
41. Jeffrey McCracken and Joseph B. White, "Ford will shed 28% of workers in North America," *Wall Street Journal*, 24 January 2006, 1A.
42. Lee Hawkins Jr., "GM plan to take toll on sales volume, personnel," *Wall Street Journal*, 28 March 2006, A3.
43. Sarah Ellison, "Colgate's fight for market share will likely erode profit," *Wall Street Journal*, 13 December 2004, C1.
44. Jack Neff, "Why some marketers turn away customers," *Advertising Age*, 14 February 2005, 1.
45. Beth Snyder Bulik, "Cool hunting goes corporate," *Advertising Age*, 1 August 2005, 3.
46. Aaron O. Patrick, "Making P&G's skin products manly," *Wall Street Journal*," 5 August 2005, B4.
47. Gina Chon, "Fuel economy has returned as a marketing tool," *Wall Street Journal*, 26 September 2005, B4.
48. Jean Halliday, "Save your energy: Marketers tout conservation," *Advertising Age*, 10 October 2005, 3.
49. Stephanie Thompson, "Nestle, Hershey figure sticks will be big sellers," *Advertising Age*, 3 October 2005, 3.
50. Sarah Ellison, "Life on the go means eating on the run, and a lot of spilling," *Wall Street Journal*, 7 June 2005, 1A.
51. Kris Oser, "Expecting? Buy those Huggies now," *Advertising Age*, 16 May 2005, 8.
52. Ernest Sander, "Pizza-delivery teams are training hard for Sunday's game," *Wall Street Journal*, 31 January 2006, 1A.
53. Bernard Ryan Jr., *It Works!* (New York: American Association of Advertising Agencies, 1991), 19.
54. Jean Halliday, "Volvo touts models' safety—and style," *Advertising Age*, 5 September 2005, 8.
55. "Five Barnburners: Febreze," *Advertising Age*, 12 December 2005, S-2.
56. Alice Z. Cuneo, "RAZR," *Advertising Age*, 7 November 2005, S-6.
57. "INSEAD profs: If you can't beat 'em, change the rules of engagement," *Point*, February 2005, 2.
58. Jack Neff, "Moving to margins in a new marketing age," *Advertising Age*, 24 July 2006, 1.
59. Rita Gunther McGrath and Ian C. MacMillan, "When in doubt simplify," *Point*, April 2005, 7.
60. Joyce M. Rosenberg, "Costs, competition help decide prices," *Atlanta Journal-Constitution*, 22 February 2005, C3.
61. Mya Frazier, "Sales may go out like last year's winter coat," *Advertising Age*, 25 April 2005, 16.
62. James B. Arndorfer and Rich Thomaselli, "United to tap draft for part of $60M direct biz," *Advertising Age*, 9 January 2006, 4.
63. Stephanie Thompson, "In-crowd: Paris Hilton, Lucky the Leprechaun," *Advertising Age*, 20 February 2006, 8.
64. Jeremy Mullman, "Blue Moon bets big on word-of-mouth," *Advertising Age*, 20 March 2006, 8.
65. Stephnie Thompson, "Frito-Lay defends its snack turf against all comers, salty or sweet," *Advertising Age*, 16 May 2005, 16.
66. Rebecca Weeks, "Buying consumers search for auto research," www.imediaconnection.com, 26 January 2006.
67. Susan Kuchinskas, "Saw it online, paid for it off," www.ecomerce-guide.com, 21 October 2005.
68. "Women's use of Internet affects purchasing decisions," www.microsoft.com/presspass/pass, 26 January 2006.
69. James B. Arndorfer, "Depending on direct: Discipline grows to $161B," *Advertising Age*, 24 October 2005, 6.
70. Michael R. Solomon, *Consumer Behavior* (Upper Saddle River, NJ: Prentice Hall, 2004), 403.

Chapter 3

p. 83   Courtesy of Shutterstock
p. 84   The TABASCO® marks, bottle and label designs are registered trademarks and servicemarks exclusively of McIlhenny Company, Aery Island, LA 70513. www.TABASCO.com
1. Cheryl Giovannoni, "Superbrands," www.superbrands.org/uk, 24 July 2006.
2. Robert Berner, "P&G. New and improved," *BusinessWeek*, 7 July 2003, 52–63.
3. Bruce Tait, "A brand new idea," *Brand Marketing*, February 2002, 23.
4. Steven Rosenbush, "Verizon's gutsy bet," *BusinessWeek*, 4 August 2003, 53.
5. Bruce Tait, "A brand new idea," *Brand Marketing*, February 2002, 23.
6. Bob Garfield, "Zune ads are infectious, but won't affect brand's success," *Advertising Age*, 26 November 2006, 52.
7. Steven Gray, "How Sara Lee spun white, grain into gold," *Wall Street Journal*, 4 April 2006, B1.
8. "Royal Crown plotting a comeback with new owners' financial support," *Atlanta Journal-Constitution*, 6 March 1994, C8.
9. Stephanie Thompson, "Kellogg positions Special K as megabrand," *Advertising Age*, 7 November 2006.
10. Patricia Callahan, "Freeze-dried berries heat up cereal dual," *Wall Street Journal*, 15 May 2003, B2.
11. Stephanie Thompson, "EZ being green: Kids line is latest Heinz innovation," *Advertising Age*, 10 July 2000, 3.
12. Charlotte Moore, "Glowing reports about the health benefits of inexpensive aspirin are still emerging," *Atlanta Journal-Constitution*, 13 May 2003, E1.
13. Antonio Marraza, "The very tangible value of the brand," www.landor.com, 2000.
14. David Martin, *Romancing the Brand* (New York: Amacon, 1989), xiv.
15. Norman Berry, "Revitalizing brands," *Viewpoint*, July–August 1987, 18.
16. Daniel Gross, "Birth of a salesman," *Fortune*, 8 August 2005, 40–59.
17. Howard, Merrell & Partners, "Introduction," 2000.
18. J. Walker Smith and Ann Clurman, *Rocking the Ages* (New York: Harper Business, 1997), 276–286.
19. Diane Crispell and Kathleen Brandenburg, "What's in a brand?" *American Demographics*, May 1993, 26–28.
20. Charlie Wrench, "Brand integration: A tough nut to crack," www.landor.com, May 2003.
21. Allen P. Adamson, *BrandSimple* (New York: Palgrave Macmillan, 2006), 10–12.
22. Alan M. Webber, "What great brands do," *Fast Company*, August–September 1997, 96–100.

Chapter 4

p. 118   Used with permission from McDonald's Corporation

1. Rex Briggs and Greg Stuart, *What Sticks* (Chicago: Kaplan, 2006), 218–219.
2. Joe Marconi, "Targets big enough to miss," *American Demographics*, October 1996, 51–52.
3. John McManus, "Street wiser," *American Demographics*, July/August 2003, 32–35.
4. Alison Stein Wellner, "Generational divide," *American Demographics*, October 2000, 56.
5. Allison Stein Wellner, "The next 25 years," *American Demographics*, April 2003, 24–31.
6. Christine Bunish, "Multicultural guide," *Advertising Age*, 3 November 2003, M1.
7. William H. Frey, "Revival," *American Demographics*, October 2003, 26–31.
8. Christine Bunish, "Multicultural guide," *Advertising Age*, 3 November 2003, M1.
9. Speech by Carl Kravetz, at Association of National Advertisers Multicultural Marketing Conference, November 13, 2006, at Fairmont Miramar Hotel, Santa Monica, CA.
10. Laurel Wentz, "New data repaints demographic picture of U.S. Hispanics," *Advertising Age*, http://adage.com/article_id=110568, 14 November 2006.
11. Chriistine Bunish, "Multicultural guide," *Advertising Age*, 3 November 2003, M1
12. "Disney's Davila: Multicultural 'not a fad,'" *Advertising Age*, 3 November 2003, M3.
13. Marcia Mogelonsky, "America's hottest markets," *American Demographics*, January 1996, 20–27.
14. Michelle Conlin, "The new gender gap," *BusinessWeek*, 26 May 2003, 74–80.
15. Tiffany Meyers, "She-Noms," *Advertising Age*, 30 October 2006, S-1-S-8.
16. James Morrow, "A place for one," *American Demographics*, November 2003, 24–29.
17. Cheryl Wetzstein, "More homes in U.S. go solo," *Washington Times*, http://washtimes.com/functions/print.php?Story, ID=20050817-123759-7286r, 17 August 2005.
18. Alison Stein Wellner, "Generational divide," *American Demographics*, October 2000, 52–58.
19. Edna Gundersen, "Where will teens taste land next?" USA Today, 22 September 2000, E1-E2.
20. Sholnn Freeman and Norihiko Shirouzu, "Toyota's Gen Y Gamble," *Wall Street Journal*, 30 July 2003, B1.
21. Gina Piccalo, "Girls just want to be plugged in-to everything," *Los Angeles Times*, www.latimes.com/business/la-et-polltween11aug11,1,1040639.story?coll=la-headlines-business, 11 August 2006.
22. Sholnn Freeman and Norihiko Shirouzu, "Toyota's Gen Y gamble," *Wall Street Journal*, 30 July 2003, B1.
23. David F. D'Alessandro, *Brand Warfare* (New York: McGraw-Hill, 2000), 38–39.
24. J. Walker Smith and Ann Clurman, *Rocking the Ages* (New York: HarperCollins, 1997), 16.
25. Philip Kotler, *Marketing Management*, 8th ed. (Upper Saddle River, NJ: Prentice Hall, 1994), 18–21.
26. Frederick E. Webster Jr., "Executing the new marketing concept," *Marketing Management*, 3, no. 1, 9–16.
27. Kevin Maney, "Tomorrow's super bar codes create today's nervous Nellies," *USA Today*, 8 October 2003, 3B.
28. Robert C. Blattberg, Thomas Buesing, and Subrata K. Sen, "Segmentation strategies for new national brands," *Journal of Marketing*, Fall 1980, 60.
29. David J. Lipke, "Head trips," *American Demographics*, October 2000, 38.
30. Rebecca Piirto Heath, "The frontier of psychographics," *American Demographics*, July 1996, 40.
31. Kevin J. Clancy and Robert S. Shulman, *The Marketing Revolution* (New York: Harper Business, 1991), 63.
32. Jack Trout, *Differentiate or Die* (New York: John Wiley & Sons, 2000), 185.
33. Alvin Achenbaum, "Understanding niche marketing," *Adweek*, 1 December 1986, 62.
34. Ira P. Scheiderman, "Niche marketers should follow old rules," *BrandMarketing*, August 2000, 6.
35. Jeff Neff, "Huggies Little Swimmers tests out a new niche," *Advertising Age*, 25 August 1997, 8.
36. Lisa Sanders, "Startup shop Amalgamated targets big-spending Bobos," *Advertising Age*, 9 September 2003, 89.
37. Kevin J. Clancy and Robert S. Shulman, *The Marketing Revolution* (New York: Harper Business, 1991), 84–87.
38. Jack Trout and Al Ries, *The Positioning Era* (New York: Ries Cappiello Colwell, 1973), 38–41.
39. David A. Aaker, *Managing Brand Equity* (New York: The Free Press, 1991), 114–115.
40. Philip Kotler, *Kotler on Marketing* (New York: The Free Press, 1999), 57–58.
41. David N. Martin, *Be the Brand* (Richmond: New Marketplace Books, 2000), 88–98.
42. Scott Leith, "For a limited time," *Atlanta Journal-Constitution*, 9 September 2003, C1.
43. Marti Barletta,"Targeting a powerhouse female demographic: Older women," *Advertising Age*, ID: AAR01E, advertisingage.com, 10 October 2005.
44. Jeffry Scott, *Atlanta Journal*, July 2, p. 13, 2001.
45. Acxiom, www.acxiom.com/default.aspx?ID=2521&DisplayID=18, 12 November 2006.

Chapter 5

p. 157   Courtesy of Shutterstock
p. 158   Courtesy of Tropicana Products, Inc.

1. Podcast, The craziest ads guys in America," *BusinessWeek*, www.businessweek.com, 22 May 2006.
2. "We've been here before," *Graphic Design:USA*, September 2000, 70.
3. James Melvin Lee, *History of American Journalism*, rev. ed. (Boston: Houghton Mifflin, 1933), 74.
4. Ken Roman and Jane Maas, *How to Advertise* (New York: St. Martin's Press, 2003), 216.
5. Ann Cooper, "Bernbach's children come of age," *Adweek*, 25 March 1996, 33–36.
6. Daniel Gross, "The scramble on Mad. Ave, *Fortune*, 8 August 2005, 63–64.
7. Jeff Weiner, "Anxious ranks," *Agency*, Spring 1994, 42.
8. Suzanne Vranica, "Marketers shop for fresh creativity," *Wall Street Journal*, 28 July 2003, B3.
9. Mark Gleason, "Agency nets puzzle over brand identity," *Advertising Age*, 6 May 1996, 15.
10. Jan Larson, "It's a small world, after all," *Marketing Tools*, September 1997, 47–51.
11. Ken Roman and Jane Maas, *How to Advertise* (New York: St. Martin's Press, 2003), 43–44.
12. "How does global marketing benefit consumers?" *Adweek*, 17 November 2003, 96.
13. "Coke seeks ad formula with global appeal," *Atlanta Journal-Constitution*, 18 November 1991, A5.
14. Ashish Banerjee, "Global campaigns don't work; multinationals do," *Advertising Age*, 18 April 1994, 23.
15. Catharine P. Taylor, "Are holding companies obsolete?" *Adweek*, 9 June 2003, 30–31.
16. Claire Atkinson, "Publicis networks switch to client-based accounting," *Advertising Age*, 31 March 2003, 8.
17. Lisa Sanders and Jean Halliday, "GM hammers agency costs," *Advertising Age*, 17 November 2003, 1.
18. Noreen O'Leary, "The 30-second spot is dead; long live the 30-second spot," *Adweek*, 17 November 2003, 12–14.
19. Interview with Kristen Kyle, 5 December 2000.
20. Terrence Poltrack, "Pay dirt," *Agency*, July/August 1991, 20–25.

21. Stan Beals, "Fresh approaches to agency compensation," *Advertising Age*, 29 August 1994, 20.

22. Leon Stafford, "Tourism officials barter to stretch tight advertising budgets," *Atlanta Journal-Constitution*, 15 May 2003, D1.

23. David Aaker, "The agency as brand architect," *American Advertising*, Spring 1996, 18–21.

Chapter 6

p. 194   Courtesy of Chick-fil-A

1. Ken Bernhardt, "New consumer is a savvy user of new media," *Atlanta Business Chronicle*, 28 July 2006, 3B.

2. Christopher Vollmer, John Frelinghuysen, and Randall Rothenberg, "The future of advertising is now," *Strategy+Business*, Summer 2006, 38–51.

3. Kate MacArthur, "Wendy's Restructures Marketing Unit Amid Layoffs Wendy's Restructures Marketing Unit Amid Layoffs, "July 26, 2006/ http://adage.com/article?article_id=110759

4. Jack Neff, "P&G recategorizes marketing directors," *Advertising Age*, 31 March 2003, 6.

5. Scott Hume, "Integrated marketing: Who's in charge here?" *Advertising Age*, 23 March 1993, 3.

6. William N. Swain, "An exploratory assessment of the IMC PARADIGM: Where are we, and where do we go from here," *Integrated Marketing Communication Research Journal*, 9, Spring 2003, 3–11.

7. William N. Swain, "An exploratory assessment of the IMC PARADIGM: Where are we, and where do we go from here," *Integrated Marketing Communication Research Journal*, 9, Spring 2003, 3–11.

8. Don Schultz, "Managers still face substantial IMC questions," *Marketing News*, 27 September 1993, 10.

9. Don E. Schultz, "Managers still face substantial IMC questions," *Marketing News*, 27 September 1993, 10.

10. Marian Burk Wood, "Clear IMC goals build strong relationships," *Marketing News*, 23 June 1997, 11.

11. Al Ries, "Why marketing people get it wrong," AdAge.com, 17 March 2003.

12. Leslie H. Moeller, Sharat K. Mathur, and Randall Rothenberg, "The better half: The artful science of ROI marketing," *Strategy[plsu]Business*, Spring 2003, 32–45.

13. Rex Briggs and Greg Stuart, *What Sticks* (Chicago: Kaplan, 2006), 213–215.

14. Twenty-Sixth Gallagher Report Consumer Advertising Survey.

15. Steve McKee, "Best foot forward from the start," *BusinessWeek*, 17 April 2006.

16. Dean Foust, "Queen of pop," *BusinessWeek*, 7 August 2006, 44–53.

17. Louise Story, *New York Times*, www.nytimes.com, 2 November 2006.

18. Christopher Vollmer, John Frelinghuysen, Randall Rothenberg, "The future of advertising is now," *Strategy+Business*, Summer 2006, 38–51.

19. Michele Gershberg, "U.S. advertising goes digital to track ads," *USA TODAY*, www.usatoday.com, 14 February 2005.

20. Susan Kuchinskas, "Brave new world," *Adweek*, 25 September 2006, SR 6–7.

21. William M. Bulkeley, "Marketers scan blogs for brand insights," *Wall Street Journal*, 23 June 2005, B1.

22. Delooitte.com., January 15, 2007.

23. Stefano Hatfield, "Testing on trial," Creativity, October 2003,30.

24. Joe Mandee, "How far is too far?" *Agency*, May/June 1991, 9.

25. Eleftheria Parpis, "Moore to come," *Adweek*, 18 September 2000, 28.

26. Lisa Sanders, "Ford ad chief hails content convergence," *Advertising Age*, 18 April 2003, 3.

27. NissanUSA.com/7 days/

28. asoy.com, January 6, 2007

29. Stewart Elliott, "Advertiser-agency relationships turn a bit brighter," *New York Times*, 6 November 2006, www.nytimes.com, 11 November 2006.

30. Jeff Neff, "Recently named Clorox CEO sets sights on trade marketing," *Advertising Age*, www.adage.com, 31 August 2006.

31. Karen Benezra, "Sea change: Agencies diversify to regain client trust," *Adweek*, 19 April 1999, 42–43.

32. Jennifer Comiteau, "Power play," *Adweek*, 10 June 1996, 33–38.

33. Laura Petrecca, "The year in review: Is it a record pace?" *Advertising Age*, 2 June 1997, 1.

34. Suzanne Vranica, "Marketers shop for fresh creativity," *Wall Street Journal*, 28 July 2003, B3.

35. Russell H. Coilley, Defining Advertising Goals for Measured Effectiveness (New york:Association of National Advertisers publicaion).

36. Jack Neff, "Half of your advertising isn't wasted-just 37%," *Advertising Age*, 7 August 2006, 1.

37. Tom Patty, "Mastering the New Five P's of Marketing," TBWA/Chiat/Day Web site, 1997.

Chapter 7

p. 229   Courtesy of Shutterstock

p. 230   Courtesy of Shutterstock

1. Advertising Age, 26 June 2006, S-8.

2. From http://publications.mediapost.com/index.cfm?fuseaction5Articles.showArticle&art_aid545105.

3. Rich Thomaselli, "Reebok's Terry Tate set to play dirty bass," Advertising Age, 21 April 2003, 4, 48.

4. Erwin Ephron, "Preventing Dis-Engagement," www.ephrononmedia.com, 8 May 2006

5. Matthew Creamer, "Lazarus wants media back at the table," Advertising Age, 20 November 2006, 25.

6. "The state of the agency," Adweek, 17 November 2003, 70–71.

7. Andrew McMains, "Different paths but one idea: Reclaim media strategy," Adweek, 21 August 2006, 8.

8. Erwin Ephron, "A new media-mix strategy," Advertising Age, 28 February 2000, S10.

9. W. Ronald Lane, Karen W. King, and J. Thomas Russell, "Chris Oberholtzer Viewpoint 7.2," in Kleppner's Advertising Procedure, 16th ed. (Pearson Prentice Hall, 2005), 219.

10. Mickey Marks, "Millennial satiation," Advertising Age, 14 February 2000, S16.

11. Erwin Ephron, "A new media-mix strategy," Advertising Age, 28 February 2000, S10.

12. From www.claritas.com, accessed 15 November 2006.

13. Allen Brivic, What Every Account Executive Should Know About Media (American Association of Advertising Agencies, 1989), 14.

Chapter 8

p. 256   Courtesy of Shutterstock

1. David Fisher and Marshall Jon Fisher, *Tube: The Invention of Television* (Washington: Counterpoint, 1996), 22.

2. From www.tvb.org/rcentral/MediaTrendsTrack/tvbasics/39_Consumers_Allocate.asp, 3 January 2007.

3. From www.tvb.org/nav/build_frameset.asp, 4 January 2007.

4. Barry L. Sherman, *The Television Standard* (New York: Gerson Lehrman Group, 1999), 2.

5. Based on numbers reported in *Advertising Age*, 26 June 2006, S-11. Source: Robert Coen's Media Analysis at Universal McCann.

6. Jane Dalzell, "Who's on first," *Advertising Age, 50 Years of TV Advertising*, Spring 1995, 8.

7. Clarence Page, "A bridge to the new media century," *The Park Distinguished Visitors Series* (Ithaca, NY: Ithaca College, 2000), 6.

8. From www.tvb.org/nav/build_frameset.asp, 4 January 2007.

9. Andrew Green, "Clutter crisis countdown," *Advertising Age*, 21 April 2003, 22.

10. Brian Steinberg and Suzanne Vranica, "Madison Avenue sifts through 'clutter,'" *Wall Street Journal Online*, www.wsj.com/article/SB116778101889165317, 7 January 2007.

11. Scott Woolley, "Zap," *Forbes Magazine*, 29 September 2003, 77.

12. From www.tvb.org/nav/build_frameset.asp, 4 January 2007.

13. Brian Steinberg and Suzanne Vranica, "Madison Avenue sifts through 'clutter,'" *Wall Street Journal Online*, www.wsj.com/article/SB116778101889165317, 7 January 2007.

14. Scott Woolley, "Zap," *Forbes Magazine*, 29 September 2003, 77.
15. Steve McClellan, www.adweek.com/aw/search/article_display. jsp?vnu_content_id=1001096022, 20 September 2006. Source: TNS Media Intelligence.
16. Ibid.
17. "Mil-a-minute TV not all bad," *Advertising Age*, 23 September 1996, 28.
18. The term *scatter plan* has two definitions. The first refers to buying a group of spots across a number of programs. The second refers to those spots that are still available after the up-front buying season is completed.
19. From www.fcc.gov/ownership/rules.html, accessed 15 January 2007.
20. *Advertising Age*, 26 June 2006, S-8. Source: Robert Coen's Media Analysis at Universal McCann.
21. Claire Atkinson, "He got game," *Advertising Age*, 7 March 2005, S-4.
22. Cynthia Littleton, "ABC inks long-term *Wheel/Jeopardy* deals," *TV Guide*, www.tvgen.com, 21 October 1998.
23. Adapted from Joe Mandese, "Syndie stars easy to find," *Advertising Age*, 17 January 2000, S4.
24. "1995 cable TV facts," a publication of the Cable Advertising Bureau, 72.
25. Fern Siegel, "Magazine Rack: Nick Jr. Family Magazine," MediaPost Publications e-newsletter, magazinerack@mediapost.com, 16 August 2006.
26. "What is it about TV? Publishing makes the one magazine spin-off of a TV property succeed, while others fail miserably," Real Media Riffs, Mediapost, 11 September 2003, www.mediapost.com.
27. "A guide to cable interconnects 2001/2002," *Advertising Age*, 1 October 2001, A3.
28. Source: www.tvb.org, as found on www.mediainfocenter.org/television/size/cable_vcr.asp, 29 December 2006.
29. From www.marketingvox.com/archives/2006/05/04/jupiter_dvr_ad_skipping_threatens_8b_in_advertising/, accessed 5 January 2007.
30. Jack Loechner, "Adults in DVR households read more, surf more and watch TV more," from http://publications.mediapost.com/index.cfm?fuseaction=Articles.showArticleHomePage&art_aid=46723, accessed 17 August 2006.
31. Sheree R. Curry, "Place it in post," from http://publications.mediapost.com/index.cfm?fuseaction=Articles.showArticle&art_aid=44756&art_type=100, accessed 14 July 2006.
32. David Goetzl, "ABC's 'Miracle Workers' worked miracles, deemed best product placement of '06," http://publications.mediapost.com/index.cfm?fuseaction=Articles.showArticleHomePage&art_aid=53476, accessed 8 January 2007.
33. Ibid.
34. Sheree R. Curry, "Place it in post," http://publications.mediapost.com/index.cfm?fuseaction=Articles.showArticle&art_aid=44756&art_type=100, accessed 14 July 2006.
35. Paul J. Gough, "New TV ratings system tracks product placement, sponsorship," *MediaPost's Media Daily News*, www.mediapost.com, 28 October 2003.
36. Information in this section is from Nielsen Media Research.

Chapter 9
p. 288   Courtesy of XM Satellite Radio
1. "Nielsen begins ratings; 'Lux,' 'Lone Ranger' lead," *Advertising Age*, 19 April 1999, 89.
2. http://tvb.org/nav/build_frameset.asp?url=/rcentral/viewertrack/weekly/2006-07/a18-49/a18-49.asp?ms=?oct_29-2006.asp, 5 November 2006. *Source:* Nielsen Galaxy Lightning 9/19/05–5/24/06, Ad-Supported Subscription TV only. Programming under 25 minutes excluded.
3. www.rab.com/public/media/2006RMG&FB-LR.pdf.

4. www.crutchfieldadvisor.com/ISEOrgbtcspd/learningcenter/car/hdradio.html. Accessed 11 November 2006.
5. www.adweek.com/aw/search/article_display.jsp?schema=vnu1&vnu_content_id=1001614304. Accessed 5 December 2005.
6. "How Can I Stand Out from the Competition?" www.rab.com, 24 May 2000.
7. "What Happens When the Spots Come On: The Impact of Commercials on the Radio Audience," www.arbitron.com, 28 October 2006.
8. www.adweek.com/aw/search/article_display.jsp?schema=vnu1&vnu_content_id=1001614304. Accessed 5 December 2005.
9. www.newsgeneration.com/radio_resources/by_state.htm. Accessed 1 December 2006.
10. "Ad Spending Totals by Media," *Advertising Age*, 26 June 2006, S-8. Source: Robert Coen's Media Analysis at Universal McCann.
11. "Ad Spending Totals by Media," *Advertising Age*, 26 June 2006, S-8. Source: Robert Coen's Media Analysis at Universal McCann.
12. "Top U.S Advertisers in 10 MediaAd Spending Totals by Media," *Advertising Age*, 26 June 2006, S-11. Source: Robert Coen's Media Analysis at Universal McCann.
13. www.arbitron.com/radio_stations/mm001050.asp, 16 November 2006.
14. Arbitron/Edison Media Research Internet and Multimedia 2006: On-Demand Media Explodes, www.arbitron.com. Accessed 20 November 2006.
15. www.arbitron.com/national_radio/radar.htm, 5 November 2006.
16. www.arbitron.com/portable_people_meters/thesystem_ppm.htm, 30 October 2006.
17. "Top U.S Advertisers in 10 MediaAd Spending Totals by Media," *Advertising Age*, 26 June 2006, S-11. Source: Robert Coen's Media Analysis at Universal McCann.
18. www.arbitron.com//hispanicradiotoday06. Accessed 5 November 2006.
19. www.arbitron.com/downloads/Black_Radio_Today_06.pdf.

Chapter 10
p. 310   Courtesy of Shutterstock
1. *The Source. Newspapers by the Numbers*, www.naa.org/thesource.
2. *The Source. Newspapers by the Numbers* (Business Analysis and Research), NAA, www.naa.org, 1 December 2006.
3. *The Source. Newspapers by the Numbers* (Editor and Publisher), NAA, www.naa.org, 1 December 2006.
4. Marc Gunther, "Publish or perish?" *Fortune*, 10 January 2000, 148.
5. NAA/Universal McCann, *The Source. Newspapers by the Numbers*, www.naa.org, 1 December 2006.
6. U.S. Department of Commerce; NAA, *The Source. Newspapers by the Numbers*, www.naa.org, 1 December 2006.
7. Adapted from Leo Bogart, "Newspapers," *Media Studies Journal*, Spring/Summer 1999, 68.
8. "How to reach 141.6 million people," *Advertising Age*, 13 October 2003, N3.
9. Steve McClellan, "Newspaper biz evolves too slowly for ad buyers," *AdWeek*, 8 January 2007, 8.
10. NAA/Universal McCann, *The Source. Newspapers by the Numbers*, www.naa.org, 1 December 2006.
11. CareerBuilder.com, www.careerbuilder.com, 2 January 2007.
12. "The history of ABC," www.accessabc.com/press/Introduction.pdf, 11 March 2007.
13. From www.naa.org/info/facts04/weeklynewspapers.html, 12 September 2006.

Chapter 11
p. 338   Courtesy of LWA-Stephen Welstead. Shutterstock
1. Unless otherwise noted, the source of information in this chapter is the Magazine Publishers of America: www.magazine.org.

2. From www.magazine.org. Source: *National Directory of Magazines* (Oxford Communications, 2006).

3. Aimee Deeken, "Service upgrades," *Mediaweek*, 2 December 2002, 45–46.

4. *Advertising Age*, 23 October 2006, S-2, S-13.

5. James Playsted Wood, *Magazines in the United States* (New York: The Ronald Press Company, 1949), 104.

6. From www.magazine.org. Source: PricewaterhouseCoopers' Financial Survey, 2005.

7. www.magazine.org. Source: Hall's Magazine Reports, 2006.

8. "High circulation costs stymie magazine growth opportunities," *Advertising Age*, 14 February 2000, S14.

9. "Taking charge of America's newsstand," *Advertising Age*, 6 October 2003, 38.

10. Robert Coen's Media Analysis at Universal McCann. Based on numbers reported in *Advertising Age*, 26 June 2006, S-11.

11. From www.mediaweek.com/mw/news/print/article_display. jsp?vnu_content_id=1002157655, accessed 15 March 2006.

12. From www.magazine.org. Source: Affinity's VISTA Print Effectiveness Rating Service, 2006.

13. www.magazine.org. Source: MRI, Fall 2005.

14. From www.mediapost.com/articleId=212870, 26 July 2003.

15. Jon Fine, "Regional titles form ad network," *Advertising Age*, 1 September 2003, 8.

16. From www.hearst.com/magazines/property/group/ custsol.htm, accessed 4 January 2007.

17. Hassan Fattah, "Custom publishing grows up," *American Demographics*, July/August 2002, 26.

18. Sarah Ellison, "Good Housekeeping touts its test lab to seek new readers' seal of approval," *Wall Street Journal Online*, http://online.wsj.com/article/SB116052613652288766.html, 11 October 2006.

19. Ann Marie Kerwin, "Time Inc. buys sampling biz to help bolster 'Parenting,'" *Advertising Age*, 2 November 1998, 6.

20. Stuart Elliot, "Read the magazine, then eat the meal," www.nytimes.com/2005/ 08/30/business/media/30adco.html?adxnnl=1&adxnnlx= 1126012136-rFrdNG+/gI+RIYZKlpgN6Q&pagewanted=print, 30 August 2005.

21. Steve McClellan, "MediaVest exec: Print is not enough," www.adweek.com/aw/specials/advertising_week/article_disp lay.jsp?vnu_content_id=1003157368, accessed 27 September 2006.

22. David S. Hirschman, "Web first, print later," www.mediabistro. com/articles/cache/a7139.asp, accessed 15 March 2006.

23. Matthew Rose, "In fight for ads, publishers often overstate their sales," *Wall Street Journal*, 6 August 2003, A1, 10.

24. www.newsweekmediakit.com/newsite/us/editions/ national.shtml, accessed 2 January 2007.

25. "Research brief: B2B media and trade shows most important to executives," Center for Media Research E-Newsletter (research@mediapost.com), 3 August 2006.

26. "The value and role of corporate advertising for business-to-business marketers," *Cahners Advertising Research Report*, #2000.15.

27. "Advertising effectiveness in business-to-business markets," www.reedbusiness.com, 18 September 2006.

28. Marc Spiegler, "Hot media buy: The farm report," *American Demographics*, October 1995, 18.

Chapter 12

p. 382   Courtesy of James Estrin/The New York Time. Redux Pictures; AP Wide World Photos; Andrew Hetherington. Redux Pictures

1. Unless otherwise noted, material for this chapter was provided by the Outdoor Advertising Association of America.

2. www.census.gov/Press-Release/www/releases/archives/ american_community_survey_acs/004489.html, accessed 30 March 2005.

3. Eugene Morris, "O-O-H—Media's plain Jane sister," *Inside Out of Home*, January 2000, 7.

4. Carol Krol, "Life after tobacco," *Advertising Age*, 19 April 1999, 48.

5. www.oaaa.org/government/codes.asp, accessed 22 December 2006.

6. Erwin Ephron, "About the medium," Outdoor Advertising Association of America, www.oaaa.org, accessed 11 November 2003.

7. "Wall to wall walls," *Inside Out of Home*, April 1999, 1.

8. "Creating award winning outdoor," www.oaaa.org, accessed 12 December 2006.

9. Normandy Madden, "Adidas introduces human billboards," *Advertising Age*, 1 September 2003, 11.

10. www.tabonline.com/thenewaudit.aspx, accessed 3 January 2007.

11. www.mediaweek.com/mw/news/media_agencies/article_ display.jsp?vnu_content_id=1002837875, accessed 13 July 2006

12. www.smrb.com, accessed 12 January 2007

13. www.oaaa.org/outdoor/councils/transit.asp, accessed 11 November 2003.

14. "Transit TV: A really mobile medium," http://publications. mediapost.com/index.cfm?fuseaction=Articles.san&s= 39071&Nid=18225&p=342208.

15. www.oaaa.org/outdoor/councils/furniture.asp, accessed 11 November 2003.

16. "Eller goes whole hog to promote transit shelter O-O-H," *Inside Out of Home*, April 1998, 4.

17. "Deals strengthen gym media muscle," www.brandweek.com/ bw/news/sportsent/article_display.jsp?vnu_content_id= 1002236559, accessed 27 March 2006.

18. "Reaching the unreachable," *Marketing Magazine*, 1 August 2005.

19. "Charmin rolls out 20 restrooms in Times Square," *USA Today*, 22 November 2006, 6A; and "P&G brings potty to parties," *Advertising Age*, 17 February 2003.

20. "Garbage trucks: The new hot spot for advertisers," http://adage.com/article?article_id=114665, accessed 31 January 2007.

21. "'Desperate' for suds, duds," http://hollywoodreporter.com/thr/television/brief_display.js p?vnu_content_id=1001021171, accessed 25 August 2005.

22. "For CBS's fall lineup, check inside your refrigerator," www.nytimes.com/2006/07/17/business/media/17adco. html?_r=1&oref=slogin, accessed 17 July 2006.

23. Abbey Klassen, "The hottest out-of-home technologies," http://adage.com/mediaworks/article?article_id-112204, accessed 3 October 2006.

Chapter 13

p. 408   Courtesy of eBay, Inc.

1. "First-time vehicle buyers eschew traditional media," www.business-journal.com/AutoMediaObsolete.asp, accessed 31 January 2006.

2. Robert McKim, "Strengthen affinities with spiral branding," *DMNews*, 19 June 2000, 32.

3. Gavin O'Malley, "Sixty percent of wired homes now use broadband," http://adage.com/digital/article?article_id+ 110500, 14 July 2006.

4. Nielsen/NetRatings, www.internetworldstats.com/am/ us.htm, accessed 31 January 2007.

5. Joe Mandese, "Ad execs see TV budgets moving into online video," http://publications.mediapost.com/index.cfm? fuseaction=Articles.san&s=51103&Nid=25091&p=342208, 14 November 2006.

6. Jane Black, "No complaints in the online ad biz," from www.businessweek.com:technology/content/jul2003/ tc20030725_1182_tc055.htm? tc, accessed 29 July 2003.

7. Mark Walsh, "eMarketer: Online ad spending growth to slow," http://publications.mediapost.com, accessed 27 February 2007.

8. Bill Hopkins and Britton Manasco, "The new technologies of marketing," *DMNews*, 22 May 2000, 51.

9. Steve Diller, "Direct marketing's role in a new society," *DMNews*, 1 May 2000, 22.

10. Jeff Neff, "Spam research reveals disgust with pop-up ads," *Advertising Age*, 25 August 2003, 1, 21.
11. H. Robert Wientzen, "Tackling the spam issue," www.the-dma.org/memberguide/tacklingspam.shml, accessed 6 January 2004.
12. Association of National Advertisers (ANA), www.ana.net, accessed 14 October 2003.
13. Zachary Rodgers, "Financial services customers warmed by e-mail," http://cyberatlas.internet.com, accessed 8 December 2003.
14. David Goetzl, "Nissan backs online series *StarTomorrow*," http://publications.mediapost.com/index.cfm?fuseaction= Articles.san&s=45549&Nid=21709&p=342208, accessed 14 July 2006.
15. "CBS to invest in virtual designer Electric Sheep," www.reuters.com/article/internetNews/idUSN2518789120070226, accessed 26 February 2007.
16. "Interact & integrate," *Advertising Age*, 19 June 2000, S40.
17. Rebecca Flass, "Web supplants TV as teen media hub," www.mediaweek.com, accessed 30 August 2003.
18. Rebecca Gardyn, "Born to be wired," *American Demographics*, April 2003, 14.
19. Flass, "Web supplants TV as teen media hub."
20. "New white paper from online publishers association identifies, examines and characterizes Internet dayparts," www.online-publishers.org, accessed 6 February 2003.
21. "Ad Age agency of the year: The consumer," http://adage.com/article.php?article_id=114132, accessed 8 January 2007.
22. Stuart Elliott, "Online, P & G gets a little crazy," www.nytimes.com/2006/12/14/business/media/14adco.html?_r=1&oref= slogin, 14 December 2006, accessed 14 December 2006.
23. Lorne Manly, "Brewtube" www.nytimes.com/2007/02/04/magazine/04BudTV.t..html?ei=5070&en=8blab52834e02277& 1171429200&emc=etal, 4 February 2007, accessed 4 February 2007.
24. Tobi Elkin, "Piper Jaffray dubs emerging media trend 'communitainment'," http://publications.mediapost.com/index.cfm?fuseaction=Articles.san&s=56065&Nid=27757& p=342208 Accessed 26 February 2007.
25. "Nike, Google kick off social-networking site," www.businessweek.com/technology/content/mar2006/tc20060320_591107.htm?chan=technology_technology+ index+page_internet, 20 March 2006.
26. *Direct Marketing Course Rationale*, a publication of the Direct Marketing Educational Foundation, 1.
27. Jeff Caplan, "Predictive data: It's the real-time thing," *DMNews*, 24 May 1999, 34.
28. Denny Hatch, "Making DRTV work for you," *Target Marketing*, September 1999, 76.
29. National Trust for Historic Preservation, www.nationaltrust.org/help/mail_order_home.html, 5 January 2003.
30. Jack Schmid and Steve Trollinger, "Who's making the Net work?" *Target Marketing*, June 1999, 73.
31. "Ad spending totals by media," *Advertising Age* 26 June 2006, S-8.
32. Lewis Rashmir, "The first compiler was Charles Groves," *DMNews*, 15 February 1993, 35.

Chapter 14

p. 438   © 2006. Used with permission from DaimlerChrysler Corporation
1. David Vacek and Richard Sale, "100 years of promotion," *PROMO*, August 1998, 142.
2. Betsy Spethmann, "Is advertising dead?" *PROMO*, September 1998, 32.
3. Peter Breen, "Seeds of change," *PROMO*, May 2000, A5.
4. Russell Bowman and Paul Theroux, "By the book," *PROMO*, March 2000, 95.
5. From www.partnerslevit.com/ConferenceRoom/Sales_ Promotions_and_ Sweepstak/sales_promotions_and_ sweepstak.html.

6. From http://promomagazine.com/research/industrytrends/marketing_riding_tid.
7. Stephanie Thompson, "Despite tough third quarter, will still emphasize in-store," AdAge.com, 16 October 2006.
8. Steve McClellan, "Study: Sponsorships yield superior ROI," *Adweek*, 8 January 2007, 7.
9. J. Jeffrey Inman and Russell S. Winer, "Where the rubber meets the road: A model of in-store consumer decision making," Working Paper, Marketing Science Institute, October 1998, 25.
10. "Out of sight, out of mind," *PROMO*, March 1996, 16.
11. Richard Sele, "The display police," *PROMO*, March 1999, 80.
12. Kate Bertrand, "Premiums prime the market," *Advertising Age*, May 1998, S6.
13. David Vacek, "Getting in gear," *PROMO*, May 1998, S5.
14. "Rewarding the faithful," promomagzine.com, April 1, 2006.
15. Andrew Scott, "The new frontier," *PROMO*, 1 April 2005, 23.
16. David Goetzl, "Card me: Anheuser-Busch kicks off Bud.TV post-Super Bowl with age verification system," MediaPost.com, 23 January 2007.
17. Patricia Joyce, "NFL players send voice messages," *PROMO*, http://promomagazine.com/news/nfl_players, 24 January 2007.
18. Andrew Hampp, "Chipotle picks its YouTube winners: Inside view of a consumer-generated campaign" AdAge.com, 14 November 2006.
19. Katherine M. Joyce, "Flipping the coin," http://promomagazine.com, 16 January 2007.
20. Unless otherwise noted, material in this section was provided by the Promotional Products Association International.
21. Research by Louisiana State University and Glenrich Business Studies reported in www.ppai.org.
22. Andrew Scott, "Try me," promomagazine.com/industry trends/ April 21, 2006.
23. Kathleen M. Joyce, "Overview 2006: Higher gear," promomagazine.com, April 9, 2007.
24. Amy Johannes, "Playing the Game," Promomagazine/research/industry trends/ April 9, 2007
25. Ira Teinowitz, "Marketers yield to sweepstakes curbs," *Advertising Age*, 24 May 1999, 61.
26. Yellow Pages I.M.A., www.Yellowpagesima.org/advertising/aboutcfm, 30 Ocotber 2003.
27. Matthew Kinsman, "Signs of life," http://promomagazine.com/ar/marketing_signs_life/index.htm, 4 February 2004.
28. Paul Nolan and Vincent Alonzo, "Making the mark," *Incentive*, August 1999, 30.

Chapter 15

p. 473   Courtesy of Shutterstock
p. 474   Courtesy of J. M. Smucker Company
1. Sergio Zyman, *The End of Marketing as We Know It* (New York: HarperCollins, 1999), 62.
2. CMOR, www.cmor.org/resp_coop_news1003_2.htm, 2 December 2003.
3. Jon Steel, *Truth, Lies & Advertising* (New York: John Wiley & Sons, 1998), 36.
4. Ibid., 43.
5. David Goetzl, "O&M turns reality TV into research tool," *Advertising Age*, 10 July 2000, 6.
6. Tobi Elkin, "Product pampering," *Brandweek*, 16 June 1997, 28–40.
7. Natalie Perkins, "Zeroing in on consumer values," *Advertising Age*, 22 March 1993, 23.
8. "Schwarzenegger campaign uses data on consumer buying habits to identify supporters," www.iht.com/articles/ap/2006/10/26/america/NA_POL_US_Schwarzenegger.php, 27 October 2006.
9. "Phil Lempert—Facts, figures & the future," PhilLempertFactsFiguresTheFuture@mail.subscribermail.com, *FMI/ACNielsen/Lempert E-Newsletter*, 14 November 2005.
10. James A. Bayton, "Motivation, cognition, learning—Basic factors in consumer behavior," *Journal of Marketing*, January 1958, 282.

11. Melanie Wells, "In search of the buy button," *Forbes*, 1 September 2003, 62–66, 70.
12. SRI Consulting Business Intelligence, www.sric-bi.com/VALS, 9 September 2006.
13. Yankelovich, www.yankelovich.com, 10 December 2003.
14. Christine Hansen, "Brainscan," *Deliver*—a magazine for marketers, November 2006, 18–23.
15. Ibid.
16. Ibid.
17. Ibid.
18. Jean Halliday, "Automakers involve consumers," *Advertising Age*, 31 January 2000, 82.
19. Kathleen Sampey, "Nikon widens target to capture casual shooters," *Adweek*, 26 May 2003, 9.
20. Jim Aitchison, *Cutting Edge Advertising* (Singapore: Prentice-Hall, 1999), 28–29.
21. PACT—Positioning Advertising Copy Testing, The PACT Agencies Report 1982, 6–25.
22. Lisa Sanders and Jack Neff, "Copy tests under fire from new set of critics," *Advertising Age*, 9 June 2003, 6.
23. Ibid.

Chapter 16

p. 500   Courtesy of Mayfield Dairies

1. "Great advertising—It's simply a must," *Viewpoint*, January 1999, 12–13.
2. Kenneth Roman and Jane Maas, *How to Advertise*, 3rd ed. (New York: St. Martin's Press, 2003), 215.
3. Jack Myers, "Can the rules of research change?" http://blogs.mediapost.com/tv_board/?p=8, 5 January 2007.
4. Lisa Sanders, "Ignore the research and trust your gut, Euro's David Jones tells Idea Conference to take back creativity from consumers," adage_daily@adage.com, 8 November 2006.
5. Jim Aitchison, *Cutting Edge Advertising* (Singapore: Prentice-Hall, 1999), 31–35.
6. Stefano Hatfield, "World's hot shop is in Paris, and it's Veruroegen's TBWA," *Advertising Age*, 4 August 2003, 16.
7. Luke Sullivan, *Hey Whipple, Squeeze This: A Guide to Creating Great Ads* (New York: John Wiley & Sons, 1998), 60–65.
8. John Hegarty, "My apologies for this letter being so long. Had I more time it would have been shorter," *Creativity*, March 1997, 12.
9. Jim Aitchison, *Cutting Edge Advertising* (Singapore: Prentice-Hall, 1999), 31–35.
10. Ron Huey, interviews by W. Ronald Lane, September 1994, September 1997, August 2003, October 2006.
11. David Martin, *Romancing the Brand* (New York: Amacom, 1989), 134–36.
12. From an American Association of Advertising Agencies speech, 17 May 1980.
13. Dick Costello, "The big picture," *Adweek*, 29 March 1999, 25.
14. The term *copy* is a carryover from the days in printing when a compositor, given a manuscript to set in type, was told to copy it. Before long, the manuscript itself became known as copy. In the creation of a printed advertisement, copy refers to all the reading matter in the advertisement. However, in the production of print advertising, copy refers to the entire subject being reproduced—words and pictures alike. This is one of those instances in advertising when the same word is used in different senses, a practice that all professions and crafts seem to enjoy because it bewilders the uninitiated.
15. Luis Bassar, "Creative paths to great advertising," *Viewpoint*, September/October 1991, 23–24.
16. Steve Lance and Jeff Woll, *The Little Blue Book of Advertising* (New York: Penguin Group, 2006), 189.
17. Steve Lance and Jeff Woll, *The Little Blue Book of Advertising* (New York: Penguin Group, 2006), 184–86.
18. Michael McCarthy, "American Express sticks with tradition of celebrity pitches," *USA Today*, 7 March 2005.
19. Dean Rieck, "Build consumer confidence with testimonials," *DM News*, 8 February 1999, 12.
20. Kevin Roberts, "Emotional rescue" (speech presented at The AdTech Conference, San Francisco, May 2000).
21. Leslie Picot-Zane, "Is advertising too emotional?" www.centerforemotionalmarketing.com, 9 January 2006.
22. From www.ftc.gov/bcp/policystmt/ad-compare.htm.
23. Michael McCarthy, "Imagination at work for GE," *USA Today*, 5 May 2003, 7B.
24. Jon Steel, *Truth, Lies, and Advertising* (New York: John Wiley & Sons, 1998), 141.
25. *Starch Tested Copy*, a publication of Roper Starch Worldwide.
26. Gavin O'Malley, "Digital marketer of the year: Nike," *Advertising Age*, 16 October 2006.
27. From http://money.cnn.com/magazines/fortune/fortune_archive/2006/10/02/8387416/index.
28. Barbara Lippert, "Animal husbandry," *Adweek*, 12 June 2006, 20.
29. Maxine Clark, *The Bear Necessities of Business* (Hoboken, NJ: John Wiley & Sons, 2006), 334–36.
30. Teressa Lezzi, "Getting game," *Creativity*, March 2005, 22–24.

Chapter 17

p. 534   © Carnival, Inc., 2006

1. John Butler, "Want to make art?" *Adweek*, 26 May 2003, 20.
2. Noreen O'Leary, "Does creative count?" *Adweek*, 11 December 2000, 32.
3. George Parker, *MadScam* (New York: Entrepreneur Media, 2007), 98.
4. Ryan Underwood, "Ruling the roost," *Fast Company*, April 2005, 70.
5. Kate MacArthur, "FCB's Taco Bell success might give it edge in KFC review," *Advertising Age*, 5 August 2003, 2.
6. Roper Starch Worldwide, Inc., *Starch Tested Copy* 5 (no. 3, 4).
7. Jim Aitchison, *Cutting Edge Advertising* (Singapore: Prentice-Hall, 1999), 112–65.
8. Jim Aitchison, *Cutting Edge Advertising* (Singapore: Prentice-Hall, 1999), 189.
9. From www.pantone.com/pages/pantone/Pantone.aspx?pg=19382&ca=29, 4 January 2007.
10. "Annual color forecast," *Graphic Design: USA*, June 2003, 61–80.
11. Ilene Strizver, "Do you believe in magic?" *HOW*, February 2007, 60–63.
12. Cahners Advertising Research Report (CARR) No. 118.5 (Newton, MA: Cahners, n.d.), 4.
13. "Art directing photography," *Art Direction*, March 1993, 42–54.
14. Jim Aitchison, *Cutting Edge Advertising* (Singapore: Prentice-Hall, 1999), 243–44.
15. "Stock visual decisions," *Graphic Design: USA*, 128.

Chapter 18

p. 560   Courtesy of McRae Communications

1. Allan Haley, "What's your type?" *STEP*, May/June 2003, 83.
2. Allan Haley, "Using all capitals is a graphic oxymoron," *U & lc*, Fall 1991, 14–15.
3. Richard M. Adams II, "Color-proofing systems," *Pre*, March/April 1994, 55–59.
4. William Ryan and Theodore Conover, *Graphic Communications Today*, 4th ed. (Clifton Park, NY: Thomson, 2004), 308–9.

Chapter 19

p. 588   Courtesy of Blattner Brunner, Pittsburgh, Atlanta, Washington

1. David Goetzl, "Converse's ChuckTaylor's," MediaDailyNew@MediaPost, January 2, 2007.
2. Kate MacArthur, "Subway sales so strong marketer delays new ads," *Advertising Age*, 19 June 2000, 8.
3. "TV advertising still has a future," The Guradian/Adverblog, August 2, 2005.
4. "Entertained by commercials," *American Demographics*, November 1997, 41.

5. Paul Farhi, "The frat house is now closed," *Washington Post*, 31 December 2005, C01.
6. Colin Bessonette, "Q&A on the news," *Atlanta Journal*, 1 January 1996, A2.
7. "Peyton Manning: The NFL's Anna Kournikova?" TMZ.com, 14 August 2006.
8. Cyndee Miller, "Celebrities hot despite scandals," *Marketing News*, 28 March 1994, 1–2.
9. Michael Goldman, "Legato's Laboratory," *Millimeter*, September 2005, 31–36.
10. Joseph Jaffe, *Life After the 30-seond Spot* (Hoboken, NJ: Wiley, 2005), 101.
11. Steve Lance and Jeff Woll, *The Little Blue Book of Advertising* (New York: Penguin Group, 2006), 166–167.
12. *Music—How to Use It for Commercial Production*, a publication of the Television Bureau of Advertising, New York.
13. Stefano Hatfield, "Music to watch sales by," *Creativity*, July 2003, 34–35.
14. Rick Lyon, "The circle game," *Creativity*, September 1997, 18.
15. Warren Burger, "Action fever," *Creativity*, June 2000, 47–49.
16. Fred Cisterna, "Motorola Transformer," *Creativity*, March 2005, 47.
17. Michael Spier, "Why CGI?" *Millimeter*, May 1997, 93–100.
18. Beth Jacques, "The do's and don'ts of mixing animation and live action," *Millimeter*, April 1994, 77–82.
19. Bart Cleveland, "Producing quality TV spots on a shoestring," Adage.com/small agency, 27 July 2006.
20. American Federation of Television & Radio Artists, www.aftra.org/member/irates.html, 15 January 2004.
21. American Association of Advertising Agencies, news release, 13 December 2003.
22. "AAAA Survey Finds 3 Percent Drop in Cost to Produce 30-Second TV Commercials," American Association of Advertising Agencies, news release, December 2001.
23. Bootsie Battle, "Approval system speeds projects," *Millimeter*, August 2003, 61–62.
24. Association of National Advertisers, news release, 11 March 2003.
25. Randy Kilgore, "Online Video Advertising: The Myth of the Inventory Drought," MediaPost, 20 November 2006.

Chapter 20

p. 622   Courtesy of Karen King

1. Steve Lance and Jeff Woll, *The Little Blue Book of Advertising* (Chicago: Kaplan Publishing, 2006), 211.
2. Tom Monahan, "Advertising," *Communication Arts*, July 1994, 198.
3. Erik Gruenwedel, "Net radio daze," *Adweek*, 1 May 2000, IQ26–27.
4. J. Patrick Coolican, "Jingles drop out of favor," The Associated Press, September 5, 2006.
5. Chris Reidy, "Experienced musician for hire," *Boston Globe*, 5 November 2006, B.1.
6. Aaaron Baar, "Advertising saves the radio star," *Adweek*, 6 November 2006, 12–13.
7. Stuart Elliott, "Bringing back the Slinky," www.newyorktimes.com, 3 May 2005.
8. Bruce Bendinger, *The Copy Workshop Workbook* (Chicago: Bruce Bendinger Creative Communications, Inc., 1988), 214.
9. Mike Tierney, "Radio ads that fly under the radar," *Atlanta Journal-Constitution*, 17 July 2005, Q1–4.

Chapter 21

p. 642   Folks Southern Kitchen

1. Beth Snyder Bulik, "The brand police," *Business* 2.0, 28 November 2000, 144–148.
2. Roger Sametz, "Moving from corporate identity to brand identity: A great logo only gets you so far," www.sametz.com, 20 January 2004.

3. www.Lippincottmercer.com, 1 February 2004.
4. "The Lanham Act: Alive and well after 50 years," International Trademark Association, www.inta.org/lanham.htm, 20 June 2000.
5. Allen P. Adamson, *BrandSimple* (New York: Palgrave McMillan, 2006) 114–115.
6. Richard A. Costello, "Focus on the brand," *The Advertiser*, Spring 1993, 11–18.
7. Michael E. Kannell, "Judge sides with BellSouth on copyright," *Atlanta Journal-Constitution*, 10 September 1997, C2.
8. Judy Artunian, "Change of name can come with risk," *Chicago Tribune*, 19 May 2006, B-1.
9. Allen P. Adamson, *BrandSimple* (New York: Palgrave McMillan, 2006) 160.
10. Daniel L. Doden, "Selecting a brand name that aids marketing objectives," *Advertising Age*, 5 November 1990, 34.
11. Al Ries and Laura Ries, *The Immutable Laws of Internet Branding* (New York: HarperBusiness, 2000), 59–70.
12. Julie Cottineau, *Interbrand Special Report: The 'Name Game,'* 2002.
13. Richard Linnett, "Anderson's accenture gets $175 mil ad blitz," *Advertising Age*, 4 December 2000, 20.
14. David Goetzl, "Delta flies toward $1 billion in Web sales," *Advertising Age*, 11 September 2000, 54–56.
15. www.brandchannel.com/papers_review.asp?sp_id=1270, 12 January 2007.
16. Wendy Jedlicka, "Packaging," *Communication Arts*, March/April 2000, 111.
17. www.edf_org/edf/atissue/vol4–1, 22 January 2004.
18. Betsy McKay, "Pepsi's new marketing dance: Can can," *Wall Street Journal*, 12 January 2007, B3.
19. Frank Tobolski, "Package design requires research," *Marketing News*, 6 June 1994, 4.
20. Terry Lofton, "If your brand's number two, get with the package program," *Brandweek*, 27 June 1994, 26.
21. www.packagedesignmag.com/issues/2006.11/designers.corner.shtml
22. Allen Adamson, "Future of branding based on current trends," *Landor.com*, 21 January 2004.
23. Allen Adamson, "Future of branding based on current trends," www.landor.com/index.cfm?fuseaction=cBranding.getArticle&storyid=264, 12 March 2004.

Chapter 22

p. 676   Courtesy of Blattner Brunner, Pittsburgh, Atlanta, Washington

1. Theresa Howard, "Burger King appeals to young workers with 'Your Way' ads," *USA TODAY*, 18 April 2005, M2.
2. Kenneth Roman and Jane Maas, *How to Advertise* (New York: St. Martin's Press, 2003), 48–49.
3. Andrew McMains, "First Snickers work from TBWA/C/D," *Adweek*, 12 June 2006, 8.
4. Ann M. Mack, "Web ads score on recognition factor," *Adweek*, 19 January 2004, 12.
5. Kenneth Roman and Jane Maas, *The New How to Advertise* (New York: St. Martin's Press, 1992), 71–78.
6. Lisa Siracuse, "Looks aren't everything: An examination of brand personality," *Integrated Marketing Communications Research Journal*, Spring 1997, 38–39.
7. Marc Graser, "Totota hits touch points as it hawks Yaris to youth," *Advertising Age*, 1 May 2006, 28.
8. "Being true to Dew," *Brandweek*, 24 April 2000, 28–31.
9. Gary Levin, "Tracing ads' impact," *Advertising Age*, 4 November 1991, 49.

Chapter 23

p. 705   Courtesy of Shutterstock
p. 706   Courtesy of Homer LLC

1. "The biggest moments in the last 75 years of advertising history," *Advertising Age*, 28 March 2005, 12.

2. Clayton Collins, "Status of U.S. brands slips globally among teens," *Christian Science Monitor*, as reported in *Advertising Age*, 27 February 2006, 26.

3. "The world's largest cities," *Atlanta Journal-Constitution*, 16 November 2005, D3.

4. Deborah Ball, "Women in Italy like to clean but shun the quick and easy," *Wall Street Journal*, 25 April 2006, 1A.

5. Susanna Howard, "P&G, Unilever court the world's poor," *Wall Street Journal*, 1 June 2005, B5A.

6. R. Craig Endicott, "Global spending at Top 100: $94 billion," *Advertising Age*, 14 November 2005, 29.

7. Normandy Madden, "Reaching China's youth a balancing act," *Advertising Age*, 6 June 2005, 14.

8. "Invasion of the Chinese clones," www.driving.timesonline.co.uk January 30, 2006.

9. "The best product designs of 2005," www.businessweek.com, 4 July 2005.

10. "Glocalization," www.en.wikipedia.org, 30 January 2006.

11. "Glocalization," www.searchcio.techtarget.com, 30 January 2006.

12. Mark Landler and Michael Barbaro, "No, not always," *New York Times*, 2 August 2006, C1.

13. Jared Diamond, *Collapse* (New York: Penguin Books, 2005), 495.

14. Chris Paterson, "Satellite," www.museum.TV/archives, 31 January 2006.

15. "Background: Global Internet Solutions," www.tvpress.com, 31 January 2006.

16. Barry Silverstein, "Going global with Internet marketing," www.clickz.com, 30 January 2006.

17. Elizabeth Lloyd, "Marketing to the global inbox," www.imediaconnection.com, 31 January 2006.

18. Deborah Ball, "Italian challenge, water everywhere, but not on the go," *Wall Street Journal*, 23 May 2005, 1A.

19. Eric Pfanner, "On advertising: Ad agencies see revenue in Ramadan," www.nytimes.com, 3 October 2005.

20. Aaron O. Patrick, "World Cup's advertisers hope one size fits all," *Wall Street Journal*, 28 March 2006, B7.

21. Cecilie Rohweddere, "Wal-Mart's big goal," *Wall Street Journal*, 7 June 2006, B1.

22. John Galvin, "The world on a string," *Point*, February 2005, 13.

23. "Starbucks calls China its top growth focus," *Wall Street Journal*, 14 February 2006, B4.

24. Erin White and Sarah Ellison, "Unilever ads offer a tribute to dirt," *Wall Street Journal*, 2 June 2003, B3.

25. John H. Dunning and Sangeeta Bansal, "The cultural sensitivity of the eclectic paradigm," *Multinational Business Review*, Spring 1997, www.findarticles.com, 1 February 2006.

26. "Marketing and Image Consulting," www.multilingualplanet.com, 1 February 2006.

27. Scott Donaton, "Partners are for dances. To Thrive, big agencies need to provide ideas," *Advertising Age*, 9 May 2005, 34.

28. "WPP buys J. Walter Thompson," *Advertising Age*, 21 March 2005, 12.

29. Andrew McMains, "Debunking the consolidation myth," www.adweek.com, 20 February 2006.

30. Laurel Wentz, "Talking dirty for detergents leads executive to 'brand conversation,'" *Advertising Age*, 17 October 2005, 42.

31. Kate Macarthur, "This woman scares big agencies," *Advertising Age*, 25 April 2005, 1.

32. Cara B. Dipasquale, "Making data more relevant at Wunderman, byte by byte," *Advertising Age*, 2 September 2002, 24.

33. Susan P. Douglas and C. Samuel Craig, "International advertising," www.pages.stern.nyu.edu, 2 February 2006.

34. Geoffrey A. Fowler, "China bans Nike's LeBron ad as offensive to nation's dignity," *Wall Street Journal*, 7 December 2004, B4.

35. Normandy Madden, "How China buys and sells TV," *Advertising Age*, 8 May 2006, 26.

36. Ira Teinowitz, "International advertising code revised," *Advertising Age*, 23 January 2006, 3.

37. Laurel Wentz, "Pop stops kids' marketing in Europe," *Advertising Age*, 30 January 2006, 8.

38. Doreen Carvajal, "Processed foods? Read this, France says," *International Herald Tribune*, October 2, 2005, www.iht.com, 3 February 2006.

39. Lewis Rose and John Feldman, *Internet Marketing*, quoted at www.usability.com, 3 February 2006.

40. "Tips for tapping China's explosive growth," *Advertising Age*, 16 January 2006, 10.

41. Bradley Johnson, "Looking to experience a foreign culture? Plan a vacation to California," *Advertising Age*, 21 August 2006, 17.

42. Brad Edmondson, "America, new & improved," *Advertising Age*, 2 January 2006, 31.

43. Carol Hymowitz, "In a global economy, it's no longer about how many employees you have in this group and that group. It's a lot more complicated—and if you do it right, a lot more effective," *Wall Street Journal*, 14 November 2005, R1.

44. Laurel Wentz, "Marketers hone focus on minorities," *Advertising Age*, 1 November 2004, 55.

45. Mike Beirne, "Reports: African-American buying power soaring," www.brandweek.com, 23 February 2006.

46. Laurel Wentz, "Multicultural? No, Mainstream," *Advertising Age*, 2 May 2005, 3.

47. Alex Lopez Negrete, "Marketers, don't assimilate your Hispanic ads," *Advertising Age*, 31 October 2005, 25.

48. Tiffany Meyers, "Cultural mosaic," *Advertising Age*, 13 March 2006, S-1.

49. Jeremy Mullman, *Advertising Age*, 14 August 2006, 11.

50. Brooks Barnes, "Getting 'Housewives' to speak Spanish can turn desperate," *Wall Street Journal*, 13 December 2005, 1a.

51. Brooks Barnes, "U.S. networks try crafting their own Spanish-style soaps," *Wall Street Journal*, 5 January 2006, A13.

52. www.sitv.com, FAQ.

53. Kate MacArthur, "Taco Bell tries to solve its Hispanic conundrum," *Advertising Age*, 4 September 2006, 36.

54. Ann Zimmerman, "Wal-Mart's Hispanic outreach," *Wall Street Journal*, 31 May 2005, B9.

55. "New age media concepts and Hispanic advertising," www.namct.com, 9 February 2006.

56. Lee Hawkins, Jr., "Behind GM's slide: Bosses misjudged new urban tastes," *Wall Street Journal*, 8 March 2006, 1A.

57. Brian Steinberg, "P&G brushes up iconic image of 'Crest Kid' in new campaign," *Wall Street Journal*, 29 March 2005, B9.

58. Amy Chozich, "Marketers join Cinco de Mayo party," *Wall Street Journal*, 4 May 2005, B8.

59. Lauren Wentz, "Marketers move popular brands north of border," *Advertising Age*, 16 May 2005, 49.

60. Laurel Wentz, "Survey: Hispanics 'passionate' about shopping," *Advertising Age*, 18 July 2005, 29.

61. Mercedes M. Cardona, "Ikea, Circuit City stores go bilingual," *Advertising Age*, 3 January 2005, 19.

Chapter 24

p. 748   Courtesy of Consol Energy

1. www.lucidcafe.com, 14 February 2006.

2. www.blupete.com, 14 February 2006.

3. Alan Murray, "Will 'social responsibility' harm business?" *Wall Street Journal*, 18 May 2005, A2.

4. "Corporate social responsibility: Good citizenship or investor rip-off?" *Wall Street Journal*, 9 January 2006, R6.

5. Rance Crane, "Now here's a radical theory: Ads last bastion of honesty," *Advertising Age*, 1 July 2002, 32.

6. Stephanie Thompson, "Cereal consortium tests TV effort," *Advertising Age*, 15 July 2002, 6.

7. David M. Potter, *People of Plenty: Economic Abundance and the American Character* (Chicago: University of Chicago Press, 1954), 188.

8. Michael R. Solomon, *Consumer Behavior* (Upper Saddle River, NJ: Pearson Prentice-Hall, 2004), 562.

9. Naomi Klein, *No Logo* (New York: Picador, 2002), 28.
10. Kim Sheehan, *Controversies in Contemporary Advertising* (Thousand Oaks, CA: 2004), 25.
11. www.ftc.gov/bcp/privacy/wkshp97, 15 February 2006.
12. www.howstuffworks.com, 15 February 2006.
13. www.commercialalert.org, 15 February 2006.
14. "Vance Packard's 'hidden persuaders'," *Advertising Age*, 7 March 2005, 14.
15. Marilyn Gardner, "Body by Madison Avenue," www.csmonitor.com, 24 November 1999.
16. Rosie Murray, "Adland pulls plug on man's lustful ineptitude," www.telegraph.co.uk, 22 August 2005.
17. Rich Thomaselli, "Beauty's new, er, face," *Advertising Age*, 15 August 2005, 1.
18. Rich Thomaselli, "Erection ejection: NFL bans Levitra and rivals," *Advertising Age*, 9 January 2006.
19. James B. Arndorfer, "Raising their spirits," *Advertising Age*, February 14, 2005, S-1.
20. Matthew Grimm, "A spirited debate," *American Demographics*, April 2002, 48.
21. Abbey Klasssen, "Clear Channel loses despite gains," *Advertising Age*, 15 August 2005, 8.
22. "Its all about results," www.adcouncil.org, 16 February 2006.
23. Carol Hymowitz, "Asked to be charitable, more CEOs seek to aid their business as well," *Wall Street Journal*, 22 February 2005, B1.
24. Laura Raines, "Corporate Citizens," *Atlanta Journal-Constitution*, 20 August 2006, G1.
25. "Cause market forum," a supplement to *Advertising Age*, 28 July 2003, 2.
26. James Tenser, "The new Samaritans," *Advertising Age*, 12 June 2006, S-1.
27. Rich Thomaselli, "Steady ratings for 'dLife' get marketers' attention," *Advertising Age*, 16 January 2006, 8.
28. www.gradethenews.org/dreamhost, 17 February 2006.
29. Mathew Creamer, "Ad-pull edicts elicit nary a whimper of protest," *Wall Street Journal*, 30 May 2005, 3.
30. "The family friendly programming forum," www.ana.net, 17 February 2006.
31. Gail Schiller, "Advertisers get piece of local news shows," www.hollywoodreporter.com, 16 March 2006.
32. "News is no place for shady shills," *Advertising Age*, 25 April 2005, 32.
33. Al Tompkins, "Balancing business pressure and journalism values," www.poynter.org, 17 February 2006.
34. Brian Steinberg, "Magazine editors buck marketers," *Wall Street Journal*, 17 October 2005, B3.
35. "Advertisers rush to insert products into video games," *Atlanta Journal-Constitution*, 22 May 2005, F9.
36. Ira Teinowitz, "FTC whacks professor wonder," www.adage.com, 17 April 2002.
37. Ira Teinowitz, "Tobacco firms must air spots, judge says," www.tvweek.com, 18 August 2006.
38. Christopher Conkey, "DirecTV to pay $5.3 million for calling consumers on the 'Do Not Call' list," *Wall Street Journal*, 14 December 2005, D1.
39. For a more complete listing of FTC Rules and Guidelines refer to www.ftc.gov.
40. Arthur Winston, "How to define the concept 'free' via the FTC," *DM News*, 24 June 1996, 15.
41. Ivan Preston, *The Tangled Web They Weave* (Madison, WI: University of Wisconsin Press, 1994), 103.
42. "FTC guides concerning use of endorsements and testimonials in advertising," www.ftc.gov, 16 April 2000.
43. Rich Thomaselli, "FDA scrutiny threatens DTC media bonanza," *Advertising Age*, 25 April 2005, 1.
44. Andrew B. Lustigman, "DMPEA gives USPS sweeping powers," *DM News*, 6 December 1999, 14.
45. Stephen R. Bergerson, "Supreme Court strikes a blow for commercial speech," *American Advertising*, Summer 1993, 24.
46. "High court's hard line on ad bans," *Advertising Age*, 20 May 1996, 57.
47. "Advertising alcoholic beverages," *Advertising Topics*, a publication of the Council of Better Business Bureaus, May 1996, 2.
48. "High court overturns broadcasting ban on gambling advertising," *Advertising Topics*, 14 July 1999, 1.
49. Richard Carelli, "Supreme Court rejects ban on casino ads," www.nytimes.com, 14 June 1999.
50. Linda Greenhouse, "Justices strike down ban on casino gambling ads," www.nytimes.com, 15 June 1999.
51. Ira Teinowitz, "Ad, food groups indignant," *Advertising Age*, 23 January 2006, 25.
52. *United States et al. v. United Foods, Inc.*, www.law.umkc.edu, 10 February 2006.
53. Candiss Baksa Vibbert, "Freedom of speech and corporations: Supreme Court strategies for the extension of the First Amendment," *Communications*, Vol. 12, 1990, 26.
54. Boris Becker and Dennis O. Kaldenberg, "To advertise or not to advertise? Advertising expenditures by professionals," *Proceedings of the American Academy of Advertising*, 1995, Charles S. Madden, ed.
55. Rosalind C. Truitt, "The cases for commercial speech," *Presstime*, March 1996, 31.
56. www.ftc.gov, 13 February 2006.
57. "Blockbuster to reimburse consumers for late fees," *Advertising Age*, 4 April 2005, 18.
58. *Wall Street Journal*, January 19, 2006, D4.
59. "Judge trims Gillette claims," www.consumeraffairs.com, 13 February 2006.
60. www.encarta.msn.com/encyclopedia, 13 February 2006.
61. "NBC, CBS to drop some of Miller's ads," *Atlanta Journal-Constitution*, 18 December 2004, F3.
62. Abbey Klassen, "Toy industry looks to tots for boost," *Advertising Age*, 28 February 2005, 8.
63. "Screen advertisement: A guide for the media," www.ftc.gov, issued September 1998.
64. John R. Wilke, "FTC asks media to reject false ads," *Wall Street Journal*, 20 November 2002, A3.
65. "FTC cites drop in fraudulent diet ads," *Advertising Age*, 7 February 2005, 16.
66. "*The Sporting News* and DOJ agree to $7.2m settlement regarding acceptance of offshore gambling site ads," www.manatt.com, 10 March 2006.
67. Rich Thomaselli, "Drug industry ad code seen as negotiating play," *Advertising Age*, 8 August 2005, 8.
68. Caroline Wilbert, "Beverage industry ads tout new school policy," *Atlanta Journal-Constitution*, 13 October 2005, F1.
69. "Basic principles of the Better Business Bureau Code of Advertising," www.bbb.org, 19 June 2002.
70. "National Advertising Review Council," *Advertising Age*, 28 March 2005, 12.
71. Statement from the NAD, www.narc.org, 14 February 2006.
72. www.iom.edu, 14 February 2006.
73. Ira Teinowitz and Stephanic Thompson, "CARU's medicine hard to swallow," *Advertising Age*, 28 November 2005, 3.

INDEX